7-11(36)
18 (44)

D1575624

6-6-08 (3)

Indian Prairie Public Library District
401 Plainfield Road
Darien, Illinois 60561

BEST AMERICAN PLAYS

SIXTH SERIES—1963–1967

by JOHN GASSNER

BEST AMERICAN PLAYS SERIES

25 BEST PLAYS OF THE MODERN AMERICAN THEATRE: *Early Series, 1916-1929*

20 BEST PLAYS OF THE MODERN AMERICAN THEATRE: *1930-1939*

BEST PLAYS OF THE MODERN AMERICAN THEATRE: *Second Series, 1939-1946*

BEST AMERICAN PLAYS: *Third Series, 1945-1951*

BEST AMERICAN PLAYS: *Fourth Series, 1951-1957*

BEST AMERICAN PLAYS: *Supplementary Volume, 1918-1958*

20 BEST EUROPEAN PLAYS ON THE AMERICAN STAGE

BEST AMERICAN PLAYS: *Fifth Series, 1957-1963*

BEST PLAYS OF THE EARLY AMERICAN THEATRE: *From the Beginning to 1916*

(in association with Mollie Gassner)

THEATRE AT THE CROSSROADS

FORM AND IDEA IN THE MODERN THEATRE

THE THEATRE IN OUR TIMES

HUMAN RELATIONS IN THE THEATRE

COMEDIES OF MOLIÈRE

ENGLISH COMEDIES

BEST FILM PLAYS OF 1945 (with Dudley Nichols)

BEST FILM PLAYS OF 1943-44 (with Dudley Nichols)

TWENTY BEST FILM PLAYS (with Dudley Nichols)

GREAT FILM PLAYS (with Dudley Nichols)

OUR HERITAGE OF WORLD LITERATURE (with Stith Thompson)

PRODUCING THE PLAY

MASTERS OF THE DRAMA

A TREASURY OF THE THEATRE (3 volumes)

INTRODUCING THE DRAMA (with Morris Sweetkind)

THE LIBRARY OF WORLD DRAMA (General editor, 12 volumes)

by CLIVE BARNES

BALLET IN BRITAIN SINCE THE WAR

FREDERICK ASHTON AND HIS BALLETS

DANCE SCENE—U.S.A.

Best American Plays

SIXTH SERIES 1963–1967

Edited by

John Gassner and Clive Barnes

WITH AN INTRODUCTION
AND PREFACES TO THE PLAYS BY

Clive Barnes

Darien Public Library
7516 Cass Ave.
Darien, IL 60559

Crown Publishers, Inc., NEW YORK

ACKNOWLEDGMENTS

ACKNOWLEDGMENT is due to the following for their excellent cooperation in preparation of this volume: Atheneum Publishers; The Dial Press; Doubleday & Company; The Drama Book Specialists; Farrar, Straus & Giroux, Inc.; Houghton Mifflin Company; Random House, Inc.; The Sterling Lord Agency; The Viking Press; and Yale University Press.

NOTE: All plays contained in this volume are fully protected under the copyright laws of the United States of America, the British Empire, including the Dominion of Canada, and all other countries of the Copyright Union. Permission to reproduce, wholly or in part, by any method, must be obtained from the copyright owners or their agents. (See notices at the beginning of each play.)

© 1971 BY CROWN PUBLISHERS, INC.
LIBRARY OF CONGRESS CATALOG CARD NUMBER: 57–12830
ISBN: 0-517-509512
PRINTED IN THE UNITED STATES OF AMERICA
PUBLISHED SIMULTANEOUSLY IN CANADA BY GENERAL PUBLISHING COMPANY LIMITED
10 9 8 7 6 5 4 3

TABLE OF CONTENTS

PREFACE

ONCE IN A WHILE you will read something that is so apt in its sentiment, and so felicitous in its phrasing, that to try to improve on it would be more like crushing lilies than gilding them. The other day, having read Brooks Atkinson's splendid and affectionate tribute to his world, *Broadway,* my eye encountered among the Acknowledgments a tribute to the late John Gassner. And, as it cannot be bettered, with respect I quote it. "But no one [John Gassner] has served the theatre with so much insight, erudition, kindness and good will. When he died in 1967, he left permanently an empty niche."

John Gassner was tireless in his work for the theatre. At the time of his death he was Sterling Professor of Playwriting and Dramatic Literature at Yale University. He served on the Pulitzer Prize jury for many years, and for thirty years he was among America's most distinguished critics. And he was also editor of the Best Plays series—anthologies that have over the years won the respect of students, scholars, and lovers of the theatre.

It was my misfortune that I never met Professor Gassner, although I have had the pleasure of meeting his charming wife, Mollie, and a great deal about a man can be seen through his wife. In any event, Gassner's work stands for all to see. First, perhaps, there is his *Masters of the Drama.* Of this, Mr. Atkinson wrote: "Apart from the scope of the information it contains, it always amazes me because it is written throughout in a style of sustained enjoyment." That same quality of "sustained enjoyment" also illuminated his theatre reviews, which can be seen in his major collections, *The Theatre in Our Times, Theatre at the Crossroads,* and *Dramatic Soundings,* the latter published posthumously and gathered together by Glenn Loney. It can also be seen in his earlier collections in this series—enjoyment, of course, but also an enviable catholicity of taste.

When Herbert Michelman of Crown Publishers and a good friend of Gassner's approached me to take on the series, my first reaction was one of panic. But eventually I agreed, partly because Gassner was a man whose work I admired, and partly because it was a series that I used myself and that I felt should continue. We have a need for such a collection. But the making of such a collection is not always easy.

Looking back at the previous play series, as I had to when editing a four-volume set, *50 Best Plays of the American Theatre,* an anthology drawn from the earlier volumes in the series, I was struck both by the sagacity of Professor Gassner's choice and the breadth of his taste.

Before he died, Gassner had already planned this present volume, although the final choice of plays had yet to be settled upon. For various reasons some plays were unavailable, so, in the end, about half the plays have been chosen by Gassner and about half by myself. It is my hope that no one will be able to tell which half is which.

To become the foster father of a series as distinguished as this is an awesome responsibility, and this responsibility is not lessened by the remarkable changes, economically, institutionally, and aesthetically that we are now witnessing. However, I hope this series will continue to be in the future what it has been in the past, not just a collection of plays all well worth having, but also a temperature reading of the American theatre at a given time.

Although the dramatic and literary quality of the plays must always be the prime consideration, I think there was one other factor that also played a part in Gassner's choices. He wanted the series to be typical of their time so that these plays can be taken not only as examples of the quality of American playwriting during the period, but also as representative of the type of theatre being given.

The next volume in the series will be another *Best European Plays on the American Stage,* and then a Seventh Series of *Best Plays.* The format remains the same; only the taste and judgment formulating the choices will have changed, and here, at least to the best of my abilities, I shall try to emulate my distinguished predecessor.

CLIVE BARNES

INTRODUCTION

by Clive Barnes

LIFE IS changing with a rapidity that we can more easily sense than notice. Preparing this volume which records American plays from 1963 to 1967 presented in the New York theatre, I soon became aware that I was already dealing with history. So much has happened in the world and in the theatre since these plays—all, I think, typical of their period—were first produced.

I think the plays here represented are, for the most part, very good. I freely confess that there were two plays we wanted—Arthur Miller's *Incident at Vichy* and, even more, Jean-Claude van Itallie's *America Hurrah!*—that we could not get for copyright reasons. It would have been pleasant—if only for old time's sake—to have had Miller included, but the Van Itallie represented something quite different. It represented a link between this volume—the Sixth Series of *Best American Plays*—and the next volume, which is almost bound to be a controversial Seventh Series. Yet the picture is clear enough.

Looking at this Sixth Series and comparing it with its predecessors, I am very tempted to say that this is the best, the most distinguished collection. This, of course, reflects no credit on the editors. Yet it is interesting—possibly dangerously revealing—that at a time when Broadway has been complaining that things are getting worse than they have ever been and that profits are lower than they ever were, American playwrights have still managed to turn out some of their best works. You will admittedly find a few golden potboilers here—and the theatre needs them—but I think you will also find writing fit to be compared with plays anywhere in the world.

This special period we have under discussion was quite clearly a period of transition, a period of change. Here you are looking at a time when the entire Broadway scene was being questioned, by nothing more or less pertinent than its economic viability.

Here in New York we have had a benign confidence in Broadway's ability to make a buck. We have seen entrepreneurs (which is classy French for producers) sweep down on the American theatre, make a bundle, and sweep up before anyone noticed. And we rightly felt that this was not too bad. If a man can offer a show that enlivens the hearts of the populace, well, the man deserves to have a few bucks left after tax and social security deductions.

Nowadays, however, Broadway has become an exceptionally risky business. Spiraling costs and spiraling ticket prices have made Broadway producers increasingly wary of experiment. A musical can easily lose half a million dollars, or even more, in just one memorable night. In the face of this, caution becomes all, and success itself is put at a premium.

The playwright finds himself denied the most precious freedom of all to an artist—the freedom to fail. No one can do any really experimental work on Broadway anymore, and what is of most interest right now is almost always imported from elsewhere. Broadway has become a shop window for the theatre rather than a workshop for the theatre, and with rising prices it nowadays seems uncertain how long Broadway can maintain even this position.

The period we have here still maintained something of the old Broadway buoyancy, but change was imminent, and indeed, looking back it can be seen that the change had in many ways already started. For example, Broadway was already heavily committed to its importation policy. More and more of the most theatrically daring plays were imports.

Think of some of the best imported plays of the period in roughly the order in which they appeared (most of them On-Broadway but a few Off-Broadway): Harold Pinter's *The Collection*, Max Frisch's *Andorra*, Bertolt Brecht's *Mother Courage*, Charles Dyer's *Rattle of a Simple Man*, Jean Anouilh's *The Rehearsal*, Arnold Wesker's *Chips with Everything*, James Saunders's *Next Time I'll Sing to*

You, Rolf Hochhuth's *The Deputy*, Ann Jellicoe's *The Knack*, Friedrich Dürrenmatt's *The Physicists*, Jean Anouilh's *Poor Bitos*, Peter Shaffer's *The Royal Hunt of the Sun*, John Osborne's *Inadmissible Evidence*, Peter Weiss's *The Persecution and Assassination of Marat as Performed by the Inmates of the Asylum of Charenton Under the Direction of the Marquis de Sade*, Brian Friel's *Philadelphia, Here I Come!*, Frank Marcus's *The Killing of Sister George*, Harold Pinter's *The Homecoming*, and Peter Shaffer's *Black Comedy*.

This I suggest is an impressive list, and it is more important that these plays for the most part are not only good but they tend to be a little more adventurous, a little more demanding, than the average Broadway fare. I have a feeling—indeed it is more than a feeling for it has been confirmed by conversations with many Broadway producers—that such plays as *Marat/Sade* or *The Homecoming*, while perfectly successful in Broadway terms, could never have been actually created on Broadway. It would have been impossible to finance them from theatrical investors. These two plays were actually imported productions—both, as it happens, from Britain's Royal Shakespeare Company. Only their overseas successes permitted their Broadway productions.

The intention of the Broadway theatre is to make a profit. Now considering how rarely it achieves such a laudable end this may sound almost humorous, but enough fortunes have been made on Broadway to encourage stage-struck investors who, in their more soft-bitten moments, can always comfort themselves that just once their investment will not merely be another tax loss but a bonanza shot bringing back enormous profits. Yet when the investors are in their hard-bitten mood they are more likely to ask the producer who is trying to raise the money for some guarantee of the show's success.

You can no more guarantee the success of a Broadway show than promise to predict successfully the result of a horse race; indeed the two activities, theatrical production and horse racing, seem in many respects to have a remarkable lot in common. The basic animal is the thing the backer—in both instances—puts his money on, but luck, even the quality of the competition, play their parts in both cases. And then there is the matter of form.

Most backers and I suspect quite a few producers are not good "playreaders." They take a script and yet still are not able to envisage it on a stage. Now, if they can see the show, either in London, or in the American regional theatre, then they no longer have the problem of visualizing the play performance. Furthermore, its success with other audiences and other critics does also provide a guide to the play's possible running form in New York. So if you are an American playwright and you have an unusual or adventurous play to present, you might do best to have it staged in London first, which is precisely what, in 1969, Arthur Kopit did with his *Indians*, which was given by both the Royal Shakespeare Company in London and the Arena Stage in Washington, D.C., before it came to Broadway.

During this period the economic factors were changing. Other things were happening as well, and these have been reflected in the present volume. For example, we saw the beginning of the rise of the black theatre—and this was not just black theatre for white folks, such as *Porgy and Bess* or *Anna Lucasta;* this was beginning to be black theatre for black folks. There are representative black plays in the present selection, three of them, for the first time in the series.

In subsequent seasons the black theatre became more and more important, being used partly as a political platform—becoming perhaps the most strongly oriented political theatre to exist in America since the Group Theatre of the 1930s. It is amazing how quickly the theatre manages to catch up with its reflection of society and society's tastes and mores.

Today, as I write, we have become so used to the permissive theatre that we accept not just without protest but almost without notice the use of a four-letter expletive in a Julie Harris comedy or a Richard Rodgers musical. And stage nudity is felt nowadays to be hardly worth critical comment.

What might be called the de-escalation of theatrical obscenity has happened so fast that it has taken everyone by surprise. Do you know that when Ben Hecht and Charles MacArthur's *The Front Page* made its first appearance in 1928, my illustrious predecessor as drama critic of the *New York Times,* Brooks Atkinson, complained, and rightly so, in context, of the language. He particularly objected to the use of the word "sonofabitch." Profanity has gone further.

I called this the de-escalation of obscenity, yet it might be thought that the reverse phrase is the more appropriate. But in a very real sense it is truly de-escalation. A playwright uses a profanity, a blasphemy, a vulgarism, or an obscenity to create a certain effect. However, as the threshold value of public susceptibility to shock has gone up and up, so the shock value of such words has gone down and down.

There is a perfect theatrical example of this law of diminishing shocks in the story of Eliza Doolittle. When Shaw in 1912 wanted to startle his audience in *Pygmalion,* he had Eliza use the then taboo word "bloody." Even in 1938, when the film version was made by Gabriel Pascal, the word still maintained its power to shock and was left unchanged. However, by 1956, when Alan Jay Lerner wanted to create a similar effect of shock in the musical version of the play, *My Fair Lady,* he used the word "arse." Only the other day I asked Alan Jay Lerner what word he would substitute now to create the same effect. He grinned affably, and admitted that that kind of effect was probably today outside of the playwright's range!

So times move—and the *Best Plays* series is, in one instance, offering its first four-letter words. (Well, not precisely its first four-letter words, but its first four-letter words intended as four-letter words rather than words that happen to have four letters.) There is no apology possible here. In our next series, it will be difficult to find plays without four-letter words in them.

Recently a perfectly ordinary, nice-sounding man wrote me a friendly letter from the Middle West. He said he was bringing his family into New York for a vacation and could I recommend some good plays that did not feature obscenity, nudity or, what he called, "moral indulgence." I gulped, thought hard, and sent him to *You're a Good Man, Charlie Brown,* and hoped for the best.

Nudity? No this series does not yet offer the Nudest Best Plays. However, during the period in question, we did have the first Broadway stage nudity—but it came in a European play that was not eligible for this collection, Peter Weiss's *Marat/Sade.* Here in Peter Brook's bril-liant staging the New York theatre audience got its first, but not last, view of a naked human posterior—in this instance, male. It was a sign of the times.

What is in fact the latest play in this volume, Robert Anderson's *You Know I Can't Hear You When the Water's Running,* was first given in March 1967. It was an omnibus title for four playlets, the first being called *The Shock of Recognition.* It involved a playwright requesting, for the purposes of realism, an actor to appear stark naked on stage. The premise of the joke was that the audience would instantly find such a request ludicrous. Within little more than a year nudity was all but a commonplace On-Broadway, Off-Broadway and Off-Off-Broadway. *Hair,* with its nude be-in scene, was one sign during the 1967–1968 season. The following year came *Oh! Calcutta!,* the revue that was not about economic conditions in Mother India.

Another first in this current *Best Plays* series is the introduction of a couple of musicals amid what are—frequently laughingly—called legitimate plays. So the series has opened itself to illegitimacy, and perhaps not too soon.

One of the major glories of the American theatre from *The Black Crook* onward has been the strength and power of its musical comedy. Indeed, what began as a musical comedy, an offshoot of the European operetta tradition, has evolved into a distinctively indigenous American form.

There are certain difficulties in *printing* a musical. At their very best these represent what Richard Wagner termed a *Gesamstkunstwerk,* where all the parts add up equally to the whole, and no part has a complete existence apart. Some of the books and lyrics of the very best musicals would not stand up very well in the cold light of the printed word. This is true enough, but we feel that the two examples we are giving here—*Fiddler on the Roof* and *The Fantasticks*—do have a literary quality apart from the music that collaborated with it.

It is also a matter of historic record—a concern that must always be kept in mind in these continuing annals of the American theatre—that the book of important musicals should occasionally be preserved. I merely ask that they be read with sympathy, and an understanding of what they are. These are not plays but the febrile, heaving skeletons of the musical theatre. They were fleshed out by music, but they have their own fever, their own strength, and, I think, their own validity. They are also object lessons to people who want to write the books of musicals, and gently persuasive reminders for people who want to remember the musicals they have loved.

The Fantasticks, together with LeRoi Jones's *The Toilet,* is also another first for the series, our first Off-Broadway plays. Originally the Off-Broadway theatre was fundamentally a showcase for actors. Usually the plays were old, although the actors were new. Later, the playwright caught on to Off-Broadway's possibilities. Then, with the rising costs and diminishing opportunities of Broadway, a great deal of the creative action moved over. Today the Off-Broadway theatre is becoming more and more significant, at least for the time being.

I have already mentioned Broadway's necessary abdication of the role of experimenter and leader. Curiously enough, something of the same problems are now overtaking Off-Broadway. The costs of Off-Broadway have also been mounting, and indeed will increase with the agreement reached at the end of 1970 with Actors Equity. The future for Off-Broadway, with its comparatively small theatres and severely reduced earning capacity, may prove at first as hazardous and then as safe as the future for Broadway. Off-Broadway has come of age. Any self-respecting angel can lose a fortune on it.

This is the future—although there were barely rumbles of it in the period under review—and it may mean an increasing importance given to Off-Off-Broadway, a free-for-all theatrical jungle that has proliferated into the basements, attics, lofts, and backyards of the city, and is apparently here to stay. Off-Off-Broadway is still a place where a playwright can starve with dignity while an actor does his own thing. And it is becoming an increasingly aware, increasingly active, scene.

Had it not been for Arthur Miller's agents, or publishers, or copyright holders, or assorted friends or enemies, we might have had another first for the series in Mr. Miller's extraordinarily dull but extraordinarily worthy *Incident at Vichy.* This was intended to be our first institutional play. However, you have not missed too much with the play, and you are in any event going to get the lesson that it provides, or

does not provide, for institutional theatre.

When we can finally see this period from a decent perspective of time, I think the rise of the institutional theatre will be seen to be its most important development. And *Incident at Vichy* was given by the Lincoln Center Repertory Company—one of our first institutional theatres. It flopped, but it was historically important.

Institutional theatre is theatre that does not intend to make a profit, which sets it in a class apart from Broadway, which, quite unsuccessfully as it happens, does intend to make a profit. There have been high-minded, low-sighted, and short-winded theatres aimed at art for its own sake for many years in New York. But it was around now that people really began to consider the theatre as a social art, and to wonder whether it could exist without subsidy.

Incident at Vichy was one of the first offerings of the Lincoln Center Repertory Company when it was in its first manifestation at the ANTA Theatre off Washington Square—before it in fact moved to Lincoln Center. The checkered and lurid history of the Lincoln Center Repertory from then until now need not concern us. But the idea of a classic repertory company in New York—supported largely from public funds—is extremely important.

Already at this time two other institutional theatres existed in New York—Joseph Papp's New York Shakespeare Festival, giving free Shakespeare of high standard in Central Park every summer, and Theodore Mann's Circle-in-the-Square. During the following period, the institutional theatre became more and more important, and the whole idea of a theatre based on profit came under scrutiny if not actual suspicion.

This then was a period of enormous change. The plays being produced were different. The old menopausal Broadway comedies intended to massage and soothe the eroded psyches of their middle-aged audiences were slowly losing favor. This kind of "assurance" play—the kind of play that calms a man rather than excites him—was being given both free and efficiently on television. And during this period—and even more during the subsequent period—plays that at one time would have ticked over merrily to the sound of money were compared with free television and obviously found wanting.

There were, of course, things that television just could not do, and it seemed that the big, splashy musical found a special place in the entertainment scene. But all in all it was the beginning of a time of re-assessment, of reevaluation of what the theatre meant to the people, and what the people meant to the theatre.

The plays you will find in this volume are not eternal masterpieces (it may well be that the tiny, pregnant O'Neill will turn out to be the most enduring of the lot), but in this kind of collection we are not offering great plays of all time but rather the best plays of a specific period. They can all, I hope, be read with pleasure, and they all offer us a vignette of our society at a specific time.

These were the best American plays of their period and they possess a sociological as well as artistic interest. Personally I must say that looking back at the plays and the years that produced them I do think that they offer a fairly accurate picture. And it is a good bunch.

I admire the humanistically involved wit of Simon—and we have one of his best plays in this collection—and the theatrical magic and intensity of Albee. We have many other plays here—for example, Broadway's biggest mistake, probably one of the finest plays ever to fail on Broadway, and a play I am particularly proud to include, Saul Bellow's *The Final Analysis*. (Come back to us, Mr. Bellow, and you too, James Baldwin.)

Admittedly, what we are dealing with in such collections is the enormously important small change of drama. The people here are not the Shakespeares, Molières, or O'Neills of this world (except in one obvious instance); these are the playwrights who make our theatrical journey viable and lovable. These are plays that give importance to our theatre, while not always being of importance in themselves.

It is a curious aspect of our theatre in that, unlike all of the other performing arts, we live on the moment, thrive on immediacy. Take music, for example. Imagine what would happen if the music repertory became like the theatrical repertory. Imagine going to concerts in which, absolutely invariably, 95 percent of the music had been composed within the past five years. Imagine the same situation in dance or in opera. In those arts a classical repertory is understood and respected. Perhaps too much understood and too much respected.

The freshness of drama does lead to a certain brashness and rawness, but it also leads to an adventurousness and a certain special felicity to our times. You have to love and respect the newness of the theatre, and accept that that newness offers a contemporary awareness that far offsets this disadvantage of its continual and continuous inability to match up with the masterpieces of the past.

Despite the mandarin claims of certain foolish critics, the theatre is not in the masterpiece-making business. Shakespeare, Molière, Sophocles, Ibsen, and all the rest were literally fantastic freaks. They, and another dozen or so, are more meaningful to us than any other playwrights. They have changed our minds, formed our tastes, and enriched our hearts. Most plays are not like that. But the theatre works on various levels, and if its small things are done well, we can enjoy their temporary relevance almost as much as the timelessness of those who have outlived temporary relevance to progress into an accepted and profound state of classicism.

There is one last point I must make, although I have hinted at it earlier, and it is probably inherent in the total overview of this period. This was really and truly the period when the commercial theatre started to die. This was the beginning of Broadway's malaise not as an artistic unit but as an economic viability.

The American theatre is a luxury that the American people are going to have to decide whether or not it wants. I find it difficult to imagine any society, in the present terms of Western civilization, bereft of a theatre. Yet America's basic way of paying for that theatre—a lot of rich people pouring money into failures in the hope that the occasional hit will make them even richer—is today, here and now, unrealistic and impossible.

Historically, there has never been a really great theatre that has paid for itself. In America at the present time, and you can see the picture just about as well in this crystallized dramatic portrait of five years ago, we have the chance to build a great theatre that will enliven our hearts and leave a time-marker to the memory of our generation. But this cannot be done in commercial terms.

The longer I live in the theatre as an ordinary, day-to-day working critic, the more I become convinced that we must have massive public subsidy to survive and create. The profit motive is of very little use to the arts.

The profit motive leads to the lowest-common-denominator in the arts. And we all know what lowest-common-denominator art is: it is television, the one totally democratic art that the world has yet conceived. Yet there is a need for opportunities that go beyond the range of instant popularity, charts, ratings, box-office returns, and celebrity as sudden as sudden death. We need a theatre that is part of our lives, a simple asset in our cultural environment, our spiritual landscape.

We must forget the puritanical notion that a play has to get back at the box-office what it is worth to our emotional enrichment. It cannot. There are some activities known to men that have to be paid for by the community at large. The theatre is one of them.

Looking at this volume of *Best Plays*— yes, and looking at what will be the next *Best Plays* volume (which honestly is going to be fascinating in its range, variety, and social commitment and dissension)— you can see enormous qualities and virtues. But we are slowly running out of steam. The theatre is either going to get massive financial help (from the state, from foundations, from almost anyone with moderately hard cash) or it is going to die. The theatre is a loss operation like education or welfare. It is an amenity of life, an enrichment of existence, a bright flower growing in our urban ghettos. If we want to call the tune, we were going to have to pay the piper. Support your local theatre. If you don't, if your congressman doesn't, if your mayor doesn't, if your governor doesn't, if your senator doesn't, if your President doesn't—I hate to say it, but even if your Vice-President doesn't— the theatre cannot possibly survive.

Yet, of course, we all know the theatre will survive, must survive. Human existence would be unthinkable without the theatre, and today people all over the world are different because of the theatre. There will be good seasons and bad seasons, good times and bad times, new ways of financing, new sponsors, new subsidies, new hopes. An America without its theatre would be a devitalized America. For all the need for caution, there is still no need for gloom. Already the next volume in this series is being planned, and the volumes after that are still in the always capable hands of America's playwrights of today, tomorrow, and the day after.

BEST AMERICAN PLAYS

SIXTH SERIES—1963–1967

TINY ALICE

Edward Albee

For NOEL FARRAND

First presented by Richard Barr–Clinton Wilder at the Billy Rose Theatre in New York City on December 29, 1964, with the following cast:

LAWYER William Hutt   BUTLER John Heffernan
CARDINAL Eric Berry   MISS ALICE Irene Worth
JULIAN John Gielgud

Directed by Alan Schneider
Sets by William Ritman
Gowns by Mainbocher
Lighting by Martin Aronstein

TINY ALICE, a play by Edward Albee.
Reprinted by permission of the author and Atheneum Publishers.
Copyright © 1965 by Edward Albee.
All rights reserved.

CAUTION: Professionals and amateurs are hereby warned that *Tiny Alice,* being fully protected under the Copyright Laws of the United States of America, the British Empire, including the Dominion of Canada, and all other countries of the Berne and Universal Copyright Conventions, is subject to royalty. All rights, including professional, amateur, motion picture, recitation, lecturing, public reading, radio and television broadcasting, and the rights of translation into foreign languages, are strictly reserved. Particular emphasis is laid on the question of readings, permission for which must be secured from the author's agent in writing. All inquiries should be addressed to the William Morris Agency, 1740 Broadway, New York, N.Y.

EDWARD ALBEE was born, according to *Who's Who in America,* on March 12, 1928. He does not say where he was born, and it appears that he knows neither this, nor the names of his parents. It seems he was in Washington, D.C., soon after his birth, and when he was two weeks old he was brought to New York City to be adopted by Mr. and Mrs. Reed Albee. Mr. Albee was the son of the famous figure in vaudeville Edward F. Albee, who headed the Keith-Albee theatre circuit. The young Edward was born rich, and had to find poverty the hard way.

Albee's childhood appears to have been varied, not to say tempestuous. He was brought up in his parents' home in Larchmont, one of the lusher suburbs of New York. He went for schooling to Lawrenceville, Valley Forge Military Academy (which is an odd thought), and Choate. After high school graduation he toyed with the idea of college, and spent a year and half at Trinity College, Hartford, before becoming that institution's most distinguished dropout.

His early years were varied—copy boy, telegraph boy, working at a lunch counter, army—and after the age of twenty they were slightly cushioned by a legacy from his grandmother, giving him fifty dollars a week. He wrote poetry, novels, and short stories until his attention was taken by the theatre. "With the exception," he once wrote, "of a three-act sex farce I composed when I was twelve—the action of which occurred aboard an ocean liner, the characters of which were, for the most part, English gentry, and the title was, for some reason that escapes me now, *Aliqueen*—with the exception of that, *The Zoo Story* (1958), *The Death of Bessie Smith* and *The Sandbox* (both 1959), are my first three plays."

Oddly enough *The Zoo Story,* Albee's very first play, was first produced in Berlin and in German. The date was September 28, 1959, and it was not until January 14 of the next year that it was produced in America, Off-Broadway in New York, of course. It was a success. It was on a double bill with Samuel Beckett's *Krapp's Last Tape.* His next plays were equally successful. In the beginning of 1961 he produced *The American Dream,* which led to his canonization—premature, as it happened—as the American saint of the theatre of the absurd.

Fame came to Albee at the Billy Rose Theatre on October 13, 1962. It was perhaps not entirely unexpected. The play was *Who's Afraid of Virginia Woolf?* It became the surprise hit of the season. It made Albee the most talked-about American playwright since Arthur Miller and Tennessee Williams.

A savage domestic comedy of untamed domesticity, *Virginia Woolf* understandably attracted a few detractors. But Albee now started to produce a major play a year—some original, but usually he alternated the originals with adaptations from other writers. It was a productive period, embracing failures and successes, or an experiment in *Box-Mao-Box* of the drama as an extension of music, and Albee did not miss a season until that of 1969/70. Then he took a deserved sabbatical.

Of all Albee's plays, perhaps the most controversial (although not the most talked about, for that distinction belongs to *Virginia Woolf*) has been *Tiny Alice.* First given at the Billy Rose Theatre on December 29, 1964, with a cast distinguished enough to include John Gielgud and Irene Worth, *Tiny Alice* caused a distinct critical stir, and soon divided New York cocktails into two camps, those who thought they understood it but didn't like it, and those who liked it but didn't understand it. The situation became so fraught that on March 22, 1965, Albee took the unusual course of calling a press conference to tell the world just what *Tiny Alice* was about. It was, he claimed, "a perfectly straightforward story." A journalist present, hearing this claim, remarked: "And for this he had to have a press conference?"

What *Tiny Alice* is about is clear enough. What *Tiny Alice* means is admittedly a darker matter. But Mr. Albee is such a skillful playwright—admittedly here, there is the opening scene that seems at first blush largely irrelevant to the main purpose and certainly at the end the hero takes an unconscionable time a-dying—that he holds the audience's interest like a master conjurer.

The play is about, at least so I imagine, the surprise and necessity of martyrdom. The action of the play is perfectly clear. A lay priest named Julian is nominated by a cardinal to go to the house of a Miss Alice, who through the intermediary of her lawyer has offered the church two billion dollars spread over a twenty-year period.

Miss Alice, who has previously had affairs with both her butler and her lawyer, seduces Julian and subsequently marries him. After the ceremony the lawyer shoots Julian, and Miss Alice goes off with the butler and the lawyer, leaving Julian to die in peace. So much so good.

There is, of course, less to this allegory than meets the mind. Mr. Albee is a playwright not a metaphysician, and ideas of illusion and reality that spin through the play owe ambivalently almost as much to literature as to life. But no harm, in this instance, for this echoing ambiguity is the play's very texture.

Julian, with all the personal tragedy of predestination, is unexpectedly sacrificed, not, as he expects, to a real cause, a real god, but to the image of that cause or that god. And at the end of this strangely placed tragedy, he is forced to admit that it was the illusion that he really sought all the time.

Alice, her lawyer, and her butler are apparently the guardians of some aspect of his ideals. But not—although he does not realize this—the real guardians, merely surrogates for them. Alice lives in a huge rambling castle. In the library of this castle is a model of the castle (and in the library of that model is another model of the castle and in the . . . but that we never know) which is termed "the Wonder of the World." This then is perhaps the microcosm, but it is the small world, this illusory model that is real.

Alice is merely the image of reality, the surrogate priestess for the tiny Alice that dwells within the tiny world of truth—and, of course, who knows, tiny Alice may be a substitute for an even tinier Alice, locked in that tinier model. Illusion and reality are questions of degree, or perhaps angles of perspective, and the only surprising thing about everyday martyrdom is the price offered and the value received.

AUTHOR'S NOTE

It has been the expressed hope of many that I would write a preface to the published text of *Tiny Alice,* clarifying obscure points in the play—explaining my intention, in other words. I have decided against creating such a guide because I find—after reading the play over—that I share the view of even more people: that the play is quite clear. I will confess, though, that *Tiny Alice* is less opaque in reading than it would be in any single viewing. One further note: this printed text of *Tiny Alice* represents the complete play. Some deletions—mainly in the final act—were made for the New York production; and while I made the deletions myself, and quite cheerfully, realizing their wisdom in the particular situation, I restore them here with even greater enthusiasm.

ACT ONE

Scene One

The CARDINAL's *garden. What is needed . . . ? Ivy climbing a partial wall of huge stones? An iron gate? Certainly two chairs —one, the larger, obviously for His Eminence; the other, smaller—and certainly an elaborate birdcage, to stage left, with some foliage in it, and two birds, cardinals . . . which need not be real.*

At rise, the LAWYER *is at the birdcage, talking to the birds.*

——

LAWYER. Oomm, yoom, yoom, um? Tick-tick-tick-tick-tick. Um? You do-do-do-do-do-um? Tick-tick-tick-tick-tick-tick-tick-um? (*He raises his fingers to the bars.*) Do-do-do-do-do-do-do? Aaaaaawwwww! Oomm, yoom, yoom, um?

(*The* CARDINAL *enters from stage right—through the iron gates?—unseen by the* LAWYER, *who repeats some of the above as the* CARDINAL *moves toward center.*)

CARDINAL (*finally; quietly amused*). Saint Francis?

LAWYER (*swinging around; flustered; perhaps more annoyed than embarrassed at being discovered*). Your Eminence!

CARDINAL. Our dear Saint Francis, who wandered in the fields and forests, talked to all the . . .

LAWYER (*moving to kiss the ring*). Your Eminence, we appreciate your kindness in taking the time to see us; we know how heavy a schedule you . . .

CARDINAL (*silencing him by waving his ring at him; the* LAWYER *kneels, kisses the ring, rises*). We are pleased . . . we are pleased to be your servant (*Trailing off.*) . . . if . . . we can be your servant. We addressed you as Saint Francis . . .

LAWYER (*properly mumbling*). Oh, but surely . . .

CARDINAL. . . . as Saint Francis . . . who did talk to the birds so, did he not. And here we find *you,* who talk not only to the birds but to (*With a wave at the cage.*)—you must forgive us—to cardinals as well. (*Waits for reaction, gets none, tries again.*) . . . To cardinals? As well?

LAWYER (*a tight smile*). We . . . we understood.

CARDINAL (*he, too*). Did we.

(*A brief silence, as both smiles hold.*)

LAWYER (*to break it, moving back to-ward the cage*). We find it droll—if altogether appropriate in this setting—that there should be two cardinals . . . uh, together . . . (*Almost a sneer.*) . . . in conversation, as it were.

CARDINAL (*the smile again*). Ah, well, they are a comfort to each other . . . companionship. And they have so much to say. They . . . understand each other so much better than they would . . . uh, *other* birds.

LAWYER. Indeed. And so much better than they would understand saints?

CARDINAL (*daring him to repeat it, but still amused*). Sir?

LAWYER (*right in*). That cardinals understand each *other* better than they understand saints.

CARDINAL (*not rising to it*). Who is to say? Will you sit?

LAWYER (*peering into the cage*). They are extraordinary birds . . . cardinals, if I may say so. . . .

CARDINAL (*through with it*). You push it too far, sir. Will you join us?

(*He moves to his chair, sits in it.*)

LAWYER (*brief pause, then surrender; moves to the other chair*). Of course.

CARDINAL (*a deep sigh*). Well. What should we do now? (*Pause.*) Should we clap our hands (*Does so, twice.*) . . . twice, and have a monk appear? A very old monk? With just a ring of white hair around the base of his head, stooped, fast-shuffling, his hands deep in his sleeves? Eh? And should we send him for wine? Um? Should we offer you wine, and should we send him scurrying off after it? Yes? Is that the scene you expect now?

LAWYER (*very relaxed, but pointed*). It's so difficult to know what to expect in a Cardinal's garden, Your Eminence. An old monk would do . . . or—who is to say?—perhaps some good-looking young novice, all freshly scrubbed, with big working-class hands, who would . . .

CARDINAL (*magnanimous*). We have both in our service; if a boy is more to your pleasure . . .

LAWYER. I don't drink in the afternoon, so there is need for neither . . . unless Your Eminence . . . ?

CARDINAL (*his eyes sparkling with the joke to come about his nature*). We are known to be . . . ascetic, so we will have none of it. Just . . . three cardinals . . . and Saint Francis.

LAWYER. Oh, not Saint Francis, not a saint. Closer to a king; closer to Croesus. That was gibberish I was speaking to the cardinals—and it's certainly not accepted that Saint Francis spoke gibberish to his . . . parishioners . . . intentional gibberish or otherwise.

CARDINAL. It is not accepted; no.

LAWYER. No. May I smoke?

CARDINAL. Do.

LAWYER (*lights up*). Closer to Croesus; to gold; closer to wealth.

CARDINAL (*a heavy, weary sigh*). Aahhhh, you *do* want to talk business, don't you?

LAWYER (*surprisingly tough*). Oh, come on, Your Eminence: (*Softer.*) Do you want to spend the afternoon with me, making small talk? Shall we . . . shall we talk about . . . times gone by?

CARDINAL (*thinks about it with some distaste*). No. No no; we don't think so. It wouldn't do. It's not charitable of us to say so, but when we were at school we did loathe you so.

(*Both laugh slightly.*)

LAWYER. Your Eminence was not . . . beloved of everyone himself.

CARDINAL (*thinking back, a bit smugly*). Ah, no; a bit out of place; out of step.

LAWYER. A swine, I thought.

CARDINAL. And we you.

(*Both laugh a little again.*)

LAWYER. Do you ever slip?

CARDINAL. Sir?

LAWYER. Mightn't you—if you're not careful—(*Tiny pause.*) lapse . . . and say *I* to me . . . not we?

CARDINAL (*pretending sudden understanding*). Ah ha! Yes, we under*stand*.

LAWYER. Do we, do we.

CARDINAL. We do. We—and here we speak of our*selves* and not of our station— we . . . *we* reserve the first-person singular for intimates . . . and equals.

LAWYER. . . . And your superiors.

CARDINAL (*brushing away a gnat*). The case does not apply.

LAWYER (*matter-of-factly; the vengeance is underneath*). You'll grovel, Buddy. (*Slaps his hip hard.*) As automatically and naturally as people slobber on that ring of yours. As naturally as that, I'll have you do your obeisance. (*Sweetly.*) As you used to, old friend.

CARDINAL. We . . . (*Thinks better of what he was about to say.*) You *were* a swine at school. (*More matter-of-factly.*)

A cheat in your examinations, a liar in all things of any matter, vile in your personal habits—unwashed and indecent, a bully to those you could intimidate and a sycophant to everyone else. We remember you more clearly each moment. It is law you practice, is it not? We find it fitting.

LAWYER (*a mock bow, head only*). We are of the same school, Your Eminence.

CARDINAL. And in the same class . . . but not *of*. You have come far—in a worldly sense . . . from so little, we mean. (*Musing.*) The law.

LAWYER. I speak plainly.

CARDINAL. You are plain. As from your beginnings.

LAWYER (*quietly*). Overstuffed, arrogant, pompous son of a profiteer. And a whore. You are in the Church, are you not? We find it fitting.

CARDINAL (*a burst of appreciative laughter*). You're *good*! You *are*! Still! Gutter, but good. But, in law . . . (*Leaves it unfinished with a gesture.*) Ah! It comes back to us; it begins to. What did we call you at school? What name, what nickname did we have for you . . . all of us? What term of simple honesty and . . . rough affection did we have for you? (*Tapping his head impatiently.*) It comes back to us.

LAWYER (*almost a snarl*). We had a name for you, too.

CARDINAL (*dismissing it*). Yes, yes, but we forget it.

LAWYER. Your Eminence was not always so . . . eminent.

CARDINAL (*remembering*). Hy-e . . . (*Relishing each syllable.*) Hy-e-na. Hy. E. Na. We recall.

LAWYER (*close to breakthrough anger*). We are close to Croesus, Your Eminence. I've brought gold with me . . . (*Leans forward.*) money, Your Eminence.

CARDINAL (*brushing it off*). Yes, yes; later. Hy-e-na.

LAWYER (*a threat, but quiet*). A great deal of money, Your Eminence.

CARDINAL. We hear you, and we will discuss your business shortly. And why did we call you hyena . . . ?

LAWYER (*quiet threat again*). If Croesus goes, he takes the gold away.

CARDINAL (*outgoing*). But, Hyena, you are not Croesus; you are Croesus' emissary. You will wait; the gold will wait.

LAWYER. Are you certain?

CARDINAL (*ignoring the last*). Ah, yes, it was in natural science class, was it not? (*The* LAWYER *rises, moves away a little.*) Was it not?

LAWYER. Considering your mother's vagaries, you were never certain of your true father . . . were you?

CARDINAL. Correct, my child: considering one's mother's vagaries, one was never certain of one's true father . . . was one? But then, my child, we embraced the Church; and we *know* our true father. (*Pause; the* LAWYER *is silent.*) It was in natural science class, eleven five until noon, and did we not discover about the hyena . . .

LAWYER. More money than you've ever seen!

CARDINAL (*parody; cool*). Yum-yum. (*Back to former tone.*) Did we not discover about the hyena that it was a most resourceful scavenger? That, failing all other food, it would dine on offal . . .

LAWYER (*angrier*). Millions!

CARDINAL (*pressing on*). . . . and that it devoured the wounded and the dead? We found that last the most shocking: the dead. But we were young. And what horrified us most—and, indeed, what gave us all the thought that the name was most fitting for yourself—

LAWYER (*ibid.*). Money!

CARDINAL. . . . was that to devour its dead, scavenged prey, it would often chew into it . . .

LAWYER. MONEY, YOU SWINE!

CARDINAL (*each word rising in pitch and volume*). . . . chew into it THROUGH THE ANUS????

(*Both silent, breathing a little hard.*)

LAWYER (*finally; softly*). Bastard.

CARDINAL (*quietly, too*). And now that we have brought the past to mind, and remembered what we could not exactly, shall we . . . talk business?

LAWYER (*softly; sadly*). Robes the color of your mother's vice.

CARDINAL (*kindly*). Come. Let us talk business. You are a businessman.

LAWYER (*sadly again*). As are you.

CARDINAL (*as if reminding a child of something*). We are a Prince of the Church. Do you forget?

LAWYER (*suddenly pointing to the cage; too offhand*). Are those two lovers? Do they mate?

CARDINAL (*patronizing; through with games*). Come; let us talk business.

LAWYER (*persisting*). Is it true? Do they? Even cardinals?

CARDINAL (*a command*). If you have money to give us . . . sit down and give it.

LAWYER. To the lay mind—to the cognoscenti it may be fact, accepted and put out of the head—but to the lay mind it's speculation . . . voyeuristic, perhaps, and certainly anti-Rome . . . mere speculation, but whispered about, even by the school children—indeed, as you must recall, the more . . . urbane of us wondered about the Fathers at school . . .

CARDINAL. . . . the more wicked . . .

LAWYER. . . . about their vaunted celibacy . . . among one another. Of course, we were at an age when everyone diddled everyone else . . .

CARDINAL. Some.

LAWYER. Yes, and I suppose it was natural enough for us to assume that the priests did too.

CARDINAL (*as if changing the subject*). You have . . . fallen away from the Church.

LAWYER. And into the arms of reason.

CARDINAL (*almost thinking of something else*). An unsanctified union: not a marriage: a whore's bed.

LAWYER. A common-law marriage, for I am at law and, as you say, common. But it is quite respectable these days.

CARDINAL (*tough; bored with the church play-acting; heavy and tired*). All right; that's enough. What's your business?

LAWYER (*pacing a little, after an appreciative smile*). My employer . . . wants to give some of her money to the Church.

CARDINAL (*enthusiastic, but guarded*). Does she!

LAWYER. Gradually.

CARDINAL (*understanding*). *Ah*-ha.

LAWYER (*offhand*). A hundred million now.

CARDINAL (*no shown surprise*). And the rest gradually.

LAWYER. And the same amount each year for the next twenty—a hundred million a year. She is not ill; she has no intention of dying; she is quite young, youngish; there is no . . . rush.

CARDINAL. Indeed not.

LAWYER. It is that she is . . . overburdened with wealth.

CARDINAL. And it weighs on her soul.

LAWYER. Her soul is in excellent repair. If it were not, I doubt she'd be making the gesture. It is, as I said, that she is over-burdened with wealth, and it . . . uh . . .

CARDINAL (*finding the words for him*). . . . piles up.

LAWYER (*a small smile*). . . . and it is . . . wasted . . . lying about. It is one of several bequests—arrangements—she is making at the moment.

CARDINAL (*not astonishment, but unconcealed curiosity*). One of several?

LAWYER. Yes. The Protestants as well, the Jews . . . hospitals, universities, orchestras, revolutions here and there . . .

CARDINAL. Well, we think it is a . . . responsible action. She is well, as you say.

LAWYER. Oh, yes; very.

CARDINAL We are . . . glad. (*Amused fascination.*) How did you become her . . . lawyer, if we're not intruding upon . . . ?

LAWYER (*brief pause; tight smile*). She had a dossier on me, I suppose.

CARDINAL. It must be a great deal less revealing than ours . . . than our dossier on you.

LAWYER. Or a great deal *more* revealing.

CARDINAL. For her sake, and yours, we hope so.

LAWYER. To answer your question: I am a very good lawyer. It is as simple as that.

CARDINAL (*speculating on it*). You *have* escaped prison.

LAWYER. I've done nothing to be imprisoned for.

CARDINAL. Pure. You're pure. You're ringed by stench, but you're pure. There's an odor that precedes you, and follows after you're gone, but you walk in the eye of it . . . pure.

LAWYER (*contemptuous*). Look, pig, I don't enjoy you.

CARDINAL (*mockingly; his arms wide as if for an embrace*). School chum!

LAWYER. If it were not my job to . . .

CARDINAL (*abruptly*). Well, it is! Do it!

LAWYER (*a smile to a hated but respected adversary*). I've given you the facts: a hundred million a year for twenty years.

CARDINAL. But . . . ?

LAWYER (*shrugs*). That's all.

CARDINAL (*stuttering with quiet excitement*). Y-y-y-y-yes, b-b-but shall I just go to the *house* and pick it up in a *truck*?

LAWYER (*great heavy relief*). AAAAAAA-HHHHHHHHHHHHHHHH.

CARDINAL (*caught up short*). Hm? (*No reply.*) HM???

LAWYER. Say it again. Say it once again for me.

CARDINAL (*puzzled, suspicious*). What? Say what?

LAWYER (*leaning over him*). Say it again; repeat what you said. It was a sweet sound.

CARDINAL (*shouting*). SAY WHAT!

LAWYER (*cooing into his ear*). "Yes, but shall I just go to the house and pick it up in a truck?"

CARDINAL (*thinks on it a moment*). Well, perhaps there was a bit . . . perhaps there was too much levity there . . . uh, if one did not know one . . .

LAWYER (*coos again*). . . . "But shall *I* just go to the house . . ."

CARDINAL. Wh . . . NO!

LAWYER (*sings it out*). Shall IIIIIII just go!

CARDINAL (*cross*). No! We . . . we did not say that!

LAWYER. IIIIIIIIIIIIII.

CARDINAL (*a threat*). We did not say "I."

LAWYER (*almost baby talk*). We said I. Yes, we did; we said I. (*Suddenly loud and tough.*) We said I, and we said it straight. I! I! I! By God, we picked up our skirts and lunged for it! IIIIIII! Me! Me! Gimme!

CARDINAL (*full shout*). WE SAID NO SUCH THING!

LAWYER (*oily imitation*). We reserve the first-person singular, do we not, for . . . for intimates, equals . . . or superiors. (*Harsher.*) Well, my dear, you found all three applying. Intimate. How close would we rub to someone for all that wealth? As close as we once did?

CARDINAL (*not wanting to hear, but weak*). Leave . . . leave off.

LAWYER (*pressing*). Equals? Oh, money equals anything you want. Levels! LEVELS THE EARTH! AND THE HEAVENS!

CARDINAL. ENOUGH!!

LAWYER (*the final thrust*). . . . Or superiors. Who is superior, the one who stands on the mount of heaven? We think not! We have come down off our plural . . . when the stakes are high enough . . . and the hand, the kissed hand palsies out . . . FOR THE LOOT!!

CARDINAL (*hissed*). Satan!

LAWYER (*after a pause*). Satan? You would believe it . . . if you believed in

God. (*Breaks into—for lack of a better word—Satanic laughter, subsides. Patronizing now.*) No, poor Eminence, you don't have to drive a truck around to the back door for it. We'll get the money to you . . . to your . . . people. Fact, I don't want you coming 'round . . . at all. Clacketing through the great corridors of the place, sizing it up, not content with enough wealth to buy off the first two hundred saints picked out of a bag, but wondering if *it* mightn't get thrown into the bargain as a . . . summer residence, perhaps . . . uh, after she dies and scoots up to heaven.

CARDINAL (*on his feet, but shaky, uncertain*). This . . . uh . . .

LAWYER. . . . interview is terminated?

CARDINAL (*quietly*). This is unseemly talk.

LAWYER (*vastly, wryly amused*). Oh? Is it?

CARDINAL (*a mechanical toy breaking down*). We will . . . we will forgive your presumption, your . . . excess . . . excuse, yes . . . excuse? . . . We will . . . overlook your . . . (*A plea is underneath.*) Let us have no more of this talk. It *is* unseemly.

LAWYER (*businesslike; as if the preceding speech had not happened*). As I said, I don't want you coming 'round . . . bothering her.

CARDINAL (*humble*). I would not bother the lady; I have not met her. Of course, I would very much like to have the pleasure of . . .

LAWYER. We slip often now, don't we.

CARDINAL (*very soul-weary*). Pardon?

LAWYER. The plural is gone out of us, I see.

CARDINAL. Ah. Well. Perhaps.

LAWYER. Regird yourself. We *are* about terminated. (*Quick, insulting finger-snaps.*) Come! Come! Back up; back on your majesty! Hup!

CARDINAL (*slowly, wearily coming back into shape*). Uh . . . yes . . . of—of course. We, uh, we shall make any arrangements you wish . . . naturally. We . . . we have no desire to intrude ourselves upon . . . uh . . . upon . . .

LAWYER. Miss Alice.

CARDINAL. Yes; upon Miss Alice. If she . . . if Miss Alice desires privacy, certainly her generosity has earned it for her. We . . . would not intrude.

LAWYER. You *are* kind. (*Fishing in a pocket for a notebook.*) What . . . is . . . your . . . secretary's . . . name . . . I think I have it . . . right . . . (*Finds notebook.*)

CARDINAL. Brother . . .

LAWYER. Julian! Is that not right?

CARDINAL. Yes, Brother Julian. He is an old friend of ours; we . . .

LAWYER. Rather daring of you, wasn't it? Choosing a lay brother as your private secretary?

CARDINAL (*a combination of apology and defiance*). He is an old friend of ours, and he has served the . . .

LAWYER (*praising a puppy*). You are adventurous, are you not?

CARDINAL. He has been assigned many years to the . . .

LAWYER (*waving his notebook a little*). We have it; all down; we know.

CARDINAL (*a little sadly*). Ah-ha.

LAWYER. Yes. Well, we will send for your . . . Brother Julian. . . . To clear up odds and ends. Every bank has its runners. We don't ask vice presidents to . . . fetch and carry. Inform Your Brother Julian. We will send for him.

(LAWYER *exits.*)

CARDINAL (*to the exiting figure*). Yes, we . . . will. (*Stands still, looks at the ground, tired, looks at his sleeves, his fingernails, his ring, up, out, over. Sighs, looks at the cage. Smiles slightly, moves to the cage, the fingers of his left hand fluttering at it.*) Do . . . do you . . . do you have much to say to one another, my dears? Do you? You find it comforting? Hmmmmmmm? Do you? Hmmmm? Do-do-do-do-do-do-do-do? Hmmmmmm? Do?

CURTAIN

SCENE TWO

The library of a mansion—a castle. Pillared walls, floor-to-ceiling leather-bound books. A great arched doorway, rear center. A huge reading table to stage left—practical. A phrenological head on it. To stage right, jutting out of the wings, a huge doll's-house model of the building of which the present room is a part. It is as tall as a man, and a good deal of it must be visible from all parts of the audience. An alternative—and perhaps more practical—would be for the arched doorway to be either left or right, with bookshelves to both sides of the set, coming toward the center, and to have the entire doll's house in the rear wall, in which case it could be smaller—say, twelve feet long and proportionately high. At any rate, it is essential.

At rise, JULIAN *is alone on stage, looking at the house.*

JULIAN (*after a few moments of head-shaking concentration*). Extraordinary . . . extraordinary.

BUTLER (*after entering, observing* JULIAN, *not having heard him*). Extraordinary, isn't it?

JULIAN (*mildly startled*). Uh . . . yes, unbelievable . . . (*Agreeing.*) Extraordinary.

BUTLER (*who moves about with a kind of unbutlerlike ease*). I never cease to wonder at the . . . the fact of it, I suppose.

JULIAN. The workmanship . . .

BUTLER (*a mild correction*). That someone would do it.

JULIAN (*seeing*). Yes, yes.

BUTLER. That someone would . . . well, for heaven's sake, that someone would build . . . (*Refers to the set.*) . . . *this* . . . castle? . . . and then . . . duplicate it in such precise minature, so exactly. Have you looked through the windows?

JULIAN. No, I . . .

BUTLER. It is exact. Look and see.

JULIAN (*moves even closer to the model, peers through a tiny window*). Why . . . why, YES. I . . . there's a great . . . baronial dining room, even with tiny candlesticks on the tables!

BUTLER (*nodding his head, a thumb back over his shoulder*). It's down the hall, off the hallway to the right.

JULIAN (*the proper words won't come*). It's . . . it's . . .

BUTLER. Look over here. There; right there.

JULIAN (*peers*). It's . . . it's this *room!* This room we're *in!*

BUTLER. Yes.

JULIAN. Extraordinary.

BUTLER. Is there anyone there? Are we there?

JULIAN (*briefly startled, then laughs, looks back into the model*). Uh . . . no. It seems to be quite . . . empty.

BUTLER (*a quiet smile*). One feels one should see one's self . . . almost.

JULIAN (*looks back to him; after a brief,*

thoughtful pause). Yes. That would be rather a shock, wouldn't it?

BUTLER. Did you notice . . . did you notice that there is a model within that room in the castle? A model of the model?

JULIAN. I . . . I did. But . . . I didn't register it, it seemed so . . . continual.

BUTLER (*a shy smile*). You don't suppose that within that tiny model in the model there, there is . . . another room like this, with yet a tinier model within it, and within . . .

JULIAN (*laughs*). . . . and within and within and within and . . . ? No, I . . . rather doubt it. It's remarkable craftsmanship, though. Remarkable.

BUTLER. Hell to clean.

JULIAN (*conversational enthusiasm*). Yes! I should think so! Does it open from . . .

BUTLER. It's sealed. Tight. There is no dust.

JULIAN (*disappointed at being joked with*). Oh.

BUTLER. I was sporting.

JULIAN. Oh.

BUTLER (*straight curiosity*). Did you mind?

JULIAN (*too free*). I? No!

BUTLER (*doctrine, no sarcasm*). It would almost be taken for granted—one would think—that if a person or a person's surrogate went to the trouble, *and* expense, of having such a dream toy made, that the person *would* have it sealed, so that there'd be no dust. Wouldn't one think.

JULIAN (*sarcasm and embarrassment together*). One would think.

BUTLER (*after a pause, some rue*). I have enough to do as it is.

JULIAN (*eager to move on to something else*). Yes, yes!

BUTLER. It's enormous . . . (*A sudden thought.*) even for a castle, I suppose. (*Points to the model.*) Not that. (*Now to the room.*) This.

JULIAN. Endless! You . . . certainly you don't work alone.

BUTLER. Oh, Christ, no.

JULIAN (*reaffirming*). I would have thought.

BUTLER (*almost daring him to disagree*). Still, there's enough work.

JULIAN (*slightly testy*). I'm *sure.*

(*A pause between them.*)

BUTLER (*for no reason, a sort of "Oh, what the hell"*). Heigh-ho.

JULIAN. Will there be . . . someone? . . . to see me? . . . soon?

BUTLER. Hm?

JULIAN. Will there be someone to see me soon! (*After a blank stare from the other.*) You announced me? I trust?

BUTLER (*snapping to*). Oh! Yes! (*Laughs.*) Sorry. Uh . . . yes, there will be someone to see you soon.

JULIAN (*attempt at good-fellowship*). Ah, good!

BUTLER. Are you a priest?

JULIAN (*self-demeaning*). I? No, no . . .

BUTLER. If not Catholic, Episcopal.

JULIAN. No . . .

BUTLER. What, then?

JULIAN. I am a lay brother. I am not ordained.

BUTLER. You are *of* the cloth but have not taken it.

JULIAN (*none too happy*). You *could* say that.

BUTLER (*no trifling*). One *could* say it, and quite accurately. May I get you some ice water?

JULIAN (*put off and confused*). No!

BUTLER (*feigns apology*). Sorry.

JULIAN. You must forgive me. (*Almost childlike enthusiasm.*) This is rather a big day for me.

BUTLER (*nods understandingly*). Iced tea.

JULIAN (*laughs*). No . . . nothing, thank you . . . uh . . . I don't have your name.

BUTLER. Fortunate.

JULIAN. No, I meant that. . . .

BUTLER. Butler.

JULIAN. Pardon?

BUTLER. Butler.

JULIAN. Yes. You . . . you *are* the butler, are you not, but . . .

BUTLER. Butler. My name is Butler.

JULIAN (*innocent pleasure*). How extraordinary!

BUTLER (*putting it aside*). No, not really. Appropriate: Butler . . . butler. If my name were Carpenter, and I were a butler . . . or if I *were* a carpenter, and my name were Butler . . .

JULIAN. But *still* . . .

BUTLER. . . . it would not be so appropriate. And think: if I were a woman, and had become a chambermaid, say, and my name were Butler . . .

JULIAN (*anticipating*). . . . you would be in for some rather tiresome exchanges.

BUTLER (*cutting, but light*). None more than this.

JULIAN (*sadly*). Aha.

BUTLER (*forgiving*). Coffee, then.

JULIAN (*as if he can't explain*). No. Nothing.

BUTLER (*semi-serious bow*). I am at your service.

(LAWYER *enters.*)

LAWYER. I, too.

JULIAN. Ah!

LAWYER. I'm sorry to have kept you waiting, but . . .

JULIAN. Oh, no, no . . .

LAWYER. . . . I was conferring with Miss Alice.

JULIAN. Yes.

LAWYER (*to* BUTLER; *no fondness*). Dearest.

BUTLER (*to* LAWYER; *same*). Darling.

LAWYER (*to* JULIAN). Doubtless, though, you two have . . . (*Waves a hand about.*)

JULIAN. Oh, we've had a most . . . unusual . . .

LAWYER (*to* BUTLER, *ignoring* JULIAN's *answer*). You've offered our guest refreshments?

JULIAN. Brother Julian.

BUTLER. Ice water, iced tea, and coffee— hot assumed, I imagine—none taken.

LAWYER. Gracious! (*Back to* JULIAN.) Port, perhaps. Removed people take port, I've noticed.

JULIAN (*more to please than anything*). Yes. Port. Please.

LAWYER (*to* BUTLER). Port for . . .

JULIAN. Julian—Brother Julian.

LAWYER (*slightly patronizing*). I *know*. (BUTLER *goes to a sideboard.*) I would join you, but it is not my habit to drink before sundown. Not a condemnation, you understand. One of my minor disciplines.

BUTLER (*generally, looking at the bottle*). The port is eighteen-oh-six. (*To the* LAWYER.) How do they fortify wines, again?

JULIAN. Alcohol is added, more alcohol . . . at the time of casking. Fortify . . . strengthen.

BUTLER. Ah, yes.

LAWYER (*to* JULIAN). Of course, your grandfather was a vintner, was he not.

JULIAN. Goodness, you . . . you have my history.

LAWYER. Oh, we do. Such a mild life . . . save those six years in your thirties

Darien Public Library
7516 Cass Ave.
Darien, IL. 60559

which are . . . blank . . . in our report on you.

JULIAN (*a good covering laugh*). Oh, they were . . . mild, in their own way. Blank, but not black.

LAWYER. Will you fill them for us? The blank years?

JULIAN (*taking the glass from* BUTLER). Thank you. (*The laugh again.*) They were nothing.

LAWYER (*steelier*). Still, you will fill them for us.

JULIAN (*pleasant, but very firm*). No.

BUTLER. Gracious!

LAWYER. Recalcitrance, yes . . . well, we must have our people dig further.

JULIAN. You'll find nothing interesting. You'll find some . . . upheaval, but . . . waste, mostly. Dull waste.

LAWYER. The look of most of our vices in retrospect, eh?

BUTLER (*light*). I have fleshpot visions: carousals, thighs and heavy perfume. . . .

LAWYER (*to* BUTLER). It's in your mind, fitting, a mind worthy of your name. (*To* JULIAN.) Did you two . . . did he tell you his name, and did you two have a veritable badminton over it? Puns and chuckles?

JULIAN. We . . . labored it a bit, I more than . . . Butler, it would appear.

BUTLER. I was churlish, I'm sorry. If there weren't so many of *you* and only one of *me* . . .

JULIAN. Oh, now . . .

LAWYER (*still on it*). You're not going to tell me about those six years, eh?

JULIAN (*stares at him for a moment, then says it clearly, enunciating*). No.

(LAWYER *shrugs.*)

BUTLER. May I have some port?

LAWYER (*slightly incredulous*). Do you *like* port?

BUTLER. Not very, but I thought I'd keep him company while you play police.

LAWYER (*shrugs again*). It's not my house. (*Turns to* JULIAN.) One can't say, "It's not my castle," can one? (*Back to* BUTLER.) If you think it's proper.

BUTLER (*getting himself some*). Well, with the wine cellar stacked like a munitions dump, and you "never having any" until the barn swallows start screeping around . . .

LAWYER. There's no such word as screep.

BUTLER (*shrugs*). Fit.

JULIAN. I think it has a nice onomatopoetic ring about it . . .

LAWYER (*down to business, rather rudely*). Your buddy told you why we sent for you?

JULIAN (*offended, but pretending confusion*). My . . . buddy?

LAWYER. Mine, really. We were at school together. Did he tell you that? (*As* JULIAN *intentionally looks blank.*) His Eminence.

JULIAN. Ah!

LAWYER (*imitation*). Ah! (*Snapped.*) Well? Did he?

JULIAN (*choosing his words carefully, precisely*). His Eminence informed me . . . generally. He called me into his . . .

LAWYER. . . . garden . . .

JULIAN. . . . garden . . . which is a comfortable office in summer . . .

BUTLER. Ninety-six today.

JULIAN (*interested*). Indeed!

BUTLER. More tomorrow.

LAWYER (*impatiently*). Called you into his garden.

JULIAN. And—sorry—and . . . told me of the high honor which he had chosen for me.

LAWYER (*scoffing*). He. Chosen. You.

JULIAN. Of . . . your lady's most . . .

LAWYER. Miss Alice.

JULIAN. Of Miss Alice's—sorry, I've not met the lady yet, and first names—of her overwhelming bequest to the Church . . .

LAWYER. Not a bequest; a bequest is made in a will; Miss Alice is not dead.

JULIAN. Uh . . . grant?

LAWYER. Grant.

JULIAN (*taking a deep breath*). Of her overwhelming grant to the Church, and of my assignment to come here, to take care of . . .

LAWYER. Odds and ends.

JULIAN (*shrugs one shoulder*). . . . if you like. "A few questions and answers" was how it was put to me.

BUTLER (*to* LAWYER, *impressed*). He's a lay brother.

LAWYER (*bored*). We *know*. (*For* JULIAN's *benefit.*) His Eminence—buddy . . .

JULIAN (*natural, sincere*). Tch-tch-tch-tch-tch . . .

LAWYER. He was my buddy at school . . . if you don't mind. (*Beginning, now, to* BUTLER, *but quickly becoming general.*) His Eminence—though you have never met him, Butler, seen him, perhaps—is a most . . . eminent man; and bold, very bold; behind—or, underneath—what would seem to be a solid rock of . . . pomposity, sham, peacocking, there is a . . . flows a secret river . . . of . . .

BUTLER (*for* JULIAN's *benefit*). This is an endless metaphor.

LAWYER. . . . of unconventionality, defiance, even. Simple sentences? Is that all you want? Did you know that Brother Julian here is the only lay brother in the history of Christendom assigned, chosen, as secretary and confidant to a Prince of the Church? Ever?

JULIAN (*mildly*). That is not known as fact.

LAWYER. Name others!

JULIAN. I say it is not known as fact. I grant it is not usual—my appointment as secretary to His Eminence. . . .

LAWYER (*faint disgust*). An honor, at any rate, an unusual honor for a lay brother, an honor accorded by a most unusual Prince of the Church—a prince of a man, in fact—a prince whose still waters . . . well, you finish it.

BUTLER (*pretending puzzlement as to how to finish it*). . . . whose still waters . . .

JULIAN. His Eminence is, indeed, a most unusual man.

LAWYER (*sourly*). I said he was a prince.

BUTLER (*pretending to be talking to himself*). . . . run quiet? Run deep? Run *deep! That's* good!

LAWYER. Weren't there a few eyebrows raised at your appointment?

JULIAN. There . . . I was not informed of it . . . if there were. His Eminence would not burden me. . . .

LAWYER (*still to* JULIAN, *patronizing*). He is really Santa Claus; we know.

JULIAN (*rising to it*). Your animosity toward His Eminence must make your task very difficult for you. I must say I . . .

LAWYER. I have learned . . . (*Brief pause before he says the name with some distaste.*) Brother Julian . . . never to confuse the representative of a . . . thing with the thing itself.

BUTLER. . . . though I wonder if you'd intended to get involved in *two* watery metaphors there: underground river, and still waters.

LAWYER (*to* BUTLER). No, I had not. (*Back to* JULIAN.) A thing with its representative. Your Cardinal and I loathe one another, and I find him unworthy of contempt. (*A hand up to stop any coming objection.*) A cynic and a hypocrite, a

posturer, but all the same the representative of an august and revered . . . body.

JULIAN (*murmured*). You are most unjust.

LAWYER (*as if he were continuing a prepared speech*). Uh . . . revered body. And Rome, in its perhaps wily—though certainly inscrutable—wisdom, Rome has found reason to appoint that wreckage as its representative.

JULIAN. Really, I can't permit you to talk that way.

LAWYER. You will permit it, you're under instructions, you have a job to do. In fact, you have this present job be*cause* I cannot stand your Cardinal.

JULIAN. He . . . he did not tell me so.

LAWYER. *We* tell you so.

(JULIAN *dips his head to one side in a "perhaps it is true" gesture.*)

And it is so.

JULIAN. I will not . . . I will not concern myself with . . . all this.

BUTLER (*quite to himself*). I don't *like* port.

LAWYER (*to* BUTLER). Then don't drink it. (*To* JULIAN.) You're quite right: bow your head, stop up your ears and do what you're told.

JULIAN. Obedience is not a fault.

LAWYER. Nor always a virtue. See Fascism.

JULIAN (*rather strong for him*). Perhaps we can get on with our business. . . .

LAWYER (*he, too*). You don't want to take up my time, or your own.

JULIAN. Yes.

BUTLER (*putting down glass*). Then I won't drink it.

LAWYER (*to* JULIAN, *briskly, as to a servant*). All right! I shall tell Miss Alice you've come—that the drab fledgling is pecking away in the library, impatient for . . . food for the Church.

JULIAN (*a tight smile, a tiny formal bow*). If you would be so kind.

LAWYER (*twisting the knife*). I'll find out if she cares to see you today.

JULIAN (*ibid.*). Please.

LAWYER (*moving toward the archway*). And, if she cares to, I will have you brought up.

JULIAN (*mild surprise, but not a question*). Up.

LAWYER (*almost challenging him*). Up. (*Pause.*) You will not tell us about the six years—those years blank but not black . . . the waste, the dull waste.

JULIAN (*small smile*). No.

LAWYER (*he, too*). You will . . . in time. (*To* BUTLER.) Won't he, Butler? Time? The great revealer?

(LAWYER *exits.*)

JULIAN (*after the* LAWYER *is gone; no indignation*). Well.

BUTLER (*offhand*). Nasty man.

JULIAN (*intentionally feigning surprise*). Oh? (HE *and* BUTLER *laugh.*) Up.

BUTLER. Sir?

JULIAN. Up.

BUTLER. Oh! Yes! She . . . (*Moves to the model.*) has her apartments up . . . here. (*He points to a tower area.*) Here.

JULIAN. A-ha.

BUTLER (*straightening things up*). About those six years . . .

JULIAN (*not unfriendly, very matter-of-fact*). What of them?

BUTLER. Yes, what of them?

JULIAN. Oh . . . (*Pause.*) I . . . I lost my faith. (*Pause.*) In God.

BUTLER. Ah. (*Then a questioning look.*)

JULIAN. Is there more?

BUTLER. *Is* there more?

JULIAN. Well, nothing . . . of matter. I . . . declined. I . . . shriveled into myself; a glass dome . . . descended, and it seemed I was out of reach, unreachable, finally unreaching, in this . . . paralysis, of sorts. I . . . put myself in a mental home.

BUTLER (*curiously noncommittal*). Ah.

JULIAN. I could not reconcile myself to the chasm between the nature of God and the use to which men put . . . God.

BUTLER. Between your God and others', your view and theirs.

JULIAN. I said what I intended: (*Weighs the opposites in each hand.*) It is God the mover, not God the puppet; God the creator, not the God created by man.

BUTLER (*almost pitying*). Six years in the loony bin for semantics?

JULIAN (*slightly flustered, heat*). It is not semantics! Men create a false God in their own image, it is easier for them! . . . It is not . . .

BUTLER. Levity! Forget it!

JULIAN. I . . . yes.

(*A chime sounds.*)

BUTLER. Miss Alice will see you. I will take you up.

JULIAN. Forgive me . . . I . . .

BUTLER (*moves toward archway*). Let me show you up.

JULIAN. You *did* ask me.

BUTLER (*level*). Yes, and you told me.

JULIAN (*an explanation, not an apology*). My faith and my sanity . . . they are one and the same.

BUTLER. Yes? (*Considers it.*) A-ha. (*Smiles noncommittally.*) We must not keep the lady waiting.

(*They begin exiting,* BUTLER *preceding* JULIAN.)

CURTAIN

SCENE THREE

An upstairs sitting room of the castle. Feminine, but not frilly. Blues instead of pinks. Fireplace in keeping with the castle. A door to the bedroom in the rear wall, stage left; a door from the hallway in the side wall, stage left.

At rise, MISS ALICE *is seated in a wing chair, facing windows, its back to the audience; the* LAWYER *is to one side, facing her.*

————

LAWYER (*pause, he has finished one sentence, is pondering another*). . . . Nor is it as simple as all that. The instinct of giving may die out in our time—if you'll grant that giving is an instinct. The government is far more interested in taking, in regulated taking, than in promoting spontaneous generosity. Remember what I told you—what we discussed—in reference to the charitable foundations, and how . . . (*A knock on the hall door.*) That will be our bird of prey. Pray. P-R-A-Y. What a pun I could make on that; bird of pray. Come in.

(*The hall door opens;* BUTLER *precedes* JULIAN *into the room.*)

BUTLER. Brother Julian, who *was* in the library, is now here.

LAWYER. So he is. (*To* JULIAN, *impatiently.*) Come in, *come* in.

JULIAN (*advancing a little*). Yes . . . certainly.

BUTLER. May I go? I'm tired.

LAWYER (*grandly*). By all means.

BUTLER (*turns to go*). Thank you. (*To* JULIAN.) Goodbye.

JULIAN. Goodb . . . I'll . . . we'll see one another again?

BUTLER. Oh. Yes, probably. (*As he exits.*) Goodbye, everybody.

LAWYER (*after* BUTLER *exits, chuckles*). What is it the nouveaux riches are always saying? "You can't get good servants nowadays"?

JULIAN. He seems . . .

LAWYER (*curt*). He is very good. (*Turns to the chair.*) Miss Alice, our Brother Julian is here. (*Repeats it, louder.*) OUR BROTHER JULIAN IS HERE. (*To* JULIAN.) She's terribly hard of hearing. (*To* MISS ALICE.) DO YOU WANT TO SEE HIM? (*To* JULIAN.) I think she's responding. Sometimes . . . well, at her age and condition . . . twenty minutes can go by . . . for her to assimilate a sentence and reply to it.

JULIAN. But I thought . . . His Eminence said she was . . . young.

LAWYER. SHHHHHHHH! She's moving.

(MISS ALICE *slowly rises from her chair and comes around it. Her face is that of a withered crone, her hair gray and white and matted; she is bent; she moves with two canes.*)

MISS ALICE (*finally, with a cracked and ancient voice, to* JULIAN). Hello there, young man.

LAWYER (*as* JULIAN *takes a step forward*). Hah! Don't come too close, you'll unnerve her.

JULIAN. But I'm terribly puzzled. I was led to believe that she was a young woman, and . . .

MISS ALICE. Hello there, young man.

LAWYER. Speak to her.

JULIAN. Miss . . . Miss Alice, how do you do?

LAWYER. Louder.

JULIAN. HOW DO YOU DO?

MISS ALICE (*to* LAWYER). How do I do *what*?

LAWYER. It's a formality.

MISS ALICE. WHAT!?

LAWYER. IT IS A FORMALITY, AN OPENING GAMBIT.

MISS ALICE. Oh. (*To* JULIAN.) How do *you* do?

JULIAN. Very well . . . thank you.

MISS ALICE. WHAT!?

JULIAN. VERY WELL, THANK YOU.

MISS ALICE. Don't you scream at me!

JULIAN (*mumbled*). Sorry.

MISS ALICE. WHAT!?

JULIAN. SORRY!

MISS ALICE (*almost a pout*). Oh.

LAWYER (*who has enjoyed this*). Well, I think I'll leave you two now . . . for your business. I'm sure you'll have a . . .

JULIAN (*an attempted urgent aside to the* LAWYER). Do you think you . . . shouldn't you be here? You've . . . you've had more experience with her, and . . .

LAWYER (*laughing*). No, no, you'll get along fine. (*To* MISS ALICE.) I'LL LEAVE YOU TWO TOGETHER NOW. (MISS ALICE *nods vigorously.*) HIS NAME IS BROTHER JULIAN, AND THERE ARE SIX YEARS MISSING FROM HIS LIFE. (*She nods again.*) I'LL BE DOWNSTAIRS. (*Begins to leave.*)

MISS ALICE (*when the* LAWYER *is at the door*). Don't steal anything.

LAWYER (*exiting*). ALL RIGHT!

JULIAN (*after a pause, begins bravely, taking a step forward*). Perhaps you should sit down. Let me . . .

MISS ALICE. WHAT!?

JULIAN. PERHAPS YOU SHOULD SIT DOWN!

MISS ALICE (*not fear; malevolence*). Keep away from me!

JULIAN. Sorry. (*To himself.*) Oh, really, this is impossible.

MISS ALICE. WHAT!?

JULIAN. I SAID THIS WAS IMPOSSIBLE.

MISS ALICE (*thinks about that for a moment, then*). If you're a defrocked priest, what're you doing in all that? (*Pointing to* JULIAN'*s garb.*)

JULIAN. I AM NOT A DEFROCKED PRIEST, I AM A LAY BROTHER. I HAVE NEVER BEEN A PRIEST.

MISS ALICE. What did you drink downstairs?

JULIAN. I had a glass of port . . . PORT!

MISS ALICE (*a spoiled, crafty child*). You didn't bring *me* one.

JULIAN. I had no idea you . . .

MISS ALICE. WHAT!?

JULIAN. SHALL I GET YOU A GLASS?

MISS ALICE. A glass of *what*.

JULIAN. PORT. A GLASS OF PORT.

MISS ALICE (*as if he were crazy*). What for?

JULIAN. BECAUSE YOU . . . (*To himself again.*) Really, this *won't* do.

MISS ALICE (*straightening up, ridding herself of the canes, assuming a normal voice*). I agree with you, it won't do, really.

JULIAN (*astonishment*). I beg your pardon?

MISS ALICE. I said it won't do at all.

(SHE *unfastens and removes her wig, unties and takes off her mask, becomes*

herself, as JULIAN *watches, openmouthed.*)
There. Is that better? And you needn't
yell at me any more; if anything, my hearing is *too* good.

JULIAN (*slightly put out*). I . . . I don't
understand.

MISS ALICE. Are you annoyed?

JULIAN. I suspect I will be . . . might
be . . . after the surprise leaves me.

MISS ALICE (*smiling*). Don't be; it's only
a little game.

JULIAN. Yes, doubtless. But why?

MISS ALICE. Oh, indulge us, please.

JULIAN. Well, of course, it would be my
pleasure . . . but, considering the importance of our meeting . . .

MISS ALICE. Exactly. Considering the importance of our meeting.

JULIAN. A . . . a test for me.

MISS ALICE (*laughs*). No, not at all, a
little lightness to counter the weight.
(*Mock seriousness.*) For we are involved
in weighty matters . . . the transfer of
millions, the rocking of empires. (*Normal, light tone again.*) Let's be comfortable, shall we? Swing my chair around.
(JULIAN *moves to do so.*) As you can see
—you *can,* I trust—I'm *not* a hundred and
thirteen years old, but I *do* have my crotch-
ets, even now: I have chairs everywhere
that are mine—in each room . . . a chair
that is mine, that I alone use.

JULIAN (*moving the chair*). Where
would you . . .

MISS ALICE (*lightly*). Just . . . swing it
. . . around. You needn't move it. Good.
Now, sit with me. (*They sit.*) Fine. In the
dining room, of course, there is no question—I sit at the head of the table. But, in
the drawing rooms, or the library, or whatever room you wish to mention, I have a
chair that I consider my possession.

JULIAN. But you possess the entire . . .
(*Thinks of a word.*) establishment.

MISS ALICE. Of course, but it is such a
large . . . establishment that one needs
the feel of specific possession in every . . .
area.

JULIAN (*rather shy, but pleasant*). Do
you become . . . cross if someone acci-
dentally assumes your chair, one of your
chairs?

MISS ALICE (*thinks about it, then*). How
odd! Curiously, it has never happened, so
I cannot say. Tell me about yourself.

JULIAN. Well, there isn't much to say
. . . much that isn't already known. Your

lawyer would seem to have assembled a
casebook on me, and . . .

MISS ALICE. Yes, yes, but not the things
that would interest him, the things that
would interest me.

JULIAN (*genuine interest*). And what
are they?

MISS ALICE (*laughs again*). Let me see.
Ah! Do I terrify you?

JULIAN. You *did,* and you are still . . .
awesome.

MISS ALICE (*sweetly*). Thank you. Did
my lawyer intimidate you?

JULIAN. It would seem to be his nature
—or his pleasure—to intimidate, and . . .
well, I am, perhaps, more easily intimidated than some.

MISS ALICE. Perhaps you are, but he *is* a
professional. And how did you find Butler?

JULIAN. A gentle man, quick . . . but
mostly gentle.

MISS ALICE. Gentle, yes. He was my lover
at one time. (*As* JULIAN *averts his head.*)
Oh! Perhaps I shouldn't have told you.

JULIAN. No, forgive me. Things sometimes . . . are so unexpected.

MISS ALICE. Yes, they are. I am presently
mistress to my lawyer—the gentleman
who intimidated you so. He is a pig.

JULIAN (*embarrassed*). Yes, yes. You
have . . . never married.

MISS ALICE (*quiet amusement*). Alas.

JULIAN. You are . . . not Catholic.

MISS ALICE (*the same*). Again, alas.

JULIAN. No, it is fortunate you are not.

MISS ALICE. I am bored with my present
lover.

JULIAN. I . . . (*Shrugs.*)

MISS ALICE. I was not soliciting advice.

JULIAN (*quiet laugh*). Good, for I have
none.

MISS ALICE. These six years of yours.

JULIAN (*says it all in one deep breath*).
There is no mystery to it, my faith in God
left me, and I committed myself to an asylum. (*Pause.*) You see? Nothing to it.

MISS ALICE. What an odd place to go to
look for one's faith.

JULIAN. You misunderstand me. I did
not go there to *look* for my faith, but because *it* had left me.

MISS ALICE. You tell it so easily.

JULIAN (*shrugs*). It is easy to tell.

MISS ALICE. Ah.

JULIAN (*giggles a little*). However, I

would not tell your present . . . uh, your lawyer. And that made him quite angry.

MISS ALICE. Have you slept with many women?

JULIAN (*carefully*). I am not certain.

MISS ALICE (*tiny laugh*). It is an easy enough thing to determine.

JULIAN. Not so. For one, I am celibate. A lay brother—you must know—while not a priest, while not ordained, is still required to take vows. And chastity is one of them.

MISS ALICE. A dedicated gesture, to be sure, celibacy without priesthood . . . but a melancholy one, for you're a handsome man . . . in your way.

JULIAN. You're kind.

MISS ALICE. But, tell me: why did you not become a priest? Having gone so far, I should think . . .

JULIAN. A lay brother serves.

MISS ALICE. . . . but is not ordained, is more a servant.

JULIAN. The house of God is so grand . . . (*Sweet apologetic smile.*) it needs many servants.

MISS ALICE. How humble. But is that the only reason?

JULIAN. I am not wholly reconciled. Man's God and mine are not . . . close friends.

MISS ALICE. Indeed. But, tell me, how are you not certain that you have slept with a woman?

JULIAN (*with curiosity*). Shall I tell you? We have many more important matters. . . .

MISS ALICE. Tell me, please. The money will not run off. Great wealth is patient.

JULIAN. I would not know. Very well. It's good for me, I think, to talk about it. The institution . . . to which I committed myself—it was deep inland, by the way— was a good one, good enough, and had, as I am told most do, sections—buildings, or floors of buildings—for patients in various conditions . . . some for violent cases, for example, others for children. . . .

MISS ALICE. How sad.

JULIAN. Yes. Well, at any rate . . . sections. Mine . . . my section was for people who were . . . mildly troubled—which I found ironic, for I have never considered the fleeing of faith a mild matter. Nonetheless, for the mildly troubled. The windows were not barred; one was allowed utensils, and one's own clothes. You see,

escape was not a matter of urgency, for it was a section for mildly troubled people who had committed themselves, and should escape occur, it was not a danger for the world outside.

MISS ALICE. I understand.

JULIAN. There was a period during my stay, however, when I began to . . . hallucinate, and to withdraw, to a point where I was not entirely certain when my mind was tricking me, or when it was not. I believe one would say—how is it said?—that my grasp on reality was . . . tenuous—occasionally. There was, at the same time, in my section, a woman who, on very infrequent occasions, believed that she was the Virgin Mary.

MISS ALICE (*mild surprise*). My goodness.

JULIAN. A quiet woman, plain, but soft features, not hard; at forty, or a year either side, married, her husband the owner of a dry-goods store, if my memory is correct; childless . . . the sort of woman, in short, that one is not aware of passing on the street, or in a hallway . . . unlike you— if you will permit me.

MISS ALICE (*smiles*). It may be I am . . . noticeable, but almost never identified.

JULIAN. You shun publicity.

MISS ALICE. Oh, indeed. And I have few friends . . . that, too, by choice. (*Urges him on with a gesture.*) But please . . .

JULIAN. Of course. My hallucinations . . . were saddening to me. I suspect I should have been frightened of them—as well as by them—most people are, or would be . . . by hallucinations. But I was . . . saddened. They were, after all, provoked, brought on by the departure of my faith, and this in turn was brought on by the manner in which people mock God. . . .

MISS ALICE. I notice you do not say you lost your faith, but that it abandoned you.

JULIAN. Do I. Perhaps at bottom I had lost it, but I think more that I was confused . . . *and* intimidated . . . by the world about me, and let slip contact with it . . . with my faith. So, I was *sad*dened.

MISS ALICE. Yes.

JULIAN. The periods of hallucination would be announced by a ringing in the ears, which produced, or was accompanied by, a loss of hearing. I would hear people's voices from a great distance and through the roaring of . . . surf. And my body would feel light, and not mine, and I would float—no, glide.

MISS ALICE. There was no feeling of terror in this? I would be beside myself.

JULIAN. No, as I said, sadness. Aaaaahhh, I would think, I am going from myself again. How very, very sad . . . everything. Loss, great loss.

MISS ALICE. I understand.

JULIAN. And when I was away from myself—never far enough, you know, to . . . blank, just to . . . fog over—when I was away from myself I could not sort out my imaginings from what was real. Oh, sometimes I would say to a nurse or one of the attendants, "Could you tell me, did I preach last night? To the patients? A fire-and-brimstone lesson. Did I do that, or did I imagine it?" And they would tell me, if they knew.

MISS ALICE. And did you?

JULIAN. Hm? . . . No, it would seem I did not . . . to their knowledge. But I was never sure, you see.

MISS ALICE (*nodding*). No.

JULIAN (*a brief, rueful laugh*). I imagined so many things, or . . . did so many things I thought I had imagined. The uncertainty . . . you know?

MISS ALICE (*smiles*). Are you sure you're not describing what passes for sanity?

JULIAN (*laughs briefly, ruefully*). Perhaps. But one night . . . now, there! You see? I said "one night," and I'm not sure, even now, whether or not this thing happened or, if it did not happen, it did or did not happen at noon, or in the morning, much less at night . . . yet I say night. Doubtless one will do as well as another. So. One *night* the following either happened or did not happen. I was walking in the gardens—or I imagined I was walking in the gardens—walking in the gardens, and I heard a sound . . . sounds from near where a small pool stood, with rosebushes, rather overgrown, a formal garden once, the . . . the place had been an estate, I remember being told. Sounds . . . sobbing? Low cries. And there was, as well, the ringing in my ears, and . . . and fog, a . . . a milkiness, between myself and . . . everything. I went toward the cries, the sounds, and . . . I, I fear my description will become rather . . . vivid now. . . .

MISS ALICE. I am a grown woman.

JULIAN (*nods*). Yes. (*A deep breath.*)

The . . . the woman, the woman I told you about, who hallucinated, herself, that she was the Virgin . . .

MISS ALICE. Yes, yes.

JULIAN. . . . was . . . was on a grassy space by the pool—or this is what I imagined—on the ground, and she was in her . . . a nightdress, a . . . gossamer, filmy thing, or perhaps she was not, but there she was, on the ground, on an incline, a slight incline, and when she saw me—or sensed me there—she raised her head, and put her arms . . . (*Demonstrates.*) . . . out, in a . . . supplication, and cried, "Help me, help me . . . help me, oh God, God, help me . . . oh, help, help." This, over and over, and with the sounds in her throat between. I . . . I came closer, and the sounds, her sounds, her words, the roaring in my ears, the gossamer and the milk film, I . . . a ROAR, AN OCEAN! Saliva, perfume, sweat, the taste of blood and rich earth in the mouth, sweet sweaty slipping . . . (*Looks to her apologetically, nods.*) . . . ejaculation. (*She nods.*) The sound cascading away, the rhythms breaking, everything slowly, limpid, quieter, damper, soft . . . soft, quiet . . . done.

(*They are both silent.* MISS ALICE *is gripping the arms of her chair;* JULIAN *continues softly.*)

I have described it to you, as best I can, as it . . . happened, or did not happen.

MISS ALICE (*curiously . . . dispassionately*). I . . . am a very beautiful woman.

JULIAN(*after a pause which serves as reply to her statement*). I must tell you more, though. You *have* asked me for an entirety.

MISS ALICE. And a very rich one.

JULIAN (*brief pause, nods*). As I mentioned to you, the woman was given to hallucinations as well, but perhaps I should have said that being the Virgin Mary was merely the strongest of her . . . delusions; she . . . hallucinated . . . as well as the next person, about perfectly mundane matters, too. So it may be that now we come to coincidence, or it may not. Shortly—several days—after the encounter I have described to you—the encounter which did or did not happen—the woman . . . I do not know which word to use here, either descended or ascended into an ecstasy, the substance of which was that she was with child . . . that she was pregnant with the Son of God.

MISS ALICE. And I live here, in all these rooms.

JULIAN. You don't laugh? Well, perhaps you will, at *me*. I was . . . beside myself, for I assumed the piling of delusion upon delusion, though the chance of there being fact, happening, there somewhere . . . I went to my . . . doctor and told him of my hallucination—if indeed that is what it was. He told me, then . . . that the woman had been examined, that she was suffering from cancer of the womb, that it was advanced, had spread. In a month, she died.

MISS ALICE. Did you believe it?

JULIAN (*small smile*). That she died?

MISS ALICE. That you spoke with your doctor.

JULIAN (*pause*). It has never occurred to me until this moment to doubt it. He has informed me many times.

MISS ALICE. Ah?

JULIAN. I *do see* him . . . in reality. We have become friends, we talk from time to time. Socially.

MISS ALICE. Ah. And was it he who discharged you from . . . your asylum?

JULIAN. I was persuaded, eventually, that perhaps I was . . . overconcerned by hallucination; that some was inevitable, and a portion of that—even desirable.

MISS ALICE. Of course.

JULIAN (*looking at his hands*). Have I answered your question? That I am not . . . sure that I have slept with a woman.

MISS ALICE (*puzzling . . . slowly*). I don't . . . know. Is the memory of something having happened the same as it having happened?

JULIAN. It is not the nicest of . . . occurrences—to have described to you.

MISS ALICE (*kindly*). It was many years ago. (*Then, an afterthought.*) Was it not?

JULIAN. Yes, yes, quite a while ago.

MISS ALICE (*vaguely amused*). I am rich and I am beautiful and I live here in all these rooms . . . without relatives, with a . . . (*Wry.*) companion, from time to time . . . (*Leans forward, whispers, but still amused.*) . . . and with a secret.

JULIAN. Oh? (*Trying to be light, too.*) And may I know it? The secret?

MISS ALICE. I don't know yet.

JULIAN (*relaxing*). Ah-ha.

MISS ALICE (*sudden change of mood, to brisk, official, cool*). Well then. You're here on business, not for idle conversation, I believe.

JULIAN (*confused, even a little hurt*). Oh . . . yes, that's . . . that's right.

MISS ALICE. You have instruction to give me—not formal, I'm not about to settle in your faith. Information, facts, questions and answers.

JULIAN (*slightly sour*). Odds and ends, I believe.

MISS ALICE (*sharp*). To you, perhaps. But important if you're to succeed, if you're not to queer the whole business, if you're not to . . .

JULIAN. Yes, yes!

MISS ALICE. So you'll be coming back here . . . when I wish to see you.

JULIAN. Yes.

MISS ALICE. Several times. It might be better if you were to move in. I'll decide it.

JULIAN. Oh . . . well, of course, if you think . . .

MISS ALICE. I think. (JULIAN *nods acquiescence.*) Very good. (*She rises.*) No more today, no more now.

JULIAN (*up, maybe retreating a little*). Well, if you'll let me know when . . .

MISS ALICE. Come here.

(JULIAN *goes to her; she takes his head in her hands, kisses him on the forehead, he registers embarrassment, she laughs, a slightly mocking, unnerving laugh.*)

Little recluse. (*Laughs again.*)

JULIAN. If you'll . . . advise me, or His Eminence, when you'd like me to . . .

MISS ALICE. Little bird, pecking away in the library. (*Laughs again.*)

JULIAN. I'm . . . disappointed you find me so . . . humorous.

MISS ALICE (*cheerful, but not contrite*). Oh, forgive me, I live so alone, the oddest things cheer me up. You . . . cheer me up. (*Holds out her hand to be kissed.*) Here. (JULIAN *hesitates.*) Ah-ah-ah, he who hesitates loses all.

(JULIAN *hesitates again, momentarily, then kisses her hand, but kneeling, as he would kiss a Cardinal's ring.* MISS ALICE *laughs at this.*)

Do you think I am a Cardinal? Do I look like a Prince? Have you never even kissed a woman's hand?

JULIAN (*back on his feet, evenly*). No. I have not.

MISS ALICE (*kindlier now*). I'll send for

you, we'll have . . . pleasant afternoons, you and I. Goodbye.

(MISS ALICE *turns away from* JULIAN, *gazes out a window, her back to the audience.* JULIAN *exits. The* LAWYER *enters the set from the bedroom door.*)

LAWYER (*to* MISS ALICE, *a bit abruptly*). How did it go, eh?

MISS ALICE (*turns around, matter-of-factly*). Not badly.

LAWYER. You took long enough.

(MISS ALICE *shrugs.*)

When are you having him again?

MISS ALICE (*very wickedly*). On business, or privately?

LAWYER. Don't be childish.

MISS ALICE. Whenever you like, whenever you say. (*Seriously.*) Tell me honestly, do you really think we're wise?

LAWYER. Wise? Well, we'll see. If we prove not, I can't think of anything standing in the way that can't be destroyed. (*Pause.*) Can you?

MISS ALICE (*rather sadly*). No. Nothing.

CURTAIN

ACT TWO

SCENE ONE

The library—as of Act One, Scene Two. No one on stage. Evening. MISS ALICE *hurtles through the archway, half running, half backing, with the* LAWYER *after her. It is not a chase; she has just broken from him, and her hurtling is the result of sudden freeing.*

MISS ALICE (*just before and as she is entering; her tone is neither hysterical nor frightened; she is furious and has been mildly hurt*). KEEP . . . GO! GET YOUR . . . LET GO OF ME (*She is in the room.*) KEEP OFF! KEEP OFF ME!

LAWYER (*excited, ruffled, but trying to maintain decorum*). Don't be hysterical, now.

MISS ALICE (*still moving away from him, as he comes on*). KEEP . . . AWAY. JUST STAY AWAY FROM ME.

LAWYER. I said don't be hysterical.

MISS ALICE. I'll *show* you hysteria. I'll give you *fireworks!* KEEP! Keep away.

LAWYER (*soothing, but always moving in on her*). A simple touch, an affectionate hand on you; nothing more . . .

MISS ALICE (*quiet loathing*). You're degenerate.

LAWYER (*steely*). An affectionate hand, in the privacy of a hallway . . .

MISS ALICE (*almost a shriek*). THERE ARE PEOPLE!!

LAWYER. Where? There are no people.

MISS ALICE (*between her teeth*). There are people.

LAWYER (*feigning surprise*). There are no people. (*To a child.*) Ahh! (*Walks toward the model, indicates it.*) Unless you mean all the little people running around inside here. Is that what you mean?

MISS ALICE (*a mirthless, don't-you-know-it laugh*). Hunh-hunh-hunh-hunh.

LAWYER. Is that who you mean? All the little people in here? (*Change of tone to normal, if sarcastic.*) Why don't we show them a few of your tricks, hunh?

MISS ALICE (*moving away, clenched teeth again*). Keep . . . away . . . from . . . me.

LAWYER (*without affection*). To love is to possess, and since I desire to possess you, that must mean conversely that I love you, must it not. Come here.

MISS ALICE (*with great force*). PEOPLE!

LAWYER. Your little priest? Your little Julian? He is not . . .

MISS ALICE. He is not a priest!

LAWYER. No. And he is not nearby—momentarily! (*Hissed.*) I am sick of him here day after day, sick of the time you're taking. Will you get it done with!

MISS ALICE. No! He will be *up.*

LAWYER. Oh, for Christ's sake, he's a connoisseur; he'll be nosing around the goddam wine cellar for hours!

MISS ALICE. He will be *up.* (*Afterthought.*) Butler!

LAWYER (*advancing*). Butler? Let him watch. (*A sneer.*) Which is something I've been meaning to discuss with you for the longest time now. . . .

MISS ALICE (*calm, quivering hatred; almost laughing with it*). I have a loathing for you that I can't *describe.*

LAWYER. You were never one with words. (*Suddenly brutal.*) NOW, COME HERE.

MISS ALICE (*shrugs*). All right. I won't react, I promise you.

LAWYER (*beginning to fondle her*). Won't react . . . indeed.

(*During this next,* MISS ALICE *is backed up against something, and the* LAWYER *is calmly at her, kissing her neck, fondling her. She is calm, and at first he seems amused.*)

MISS ALICE. What causes this loathing I have for you? It's the *way* you have, I suppose; the clinical way; methodical, slow . . .

LAWYER. . . . thorough . . .

MISS ALICE. . . . uninvolved . . .

LAWYER. . . . oh, very involved . . .

MISS ALICE. . . . impersonality in the most personal things . . .

LAWYER. . . . your passivity is exciting . . .

MISS ALICE. . . . passive only to some people . . . (*He nips her.*) ow.

LAWYER. A little passion; good.

MISS ALICE (*as he continues fondling her; perhaps by the end he has her dress off her shoulders*). With so much . . . many things to loathe, I must choose carefully, to impress you most with it.

LAWYER. Um-humh.

MISS ALICE. Is it the hair? Is it the hair on your back I loathe most? Where the fat lies, on your shoulderblades, the hair on your back . . . black, ugly? . . .

LAWYER. But too short to get a hold on, eh?

MISS ALICE. Is it that—the back hair? It could be; it would be enough. Is it your . . . what is the polite word for it . . . your sex?

LAWYER (*mocking*). Careful now, with a man's pride.

MISS ALICE. Ugly; that too—ugly.

LAWYER (*unruffled*). Better than most, if you care for a *man* . . .

MISS ALICE. . . . ugly coarse uncut ragged . . . PUSH!

LAWYER. Push . . . yes . . .

MISS ALICE. . . . selfish, hurtful, ALWAYS! OVER AND OVER!

LAWYER. You like it; it feels good.

MISS ALICE (*very calm and analytical*). But is that what I loathe most? It could be; that would be enough, too.

LAWYER. . . . oh, what a list . . .

MISS ALICE. But I think it is most the feel of your skin . . . (*Hard.*) that you can't sweat. (*He stiffens some.*) That your body is as impersonal as your . . . self—dry, uncaring, rubbery . . . dead. Ah . . . there . . . that is what I loathe about you most: you're dead. Moving pushing selfish dry dead. (*Brief pause.*) Does that hurt? Does something finally, beautifully hurt?

(*Self-mocking laugh.*) Have I finally gotten . . . into you?

LAWYER (*a little away from her now*). Insensitive, still, aren't you, after all this time. Does it hurt? Does something finally hurt?

MISS ALICE. . . . deep, gouging hurt?

LAWYER. Everything! Everything in the day and night, eating, resting, walking, rutting, everything! Everything *hurts*.

MISS ALICE. Awwwwww.

LAWYER. Inside the . . . sensibility, everything hurts. Deeply.

MISS ALICE (*ridiculing*). And is that why I loathe you?

LAWYER (*a quiet, rueful laugh*). Probably. (*Quickly back to himself.*) But you, little playmate, you're what I want now. GIVE!

MISS ALICE. If Julian comes in here . . .

LAWYER (*shoves her*). Are you playing it straight, hunh? Or do you like your work a little bit, hunh? (*Again.*) Do you enjoy spreading your legs for the clergy? (*Again.*) Hunh?

MISS ALICE. STOP! . . . YOU!

LAWYER. Is that our private donation to the Church? Our own grant? YES? (*Begins to hurt her arm.*) Are we planning to turn into a charitable, educational foundation?

MISS ALICE (*in pain*). My arm!

(*BUTLER enters, unnoticed; watches.*)

LAWYER (*hard and very serious*). Don't you dare mess this thing up. You behave the way I've told you; you PLAYACT. You do your part; STRAIGHT.

BUTLER (*calmly*). Brother Julian . . .

MISS ALICE. Butler! Help me!

BUTLER (*as the LAWYER releases her*). . . . has now examined the wine cellar, with awe and much murmuring, and will be with us presently. He's peeing. So I suggest—unless you're doing this for his benefit—uh, you stop.

MISS ALICE (*as she and the LAWYER pull themselves together*). He hurt me, Butler.

BUTLER (*calmly, as if reminding her*). Often. (*To the LAWYER, with mock friendliness.*) Up to your old tricks, eh?

LAWYER (*dusting himself off*). She is . . . not behaving.

BUTLER (*very noncommittal*). Ah me.

MISS ALICE (*under her breath, to the LAWYER*). Savage! (*Realizes.*) Both of you!

LAWYER (*laughs*). The maiden in the shark pond.

MISS ALICE. He thinks I'm sleeping with Julian. (*To* LAWYER.) You poor jealous . . .

BUTLER. Are you?

MISS ALICE (*indignant*). No! (*Almost sad about it.*) No, I am not.

LAWYER. She is!

MISS ALICE. I said I am not!

BUTLER. Are you going to?

MISS ALICE (*after a pause; to* LAWYER). Am I going to? Am I going to . . . spread my legs for the clergy? Enjoy my work a little? Isn't that what you'd have me do? To not mess it up? To play my part straight? Isn't that what you'll HAVE ME DO?

LAWYER. You don't need urging! . . .

BUTLER. Now, children . . .

MISS ALICE. When the time comes? Won't you have me at him? Like it or not? Well . . . I will like it!

(*A little hard breathing from* MISS ALICE *and the* LAWYER.)

BUTLER. Something *should* be done about the wine cellar. I've noticed it—as a passerby would—but Brother Julian pointed out the extent of it to me: bottles have burst, are bursting, corks rotting . . . something to do with the temperature or the dampness. It's a shame, you know.

MISS ALICE (*surprisingly shrill*). Well, fix it!

BUTLER (*ignoring her tone*). Some great years, popping, dribbling away, going to vinegar under our feet. There is a Mouton Rothschild—one I'm especially fond of—that's . . .

LAWYER (*pacifying*). Do. Do . . . fix it.

BUTLER (*shakes his head*). Going. All of it. Great shame.

LAWYER. Yes, yes.

BUTLER (*brightly*). Nice thing about having Julian here so much . . . he's helpful. Wines, plants . . . do you know, he told me some astonishing things about ferns. We were in the solarium . . .

MISS ALICE (*quiet pleading*). Please . . . stop.

BUTLER. Oh. Well, it's nice having him about.

LAWYER (*sour*). Oh, we'll be a foursome very soon.

MISS ALICE (*brightly*). Yes.

LAWYER (*with a mirthless smile*). Warning.

BUTLER (*cheerful again*). It *would* be a great deal more sensible than . . . puttering out here every day. We could put him over the chapel! Now, that's a splendid idea. He likes the chapel, he said, not resonant, too small or something, wrong angles, but he likes it . . .

MISS ALICE. When he moves here . . .

LAWYER. He will move here when I say —and as I say.

MISS ALICE (*fake smile*). We shall see.

LAWYER (*still offhand*). We shall not see.

JULIAN (*offstage*). Halloo!

BUTLER. In . . . in here.

MISS ALICE (*sotto voce to the* LAWYER). You say we shall not see? *Shall* we?

LAWYER (*as above*). Warning.

(JULIAN *enters.*)

JULIAN. Ah! There you all are.

LAWYER. *We* had wondered where *you* were.

MISS ALICE (*reminding a child*). You usually find us here after dinner.

JULIAN. Yes, and a superb dinner.

LAWYER. . . . and then Butler reminded us that you were in the cellar.

JULIAN (*sincere, but prepared*). Miss Alice, your . . . home possesses two things that, were I a designer of houses—for the very wealthy, of course—I would put in all my designs.

MISS ALICE (*smiling*). And what are they?

LAWYER (*to* MISS ALICE, *mildly mocking* JULIAN). Can't you guess?

MISS ALICE (*charmingly*). Of course I can guess, but I want Julian to have the pleasure of saying it.

JULIAN. A chapel and a wine cellar.

MISS ALICE (*agreeing, but is she making light fun?*). Yes.

LAWYER. We hear, though, that the wine cellar is a wreck. And aren't there cobwebs in the chapel, too?

JULIAN (*light but standing up to him*). One or two spiders have been busy around the altar, and the organ is . . . in need of use . . .

LAWYER (*very funny to him*). HUNH!

JULIAN (*choosing to ignore it*). . . . but it *is* a chapel, a good one. The wine cellar, however . . . (*Shakes his head.*) . . . great, great shame.

BUTLER. Exactly my words.

MISS ALICE. Well, we must have it tended to—and especially since you are our guest so frequently these days, and enjoy good wines.

JULIAN. I would call someone in, a specialist, if I were you.

LAWYER (*patronizing*). Why? Can't you take care of it? Your domain?

JULIAN (*quietly*). The chapel, more, I should think.

BUTLER. Where does the Church get its wine . . . for Communion and the like?

JULIAN. Oh, it is grown, *made* . . . grown, the grapes, harvested, pressed . . . by, by monks.

LAWYER (*false heartiness*). A regular profit-making setup, the Church.

JULIAN (*quietly, as usual*). Self-sustaining . . . in some areas.

LAWYER. But not in others, eh? Sometimes the old beggar bell comes out, doesn't it? Priest as leper.

MISS ALICE (*mildly to the* LAWYER). It *is* true: you are not fit for God's sight.

BUTLER (*to the* LAWYER; *cheerfully interested*). Is that *so!* I wasn't sure.

LAWYER (*to* MISS ALICE, *feigning curiosity and surprise*). Who whispered it to you?

MISS ALICE (*indicating* JULIAN; *semi-serious*). My confessor.

LAWYER (*a sneer; to* JULIAN). *Did* you? And so *you* object, as well? To my mention of the Church as solicitor.

JULIAN. In England I believe *you* would be referred to as solicitor.

LAWYER. No, I would not. And we are not in England . . . are we?

BUTLER. This *place* was . . . in England.

MISS ALICE (*as if suddenly remembering*). Yes, it was! Every stone, marked and shipped.

JULIAN. Oh; I had thought it was a replica.

LAWYER. Oh no; that would have been too simple. Though it *is* a replica . . . in its way.

JULIAN. Of?

LAWYER (*pointing to the model*). Of that.

(JULIAN *laughs a little; the* LAWYER *shrugs.*)

Ah well.

JULIAN (*to* MISS ALICE). Did your . . . did your father have it . . . put up? (*A parenthesis.*) It suddenly occurred to me that I know nothing of your family, though I . . . I don't mean to pry . . .

MISS ALICE (*a private laugh*). No, we must not . . . well, should we say that?

That my father put it up? No. Let us not say that.

BUTLER (*To* JULIAN, *pointing first to the model, then to the room*). Do you mean the model . . . or the replica?

JULIAN. I mean the . . . I mean . . . what we are in.

BUTLER. *Ah*-ha. And which is that?

JULIAN. That we are in?

BUTLER. Yes.

LAWYER (*to* JULIAN). You are clearly not a Jesuit. (*Turning.*) Butler, you've put him in a clumsy trap.

BUTLER (*shrugging*). I'm only a servant.

LAWYER (*to* JULIAN, *too sweetly*). You needn't accept his alternative . . . that since we are clearly not in a model we must be in a replica.

BUTLER (*vaguely annoyed*). Why must he not accept that?

MISS ALICE. Yes. Why not?

LAWYER. I said he did not *need* to accept the alternative. I did not say it was not valid.

JULIAN (*cheerfully*). I will not accept it; the problem is only semantic.

BUTLER (*perhaps too consoling*). Well, yes; that's what I would have thought.

LAWYER. Not necessarily, though. Depends, doesn't it, on your concept of reality, on the limit of possibilities. . . .

MISS ALICE (*genuinely put off*). Oh, Lord!

LAWYER. There are no limits to possibi . . . (*Suddenly embarrassed.*) I'm . . . I'm sorry.

MISS ALICE (*to* JULIAN, *but at the* LAWYER). He starts in, he *will;* give him the most sophomoric conundrum, and he'll bore you to death.

LAWYER (*violently*). I! Will! Not!

JULIAN (*to break the silence*). Well . . . perhaps I'm at fault here.

MISS ALICE (*quietly, kindly*). How could you be? . . . Dear Julian.

LAWYER (*to* MISS ALICE; *burning*). I thought I had educated you; I thought I had drilled you sufficiently in matters of consequence; (*Growing louder.*) I thought I had made it clear to you the way you were to behave.

JULIAN. Perhaps I should leave now; I think that . . .

LAWYER. DON'T INTERRUPT ME!

(*Glares at* JULIAN, *who moves off to the model.*)

MISS ALICE (*to the* LAWYER; *calmly*). You forget your place.

LAWYER (*clearly trying to get hold of himself*). I . . . you . . . are quite right . . . Miss Alice, and abstractions *are* upsetting.

MISS ALICE (*to the* LAWYER; *patiently*). Perhaps you'll go home now.

BUTLER (*cheerfully*). Shall I have your car brought around?

LAWYER (*trying to be private in public*). I . . . I thought that with so much to attend to, I might . . . spend the night. Of course, if you'd rather I didn't . . .

(*Leaves it unfinished.* MISS ALICE *smiles enigmatically.*)

BUTLER (*pretending to think the remark was for him*). I don't *mind* whether you do or not.

JULIAN (*peering at the model, rather amazed*). Can it . . . can it be?

LAWYER. In the heat of . . . I, I forgot myself.

MISS ALICE (*patronizingly sweet*). Yes.

LAWYER (*matter-of-fact*). You will forgive me.

MISS ALICE (*toying*). Oh?

BUTLER. Shall I have his car brought around?

LAWYER (*sudden softening*). Let me stay.

JULIAN (*shy attempt at getting attention*). Please . . .

MISS ALICE (*malicious pleasure in it*). I don't know . . .

JULIAN (*more urgently*). Please!

LAWYER (*bitter*). As you wish, of course.

(*Swings his hand back as if to strike her; she flinches.*)

JULIAN. PLEASE!

BUTLER (*patiently amused curiosity*). What *is* it, for heaven's sake?

JULIAN (*pointing to the model*). The model is . . . on fire; it's on fire!

BUTLER (*urgent dropping of butlerish attitudes*). Where!

LAWYER. Good Christ!

MISS ALICE. Quick!

(*The* LAWYER *and* BUTLER *rush to the model.*)

BUTLER. *Where,* for Christ's sake!

JULIAN (*jostled*). In the . . . over the . . .

LAWYER. Find it!

BUTLER (*peering into various windows with great agitation*). It's . . . it's the . . . where the hell is it! . . . It's the . . . chapel! The chapel's burning!

MISS ALICE. Hurry!

BUTLER. Come on! Let's get to it! (*Begins to run out of the room.*) Are you coming? Julian!

JULIAN (*confused, but following*). But I . . . but . . . yes, of course.

(JULIAN *and* BUTLER *run out.*)

MISS ALICE (*to the* LAWYER *as he hangs back*). We're burning down! Hurry!

LAWYER (*comes up to her, grabs her by the wrist, forces her to the ground, keeps hold*). Burning down? Consumed? WHY NOT! Remember what I told you. Watch . . . your . . . step!

(*He runs out after the others.* MISS ALICE *is left alone; maybe we hear one or two diminishing shouts from the others, offstage. Finally, silence.* MISS ALICE *doesn't rise from the floor, but gradually assumes a more natural position on it.*)

MISS ALICE (*she alternates between a kind of incantation-prayer and a natural tone*).

(*Prayer*)

Let the fire be put out. Let the chapel be saved; let the fire not spread; let us not be consumed.

(*Natural*)

He hurt me. My wrist hurts. Who was the boy when I was little hurt my wrist? I don't remember.

(*Prayer*)

Let the fire not spread; let them be quick.

(*Natural*)

YOU PIG!

(*Softly, almost a whine*)

You hurt my wrist.

(*Imitates the* LAWYER'*s tone*)

Watch . . . your . . . step.

(*Prayer*)

Oh God, I have watched my step. I have . . . trod . . . so carefully.

(*Natural and weary*)

Let it all come down—let the whole place . . . go.

(*She must now, when using a natural tone, almost give the suggestion of talking to someone in the model. Natural.*)

I don't mean that. I don't remember his name . . . or his face; merely the hurt . . . and that continues, the hurt the same, the name and the face changing, but it doesn't matter. Let them save it.

(*Prayer*)

Let them save it. Don't . . . destroy. Let them save the resonance.

(*Natural*)

Increase it. Julian says there is no reson-
ance, that it's not right.
(*Prayer*)
Let the resonance increase.
(*Natural; a little-girl tone*)
I have tried very hard to be careful, to
obey, to withhold my . . . nature? I have
tried so hard to be good, but I'm . . . such
a stranger . . . here.
(*Prayer*)
I have tried to obey what I have not under-
stood, understanding that I must obey.
Don't destroy! I have tried! TRIED.
(*Natural*)
Is that the way about hurt? That *it* does
not change . . . but merely its agents?
(JULIAN *appears, unseen by* MISS ALICE.)
(*Natural, still*)
I will hold on.
(*Sweetly, apologetically*)
I will try to hold on.
(*Prayer*)
I will try to hold on!
(*Natural*)
Please, please . . . if you *do* . . . be gen-
erous and gentle with me, or . . . just
gentle.

JULIAN (*softly, a little sadly*). I don't
understand anything. The chapel was in
flames.

MISS ALICE. Yes.

JULIAN. . . . and yet . . . I saw the fire
here in the model . . . and yet . . . the
real chapel was in flames. We put it out.
And now the fire here is out as well.

MISS ALICE (*preceded by a brief, hysterical laugh*). . . . yes.

JULIAN (*underneath the wonder, some
fear*). I don't understand.

MISS ALICE (*she is shivering a little*). It's
very hard. Is the chapel saved?

JULIAN (*his attention on the model*).
Hm? Oh, yes . . . partially, mostly. The
. . . the boards, floorboards, around the
altar were . . . gave way, were burned
through. The altar . . . sank, some, angled down into the burned-through floor.
Marble.

MISS ALICE (*almost a whisper*). But the
fire is out.

JULIAN. Yes. Out. The spiders, burned
to a crisp, I should say, curled-up, burned
balls. (*Asking the same question.*) I . . .
I don't understand.

MISS ALICE (*vaguely to the model*). It is
all well. We are not . . . consumed.

JULIAN. Miss Alice? Why, why did it

happen that way—in both dimensions?

MISS ALICE (*her arms out to him*). Help
me.

(JULIAN *goes to her, lifts her by the
arms; they stand, at arm's length, holding
hands, facing each other.*)

JULIAN. Will you . . . tell me anything?

MISS ALICE (*a helpless laugh, though
sad*). I don't know anything.

JULIAN. But you were . . . (*Stops.*)

MISS ALICE (*pleading*). I don't *know*
anything.

JULIAN (*gently, to placate*). Very well.

MISS ALICE (*coming closer to him*).
Come stay.

JULIAN. Miss Alice?

MISS ALICE. Come stay here. It will . . .
be easier. For you.

JULIAN (*concern, not anger*). Did he
hurt you?

MISS ALICE. Easier than going back and
forth. And for me, too.

JULIAN. Did he?

MISS ALICE (*after a pause and a sad
smile*). Some. You're shivering, Julian.

JULIAN. No, Miss Alice, it is *you* . . .
you are shivering.

MISS ALICE. The Cardinal will agree to it.

JULIAN (*looking toward the model*).
Yes, I . . . suppose so.

MISS ALICE. Are you frightened, Julian?

JULIAN. Why, no, I . . . I *am* shivering,
am I not?

MISS ALICE. Yes.

JULIAN. But I am not . . . yes, I suppose I am . . . frightened.

MISS ALICE. Of what, Julian?

JULIAN (*looks toward the model again*).
But there is . . . (*Back.*) . . . of what.

MISS ALICE. Yes.

JULIAN (*knowing there is*). Is there anything to be frightened of, Miss Alice?

MISS ALICE (*after a long pause*). Always.

CURTAIN

SCENE TWO

*The library—as of Act One, Scene Two.
The* BUTLER *is on stage. The* LAWYER *enters
immediately, angry, impatient.*

LAWYER. Well, where are they today?

BUTLER (*calm, uninvolved*). Hm? Who?

LAWYER. WHERE IS SHE! Where is she off
to now?

BUTLER. Miss Alice? Well, I don't really know. (*Thinks about it.*) You look around?

LAWYER. They're not here.

BUTLER. You don't think they've eloped, do you?

LAWYER. Do you know!

BUTLER. They're moving together nicely; the fire in the chapel helped, I thought, though maybe it was intended to . . . brought them closer.

LAWYER. Where are they!

BUTLER. They spend so much time together now; everything on schedule.

LAWYER. Where have they gone!

BUTLER. I don't *know;* really. Out walking? In the gardens? Driving somewhere? Picnicking, maybe? Cold chicken, cheese, a Montrachet under an elm? I don't *know* where they are.

LAWYER. Don't you watch them?

BUTLER. Keep one eye peeled? Can't she take care of herself? She knows her business. (*Pause; then, quietly meaningful.*) Doesn't she. (*No answer.*) Doesn't she.

LAWYER. You should watch them. We don't want . . . error. She is . . .

BUTLER. Human? Yes, and clever, too . . . isn't she. *Good* at it, wrapping around fingers, enticing. I recall.

LAWYER. *Too* human; not playing it straight.

BUTLER. Enjoying her work a little? They're not sleeping together yet.

LAWYER. NO! NOT YET!

BUTLER (*a quiet warning*). Well, it won't bother you when they do . . . will it.

LAWYER (*matter-of-factly*). I, too: human.

BUTLER. Human, but dedicated.

LAWYER (*quiet, sick loathing*). He doesn't deserve her.

BUTLER (*kindly*). Well, he'll not have her long.

LAWYER (*weary*). No; not long.

BUTLER. On . . . and on . . . we go.

LAWYER (*sad*). Yes.

BUTLER (*too offhand, maybe*). I've noticed, you've let your feelings loose lately; too much: possessiveness, jealousy.

LAWYER. I'm *sorry.*

BUTLER. You used to be so good.

LAWYER. I'm SORRY!

BUTLER. It's all right; just watch it.

LAWYER. Attrition: the toll time takes.

BUTLER. I watch you carefully—you, too

—and it's the oddest thing: you're a cruel person, straight through; it's not cover; you're hard and cold, saved by dedication; just that.

LAWYER (*soft sarcasm*). Thank you.

BUTLER. You're welcome, but what's happened is you're acting like the man you wish you were.

LAWYER. Yes?

BUTLER. Feeling things you can't feel. Why don't you mourn for what you are? There's lament enough there.

LAWYER (*a sad discovery*). I've never liked you.

BUTLER (*a little sad, too*). I don't mind. We get along. The three of us.

LAWYER. She's *using* Julian! To humiliate me.

BUTLER (*nodding*). Of course. Humiliate; not hurt. Well, let her do her job the way she wants; she'll lead him, bring him around to it.

LAWYER. But she *cares* for him.

BUTLER. *Of* course; human, a woman. Cares, but it won't get in the way. Let her use what she can. It will be done. Don't you think it's time you went to see His Holiness again?

LAWYER. Eminence, not Holiness. You think it's time I went again? Yes; well, it *is* time. You come, too.

BUTLER (*mildly taunting*). But shouldn't I stay here . . . to watch? To fill you in on the goings on? To let you be the last to know?

LAWYER. YOU COME! To back me up, when I want emphasis.

BUTLER. In the sense that my father used the word? Wants emphasis: lacks emphasis?

LAWYER. No. The touch of the proletarian: your simplicity, guilelessness . . .

BUTLER. Aw . . .

LAWYER. His Eminence is a pompous ass.

BUTLER. Stupid? I doubt *that.*

LAWYER. Not stupid; an ass.

BUTLER. Cardinals aren't stupid; takes brains to get there; no jokes in the Church.

LAWYER. Pompous!

BUTLER. Well, in front of you, maybe. Maybe has to wear a face; you're not easy. What will you tell him?

LAWYER. What will I tell him? Tell me.

BUTLER. All right. You play Cardinal, I'll play you.

LAWYER (*goes into it eagerly; with a*

laugh). Ah, two of you. We are doubly honored. Will you not sit?

BUTLER. Really? Like that?

LAWYER. And how is our Brother Julian faring . . . in the world of the moneyed and the powerful?

BUTLER. No. Really?

LAWYER. Really! And can we be of service to you, further service?

BUTLER. Maybe.

LAWYER. Maybe? Ah?

BUTLER. Yes, your Brother Julian is going to be taken from you.

LAWYER. Our Brother Julian? Taken? From us?

BUTLER. Come on, Your Eminence.

LAWYER. This is a . . . preposterous . . . We . . . we don't understand you.

BUTLER. Isn't the grant enough? Isn't a hundred million a year for twenty years enough? For one man? He's not even a priest.

LAWYER (*as the* CARDINAL). A man's soul, Sir! (*Himself.*) Not his soul, mustn't say that to him.

BUTLER (*musing*). Shall we be dishonest? Well, then, I suppose you'll have to tell him more. Tell him the whole thing.

LAWYER (*himself*). I will like that. It will blanch his goddam robes . . . turn 'em white.

BUTLER (*chuckles*). Nice when you can enjoy your work, isn't it? Tell him that Julian is leaving him. That Julian has found what he's after. (*Walks to the model, indicates it.*) And I suppose you'd better tell him about . . . this, too.

LAWYER. The wonders of the world?

BUTLER. I think he'd better know . . . about this.

LAWYER. Shatter.

BUTLER. And, you know what I think would be a lovely touch?

LAWYER (*a quiet smile that is also a grimace*). Tell me.

BUTLER. How eager you are. I think it would be a lovely touch were the Cardinal to marry them, to perform the wedding, to marry Julian to . . .

LAWYER. Alice.

BUTLER. *Miss* Alice.

LAWYER. Alice!

BUTLER. Well, all right; one through the other. But have him marry them.

LAWYER (*smiles a little*). It would be nice.

BUTLER. *I* thought so.

LAWYER. But *shall* we tell him the whole thing? The Cardinal? What is happening?

BUTLER. How much can he take?

LAWYER. He is a man of God, however much he simplifies, however much he worships the symbol and not the substance.

BUTLER. Like everyone.

LAWYER. Like most.

BUTLER. Julian can't stand that; he told me so: men make God in their own image, he said. Those six years I told you about.

LAWYER. Yes. When he went into an asylum. YES.

BUTLER. It was—because he could not stand it, wasn't it? The use men put God to.

LAWYER. It's perfect; wonderful.

BUTLER. Could not reconcile.

LAWYER. No.

BUTLER. God as older brother, scout leader, couldn't take that.

LAWYER. And still not reconciled.

BUTLER. Has pardoned men, I think. Is walking on the edge of an abyss, but is balancing. Can be pushed . . . over, back to the asylums.

LAWYER. Or over . . . to the Truth (*Addressing* JULIAN, *as if he were there; some thunder in the voice.*) God, Julian? Yes? God? *Whose* God? Have you pardoned men their blasphemy, Julian? Have you forgiven them?

BUTLER (*quiet echoing answers; being* JULIAN). No, I have not, have not really; have *let* them, but cannot accept.

LAWYER. Have not forgiven. No, Julian. Could you ever?

BUTLER (*ibid.*). It is their comfort; my agony.

LAWYER. Soft God? The servant? Gingerbread God with the raisin eyes?

BUTLER (*ibid.*). I cannot accept it.

LAWYER. Then don't accept it, Julian.

BUTLER. But there is *some*thing. There is a *true* God.

LAWYER. There is an abstraction, Julian, but it cannot be understood. You cannot worship it.

BUTLER (*ibid.*). There is more.

LAWYER. There is Alice, Julian. That can be understood. Only the mouse in the model. Just that.

BUTLER (*ibid.*). There must be more.

LAWYER. The mouse. Believe it. Don't personify the abstraction, Julian, limit it, demean it. Only the mouse, the toy. And that does not exist . . . but is all that can be worshiped. . . . Cut off from it, Julian, ease yourself, ease off. No trouble now; accept it.

BUTLER (*talking to* JULIAN *now*). Accept it, Julian; ease off. Worship it . . .

LAWYER. Accept it.

BUTLER (*after a pause; normal again*). Poor, poor Julian.

LAWYER (*normal, too*). He can make it.

BUTLER. I hope he can.

LAWYER. If not? (*Shrugs.*) Out with him.

BUTLER (*pause*). You cannot tell, the Cardinal . . . that.

LAWYER (*weary*). The benefits to the Church.

BUTLER. Not simply that.

LAWYER. And a man's soul. If it be saved . . . what matter how?

BUTLER. Then we'd best go to him.

LAWYER. Yes.

BUTLER. Leave Julian to Miss Alice; he is in good hands.

LAWYER (*quiet, sick rage rising*). But his hands . . . on her.

BUTLER (*soothing*). Temporary . . . temporal. You'll have her back.

LAWYER (*rises*). All right.

BUTLER. Let's go.

LAWYER (*walks to the model, addresses it; quietly, but forcefully; no sarcasm*). Rest easy; you'll have him . . . Hum; purr; breathe; rest. You will have your Julian. Wait for him. He will be yours.

CURTAIN

SCENE THREE

MISS ALICE's *sitting room, as of Act One, Scene Three.* JULIAN *is on stage, near the fireplace, carries a riding crop; the door to the bedroom is ajar.*

JULIAN (*after a moment; over his shoulder*). It was fun, Miss Alice; it was fun.

MISS ALICE (*from behind the door*). What, Julian?

JULIAN (*turns*). It was . . . I enjoyed it; very much.

MISS ALICE (*her head appearing from behind the door*). Enjoyed what?

JULIAN. Riding; it was . . . exhilarating.

MISS ALICE. I would never have thought you rode. You were good. (*Disappears.*)

JULIAN (*a small, self-deprecating laugh*). Oh. Yes. When I was young—a child—I knew a family who . . . kept horses, as a pastime, not as a business. They were moneyed—well, had *some*. It was one of their sons who was my playmate . . . and we would ride.

MISS ALICE (*still behind the door*). Yes.

JULIAN. You remember, you know how seriously children talk, the cabalas we have . . . had. My friends and I would take two hunters, and we would go off for hours, and talk ourselves into quite a state— mutually mesmerizing, almost an hysteria. We would forget the time, and bring the animals back quite lathered. (*Laughs.*) We would be scolded—no: cursed *out*— by one groom or another; usually by a great dark Welshman—a young fellow who always scowled and had—I remember it clearly, for I found it remarkable—the hairiest hands I have ever seen, with hair —and this is what I found most remarkable—tufts of coarse black hair on his thumbs. (*Looks at his own thumbs.*) Not down, or a few hairs, which many of us have, but tufts. This Welshman.

MISS ALICE (*head appearing again*). D. H. Lawrence.

JULIAN. Pardon?

MISS ALICE (*appearing, wearing a black negligee with great sleeves*). "Love on the Farm." Don't you know it?

(*Circles him as she recites it; mock-stalks him.*) "I hear his hand on the latch, and rise from my chair
Watching the door open . . .
He flings the rabbit soft on the table board
And comes toward me: he! the uplifted sword
Of his hand against my bosom! . . .
. . . With his hand he turns my face to him
And caresses me with his fingers that still smell grim
Of rabbit's fur! . . .
And down his mouth comes on my mouth! and down
His bright dark eyes over me . . .
. . . his lips meet mine, and a flood
Of sweet fire sweeps across me, so I drown
Against him, die and find death good!"
(*Cocks her head, smiles.*)
No?

JULIAN (*embarrassed*). That was . . . not quite my reaction.

MISS ALICE (*a great, crystal laugh*). No!

Silly Julian! No. (*Conspiratorial.*) That was a verse I knew at school, that I memorized. "And down his mouth comes on my mouth." Oh! That would excite us so . . . at school; things like that. (*Normal tone; a shrug, a smile.*) Early eroticism; mental sex play.

JULIAN (*still embarrassed*). Yes.

MISS ALICE. I've embarrassed you!

JULIAN. No! No!

MISS ALICE. Poor Julian; I have. And you were telling me about horseback riding.

JULIAN. No, I was telling you about the groom, as far as that goes. And I suppose . . . yes, I suppose . . . those thumbs were . . . erotic for *me*—at that time, if you think about it; mental sex play. Unconscious.

MISS ALICE (*sweetly, to divert him*). It *was* fun riding. *Today.*

JULIAN. Yes!

MISS ALICE. I am fond of hair—man's body hair, except that on the back. (*Very offhand.*) Are you hairy, Julian?

JULIAN. I . . . my chest is rather nice, but my arms are . . . surprisingly hairless.

MISS ALICE. And you have no back hair.

JULIAN. Well . . . do you really wish to know?

MISS ALICE (*with a laugh*). Yes!

JULIAN (*nods in acquiescence*). I have no . . . back hair, in the usual sense—of the shoulders . . .

(MISS ALICE *nods.*) . . . but there is hair, at the small of the back . . . rising.

MISS ALICE. Yes, yes, well, *that* is nice. (*Laughs, points to the crop.*) You're carrying the crop. Are you still in the saddle?

JULIAN (*laughing; shyly brandishing the crop*). Are you one of Mr. Lawrence's ladies? Do you like the smell of saddle soap, and shall I take my crop to you?

MISS ALICE (*briefest pause; testing*). Would you?

JULIAN (*halfhearted laugh*). MISS ALICE!

MISS ALICE. Nobody does things naturally any more—so few people have the grace. A man takes a whip to you—a loving whip, you understand—and you *know*, deep and sadly, that it's imitation—literary, seen. (*Intentionally too much.*) No one has the natural graces any more.

JULIAN (*putting the crop down; quietly*). I have . . . not whipped . . .

MISS ALICE. But surely you have.

JULIAN (*an apology*). I do not recall.

MISS ALICE (*expansive*). Oh, my Julian! How many layers! Yes?

JULIAN. We . . . simplify our life . . . as we grow older.

MISS ALICE (*teasing him*). But from understanding and acceptance; not from . . . emptying ourselves.

JULIAN. There are many ways.

MISS ALICE (*showing her outfit*). Do you like this?

JULIAN. It is most . . . becoming.

MISS ALICE (*giggles*). We're dressed quite alike.

JULIAN (*he, too*). But the effect is not the same.

MISS ALICE. No. It *is* easier for you living here . . . isn't it?

JULIAN. It's . . . more than a person could want—or *should* want, which is something we must discuss.

MISS ALICE (*sensing a coming disappointment*). Oh . . .

JULIAN. Really.

MISS ALICE (*not pleasantly*). What do we do wrong?

JULIAN. One of the sins is gluttony . . .

MISS ALICE. Are you getting a belly?

JULIAN (*smiles, but won't be put off*). . . . and it has many faces—or many bellies, if you wish. It's a commonplace that we can have too much of things, and I have too much . . . of comfort, of surroundings, of ease, of kindness . . . of happiness. I am filled to bursting.

MISS ALICE (*hard*). I think perhaps you misunderstand why you're here. You're *not* here to . . . to indulge yourself, to . . .

JULIAN (*tight-lipped*). I'm aware of that.

MISS ALICE. . . . to . . . to ease in. You're here in service to your *Church.*

JULIAN. I've not lost sight of my function.

MISS ALICE. I wonder!

JULIAN (*really quite angry*). And *I* wonder! What's being *done* to me. Am I . . . am I being temp—tested in some fashion?

MISS ALICE (*jumping on it*). Tempted?

JULIAN. Tested in some fashion?

MISS ALICE. TEMPTED?

JULIAN. BOTH! Tested! What! My . . . my sincerity, my . . . my other cheek? You have allowed that . . . that *man*, your . . . your lover, to . . . ridicule me. You have per*mit*ted it.

MISS ALICE. I? Permit?

JULIAN. You have allowed him to abuse me, my position, his, the Church; you have tolerated it, and *smiled*.

MISS ALICE. Tolerate!

JULIAN. And smiled. WHY AM I BEING TESTED! . . . And why am I being tempted? By luxury, by ease, by . . . content . . . by things I do not care to discuss.

MISS ALICE (*unsympathetic*). You're answerable to your own temptations.

JULIAN. Yes?

MISS ALICE (*singsong and patronizing*). Or God is.

(JULIAN *snorts*.) No? God is not? Is not answerable?

JULIAN. Knows. But is not answerable. I.

MISS ALICE (*softening some*). Then *be* answerable.

JULIAN. To my temptations, I am (*To himself more than to her*.) It would be so easy to . . . fall in, to . . . accept these surroundings. Oh, life would speed by!

MISS ALICE. With all the ridicule?

JULIAN. That aside.

MISS ALICE. You *have* a friend here . . . as they put it.

JULIAN (*smiles*). Butler. Yes; he's nice.

MISS ALICE (*a little laugh*). I meant me.

JULIAN. Well, of *course*. . . .

MISS ALICE. Or, do you think of me otherwise? Do *I* tempt you?

JULIAN. You, Miss Alice?

MISS ALICE. Or, is it merely the fact of temptation that upsets you so?

JULIAN. I have longed . . . to be of great service. When I was young—and very prideful—I was filled with a self-importance that was . . . well disguised. Serve. That was the active word: I would serve! (*Clenches his fist*.) I would serve, and damn anyone or anything that stood in my way. I would shout my humility from the roof and break whatever rules impeded my headlong rush toward obedience. I suspect that had I joined the Trappist order, where silence is the law, I would have chattered about it endlessly. I was impatient with God's agents, and with God, too, I see it now. A . . . novice porter, ripping suitcases from patrons' hands, cursing those who preferred to carry some small parcel for their own. And I was blind to my pride, and intolerant of any who did not see me as the humblest of men.

MISS ALICE (*a little malice*). You phrase it so; I suspect you've said it before.

JULIAN. Doubtless I have. Articulate men often carry set paragraphs.

MISS ALICE. Pride still.

JULIAN. Some.

MISS ALICE. And how did your ambition sit?

JULIAN. Ambition? Was it?

(MISS ALICE *displays a knee casually;* JULIAN *jumps*.) What are you doing!

MISS ALICE (*vague flirting*). I'm . . . sorry.

JULIAN. Well. Ambition, yes, I suppose —ambition to be nothing, to be least. Most obedient, humblest. How did it sit? For some, patiently, but not well. For me? Even less well. But I . . . learned.

MISS ALICE. To . . . subside. Is that the simplification you mentioned before? Of your life. To subside . . . and vanish; to leave no memory.

JULIAN. No; I wish to leave a . . . memory—of work, of things done, I've told you; I wish to be of great service, to move great events; but when it's all time for crediting, I'd like someone to say no more than "Ah, wasn't there someone involved in this, who brought it all about? A priest? Ah-*ha*, a *lay* brother—was that it." (*Smiles*.) Like that. The memory of someone who helped.

MISS ALICE (*pauses, then laughs*). You're lying!

JULIAN. I?

(*Then they both laugh, like conspiratorial children*.)

MISS ALICE. Every monster was a man first, Julian; every dictator was a colonel who vowed to retire once the revolution was done; it's so easy to postpone elections, little brother.

JULIAN. The history of the Church . . .

MISS ALICE. The history of the Church shows half its saints were martyrs, martyred either for the Church, or by it. The chronology is jammed with death-seekers and hysterics: the bloodbath to immortality, Julian. Joan was only one of the suicides.

JULIAN (*quivering with intensity*). I WISH TO SERVE AND . . . BE FORGOTTEN.

MISS ALICE (*comes over, strokes his cheek*). Perhaps you will, Julian.

(*He takes her hand, kisses it, puts it back on his cheek*.)

Yes?

JULIAN (*guiltily*). I wish to be of service. (*A little giggle.*) I *do*.

MISS ALICE. And be forgotten.

JULIAN. Yes.

MISS ALICE (*stroking his head*). Not even remembered a little? By some? As a gentle man, gentle Julian . . .

JULIAN. Per . . . perhaps.

MISS ALICE. . . . my little lay brother and expert on wines; my little horseback rider and crop switcher . . .

JULIAN (*as she ruffles his hair*). Don't . . . do that.

MISS ALICE (*ruffles harder*). My little whipper, and RAPIST?

JULIAN (*rising, moving away*). DON'T!

MISS ALICE (*pouting, advancing*). Julian . . .

JULIAN. No, now; no.

MISS ALICE (*still pouting*). Julian, come kiss me.

JULIAN. Please!

MISS ALICE (*singsong*). Come kiss.

JULIAN (*a plea*). Miss Alice . . . Just . . . let me do my service, and let me go.

MISS ALICE (*abruptly to business; not curt, though*). But you're *doing* great service. Not many people have been put in the position you've been graced by—not many. Who knows—had some lesser man than you come, some bishop, all dried and salted, clacketing phrases from memory, or . . . one of those insinuating super-salesmen your Church uses, had one of them come . . . who knows? Perhaps the whole deal would have gone out the window.

JULIAN. Surely, Miss Alice, you haven't been playing games with . . . so monumental a matter.

MISS ALICE. The rich are said to be quixotic, the very wealthy cruel, overbearing; who is to say—might not vast wealth, the insulation of it, make one quite mad? Games? Oh, no, my little Julian, there are no games played here; this is for keeps, and in dead earnest. There *are* cruelties, for the insulation breeds a strange kind of voyeurism; and there is impatience, too, over the need to accomplish what should not be explained; and, at the end of it, a madness of sorts . . . but a triumph.

JULIAN (*hands apart*). Use me, then . . . for the triumph.

MISS ALICE (*moving on him again*). You are *being* used, my little Julian. *I* am being used . . . my little Julian. You want to be . . . employed, do you not? Sacrificed, even?

JULIAN. I have . . . there are no secrets from you, Miss Alice . . . I have . . . dreamed of sacrifice.

MISS ALICE (*she touches his neck*). Tell me.

JULIAN. You mustn't do . . . it is not wise . . .

MISS ALICE. Tell me.

(*She will circle him, touch him occasionally, kiss the back of his neck once during the next speech.*)

JULIAN. Still my pride . . . a vestige of it.

(*He becomes quite by himself during this; unaware of her.*)

Oh, when I was still a child, and read of the Romans, how they used the saints as playthings—enraged children gutting their teddy bears, dashing the head of their doll against the bedpost, I could . . . I could entrance myself, and see the gladiator on me, his trident fork against my neck, and hear, even hear, as much as feel, the prongs as they entered me; the . . . the beast's saliva dripping from the yellow teeth, the slack sides of the mouth, the . . . sweet, warm breath of the lion; great paws on my spread arms . . . even the rough leather of the pads; and to the point of . . . as the great mouth opened, the breath no longer warm but hot, the fangs on my jaw and forehead, positioned . . . IN. And as the fangs sank in, the great tongue on my cheek and eye, the splitting of the bone, and the *blood* . . . just before the great sound, the coming dark and the silence. I could . . . experience it all. And was . . . engulfed. (*A brief laugh, but not breaking the trance.*) Oh, martyrdom. To be that. To be able . . . to be that.

MISS ALICE (*softly, into his ear; he does not hear it*). Marry me, Julian.

JULIAN. The . . . death of the saints . . . was always the beginning of their lives. To go bloodstained and worthy . . . upward. I could feel the blood on my robes as I went; the smell of the blood, as intense as paint . . . and warm . . . and painless.

MISS ALICE. Marry me.

JULIAN. "Here. I have come. You see my robes? They're red, are they not? Warm? And are not the folds caught together . . . as the blood coagulates? The . . . fingers of my left hand—of both!— are . . . are hard to move apart, as the blood holds finger to finger. And there is a wound in me, the warm dark flow . . . runs down my belly . . . to . . . bathing my groin. You see? I have come . . . bloodstained and worthy."

MISS ALICE. Marry me.

JULIAN (*still self-tranced*). Bathed . . . my groin. And as the thumbs of the gladiator pressed . . . against . . . my neck, I . . . as the lion's belly pressed on my chest, I . . . as the . . . I . . . or as the woman sank . . . on the mossy hillock by the roses, and the roar is the crunching growls is the moan is the sweat-breathing is the . . .

MISS ALICE (*behind him, her arms around his neck, on his chest*). . . . sweat-breathing on the mossy hillock and the white mist in the perfumes . . .

JULIAN. . . . fumes . . . lying . . . on the moss hill in the white filmy gladiator's belly pressing on the chest fanged and the soft hard tongue and the *blood* . . . ENTERS . . . (*Lurches from the chair.*) . . . STOP! . . . THAT!

MISS ALICE (*coming at him slowly*). Come to Alice, Julian, in your sacrifice . . .

JULIAN (*moving away, but helpless*). Stay . . . away . . . stay.

MISS ALICE. . . . give yourself to her, Julian . . .

JULIAN. . . . a . . . away . . .

MISS ALICE (*sweetly singsong*). Come marry Alice, she wants you so; she says she wants you so, come give yourself to Alice; oh, Alice needs you and your sacrifice . . .

JULIAN. . . . no . . . no . . .

MISS ALICE. . . . Alice says she wants you, come to Alice, Alice tells me so, she wants you, come to Alice . . .

JULIAN. . . . no . . . sacrifice . . .

MISS ALICE. Alice tells me so, instructs me, come to her.

(MISS ALICE *has her back to the audience,* JULIAN *facing her, but at a distance; she takes her gown and, spreading her arms slowly, opens the gown wide; it is the unfurling of great wings.*)

JULIAN (*shaking, staring at her body*). . . . and . . . sacrifice . . . on the altar of . . .

MISS ALICE. Come . . . come . . .

JULIAN. . . . the . . . Lord . . . God . . . in . . . Heaven . . .

MISS ALICE. Come . . .

(JULIAN *utters a sort of dying cry and moves, his arms in front of him, to* MISS ALICE; *when he reaches her, she enfolds him in her great wings.*)

MISS ALICE (*soothing*). You will be hers; you will sacrifice yourself to her . . .

JULIAN (*muffled*). Oh my God in heaven . . .

MISS ALICE (*her head going back, calling out*). Alice . . . Alice? . . .

JULIAN (*slowly kneeling within the great wings*). . . . in . . . my . . . sacrifice . . .

MISS ALICE (*still calling out*). He will be yours! He will be yours! AAALLLIIICCCEEE!

CURTAIN

ACT THREE

The library, as of Act One, Scene Two. No one on stage. After a moment or so, BUTLER *enters, carrying what looks to be a pile of gray sheets. They are clearly quite heavy. He sets them down on a table, straightens his shoulders from the effort, looks at various chairs, turns to counting the pile.* JULIAN *enters, at more than a casual pace, dressed in a suit.*

———

JULIAN. Butler!

BUTLER. (*deliberate pause; then*). . . . four . . . five . . . six . . . (*Pretending suddenly to see* JULIAN.) Oh! Hello there.

JULIAN. Where . . . I . . . I feel quite *lost.*

BUTLER (*no comment*). Why?

JULIAN (*agitation underneath*). Well, uh . . . I will confess I haven't participated in . . . been married before, but . . . I can't imagine it's usual for everyone to disap*pear.*

BUTLER. Has everyone?

JULIAN. Yes! (*Quieter.*) Yes, I . . . per—perhaps His Eminence is occupied, or has *business*—that's it!—has business with . . . but—but why *she* should . . . There I was . . . one moment married, flooded with white, and . . . then . . . the next alone. Quite alone, in the . . . echoes.

BUTLER. There is an echo, sometimes, all through it, down every long hall, up in the huge beams . . .

JULIAN. But to be left alone!

BUTLER. Aren't you used to that?

JULIAN. Suddenly!

BUTLER (*sad smile*). Like a little boy?

When the closet door swings shut after him? Locking him in the dark?

JULIAN. Hm? Yes . . . yes, like that. (*Shudders a little.*) Terrifying.

BUTLER. And it's always remote, an attic closet, where one should not have been, where no one can hear, and is not likely to come . . . for a very long time.

JULIAN (*asking him to stop*). Yes!

BUTLER (*to the sheets again counting them*). We learn so early . . . are *told,* where not to go, the things we should not do. And there's often a reason.

JULIAN. And *she* vanished as well.

BUTLER. Who?

JULIAN. My . . . my wife.

BUTLER. And who is that?

JULIAN (*as if* BUTLER *had forgotten everything*). Miss Alice!

BUTLER. Ah. Really?

JULIAN. Butler, you saw the wedding!

BUTLER (*puzzles it a moment*). Quite so; I did. We . . . Well. Perhaps Miss Alice is changing.

JULIAN. She *must* be; of course. But . . . for everyone to . . . vanish, as if I'd turned my back for a *moment,* and an hour elapsed, or a . . . dimension had . . .

BUTLER (*passing it over*). Yes, a dimension—well, that happens.

JULIAN (*still preoccupied*). Yes, she must be . . . upstairs. What . . . what are you doing?

BUTLER. What?

JULIAN. What are those?

BUTLER These? (*Looks at them.*) Uh . . . sheets, or covers, more accurately.

JULIAN (*still quite nervous, staying away*). What are they for?

BUTLER. To . . . cover.

JULIAN (*ibid.*). Cover *what!*

BUTLER. Oh . . . nothing; no matter. Housework, that's all. One of my labors.

JULIAN. I . . . I would have thought you'd have champagne . . . ready, that you'd be busy with the party. . . .

BUTLER. One does *many* things. You'll have your champagne, sir, never fear.

JULIAN. I'm sorry; I . . . I was so upset.

BUTLER. Yes.

JULIAN (*attempting a joke*). After all, I've not been married before.

BUTLER. No.

JULIAN. And the procedures are a little . . . well, you know.

BUTLER. Yes.

JULIAN. . . . *still* . . .

BUTLER. Yes.

JULIAN. It all *does* seem odd.

BUTLER. Marriage is a confusing business.

JULIAN. Have . . . have you been . . . married?

(BUTLER *gives a noncommittal laugh as answer.*)

I . . . I don't know if marriage is, but certainly the circumstances surrounding this *wedding* are rather . . .

BUTLER (*a fairly chilling smile*).

Special people, special problems.

JULIAN (*hurt*).

Oh. Well . . . yes.

BUTLER (*disdainful curiosity*).

Do you . . . *feel* married?

JULIAN (*withdrawn*). Not having been, I cannot say. (*Pause.*) Can I?

BUTLER.

(*Takes one of the sheets, opens it with a cracking sound, holds it in front of him, a hand on each shoulder.*)

No. (*Puts it to one side.*) I suppose not.

JULIAN. No. I wonder if . . . I wonder if you could go upstairs, perhaps, and see if Miss Alice . . . my *wife* . . . is . . .

BUTLER. No. (*Then, rather stern.*) I have much too much work to do. (*Cheerful.*) I'll get you some champagne, though.

JULIAN (*rather removed*). No, I'll . . . wait for the others, if they haven't all . . . disappeared.

BUTLER (*noncommittal*). To leave you alone with your bride, on your wedding night? No; not yet.

JULIAN (*for something to say, as much as anything, yet hopeful of an answer, or an explanation*). Miss Alice . . . chose not to invite . . . friends . . . to the ceremony.

BUTLER (*chuckle*). Ah, no. Alice . . . *Miss* Alice does not have friends; admirers, yes. Worshipers . . . but not buddies.

JULIAN (*puzzled*). I asked her why she had not, and she replied . . .

BUTLER (*improvising*). . . . . it is you, Julian, who are being married . . . ?

JULIAN (*too self-absorbed to be surprised*). Yes; something like that.

BUTLER. Your wife is . . . something of a recluse.

JULIAN (*hopeful*). But so outgoing!

BUTLER. Yes? Well, then; you will indeed have fun. (*Mock instructions.*) Uncover the chandeliers in the ballroom! Lay on some footmen! Unplug the fountains! Trim the maze!

JULIAN (*more or less to himself*). She *must* have friends . . . (*Unsure.*) must she not?

BUTLER (*stage whisper*). I don't know; no one has ever asked her.

JULIAN (*laughing nervously*). Oh, indeed!

(MISS ALICE *comes hurriedly into the room; she has on a suit. She sees only* BUTLER *first.*)

MISS ALICE. Butler! Have you seen . . . ? (*Sees* JULIAN.) Oh, I'm . . . sorry. (*She begins to leave.*)

JULIAN. There you are. No, wait; wait!

(*But* MISS ALICE *has left the room. In need of help.*)

I find everything today puzzling.

BUTLER (*about to give advice*). Look . . . (*Thinks better of it.*)

JULIAN. Yes?

BUTLER (*shrugs*). Nothing. The wages of a wedding day.

JULIAN. Are you my friend?

BUTLER (*takes a while to think about the answer*). I am; yes, but you'll probably think not.

JULIAN. Is something being kept from me?

BUTLER (*after a pause*). You loathe sham, do you not?

JULIAN. Yes.

BUTLER. As do we all . . . most of us. You are dedicated to the reality of things, rather than their appearance, are you not?

JULIAN. Deeply.

BUTLER. As are . . . some of us.

JULIAN. It was why I retreated . . . withdrew . . . to the asylum.

BUTLER. Yes, yes. And you are devout.

JULIAN. You know that.

BUTLER. When you're locked in the attic, Julian, in the attic closet, in the dark, do you care who comes?

JULIAN. No. But . . .

BUTLER (*starts to leave*). Let me get the champagne.

JULIAN. Please!

BUTLER. So that we all can toast.

(*As* BUTLER *leaves, the* CARDINAL *enters.*) Ah! Here comes the Church.

JULIAN (*going to the* CARDINAL, *kneeling before him, kissing his ring, holding the ring hand afterward, staying kneeling*). Your Eminence.

CARDINAL. Julian. Our dear Julian.

BUTLER. Have you caught the bride?

CARDINAL. No. No. Not seen her since the . . . since we married her.

JULIAN. It was good of you. I suspect she will be here soon. Butler, would you . . . go see? If she will come here? His Eminence would . . . Now do be good and go.

(BUTLER *exits.*) He has been a great help. At times when my service has . . . perplexed me, till I grew despondent, and wondered if perhaps you'd not been mistaken in putting such a burden . . .

CARDINAL (*not wanting to get into it*). Yes, yes, Julian. We have *resolved* it.

JULIAN. But then I judge it is God's doing, this . . . wrenching of my life from one light to another . . .

CARDINAL. . . . Julian . . .

JULIAN. . . . though not losing God's light, joining it with . . . my new. (*He is like a bubbling little boy.*) I can't tell you, the . . . radiance, humming, and the witchcraft, I think it must be, the ecstasy of this light, as *God*'s exactly; the transport the same, the lifting, the . . . the sense of service, and the EXPANSION . . .

CARDINAL. . . . Julian . . .

JULIAN. . . . the blessed wonder of service with a renewing, not an ending joy— that joy I thought possible only through martyrdom, now, now the sunlight is no longer the hope for glare and choking in the dust and plummeting, but with cool and green and yellow dappled . . . perfumes . . .

CARDINAL (*sharply*). Julian!

JULIAN (*little-boy smile*). Sir.

CARDINAL (*evading* JULIAN's *eyes*). We sign the papers today, Julian. It's all arranged, the grant is accomplished; through your marriage . . . your service.

JULIAN (*puzzlement*). Father?

CARDINAL (*barely keeping pleasure in his voice*). And isn't it wonderful: that you have . . . found yourself such great service and such . . . exceeding happiness, too; that God's way has brought such gifts to his servant, and to his servant's servant as well.

JULIAN (*puzzled*). Thank you . . . Your Eminence.

CARDINAL (*sadly*). It is your wedding day, Julian!

JULIAN (*smiles, throws off his mood*). Yes, it is! It's my wedding day. And a day of glory to God, that His Church has been blessed with great wealth, for the suffering of the world, conversion and the pronouncement of His Glory.

CARDINAL (*embarrassed; perfunctory*). Praise God.

JULIAN. That God has seen fit to let me be His instrument in this undertaking, that God . . .

CARDINAL. Julian. (*Pause.*) As you have accepted what has happened . . . removed, so far removed from . . . any thought . . . accept what . . . *will* happen, *may* happen, with the same humility and . . .

JULIAN (*happily*). It is my service.

CARDINAL (*nods*). Accept what may come . . . as God's will.

JULIAN. Don't . . . don't frighten me. Bless me, Father.

CARDINAL (*embarrassed*). Julian, please . . .

JULIAN (*on his knees before the* CARDINAL). Bless me?

CARDINAL (*reluctantly; appropriate gestures*). In the name of the Father and of the Son and the Holy Ghost . . .

JULIAN. . . . Amen . . .

CARDINAL. . . . Amen. You *have* . . . confessed, Julian?

JULIAN (*blushing, but childishly pleased*). I . . . I have, Father; I have . . . confessed, and finally, to sins more real than imagined, but . . . but they are not sins, are they, in God's name, done in God's name, Father?

CARDINAL. May the presence of our Lord Jesus Christ be with you always . . .

JULIAN. . . . to . . . to shield my eyes from too much light, that I may be always worthy . . .

CARDINAL. . . . to light your way for you in the darkness . . .

JULIAN. . . . dark, darkness, Father? . . .

CARDINAL. . . . that you may be worthy of whatever sacrifice, unto death itself . . .

JULIAN. . . . in all this light! . . .

CARDINAL. . . . is asked of you; that you may accept what you do not understand . . .

JULIAN (*a mild argument*). But, Father . . .

CARDINAL. . . . and that the Lord may have mercy on your soul . . . as, indeed, may He have on us all . . . all our souls.

JULIAN. . . . A . . . Amen?

CARDINAL (*nodding*). Amen.

LAWYER (*entering*). Well, well. Your Eminence. Julian. Well, you are indeed a fortunate man, today. What more cheering sight can there be than Frank Fearnought, clean-living, healthy farm lad, come from the heartland of the country, from the asylums—you see, I know—in search of fame, and true love—never fortune, of course.

JULIAN. . . . Please . . .

LAWYER. And see what has happened to brave and handsome Frank: he has found what he sought . . . true . . . love; *and* fortune—to his surprise, for wealth had never crossed his pure mind; and fame? . . . Oooooh, there will be a private fame, perhaps.

CARDINAL. *Very* pretty.

LAWYER. And we are dressed in city ways, too, are we not? No longer the simple gown of the farm lad, the hems trailing in the dung; no; now we are in city clothes . . . banker's clothes.

JULIAN. These are proper clothes.

LAWYER. As you will discover, poor priestlet, poor former priestlet. Dressed differently for the sacrifice, eh?

JULIAN. I . . . think I'll . . . look for Miss . . . for my wife.

LAWYER. Do.

CARDINAL. Oh, yes, Julian; please.

JULIAN (*kneels, kisses the ring again*). Your Eminence. (*To the* LAWYER, *mildly.*) We are both far too old . . . are we not . . . for all that?

(JULIAN *exits.*)

CARDINAL (*after* JULIAN *leaves*). Is cruelty a lesson you learned at your mother's knee? One of the songs you were taught?

LAWYER. One learns by growing, as they say. I have fine instructors behind me . . . yourself amongst them. (*A dismissing gesture.*) We have no time. (*Raises his briefcase, then throws it on a table.*) All here. (*Great cheerfulness.*) All here! The grant: all your money. (*Normal tone again.*) I must say, your Church lawyers are picky men.

CARDINAL. Thorough.

LAWYER. Picky. Humorless on small matters, great wits on the major ones; ribald over the whole proposition.

CARDINAL (*mumbling*). . . . hardly a subject for ribaldry . . .

LAWYER. Oh, quite a dowry, greatest marriage settlement in history, *mother* church indeed . . . things like that.

CARDINAL (*unhappily*). Well, it's all over now . . .

LAWYER. Almost.

CARDINAL. Yes.

LAWYER. Cheer up; the price was high enough.

CARDINAL. Then it is . . . really true? About . . . *this*? (*Points at the model.*)

LAWYER. I haven't time to lie to you.

CARDINAL. Really . . . true.

LAWYER (*moving to the model*). Really. Can't you accept the wonders of the world? Why not of this one, as well as the other?

CARDINAL. We should be . . . getting on.

LAWYER. Yes. (*Points to a place in the model.*) Since the wedding was . . . *here* . . . and we are (*Indicates the room they are in*) here . . . we have come quite a . . . dimension, have we not?

(*The* LAWYER *moves away from the model to a table, as the* CARDINAL *stays at the model.*)

CARDINAL (*abstracted*). Yes. A distance.

(*Turns, sees the* LAWYER *open a drawer, take out a pistol and check its cartridges.*) What . . . what are you doing? (*Moves toward the* LAWYER, *slowly.*)

LAWYER. House pistol.

CARDINAL. But what are you doing?

LAWYER (*looking it over carefully*). I've never shot one of these things . . . pistols. (*Then, to answer.*) I'm looking at it . . . to be sure the cartridges are there, to see that it is oiled, or whatever is done to it . . . to see how it functions.

CARDINAL. But . . .

LAWYER (*calmly*). You know we may have to shoot him; you know that may be necessary.

CARDINAL (*sadly and softly*). Dear God, no.

LAWYER (*looking at the gun*). I suppose all you do is . . . pull. (*Looks at the* CARDINAL.) If the great machinery threatens . . . to come to a halt . . . the great axis on which all turns . . . if it needs oil . . . well, we lubricate it, do we not? And if blood is the only oil handy . . . what is a little blood?

CARDINAL (*false bravura*). But that will not be necessary. (*Great empty quiet loss.*) Dear God, let that not be necessary.

LAWYER. Better off dead, perhaps. You know? Eh?

CARDINAL. The making of a martyr? A saint?

LAWYER. Well, let's make that saint when we come to him.

CARDINAL. Dear God, let that not be necessary.

LAWYER. Why not? Give me *any* person . . . a martyr, if you wish . . . a saint . . . He'll take what he gets for . . . what he wishes it to be. AH, it is what I have always wanted, he'll say, looking terror and betrayal straight in the eye. Why not: face the inevitable and call it what you have always wanted. How to come out on top, going under.

(JULIAN *enters.*)

LAWYER. Ah! There you are. Still not with Miss Alice!

JULIAN. I seem not to be with anyone.

LAWYER (*smile*). Isn't that odd?

JULIAN (*turning away, more to himself*). I would have thought it so.

CARDINAL (*hearty, but ill at ease*). One would have thought to have it all now—corks popping, glasses splintering in the fireplace . . .

LAWYER. When Christ told Peter—so legends tell—that he would found his church upon that rock, He must have had in mind an island in a sea of wine. How firm a foundation in the vintage years . . .

(*We hear voices from without; they do, too.*)

MISS ALICE (*offstage*). I don't *want* to go in there . . .

BUTLER (*offstage*). You *have* to come in, now . . .

MISS ALICE (*offstage*). I won't go *in* there. . . .

BUTLER (*offstage*). Come along now; don't be a child. . . .

MISS ALICE (*offstage*). I . . . won't . . . go . . .

(BUTLER *appears; two champagne bottles in one hand, pulling* MISS ALICE *with the other.*)

BUTLER. Come along!

MISS ALICE (*as she enters; sotto voce*). I don't want to . . .

(*As she sees the others see her, she stops talking, smiles, tries to save the entrance.*)

BUTLER. Lurking in the gallery, talking to the ancestral wall, but I found her.

MISS ALICE. Don't be silly; I was . . . (*Shrugs.*)

BUTLER (*shrugs, too*). Suit yourself. Champagne, everybody!

JULIAN. Ah! Good. (*Moving toward* MISS ALICE.) Are you all right?

MISS ALICE (*moves away from him; rather impatiently*). Yes.

CARDINAL. But you've changed your clothes, and your wedding gown was . . .

MISS ALICE. . . . two hundred years old . . .

LAWYER. . . . fragile.

CARDINAL. Ah!

(*Something of a silence falls. The other characters are away from* JULIAN; *unless otherwise specified, they will keep a distance, surrounding him, but more than at arm's length. They will observe him, rather clinically, and while this shift of attitude must be subtle, it must also be evident.* JULIAN *will grow to knowledge of it, will aid us, though we will be aware of it before he is.*)

JULIAN (*to break the silence*). Well, shall we have the champagne?

BUTLER. Stay there! (*Pause.*) I'll bring it.

CARDINAL. Once, when we were in France, we toured the champagne country . . .

LAWYER (*no interest*). Really.

CARDINAL. Saw the . . . mechanics, so to speak, of how it was done. . . .

LAWYER. Peasants? Treading?

CARDINAL (*laughs*). No, no. That is for woodcuts.

(*The cork pops.*)

Ah!

BUTLER. Nobody move! I'll bring it to you all.

(*Starts pouring into glasses already placed to the side.*)

MISS ALICE (*to the* LAWYER). The ceremony.

(*He does not reply.*) The ceremony!

LAWYER (*overly sweet smile*). Yes. (*To them all.*) The ceremony.

CARDINAL. Another? Must we officiate?

LAWYER. No need.

JULIAN (*a little apprehensive*). What . . . ceremony is this?

BUTLER (*his back to them*). There's never as much in a champagne bottle as I expect there to be; I never learn. Or, perhaps the glasses are larger than they seem.

LAWYER (*ironic*). When the lights go on all over the world . . . the true world. The ceremony of Alice.

JULIAN (*to* MISS ALICE). What is this about?

(*She nods toward the* LAWYER.)

LAWYER. Butler? Are you poured?

BUTLER (*finishing; squeezing the bottle*). Yeeeeesssss . . .

LAWYER. Pass.

BUTLER (*starts passing the tray of glasses*). Miss Alice.

MISS ALICE (*strained*). Thank you.

BUTLER (*starts toward* JULIAN, *changes his mind, goes to the* CARDINAL). Your Eminence?

CARDINAL. Ahhh.

BUTLER (*starts toward* JULIAN *again, changes his mind, goes to the* LAWYER). Sweetheart?

LAWYER. Thank you.

BUTLER (*finally goes to* JULIAN, *holds the tray at arm's length; speaks, not unkindly*). Our Brother Julian.

JULIAN (*shy friendliness*). Thank you, Butler.

LAWYER. And now . . .

BUTLER (*moving back to the table with the tray*). Hold on; I haven't got mine yet. It's over here.

JULIAN. Yes! Butler must drink with us. (*To* MISS ALICE.) Don't you think so?

MISS ALICE (*curiously weary*). Why not? He's family.

LAWYER (*moving toward the model*). Yes; what a large family you have.

(*The* LAWYER *would naturally have to pass near* JULIAN; *pauses, detours.*)

JULIAN. I'm sorry; am . . . am I in your way?

LAWYER (*continues to the model*). Large family, years of adding. The ceremony, children. The ceremony of Alice.

(*The others have turned, are facing the model. The* LAWYER *raises his glass.*)

To Julian and his bride.

CARDINAL. Hear, hear.

JULIAN (*blushing*). Oh, my goodness.

LAWYER. To Julian and his bride; to Alice's wisdom, wealth and whatever.

BUTLER (*quietly, seriously*). To Alice.

MISS ALICE. To Alice.

(*Brief pause; only* JULIAN *turns his head, is about to speak, but . . .*)

LAWYER. To their marriage. To their binding together, acceptance and worship . . . received; accepted.

BUTLER. To Alice.

LAWYER. To the marriage vow between them, which has brought joy to them both, and great benefit to the Church.

CARDINAL. Amen.

MISS ALICE. To Alice.

(*Again only* JULIAN *responds to this; a half turn of the head.*)

LAWYER. To their house.

BUTLER, MISS ALICE and CARDINAL (*not quite together*). To their house.

JULIAN (*after them*). To their house.

LAWYER. To the chapel wherein they were bound in wedlock.

(*A light goes on in a room in the model.* JULIAN *makes sounds of amazement; the others are silent.*)

To their quarters.

(*Light goes on upstairs in the model.*)

To the private rooms where marriage lives.

BUTLER. To Alice.

MISS ALICE. To Alice.

(*To which* JULIAN *does not respond this time.*)

LAWYER. And to this room . . . (*Another light goes on in the model.*) in which they are met, in which we are met . . . to celebrate their coming together.

BUTLER. Amen.

LAWYER. A union whose spiritual values shall be uppermost . . .

MISS ALICE. That's enough . . .

LAWYER. . . . whose carnal side shall . . .

MISS ALICE. That's enough!

JULIAN. May . . . May I?

(*It is important that he stay facing the model, not* MISS ALICE. BUTLER, *who is behind him, may look at him; the* CARDINAL *will look to the floor.*)

May I . . . propose. To the wonders . . . which may befall a man . . . least where he is looking, least that he would have thought; to the clear plan of that which we call chance, to what we see as accident till our humility returns to us when we are faced with the mysteries. To all that which we really want, until our guile and pride . . .

CARDINAL (*still looking at the floor*). . . . Julian . . .

JULIAN. . . . betray us? (*Looks at the* CARDINAL; *pauses, goes on, smiling sweetly.*) My gratitude . . . my wonder . . . and my love.

LAWYER (*pause*). Amen?

JULIAN. Amen.

LAWYER (*abruptly turning*). Then, if we're packed, let us go.

BUTLER (*not moving*). Dust covers.

JULIAN (*still smiling*). Go?

CARDINAL (*to delay*). Well. *This* champagne glass seems smaller than one would have guessed; it has emptied itself . . . on one toast!

LAWYER. I recall. Suddenly I recall it.

When we were children. (*Quite fascinated with what he is saying.*) When we were children and we would gather in the dark, two of us . . . any two . . . on a swing, side porch, or by the ocean, sitting backed against a boulder, and we would explore . . . those most private parts, of one another, any two of us . . . (*Shrugs.*) boy, girl, how—when we did it—we would talk of other things . . . of our schoolwork, or where we would travel in the summer. How, as our shaking hands passed under skirts or undid buttons, sliding, how we would, both of us, talk of other things, whispering, our voices shaking as our just barely moving hands. (*Laughs, points to the* CARDINAL.) Like you! Chattering there on the model! Your mind on us and what is happening. Oh, the subterfuges.

MISS ALICE. I am packed.

JULIAN (*still off by himself*). Packed? . . . Miss Alice? . . .

MISS ALICE (*to the* LAWYER; *cold*). May we leave soon?

JULIAN. Miss . . . Alice?

MISS ALICE. May we?

LAWYER (*pause*). Fairly.

JULIAN (*sharp*). Miss Alice!

MISS ALICE (*turns toward him; flat tone; a recitation*). I'm very happy for you, Julian, you've done well.

JULIAN (*backing away from everyone a little*). What is . . . going on . . . here? (*To* MISS ALICE.) Tell me!

MISS ALICE (*as if she is not interested*). I am packed. We are going.

JULIAN (*sudden understanding*). Ah! (*Points to himself.*) *We* are going. But where? You . . . didn't tell me we . . . we were . . .

MISS ALICE (*to the* LAWYER, *moving away*). Tell him.

JULIAN. . . . going somewhere. . . .

MISS ALICE (*quite furious*). Tell him!

LAWYER (*about to make a speech*). Brother Julian . . .

JULIAN (*strained*). I am no longer Brother.

LAWYER (*oily*). Oh, are we not all brothers?

JULIAN (*to* MISS ALICE; *with a half-hearted gesture*). Come stand by me.

MISS ALICE (*surprisingly little-girl fright*). No!

LAWYER. Now. Julian.

CARDINAL. Order yourself, Julian.

JULIAN (*to the* CARDINAL). Sir?

LAWYER (*sarcasm is gone; all is gone, save fact*). Dear Julian; we all serve, do we not? Each of us his own priesthood; publicly, some, others . . . within only; but we all do—what's-his-name's special trumpet, or clear lonely bell. Predestination, fate, the will of God, accident . . . All swirled up in it, no matter what the name. And being man, we have invented choice, and have, indeed, gone further, and have catalogued the underpinnings of choice. But we do not know. Anything. End prologue.

MISS ALICE. Tell him.

LAWYER. No matter. We are leaving you now, Julian; agents, every one of us—going. We are leaving you . . . to your accomplishment: your marriage, your wife, your . . . special priesthood.

JULIAN (*apprehension and great suspicion*). I . . . don't know what you're talking about.

LAWYER (*unperturbed*). What is so amazing is the . . . coming together . . . of disparates . . . left-fielding, out of the most unlikely. Who would have thought, Julian? Who would have thought? You have brought us to the end of our service here. We go on; you stay.

BUTLER. May I begin to cover?

MISS ALICE. Not yet. (*Kindly.*) Do you understand, Julian?

JULIAN (*barely in control*). Of course not!

MISS ALICE. Julian, I have tried to be . . . her. No; I have tried to be . . . what I thought she might, what might make you happy, what you might use, as a . . . what?

BUTLER. *Play* God; go on.

MISS ALICE. We must . . . represent, draw pictures, reduce or enlarge to . . . to what we can understand.

JULIAN (*sad, mild*). But I have fought against it . . . all my life. When they said, "Bring the wonders down to me, closer; I cannot see them, touch; nor can I believe." I have fought against it . . . all my life.

BUTLER (*to MISS ALICE; softly*). You see? No good.

MISS ALICE (*shrugs*). I have done what I can with it.

JULIAN. All my life. In and out of . . . confinement, fought against the symbol.

MISS ALICE. Then you should be happy now.

CARDINAL. Julian, it has been your desire always to serve; your sense of mission . . .

LAWYER. We are surrogates; *our* task is done now.

MISS ALICE. Stay with her.

JULIAN (*horror behind it; disbelieving*). Stay . . . with . . . her?

MISS ALICE. Stay with her. Accept it.

LAWYER (*at the model*). Her rooms are lighted. It is warm, there is enough.

MISS ALICE. Be content with it. Stay with her.

JULIAN (*refusing to accept what he is hearing*). Miss Alice . . . I have married you.

MISS ALICE (*kind, still*). No, Julian; you have married *her* . . . through me.

JULIAN (*pointing to the model*). There is nothing there! We are *here*! There is no one *there*!

LAWYER. *She* is there . . . we believe.

JULIAN (*to MISS ALICE*). I have *been* with *you*!

MISS ALICE (*not explaining; sort of dreamy*). You have felt her warmth through me, touched her lips through my lips, held hands, through mine, my breasts, hers, lain on her bed, through mine, wrapped yourself in her wings, your hands on the small of her back, your mouth on her hair, the voice in your ear, hers not mine, all hers; her. You are hers.

CARDINAL. Accept.

BUTLER. Accept.

LAWYER. Accept.

JULIAN. THERE IS NO ONE THERE!

MISS ALICE. She is there.

JULIAN (*rushes to the model, shouts at it*). THERE IS NOTHING THERE! (*Turns to them all.*) THERE IS NOTHING THERE!

CARDINAL (*softly*). Accept it, Julian.

JULIAN (*all the power he has*). ACCEPT IT!

LAWYER (*quietly*). All legal, all accomplished, all satisfied, that which we believe.

JULIAN. Accept!

BUTLER. . . . that which is done, and may not be revoked.

CARDINAL (*with some difficulty*). . . . yes.

JULIAN. WHAT AM I TO ACCEPT!

LAWYER. An act of faith.

JULIAN (*slow, incredulous*). An . . . act . . . of . . . faith!

LAWYER (*snaps his fingers at the CARDINAL*). Buddy?

CARDINAL. Uh . . . yes, Julian, an . . . act of faith, indeed. It is . . . believed.

LAWYER (*deadly serious, but with a small smile*). Yes, it is . . . believed. It is what we believe, therefore what we know. Is that not right? Faith is knowledge?

CARDINAL. An act of faith, Julian, however we must . . .

JULIAN (*horror*). FAITH!?

CARDINAL. . . . in God's will . . .

JULIAN. GOD'S! WILL!

CARDINAL (*as if his ears are hurting, sort of mumbling*). Yes, Julian, you see, we must accept, and . . . be glad, yes, be glad . . . our ecstasy.

JULIAN (*backing off a little, shaking his head*). I have not come this distance . . .

CARDINAL (*moving toward him a little*). Julian . . .

JULIAN. Stay back! I have not come this long way . . . have not—in all sweet obedience—walked in these . . . (*Realizes he is differently dressed.*) those robes . . . to be MOCKED.

LAWYER. Accept it, Julian.

JULIAN. I have not come this long *way!*

BUTLER. Yes; oh, yes.

JULIAN. I HAVE NOT!

MISS ALICE (*kindly*). Julian . . . dear Julian; accept.

JULIAN (*turns toward her, supplicating*). I have not worn and given up for . . . for mockery; I have not stretched out the path of my life before me, to walk on straight, to be . . .

MISS ALICE. Accept.

JULIAN. I have not fought the nightmares—and the waking demons, yes—and the years of despair, those, too . . . I have not accepted *half,* for *nothing.*

CARDINAL. For everything.

MISS ALICE. Dear Julian; accept. Allow us all to rest.

JULIAN (*a child's terror of being alone*). NO!

MISS ALICE (*still kind*). You must.

BUTLER. No choice.

JULIAN. I have . . . have . . . given up everything to gain everything, for the sake of my faith and my peace; I have allowed and followed, and sworn and cherished, but I have *not,* have *not* . . .

MISS ALICE. Be with her. Please.

JULIAN. For halluci*nation?* I HAVE DONE WITH HALLUCINATION.

MISS ALICE. Then have done with for-gery, Julian; accept what's real. I am the . . . illusion.

JULIAN (*retreating*). No . . . no no no, oh no.

LAWYER (*quietly*). All legal, all accomplished, all satisfied, that which we believe.

MISS ALICE. All done.

JULIAN (*quite frightened*). I . . . choose . . . *not.*

CARDINAL. There is no choice here, Julian. . . .

LAWYER. No choice at all.

MISS ALICE (*hands apart*). All done.

(JULIAN *begins backing toward the model; the* LAWYER *begins crossing to the desk wherein he has put the gun.*)

BUTLER (*quietly*). I *must* cover now; the cars are waiting.

JULIAN. No . . . no . . . I WILL NOT ACCEPT THIS.

LAWYER (*snaps for the* CARDINAL *again*). Buddy . . .

CARDINAL. We . . . (*Harder tone.*) I *order* you.

LAWYER (*smile*). There. Now will you accept?

JULIAN. I . . . cannot be so mistaken, to have . . . I cannot have so misunderstood my life; I cannot have . . . was I sane *then?* Those *years?* My time in the *asylum?* WAS THAT WHEN I WAS RATIONAL? THEN?

CARDINAL. Julian . . .

LAWYER (*taking the gun from the drawer, checking it; to the* CARDINAL). Don't you teach your people anything? Do you let them improvise? *Make* their Gods? *Make* them as they *see* them?

JULIAN (*rage in the terror*). I HAVE ACCEPTED GOD.

LAWYER (*turns to* JULIAN, *gun in hand*). Then accept his works. Resign yourself to the mysteries . . .

MISS ALICE. . . . to greater wisdom.

LAWYER. Take it! Accept what you're given.

MISS ALICE. Your priesthood, Julian—full, at last. Stay with her. Accept your service.

JULIAN. I . . . cannot . . . accept . . . this.

LAWYER (*aims*). Very well, then.

JULIAN. I have not come this . . . given up so much for . . .

BUTLER. Accept it, Julian.

MISS ALICE. Stay with her.

JULIAN. No, no, I will . . . I will go

back! I will . . . go *back* to it. (*Starts backing toward the stairs.*) To . . . to . . . I will go back to the asylum.

LAWYER. Last chance.

MISS ALICE. Accept it, Julian.

JULIAN. To . . . my asylum. MY! ASYLUM! My . . . my refuge . . . in the world, from all the demons waking, my . . . REFUGE!

LAWYER. Very well then.

(*Shoots. Then silence.* JULIAN *does not cry out, but clutches his belly, stumbles forward a few steps, sinks to the floor in front of the model.*)

MISS ALICE (*softly, with compassion*). Oh, Julian. (*To the* LAWYER; *calm.*) He would have stayed.

LAWYER (*to* MISS ALICE, *shrugging*). It was an accident.

JULIAN. Fa . . . ther?

MISS ALICE. Poor Julian. (*To the* LAWYER.) You did not have to do that; I could have made him stay.

LAWYER. Perhaps. But what does it matter . . . one man . . . in the face of so much.

JULIAN. Fa . . . ther?

BUTLER (*going to* JULIAN). Let me look.

MISS ALICE (*starting to go to him*). Oh, poor Julian . . .

LAWYER (*stopping her*). Stay where you are.

(BUTLER *goes to* JULIAN *while the others keep their places.* BUTLER *bends over him, maybe pulling his head back.*)

BUTLER. Do you want a doctor for him?

LAWYER (*after a tiny pause*). Why?

BUTLER (*straightening up*). . . . Because . . .

LAWYER. Yes?

BUTLER (*quite matter-of-fact*). Because he will bleed to death without attention?

JULIAN (*to the* CARDINAL). Help . . . me?

(*In answer, the* CARDINAL *looks back to the* LAWYER, *asking a question with his silence.*)

LAWYER (*after a pause*). No doctor.

BUTLER (*moving away*). No doctor.

MISS ALICE (*to the* LAWYER; *great sadness*). No?

LAWYER (*some compassion*). No.

JULIAN. Father!

CARDINAL (*anguished*). Please, Julian.

JULIAN (*anger through the pain*). In the sight of God? You dare?

LAWYER. Or in the sight of man. He

dares. (*Moves to the table, putting the gun away, taking up the briefcase.*)

JULIAN (*again*). You dare!?

(BUTLER *goes to cover something.*)

LAWYER (*taking the briefcase to the* CARDINAL). There it is, all of it. All legal now, the total grant: two billion, kid, twenty years of grace for no work at all; no labor . . . at least not yours. (*Holds the briefcase out.*) There . . . take it.

CARDINAL. We do not . . . fetch and carry. And have not acquiesced . . . (*Indicates briefcase.*) For *this*.

JULIAN (*weak again*). Father?

LAWYER. Not God's errand boy?

CARDINAL. God's; not yours.

LAWYER. *Who* are the Gods?

JULIAN (*pain*). God in heaven!

MISS ALICE. Poor Julian!

(*Goes to him; they create something of a Pietà.*)

Rest back; lean on me.

LAWYER (*withdrawing his offer of the briefcase*). Perhaps your *new* secretary can pick it up. You *will* go on, won't you—red gown and amethyst, until the pelvic cancer comes, or the coronary blacks it out, all of it? The good with it, and the evil? (*Indicates* JULIAN.) Even this? In the final mercy?

(*The* CARDINAL *looks straight ahead of him for a moment, hesitates, then walks out, looking neither left nor right.*)

BUTLER (*calling after him, halfhearted and intentionally too late*). Any of the cars will do . . . (*Trailing off.*) . . . as they're all hired.

JULIAN. Who . . . who left? Who!

MISS ALICE (*comforting him*). You're shivering, Julian . . . so.

JULIAN (*almost a laugh*). Am I?

LAWYER (*still looking after the departed* CARDINAL). Once, when I was at school —our departed reminds me—once, when I was at school, I was writing poetry— well, no, poems, which were published in the literary magazine. And each issue a teacher from the English Department would criticize the work in the school newspaper a week or two hence.

MISS ALICE (*to* JULIAN). A blanket?

JULIAN. No. Hold close.

LAWYER. And one teacher, who was a wag and was, as well, a former student, wrote of one of my poems—a sonnet, as I recall—that it had all the grace of a walking crow.

MISS ALICE (*ibid.*). I don't want to hurt.

JULIAN. Closer . . . please. Warmth.

LAWYER. I was green in those years, and, besides, I could not recall how crows walked.

MISS ALICE (*ibid.*). How like a little boy you are.

JULIAN. I'm lonely.

LAWYER. Could not recall that I had ever *seen* a crow . . . walking.

MISS ALICE. Is being afraid always the same—no matter the circumstances, the age?

JULIAN. It is the attic room, always; the closet. Hold close.

LAWYER (*fully aware of the counterpoint by now, aiding it*). And so I went to see him—the wag—about the walking crow . . . the poem, actually.

BUTLER (*putting a cover on something*). Crows don't walk much . . .

JULIAN. . . . and it is very dark; always. And no one will come . . . for the longest time.

MISS ALICE. Yes.

LAWYER. Yes; that is what he said—sitting with his back against all the books, "Crows don't walk much . . . if they can help if . . . if they can fly."

JULIAN. No. No one will come.

BUTLER (*snapping open a cover*). I could have told you that; surprised you didn't know it. Crows walk around a lot only when they're sick.

LAWYER. "Santayanian finesse."

JULIAN. No one will come . . . for the longest time; if ever.

MISS ALICE (*agreeing*). No.

LAWYER. That was the particular thing: "Santayanian finesse." He said that had . . . all the grace of a walking crow.

BUTLER (*rubbing something for dust*). Bright man.

LAWYER (*to* BUTLER). I don't know; he stayed on some years after I left—after our walking bird and I left—then went on to some other school. . . . (*To* MISS ALICE, *immediately.*) Are you ready to go?

MISS ALICE (*looking up; sad irony*). Am I ready to go on with it, do you mean? To move to the city now before the train trip south? The private car? The house on the ocean, the . . . same mysteries, the evasions, the perfect plotting? The removed residence, the Rolls twice weekly into the shopping strip . . . all of it?

LAWYER. Yes. All of it.

MISS ALICE (*looks to* JULIAN, *considers a moment*). Are you warm now?

JULIAN. Yes . . . and cold.

MISS ALICE (*looks up to the* LAWYER, *smiles faintly*). No.

LAWYER. Then get up and come along.

MISS ALICE (*to the* LAWYER). And all the rest of it?

LAWYER. Yes.

MISS ALICE. The years of it . . . to go on? For how long?

LAWYER. Until we are replaced.

MISS ALICE (*with a tiny, tinkling laugh*). Oh God.

LAWYER. Or until everything is desert (*Shrugs.*) . . . on the chance that *it* runs out before *we* do.

BUTLER (*examining the phrenological head*). I have never even examined phrenology.

LAWYER. But more likely till we are replaced.

JULIAN (*with a sort of quiet wonder*). I am cold at the core . . . where it burns most.

MISS ALICE (*sad truth*). Yes. (*Then to the* LAWYER.) Yes.

LAWYER (*almost affectionately*). So, come now; gather yourself.

MISS ALICE (*restrained pleading*). But, he is still . . . ill . . .

JULIAN (*to* MISS ALICE, *probably, but not at her*). You wish to go away now?

MISS ALICE (*to the* LAWYER). You see how he takes to me? You see how it *is* natural? Poor Julian.

LAWYER. Let's go.

MISS ALICE (*to* JULIAN). I *must* go away from you now; it is not that I wish to. (*To* BUTLER.) Butler, I have left my wig, it is upstairs . . .

BUTLER (*rather testy*). I'm sorry, I'm covering, I'm busy.

LAWYER (*turning to go*). Let me; it's such a pretty wig, becomes you so. And there are one or two other things I'd like to check.

MISS ALICE (*sad smile*). The pillowcases? Put your ear against them? To eavesdrop? Or the sheets? To see if they're still writhing?

(*The* LAWYER *almost says something, thinks better of it, exits.*)

Poor Julian.

BUTLER. Then we all are to be together.

MISS ALICE (*small laugh*). Oh God, you heard him: forever.

BUTLER. I like it where it's warm.

MISS ALICE. I dreaded once, when I was in my teens, that I would grow old, look back, over the precipice, and discover that I had not lived my life. (*Short abrupt laugh.*) Oh Lord!

JULIAN (*now a semi-coma, almost sweet*). How long wilt thou forget me, O Lord? Forever?

BUTLER. We live *something.*

MISS ALICE. Yes.

JULIAN. How long wilt thou hide thy face from me?

BUTLER (*to* JULIAN). Psalm Thirteen.

MISS ALICE (*to* JULIAN). Yes?

JULIAN. Yes.

BUTLER. How long shall my enemy be exalted over me?

JULIAN. Yes.

MISS ALICE. Not long.

BUTLER (*looking at a cover*). Consider and hear me, O Lord, my God.

JULIAN. What does it mean if the pain . . . ebbs?

BUTLER (*considered; kindly*). It means the agony is less.

MISS ALICE. Yes.

JULIAN (*rueful laugh*). Consciousness, then, is pain. (*Looks up at* MISS ALICE.) All disappointments, all treacheries. (*Ironic laugh.*) Oh, God.

BUTLER. Why are we taking separate cars, then?

MISS ALICE. Well, I might ride rubbing hips on either side with a different lover, bouncing along, but . . . Alice, Miss Alice would not. (*Pause.*) Would I? I would not do that. She.

BUTLER. I love you . . . not her. Or . . . quite differently.

MISS ALICE. Shhhh . . .

BUTLER. For ages, *I* look at the sheets, listen to the pillowcases, when they're brought down, sidle into the laundry room . . .

MISS ALICE. Don't.

(JULIAN *makes a sound of great pain.*) Oh! . . . Oh! . . .

JULIAN (*commenting on the pain*). Dear . . . God . . . in . . . heaven . . .

MISS ALICE. Calm; be calm now.

BUTLER (*wistful*). But you pass through everyone, everything . . . touching just briefly, lightly, passing.

MISS ALICE. My poor Julian. (*To the model.*) Receive him? Take him in?

JULIAN (*a little boy, scared*). Who are you talking to?

MISS ALICE (*breathing it*). Alice . . .

JULIAN. Alice? Ah.

BUTLER. Will we be coming back . . . when the weather changes?

MISS ALICE (*triste*). Probably.

JULIAN (*confirming the previous exchange*). Alice?

MISS ALICE. Yes.

JULIAN. Ah.

BUTLER (*understanding what he has been told*). Ah.

(*The* LAWYER *enters with* MISS ALICE'S *wig.*)

LAWYER. Bed stripped, mothballs lying on it like hailstones; no sound, movement, nothing.

(*Puts the wig on the phrenological head.*)

Do you want company, Julian? Do you want a friend? (*To* MISS ALICE.) Looks nice there. Leave it; we'll get you another. Are you ready to go?

MISS ALICE (*weary*). You want me to go now?

LAWYER (*correcting her*). Come.

MISS ALICE. Yes. (*Begins to disengage herself.*) Butler, come help me; we can't leave Julian just . . .

BUTLER. Yes. (*Moves to help her.*)—

JULIAN (*as they take him by the arm*). Don't do that!

MISS ALICE. Julian, we must move you . . .

JULIAN. Don't.

LAWYER (*without emotion*). Leave him where he is.

JULIAN. Leave me . . . be.

(*He slides along the floor, backing up against the model.*)

Leave me . . . where I am.

LAWYER. Good pose: leave him there.

BUTLER (*getting a chair cushion*). Cushion.

JULIAN. All . . . hurts.

BUTLER (*putting the cushion behind him*). Easy . . .

JULIAN. ALL HURTS!!

MISS ALICE (*coming to him*). Oh, my poor Julian . . .

JULIAN (*surprisingly strong, angry*). LEAVE ME!

(MISS ALICE *considers a moment, turns, leaves.*)

LAWYER (*walks over to* JULIAN, *regards him; almost casually*). Goodbye.

JULIAN (*softly, but a malediction*). Instrument!

LAWYER (*turns on his heel, walks out, saying as he goes*). Butler?

(*Exits.*)

BUTLER (*as* LAWYER *goes; abstracted*). Yes . . . dear.

JULIAN (*half laughed, pained incredulity*). Good . . . bye!

BUTLER (*looks about the room*). All in order, I think.

JULIAN (*wistful*). Help me?

BUTLER. My work done.

JULIAN. No?

(BUTLER *regards* JULIAN *for a moment, then walks over, bends, kisses* JULIAN *on the forehead, not a quick kiss.*)

BUTLER. Goodbye, dear Julian.

(*As* BUTLER *exits, he closes the doors behind him.*)

JULIAN (*alone, for a moment, then, whispered*). Goodbye, dear Julian. (*Pause.*) Exit . . . all. (*Softly.*) Help me . . . come back, help me. (*Pause.*) HELP ME! (*Pause.*) No . . . no help. Kiss. A kiss goodbye, from . . . whom? . . . Oh. From, from one . . . an . . . arms: around me; warming. COME BACK AND HELP ME. (*Pause.*) If only to stay *with* me, while it . . . *if* . . . while it happens. For . . . you, you would not have left me if it . . . were not . . . would you? No. (*Calling to them.*) I HAVE NEVER DREAMED OF IT. NEVER . . . IMAGINED . . . (*To himself again.*) what it would be like. (*As if they were near the door.*) I died once, when I was little . . . almost, running, fell past jagged iron, noticed . . . only when I . . . tried to get up, that my leg, left, was torn . . . the whole thigh *and* calf . . . down. Such . . . *searing* . . . pain? Sweet smell of blood, screaming at the sight of it, so *far* . . . away from the house, and in the field, all hot . . . and yellow, white in the sun. COME BACK TO ME. Sunday, and my parents off . . . somewhere, only my grandfather, and he . . . OFF: SOMEWHERE: mousing with the dog. All the way down . . . bone, flesh, meat, moving. Help me, Grandfather! "Ere I die, ere life ebbs." (*Laughs softly.*) Oh, Christ. (*Little boy.*) Grandfather? Mousing? Come to me: Julian bleeds, leg torn, from short pants to shoe, bone, meat open to the sun; come to him. (*Looks at the model, above and behind him.*) Ahhhh. Will no one come? (*Looks at the ceiling.*) High; high

walls . . . summit. (*Eyes on his leg.*) Belly . . . not leg. Come, grandfather! Not leg, belly! Doublebutton. Pinpoint, searing . . . pain? "If you . . . if you die." Are you sleeping, not mousing? Sleeping on the sunporch? Hammocking? Yes. "If I die before *you* wake, will the Lord deign *your* soul take?" Grandfather? (*Cry of pain, then.*) Oh . . . GOD! "I come to thee, in agony." (*Cry to the void.*) HELP . . . ME! (*Pause.*) No help. Stitch it up like a wineskin! Hold the wine in. Stitch it up. (*Sweet reminiscence.*) And every day, put him in the sun, quarter over, for the whole stitched leg . . . to bake, in the healing sun. Green? Yes, a little, but that's the medicine. And keep him out of the fields, chuckle, chuckle. And every day, swinging in the sun, baking; good. Aching all the while, but good. The cat comes, sniffs it, won't stay. Finally . . . stays; lies in the bend, doubling it, purring, breathing, soaking in the sun, as the leg throbs, aches, heals. "How will I know thee, O Lord, when I am in thy sight? How will I know thee?" By my *faith*. Ah, I see. (*Furious, shouting at the roof.*) BY FAITH? THE FAITH I HAVE SHOWN THEE? BENT MYSELF? What may we avoid! Not birth! Growing up? Yes. Maturing? Oh, *God!* Growing old, and? . . . yes, growing old; but not the last; merely when. (*Sweet sing-song.*) But to live again, be born once more, sure in the sight of . . . (*Shouts again.*) THERE IS NO ONE! (*Turns his head toward the closed doors, sadly.*) Unless you are listening there. Unless you have left me, tiptoed off some, stood whispering, smothered giggles, and . . . silently returned, your ears pressed against, or . . . or one eye into the crack so that the air smarts it sifting through. HAVE YOU COME BACK? HAVE YOU NOT LEFT ME? (*Pause.*) No. No one. Out in the night . . . nothing. Night? No; what then? IS IT NIGHT . . . OR DAY? (*Great weariness.*) Or does it matter? No. How long wilt thou forget me, O Lord? Forever? How long wilt thou hide thy face from me? How long shall my enemy . . . I . . . can . . . barely . . . feel. Which is a sign. A change, at any rate. (*To the rooftops again.*) I DO NOT UNDERSTAND, O LORD, MY GOD, WHAT THOU WILT HAVE OF ME! (*More conversational.*) I have never dreamed of it, never imagined what it would be like. I have—oh, yes—dwelt

(*Laughs at the word.*) . . . dwelt . . . on the *fact* of it, the . . . principle, but I have not imagined dying. Death . . . yes. Not being, but not the act of . . . dying? ALICE!? (*Laughs softly.*) Oh, Alice, why hast *thou* forsaken me? (*Leans his head back to see the model.*) Hast thou? Alice? *Hast* thou forsaken me . . . with . . . all the others? (*Laughs again.*) Come bring me my slippers and my pipe, and push the dog into the room. Bring me my slippers, the sacramental wine, (*Little boy.*) my cookie? (*Usual again.*) . . . come bring me my ease, come sit with me . . . and watch me as I die. Alice? ALICE!? (*To himself.*) There is nothing; there is no one. (*Wheedling a little.*) Come talk to me; come sit by my right hand . . . *on* the one hand . . . come sit with me and hold my . . . what? Then come and talk; tell me how it goes, Alice. (*Laughs.*) "Raise high the roofbeam, for the bridegroom comes." Oh, what a priesthood is this! Oh, what a range of duties, and such parishioners, and such a chapel for my praise. (*Turns some, leans toward the model, where the chapel light shines.*) Oh, what a priesthood, see my chapel, how it . . .

(*Suddenly the light in the chapel in the model goes out.* JULIAN *starts, makes a sound of surprise and fear.*)

Alice? . . . God? SOMEONE? Come to Julian as he . . . ebbs.

(*We begin to hear it now, faintly at first, slowly growing, so faintly at first it is subliminal: the heartbeat . . . thump thump . . . thump thump . . . And the breathing . . . the intake taking one thump-thump, the exhaling the next.* JULIAN *neither senses nor hears it yet, however.*)

Come, comfort him, warm him. He has not been a willful man . . . Oh, willful in his . . . cry to serve, but gentle, would not cause pain, but bear it, *would* bear it . . . has, even. Not much, I suppose. One man's share is not . . . another's burden. (*Notices the wig on the phrenological head; crawls a bit toward it; half kneels in front of it.*) Thou art my bride? Thou? For thee have I done my life? Grown to love, entered in, bent . . . accepted? For thee? Is that the . . . awful humor? Art thou the true arms, when the warm flesh I touched . . . rested against, was . . . nothing? And *she* . . . was not real? Is thy stare the true look?

Unblinking, outward, through, to some horizon? And her eyes . . . warm, accepting, were they . . . not real? Art thou my bride? (*To the ceiling again.*) Ah God! Is that the humor? THE ABSTRACT? . . . REAL? THE REST? . . . FALSE? (*To himself, with terrible irony.*) It is what I have wanted, have insisted on. Have nagged . . . for (*Looking about the room, raging.*) IS THIS MY PRIESTHOOD, THEN? THIS WORLD? THEN COME AND SHOW THYSELF! BRIDE? GOD?

(*Silence; we hear the heartbeats and the breathing some.*)

SHOW THYSELF! I DEMAND THEE! (JULIAN *crawls back toward the model; faces it, back to the audience, addresses it.*) SHOW THYSELF! FOR THEE I HAVE GAMBLED . . . MY SOUL? I DEMAND THY PRESENCE. ALICE!

(*The sounds become louder now, as, in the model, the light fades in the bedroom, begins to move across an upper story.* JULIAN's *reaction is a muffled cry.*)

AGHHH! (*On his hands and knees he backs off a little from the model, still staring at it.*) You . . . thou . . . art . . . coming to me? (*Frightened and angry.*) ABSTRACTION? . . . ABSTRACTION! . . . (*Sad, defeated.*) Art coming to me. (*A shivered prayer, quick.*) How long wilt thou forget me, O Lord? Forever? How long wilt thou hide thy face from me? . . . Consider and hear me, O Lord, my God. (*Shouted now.*) CONSIDER AND HEAR ME, O LORD, MY GOD. LIGHTEN MY EYES LEST I SLEEP THE SLEEP OF DEATH.

(*The lights keep moving; the sounds become louder.*). BUT I HAVE TRUSTED IN THY MERCY, O LORD. HOW LONG WILT THOU FORGET ME? (*Softly, whining.*) How long wilt thou hide thy face from me? COME, BRIDE! COME, GOD! COME!

(*The breathing and heartbeats are much, much louder now. The lights descend a stairway in the model.* JULIAN *turns, backs against the model, his arms way to the side of him.*)

Alice? (*Fear and trembling.*) Alice? ALICE? MY GOD, WHY HAST THOU FORSAKEN ME?

(*A great shadow, or darkening, fills the stage; it is the shadow of a great presence filling the room. The area on* JULIAN *and around him stays in some light, but, for the rest, it is as if ink were moving through paper toward a focal point. The sounds become enormous.* JULIAN *is aware of the presence in the room, "sees" it, in the sense that his eyes, his head move to all areas of the room, noticing his engulfment. He almost-whispers loudly.*)

The bridegroom waits for thee, my Alice . . . is thine. O Lord, my God, I have awaited thee, have served thee in thy . . . ALICE? (*His arms are wide, should resemble a crucifixion. With his hands on the model, he will raise his body some, backed full up against it.*) ALICE? . . . GOD?

(*The sounds are deafening.* JULIAN *smiles faintly.*) I accept thee, Alice, for thou art come to me. God, Alice . . . I accept thy will.

(*Sounds continue.* JULIAN *dies, head bows, body relaxes some, arms stay wide in the crucifixion. Sounds continue thusly: thrice after the death . . . thump thump thump thump thump thump. Absolute silence for two beats. The lights on* JULIAN *fade slowly to black. Only then, when all is black, does the curtain slowly fall.*)

BLUES FOR MISTER CHARLIE

James Baldwin

To the memory of
MEDGAR EVERS,
and his widow and his children,
and
to the memory of the dead children of Birmingham.

First presented by the Actors Studio, Inc., on April 23, 1964, at the Anta Theatre, New York City, with the following cast:

(In order of appearance)

DISC JOCKEY Frankie (Downbeat) Brown
LYLE BRITTEN Rip Torn
RICHARD HENRY Al Freeman, Jr.
REV. MERIDIAN HENRY Percy Rodriguez
TOM Wayne Grice
ARTHUR Clyde Williams
KEN Otis Young
MOTHER HENRY Rosetta LeNoire
JUANITA Diana Sands
PETE Lincoln Kilpatrick
LORENZO David Baldwin
PARNELL Pat Hingle
JO BRITTEN Ann Wedgeworth
PAPA D. John McCurry
HAZEL Pat Randall

SUSAN Patricia Quinn
RALPH Ralph Waite
ELLIS Joe Don Baker
LILLIAN Ann Hennessey
REV. PHELPS Bill Moor
JUDGE Ralph Waite
COURT STENOGRAPHER Pat Corley
THE STATE Dick Bradford
COUNSEL FOR THE BEREAVED Otis Young
TROMBONIST Grachan Moncur III
DRUMMER Frankie (Downbeat) Brown
TOWNSPEOPLE Billie Allen, Pat Corley,
Grachan Moncur III,
Bill Moor, Pearl Reynolds

Directed by Burgess Meredith
Design and lighting by Feder
Musical Coordinator, Robert Cordier
Assistants to the Director, Ira Cirker, Talley Beatty
Special Consultant, Jerome Smith
Executive Assistant, Richard R. Chandler

Copyright © 1964 by James Baldwin.
All rights reserved.
Used by permission of The Dial Press.

It is a curious thing that for years the black playwright did not have any very significant role to play in the American theatre. That is, it is curious until you examine the simple whys and wherefores, and the pattern of political, and by inference, theatrical power. The theatre could legitimately have been used as a means of black protest except for the evident fact that there was no real black theatre.

In 1858 William Wells Brown wrote *The Escape, or a Leap to Freedom,* which is generally regarded as the first black play written in America. Satirically critical of slavery, the play was never, so far as is known, produced, but Brown gave lecture readings of it, and apparently of other plays. In the years that followed, other plays by black playwrights were written, some were even given on Broadway, such as Frank Wilson's *Meek Mose,* in 1928. In 1935 Langston Hughes, the first really successful black playwright, offered *Mulatto,* which ran on Broadway for more than two years. But it was not until our own immediate time that the black theatre became a real and evident part of the American theatrical scene.

Three of the first writers to impress themselves on the American consciousness (and perhaps I mean here the white American consciousness), were Lorraine Hansberry, LeRoi Jones, and James Baldwin, all represented in this volume. Baldwin, simply because he was a famous novelist, was perhaps the most impressive.

James Baldwin was born on August 2, 1924, the son of a Harlem minister, and the eldest of nine children. He graduated from a New York high school in 1942 and for the next six years or so he did many, many jobs, most of them menial: elevator operator, dishwasher, file clerk, etc., etc. In 1948 Baldwin left for Europe.

For nearly ten years Baldwin based himself in Paris, although he traveled to many parts of Europe, only coming back to America for the occasional business trip. His first novel, *Go Tell It on the Mountain,* was published in 1953, followed two years later by a series of very provocative and brilliant essays, *Notes of a Native Son.* In 1956 he published *Giovanni's Room,* the novel that established his reputation. It was while he was in Paris, in the early 1950s, that Baldwin wrote his first play, *The Amen Corner.* In 1957 his exile ended and he returned home to New York City to fight for his beliefs on his home turf.

Baldwin has been a much-abused, much-praised, and now perhaps much-neglected black writer. He has always been conscious of his existence as an American as well as a black man, and as a writer he finds it difficult to be intolerant. He has great humanity and a very uncompromising honesty that just now, at our poised 1971 present, seems not to be particularly popular with either black or white.

His father was a preacher, and Baldwin himself once considered preaching as a career. It is from this perhaps—those Harlem churches of hellfire and promise—that the young Baldwin got his first insight into the nature of the theatre. He has a concept of the theatre that is both alive and totally real, and yet, at times, oddly unsophisticated.

Blues for Mister Charlie is his best-known play to date. At the end of 1958, soon after Baldwin's return to New York, Elia Kazan asked him if he wanted to work in the theatre. At first he hesitated, not seeing the relevance of the theatre as an art form, but at last he relented, and *Blues for Mister Charlie,* which, staged by Burgess Meredith, opened at the ANTA Theatre on April 23, 1964, was the result.

There is enough of the preacher in Baldwin for him to see the theatre as a great pulpit. The germ of his play came, as he admits, "very loosely indeed" from the 1955 murder in Mississippi of a Negro youth, Emmett Till. And it is no mistake that the play is dedicated to the civil rights martyr Medgar Evers.

The play then is about a racial murder. Its form shows the influence of a religious meeting, and its substance is humanist. The interesting thing is the compassion that Baldwin shows for the white racist murderer, the despicable "Mister Charlie." He once said: "I'm not a nigger, I am a man, but if you think I'm a nigger, it means you need it."

This is Baldwin's concept—we need to feel guilt even for the guilty. Writing about the white murderer, in an introduction to the play, Baldwin said: "If it is true, and I believe it is, that all men are brothers, then we have the duty to try to understand this wretched man; and while we cannot hope to liberate him, begin working toward the liberation of his children." You see, James Baldwin is that now pitifully rare thing, the black liberal, and in present political rhetoric there is only one thing worse than a white liberal and that is a black liberal. But Baldwin is also a playwright and a novelist who has a good chance of surviving any rhetoric or rhetorical positions.

AUTHOR'S NOTES

This play has been on my mind—has been bugging me—for several years. It is unlike anything else I've ever attempted in that I remember vividly the first time it occurred to me; for in fact, it did not occur to me, but to Elia Kazan. Kazan asked me at the end of 1958 if I would be interested in working in the Theatre. It was a generous offer, but I did not react with great enthusiasm because I did not then, and don't now, have much respect for what goes on in the American Theatre. I am not convinced that it *is* a Theatre; it seems to me a series, merely, of commercial speculations, stale, repetitious, and timid. I certainly didn't see much future for me in that frame-work, and I was profoundly unwilling to risk my morale and my talent—my life—in endeavors which could only increase a level of frustration already dangerously high.

Nevertheless, the germ of the play persisted. It is based, very distantly indeed, on the case of Emmett Till—the Negro youth who was murdered in Mississippi in 1955. The murderer in this case was acquitted. (His brother, who helped him do the deed, is now a deputy sheriff in Rulesville, Mississippi.) After his acquittal, he recounted the facts of the murder—for one cannot refer to his performance as a confession—to William Bradford Huie, who wrote it all down in an article called "Wolf Whistle." I do not know why the case pressed on my mind so hard—but it would not let me go. I absolutely dreaded committing myself to writing a play—there were enough people around already telling me that I couldn't write novels—but I began to see that my fear of the form masked a much deeper fear. That fear was that I would never be able to draw a valid portrait of the murderer. In life, obviously, such people baffle and terrify me and, with one part of my mind at least, I hate them and would be willing to kill them. Yet, with another part of my mind, I am aware that no man is a villain in his own eyes. Something in the man knows—*must* know—that what he is doing is evil; but in order to accept the knowledge the man would have to change. What is ghastly and really almost hopeless in our racial situation now is that the crimes we have committed are so great and so unspeakable that the acceptance of this knowledge would lead, literally, to madness. The human being, then, in order to protect himself, closes his eyes, compulsively repeats his crimes, and enters a spiritual darkness which no one can describe.

But if it is true, and I believe it is, that all men are brothers, then we have the duty to try to understand this wretched man; and while we probably cannot hope to liberate him, begin working toward the liberation of his children. For we, the American people, have created him, he is our servant; it is we who put the cattle-prodder in his hands, and we are responsible for the crimes that he commits. It is we who have locked him in the prison of his color. It is we who have persuaded him that Negroes are worthless human beings, and that it is his sacred duty, as a white man, to protect the honor and purity of his tribe. It is we who have forbidden him, on pain of exclusion from the tribe, to accept his beginnings, when he and black people loved each other, and rejoice in them, and use them; it is we who have made it mandatory—honorable—that white father should deny black son. These are grave crimes indeed, and we have committed them and continue to commit them in order to make money.

The play then, for me, takes place in Plaguetown, U.S.A., now. The plague is race, the plague is our concept of Christianity: and this raging plague has the power to destroy every human relationship. I once took a short trip with Medgar Evers to the back-woods of Mississippi. He was investigating the murder of a Negro man by a white storekeeper which had taken place months before. Many people talked to Medgar that night, in dark cabins, with their lights out, in whispers; and we had been followed for many miles out of Jackson, Mississippi, not by a lunatic with a gun, but by state troopers. I will never forget that night, as I will never forget Medgar—who took me

49

to the plane the next day. We promised to see each other soon. When he died, something entered into me which I cannot describe, but it was then that I resolved that nothing under heaven would prevent me from getting this play done. We are walking in terrible darkness here, and this is one man's attempt to bear witness to the reality and the power of light.

ACT ONE

*Mutiple set, the skeleton of which, in
the first two acts, is the Negro church,
and, in the third act, the courthouse. The
church and the courthouse are on opposite
sides of a southern street; the audience
should always be aware, during the first
two acts, of the dome of the courthouse
and the American flag. During the final
act, the audience should always be aware
of the steeple of the church, and the cross.*

*The church is divided by an aisle. The
street door upstage faces the audience. The
pulpit is downstage, at an angle, so that
the minister is simultaneously addressing
the congregation and the audience. In the
third act, the pulpit is replaced by the witness stand.*

*This aisle also functions as the division
between* WHITETOWN *and* BLACKTOWN. *The
action among the blacks takes place on one
side of the stage, the action among the
whites on the opposite side of the stage—
which is to be remembered during the
third act, which takes place, of course, in
a segregated courtroom.*

This means that RICHARD'S *room,* LYLE'S
store, PAPA D.'S *joint,* JO'S *kitchen, etc., are
to exist principally by suggestion, for these
shouldn't be allowed to obliterate the
skeleton, or, more accurately, perhaps, the
framework, suggested above.*

*For the murder scene, the aisle functions
as a gulf. The stage should be built out, so
that the audience reacts to the enormity of
this gulf, and so that* RICHARD, *when he
falls, falls out of sight of the audience, like
a stone, into the pit.*

In the darkness we hear a shot.

Lights up slowly on LYLE, *staring down
at the ground. He looks around him, bends
slowly and picks up* RICHARD'S *body as
though it were a sack. He carries him upstage drops him.*

———

LYLE. And may every nigger like this
nigger end like this nigger—face down in
the weeds!

(*Exits.* BLACKTOWN: *The church. A
sound of mourning begins.* MERIDIAN, TOM,
KEN, *and* ARTHUR.)

MERIDIAN. No, no, no! You have to say
it like you mean it—the way they really
say it: nigger, nigger, nigger! *Nigger!*
Tom, the way *you* saying it, it sounds like
you just *might* want to make friends. And

that's not the way they sound out there.
Remember all that's happened. Remember
we having a funeral here—tomorrow
night. Remember why. Go on, hit it again.

TOM. You dirty nigger, you no-good
black bastard, what you doing down here,
anyway?

MERIDIAN. That's much better. Much,
much better. Go on.

TOM. Hey, boy, where's your mother?
I bet she's lying up in bed, just a-pumping
away, ain't she, boy?

MERIDIAN. *That's* the way they sound!

TOM. Hey, boy, how much does your
mother charge? How much does your sister charge?

KEN. How much does your *wife* charge?

MERIDIAN. Now you got it. You really
got it now. That's them. Keep walking,
Arthur. *Keep walking!*

TOM. You get your ass off these streets
from around here, boy, or we going to do
us some cutting—we're going to cut that
big, black thing off of you, you hear?

MERIDIAN. Why you all standing around
there like that? Go on and get you a
nigger. Go on!

(*A scuffle.*)

MERIDIAN. All right. All right! Come on,
now. Come on.

(KEN *steps forward and spits in* ARTHUR'S
face.)

ARTHUR. You black s.o.b., what the hell
do you think you're doing? You mother—!

MERIDIAN. Hey, hold it! Hold it! Hold
it!

(MERIDIAN *wipes the boy's face. They are
all trembling.*)

(MOTHER HENRY *enters.*)

MOTHER HENRY. Here they come. And it
looks like they had a time.

(JUANITA, LORENZO, PETE, JIMMY, *all Negro, carry placards, enter, exhausted and
disheveled, wounded;* PETE *is weeping. The
placards bear such legends as* Freedom
Now, We Want The Murderer, One Man,
One Vote, *etc.*)

JUANITA. We shall overcome!

LORENZO. We shall not be moved!
(*Laughs.*) We were moved tonight,
though. Some of us has been moved to
tears.

MERIDIAN. Juanita, what happened?

JUANITA. Oh, just another hometown
Saturday night.

MERIDIAN. Come on, Pete, come on, old
buddy. Stop it. Stop it.

LORENZO. I don't blame him. I do not blame the cat. You feel like a damn fool standing up there, letting them white mothers beat on your ass—shoot, if I had my way, just once—stop crying, Pete, goddammit!

JUANITA. Lorenzo, you're in church.

LORENZO. Yeah. Well, I wish to God I was in an arsenal. I'm sorry, Meridian, Mother Henry—I don't mean that for you. I don't understand you. I don't understand Meridian here. It was his son, it was your grandson, Mother Henry, that got killed, butchered! Just last week, and yet, here you sit—in this—this—the house of this damn almighty God who don't care what happens to nobody, unless, of course, they're white. Mother Henry, I got a lot of respect for you and all that, and for Meridian, too, but that white man's God is *white*. It's that damn white God that's been lynching us and burning us and castrating us and raping our women and robbing us of everything that makes a man a man for all these hundreds of years. Now, why we sitting around here, in *His* house? If I could get my hands on Him, I'd pull Him out of heaven and drag Him through this town at the end of a rope.

MERIDIAN. No, you wouldn't.

LORENZO. I wouldn't? Yes, I would. Oh, yes, I would.

JUANITA. And then you wouldn't be any better than they are.

LORENZO. I don't want to be better than they are, why should I be better than they are? And better at what? Better at being a doormat, better at being a corpse? Sometimes I just don't know. We've been demonstrating—*non-violently*—for more than a year now and all that's happened is that now they'll let us into that crummy library downtown which was obsolete in 1897 and where nobody goes anyway; who in this town reads books? For that we paid I don't know how many thousands of dollars in fines, Jerome is still in the hospital, and we all know that Ruthie is never again going to be the swinging little chick she used to be. Big deal. Now we're picketing that great movie palace downtown where I wouldn't go on a bet; I can live without Yul Brynner and Doris Day, thank you very much. And we *still* can't get licensed to be electricians or plumbers, we still can't walk through the park, our kids still can't use the swimming pool in town. We still can't vote, we can't even get registered. Is it worth it? And these people trying to kill us, too? And we ain't even got no guns. The cops ain't going to protect us. They call up the people and tell them where we are and say, "Go get them! They ain't going to do nothing to you—they just dumb niggers!"

MERIDIAN. Did they arrest anybody tonight?

PETE. No, they got their hands full now, trying to explain what Richard's body was doing in them weeds.

LORENZO. It was wild. You know, all the time we was ducking them bricks and praying to *God* we'd get home before somebody got killed— (*Laughs.*) I had a jingle going through my mind, like if I was a white man, dig? and I had to wake up every morning singing to myself, "Look at the happy nigger, he doesn't give a damn, thank God I'm not a nigger—"

TOGETHER. "—*Good Lord, perhaps I am!*"

JUANITA. You've gone crazy, Lorenzo. They've done it. You have been unfitted for the struggle.

MERIDIAN. I cannot rest until they bring my son's murderer to trial. That man who killed my son.

LORENZO. But he killed a nigger before, as I know all of you know. Nothing never happened. Sheriff just shovelled the body into the ground and forgot about it.

MERIDIAN. Parnell will help me.

PETE. Meridian, you know that *Mister* Parnell ain't going to let them arrest his ass-hole buddy. I'm sorry, Mother Henry!

MOTHER HENRY. That's all right, son.

MERIDIAN. But I think that Parnell has proven to be a pretty good friend to all of us. He's the only white man in this town who's ever *really* stuck his neck out in order to do—to do right. He's *fought* to bring about this trial—I can't tell you how hard he's fought. If it weren't for him, there'd be much less hope.

LORENZO. I guess I'm just not as nice as you are. I don't trust as many people as you trust.

MERIDIAN. We can't afford to become too distrustful, Lorenzo.

LORENZO. We can't afford to be too trusting, either. See, when a white man's a *good* white man, he's good because he wants *you* to be good. Well, sometimes I just might want to be *bad*. I got as much right to be bad as anybody else.

MERIDIAN. No, you don't.

LORENZO. Why not?

MERIDIAN. Because you know better.

(PARNELL *enters*.)

PARNELL. Hello, my friends. I bring glad tidings of great joy. Is that the way the phrase goes, Meridian?

JUANITA. Parnell!

PARNELL. I can't stay. I just came to tell you that a warrant's being issued for Lyle's arrest.

JUANITA. They're going to arrest him? Big Lyle Britten? I'd love to know how you managed *that*.

PARNELL. Well, Juanita, I am not a *good* man, but I have my little ways.

JUANITA. And a whole lot of folks in this town, baby, are not going to be talking to you no more, for days and days and *days*.

PARNELL. I hope that you all will. I may have no other company. I think I should go to Lyle's house to warn him. After all, I brought it about and he *is* a friend of mine—and then I have to get the announcement into my paper.

JUANITA. So it *is* true.

PARNELL. Oh, yes. It's true.

MERIDIAN. When is he being arrested?

PARNELL. Monday morning. Will you be up later, Meridian? I'll drop by if you are —if I may.

MERIDIAN. Yes. I'll be up.

PARNELL. All right, then. I'll trundle by. Good night all. I'm sorry I've got to run.

MERIDIAN. Good night.

JUANITA. Thank you, Parnell.

PARNELL. Don't thank me, dear Juanita. I only acted—as I believed I had to act. See you later, Meridian.

(PARNELL *exits*.)

MERIDIAN. I wonder if they'll convict him.

JUANITA. Convict him. Convict him. You're asking for heaven on earth. After all, they haven't even *arrested* him yet. And, anyway—why *should* they convict him? Why him? He's no worse than all the others. He's an honorable tribesman and he's defended, with blood, the honor and purity of his tribe!

(WHITETOWN. LYLE *holds his infant son up above his head*.)

LYLE. Hey old pisser. You hear me, sir? I expect you to control your bladder like a *gentleman* whenever your Papa's got you on his knee.

(JO *enters*.)

He got a mighty big bladder, too, for such a little fellow.

JO. I'll tell the world he didn't steal it.

LYLE. You mighty sassy tonight.

(*Hands her the child.*)

Ain't that right, old pisser? Don't you reckon your Mama's getting kind of sassy? And what do you reckon I should do about it?

(JO *is changing the child's diapers.*)

JO. You tell your Daddy he can start sleeping in his own bed nights instead of coming grunting in here in the wee small hours of the morning.

LYLE. And you tell your Mama if she was getting her sleep like she should be, so she can be alert every instant to your needs, little fellow, she wouldn't *know* what time I come—*grunting* in.

JO. I got to be alert to *your* needs, too. I think.

LYLE. Don't you go starting to imagine things. I just been over to the store. That's all.

JO. Till three and four o'clock in the morning?

LYLE. Well, I got plans for the store, I think I'm going to try to start branching out, you know, and I been—making plans.

JO. You thinking of branching out *now*? Why, Lyle, you know we ain't *hardly* doing no business *now*. Weren't for the country folks come to town every Saturday, I don't know *where* we'd be. This ain't no time to be branching *out*. We barely holding *on*.

LYLE. Shoot, the niggers'll be coming back, don't you worry. They'll get over this foolishness presently. They already weary of having to drive forty-fifty miles across the state line to get their groceries —a lot of them ain't even got cars.

JO. Those that don't have cars have *friends* with cars.

LYLE. Well, friends get weary, too. Joel come in the store a couple of days ago—

JO. Papa D.? He don't count. You can always wrap him around your little finger.

LYLE. Listen, will you? He come in the store a couple of days ago to buy a sack of flour and he *told* me, he say, The niggers is *tired* running all over creation to put some food on the table. Ain't nobody going to keep on driving no forty-fifty miles to buy no sack of flour—what you mean when you say Joel don't count?

JO. I don't mean nothing. But there's something wrong with anybody when his own people don't think much of him.

LYLE. Joel's got good sense, is all. I think more of him than I think of a lot of white men, that's a fact. And he knows what's right for his people, too.

JO (*puts son in crib*). Well. Selling a sack of flour once a week ain't going to send this little one through college, neither. (*A pause.*) In what direction were you planning to branch out?

LYLE. I was thinking of trying to make the store more—well, more colorful. Folks like color—

JO. You mean, niggers like color.

LYLE. Dammit, Jo, I ain't in business just to sell to niggers! Listen to me, can't you? I thought I'd dress it up, get a new front, put some neon signs in—and, you know, we got more space in there than we use. Well, why don't we open up a line of ladies' clothes? Nothing too fancy, but I bet you it would bring in a lot more business.

JO. I don't know. Most of the ladies I know buy their clothes at Benton's, on Decatur Street.

LYLE. The niggers don't—anyway, we could sell them the same thing. The white ladies, I mean—

JO. No. It wouldn't be the same.

LYLE. Why not? A dress is a dress.

JO. But it sounds better if you say you got it on Decatur Street! At Benton's. Anyway—where would you get the money for this branching out?

LYLE. I can get a loan from the bank. I'll get old Parnell to co-sign with me, or have him get one of his rich friends to co-sign with me.

JO. Parnell called earlier—you weren't at the store today.

LYLE. What do you mean, I wasn't at the store?

JO. Because Parnell called earlier and said he tried to get you at the store and that there wasn't any answer.

LYLE. There wasn't any business. I took a walk.

JO. He said he's got bad news for you.

LYLE. What kind of bad news?

JO. He didn't say. He's coming by here this evening to give it to you himself.

LYLE. What do you think it is?

JO. I guess they're going to arrest you?

LYLE. No, they ain't. They ain't gone crazy.

JO. I think they might. We had so much trouble in this town lately and it's been in all the northern newspapers—and now, this—this dead boy—

LYLE. They ain't got no case.

JO. No. But you was the last person to see that crazy boy—alive. And now everybody's got to thinking again—about that other time.

LYLE. That was self-defense. The Sheriff said so himself. Hell, I ain't no murderer. They're just some things I don't believe is right.

JO. Nobody never heard no more about the poor little girl—his wife.

LYLE. No. She just disappeared.

JO. You never heard no more about her at all?

LYLE. How would I hear about her more than anybody else? No, she just took off —I believe she had people in Detroit somewhere. I reckon that's where she went.

JO. I felt sorry for her. She looked so lost those last few times I saw her, wandering around town—and she was so young. She was a pretty little thing.

LYLE. She looked like a pickaninny to me. Like she was too young to be married. I reckon she *was* too young for him.

JO. It happened in the store.

LYLE. Yes.

JO. How people talked! That's what scares me now.

LYLE. Talk don't matter. I hope you didn't believe what you heard.

JO. A lot of people did. I reckon a lot of people still do.

LYLE. *You* don't believe it?

JO. No. (*A pause.*) You know—Monday morning—we'll be married one whole year!

LYLE. Well, can't nobody talk about *us.* That little one there ain't but two months old.

(*The door bell rings.*)

JO. That's Parnell.

(*Exits.*)

(LYLE *walks up and down, looks into the crib.* JO *and* PARNELL *enter.*)

LYLE. It's about time you showed your face in here, you old rascal! You been so busy over there with the niggers, you ain't got time for white folks no more. You sure you ain't got some nigger wench over there on the other side of town? Because, I declare—!

PARNELL. I apologize for your husband, Mrs. Britten, I really do. In fact, I'm afraid I must deplore your taste in men. If I had only seen you first, dear lady, and if you had found me charming, how much suffering I might have prevented! Yet got anything in this house to drink? Don't tell me you haven't, we'll both need one. Sit down.

LYLE. Bring on the booze, old lady.

(JO *brings ice, glasses, etc.; pours drinks.*)

What you been doing with yourself?

PARNELL. Well, I seem to have switched territories. I haven't been defending colored people this week, I've been defending you. I've just left the Chief of Police.

LYLE. How is the old bastard?

PARNELL. He seems fine. But he really *is* an old bastard. Lyle—he's issuing a warrant for your arrest.

LYLE. He's going to arrest *me?* You mean, he believes I killed that boy?

PARNELL. The question of what he believes doesn't enter into it. This case presents several very particular circumstances and these circumstances force him to arrest you. I think we can take it for granted that he wouldn't arrest you if he could think of some way not to. *He wouldn't* arrest anybody except blind beggars and old colored women if he could think of some way not to—he's bird-brained and chicken-hearted and big-assed. The charge is murder.

JO. Murder!

LYLE. Murder?

PARNELL. Murder.

LYLE. I ain't no murderer. You know that.

PARNELL. I also know that somebody killed the boy. Somebody put two slugs in his belly and dumped his body in the weeds beside the railroad track just outside of town. Somebody did all that. We pay several eminent, bird-brained, chicken-hearted, big-assed people quite a lot of money to discourage such activity. They never do, in fact, discourage it, but, still —we must find the somebody who killed that boy. And you, my friend, according to the testimony of Joel Davis, otherwise known as Papa D., were the last person to see the boy alive. It is also known that you didn't like him—to say the least.

LYLE. Nobody liked him.

PARNELL. Ah. But it isn't nobody that killed him. *Somebody* killed him. We must find the somebody. And since you were the last person to see him alive, we must arrest you in order to clear you—or convict you.

LYLE. They'll never convict me.

PARNELL. As to that, you may be right. But you *are* going to be arrested.

LYLE. When?

PARNELL. Monday morning. Of course, you can always flee to Mexico.

LYLE. Why should I run away?

PARNELL. I wasn't suggesting that you should run away. If you did, I should urge your wife to divorce you at once, and marry me.

JO. Ah, if that don't get him out of town in a hurry, I don't know what will! The man's giving you your chance, honey. You going to take it?

LYLE. Stop talking foolishness. It looks bad for me, I guess. I swear, I don't know what's come over the folks in this town!

PARNELL. It doesn't look good. In fact, if the boy had been white, it would look very, *very* bad, and your behind would be in the jailhouse now. What do you mean, you don't understand what's come over the people in this town?

LYLE. Raising so much fuss about a nigger—and a northern nigger at that.

PARNELL. He was born here. He's Reverend Meridian Henry's son.

LYLE. Well, he'd been gone so long, he might as well have been a northern nigger. Went North and got ruined and come back here to make trouble—and they tell me he was a dope fiend, too. What's all this fuss about? He probably got killed by some other nigger—they do it all the time —but ain't nobody even thought about arresting one of *them*. Has niggers suddenly got to be *holy* in this town?

PARNELL. Oh, Lyle, I'm not here to discuss the sanctity of niggers. I just came to tell you that a warrant's being issued for your arrest. *You* may think that a colored boy who gets ruined in the North and then comes home to try to pull himself together deserves to die—*I* don't.

LYLE. You sound like you think I got something against colored folks—but I don't. I never have, not in all my life. But I'll be damned if I'll mix with them. That's all. I don't believe in it, and that's *all*. I don't want no big buck nigger lying up next to Josephine and that's where all this will lead to and you know it as well as I do! I'm against it and I'll do anything I have to do to stop it, yes, I will!

PARNELL. Suppose *he*—my godson there —decides to marry a Chinese girl. You know, there are an awful lot of Chinese girls in the world—I bet you didn't know that. Well, there are. Let's just say that he grows up and looks around at all the pure white women, and—saving your presence, ma'am—they make him want to puke and he decides to marry a pure Chinese girl instead. What would you do? Shoot him in order to prevent it? Or would you shoot her?

LYLE. Parnell, you're my buddy. You've *always* been my buddy. You know more about me than anybody else in the world. What's come over you? You—you ain't going to turn against me, are you?

PARNELL. No. No, I'll never turn against you. I'm just trying to make you think.

LYLE. I notice you didn't marry no Chinese girl. You just never got married at all. Women been trying to saddle old Parnell for I don't know how long—I don't know what you got, old buddy, but I'll be damned if you don't know how to use it! What about this present one— Loretta—you reckon you going to marry her?

PARNELL. I doubt it.

JO. Parnell, you're just awful. Awful!

PARNELL. I think I'm doing her a favor. She can do much better than me. I'm just a broken-down newspaper editor—the editor of a newspaper which *nobody* reads— in a dim, grim backwater.

LYLE. I thought you liked it here.

PARNELL. I don't like it here. But I love it here. Or maybe I don't. I don't know. I must go.

LYLE. What's your hurry? Why don't you stay and have pot-luck with us?

PARNELL. Loretta is waiting. I must have pot-luck with *her*. And then I have errands on the other side of town.

LYLE. What they saying over there? I reckon they praying day and night for my ass to be put in a sling, ain't they? Shoot, I don't care.

PARNELL. Don't. Life's much simpler that way. Anyway, Papa D.'s the only one doing a whole lot of talking.

JO. I told you he wasn't no good, Lyle, I told you!

LYLE. I don't know what's got into him! And we been knowing each other all these years! He must be getting old. You go back and tell him I said he's got it all *confused*—about me and that boy. Tell him you talked to me and that *I* said he must have made some mistake.

PARNELL. I'll drop in tomorrow, if I may. Good night, Jo, and thank you. Good night, Lyle.

LYLE. Good night, old buddy.

JO. I'll see you to the door.

(JO *and* PARNELL *exit.* LYLE *walks up and down.*)

LYLE. Well! *Ain't* that something! But they'll never convict me. Never in this world. (*Looks into crib.*) Ain't that right, old pisser?

(BLACKTOWN. *The church, as before.*)

LORENZO. And when they bring him to trial, I'm going to be there every day— right across the street in that courthouse— where they been dealing death out to us for all these years.

MOTHER HENRY. I used to hate them, too, son. But I don't hate them no more. They too pitiful.

MERIDIAN. No witnesses.

JUANITA. Meridian. Ah, Meridian.

MOTHER HENRY. You remember that song he used to like so much?

MERIDIAN. I sing because I'm happy.

JUANITA. I sing because I'm free.

PETE. For his eye is on the sparrow—

LORENZO. And I know he watches—me. (*Music, very faint.*)

JUANITA. There was another song he liked—a song about a prison and the light from a train that shone on the prisoners every night at midnight. I can hear him now: Lord, you wake up in the morning. You hear the ding-dong ring—

MOTHER HENRY. He had a beautiful voice.

LORENZO. Well, he was pretty tough up there in New York—till he got busted.

MERIDIAN. And came running home.

MOTHER HENRY. Don't blame yourself, honey. Don't blame yourself!

JUANITA. You go a-marching to the table, you see the same old thing—

JIMMY. All I'm going to tell you: knife, a fork, and a pan— (*Music stronger.*)

PETE. And if you say a thing about it—

LORENZO. You are in trouble with the man.

(*Lights dim in the church. We discover* RICHARD, *standing in his room, singing. This number is meant to make vivid the* RICHARD *who was much loved on the Apollo Theatre stage in Harlem, the* RICHARD *who was a rising New York star.*)

MERIDIAN. No witnesses!

(*Near the end of the song,* MOTHER HENRY *enters, carrying a tray with milk, sandwiches, and cake.*)

RICHARD. You treating me like royalty, old lady—I ain't royalty. I'm just a raggedy-assed, out-of-work, busted musician. But I sure can sing, can't I?

MOTHER HENRY. You better learn some respect, you know that neither me nor your father wants that kind of language in this house. Sit down and eat, you got to get your strength back.

RICHARD. What for? What am I supposed to do with it?

MOTHER HENRY. You stop that kind of talk.

RICHARD. Stop that kind of talk, we don't want that kind of talk! Nobody cares what people feel or what they think or what they do—but stop that kind of talk!

MOTHER HENRY. Richard!

RICHARD. All right. All right. (*Throws himself on the bed, begins eating in a kind of fury.*) What I can't get over is—what in the world am I doing *here*? Way down here in the ass-hole of the world, the deep, black, funky South.

MOTHER HENRY. You were born here. You got folks here. And you ain't got no manners and you *won't* learn no sense and so you naturally got yourself in trouble and had to come to your folks. You lucky it wasn't no worse, the way you go on. You want some more milk?

RICHARD. No, old lady. Sit down.

MOTHER HENRY. I ain't got time to be fooling with you. (*But she sits down.*) What you got on your mind?

RICHARD. I don't know. How do you stand it?

MOTHER HENRY. Stand what? You?

RICHARD. Living down here with all these nowhere people.

MOTHER HENRY. From what I'm told and from what I see, the people you've been among don't seem to be any better.

RICHARD. You mean old Aunt Edna? She's all right, she just ain't very bright, is all.

MOTHER HENRY. I am not talking about Edna. I'm talking about all them other folks you got messed up with. Look like you'd have had better sense. You hear me?

RICHARD. I hear you.

MOTHER HENRY. That all you got to say?

RICHARD. It's easy for you to talk, Grandmama, you don't know nothing about New York City, or what can happen to you up there!

MOTHER HENRY. I know what can happen to you anywhere in this world. And I know right from wrong. We tried to raise you so you'd know right from wrong, too.

RICHARD. We don't see things the same way, Grandmama. I don't know if I really *know* right from wrong—I'd like to, I always dig people the most who know *anything,* especially right from wrong!

MOTHER HENRY. You've had yourself a little trouble, Richard, like we all do, and you a little tired, like we all get. You'll be all right. You a young man. Only, just try not to *go* so much, try to calm down a little. Your Daddy loves you. You his only son.

RICHARD. That's a good reason, Grandmama. Let me tell you about New York. You ain't never been North, have you?

MOTHER HENRY. Your Daddy used to tell me a little about it every time he come back from visiting you all up there.

RICHARD. Daddy don't know nothing about New York. He just come up for a few days and went right on back. That ain't the way to get to know New York. No ma'am. He *never* saw New York. Finally, I realized he wasn't never *going* to see it—you know, there's a whole lot of things Daddy's never seen? I've seen more than he has.

MOTHER HENRY. All young folks thinks that.

RICHARD. Did *you?* When you were young? Did you think you knew more than your mother and father? But I bet you really did, you a pretty shrewd old lady, quiet as it's kept.

MOTHER HENRY. No, I didn't think that. But I thought I could find *out* more, because *they* were born in slavery, but *I* was born free.

RICHARD. *Did* you find out more?

MOTHER HENRY. I found out what I had to find out—to take care of my husband and raise my children in the fear of God.

RICHARD. You know I don't believe in God, Grandmama.

MOTHER HENRY. You don't know what you talking about. Ain't no way possible for you not to believe in God. It ain't up to you.

RICHARD. Who's it up to, then?

MOTHER HENRY. It's up to the life in you —the life in you. *That* knows where it comes from, *that* believes in God. You doubt me, you just try holding your breath long enough to die.

RICHARD. You pretty smart, ain't you? (*A pause.*) I convinced Daddy that I'd be better off in New York—and Edna, she convinced him too, she said it wasn't as tight for a black man up there as it is down here. Well, that's a crock, Grandmama, believe me when I tell you. At first I thought it was true, hell, I was just a green country boy and they ain't got no signs up, dig, saying you can't go here or you can't go there. No, you got to find that out all by your lonesome. But—for a while —I thought everything was swinging and Edna, she's so dizzy she thinks everything is *always* swinging, so there we were—like *swinging*.

MOTHER HENRY. I know Edna got lost somewhere. But, Richard—why didn't *you* come back? You knew your Daddy wanted you back, your Daddy and me both.

RICHARD. I didn't want to come back here like a whipped dog. One whipped dog running to another whipped dog. No, I didn't want that. I wanted to make my Daddy proud of me—because, the day I left here, I sure as hell wasn't proud of *him.*

MOTHER HENRY. Be careful, son. Be careful. Your Daddy's a fine man. Your Daddy loves you.

RICHARD. I know, Grandmama. But I just wish, that day that Mama died, he'd took a pistol and gone through that damn white man's hotel and shot every son of a bitch in the place. That's right. I wish he'd shot them dead. I been dreaming of that day ever since I left here. I been dreaming of my Mama falling down the steps of that hotel. *My* Mama. I never believed she fell. I *always* believed that some white man pushed her down those steps. And I know that Daddy thought so, too. But he wasn't there, he didn't know, he couldn't say nothing, he couldn't *do* nothing. I'll never forget the way he looked—whipped, whipped, whipped, whipped!

MOTHER HENRY. She fell, Richard, she *fell*. The stairs were wet and slippery and she *fell*.

RICHARD. My mother *fell* down the steps of that damn white hotel? My mother was *pushed*—you remember yourself how them white bastards was always sniffing around my mother, *always* around her—because she was pretty and *black!*

MOTHER HENRY. Richard, you can't start walking around believing that all the suffering in the world is caused by white folks!

RICHARD. I can't? Don't tell me I can't. I'm going to treat everyone of them as though they were responsible for all the crimes that ever happened in the history of the world—oh, yes! They're responsible for all the misery *I've* ever seen, and that's good enough for me. It's because my Daddy's got no power that my Mama's dead. And he ain't got no power because he's *black*. And the only way the black man's going to *get* any power is to drive all the white men into the sea.

MOTHER HENRY. You're going to make yourself sick. You're going to make yourself sick with hatred.

RICHARD. No, I'm not. I'm going to make myself well. I'm going to make myself *well* with hatred—what do you think of that?

MOTHER HENRY. It can't be done. It can never be done. Hatred is a poison, Richard.

RICHARD. Not for me. I'm going to learn how to drink it—a little every day in the morning, and then a booster shot late at night. I'm going to remember everything. I'm going to keep it right here, at the very top of my mind. I'm going to remember Mama, and Daddy's face that day, and Aunt Edna and all her sad little deals and all those boys and girls in Harlem and all them pimps and whores and gangsters and all them cops. And I'm going to remember all the dope that's flowed through my veins. I'm going to remember everything —the jails I been in and the cops that beat me and how long a time I spent screaming and stinking in my own dirt, trying to break my habit. I'm going to remember all that, and I'll get well. I'll get well.

MOTHER HENRY. Oh, Richard. Richard. Richard.

RICHARD. Don't Richard *me*. I tell you, I'm going to get *well*.

(*He takes a small, sawed-off pistol from his pocket.*)

MOTHER HENRY. Richard, what are you doing with that gun?

RICHARD. I'm carrying it around with me, that's what I'm doing with it. This gun goes everywhere I go.

MOTHER HENRY. How long have you had it?

RICHARD. I've had it a long, long time.

MOTHER HENRY. Richard—you never—?

RICHARD. No. Not yet. But I will when I have to. I'll sure as hell take one of the bastards with me.

MOTHER HENRY. Hand me that gun. Please.

RICHARD. I can't. This is all that the man understands. He don't understand nothing else. *Nothing else!*

MOTHER HENRY. Richard—your father— think of your father—

RICHARD. Don't tell him! You hear me? (*A pause.*) Don't tell him!

MOTHER HENRY. Richard. Please.

RICHARD. Take the tray away, old lady. I ain't hungry no more.

(*After a moment,* MOTHER HENRY *takes the tray and exits.* RICHARD *stretches out on the bed.*)

JUANITA (*off*). Meridian? Mother Henry? Anybody home in this house? (*Enters.*) Oh! Excuse me.

RICHARD. I think they might be over at the church. I reckon Grandmama went over there to pray for my soul.

JUANITA. Grandmama?

RICHARD. Who are you? Don't I know you?

JUANITA. Yes. I think you might.

RICHARD. Is your name Juanita?

JUANITA. If your name is Richard.

RICHARD. I'll be damned.

JUANITA. Ain't you a mess? So you finally decided to come back here—come here, let me hug you! Why, you ain't hardly changed at all—you just a little taller but you sure didn't gain much weight.

RICHARD. And I bet you the same old tomboy. You sure got the same loud voice —used to be able to hear you clear across this town.

JUANITA. Well, it's a mighty small town, Richard, that's what you always said—and the reason my voice got so loud so early, was that I started screaming for help right quick.

(*Pete enters.*)

Do you know Pete Spivey? He's someone come on the scene since you been gone. He's going to school down here, you should pardon the expression.

RICHARD. How do you do, man? Where you from?

PETE. I'm from a little place just outside Mobile.

RICHARD. Why didn't you go North, man? If you was going to make a *move*. *That's* the place. You get lost up there and I guarantee you some swinging little chick is sure to find you.

JUANITA. We'll let that pass. Are you together? Are you ready to meet the day?

RICHARD. I am *always* together, little sister. Tell me what you got on your mind.

PETE. We thought we'd just walk around town a little and maybe stop and have a couple of drinks somewhere. Or we can drive. I got a car.

RICHARD. I didn't think I'd never see you no more, Juanita. You been here all this time?

JUANITA. I sure have, sugar. Just waiting for you to come home.

RICHARD. Don't let this chick upset you, Pete. All we ever did was climb trees together.

PETE. She's had me climbing a few trees, too. But we weren't doing it together.

(PAPA D.'s JUKE JOINT: *Juke box music, loud. Less frantic than* RICHARD's *song. Couples dancing, all very young, doing very lively variations of the "Twist," the "Wobble," etc.* PAPA D. *at the counter. It is now early evening.* JUANITA, PETE *and* RICHARD *enter.*)

JUANITA. How you making it, Papa D.? We brought someone to see you—you recognize him?

PAPA D. It seems to me I know your face, young man. Yes, I'm *sure* I know your face. Now, wait a minute, don't tell me—you ain't Shirelee Anderson's boy, are you?

RICHARD. No. I remember Shirelee Anderson, but we ain't no kin.

PETE. Try again, Papa D.

PAPA D. You your father's boy. I just recognized that smile—you Reverend Henry's son. Well, how you doing? It's nice to have you back with us. You going to stay awhile?

RICHARD. Yes sir. I think I'll be around for a while.

PAPA D. Yeah, I remember you little old string bean of a boy, full of the devil. How long you been gone from here?

RICHARD. Almost eight years now. I left in September—it'll be eight years next month.

PAPA D. Yeah—how's your Daddy? And your Grandmother? I ain't seen them for a while.

PETE. Ain't you been going to church, Papa D.?

PAPA D. Well, you know how it is. I try, God *knows* I try!

RICHARD. They fine, Papa D.

PAPA D. You all don't want nothing to eat?

RICHARD. We'll think about it.

(*They sit down.*)

PETE. Old Papa D. got something on everybody, don't he?

JUANITA. You better believe it.

RICHARD. He's kind of a Tom, ain't he?

PETE. Yeah. He *talks* about Mister Charlie, and he *says* he's with us—us kids—but he ain't going to do nothing to offend him. You know, he's still trading with Lyle Britten.

RICHARD. Who's Lyle Britten?

PETE. Peckerwood, owns a store nearby. And, man, you ain't *seen* a peckerwood until you've seen Lyle Britten. Niggers been trading in his store for years, man, I wouldn't be surprised but if the cat was rich—but that man still expects you to step off the sidewalk when he comes along. So we been getting people to stop buying there.

JUANITA. He shot a colored man a few years back, shot him dead, and wasn't nothing never said, much less done, about it.

PETE. Lyle had been carrying on with this man's wife, dig, and, naturally, Old Bill—his name was Bill Walker, everybody called him Old Bill—wanted to put a stop to it.

JUANITA. She was a pretty little thing—real little and real black.

RICHARD. She still around here?

PETE. No. She disappeared. She went North somewhere.

RICHARD. Jive mothers. They can rape and kill our women and we can't do nothing. But if we touch one of their dried-up, pale-assed women, we get our nuts cut off. You remember that chick I was telling you about earlier, lives in Greenwich Village in New York?

PETE. What about her?

RICHARD. She's *white,* man. I got a whole *gang* of white chicks in New York. That's *right*. And they can't get enough of what little Richard's got—and I give it to them, too, baby, believe me. You say black people ain't got no dignity? Man, you ought to watch a white woman when she want you to give her a little bit. They will do anything, baby *anything*! Wait—I got some pictures. That's the one lives in the Village. *Ain't* she fine? I'd hate to tell you where I've had that long yellow hair. And, dig this one, this is Sandy, her old man works on Wall Street—

PETE. We're making Juanita nervous.

JUANITA. Don't worry about *me*. I've been a big girl for a *long* time. Besides, I'm studying abnormal psychology. So please feel free. Which one is this? What does *her* father do?

RICHARD. That's Sylvia. I don't know what her father does. She's a model. She's loaded with loot.

PETE. You take money from her?

RICHARD. I take their money and they love it. Anyway, they ain't got nothing else to do with it. Every one of them's got some piss-assed, faggotty white boy on a string somewhere. They go home and marry him, dig, when they can't make it with me no more—but when they want some *loving,* funky, down-home, bring-it-on-here-and-put-it-on-the-table style—

JUANITA. They sound very sad. It must be very sad for you, too.

RICHARD. Well, I want *them* to be sad, baby, I want to screw up *their* minds *forever*. But why should *I* be so sad? Hell, I was swinging, I just about had it made. I had me some fine chicks and a fine pad and my car, and, hell, I was on my way! But then—then I screwed up.

JUANITA. We heard you were sick.

RICHARD. Who told you I was sick?

JUANITA. Your father. Your grandmother. They didn't say what the sickness was.

(PAPA D. *passes their table.*)

RICHARD. Hey, Papa D., come on over here. I want to show you something.

(PAPA D. *comes over.*)

Hey, look at these, man, look! Ain't they some fine chicks? And you know who

each one of them calls: *Baby! Oh, baby?*
That's right. You looking at the man.

PAPA D. Where'd you steal those pictures,
boy?

RICHARD (*laughs*). *Steal* them! Man, I
ain't got to steal girls' pictures. I'm telling
you the truth!

PAPA D. Put them pictures away. I
thought you had good sense.

(*He goes back to the counter.*)

RICHARD. Ain't that a bitch. He's scared
because I'm carrying around pictures of
white girls. That's the trouble with niggers. They all scared of the man.

JUANITA. Well, I'm *not* scared of the
man. But there's just no point in running
around, asking—

PETE. —to be lynched.

RICHARD. Well, okay, I'll put my pictures
away, then. I sure don't want to upset nobody.

PETE. Excuse me. I'll be back.

(*Exits.*)

RICHARD. You want to dance?

JUANITA. No. Not now.

RICHARD. You want something to eat?

JUANITA. No. Richard?

RICHARD. Yeah?

JUANITA. Were you *very* sick?

RICHARD. What d'you want to know for?

JUANITA. Like that. Because I used to be
your girl friend.

RICHARD. You was more like a boy than
a girl, though. I couldn't go nowhere without you. You were determined to get your
neck broken.

JUANITA. Well, I've changed. I'm now
much more like a girl than I am like a
boy.

RICHARD. You didn't turn out too bad,
considering what you had to start with.

JUANITA. Thank you. I guess.

RICHARD. How come you ain't married
by now? Pete, now, he seems real fond of
you.

JUANITA. He *is* fond of me, we're
friends. But I'm not in any hurry to get
married—not now. And not here. I'm not
sure I'm going to stay here. I've been
working very hard, but next year I think
I'll leave.

RICHARD. Where would you go?

JUANITA. I don't know. I had always intended to go North to law school and then
come back down here to practice law—
God knows this town could stand it. But,
now, I don't know.

RICHARD. It's rough, huh?

JUANITA. It's not that so much. It *is*
rough—are you all right? Do you want
to go?

RICHARD. No, no. I'm all right. Go on.
(*A pause.*) I'm all *right*. Go on.

JUANITA. It's rough because you can't
help being scared. I don't want to die—
what was the matter with you, Richard,
what were you sick with?

RICHARD. It wasn't serious. And I'm
better now.

JUANITA. Well, no, that's just it. You're
not really better.

RICHARD. How do you mean?

JUANITA. I watch you—

RICHARD. *Why* do you watch me?

JUANITA. I care about you.

RICHARD. You care about me! I thought
you could hold your liquor better than
that, girl.

JUANITA. It's not liquor. Don't you believe that anyone can care about you?

RICHARD. Care about me! Do you know
how many times chicks have told me that?
That they *cared* about me?

JUANITA. Well. This isn't one of those
times.

RICHARD. I was a junkie.

JUANITA. A what?

RICHARD. A junkie, a dope addict, a hophead, a mainliner—a dope fiend! My arms
and my legs, too, are full of holes!

JUANITA. I asked you tell *me*, not the
world.

RICHARD. Where'd Pete go?

JUANITA. He's dancing.

RICHARD. You want to dance?

JUANITA. In a minute.

RICHARD. I got hooked about five years
ago. See, I couldn't stand these chicks I
was making it with, and I was working
real hard at my music, and, man, I was
lonely. You come off a gig, you be tired,
and you'd already taken as much shit as
you could stand from the managers and
the people in the room you were working
and you'd be off to make some down
scene with some pasty white-faced bitch.
And so you'd make the scene and somehow you'd wake up in the morning and
the chick would be beside you, alive and
well, and dying to make the scene again
and somehow you'd managed not to stran-
gle her, you hadn't beaten her to death.
Like you wanted to. And you get out of
there and you carry this pain around in-

side all day and all night long. No way to beat it—no *way*. No matter how you turned, no matter what you did—no *way*. But when I started getting high, I was cool, and it didn't bother me. And I wasn't lonely then, it was all right. And the chicks —I could handle them, they couldn't reach me. And I didn't know I was hooked— until I was *hooked*. Then I started getting into trouble and I lost a lot of gigs and I had to sell my car and I lost my pad and most of the chicks, they split, naturally— but not all of them—and then I got busted and I made that trip down to Lexington and—here I am. Way *down* upon the Swanee River. But I'm going to be all right. You can bet on it.

JUANITA. I'd like to do better than that. I'd like to see to it.

RICHARD. How?

JUANITA. Well, like I used to. I won't let you go anywhere without me.

RICHARD. You *still* determined to break your neck.

JUANITA. Well, it's a neck-breaking time. I wouldn't like to appear to be above the battle.

RICHARD. Do you have any idea of what you might be letting yourself in for?

JUANITA. No. But you said you were lonely. And I'm lonely, too.

(LYLE *enters, goes to the counter. His appearance causes a change in the atmosphere, but no one appears to stop whatever they are doing.*)

LYLE. Joel, how about letting me have some change for cigarettes? I got a kind of long drive ahead of me, and I'm out.

PAPA D. Howdy, Mister Lyle, how you been? Folks ain't been seeing much of you lately.

LYLE (*laughs*). That's the truth. But I reckon old friends just stays old friends. Ain't that right?

PAPA D. That's right, Mister Lyle.

JUANITA. That's Lyle Britten. The one we were talking about before.

RICHARD. I wonder what he'd do if I walked into a white place.

JUANITA. Don't worry about it. Just stay out of white places—believe me!

RICHARD (*laughs*). Let's TCB—that means taking care of business. Let's see if I can dance.

(*They rise, dance. Perhaps she is teaching him the "Fight," or he is teaching her the "Pony"; they are enjoying each other.*

LYLE *gets his change, gets cigarettes out of the machine, crosses to the counter, pauses there to watch the dancers.*)

LYLE. Joel, you know I ain't never going to be able to dance like that.

PAPA D. Ain't nothing to it. You just got to be supple, that's all. I can *yet* do it.

(*Does a grotesque sketch of the "Twist."*)

LYLE. Okay, Joel, you got it. Be seeing you now.

PAPA D. Good night, Mister Lyle.

(*On* LYLE's *way out, he jostles* JUANITA. RICHARD *stops, holding* JUANITA *at the waist.* RICHARD *and* LYLE *stare at each other.*)

LYLE. Pardon me.

RICHARD. Consider yourself pardoned.

LYLE. You new around here?

PAPA D. He just come to town a couple of days ago, Mister Lyle.

RICHARD. Yeah. I just come to town a couple of days ago, Mister Lyle.

LYLE. Well. I sure hope your stay'll be a pleasant one.

(*Exits.*)

PETE. Man, are you *anxious* to leave this world? Because he wouldn't think nothing of helping you out of it.

RICHARD. Yeah. Well, I wouldn't think nothing of helping him out of it, neither. Come on, baby, record's going to waste— let's TCB.

(*They dance.*)

So you care about me, do you? Ain't that a bitch?

(THE CHURCH. PETE *and* JUANITA, *a little apart from the others.*)

PETE. Why have you been avoiding me? Don't answer that. You started going away from me as soon as Richard came to this town. Now listen, Richard's dead but you still won't turn to me. I don't want to ask you for more than you can give, but why have you locked me out? I *know*—you liked me. We had nice times together.

JUANITA. We did. I *do* like you. Pete, I don't know. I wish you wouldn't ask me now. I wish *nobody* would ask me for anything now!

PETE. Is it because of Richard? Because if that's what it is, I'll wait—I'll wait until you know inside you that Richard's dead, but you're alive, and you're *supposed* to live, and I love you.

JUANITA. When Richard came, he—*hit* —me in someplace where I'd never been touched before. I don't mean—just physically. He took all my attention—the deepest attention, maybe, that one person can give another. He needed me and he made a difference for me in this terrible world —do you see what I mean? And—it's funny—when I was with him, I didn't think of the future, I didn't dare. I didn't know if I could be strong enough to give him what he needed for as long as he would need it. It only lasted four or five days, Pete—four or five days, like a storm, like lightning! And what I saw during that storm I'll always see. Before that—I thought I knew who I was. But now I know that there are more things in me than I'll ever understand—and if I can't be faithful to myself, I'm afraid to promise I'll be faithful to one man!

PETE. I need you. I'll be faithful. That helps. You'll see.

JUANITA. So many people need so much!

PETE. So do you. So do I, Juanita. You take all my attention. My deepest attention.

JUANITA. You probably see things that I think are hidden. You probably think I'm a fool—or worse.

PETE. No. I think there's a lot of love in you, Juanita. If you'll let me help you, we can give it to the world. You can't give it to the world until you find a person who can help you—love the world.

JUANITA. I've discovered that. The world is a loveless place.

PETE. Not yet—

(*The lights of a car flash in their faces. Silence. They all listen tensely as the lights of another car approach, then pass; they watch the lights disappear. The telephone rings in the office.* MOTHER HENRY *goes off to answer it. They listen to the murmur of* MOTHER HENRY's *voice.* MOTHER HENRY *enters.*)

MOTHER HENRY. That was Freddy Roberts. He say about two-thirty his dog started to barking and woke him up and he let the dog out on the porch and the dog run under the porch and there was two white men *under* Freddy's porch, fooling around with his gas pipes. Freddy thinks the dog bit one of them. He ran inside to get him his rifle but the rifle jammed and the men got away. He wanted to warn us, maybe they might come prowling around here.

LORENZO. Only we ain't got no rifles.

JUANITA. It was the dog that woke him up? I'll bet they come back and kill that dog!

JIMMY. What was they doing under the man's house, messing around with his gas pipes, at that hour of the morning?

PETE. They was fixing to blow up his house. They *might* be under your house, or *this* house, right now.

LORENZO. The real question is why two white men feel safe enough to come to a black neighborhood after dark in the first place. If a couple of them get their heads blown off, they won't feel so goddamn courageous!

JUANITA. I better call home.

(*Exits into office.*)

PETE. Will you have your mother call my house?

LORENZO. And have *his* mother call *my* house?

JIMMY. And tell all the people that don't have rifles or dogs to stay off their porches!

LORENZO. Tell them to fall on their knees and use their Bibles as breast-plates! Because I know that each and every one of them got *Bibles!* (MERIDIAN *has walked to the church door, stands looking off.*)

LORENZO. Don't they, Meridian?

MOTHER HENRY. Hush.

(*We hear* JUANITA's *voice, off. Then silence falls. Lights dim on the students until they are in silhouette. Lights up on* MERIDIAN. *We hear* RICHARD's *guitar, very lonely, far away.*)

(*A car door slams. The voices of young people saying good night.* RICHARD *appears, dressed as we last saw him.*)

RICHARD. Hello, Daddy. You still up?

MERIDIAN. Yeah. Couldn't sleep. How was your day?

RICHARD. It was all right. I'd forgotten what nights down here were like. You never see the stars in the city—and all these funny country sounds—

MERIDIAN. Crickets. And all kinds of bugs and worms, running around, busy, shaking all the bushes.

RICHARD. Lord, if I'd stayed here, I guess I might have married old Juanita by now, and we'd have a couple of kids and I'd be sitting around like this *every* night. What a wild thought.

MERIDIAN. You can still marry Juanita. Maybe she's been waiting for you.

RICHARD. Have you ever thought of marrying again?

MERIDIAN. I've thought of it.

RICHARD. Did you ever think of marrying Juanita?

MERIDIAN. Why do you ask me that?

RICHARD. Because I'd like to know.

MERIDIAN. *Why* would you like to know?

RICHARD. Why would you like to hide it? I'd like to know because I'm a man now, Daddy, and I can ask you to tell me the truth. I'm making up for lost time. Maybe you should try to make up for lost time too.

MERIDIAN. Yes. I've thought of marrying Juanita. But I've never spoken of it to her.

RICHARD. That's the truth?

MERIDIAN. Yes.

RICHARD. Why didn't you tell me the truth way back there? Why didn't you tell me my mother was murdered? She was pushed down them steps.

MERIDIAN. Richard, your mother's dead. People die in all kinds of ways. They die when their times comes to die. Your mother loved you and she was gone—there was nothing more I could do for her. I had to think of you. I didn't want you to be—poisoned—by useless and terrible suspicions. I didn't want to wreck your life. I knew your life was going to be hard enough. So, I let you go. I thought it might be easier for you—if I let you go. I didn't want you to grow up in this town.

RICHARD. But there was something else in it, too, Daddy. You didn't want me to look at you and be ashamed of you. And you didn't know what was in my eyes, you couldn't stand it, I could tell from the way you looked at me sometimes. That was it, wasn't it?

MERIDIAN. I thought it was better. I suppose I thought it was all over for me, anyway. And I thought I owed it to your mother and to girls like your mother, to try—try to change, to purify this town, where she was born, and where we'd been so happy, and which she loved so much. I was wrong, I guess. I was wrong.

RICHARD. You've just been a public man, Daddy, haven't you? Since that day? You haven't been a private man at all.

MERIDIAN. No. I haven't. Try to forgive me.

RICHARD. There's nothing to forgive. I've been down the road a little bit. I know what happened. I'm going to try again, Daddy.

(*A pause.* RICHARD *takes out the gun.*)

Here. Grandmama saw this this morning and she got all upset. So I'll let you hold it for me. You keep it till I ask you for it, okay? But when I ask you for it, you got to give it to me. Okay?

MERIDIAN (*takes the gun*). Okay. I'm proud of how you've come through—all you've had to bear.

RICHARD. I'm going to get some sleep. You coming over to the house now?

MERIDIAN. Not yet.

RICHARD. Good night. Say, Daddy?

MERIDIAN. Yeah?

RICHARD. You kind of like the idea of me and Juanita getting together?

MERIDIAN. Yeah. I think it's a fine idea.

RICHARD. Well, I'm going to sleep on it, then. Good night.

MERIDIAN. Good night.

(RICHARD *exits.*)

(*After* RICHARD*'s exit, the lights come up on the students.*)

JUANITA. Lord it's gone and started raining.

PETE. And you worried about your hair.

JUANITA. I am *not* worried about my hair. I'm thinking of wearing it the way God arranged it in the first place.

LORENZO. Now, now, Mau-Mau.

PETE. This chick is going through some weird changes.

MERIDIAN. That's understandable. We all are.

JIMMY. Well, we'll see you sometime tomorrow. It promises to be a kind of *active* day.

MERIDIAN. Yes, we've got some active days ahead of us. You all better get some sleep.

JUANITA. How're you getting home, Jimmy?

JIMMY. Pete's driving us all home.

JUANITA. And then—are you going to drive all the way to your house alone, Pete?

PETE. You're jumpy tonight. I'll stay at Lorenzo's house.

LORENZO. You can call your house from there.

MOTHER HENRY. You get some sleep, too, Meridian, it's past three o'clock in the morning. Don't you stay over here much longer.

MERIDIAN. No, I won't. Good night, all.

MOTHER HENRY. Good night, children. See you in the morning, God willing.

(*They exit.* MERIDIAN *walks to the pul-*

pit, puts his hand on the Bible. PARNELL *enters.*)

PARNELL. I hear it was real bad tonight.

MERIDIAN. Not as bad as it's going to get. Maybe I was wrong not to let the people arm.

PARNELL. If the Negroes were armed, it's the Negroes who'd be slaughtered. You know that.

MERIDIAN. They're slaughtered anyway. And I don't know that. I thought I knew it—but now I'm not so sure.

PARNELL. What's come over you? What's going to happen to the people in this town, this church—if you go to pieces?

MERIDIAN. Maybe they'll find a leader who can lead them someplace.

PARNELL. Somebody with a gun?

(MERIDIAN *is silent.*)

Is that what you mean?

MERIDIAN. I'm a Christian. I've been a Christian all my life, like my Mama and Daddy before me and like their Mama and Daddy before them. Of course, if you go back far enough, you get to a point *before* Christ, if you see what I mean, *B.C.* —and at that point, I've been thinking, black people weren't raised to turn the other cheek, and in the hope of heaven. No, then they didn't have to take low. Before Christ. They walked around just as good as anybody else, and when they died, they didn't go to heaven, they went to join their ancestors. My son's dead, but he's not gone to join his ancestors. He was a sinner, so he must have gone to hell —if we're going to believe what the Bible says. Is that such an improvement, such a mighty advance over B.C.? I've been thinking, I've had to think—would I have *been* such a Christian if I hadn't been born black? Maybe I *had* to become a Christian in order to have any dignity at all. Since I wasn't a man in men's eyes, then I could be a man in the eyes of God. But that didn't protect my wife. She's dead, too soon, we don't really know how. That didn't protect my son—he's dead, we know how too well. That hasn't changed this town—this town, where you couldn't find a white Christian at high noon on Sunday! The eyes of God—maybe those eyes are blind—I never let myself think of that before.

PARNELL. Meridian, you can't be the man who gives the signal for the holocaust.

MERIDIAN. Must I be the man who watches while his people are beaten, chained, starved, clubbed, butchered?

PARNELL. You used to say that your people were all the people in the world—all the people God ever made, or would make. You said your race was the human race.

MERIDIAN. The human race!

PARNELL. I've never seen you like this before. There's something in your tone I've never heard before—rage—maybe hatred—

MERIDIAN. You've heard it before. You just never recognized it before. You've heard it in all those blues and spirituals and gospel songs you claim to love so much.

PARNELL. I was talking about *you*—not your history. I have a history, too. And don't be so sure I've never heard that sound. Maybe I've never heard anything else. Perhaps my life is also hard to bear.

MERIDIAN. I watched you all this week up at the Police Chief's office with me. And you know how to handle him because you're sure you're better than he is. But you both have more in common with each other than either of you have with me. And, for both of you—I watched this, I never watched it before—it was just a black boy that was dead, and that was a problem. He saw the problem one way, you saw it another way. But it wasn't a *man* that was dead, not my *son*—you held yourselves away from *that!*

PARNELL. I may have sounded—cold. It was not because I felt cold. There was no other way to sound, Meridian. I took the only tone which—it seemed to me—could accomplish what we wanted. And I *do* know the Chief of Police better than you —because I'm white. And I can make him listen to me—because I'm white. I don't know if I think I'm so much better than he is. I know what we have done—and do. But you must have mercy on us. We have no other hope.

MERIDIAN. You have never shown us any mercy at all.

PARNELL. Meridian, give me credit for knowing you're in pain. We are two men, two friends—in spite of all that could divide us. We have come too far together, there is too much at stake, for you to become black now, for me to become white. Don't accuse me. Don't accuse me. *I* didn't do it.

MERIDIAN. So was my son—innocent.

PARNELL. Meridian—when I asked for mercy a moment ago—I meant—please—please try to understand that it is not so easy to leap over fences, to give things up —all right, to surrender privilege! But if you were among the privileged you would know what I mean. It's not a matter of trying to hold *on;* the things, the privilege —are part of you, are *who* you are. It's in the *gut.*

MERIDIAN. Then where's the point of this struggle, where's the hope? If Mister Charlie can't change—

PARNELL. Who's Mister Charlie?

MERIDIAN. You're Mister Charlie. *All* white men are Mister Charlie!

PARNELL. You sound more and more like your son, do you know that? A lot of the colored people here didn't approve of him, but he said things they longed to say—said right out loud, for all the world to hear, how much he despised white people!

MERIDIAN. He didn't say things *I* longed to say. Maybe it was because he was my son. I didn't care *what* he felt about white people. I just wanted him to live, to have his own life. There's something you don't understand about being black, Parnell. If you're a black man, with a black son, you have to forget all about white people and concentrate on trying to save your child. That's why I let him stay up North. I was wrong, I failed, I failed. Lyle walked him up the road and killed him.

PARNELL. We don't *know* Lyle killed him. And Lyle denies it.

MERIDIAN. Of course, he denies it—what do you mean, we don't *know* Lyle killed him?

PARNELL. We *don't* know—all we can say is that it looks that way. And circumstantial evidence is a tricky thing.

MERIDIAN. *When* it involves a white man killing a black man—if Lyle didn't kill him, Parnell, who did?

PARNELL. I don't *know.* But we don't know that Lyle did it.

MERIDIAN. Lyle doesn't deny that he killed Old Bill.

PARNELL. No.

MERIDIAN. And we know how Lyle feels about colored people.

PARNELL. Well, yes. From your point of view. But—from another point of view—Lyle hasn't got anything *against* colored people. He just—

MERIDIAN. He just doesn't think they're human.

PARNELL. Well, even *that's* not true. He doesn't think they're *not* human—after all, I know him, he's hot-tempered and he's far from being the brightest man in the world—but he's not mean, he's not cruel. He's a poor white man. The poor whites have been just as victimized in this part of the world as the blacks have ever been!

MERIDIAN. For God's sake spare me the historical view! Lyle's responsible for Richard's death.

PARNELL. But, Meridian, we can't, even in our own minds, *decide* that he's guilty. We have to operate the way justice *always* has to operate and give him the benefit of the doubt.

MERIDIAN. *What* doubt?

PARNELL. Don't you see, Meridian, that now you're operating the way white people in this town operate whenever a colored man's on trial?

MERIDIAN. When was the last time one of us was on *trial* here, Parnell?

PARNELL. That *can't* have anything to do with it, it *can't.* We must forget about all —*all* the past injustice. We have to start from scratch, or do our best to start from scratch. It isn't vengeance we're after. Is it?

MERIDIAN. I don't want vengeance. I don't want to be paid back—anyway, I couldn't be. I just want Lyle to be made to know that what he did was evil. I just want this town to be forced to face the evil that it countenances and to turn from evil and do good. That's why I've stayed in this town so long!

PARNELL. But if Lyle didn't do it? Lyle is a friend of mine—a strange friend, but a friend. I love him. I know how he suffers.

MERIDIAN. *How* does he suffer?

PARNELL. He suffers—from being in the dark—from having things inside him that he can't name and can't face and can't control. He's not a wicked man. I know he's not, I've known him almost all his life! The face he turns to you, Meridian, isn't the face he turns to me.

MERIDIAN. Is the face he turns to you more real than the face he turns to me? *You* go ask him if he killed my son.

PARNELL. They're going to ask him that in court. That's why I fought to bring about this trial. And he'll say no.

MERIDIAN. I don't care what he says in court. You go ask him. If he's your friend, he'll tell you the truth.

PARNELL. No. No, he may not. He's—he's maybe a little afraid of me.

MERIDIAN. If you're *his* friend, you'll know whether he's telling you the truth or not. Go ask him.

PARNELL. I can't do it. I'm his friend. I can't betray him.

MERIDIAN. But you can betray *me?* You *are* a white man, aren't you? Just another white man—after all.

PARNELL. Even if he says yes, it won't make any difference. The jury will never convict him.

MERIDIAN. Is that why you fought to bring about the trial? I don't care what the jury does. I know he won't say yes to them. He won't say yes to me. But he might say yes to you. You say we don't know. Well, I've got a right to know. And I've got the right to ask you to find out—since you're the only man who *can* find out. And *I've* got to find out—whether we've been friends all these years, or whether I've just been your favorite Uncle Tom.

PARNELL. You know better than that.

MERIDIAN. I don't know, Parnell, any longer—any of the things I used to know. Maybe I never knew them. I'm tired. Go home.

PARNELL. You don't trust me anymore, do you, Meridian?

MERIDIAN. Maybe I never trusted you. I don't know. Maybe I never trusted myself. Go home. Leave me alone. I must look back at my record.

PARNELL. Meridian—what you ask—I don't know if I can do it for you.

MERIDIAN. I don't want you to do it for me. I want you to do it for you. Good night.

PARNELL. Good night.

(PARNELL *exits.* MERIDIAN *comes downstage. It is dawn.*)

MERIDIAN. My record! Would God—would *God*—would God I had died for thee—my son, my son!

CURTAIN

ACT TWO

WHITETOWN: *The kitchen of* LYLE's *house. Sunday morning. Church bells. A group of white people, all ages, men and women.*

JO *and an older woman,* HAZEL, *have just taken a cake out of the oven.* HAZEL *sets it out to cool.*

———

HAZEL. It's a shame—having to rush everything this way. But it can't be helped.

JO. Yes. I'm just so upset. I can't help it. I know it's silly. I know they can't do nothing to Lyle.

HAZEL. Girl, you just put all those negative thoughts right out of your mind. We're going to have your little anniversary celebration *tonight* instead of *tomorrow* night because we have reason to believe that *tomorrow* night your husband might be called away on business. Now, you think about it that way. Don't you go around here with a great long face, trying to demoralize your guests. I won't have it. You too young and pretty for that.

LILLIAN. Hallelujah! I *do* believe that I have finally mastered this recipe.

SUSAN. Oh, good! Let me see.

LILLIAN. I've only tried it once before, and it's real hard. You've got to time it just right.

SUSAN. I have tried it and tried it and it never comes out! But yours is wonderful! We're going to eat tonight, folks!

RALPH. You supposed to be cooking something, too, ain't you?

SUSAN. I'm cooking our contribution later, at our own house. We got enough women here already, messing up Jo's kitchen.

JO. I'm just so glad you all come by I don't know what to do. Just go ahead and mess up that kitchen, I got lots of time to clean it.

ELLIS. Susan's done learned how to cook, huh?

RALPH. Oh, yeah, she's a right fine cook. All you got to do is look at me. I never weighed this much in my life.

ELLIS. Old Lyle's done gained weight in this year, too. Nothing like steady home cooking, I guess, ha-ha! It really don't seem like it was a year ago you two got married. Declare, I never thought Lyle was going to jump up and do that thing. But old Jo, here, she hooked him.

REV. PHELPS. Well, I said the words over them, and if I ever saw a happy man in my life, it was Big Lyle Britten that day.

Both of them—there was just a light shining out of them.

GEORGE. I'd propose a toast to them, if it wasn't so early on a Sunday, and if the Reverend wasn't here.

REV. PHELPS. Ain't nothing wrong with toasting happy people, no matter what the day or hour.

ELLIS. You heard the Reverend! You got anything in this house we can drink to your happiness in, Mrs. Britten?

JO. I'm pretty sure we do. It's a pity Lyle ain't up yet. He ain't never slept through this much racket before.

ELLIS. No ma'am, he ain't never been what you'd call a heavy sleeper. Not before he passed out, ha-ha! We used to have us some times together, him and me, before he got him some sense and got married.

GEORGE. Let him sleep easy. He ain't got no reason not to.

JO. Lyle's always got his eye on the ball, you know—and he's just been at that store, night after night after night, drawing up plans and taking inventory and I don't know what all—because, come fall, he's planning to branch out and have a brand new store, just about. You all won't recognize the place, I guarantee you!

ELLIS. Lyle's just like his Daddy. You can't beat him. The harder a thing is, well, the surer you can be that old Lyle Britten will do it. Why, Lyle's Daddy never got old—*never!* He was drinking and running after women—and getting them, too!—until just before they put him in his grave. I could tell you stories about the old man, boy—of course, I can't tell them now, on a Sunday morning, in front of all these women!

JO. Here you are, gentlemen. I hope you all drink bourbon.

RALPH. Listen to her!

GEORGE. Ladies! Would you all like to join us in a morning toast to the happy and beloved and loving couple, Mr. and Mrs. Lyle Britten, on the day immediately preceding their first wedding anniversary?

ELLIS. The bridegroom ain't here because he's weary from all his duties, both public and private. Ha-ha! But he's a good man, and he's done a lot for us, and I know you all know what I'm talking about, and I just feel like we should honor him and his lovely young wife. Ladies! Come on, Reverend Phelps says it's all right.

SUSAN. Not too much for me, Ralph.

LILLIAN. I don't think I've ever had a drink at this hour of a Sunday morning, and in the presence of my pastor!

(*They pour, drink, and sing* "For He's a Jolly Good Fellow.")

HAZEL. Now you've started her to crying, naturally. Here, honey, you better have a little drink yourself.

JO. You all have been *so* wonderful. I can't imagine how Lyle can go on sleeping. Thank you, Hazel. Here's to all of you!

(*Drinks.*) Listen. They're singing over there now.

(*They listen.*)

HAZEL. Sometimes they can sound so nice. Used to take my breath away when I was a girl.

ELLIS. What's happened to this town? It was peaceful here, we all got along, we didn't have no trouble.

GEORGE. Oh, we had a little trouble from time to time, but it didn't amount to a hill of beans. Niggers was all right then, you could always get you a nigger to help you catch a nigger.

LILLIAN. That's right. They had their ways, we had ours, and everything went along the way God intended.

JO. I've never been scared in this town before—never. They was all like my own people. I never knew of anyone to mistreat a colored person—have you? And they certainly didn't *act* mistreated. But now, when I walk through this town—I'm scared—like I don't know what's going to happen next. How come the colored people to hate us so much, all of a sudden? We *give* them everything they've got!

REVEREND PHELPS. Their minds have been turned. They have turned away from God. They're a simple people—warmhearted and good-natured. But they are very easily led, and now they are harkening to the counsel of these degenerate Communist race-mixers. And they don't know what terrible harm they can bring on themselves—and on us all.

JO. You can't tell what they're thinking. Why, colored folks you been knowing all your life—you're almost afraid to hire them, almost afraid to *talk* to them—you don't know what they're thinking.

ELLIS. *I* know what they're thinking.

SUSAN. We're not much better off than the Communist countries—that's what Ralph says. *They* live in fear. They don't want us to teach God in our schools—you send your child to school and you don't know *what* kind of Godless atheist is going to be filling the little one's mind with all *kinds* of filth. And he's going to believe it, of course, kids don't know no better. And now they tell us we got to send our kids to *school* with niggers— why, everybody *knows* that ain't going to work, won't nobody get no education, white *or* black. Niggers can't learn like white folks, they ain't got the same *interests*.

ELLIS. They got one interest. And it's just below the belly button.

GEORGE (*laughs*). You know them yellow niggers? Boy, ain't they the worst kind? Their own folks don't want them, don't nobody want them, and you *can't* do nothing with them—you might be able to scare a black nigger, but you can't do nothing with a yellow nigger.

REVEREND PHELPS. That's because he's a mongrel. And a mongrel is the lowest creation in the animal kingdom.

ELLIS. Mrs. Britten, you're married and all the women in this room are married and I know you've seen your husband without no clothes on—but have you seen a nigger without no clothes on? No, I guess you haven't. Well, he ain't like a white man, Mrs. Britten.

GEORGE. That's right.

ELLIS. Mrs. Britten, if you was to be raped by an orang-outang out of the jungle or a *stallion,* couldn't do you no worse than a nigger. You wouldn't be no more good for nobody. I've *seen* it.

GEORGE. That's *right.*

RALPH. That's why we men have got to be so vigilant. I tell you, I have to be away a lot nights, you know—and I bought Susan a gun and I taught her how to use it, too.

SUSAN. And I'm a pretty good shot now, too. Ralph says he's real proud of me.

RALPH. She's just like a pioneer woman.

HAZEL. I'm so glad Esther's not here to see this. She'd die of shame. She was the sweetest colored woman—you remember her. She just about raised us, used to sing us to sleep at night, and she could tell just the most beautiful stories—the kind of stories that could scare you and make you laugh and make you cry, you know? Oh, she was wonderful. I don't remember a cross word or an evil expression all the time she was with us. She was always the same. And I believe she knew more about me than my own mother and father knew. I just told her everything. Then, one of her sons got killed—he went bad, just like this boy they having a funeral for here tonight—and she got sick. I nursed her, I bathed that woman's body with my own hands. And she told me once, she said, "Miss Hazel, you are just like an angel of light." She said, "My own couldn't have done more for me than you have done." She was a wonderful old woman.

JO. I believe I hear Lyle stirring.

SUSAN. Mrs. Britten, somebody else is coming to call on you. My! It's that Parnell James! I wonder if he's sober this morning. He never *looks* sober.

ELLIS. He never acts it, either.

(PARNELL *enters.*)

PARNELL. Good morning, good people! Good morning, Reverend Phelps! How good it is to see brethren—and sistren— walking together. Or, in this case, standing together—something like that, anyway; my Bible's a little rusty. Is church over already? Or are you having it here? Good morning, Jo.

JO. Good morning, Parnell. Sit down, I'll pour you a cup of coffee.

GEORGE. You look like you could use it.

REV. PHELPS. We were all just leaving.

PARNELL. Please don't leave on my account, Reverend Phelps. Just go on as you were, praying or singing, just as the spirit may move you. I *would* love that cup of coffee, Jo.

ELLIS. You been up all night?

PARNELL. Is that the way I look? Yes, I *have* been up all night.

ELLIS. Tom-catting around, I'll bet. Getting drunk and fooling with all the women.

PARNELL. Ah, you flatter me. And in games of chance, my friend, you have no future at all. I'm sure you always lose at poker. So *stop betting.* I was not tomcatting, I was at home, working.

GEORGE. You been over the way this morning? You been at the nigger funeral?

PARNELL. The funeral takes place this evening. And, yes, I will be there. Would you care to come along? Leaving your baseball bat at home, of course.

JO. We heard the singing—

PARNELL. Darkies are always singing.

You people know that. What made you think it was a funeral?

JO. Parnell! You are the limit! Would anybody else like a little more coffee? It's still good and hot.

ELLIS. We heard that a nigger got killed. That's why we thought it was a funeral.

GEORGE. They bury their dead over the way, don't they?

PARNELL. They do when the dogs leave enough to bury, yes.

(*A pause.*)

ELLIS. Dogs?

PARNELL. Yes—you know. Teeth. Barking. Lots of noise.

ELLIS. A lot of people in this town, Parnell, would like to know exactly where you stand, on a lot of things.

PARNELL. That's exactly where I stand. On a lot of things. Why don't you read my paper?

LILLIAN. I wouldn't filthy my hands with that Communist sheet!

PARNELL. Ah? But the father of your faith, the cornerstone of that church of which you are so precious an adornment, was a communist, possibly the first. He may have done some tom-catting. We *know* he did some drinking. And he knew a lot of—loose ladies and drunkards. It's all in the Bible, isn't it, Reverend Phelps?

REV. PHELPS. I won't be drawn into your blasphemous banter. Ellis is only asking what many of us want to know—are you with us or against us? And he's telling you what we all feel. We've put up with your irresponsibility long enough. We won't tolerate it any longer. Do I make myself clear?

PARNELL. Not at all. If you're threatening me, be specific. First of all, what's this irresponsibility that you won't tolerate? And if you aren't going to tolerate it, what *are* you going to do? Dip me in tar and feathers? Boil me in oil? Castrate me? Burn me? Cover yourselves in white sheets and come and burn crosses in front of my house? Come on, Reverend Phelps, don't stand there with your mouth open, it makes you even more repulsive than you are with it closed, and all your foul, graveyard breath comes rushing out, and it makes me want to vomit. Out with it, boy! What's on your mind?

ELLIS. You got away with a lot of things in this town, Parnell, for a long time, because your father was a big man here.

PARNELL. One at a time. I was addressing your spiritual leader.

SUSAN. He's *worse* than a nigger.

PARNELL. I take that as a compliment. I'm sure no man will ever say as much for you. Reverend Phelps?

REV. PHELPS. I think I speak for us all—for *myself* and for us all, when I say that our situation down here has become much too serious for flippancy and cynicism. When things were more in order here, we didn't really mind your attitude, and your paper didn't matter to us, we never read it, anyway.

ELLIS. We knew you were just a spoiled rich boy, with too much time on his hands that he didn't know what to do with.

REV. PHELPS. And so you started this paper and tried to make yourself interesting with all these subversive attitudes. I honestly thought that you would grow out of it.

GEORGE. Or go North.

REV. PHELPS. I know these attitudes were not your father's attitudes, or your mother's. I was very often invited to your home when they were alive—

PARNELL. How well I remember! What attitudes are you speaking of?

HAZEL. Race-mixing.

PARNELL. *Race-mixing!* Ladies and gentlemen, do you think anybody gives a good goddamn who you sleep with? You can go down to the swamps and couple with the snakes, for all I care, or for all anybody else cares. You may find that the snakes don't want you, but that's a problem for you and the snakes to work out, and it might prove astonishingly simple—the working out of the problem, I mean. I've never said a word about race-mixing. I've talked about social justice.

LILLIAN. That sounds Communistic to me!

PARNELL. It means that if I have a hundred dollars, and I'm black, and you have a hundred dollars, and you're white, I should be able to get as much value for *my* hundred dollars—my black hundred dollars—as you get for your *white* hundred dollars. It also means that I should have an equal opportunity to *earn* that hundred dollars—

ELLIS. Niggers can get work just as well as a white man can. Hell, *some* niggers make *more* money than me.

PARNELL. Some niggers are smarter than

you, Ellis. Much smarter. And much nicer. And niggers *can't* get work just as well as a white man can, and you know it.

ELLIS. What's stopping them? They got hands.

PARNELL. Ellis, you don't really work with your *hands*—you're a salesman in a shoe store. And your boss wouldn't give that job to a nigger.

GEORGE. Well, goddammit, white men come before niggers! They *got* to!

PARNELL. Why?

(LYLE *enters.*)

LYLE. What's all this commotion going on in my house?

JO. Oh, Lyle, good morning! Some folks just dropped in to see you.

LYLE. It sounded like they was about to come to blows. Good morning, Reverend Phelps, I'm glad to see you here. I'm sorry I wasn't up, but I guess my wife might have told you, I've not been sleeping well nights. When I *do* go to sleep, she just lets me sleep on.

REV. PHELPS. Don't you apologize, son —we understand. We only came by to let you know that we're with you and every white person in this town is with you.

JO. Isn't that nice of them, Lyle? They've been here quite a spell, and we've had *such* a nice time.

LYLE. Well, that *is* mighty nice of you, Reverend, and all of you—hey there, Ellis! Old George! And Ralph and Susan—how's married life suit you? Guess it suits you all right, ain't nobody seen you in months, ha-ha! Mrs. Proctor, Mrs. Barker, how you all? Hey! Old Parnell! What you doing up so early?

PARNELL. I was on my way to church, but they seemed to be having the meeting here. So I joined the worshippers.

LYLE. On your way to church, that's a good one. Bet you ain't been to bed yet.

PARNELL. No, I haven't.

LYLE. You folks don't mind if I have a little breakfast? Jo, bring me something to eat! Susan, you look mighty plump and rosy, you ain't keeping no secrets from us, are you?

SUSAN. I don't think so, Lyle.

LYLE. I don't know, you got that look— like a real ripe peach, just right for eating. You ain't been slack in your duty, have you, Ralph? Look at the way she's blushing! I guess you all right, boy.

ELLIS. You know what time they coming for you tomorrow?

LYLE. Sometime in the morning, I reckon. I don't know.

REV. PHELPS. I saw the Chief of Police the other day. He really doesn't want to do it, but his hands are tied. It's orders from higher up, from the North.

LYLE. Shoot, I know old Frank don't want to arrest me. I understand. I ain't worried. I know the people in this town is with me. I got nothing to worry about.

ELLIS. They trying to force us to put niggers on the jury—that's what I hear. Claim it won't be a fair trial if we don't.

HAZEL. Did you *ever* hear anything like that in your *life*?

LYLE. Where they going to find the niggers?

ELLIS. Oh, I bet your buddy, Parnell, has got that all figured out.

LYLE. How about it, Parnell? You going to find some niggers for them to put on that jury?

PARNELL. It's not up to me. But I might recommend a couple.

GEORGE. And how they going to get to court? You going to protect them?

PARNELL. The police will protect them. Or the State troopers—

GEORGE. That's a good one!

PARNELL. Or Federal marshals.

GEORGE. Look here, you really think there should be niggers on that jury?

PARNELL. Of course I do, and so would you, if you had any sense. For one thing, they're forty-four percent of the population of this town.

ELLIS. But they don't vote. Not most of them.

PARNELL. Well. That's also a matter of interest to the Federal government. Why *don't* they vote? They got hands.

ELLIS. You claim Lyle's your buddy—

PARNELL. Lyle *is* my buddy. That's why I want him to have a fair trial.

HAZEL. I can't listen to no more of this, I'm sorry, I just can't. Honey, I'll see you all tonight, you hear?

REV. PHELPS. We're all going to go now. We just wanted to see how you were, and let you know that you could count on us.

LYLE. I sure appreciate it, Reverend, believe me, I do. You make me feel much better. Even if a man knows he ain't done no wrong, still, it's a kind of troublesome spot to be in. Wasn't for my good Jo, here,

I don't know what I'd do. Good morning, Mrs. Barker. Mrs. Proctor. So long, George, it's been good to see you. Ralph, you take good care of Susan, you hear? And name the first one after me—you might have to bring it on up to the jail house so I can see it.

SUSAN. Don't think like that. Everything's going to be all right.

LYLE. You're sure?

SUSAN. I guarantee it. Why they couldn't —*couldn't*—do anything to you!

LYLE. Then I believe it. I believe *you*.

SUSAN. You keep right on believing.

ELLIS. Remember what we said, Parnell.

PARNELL. So long, Ellis. See you next Halloween.

LYLE. Let's get together, boy, soon as this mess is over.

ELLIS. You bet. This mess is just about over now—we ain't going to let them prolong it. And I know just the thing'll knock all this clear out of your mind, this, and everything else, ha-ha! Bye-bye, Mrs. Britten.

JO. Goodbye. And thanks for coming!

(HAZEL, LILLIAN, SUSAN, RALPH, ELLIS, REVEREND PHELPS, *and* GEORGE *exit*.)

LYLE. They're nice people.

JO. Yes. They are.

PARNELL. They certainly think a lot of you.

LYLE. You ain't jealous, are you, boy? No. We've all had the same kind of trouble—it's the kind of trouble you wouldn't know about, Parnell, because you've never had to worry about making your living. But me! I been doing hard work from the time I was a puppy. Like my Mama and Daddy before me, God rest their souls, and their Mama and Daddy before them. They wore themselves out on the land— the land never give them nothing. Nothing but an empty belly and some skinny kids. I'm the only one growed up to be a man. That's because I take after my Daddy—he was skinny as a piece of wire, but he was hard as any rock. And stubborn! Lord, you ain't never seen nobody so stubborn. He should have been born sooner. Had he been born sooner, when this was still a free country, and a man could really *make* some money, I'd have been born rich as you, Parnell, maybe even richer. I tell you—the old man struggled. He worked harder than any nigger. But he left me this store.

JO. You reckon we going to be able to leave it to the little one?

LYLE. We're going to leave him more than that. That little one ain't going to have nothing to worry about. I'm going to leave him as rich as old Parnell here, and he's going to be educated, too, better than his Daddy; better, even, than Parnell!

PARNELL. You going to send him to school in Switzerland?

LYLE. *You* went there for a while, didn't you?

JO. That's where Parnell picked up all his wild ideas.

PARNELL. Yes. Be careful. There were a couple of African princes studying in the school I went to—they did a lot more studying than I did, I must say.

LYLE. African princes, huh? What were they like? Big and black, I bet, elephant tusks hanging around their necks.

PARNELL. Some of them wore a little ivory, on a chain—silver chain. They were like everybody else. Maybe they thought they were a little *better* than most of us —the Swiss girls certainly thought so.

LYLE. The *Swiss* girls? You mean they didn't have no women of their own?

PARNELL. Lots of them. Swiss women, Danish women, English women, French women, Finns, Russians, even a couple of Americans.

JO. I don't believe you. Or else they was just trying to act like foreigners. I can't stand people who try to act like something they're not.

PARNELL. They were just trying to act like women—poor things. And the Africans were men, no one had ever told them that they weren't.

LYLE. You mean there weren't no African women around at *all*? Weren't the Swiss people kind of upset at having all these niggers around with no women?

PARNELL. They didn't seem to be upset. They seemed delighted. The niggers had an awful lot of money. And there weren't many African girls around because African girls aren't educated the way American girls are.

JO. The American girls didn't *mind* going out with the Africans?

PARNELL. Not at all. It appears that the Africans were excellent dancers.

LYLE. I won't never send no daughter of mine to Switzerland.

PARNELL. Well, what about your son?

He might grow fond of some little African princess.

LYLE. Well, that's different. I don't care about that, long as he leaves her over there.

JO. It's *not* different—how can you say that? White men ain't got no more business fooling around with black women than—

LYLE. Girl, will you stop getting yourself into an uproar? Men is different from women—they ain't as delicate. Man can do a lot of things a woman can't do, you know that.

PARNELL. You've heard the expression, sowing wild oats? Well, all the men we know sowed a lot of wild oats before they finally settled down and got married.

LYLE. That's right. Men *have* to do it. They ain't like women. Parnell is *still* sowing his wild oats—I sowed mine.

JO. And a woman that wants to be a decent woman just has to—*wait*—until the men get tired of going to bed with—harlots!—and decide to settle down?

PARNELL. Well, it sounds very unjust, I know, but that's the way it's always been. I *suppose* the decent women were waiting —though nobody seems to know *exactly* how they spent the time.

JO. Parnell!

PARNELL. Well, there *are* some who waited too long.

JO. Men ought to be ashamed. How can you blame a woman if she—goes wrong? If a decent woman can't find a decent man —why—it must happen all the time—they get tired of waiting.

LYLE. Not if they been raised right, no sir, that's what my Daddy said, and I've never known it to fail. And look at you— *you* didn't get tired of waiting. Ain't nobody in this town ever been able to say a word against you. Man, I was so scared when I finally asked this girl to marry me. I was afraid she'd turn me out of the house. Because I had been pretty wild. Parnell can tell you.

JO. I had heard.

LYLE. But she didn't. I looked at her, it seemed almost like it was the first time —you know, the first time you really *look* at a woman?—and I thought, I'll be damned if I don't believe I can make it with her. I believe I can. And she looked at me like she loved me. It was in her eyes. And it was just like somebody had lifted a great big load off my heart.

JO. You shouldn't be saying these things in front of Parnell.

LYLE. Why not? I ain't got no secrets from Parnell—he knows about men and women. Look at her blush! Like I told you. Women is more delicate than men.

(*He touches her face lightly*.)

I know you kind of upset, sugar. But don't you be nervous. Everything's going to be all right, and we're going to be happy again, you'll see.

JO. I hope so, Lyle.

LYLE. I'm going to take me a bath and put some clothes on. Parnell, you sit right there, you hear? I won't be but a minute.

(*Exits*.)

JO. What a funny man he is! It don't do no good at all to get mad at him, you might as well get mad at that baby in there. Parnell? Can I ask you something?

PARNELL. Certainly.

JO. Is it true that Lyle has no secrets from you?

PARNELL. He said that *neither* of you had any secrets from me.

JO. Oh, don't play. Lyle don't know a thing about women—what they're really like, to themselves. Men don't know. But I want to ask you a serious question. Will you answer it?

PARNELL. If I can.

JO. That means you won't answer it. But I'll ask it, anyway. Parnell—was Lyle —is it true what people said? That he was having an affair with Old Bill's wife and that's why he shot Old Bill?

PARNELL. Why are you asking me that?

JO. Because I have to know! It's true, isn't it? He had an affair with Old Bill's wife—and he had affairs with lots of colored women in this town. It's *true*. Isn't it?

PARNELL. What does it matter who he slept with before he married you, Jo? I know he had a—lot of prostitutes. Maybe some of them were colored. When he was drunk, he wouldn't have been particular.

JO. He's never talked to you about it?

PARNELL. Why would he?

JO. Men talk about things like that.

PARNELL. Men often joke about things like that. But, Jo—what one man tells another man, his friend—can't be told to women.

JO. Men certainly stick together. I wish women did. All right. You can't talk about Lyle. But tell me this. Have *you* ever had an affair with a colored girl? I don't mean a—a *night*. I mean, did she mean something to you, did you like her, did you— love her? Could you have married her—I mean, just like you would marry a white woman?

PARNELL. Jo—

JO. Oh! Tell me the truth, Parnell!

PARNELL. I loved a colored girl, yes. I think I loved her. But I was only eighteen and she was only seventeen. I was still a virgin. I don't know if she was, but I think she was. A lot of the other kids in school used to drive over to niggertown at night to try and find black women. Sometimes they bought them, sometimes they frightened them, sometimes they raped them. And they were proud of it, they talked about it all the time. I couldn't do that. Those kids made me ashamed of my own body, ashamed of everything I felt, ashamed of being white—

JO. Ashamed of being white.

PARNELL. Yes.

JO. How did you meet—this colored girl?

PARNELL. Her mother worked for us. She used to come, sometimes, to pick up her mother. Sometimes she had to wait. I came in once and found her in the library, she was reading Stendhal. *The Red and The Black*. I had just read it and we talked about it. She was funny—very bright and solemn and very proud—and she was *scared*, scared of me, but much too proud to show it. Oh, she was funny. But she was bright.

JO. What did she look like?

PARNELL. She was the color of gingerbread when it's just come out of the oven. I used to call her Ginger—later. Her name was really Pearl. She had black hair, very black, kind of short, and she dressed it very carefully. Later, I used to tease her about the way she took care of her hair. There's a girl in this town now who reminds me of her. Oh, I loved her!

JO. What happened?

PARNELL. I used to look at her, the way she moved, so beautiful and free, and I'd wonder if at night, when she might be on her way home from someplace, any of those boys at school had said ugly things to her. And then I thought that I wasn't any better than they were, because I thought my own thoughts were pretty awful. And I wondered what she thought of me. But I didn't dare to ask. I got so I could hardly think of anyone but her. I got sick wanting to take her in my arms, to take her in my arms and love her and protect her from all those other people who wanted to destroy her. She wrote a little poetry, sometimes she'd show it to me, but she really wanted to be a painter.

JO. What happened?

PARNELL. Nothing happened. We got so we told each other everything. She was going to be a painter, I was going to be a writer. It was our secret. Nobody in the world new about her *inside*, what she was like, and how she dreamed, but me. And nobody in the world knew about *me* inside, what I wanted, and how I dreamed, but her. But we couldn't look ahead, we didn't dare. We talked about going North, but I was still in school, and she was still in school. We couldn't be seen anywhere together—it would have given her too bad a name. I used to see her sometimes in the movies, with various colored boys. She didn't seem to have any special one. They'd be sitting in the balcony, in the colored section, and I'd be sitting downstairs in the white section. She couldn't come down to me, I couldn't go up to her. We'd meet some nights, late, out in the country, but— I didn't want to take her in the bushes, and I couldn't take her anywhere else. One day we were sitting in the library, we were kissing, and her mother came in. That was the day I found out how much black people can hate white people.

JO. What did her mother do?

PARNELL. She didn't say a word. She just looked at me. She just looked at me. I could see what was happening in her mind. She knew that there wasn't any point in complaining to my mother or my father. It would just make her daughter look bad. She didn't dare tell her husband. If he tried to do anything, he'd be killed. There wasn't anything she could do about me. I was just another horny white kid trying to get into a black girl's pants. She looked at me as though she were wishing with all her heart that she could raise her hand and wipe me off the face of the earth. I'll never forget that look. I still see it. She walked over to Pearl and I thought she was going to slap her. But she didn't. She took her by the hand, very sadly, and all she said was, "I'm ready to go now. Come on." And she took Pearl out of the room.

JO. Did you ever see her again?

PARNELL. No. Her mother sent her away.

JO. But you forgot her? You must have had lots of other girls right quick, right after that.

PARNELL. I never forgot her.

JO. Do you think of her—even when you're with Loretta?

PARNELL. Not all of the time, Jo. But some of the time—yes.

JO. And if you found her again?

PARNELL. If I found her again—yes, I'd marry her. I'd give her the children I've always wanted to have.

JO. Oh, Parnell! If you felt that way about her, if you've felt it all this time!

PARNELL. Yes. I know. I'm a renegade white man.

JO. Then Lyle could have felt that way about Old Bill's wife—about Willa Mae. I know that's not the way he feels about me. And if he felt that way—he could have shot Old Bill—to keep him quiet!

PARNELL. Jo!

JO. Yes! And if he could have shot Old Bill to keep him quiet—he could have killed that boy. He could have killed that boy. And if he did—well—that *is* murder, isn't it? It's just nothing but murder, even if the boy *was* black. Oh, Parnell! Parnell!

PARNELL. Jo, please. Please, Jo. Be quiet.

LYLE (*off*). What's all that racket in there?

PARNELL. I'm telling your wife the story of my life.

LYLE (*off*). Sounds pretty goddamn active.

PARNELL. You've never asked him, have you, Jo?

JO. No. No. No.

PARNELL. Well, *I* asked him—

JO. When?

PARNELL. Well, I didn't really *ask* him. But he said he didn't do it, that it wasn't true. You heard him. He wouldn't lie to me.

JO. No. He wouldn't lie to you. They say some of the niggers have guns—did you hear that?

PARNELL. Yes. I've heard it. But it's not true.

JO. *They* wouldn't lie to you, either? I've just had too much time to worry, I guess—brood and worry. Lyle's away so often nights—he spends so much time at that store. I don't know what he does

there. And when he comes home, he's just dead—and he drops right off to sleep.

(LYLE *enters, carrying the child.*)

Hi, honey. What a transformation. You look like you used to look when you come courting.

LYLE. I sure didn't come courting carrying no baby. He was awake, just singing away, and carrying on with his toes. He acts like he thinks he's got a whole lot of candy attached to the end of his legs. Here. It's about time for him to eat, ain't it? How come you looking at me like that? Why you being so nice to me, all of a sudden?

PARNELL. I've been lecturing her on the duties of a wife.

LYLE. That so? Well, come on, boy, let's you and me walk down the road a piece. Believe I'll buy you a drink. You ain't ashamed to be seen with me, I hope?

PARNELL. No, I'm not ashamed to be seen with you.

JO. You going to be home for supper?

LYLE. Yeah, sugar. Come on, Parnell.

JO. You come, too, Parnell, you and Loretta, if you're free. We'd love to have you.

PARNELL. We'll try to make it. So long, Jo.

JO. So long.

(*They exit.* JO *walks to the window. Turns back into the room, smiles down at the baby. Sings.*)

> Hush, little baby, don't say a
>   word,
> Mama's going to buy you a
>   mocking bird—

But you don't want no mocking bird right now, do you? I know what you want. You want something to eat. All right, Mama's going to feed you.

(*Sits, slowly begins to unbutton her blouse. Sings.*)

> If that mocking bird don't sing,
> Mama's going to buy you a dia-
>   mond ring.

(LYLE'S STORE: *Early evening. Both* LYLE *and* PARNELL *are a little drunk.*)

LYLE. Didn't you ever get like that? Sure, you must have got like that sometimes—just restless! You got everything you need and you can't complain about nothing—and yet, look like, you just can't be satisfied. Didn't you ever get like that? I swear, men is mighty strange! I'm kind of restless now.

PARNELL. What's the matter with you? You worried about the trial?

LYLE. No, I ain't worried about the trial. I ain't even mad at you, Parnell. Some folks think I should be, but I ain't mad at you. They don't know you like I know you. I ain't fooled by all your wild ideas. We both white and we both from around here, and we been buddies all our lives. That's all that counts. I know you ain't going to let nothing happen to me.

PARNELL. That's good to hear.

LYLE. After all the trouble started in this town—but before that crazy boy got himself killed, soon after he got here and started raising all that hell—I started thinking about her, about Willa Mae, more and more and more. She was too young for him. Old Bill, he was sixty if he was a day, he wasn't doing her no good. Yet and still, the first time I took Willa Mae, I had to fight her. I swear I did. Maybe she was frightened. But I never had to fight her again. No. It was good, boy, let me tell you, and she liked it as much as me. Hey! You still with me?

PARNELL. I'm still with you. Go on.

LYLE. What's the last thing I said?

PARNELL. That she liked it as much as you—which I find hard to believe.

LYLE. Ha-ha! I'm telling you. I never had it for nobody bad as I had it for her.

PARNELL. When did Old Bill find out?

LYLE. Old Bill? He wouldn't never have thought nothing if people hadn't started poisoning his mind. People started talking just because my Daddy wasn't well and she was up at the house so much because somebody had to look after him. First they said she was carrying on with *him*. Hell, my Daddy would sure have been willing, but he was far from able. He was really wore out by that time and he just wanted rest. Then people started to saying that it was me.

PARNELL. Old Bill ever talk to you about it?

LYLE. How was he going to talk to me about it? Hell, we was right good friends. Many's the time I helped Old Bill out when his cash was low. I used to load Willa Mae up with things from the kitchen just to make sure they didn't go hungry.

PARNELL. Old Bill never mentioned it to you? Never? He never gave you any reason to think he knew about it?

LYLE. Well, I don't know what was going on in his *mind,* Parnell. You can't never see what's in anybody else's *mind*—you know that. He didn't *act* no different. Hell, like I say, she was young enough to be his granddaughter damn near, so I figured he thought it might be a pretty good arrangement—me doing *his* work, ha-ha! because *he* damn sure couldn't do it no more, and helping him to stay alive.

PARNELL. Then why was he so mad at you the last time you saw him?

LYLE. Like I said, he accused me of cheating him. And I ain't never cheated a black man in my life. I hate to say it, because we've always been good friends, but sometimes I think it might have been Joel—Papa D.—who told him that. Old Bill wasn't too good at figuring.

PARNELL. Why would Papa D. tell him a thing like that?

LYLE. I think he might have been a little jealous.

PARNELL. Jealous? You mean, of you and Willa Mae?

LYLE. Yeah. He ain't really an old man, you know. But I'm sure he didn't mean—for things to turn out like they did. (*A pause*.) I can still see him—the way he looked when he come into this store.

PARNELL. The way *who* looked when he came into this store?

LYLE. Why—Old Bill. He looked crazy. Like he wanted to kill me. He *did* want to kill me. Crazy nigger.

PARNELL. I thought you meant the other one. But the other one didn't die in the store.

LYLE. Old Bill didn't die in the store. He died over yonder, in the road.

PARNELL. I thought you were talking about Richard Henry.

LYLE. That crazy boy. Yeah, he come in here. I don't know what was the matter with him, he hadn't seen me but one time in his life before. And I treated him like —like I would have treated *any* man.

PARNELL. I heard about it. It was in Papa D.'s joint. He was surrounded by niggers—or *you* were—

LYLE. He was dancing with one of them crazy young ones—the real pretty nigger girl—what's her name?

PARNELL. Juanita.

LYLE. That's the one. (*Juke box music, soft. Voices. Laughter*.) Yeah. He looked at me like he wanted to kill me. And he insulted my wife. And I hadn't never done him no harm. (*As above, a little stronger.*) But I been thinking about it. And you know what I think? Hey! You gone to sleep?

PARNELL. No. I'm thinking.

LYLE. What you thinking about?

PARNELL. Us. You and me.

LYLE. And what do you think about us —you and me? What's the point of thinking about us, anyway? We've been buddies all our lives—we can't stop being buddies now.

PARNELL. That's right, buddy. What were you about to say?

LYLE. Oh. I think a lot of the niggers in this town, especially the young ones, is turned bad. And I believe they was egging him on.

(*A pause. The music stops.*)

He come in here one Monday afternoon. Everybody heard about it, it was all over this town quicker'n a jack-rabbit gets his nuts off. You just missed it. You'd just walked out of here.

(LYLE *rises, walks to the doors and opens them. Sunlight fills the room. He slams the screen doors shut; we see the road.*)

JO (*off*). Lyle, you want to help me bring this baby carriage inside? It's getting kind of hot out here now.

PARNELL. Let *me.*

(LYLE *and* PARNELL *bring in the baby carriage.* JO *enters.*)

JO. My, it's hot! Wish we'd gone for a ride or something. Declare to goodness, we ain't got no reason to be sitting around this store. Ain't nobody coming in here— not to *buy* anything, anyway.

PARNELL. I'll buy some bubble gum.

JO. You know you don't chew bubble gum.

PARNELL. Well, then, I'll buy some cigarettes.

JO. Two cartons, or three? It's all right, Parnell, the Britten family's going to make it somehow.

LYLE. Couple of niggers coming down the road. Maybe they'll drop in for a Coke.

(*Exits, into back of store.*)

JO. Why, no, they won't. Our Cokes is *poisoned.* I get up every morning before daybreak and drop the arsenic in myself.

PARNELL. Well, then, I won't have a Coke. See you, Jo. So long, Lyle!

LYLE (*off*). Be seeing you!

(PARNELL *exits. Silence for a few seconds. Then we hear* LYLE *hammering in the back.* JO *picks up a magazine, begins to read. Voices.* RICHARD *and* LORENZO *appear in the road.*)

RICHARD. Hey, you want a Coke? I'm thirsty.

LORENZO. Let's go on a little further.

RICHARD. Man, we been walking for *days,* my mouth is as dry as that damn dusty road. Come on, have a Coke with me, won't take but a minute.

LORENZO. We don't trade in there. Come on—

RICHARD. Oh! Is this the place? Hell, I'd like to get another look at the peckerwood, ain't going to give him but a dime. I want to get his face fixed in my *mind,* so there won't be no time wasted when the time comes, you dig? (*Enters the store.*) Hey, Mrs. Ofay Ednolbay Ydalay! you got any Coca Cola for sale?

JO. What?

RICHARD. Coke! Me and my man been toting barges and lifting bales, that's right, we been slaving, and we need a little cool. Liquid. Refreshment. Yeah, and you can take that hammer, too.

JO. Boy, what do you want?

RICHARD. A Coca Cola, ma'am. Please ma'am.

JO. They right in the box there.

RICHARD. Thank you kindly. (*Takes two Cokes, opens them.*) Oh, this is fine, *fine.* Did you put them in this box with your own little dainty dish-pan hands? Sure makes them taste *sweet.*

JO. Are you talking to me?

RICHARD. No ma'am, just feel like talking to myself from time to time, makes the time pass faster. (*At screen door.*) Hey, Lorenz, I got you a Coke.

LORENZO. I don't want it. Come on out of there.

JO. That will be twenty cents.

RICHARD. *Twenty* cents? All right. Don't you know how to say please? All the women *I* know say please—of course, they ain't as pretty as you. I ain't got twenty cents, ma'am. All I got is—twenty dollars!

JO. You ain't got nothing smaller?

RICHARD. No ma'am. You see, I don't never carry on me more cash than I can afford to *lose.*

JO. Lyle! (LYLE *enters, carrying the hammer.*) You got any change?

LYLE. Change for a twenty? No, you know I ain't got it.

RICHARD. You all got this big, fine store and all—and you ain't got change for *twenty* dollars?

LYLE. It's early in the day, boy.

RICHARD. It ain't that early. I thought white folks was rich at *every* hour of the day.

LYLE. Now, if you looking for trouble, you just might get it. That boy outside—ain't he got twenty cents?

RICHARD. That boy outside is about twenty-four years old, and he ain't got twenty cents. Ain't no need to ask him.

LYLE (*at the door*). Boy! You got twenty cents?

LORENZO. Come on out of there, Richard! I'm tired of hanging around here!

LYLE. Boy, didn't you hear what I asked you?

LORENZO. Mister Britten, I ain't *in* the store, and I ain't *bought* nothing in the store, and so I ain't *got* to tell you whether or not I got twenty cents!

RICHARD. Maybe your wife could run home and get some change. You *got* some change at home, I know. Don't you?

LYLE. I don't stand for nobody to talk about my wife.

RICHARD. I only said you was a lucky man to have so fine a *wife*. I said maybe she could run *home* and look and see if there was any change—in the *home*.

LYLE. I seen you before some place. You that crazy nigger. You ain't from around here.

RICHARD. You *know* you seen me. And you remember where. And when. I was born right here, in this town. I'm Reverend Meridian Henry's son.

LYLE. You say that like you thought your Daddy's name was some kind of protection. He ain't no protection against *me* —him, nor that boy outside, neither.

RICHARD. I don't need no protection, do I? Not in my own home town, in the good old USA. I just dropped by to sip on a Coke in a simple country store—and come to find out the joker ain't got enough bread to change twenty dollars. Stud ain't got *nothing*—you people been spoofing the public, man.

LYLE. You put them Cokes down and get out of here.

RICHARD. I ain't finished yet. And I ain't changed my bill yet.

LYLE. Well, I ain't going to change that bill, and you ain't going to finish them Cokes. You get your black ass out of here —go on! If you got any sense, you'll get your black ass out of this town.

RICHARD. You don't own this town, you white mother-fucker. You don't *even* own twenty dollars. Don't you raise that hammer. I'll take it and beat your skull to jelly.

JO. Lyle! Don't you fight that boy! He's crazy! I'm going to call the Sheriff! (*Starts toward the back, returns to counter.*) The baby! Lyle! Watch out for the baby!

RICHARD. A baby, huh? How many times did you have to try for it, you no-good, ball-less peckerwood? I'm surprised you could even get it up—look at the way you sweating now.

(LYLE *raises the hammer.* RICHARD *grabs his arm, forcing it back. They struggle.*)

JO. Lyle! The baby!

LORENZO. Richard!

(*He comes into the store.*)

JO. Please get that boy out of here, get that boy out of here—he's going to get himself killed.

(RICHARD *knocks the hammer from* LYLE'*s hand, and knocks* LYLE *down. The hammer spins across the room.* LORENZO *picks it up.*)

LORENZO. I don't think your husband's going to kill no more black men. Not to-day, Mrs. Britten. Come on, Richard. Let's go.

(LYLE *looks up at them.*)

LYLE. It took two of you. Remember that.

LORENZO. I didn't lay a hand on you, Mister Britten. You just ain't no match for —a *boy*. Not without your gun you ain't. Come on, Richard.

JO. You'll go to jail for this! You'll go to jail! For years!

LORENZO. We've been in jail for years. I'll leave your hammer over at Papa D.'s joint—don't look like you're going to be doing no more work today.

RICHARD (*laughs*). Look at the mighty peckerwood! On his *ass,* baby—and his woman watching! Now, who you think is the better man? Ha-ha! The master race! You let me in that tired white chick's drawers, she'll know who's the master! Ha-ha-ha!

(*Exits.* RICHARD'*s laughter continues in the dark.* LYLE *and* PARNELL *as before.*)

LYLE. Niggers was laughing at me for days. Everywhere I went.

PARNELL. You never did call the Sheriff.

LYLE. No.

(PARNELL *fills their glasses. We hear singing.*)

PARNELL. It's almost time for his funeral.

LYLE. And may every nigger like that nigger end like that nigger—face down in the weeds!

(*A pause.*)

PARNELL. Was he lying face down?

LYLE. Hell, yeah, he was face down. Said so in the papers.

PARNELL. Is that what the papers said? I don't remember.

LYLE. Yeah, that's what the papers said.

PARNELL. I guess they had to turn him over—to make sure it was him.

LYLE. I reckon. (*Laughs.*) Yeah. I reckon.

PARNELL. You and me are buddies, huh?

LYLE. *Yeah,* we're buddies—to the end!

PARNELL. I always wondered why you wanted to be my buddy. A lot of poor guys hate rich guys. I always wondered why you weren't like that.

LYLE. I ain't like that. Hell, Parnell, you're smarter than me. I know it. I used to wonder what made you smarter than me. I got to be your buddy so I could find out. Because, hell, you didn't seem so different in *other* ways—in spite of all your *ideas.* Two things we always had in common—liquor and poon-tang. We couldn't get enough of neither one. Of course, your liquor might have been a little better. But I doubt if the other could have been any better!

PARNELL. Did you find out what made me smarter?

LYLE. Yeah. You richer!

PARNELL. I'm richer! That's all you got to tell me—about Richard Henry?

LYLE. Ain't nothing more to tell. Wait till after the trial. You won't have to ask me no more questions then!

PARNELL. I've got to get to the funeral.

LYLE. Don't run off. Don't leave me here alone.

PARNELL. You're supposed to be home for supper.

LYLE. Supper can wait. Have another drink with me—be my buddy. Don't leave me here alone. Listen to them! Singing and praying! Singing and praying and laughing behind a man's back!

(*The singing continues in the dark.* BLACKTOWN: *The church, packed.* MERIDIAN *in the pulpit, the bier just below him.*)

MERIDIAN. My heart is heavier tonight than it has ever been before. I raise my voice to you tonight out of a sorrow and a wonder I have never felt before. Not only I, my Lord, am in this case. Everyone under the sound of my voice, and many more souls than that, feel as I feel, and tremble as I tremble, and bleed as I bleed. It is not that the days are dark—we have known dark days. It is not only that the blood runs down and no man helps us; it is not only that our children are destroyed before our eyes. It is not only that our lives, from day to day and every hour of each day, are menaced by the people among whom you have set us down. We have borne all these things, my Lord, and we have done what the prophets of old could not do, we have sung the Lord's song in a strange land. In a strange land! What was the sin committed by our forefathers in the time that has vanished on the other side of the flood, which has had to be expiated by chains, by the lash, by hunger and thirst, by slaughter, by fire, by the rope, by the knife, and for so many generations, on these wild shores, in this strange land? Our offense must have been mighty, our crime immeasurable. But it is not the past which makes our hearts so heavy. It is the present. Lord, where is our hope? Who, or what, shall touch the hearts of this headlong and unthinking people and turn them back from destruction? When will they hear the words of John? *I know thy works, that thou art neither cold nor hot: I would that thou wert cold or hot. So, then because thou art lukewarm and neither cold nor hot, I will spew thee out of my mouth. Because thou sayest, I am rich and increased with goods, and have need of nothing; and knowest not that thou art wretched and miserable and poor and blind and naked.* Now, when the children come, my Lord, and ask which road to follow, my tongue stammers and my heart fails. I will not abandon the land—this strange land, which is my home. But can I ask the children forever to sustain the cruelty inflicted on them by those who have been their masters, and who are now, in very truth, their kinfolk, their brothers and their sisters and their parents? What hope is there for a people who deny their deeds and disown their kinsmen and who do so in the name of purity and love, in the name of Jesus Christ? What a light, my Lord, is needed to conquer so mighty a darkness! This darkness rules in us, and grows, in black and white alike. I have set my face against the darkness, I will not let it conquer me, even though it will, I know, one day, destroy this body. But, my Lord, what of the children? What shall I tell the children? I must be with you, Lord, like Jacob, and wrestle with you until the light appears—I will not let you go until you give me a sign! A sign that in the terrible Sahara of our time a fountain may spring, the fountain of a true morality, and bring us closer, oh, my Lord, to that peace on earth desired by so few throughout so many ages. Let not our suffering endure forever. Teach us to trust the great gift of life and learn to love one another and dare to walk the earth like men. Amen.

MOTHER HENRY. Let's file up, children, and say goodbye.

(*Song:* "Great Getting-Up Morning." MERIDIAN *steps down from the pulpit.* MERIDIAN, LORENZO, JIMMY, *and* PETE *shoulder the bier. A disheveled* PARNELL *enters. The Congregation and the Pallbearers file past him.* JUANITA *stops.*)

JUANITA. What's the matter, Parnell? You look sick.

PARNELL. I tried to come sooner. I couldn't get away. Lyle wouldn't let me go.

JUANITA. Were you trying to beat a confession out of him? But you look as though he's been trying to beat a confession out of you. Poor Parnell!

PARNELL. Poor Lyle! He'll never confess. Never. Poor devil!

JUANITA. Poor devil! You weep for Lyle. You're luckier than I am. I can't weep in front of others. I can't say goodbye in front of others. Others don't know what it is you're saying goodbye to.

PARNELL. You loved him.

JUANITA. Yes.

PARNELL. I didn't know.

JUANITA. Ah, you're so lucky, Parnell. I know you didn't know. Tell me, where do you live, Parnell? How can you not know all of the things you do not know?

PARNELL. Why are you hitting out at me? I never thought you cared that much about me. But—oh, Juanita! There are so many things I've never been able to say!

JUANITA. There are so many things you've never been able to hear.

PARNELL. And—you've tried to tell me some of those things?

JUANITA. I used to watch you roaring through this town like a St. George thirsty for dragons. And I wanted to let you know you haven't got to do all that; dragons aren't hard to find, they're everywhere. And nobody wants you to be St. George. We just want you to be Parnell. But, of course, that's much harder.

PARNELL. Are we friends, Juanita? Please say that we're friends.

JUANITA. Friends is not exactly what you mean, Parnell. Tell the truth.

PARNELL. Yes. I've always wanted more than that, from you. But I was afraid you would misunderstand me. That you would feel that I was only trying to exploit you. In another way.

JUANITA. You've been a grown man for a long time now, Parnell. You ought to trust yourself more than that.

PARNELL. I've been a grown man far too long—ever to have dared to dream of offering myself to you.

JUANITA. Your age was never the question, Parnell.

PARNELL. Was there ever any question at all?

JUANITA. Yes. Yes. Yes, once there was.

PARNELL. And there isn't—there can't be —anymore?

JUANITA. No. That train has gone. One day, I'll recover. I'm sure that I'll recover. And I'll see the world again—the marvelous world. And I'll have learned from Richard—how to love. I must. I can't let him die for nothing.

(*Juke box music, loud. The lights change, spot on* PARNELL's *face.* JUANITA *steps across the aisle.* RICHARD *appears. They dance.* PARNELL *watches.*)

CURTAIN

ACT THREE

Two months later. The courtroom.
The courtroom is extremely high, domed, a blinding white emphasized by a dull, somehow ominous gold. The judge's stand is center stage, and at a height. Sloping down from this place on either side, are the black and white TOWNSPEOPLE: *the*

JURY; PHOTOGRAPHERS *and* JOURNALISTS *from all over the world; microphones and TV cameras. All windows open: one should be aware of masses of people outside and one should sometimes hear their voices—their roar—as well as singing from the church. The church is directly across the street from the courthouse, and the steeple and the cross are visible throughout the act.*

Each witness, when called, is revealed behind scrim and passes through two or three tableaux before moving down the aisle to the witness stand. The witness stand is downstage, in the same place, and at the same angle as the pulpit in Acts One and Two.

Before the curtain rises, song: "I Said I Wasn't Going To Tell Nobody, But I Couldn't Keep It To Myself."

The JUDGE's *gavel breaks across the singing, and the curtain rises.*

———

CLERK (*calling*). Mrs. Josephine Gladys Britten!

(JO, *serving coffee at a church social. She passes out coffee to invisible guests.*)

JO. Am I going to spend the rest of my life serving coffee to strangers in church basements? Am I?—Yes! Reverend Phelps was truly noble! As *usual!*—Reverend Phelps has been married for more than twenty years. Don't let those thoughts into your citadel! You just remember that the mind is a citadel and you can keep out all troubling thoughts!—My! Mrs. Evans! you are certainly a sight for sore eyes! I don't know how you manage to look so unruffled and *cool* and *young!* With all those *children*. And Mr. Evans. How are you tonight?—She has a baby just about every year. I don't know how she stands it. Mr. Evans don't look like that kind of man. You sure can't tell a book by its cover. Lord! I wish I was in my own home and these were *my* guests and my husband was somewhere in the room. I'm getting old! Old! Old maid! *Maid!*—Oh! Mr. Arpino! You taken time out from your engineering to come visit here with us? It sure is a pleasure to have you!—My! He is big! and dark! Like a Greek! or a Spaniard! Some people say he might have a touch of nigger blood. I don't believe that. He's just—*foreign*. That's all. He needs a hair cut. I wonder if he's got hair like that all *over* his body? Remember that your mind is a

citadel. A citadel. Oh, Lord, I'm tired of serving coffee in church basements! I want, I want—Why, good evening, Ellis! And Mr. Lyle Britten! We sure don't see either of *you* very often! Why, Mr. Britten! You know you don't mean that! You come over here just to see little old *me*? Why, you just go right ahead and drink that coffee, I do believe you need to be sobered up!

(*The light changes.*)

REVEREND PHELPS (*voice*). Do you, Josephine Gladys Miles, take this man, Lyle Britten, Jr., as your lawfully wedded husband, to have and to hold, to love and to cherish, in sickness and in health, till death do you part?

JO. I do. I *do!* Oh, Lyle. I'll make you the best wife any man ever had. I *will*. Love me. Please love me. Look at me! *Look* at me! He *wanted* me. He wanted *me!* I am—Mrs. Josephine Gladys Britten!

(*The light changes again, and* JO *takes the stand. We hear the baby crying.*)

BLACKTOWN. Man, that's the southern white lady you supposed to be willing to risk death for!

WHITETOWN. You know, this is a kind of hanging in reverse? Niggers out here to watch us being hanged!

THE STATE. What is your relationship to the accused?

JO. I am his wife.

THE STATE. Will you please tell us, in your own words, of your first meeting with the deceased, Richard Henry?

WHITETOWN. Don't be afraid. Just tell the truth.

BLACKTOWN. Here we go—down the river!

JO. Well, I was in the store, sitting at the counter, and pretty soon this colored boy come in, loud, and talking in just the most awful way. I didn't recognize him, I just knew he wasn't one of *our* colored people. His language was something awful, awful!

THE STATE. He was insulting? Was he insulting, Mrs. Britten?

JO. He said all kinds of things, dirty things, like—well—just like I might have been a colored girl, that's what it sounded like to me. Just like some little colored girl he might have met on a street corner and wanted—wanted to—for a night! And I was scared. I hadn't seen a colored boy act like him before. He acted like he was drunk or crazy or maybe he was under the influence of that dope. I never knew nobody to be *drunk* and act like him. His eyes was just going and he acted like he had a fire in his belly. But I tried to be calm because I didn't want to upset Lyle, you know—Lyle's mighty quick-tempered —and he was working in the back of the store, he was hammering—

THE STATE. Go on, Mrs. Britten. What happened then?

JO. Well, he—that boy—wanted to buy him two Cokes because he had a friend outside—

THE STATE. He brought a friend? He did not come there alone? Did this other boy enter the store?

JO. No, not then he didn't—I—

BLACKTOWN. Come on, bitch. We *know* what you going to say. Get it over with.

JO. I—I give him the two Cokes, and he —tried to grab my hands and pull me to him, and—I—I—he pushed himself up against me, real close and hard—and, oh, he was just like an animal, I could—smell him! And he tried to kiss me, he kept whispering these awful, filthy things and I got scared, I yelled for Lyle! Then Lyle come running out of the back—and when the boy seen I wasn't alone in the store, he yelled for this other boy outside and this other boy come rushing in and they both jumped on Lyle and knocked him down.

THE STATE. What made you decide not to report this incident—this unprovoked assault—to the proper authorities, Mrs. Britten?

JO. We've had so much trouble in this town!

THE STATE. What sort of trouble, Mrs. Britten?

JO. Why, with the colored people! We've got all these northern agitators coming through here all the time, and stirring them up so that you can't hardly sleep nights!

THE STATE. Then you, as a responsible citizen of this town, were doing your best to keep down trouble? Even though you had been so brutally assaulted by a deranged northern Negro dope addict?

JO. Yes. I didn't want to stir up no more trouble. I *made* Lyle keep quiet about it. I thought it would all blow over. I knew the boy's Daddy was a preacher and that he would talk to the boy about the way he was behaving. It was all over town in a second, anyway! And look like all the col-

ored people was on the side of that crazy boy. And Lyle's always been real good to colored people!

(*Laughter from* BLACKTOWN.)

THE STATE. On the evening that the alleged crime was committed—or, rather, the morning—very early on the morning of the 24th of August—where were you and your husband, Mrs. Britten?

JO. We were home. The next day we heard that the boy was missing.

COUNSEL FOR THE BEREAVED. Doesn't an attempt at sexual assault seem a rather strange thing to do, considering that your store is a public place, with people continually going in and out; that, furthermore, it is located on a public road which people use, on foot and in automobiles, all of the time; and considering that your husband, who has the reputation of being a violent man, and who is, in your own words, "mighty quick tempered," was working in the back room?

JO. He didn't know Lyle was back there.

COUNSEL FOR THE BEREAVED. But he knew that someone was back there, for, according to your testimony, "He was hammering."

JO. Well, I told you the boy was crazy. He had to be crazy. Or he was on that dope.

BLACKTOWN. You ever hear of a junkie trying to rape anybody?

JO. *I didn't say rape!*

COUNSEL FOR THE BEREAVED. Were you struggling in Mr. Henry's arms when your husband came out of the back room, carrying his hammer in his hand?

JO. No. I was free then.

COUNSEL FOR THE BEREAVED. Therefore, your husband had only *your* word for the alleged attempted assault! *You* told him that Richard Henry had attempted to assault you? Had made sexual advances to you? Please answer, Mrs. Bitten!

JO. Yes. I had—I had to—tell him. I'm his wife!

COUNSEL FOR THE BEREAVED. And a most loyal one. You told your husband that Richard Henry had attempted to assault you and then begged him to do nothing about it?

JO. That's right.

COUNSEL FOR THE BEREAVED. And though he was under the impression that his wife had been nearly raped by a Negro, he agreed to forgive and forget and do nothing about it? He agreed neither to call the law, nor to take the law into his own hands?

JO. Yes.

COUNSEL FOR THE BEREAVED. Extraordinary. Mrs. Britten, you are aware that Richard Henry met his death sometime between the hours of two and five o'clock on the morning of Monday, August 24th?

JO. Yes.

COUNSEL FOR THE BEREAVED. In an earlier statement, several months ago, you stated that your husband had spent that night at the store. You now state that he came in before one o'clock and went to sleep at once. What accounts for this discrepancy?

JO. It's natural. I made a mistake about the time. I got it mixed up with another night. He spent so many nights at that store!

JUDGE. The witness may step down.

(*Jo leaves the stand.*)

CLERK (*calls*). Mr. Joel Davis!

(*We hear a shot.* PAPA D. *is facing* LYLE.)

LYLE. Why'd you run down there this morning, shooting your mouth off about me and Willa Mae? Why? You been bringing her up here and taking her back all this time, what got into you this morning? Huh? You jealous, old man? Why you come running back here to tell me everything he said? To tell me how he cursed me out? Have you lost your mind? And we been knowing each other all this time. I don't understand you. She ain't the only girl you done brought here for me. Nigger, do you hear me talking to you?

PAPA D. I didn't think you'd shoot him, Mr. Lyle.

LYLE. I'll shoot any nigger talks to me like that. It was self defense, you hear me? He come in here and tried to kill me. You hear me?

PAPA D. Yes. Yes sir. I hear you, Mr. Lyle.

LYLE. That's right. You don't say the right thing, nigger, I'll blow your brains out, too.

PAPA D. Yes sir, Mr. Lyle.

(*Juke box music.* PAPA D. *takes the stand.*)

WHITETOWN. He's worked hard and saved his money and ain't never had no trouble—why can't they all be like that?

BLACKTOWN. Hey, Papa D.! You can't be walking around here without no handkerchief! You might catch cold—after all *these* years!

PAPA D. Mr. Lyle Britten—he is an *oppressor*. That is the only word for that man. He ain't never give the colored man no kind of chance. I have tried to reason with that man for *years*. I say, Mr. Lyle, look around you. Don't you see that most white folks have changed their way of thinking about us colored folks? I say, Mr. Lyle, we ain't slaves no more and white folks is ready to let us have our chance. Now, why don't you just come on up to where *most* of your people are? and we can make the South a fine place for all of us to live in. That's what I say—and I tried to keep him from being so *hard* on the colored—because I sure do love my people. And I was the closest thing to Mr. Lyle, couldn't nobody else reason with him. But he was *hard*—hard and stubborn. He say, "My folks lived and died this way, and this is the way I'm going to live and die." When he was like that couldn't do nothing with him. I know. I've known him since he was born.

WHITETOWN. He's always been real good to you. You were friends!

BLACKTOWN. You loved him! Tell the truth, mother—tell the truth!

PAPA D. Yes, we were friends. And, yes, I loved him—in my way. Just like he loved me—in his way.

BLACKTOWN. You knew he was going to kill that boy—didn't you? If you knew it, why didn't you stop him?

PAPA D. Oh. Ain't none of this easy. What it was, both Mr. Lyle Britten and me, we both love money. And I did a whole lot of things for him, for a long while. Once I had to help him cover up a killing—colored man—I was in too deep myself by that time—you understand? I know you all understand.

BLACKTOWN. Did he kill that boy?

PAPA D. He come into my joint the night that boy died. The boy was alone, standing at the juke box. We'd been talking—(RICHARD, *in the juke box light.*) If you think you've found all that, Richard—if you think you going to be well now, and you found you somebody who loves you—well, then, I would make tracks out of here. I would—

RICHARD. It's funny, Papa D. I feel like I'm beginning to understand my life—for the first time. I can look back—and it doesn't hurt me like it used to. I want to get Juanita out of here. This is no place for her. They're going to kill her—if she stays here!

PAPA D. You talk to Juanita about this yet?

RICHARD. No. I haven't talked to nobody about it yet. I just decided it. I guess I'm deciding it now. That's why I'm talking about it now—to you—to see if you'll laugh at me. Do you think she'll laugh at me?

PAPA D. No. She won't laugh.

RICHARD. I know I can do it. I know I can do it!

PAPA D. That boy had good sense. He was wild, but he had good sense. And I couldn't blame him too much for being so wild, it seemed to me I knew how he felt.

RICHARD. Papa D., I been in pain and darkness all my life. All my life. And this is the first time in my life I've ever felt—maybe it isn't all like that. Maybe there's more to it than that.

PAPA D. Lyle Britten come to the door—(LYLE enters.) He come to the door and he say—

LYLE. You ready for me now, boy? Howdy, Papa D.

PAPA D. Howdy, Mr. Lyle, how's the world been treating you?

LYLE. I can't complain. You ready, boy?

RICHARD. No. I ain't ready. I got a record to play and a drink to finish.

LYLE. You about ready to close, ain't you, Joel?

PAPA D. Just about, Mr. Lyle.

RICHARD. I got a record to play. (Drops coin: juke box music, loud.) And a drink to finish.

PAPA D. He played his record. Lyle Britten never moved from the door. And they just stood there, the two of them, looking at each other. When the record was just about over, the boy come to the bar—he swallowed down the last of his drink.

RICHARD. What do I owe you, Papa D.?

PAPA D. Oh, you pay me tomorrow. I'm closed now.

RICHARD. What do I owe you, Papa D.? I'm not sure I can pay you tomorrow.

PAPA D. Give me two dollars.

RICHARD. Here you go. Good night, Papa D. I'm ready, Charlie.

(Exits.)

PAPA D. Good night, Richard. Go on home now. Good night, Mr. Lyle. Mr. Lyle!

LYLE. Good night, Joel. You get you some sleep, you hear? (Exits.)

PAPA D. Mr. Lyle! Richard! And I never saw that boy again. Lyle killed him. He killed him. I know it, just like I know I'm sitting in this chair. Just like he shot Old Bill and wasn't nothing never, never, never done about it!

JUDGE. The witness may step down.

(PAPA D. leaves the stand.)

CLERK (calls). Mr. Lorenzo Shannon!

(We hear a long, loud, animal cry, lonely and terrified: it is PETE, screaming. We discover LORENZO and PETE, in jail. Night. From far away, we hear Students humming, moaning, singing: "I Woke Up This Morning With My Mind Stayed On Freedom.")

PETE (stammering). Lorenzo? Lorenzo. I was dreaming—dreaming—dreaming. I was back in that courtyard and Big Jim Byrd's boys was beating us and beating us and beating us—and Big Jim Byrd was laughing. And Anna Mae Taylor was on her knees, she was trying to pray. She say, "Oh, Lord, Lord, Lord, come and help us," and they kept beating on her and beating on her and I saw the blood coming down her neck and they put the prods to her, and, oh, Lorenzo! people was just running around, just crying and moaning and you look to the right and you see somebody go down and you look to the left and you see somebody go down and they was kicking that woman, and I say, "That woman's going to have a baby, don't you kick that woman!" and they say, "No, she ain't going to have no baby," and they knocked me down and they got that prod up between my legs and they say, "You ain't going to be having no babies, neither, nigger!" And then they put that prod to my head—ah! ah!—to my head! Lorenzo! I can't see right! What have they done to my head? Lorenzo! Lorenzo, am I going to die? Lorenzo—they going to kill us all, ain't they? They mean to kill us all—

LORENZO. Be quiet. Be quiet. They going to come and beat us some more if you don't be quiet.

PETE. Where's Juanita? Did they get Juanita?

LORENZO. I believe Juanita's all right. Go to sleep, Pete. Go to sleep. I won't let you dream. I'll hold you.

(LORENZO *takes the stand*.)

THE STATE. Did you accompany your late and great friend, Richard Henry, on the morning of August 17, to the store which is owned and run by Mr. and Mrs. Lyle Britten?

LORENZO. We hadn't planned to go there —but we got to walking and talking and we found ourselves there. And it didn't happen like she said. He picked the Cokes out of the box himself, he came to the door with the Cokes in his hand, she hadn't even moved, she was still behind the counter, he never touched that dried out little peckerwood!

WHITETOWN. Get that nigger! Who does that nigger think he is!

BLACKTOWN. Speak, Lorenzo! Go, my man!

THE STATE. You cannot expect this courtroom to believe that so serious a battle was precipitated by the question of twenty cents! There was some other reason. What was this reason? Had he—and you—been drinking?

LORENZO. It was early in the day, Cap'n. We ain't rich enough to drink in the daytime.

THE STATE. Or *smoking*, perhaps? Perhaps your friend had just had his quota of heroin for the day, and was feeling jolly— in a mood to *prove* to you what he had already suggested with those filthy photographs of himself and naked white women!

LORENZO. I never saw no photographs. White women are a problem for white men. We had not been drinking. All we was smoking was that same goddamn tobacco that made *you* rich because we picked it for you for nothing, and carried it to market for you for nothing. And I *know* ain't no heroin in this town because none of you mothers need it. You was *born* frozen. Richard was better than that. I'd rather die than be like you, Cap'n, but I'd be *proud* to be like Richard. That's all I can tell you, Mr. Boss-Man. But I know he wasn't trying to rape nobody. Rape!

THE STATE. Your Honor, will you instruct the witness that he is under oath, that this is a court of law, and that it is a serious matter to be held in contempt of court!

LORENZO. More serious than the chain gang? *I* know I'm under oath. If there was any reason, it was just that Richard couldn't stand white people. *Couldn't*

stand white people! And, 'now, do you want me to tell you all that I know about *that*? Do you think you could stand it? You'd cut my tongue out before you'd let me tell you all that I know about *that*!

COUNSEL FOR THE BEREAVED. You are a student here?

LORENZO. In my spare time. I just come off the chain gang a couple of days ago. I was trespassing in the white waiting room of the bus station.

COUNSEL FOR THE BEREAVED. What are you studying—in your spare time—Mr. Shannon?

LORENZO. History.

COUNSEL FOR THE BEREAVED. To your knowledge—during his stay in this town— was the late Mr. Richard Henry still addicted to narcotics?

LORENZO. No. He'd kicked his habit. He'd paid his dues. He was just trying to live. And he almost made it.

COUNSEL FOR THE BEREAVED. You were very close to him?

LORENZO. Yes.

COUNSEL FOR THE BEREAVED. To your knowledge—was he carrying about obscene photographs of himself and naked white women?

LORENZO. To my knowledge—and I would know—no. The only times he ever opened a popular magazine was to look at the Jazz Poll. No. They been asking me about photographs they say he was carrying and they been asking me about a gun I never saw. No. It wasn't like that. He was a beautiful cat, and they killed him. That's all. That's *all*.

JUDGE. The witness may step down.

LORENZO. Well! I thank you kindly. *Suh!* (LORENZO *leaves the stand*.)

CLERK (*calls*). Miss Juanita Harmon!

(JUANITA *rises from bed; early Sunday morning*.)

JUANITA. He lay beside me on that bed like a rock. As heavy as a rock—like he'd fallen—fallen from a high place—fallen so far and landed so heavy, he seemed almost to be sinking out of sight—with one knee pointing to heaven. My God. He covered me like that. He wasn't at all like I thought he was. He fell on—fell on me— like life and death. My God. His chest, his belly, the rising and the falling, the moans. How he clung, how he struggled—life and death! Life and death! Why did it all seem to me like tears? That he came to me, clung to me, plunged into me, sobbing, howling, bleeding, somewhere inside his chest, his belly, and it all came out, came pouring out, like tears! My God, the smell, the touch, the taste, the sound, of anguish! Richard! Why couldn't I have held you closer? Held you, held you, borne you, given you life again! Have made you be born again! Oh, Richard. The teeth that gleamed, oh! when you smiled, the spit flying when you cursed, the teeth stinging when you bit—your breath, your hands, your weight, my God, when you moved in me! Where shall I go now, what shall I do? Oh. Oh. Oh. Mama was frightened. Frightened because little Juanita brought her first real lover to this house. I suppose God does for Mama what Richard did for me. Juanita! I don't care! I don't care! Yes, I want a lover made of flesh and blood, of flesh and blood, like me, I don't want to be God's mother! He can *have* His icy, snow-white heaven! If He is somewhere around this fearful planet, if I ever see Him, I will spit in His face! In God's face! How *dare* He presume to judge a living soul! A living soul. Mama is afraid I'm pregnant. Mama is afraid of so much. I'm not afraid. I hope I'm pregnant. I *hope* I am! One more illegitimate black baby—that's right, you jive mothers! And I am going to raise my baby to be a man. A *man*, you dig? Oh, let me be pregnant, let me be pregnant, don't let it all be gone! A man. Juanita. A man. Oh, my God, there are no more. For me. Did this happen to Mama sometime? Did she have a man sometime who vanished like smoke? And left her to get through this world as best she could? Is that why she married my father? Did this happen to Mother Henry? Is this how we all get to be mothers—so soon? of helpless men—because all the other men perish? No. No. No. No. What is this world like? I will end up taking care of some man, some day. Help me do it with love. Pete. Meridian. Parnell. We have been the mothers for them all. It must be dreadful to be Parnell. There is no flesh he can touch. All of it is bloody. Incest everywhere. Ha-ha! You're going crazy, Juanita. Oh, Lord, don't let me go mad. Let me be pregnant! Let me be pregnant!

(JUANITA *takes the stand. One arm is in a sling.*)

BLACKTOWN. Look! You should have seen her when she *first* come out of jail! Why we always got to love *them*? How come it's *us* always got to do the loving? Because you *black*, mother! Everybody knows we *strong* on loving! Except when it comes to our women.

WHITETOWN. Black slut! What happened to her arm? Somebody had to twist it, I reckon. She looks like she might be a right pretty little girl—why is she messing up her life this way?

THE STATE. Miss Harmon, you have testified that you were friendly with the mother of the deceased. How old were you when she died?

JUANITA. I was sixteen.

THE STATE. Sixteen! You are older than the deceased?

JUANITA. By two years.

THE STATE. At the time of his mother's death, were you and Richard Henry considering marriage?

JUANITA. No. Of course not.

THE STATE. The question of marriage did not come up until just before he died?

JUANITA. Yes.

THE STATE. But between the time that Richard Henry left this town and returned, you had naturally attracted other boy friends?

BLACKTOWN. Why don't you come right out and ask her if she's a virgin, man? Save you time.

WHITETOWN. She probably pregnant right now—and don't know who the father is. That's the way they are.

THE STATE. The departure of the boy and the death of the mother must have left all of you extremely lonely?

JUANITA. It can't be said to have made us any happier.

THE STATE. Reverend Henry missed his wife, you missed your playmate. His grief and your common concern for the boy must have drawn you closer together?

BLACKTOWN. Oh, man! Get to *that*!

WHITETOWN. That's right. What about that liver-lipped preacher?

THE STATE. Miss Harmon, you describe yourself as a student. Where have you spent the last few weeks?

JUANITA. In jail! I was arrested for—

THE STATE. I am not concerned with the reasons for your arrest. How much time, all told, have you spent in jail?

JUANITA. It would be hard to say—a long time.

THE STATE. Excellent preparation for your future! Is it not true, Miss Harmon, that before the late Richard Henry returned to this town, you were considering marriage with another so-called student, Pete Spivey? Can you seriously expect this court to believe anything you now say concerning Richard Henry? Would you not say the same thing, and for the same reason, concerning the father? Concerning Pete Spivey? And how many others!

WHITETOWN. That's the way they are. It's not their fault. That's what they want us to integrate with.

BLACKTOWN. These people are sick. Sick. Sick people's been known to be made well by a little shedding of blood.

JUANITA. I am not responsible for your imagination.

THE STATE. What do you know of the fight which took place between Richard Henry and Lyle Britten, at Mr. Britten's store?

JUANITA. I was not a witness to that fight.

THE STATE. But you had seen Richard Henry before the fight? Was he sober?

JUANITA. Yes.

THE STATE. You can swear to that?

JUANITA. Yes, I can swear to it.

THE STATE. And you saw him after the fight? Was he sober then?

JUANITA. Yes. He was sober then. (*Courtroom in silhouette.*) I heard about the fight at the end of the day—when I got home. And I went running to Reverend Henry's house. And I met him on the porch—just sitting there.

THE STATE. You met whom?

JUANITA. I met—Richard.

(*We discover* MERIDIAN.)

MERIDIAN. Hello, Juanita. Don't look like that.

JUANITA. Meridian, what happened today? Where's Richard?

MERIDIAN. He's all right now. He's sleeping. We better send him away. Lyle's dangerous. You know that. (*Takes* JUANITA *in his arms; then holds her at arm's length.*) You'll go with him. Won't you?

JUANITA. Meridian—oh, my God.

MERIDIAN. Juanita, tell me something I have to know. I'll never ask it again.

JUANITA. Yes, Meridian—

MERIDIAN. Before he came—I wasn't just making it all up, was I? There was something at least—beginning—something

dimly possible—wasn't there? I thought about you so much—and it was so wonderful each time I saw you—and I started hoping as I haven't let myself hope, oh, for a long time. I knew you were much younger, and I'd known you since you were a child. But I thought that maybe that didn't matter, after all—we got on so well together. I wasn't making it all up, was I?

JUANITA. No. You weren't making it up—not all of it, anyway, there was something there. We were lonely. You were hoping. I was hoping, too—oh, Meridian! Of all the people on God's earth I would rather die than hurt!

MERIDIAN. Hush, Juanita. I know that. I just wanted to be told that I hadn't lost my mind. I've lost so much. I think there's something wrong in being—what I've become—something really wrong. I mean, I think there's something wrong with allowing oneself to become so lonely. I think that I was proud that I could bear it. Each day became a kind of test—to see if I could bear it. And there were many days when I couldn't bear it—when I walked up and down and howled and lusted and cursed and prayed—just like any man. And I've been—I haven't been as celibate as I've seemed. But my confidence—my confidence—was destroyed back there when I pulled back that rug they had her covered with and I saw that little face on that broken neck. There wasn't any blood—just water. She was soaked. Oh, my God. My God. And I haven't trusted myself with a woman since. I keep seeing her the last time I saw her, whether I'm awake or asleep. That's why I let you get away from me. It wasn't my son that did it. It was me. And so much the better for you. And him. And I've held it all in since then—what fearful choices we must make! In order not to commit murder, in order not to become too monstrous, in order to be some kind of example to my only son. Come. Let me be an example now. And kiss you on the forehead and wish you well.

JUANITA. Meridian. Meridian. Will it always be like this? Will life always be like this? Must we always suffer so?

MERIDIAN. I don't know, Juanita. I know that we must bear what we must bear. Don't cry, Juanita. Don't cry. Let's go on on.

(*Exits.*)

JUANITA. By and by Richard woke up and I was there. And we tried to make plans to go, but he said he wasn't going to run no more from white folks—never no more! —but was going to stay and be a man—a *man!*—right here. And I couldn't *make* him see differently. I knew what he meant, I knew how he felt, but I didn't want him to die! And by the time I persuaded him to take *me* away, to take *me* away from this terrible place, it was too late. Lyle killed him! Lyle killed him! Like they been killing all our men, for years, for generations! Our husbands, our fathers, our brothers, our sons!

JUDGE. The witness may step down.

(JUANITA *leaves the stand. Mother Henry helps her to her seat.*)

This court is adjourned until ten o'clock tomorrow morning.

(*Chaos and cacophony. The courtroom begins to empty. Reporters rush to phone booths and to witnesses. Light bulbs flash. We hear snatches of the Journalists' reports, in their various languages. Singing from the church. Blackout. The next and last day of the trial. Even more crowded and tense.*)

CLERK (*calls*). Mrs. Wilhelmina Henry!

(MOTHER HENRY, *in street clothes, walks down the aisle, takes the stand.*)

THE STATE. You are Mrs. Wilhelmina Henry?

MOTHER HENRY. Yes.

THE STATE. Mrs. Henry, you—and your husband, until he died—lived in this town all your lives and never had any trouble. We've always gotten on well down here.

MOTHER HENRY. No white man never called my husband Mister, neither, not as long as he lived. Ain't no white man never called *me* Mrs. Henry before today. I had to get a grandson killed for that.

THE STATE. Mrs. Henry, your grief elicits my entire sympathy, and the sympathy of every white man in this town. But is it not true, Mrs. Henry, that your grandson arrived in this town armed? He was carrying a gun and, apparently, had carried a gun for years.

MOTHER HENRY. I don't know where you got that story, or why you keep harping on it. *I* never saw no gun.

THE STATE. You are under oath, Mrs. Henry.

MOTHER HENRY. I don't need you to tell me I'm under oath. I been under oath all my life. And I tell you, I never saw no gun.

THE STATE. Mrs. Henry, did you ever see your grandson behaving strangely—as though he were under the influence of strong drugs?

MOTHER HENRY. No. Not since he was six and they pulled out his tonsils. They gave him ether. *He* didn't act as strange as his Mama and Daddy. He just went on to sleep. But they like to had a fit. (RICHARD's *song.*) I remember the day he was born. His mother had a hard time holding him and a hard time getting him here. But here he come, in the wintertime, late and big and loud. And my boy looked down into his little son's face and he said, "God give us a son. God's give us a son. Lord, help us to raise him to be a good strong man."

JUDGE. The witness may step down.

CLERK (*calls*). Reverend Meridian Henry!

(*Blackout.* MERIDIAN, *in Sunday School. The class itself, predominately adolescent girls, is in silhouette.*)

MERIDIAN.—And here is the prophet, Solomon, the son of David, looking down through the ages, and speaking of Christ's love for His church. (*Reads.*) How fair is thy love, my sister, my spouse! How much better is thy love than wine! and the smell of thine ointments than all spices! (*Pause. The silhouette of girls vanishes.*) Oh, that it were one man, speaking to one woman!

(*Blackout.* MERIDIAN *takes the stand.*)

BLACKTOWN. I wonder how he feels now about all that turn-the-other-cheek jazz. His son sure didn't go for it.

WHITETOWN. That's the father. Claims to be a preacher. He brought this on himself. He's been raising trouble in this town for a long time.

THE STATE. You are Reverend Meridian Henry?

MERIDIAN. That is correct.

THE STATE. And you are the father of the late Richard Henry?

MERIDIAN. Yes.

THE STATE. You are a minister?

MERIDIAN. A Christian minister—yes.

THE STATE. And you raised your son according to the precepts of the Christian church?

MERIDIAN. I tried. But both my son and I had profound reservations concerning the behavior of Christians. He wondered why they treated black people as they do. And I was unable to give him—a satisfactory answer.

THE STATE. But certainly you—as a Christian minister—did not encourage your son to go armed?

MERIDIAN. The question never came up. He was not armed.

THE STATE. He was not armed?

MERIDIAN. No.

THE STATE. You never saw him with a gun? Or with any other weapon?

MERIDIAN. No.

THE STATE. Reverend Henry—are you in a position to swear that your son never carried arms?

MERIDIAN. Yes. I can swear to it. The only time the subject was ever mentioned he told me that he was stronger than white people and he could live without a gun.

BLACKTOWN. I bet he didn't say how.

WHITETOWN. That liver-lipped nigger is lying. He's lying!

THE STATE. Perhaps the difficulties your son had in accepting the Christian faith is due to your use of the pulpit as a forum for irresponsible notions concerning social equality, Reverend Henry. Perhaps the failure of the son is due to the failure of the father.

MERIDIAN. I am afraid that the gentleman flatters himself. I do not wish to see Negroes become the equal of their murderers. I wish us to become equal to ourselves. To become a people so free in themselves that they will have no need to—fear—others—and have no need to murder others.

THE STATE. You are not in the pulpit now. I am suggesting that you are responsible—directly responsible!—for your son's tragic fate.

MERIDIAN. I know more about that than you do. But you cannot consider my son's death to have been tragic. For you, it would have been tragic if he had lived.

THE STATE. With such a father, it is remarkable that the son lived as long as he did.

MERIDIAN. Remarkable, too, that the father lived!

THE STATE. Reverend Henry—you have been a widower for how many years?

MERIDIAN. I have been a widower for nearly eight years.

THE STATE. You are a young man still?

MERIDIAN. Are you asking me my age? I am not young.

THE STATE. You are not old. It must have demanded great discipline—

MERIDIAN. To live among you? Yes.

THE STATE. What is your relationship to the young, so-called student, Miss Juanita Harmon?

MERIDIAN. I am her old friend. I had hoped to become her father-in-law.

THE STATE. You are nothing more than old friends?

WHITETOWN. That's right. Get it out of him. Get the truth out of him.

BLACKTOWN. Leave the man *something*. Leave him something!

THE STATE. You have been celibate since the death of your wife?

BLACKTOWN. He never said he was a monk, you jive mother!

WHITETOWN. Make him tell us all about it. *All* about it.

MERIDIAN. Celibate? How does my celibacy concern you?

THE STATE. Your Honor, will you instruct the witness that he is on the witness stand, not I, and that he must answer the questions put to him!

MERIDIAN. *The questions put to him!* All right. Do you accept this answer? I am a man. A *man!* I tried to help my son become a man. But manhood is a dangerous pursuit, here. And that pursuit undid him because of *your* guns, *your* hoses, *your* dogs, *your* judges, *your* law-makers, *your* folly, *your* pride, *your* cruelty, *your* cowardice, *your* money, *your* chain gangs, and *your* churches! Did you think it would endure forever? that we would pay for *your* ease forever?

BLACKTOWN. Speak, my man! Amen! Amen! Amen! Amen!

WHITETOWN. Stirring up hate! Stirring up hate! A *preacher*—stirring up hate!

MERIDIAN. Yes! I *am* responsible for the death of my son. I—hoped—I prayed—I struggled—so that the world would be different by the time he was a man than it had been when he was born. And I thought that—then—when he looked at me—he would think that I—his father—had helped to change it.

THE STATE. What about those photographs your son carried about with him? Those photographs of himself and naked white women?

BLACKTOWN. Man! Would I love to look in *your* wallet!

WHITETOWN. Make him tell us about it, make him tell us *all* about it!

MERIDIAN. Photographs? My son and naked white women? He never mentioned them to me.

THE STATE. You were closer than most fathers and sons?

MERIDIAN. I never took a poll on most fathers and sons.

THE STATE. You never discussed women?

MERIDIAN. We talked about his mother. She was a woman. We talked about Miss Harmon. *She* is a woman. But we never talked about dirty pictures. We didn't need that.

THE STATE. Reverend Henry, you have made us all aware that your love for your son transcends your respect for the truth or your devotion to the church. But— luckily for the truth—it is a matter of public record that your son was so dangerously deranged that it was found necessary, for his own sake, to incarcerate him. It was at the end of that incarceration that he returned to this town. We know that his life in the North was riotous—he brought that riot into this town. The evidence is overwhelming. And yet, you, a Christian minister, dare to bring us this tissue of lies in defense of a known pimp, dope addict, and rapist! You are yourself so eaten up by race hatred that no word of yours can be believed.

MERIDIAN. Your judgment of myself and my motives cannot concern me at all. I have lived with that judgment far too long. The truth cannot be heard in this dreadful place. But I will tell you again what I know. I know why my son became a dope addict. I know better than you will ever know, even if I should explain it to you for all eternity, how I am responsible for that. But I know my son was not a pimp. He respected women far too much for that. And I know he was not a rapist. Rape is hard work—and, frankly, I don't think that the alleged object was my son's type at all!

THE STATE. And you are a minister?

MERIDIAN. I think I may be beginning to become one.

JUDGE. The witness may step down.

(*Meridian leaves the stand.*)

CLERK (*calls*). Mr. Parnell James!

(PARNELL *in his bedroom, dressed in a bathrobe. Night.*)

PARNELL. She says I called somebody else's name. What name could I have called? And she won't repeat the name. Well. That's enough to freeze the blood and arrest the holy, the liberating orgasm! Christ, how weary I am of this dull calisthenic called love—with no love in it! What name could I have called? I hope it was—a *white* girl's name, anyway! Ha-ha! How still she became! And I hardly realized it, I was too far away—and then it was too late. And she was just looking at me. Jesus! To have somebody just looking at you—just looking at you—like that— at such a moment! It makes you feel—like you woke up and found yourself in bed with your mother! I tried to find out what was wrong—poor girl! But there's nothing you can say at a moment like that—really nothing. You're caught. Well, haven't I kept telling her that there's no future for her with me? There's no future for me with anybody! But that's all right. What name could I have called? I haven't been with anybody else for a long time, a long time. She says I haven't been with her, either. I guess she's right. I've just been using her. Using her as an anchor—to hold me here, in this house, this bed—so I won't find myself on the other side of town, ruining my reputation. *What* reputation? They all know. I swear they all *know*. Know what? What's there to know? So you get drunk and you fool around a little. Come on, Parnell. There's more to it than that. That's the reason you draw blanks whenever you get drunk. Everything comes out. Everything. They see what you don't dare to see. What name could I have called? Richard would say that you've got—black fever! Yeah, and he'd be wrong—that long, loud, black mother. I wonder if she's asleep yet—or just lying there, looking at the walls. Poor girl! All your life you've been made sick, stunned, dizzy, oh, Lord! driven half mad by blackness. Blackness in front of your eyes. Boys and girls, men and women— you've bowed down in front of them all! And then hated yourself. Hated yourself for debasing yourself? Out with it, Parnell! The nigger-lover! Black boys and girls! I've wanted my hands full of them, wanted to drown them, laughing and dancing and making love—making love—

wow!—and be transformed, formed, liberated out of this grey-white envelope. Jesus! I've always been afraid. Afraid of what I saw in their eyes? They don't love me, certainly. You don't love them, either! Sick with a disease only white men catch. Blackness. What is it like to be black? To look out on the world from *that* place? I give nothing! How dare she say that! My girl, if you knew what I've given! Ah. Come off it, Parnell. To *whom* have you given? What name did I call? What name did I call?

(*Blackout.* PARNELL *and* LYLE. *Hunting on* PARNELL'S *land.*)

LYLE. You think it's a good idea, then? You think she won't say no?

PARNELL. Well, you're the one who's got to go through it. *You've* got to ask for Miss Josephine's hand in marriage. And then you've got to live with her—for the rest of your life. Watch that gun. I've never seen you so jumpy. I might say it was a good idea if I thought she'd say no. But I think she'll say yes.

LYLE. Why would she say yes to me?

PARNELL. I think she's drawn to you. It isn't hard to be—drawn to you. Don't you know that?

LYLE. No. When I was young, I used to come here sometimes—with my Daddy. He didn't like *your* Daddy a-*tall*! We used to steal your game, Parnell—you didn't know that, did you?

PARNELL. I think I knew it.

LYLE. We shot at the game and your Daddy's overseers shot at us. But we *got* what *we* came after. *They* never got *us*!

PARNELL. You're talking an awful lot today. You nervous about Miss Josephine?

LYLE. Wait a minute. You think I ought to marry Jo?

PARNELL. I don't know who anybody should marry. Do you want to marry Jo?

LYLE. Well—I got to marry somebody. I got to have some kids. And Jo is—*clean!*

(*Parnell sights, shoots.*)

PARNELL. Goddamn!

LYLE. Missed it. Ha-ha!

PARNELL. It's probably somebody's mother.

LYLE. Watch. (*Sights, shoots.*) *Ha-ha!*

PARNELL. Bravo!

LYLE. I knew it! Had my name written on it, just as pretty as you please! (*Exits, returns with his bird.*) See? My Daddy

taught me well. It was sport for you. It was life for us.

PARNELL. I reckon you shot somebody's baby.

LYLE. I tell you—I can't go on like this. There comes a time in a man's life when he's got to have him a little—peace.

PARNELL. You mean calm. Tranquility.

LYLE. Yeah. I didn't mean it like it sounded. You thought I meant—no. I'm tired of—

PARNELL. Poon-tang.

LYLE. How'd you know? You tired of it, too? Yeah. I want kids.

PARNELL. Well, then—marry the girl.

LYLE. She ain't a girl no more. It might be her last chance, too. But, I swear, Parnell, she might be the only virgin left in this town. The only *white* virgin. I can vouch for the fact ain't many black ones.

PARNELL. You've been active, I know. Any kids?

LYLE. None that I know of. Ha-ha!

PARNELL. Do you think Jo might be upset—by the talk about you and Old Bill? She's real respectable, you know. She's a *librarian*.

LYLE. No. Them things happen every day. You think I ought to marry her? You really think she'll say yes?

PARNELL. She'll say yes. She'd better. I wish you luck. Name the first one after me.

LYLE. No. You be the godfather. And my best man. I'm going to name the first one after my Daddy—because he taught me more about hunting on your land than *you* know. I'll give him your middle name. I'll call him Lyle Parnell Britten, Jr!

PARNELL. If the girl says yes.

LYLE. Well, if she says no, ain't no problem, is there? We know where to go when the going gets rough, don't we, old buddy?

PARNELL. Do we? Look! Mine?

LYLE. What'll you bet?

PARNELL. The price of your wedding rings.

LYLE. You're on. Mine? *Mine!*

(*Blackout.* PARNELL *walks down the aisle, takes the stand.*)

WHITETOWN.

Here comes the nigger-lover!

But I bet you one thing—he knows more about the truth in this case than anybody else.

He ought to—he's with them all the time.

It's sad when a man turns against his own people!

BLACKTOWN.

Let's see how the Negro's friend comes through!

They been waiting for *him*—they going to tear his behind *up!*

I don't trust him. I *never* trusted him!

Why? Because he's *white,* that's why!

THE STATE. You were acquainted with the late Richard Henry?

PARNELL. Of course. His father and I have been friends all our lives.

THE STATE. Close friends?

PARNELL. Yes. Very close.

THE STATE. And what is your relationship to the alleged murderer, Mr. Lyle Britten?

PARNELL. We, also, have been friends all our lives.

THE STATE. Close friends?

PARNELL. Yes.

THE STATE. As close as the friendship between yourself and the dead boy's father?

PARNELL. I would say so—it was a very different relationship.

THE STATE. Different in what respect, Mr. James?

PARNELL. Well, we had different things to talk about. We did different things together.

THE STATE. What sort of different things?

PARNELL. Well—hunting, for example—things like that.

THE STATE. You never went hunting with Reverend Henry?

PARNELL. No. He didn't like to hunt.

THE STATE. He told you so? He told you that he didn't like to hunt?

PARNELL. The question never came up. We led very different lives.

THE STATE. I am gratified to hear it. Is it not true, Mr. James, that it is impossible for any two people to go on a hunting trip together if either of them has any reason at all to distrust the other?

PARNELL. Well, of course that would have to be true. But it's never talked about —it's just understood.

THE STATE. We can conclude, then, that you were willing to trust Lyle Britten with your life but did not feel the same trust in Reverend Henry?

PARNELL. Sir, you may not draw any such conclusion! I have told you that Reverend Henry and I led very different lives!

THE STATE. But you have been friends all your lives. Reverend Henry is also a southern boy—he, also, I am sure, knows and loves this land, has gone swimming and fishing in her streams and rivers, and stalked game in her forests. And yet, close as you are, you have never allowed yourself to be alone with Reverend Henry when Reverend Henry had a gun. Doesn't this suggest some *lack*—in your vaunted friendship?

PARNELL. Your suggestion is unwarranted and unworthy. As a soldier, I have often been alone with Negroes with guns, and it certainly never caused me any uneasiness.

THE STATE. But you were fighting a common enemy then. What was your impression of the late Richard Henry?

PARNELL. I liked him. He was very outspoken and perhaps tactless, but a very valuable person.

THE STATE. How would you describe his effect on this town? Among his own people? Among the whites?

PARNELL. His effect? He was pretty well liked.

THE STATE. That does not answer my question.

PARNELL. His effect was—kind of unsettling, I suppose. After all, he had lived in the North a long time, he wasn't used to—the way we do things down here.

THE STATE. He was accustomed to the way things are done in the North—where he learned to carry arms, to take dope, and to couple with white women!

PARNELL. I cannot testify to any of that, sir. I can only repeat that he reacted with great intensity to the racial situation in this town, and his effect on the town was, to that extent, unsettling.

THE STATE. Did he not encourage the Negroes of this town to arm?

PARNELL. Not to my knowledge, sir, no. And, in any case, they are not armed.

THE STATE. You are in a position to reassure us on this point?

PARNELL. My friends do not lie.

THE STATE. You are remarkably fortunate. You are aware of the attitude of the late Richard Henry toward white women? You saw the photographs he carried about with him?

PARNELL. We never discussed women. I never saw the photographs.

THE STATE. But you knew of their existence?

PARNELL. They were not obscene. They were simply snapshots of people he had known in the North.

THE STATE. Snapshots of white women?

PARNELL. Yes.

THE STATE. You are the first witness to admit the existence of these photographs, Mr. James.

PARNELL. It is very likely that the other witnesses never saw them. The boy had been discouraged, very early on, from mentioning them or showing them about.

THE STATE. Discouraged by whom?

PARNELL. Why—by—me.

THE STATE. But you never saw the photographs—

PARNELL. I told him I didn't want to see them and that it would be dangerous to carry them about.

THE STATE. He showed these photographs to you, but to no one else?

PARNELL. That would seem to be the case, yes.

THE STATE. What was his motive in taking you into his confidence?

PARNELL. Bravado. He wanted me to know that he had white friends in the North, that—he had been happy—in the North.

THE STATE. You did not tell his father? You did not warn your close friend?

PARNELL. I am sure that Richard never mentioned these photographs to his father. He would have been too ashamed. Those women were beneath him.

THE STATE. A white woman who surrenders to a colored man is beneath all human consideration. She has wantonly and deliberately defiled the temple of the Holy Ghost. It is clear to me that the effect of such a boy on this town was irresponsible and incendiary to the greatest degree. Did you not find your close friendship with Reverend Henry somewhat strained by the son's attempt to rape the wife of your other close friend, Lyle Britten?

PARNELL. This attempt was never mentioned before—before today.

THE STATE. You are as close as you claim to the Britten family and knew nothing of this attempted rape? How do you explain that?

PARNELL. I cannot explain it.

THE STATE. This is a court of law, Mr. James, and we will have the truth!

WHITETOWN. Make him tell the truth!

BLACKTOWN. Make him tell the truth!

THE STATE. How can you be the close friend you claim to be of the Britten family and not have known of so grave an event?

PARNELL. I—I knew of a fight. It was understood that the boy had gone to Mr. Britten's store looking for a fight. I—I cannot explain *that,* either.

THE STATE. Who told you of the fight?

PARNELL. Why—Mr. Britten.

THE STATE. And did not tell you that Richard Henry had attempted to assault his wife? Come, Mr. James!

PARNELL. We were all very much upset. Perhaps he was not as coherent as he might have been—perhaps I failed to listen closely. It was my assumption that Mrs. Britten had misconstrued the boy's actions —he had been in the North a long time, his manner was very free and bold.

THE STATE. Mrs. Britten has testified that Richard Henry grabbed her and pulled her to him and tried to kiss her. How can those actions be misconstrued?

PARNELL. Those actions are—quite explicit.

THE STATE. Thank you, Mr. James. That is all.

JUDGE. The witness may step down.

(PARNELL *leaves the stand.*)

BLACKTOWN. What do you think of our fine friend *now?* He didn't do it to us rough and hard. No, he was real gentle. I hardly felt a thing. Did you? You can't never go against the word of a white lady, man, not even if you're white. Can't be done. He was sad. *Sad!*

WHITETOWN. It took him long enough! He did his best not to say it—can you imagine! So her story was true—after all! I hope he's learned his lesson. We been trying to tell him—for years!

CLERK (*calls*). Mr. Lyle Britten!

(LYLE, *in the woods.*)

LYLE. I wonder what he'll grow up to look like. Of course, it might be a girl. I reckon I wouldn't mind—just keep on trying till I get me a boy, ha-ha! Old Miss Josephine is something, ain't she? I really struck oil when I come across her. She's a nice woman. And she's *my* woman—I ain't got to worry about *that* a-tall! You're making big changes in your life, Lyle, and you got to be ready to take on this extra responsibility. Shoot, I'm ready. I know what I'm doing. And I'm going to work harder than I've ever worked before in my life to make Jo happy—and keep her happy—and raise our children to be fine men and women. Lord, you know I'm not a praying man. I've done a lot of wrong things in my life and I ain't never going to be perfect. I know You know that. I know You understand that. But, Lord, hear me today and help me to do what I'm supposed to do. I want to be as strong as my Mama and Daddy and raise my children like they raised me. That's what I want, oh Lord. In a few years I'll be walking here, showing my son these trees and this water and this sky. He'll have his hand in my hand, and I'll show him the world. Isn't that a funny thing! He don't even exist yet—he's just an egg in his mother's belly, I bet you couldn't even find him with a microscope—and I put him there—and he's coming out soon—with fingers and toes and eyes—and by and by, he'll learn to walk and talk—and I reckon I'll have to spank him sometime —if he's anything like me, I know I will. Isn't that something! My son! Hurry up and get here, so I can hug you in my arms and give you a good start on your long journey!

(*Blackout.* LYLE, *with* PAPA D. *Drunk. Music and dancing.*)

LYLE. You remember them days when Willa Mae was around? My mind's been going back to them days. You remember? She was a hot little piece, I just had to have some of that, I just *had* to. Half the time she didn't wear no stockings, just had them brown, round legs just moving. I couldn't keep my eyes off her legs when she didn't wear no stockings. And you know what she told me? You know what she told me? She said there wasn't a nigger alive could be as good to her as me. That's right. She said she'd like to *see* the nigger could do her like I done her. You hear me, boy? That's something, ain't it? Boy—she'd just come into a room sometimes and my old pecker would stand up at attention. You ain't jealous, are you, Joel? Ha-ha! You never did hear from her no more, did you? No, I reckon you didn't. Shoot, I got to get on home. I'm a family man now, I got—great responsibilities! Yeah. Be seeing you, Joel. You don't want to close up and walk a-ways with me, do you? No, I reckon you better not. They

having fun. Sure wish I could be more like you all. Bye-bye!

(*Blackout. As* LYLE *approaches the witness stand, the lights in the courtroom dim. We hear voices from the church, singing a lament. The lights come up.*)

JUDGE. Gentlemen of the jury, have you reached a verdict?

FOREMAN. We have, Your Honor.

JUDGE. Will the prisoner please rise?

(LYLE *rises.*)

Do you find the defendant, Mr. Lyle Britten, guilty or not guilty?

FOREMAN. Not guilty, Your Honor.

(*Cheering in* WHITETOWN. *Silence in* BLACKTOWN. *The stage is taken over by Reporters, Photographers, Witnesses, Townspeople.* LYLE *is congratulated and embraced.* BLACKTOWN *files out silently, not looking back.* WHITETOWN *files out jubilantly, and yet with a certain reluctance. Presently, the stage is empty, except for* LYLE, JO, MOTHER HENRY, MERIDIAN, PARNELL, JUANITA, *and* LORENZO.)

JO. Let's get out of here and go home. We've been here just for days. I wouldn't care if I *never* saw the insides of a courtroom again! Let's go home, sugar. We got something to celebrate!

JUANITA. We, too, must go—to another celebration. We're having a prayer meeting on the City Hall steps.

LORENZO. Prayer meeting.

LYLE. Well, it was touch and go there for awhile, Parnell, but you sure come through. I knew you would.

JO. Let's go, Lyle. The baby's hungry.

MERIDIAN. Perhaps now you can ask him to tell you the truth. He's got nothing to lose now. They can't try him again.

LYLE. Wasn't much sense in trying me now, this time, was there, Reverend? These people have been knowing me and my good Jo here all our lives, they ain't going to doubt us. And you people—you people—ought to have better sense and more things to do than running around stirring up all this hate and trouble. *That's* how your son got himself killed. He listened to crazy niggers like you!

MERIDIAN. Did you kill him?

LYLE. They just asked me that in court, didn't they? And they just decided I didn't, didn't they? Well, that's good enough for me and all those white people and so it damn sure better be good enough for you!

PARNELL. That's no answer. It's not good enough for me.

LYLE. What do you mean, that's no answer? Why isn't it an answer? Why isn't it good enough for you? You know, when you were up on the stand right now, you acted like you doubted my Jo's word. You got no right to doubt Jo's word. You ain't no better than she is! You ain't no better than me!

PARNELL. I am aware of that. God knows I have been made aware of that—for the first time in my life. But, as you and I will never be the same again—since our comedy is finished, since I have failed you so badly —let me say this. I did not doubt Jo's word. I knew that she was lying and that you had made her lie. That was a terrible thing to do to her. It was a terrible thing that I just did to you. I really don't know if what I did to Meridian was as awful as what I did to you. I don't expect forgiveness, Meridian. I only hope that all of us will suffer past this agony and horror.

LYLE. What's the matter with you? Have you forgotten you a white man? A white man! My Daddy told me not to *never* forget I was a white man! Here I been knowing you all my life—and now I'm ashamed of you. Ashamed of you! Get on over to niggertown! I'm going home with my good wife.

MERIDIAN. What was the last thing my son said to you—before you shot him down —like a dog?

LYLE. Like a dog! You a smart nigger, ain't you?

MERIDIAN. What was the last thing he said? Did he beg you for his life?

LYLE. *That* nigger! He was too smart for that! He was too full of himself for that! He must have thought he was white. And I gave him every chance—every chance—to live!

MERIDIAN. And he refused them all.

LYLE. Do you know what that nigger said to me?

(*The light changes, so that everyone but* LYLE *is in silhouette.* RICHARD *appears, dressed as we last saw him, on the road outside* PAPA's *joint.*)

RICHARD. I'm ready. Here I am. You asked me if I was ready, didn't you? What's on your mind, white man?

LYLE. Boy, I always treated you with respect. I don't know what's the matter with you, or what makes you act the way

you do—but you owe me an apology and I come out here tonight to get it. I mean, I ain't going away without it.

RICHARD. *I* owe *you* an apology! That's a wild idea. What am I apologizing for?

LYLE. You know, you mighty lucky to still be walking around.

RICHARD. So are you. White man.

LYLE. I'd like you to apologize for your behavior in my store that day. Now, I think I'm being pretty reasonable, ain't I?

RICHARD. You got anything to write on? I'll write you an IOU.

LYLE. Keep it up. You going to be laughing out of the other side of your mouth pretty soon.

RICHARD. Why don't you go home? And let me go home? Do we need all this shit? Can't we live without it?

LYLE. Boy, are you drunk?

RICHARD. No, I ain't drunk. I'm just tired. Tired of all this fighting. What are you trying to prove? What am *I* trying to prove?

LYLE. I'm trying to give you a break. You too dumb to take it.

RICHARD. I'm hip. You been trying to give me a break for a great, long time. But there's only one break I want. And you won't give me that.

LYLE. What kind of break do you want, boy?

RICHARD. For you to go home. And let me go home. I got things to do. I got— lots of things to do!

LYLE. I got things to do, too. I'd like to get home, too.

RICHARD. Then why are we standing here? Can't we walk? Let me walk, white man! Let me walk!

LYLE. We can walk, just as soon as we get our business settled.

RICHARD. It's settled. You a man and I'm a man. Let's walk.

LYLE. Nigger, you was born down here. Ain't you never said sir to a white man?

RICHARD. No. The only person I ever said sir to was my Daddy.

LYLE. Are you going to apologize to me?

RICHARD. No.

LYLE. Do you want to live?

RICHARD. Yes.

LYLE. Then you know what to do, then, don't you?

RICHARD. Go home. Go home.

LYLE. You facing my gun. (*Produces it.*)

Now, in just a minute, we can both go home.

RICHARD. You sick mother! Why can't you leave me alone? White man! I don't want nothing from you. You ain't got nothing to give me. You can't eat because none of your sad-assed chicks can cook. You can't talk because won't nobody talk to you. You can't dance because you've got nobody to dance with—don't you know I've watched you all my life? *All my life!* And *I* know your women, don't you think I don't—better than you!

(*Lyle shoots, once.*)

Why have you spent so much time trying to kill me? Why are you always trying to cut off *my* cock? You worried about it? Why?

(LYLE *shoots again.*)

Okay. Okay. Okay. Keep your old lady home, you hear? Don't let her near no nigger. She might get to like it. You might get to like it, too. Wow!

(RICHARD *falls.*)

Juanita! Daddy! *Mama!*

(*Singing from the church. Spot on* LYLE.)

LYLE. I had to kill him then. I'm a white man! Can't nobody talk that way to *me!* I had to go and get my pick-up truck and load him in it—I had to carry him on my back—and carry him out to the high weeds. And I dumped him in the weeds, face down. And then I come on home, to my good Jo here.

JO. Come on, Lyle. We got to get on home. We got to get the little one home now.

LYLE. And I ain't sorry. I want you to know that I ain't sorry!

JO. Come on, Lyle. Come on. He's hungry. I got to feed him.

(JO *and* LYLE *exit.*)

MOTHER HENRY. We got to go now, children. The children is already started to march.

LORENZO. Prayer!

MERIDIAN. You know, for us, it all began with the Bible and the gun. Maybe it will end with the Bible and the gun.

JUANITA. What did you do with the gun, Meridian?

PARNELL. You have the gun—Richard's gun?

MERIDIAN. Yes. In the pulpit. Under the Bible. Like the pilgrims of old.

(*Exits.*)

MOTHER HENRY. Come on, children.

(*Singing.*)

(PETE *enters.*)

PETE (*stammers*). Are you ready, Juanita? Shall we go now?

JUANITA. Yes.

LORENZO. Come here, Pete. Stay close to me.

(*They go to the church door. The singing swells.*)

PARNELL. Well.

JUANITA. Well. Yes, Lord!

PARNELL. Can I join you on the march, Juanita? Can I walk with you?

JUANITA. Well, we can walk in the same direction, Parnell. Come. Don't look like that. Let's go on on.

(*Exits.*)

(*After a moment,* PARNELL *follows.*)

CURTAIN

THE LAST ANALYSIS

Saul Bellow

To my son ADAM, who had
a great time in the Belasco Theatre.

First presented by Stevens Productions, Inc., Bonfils-Seawell Enterprises, and David Oppenheim on October 1, 1964, at the Belasco Theatre, New York City, with the following cast:*

(In order of appearance)

PHILIP BUMMIDGE Sam Levene
SHELDON Charles Boaz
LEWIS MOTT Sully Michaels
IMOGEN Alix Elias
WINKLEMAN Leon Janney
FIRST TECHNICIAN Walter Williams
SECOND TECHNICIAN Ed Bordo
THIRD TECHNICIAN Philip Pruneau
MADGE Lucille Patton
MAX Anthony Roberts

PAMELA Ann Wedgeworth
ANTIQUE DEALER Ted Schwartz
AUFSCHNITT Will Lee
BELLA Tresa Hughes
STICKLES Bert Conway
MESSENGER Ted Schwartz
TANTE FRUMKAH Minerva Pious
FIDDLEMAN Michael Vale
KALBFUSS James Dukas

Directed by Joseph Anthony
Setting and lighting by David Hays
Costumes by Ann Roth

THE LAST ANALYSIS by Saul Bellow.
Copyright © 1965 by Saul Bellow.
All rights reserved.
Reprinted by permission of The Viking Press, Inc.

This play in its printed form is designed for the reading public only. All dramatic rights in it are fully protected by copyright, and no public or private performance—professional or amateur—may be given without the written permission of the author and the payment of royalty. As the courts have also ruled that the public reading of a play constitutes a public performance, no such reading may be given except under the conditions stated above. Anyone disregarding the author's rights renders himself liable to prosecution. Communications

* The cast of characters was amended in later versions.

regarding these rights should be addressed to the author's representative, Toby Cole, 234 West 44th Street, New York, N.Y. 10036.

COMPARATIVELY few of America's best novelists have tried their hand at playwriting. One such is Saul Bellow, although he, after a disappointing attempt on Broadway with *The Last Analysis,* seems, at least for the moment, to have regrettably lost heart.

Bellow, who teaches at the University of Chicago, as well as writes, was born on July 10, 1915, in Lachine, Quebec. His father, Abraham Bellow, had emigrated to Canada from Saint Petersburg, Russia, two years earlier. A businessman, the elder Bellow took his family first to Montreal, and then, in 1924, they all crossed the border and settled in Chicago, where Saul Bellow was brought up. He entered the University of Chicago in 1933, moving to Northwestern University two years later, where he graduated in anthropology and sociology in 1937.

Having decided to write he worked, briefly before service in World War II, in the editorial department of the Encyclopaedia Britannica. His first novel, *Dangling Man,* was published in 1944, and although favorably received for a first work, it was not really until 1953, with the publication of *The Adventures of Augie March,* an almost picaresque novel of a young Jewish boy growing up in Chicago, that his reputation was firmly established. In 1964 he published what is probably his finest work to date, *Herzog,* a long discursive and deeply personal novel about an academic trying to equate himself with his world.

Anyone acquainted with Bellow's literary style is likely to have noticed his swift and sure command of dialogue, and his insight into character and the motivations of character. It was apparently the playwright Lillian Hellman who first suggested that Bellow try to write plays, pointing out that his brief novel, *Seize the Day,* published in 1956, would be very suitable for dramatic adaptation.

The Last Analysis opened on October 1, 1964, and closed very rapidly afterward. For Bellow it was a dispiriting experience. In the words of the critic Robert Brustein, writing on the play in the *New Republic:* "There is an awful lot of noise issuing from the stage of the Belasco these days, but the loudest explosion of all can be heard only with the inner ear: it comes from the head-on collision of a gifted writer, Saul Bellow, with the crassness and incompetence of the whole commercial theater system."

Miscast, underdirected, in addition to being at times admittedly overwritten, Mr. Bellow's play hardly stood a fair chance. It should be pointed out here that what is being published is not the play that opened at the Belasco, but a revised version that has yet to be staged in New York. In an author's note to the first complete printed edition (sections of the play were originally published in the *Partisan Review* in 1962) Bellow makes this clear. After referring to the original production, Bellow writes: "The present version makes use of some of the timbers of that shipwreck, but much of it is entirely new."

Despite the obvious disappointment of this Broadway failure, Bellow seems not to have been entirely cast down. As he says below, he gained a great deal from it.

In 1965, two of Bellow's shorter plays, *The Wen* and *Orange Soufflé,* were staged by the Traverse Theatre in Edinburgh, and later the same year they were produced in London. But, most unfortunately, it seems as if the enormously gifted writer is now shying clear of the stage.

The extent of this loss to the American theatre can be seen by anyone reading *The Last Analysis.* Because of its wild and riotous subject matter—a fading comedian, Bummidge, arranges to have his final psychiatric analysis put on closed-circuit TV—the play has frequently been taken as a spoof of Freudian psychology. But Bellow himself, in a 1964 interview with the *Saturday Review,* described it as "a satire on intellectual solemnity, on the metaphors that capture the imagination." This seems a fair description; in any event this exhilarating play is precisely what Bellow called its Broadway debacle—"an enriching experience."

AUTHOR'S NOTE

An earlier version of *The Last Analysis,* produced by Roger Stevens, directed by Joseph Anthony, with Sam Levene, Tresa Hughes, Leon Janney, and Lucille Patton in the principal roles, opened at the Belasco Theatre, New York City, in September 1964,* and closed after a short run. The present version makes use of some of the timbers of that shipwreck, but much of it is entirely new. I have dropped several characters, written one new part, attempted to simplify the cluttered and inconsequent plot, which puzzled the audience (and even the playwright), and tried to eliminate pointless noises and distracting bits of business. I have heard the Middlebrow defined as one who makes every loss yield a profit, but at the risk of acquiring a bad name, I feel obliged to say that a Broadway failure can be an enriching experience. The rehearsals, the previews, the cold and peevish first-night audience, the judgments of the critics, were of the greatest value to me.

The Last Analysis is not simply a spoof of Freudian psychology, though certain analysts touchily interpreted it as such. Its real subject is the mind's comical struggle for survival in an environment of Ideas—its fascination with metaphors, and the peculiarly literal and solemn manner in which Americans dedicate themselves to programs, fancies, or brainstorms. In *The Last Analysis* a clown is driven to thought, and, like modern painters, poets, and musicians before him, turns into a theoretician. I have always had a weakness for autodidacts and amateur philosophers and scientists, and enjoy observing the democratic diffusion of high culture. Regrettably, the Broadway version neglected the *mental* comedy of Bummidge and his family, and I have tried to restore it.

* PUBLISHER'S NOTE: The actual opening date was October 1, 1964.

CAST OF CHARACTERS

BUMMIDGE. A former star whose popularity has declined, now his own psychiatrist. I think of Bummidge as a large man, or at least a stout one. Nearing sixty, he is still eagerly mapping programs and hatching new projects. Half ravaged, half dignified, earnest when he is clowning and clowning when he means to be earnest, he represents the artist who is forced to be his own theoretician. The role requires great subtlety and charm, and extraordinary mimetic powers.

WINKLEMAN. Bummidge's cousin. A lawyer, authoritative and realistic, he has a deep voice, and a slightly oracular style. He has adopted, as Mott points out, the Harvard Club manner.

BELLA. Bummidge's estranged wife. Not as estranged as he would like her to be. Bella is proud of her businesslike ways, her air of command. She is an aggressive, hammering woman, large and masculine, elaborately made up and wearing a bottle-green suit trimmed in fox fur, and spike-heeled shoes. She carries a whopping patent-leather purse.

MADGE. Bummidge's sister. The businesswoman, thinly disguised as a Westchester matron.

MAX. Bummidge's son is in his mid-thirties. Impeccably tailored, manicured, barbered, he is nevertheless the Angry Young Man.

AUNT VELMA. Bummidge's ancient aunt and midwife. At the edge of the grave, and tottering, she is still aggressive. Wears horn-rimmed glasses and smokes cigars.

IMOGEN. Bummidge's secretary. A little darling, the utterly credulous ingénue. Bummidge's relation to her is entirely fatherly.

PAMELA. Bummidge's paramour. The relationship has obviously faded. She does not expect to get much more from him and is tired of humoring him. Her face is masklike, with raised brows and prim, bland lips. She has a thin figure and is dressed in a modest suit.

LOUIE MOTT. Bummidge's old pal, the television technician, is desperately trying to keep youthful. He wears College Shop clothing—a turtle-necked shirt and white buckskin shoes.

BERTRAM. Bummidge's scientific collabora-tor, formerly a ratcatcher. A slender, elderly, terribly smiling man with high color and false teeth.

GALLUPPO. A private detective. Stocky, shifty, corrupt-looking, he chews a toothpick, at which he occasionally sniffs furtively.

AUFSCHNITT. The little Viennese tailor. The part was played to perfection by Mr. Will Lee at the Belasco Theatre.

FIDDLEMAN. An impresario. He wears a colored vest, has ducal grand manners in the Hollywood style, and speaks very impatiently.

A TECHNICIAN

A MESSENGER

ACT ONE

A two-story loft in a warehouse on the West Side of New York, brightly lighted by a studio window. Upstage left, a door to the fire escape. There are also exits to the library, stage right, and through an old-fashioned fire door, stage left. At the back of stage right is a little iron staircase leading to a small balcony. The bathroom door is at stage left. Characters arriving from the street enter through an elevator door, stage right.

*The stage is not cluttered. It is hung with bright fabrics, though they are by no means new. The inhabitant of this loft is obviously eccentric. He keeps an old barber chair, downstage right, and an elegant old sofa such as an analyst of the Vienna school might have used, downstage left. The posters on the wall go back to the twenties and thirties—*BUMMY, THE OLD TRILBY THEATRE. ZANY BUMMIDGE OF THE FOLLIES. KING OF THE CLOWNS. BUMMY WE LOVE YOU. *Television equipment has been coming in. Obviously, a broadcast is being prepared. There is a floodlamp on the wall, downstage right, in position to cover the barber chair. Near the sofa is a bust of Sigmund Freud. Behind it, bookcases with learned-looking tomes and journals. In center stage is a movable platform.*

At curtain, we discover BUMMIDGE *lying in the barber chair, completely covered by a sheet. Imogen sits by her desk on a swivel chair, legs crossed, eagerly transcribing notes from a stenographic pad to large file cards. Enter* WINKLEMAN.

WINKLEMAN. Imogen, where's my cousin? Oh, there. Now, Bummy—

IMOGEN. Please, Lawyer Winkleman. I just got him to rest. The strain of today's broadcast is twisting his nerves.

WINKLEMAN (*looking about*). Ah, television equipment. But not the real thing. Only closed-circuit. There was a time when my cousin Bummidge was king of the networks—the greatest comedian of his time. Now look at him, almost destroyed by his ideas, mental experiments —homebrewed psychoanalysis. Poor has-been.

(BUMMIDGE *quivers under the sheet.*)

He spends his days in an old loft with his colleagues—(*A gesture at* IMOGEN.)— acting out his neuroses. His traumas. The psychological crises of his life. It's very painful.

IMOGEN. It's almost deliberate, Mr. Winkleman, the way you refuse to understand.

WINKLEMAN. What's to understand?

BUMMIDGE (*tears off the sheet*). Don't waste your time, Imogen. He pretends to be a genuine lowbrow, a plebeian. *You* know, Winkie, why I act out my past life.

WINKLEMAN (*with heavy irony*). Yeah, self-knowledge.

BUMMIDGE. If a man like me needs insight, why should he go to some punk? I have my own method—*Existenz*-Action-Self-analysis.

WINKLEMAN. Once you were in a class with Bert Lahr, Groucho Marx. Now I foresee you waiting in an alley for a handout of dried eggs from Federal Surplus.

IMOGEN (*to* BUMMIDGE). Finish your rest. You have to have it.

WINKLEMAN. Lowbrow! For you no brow could ever be high enough. Some people are social climbers. You are a mental climber. I'm not against thought, but you're a comic, not a scientist. Is this a time to plunge into theory? Originality? Delirium! And now, with a secretary who used to be a bunny in the Playboy Club, and a collaborator who used be a rat-catcher . . . now you spend your last dough on a closed-circuit TV broadcast to a bunch of specialists at the American Psychiatric Association. How was it arranged? Whom did you bribe on the Program Committee?

BUMMIDGE (*nettled*). Bribe? They jumped at the chance to see my work.

IMOGEN. Rest . . . I don't know how his organism stands the strain. (*She draws the sheet over him.*)

WINKLEMAN. And whose equipment is this? (*Reads label.*) Diamond Electronics. I thought so. Louie Mott, your old Hungarian sidekick and errand boy. That swindler. Bummy, listen to me. We have ties. Why, my mother brought you into the world.

BUMMIDGE (*sits up*). Oh, Aunt Velma! That ancient thing, she still exists. She delivered me. She could clue me into the Unconscious in a dozen places. Where is she?

WINKLEMAN. Very busy, in her old age. She said you telephoned her.

IMOGEN. You haven't rested, haven't eaten in two weeks. You must relax a while before you face the cameras.

BUMMIDGE (*as she begins to cover him again*). Today my powers must be at their peak. I must convince everyone.

(*Enter* MOTT.)

MOTT. Well, my assistant is here. We can hook up the equipment. But first there's one matter to be took up—money, the balance.

(BUMMIDGE *pulls the sheet over his head.*)

WINKLEMAN. I knew you'd be mixed up in this, you devious Hungarian. Whenever he's on the brink of disaster, you're always right behind him.

MOTT. Go blow it out, Winkleman. I stood by him for years.

WINKLEMAN. Only because there were broads around.

MOTT. Wink the Fink!

WINKLEMAN. And now this TV racket. I bet you can't transmit to the Waldorf.

MOTT. I could transmit all the way to China, if I wanted. Look at this citation from the College of Surgeons. I filmed the heart operations at Rochester, you ambulance-chaser!

WINKLEMAN. Sex maniac! Deviant!

MOTT. Maybe you fool your pals at the Harvard Club, but not me. I know about your old-peoples'-home racket.

(WINKLEMAN *flinches.*)

IMOGEN. Nursing home?

MOTT. You bet. Cousin Winkie bought an old luxury hotel and filled it with ancient, senile old-folks.

WINKLEMAN. Perfectly legitimate. The old Ravenna Towers. Gorgeous! A work of art. The space, the gilt cornices. The doorknobs themselves are priceless.

MOTT. Three bunks to a single room. And your old lady is like the camp commandant.

(WINKLEMAN *is glaring.*)

BUMMIDGE. Imogen—tell them to wrangle outside.

MOTT. Bummy, the office insists on the final payment. Five grand.

IMOGEN. What about the thirty-five thousand he already paid you?

MOTT. I can't help it. And no funny stuff, Bummy.

BUMMIDGE (*sits up, the sheet clutched at his throat*). I thought you were pulling with me, Louie. I've invited all those distinguished people. They want to see the results of my research.

MOTT. Okay, fine. But the office . . .

BUMMIDGE (*earnest*). Don't sell out to the bookkeepers. This is of universal significance.

IMOGEN. I'll look for the checkbook.

(BUMMIDGE *detains her.*)

BUMMIDGE. Wink. (*Beckons him near, speaks sotto voce.*) Let me have the dough for a few days.

WINKLEMAN. Cousin, you're joking.

BUMMIDGE. Why joking? I need it. You made millions on me.

WINKLEMAN. Ancient history! That was when you let me do the thinking. I'd like to help. But I have my principles, too, just like you.

BUMMIDGE. O, money! O, Plutus! O, Mammon!

WINKLEMAN. Is anything more horrible than a solemn buffoon. Where are your savings?

BUMMIDGE. In the separation Bella cleaned me out. Two millions.

WINKLEMAN. You made her furious. Your mistresses used her charge accounts.

BUMMIDGE. Don't you know what Freud says about gold? What does the color remind you of?

WINKLEMAN. Try giving Louie here— (*Gestures.*)—the other substance. See if he'll take it.

BUMMIDGE. For thirty years you sold me to the lousy public like dry cereal.

WINKLEMAN. Lousy? You lost your touch. They stopped laughing.

BUMMIDGE. I can make those apes laugh any time. At will. (*Pause.*) It's just that I can't stand the sound they make. And I

feel hit by the blast of sickness from their lungs. It makes me shrink.

WINKLEMAN. And you're going to cure the ravaged psyche of the mass. Poor cousin!

BUMMIDGE. You exploited me. Dragged me down into affluence.

MOTT. Let's not forget that check.

IMOGEN (*crossing to desk*). You see me looking for it, don't you?

BUMMIDGE. You made me change my name. Lead a false life. Maybe an actor must—I'll give you that much. But— (*with fervor*)—now I want insight. Value. I'll die without value. And finally I've succeeded in getting off the mere surface of life. Wink, back me today.

WINKLEMAN (*wraps himself in his coat and sits on couch*). You're not the only one in trouble.

IMOGEN. I came to Mr. Bummidge's door with a questionnaire. Instead of answering my questions, he took me by the hand and said, "My dear, what do you consider funny?"

MOTT. What did you say?

IMOGEN. I just said, "Me, coming to your door to ask if you eat soup." And he laughed, and hired me. I believe in him. (*Her hand is on her breast.*) Mr. Winkleman, leading scientists have agreed to watch. Doctor Gumplovitch, Doctor Ratzenhofer, the giants of American psychiatry. And people from Princeton and Johns Hopkins, the Ford Foundation. They know they're dealing with a great artist.

MOTT. I'm waiting!

BUMMIDGE. Calm! (*Throws himself back in the chair.*)

MOTT. Here's a check. Fill it in. Five zero zero zero and no one hundred cents.

(IMOGEN *writes.*)

WINKLEMAN. Between Bella, and his son Max, and his broads, especially the present one, Pamela, the ex-chorus girl, I figure he's been taken for ten million. Your sister Madge and I are worried. Your real friends.

MOTT. Let's have the signature, now.

BUMMIDGE (*as he signs*). Imogen, we must check out a few things. Where's Bertram? And Kalbfuss! Make sure Kalbfuss will be watching me. Phone his shop.

WINKLEMAN. Kalbfuss? Shop?

(*Enter a* TECHNICIAN, *pushing a television camera.*)

TECHNICIAN (*to* MOTT). Louie, is this the

joint? The floor doesn't look solid enough. These boards waggle like loose teeth. (*Seeing* IMOGEN.) Well—hello, Miss.

IMOGEN. Bertram went to the Waldorf to see about the canapés and champagne.

WINKLEMAN. Champagne? And who is this Kalbfuss—the lord high egghead? (*Speaking to the* TECHNICIAN *and then to* IMOGEN.) Earnestness has been the ruin of my cousin. High-mindedness. The suckers had their mouths open for yucks—he fed them Aristotle, Kierkegaard, Freud. Who needs another homemade intellectual? One more self-nominated boring intellectual, sick with abstractions? An American intellectual?

TECHNICIAN (*pushing equipment before him*). Look out, friend.

WINKLEMAN. Reading! This man hid books in his dressing room. Huge volumes, thick journals. Booksellers were like dope-pushers to him. He was like a junkie —on thought.

IMOGEN. All I can say is that he's done great things for my mental development. He saw more than these externals. No other man has ever been willing to look past them.

(*The* TECHNICIAN *whistles at her.*)

MOTT (*sniffing her*). She's like a mound of nectarines— Business first. I'll run down to the bank. (*Exit.*)

BUMMIDGE. Oh! (*Sits up.*) The time is short. I've got so much mental preparation to make, and I'm hampered, hindered, held back, obstructed, impeded, impaired. (*To* WINKLEMAN.) Where is your mother? I need those sagging bones. I want her here today. (*Crossing stage.*) And Bertram —Kalbfuss. He's crucial. Come, Imogen. (*Exit stage right.*)

(*As* IMOGEN *follows, the* TECHNICIAN *pinches her.*)

IMOGEN. Yes, Mr. Bummidge. (*To* TECHNICIAN.) Please! (*Exit.*)

WINKLEMAN. No matter what Bummy masterminded, no matter what he brewed, I could make use of it. It brought me a buck, and a tax-clean buck, too. With phantasmagoria like his there's only one thing to do: sell them! When he wanted to weave rugs, I put him into a Fifth Avenue window. If he wanted to paint action pictures, play the organ like Albert Schweitzer, I'd make a deal. But now he's lost his image with the public, he's confused the Plain Man, and that's the sonofabitch that pays for the whole show. . . . I admit I also have a bad character. It's true, I no longer care who lives and who dies. Still, I have to pursue my own way. It's a job, and jobs have to be done. And I'm in trouble myself. He's not the only one. (*Moves upstage and right.*) He doesn't know it yet, but he's going to save the day for me, as he's done before. Keep sharp, look sharp, Winkie. Lurk offshore. Rush in at the right moment and grab Bummy again. Hide, wait, listen, haunt the fringes, you'll get benefits. And now, a little oxygen for the system—(*Inhales.*)—and submerge. (*Exit, holding his nose like a swimmer.*)

(*Enter* BUMMIDGE *with a timer.*)

BUMMIDGE. Hours and minutes! No time. Curse that interfering Winkleman. I know he wants to exploit me. He and my sister Madge, they always work together. There's some intrigue. (*He wipes them away with a gesture.*) Now I am alone. (*Puts the timer on the platform, center.*) Ultimate reality—that's what we want. Deep, deep and final. The truth which daily life only distorts. Okay, Bummy. (*Sits on platform.*) What's on your mind? Come, boy, let's have it. Begin with the dreams you dreamt last night. Sleep is dotted with madness. Each dream is a tiny psychosis. The sleeper is a tranquil criminal. All right—the dreams. . . . What I dreamt! A huge white animal climbed into my bed. I thought, "A polar bear." I looked again and saw pig's feet. A white sow. But wait—I didn't do anything to her. A nursing pig. What's the symbolism of it? (*Ponders, then shrugs.*) I thought, "Live and let live. Let her lie there." I moved over on the diagonal. Part of my basic submissiveness. At least I didn't have to make love to her. But the dream, the dream! The pig squirmed and writhed like a phantom knockwurst, and turned into a fat, enormous man in a baggy sweater with little candy milk bottles sewn in rows. Like Hermann Goering with his medals. But was this fat man a man? In the unconscious, to be obese is female. Oh, that unconscious! Is it ever cunning! Repression! The power of the Id! This was a male with breasts. (*Rises.*) I want notes on this, for the record. (*Calls.*) Imogen! Is that girl slipping, libido-wise? Wait, there's more. (*Crosses over and sits on his analytic sofa.*) Then he/she lay in bed with me, shaking, and all the little bottles clinked and jingled. He/she was laughing. (*Laughs in several keys, assuming various characters.*) He-he-he! Ha! Hoo-hoo-hoo! That laughter! (*Now he is grave.*) A nightmare. The creature mocked me. I'm afraid I may not be taken seriously in the field of science. And I no longer know what laughter is. I've lost my bearings and it all sounds wrong to me. In the dream I threw a fit. I puffed up with rage like a squid. My psyche let out angry ink. I almost levitated from the bed. And I cried out in many tongues—"*Nefesh, Ish. Ecce homo. Ho thanatos,*" in Hebrew, Latin, Greek, and bared my chest in the dead eye of the floating moon. Seen through the skylight. And . . . (*He staggers a bit.*)

(*Enter* IMOGEN, *with the* TECHNICIAN *close behind her.*)

IMOGEN. Please! You must let me alone!

BUMMIDGE. Imogen, is this one of your sexual lapses?

IMOGEN. Of course not, Mr. Bummidge.

BUMMIDGE (*to the* TECHNICIAN). I'm going to request that you leave this broad alone.

TECHNICIAN. *I,* let *her* alone? (*Laughs.*) Do I wear lipstick, use perfume, waggle my behind? *She* does it.

BUMMIDGE. Such random eroticism is a bad sign. Is your home life so inadequate that you become inflamed before dinner? (*The* TECHNICIAN *laughs.* BUMMIDGE *is enraged.*) Listen to that laugh. Is that neurotic, or is that neurotic? Boy, what decadence! Malignancy in the marrow of society. (*Sits in barber chair.*)

TECHNICIAN (*to* IMOGEN). Is he serious? (*Laughs.*) Is that Bummidge the comedian? He's lost his marbles. (*Exit.*)

BUMMIDGE. You'd better adjust yourself a bit.

(IMOGEN *turns her back to* BUMMIDGE. *He buttons her dress.*)

IMOGEN. It makes me so unhappy. I try to communicate with people, but they only pay attention to my body.

BUMMIDGE (*sympathetic*). Ah, yes.

IMOGEN (*sits on his knee, filially*). That's why I understand when you try to speak seriously, and they insist on treating you like a hambone comedian. They don't know how profound you are.

BUMMIDGE (*he has picked up a hand mirror and is grimacing into it*). I look frightful. Can people accept my message of sanity and health if I look like death or madness?

IMOGEN. But you're making faces before you look.

BUMMIDGE (*to the mirror*). Come on, you! I know your lousy tricks! Humankind must tear itself away from its nonsense.

IMOGEN. I just know you'll win today. It's bound to be a triumph. I feel it.

BUMMIDGE (*eager*). You think so? Thank you, Imogen. You help me bear my burden. What time is it?

IMOGEN. Two-oh-nine.

(*Both rise quickly.*)

BUMMIDGE. Even time is my enemy today. (*Crosses stage.*) I haven't decided on an opening for my TV appearance. What music shall we begin with?

IMOGEN (*looking through records*). Well, we have Wagner, Grieg, and here's "Les Sylphidees."

BUMMIDGE (*stands beside bust of Freud*). Where shall I stand? Here? Maybe with this bust of Freud. Just the two of us. I'll wear a special coat I designed. Aufschnitt is bringing it. He'll want money too.

IMOGEN. Here's classical guitar music.

BUMMIDGE. No, something wilder. Music to denote that I've roused the sleeping Titans of the instincts. Wham! Crash! Thunder! Remember who'll be watching at the Waldorf. I've invited not only psychologists and analysts, but artists, too, and comedians. I want the comedians to see how the analysts laugh. I want the analysts to see how seriously the comedians take me. I must reach everyone. Everything. Heart, reason, comic spirit. I have something tremendous to say. I want to persuade them. Move them. Stun them. . . . Oh, Imogen, I'm frightened. My fingers are freezing.

IMOGEN (*chafing his hands*). You'll do it.

(*She begins to drape the barber chair with tapestries.*)

BUMMIDGE. The enterprise is bigger than me, but there's nobody else to do it. What are these fabrics?

IMOGEN. For a papal-throne effect.

BUMMIDGE. I've also invited the clergy. Where is Bertram? Louie—at the bank with my bad check. I must raise the money. Meantime, my schedule. My inner self. Oh-oh—my sordid sister.

(*Exit* IMOGEN, *as* MADGE *enters.* MADGE *is*

conservatively dressed; the matron from New Rochelle is what she tries to be.)

MADGE. Well, Bummy, what's all the excitement?

BUMMIDGE (*at first trying to charm her*). Madge, dear, what a surprise! But I knew you'd come.

MADGE. Naturally. You were weeping on the phone. I thought you were dying. How nice to see TV equipment again. A reminder of your former greatness.

BUMMIDGE (*more charm*). Madge, I've missed you. You have Mama's sense of humor.

MADGE. The good old days! The big time, the celebrities, the beautiful trips. I'm often sorry for you, Philip.

BUMMIDGE. You think I goofed.

MADGE. Are you as prosperous in psychoanalysis as you were in show business?

BUMMIDGE. How's Harold?

MADGE (*indifferently*). The same. (*They kiss.*)

BUMMIDGE. Madge, I need five thousand dollars.

MADGE (*laughs*). Oh, Bummy!

BUMMIDGE (*behaves oddly when she laughs; puts his ear to her chest like a physician*). That makes you laugh? Laugh again.

MADGE (*pushing him off*). First you read these books, then you turn into a mad scientist. You have to broadcast your message on closed-circuit. . . .

BUMMIDGE. Any minute, Louie Mott will be back from the bank with a bad check.

MADGE. You're putting me on. It's just your idiosyncrasy to live in this warehouse and play psychologist with a dumb doll and a ratcatcher. You didn't let Max and Bella and Pamela take *every*thing!

BUMMIDGE. Why leave yourself off the list? Madge, we're siblings. Sib-lings! From the same womb. It's not like being registered in the same hotel, different nights.

MADGE. I'm grateful to you for what little I have. But don't forget *my* problems. Why, Harold alone—first his prostate, then his coronary, then his eyes!

BUMMIDGE. I wish I were a modest failure like Harold—no broad perspectives, no ideas, adrift with bifocals. All I'm asking is five—

MADGE (*laughs*). Peanuts, to a former millionaire.

BUMMIDGE. Your laughter fascinates me. Mama had a throaty laugh. Yours has little screams and cries in it. (*Imitates.*) But don't make a poor mouth. (*Seizes her wrist.*) You took your diamonds off in the street. I can see the marks.

MADGE (*jerks away her arm*). Your sister will show you how broke she is. My very slip is torn. (*She shows the lace of her slip; it hangs loose.*)

BUMMIDGE (*voice rising*). Oh, my Lord! Your underwear. (*Fingers it.*) Your underwear!

MADGE. Now even you can understand how it is.

BUMMIDGE. Wait! What's happening. My unconscious is trying to tell me something. What, you primitive devil—guilt? Lust? Crime? Tell me! (*Prods his head.*)

MADGE. I hope you're satisfied.

BUMMIDGE. I hear the groaning past—like a bass fiddle. (*He makes deep sounds in his throat.*) Madge, you've mobilized ancient emotions.

MADGE. I can't stay.

BUMMIDGE (*clinging to the lace*). Wait! (*They both tug.*)

MADGE. Let go my slip.

BUMMIDGE. Answer some questions about Williamsburg, where we lived behind the store.

MADGE. Hideous place. I was ashamed to bring a boy to the house.

BUMMIDGE. The scene of my infancy.

MADGE. So, put up a plaque—you're tearing my clothing, Bummy.

BUMMIDGE (*now on his knees*). I'm on an expedition to recover the forgotten truth. Madge, you have no idea what human beings really are; the stages of the psyche—polymorphous, oral, anal, narcissistic. It's fantastic, intricate, complicated, hidden. How can you live without knowing? Madge, look deep! Infinite and deep!

MADGE. You want me to be as confused as yourself? Get out from under my skirt. Freud is passé. Even I know it. (*Rises in haste.*)

BUMMIDGE (*tearing the lace from her slip*). I need this. (*Puts it to his nose.*)

MADGE. You're stripping me!

BUMMIDGE (*rises*). It's coming back to me. Ah! A sealed door has burst open. Dusty light is pouring out. Madge—Madge!

MADGE. I'm leaving.

BUMMIDGE (*stops her*). No. You have to

share this with me—this trauma you gave me at eleven. You caught me fooling with the things in your dresser. We'll re-enact it. Eleven and thirteen. You catch me. Scream for Mama.

MADGE. No, I won't.

BUMMIDGE (*stamps his foot*). You will. You owe it to me. You damaged me. (*Changing tone.*) It'll do you good, too.

MADGE. It's crazy. Twenty-four hours a day, I have to defend myself from insanity.

BUMMIDGE (*leading her to his desk*). This is the dresser. You surprise me as I fondle your step-ins. Clutch my arm and shout *Mama, Mama!*

(*During the following action,* MAX, IMOGEN, BERTRAM, *and* WINKLEMAN *enter and watch.* BUMMIDGE *in pantomime opens a drawer and feels silks with adolescent lasciviousness.* MADGE *falls on him from behind with a sudden cry.*)

MADGE. Mama! Mama!

BUMMIDGE. That's not right. Give it more. Again, and use your nails, too.

MADGE. Mama!

BUMMIDGE. You're beginning to have that bitchy tone I remember. But more.

MADGE (*piercing*). Ma!

BUMMIDGE. More yet. (*Pinches her.*)

MADGE (*fiercely*). You nasty, sneaking little bastard.

BUMMIDGE (*triumphant*). The old Madge. You can hear it yourself.

MADGE (*inspired*). Look what I caught him doing, Mama. I'm the daughter, the only daughter, and I have no privacy in this filthy, foul, horrible hole. Look what I caught him doing. He'll end up with the whores yet. Dirty, snotty, cockeyed little poolroom bum!

BUMMIDGE (*squatting*). Right—right! And I crouch there, trapped, quivering, delight turning to horror. I'm the human Thing—the peculiar beast that feels shame. And now Mama's swinging at me.

(*He ducks.* MADGE *swipes at him with a broom.*)

Don't hit me.

MADGE (*shaken*). Who *am* I, anyway?

WINKLEMAN. If this isn't spooky. Playing with dead relatives.

MAX (*angry*). Hey, what about a minute for a living relative? It's me, your son, your only child. Remember? You damn well will. I'll see to that.

BUMMIDGE. One generation at a time. Bertram, did you see this?

BERTRAM. I sure did. You're all shook up.

BUMMIDGE. A petticoat. Lace. Hem. I was hemmed in. A boy's awakening sex cruelly suppressed. A drawer. Drawer—coffin—death. Poor things that we are. Binding with briars the joys and desires. Madge, you see how I work?

MADGE (*matronly composure beginning to return*). Ridiculous!

MAX. That's what I say. A crude joke.

BUMMIDGE (*turns to him*). Can you tell me what a joke is? (*He starts to leave.*)

MAX. Stay here. Once and for all, we're going to have it out.

BUMMIDGE. Come, Bert—Imogen. Help . . . upstairs. Consultation . . .

MAX. Pop, I warn you. . . .

IMOGEN. An artist like your father is entitled to respect.

MAX. Artist? Feet of clay, all the way up to the ears.

BUMMIDGE. Wink. Your mother. Tante Velma. Bring her.

(*Exit with* IMOGEN *and* BERTRAM, *smelling* MADGE'*s lace.*)

WINKLEMAN. Would anyone pay to see him carry on like this?

MAX. An obsolete comedian? His generation is dead. Good riddance to that square old stuff. . . . What are you doing here, Winkie—you want to con something out of him?

WINKLEMAN. How delightful to hear a youthful point of view.

MAX (*to* MADGE). And what's your angle? You didn't come to give him a glass of Yiddisher tea.

MADGE. I'm his agent still. And Wink's his lawyer.

MAX. Parasites, germs and viruses. You two, and Pamela, the famous Southern choreographer . . .

MADGE. You went through quite a chunk of money yourself. Well, your mother took Bummy's millions; what do you want with him?

MAX. Yesterday my old man raised thirty-five thousand on the property in Staten Island. It's mine in trust. He's spending it on this TV production. . . . Pathetic show-off slob. But I'm going to stop him.

(*Exit angry and determined.*)

WINKLEMAN. What's he up to? He probably owes his bookie. He's forever in a booth having long phone conversations with crooks. Dimes are like goof pills to him. I'm glad I never had a son, never married.

MADGE. Why didn't you?

WINKLEMAN. I know my married friends lead *lovely* lives. But me? (*An elaborate sigh, mocking himself and* MADGE.) There's an old poem—

> To hold a horse, you need a
> rein,
> To hold an elephant, a chain,
> To hold a woman, you need a
> heart. . . .

MADGE. Everyone has a heart.

WINKLEMAN. Every restaurant serves potatoes. (*Pause.*) We served too many potatoes to the old people. Now we're in trouble.

MADGE. Does Bummy suspect anything?

WINKLEMAN. So far I've kept it out of the news. Eight cases of malnutrition. If the inspector breaks it to the papers we're ruined. I socked a quarter of a million into this. I told you we couldn't feed 'em on a buck a day.

MADGE. We could, but your mother took kickbacks on meat, eggs, bread, milk. Face it, she starved them.

WINKLEMAN (*opens a newspaper*). You gave her a hopeless budget. Look at these prices. Pot roast sixty-eight cents. Ground meat forty-three cents. And what about special diets? Some of these people have diabetes, anemia.

MADGE. Why waste time here? I know, we need a lump of money to bribe our way out of a scandal. (*Pause.*) Only think, we used to get half a million a year out of Bummy. But that was before he shot his bolt.

WINKLEMAN. Still, he's never lost his audience sense.

MADGE. He did. He turned solemn, boring, a Dutch uncle, a scold.

WINKLEMAN. Scolding is a career too. Some of our biggest idealists made a fortune, scolding.

MADGE. He should have stuck to his nonsense.

WINKLEMAN. But that's just it. The great public is tired of the old nonsense-type nonsense. It's ready for serious-type nonsense. This psychological set-up is just the thing for a comeback. I would have given him the five thousand.

MADGE. Are you out of your head? Today? When we need every penny?

WINKLEMAN. I still say cooperate. I don't know what those highbrows at the Waldorf will think of his shenanigans, but what would Madison Avenue think?

MADGE (*pondering*). You always were a thoughtful, imaginative angler.

WINKLEMAN (*bows, acknowledging the compliment*). I've been in touch with Fiddleman.

MADGE (*thunderstruck*). Fiddleman! But he wrote Bummy off years ago.

WINKLEMAN. At this moment, Fiddleman, kingpin impresario, bigger than Hurok, is in his limousine en route to the Waldorf to watch the telecast at my invitation. Don't forget, those people are up against it for novelty. A billion-dollar industry, desperate for innovation. It fears death. It has to come up with something big, original, every month.

MADGE. Maybe. But would Bummy go commercial again? He's half nuts over Freud. Just as Freud becomes old hat.

WINKLEMAN. But on the lower levels the social order is just catching up with psychoanalysis. The masses want their share of insight. Anyway, put a five-million-dollar contract under Bummy's nose, and see what happens.

MADGE. Five! My commission is ten per cent. . . . Winkie, I'm sure he still has money stashed away. In this joint, too.

WINKLEMAN. Crafty he's always been.

MADGE. He'd never hide it. He always loved "The Purloined Letter." He'd put his dough in an obvious place. For instance, what's this old valise?

WINKLEMAN. Open it.

MADGE. It's locked. Chained to this barber chair.

WINKLEMAN. He's his own bag man. This is his loot.

MADGE. Tip the chair, and I'll slip the chain out.

WINKLEMAN. Theft? Me? I'm a lawyer. I may be disbarred as it is.

MADGE. Calling me poor-mouth.

WINKLEMAN. Reading me sermons on anality. Ha-ha! That nut. He has charm. You must admit it.

(*Shouting is heard above.*)

My ridiculous cousin. What's he yelling about?

MADGE. Let's have a talk.

(*They go. Enter* BERTRAM *and* IMOGEN, *supporting* BUMMIDGE.)

BERTRAM. Lucky I heard you. You almost fell out of the window.

IMOGEN. Why did you lean out so far?

BUMMIDGE. I saw Louie coming from the bank. Bertram, stall him. Keep the equipment coming.

BERTRAM. I'll do what I can. (*Exit.*)

BUMMIDGE (*calling after* BERTRAM). Bring me a sandwich. Imogen, where's the schedule? (*Reads schedule.*) Dreams. Madge. Aunt Velma. Couch work. I haven't done the couch work. Before the broadcast, I must. There's still a big block. (*Brings out a screen and places it at the head of the couch.*)

IMOGEN. You haven't eaten, haven't shaved.

BUMMIDGE. I can't stop. Must barrel through. This may be one of those central occasions in the history of civilization. I claim nothing personally. I'm the instrument of a purpose beyond ordinary purpose. I may be the only man on the Eastern Seaboard with a definitely higher purpose. What a thing to get stuck with!

IMOGEN. Ready for the session. (*Sits with stenographic pad.*) Number eight-one-oh-eight.

BUMMIDGE (*lying down*). Eight-one-oh-eight. (*Mutters.*) One-oh-eight. (*Rises.*) Imogen, I can't do this alone. I must call in the analyst.

IMOGEN. I understand. The tension must be frightful.

BUMMIDGE (*goes behind the screen and emerges as the analyst, in horn-rimmed smoked glasses*). Well, Mr. Bummidge, how is the psyche today? Lie down, stretch out. How do you intend to proceed? I leave you complete freedom of choice, as an analyst should.

(*Throughout this scene, he wears glasses as the analyst. Removing them, he is the patient.*)

BUMMIDGE (PATIENT). Doctor, things are not good. Last night I dreamed of a male with breasts. After this I found myself in a swimming pool, not swimming, not wet. An old gentleman with a long beard floats by. Such a long white beard, and rosy cheeks.

BUMMIDGE (ANALYST). The material is quite mixed. Water stands for the amniotic bag-of-waters. A beard refers to the father-figure.

BUMMIDGE (PATIENT). I have to tell you, Doctor, I'm fed up with these boring figures in my unconscious. It's always Father, Mother. Or again, breast, castration, anx-iety, fixation to the past. I am desperately bored with these things, sick of them!

BUMMIDGE (ANALYST). You're sick *from* them. Of course. We are all sick. That is our condition. Man is the sick animal. Repression is the root of his madness, and also of his achievements.

BUMMIDGE (PATIENT). Oh, Doctor, why can't I live without hope, like everybody else?

BUMMIDGE (ANALYST). Mr. Bummidge, you are timid but obstinate. Exceptional but commonplace. Amusing but sad. A coward but brave. You are stuck. The Id will not release you to the Ego, and the Ego cannot let you go to the Id.

BUMMIDGE (PATIENT). No resolution?

BUMMIDGE (ANALYST). Perhaps. If you can laugh. But face the void of death. Why do you dream of your father?

BUMMIDGE (PATIENT). But was it Papa? Papa had no beard. In his last illness, he shaved his mustache. (*Sits.*) I was shocked by this. Pa . . . oh, Pa, your lip is so white. Age and weakness have suddenly come over you. Too feeble to count out the *Daily Mirrors*. Mustache gone, face changed, your eyes are so flat, they show death. Death, what are you doing to Papa? You can't . . . Is this the mighty hero I feared? Him with the white lip? Papa, don't go from us.

BUMMIDGE (ANALYST). Don't be deceived by surface feelings, Mr. Bummidge. Remember—ambivalence. You may not really feel compassion. An old enemy and rival is going down. In your heart you also exulted. Maybe you wanted him to live only to see your success.

BUMMIDGE (PATIENT). I don't believe it.

IMOGEN (*applauding*). Good!

BUMMIDGE (PATIENT). You're a hard-nosed man. Why do you prefer the ugliest interpretations? Why do you pollute all my good impulses?

(*Enter* BERTRAM *with a sandwich.*)

I loved my old father. . . . I want to weep.

IMOGEN. He's giving it to himself today.

BUMMIDGE (ANALYST). Did I invent the human species? It can't be helped. I want to cry, too.

BUMMIDGE (PATIENT). My father couldn't bear the sight of me. I had adenoids, my mouth hung open—was that a thing to beat me for? I liked to hum to myself while eating—was that a thing to beat me for? I loved to read the funnies—is that any reason to whip a child? (*Looks into sandwich and mutters to* BERTRAM.) More mustard. (*His voice rises.*) Killjoy! A human life was in my breast, you old killjoy. You attacked all my pleasure sources. But I fought. I hid in the cellar. I forged your signature on my report card. I ate pork. I was a headliner at the good old Trilby. The good-for-nothing became a star and earned millions, making people laugh—all but Papa. He never laughed. What a peevish face. Laugh, you old Turk. Never! Censure. Always censure. Well, you grim old bastard, I made it. You're dead, and I'm still jumping. What do I care for your grave? Let Madge look after it. Down goes the coffin. Down. The hole fills with clay. But Bummidge is still spilling gravy at life's banquet, and out front they're laughing fit to bust. (*He laughs, close to tears.*) Yes, I am that crass man, Bummidge. Oh, how foul my soul is! I have the Pagliacci gangrene. Ha, ha, ha —weep, weep, weep! (*Buries his face in his hands.*)

BUMMIDGE (ANALYST). Do you see the Oedipal strain in this situation? What of your mother?

BUMMIDGE (PATIENT). I saw I'd have Mama to myself. *She* laughed. Oh what a fat throaty laugh she had. Her apron shook.

BUMMIDGE (ANALYST). But what did you want with your mother?

BUMMIDGE (PATIENT). You mean the mother who bathed me in the little tin tub by the kitchen stove? Oh, Doctor, what are you suggesting?

BUMMIDGE (ANALYST). Don't repress the poisonous truth. Go deeper.

BUMMIDGE (PATIENT). How deep?

BUMMIDGE (ANALYST). As deep as you can.

BUMMIDGE (PATIENT). Will there ever be a bottom?

BUMMIDGE (ANALYST). Does the universe have a bottom?

BUMMIDGE (PATIENT). How can I bear it? I, too, am blind. Like Oedipus, far gone in corrupt habits. Oh, hubris! I put a rose bush on Mama's grave. But Papa's grave is sinking, sinking. Weeds cover the tombstone. Oh, shame, Jocasta! (*Collapses on the sofa.*)

IMOGEN. Oh, Mr. Bummidge, marvelous!

BERTRAM. Quite extraordinary. If you perform like this on television, the analysts will give you an ovation.

IMOGEN. He ought to have the Nobel Prize. I think psychology is worth every sacrifice. I love it more and more.

BUMMIDGE. My whole brain is like a sea of light. (*He unlocks the valise. Now* BUMMIDGE *the patient puts twenty dollars on the chair.*) This is one point on which I can't break with orthodox Freudianism. You must pay the analyst.

(*Enter* MADGE.)

MADGE. What is this?

BUMMIDGE (ANALYST) (*picks up the money*). Thank you.

BERTRAM. Better lock up the doctor's money.

IMOGEN. Bank it for him.

BUMMIDGE. He prefers it this way.

(*Exit* BUMMIDGE, *with* BERTRAM *and* IMOGEN.)

MADGE (*going rapidly to the bag*). Money. Loaded.

(*Enter* MOTT.)

MOTT (*angry, shaken*). Boy, is he dishonest! Bummy! Where is he, your brother? He wrote a bad check.

MADGE. Oh, the poor kid. Stalling for a little time.

MOTT. I wouldn't believe the teller. No funds! "What?" I said—Bummy complains there are no more real underlings. Just bureaucrats, full of aggression.

MADGE (*soothing*). You won't pull out because of a few dollars. This broadcast is too important, Louie.

MOTT. No sweet talk, please. It's too late. Thirty years ago you turned me down flat.

MADGE (*shades of youthful allure*). I was a foolish girl. I thought you were attacking me. I'd be smarter now, maybe. You're still so youthful.

MOTT. Excuse me. . . . I didn't mean . . . I think you're lovely. Don't get me wrong. . . . I used to get such a flash when I saw you—in the old days.

MADGE (*with, alas, antiquated wiles*). You're a dear, Louie. Louie, we mustn't let my brother down. He's been a true friend. He saved you from those Boston hoodlums during Prohibition.

MOTT. True. I was in the dehydrated-wine business. Dry, purple bricks. Add water, make wine. Boston Blackie tried to muscle me out.

MADGE. Bummy saved you.

MOTT. Yes, true. I don't deny it. I tell everybody. But . . .

MADGE. He's always helped you. Staked you six different times. Covered for you with women. Even got you this little electronics racket.

MOTT. I admit that. He paid for the course. Enrolled me personally.

MADGE. Don't cry. I know how emotion tears your Hungarian heart.

MOTT (*moved*). Bummy says I suffer from moral dizziness. No roots. Only loose wires. It's all true. But when he gives bad checks . . .

MADGE. Louie, I myself will make it good.

MOTT. You? (*All business again.*) Sorry . . . but not in trade. I have to have cash.

MADGE (*stung*). Don't be nasty! (*Recovers.*) Old friend, I'll let you in on a good thing. We have people watching at the Waldorf. Fiddleman . . .

MOTT (*impressed*). Leslie—the impresario?

MADGE. You know my brother still has greatness in him. He's due for a revival. He'll be bigger than ever. I want you to pipe the performance not only to the scientists but also to an adjoining suite. NBC, CBS, MCA will be watching. With sponsors. The biggest.

MOTT. Is that so? That's clever. Can do. But the money . . .

MADGE. You'll be cut in. There's money for all. I guarantee it. (*She lightly kicks* BUMMIDGE's *bag.*) You want it in black and white?

(*Enter* TECHNICIAN.)

TECHNICIAN. Well, what gives?

MOTT (*wavers, then decides*). We work. Start hooking up.

(MADGE *and* MOTT *shake hands. Exit* MADGE, *right. Enter* BUMMIDGE, *now wearing trousers and a T shirt.* MAX *follows him.*)

BUMMIDGE. Max, don't be destructive.

MAX. Take this crap out.

BUMMIDGE. Oh, Louie. Don't let me down over a few bucks. I know the check was rubber, but—

MOTT. It was a lousy thing to do. But I've thought it over and decided to do the big thing. You have another hour to raise the dough.

BUMMIDGE (*sincerely grateful*). Oh, you generous heart.

MAX (*seizing a cable*). You won't squander my inheritance.

(*He and* BUMMIDGE *and* MOTT *tug at cable.*)

TECHNICIAN. That line is hot. Watch it!

(*The fuses blow. The stage is plunged into darkness. Green and red sparks fly.* BUMMIDGE *screams.*)

BUMMIDGE. My son wants to electrocute me!

MOTT. He blew everything.

BUMMIDGE. Ruined! Lights, lights! Imogen! Bertram!

MOTT. My flashlight! We have to find the fusebox.

(BUMMIDGE *lights a candle,* MOTT *holding a flashlight.* MOTT *and* TECHNICIAN *run out.*)

BUMMIDGE. What the Christ do you think you're doing?

MAX. You're not throwing my dough out the window. I need it today. And the hell with your originality.

BUMMIDGE. Every moment is precious. Guests are waiting at the Waldorf—eminent people.

MAX. Sure, you're the center of everything. Everybody has to wait. You breathe all the air, eat all the food, and lay all the women.

BUMMIDGE (*alters his tone*). Poor child, master this Oedipal hate and love. You're no kid. You mustn't waste fifty years distorting simple facts. Your father is only flesh and blood. Reason is your only help. Think, Max, think for dear life.

MAX. You think. Why wouldn't you be Bella's husband, the public's favorite?

BUMMIDGE. You mean a nice, square, chuckling Santa Claus to entertain the expense-account aristocracy with gags.

MAX. What else are you good for?

BUMMIDGE. I'm all for the emancipation of youth. Even at your age. Fight with authority, yes. But what good is that doggish look, that cool, heavy, sullen expression? My boy, this war of fathers and sons is a racket. Humankind has a horrible instinct for complaint. It's one whole section of the death instinct.

MAX. If we're going to have one of these high-level theoretical talks, you might start by zipping your fly.

BUMMIDGE. Is it open? It isn't worth a glance.

MAX. Showoff! You want to be the great

stud. And I'm just a sample of your marvelous work.

BUMMIDGE. Not true. You're still just one of these child fanatics.

MAX. You made me drive you and that choreographer to Boston on *business*. Well, she was giving me the high sign.

BUMMIDGE. Pamela? Why, you crumb. You—you ex-sperm, you.

MAX. Old egomaniac!

BUMMIDGE. Quick, before you provoke me to terrible violence, what do you want?

MAX. You grabbed my property on Staten Island. That's theft. You owe me a good start in life.

BUMMIDGE. You've had six, seven starts.

MAX (*in earnest*). Come clean with me. What's the reason for this analysis? You latch on to everybody who knocks at the door—delivery boys, ratcatchers, bill collectors. You make them act out psychological situations. Are you kidding your way to God? What makes a comic think he can cure human perversity? It'll only take different forms. If you change your vices, is that progress?

BUMMIDGE. *Only* a comic. Bummidge—he doesn't know Greek or calculus. But he knows what he knows. Have you ever watched audiences laughing? You should see how monstrous it looks; you should listen from my side of the footlights. Oh, the despair, my son! The stale hearts! The snarling and gasping! (*He imitates various kinds of laughter—snarling, savage, frightening, howling, quavering.*) "Ha, ha —I am a cow, a sheep, a wolf, a rat. I am a victim, a killer. Ha, ha—my soul is corked up forever. Let me out. My spirit is famished. I twist, and rub. Ha, ha, ha, I'm an impostor. Can't you see? Catch me, please. No, it's too late. Life has no meaning. Ha, ha, ha, ha, ha!"

MAX. Why take it on yourself? Do your work, draw your dough, and to hell with it.

BUMMIDGE. My work? It's being stolen from me. Sophistication is putting me out of business. Everybody is kidding, smiling. Every lie looks like a pleasantry. Destruction appears like horseplay. Chaos is turned into farce, because evil is clever. It knows you can get away with murder if you laugh. Sadism makes fun. Extermination is a riot. And this is what drives clowns to thought. (*Gravely.*) To thought.

MAX. Why, you have a lump in your throat, Dad.

BUMMIDGE. Max! You called me Dad. Max!

MAX. Pa! (*They are about to embrace. He turns.*) It's just an expression—don't get all shook up.

BUMMIDGE. But you said it. My son!

MAX. Oh . . . everybody's "Dad."

BUMMIDGE. Except your father.

MAX. Don't confuse everything. I'm here to talk business. Listen, Bummy, there's a shipment of toasters from Czechoslovakia, refused by the importer because the cords are faulty. I know where to put my hands on the right Japanese-made cords, and there's an importer from Honduras, waiting.

BUMMIDGE. What have I begotten?

MAX. Another father would be proud. I beat those Czechs down to nothing. Ten grand today gets me thirty tomorrow. For twenty I can buy into a frozen-lasagne operation. All I want from you is three grand. Deduct it from the thirty-five you stole from me.

BUMMIDGE. In other words, you have seven and need three. Max—(*Shifting his chair closer confidentially.*)—why don't you lend me five and take my note for thirty?

MAX (*recoiling*). What, invest in your fantasies?

BUMMIDGE. Me you accuse of fantasy? You with the toasters and the guys from Honduras and Japan who'll make you a fortune in lasagne?

MAX. Is that worse than this giant insanity about psychoanalysis and comedy—this Tower of Babel you're building single-handed? You think you're a new Moses?

BUMMIDGE. In the sandbox I watched over you. In the incubator I read to you.

MAX. Lucky I couldn't understand. You would have addled my brains, too.

BUMMIDGE. I wanted to lead you out of the realm of projections into the light of sanity. But you prefer the institutionalized psychosis of business.

MAX. Old lunatic!

BUMMIDGE. You may not be my child. Men have been tricked before.

MAX. Profound old fart!

BUMMIDGE. Spirochete! Filterable virus! Go bug your mother!

(*Lights go on.*)

MAX. You wait. I'll show you what

things are really like. I'll open your eyes about that Pamela broad; I'll plow you. You hocked my building. (*Jumps up and down in a tantrum.*) You could go to jail.

BUMMIDGE. From a winged boy into a tailored vulture.

MAX. I may have you committed. . . . You wait, I'll be back with a warrant. An injunction. There'll be no telecast. (*In running out he bumps into* MOTT, TECHNICIAN, *and* BERTRAM.) Get out of my way! (*Exit.*)

TECHNICIAN. What's eating him?

BUMMIDGE. My son has wounded me. Wounded me. (*Exit.*)

MOTT. Tough!

(*He and* TECHNICIAN *go about their work.* BERTRAM *is curious, watching.*)

BERTRAM. It all connects, eh? And you'll beam the lecture to the Waldorf?

MOTT. I could transmit it to Iceland, if I wanted . . . I wonder how Bummy'll be.

BERTRAM. Brilliant.

MOTT. Didn't you first come here as the exterminator?

BERTRAM. As soon as I saw the place I realized there were rats. You ask me how? I feel the molding, the baseboards. Rats have greasy fur, and they always run along the wall. Also, a rat drops many pellets.

MOTT. Ugh!

BERTRAM. The expert can date these pellets accurately. By a gentle squeeze of thumb and forefinger. Infallible. He also puts an ear to the wall. Rats must gnaw to survive. Otherwise the fangs'd get too long to chew with, their mouths would lock, and they'd starve. Bummy and I have scientific interests in common. What now?

TECHNICIAN. We hook the A line to this camera.

BERTRAM. Bummy and I hit it off right away. I got involved in psychotherapy. He showed me that to go around killing rats meant I must be compulsive, obsessional. The rat often symbolizes the child, as in the "Pied Piper." The rat also stands for a primordial mystery. Earth mystery. Chthonic. But most of all, my sense of humor fascinated Bummy. I don't laugh at jokes.

MOTT (*curious*). Never?

BERTRAM. I can't. I'm too neurotic. (*He stands between* MOTT *and the* TECHNICIAN.) I have no sense of humor. I only have occasion to laugh.

TECHNICIAN. When does that happen?

BERTRAM. Mainly when I'm tickled.

(*They tickle him. He laughs horribly. They are aghast.*)

MOTT. Stop! Stop it!

BERTRAM. I know. It's pathological. Tickling shouldn't make a normal person laugh.

TECHNICIAN. Let's see.

(*He and* MOTT *solemnly tickle each other.*)

MOTT. I'm knocking myself out trying to understand about the broadcast. Bummy loves big gestures. Does he want to be a college professor?

(*Enter* IMOGEN.)

IMOGEN. Mr. Bummidge doesn't realize how fast time is passing.

(*Enter* BUMMIDGE.)

BUMMIDGE. To understand Max, I must revisit *my* father.

MOTT (*a bit shocked*). But he's dead. . . .

BUMMIDGE. In the unconscious, Louie, there is no time, no logic, and no death.

TECHNICIAN. We need a sound level.

MOTT. I'll set up these lights.

BUMMIDGE. Bertram, you'll play Father. We live behind the candy store in Williamsburg. . . . It was so dark there. Dark. And poverty.

MOTT (*as he works with lights*). Here goes the poor-childhood routine, again. How he fetched wood and coal. Was beaten. Peddled papers. Froze his ears. How there was never real toilet paper in the house, only orange wrappers.

BUMMIDGE. Papa wouldn't allow me to have candy. I stole. I'd wolf down the stale chocolates, choking. Now Bert, as Papa, you discover a Mary Jane wrapper floating in the toilet. You clutch my ear and cry out, "Thief! Goniff!"

BERTRAM (*taking* BUMMIDGE *by the ear*). Thief—goniff.

IMOGEN. I wouldn't want Bertram to pinch my ear.

BUMMIDGE. Harder, Bert. Don't just squeeze—twist. It's essential to feel the pain.

BERTRAM (*warningly*). It's not a good idea to encourage my cruelty.

MOTT. Go on, Bert, turn it on.

(BERTRAM, *face transformed, twists.* BUMMIDGE *screams.*)

BUMMIDGE. That's it! Unbearable! (*Sinks to his knees.*) I haven't felt such agony in forty years. (*Supplicating.*) Papa, Papa! Don't! I'm only a child. I have an innocent craving for sweets. It's human nature. I inherit it from you. Papa, it's the pleasure principle. Jung and Freud would agree.

IMOGEN. He's read simply everything.

BERTRAM. Mine son stealing?

BUMMIDGE (*rises*). No, Bert, Papa had a ballsy voice. (*Imitates his father.*) "By thirteen I was already in the sweat shop, brought home pay. God helped, I got this lousy business. All day buried behind a dark counter with broken feet; with gall bladder; blood pressure. I sell egg-cream, mushmellows, cheap cigars, gumballs—all kinds of *dreck*. But you, your head lays in idleness? Play? Fun? Candy? You'll be a *mensch* or I'll kill you." (*Himself again.*) Desire pierced my glands and my mouth watered. I heard a subversive voice that whispered, "Joy, joy!" It made a criminal of me. (*Reflecting.*) A humorless savage, he was. But I loved him. Why won't my son love me? My father whipped me. (*Bending, he canes himself.*)

MOTT. Now he's a flagellant?

BUMMIDGE (*kneeling, head to the floor*). Flogged.

IMOGEN. Oh, dear, he'll have an attack of Humanitis.

TECHNICIAN. What's Humanitis?

BERTRAM. It's when the human condition is suddenly too much for you.

BUMMIDGE (*sitting on floor*). When he punished me, I took myself away and left an empty substitute in his hands. (*Crawls toward exit, sits again.*) I let myself be punished in effigy. I split up into fragments. There were two, four, an army, and the real Bummidge gets lost. I couldn't keep track. My self got lost. But where is the *me* that is me? What happened to it? (*Rises slowly.*) That was the beginning of my comic method.

(*Explaining the matter to himself, he goes.* BERTRAM *helps him off.*)

IMOGEN. We'll never be ready, at this rate.

MOTT (*to* TECHNICIAN). Run down to the truck and get the rest of those cables.

(*Exit* TECHNICIAN.)

I talked the office into giving Bummy a little more time.

IMOGEN. That's kind of you.

MOTT. That's the kind of friend I am. . . . Imogen. (*Takes her hand.*) As soon as I saw you, I had like a tremendous flash!

IMOGEN (*trying to free her hand*). Mr. Mott!

MOTT. You're my erotic type.

IMOGEN. Don't, Mr. Mott. I can't bear to be a sexy joke. I really am a serious person.

MOTT. This *is* serious. I'm a mature man, mature and single. Most important, I'm youthful. Most mature men in New York are married. The rest are queer, crazy, infected, dangerous. But I—

IMOGEN. No, no. Someone's coming. (*Flees.*)

MOTT. Wait!

(*Exits in pursuit. Enter* PAMELA. *She is, like* MADGE, *highly respectable in appearance, wears a knit suit, a modest hat; she has a slight Southern accent.*)

PAMELA. Bummy? Where are you, dear? (*Looks for him.*) I've come to be with you on this important day. (*Seeing she is alone.*) It's sure to be a bomb. Then what? Then we can stop pretending. I can't wait. Love, science. "Oh, value, value. I'll die without value." What a drag it's turned into. (*Listens.*) Footsteps? I'll surprise him.

(*She steps behind the screen.* MADGE *and* WINKLEMAN *enter.*)

WINKLEMAN. It's set, at the Waldorf. The networks, the agencies—Fiddleman. Phew. It took plenty of doing. Fiddleman will phone, the instant the broadcast is over.

MADGE. Bummy's got to get us off the hook. And listen, I saw Bella at Columbus Circle, waiting for a bus. With all her money, she won't take a taxi.

WINKLEMAN. Was she coming here?

MADGE. Where else? What a tough old broad she's become, loud, brassy, suspicious. She'll throw a monkey wrench in the works if she can.

WINKLEMAN. My contact, the inspector, said he'd wait one day. Tomorrow, at the latest, we have to bribe him. Does Bella know we're in a tight spot?

MADGE. She has everyone followed, investigated. She must suspect. How much is that guy holding us up for? . . . I still wonder about this valise of Bummy's. Could I work my hand in? Is it money? Winkie, it is—it is money!

(PAMELA *now steps out.* MADGE's *wrist is caught in the valise.*)

WINKLEMAN (*trying to cover*). Why, it's Pamela.

PAMELA. Shall we play peek-a-boo? I love

to catch people red-handed. Such a luxurious feeling.

MADGE. Help me.

(*With* PAMELA *and* WINKLEMAN *tugging,* MADGE *frees her hand, and falls backward.*)

PAMELA. You'll have to cut me in. Let's not waste time lying. I understand what you're up to. If Bummy gets offers, you'll need my help, my persuasive powers.

MADGE (*as she and* WINKLEMAN *exchange glances, shrug, accept the inevitable*). Okay.

PAMELA. Life isn't easy for a person like me. If we can put Bummy back in the big time I can lead the respectable life I've always longed for. I'll find out what he's got in this bag. He must carry the keys. Come, let's work out the details.

(*She and* MADGE *go off.*)

WINKLEMAN. Why didn't I retire two years ago, when I was ahead? Lead a quiet life? Write the Comedy Humane of New York? Maybe I was afraid to be left alone with my distorted heart. Oh, here comes my cousin. (*Exit.*)

(BUMMIDGE *and* BERTRAM *enter.* BUMMIDGE *is holding a child's potty.*)

BUMMIDGE. Bert, this was a real piece of luck. This is just like the one Mama sat me on. It will help me to re-enter my infancy.

BERTRAM. You won't sit on that during the broadcast, will you?

BUMMIDGE. I'm not sure. But the Ego has hung a veil, the veil of infantile amnesia, over the earliest facts of life. I have to tear it down. See the bare truth . . .

BERTRAM. Can it be done?

BUMMIDGE. Shush! (*Finger to lips.*) A quiet corner. A bit of reverie. We were all *body* once. Then we split.

BERTRAM. The trauma . . .

(PAMELA *comes in.*)

BUMMIDGE. O Trauma. O Regression— Sublimation! I think this is a good spot.

(*He squats behind the sofa, so that only his head is visible.*)

BERTRAM (*catching sight of* PAMELA). Don't get settled yet.

BUMMIDGE. The mighty of the earth have put us in this position, and it's from here we must make our stand. This is a very small pot.

(BERTRAM *whispers to him.*)

Why didn't you say so?

BERTRAM. Get a grip on yourself.

PAMELA. Lover?

BUMMIDGE (*leaps up*). Just as I was beginning to feel something. Bert, go clear everything with Mott. There's still that headache about the money. Where's Aufschnitt with the coat? If these people trip me up before the broadcast, I'll murder them, cut my throat, and set fire to the building.

(*Exit* BERTRAM.)

PAMELA. What are you doing?

BUMMIDGE. Therapy, dear. Therapy. I didn't expect to see you.

PAMELA. On a day like this? I came to help.

BUMMIDGE. Help? You? That's a new one. Where have you been?

PAMELA. Thinking of you. Of your ideas. Our future. (*Sits on sofa.*)

BUMMIDGE (*pulling up a chair beside her*). Where were you last night? I phoned and phoned.

PAMELA. Why, darling, I was visiting Mother. You forgot.

BUMMIDGE. That madam? The hell you were.

PAMELA. We went out to U.S. One for a pizza pie. I told her how mad I am for you, and how happy we'd be if you became a professor of dramatic psychology. I'm sure Johns Hopkins will offer you the chair.

BUMMIDGE. There are times when I wish you didn't have that vapid look. I do love you, in my peculiar way.

PAMELA. A quiet, decent life. Straight. A real home.

BUMMIDGE. I've figured out the main forms of love. A man can love a woman on the tenderness system. That's very good. Or on the lust system. That's better than nothing. Or on the pride system. That's worse than nothing.

PAMELA. My lover! (*Embracing him.*) Your stomach is rumbling.

BUMMIDGE. It isn't rumbling. It's doing free association.

PAMELA. You're brain all over. Sheer brain.

(*They rise and move toward barber chair.*)

BUMMIDGE. Sweetheart—that diamond anklet—*points*—bought when I was flush. I paid Tiffany twelve grand.

PAMELA. Kiss me, Bummy, hold me close. (*Goes through his pockets; gets the key to the valise.*)

BUMMIDGE. I could pawn it for five. Louie Mott would take it.

(*They are now back to back.* BUMMIDGE *holds* PAMELA's *ankle and removes her shoe. She, meanwhile, is opening the valise.*)

PAMELA. All my life I've looked for nothing but peace, security, quiet, but I always wind up in some absurd mixup.

BUMMIDGE. You have big feet.

PAMELA. You swept me off them like a force of nature.

BUMMIDGE (*removing the anklet*). I've got it! (*They begin to part.*)

PAMELA. It's opening. Thousands! (*Turning to face him.*) You've got thousands here.

BUMMIDGE. But earmarked for a higher purpose. I can't use them.

PAMELA. My anklet! Give it back!

BUMMIDGE. Where did you get the keys? Shut my valise.

PAMELA. You thief!

BUMMIDGE. Calling *me* a thief?

(*He shuts and locks the valise while* PAMELA *tries to recover the anklet.* LOUIE MOTT *runs in.*)

MOTT. Your wife is below—Bella.

BUMMIDGE. Keep her away. . . . I don't want to see her.

MOTT. Can't you hear her hollering?

(*Enter* BERTRAM.)

BERTRAM. Bummy, your estranged Missis!

BUMMIDGE (*to* PAMELA). You'd better go.

PAMELA. Without my jewels? Like hell I will. (*In a temper.*) I came to help you.

BUMMIDGE. The screaming, the scratching, the hairpulling—you'll kill my broadcast. My scientific demonstration—the biggest thing in my life.

PAMELA. I won't go. Get rid of her. I'll wait.

BERTRAM. Where'll we put you? In the toilet? The broom closet?

PAMELA. I'd see you dead first, you creep.

MOTT. What about the fire escape?

PAMELA. I'll wait on the fire escape a few minutes. No longer. It's going to drizzle. And give me the anklet. My diamonds!

BUMMIDGE. Later, dear, later.

(BERTRAM *and* MOTT *hurry* PAMELA *to the fire escape.*) Lock that door. Lock her out. Oh, my character has created another typical crisis. What crazy things we are! The repetition compulsion. (*To statue of Freud.*) O, Master, how deep you were! . . . Imogen! Where is she? Astray again?

That poor sexual waif. Louie, pull the shade.

(*We now see nothing of* PAMELA *but an occasional silhouette through the shade.*) How am I going to get rid of Bella?

(*Exits with* BERTRAM. *Enter* IMOGEN.)

IMOGEN. Did Mr. Bummidge call me?

MOTT. Imogen, as soon as I see you my pulses double and triple. Don't ask a man to waste such feelings.

IMOGEN (*fights him off*). Mr. Mott, don't. It's almost broadcast time.

MOTT. A flash! A red haze. And from below I get this gentle, gentle heat. Here. Feel. . . . Where's your hand?

(*Pounding at the door, right.*)

IMOGEN (*struggling*). Someone's coming.

MOTT (*all over her*). I'm oblivious!

IMOGEN. You look so . . . icky.

MOTT. It's virility. You'll be astonished. Ecstatic. Wait till you see.

(*Someone is battering the door.* MOTT, *blowing a kiss, takes off.* IMOGEN's *stockings are falling. Her dress has been pulled off the shoulders.*)

IMOGEN. How did he get to my garter belt? . . . Who is it? (*Trying to fasten her stockings.*) Coming . . .

(*She opens the door. Enter* AUFSCHNITT, *carrying a coat on a hanger and wrapped in brown paper.*)

AUFSCHNITT (*crossing*). Is Mr. Bummidge here? I am his tailor.

IMOGEN. I thought you were his wife.

AUFSCHNITT. I came with the coat for his broadcast. But, please, I need C.O.D.

(*Enter* BELLA, *large and aggressive, pushing past them into the room, outlandishly dressed. One can see that* PAMELA *has made a study of* BUMMIDGE's *wife in order to give him—or pretend to give him—all that* BELLA *could never conceivably offer.*)

BELLA. Where is he, that miserable man? And where is that cheap lay of his? I'll clobber them both. Then let them go on television with bloody faces.

AUFSCHNITT. Mrs. Bummidge, I have your husband's coat. But this time he must pay.

BELLA. I don't blame you. He wanted squalor, did he? Ugh! No self-respecting dog would throw up here. Imogen, tell him I've come. (*Sits.*)

IMOGEN. I'll try and find him. (*Exits.*)

BELLA. He's somewhere near, listening.

(*She looks for him. We see* PAMELA's *silhouette. We hear the rumble of thunder.*

Enter BERTRAM, *instructed to get rid of* BELLA.)

BERTRAM. Mrs. Bummidge, are you looking for your husband?

BELLA. So, where is the great mental wizard? Ah, it's the ratcatcher. How can he bear to have you around? You must get your suits in the morgue. They smell like it. Where is he?

BERTRAM. They're building that dam in the Nile. Abu Simbel. He wanted to have a look at those Pharaohs before the water covers them.

(*Enter* BUMMIDGE *as a little boy, playing hopscotch.*)

BELLA. So. With his psychology he's gone back to childhood. Here's our kiddy. Some people fade or subside, but not him. He'll go through every agony. How old are you, little man?

BUMMIDGE. Six and a half.

BELLA (*to* BERT). I wish he had gone to Ethiopia, you stooge. (*To* BUMMIDGE.) And are you a good little boy?

BUMMIDGE. Oh, yes, otherwise my parents hit me with rulers. They slash me with straps. So I am.

BELLA. And what are you going to be when you grow up?

BUMMIDGE. With wings, but on foot like a goose.

AUFSCHNITT. Mr. Bummidge, are you ready for the coat?

BUMMIDGE (*looks at coat, pleased*). Ah!

AUFSCHNITT. So pay me.

BUMMIDGE (*face changing, he examines the coat*). What kind of a garment do you call this? Is that a buttonhole? Aufschnitt, have you lost all pride in your work?

AUFSCHNITT. Pride I can't eat. Pride doesn't pay the rent.

(BUMMIDGE *stands on the platform as* AUFSCHNITT *fits the coat, a garment resembling the one worn by the late Mr. Nehru.*)

BUMMIDGE. Affluence is finished. People are poor again. I've paid you thousands.

AUFSCHNITT. Not a cent in two years. In two years! What do I know from affluence!

BELLA (*laughing at* BUMMIDGE *in his coat*). Look at that! What a freak he is! Now you'll pay what—sixty G's—to play the psychiatrist to that howling gang at the Waldorf.

BUMMIDGE. Who's howling? Have you been there?

BELLA. Certainly, and a rummier bunch I never saw. Gobbling up the caviar and lushing champagne. Who *are* those scientists? (*She puts her purse on chair near him and strides about.*)

BUMMIDGE (*when her back is turned examines her purse*). You saw the gate-crashers. You have to expect some of that at every affair. Now Bella, sweetheart . . .

BELLA (*snatches away her purse, shouting*). Don't you pull that sweetheart stuff on me, after my years of misery! I'll never let you snow me again.

BUMMIDGE (*angrily, pursuing her about stage as* AUFSCHNITT *tries to fit the coat*). Then what do you want? These fights with me are your bread and meat.

BELLA. I've come. I have my reasons, never mind. Legally I'm still your wife.

BUMMIDGE. You took everything. Two million dollars' worth of property. I have to squabble with ingrate buttonhole makers.

AUFSCHNITT (*running after him*). Don't move your arms too much. It's a rush job. The seams are weak.

BELLA. I had to stop you from squandering every last cent on broads. Especially this last one—the choreographer. A fancy word for whore.

BUMMIDGE (*again on the platform*). Don't talk like that. She loves me.

BELLA. Love? Don't talk to me about love. I've seen the bills.

(*The* TECHNICIAN *enters with a kit and begins to apply make-up to* BUMMIDGE'S *face.*)

TECHNICIAN. Let's see you under the lights. Your skin is peculiar.

BELLA. You took her to Europe on that disastrous tour of old opera houses. Me you left behind. You think Pamela loves you for your personality? For your brilliant mind? For your bad bridgework? And your belching, and getting up ten times a night to pee, so a person can't sleep? Is that what she loves you for? (*Her eye is caught by an open newspaper.*) Oh, General Electric, down three-eighths.

BUMMIDGE (*smoothing the front of his coat*). Bella, you're distracting me from my great purpose. Keep the two millions, but stop bothering me.

TECHNICIAN. Let me see what I can do with this complexion of yours.

(*He drags a complaining* BUMMIDGE *to the barber chair.*)

BELLA. You sent me on phony errands to clear the decks for your orgies. I was a prisoner for six months on that milk farm in Wisconsin.

BUMMIDGE. Overweight. We had to think of your blood pressure.

BELLA. You put a pistol in my night table to suggest suicide.

BUMMIDGE. Maybe I wanted you to shoot me. (*To* TECHNICIAN.) I want you to emphasize the serenity of my brow and my eyes. Let's eliminate this clownish slant.

BELLA (*as she comes over to the barber chair we hear a rumble of thunder*). Bummy, tell me the truth. What's going to happen? I can't understand. I'm just an old-fashioned, goodhearted broad, an ordinary, practical, loyal woman.

BUMMIDGE (*to* TECHNICIAN). Recognize the party line?

(*The* TECHNICIAN *makes a broad grimace of agreement, but continues working.*)

BELLA. At one time, to me, you were everything. Why don't you explain it to me? . . . I think we're going to have a thundershower.

BUMMIDGE (*with an anxious glance toward the fire escape*). Listen, Bella, in eighteen fifty-nine Darwin published *The Origin of Species;* nineteen hundred, Freud came out with *The Interpretation of Dreams.*

BELLA. For God's sake, Bummy, have a little pride. Don't go tell those intellectuals what they already know. Elementary. They'll laugh at you.

BUMMIDGE. They know *nothing* about laughing. That's my field. . . . Bella, there's something I can't forgive you. Never. (*Leaves the chair.*)

BELLA (*follows him*). What, now? What?

BUMMIDGE. You want to be a business power, a tycoon. Well, you took the old building where I played in youth, the Trilby Theatre, and rented it for a meat market. Where names like "Bummidge," like "Jimmy Savo," used to be on the marquee, we now have "The Kalbfuss Palace of Meats. Pork Butts Today."

BELLA (*giving no ground*). So what?

BUMMIDGE. I'm going to restore it, rededicate it to comedy.

BELLA. Brink back vaudeville?

BUMMIDGE. No. I want to open it to the public. I want to make it a theatre of the soul. Let people come off the street to practice my *Existenz*-Action-Self-analysis. Tickets at modest prices. Let the public step up and work with me—my method.

BELLA. You want to bring psychoanalysis to the vaudeville stage?

BUMMIDGE. You can't get the whole public on the couch. Theories have to be socially active, broad. The couch is for higher-income brackets. Bella, people make a career of their problems, a racket of their characters, an occupation of their personality traits. Take yourself, for instance. (*Parodies her.*) "An old-fashioned, good-hearted broad. To me you were everything." . . . How you belt it out! The throbbing heart! And love! Jesus, what a production you make of love! Warfare, that's what you really love. You spend your whole life playing the dramatic values of your Devotion, your Fate, your Sacrifice and Struggles. What corn! Aren't you ashamed of yourself? Bella, only laughter can save you from this. Such elaboration of personality is a joke.

BELLA (*stunned by this*). Reopen the Trilby. That's Utopian. Crazy. . . . Oh, one man's jokes are another man's theories. I don't get it.

BUMMIDGE. In this valise I have almost enough to buy the lease from Kalbfuss. Oh, Lord, and I have to scrape up the balance for Louie. (*Runs to desk.*) Somewhere in this mess is the receipt from Tiffany's. (*Pulls out drawers.*) Ah, here. More than I thought. Fourteen thousand.

AUFSCHNITT. I don't dare leave this coat without you pay me. My wife warned me.

BUMMIDGE. Bella, maybe you've got a few bucks.

BELLA. A headache from your theories, that's what I've got.

(*Enter* BERTRAM.)

Do you have aspirins in the medicine chest? I'm sure you have rats in that bathroom. Where's the light? (*Exits.*)

BERTRAM. I'll show you. . . . Rats?

AUFSCHNITT. Mr. Bummidge, you say plain, ordinary people could understand your psychology? I have plenty of trouble in my family. A sad daughter who won't even get out of bed.

BUMMIDGE. Single?

AUFSCHNITT. The bed or the daughter? . . . Both single.

(*Enter* IMOGEN.)

BUMMIDGE. Perhaps you and I could work together. Free of charge, of course.

AUFSCHNITT. For nothing?

IMOGEN. Mr. Bummidge, you have very little time.

BUMMIDGE. For instance.

IMOGEN. He's never too busy to hold out a hand to misery.

BUMMIDGE. Now Aufschnitt, listen to me.

IMOGEN. It's started to rain.

BUMMIDGE. Bertram, find an umbrella for you-know-who. Aufschnitt, I am six years old. My parents have bought me my first pair of galoshes for school. Gleaming black rubber, and such a delicious smell. They make beautiful tracks in the snow. But my mother warns me—the usual: We are poor people. You lose everything. Don't you come home without those galoshes. Papa will kill you stone dead!

(BERTRAM *frantically looks for an umbrella.* PAMELA *tries to make herself heard through the glass door.* BERTRAM *can find nothing but a little girl's pink parasol. When he opens the door a crack,* PAMELA *tries to fight her way in. He succeeds in locking the door.*)

BERTRAM. It's raining out there. A regular monsoon.

BUMMIDGE. Listen, Aufschnitt, my first-grade teacher, Miss Farnum, was a youthful rhubarb blonde. You be Miss Farnum, and I'll be six.

AUFSCHNITT. What should I do?

BUMMIDGE. Act and feel like my teacher.

(*Enter* MAX *and a private detective,* MR. GALLUPPO.)

MAX. Pop, Mr. Galluppo, here, is my lawyer, a private investigator.

BUMMIDGE. He looks like a blackmailer. I have no time for this.

MAX. Listen to his report.

GALLUPPO (*gazing about*). So this is what happens to stars in retirement. Substandard housing.

AUFSCHNITT. I'm not sure I can imitate a young teacher in a long dress.

BUMMIDGE. Of course you can. Do it for your daughter. This can help her. Like this. (*Enacts Miss Farnum.*)

AUFSCHNITT. Like this? (*He tries.*)

BUMMIDGE. Quite good for a first effort.

AUFSCHNITT. How could it help my poor daughter Joy?

BUMMIDGE. Concentrate with me, Aufschnitt. The other kids with their sheepskins and boots have gone home. But where are my galoshes?

(*He and* AUFSCHNITT *hunt under chairs for the galoshes.*)

MAX (*to* GALLUPPO). Give your report on his friend Pamela. Where was she last night?

GALLUPPO. In premises at Six-Y Jones Street. She had relations with a gentleman of the other sex. Every night a different person.

BUMMIDGE (*with some hauteur*). You must have the wrong party. Miss Sillerby is an artist from a distinguished Southern family. (*To* AUFSCHNITT.) Now, Miss Farnum, I'm in a terrible spot. First you scold me. Then you make fun of me. You stick out your tongue. I start to bawl. . . . Max, why do you do this?

AUFSCHNITT. Now little boy, you'd better not cry.

(*Enter* MOTT. *The* TECHNICIAN *appears above.*)

MOTT. We've got to have a sound level, Bummy. Swing out the boom, John.

GALLUPPO. Is this a photo of the party in question?

MAX. You bet. Show it to my father.

IMOGEN (*trying to interpose herself*). Oh, don't do that. You'll upset everything.

BUMMIDGE. That's what he wants to do. (GALLUPPO *shows photo to* AUFSCHNITT, *who can't bear to look.*)

AUFSCHNITT. Why me? I don't recognize these people. They have no clothes on.

GALLUPPO. Monday with a Wall Street broker. Tuesday with a bartender. Wednesday the super of her building.

BUMMIDGE. I'm crying over my galoshes. I'm not a day over six.

AUFSCHNITT. What a little crybaby! (*Puts out his tongue.*)

BUMMIDGE. She tried to make me laugh at my dread. I hated her for it. But she was right. She tried to teach me to reject ridiculous pain. (*He pounds at door of the fire escape, where we see* PAMELA'S *anguished figure in silhouette.*)

TECHNICIAN. What's he doing? What goes on?

IMOGEN. It's a cloudburst. They always affect him.

MOTT. Let's try those lights. Bert, give a hand here. Bummy, you've got only twenty minutes.

BUMMIDGE. What? (*Shakes his fist at door, then turns from it.*) Louie, take these rocks. Tiffany's. Here's the receipt. Worth eight grand at least. Oh Bummidge, you sucker, you patsy, you mark! Max, take this snooper away. It's nearly time for my broadcast. Louie, let's go.

AUFSCHNITT. Crybaby! Crybaby!

BUMMIDGE. I should have laughed, not wept. (*Tries laughter.*)

MAX. There'll be no broadcast.

(*Enter* BELLA.)

Mother, what are you doing here?

BELLA (*pointing to* GALLUPPO). Where did he come from? Does he do work for you too? I pay him fat fees. He takes from us both for the same information, I bet.

GALLUPPO. I didn't know you was related.

AUFSCHNITT. Crybaby! Crybaby!

BELLA. Shut up! My head is splitting.

(*Enter* WINKLEMAN *and* MADGE.)

I knew they'd show up!

TECHNICIAN (*holding up microphone*). Let's hear you speak a word or two.

BUMMIDGE. Help! Help!

(GALLUPPO *forces him to look at the photo.*)

Oh, the bitch!

(*There is a sharp rapping at the door. Lights are tested. Cables are draped over furniture. Enter a messenger.*)

What do you want?

MESSENGER. Western Union.

IMOGEN. I'll take the wire.

(*Enter* AUNT VELMA *in a wheelchair. She carries a cane.*)

WINKLEMAN. Here's Mother.

BUMMIDGE. Tante Velma! She's come!

VELMA. Why is it so crowded and noisy?

BUMMIDGE. You were midwife at my birth. From the sightless universe into your hands!

(*Telephone rings.*)

Bertram, answer.

BERTRAM. Shouldn't I open that door?

BELLA. Is that a woman screaming somewhere?

BUMMIDGE. The wind! Wind and rain!

MADGE (*persuasive, cooperative*). Now listen to me, Bummy.

BUMMIDGE (*mistaking her tone*). You and Kinkie are plotting against me. A conspiracy.

MADGE. But that's just paranoid.

AUFSCHNITT. You must pay me or I can't let you have the coat. (*Tries to remove it.*)

BUMMIDGE. Bella, won't you get this needle-pusher off my back?

BELLA. How much?

AUFSCHNITT. One twenty-five.

MAX (*tries to stop her*). Mother, don't.

BELLA (*fishing money out of her bosom*). You've ruined my life, but thank God I'm comfortably ruined.

BERTRAM. It's Doctor Ratzenhofer on the phone. He says how long will the broadcast be? He has appointments.

BUMMIDGE. Oh, Doctor Ratzenhofer?

WINKLEMAN. How can you start in all this chaos?

MOTT. How do I know these diamonds aren't paste?

IMOGEN. The wire is from Kalbfuss. He's standing by.

BUMMIDGE. Kalbfuss! (*Throws his arms upward.*) Thank heaven for his loyalty.

AUFSCHNITT. The seams! The seams are opening!

BELLA. There are the fruits of my husband's originality. Confusion!

VELMA (*rapping with her cane*). I think this floor is sagging.

BUMMIDGE. A mere symbol, Tante.

WINKLEMAN. Look here, Cousin, you've got Madge and me all wrong.

BELLA (*pushing forward*). We know about you. Starving old people. Conditions worse than Andersonville. Investigations. The whole story about to break. A hell of a note.

BUMMIDGE. You've all come to prevent my broadcast.

MAX. That's right.

GALLUPPO (*pulling out a paper*). I have a restraining order.

BELLA (*to* MAX). Don't try to shaft your father. He's got it coming from me.

BUMMIDGE. You want to make a farce of my serious intentions. But someone has to do something. Even if that someone is only me.

(MOTT *is about to hit the diamonds with a hammer to see if they are real.*)

Hold it!

(BUMMIDGE *restrains* MOTT. *There is silence. Then* BUMMIDGE *laughs strangely.*)

Ladies and gentlemen, I invite you to witness a typical moment of human existence, showing mankind as it makes the most of its universal opportunities, amid all the miracles of light and motion. . . .

(*The next group of speeches is spoken together, jumbled.*)

MAX. Now he's Cassandra.

MADGE. I never know what he's talking about. Let's start.

VELMA. Why did I even come? Family feeling? Big deal!

GALLUPPO. Fifty bucks an hour, I charge.

WINKLEMAN. We can't let this go on!

(*They fall silent.*)

BUMMIDGE (*violently*). Stop! Why are you here? I am your food, your prey. You have filled my life with stench and noise; dogged me night and day; lived on me like green fungus on pumpernickel. But you won't be happy till I'm crucified? You, a Roman crowd? I, an Asiatic slave?

MAX. Man, now he's on the Jesus kick.

BUMMIDGE (*holds up both hands, fingers widely spread*). Shall I submit?

WINKLEMAN (*trying vainly to soothe him*). Please come off it, Bummy. Don't be carried away.

MADGE. You'll forget your purpose.

VELMA. This is New York. Nineteen sixty-five A.D.

BUMMIDGE. All right, where is that staple gun? Imogen. (*He stands on the desk. IMOGEN approaches with the stapler.*) Staple Bummidge to the wall.

(IMOGEN *hesitates*. BERTRAM *staples* BUMMIDGE's *cuffs. His arms are outstretched.*)

MAX. The martyrdom bit!

WINKLEMAN. Wasted! He's using up his energy before the broadcast. Wait, Bummy.

MADGE. Save it for the cameras.

TECHNICIAN. I'm impressed.

GALLUPPO. Maybe I am a lousy crook, a double-dealing fink, but this is blasphemy.

IMOGEN. Not with Mr. Bummidge. It's real! Can't you see he's in pain? He's having an attack of Humanitis. Catch him.

BELLA. No, Bummy, no! I take it all back.

(PAMELA, *drenched, with the parasol, has forced her way in. She is gasping.*)

MOTT. We got just a little time before the broadcast. (*To* TECHNICIAN.) Let's take a five-minute break.

(*They kneel and shoot dice.*)

BELLA (*as* PAMELA *collapses at* BUMMIDGE's *feet*). There's the whore in the picture. Now we got the full cast.

MOTT. Okay. Roll 'em.

BUMMIDGE. Forgive them, Father, for, for . . . What comes next?

CURTAIN

ACT TWO

Minutes later: BUMMIDGE *has been extricated from his coat, which hangs empty on* the wall. *Onstage are* PAMELA, *who has wrapped herself, shivering, in the tapestry on the barber chair;* AUFSCHNITT, *who is taking down the coat in order to mend it;* MADGE, *explaining the situation to* MAX *and* GALLUPPO. BELLA *appears skeptical but is really (as always) passionately in pursuit of her life's project: involvement with her husband's magical peculiarities.* TANTE VELMA, *legs boldly crossed, sits in her wheelchair smoking a cigar and studying business documents. Her kindly old eyeglasses have been pushed up on her forehead; without them she looks tough and severe.* MOTT *is looking at his wristwatch.*

MOTT. We may have to call it all off.

MADGE. Nonsense! Too much is riding on Bummy for us all. Max understands now.

MAX. I see what you mean. I get it. He's going to do this anyway. We can't overcome his peculiar ideas, so we exploit them instead. Smart.

BELLA. You *think* you can outsmart him. Wait. You'll see how shifty and shrewd he is.

MADGE. Winkie is in the library with him, explaining that we offer full cooperation. All of us.

GALLUPPO. But what will CBS, NBC, MCA, Fiddleman, and the rest see in his shenanigans?

MAX. Madge and Winkie are right. There's nothing so extreme or kookie that the mass media won't try to use it. We talk of atomic explosion and population explosion, but in the twentieth century there's also an explosion of consciousness. Society needs the imagination of its most alienated members. They want to defy it? It doesn't care. It pays them millions. Money reconciles all tendencies.

VELMA. You're your father's son. You sound like him.

PAMELA. I'm soaked to the skin.

BELLA (*acid*). Undress. By now everybody knows how you look in the nude.

PAMELA. Without your corsets, you must be like a sea cow.

BELLA. The government should label people the way it does meat—prime, choice, and dog food.

PAMELA. You have a plain label—the ball-breaking wife.

(BELLA *is about to strike* PAMELA *with her purse;* PAMELA *prepares to defend her-*

self with her high-heeled shoe; MAX *re-strains his mother.*)

MOTT. Minutes ticking away!

VELMA (*to* AUFSCHNITT *as he passes with the coat*). And what's he doing?

AUFSCHNITT. Mending the raiment. (*Exits.*)

MAX. The thing is, what will I get out of it?

MADGE. You? You're the heir.

VELMA. With Papa in the big money again? And doting on his sonny boy? Ha, ha!

PAMELA. So far, I've lost my anklet.

(MOTT *covertly lifts it from his pocket and looks at it.*)

MADGE (*suspicious*). Louie . . .

(*Enter* IMOGEN *and* BERTRAM. BERTRAM *carries an infant in his arms.*)

BERTRAM. Bummy wanted to see a little child. Where is he?

(*Enter* BUMMIDGE *with* WINKLEMAN.)

IMOGEN. Mr. Bummidge—an infant!

BUMMIDGE (*excited*). Undress it. I must see the original human material. The essential thing.

BELLA (*taking charge*). This child could use a clean diaper.

BERTRAM. Her mother is an alcoholic. I had to give her a twenty-dollar deposit.

IMOGEN. In the bar, across the street.

BUMMIDGE (*enraptured*). Look at this freedom! How the little belly rises and falls. The state of Nature! Life drifts into the infant. . . . (*Laves himself with air.*) Drifts, drifts. Precious, blessed infancy. Everything loathsome about the human species is forgiven time after time, and with every child we begin again.

GALLUPPO. I don't dig it.

IMOGEN (*explaining*). Heaven lies about us in our infancy. Then comes repression. We lose Eternity. We get shut up in Time.

VELMA (*gestures with her cigar, looks upward*). Big deal. I delivered thousands of them, poor things.

MOTT. Bummy, it's practically zero hour.

(AUFSCHNITT *enters with the coat.*)

BUMMIDGE. Take the baby, Bertram. Wait, I must have one last look. (*He looks tenderly at the infant, as if to memorize it.*)

AUFSCHNITT. I fixed the seams.

BERTRAM. I'm out of pocket twenty bucks.

BUMMIDGE (*as he is getting into the coat, looks at* BELLA). Bella . . .

BELLA. On twenty bucks the mother'll go on a two-day binge. Oh, well . . . (*Digs again into her bosom.*)

(BERTRAM *takes money and goes, with the infant under one arm.*)

PAMELA (*comes forward*). Bummy, I have to have dry clothes. And where's my anklet?

BUMMIDGE (*hurries to large wicker clothes hamper, opens it*). Here's something for you. (*Struck by an idea.*) There's something here for each of you. . . . Ah, yes. For each and every one. Marvelous! You'll all participate with me in the broadcast. Louie, throw away the old format.

WINKLEMAN. Ad lib? Now? But Bummy —think!

BUMMIDGE. I've never been so lucid. That little infant shows me the way. All impulse. Impulse is the soul of freedom. My deeper self is telling me what to do. (*Clutches his head, but smilingly.*)

PAMELA (*unfolding the garment*). Why, this is nothing but a burlesque stripper's outfit!

BUMMIDGE (*to* WINKLEMAN). You said everyone would stand behind me.

MADGE. To a man! I remember Doctor Ehrlich and the magic bullet.

WINKLEMAN. And Semmelweiss, and Pasteur!

MOTT. Don't forget Richard Nixon. How against him they all were until he went on television with that little dog.

BUMMIDGE. And Pamela? You, too?

PAMELA (*somewhat reluctant*). Yes, Bummy. You'll give back my diamonds, won't you? (*Exits.*)

BUMMIDGE (*as he watches her go*). The forms—the many forms that suffering takes. The compulsion to suffer. But for each and every one of these there is a method to evade suffering. Delusion. Intoxication. Ecstasy. And comedy. I must remember that for the broadcast. Now listen, all of you. I'm going back to my sources and you'll all wear costumes and step forward as I call on you. Imogen, hand them out. Louie, the hoodlum you were during Prohibition.

(MOTT *goes to change.*)

Madge, this flapper's dress with fringes.

(MADGE *goes.*)

Max, you'll represent my father. You resemble him.

(MAX *puts on a shopkeeper's apron and a broad-brimmed hat.*)

Bella, a bridal gown.

(BELLA *goes.*)

Winkie. These rompers.

WINKLEMAN. Must I?

BUMMIDGE. Your cooperation is essential.

(WINKLEMAN *goes.*)

There's a reason why they're all so obliging, Woe unto you when all men shall speak well of you.

(*Enter* BERTRAM.)

But it's woe anyway, wherever you look. Imogen, dear, will you assist?

IMOGEN. Of course, Mr. Bummidge.

VELMA. Where do I come in?

BUMMIDGE. Give the old bat this hat with fruit. Bertram, in my unconscious it turns out you have female characteristics. Wear this dress.

BERTRAM (*accepting*). Female? Curious!

BUMMIDGE. Isn't it? (*He marvels briefly.*)

IMOGEN. Mr. Bummidge, are you sure you know what you're doing?

BUMMIDGE. It is the right thing, my child—whatever *that* is. I feel inward confidence. Aufschnitt . . .

AUFSCHNITT. Am I in the broadcast too? I've never been on television.

BUMMIDGE. Man! That's who you'll be. Repressed, civilized Man. Poor humankind in bondage. Thread in your fingers and chains on your feet.

GALLUPPO. And me?

BUMMIDGE. Sly, smiling, menacing . . . I have it! Bella's father. Grinning, then violent. Yes!

(*Enter* TECHNICIAN.)

TECHNICIAN. Where's the opening setup?

(*Enter* MOTT *dressed as a neighborhood tough.*)

MOTT. Places! Let's have lights.

BUMMIDGE. Louie, iris in on me here, by this statue of Freud.

IMOGEN. I'm dying of excitement!

MOTT. Time! Five, four, three, two, one —you're on.

BUMMIDGE (*begins an attempt at smiling refinement*). Ladies and gentlemen of the psychiatric world. Honored guests. You know me, of course, as a comedian. But today I invite you to put away that old image. Look at this person, one of yourselves, a human being. See this hair, these eyes, these wattles, stubby hands, a heart that beats: Philip Bummidge, sixty years old. Sixty-one years ago I was literally nothing. I was merely possible. Then I

was conceived, and became inevitable. When I die, I shall be *im*possible. Meanwhile, between two voids, past and future, I exist. Medically, I seem quite sound, though not in my first youth. Strong as a horse. (*Feels his muscles.*) Twenty-twenty vision. (*Pulls down his underlids.*) Powerful lungs. (*Shouts.*) Hoy! (*Pauses.*) Nothing wrong with the organism, hey? But up here. (*Suddenly gloomy.*) My mind! Inside my skull. My feelings, my emotions. (*Quite tragically.*) My personality, my mind! My mind has a will of its own. This psyche of mine is an outlaw. Can this be the normal human state? Is this what we are meant to be? Oh, my character! How did I ever get stuck with these monstrous peculiarities? Why so vivid within, so dead outside? I feel like a museum of all the perversity, sickness, and ugliness of mankind. Oh, Death, take me or leave me, but don't haunt me any more. But you see, ladies and gentlemen, brothers and sisters, it's because of death that we are individuals. Organisms without death have no true identity. But we are what we are owing to our morbidity. (*In earnest.*) I bless the day when I discovered how abnormal I was. I read all the books and, never forgetting that I was an actor, a comedian, I formed my own method. I learned to obtain self-knowledge by doing what I best knew how to do, acting out the main events of my life, dragging repressed material into the open by sheer force of drama. I'm not solely a man but also a man who is an artist, and an artist whose sphere is comedy. Though the conditions may be impossible, laughter in decay, there is nothing else for me to do but face those real conditions. (*The lecturer.*) A general increase of consciousness in civilized people accompanied by a decrease in the value they attach to themselves and one another is a prime condition. (*Dissatisfied with his own pomposity.*) But rather than lecture, I prefer to illustrate. Let me introduce, briefly, certain friends and relatives.

(*In the following scene, people come forward as called, in their costumes.*)

This is Aunt Velma, who delivered me. This, my tender bride. This is my son, who will represent my father. This proper lady is my sister. This is my colleague, Bertram, a mother figure.

(*Enter* WINKLEMAN *in a Lord Fauntleroy costume.*)

Oh, yes, this is my cousin Winkie, whose mother always dressed him absurdly.

WINKLEMAN. Excuse these knickers—one must humor a client, a man of genius with brilliant ideas.

(*Enter* PAMELA, *wearing her strip-tease costume.*)

BUMMIDGE. This little lady has offered to represent the grandeur and misery of the erotic life. She's something of an expert on this subject. These unfortunates are part of me, and I of them. Now, my method, on the most elementary level, opens a channel to the past. Like that old song (*sings*) "*I'm just a kid again, doin' what I did again.*"

(*All sing in chorus. He leads them forward. The group stands about him.*)

I am convinced that lies are bad art. I reclaim my freedom by acting. I tear down the Bastille of censorship and distortion. No more isolation. Break out of jail! We must leap beyond repression. But look at these miserable creatures. I shall start with one of them, my old aunt. (*Wheels her forward.*) Tante, you bridge many generations, and you have a long memory.

VELMA. Like an old filing case, I am.

BUMMIDGE. Was mine a difficult birth?

VELMA. On your father's scales you weighed fourteen pounds. You gave lots of pain. It was tough, but I pulled you through.

BUMMIDGE (*to camera*). She thinks she's being funny. (*To her.*) Now, when was I weaned?

VELMA. Late. On the way to Prospect Park, on your mama's lap, your feet were dragging on the floor of the streetcar. You didn't want the breast and your mama said, "All right, I'll give it to the conductor."

BUMMIDGE (*to camera*). An old gag. She's full of them. They're really sadistic threats in comic form. Now, when was I toilet-trained?

VELMA. My sister and I kept clean houses. As soon as you could sit up.

BUMMIDGE (*somberly*). This is very bad!

MADGE. Was it so serious?

BUMMIDGE. Ah, Madge—my sister, my poor companion in abuse. Terrible! They ruined us. This is horrible information.

BELLA. Don't take it so hard.

BUMMIDGE. I never had a chance. How can I hold my head up?

VELMA. But nobody could keep you clean. You made in your pants. You were a wild, disobedient boy, like your Uncle Mitchell.

BUMMIDGE. Yes, tell everyone about him. (*To television audience.*) She thinks she's irresistible.

VELMA. He played baseball. Shortstop. The bus with his team fell in the Passaic River. It damaged his brains. On the Sea Beach Express, he exposed himself to some girls from the shirtwaist factory.

BUMMIDGE (*to camera*). This is her lifelong patter. Old lobster shells of wit. The meat is gone. Tell the people more. . . .

VELMA. Then there was Uncle Harold. He was a saxophone performer. On the Weehawken Ferry. During the War, he passed the hat for the boys Over There.

MAX. But he put the money in his own pocket.

VELMA. He needed a start in business. That branch of the family did all right. Furthermore . . .

BUMMIDGE. Enough. She comes on like a charming old thing. From her jokes, you'd never guess what viciousness there was in her.

(VELMA *spreads her mouth with her fingers and makes a horrid face at him.*)

WINKLEMAN (*sternly*). Mother! On the air!

VELMA. Should I say more? Should I tell about Aunt Rose? (*Parodying her own family sentiments.*) All Perth Amboy listened in the street when she sang. Such a woice!

BUMMIDGE. No, enough. Take her away, Winkie.

VELMA. Give me a light, my child. (*Cigar, again.*)

BUMMIDGE. Infinite sadness salted with jokes. But . . . (*Lecturing.*) My method —as follows: I have trained myself to re-enter any phase of my life, at will. By bouncing a ball, rolling a hoop, sucking my thumb, I become a child. When I want to visit the remote parts of my mind, I take to the couch. (*Lies down.*) Doctor, I had a dream. (*As analyst.*) Tell me all about it. (*As patient.*) I dreamt I was at sea in an old shoebox. (*Rising.*) Thus, ladies and gentlemen, I was able to isolate a hard core of problems, by adapting the methods of Freud—that Genius! (*Turns emotion-*

ally to bust.) The disease I discovered in myself, I call Humanitis. An emotional disorder of our relation to the human condition. Suddenly, being human is too much for me. I faint, and stagger. (*He enacts the sick man. Holds dialogue with himself.*) "What's the matter, Bummidge? Don't you like other human beings?" "Like them! I adore them! Only I can't bear them." "I love 'em like a dog. So ardent, so smoochy. Wagging my tail. This sick, corrupt emotion leaks out of me." I don't have the strength to bear my feelings. (*Lecturing.*) This is the weakness of my comedy. When the laughing stops, there's still a big surplus of pain.

BERTRAM. He's going to explain about the Pagliacci gangrene.

BUMMIDGE. The Pagliacci gangrene! Caused as all gangrene is by a failure of circulation. Cut off by self-pity. Passivity. Fear. Masochistic rage. Now (*smiling and bowing*) I shall ask you to follow me into the library, where I have prepared an exhibit of charts and diagrams.

(*Exits, followed by the* TECHNICIAN *with camera and by* MOTT.)

GALLUPPO. You think you sell this? I'd walk out. Worst show I ever saw.

MAX. It's like a lecture at the New School, but crazier.

IMOGEN. Every word of it is clear to me.

BERTRAM. Plain as day.

WINKLEMAN. Take it from me, the industry is hard up for novelty. There is something here for the great public. (*Desperate.*) It's got to work.

MAX. If it doesn't, I've lost out on one of the biggest deals that ever came my way. My mother turned it down.

BELLA. Damn right I did.

PAMELA. I want my jewels back, at least. In this getup I deserve some consideration.

BELLA. It's a miracle you can keep them on those skinny wrists and ankles.

PAMELA. Better to be petite than built like a lady wrestler.

BELLA. Petite! Dry bones. You could do a fan dance with fly swatters.

(*They begin to fight.*)

GALLUPPO. Here, break it up. (*Takes a police grip on* PAMELA.)

MADGE. A cat fight is all we need. For heaven's sake, you've got to keep in line. If this fails, Winkie and I stand to lose a fortune.

BERTRAM. Bummy won't fail.

WINKLEMAN (*sweating, he tries to persuade them*). Freud has filtered down to the broad masses. He used to belong to the intellectuals and the upper middle class, but now the proles demand their share of this. As the standard of living rises, people claim the privilege of sickness, formerly one of the aristocratic prerogatives.

VELMA. Listen to my son! I had only one, but with the brains of five.

WINKLEMAN. Look! There's all this machinery of entertainment, publicity. A billion-dollar industry with administration, bureaucracy. It needs fresh material every week. And out there are millions of Americans, asking for nourishment. Bread. The industry gives 'em every substitute it can invent. Faith. I ask you to have a little faith. Haven't I always marketed whatever Bummy dreamed up?

IMOGEN. Mr. Bummidge isn't interested in being marketed.

MADGE. Isn't he? We'll see about that.

VELMA. Wheel me back. Here he comes.

(TECHNICIAN, *led by* MOTT, *comes in with camera.*)

MOTT. One side. Clear it. Get Bummidge as he enters the doorway. Go, camera.

BUMMIDGE. Such, my friends, is the Pagliacci gangrene, crying as you laugh, but making a fortune meanwhile. Now let us have a brief look at my career. At twenty I sing and dance at the Old Trilby. (*Sings and shuffles.*)

"Oh I went to school with Maggie Moiphy
And Maggie Moiphy went to school with me-e-e.
I tried to get the best of Maggie Moiphy,
But the sonofagun, she got the best of me."

(*Another routine.*)

"Lady, lady, put out your can
I think I hear the garbage man."

(*As lady, answering.*)

"But Mister, I don't want any garbage."

(*Lecturing again.*)

By 1927 we're at the top of our fields, Coolidge and me. I tap-dance in the White House portico. (*Hoofing.*)

BELLA. I almost burst with pride.

BUMMIDGE (*strutting*). Three agents, two bodyguards, a fleet of Dusenbergs.

Five paternity suits in one year. My own cigar vault at Dunhill's next to the Prince of Wales. I charter the Twentieth Century to take me to Saratoga for the races. People laugh at everything I say. "Nice day." (*To group.*) Laugh!

(*They laugh uproariously.*)

You see how it worked. "Nice day."

(*They laugh again. He sneezes.*)

AUFSCHNITT. *Gesundheit.*

BUMMIDGE. Now a dark subject. I should like to reenact the circumstances of my marriage. I shall represent myself. Bella— Bella . . .

BELLA (*pushed forward*). Yes.

BUMMIDGE. You be Bella. The other characters will emerge as they are needed. Now, Bella, what were the first words that kicked us off into matrimony?

BELLA. The first words? It was on the telephone. I need a telephone.

(IMOGEN, *stooping, out of the way of camera, brings two phones. They ring.* BUMMIDGE *and* BELLA, *back to back, converse.*)

BUMMIDGE. Yes? Hello?

BELLA (*breathless*). Philip?

BUMMIDGE. Yes?

BELLA. I have bad news. I'm six weeks late.

BUMMIDGE. What? What was that?

BELLA. Late! You know what I'm talking about. Do I have to draw a picture?

BUMMIDGE (*to camera*). I wouldn't have understood the picture, either. (*To telephone.*) From that? We were just fooling. We didn't even undress.

BELLA. I admit there wasn't much to it.

MAX. They won't spare me a single detail!

BUMMIDGE. I'll come right over. (*Hangs up and speaks to camera.*) Passion on a grand scale is always safe. It's that miserable, neurotic poking around that causes trouble.

PAMELA. How can he be sure she didn't do it on purpose?

BUMMIDGE. The time is now a beautiful afternoon in May. The Trifflers are having a little party in the garden.

GALLUPPO. We Trifflers are rising in the world.

MADGE. Rising into the upper lower middle class of Brooklyn.

VELMA. Lovely house. Mission-style apricot stucco.

BUMMIDGE. I am sniffing lilacs, unaware

that Bella has told her parents she's knocked up. Suddenly old Triffler swoops down and says, "What did you do to my child?"

GALLUPPO (*as old Triffler*). What did you do to my child!

BUMMIDGE (*coaching*). "This you do to a father?"

GALLUPPO. This you do to a father?

BELLA. I stood under the weeping willow, when my mother ran up. (*Tapping* BERTRAM.) She hissed, "Arnold, a houseful of guests! Not now!"

BERTRAM. Arnold, a houseful of guests. Not now.

MADGE. My opinion was that they were framing him. Bella was an aggressive girl.

BELLA (*hotly*). A lot you know! But I recall the moment. My mother shouted—

VELMA. I was there. Your mother shouted, "He's so coarse! Couldn't it be a nice refined boy, you tramp? His habits are filthy. He cleans his ears in public and looks at the wax."

BELLA. She didn't call me tramp!

BUMMIDGE. She did. And she said, "Look how bad his skin is. He must have syphilis."

BELLA. She warned me you'd be a selfish husband. A hypochondriac. A tyrant. And you were. I told Mama, "He's everything you say."

MADGE. But you weren't getting any younger.

BELLA (*fiercely*). I was just a kid. My heart told me to marry him.

MADGE. Her heart! She was out to here, already. (*Indicates a swollen belly.*)

BUMMIDGE. Bella, you love melodrama, and you're happy when the materials of your personality turn into soap opera. You do have a sense of humor, of a grim sort, but you've neglected it.

BELLA. This proves my suffering never touched your heart. You didn't care.

BUMMIDGE. I said to Mama Triffler, "Don't you think I'm too immature to marry? I'm not ready yet."

BELLA. And you started to blubber.

BUMMIDGE. And then you hit me.

BELLA. I said, "Coward! I'll give you something to cry about!" (*She strikes him.*)

BUMMIDGE (*reels*). Ow! (*Angry.*) This was harder than the first time. (*Holding his cheek.*) This is very rich material.

BELLA. You tried to escape out the gate.

"You people are railroading me." We were a respectable family, till we met you. You twisted our behavior into comedy.

MAX. That sounds like the truth.

BUMMIDGE. Your so-called respectability was comical without twisting. Your father tried to throttle me, is that respectable? (*To* GALLUPPO.) Choke me.

GALLUPPO. Wait a minute. What's my responsibility if there's an injury? There's a legal point, here.

BUMMIDGE (*commanding*). My method requires reliving. Choke me.

BELLA. You were just slapped.

(*A* MESSENGER *has just entered the scene.*)

BUMMIDGE (*frantic*). I must have closure. We're on the air. You have to obey me.

GALLUPPO. No!

BUMMIDGE. Somebody— (*To* MESSENGER.) *You* choke me.

MADGE (*pushing the* MESSENGER *forward*). Choke him, and get it over with.

BELLA. Bummy, with all those intellectuals watching, don't be a goddamn jerk!

BUMMIDGE (*on his toes, rigid*). Choke me!

MESSENGER (*to* VELMA). Hold this!

(*He brutally chokes* BUMMIDGE, *who falls to his knees.* BELLA, BERTRAM, *and* MOTT *try to drag him away from his victim.*)

WINKLEMAN. His face is getting purple.

IMOGEN. Enough! Stop!

MOTT (*he and* BERT *with difficulty pry the* MESSENGER'S *fingers loose*). This fellow's a killer.

BERTRAM. Who taught you to take life like that?

MESSENGER. He asked for it. I have to grab all opportunities.

MAX. Pop, are you all right?

BUMMIDGE (*feebly*). Tip the boy. . . .

IMOGEN. It's a telegram from Mr. Fiddleman.

MADGE (*grabbing wire*). For Winkleman.

MESSENGER. What's this, a TV show? Is that Bummy? The comic?

WINKLEMAN (*reading*). Great interest, so far.

MADGE. Oh, Winkie!

(MOTT *and* BERTRAM *throw the* MESSENGER *out.*)

BUMMIDGE (*to cameras*). This choking was an orgastic experience, almost. Suffering and agony can be repressive forms of gratification. Under conditions of general repression, that is how it works out. Under these conditions, man conceives the project of changing the external world, and the project of changing himself. There is no other creature that aims to change itself, or discover another kind of life. From top to bottom, each man rejects himself, denies what he is, and doesn't even know it. (*He laughs. He pushes the others and forces them to laugh with him.*) Isn't that funny? (*General laughter.*) You, too, Bert.

BERTRAM (*tries to laugh*). Heh, heh!

BUMMIDGE. Bertram is far too sick to laugh. . . . But now, my father has learned of my transgression with Bella, and waits for me on the stoop.

MAX (*as* FATHER). Outcast! Now you'll marry? On what?

BUMMIDGE. His favorite punishment was to strike me under the nose with his forefinger. Exceedingly castrating. My mother and sister weep in the background, and I am struck.

(MAX *flicks him under the nose.*)

Ow! That hurt. How did you learn to do it? (*He has a nosebleed.*) You see the technique? My father struck me, and now my son . . . My nose! Oh, I'm bleeding! Give me something! Someone! A rag! Ice! Let me smell vinegar! Bella . . . I'm bleeding. I'm undone!

(BELLA *gives him a handkerchief. He collapses in barber chair.*)

MADGE. Just as things were going good. Take the camera off him.

MOTT. Somebody—do something.

AUFSCHNITT (*in the center of the stage, stunned, frightened as the camera turns on him*). Ladies and gentlemen, my name is Gerald Aufschnitt. I was born in Vienna, also the home of Mr. Freud. I am now Mr. Bummidge's tailor for thirty years. What a wonderful person. He helps me with my troubles. My daughter's troubles, too. I make his costumes in my little shop on Columbus Avenue. He asked me to play in his show. I was just man, in the grip of relentless suppressions. I was never in a show before. How do I look?

MADGE. It's a fiasco. Wink, get on camera.

WINKLEMAN. Good evening. Yes, we are relatives. Were playmates. My cousin is a man of genius. Without him, my life would have been very empty. It is becoming rare for any person to need any other specific person. I mean, usually, if death removes the one before you, you can always get another. And if you die, it might be much the same to the rest. The parts are interchangeable. But Bummidge is *needed*. . . .

MADGE. Get off with that stuff.

MAX. Pamela! Dance—bumps, grinds—anything!

(BERTRAM *is now before the camera*.)

BERTRAM. By profession I was a zoologist, but got into the exterminating business. For every one of us, there is a rat. One to one. We seldom realize that rats are part of civilization. Rats came from Europe. They couldn't cross the continent until there was enough garbage from the covered wagons. They were pioneers, too. Mr. Bummidge understands. He has taken me on for training and study. He feels I tried to overcome my Oedipal problem by becoming father to myself. That is why I am so stern, why the rats are like children to me, and why I do not laugh. Unless tickled.

(MOTT *tickles him and* BERTRAM *laughs horribly. They push him from the spotlight*.)

MADGE. Pamela, take over.

(PAMELA *performs, something between modern dance and burlesque*.)

BELLA. It's a disaster! This broad will ruin him. I always said it.

BUMMIDGE (*rising from chair*). The bleeding has stopped. Where's the camera? Ladies and gentlemen, a violent father often has terrible effects on a son, if the son idolizes strength. (*He goes toward* MAX *but finds himself entangled in the arms and legs of* PAMELA.) Age twelve. I lose my virginity, as they say. Seduced on the counter of a dairy restaurant by a certain Mrs. Friedmacher. . . . (*Extricates himself*.) Locked in my bosom, a child, a little child who weeps. But now I am ten. The perils of reality surround the boy. He flirts with death on the fire escape, on the back of the trolley. Disease is trying to infect me. Time waits to consume me. The Id wants to detain me in infancy till I become like an ancient Mongolian idiot, old, wrinkled, yellow. I run and hide, steal, lie, cheat, hate, lust. Thus . . . my pursuit of happiness!

MADGE. Winkie, if he rambles on like this, we're sunk.

BUMMIDGE. And now I ask you to witness a pair of solemn events. At this moment I am yet unborn. We are behind the candy store in Williamsburg. A January night. (*Counts on his fingers*.) It must have been January. I don't exist. (*Covers his eyes*.) Oh, blackness, blackness, and frost. The stove is burning. A brass bedstead. And here they are. (*Points*.) My parents, male and female. Two apparitions. Oh! (*He turns away*.)

MADGE. When? Papa and Mama! What's he talking! Bummy, there are limits!

VELMA. Of such things the law should prohibit viewing. Even on closed-circuit.

BUMMIDGE (*pushes* MADGE *aside*). My little sister is sleeping. Unaware. And then—(*Pointing a trembling hand*.)—my father takes . . . And my mother . . . Oh, no, Mama, no! Pa! Ma! Wait! Hold it! Consider! Oh, don't do this to me. (*To the audience*.) It's the Primal Scene. Nobody can come between them. The action of Fate. I am being conceived. No, no, no, no, no! Pray, little Philip Bomovitch. Oh, pray! (*On his knees*.) But it's too late. My number is up! Bang! (*Claps hands to head*.) I'm doomed now to be born. May God have mercy on my soul—on all our souls.

WINKLEMAN. Brother! Even the old name, Bomovitch.

BUMMIDGE (*rising, before camera*). And now, ladies and gentlemen all . . . I will ask you to observe the projection of another most significant event. I shall try to penetrate the mystery of birth. I do this in the hope of renewal, or rebirth. This is the climax of my method. I invite you to watch a playlet which attempts to bring together the ancient and the avant-garde. (*To group*.) I have parts for all of you.

WINKLEMAN. Oh, God, now he's a playwright. Meantime, disaster waits for me.

MADGE. I've staked everything on this!

GALLUPPO (*to* MAX). You'll get a bill from me, buddy-boy.

IMOGEN. Here are the parts, Mr. Bummidge.

BUMMIDGE. Hand them out.

PAMELA. I thought it was all impulse.

(*A black cloth has been prepared on the sofa, midstage. There are holes in this cloth for the heads of the chorus. The company dons the cloth,* IMOGEN *assisting,* BUMMIDGE *supervising*.)

MAX. What is this?

BELLA. A Greek chorus?

GALLUPPO. Why am I the Second Voice?

VELMA. I'm no Greek.

(*Final adjustments of the black cloth are made.*)

BUMMIDGE. The title of this presentation is "The Upper Depths," or "The Birth of Philip Bomovitch." Ready . . . get set . . . Go. (*Lies on the sofa.*)

BELLA (*reading*). The babe is in the womb now.

WOMEN. What far-off force presides over this curious particle of matter?

VELMA. O Kronos!

MOTT (*to* TECHNICIAN). Who the hell is this Kronos?

VELMA. Speak, Tiresias. Speak, holy hermaphrodite. Blind, you know the darkness best. (*Continues to smoke her cigar.*)

MEN. The cells of the babe divide.

WINKLEMAN. Seeming chaos. A terrible order.

GALLUPPO. Iron. Proteins.

MAX. The swift enzymes. Transistors of flesh.

PAMELA. Matter torn away from other forms of being.

ALL. Will this be nothing but finite, mortal man?

BELLA. His eyes.

MADGE. Tongue.

PAMELA. Genitalia.

VELMA. His liver.

WINKLEMAN. And his nerves.

MAX. And within the soft skull, a soft mass of white cells which will judge the world.

BELLA. O Transfiguration!

ALL. He is being created.

GALLUPPO. Merely to jest? So that other animals may grin?

MAX. But there is no unmetaphysical calling.

PAMELA. And what is the mother doing? Does she go stately through the slums? Is her mind upon the gods? Does she understand what she is carrying?

MADGE. Not she. No thought, no prayer, no wine, no sacrifices. Only herring, potatoes, tea, cards, gossip, newspaper serials. How far is this Daughter of Man from authentic Being.

WINKLEMAN. The unborn Bummidge, afloat in Stygian darkness.

(BUMMIDGE *floats like an embryo.*)

ALL. He's folding, unfolding, refolding. Now he's a fish.

(BUMMIDGE *enacts the fish.*)

MAX. Dimly he beholds the geologic periods.

GALLUPPO *and* MADGE. The vacant lifeless seas.

BELLA *and* MAX. Things that crawl.

VELMA *and* WINK. The ferns, the lumbering beasts.

MAX. From stone, from brine, sucking the seething power of the sun.

PAMELA. Now appears the backbone.

GALLUPPO. The gills.

WINKLEMAN. He's a reptile.

MADGE. A mammal. Higher. Up the vertebrate tree.

ALL. Up! Up! This thing is evolving into a man.

(BUMMIDGE *stands.*)

VELMA. Reason.

WINKLEMAN. Self-regard. Tragic apprehension. Comic knowledge.

BUMMIDGE (*getting back on sofa*). It's great in here. I like it.

BELLA. Blind and dumb, the babe. Sheer happiness—Nirvana!

GALLUPPO. But it can't last. The pains are starting.

ALL. Contractions.

(BUMMIDGE *sits up on sofa. The chorus makes the cloth billow behind him, by degrees more violently.*)

WINKLEMAN. Fifteen.

ALL. Ba-ba-ba-baboom!

WINKLEMAN. Ten.

ALL. Ba-ba-ba-baboom!

WINKLEMAN. Eight!

ALL. Ba-ba-ba-baboom!

WINKLEMAN. Four.

ALL. Ba-ba-ba-baboom!

WINKLEMAN. Two.

ALL. Ba-ba-ba-baboom!

(*The violent swelling of the cloth has put* BUMMIDGE *on his feet.*)

BUMMIDGE. Oh, Mother! Our time has come. (*Knocks as if on a door.*) Mother! (*Stamps his foot.*) Mother! The bag is broken. (*Sharp cry.*) Help! I'm grounded in here. Oh, terror, rage, suffocation! This is expulsion. I hear screams. I'd scream, too, if I could breathe. Tante Velma has me by the head, dragging me, dragging me. Take it easy, Tante—I'm choking. Choking. Air, air, give me air. Agony to my lungs! Oxygen! The light is scalding my eyes. (*Newborn, with wrinkled blind face and clenched poor hand, he slaps himself on the behind and gives the feeble in-*

fant cry.) Eh . . . Ehh! (*He squalls like a newborn infant.*)

BELLA. It tears your heart to hear that cry.

MAX. A tyrant. Utterly helpless. Absolute from weakness.

PAMELA. They cut the cord.

(BUMMIDGE *looks about.*)

WOMEN. So this is the world?

MEN. It is the Kingdom of Necessity.

ALL. *Sein! Dasein! Bewusstsein!*

(IMOGEN *presses an inflated balloon to his mouth.*)

BELLA. The breast. She holds him in her arms.

ALL. Bliss.

BELLA. He breathes. He suckles.

ALL. Bliss.

BUMMIDGE. Where do I end, and where does the world begin? I must be the world myself. I'm it. It's me.

MAX. A little moment of omnipotence.

(IMOGEN *pulls away the balloon, which is attached to a long string.*)

BUMMIDGE. So *that's* the way it is!

WINKLEMAN. Only the first lesson of reality.

BUMMIDGE (*raging*). Give it back!

(*The chorus now reads him a lesson.*)

MADGE. Strife.

PAMELA. Disappointment.

BELLA. Loss.

GALLUPPO. Law.

VELMA. Thou shalt not.

MADGE. Thou shalt not covet.

PAMELA. Stifle those horrible needs.

MAX. Bow your head as all mankind must, and submit to your burden.

WINKLEMAN. The war has begun between the instincts of life and the instincts of death.

ALL. *Ave atque vale . . .*

(*With this incantation they go off.*)

BUMMIDGE. Oh, my friends. Men, women, brothers, sisters, all . . . (*He crawls forward.*) You see me now in swaddling clothes. I thought I was born to life, to joy. Not so. I am a sad, vain, tangled thing. I cannot rest in any state. Would it have been better never to be summoned into this world? Should I pray to cease being? I was born once. Can I be born again from my own empty heart? I am one of certain voices entering the world, and have not spoken as I should. I chose to serve laughter, but the weight of suffering overcame me time and again.

As I rose to my unsteady feet—(*Rises.*)—I heard the sins of history shouted in the street.

BERTRAM. The *Titanic,* sinking.

AUFSCHNITT. Clemenceau goes to the front.

MOTT. Lenin reaches Finland.

(*Sound of bells.*)

BUMMIDGE. Armistice Day, nineteen eighteen. From the abyss of blood, the sirens of peace. I have a vision of bandaged lepers screaming, "Joy, joy!" Twenty million mummy bundles of the dead grin as the child, Philip Bummidge, intuits the condition of man and succumbs for the first time to Humanitis, that dread plague. Being human is too much for flesh and blood. . . .

IMOGEN. He's having one of his attacks.

MAX. Jesus, Pop.

(BUMMIDGE *sinks into his barber chair, covers himself with the sheet.*)

What is he doing?

IMOGEN (*before the camera*). Mr. Bummidge foresaw he might be overcome during this broadcast, being a highly emotional man. As his colleagues, Bertram and I are prepared to spell out essential parts of his program.

BERTRAM (*reading*). "The spirit of Gargantua was captured by totalitarianism. When lampshades are made of human skin, we see that fun is very big in hell."

IMOGEN (*reading*). "Farce follows horror into darkness. Deeper, deeper."

BERTRAM (*reading*). "Sores and harsh pains, despair and death—those raise loud, brutal laughter."

IMOGEN (*reading*). "And what minor follies are there for the comedian to work with? If he tries to be an extremist, he finds the world is far more extreme than he can ever be."

BERTRAM (*reading*). "As the social order extends its monopoly of power, it takes over the fields of fantasy and comedy. It makes all the best jokes."

IMOGEN (*reading*). "Illuminated by Freudian and other studies, Bummidge tries to understand the situation." (*With a soft and graceful gesture of her arm, indicates the figure of* BUMMIDGE *covered by the cloth.*)

BERTRAM (*reading*). "For the spirit of man must preserve itself."

IMOGEN (*reading*). "And can preserve

itself only upon a higher level than any yet attained."

BERTRAM (*reading*). "Investigators of sleep know that if you keep people from having dreams at night they begin to be crazy."

IMOGEN (*reading*). "And what is true of dreams is true of laughter, too. They come from the same source in the unconscious."

BERTRAM (*reading*). "So wit and comedy have to be recovered. So the social order does not keep the monopoly."

IMOGEN (*reading*). "Therefore, Philip Bummidge, with this bag of money, his last savings, intends to buy, from Franklin Kalbfuss, the Trilby Theatre, which he has made into a butcher shop, and establish there a center, an academy or conservatory of comic art based on the latest psychological principles."

BERTRAM (*reading*). "The characters we are so proud of having, the personalities we show off, the conflicts about which we are so serious (little monsters of vanity that we are, fascinated by the dead matter produced by Ego and Superego), these are the materials of the new comedy. To disown the individual altogether is nihilism, which isn't funny at all. But suppose all we fumblers and bumblers, we cranks and creeps and cripples, we proud, sniffing, ragged-assed paupers of heart and soul, sick with every personal vice, rattled, proud, spoiled, and distracted—suppose we look again for the manhood we are born to inherit."

MAX. The Trilby! He's out of his head, completely. I may have to commit him.

BUMMIDGE (*rising*). I shall now die to the old corn. (*He begins to parody old routines.*) "Do you file your fingernails?" "No, I throw them away."

MAX. He thinks he's back in burlesque.

BUMMIDGE. "Why did the chicken cross the road?" "That was no chicken, Jack, that was my life."

PAMELA (*who has been in the wings, and now enters*). He's flipped.

MADGE (*also coming forward*). His mind was never strong.

BUMMIDGE. "What did the monkey say when he peed on the cash register?" "This is going to run into money. . . ." Farewell, old jokes. (*Waving his arms.*) Fly away, flap-flap, like clumsy old chickens. I am sinking . . . sinking . . .

(BELLA *comes forward, curious, from the wings.* WINKLEMAN *follows.*)

BELLA. What's happening to him?

WINKLEMAN. He looks as if he's dying. . . . Is he?

PAMELA. I never could be sure of anything, with him.

BUMMIDGE (*crawls into the wardrobe basket*). The dark night of my soul has begun. Oh, Lazarus, we are brothers. I die of banality. Lay me in this mirthless tomb, and cover me with corn. Let me hear the laughter of evil for the last time. Oh, demons who murder while guffawing, I have succumbed. (*Reaches for the lid of the basket.*) Consummatum est. It is ended. (*Shuts the top of the basket. He emerges seconds later from the back of the wicker wardrobe trunk.*) But I am Lazarus. I was sick unto death, died, and was buried. Now I await resurrection . . . the word, "Come forth, Lazarus." . . . (*He waits.*) Will no one speak? (*Waits.*) No one? (*Faintly, appealing.*) Someone has got to speak!

IMOGEN (*timidly raising her hand like a schoolgirl*). Come forth, Lazarus.

(BUMMIDGE *rises slowly.*)

BERTRAM. He's being reborn.

BELLA (*bossy, but stirred as well*). Come forth . . . okay already, come forth!

(*They break into Handel's "Hallelujah Chorus" and modulate into the anthem "America the Beautiful."* WINKLEMAN *brings in an American flag.* BUMMIDGE *is raised to the top of the wardrobe trunk.*)

MOTT. Cut . . . time. Time. Cut.

IMOGEN. He kept talking about the Last Analysis. Now I know what he meant. Mr. Bummidge! He's white, fainting. Help!

WINKLEMAN. I'll change and be back immediately. (*Exits.*)

MOTT. What sense of timing! Better than a clock. The broadcast is over.

PAMELA. I have to get out of this costume. Bert, lend me that dress. And I want my diamonds back. Who has them?

MAX (*bending over him*). What's the matter, Dad, is it for real?

BELLA. He's out cold. Emotion really overcame him. Loosen his collar.

TECHNICIAN. Well, that's it. Save the lights. Wrap it up.

BERTRAM. Louie and I will put Bummidge to bed.

(*They carry him out.* PAMELA *follows,*

unbuttoning BERTRAM's *dress from back*.)

MAX (*hurries to telephone*). I've got to see if my deal is still on.

MADGE. No. We're waiting for Fiddleman to call.

(*She and* MAX *pull at the phone. The wire is torn loose*.)

See what you've done! It's disconnected.

MAX. I? You did it!

MADGE. All these preparations. All these shenanigans, and you have to eff it all up. How will Fiddleman reach us?

IMOGEN. And Doctor Ratzenhofer, Doctor Gumplovitch. Mr. Bummidge will be very upset.

MAX. I'll run down, make my call, and phone a repairman. (*Exits*.)

BELLA. It was a fiasco anyway. Pathetic Bummy's always been. It's his charm—boorish and touching, also. But who could take this seriously?

IMOGEN. I have to tell him what's happening, as soon as he comes out of it. (*Exits*.)

MADGE. Bella, I'm bound to agree. And it's a sad, dismal day for me, too. I don't know what we'll do.

BELLA. I know, you hoped to hush up the scandal. That would take dough. But why did you starve those old people?

MADGE. It was Aunt Velma, chiseling. Malnutrition! I didn't know it was that bad. Handling the aged is a hell of a problem.

BELLA. I'd throw you and Winkie to them. Let them prod you to death with crutches and canes.

MADGE. Bella, help. We'll cut you in. You're a business woman. Handled right, this is a really profitable racket.

BELLA. I wouldn't have the heart for it, it's too sordid. . . . Make me a proposition.

MADGE. We have to move fast. There's an inspector who threatens to leak the story to the papers.

BELLA. Throw Aunt Velma to the wolves. Let her take the rap. A year in jail is just what she needs.

MADGE. No, Winkie is sentimental about his mother. . . . Anyway, I agree Bummy washed out. Fiddleman could *never* go for this stuff.

(*Police sirens are heard*.)

What is that?

BELLA. Sounds to me like the cops.

MADGE. Bella, whom do you suppose they want? Us?

BELLA. Get a grip on yourself. . . . What a chunk of money he blew on this today.

(*Enter* WINKLEMAN *in his own clothing*.)

WINKLEMAN. The police are making a terrible racket in the street. Has anyone telephoned?

MADGE. Max tore the wires out. I thought he was going to strike me. Today I wouldn't have minded so much.

BELLA. Winkleman, you know as well as I do Bummy's performance was a bomb.

WINKLEMAN. Ripped out the phone, you say! Fiddleman did send a wire, but that was early. I agree—that broadcast must have emptied the Waldorf. A man of genius turned into a crank is a painful sight. So foolish. And what is his big idea? The Trilby Theatre! So figmentary, improbable, Utopian. I really can't stand these Utopians. I could be sorry for him if I wasn't in such a mess myself.

(*Enter* FIDDLEMAN, *the great impresario*.)

MADGE. Fiddleman!

FIDDLEMAN. I'm here with a police escort.

WINKLEMAN. Now don't be sore, Mr. Fiddleman, we meant it for the best.

BELLA. What are you doing here, Leslie?

FIDDLEMAN. What are you asking? Didn't Winkleman get my wire? I'm here because of Bummy.

WINKLEMAN. Accept my apologies. We had no idea he was so twisted in his mind.

MADGE. Those insane theories.

FIDDLEMAN. What are you talking! I couldn't get you on the phone. He was a sensation!

MADGE. Please, Mr. Fiddleman, don't put us on.

WINKLEMAN. We admit it was a mistake. We're crushed already. Then why punish us with bitter jokes?

FIDDLEMAN. Would I waste time on jokes? This is no joke. He wowed everybody!

BELLA. I can't believe it. From here it looked like a monstrosity. But that's because we're not artists. Bummy is one, so the thing had form.

MADGE. So that's what happened. (*Incredulous, then brightening*.) Winkie.

WINKLEMAN. It worked. I'm vindicated. We're still with it. He'll pull us out of the ditch. (*Lays about with an imaginary whip*.) Pull, dammit, pull!

MADGE. We are saved!

WINKLEMAN. I'll go and fetch him.

MADGE. No, wait.

WINKLEMAN. Yes! Bide our time until we figure out the best way to handle this.

MADGE. How?

WINKLEMAN. I'm thinking. My heart is kicking like a child in the womb. Just because you're corrupt is no reason to quit. I know that now.

FIDDLEMAN. You know I was skeptical. Bummy? A has-been, a waste of time. But everybody was floored by him. The scientists? Don't even ask. And the show-business people, their mouths dropped open. Personally, the fellow just stormed my heart—right here. But what's with your phone? I got a squad-car escort from the police department.

BELLA. Tell us how it came over.

FIDDLEMAN. Beautiful. And the whole Waldorf was in those rooms. Everybody in New York, from caveman to egghead. What excitement! Since Valentino's funeral, I haven't seen such a spontaneous mob. Women kissed the television screens. And strangers were hugging and dancing. They wept with laughter, or else they grinned as they were sobbing—sometimes it's hard to tell. The place was like the deck of the *Titanic*.

BELLA. How could we doubt him? But it's like being in the orchestra. You play oompa-oompa-oompa, but out front it's Beethoven.

MADGE. Winkleman, are you thinking?

WINKLEMAN. I am. With all my might I am!

FIDDLEMAN. And when he was born, people were like fish in a net. Stripers, flounders, lobsters—gasping.

MADGE. What kind of money is there in it?

BELLA. Let Leslie finish.

FIDDLEMAN. Some of the toughest crooks in the industry broke up when he said that about being born from an empty heart. They started gushing tears. In a way it was repulsive.

WINKLEMAN. From excess to excess.

FIDDLEMAN. Anyway, the networks, the public, the nation, the American people—they're all his. Where is Bummy?

BELLA. Resting.

(*Enter* MESSENGER.)

MESSENGER. I'm back.

BELLA. I'll take that wire.

WINKLEMAN. I'm his lawyer.

MADGE. —His agent. Give it here. (*Opens.*) It's signed Kalbfuss.

(WINKLEMAN *drops a coin in the* MESSENGER'*s hat. Exit* MESSENGER.)

BELLA. Kalbfuss. The butcher who rents the old Trilby property.

FIDDLEMAN. What was that they said about the Trilby, that sagging old joint? It goes back to the Civil War. They used to have boxes with fruits and fiddles on their bellies, like marzipan.

WINKLEMAN. Forget it. . . . Madge, what does the butcher say? Maybe he'll kill the deal.

MADGE (*reading*). "Master, I did not know you were a great genius. Will give lease to property on your terms. A shrine. Should be preserved."

BELLA. He doesn't want it preserved but reopened as a theatre of the soul.

FIDDLEMAN (*loudly*). For Christ sakes! (*Softening his tone.*) What kind of *shtuss* is this from a woman like you, Bella?

BELLA. I'm just repeating what he said. You heard him. A theatre of the soul. People will come up from the audience and Bummy will work with them. They will act out pieces of life. Bummy thinks a man's character is a lot of old junk—rusty bedsprings, busted axles. We should stop carrying all this ridiculous scrap metal around, we—

FIDDLEMAN. Don't get all wound up. What's he going to run at the Trilby, a sanatorium?

MADGE. I pictured a mental spa.

WINKLEMAN. Is that the whole wire?

MADGE. There's more. (*Reads.*) "May I be allowed to work with you? My only wish. A man of blood. Living from dead beasts. Who wishes to be redeemed." Signed "Franklin Kalbfuss."

FIDDLEMAN. You see how he moves the people? A butcher! A lousy butcher!

BELLA. Everybody waiting, waiting, waiting for emotional truth. For even a little sign.

WINKLEMAN. And can recognize it only in absurd form. Now, Fiddleman, we have to move fast. You must have some ideas.

FIDDLEMAN. A hundred million dollars' worth.

(*Enter* BERTRAM, *carrying covered dishes.*)

BELLA. How's Bummy?

BERTRAM. Reviving. Breathing hard, but coming around.

FIDDLEMAN. Who's this?

BERTRAM. I prepared a little spread for after the broadcast. Chopped liver. With my own hands. Try some.

BELLA. Never!

FIDDLEMAN. I already got proposals, option checks. Sponsors were there. Here's one from King Cigarettes—two hundred and fifty grand. Chicken feed. Here's from Imperial Deodorants, half a million.

MADGE. Against what? Give it here.

WINKLEMAN. Let me see this.

BELLA. You must have something in mind, Leslie.

FIDDLEMAN. Of course, I saw it like a flash. Have him do his psychotherapy on TV with famous people—Casey Stengel, Marlon Brando, Artie Shaw.

WINKLEMAN. We'll be smart this time. Incorporate. Put everybody on the payroll. The company will buy real estate to take advantage of depreciation. . . .

BELLA. You'll sell him your lousy old-people's home and get out of the hole yourself. That's an inspiration straight from the sewer. How can you do it to him?

MADGE. Bella, be serious. This is a business discussion.

(*Enter* BUMMIDGE, *led by* IMOGEN; MOTT, PAMELA, *and* MAX *drift in soon after*.)

BUMMIDGE. Imogen, I feel very vague . . . awfully peculiar.

FIDDLEMAN (*confronting him*). Bummy, look. Who is this? *I* am here in *your* house. Do you know what it means?

BUMMIDGE (*shaking his head*). No. I don't understand.

WINKLEMAN. Come off it! Leslie Fiddleman!

BELLA. Bummy, you were right, and you only.

WINKLEMAN. Not he only. I said he'd make this comeback.

MAX. Comeback? I thought it was a bomb.

MADGE. No. It worked. See for yourself. Here's Fiddleman.

MOTT. So that's why the limousine is downstairs, and the cops, and the big crowd. Bummy, do you hear? We won the sweepstakes! (*To* FIDDLEMAN.) How was the reception? I must have sent a terrific picture.

PAMELA. Oh, lover, I'm so happy for you.

BELLA. We could have been the greatest family in America, on the cover of *Time,* if only the whores let him alone.

MAX. Pop doesn't seem to get it.

PAMELA. The broadcast was a smash.

IMOGEN. What about the scientific reaction?

FIDDLEMAN. There are about fifty of those longhaired guys trying to get in. I asked the cops to hold 'em back awhile.

IMOGEN. That isn't fair! It was all meant for them.

MAX. We've got business. Keep 'em out. Let the family settle first.

BERTRAM. Bummy, you do look strange.

BUMMIDGE. The grave . . .

MOTT. What does he mean?

BERTRAM. He's referring to Lazarus.

BUMMIDGE. I still feel deathy. I feel both old and new.

MADGE. You stunned everybody.

PAMELA. No more living in filth. What a future lies before us!

(BUMMIDGE *eyes her strangely; he seems far removed from them all.*)

FIDDLEMAN. Bummy, what's with the fish eye? Am I a stranger? We've known each other forty years.

BUMMIDGE. Is that so? (*Curiously distant.*) If you say so.

FIDDLEMAN. Of course I say. Since Boys High, on the gymnastic team. You got amnesia?

BUMMIDGE. All that was familiar is strange, and the strange is familiar. Life and death are two slopes under me. I can look down one side or the other. What was I before?

MADGE. Before, during, and after—a buffoon! Bummy dear, please don't fool around. There's so much at stake.

BUMMIDGE. A buffoon! Oh, how unfortunate. Forcing laughs, you mean? Sucking up to the paying public? Oh, my!

MAX. Now, Father! Are you serious?

BELLA. Yes, what is this, Bummy? Are you pulling something?

FIDDLEMAN. What's with him?

IMOGEN. He's gone through rebirth. He may not be the same person now.

BUMMIDGE (*mysteriously remote*). That . . . is the truth.

MADGE. Let's see if he'll deny his own sister.

MAX. Or me.

WINKLEMAN. Let me handle it.

(*All close in about* BUMMIDGE.)

BUMMIDGE. Please—please don't crowd.

Oh, don't touch! It makes me cold in the bowels. I feel you breathing on me. See how my skin is wincing. (*He shrinks, draws up his shoulders, warms hands between his thighs.*)

BERTRAM. Step back, step back here. Give him air.

PAMELA (*to* BERTRAM). Hands off! (*To* BUMMIDGE.) You always liked me to touch you.

FIDDLEMAN. What is he? Putting us on?

MAX. He's trying to get away with something.

IMOGEN. Oh, what an unfair accusation.

BUMMIDGE. I'm not the person I was. Something has happened.

MOTT. Like what?

BUMMIDGE. I am drenched with new meaning. Wrapped in new mystery.

MAX. Oh, can it, Pop!

BUMMIDGE. Pop? (*He is mildly curious.*)

MADGE. Well, who are you?

BUMMIDGE. I'm waiting to find out. Chaos swallowed me up, now I am just coming out again.

MOTT. That sounds just great. You can use it in a show. Say, Mr. Fiddleman— anything specific?

WINKLEMAN (*showing him the checks*). A little option money.

MAX. Real dough? Let's see.

PAMELA. Show me those.

BELLA. Come on, Bummy—*you* know what's happening. The networks want you back.

IMOGEN (*she has found the butcher's wire*). A telegram came from Mr. Kalbfuss. He offers you the Trilby.

BUMMIDGE (*we can't be sure how much he understands*). The Trilby?

FIDDLEMAN. The old vaudeville dump where you used to perform. You said you wanted it back as a theatre of the soul, or something.

BUMMIDGE. Of the soul . . . I don't know what you're doing here. I wish you'd all go. I feel life drifting into me. Drift, drift. (*Laves his bosom with air.*)

MAX. He wants to drive us nuts!

IMOGEN. Don't you understand? He's been transfigured.

MADGE. As a school kid he'd pretend to be blind. He'd stare right through you and he'd stagger around. A whole week he made me feed him with a spoon.

BUMMIDGE. I have attained rebirth. I am in a pure condition which cannot be exploited. Noli me tangere. Noli, noli, noli . . .

FIDDLEMAN (*to others*). Can you guess how much my time is worth? Come on. A figure. Five hundred an hour? Ha! Guess again. I can't stick around here.

BUMMIDGE. I am not certain who I am. . . .

BELLA. We'll tell you. We'll straighten you out. Don't you worry, kid.

BUMMIDGE. Oh, fallen man, as you lie suffering in the profane, longing for what is absolutely real . . .

WINKLEMAN. Now he's a sage. I think I get it. You don't know who you are?

BUMMIDGE. But I do know who I am *not*. How many of you can say that?

PAMELA. Bummy, I am Pamela who loves you heart and soul.

BUMMIDGE (*viewing her*). Souls? Hearts? You?

PAMELA. How can you pretend not to know me?

BUMMIDGE. Pretend? (*To* IMOGEN.) Imogen, take a note. Write, "Weeping is the mother of music."

IMOGEN (*writing*). Yes, Mr. Bummidge.

MOTT. For God's sake!

FIDDLEMAN. He thinks he'll bring me to my knees. Not these knees. Never.

PAMELA. Maybe I deserve to be treated like this. All I know is I love you.

BUMMIDGE. A note, Imogen, a note: "Is pleasure the true object of desire? This may be the great modern error. We will revise Freud some more—respectfully."

PAMELA. Please look at me, dearest Bummy.

BUMMIDGE. I can't see clearly. It's like I have drops of argyrol in my eyes.

PAMELA. Look.

BUMMIDGE. I'll try.

PAMELA. What do you see?

BUMMIDGE. I'm not sure.

PAMELA. I want you to see me, dearest.

BUMMIDGE. Ah, yes.

PAMELA (*trying to control her vexation*). Yes what?

BUMMIDGE. Yes, of course.

PAMELA. What do you see?

BUMMIDGE. A bed. A king-sized bed. And a photograph on the wall. Is it a graduation picture? Is it an ikon?

PAMELA. Darling, a picture of *you!*

BUMMIDGE. Oh, I know who *you* are. You are the desire I tried very hard to have. How do you do?

PAMELA. Our love!

BUMMIDGE. "Love," but not right. Love, sweet but grimy. Like—I have it. Like eating ice cream from a coal scuttle.

PAMELA. You break my heart, Bummy!

BUMMIDGE. Imogen, a note: "Wouldn't it be better to have a rutting season? Once a year, but the real thing? When the willows turn yellow in March? But only animals are innocent." (*To* PAMELA.) O phantom of erections past, farewell! Bertram, show this lady out. (*He takes the bracelet from* MOTT's *pocket and puts it in* PAMELA's *hand.*)

PAMELA. I won't go. (*She resists Bertram and remains.*)

BELLA. I don't blame you, Bummy. It's high time, too. You don't know her, that's right. But you damn well know me.

BUMMIDGE. I faintly recall . . .

BELLA. The devotion of a wife.

BUMMIDGE. Something unpleasant. Like noisy supervision. Like suffocation for my own good. No, like West Point with a marriage license.

BELLA. What do you mean, West Point!

BUMMIDGE. "A-tten-shun! Inspec-shun! Let's see your nails. Your necktie. Your cuffs. Your heels. Your handkerchief. Lipstick? Where have you been? What did you do? Open your fly—hup-two-three-four. The greatest in America!" Bertram, will you escort this lady to the street?

BELLA. Put a rat-catching hand on me and I'll kick you in the head. (*She remains.*)

MAX. And what about me?

BUMMIDGE. You? I am newborn. . . .

MAX. Aren't you a little infantile for a father?

BUMMIDGE. Aren't you a little old to be still a son? (*To* WINKLEMAN.) I seem to remember you.

WINKLEMAN. You should. I made you great. And I'll make you greater than ever. I'll put you back to work. Because you've made a new discovery. And you have no time to think of the administration, Bummy. You're too creative. Leave it all to me. Please! Be sensible, I beg you.

BUMMIDGE. I definitely remember you. You make linoleum out of roses. You walk over my soul with gritty shoes. Yes, and you have a strange tic. You tell false falsehoods.

BELLA. Some rose!

BUMMIDGE. I may not be the bud of a

flower, but neither am I an old rubber plant. (*To* MADGE.) And you, Madam . . . I believe we once played cards together. You got into the habit of cheating, and you cheated and you cheated and you cheated. . . . A note, Imogen.

IMOGEN. Ready, Mr. Bummidge.

BUMMIDGE. "How does the lonely cactus thrive in deserts dry."

MOTT. Bummy, have you flipped?

BUMMIDGE. "It has a mystery to guard. Otherwise, why stand in the sun—why buck the drought, why live with vultures and tarantulas?"

FIDDLEMAN. And me, Fiddleman?

BUMMIDGE (*hand to brow*). Pardon?

FIDDLEMAN. Where are those damn checks—give 'em here. (*Snatches them from* PAMELA *and* MOTT *and thrusts them on* BUMMIDGE.)

BUMMIDGE (*examining them*). Are these yours? I don't want them. Imogen, what I want to know is, where are my colleagues? Where are Doctors Gumplovitch and Ratzenhofer and the others?

IMOGEN. Trying to get up to see you. The police are holding them back.

BUMMIDGE. Police? . . . A note: "They say that tragedy makes us look better and comedy worse than we are. But that is puzzling. In the first place, what are we? And in the second place, what is worse?"

WINKLEMAN. Bummy wants to dump his friends, to try to make it as an intellectual. Yes, he's aiming very high. He wants power. Oh, cousin, look out. You'll shoot yourself in the foot. You shouldn't turn your back on us. In spite of everything, we love you.

BERTRAM. Isn't anybody going to taste my liver?

FIDDLEMAN. All right, Bummy. You've had your fun with me. I am shivering with insults. But okay. Now talk turkey. Those checks are nothing. We'll make millions. You'll be the biggest thing that ever hit the channels. A giant, a healer, a prophet. The man who went down into the hell of modern life and took comedy by the hand and brought it back again to every living room and bar in America. You want the old Trilby? I'll fix it for you. Sumptuous. New everything. Gold urinals, if you like. With the most advanced television equipment, and every night capacity houses.

BUMMIDGE. You make me recall the life I once agreed to live. All that I used to do, when only wind and fury could make flimsy things succeed. With forced breath and tired nerves. And an audience smelling like a swamp of martinis and half-digested steak. Well, of course it earned millions. (*Looks at checks again.*) The world *is* hard up for original inventions.

BERTRAM. Emerson, or was it Elbert Hubbard, said if you invented a better rat trap the world would beat a path to your door.

BUMMIDGE. Or you will be sucked out of your doorway, deep into the boundless universe, as by a vacuum cleaner. So—(*to Fiddleman*)—as Aristotle said . . .

WINKLEMAN. My God—Madge, I think it's hopeless!

BUMMIDGE. As Aristotle said . . .

WINKLEMAN. Wait, you're overexcited. Sit down. I'll handle it. (*Helplessly.*) Aristotle . . .

BUMMIDGE. As *he* said, get out of here! (*Tears up checks.*) Beat it, the whole gang of you.

MOTT. What?

MAX. No, Father. . . .

MADGE. Are you crazy?

WINKLEMAN. I can't desert you. Abuse me all you like, but I'm too loyal.

BUMMIDGE. Without me you are ruined.

MADGE. Yes, and me. Your sister, I'm losing everything.

BUMMIDGE. Bertram, Bertram, throw them all out.

ALL. No. Keep your hands off. I've got old files. I'll sue.

BUMMIDGE. You compel me to take measures? You refuse to let me be? Bertram, the net.

BERTRAM. Right!

BELLA. What's happening—what is this?

(*A device appears above.* BELLA, PAMELA, WINKLEMAN, MOTT, MADGE, FIDDLEMAN, *and* MAX *stare up.*)

WINKLEMAN. A net! Duck! Look out!

(*All are caught in the net.* BERTRAM *runs up like the ratcatcher he is to see what he has trapped.*)

BUMMIDGE (*dancing about in excitement*). Out, out! Drag 'em out!

BELLA. You lunatic!

MADGE. He's going to kill us!

IMOGEN. Don't hurt them, Mr. Bummidge, don't hurt them.

WINKLEMAN. Don't destroy a lifelong relationship.

BUMMIDGE. You came between me and my soul. Drag 'em away, Bertram. (*Jubilant.*) Oh, I can't bear to see them suffering. Ha, ha! They break my heart, throw them out.

FIDDLEMAN. I'll bring an action.

PAMELA. Oh, help me!

(BERTRAM *and* BUMMIDGE *drag all in the net through the doorway.* BUMMIDGE *slams the door, and then does a dance with* IMOGEN.)

BUMMIDGE. A new life. A new man. I really am reborn. (*Sprinkles water on his head from water jug.*) I baptize myself.

(BERTRAM *enters from other side.*)

BERTRAM. It worked. Technically perfect.

BUMMIDGE. Just perfect. I could vault over clouds.

BERTRAM (*looking down at scraps of paper*). You tore up nearly a million bucks.

IMOGEN. It had to be done. Bertram, you know it.

BUMMIDGE. No, no, Imogen. I wanted to do it. I did it of my own free will. (*Thinking.*) Or did those people force freedom on me? Now, where is the butcher's telegram? We have things to do. Work, work! Onwards, to the Trilby. We have to tear up the floors and purge the smell of blood. Go, Imogen, and let in my scientific colleagues. They've been waiting. I will put on my toga. The Trilby will be run like Plato's academy. (*Puts on toga, arranges folds.*) The Bummidge Institute of Nonsense. We deserve a modern skyscraper like the United Nations, but the poor, the sad, the bored and tedious of the earth will trust us better for beginning so humbly. And we will train people in the Method and send them as missionaries to England, to Germany, to all those bleak and sadistic countries. I am so moved! What a struggle I've had. It took me so long to get through the brutal stage of life. And when I was through with it, the mediocre stage was waiting for me. And now that's done with, and I am ready for the sublime. (*He raises his arms in a great gesture.*)

CURTAIN

HOGAN'S GOAT

William Alfred

A. M. D. G.
for
JOHN and MÁIRE SWEENEY
with love.

First presented by the American Place Theatre (Wynn Handman, artistic director) in association with Norman Kean, in New York City, on November 11, 1965, with the following cast:

(In order of appearance)

MATTHEW STANTON, *leader of the Sixth Ward of Brooklyn* Ralph Waite

KATHLEEN STANTON, *his wife* Faye Dunaway

JOHN "Black Jack" HAGGERTY, *Assistant Ward Leader* Roland Wood

PETEY BOYLE, *a hanger-on of Stanton's* Cliff Gorman

BESSIE LEGG, *a back-room girl* Michaele Myers

MARIA HAGGERTY, *"Black Jack's" wife, the Stantons' janitor* Grania O'Malley

FATHER STANISLAUS COYNE, *Pastor of St. Mary Star of the Sea* Barnard Hughes

FATHER MALONEY, *Pastor of the All-night Printers' Church* John Dorman

EDWARD QUINN, *Mayor of Brooklyn* Tom Ahearne

JAMES "Palsy" MURPHY, *Boss of the city of Brooklyn* Conrad Bain

BILL, *a hanger-on of Quinn's* Luke Wymbs

ANN MULCAHY, *Father Coyne's housekeeper* Agnes Young

JOSEPHINE FINN, *Maria Haggerty's niece* Tresa Hughes

BOYLAN, *a policeman* Tom Crane

A DOCTOR David Dawson

CONSTITUENTS: Stan Sussman, *piano;* Eileen Fitzpatrick, Jack Fogarty, John Hoffmeister, Monica MacCormack, Michael Murray, Bruce Waite, Albert Shipley·

Directed by Frederick Rolf
Scenery, lighting, and costumes by Kert Lundell

Copyright © 1958, 1966 by William Alfred.
All rights reserved.
Reprinted by permission of Farrar, Straus & Giroux, Inc.

NOTE: All rights, including professional, amateur, dramatic, motion-picture, recitation, lecturing, public-reading, radio and television broadcasting, are strictly reserved and no portion of this play may be performed without express written permission. Inquiries about such rights should be addressed to the author's dramatic agent, Miss Toby Cole, 234 West 44 Street, Suite 700, Sardi Building, New York, New York, 10036.
Almost all of the place names in this play really exist; but none of these characters has ever lived except in my own mind. Any resemblance to any person living or dead is purely coincidental.

WILLIAM ALFRED is not entirely the stock figure one imagines when thinking of a playwright. He is fundamentally an academic, and, it seems, proud of it. He was born in New York City on August 16, 1922. He took his B.A. at Brooklyn College in 1948, his M.A. at Harvard a year later, and his Ph.D. in 1954. That same year he joined the faculty of Harvard University, becoming a professor of English in 1963. His first play, *Agamemnon,* came in 1954 and two years later this was followed by his best-known work, *Hogan's Goat.*

Although written in 1956, *Hogan's Goat* had to wait a long time before it saw the professional stage. In 1965 it was given a production by Wynn Handman's American Place Theatre, a New York institution devoted to the encouragement of the American playwright, and offering new plays on a subscription basis to a highly sophisticated audience. *Hogan's Goat* was first produced at the American Place on November 11, 1965, and its success was such that it transferred to an Off-Broadway theatre, where it enjoyed a considerable run. One piece of incidental intelligence about this production is that it gave the first big chance to young Faye Dunaway, who was later to find fame as Bonnie in Arthur Penn's movie *Bonnie and Clyde.*

Mr. Alfred has continually sought to combine his two careers, and he is probably the only writer in the world to be a member of both the Medieval Academy and the Dramatists Guild. Both of his published plays are in verse, and he has a reputation as a poet, from 1942 to 1944 being associate editor of *American Poet,* and subsequently the author of a new verse translation of *Beowulf.*

He has had poems published in *The Hudson Review, Commonweal,* and has won the Atlantic Monthly Poetry Prize and the Harvard Monthly Prize. As a poet he has been influenced by Archibald MacLeish, who recommended him for the Amy Lowell Traveling Poetry Scholarship, with which he spent a full year in London, where he completed the first draft of *Hogan's Goat.* Although he continued to work for the theatre, Mr. Alfred's next production was *Cry for Us All,* a musical version of *Hogan's Goat.* First produced on Broadway on April 8, 1970, the book was by Mr. Alfred in collaboration with Albert Marre, the producer and director of the musical, and for the lyrics Mr. Alfred was joined by an advertising copywriter, Phyllis Robinson. The production was not generally well received and closed after a few performances.

Like his mentor, Mr. MacLeish, Mr. Alfred is a rare figure in the American drama in that his plays are written in verse. *Hogan's Goat* is set in the Brooklyn of 1890, and is concerned with the none too poetic subject of local politics in that Irish-dominated world. The story was apparently suggested to Mr. Alfred by his great-grandmother, Anna Marie Egan, who often told him stories of her early life in County Mayo, Ireland, and it was one of these, about a politician who risked his career by marrying his first cousin outside the church, which provided the inspiration for *Hogan's Goat.*

ACT ONE

Ten o'clock, the evening of Thursday,
April 28, 1890. The parlor of Matthew
Stanton's flat on the second floor of his
house on Fifth Place, Brooklyn. The set
is on two levels, the lower level containing
the kitchen of the Haggertys, which is
blacked out. To stage right there is a steep,
narrow staircase. Enter MATTHEW STANTON,
carrying a bottle of champagne. He is a
handsome, auburn-haired man in his late
thirties, dressed carefully in a four-but-
toned suit of good serge, and a soft black
hat. He bounds up the stairs and into his
flat, and throws his hat on a chair and
hides the bottle of champagne behind the
sofa. The furnishings of the room are in
period: the chairs are tufted and fringed,
the mantelpiece covered with a lambre-
quin, the window heavily draped.

———

STANTON
Katie? Katie! Where the devil are you?
Come on out in the parlor.
(*Enter* KATHLEEN STANTON, *closing
the door behind her. She is tall and
slim and dressed in a black broadcloth
suit which brings out the redness of
her hair and the whiteness of her
skin*)

KATHLEEN
I wish you wouldn't take those stairs so
fast;
They're wicked: you could catch your foot
and fall—
I had a bit of headache and lay down.
Why, Mattie darling, what's the matter
with you?
You're gray as wasps' nests.

STANTON
                     I'm to be the mayor!
No more that plug who runs the Court
Café
And owes his ear to every deadbeat sport
With a favor in mind and ten cents for
a ball,
But mayor of Brooklyn, and you the may-
or's lady.
They caught Ned Quinn with his red fist
in the till,
The Party of Reform, I mean, and we
"Are going to beat their game with resti-
tution

And self-reform." Say something, can't
you, Kate!
(KATHLEEN *sits down heavily, and
puts her hand to her temple*)

KATHLEEN
Oh, Mattie, Mattie.

STANTON
                 Jesus! Are you crying?
I've what I wanted since I landed here
Twelve years ago, and she breaks into
tears.

KATHLEEN
It's that I'm—

STANTON
           What? You're what?

KATHLEEN
                      Afraid.

STANTON
                    Kathleen,
Now please don't let's go into that again.

KATHLEEN
Would you have me tell you lies?

STANTON
                  I'd have you brave.
(KATHLEEN *rises angrily, and strides
towards the bedroom*)
Where are you going, Kate? To have a
sulk?
Wait now, I'll fix a sugar teat for you,
Unless, of course, you'd rather suck your
thumb,
Brooding in your room—

KATHLEEN
                I have the name!
As well to have the game!

STANTON
                It's riddles, is it?

KATHLEEN
Riddles be damned! You think me idiotic;
I might as well fulfill your good opinion—
(STANTON *walks toward her*)
Come near me, and I'll smash your face
for you.
(STANTON *embraces her*)

STANTON

You're terrible fierce, you are. I wet me
pants.

KATHLEEN

You clown, you'll spring my hairpins.
Mattie, stop.

STANTON

Are these the hands are going to smash
my face?
They're weak as white silk fans . . . I'm
sorry, Kate:
You made me mad. And you know why?

KATHLEEN

                                I do.
You're as afraid as I.

STANTON

                     I am. I am.
You know me like the lashes of your
eye—

KATHLEEN

That's more than you know me, for if you
did,
You'd see what these three years have
done to me—
    (STANTON *breaks away from her*)
Now it's my turn to ask you where you're
going.

STANTON

I begged you not to bring that up again.
What can I do?

KATHLEEN

             You can tell Father Coyne,
And ask him to apply for dispensation,
And we can be remarried secretly.

STANTON

Now?

KATHLEEN

       Yes, Matt, now. Before it is too late.
We aren't married.

STANTON

            What was that in London,
The drunkard's pledge I took?

KATHLEEN

           We're Catholics, Matt.
Since when can Catholics make a valid
marriage
In a city hall? You have to tell the priest—

STANTON

Shall I tell him now? Do you take me for
a fool
To throw away the mayor's chair for that?

KATHLEEN

I slink to Sunday Mass like a pavement
nymph.
It's three years now since I made my
Easter Duty,
Three years of telling Father Coyne that
we
Receive at Easter Mass in the Cathedral,
Mortal Sin on Mortal Sin, Matt. If I died,
I'd go to Hell—

STANTON

           I think the woman's crazy!

KATHLEEN

Don't you believe in God?

STANTON

               Of course, I do.
And more, my dear, than you who think
that He
Would crush you as a man would crush
a fly
Because of some mere technical mistake—

KATHLEEN

Mere technical mistake? It's that now,
is it?
A blasphemous marriage, three years' fornication,
And now presumption—Technical mistake!
    (KATHLEEN *takes a cigarette out of a
box on the table and lights it.*)

STANTON

I wish you wouldn't smoke them cigarettes.
High-toned though it may be in France
and England,
It's a whore's habit here.
    (*Pause*)

KATHLEEN

             "Those cigarettes."
Don't try to hurt me, Matt. You know you
can,
As I know I can you.

STANTON

           What do you want!

KATHLEEN

I want to be your wife without disgrace.
I want my honor back. I want to live
Without the need to lie. I want you to
keep faith.

STANTON

Not now! Not now!

KATHLEEN

You've said that for three years.
What is it you're afraid of?

STANTON

Losing out.
You do not know these people as I do.
They turn upon the ones they make most
of.
They would on me, if given half a chance.
And if it got around that we were married
In an English City Hall, lose out we
would.

KATHLEEN

Matt, losing out? What profit for a man
To gain the world, and lose his soul?

STANTON

His soul!
That's Sunday school! That's convent
folderol,
Like making half-grown girls bathe in
their drawers
To put the shame of their own beauty in
them,
And break their lives to bear the Church's
bit.
We are not priests and nuns, but men
and women.
The world religious give up is our world,
The only world we have. We have to win
it
To do the bit of good we all must do;
And how are we to win the world unless
We keep the tricky rules its games are
run by?
Our faith is no mere monastery faith.
It runs as fast as feeling to embrace
Whatever good it sees. And if the good
Is overgrown with bad, it still believes
God sets no traps, the bad will be cut
down,
And the good push through its flowering
to fruit.
Forget your convent school. Remember,
Katie,

What the old women in the drowned
boreens
Would say when cloudbursts beat their
fields to slime,
And the potatoes blackened on their stalks
Like flesh gone proud. "Bad times is
right," they'd say,
"But God is good: apples will grow
again."
What sin have we committed? Marriage,
Kate?
Is that a sin?

KATHLEEN

It is with us.

STANTON

Because
You feel it so. It isn't. It's but prudence.
What if they should make a scandal of us?

KATHLEEN

Could we be worse off than we are?

STANTON

Kathleen!

KATHLEEN

Could we be worse off than we are, I said?

STANTON

Could we! We could. You don't know
poverty.
You don't know what it is to do without,
Not fine clothes only, or a handsome
house,
But men's respect. I do. I have been poor.
"Mattie, will you run down to the corner,
And buy me some cigars" or "Mattie, get
This gentleman a cab." Nine years, I
served
Ned Quinn and Agnes Hogan, day by day,
Buying my freedom like a Roman slave.
Will you ask me to put liberty at stake
To ease your scrupulous conscience? If
you do,
You're not the woman that I took you for
When I married you. Have you no cour-
age, Kate?

KATHLEEN

Will you lecture me on courage? Do you
dare?
When every time I walk those stairs to
the street
I walk to what I know is an enemy camp.

I was not raised like you. And no offense,
Please, Mattie, no offense. I miss my home.
Whore's habit it may be to smoke, as you
    say,
But it brings back the talk we used to
    have
About old friends, new books, the Lord
    knows what,
On our first floor in Baggot Street in
    Dublin.
This following you think so much about,
We live in Mortal Sin for fear you'll lose
    it,
I never knew the likes of them to talk to,
Person to person. They were cooks and
    maids,
Or peasants at the country houses, Matt.
All they can find to talk of, servants' talk,
Serfs' talk, eternal tearing down.
I'm like a woman banished and cut off.
I've you and May in the flat downstairs.
    That's all.
Don't tell me I don't know what poverty
    is.
What bankruptcy is worse than loneliness.
They say the sense of exile is the worst
Of all the pains that torture poor damned
    souls.
It is that sense I live with every day.

STANTON

Are you the only exile of us all?
You slept your crossing through in a rose-
    wood berth
With the swells a hundred feet below
    your portholes,
And ate off china on a linen cloth,
With the air around you fresh as the first
    of May.
I slept six deep in a bunk short as a coffin
Between a poisoned pup of a seasick boy
And a slaughtered pig of a snorer from
    Kildare,
Who wrestled elephants the wild nights
    through,
And sweated sour milk. I wolfed my
    meals,
Green water, and salt beef, and wooden
    biscuits,
On my hunkers like an ape, in a four-foot
    aisle
As choked as the one door of a burning
    school.
I crossed in mid-December: seven weeks
Of driving rain that kept the hatches bat-
    tened

In a hold so low of beam a man my height
Could never lift his head. And I couldn't
    wash.
Water was low; the place was like an
    icehouse;
And girls were thick as field mice in a
    haystack
In the bunk across. I would have died of
    shame,
When I stood in the landing shed of this
    "promised land,"
As naked as the day I first saw light,
Defiled with my own waste like a dying
    cat,
And a lousy red beard on me like a
    tinker's,
While a bitch of a doctor, with his nails
    too long,
Dared tell me: "In Amurrica, we bathe!"
I'd have died with shame, had I sailed
    here to die.
I swallowed pride and rage, and made a
    vow
The time would come when I could spit
    both out
In the face of the likes of him. I made a
    vow
I'd fight my way to power if it killed me,
Not only for myself, but for our kind,
For the men behind me, laughing out of
    fear,
At their own shame as well as mine, for
    the women,
Behind the board partition, frightened
    dumb
With worry they'd be sent back home to
    starve
Because they'd dirty feet. I was born again.
It came to me as brutal as the cold
That makes us flinch the day the mid-
    wife takes
Our wet heels in her fist, and punches
    breath
Into our dangling carcasses: Get power!
Without it, there can be no decency,
No virtue and no grace. I have kept my
    vow.
The mayor's chair is mine but for the
    running.
Will you have me lose it for your convent
    scruples?
    (*Pause*)

KATHLEEN

You never told me that about your landing.

STANTON

There's many things I never told you,
Kate.
I was afraid you'd hold me cheap.

KATHLEEN

Oh, Mattie,
Don't you know me yet?

STANTON

Stand by me.
Stand by me, Kate. The next four days
count hard.
By Sunday next, I'll have won all or lost.

KATHLEEN

What's Sunday next?

STANTON

The Clambake for Quinn's birthday:
We're to make things up between us and
make the announcement
On the steamer voyage to Seagate Sunday
evening.
Stand by me, Kate. As sure as God's my
judge
The minute I get into City Hall
The first thing I will do is call the priest,
And ask him to make peace with God
for us.
Stand by me, Kate.

KATHLEEN

I will though it costs my life.
(STANTON *kisses her*)

STANTON

God stand between us and all harm! There
now!
I've wiped those words from your lips.
—Oh, where's my mind!
I've brought champagne, and it's as warm
as tears.
Go get the glasses.
(KATHLEEN *takes two glasses down
from a cupboard.* STANTON *opens the
champagne and pours it. They touch
glasses.*)
Let the past be damned,
The dead bury the dead. The future's ours.

CURTAIN

ACT TWO

*Eleven o'clock the same night. The back
room of Stanton's saloon, The Court Café.*

*To stage left, glass-paned double doors cut
the room off from the bar, from which a
hum of voices can be heard. To stage
right, the Ladies' Entrance. Next to it,
a square piano with a pot of dead fern on
it. Around the room, squat round tables
and bent iron chairs. Stage center, around
one of the tables, with whiskeys in front
of them, three people. At the head,* JOHN
"BLACK JACK" HAGGERTY, *in his late sixties,
wearing his Sunday clothes, his hair parted
in the middle and swagged over his eyebrows in dove's wings, his handlebar mustache repeating the design. Both hair and
mustache are dyed an improbable black.
To Haggerty's left,* PETEY BOYLE, *a young
tough in his twenties, his heavy hair parted
in the middle and combed oilily back, the
teeth marks of the comb still in it. His
rachitic frame is wiry as a weed; and he is
dressed in a Salvation Army suit that
droops in the seat, balloons at the knees
and elbows. Next to Boyle, but facing the
audience,* BESSIE LEGG, *a blond girl in her
late twenties or early thirties, her hair in
a pompadour under a Floradora hat that
looks like an ostrich nest, a long feather
boa on, together with many strands of
glass beads, and rings on every finger but
her thumbs, all cheap. Her doll's face is
a bit crumpled, but there is no petulance
in it, merely jocose self-indulgence. There
is a crepe-paper shamrock tacked to the
piano, and four sprung tapes of green and
gold crepe paper run from the corners of
the room and belly over the table in a
haphazardly celebrative way.*

HAGGERTY

That Walsh from Albany was no man's
fool.
The first thing that he asked about was
Ag Hogan,
And then about Matt's temper, you know,
the time
He nearly broke Tim Costigan in two
For calling him Hogan's Goat. But at last
we cleared Matt.

BOYLE

Bess, Black Jack thinks the nomination'll
stand!

HAGGERTY

Stop your tormenting, Petey. Of course,
it will.
Amn't I Assistant Leader of this Ward

And head of the Matthew Stanton Asso-
ciation?
And isn't Palsy Murphy Boss of Brooklyn
And head of the Edward Quinn Associa-
tion?
Walsh said that Father Coyne and the
both of us
Would constitute a due and legal caucus;
And he's the representative of the Party,
He ought to know.

BESSIE
          Yeah? When does Quinn find out?

HAGGERTY
Tomorrow morning. It has to be told him
fast.
We're to break the news Matt's nominated
Sunday
At the Clambake for Quinn's birthday
down in Seagate.

BOYLE
Is both Associations going on this Clambake?

HAGGERTY
Yes. Murphy's got the job of telling Quinn
And getting him to make things up with
Matt.

BOYLE
That's a moonlight voyage we'll all be see-
ing stars.
It'll make the riot on the *Harvest Queen,*
When that Alderman knifed that guy in
'87,
Look like a slapping match in St. Mary's
schoolyard.
Quinn ain't never giving up to no Stan-
ton
In no four days.

BESSIE
               Dust off your steel derby,
Or your head will be all lumps like a bag
of marbles.

BOYLE
You tell him, kid. I'll hold the baby.

HAGGERTY
                         Lord!
What a pair of lochremauns! That's why
Murphy's Boss:
He could talk a Hindu out of a tiger's
mouth.

He'll find some cosy way to break the
news,
And Quinn will purr like a kitten.
          (*Enter* MARIA HAGGERTY *through the
          Ladies' Entrance. She is a tall, raw-
          boned woman in her late sixties, with
          loose-stranded iron-gray hair pulled
          back around a center part in a tight
          bun. She wears a rusty black toque,
          and a long black woolen coat with a
          frayed hem, and is carrying a large
          handbag, which she sets down on the
          floor as she settles wearily into the
          chair to stage right of Haggerty, her
          husband.*)

MARIA
                    Ah, there you are!
How are you, Mrs. Legg? How are you,
Petey?
I thought you might be waiting here for
Matt,
When Josie told me. Why is it so secret?

HAGGERTY
It won't be secret long with Josie Finn
Trumpeting it from here to Fulton Ferry
Like an elephant in heat. Quinn doesn't
know yet.
That's why it's so secret.

MARIA
               What's that you're drinking?

HAGGERTY
Whiskey and water, May.

MARIA
                    Give Ma a swallow.

HAGGERTY
Great God in Heaven, drink it all, why
don't you!
We're met to celebrate Matt Stanton's
luck.
Corner-boy Boyle and Bessie the balloon
brain
See trouble in store undreamed by Albany,
And my wife drags in here with a puss
on her
Like a lead-horse on a hearse. What's the
matter with you?

MARIA
I'm sure I'm glad for Matt's sake. He's
worked hard,

And he's been good, giving us the flat and
all.
But in a way, you know, Ned Quinn is
right:
Matt's hard on people, harder than he
should be.
He's a lot to answer for before he dies.

BESSIE
You mean Ag Hogan?

MARIA
    Yes, I do.

BESSIE
       Poor girl.
When I was there this morning, she
looked awful.

MARIA
She'll never live to comb out a gray head.
I've just now come from giving her her
tea,
In that coffin of a furnished room in Smith
Street.
I looked at the cheesecloth curtains hung
on strings;
And I thought of all those velvet-muffled
windows,
Those carpets red as blood and deep as
snow,
Those tables glistening underneath the
lamps
Like rosy gold, in her big house in Sea-
gate.
And I said to myself, if it weren't for
Agnes Hogan,
Matt would be a grocery clerk at Nolan's,
And not the owner of The Court Café.
And candidate for mayor; and there she
lies,
Flat on her back with two beanbags of
buckshot
On her shriveled breasts, to chain her to
the mattress,
As if she could move, her eyes in a black
stare
At the white paint peeling off that iron
bedstead,
Like scabs of a rash; and he never once
comes near her,
For fear, I suppose, they'd call him
Hogan's Goat,
And his missis might find out about their
high jinks.
And yet if Matt were any kind of man,
Wouldn't he go and take her in his arms,

And say, "You hurt me bad three years
ago;
But I hurt you as bad. Forgive and forget."
Maybe it's because the girl's my niece,
But I think I'd feel the same if she were
not.

HAGGERTY
Be that as may be, what has passed be-
tween them
Is their affair. It isn't ours to judge,
Especially after all Matt's done for us—
And you'll set this one thinking how Tom
Legg
Left her in the lurch in Baltic Street,
And spraying us all like a drainpipe in a
downpour,
If you keep up that way. Sure, what's past
is past.
What can't be remedied must be endured.

BESSIE
Say, listen here, Napoleon the Turd,
Legg never found me in no bed with no
one,
Like Matt done Ag, if that's what you're
implying.

HAGGERTY
How could he, when he worked in the
subway nights,
And was so blind he couldn't tie his shoes
Without his nose to the eyelets, his rump
in the air,
Like a startled ostrich.

BESSIE
    Say that again, I dare you!

HAGGERTY
No matter now. It served what it was
meant to:
Better glares than tears—
 (*A loud shout from the bar. Applause,
 cheers and singing. Enter* STANTON
 *from the bar with a crowd around
 him, singing. The four at the table
 join in.*)

EVERYBODY
He'll make a jolly good mayor!
He'll make a jolly good mayor!
He'll make a jolly good mayor!
Which nobody can deny!

HAGGERTY
Speech, Mattie, speech!

STANTON
                    Thanks all! What will I say!
It's me who should be singing songs to
    you,
Not you to me. And I don't know how
    you've learned
That I'm to run for mayor. It's a secret.
Ask the man who told you if it isn't,
Jack Haggerty—
    (*Applause*)
                    When I returned from England
Three years ago with my new wife, I
    thought
My chances to get back into the Party
Were gone for good. Yet in those three
    short years
You stuck by me so fast, the Party made
    me
Leader of the Ward in which the mayor
I had a falling-out with lives; and now
You're bent on giving me his place.
Ned Quinn—
    (*Booing and hissing.* PETEY BOYLE
    *jumps on a table, puts one fist on his
    hip, throws his head back insolently,
    and sings, in a nasal imitation of John
    McCormack. Enter* FATHER COYNE, *un-
    noticed, through the Ladies' Entrance,
    wearing his biretta and an old black
    overcoat shorter than his cassock.*)

BOYLE
Is it Ned Quinn you mean? } *repeat*
Says the Shan Van Vocht,
He's in Fogarty's shebeen
Drinking bourbon with some } *repeat*
    quean,
Says the Shan Van Vocht.
Let him drink it to the dregs, } *repeat*
Says the Shan Van Vocht.
For the goose that lays gold eggs
Lays no more for hollow legs, } *repeat*
Says the Shan Van Vocht.
    (*Applause and laughter.* BOYLE *mo-
    tions for silence and sings.*)

BOYLE
Go and tell that swindler!
    (BOYLE *points to* HAGGERTY.)

HAGGERTY
Go and tell that swindler!
    (HAGGERTY *points to* BESSIE.)

BESSIE
Go and tell that swindler!

BOYLE
What the Shan Van Vocht has said!
    (BOYLE *apes a choir director.*)

EVERYBODY
What the Shan Van Vocht has said!
    (*Laughter and applause.* FATHER COYNE
    *angrily jostles his way to stage center,
    the people shamefacedly making way
    for him.*)

FATHER COYNE
For shame! For shame! Have you no
    charity?
Don't turn upon the man, but on his sin.

HAGGERTY
Father! Sit down. I thought you'd be in
bed.

FATHER COYNE
I couldn't sleep. I thought I'd come by
here
And have a word with Matt alone.

BOYLE
                    A word or a drink?

FATHER COYNE
What's that you say, Pete Boyle? Speak
up, why don't you,
And show them how malicious you can
be,
And you so drunk!

BOYLE
                    I didn't mean no harm.

FATHER COYNE
You meant no harm! You're all of you
alike.
You talk to preen your wit or flex your
pride,
Not to lay bare your hearts or tell God's
truth.
Words have more force than blows. They
can destroy.
Would you punch an old man's face to
test your arm?
Answer me, Pete Boyle.

BOYLE
                    You know I wouldn't.

FATHER COYNE
You did as much to me.

BOYLE

I'm sorry, Father.

FATHER COYNE

I hope you are, my son. Don't look so
pious,
The rest of you. You're just as bad as him,
Dancing around the ruin of Quinn's name
Like a pack of savages. Do you know the
story
The Rabbis set down centuries ago
Beside the part in Exodus where the Jews
Are shown exulting over the drowned
troops
Of Pharaoh on the shores of the Red Sea?
The angels, says the story, joined their
voices
With those of the men below. And God
cried out:
"What reason is there to hold jubilee?
The men of Egypt are my children too!"
The men of Egypt were God's enemies,
And Edward Quinn's your friend, may
God forgive you!

STANTON

That kind of justice is too heavenly
For us on earth. If we condone Ned
Quinn,
Don't we condone corruption with him,
Father?

FATHER COYNE

You know, don't you, a man can commit
theft,
And yet not be a thief by nature, Matt?
Corruption sometimes saps the choicest
men;
Sometimes it is disordered sweetness drives
A man to act contrary to what's right.
Collusion can arise from faithfulness,
And graft from bankrupt generosity.
You know I'd never ask you to condone
that.
But once he's made the city restitution,
The loss of office is enough chastisement
For Edward Quinn. You must not banish
him.
What purpose would it serve to break a
man
Who's slaved for Church and people thirty
years?

STANTON

What purpose would it serve? 'Twould
end corruption.
Corruption, Father, may be, as you say,

Disordered sweetness sometimes, but in
men
Who govern others, can we risk disorder
To save the heart it works its ferment on?
A man may cut away the seething bruise
That festers in good fruit or even flesh.
The heart's corruption poisons surgery.
The pulse of it is rapid. It pollutes
Like ratbite, and like ratbite spawns
Plagues to charge whole graveyards.
Isolate its carriers fast, I say. Disown them,
Before they can infect us with the pox
We came across the ocean to avoid,
Liberty gone blind, the death of honor!—
Would you have the big men of this city
say
That they were right in keeping us cheap
labor,
Because we are not fit for nobler service,
We dirty what we touch? Say that they
will,
And with full right, unless we dare cut
free
From these enfeebling politics of pity,
And rule the city right. Ned Quinn must
go—
      (Applause)

HAGGERTY

Hurray for Stanton! The man is right,
God bless him.
What answer, Father, can you make to
that?

FATHER COYNE

What answer, Black Jack, but the same
old answer?
Judge not, Matt Stanton, lest yourself be
judged;
Beware, Matt Stanton, lest in pointing out
The mote within your neighbor's watering
eye,
You overlook the beam that blinds your
own.

STANTON

I meant no disrespect. Forgive me, Father.

FATHER COYNE

Do not delude yourself it is offense
Has made me quote the Scripture to you,
man.
I dare not take offense. My task is love.
I have no passion save the one for souls.
Salus suprema lex, remember that,
Salvation is the law that must come first.

My cure includes both you and Edward
  Quinn.
Because it does, I have to warn you, Matt,
Do not mistake vindictiveness for justice.
I hope you take my meaning. Do you?

STANTON

                                Yes.
I'll make no move against Ned Quinn,
  I promise,
Unless he moves against me first.

FATHER COYNE

                           Good, Matt.

STANTON

For your penance, Petey, draw the priest
a beer.

FATHER COYNE

I won't tonight, Matt, thank you. I've a
  matter
I'd like to talk to you about alone.

STANTON

Sure, Father— Out, the lot of you, to the
  bar.
The drinks are on the house.

HAGGERTY

Stanton abu, boys.

BOYLE

Let the Jickies and Prods,
Says the Shan Van Vocht,
Look down on us like gods,
Says the Shan Van Vocht.
We've got Stanton, damn the odds,
Says the Shan Van Vocht.
  (*Exit* EVERYBODY *cheering. Pause.*)

FATHER COYNE

It's no good being delicate. If I tried,
I'd put your eye out, Matt, or break your
  bones.
I'll just come out and say it: go see Ag.

STANTON

Agnes Hogan, Father?

FATHER COYNE

                    Agnes Hogan.
What other Ag would I mean?

STANTON

                    I can't do that.

FATHER COYNE

You can't or you won't?

STANTON

              One knock at Aggie's door,
And Josie Finn would be scissoring down
  Fifth Place
With the wind in tatters around her, and
  at Kate's ear
Before the latch was lifted. It would all
  come out—

FATHER COYNE

It should have come out long since. Ag's
  dying, Matt.
Tell Kate about her, and go.

STANTON

             Whose fault she's dying?
Did you ever know her stop when the
  thirst was on her?
Who poured that whiskey down her four-
  teen months
Until the lungs were tattered in her
  breast?
Who landed her in Saranac?
    (*Pause*)
             She was always like that.
Whiskey, or clothes, or diamonds . . . or
  men!
You can say what you want of Jo Finn
  and her tongue,
If it wasn't for her, I'd never have found
  out
I was the goat for fair.

FATHER COYNE

            Ag was fully clothed.
And so was Quinn.

STANTON

          You didn't see them, Father.
They were leg in leg when Josie brought
  me in.
Asleep, I grant you, but his ham of a hand
Was tangled in the fullness of her hair—

FATHER COYNE

You told me that long since. What's done
  is done.
Don't let the woman die unreconciled.
Tell Kate, and go to see her.

STANTON

                Yes, but—

FATHER COYNE

What?

What can I know of love, a celibate,
Numb as a broomstick in my varnished
    parlor,
With my frightened curate jumping at
    each word,
And Ann Mulcahy to do my housekeeping
Without a whimper of complaint. What
    can I know?
Putting aside the fact that priesthood's
    marriage
To a Partner Who is always right, I know
If you don't tell Kate, there are others will,
Before the ink is dry on the campaign
    posters,
And that would be disastrous—

STANTON

Tell her what!

FATHER COYNE

Don't take that tone with me.

STANTON

I lived with her?

Shall I tell my wife I serviced Ag three
    years?

FATHER COYNE

If you're trying to shock me, Matt, you're
    being simple.
For forty years, no Saturday's gone by,
I have not sat alone from three to nine
In my confessional, and heard men spill
Far blacker things than that. Man, use
    your reason!

STANTON

I loved Ag, and kept faith.

FATHER COYNE

Who says you didn't?

STANTON

I loved her and kept faith. I did my part.
She played me false with Quinn.

FATHER COYNE

If you loved her, Matt,

How is it that you didn't marry her,
Before she, how did you put it, played
    you false?
    (*Pause*)

STANTON

Not to give you a short answer, Father,
But don't you think that's my affair?

FATHER COYNE

No, Matt.

STANTON

It's not the kind of thing you talk to
priests of.

FATHER COYNE

You're trying to make me angry, aren't
    you?
Since *you* won't tell *me* why, let me tell
    you.
You only wanted Ag for fun and games;
You didn't want her on your neck for life.
You thought she'd spoil your chances,
    didn't you?
Your chances for the mayor's chair? You
    thought,
If you married her, they'd call you
    Hogan's Goat
To the day you died. Your heart rejoiced
    when you found
The both of them in bed—

STANTON

Are you finished, Father?

FATHER COYNE

No, Matt. I'm not. Do you know why
    you're fuming?
Because you're a good man, and you feel
    ashamed,
Because I'm saying what you tell yourself:
Whatever wrong was done was on both
    sides.
The woman made you what you are to-
    day;
The woman's dying. Hogan's Goat, or not,
Pocket your pride, and tell your wife
    about her.
Go talk with Ag, and let her die in peace,
Or else you'll be her goat in the Bible
    sense,
With all her sins on your head, and the
    world a desert.
Do you think I like to say such things to
    you?
I'm trying to help you, Matt.

STANTON

I had the right

To show her no one plays Matt Stanton
    false
More than one time!

FATHER COYNE

If you'd the right, my son,

Why are you screaming at me?

STANTON
                    Because you'd have me
Destroy this new life I've been three years
    building,
Not only for myself but for my kind,
By dragging my poor wife to the room in
    my heart
Where my dead loves are waked.
        (*Pause*)

FATHER COYNE
                    Tell Kathleen, Matt.
Maybe it's that which stands between you,
    son,
And stiffens both your backs against each
    other.

STANTON
Who dares to say that something stands
    between us?
That's a pack of lies!

FATHER COYNE
                    Is it? Tell Katie, Matt—
(BOYLE *bursts through the bar door.*)

BOYLE
It's Aggie Hogan, Father.
She's dying; and she won't confess to
    your curate.
They want you.

FATHER COYNE
                    Mattie?

STANTON
                    Sacred Heart of Jesus!

FATHER COYNE
Will you come with me?

STANTON
                    I will, Father. I will.
(*Exit all three through the Ladies'
    Entrance.*)

CURTAIN

ACT THREE

*Midnight the same night. The all-night
Printers' Church in the Newspaper Row
of Brooklyn on lower Fulton Street.* STAN-
TON *kneels on a prie-dieu with a framed
baize curtain atop it.* FATHER MALONEY

*sits on the other side of the prie-dieu,
hearing his Confession.*

————

STANTON
Bless me, Father. I have sinned. Three
    years.
It is three years since I made my last Con-
    fession.
I accuse myself of lying many times.

FATHER MALONEY
How many times?

STANTON
                    God knows!

FATHER MALONEY
                    With a mind to harm?

STANTON
God knows!

FATHER MALONEY
    Take hold of yourself. What ails you!

STANTON
I did a woman wrong. Tonight she died.
Tomorrow is her wake.

FATHER MALONEY
                    What kind of wrong
Is it you did her?

STANTON
                    I . . .

FATHER MALONEY
                    What kind of wrong?

STANTON
I lived with her three years before I mar-
    ried.
They pulled the sheet over her face an
    hour ago.
The hem of it gave. It was gray as a buried
    rag.
She wouldn't have the priest. She lay
    there sweating,
And they around her with their lighted
    candles.
She glowered and said, "If such love was
    a sin,
I'd rather not make peace with God at
    all."
They pressed her hard. She shook and
    shook her head.

She kept on shaking it until she died—
Absolve her through me!

FATHER MALONEY
             You know I can't do that.

STANTON
What can you do then!

FATHER MALONEY
             Absolve *you* from *your* sin.

STANTON
Her sin is mine. Absolve the both of us.

FATHER MALONEY
Why did you leave this woman?

STANTON
                 She played me false.
I found her in the one bed with a man—
She stood on the wide porch with her hair
   down, crying.
I walked away. I heard her screaming at
   me.
She told me, go, yes go, but not to come
   back. Never.
She'd rip the clothes she bought me into
   threads
And throw them in the fire. She'd burn
   my letters,
And every bit of paper that I'd put my
   name to.
And she did . . . I'm sure she did. She
   was wild by nature.
But tonight . . . when I came back . . .
   she stretched out her hands
Like a falling child . . .

FATHER MALONEY
             Go on.

STANTON
                 And I turned away—
I cannot rest with thinking of her face
And that black look of stubborn joy on it.

FATHER MALONEY
Well for you, you can't rest. She died in
   the Devil's arms
In a glory of joy at the filthy shame to
   her flesh
You visited on her, and like all the rest,
You come to a strange priest outside your
   parish
In the mistaken hope he will not judge
   you,

But give you comfort when you need correction.
What about this other one you took up
   with
When you threw the dead one over?—

STANTON
                 Jesus, Father!

FATHER MALONEY
Don't take the name of the Lord in vain
   to me!

STANTON
I don't know why I came here in the first
   place.

FATHER MALONEY
You came here for forgiveness—

STANTON
                 From the likes of you!
For thirty years I've put up with your
   kind.
Since my First Communion. Saturday
   Confession!
Spayed mutts of men, born with no spice
   of pride,
Living off the pennies of the poor,
Huddled in their fat in basement booths,
Calling the true vaulting of the heart
Toward its desire filth and deviation,
Dragging me, and all unlike you down—

FATHER MALONEY
Whatever a noble creature like yourself
May think of me, I'm here to do God's
   work;
And since that begins with dragging you
   down to the earth
We all have come from and must all
   return to,
Drag you down I will. God lifts none but
   the humble—

STANTON
The pride steams off you like the stink of
   cancer,
And you sit there and preach humility!

FATHER MALONEY
Take care! I will deny you absolution.

STANTON
What harm! Who can absolve us but ourselves!

I am what I am. What I have done, I'd
    cause for.
It was seeing what life did to her un-
    manned me;
It was looking in her eyes as they guttered
    out
That drove me here like a scared kid from
    the bogs
Who takes the clouds that bruise the light
    for demons.
But thanks to the words from the open
    grave of your mouth
I see that fear for the wind in fog that it is
And it is killed for good. I'm my own
    man now.
I can say that for the first time in my life.
I'm free of her; and I'm free of you and
    yours.
Come what come may to me, from this
    day forward,
I'll not fall to my knees for man or God.
    (STANTON *rises, and quickly strides*
    out. FATHER MALONEY *rises.*)

FATHER MALONEY

Will you dare to turn your back on the
    living God!

CURTAIN

ACT FOUR

Ten o'clock, Friday morning, April 29,
1890. The back room of Fogarty's Saloon.
JAMES "PALSY" MURPHY *sits at a chair*
pushed well back from a table, apprehen-
sively holding a sheaf of papers in his hand.
He is a florid, rather stout man in his late
fifties, with black hair en brosse, *graying at*
the temples. MAYOR EDWARD QUINN *stands*
facing MURPHY *like a statue of a lawyer*
in a park. He is a tall, husky, big-boned
man in his seventies, bald, but with hair
growing out of his ears. He is dressed in
rumpled morning clothes.

———

QUINN

Does Matthew Stanton think he can oust
    me
By hole-in-corner meetings in school halls,
With craw thumpers and Sunday-pass-the-
    plates,
Black Jack the plug and the ga-ga Parish
    Priest
Both nodding yes to everything he says

Like slobbering dummies?— What is it
    that he said?

MURPHY

Do you want to hear?

QUINN

               Would I ask, James, if I didn't?

MURPHY

Listen then. I have . . . full notes on it.
I took down everything that Stanton said.

QUINN

Read it. Read it. Do you want applause?

MURPHY

No, Ned: attention. Here: "My dear old
    friends,
When Father Coyne asked me to speak to
    you,
He said it was about Ag Hogan's bills,
A gathering to help raise funds to pay
    them.
I never thought the purpose of this meet-
    ing
Would be political"—

QUINN

               "I never thought
The purpose of this meeting"—Father
    Coyne!
I roofed his sieve of a church and glazed
    it too;
And put a tight new furnace in its cellar.
There's not a priest you can trust!

MURPHY

Will you listen, Ned!

QUINN

               I'm listening. Go on.

MURPHY

"The Party of Reform"—

QUINN

"The Party of Reform"! Ah, yes, reform!
A Lutheran lawyer with a flytrap mouth
And a four-bit practice of litigious Swedes
In a closet rank as rats down by the river!
A lecherous broker with a swivel eye
You wouldn't trust with Grandma in a
    hack!
A tear-drawers arm in arm with a gaping
    bollocks!

MURPHY
Will you quit your interrupting!

QUINN
Read on. Read on.

MURPHY
"The Party of Reform has in its hands
Sworn affidavits on the city books"—

QUINN
Got by collusion and by audits forged
As the certificates above their parents'
beds!—

MURPHY
"The Party of Reform has in its hands
Sworn affidavits on the city books,
Drawn up from careful audit, and declar-
ing
A hidden deficit of fifteen thousand"—

QUINN
Of fifteen thousand! The unfortunates!
They couldn't even get that business right.
It's twenty thousand, Palsy, if it's a cent!
(*Glum pause*)
I'm in the treasury for twenty thousand.
(*Pause*)

MURPHY
"You say they will expose us to the public,
Unless we guarantee that Edward Quinn
Resigns as candidate in the next elec-
tion"—

QUINN
See, that's Matt's game. He's out to get my
job;
But he's not the guts to grab it like a man.
Will you listen to the cagey way he puts it:
"*You* say *they* will expose *us* to the pub-
lic!"
As sneaky as a rat in a hotel kitchen.
Don't you see the cunning of it, James?
The craft?
It's not my job he wants, but to save the
Party!
And all I did for him. I made him, James.
I picked him up when he first came to me,
Twelve years ago, when he was twenty-five
And lost his job for beating up that grocer.
He'd no knees in his pants; his coat was
slick
With grease as a butcher's thumb. He was
skin and bones.
I was sitting here in Fogarty's back room,

With poor Ag Hogan codding me, when
he
Burst in the door, and asked me for my
help.
"I'll do anything that's honest, Mr.
Quinn,"
Is what he says. He had that crooked
grin—
It reminded me of Patrick that's long dead,
Patrick, my poor brother—

MURPHY
Go on, now, Ned!
Leave out the soft-soap. He'd a crooked
grin
You knew would serve you well among
the women—

QUINN
I should have said, "Go now, and scare the
crows,
Raggedy-arse Keho; that's all you're good
for!"
But, no, there was that grin; and Ag said,
"Take him."
She loved him, the poor slob, from the day
she saw him,
Fat good it did her. "You can put him on
With Judge Muldooney," says she; "take
him, Ned,
God will bless us for it . . ."
(*Pause*)
Aggie's dead, James. Dead.

MURPHY
Yes, Ned. She is.

QUINN
Did Stanton get to see her?
(*Pause*)
Did he?

MURPHY
Yes.

QUINN
She wouldn't let me in.
(*Pause*)

MURPHY
I'm sorry, Ned.

QUINN
And Stanton's high-toned wife?
What did she say when she found out
about them?

MURPHY
She didn't, Ned. She knows that Ag
helped Matt,
But nothing else.

QUINN
                    Ah, nothing else? I see.
Where was I, Palsy?

MURPHY
                    "All I done for him,"
Fifth book, tenth chapter—

QUINN
                    Go to hell, James Murphy.
You think it's funny, do you? I'll give you
fun.
If it's jail for me, you know, it's jail for
you.
No hundred-dollar suits and fancy feeds
With tarts in Rector's drinking cold cham-
pagne
From glasses bright as ice with hollow
stems,
But tea from yellowed cups and mulligan
Foul as the odds and ends they make it
from.

MURPHY
Sure, they'll send us puddings.

QUINN
                    Are you mad, or what?
I tell you, I'm in danger. I'm in danger.
Don't shake your head. They're spoiling
for the kill.
It's in their blood.

MURPHY
                    Whose blood?

QUINN
                    Whose blood but our own.
They turn upon the strong, and pull them
down,
And not from virtue, James, but vicious
pride.
They want to hold their heads up in this
city,
Among the members of the Epworth
League,
The Church of Ethical Culture and the
Elks,
That's why they're taking sides with Ole
Olson,
Or whatever the hell his name is, and that
whore

From Wall Street in the clean pince-nez.
For thirty years
I've kept their heads above the water,
James,
By fair means or by foul. Now they've
reached the shore
They'd rather not remember how they got
there.
They want to disown me. They're a faith-
less lot,
And Matthew Stanton is the worst of all—
Read on, why don't you? What's the mat-
ter with you?
                    (*Pause*)

MURPHY
"I would not stand in this school hall be-
fore you
If Edward Quinn had not, in his full
power,
Made of me what I am. I cannot think,
Since you have shared his generosity
As long as I, that you are asking me
To help you pull him down"—

QUINN
                    Good Jesus, James!

MURPHY
"The way to cope with the Party of Re-
form's
To raise the funds to make Quinn's deficit
up.
I pledge three thousand dollars, and I ask
Each and every one of you who can
To give as much as possible. Ned Quinn
Must not live out his final days in jail
Because he was too kindly to be wise"—

QUINN
I want no handouts from the likes of him.
Will he pity me?

MURPHY
                    What's that?

QUINN
                    You heard me, James.
Will he pity me? Does he think I need his
pity!
I made him, and I can unmake him too,
And make another in his place. I'm old,
I'm far too old to live on charity
From a greenhorn that I picked up in a
barroom
To run my sweetheart's errands. Don't
you see, James?

He took Ag from me first; that's how he
    started.
He ran her roadhouse for her. "He was
    handsome!
He'd skin like milk, and eyes like stars in
    winter!"
And he was young and shrewd! She
    taught him manners:
What clothes to wear, what cutlery to be-
    gin with,
What twaddle he must speak when in-
    troduced
To the state bigwigs down from Albany.
He told her that he loved her. She ditched
    me.
I'm twenty years her senior. Then that day,
That famous Labor Day three years ago,
We'd a drink or two, you know, for old
    times' sake,
And we passed out, and that bitch Josie
    Finn
Found out about us, and brought Matt in
    on us,
Our arms around each other like two chil-
    dren.
And he spat on poor Ag's carpet, called
    her a whore,
Me a degenerate. Three years ago,
The very year he married this Kathleen,
The Lord knows who, James, from the
    Christ knows where,
In some cosy hocus-pocus there in London,
To show Ag he could do without her. He
    never spoke
To Ag at all until he found her done for,
Dying lung by lung. He'd never speak to
    me at all
If I were not in trouble.
Don't you see the triumph of it, Palsy
    Murphy!
He takes his vengeance in a show of
    mercy.
He weeps as he destroys! He's a croco-
    dile—

MURPHY
Ned, I . . .

QUINN
        Ned what?

MURPHY
        I hope you won't be hurt.
We on the Party board agree with Matt.
We feel the time has come for some new
    blood—

QUINN
"We on the Party board agree with Matt"!
Now it comes out at last! It all comes out!
You and your pack of lies, your trumped-
    up story,
Pretending to be reading what he said
When you can't read a thing that hasn't
    pictures.
Did you think me such a boob I wouldn't
    know
What you and Walsh were up to here last
    night?
It made the rounds of the Ward by half
    past nine!
    (*Pause*)
Bismarck the diplomat! You goddamned
    fool,
Pouring that vat of soft-soap over me!
"Because he was too kindly to be wise"!
They'll soon be making you the editor
Of *The Messenger of the Sacred Heart.*

MURPHY
            Now, Ned—

QUINN
"Now, Ned." "Now, Ned." Shut up, or
    I'll drink your blood.
The only thing rang true in what you said
Was Stanton's offer to be noble to me.
    (*Pause*)

MURPHY
I wanted to break it easy. Matt made no
    offer.
The Party it is will cover you on the books.
But on one condition, Ned: you must re-
    sign.

QUINN
I must resign. We'll see who backs out
    first.
I didn't stay the mayor of this city
For thirty years by taking orders, James.
You tell the Party board I'll rot in prison
Before I'll let Matt Stanton take my place.
You tell the Party board I'll meet the
    debits
The Party of Reform found in the books.
You tell the Party board they'd best not
    cross me.
Don't look as if you think this all is
    blather.
There's not a one of you I can't get at,
You least of all. Remember that, James
    Murphy.

How long, do you think, that knowing
    what I know
About your money, James, and how you
    got it,
The Jesuit Fathers at St. Francis Xavier's,
With all their bon-ton notions of clean
    hands,
Would let your boys play soldier in their
    yard?
Don't glare like that at me. You tell the
    board
What I have said. I meant it, every word.

MURPHY

The Party will disown you!

QUINN

                   Let them try!
I'll grease the palm of every squarehead
    deadbeat
From Greenwood Cemetery to the Nar-
    rows
Who'll stagger to the polls for three
    months' rent,
I'll buy the blackface vote off all the fences
Down Fulton Street from Hudson Ave-
    nue.
I'll vote from every plot in Holy Cross
With an Irish headstone on it. I'll win this
    fight—

MURPHY

I'll telegraph to Albany. I warn you!

QUINN

Damn Albany! Get out of here. Get out!
    (*Exit* MURPHY *stage left.* QUINN *walks
    over to the bar door to stage right.*)
Hey, Bill.
    (*Enter* BILL, *a wiry bowlegged man
    about seventy who has the look of a
    drunk.*)
Go down to one-o-seventy Luqueer Street,
And get me Josie Finn—On second
    thought,
Best wait till noon and collar me some
    schoolboy
To run the errand for me. If they saw you,
They'd know 'twas I that wanted her. And
    yes!
Send to Fitzsimmons and Rooney for a
    wreath,
A hundred-dollar wreath, and have them
    spell
This message out in them gold-paper let-
    ters

On a silk-gauze band: "For Agnes Mary
    Hogan,
Gone but not forgotten." Look alive!

CURTAIN

ACT FIVE

*Eight o'clock the same evening. The
Haggertys' kitchen, beneath the Stantons'
parlor in the double set. The kitchen table and chairs are of cheap oak, varnished
and revarnished until they looked charred
and blistered. The chairs are unmatched,
and of the "Queen Anne" style, jerrybuilt
replicas of a bad idea of eighteenth-century
furniture, with die-embossed designs on
the back, their seats repaired with pressed
cardboard. Behind the table stands the big
coal cooking stove, jammed into the chimney. The mantelpiece is covered with
newspaper cut into daggers of rough lace
and filled with every kind of souvenir you
could think of, yellowing letters, bills, clippings stuck behind the grimy ornaments.
To stage right of the stove, an entrance
into the three remaining rooms of the
flat, an opening hung with a single por-
tiere of heavy, warped, faded brown velour
on greasy, wooden rings. Through that
opening, from time to time, as the scene
progresses, can be heard the sound of people saying the Rosary. The door of the
flat, giving on the hall and the stairs to the
Stantons' flat, is ajar; and leaned against it
glitters Edward Quinn's appalling flower
piece. Seated to stage left of the table is
JOSIE FINN, a tall, rather handsome woman
in her late thirties, with her black hair in
a loose bun. Opposite her sits ANN MUL-
CAHY, a small, plump woman with a face
like a withered apple, red hair gone white,
and fine searching eyes. Between them, its
back to the audience, stands an empty
chair. They have cups in front of them,
and are waiting for the kettle to boil for
the tea.*

———

ANN

I'm sure Matt will have luck for burying
    Ag
And letting Maisie hold the wake down-
    stairs here
In his own house for all that past beween
    them.
    (JOSIE *nods disconsolately. Enter*

PETEY BOYLE, *swaying slightly, his hat
in his hands*.)

BOYLE
I'm sorry for your trouble, Mrs. Finn.

JOSIE
My trouble, Petey. Trouble it is for fair.
That's Aggie Hogan that's laid out in
    there,
My dead aunt's daughter, that I haven't
    talked to
For, Mother of God, I think it's three long
    years
September.

BOYLE
                If you come to crow about it,
My ass on you then, kid—

JOSIE
                            Sir, you presume!
John Haggerty!
    (BOYLE *scurries through the portiere
    to the sanctuary of the coffin.*)

ANN
Now don't be calling Jack. It will cause
    trouble.
Poor Petey Boyle was always ignorant.
He meant no harm by talking to you dirty,
Josie dear.

JOSIE
            It's not his talking dirty
Made me mad. What kind of creature
    must he take me for,
To come to crow at my own cousin's
    wake!—
You know, Ag wouldn't see me at the last?

ANN
Nor would she have the priest. She was
    crazed with pain,
In fever tantrums, don't you know, half
    dead.
She hardly knew what she was doing.

JOSIE
Ann, you're a saint.

ANN
                Now, Josie, praise is poison,
Though I thank you for the kindness that's
    behind it.

JOSIE
How can you live, remembering what
    you've done,

Unless you are a saint, or a half brute,
Like Quinn in there!

ANN
                By doing what you must;
And begging for the grace to forgive
    yourself
As well as others when you don't do right.
You just reminded me: I hope Ned's going
    soon.
It's getting on towards eight; and Matt's
    expected down.

JOSIE
Oh, Quinn knows that. Sure, Quinn
    knows everything:
Whose money's stained, and how, and
    whose is not;
Who's in whose bed, and who is not, and
    why;
Who has a shame to hide that he can use
To coat his nest with slime against the
    wind!

ANN
There's a bit of skunk in all of us, you
    know.
We stink when we're afraid or hurt. Ned's
    both.

JOSIE
Pray for me, Ann Mulcahy. I've made a
    vow
On my dead mother's grave to guard my
    tongue
And keep my temper.

ANN
                    God in Heaven help you.

JOSIE
It's up to me, not Him.

ANN
                        Ah, don't say that.
Sure, that's presumption.

JOSIE
                    Then I won't say that.
But thinking back on things I've said and
    done,
And my knees all bunions, kneeling out
    novenas,
If you think that God and all His holy
    angels
Can shut my mouth once anger oils the
    hinges,

You're more a fool than ever I took you
    for
When first I met you—
    (*Enter* FATHER COYNE, *dressed in the
    same rusty black coat and frayed
    biretta.*)

FATHER COYNE
                    Here in the nick of time!
Who's calling my lost parish's one saint
A fool to her face!

JOSIE
                    Good evening to you, Father.

FATHER COYNE
Good evening, Mrs. Finn. I'm glad to see
Your three hard years of war with the
    deceased
Has ended in some show of gallantry.
What was the fight about? Do you recall?

JOSIE
You well know that I do. But what's been
    has been.
She'd have done the same for me.

FATHER COYNE
                    I'm sure she would:
For where would be the harm in that, I
    ask you?
There'd be small danger of much conver-
    sation
To thaw your icy hearts—

ANN
                    Please, Father Coyne—

FATHER COYNE
Dear God, forgive me. I forgot you, Ann.
It's like me to fly out at Mrs. Finn
With the one soul left here I could scan-
    dalize
From Dwight Street to the steps of City
    Hall.
I'll be as gracious as St. Francis Sales
To make it up to you, Ann—Now, Mrs.
    Finn,
And how have you been ever since?

JOSIE
                    Since when?

FATHER COYNE
Since Easter Sunday three long years ago,
The last time that I saw you in my
    church!

JOSIE
There's other churches!

FATHER COYNE
                    Yes, but not this parish;
And that's where you belong—
    (ANN *touches* FATHER COYNE *on the
    sleeve and looks into his eyes.*)
                    I'm a sinful man.
Pray for me, Ann Mulcahy. I'll begin the
    beads,
Before I throw my forty years of prayer
Into the pits of Hell to best a slanderer.
Will you come with me?

ANN
                    In a minute, Father.
The kettle's on the boil.
    (*Exit* FATHER COYNE *through the por-
    tiere. Pause*)

JOSIE
                    I have the name;
As well to have the game!

ANN
                    He meant no harm.
He's torn apart with trying to talk sense
To poor Ag dying; and he struck at you
Because you brought the days back Ag
    was well.
    (*Pause*)
Will you wet the tea, while I go in and
    ask
If Ned Quinn can't be hurried just a bit.
I'm destroyed with worrying that Matt
    will come.
    (*Exit* ANN. *Sound of Rosary.* JOSIE
    *rises, and brews the tea in a large
    earthenware pot. Enter* QUINN *quietly
    through the portiere. Sound of Ro-
    sary.* JOSIE *looks up from the stove,
    directly at him, then away. Most of
    their conversation is carried on with
    averted faces.*)

QUINN
Why have they put that wedding ring on
    Ag?
    (*Pause*)

JOSIE
She asked them to. She said it was her
    mother's.
    (*Pause*)

QUINN

What harm would there be in it, I'd like
to know!

JOSIE

You'd like to know? You know damned
well what harm.
I told you no this afternoon. I meant it.
Am I your cat's-paw, do you think, Ned
Quinn,
To pull your poisoned chestnuts from the
fire
And feed them to your foes? I told you.
No.

QUINN

You didn't think that way the day you led
him
Into the room where her that's dead in
there
Lay in my arms as guiltless as a baby
In a fit of drunken warmth she took for
love!

JOSIE

More shame to me I didn't think that way!
She was my own blood, and she loved the
man;
And I tried to get between them, and
broke her heart.
It's all my fault that she lies dead in there,
No one's but mine. And she was good to
me,
And I betrayed her—Ned, she wouldn't
see me.
She wouldn't let me in the room at the
last.
They say she'd not confess her life with
Matt;
They say she would not call that life a sin.
        (*Pause*)
I'll never interfere that way again.
If it were not for me, they'd have been
married,
And there'd have been no sin. Has Ag
gone to Hell?
Do you think that, Ned? For that would
be my fault.
Have I destroyed her life forever, Ned,
In this world and the next?
        (*Pause*)

QUINN

                You're talking blather.
Ach, God's more merciful than Father
Coyne,

Be sure of that, or we'd have been roasted
black,
The whole damned lot of us, long since.
        (*Pause*)
                                Come on.
Wouldn't you like to make it up to Ag,
Jo?
Do something for her dead? That's all I'm
asking.
Shouldn't Matt pay for what he did to
her?
All that you'd need to say's a single sen-
tence,
When the Lady Duchess Kathleen Kakiak
Descends in visitation: "Mrs. Stanton,
Sure, God will bless you for your charity."
"My charity?" she'll ask. You'll say, "You
know,
Ag having lived with Matt three years and
all."
That's all you'd have to say.

JOSIE

                        What am I, Ned,
That you take me for a fool and villain
both?
Don't talk to me about your broken heart,
And how you feel you owe poor Ag re-
venge!
If she had wanted that, would she have
died
Without the sacraments to spare Matt
pain?
I know you want to drive Matt from the
running
And that you'd stop at nothing short of
murder
For one more term as lord of City Hall.
Best give it up, Ned. Fast. It will destroy
you.

QUINN

Give what up, Jo?

JOSIE

        Your pride. Your murderous pride.

QUINN

I don't know what you mean by that at all.
They're out to get me, Jo. I have to fight.
They telephoned today at half past three:
"Albany says resign or they'll destroy
you!"
I had to send a letter to that bastard
Throwing in the sponge. But I'm not
through yet;
And I'll win out. I always have before.

But if I go down, I won't go down alone.
You may call that pride, if you like. I call
     it honor.

JOSIE

No, Ned. Not honor, I know. Pride kept
     me from her.
I'd not admit the wrong was on my side,
And her with the blood of her heart on
     her shaking chin
In that· icebox of a hallroom down in
     Smith Street,
The wall at her nose. Oh, Sacred Heart of
     Jesus,
I should have flung myself on the oilcloth
     floor
And not got up until she gave me pardon.
She'd have laughed at me, and called me a
     young whale,
Or some such nonsense. She'll never laugh
     again . . .
What must Matt feel?

QUINN
               Good riddance to bad rubbish
Is what he feels!

JOSIE
               You never knew Matt, Ned,
If you think that.

QUINN
               I knew him well enough!—
You're still in love with him—

JOSIE
                         What's that to you!

QUINN
And him with the worst word in his
     mouth for you,
As he always has had!

JOSIE
               I don't believe you, Ned.

QUINN
Ah, well. Ah, well. No one believes me
     now.
Stanton's your god; and that's just as it
     should be.
You're traitors all, as fickle as the sunlight
On April Fools' Day. But there'll come a
     time
You'll say Ned Quinn was right.

JOSIE
                         What kind of thing
Is it he says of me?

QUINN
               No matter, now.
You'd not believe me if I told it you.

JOSIE
What does he say?
     (Pause)

QUINN
               For one thing that you're two-faced,
And well enough, since the face that you
     were born with's
Like a madman's arse.

JOSIE
               You son of a bitch, Ned Quinn,
That sounds like you, not him.

QUINN
                         Have it your own way.
I'm old, you know; I'm all dustmice up-
     stairs.
It's hard for me to lay my mind on recol-
     lections.
Yet it seems to me I can recall a toast
Matt drank his birthday night at Ville-
     pigue's
Two weeks before we had that fight in
     Seagate . . .
He stood there fingering that green silk
     tie
That you embroidered those gold sham-
     rocks on—

JOSIE
How do you know that I gave Matt that
     tie?

QUINN
He told me when he gave the tie to
     Petey—

JOSIE
You made that up!
     (Pause)

QUINN
               He lifted up his glass,
And laughed, and said: "Confusion to the
     devil
That's bent Jo Finn as fast around my
     neck

As a coop around a barrel; and her legs as
loose
As her lying tongue—

JOSIE

        God's curse on you for that!

QUINN

God's curse on me? I'm only telling truth.
Come to your senses, woman. He played
me false.
And Ag. And her he's married to, Kathleen.
What makes you think you are the bright
exception?

JOSIE

Because I know him for a good man, Ned.
And not a poisonous old woman of a thief,
Destroying names to keep himself in of-
fice—

QUINN

A thief, am I! I'll get what I want without
you;
And when Stanton plays you false, don't
whine to me.
    (*Enter* KATHLEEN, STANTON, *and* MUR-
    PHY. MURPHY *is carrying a case of
    liquor, which he sets on the chair
    nearest him, his eyes fixed on* QUINN
    and STANTON *confronting each other.*)

STANTON

I will not play her false, nor will I you . . .
I got your letter; and I thank you for it.
I'm sorry that my winning means your
loss.
    (*Pause.* QUINN *glares at* STANTON, *then
    takes a step towards the door.*)

MURPHY

Wait, Ned!

STANTON

    I swear, I'll see you through this trouble.
I want to be your friend again. Shake
hands.
Come on, man. And what better place than
here.
I'm sure Ag would have wanted it. Come
on—

QUINN

Good God! The goat can talk. When Ag
was living, though,
You rarely met the livestock in the house!

    (STANTON *hurls himself at* QUINN, *and
    takes him by the throat.* KATHLEEN
    screams.* JOSIE *and* MURPHY *rush to get
    between them.*)

STANTON

I'll kill him!

MURPHY

    Hold him back. Go on, Ned. Go.
Remember Ag, Matt. Please. No disrespect.
    (MURPHY *is holding* STANTON's *arms.
    *QUINN, *disengaging himself from* JO-
    SIE, *blackly looks* STANTON *up and
    down, and spits in his face. It takes
    both* MURPHY *and* KATHLEEN *to hold
    *STANTON *back.* QUINN *watches the
    struggle. Exit* QUINN *slowly.* JOSIE
    fetches a rag, and hands it to* STANTON.
    He wipes the spittle off his face and
    coat.*)

JOSIE

Pay him no heed, Matt. Sure, what need
have you
To care what a thief thinks who's been
found out—

STANTON

I'll thank you to keep out of this, Jo Finn.
You always were a one for interfering.

JOSIE

Why take things out on me? It was he spit
at you.

KATHLEEN

Mattie, Mattie, are you crazed or what?
You've hurt the woman's feelings.

STANTON

             Kate, come ahead.
Where are the Haggertys?

JOSIE

            Inside with the rest.
Inside in the parlor.
    (STANTON *takes* KATHLEEN *by the arm,
    but she holds back.*)

KATHLEEN

          Matt, beg her pardon.

STANTON

For what? For what? Don't waste your
sympathy

On that one. And stay clear of her as can
be:
She has a wicked tongue. Watch out for
her—

KATHLEEN
The woman heard you!—

STANTON
                         Devil a bit I care!
Will you come into the parlor!

KATHLEEN
                         Matt, she's crying.
(STANTON *strides over towards* JOSIE,
awkward with remorse.)

STANTON
Josie—

                Never mind. I heard you, Matt.

STANTON
                              The devil
Take you then, for your big ears!

JOSIE
                The devil take me, Matt.

KATHLEEN
Please, Mrs. Finn—

JOSIE
                         Go in now to the wake,
And let me be!
(*Pause.* MURPHY *shakes his head, and
motioning* KATHLEEN *towards the por-
tiere, holds it up for her. Exit* KATH-
LEEN, STANTON, *and* MURPHY. JOSIE
*walks to the table and picks up the
rag which* STANTON *used to wipe the
spittle off himself. In a spasm of rage,
she tears it in two and throws it on
the floor. Enter* MARIA HAGGERTY.)

MARIA
What's this that Mrs. Stanton's after saying
About a fight between her man and you?

JOSIE
I'm not the kind that would demean my-
self
By having words with the likes of him,
Maria.

MARIA
The likes of him? What is this all about?
I've never heard you talk that way of Matt.

JOSIE
I never found him out until just now.
He treated me like dirt. And who is he
To be so high and mighty—Hogan's Goat,
A fancy boy made good! Ag's fancy boy!

MARIA
You shut your mouth, or I will shut it for
you.
Matt's broken up because of Aggie's death;
That's why he lost his temper. That and
Quinn,
Bad luck be with the day I let him in here.
I'll not have you make trouble for Matt,
Jo.
I want you to come into the parlor now
And take Matt's hand.

JOSIE
                    It's he should take my hand.

MARIA
Will you come in, if he comes out to you
first?
        (*Enter* KATHLEEN *softly behind* MA-
RIA.)

JOSIE
I'll make no promises.
        (*Pause.* KATHLEEN *puts her black-
gloved hand on* MARIA's *shoulder.*
MARIA *starts, and acknowledges her
with nervous heartiness.*)

MARIA
                         Why, Mrs. Stanton!

KATHLEEN
I'd like to talk to Mrs. Finn alone.
        (*Pause*)
Maria? Just a moment or two. Alone.
        (*Exit* MARIA *reluctantly.*)
Mrs. Finn, please. Matthew meant no
harm . . .
He has a dreadful temper. You know that.
And he's like a scalded cat since yesterday
When he got the news that Agnes Hogan
died.
        (*Pause*)
He told me just how much she'd meant to
him
When he was starting out on his career.

You know that better, maybe, than myself—

JOSIE

He told you that, did he! Did he tell you
how
He lived with her three years in a state of
sin
In a love nest of a roadhouse down in
Seagate?
And the devil take the talk! Did he tell
you, too,
She drank herself consumptive for his sake
Because he threw her over three years
since,
When he'd got all he wanted from her,
missis,
And married you—
    (KATHLEEN *gasps and runs out the
    door.* JOSIE *looks straight ahead into
    the air before her face, brings both
    hands to her forehead with a slap, and
    sits swaying in her chair.*)

CURTAIN

ACT SIX

*Eleven o'clock the same evening. The
Stantons' flat. Before the curtain rises, the
sound of a scuffle and a cry.* KATHLEEN
*stands, tight with fury, a large silver hand
mirror, which she has just struck* STANTON
with, in her hand. STANTON *sits on the edge
of the couch, a handkerchief to his forehead, which is bleeding slightly.* KATHLEEN
turns her gaze from STANTON *to the floor.
With that sudden recession of energy
which follows drunken violence, she sways
and slumps, the hand with the mirror in
it hanging slackly at her side. She kicks at
the fragments of the mirror with the toe
of her shoe, as if she were puzzled by
them. She is very drunk, but on brandy;
that is, her mind is sharper than it would
seem to be.*

———

KATHLEEN

The mirror's broken.

STANTON

                Yes. That means bad luck.

KATHLEEN

I know it does. But now I can see plain,
Just as it says in First Corinthians:

When I was a child, I saw as a child does,
Saw what I loved as in a mirror darkly,
But now I see his face—

STANTON

                This night of all nights!
When I have Quinn's note resigning in
my hand!
The bitch of a Josie Finn with her snake's
tongue!—
Where have you been till now? Where did
you get it?

KATHLEEN

Did I get what, Matt?

STANTON

                The drink that's crazed you.

KATHLEEN

In your own back room with a woman
named Miss Legg.
Miss Bessie Legg. She'd yards and yards of
beads on,
And a hat like a berry patch attacked by
magpies,
And a fancy neckpiece like twelve Persian
cats
All tied together. You'd think she'd blow
away
At the first breeze with all those feathers
on her.

STANTON

How could you do a thing like that to me?
Get paralyzed for everyone to gawk at,
And with the district whore?

KATHLEEN

                She's that, is she?
Birds of a feather flock together, Matt,
And whore will meet with whore. That's
what I am.
We aren't married. We aren't. You know
that.
Isn't it the same as you and Agnes?

STANTON

                Jesus, Katie!

    (*Pause*)

KATHLEEN

Are you hurt bad, Matt?

STANTON

                It's nice of you to ask.
    (KATHLEEN *flies at him.*)

KATHLEEN
You son of a bitch, I'll kill you.
(STANTON *pinions her arms. She drops
the mirror. What began as battle ends
as embrace.*)
                              Mattie, Mattie.

STANTON
Oh, Katie, what's the matter with us both!

KATHLEEN
What can a woman say when she learns
    the man
She left her country and her God to marry
Has married her to show his cast-off mis-
    tress
That he can do without her, or even worse,
Only to earn his good name back again?

STANTON
I married you because I love you, Kate.

KATHLEEN
Then why was I the one soul in this city
Who didn't know of you and Agnes?
    Why?

STANTON
I didn't want to hurt you.

KATHLEEN
                              Well, you have—
How do I know you won't abandon me
If I don't get you what you want from life?

STANTON
Don't say such things.

KATHLEEN
            No wonder they seemed strange,
Your what-d'ya-callem's, your constituents:
They none of them could look me in the
    face
For fear they might let on. Didn't Bessie
    Legg
Tell me she thought the only reason Agnes
    Hogan
Went to bed with Quinn was to prove to
    herself
That there was someone loved her, when
    she saw
Your feelings for her dying like wet coal,
And realized she'd lost you? How do I
    know
The same thing will not happen to myself;
And people won't be saying a year from
    now,

Kate went the same way as the poor dead
    whore?

STANTON
Kate. Don't call her that.

KATHLEEN
                              Why not? Don't they?

STANTON
They don't. And don't you call her out of
    name.
You never knew her. And the talk you've
    heard
Has been about her as she was in public,
Stripping the heavy diamonds off her fin-
    gers
To keep the party going one more hour.
I knew what lay behind it. It was mine:
Her will to fullness. She contained a man
As the wind does, the first giddy days of
    spring,
When your coat blows open, and your
    blood beats hard,
As clear as ice, and warm as a chimney
    wall.
'Twas she first gave me heart to dare be
    free.
All threats turned promise when she talked
    to you.
With her on your arm, you saw your life
    before you
Like breast-high wheat in the soft dazzle
    of August.
She had a way of cupping her long hands
Around my bulldog's mug, as if I were
Some fancy fruit she'd bought beyond her
    means,
And laughing with delight. She put noth-
    ing on
She did not feel, and felt with flesh and
    soul.
I don't believe she knew what shame
    might be.
You could not resist her. *I* could not. I
    tried.
I was twenty-five years old, when first I
    met her.
I'd never . . .

KATHLEEN
                              What?

STANTON
            I was what you'd call a virgin . . .

KATHLEEN
The saints preserve us!

STANTON
                              Yes, it's funny now;
It wasn't funny then.
    (*Pause*)
                    It was she wooed me.
It seemed—Lord knows, I don't—unnat-
ural.
She was ten years my senior. But, oh, Kate,
To look at her downstairs, you'd never
know
What once she was! Her hair was bronze-
and silver
Like pear trees in full bloom, her eyes
were opal,
Her skin was like new milk, and her blue
veins
Trembled in the shimmer of her full
straight neck
Like threads of violets fallen from her hair
And filliped by the breeze. She bought me
presents:
A handmade vest of black brocaded silk,
A blond Malacca cane with a silver head
Cast like an antique statue, the Lord
knows what,
There were so many of them. And she'd
cock
That angel's head of hers, and tell me:
"You look like such a slob, Matt, I took
pity
And bought you something nice. You can
pay me back . . .
Some day.
    (*Pause*)
              I took them not to hurt her, Kate;
And when she asked me would I work for
her,
Would I run the gaming rooms in Seagate
for her,
And keep her out of trouble, I said yes;
And when she asked me would I be her
man,
I'd have said yes, but I could scarcely
breathe
Between the want and fear of her. I
nodded—
I never knew a man say no to her
Until I did myself that Labor Day
I found her in the one bed with Ned
Quinn.
I looked her in the eyes, and I said, "No!
I'll play the fancy boy to you no more."
    (*Pause*)

That's what I was, Kathleen, Ag's fancy
boy,
I was Hogan's Goat to everyone, Ag's stud.
All my high hopes for power and for office
Fell down around my ears like a spavined
roof
When I first heard them call me that—
And, Kate,
When it comes to feelings, there was my
side too:
I might have been some tethered brute in
the yard
The way she acted. That last year she
seemed bent
On driving home to me she was all I had,
Without her, I was nothing— Even after
Newark,
She never changed—

KATHLEEN
                    What happened in Newark?—

STANTON
                              Nothing!
I don't know why I brought it up in the
first place.
We had a fight. I left her. I went to Newark.
She followed me. We made it up. That's
all.
Let's not talk about it. It brings things
back.

KATHLEEN
You loved her, didn't you? You love her
still.

STANTON
Ag's dead, Kathleen. How can you love a
corpse?
And in my heart she's been that these
three years—
Part of me lay dead as a horse in the street
In that house in Seagate, till I met you in
London.
It was as if God had sent me down an
angel
To bring me back from the grave. That's
why I asked you
To marry me in that London City Hall
Without the eight weeks' wait to cry the
banns,
And come back with me right away. I
was afraid,
I was afraid I'd lose you, if I left
And waited here for you till the banns
were cried—

I swear to you, on my dead mother's grave,
As soon as the election's past, we'll marry
Right in St. Mary's Church, and damn the
    gossip!
        (*Pause*)
I didn't tell you—

KATHLEEN

                    Why?—

STANTON

                    I was ashamed
That I was ever young. I wanted you
To think I knew my way around from
    birth.

KATHLEEN
Lord help us!

STANTON

And somehow, even more, I was ashamed
That I had let her woo me like a girl,
And I could not resist her or say no
For three long years. It was that slavery
I was ashamed of most—

KATHLEEN

                    That slavery,
My dear, is love—

STANTON

                    What is it you just said?

KATHLEEN
I'm terrible drunk.

STANTON

                    Sure, don't I know that!
And if you weren't, Kate, you'd be a
    widow.
You'd have brained me good and proper
    with that mirror,
If your eye had not been blurred—

KATHLEEN

                    But I see plain!

STANTON
Come, Katie, let me help you into bed—

KATHLEEN
You never came to look for me, did you?

STANTON
I did. I couldn't find you.

KATHLEEN

                    Tell the truth!
You were too proud. You sat up here and
    waited.
You knew I would come back like a hun-
    gry cat,
Like Agnes Hogan! Call to her, why don't
    you?
She'll stiffen in the coffin at your voice
And drag herself up those dark stairs
    outside
On her bare feet! They never put shoes
    on them.
She's back to where she was before in
    Ireland:
The dirt will clog her toes!

STANTON

                    Oh, Jesus, Katie!

KATHLEEN
Don't you understand me, Mattie?

STANTON

                    Come on now, Kate.
The fire's sunk. You'll catch your death
    of cold,
If you keep up this way. Kate, come on
    to bed.

KATHLEEN
No, never!

STANTON

                    Katie, Katie, what's the matter!

KATHLEEN
I looked at her downstairs. I feel afraid.
They say death visits three before it's done.
I looked at her sewn lips, her spotted hand
With the wedding ring you never gave
    her on it.
They said it was her mother's. Poor Aggie,
    Matt!
Poor you and me!
        (*Pause.* STANTON *covers his face with
        his hands and falls to the couch.*
        KATHLEEN *suddenly throws herself on
        her knees, and embraces him around
        the waist.*)
                    I don't want liberty!
Don't leave me, Mattie, please. I feel
    afraid.
        (STANTON *uncovers his face, cups the
        back of her head in his hand, and
        kisses her temples.*)

STANTON

Toc-sha-shin-inish, my darling. Don't be talking—

KATHLEEN

It isn't God I want, it's you—

STANTON

Sh. Sh.

KATHLEEN

I wanted to go away, Matt; but I couldn't.
Those things you said about you and Ag Hogan,
About resenting how you felt for her,
They go for me— Oh, Matt, we're like twin children:
The pride is in our blood— I'd like to kill you,
Or die myself. Do you understand me, Matt!
Don't let me. I am sick with shame. I love you—
(STANTON *kisses her on the mouth, lifts her to her feet, and helps her towards the bedroom.*)

STANTON

You're crying drunk—

KATHLEEN

In vino veritas:
There's truth in drink.

STANTON

God! Now she's quoting Latin,
And me so ignorant that all I know
Is that I'm cold and want my wife beside me
Before I can feel warm again or rest.
Ag's dead, Kate, dead.
But, Katie, we're alive.
Come with me out of the cold. Ag's gone for good.

CURTAIN

ACT SEVEN

Midnight the same night. The back room of Stanton's Saloon. Stanton for Mayor is spelled out in gold-paper letters hanging from the crepe-paper streamers. BESSIE LEGG *sits at a table, looking downcast and bewildered, an empty glass before her, her*

back to the Ladies' Entrance. The door to the Ladies' Entrance swiftly opens a crack. BILL *sticks his head in and withdraws it. The door swiftly closes.* BESSIE *cranes round, sees nothing, and returns to her glum daydream. Enter* QUINN *and* BILL *through the Ladies' Entrance.*

———

BESSIE

Watch what the hell you're doing!
Creeping up on parties like the Blackhand!
Good Christ, it's you! What are you doing here?
You want to start a riot?

QUINN

Go easy, Bessie,
Or you'll have them in here. I'll tell you what to do.
Go get two doubles; and tell them at the bar
You'd like to be alone in here awhile,
You have a customer.
(QUINN *puts a ten-dollar bill on the table in front of her.*)

BESSIE

I'm through with that.

QUINN

I'm through with that, says she, and her stairs in splinters
From the armies charging up and down them nights!
Don't sit there that way with your mouth sprung open
Like a busted letter box. Go get the drinks.
(QUINN *moves out of sight of the bar. Exit* BESSIE, *opening and closing the door as if it were mined.*)

QUINN

Keep watch outside now, Bill. Give the door a kick
If you see that bastard coming. If the trunk is there,
And the box is in it, I'll pass you out the key.
(*Exit* BILL *through the Ladies' Entrance.* QUINN *walks around the room as if examining it before taking it over. Kick at the bar door.* QUINN *starts, looks towards the Ladies' Entrance, then back at the bar door. When he sees that someone is opening the door for* BESSIE, *he draws back into*

the shadows. Enter BESSIE *with two double whiskeys in her hand.*)

BESSIE

When I say private, I mean private, Percy.
Din't your mother teach you manners—
Thanks for nothing!
Pinching a person when a person's help-
less!
Shut the door or you'll get a bourbon eye-
wash.
          (*As the bar door shuts behind her,
a* MALE VOICE *chants in falsetto.*)

MALE VOICE

Remember St. Peter's,
Remember St. Paul's,
Remember the goil
You kissed in the hall!

BESSIE

Honest, if there ain't more snots than
noses,
I'm the Mother Superior at Good Shep-
herd's!
Here's your lousy drinks.
          (BESSIE *sets the doubles before herself
and* QUINN *as she sits down. She
pushes the change from the ten across
the table.* QUINN *smiles, and pushes it
back to her.*)
                         That was a ten-spot.
Them drinks were forty cents.
          (QUINN *smiles again, shakes his head,
and motions her to take the money.
She does, with a shame-faced smile.
They lift their glasses to each other
and drink.*)

QUINN

                         How are you since? . . .

BESSIE

You didn't come here for no dish of tea.

QUINN

As a matter of fact, I'd like to ask a favor;
And I missed you at the wake. That's
why I came.

BESSIE

You didn't miss me, kid. I didn't go.
Dead people make me nervous. What's
this favor?

QUINN

I hear you've been spelling out May Haggerty

Looking after Ag this past year, Bessie.
I wonder did Ag still have a cowhide
trunk?

BESSIE

A yellow leather trunk? She did.

QUINN

                         Where is it?

BESSIE

It's around the corner in her room in
Smith Street,
The Haggertys didn't have time to cart it
home.

QUINN

There's something in it that I'd like to
have,
For a keepsake, don't you know. Have
you the key?

BESSIE

The key to Ag's room? Yeah.

QUINN

                         Good. Give it here.

BESSIE

What's in this trunk you want?

QUINN

                         An onyx brooch.
It was my poor old mother's. I gave it Ag
When I first met her.

BESSIE

                         She ain't got that now.
I seen that tin box that she kept her things
in
Two days ago. That's where May got the
ring
They're burying Ag in. That was all there
was,
That and some old papers—

QUINN

                         I'd like to see those too.

BESSIE

Why?

QUINN

          Why! To make sure that there are
no receipts there
To fall into wrong hands.

BESSIE

You go ask Maisie.
I got no right to give no key to you.
Those things are hers now.

QUINN

Lord! I can't do that.
She'd go ask Matt; and then I'd never get
them!

BESSIE

I thought you wanted that thing that was
your mother's.

QUINN

I do. That onyx ring

BESSIE

You said a brooch.
There's something in that box that'll cause
trouble.
I'm going to take and give the key to
Matt.

QUINN

I wouldn't do that, child, if I were you.
Remember what you told them in the bar,
You wanted to be alone in here awhile,
You had a customer? Shall I call the cop,
What's this his name is, Boylan's on this
beat,
And have you up on lewd solicitation?
Would you like a three months' course in
sewing mailbags
In the Women's Prison? Bessie, smarten
up.
Hand me the key.
(BESSIE *rummages in her bag, then
throws the key and the change from
the drinks on the table. She rises, and
walks towards the bar door.*)
Where do you think you're going?

BESSIE

Ain't you finished with me yet?

QUINN

Sit down, my dear.
You'll not leave here till the box is in my
hands.
You'd be up the street and at Matt's ear
in no time
Like a wasp at a pear. Sit down when I
tell you to.
(BESSIE *sits down.* QUINN *opens the
door to the Ladies' Entrance. Sound
of running feet.* QUINN *closes the*

*door, returns to the table, and sits
down. He pushes the change from the
drinks back to* BESSIE.)
Would you like another drink while we're
waiting, Bessie?—

BESSIE

I wouldn't drink with you if I had the
jimjams
And every crack in the wall had a rat's
snout in it.

QUINN

I know how my morality must offend
A fine upstanding woman like yourself—
(BESSIE *throws her whiskey in* QUINN's
*face, looks terrified, then bursts into
tears. With great coolness,* QUINN *pulls
a large silk handkerchief out of his
pocket, and blots his face and clothing.*)
You always were a great one for the crying.

BESSIE

I guess I done some bum things in my life
But this is the first time that I ever ratted.

QUINN

Ratted, my dear? I don't know what you
mean.
I told you all I wanted was old receipts.
(*Sound of running.* BILL *runs through
the Ladies' Entrance and hands* QUINN
a tin box. QUINN *motions* BILL *back
out to keep watch. Exit* BILL. QUINN
*puts the box on the floor and kicks it.
It opens. He puts the box on the
table.*)
I gave that box to Ag myself. The lock
Was always window dressing. For how
could I know
When there might be something here I'd
like to see.
Will you look at this? A bundle of
scorched letters:
Matt Stanton, Esq., Care of the Gen PO,
Newark, New Jersey. That's where Mattie
went
When he slipped Ag's tether in Seagate.
And look, the necktie
That Josie made for Matt, and a dried
camellia,
And a pair of busted garnet rosaries.
And this, dear God in Heaven, look at
this,
A letter with no salutation on it

In poor Ag's pothook script. It has no date.
"You're dead to me, because I'm dead my-
self.
I have been since you left me. If you think
I mean to cause you trouble for what
you've done,
You never knew me. You've made your
dirty bed.
Lie in it now till you feel the filth in your
bones.
I—" No more. No more!—Ag always
was too proud.
She never sent it.

BESSIE
                    Put them things all back.
They don't belong to you.

QUINN
                    Wait now. Wait now.
There's a trick to this false bottom. There
it goes.
If it's not the kind of receipt I knew
would be here!
It's charred. She meant to burn it. But
you can read it.

BESSIE
Give me them things.

QUINN
                    I only want this, Bessie.
(QUINN *puts the paper in his pocket.*)
I'm through now. We can part. Don't
worry, child.
I'm putting these things in the box, and
Bill will return it
And lock the trunk and room behind him.
But mark me.
You're not to say a thing of this to Stan-
ton.
He's a worse suspicious nature than your
own;
And we've got to come, you know, to a
meeting of minds
At the Clambake on my birthday Sunday,
Bessie,
Stanton and I. It would only throw him
off
If he heard I had been going through Ag's
things.
We wouldn't want that, Bessie; would we,
child,
Any more than you'd want that stretch in
jail.
I hope you take my meaning— I must
leave you, Bessie.

(QUINN *rises with the box under his
arm, and moves towards the Ladies'
Entrance.*)

BESSIE
I hope you rot in Hell!

QUINN
                    You must love me, child,
That you should want my company forever.
(*Exit* QUINN. *Sound of a hack rolling
off.* BESSIE *grabs the money off the
table and crumples it up in her hands.
She looks at the door and at the
money. She puts the money in her
bag and bursts out crying.*)

CURTAIN

ACT EIGHT

*Twilight, the evening of Sunday, May 1,
1890. The stern of a Coney Island steamer
bound for Seagate. The lower deck is
overhung with an upper, upon which people pass from time to time. There are two
oval portraits, one of* STANTON, *the other
of* QUINN, *suspended from the railings of
the upper deck, above entrances to stage
right and stage left. Between them, there
is a large shield printed in bold Pontiac
reading* For the Public Good. *The shield
and portraits are hung over swagged bunt-
ing. On the lower deck, to stage right,
there is a table with a cluster of carpet-
seated folding chairs around it. Set off a
little from them, its back to the table,
there is a carpet-seated armchair.*

HAGGERTY, BOYLE, *and* ANN MULCAHY *are
seated at the table.* HAGGERTY *is wearing a
green-and-gold sash with* The Matthew
Stanton Association *printed on it. Enter*
MARIA HAGGERTY *with a large, loaded tea
tray, which she sets on the table. She pours
and passes the tea.*

———

MARIA
One hour more, and we'll be into Seagate.
That's what the deckhand says. I'm glad
of that.
Two hours more of sailing, I declare to
God,
And the babies all would be drunk in their
carriages.

HAGGERTY

Where's missis, May? Will I bring her
tea to her?

MARIA

No. Let her sleep. She's dozed off in
Matt's stateroom.
The brandy must have killed the queasi-
ness.

ANN

Wasn't that a grand speech Ned Quinn
made
Before Matt came, on the pier at Fulton
Street,
When he said he was glad he'd arranged
the Clambake late,
So that he could begin his voyage into the
evening,
His loyal supporters at his side to the end.

BOYLE

I'm coming. I'm coming.
And my belly's full of gin.
I hear their drunken voices calling
Old Ned Quinn.

HAGGERTY

Don't dance on Quinn's grave, Petey. It's
unlucky.
We're not through this night yet.

MARIA

           True for you there, Jack!
They've yet to make the bad blood up be-
tween them.
Father Coyne's been in Quinn's stateroom
this past hour,
And Palsy's been at Matt in the Saloon
Bar.
Quinn wants Mattie to come to *him;* and
Matt
Won't move an inch towards him till
Quinn begs his pardon
For spitting in his face at Aggie's wake.

HAGGERTY

Woman, shut up. No call to worry that
much.
If you knew politics as well as I do,
You'd see they'll both bow down to a
higher law
Before this night is out.

BOYLE

           St. Albany,
Pray for us.

HAGGERTY

           Stop your blaspheming, Petey.
I don't mean Albany, but the public
good—
    (*Enter* BESSIE LEGG, *stage right, in a
    rush.*)

BESSIE

Oh, Petey. Petey. Come to the front of the
boat.
You can see the electra light from Coney
there,
And that hotel they built like a elephant.
Why don't youse all come. God, its beautiful.
    (*Exit* BOYLE *and* BESSIE, *the* HAGGER-
    TYS *and* ANN, *stage right.*)

BOYLE

I asked me mother for fifty cents,
To see the elephant jump the fence.
He jumped so high, he touched the sky,
And never come down till the Fourt' of
July.

The Fourt' of July when he crashed to
earth
He landed near my fat Aunt Gert.
She says you lumpy pig-eyed skunk
Stay off that sauce if you get that drunk.
    (*Sound of their laughter fading. En-
    ter* QUINN *and* BILL, *with* FATHER
    COYNE *following, stage left.*)

FATHER COYNE

You'll meet with him here then?

QUINN

           Yes, Father, I will.
I'll meet with him anywhere. But he'll
come to me.

FATHER COYNE

I'll go and get him.
    (*Exit* FATHER COYNE, *stage left.* QUINN
    *stands back and looks at the shield
    and posters.*)

QUINN

           Look at that now, Billy.
Brooklyn, how are you! For the public
good!
A whore for a mayor and a spoiled nun
for his lady!
We mustn't let that happen, must we
now?—
Play lose me, Billy. Here's the lot of them.

(*Exit* BILL, *stage right. Enter* FATHER
COYNE, *followed by* MURPHY *and* STAN-
TON. STANTON *walks forward, keeping
his eyes straight ahead.* QUINN *rakes
all three of them with his eyes, then
averts his gaze from* STANTON.)

QUINN
    (*To* MURPHY)
If it isn't the Lord Beaconsfield of Brook-
    lyn
With the ten thumbs of his fine Italian
    hands
Done up in ice-cream gloves.
    (*He turns suddenly to* STANTON.)
                    How are you since?—

STANTON
I'll speak no word until he begs my par-
    don.
I told you, Father. Has he grown so old
    and silly
He thinks men can do harm without
    amends!

FATHER COYNE
Do you want him to get down on his
    knees to you!
He's lost enough already. Leave him his
    pride.

MURPHY
The food in the mouth of the voters is at
    stake,
It's bread and lard for lunch for thou-
    sands, thousands,
If this election's lost; and it will be lost
Unless you join your hands and pull to-
    gether.

QUINN
For all that's passed between us, I'll shake
    his hand,
If he will mine.

MURPHY
            Come on now, Matt. Come on.

QUINN
When he gets as old as I am, he'll under-
    stand
It was death I spat at that night at the
    wake,
And wish he'd come to terms with an old
    man's rage.
    (*Pause.* STANTON *suddenly grabs*
    QUINN'*s hand.* QUINN *gives him a*

clumsy bear hug, his face appearing
over STANTON's shoulder.)

STANTON
Go on now, Ned. You're not that old.
    You've years.
There's years of use in you.

QUINN
                        Matt boy.

MURPHY
They say that when a man shakes hands
    with his foe,
A suffering soul shoots out of Purgatory
Straight into Heaven, like a lark from a
    cage.

FATHER COYNE
What Council was it, Palsy, declared that
    dogma?

QUINN
Sister Mary Asafoetida Doyle,
His fourth-grade teacher.

MURPHY
                    To the Saloon Bar!
Drinks for all comers, and on the Party
    too!
    (MURPHY *and* FATHER COYNE *move to-
    wards the exit, stage left, with* QUINN
    and STANTON *a few paces behind
    them.*)

QUINN
You know, Matt, if you left the landing
    to me,
I could drive it home to all what terms
    we're on,
And make the kind of an occasion of it
Your missis would remember all her life.
With both the bands of our Associations
Thundering and ringing out below us
And all the voters stamping and applaud-
    ing,
I'd like to take your wife and you by the
    hand
And bring you down. A little taste of glory
Has never done a creature any harm—

STANTON
That's just the thing, maybe, might pick
    her up.
The water made her qualmish and she lay
    down—

You've never met Kathleen to talk to, have you?

Come down with me now, and I will introduce you.

> (*Exit* FATHER COYNE *and* MURPHY, QUINN *and* STANTON, *stage left. Pause. Enter* KATHLEEN *slowly, stage right. She is dressed in a black traveling suit and is wearing a large black hat. She stands looking at the wake of the steamer a moment, moves the armchair into the shadows, and sits in it, her back to the soft bustle of voices coming towards her. Pause. Enter the* HAGGERTYS, ANN MULCAHY, BOYLE, *and* BESSIE. *They do not notice* KATHLEEN. MARIA *is carrying yet another large pot of tea, and herding* HAGGERTY *before her.*)

HAGGERTY

You'll have my kidneys burst with all that tea.

MARIA

Never mind. You've a night of drink before you.

Keep moving, bullhead.

HAGGERTY

> Have a little respect.

BESSIE

Didn't I tell youse it was beautiful!

ANN

Going back to Seagate's a bit sad

With poor Ag in the ground just yesterday.

BESSIE

Yeah. Ain't it. Yeah. I wish it was Coney instead.

The shoot-the-chutes—

BOYLE

> The tunnel of love.

BESSIE

> Oh, Petey.

ANN

Will you ever forget the Clambake Aggie gave us

Three years ago, on that lovely stretch of beach!

We'd pails of clams and oysters, steamed and fresh,

And pounds of butter in round wooden tubs,

And crabs and lobsters bigger than our heads,

Chickens and potatoes, roasted corn—

BOYLE

And wagonloads of beer.

HAGGERTY

> And good beer too.

ANN

And all day long the men with accordeens

Went weaving in and out us on the sand

Till the stars were thick and near us in the sky.

MARIA

And Aggie, God have mercy on her soul,

Got skittish when they freshened up the fires,

And danced a jig on three kegs roped together,

With all them little bells she used to sew

Into the hems of her dresses ringing thin

Like birds at dawn.

> (*Pause*)

HAGGERTY

> She nearly broke her arse.

MARIA

John Haggerty!

HAGGERTY

> She did! Don't look at me so stark.

One keghead gave, and she went on her ear.

She showed us everything she had that time,

The clocks of her stockings to her knicker buttons,

Acres and acres of somersaulting drawers.

Amn't I right, Pete boy?

BOYLE

> You're right as rain.

BESSIE

You was too young to notice.

> (BOYLE *pulls the lower eyelid of his left eye down with his left forefinger.*)

BOYLE

Do you see green?—
That was the night Matt found Ag playing tigress
To Tiger Quinn.

MARIA

You shut your mouth, Pete Boyle.

BOYLE

He said she broke her ass!

HAGGERTY

That wasn't gossip.
It was a simple statement of pure fact,
To use the lawyer's parlance.

MARIA

The lawyer's parlance!
Drink your tea, you omadhaun. You're drunk.
Shut up and drink your tea.

HAGGERTY

"Ah, man! Proud man!
Dressed in a little brief authority"—
(MARIA *gives him what she'd call "one look."*)
I'm drinking it fast as I can! My mouth's destroyed!

BESSIE

You should see Pete jigging. He's the best there is.
He learned me how.

BOYLE

Get up and we'll show them, kid.

HAGGERTY

They'll show us, will they! Stand up to me there, woman,
And show them how we won the branch and bottle
On the pounded clay of every Kerry crossroads.
(MARIA *and* HAGGERTY *begin the jig with* BOYLE *and* BESSIE *doing a little shuffle all their own.* ANN *remains seated, helpless with shamefaced laughter.* KATHLEEN *rises and, standing half in the shadows, watches them with a shy smile. They are too engrossed to notice her.*)

BOYLE

He gave it to Maisie;
It near drove her crazy,

The leg of the duck!
The leg of the duck!
(*Enter* STANTON, *searching for* KATHLEEN. *He looks amused; but when he sees* KATHLEEN, *his face blackens.*)
I gave it to Bessie;
She says it was messy,
The leg of the duck!
The leg of the duck!

STANTON

What kind of song is that in front of my wife?

HAGGERTY

We didn't see her, Matt.

STANTON

Are you blind or what!
You, you narrow-back plug, with your mouth of slime,
You can slather this one all that you've a mind to,
But there are others born with a little shame!—
I'd be amazed at you two, May and Jack,
If I'd not noticed the liberties you've been taking
These past few months. There'll be an end to that.

HAGGERTY

All right. All right. There'll be an end to that . . .
Come, May and Ann, we'd best go inside now.

BOYLE

Wait; we'll come too. I'll lug these things for you.
(*All four move towards the exit to stage right.*)

KATHLEEN

Maria, dear, come back in a few minutes.
I need you. Please. I'm not myself at all.

MARIA

Yes, ma'am. Yes, ma'am.
(*Exit* BOYLE *and* BESSIE, HAGGERTY *and* MARIA.)

KATHLEEN

Beg their pardon, Mattie.
They didn't see me; and what harm if they did,
They were only dancing.

STANTON

        Things have changed now, Kate.
You have to demand respect, or you won't get it.
From this day on, they're to learn their place and keep it.
We're with them, but not of them. —Kate, I've won!
Quinn and I made up and he wants to meet you.

KATHLEEN

If that's what winning means, God help us both.

STANTON

What's the matter with you?

KATHLEEN

               It's being aboard a ship,
It's that, I suppose. When I watch the wake of the boat
Spread out like a pigeon's tail with the wind going through it,
I think of all that's left behind or canceled,
And the heart of me feels pillaged in my breast.
The farther away I go from what is past,
The more I stiffen with the sense of danger.
I look around me at all, and want to hold it:
May dancing there with her back straight as a bowstring
Despite the tug of age on all her bones,
And the dazzle of Jack's eyes as they browsed her face,
And Ann Mulcahy helpless with pure joy,
And that dusty weed of a boy and Bessie Legg,
Playing their little games like aging children.
There's not a thing that is not riches, Mattie,
And it all goes from us, darling, like those days
On the boat from England, glazed with salt and sunshine,
We melted first into light like flame and candle,
It all goes from us. Hold me, Mattie, hold me.
Don't thrust me from you as you just did them.

STANTON

Katie, I'd sooner hack the hands from my wrists
Than thrust you from me. As for what's been lost,
God in Heaven be with the days I lay
Like a bee in a lily with the ocean's glitter
Live gold on the stateroom panels. They were good.
But what's ahead, you'll not believe till you see it.
We've won! We've won, Kate! Quinn's arranged our landing:
You'll be breathing music like the saints in Heaven
As you walk ashore. But let him tell it you.
     (STANTON *kisses her*.)
What is that? Brandy, that I smell on you?

KATHLEEN

I took a glass or two for the seasickness.

STANTON

Promise me on your dead parents' grave,
You'll drink no more from this time forward, Kate.
There's no sight worse on earth than a drunken woman.
I know it to my shame, from her that's dead.
    (*Pause*)

KATHLEEN

. . . I promise, Mattie.
    (STANTON *kisses her hand*.)

STANTON

              There now. I'll get the mayor.
(*Exit* STANTON, *stage left.* BESSIE *emerges from the shadows, stage right, and hurries over to* KATHLEEN.)

BESSIE

You mind if I sit down? Remember me?

KATHLEEN

Of course, I do, Miss Legg. Please do sit down.
I'm pleased to see you.

BESSIE

             It isn't Miss. It's Mrs.

KATHLEEN

Yes. Mrs. Legg. Of course.

BESSIE

             Was he that mad
Just for that dirty song that Petey sung,

Or was it something that Quinn said to
  him
That he took out on us? You know what
  I mean.

KATHLEEN
No, I don't, Miss Legg. I don't know what
you mean.

BESSIE
Not Miss. It's Mrs.

KATHLEEN
           What would the mayor say?
Matt's just gone in to get him. They're
friends now.

BESSIE
They're friends now. Yeah. They're friends.

KATHLEEN
              What is it, please?

BESSIE
Oh, he hurted my feelings, see, the way
he talked,
And I got nervous. I'm a nervous girl.
That, and you know, what you said up
  my flat that night,
About there was some mix-up in the mar-
  riage.
It sounded so romantic when you said it,
"The man I left my God and country to
  marry."
I couldn't make it out. You was awful
  . . . you know.

KATHLEEN
If I said that, I was awful drunk indeed.
You didn't believe me, did you, Mrs.
Legg?

BESSIE
Oh, no. Oh, no. But I don't know where
  you was
Before I went and took you up my flat.
I thought that maybe Quinn got wind of
  it—

KATHLEEN
I hope you've not repeated what I said.
You haven't, have you?
    (BESSIE rises.)

BESSIE
          Excuse me. I'll be going.

KATHLEEN
Now don't be that way.

BESSIE
          What do you think I am,
Some kind of rat . . . I thought you was
  a sport.
You're like the rest . . . Oh, I seen you
  looking round
When I brought you back up my flat that
  night.
It's not my fault the place is such a mess.
I only rent it, see? It isn't mine.
And we only just got in when you passed
  out—
I mean, fell off to sleep . . . I didn't like
To make no noise . . . It's hard to keep
  things nice.
There was a time I had things beautiful.
When Legg was living with me, Legg,
  you know,
My husband . . . I passed the flat we
  used to have
On Baltic Street and Court the other day.
We lived in it two years. I kept it spot-
  less . . .
The windows all were dirty when I passed,
The windows of the flat we used to have,
I mean. All dirty . . . It nearly broke my
  heart.
I had a lovely home. I used to have . . .
Canary bird. Piano. Everything—
It's not my fault Legg left. Where he is,
  Christ knows.
Maybe he's dead. I hope to God he is,
May God forgive me, but I hope he is!
    (BESSIE *bursts into tears.* KATHLEEN
    rises and comforts her. Enter BOYLE,
    stage right.)

KATHLEEN
Oh, Bessie, Bessie, God in Heaven help us.

BOYLE
Who turned on the hydrants?

BESSIE
              Hello, Petey.
Buy me a drink or something, will you,
  ha?

BOYLE
Sure, kid, sure.
    (BOYLE *walks to the exit, stage right.*
    KATHLEEN *and* BESSIE *look at one an-*
    other.)

KATHLEEN

Goodbye.

BOYLE

You coming, Little Eva?
(*Exit* BOYLE. BESSIE *walks to the exit,
then turns to* KATHLEEN *again.*)

BESSIE

Don't worry, missis. Don't. There ain't no
call.
There ain't no one can hurt you. You're
a lady.
(*Exit* BESSIE. KATHLEEN *walks to the
rail and looks at the wake of the
steamer. Sound of a ship's bell. Enter
MARIA with a water glass of brandy.*)

DECKHAND

Seagate. Seagate. In ten minutes. Seagate.

MARIA

I brought you this.

KATHLEEN

I won't. I promised Matt—

MARIA

House devil and street saint, sure, he's
worse than Quinn!
He's down there now with Quinn playing
king of England.
He traipses up to me in the Saloon Bar
And takes my hand and thrusts ten dollars
in it.
He's not dead yet! There'll come a time
he'll see
There are some things in the world you
can't take back.
If I could get a job, we'd move. We
would—
(KATHLEEN *presses her fist to her
mouth and sinks into the armchair.*)
Good Jesus, Mrs. Stanton, what's the
matter!
Promise or no, best have a drop of this.
(KATHLEEN *downs half the glass of
brandy.*)

KATHLEEN

Promise or no.

MARIA

You'll feel the good of that.
(*Pause. Sound of ship's bell and of the
paddle churning water for the turn
inshore.*)

KATHLEEN

Do you know what I am thinking about,
Maria?
How it is this time of year back home in
Ireland.
The foxglove has come out in the boreens,
And the seals are barking on the mossy
rocks
Below Mount Brandon. On this very day,
They'll dress the loveliest girl in all the
village
In a wedding gown, and lead her to the
church
To put a crown of roses on the Virgin.
And all the children in Communion
clothes,
White suits and dresses, smilax wreaths,
pearl prayer books,
Will stand around her as she climbs the
ladder,
And sing that song that always makes me
cry:
Daughter of a mighty Father,
Maiden, patron of the May,
Angel forms around thee gather,
Macula non est in te.
Macula non est in te: Never spot was
found in thee.
(KATHLEEN *breaks into tears.*)

MARIA

Oh, Mrs. Stanton.

KATHLEEN

What's the matter with me?
My ears are ringing like a field of weeds,
Noontime in August, when the sun's raw
fire.

MARIA

I wonder is it flashes.

KATHLEEN

At my age!

MARIA

More likely kicks. Are you all together,
missis.

KATHLEEN

Am I what, Maria?

MARIA

Have you missed your term?
Don't bite your lip and blush. You're not
a nun.

KATHLEEN
No, I've not missed my term.
  (*Enter* QUINN, *stage left. He stands
  looking over at* MARIA *and* KATHLEEN,
  unnoticed by them at first.)

MARIA
                            Then it's the dead.

KATHLEEN
The dead?

MARIA
The dead. Who do you know needs
prayers?
They say that's how the dead call on the
living,
By whining in their blood.

KATHLEEN
                            Poor Agnes Hogan,
The Lord have mercy on her and preserve
her . . .
  (KATHLEEN *notices* QUINN.)
Don't look so troubled, May. I'm better
now.
You know there's a bottle of that Worth
perfume
Down in the stateroom in my reticule.
Would you bring it to me, dear, with a
handkerchief.
  (*Exit* MARIA, *stage right.* QUINN *walks
  over to* KATHLEEN.)

QUINN
Good evening to you, Mrs. Stanton. May
I?

KATHLEEN
Please do, your honor.
  (QUINN *sits down.*)

QUINN
                            Matt's stuck in the bar,
Buying drinks for all the upright voters,
So I came up alone. It would fill your eye
To see him there. You'd think he trusted
them!

KATHLEEN
God forbid he shouldn't trust them,
Mayor.

QUINN
If you think, my dear, not trusting people's
a sin,
You'd best get out of politics.

KATHLEEN
                            It's the worst sin.
Without trust, there's no faith or hope or
love.

QUINN
That kind of talk is like a penny cream
puff,
All wind and whey, and deadly when it
sours.
Trust no one. No one. Let no man too
close.
They are as quick to fury as to love.
Once give them purchase, they will pull
you down,
And for a sigh let slip, for a ruptured
smile.
They're a pack of wicked mutts that go
for shadows.
There is no reason in their ugliness,
No justice in their rage. Trust no one,
missis.

KATHLEEN
Who are "they"? Is it my husband,
Mayor,
Or old John Haggerty or Mister Murphy?
From what you say, you think the people
devils
Who've honored you as mayor of this city
For thirty years. Do you really think them
that?

QUINN
I do . . . And Stanton is the worst of
all!—

KATHLEEN
Do you think I'll sit and listen to your
slander!

QUINN
"Do you think this? Do you think this?"
Or "Don't you?"
"Faith and hope and love," and I mustn't
slander—
You're awful pious for a woman living
With your husband in a state of Mortal
Sin;
And a Mortal Sin it is for a Catholic
woman
To marry a man outside the Catholic
Church.
I don't know much religion, but I know
that,
As, I might add, do all our holy voters.
  (*Pause*)

KATHLEEN
I suppose you must have got that from
Miss Legg.

QUINN
No, my dear. From England. Where you
did it.
I've known it years. I hoped I'd not have
to use it,
But need is need. And it's not Miss. It's
Mrs.

KATHLEEN
You rejoice when people go wrong, don't
you, Mayor!

QUINN
We've no time now to talk morality.
We'll wait for Stanton, then go get Father
Coyne
And the rest, and walk down to my state-
room
And arrange what we will say. I've bought
off those accountants,
Paid back that little sum from the funds
I borrowed,
And the books are doctored. All that now
remains is
To find a way to break the joyous news
That I will run again. I think Matt should
do it!

KATHLEEN
If you're a man who'd ruin two reputa-
tions
To gain your ends, what have you done
with your life?

QUINN
What I have done with my life is my
affair!
Do you think I'll let that bastard have my
office?
I loved the woman that he took from me,
And I let her go with him, but I kept my
office.
And I heard them here in Seagate making
sport
Of all I'd done for them, but I kept mum,
And I kept my office. And I watched the
poor bitch die
While he grew high and mighty, but I
kept my office.
Keep my office I will to the day I die,
And God help those who try to take it.

KATHLEEN
                         Make sense.
The scandal about the funds is a public
fact;
But you and Mrs. Legg are the only ones
Who know about the marriage. Spare my
husband.
Spare him, Mayor. God will bless you for
it.

QUINN
Sure, that's what Aggie said when she
pleaded for him,
The first time that she met him, the poor
slob,
Did God bless her, missis?

KATHLEEN
                         They'll never let you run!
They'll gang up with the Party of Reform
And crucify you.

QUINN
                         We'll see about that, missis.
Do you think I'll let them turn their backs
on me
And turn their backs on me for the likes
of him,
A narrow-back pimp, who rose to where
he is
On the broken heart of the woman that I
loved!

KATHLEEN
Pour all the venom you want into my
ears!
The Party will stand by us! They'll stand
by us.
They'll cover us on the marriage. And
they should!
For though we were not married in the
Church,
May God forgive us, we are man and
wife!
     (Pause)

QUINN
I wouldn't be too sure of that now, missis.

KATHLEEN
What do you mean by that, you lying
devil?
     (QUINN pulls a scorched paper out of
     his pocket, and throws it into KATH-
     LEEN's lap.)

QUINN

I'm a lying devil, am I! Look at that!
Look at it, why don't you. Are you blind!
How can you be his wife when he married
　　Ag
In the Sacred Heart in Newark in '86!
　　　　(*Repeated sound of ship's bell. Peo-*
　　　　ple are gathering, preparing to get off.
　　　　Sound of winches, lowering gang-
　　　　plank. KATHLEEN *sits as if shot, the*
　　　　paper in her hands.)

DECKHAND

Seagate! Seagate! Everybody off.

KATHLEEN

All gone. All gone.
　　　　(KATHLEEN *rises suddenly, the paper*
　　　　in her hand, swaying with shock, as
　　　　if drunk. The disembarking passen-
　　　　gers look curiously at her.)
　　　　　　God damn the day I met him.
God damn this mouth that spoke him fair,
　　these eyes
That flooded my blood with his face. God
　　damn this flesh
That kindled in his arms, and this heart
　　that told me,
Say yes, say yes, to everything he asked.
It would have been better had I not been
　　born.
　　　　(QUINN *grabs the paper out of* KATH-
　　　　LEEN's *hand and puts it back into his*
　　　　pocket fast.)

QUINN

For God's sake, missis. Don't take on this
　　way.
We have to keep this quiet. There's people
　　watching.
　　　　(QUINN *runs to the table and fetches*
　　　　the half-finished glass of brandy.
　　　　KATHLEEN, *still swaying, her arms at*
　　　　her side, automatically accepts the
　　　　glass from him and, as if by reflex,
　　　　presses it to her breast. She does not
　　　　see the people who are staring at her.
　　　　Enter STANTON *with* MURPHY *and*
　　　　FATHER COYNE, *a group of voters*
　　　　around him.)

STANTON

It isn't in the courts reform must work
But in each striving heart . . .
　　　　(STANTON *sees the people staring at*
　　　　KATHLEEN *and* QUINN. *He breaks away*
　　　　from those around him and hurries

over to her. He speaks in a steely
whisper.)
Look at you. Look at you, for the love of
　　Jesus.
In front of all these people. You're owl-
　　eyed drunk,
With the bands about to fife us off the
　　boat!
I'll get Maria to help you sober up.
Quinn and I will walk ashore together.
You are not fit for decent men to be seen
　　with!
　　　　(KATHLEEN *smashes the glass to the*
　　　　floor. She speaks in a ringing voice.)

KATHLEEN

Did you think that—
Did you think that when you lied to me
　　in London,
And I let you marry me in the City Hall,
Because you said you couldn't wait for the
　　banns,
You wanted me so much! Did you think
　　that
When you had me in the bed in sacrilege
Above the corpse of your true-wedded
　　wife,
Ag Hogan!
　　　　(*Hostile reaction from the crowd. The*
　　　　sound of the bands suddenly blares
　　　　out.)

CURTAIN

ACT NINE

*Very late the same night. The double
set. There is a dim light in the hall by the
Haggertys' door; and the light in Stanton's
flat is on full. There are two trunks in the
parlor, one already locked, the other open.*
KATHLEEN *moves in and out of the bedroom, packing. Enter* FATHER COYNE *and*
MURPHY, *the* HAGGERTYS, BOYLE, *and* BESSIE.
The HAGGERTYS *and* BOYLE *are laden down
with baskets and pillows done up in
steamer blankets, and have the tired, apprehensive look of new immigrants.* HAG-
GERTY *sets down his basket and unlocks
the door.*

MARIA

Open it, can't you! He may be right be-
　　hind us.
And I'll not stand in the one hall with
　　him!—

We'll be out of here before the week is
done,
If I have to beg to do it—

FATHER COYNE
                    Now, Maria—

MARIA
Now Maria, Father? Are we saints!
If he got on his knees to me, I'd not for-
give him!

MURPHY
It's grand of you to let us wait here for
him.
You must be tired.
          (HAGGERTY opens the door.)

MARIA
                    I'll not close an eye
Until I'm out from underneath this roof!

HAGGERTY
Come in the parlor, Father. I'll light the
fire.
You're famished with the cold. May, bring
the whiskey.
Come in now, Pete. Come in all.
          (MARIA, FATHER COYNE, MURPHY,
          BOYLE, and BESSIE pass through the
          portiere, followed by HAGGERTY. Pause.
          KATHLEEN moves in and out of the
          parlor, packing. Enter STANTON. He
          runs lightly up the stairs and into the
          parlor. He looks at the trunks and
          falls into a chair. Enter KATHLEEN,
          with some clothes. She sees him, averts
          her gaze, and puts the clothes into the
          trunk.)

STANTON
Where do you think you're going!
          (KATHLEEN passes back into the bed-
          room for more clothes and returns
          with them.)
                    Answer me!

KATHLEEN
I'm going home.

STANTON
                    Your home is here with me.

KATHLEEN
You haven't even the grace to beg my
pardon!
How can you look me in the face again!

STANTON
It's I should ask that question. It's all over.
They gave the nomination back to Quinn.
He brought me to the pitch of hope and
betrayed me.
And you stood by and let him do it to me!

KATHLEEN
It ill becomes you, man, to talk betrayals.
Can you tell me whom you've known
you've not betrayed!—
You killed Ag Hogan. But you won't kill
me!

STANTON
I had the right to leave her. She played me
false—

KATHLEEN
Had you the right to marry me? The right
To cut me off from all that I hold holy?

STANTON
Would "all that you hold holy," our pre-
cious Church,
Have granted me a divorce from Agnes
Hogan,
An adulteress!—

KATHLEEN
                    What kind of man are you!
That woman died without the Sacraments
Because in her last fever she was afraid
If she confessed her sins she might betray
you.
She died cut off from God to spare you
harm.
And you have the worst word in your
mouth for her.
Do you know why? Because you're no
good, man.
You waited for your chance to throw her
over.
You saw that with her you'd be nothing.
Nothing.
You had to be the mayor of this city
And she was in the way. You married me
To make yourself respectable again.
That's the only reason.

STANTON
                    I loved . . . I loved you, Kate.
Kathleen, I've nothing left.
I need you.

KATHLEEN
                    Yes. To patch your kick-down fences.
But I have my pride too!—

STANTON
                    Go then, God damn you!
Do you think I'll kneel on the floor and
    beg your help!
I never begged for help from man or God,
And I won't now. You'll not drive me to
    my knees!

KATHLEEN
To sit and tell me you have nothing left!
No more do I! You've taken it out of me
By demanding more than anyone can give.
That's what evil is,
The starvation of a heart with nothing in it
To make the world around it nothing too.
You never begged from man or God! You
    took!
You've taken all your life without return!
You never gave yourself to a single soul
For all your noble talk. —Even in bed
You stole me blind!—

STANTON
                    Get out of here! Get out!
You're not a woman. You're a would-be
    nun!
You were from the beginning.

KATHLEEN
                    God help you, Matt.
    (KATHLEEN *closes and locks the second
    trunk, and puts on her hat.*)
I'll book my passage quickly as I can.
There's nothing in those trunks your
    money bought me.
Leave May the key. The Express will call
    for them.
I put the jewelry in the velvet box
In the top drawer of the bureau by the
    window;
And left the dresses and the sable coat
Hanging in your wardrobe. And that per-
    fume
You bought me's on the vanity.
    (KATHLEEN *walks out the door to the
    head of the stairs.*)
                    Don't look so black.
You're free now, Matt. That's what you
    always wanted.
Marry if you like.
    (KATHLEEN *almost breaks down.*)
                    I'm not your wife. I never was.

STANTON
You mean to leave me here alone!

KATHLEEN
                    I'm sorry, man;
But that's the way we all are, but for God.
    (STANTON *rushes out the door and
    grabs* KATHLEEN.)

STANTON
You'll not leave me! I'll see to that!
    (*Blackout.* KATHLEEN *screams and hits
    the bottom of the stairs.* MARIA *rushes
    into the kitchen with a kerosene lamp
    in her hand, followed by* HAGGERTY,
    FATHER COYNE, MURPHY, BOYLE, *and*
    BESSIE. BOYLE *is carrying a glass of
    whiskey.* HAGGERTY *flings open the
    door, revealing* KATHLEEN *at the foot
    of the stairs in a heap, and* STANTON
    *halfway down the flight in a near
    faint.*)

HAGGERTY
Good Jesus, May! How did it happen,
man?
Give me your whiskey, Pete. Poor Mrs.
Stanton.

KATHLEEN
Ah, Jack. And May. And is that the Father
there?
Amn't I a shame and a disgrace
To get so legless drunk I fall downstairs
Like an unwatched child—

STANTON
                    Oh, Katie. Katie, Katie.
Are you hurt bad.

KATHLEEN
                    Sh!

HAGGERTY
                    Petey, go get Boylan on the beat,
And tell him to get a doctor that's still up,
There's been an accident—

KATHLEEN
                    That's right. That's right.
I caught my heel on the baluster and fell.

BOYLE
I seen a man fall off a hoist through a hold
On Pier Sixteen down in the Erie Basin.
His head was bent that way. Her neck is
broke—

HAGGERTY

Don't stand there nattering. Go get the
doctor.
(*Exit* BOYLE, *running.*)

MURPHY

I'd best go too. I've a thing to do, I must.
(STANTON *takes* KATHLEEN *from* HAG-
GERTY *and cradles her in his arms.*)

STANTON

Will you get away from her so I can hold
her!

HAGGERTY

Be careful with her—

STANTON

Katie, you were right.
I've taken without returning all my life.
And I'd the face to call Ned Quinn cor-
rupt!
The harm I've done and called it good!
The harm!
I saw that harm in Aggie Hogan's face,
And now I see it in yours. Can you forgive
me?

KATHLEEN

Hush now, Matt darling. Toc-sha-shin-
inish:
Let others talk. We'll keep our own safe
counsel.
There's been shame enough already with-
out more—
Do you know what stopped my breath up
on the landing?
I love you still. I thought of us on the boat
from England.
There's few have been as happy as we
were—
Is that the Father there? I want the Father.
(*Enter* BOYLE *with the policeman,*
BOYLAN, *and a* DOCTOR.)

FATHER COYNE

Here I am, child. Here I am right beside
you.
(FATHER COYNE *leans over* KATHLEEN,
putting on his stole as he does so.)

KATHLEEN

Oh . . . my God . . . I am . . . heartily
sorry
For . . . having . . . offended Thee—
(STANTON *pulls* KATHLEEN *away from
the priest in a tight embrace.*)

STANTON

You're not to die!

KATHLEEN

The boat from England, Mattie . . .
(STANTON *kisses her on the mouth,
and hugs her to him, his hand on the
back of her head.*)

STANTON

Yes, we'll have that again. I'll make it up
to you.
I'll make it up. We'll go back home to
Ireland.
I'll give The Court Café to Jack to run,
And we'll go home, and take a high-
stooped house
In one of them good squares, I mean,
those squares . . .
(STANTON *loosens his embrace to look
in* KATHLEEN's *face. Her head falls to
the side.*)
Why don't you answer me? Don't turn
away!—
Where in the name of Jesus Christ's the
doctor?
(*The* DOCTOR *kneels and puts his ear
to* KATHLEEN's *chest. He rises with a
negative shudder of his head to* HAG-
GERTY. FATHER COYNE *motions* BOYLAN
and the DOCTOR *out with his head.
Exit both. Pause.*)

HAGGERTY

She's dead, you know, Matt boy.

STANTON

You're lying, man!
Do you think I have no feeling in my
flesh!
She's warm as a newborn child. We're
going home—
(STANTON *loosens his embrace again.*
KATHLEEN's *hair comes down.*)
I've sprung her hairpins on her— God in
heaven,
I was making love to nothing. She is dead.

FATHER COYNE

Get up please, son; let me finish giving her
Conditional absolution—
(STANTON *tightens his embrace on*
KATHLEEN *again and glares at the
priest like a cornered animal.*)

STANTON
                    Absolve *her*, Father!
Absolve your God, why don't you, He did
  this!
When she found out the marriage was no
  good,
She packed her trunks upstairs. She meant
  to leave me.
She never died in drink! She never fell!
I flung her down the stairs to keep her
  here.
I thought she'd sprain her ankle— Don't
  come near me.
I'll spit in your face if you come near me,
  Father—

FATHER COYNE
Go easy, son. Go easy.

HAGGERTY
                    Get up now, Matt.

FATHER COYNE
Yes, Matt. You have to follow Boylan to
  the precinct.
When there's a question of murder, it's
  the law.
    (STANTON *relinquishes* KATHLEEN *to*
    FATHER COYNE, *and rises.* STANTON
    *turns his back on his dead wife and
    the priest as if in mortal offense.*)

STANTON
Maria, lay my wife out on the bed
With some degree of decency, and spill
That bottle of the Worth perfume she
  loved
Over that bedspread that she was so proud
  of,
And sit with her until the coroner
  comes . . .
I will not have her stink, or lie alone—
    (*With great difficulty*, STANTON *brings
    himself to turn and look at his wife
    and the priest.*)
With all her sins on my head, and the
  world a desert.

(STANTON *throws his arms out in a
begging embrace and falls on his
knees. Enter* MURPHY *and* QUINN, *unnoticed by* STANTON.)
Maisie, Jack. And Petey. Bessie, Father,
Help me, for the love of Jesus, help me.
Dear God in Heaven, help me and forgive
  me.
    (*The* HAGGERTYS *rush to him and
    grasp his hands.* HAGGERTY *raises him,
    and relinquishes him to* FATHER
    COYNE.)

MURPHY
God have mercy on her. Our election's
  lost.
    (STANTON *wheels around. His eyes
    meet with* QUINN's.)

QUINN
I never meant to do this to you, Matt.
I didn't know. I never meant to do it.
I only meant to look out for my good.
I'm nobody. I'm no one, if I'm not the
  mayor.
I'm nothing, Matt. I'm nobody. I'm noth-
  ing—
    (STANTON *rakes* QUINN's *face with a
    blind man's stare. Exit* STANTON.)

FATHER COYNE
Why are you standing round like imbe-
  ciles!
Carry her up the stairs, and lay her out
As Mattie asked you to.
    (HAGGERTY *and* BOYLE *lift* KATHLEEN,
    and start up the stairs with her. MARIA
    *follows, her mouth in the crook of
    her elbow, shaking with tears.* QUINN
    and MURPHY, BESSIE *and* FATHER COYNE
    look on from below.)
                    Well you may cry!
Cry for us all while you're at it. Cry for us
  all!

                    CURTAIN

THE FANTASTICKS

Tom Jones

Suggested by a play called *Les Romanesques* by EDMOND ROSTAND

First presented by Lore Noto at the Sullivan Street Playhouse, New York City, on May 3, 1960, with the following cast:

THE MUTE	Richard Stauffer	BELLOMY	Hugh Thomas
EL GALLO	Jerry Orbach	HENRY	Thomas Bruce
LUISA	Rita Gardner	MORTIMER	George Curley
MATT	Kenneth Nelson	THE PIANIST	Julian Stein
HUCKLEBEE	William Larson	THE HARPIST	Beverly Mann

Music by Harvey L. Schmidt
Music direction and arrangements by Julian Stein
Directed by Word Baker
Production designed by Ed Wittstein
Associate Producers, Shelly Baron, Dorothy Olim, and Robert Alan Gold

© Copyright 1959 by Tom Jones and Harvey L. Schmidt.
Reprinted by permission of Drama Book Specialists/Publishers.
All rights reserved.

CAUTION: Professionals and amateurs are hereby warned that *The Fantasticks* is fully protected by the laws of copyright and is subject to royalty. All rights, including professional, amateur, motion picture, recitation, lecturing, public reading, radio and television broadcasting, the rights of translation into foreign languages, and quotation are strictly reserved. No part of this work may be used in any way without the written consent of the copyright holders. All inquiries concerning rights in the play should be addressed to the Drama Book Specialists/Publishers, 150 West 52nd Street, New York, N.Y. 10019.

ONCE upon a time—on May 3, 1960, to be precise—at a place called Sullivan Street Playhouse, in a city called New York, a musical play called *The Fantasticks* was born. And it lived happily ever after. Fantastick!

The Fantasticks is the longest-running show in the history of New York's professional theatre. And at time of writing it is still doing good business. It seems always to have been a show for lovers, and although its first generation of lovers are now bringing up families in Brooklyn or Westchester, New York has not yet run out of the type. And *The Fantasticks* continues, happily, gratefully, and still to give pleasure.

What opened on that May night a decade ago was an expansion of an earlier one-act version. The musical—Tom Jones wrote the book and lyrics and Harvey Schmidt wrote the music—was far from universally praised by the critics. The granddaddy of us all, Brooks Atkinson, writing the morning after in the *New York Times,* loved the first act but disapproved of the musical's expansion. He wrote: "Perhaps *The Fantasticks* is by nature the sort of thing that loses magic the longer it endures."

The collaboration began in 1949 at the University of Texas. Both are Texans, Tom Jones born there in 1928 and Harvey Schmidt a year later, Jones the son of a turkey farmer and Schmidt the son of a Methodist preacher. Other people at the University of Texas at that time included actors Fess Parker, Rip Torn, Pat Hingle, and the director Word Baker, who eventually was to stage *The Fantasticks.* Jones was a drama major, but Schmidt majored in art, although both were members of the University's Curtain Club, where theatrical aspirants first tried out their wings. The collaboration begun here blossomed in New York, where they worked on Julius Monk's Upstairs-at-the-Downstairs show.

Perhaps the first taste of fame came to Mr. Schmidt when, in collaboration with another University of Texas graduate, Robert Benton, he wrote *The In and Out Book,* a piece of light sociology trying to explain why some people were In and some people were, just as intangibly but just as definitely, Out. The following year *The Fantasticks* opened and Mr. Schmidt was soon to find himself an In person.

After *The Fantasticks* the team of Jones and Schmidt moved to Broadway. Their first musical was an adaptation of the play *The Rainmaker,* with a book written by the original playwright, N. Richard Nash. Called *110 in the Shade,* it opened on October 24, 1963, and ran for 330 performances. On December 5, 1966, their musical *I Do! I Do!,* based on Jan de Hartog's comedy *The Fourposter,* opened on Broadway for a run of 560 performances. Their most recent collaboration was *Celebration,* a completely original work which Tom Jones described as "an attempt at a ritual experience. With laughs. And a few naked girls." It opened on Broadway on January 22, 1969, and ran for 109 performances.

None of these later shows has matched the charm and invention, and certainly not the popularity, of *The Fantasticks.* Now for a very personal confession. Although I have, of course, read it and heard the music, I myself am possibly the only man interested in the theatre and living in New York City who has not seen *The Fantasticks.* This fact started as an accident and has continued as a joke. I once did decide to go and see it, and even write about it for my newspaper, but the management, having no wish to disturb a good thing, asked me to desist, and I desisted. I think that now I will wait for its fifteenth or twentieth birthday, or some other appropriate landmark in its career in the American theatre.

It is a charming, original piece of work that completely deserves its success. It is based, fairly lightly I think, on Edmond Rostand's *Les Romanesques.* It is a slight story —moonshine in the first act, sunlight in the second—about a boy and girl who falsely believe that their fathers would disapprove of their marriage and are, as a kind of consequence, desperately in love.

A slender, tender love tale, embellished with Schmidt's delicately evocative music. Who would have thought that it would have had the resilience to become New York's longest-running play? You never can tell for certain.

It is very difficult to make clear the style of a play. We all know what regular musicals are like, and how they are normally staged. And yet this musical is different. It has a small cast. It has no scenery to speak of. The people in it are realistic and at the same time stylized too.

This being so, I would like to preface this script with one or two notes about the concept of production. If they help you, good, if you don't need them, then that is even better.

First of all, this musical was intended ideally for an open stage—a simple space surrounded on three sides by audience. It may be played and has been played, successfully upon proscenium stages and in the round. One thing is important, however. It should be played as closely to the audience as possible, whatever kind of stage may hold it. People speak to the audience at many points. And even when characters are not "taking their case" directly to the audience, it is well for them to keep the audience specifically in mind. Thus, when the old actor in his first scene asks El Gallo to imagine him in wig and make-up, he is speaking to the audience just as much as he is to El Gallo. When the parents and the children quarrel in the beginning of Act Two, each of the four speaks often to the audience. When Luisa says "I put a little ribbon on the spot," I feel sure that she is showing her bruised arm, not to Matt or to the fathers, but to the audience. Perhaps the best way to explain it is that each actor considers the audience to be his friend. Each actor, upon entering into the play, has been given a speech directly to the audience. Therefore, each quite naturally assumes that the audience will understand him even if the other characters in the play do not.

Given this somewhat stylized premise of presentation, it is not necessary for the actors to add any theatrical icing of their own. That is to say, asides are not spoken in the melodramatic "theatrical" way, but simply and directly. And the parts should not be "spoofed," even when the romanticism becomes extreme. The people should be people, not cardboard rococo.

Point: The actors do not leave the stage, but wait outside the center of action for their turn to "come back on." Sometimes they watch the actors in the light, as in the beginning, when Luisa and Matt have their solos. Later on, after the show is underway, they simply sit on the back of the platform with their backs toward us—or upon benches upstage which have been left there for that purpose. They are soon accepted and forgotten by the audience. And their presence serves to underline the basic point of view —i.e., this is not real literally. We are players, this is a stage. You are an audience. What we do together is to create a special reality—the reality of the mind and the emotions.

Point: Lights become vastly important when there are no sets. A careful use of light will help to set up the moods and to relieve the visual sameness.

Point: Costumes should be theatrical—should have a flair—should even suggest commedia dell'arte in a way. But they should be basically contemporary. No tights, please! But B.V.D.'s are okay.

Point: The Mute should not be coy or elfin. He should not intrude with pantomime specialties. His function is essentially to function. He hands out and returns props— swiftly. He provides chairs and benches as needed. And removes them the instant we don't need to make use of them anymore. He holds up a stick to represent the wall— but only when we feel that we need it. He hangs up a multi-colored drape before "Soon It's Gonna Rain" and holds up a cardboard butterfly during the "Glen speech" of El Gallo. He should not be a butterfly himself. His job is a hard one. He must move well, have a prodigious memory and concentration for detail. His face should be pleasant— but not distracting. He is always there. We must always sense his presence and yet he must never intrude.

Point: It is difficult to indicate in a reading script all of the musical underscorings of a piece such as this without cluttering the pages with notes about notes. Also, obbligatos and vocalized sections become ludicrous in print. Therefore, I would like to suggest that the original cast album of the show, recorded by MGM (E3872OC) might be a helpful tool in clarifying any points that are not covered in detail by this script or by the music score which accompanies it.

ACT ONE

*This play should be played on a plat-
form. There is no scenery as we generally
know it, but occasionally a stick may be
held up to represent a wall. Or a cardboard
moon may be hung upon a pole to indicate
that it's night.*

*When the audience enters the audito-
rium, the platform is clearly in sight.
There is a tattered drape across the front
of it upon which is lettered "THE FAN-
TASTICKS." There is a bench down
center. And at the stage right side of the
platform there is a large box in which
the props are kept. This is the extent of the
setting, although it is desirable if possible
to have four iron poles inset near the
corners of the platform and extending up
into the ceiling. And in some proscenium
productions, you may wish to add a ladder.*

When the Overture begins, the MUTE
*comes walking on in tempo to the music.
He sees the audience and signals for the
other actors to come on.*

The BOY's *father (*HUCKLEBEE*) enters
irately, dressed in his shirt and his B.V.D.'s.
He mumbles "I know my cue!" Then he
notices the audience and makes an embarrassed bow. He is followed by the* GIRL's
*father (*BELLOMY*) who walks directly to
center with a benign smile and bows repeatedly, until* HUCKLEBEE *beckons him to
get to work. They pick up the bench from
down center and carry it out of sight behind the drape.*

The GIRL *(*LUISA*) enters in her white
petticoats and tries a couple of dance steps
on the newly polished floor. She sees the
audience, smiles, and begins to back off
stage left; then the* FATHERS *stick their
heads around from the right side of the
drape and "psst" to her that she is supposed to join them there. She does so,
pausing only long enough to bestow one
last dazzling smile at the audience.*

The BOY *(*MATT*) strides on, carrying a
tall wooden chair, which he tosses up for
the* MUTE *to catch and place upon the platform.* MATT *comes to the center, checks the
lights, checks the drape to see that it is
straight; then he smiles at the audience and
joins his fellow actors behind the lettered
drape.*

Last of all, the NARRATOR *(*EL GALLO*)
comes striding in. The* MUTE *hands him a
dashing hat which the* NARRATOR *places
rakishly on his head. Then he comes to the
center of the stage and bows grandly to
the audience. After this, the* NARRATOR *and
the* MUTE *go to either side of the lettered
drape, undo the ropes which hold it to the
poles, and drop it to the floor, revealing
the* BOY, *the* GIRL, *and the* FATHERS *in a
hastily assembled dramatic tableau. As the
music grows faster and more and more
frantic, the parents and the children break
from the tableau and rush to be ready.
Props are pulled from the prop box.* LUISA
gets her skirt; MATT *his sweater;* BELLOMY
his little checkered vest; and HUCKLEBEE
*his pants, with which he wrestles franti-
cally. The* NARRATOR *juggles three bright
oranges, and finally, as all of the actors
climb back on the platform and take their
places for the play, the* MUTE *throws bright
squares of colored paper spiraling into the
air, making the area alive with color and
movement.*

When the Overture is over, the NARRATOR
*sits upon the platform and sings directly
to the audience. Behind him, the actors
are in a relaxed informal pose on the platform—listening to him, and occasionally
singing to the audience too, asking them
to "follow."*

———

["Try to Remember"]

EL GALLO

Try to remember the kind of September
When life was slow and oh, so mellow.
Try to remember the kind of September
When grass was green and grain was
   yellow.
Try to remember the kind of September
When you were a tender and callow fel-
   low.
Try to remember, and if you remember,
Then follow.

LUISA

Follow, follow, follow, follow.

EL GALLO

Try to remember when life was so tender
That no one wept except the willow.
Try to remember when life was so tender
That dreams were kept beside your pillow.
Try to remember when life was so tender

That love was an ember about to billow.
Try to remember, and if you remember,
Then follow.

LUISA, MATT and FATHERS
Follow, follow, follow, follow.

EL GALLO
Deep in December it's nice to remember
Although you know the snow will fol-
low.
Deep in December it's nice to remember
Without a hurt the heart is hollow.
Deep in December, it's nice to remember
The fire of September that made us mel-
low.
Deep in December our hearts should re-
member,
And follow.

EL GALLO (*speaks to audience*)
Let me tell you a few things you may
want to know
Before we begin the play.
First of all, the characters:
A boy; a girl; two fathers;
And a wall.
Anything else that's needed
We can get from out of this box.

(EL GALLO *and the* MUTE *open the
large prop box stage right and remove from it a smaller prop box
which they place down stage center.*)

It's hard to know which is most important,
Or how it all began.
The Boy was born.
The Girl was born.
They grew up, quickly,
Went to school,
Became shy,
(In their own ways and for different
reasons)
Read Romances,
Studied cloud formations in the lazy after-
noon,
And instead of reading textbooks,
Tried to memorize the moon.
And when the girl was fifteen
(She was younger than the boy),
She began to notice something strange.
Her ugly duckling features
Had undergone a change.
In short, she was growing pretty;
For the first time in her whole life pretty.
And the shock so stunned and thrilled her

That she became
Almost immediately
Incurably insane.
Observe:

(MUSIC *as* LUISA *walks forward and
sits on the large wooden chair, which
the* MUTE *has thoughtfully placed just
beneath her.*)

LUISA (*to audience*)
The moon turns red on my birthday every
year and it always will until somebody
saves me and takes me back to my palace.

EL GALLO
That is a typical remark.
The other symptoms vary.
She thinks that she's a princess;
That her name must be in French,
Or sometimes Eurasian, although she isn't
sure what that is.

LUISA (*to audience*)
You see, no one can feel the way I feel
And have a father named Amos Babcock
Bellomy.

EL GALLO
She has a glue-paste necklace
Which she thinks is really real.

LUISA (*putting on the necklace which
the* MUTE *has just removed from the prop
box and given to her*)
I found it in the attic
With my Mother's name inside;
It is my favorite possession.

EL GALLO
It's her fancy.

LUISA
It's my pride.

(*Now* LUISA *talks to the accompaniment of the harp.*)

This morning a bird woke me up.
It was a lark or a peacock
Or something like that.
Some strange sort of bird that I'd never
heard.
And I said "hello"
And it vanished: flew away.
The very minute that I said "hello."
It was mysterious.

So do you know what I did?
I went over to my mirror
And brushed my hair two hundred times
    without stopping.
And as I was brushing it,
My hair turned mauve!
No, honestly! Mauve!
And then red.
And then sort of a deep blue when the sun
    hit it.

I'm sixteen years old,
And every day something happens to me.
I don't know what to make of it.
When I get up in the morning to get
    dressed,
I can tell:
Something's different.
I like to touch my eyelids
Because they're never quite the same.

(MUSIC *begins underneath her speaking.*)

Oh! Oh! Oh!
I hug myself till my arms turn blue,
Then I close my eyes and I cry and cry
Till the tears come down
And I taste them. Ah!
I love to taste my tears!
I am special.
I am special.
Please, God, please—
Don't let me be normal!

(*And, rapturously, she sings.*)

["Much More"]

I'd like to swim in a clear blue stream
Where the water is icy cold;
Then go to town in a golden gown,
And have my fortune told.
Just once.
Just once.
Just once before I'm old.
I'd like to be—not evil,
But a little worldly wise.
To be the kind of girl designed
To be kissed upon the eyes.
I'd like to dance till two o'clock,
Or sometimes dance till dawn,
Or if the band could stand it,
Just go on and on and on!
Just once,
Just once,
Before the chance is gone!

I'd like to waste a week or two,
And never do a chore,
To wear my hair unfastened
So it billows to the floor.
To do the things I've dreamed about
But never done before!
Perhaps I'm bad, or wild, or mad,
With lots of grief in store,
But I want much more than keeping
    house!
Much more!
Much more!
Much more!

(*At the end of the song,* LUISA *half swoons with ecstasy, and the* MUTE *moves the chair beneath her just as she is about to fall.*)

EL GALLO
Good.
And now the boy.
His story may be a wee bit briefer,
Because it's pretty much the same.

(MUSIC. *As* MATT *rises and stands upon the platform center, the* MUTE *opens the center prop box, gets a biology book and tosses it up to* MATT.)

MATT (*to audience*)
There is this girl.

EL GALLO
That is the essence.

MATT (*to audience*)
There is this girl.

EL GALLO (*crossing to the side and sitting*)
I warn you: it may be monotonous.

MATT
There is this girl.
I'm nearly twenty years old.
I've studied Biology.
I've had an education.
I've been inside a lab;
Dissected violets:
I know the way things are.
I'm grown-up, stable;
Willing to conform.
I'm beyond such foolish notions,
And yet—in spite of my knowledge—
There is this girl.

She makes me young again, and foolish,
And with her I perform the impossible:
I defy Biology!
And achieve ignorance!

(*He tosses the book back to the*
MUTE.)

There are no other ears but hers to hear
The explosion of my soul! There are no
other eyes but hers to make me wise, and
despite what they say of species, there is
not one plant or animal or any growing
thing that is made quite the same as she
is. It's stupid, of course, I know it. And
immensely undignified, but I do love her!

So, that's my situation in a nutshell.
I've gone mad.
My knowledge—pfft; it's vanished. And
    since that's so,
I intend to go hatter-mad, or madder.
Mad as Hamlet.
As unrestrained as Lear.
I'm going to poke my sword at shadows
And write sonnets to the moon.
And swoon
And swear
And curl my hair
And grow an enviable moustache!

And the reason, if you ask me, is
Because there is this girl.

EL GALLO
Look! There is the wall their fathers built
between their houses.

(EL GALLO *snaps his fingers and everyone moves quickly into position for
the action of the play.* LUISA *rises and
crosses upstage to sit on the long
bench upon the platform.* BELLOMY
*grabs her wooden chair, carries it to
the back of the platform, and sits on
it, his back to the audience.* HUCKLEBEE
*sits on the upstage side of the plat-
form with his back to us.* EL GALLO
*seats himself comfortably to the side,
or top of the stage right prop box.
And the* MUTE *gets a wooden stick
and stands directly up center on the
platform, holding up the stick—to
represent the wall.* LUISA *and her father are stage right of the stick;* MATT
*and his father stage left of stick.
Throughout the next scene—and in-*

deed, up until the time the MUTE *takes
away the stick, the* ACTORS *observe the
imaginary line of the wall, extending
from the* MUTE's *little stick directly
down the center line of the stage.*)

MATT (*as soon as* EVERYONE *is in place*)
They built it ages ago last month when I
came home from school. Poor fools, they
built it to keep us apart. Maybe she's
there now. I hope so—I'll see.
(*He goes up to stage left side of the
platform.*)
. . . I don't know what to call her. She's
too vibrant for a name. What shall I call
her? Juliet?

LUISA
Yes, dear!

MATT
Helena?

LUISA
Yes, dear!

MATT
And Cassandra. And Cleopatra. And Beatrice. And also Guinevere?

LUISA
What, dear?

MATT
I think she's there.
(*He climbs up on his side of the
bench.* LUISA *meanwhile is leaning
eagerly on the other side of the stick.*)
Can you hear me?

LUISA
Barely.

MATT
I've been speaking of you.

LUISA
To whom?

MATT
To them—I told them that if someone
were to ask me to describe you I would
be utterly and totally speechless, except to
say perhaps that you are Polaris or the inside of a leaf.

LUISA
Speak a little louder.

["Metaphor"]

MATT
I love you!

(*She swoons.*)

(*Singing vigorously.*)
If I were in the desert deep in sand,
 and
The sun was burning like a hot
 pom'granate:
Walking through a nightmare in the
 heat of
A summer day, until my mind was
 parch-ed!
—Then you are water!
Cool clear water!
A refreshing glass of water!

LUISA (*spoken*)
What, dear?

MATT (*spoken*)
WATER!

(*She swoons.*)

MATT
Love! You are love!
Better far than a metaphor
Can ever ever be.
Love! You are love!
My mystery—of love!

If the world was like an iceberg,
And everything was frozen,
And tears turned into icicles in the
 eye!
And snow came pouring—sleet and
 ice—
Came stabbing like a knife!
—Then you are heat!
A fire alive with heat!
A flame that thaws the iceberg with
 its heat!

LUISA (*spoken*)
Repeat.

MATT (*spoken*)
YOU ARE HEAT!
(*She swoons; then revives immedi-
ately to join him in song.*)

MATT (LUISA'*s lyrics in parentheses*)
Love! You are love! (I am love!)

Better far than a metaphor
Can ever ever be.
Love! You are love! (I am love!)
My mystery— (His mystery)
You are Polaris, the one trustworthy
 star!
You are! You are!

LUISA
I am! I am!

MATT
You are September, a special mystery
To me! To me!

LUISA
To he! To he!

MATT (*as* LUISA *does an obbligato*)
You are sunlight! Moonlight!
Mountains! Valleys!
The microscopic inside of a leaf!
My joy! My grief!
My star! My leaf!
Oh—

(*In her exuberance, she grabs his
hand* under *the stick, and he quickly
lifts it up and over the "wall."*)

BOTH
Love! You are love! (I am love!)
Better far than a metaphor
Can ever ever be!
Love! You are love! (I am love!)
My mystery— (His mystery)
Of love!

(*They reach over the top of the stick,
and embrace.*)

LUISA
Matt!

MATT
Luisa!

LUISA
Shh. Be careful.
I thought I heard a sound.

MATT
But you're trembling!

LUISA
My father loves to spy.

MATT
I know; I know.
I had to climb out through a window.
My father locked my room.

LUISA
Oh God, be careful!
Suppose you were to fall!

MATT
It's on the ground floor.

LUISA
Oh.

MATT
Still, the window's very small.
I could get stuck.

LUISA
This is madness, isn't it?

MATT
Yes, it's absolutely mad!

LUISA
And also very wicked?

MATT
Yes.

LUISA
I'm glad.

MATT
My father would be furious if he knew.

LUISA
Listen, I have had a vision.

MATT
Of disaster?

LUISA
No. Of azaleas.
I dreamed I was picking azaleas.
When all at once, this Duke—
Oh, he was very old,
I'd say he was nearly forty.
But attractive.
And very evil.

MATT
I hate him!

LUISA
And he had a retinue of scoundrels,
And they were hiding behind the rhodo-
   dendrons,
And then, all at once,
As I picked an azalea—
He leapt out!

MATT
God. I hate him!

LUISA
In my vision, how I struggled.
Like the Rape of the Sabine Women!
I cried "help."

MATT
And I was nearby!

LUISA
Yes. You came rushing to the rescue.
And, single-handed, you fight all his men,
And win—

MATT
And then—

LUISA
Celebration!

MATT
Fireworks!

LUISA
Fiesta!

MATT
Laughter!

LUISA
Our fathers give in!

MATT
We live happily ever after!

LUISA
There's no reason in the world why it
can't happen exactly like that. (*Suddenly
she stiffens*.) Someone's coming!

MATT
It's my father.

LUISA
Kiss me!

(They kiss as MUSIC *begins and* HUCKLEBEE *comes in with his pruning shears and prunes away at a massive imaginary plant. Miraculously, although the plant is just beneath the bench where the* LOVERS *are kissing,* HUCKLEBEE *is too engrossed with the pruning to look up and see the embrace.)*

HUCK
Too much moisture!
(To audience.)
There are a great many things I could tell you about myself. I was once in the Navy; that's where I learned Horticulture. Yes, I have been the world over. I've seen it all: mountain cactus, the century plant, Japanese Ivy. And exotic ports where bog-wort was sold in the open market! I'm a man of experience and there is one thing that I've learned: Too much moisture is worse than none at all. Prune a plant. Avoid water. And go easy on manure. Moderation. That's the moral. Hmmm. That's my son's foot. *(Which he was just about to clip.)*

MATT *(on the bench)*
Hello, Father.

(By now, LUISA *has ducked down on the other side of the stick.)*

HUCK
What are you doing up in that tree?

MATT
Reading verses.

HUCK
Curses.

MATT
How's that?

HUCK
I offer a father's curses
To the kind of education
That makes our children fools.
I sent this boy to school—to college
And I hope you know what that costs.
Did he learn to dig a cesspool, no.
He's up there reading verse.
(Suddenly suspicious.)
Why do I always find you
Standing beside that wall?

MATT
I'm waiting for it to fall.
Besides, I like it.
I like its lovely texture,
And its pretty little eyes.

HUCK
Walls don't have eyes!

MATT
Then what do you call—this flower?

(The MUTE *hands him a flower.)*

LUISA *(from her side)*
Sweet God, he's clever!

HUCK *(pulling* MATT *down from the bench)*
Son, you are an ass. There you sit every day, reading verses, while who knows what our neighbor is up to on the other side of that wall. He's a villain. I'll not have it! I'll strip down those branches where an enemy could climb! I'll lime that wall with bottles! I'll jag it up with glass!

LUISA
Ahh!

HUCK
What was that?

MATT
Some broken willow—some little wounded bird.

HUCK
Maybe. But walls have ears even though they don't have eyes. I'll just take a look.
*(*LUISA *crouches down fearfully as* HUCKLEBEE *starts to climb. However, he stops short of the top, and grabs his back in pain.)*
Ahh! There's that stiffness. The result of my Navy career. Here, son, you climb. You can see for me.

MATT
All right, Father.

*(*MATT *bounds up the bench and reaches down to take* LUISA *by the hand on the other side.)*

HUCK
What do you see?

MATT

I love you.

LUISA

I love you, too.

HUCK

What are you mumbling about? Get down from there if there's nothing to be seen! Down I say.

MATT

I obey. (MATT *hops down.*)

HUCK

You're an idiot. I've decided you need to be married. So I went shopping this morning and picked you out a wife.

LUISA

Ahh!

HUCK

There's that sound again.

MATT

Anguished bird.

HUCK

Weeping willow?
It may be.
But let's get back to business:
Son, I've picked you out a pearl.

MATT

And if I prefer a diamond?

HUCK

How dare you prefer a diamond
When I've just offered you a pearl!

MATT (*as his father tries to interrupt*)
Listen carefully to what I have to say.
Listen, Wall. And flowers. And willow, too.
And wounded bird. And Father, you
May as well listen too.
I will not wed by your wisdom.
I will not walk neatly into a church
And contract out to prolongate my race.
I will not go wedding in a too-tight suit
Nor be witnessed when I take my bride.
No!
(MUSIC *as he speaks.*)
I'll marry, when I marry,
In my own particular way;
And my bride shall dress in sunlight,

With rain for her wedding veil.
Out in the open,
With no one standing by.
No song except September
Being sung in the busy grass!
No sound except our heartbeats, roaring!
Like a flower alive with bees!
(*Getting faster and more and more carried away.*)
Without benefit of neighbor!
Without benefit of book!
Except perhaps her handprint
As she presses her hand in mine;
Except perhaps her imprint
As she gives me her golden hair;
In a field, while kneeling,
Being joined by the joy of life!
There!
In the air!
In the open!
That's how I plan to wive!

HUCK

Son, you need pruning. Come inside and write SIMPLICITY two hundred times without stopping. Perhaps that will improve your style.

(MATT *and* HUCKLEBEE *exit to upstage left of platform and sit, as* MUSIC *begins and* BELLOMY *enters on his side, carrying an enormous watering pail with a long spout.*)

BELL

That's right, drink away. Open up your thirsty little mouths.
(*To audience.*)
I'm her father. And believe me, it isn't easy. Perhaps that's why I love vegetables. So dependable. You plant a radish, and you know what you're about. You don't get a turnip or a cabbage, no. Plant a turnip, get a turnip; plant a cabbage, get a cabbage. While with children—I thought I had planted a turnip or at worst perhaps an avocado: something remotely useful. I'm a merchant—I sell buttons. What need do I have for a rose?—There she is. Missy, you must go inside.

LUISA

I've told you; I'm a princess.

BELL

You're a button-maker's daughter. Now, go inside as you're told. Our enemy is beyond that wall. Up to something: I can feel it! Him and his no-good son. Look out, you've stepped in my peppers. That settles it. I'll put a fence here by this wall. A high fence, with barbed stickers! An arsenal of wire!

LUISA
A fence is expensive, Papa.

BELL
Expensive? Well, I'll build it myself. Go inside; do as I tell you!
(LUISA *exits to the rear of the platform and sits.*)
Is she gone?—Ha, yes—she's gone.
(*Yodels.*)
Oh lady le di le da loo!

(*He puts his hand to his ear and we hear in the distance an answering yodel.* BELLOMY *yips with delight and rushes over to the bench as* HUCKLEBEE *does the same on his side. They scramble up the bench and noisily embrace over the "wall.")*

BELL
Hucklebee!

HUCK
Bellomy!

BELL
Neighbor!

HUCK
Friend!

BELL
How's the gout?

HUCK
I barely notice. And your asthma?

BELL
A trifle. (*Coughs.*) I endure it.

HUCK
Well, it's nearly settled.

BELL
What is?

HUCK
The marriage. They're nearly ready. I hid in the bushes to listen. Oh, it's something! They're out of their minds with love!

BELL (*front*)
Hurray.

HUCK
My son—he is fantastic!

BELL
My daughter is fantastic, too.
They're both of them mad.

HUCK
They are geese!

BELL (*to audience—making sure they get it*)
It was a clever plan we had.
To build this wall.

HUCK (*also to audience*)
Yes. And to pretend to feud.

BELL
Just think if they knew
That we wanted them wed.

HUCK
A prearranged marriage—

BELL
They'd rather be dead!

(MUSIC. BELL *climbs over the stick which the* MUTE *is still holding up to represent the wall. Once* BELL *has climbed over the stick to the other "side," the* MUTE *removes himself over to the large prop box, and we forget the wall completely until we need to suggest it again. All of which means that now the* FATHERS *are free to play this scene and song without any make-believe wall to hamper their movements. They are, in effect, now in "another part of the garden.")*

HUCK
Children!

BELL
Lovers!

HUCK
Fantasticks!

BELL
Geese!

HUCK
How clever we are.

BELL
How crafty to know.

HUCK
To manipulate children,

BELL
You merely say "no."

(*They sing.*)

["Never Say No"]

Ohhhhhhhh—
Dog's got to bark; a mule's got to bray.
Soldiers must fight and preachers must pray.
And children, I guess, must get their own way
The minute that you say no.

Why did the kids pour jam on the cat?
Raspberry jam all over the cat?
Why should the kids do something like that,
When all that we said was "no"?

HUCK
My son was once afraid to swim;
The water made him wince.
Until I said he mustn't swim;
Been swimmin' ever since!

BOTH
Been swimmin' ever since!

Ohhhhhhhh—
Dog's got to bark; a mule's got to bray.
Soldiers must fight and preachers must pray.
And children, I guess, must get their own way
The minute that you say no.

Why did the kids put beans in their ears?
No one can hear with beans in their ears.
After a while the reason appears.
They did it cause we said "no."

BELL
Your daughter brings a young man in,
Says "Do you like him, Pa?"
Just tell her he's a fool and then,
You've got a son-in-law!

BOTH
You've got a son-in-law!

Ohhhhhhhhhhhhhhhh—
Sure as a June comes right after May!
Sure as the night comes right after day!
You can be sure the devil's to pay,
The minute that you say no.
Make sure you never say—
No!

BELL
But there's one problem left.

HUCK
How to end the feud?

BELL
Exactly; you guessed it.
We mustn't let them know.

HUCK
Oh, no, if they knew—
We're finished.

BELL
We're through.

HUCK
I think I've found the answer.
It's delicious. Very theatrical.

BELL
Tell me.

HUCK
An abduction!

BELL
Who's abducted?

HUCK
Your daughter.

BELL
Who abducts her?

HUCK
A professional abductor.
I've hired the very man!

(EL GALLO, *who has throughout this
first portion of the play been seated in
the shadows at the side, steps forward
—puts on his bandit hat—and enters
the scene with a flourish.*)

EL GALLO
Gentlemen, good evening.

HUCK (*startled*)
What the devil?

BELL
Who are you?

EL GALLO
I was sent for.
(*Holds up note—one of the colored
squares from the Overture.*)
A maiden in distress.

HUCK
Of course, you are El Gallo.

(*He pronounces it American—
Gal-oh.*)

EL GALLO
El Gallo.

(*Which he pronounces Spanish—
Gayo.*)

HUCK
Oh—si, si. (*To* BELLOMY.) See, this is
what I was about to tell you. We hire this
man to assist us. He starts to kidnap your
daughter. My son runs in to save her.
Then, a battle.

(HUCK *and* EL GALLO *look at* BELL,
who doesn't seem to get it.)

EL GALLO
I allow the boy to defeat me . . .

HUCK
My son becomes a hero. . . . And the
feud is over forever.

BELL (*he finally gets it*)
Oooh! (*To* EL GALLO.) How much for such
a drama?

EL GALLO
That, Señor, depends.

BELL
On what?

EL GALLO
What else? The quality of the Rape.

BELL
The WHAT?

(*He starts to leave, but they catch
him.*)

EL GALLO
Forgive me. The attempted Rape. I know
you prefer Abduction, but the proper word
is Rape. It's short and businesslike.

HUCK
I heard her speak of Sabine Women.

BELL
Well, it doesn't sound right to me!

EL GALLO
It is though, I assure you.
As a matter of fact, it's standard.
(*Acts it out.*)
The lovers meet in secret. And so forth.
A group of villains interrupt them. And
so forth.
The boy fights off pirates, Indians, bandits.
The parents relent. Happy ending. And so
forth.
All of it quite standard.

BELL
What about the cost?

EL GALLO
Cost goes by type. In your case, I think I
would recommend a "First Class."

BELL
You mean we get a choice?

EL GALLO
Yes, of course. With regular Union rates.

(*Suddenly* EL GALLO *springs up on the
platform bench, strikes a Flamenco
pose, and sings lustily, as the* FATHERS
sit on the center prop box to listen.)

["It Depends on What You Pay"]

EL GALLO (*sings*)

Rape!
R-a-a-a-pe!
Raa-aa-aa-pe!
A pretty rape.
Such a pretty rape!

We've the obvious open schoolboy
    rape,
With little mandolins and perhaps a
    cape,
The rape by coach; it's little in re-
    quest.
The rape by day; but the rape by
    night is best.

Just try to see it,
And you will soon agree, señors,
Why invite regret,
When you can get the sort of rape
You'll never ever forget!

You can get the rape emphatic.
You can get the rape polite.
You can get the rape with Indians,
A truly charming sight.
You can get the rape on horseback,
They all say it's new and gay.
So you see the sort of rape
Depends on what you pay.
It depends on what you pay.

HUCK

The kids will love it.
It depends on what you—

BELL

Pay!

HUCK

So why be stingy,
It depends on what you—

EL GALLO
    (*dramatizing the whole thing*)

The spectacular rape, with costumes
    ordered from the East.
Requires rehearsal—and takes a dozen
    men at least.
A couple of singers
And a string
    quartet.   BELL (*spoken*). Sounds
                    expensive.
A major production—requires a set.

Just try to see it,

And you will soon si, si, señor,
Why invite regret,
When you can get the sort of rape
You'll never ever forget!

You can get the rape emphatic.
You can get the rape polite.
You can get the rape with Indians:
A truly charming sight!
You can get the rape on horseback,
They all say it's distingué!
So you see the sort of rape
Depends on what you pay.

EL GALLO AND HUCK

So you see the sort of rape
Depends on what you pay.

EL GALLO

It depends on what you pay.

HUCK

So why be stingy.
It depends on what you—

BELL

Pay, pay, pay!

HUCK

The kids will love it;
It depends on what you—

EL GALLO

The comic rape!
Perhaps it's just a trifle too unique.
    (Ha ha.)
Romantic rape.
Done while canoeing   BELL (*spoken*).
    on a moonlit creek   That's kinda
The Gothic rape!
I play Valkyrie on a bass bassoon!
The drunken rape.
It's done completely   BELL (*spoken*).
    in a cheap saloon.   Nothing cheap!
The rape Venetian—needs a blue la-
    goon.
The rape with moonlight—or with-
    out a moon.
Moonlight is expensive but it's in de-
    mand.
The military rape, it's done with
    drummers and a band.
You understand?
It's very grand!
It's done with drums and a great big
    brass band!
Yeah!
Scoobidoobi.

(EL GALLO *leads the* FATHERS *around the stage in a wild little dance as the* MUSIC *becomes momentarily boogie-woogie.*)

BELL (*speaks*)
It's so Spanish; that's why I like it!

HUCK (*speaks*)
I like it, too. Ai, yi, yi!

(*Now the* MUSIC *becomes once more Flamenco as* EL GALLO *and the* FATHERS *begin to clap their hands and click their heels in Spanish fashion as they sing.*)

EL GALLO
Just try to see it.

BELL
I see it!

HUCK
I see it!

EL GALLO
And you will soon si, si, señor.
Why—invite regret,
When you can get the sort of rape
You'll never ever forget!

FATHERS	EL GALLO
We can get the rape emphatic	Oh, rape!
We can get the rape polite.	Sweet rape.
We can get the rape with Indians	Oh, rape.
A truly charming sight.	Ah—rape—
We can get the rape on horseback,	
They all say it's new and gay.	
So you see the sort of rape	
Depends on what you pay.	
So you see the sort of rape	
Depends on what you pay.	
So you see the sort of rape	
Depends on what you pay.	
It depends on what you pay.	Ra—aa—
It depends on what you pay.	Aa—aa—
It depends on what you pay.	Aa—pe!

ALL THREE
Depends a lot
On what you—

HUCK (*speaks*)
I say they're only young once
Let's order us a First Class!

ALL THREE (*sing*)
Ra—aa—aa—pe! Ole!
EL GALLO (*with pad and pencil*)
One Rape First Class.

BELL
With trimmings!

EL GALLO (*makes note*)
With trimmings. Now, let's see—is it to be a big affair, or intimate?

BELL
We thought—just the children.

EL GALLO
I mean afterwards, at the party.

BELL
No. Just the immediate family.

EL GALLO
No guests? Perhaps a gathering on the lawn?

BELL
Too expensive. Just the immediate family will be enough.

EL GALLO
As you wish. That means the orchestra can go home. Still, big affairs are nice.

HUCK
Perhaps some other time.

EL GALLO
All right, then. You'd better go home and rehearse your parts.

(*And the* FATHERS, *as they exit, sing a short chorus of* "Depends on What You Pay," *then they sit again on the back of the platform. Perhaps the* MUTE *may even hold up the stick again for a short second while* BELL *climbs back over to his "side." At all events, when they are seated,* EL GALLO *speaks to the audience.*)

EL GALLO

La. Time is rushing. And a major production to do. I need actors—extra actors—to stage my elaborate Rape. But I'm not worried. Something will turn up. I can sense it in the air.

(DRUMBEAT *is heard from deep inside the stage right prop box.*)

There—you hear? What did I tell you?

(*The* MUTE *opens the prop box and* MORTIMER *emerges, dressed in a loin cloth and a feather, and playing a drum. He is followed at once by* HENRY, *an ancient actor down on his luck.*)

HENRY (*strikes a pose on down center box, after being helped onto it by* MORTIMER)

Sir, the Players have arrived!

EL GALLO

Señor, the Players are most welcome.

HENRY

Don't look at us like we are, sir. Please. Remove ten pounds of road dust from these aged wrinkled cheeks. See make-up caked, in glowing powder pink! Imagine a beard, full blown and blowing, like the whiskers of a bear! And hair! Imagine hair. In a box I've got all colors, so I beg you—imagine hair!—And not these clothes. Oh, no, no, no. Dear God, not rags like any beggar has. But see me in a doublet! Mortimer, fetch the doublet.

(MORTIMER *sheathes him in a worn-out doublet.*)

There—Imagine! It's torn; I know—forget it. It vanishes under light. That's it! That's the whole trick; try to see me under light! I recite. Say a cue. You'll see. I'll know it. Go on. Say one. Try me.

EL GALLO

"Friends, Romans, Countrymen."

HENRY (*who has reached the platform, stops, and crosses back to* EL GALLO)

It's what?

EL GALLO

"Friends, Romans, Countrymen."

HENRY

—Don't tell me, I can get it. Let's see. "Friends, Romans, Countrymen."

(MORTIMER *whispers it to him.*)

Why, yes! Of course! That's easy. Why didn't you pick something hard? (*Strikes a pose.*)

Friends, Romans, Countrymen—
Screw your courage to the sticking place!
And be not sick and pale with grief
That thou—her handmaidens—
Should be far more fair
Than she. . . .
How's that?

EL GALLO

Marvellous.

HENRY

Try to see it under light. I assure you it is dazzling.
I'm Henry Albertson. Perhaps you recall my Hamlet?

EL GALLO

Of course.

HENRY (*stunned*)

You remember? Would you like to see the clippings?

EL GALLO

Perhaps later.

HENRY

As you wish. I preserve them. Who knows —I may write a book someday. This is Mortimer; he does death scenes. He's been with me for forty years. Want to see one? He's an expert. Mortimer, die for the man.

(MORTIMER *dies.*)

You see! What did I tell you!—Now, down to business. You need Players?

EL GALLO

For a love scene. Have you done romantic drama?

HENRY

That, sir, is my specialty. Have you never seen my Romeo?

EL GALLO

I'm afraid not.

HENRY
Oh, well, I have the clippings. (*Starts to get them, but* EL GALLO *grabs him.*)

EL GALLO
Henry, here's the path: We'll have these players play something like the abduction of the maiden before this lover—

HENRY (*catching the spirit*)
And if he but blench!

EL GALLO
We'll stand our ground. And fight until the lot of us is downed!

HENRY
Nobly done!

MORTIMER (*rising from the dead, and speaking with a very thick cockney accent*)
Where do you want me, 'enry?

HENRY (*who has some trouble locating him through his myopic eyes*)
Hm? Oh! Off left, Mortimer. Indians are always off left.

MORTIMER
Wot's my cue?

HENRY
I'll tell you when it's time.

MORTIMER
Righto. (*He exits—offstage left.*)

HENRY (*calling out after him*)
Don't forget, Mortimer: dress the stage, dress the stage. Don't cluster up when you die.

(*To* EL GALLO)

Well, that does it, I think. I imagine we'd better hide.

EL GALLO
Oh, I nearly forgot. I promised them moonlight.

(*He snaps his fingers and a moon drops into place as the* MUTE *hangs a delicately tattered blue and green drop between the back two poles, and the stage lights become blue.*)

HENRY
Amazing!

EL GALLO
Beautiful, eh? A lover's moon—
Go ahead, Henry. I'll be right there.

(HENRY *exits, and* EL GALLO *speaks to the audience as the* MUTE *mimes the sensations and the words.*)

You wonder how these things begin.
Well, this begins with a glen.
It begins with a Season, which, for want of a better word,
We might as well call September.

(MUSIC.)

It begins with a forest where the wood-chucks woo
And leaves wax green,
And vines entwine like lovers; try to see it:
Not with your eyes, for they are wise;
But see it with your ears:
The cool green breathing of the leaves.
And hear it with the inside of your hand:
The soundless sound of shadows flicking light.
Celebrate sensation.
Recall that secret place;
You've been there, you remember:
That special place where once—
Just once—in your crowded sunlit lifetime,
You hid away in shadows from the tyranny of time.
That spot beside the clover
Where someone's hand held your hand,
And love was sweeter than the berries,
Or the honey,
Or the stinging taste of mint.
It is September,
Before a rainfall—
A perfect time to be in love.

(*At the end of the speech* MATT *and* LUISA *rise and come to the downstage edges of the platform; he on the left and she on stage right. The* MUTE *and* EL GALLO *stand above them, on the platform, watching.*)

MATT
Hello.

LUISA
Hello.

(*They gaze at each other for a minute.*)

My father is going to be very angry.

MATT
I know. So is mine.

(*The wind has begun to hum softly. They are both a little awkward and self-conscious.*)

LUISA
We've never been here at night.

MATT
No.

LUISA
It's different from the day.

MATT
Are you frightened?

LUISA
Yes; no. (*She looks at him.*) Brr. It's cold here. There's going to be a storm.

MATT
Would you like my jacket?

LUISA
No, thank you. Matt.

MATT
Yes?

LUISA
My hand is trembling.

MATT
Don't be afraid. Please.

LUISA
All right. I promise.

(EL GALLO *signals for thunder.* LUISA *rushes into* MATT's *arms as the* MUTE *throws some paper leaves into the air. Then* EL GALLO *retires to the side.*)

MATT (*soothingly*)
There, there. It's all right.

LUISA
Matt, take care of me. Teach me. I don't want to be awkward—or afraid. I love you, Matt. I want there to be a happy ending.

MATT
I promise that there will be. (*Kisses her.*) Look.

LUISA
What?

MATT (*smiles*)
My hand is trembling, too.

["Soon It's Gonna Rain"]

LUISA (*sings*)
Hear how the wind begins to whisper,
See how the leaves go streaming by.
Smell how the velvet rain is falling,
Out where the fields are warm and dry.
Now is the time to run inside and stay.
Now is the time to find a hideaway—
Where we can stay.

MATT
Soon it's gonna rain;
I can see it.
Soon it's gonna rain;
I can tell.
Soon it's gonna rain;
What are we gonna do?

Soon it's gonna rain;
I can feel it.
Soon it's gonna rain;
I can tell.
Soon it's gonna rain;
What'll we do with you?

We'll find four limbs of a tree.
We'll build four walls and a floor.
We'll bind it over with leaves.
Then duck inside to stay.

Then we'll let it rain;
We'll not feel it.
Then we'll let it rain;
Rain pell-mell.
And we'll not complain
If it never stops at all.
We'll live and love
Within our own four walls.

(*They talk now, as the* MUSIC *continues.*)

MATT
Would you like for me to show you around the castle?

LUISA
Oh, yes, please.

MATT
The lookout tower. And the throne. And
this, the family pride and joy: the ballroom!

LUISA
My, how grand.

MATT (*bows*)
Princess.

LUISA (*curtsies*)
Your highness.

> (*And they begin to dance—at first
> grand and sweeping and then more
> and more tenderly as the wind con-
> tinues to swirl in. As the thunder
> rolls again, MATT pulls her up on the
> platform and the MUTE, standing
> above and behind the drape, sprinkles
> them with paper rain.*)

MATT
We'll find four limbs of a tree.
We'll build four walls and a floor.
We'll bind it over with leaves,
Then duck inside to stay.

BOTH
Then we'll let it rain;
We'll not feel it.
Then we'll let it rain;
Rain pell-mell.
And we'll not complain
If it never stops at all.
We'll live and love
Within our castle walls.

["Rape Ballet"]

> (*At the end of the number, HENRY
> comes creeping back in. He signals
> for the audience to be quiet; then he
> speaks to the MUSICIANS.*)

HENRY
Accelerando con molto!

> (*As the MUSIC begins for the Rape
> Ballet, HENRY calls out "Swords" to
> the MUTE, who rushes to the down
> center prop box and removes four
> wooden sticks. Then HENRY calls out.*)

Indians, ready?
Indians—Rape!

> (*And MORTIMER springs out of his
> hiding place. He snatches up the as-
> tonished LUISA right before the eyes of
> the equally astonished MATT and starts
> to carry her out right. But HENRY, in
> a fury, interrupts him.*)

No, no. Off Left, damn it!

MORTIMER
All right, all right.

> (*And he faithfully totes her left. But
> now MATT has recovered himself suffi-
> ciently to interrupt their progress. He
> struggles with MORTIMER as HENRY
> grabs up the disentangled LUISA. MOR-
> TIMER rushes over. He and HENRY
> pick up the girl and try to carry her
> out—each in a different direction, of
> course. The MUTE hands MATT the
> drum sticks to MORTIMER's Indian
> drum, and MATT floors both the old
> actors with a mighty whop of the
> sticks. LUISA rushes up to her protector
> as HENRY struggles to his feet.*)

HENRY (*feeling his head*)
"A touch, a touch. I do confess it."

> (*Now, the moment is ripe for the big
> scene. HENRY rushes to the side and
> yells out: "Cavalry!" Which is the cue
> for EL GALLO to enter into the fray. EL
> GALLO sweeps on with a flourish. The
> MUTE supplies both him and MATT
> with wood swords and they begin to
> fight. During the midst of their battle,
> EL GALLO is thrown to the side and
> HENRY catches him and yells out:
> "Once more, dear friends, into the
> breach!" At this signal the MUTE sup-
> plies HENRY and MORTIMER with stick
> swords and all three "villains" sword-
> fight our young hero at once—not at
> all unlike the Douglas Fairbanks
> movies of the good old days. They
> advance. They retreat. Then—with a
> mighty push, MATT sends them all
> sprawling to the floor. MORTIMER rises
> —rushes forward—is killed dramatic-
> ally. HENRY rises—and as he charges,
> cries out—*)

HENRY
"God for Harry, England, and Saint Geo
—ough!"

(*The last word becomes a vivid "ouch"
as he is wounded and falls dead. Only
EL GALLO is left now. He and MATT
square off and have at it. For a while
it's nip and tuck as the two men fight
up and down the prop box, and upon
the platform, and clash together every
once in a while so that they stand
gritting, tooth to tooth, across the
criss-crossed sabers. In the end, EL
GALLO allows himself to be defeated
and he dies in so grand a manner that
even MORTIMER cannot resist a look of
admiration. EL GALLO dies like a diva
in the opera, rising again and again
from the floor, to give one last dramatic, agonized twitch.*)

(*When EL GALLO goes down for the
last time, the MUSIC becomes jolly and
triumphant. The young lovers rush
upon the little platform and embrace
in a pretty tableau. The FATHERS rush
in too. And embrace too. And get
upon the platform to finish off the
"Living Statues" type of tableau.*)

(*All these speeches are over MUSIC.*)

LUISA
Matt!

MATT
Luisa!

HUCK
Son!

BELL
Daughter!

HUCK (*to BELL*)
Neighbor!

BELL (*to HUCK*)
Friend!

LUISA (*to the world*)
I always knew there would be a happy
ending!

(*The MUSIC suddenly stops. They all
freeze as EL GALLO rises, rather painfully from the dead.*)

EL GALLO (*feeling his back*)
I think I pulled something.

MORTIMER
Oh, you get a bit sore at first; dying like
that. It's not the easiest thing in the business. But I like it. I've been dying for forty
years, ever since I was a boy. Ah, you
should have seen me in those days. I could
die backwards off a twenty foot cliff. People used to cry out: "Die again, Mortimer
—die again!" But of course I never did.

EL GALLO (*smiles at HENRY*)
Well, Henry. Are you off now?

HENRY
Yes. Going somewhere. There's not much
left to the old Company anymore—just
Mortimer and me. But we make out. I
recite Shakespeare. Mortimer dies. There's
usually an audience somewhere. Oh—
here's your moon.

(*HENRY hands EL GALLO the tattered
cardboard moon.*)

EL GALLO
Thank you—"Good night, Sweet Prince."

HENRY (*after first gently pushing MORTI-
MER out of "his" light*)
"And flights of angels sing thee to thy rest
—Why doth the drum come hither?" Re-
member, Mortimer, there are no small
actors—only small parts.

(*HENRY and MORTIMER step back into
the prop box, and—just before he
disappears under the lid, HENRY looks
out to the audience and speaks.*)

Remember me—in light!

(*And he is gone. EL GALLO looks at
the LOVERS and their PARENTS still
frozen on the stage. Like a choral conductor, he conducts them in the short
contrapuntal selection called "Happy
ending."*)

EL GALLO (*when they are through sing-
ing*)
Very pretty, eh?
Worthy of Watteau.
A group of living statues:
What do they call it?
A tableau.

Hmmm.
I wonder if they can hold it.
They'll try to, I suppose.
And yet it won't be easy
To hold such a pretty pose.

We'll see.
We'll leave them for a little
Then we'll see.

> (EL GALLO *and the* MUTE *hang the
> "FANTASTICKS" drape in front of
> the actors.*)

Act One is over.
It's the Intermission now.

> (*As he and the* MUTE *exit, the stage
> lights quickly* BLACKOUT.)

END ACT ONE

ACT TWO

PROLOGUE

> (*When the intermission is over, and the*
> MUSICIANS *have returned to their places,
> there is a* BLACKOUT. *During this moment
> of silence, we can hear a rustle of move-
> ment as the actors grope their way back
> into place. In the darkness, we hear a
> loud "Shhh!" answered by* LUISA's *plain-
> tive voice: "But I can't* see!" *Then a bit
> more movement. A heartfelt "Ouch" from
> the vicinity of the platform. And one final
> suppressed male "dammit" before the
> lights come up.*)
> (EL GALLO *reenters, carrying the moon,
> and smiles at the audience. Then he nods
> to the* MUTE, *who undoes the flap and
> lowers the curtain on the little platform
> stage. The* PARENTS *and the* LOVERS *are
> still there, poised in their pretty tableau.
> But they seem less graceful now, as if there
> were some pain involved in holding the
> pose so long.*)

EL GALLO (*speaks over music*)
Their moon was cardboard, fragile.
It was very apt to fray,
And what was last night scenic
May seem cynic by today.
The play's not done.
Oh, no—not quite,
For life never ends in the moonlit night;

And despite what pretty poets say,
The night is only half the day.

So we would like to truly finish
What was foolishly begun.
For the story is not ended
And the play is never done
Until we've all of us been burned a bit
And burnished by—the sun!

> (*He reverses the moon. On the other
> side is the sun. He throws it into the
> air, making daylight. Then he sits on
> the stage right prop box. And one by
> one, the* PARENTS *and the* CHILDREN
> *begin to break from the tableau. Their
> eyes sting in the hot red sun. The
> music underneath is sour—disgrun-
> tled.* LUISA *wilts first, letting her arm
> come down from the pose to rest on
> her* FATHER's *head, to his vast discom-
> fort.*)

HUCK
Whew! It's hot.

BELL
What?

HUCK
Hot!

BELL
Oh. Sssss—

> (CHORD OF MUSIC, *as they all try, un-
> successfully, to regain the pose.*)

LUISA
And now we can meet in the sunlight.

MATT
And now there is no more wall.

LUISA
Aren't we happy?

MATT
Yes. Aren't we.

> (CHORD.)

LUISA (*sitting down suddenly*)
He looks different in the sunlight.

MATT (*also sitting*)
I'm not ready to get married yet.

LUISA
I thought he was taller, somehow.

MATT
When you get right down to it, she's only the girl next door.

(CHORD.)

HUCK
Neighbor.

BELL
Friend.

HUCK
In-law.

BELL
Ugh.

(CHORD.)

HUCK
This is what we've always wanted. Our gardens are one.

BELL
We're merged.

HUCK
Related.

BELL
Amalga-

HUCK
Mated.

BELL
Well.

(CHORD. *As* MATT *and* LUISA *step down off the platform,* HUCK *gets his clippers and* BELL *his watering pail.*)

LUISA
What shall we do today?

MATT
Whatever you say.

LUISA
And tomorrow?

MATT
The same!

(CHORD.)

I wonder where that road goes.

LUISA
I'd like to swim in a clear blue stream—

(CHORD.)

HUCK (*looking testily at* BELL).
Water, water, water!

BELL
What did you say?

HUCK
I said, Water, Water, Water!

BELL
Clip, Clip, Clip!

HUCK
What?

BELL
You're clipping my cumquat!

HUCK
Rot!

(*The* MUSIC *for the quartet has begun as the four principals pace back and forth,* MATT *and* LUISA *eating plums which the* MUTE *has given to them.*)

["This Plum Is Too Ripe"]

LUISA
This plum is too ripe!

MATT
Sorry.

(MUSIC.)
Please don't watch me while I'm eating.

LUISA
Sorry.

(MUSIC.)

HUCK
You're about to drown that magnolia!

BELL
Sorry!

(MUSIC.)

You're—standing—in—my—CUMQUAT!

HUCK
SORRY!

(*And the quartet begins, first as solos,
and then as a round.*)

LUISA
Take away the golden moonbeam.
Take away the tinsel sky.
What at night seems oh so scenic,
May be cynic by and by.

MATT
Take away the painted sunset.
Take away the blue lagoon.
What at night seems oh so scenic,
May be cynic much too soon.

BELL
Take away the secret meetings.
Take away the chance to fight.
What at night seems oh so scenic
May be cynic in the light.

HUCK
Take away the sense of drama.
Take away the puppet play.
What at night seems oh so scenic
May be cynic by today.

ALL
So take it away and paint it up right!
Yes, take it away and decorate it!
So take it away, that sun is too bright!
I say that it really is a pity;
It used to be so pretty.

(*And now the round, ending with*)

MATT (*spoken*)
This plum is too ripe!

ALL
SORRY!

HUCK (*when the music is over*)
I was a fool to tear down that wall.

BELL
So was I. I hate people tromping in my
garden!

LUISA
Please. No fighting.
You see, I come like Cassandra
With a figleaf in my hand.

BELL
It was Minerva.

HUCK
And that's a plum sprout.

LUISA (*insulted*)
Well!

MATT
Don't mind them, Dear.
I think they're jealous.

HUCK (*surprised*)
Jealous?

MATT
Of us. Of our passion—and our youth.

BELL
Fantastic!

MATT
You see—they are jealous!

LUISA
It's sweet—just like drama.
Fathers always play the fool.

HUCK
I could speak, if I chose to—

MATT
Speak what?

BELL
Shh. Better not.

HUCK
No. I'll be silent.

(*To* MATT.)

But you'd better not push it much further.

MATT (*laughs*)
You forget that I'm a hero.
After all, there's my record—

LUISA
And my rape!

MATT
Ah, what swordplay! Now, that was really living!

LUISA
That handsome bandit—ah, what hands! He grabbed me—here!

(MUTE *ties ribbon on her wrist*.)

I've put a little ribbon on the spot.

MATT (*acting it out*)
Hot-blooded bandits! And I cut them down like wheat!

HUCK
I could speak, but I won't.

BELL
It's tempting, but we shouldn't.

LUISA
It should be made into an epic poem.

MATT
I'll write it.

LUISA
Or better yet—a shrine.

MATT
Divine! I'll build it.

LUISA
Where the wall was.

MATT
This very spot I heard your call, And here beside our fathers' wall, I drew my sword and slew them all, How many—twenty?

LUISA
Thirty!

MATT
Yes—Or even thirty-two. And every one there was to slay, I slew!

(*And* LUISA *swoons in his arms*.)

HUCK
Ass.

MATT
I beg your pardon?

HUCK
I say that you're an ass!

MATT (*laughs*)
Charming!

LUISA (*also laughing*)
Isn't it? He behaves like a pantaloon!

HUCK
By God, that does it!

BELL
Wait!

HUCK
No. I'm no pantaloon! You think that walls come tumbling down? You think that brigands find an open gate— The way prepared—You think it's Fate?

MATT
What do you mean?

HUCK
You think that fathers play the fool To children barely out of school?

LUISA
They do in books.

HUCK
In books, maybe. It's not the same in reality. No, children— Children act on puppet stages Prepared by parents' hard-won wages.

(EL GALLO *hands bill to* BELL, *who nearly faints when he sees it*.)

Or do you think such things can be? You think a First Class Rape comes free!

(BELL *hands bill to* HUCK.)

By God, look at that; it's the villain's fee!

MATT
What is this?

BELL
An itemized bill for your pretty little Rape.

LUISA
But the feud?

HUCK
We arranged it.

MATT
And the wall?

BELL
Built to fall.

MATT
I don't believe it.

HUCK
Read on, Macduff!

MATT (*reads*)
"Item—a silver piece for actor to portray Indian Raiding Party—body paint included."
"Item—a piece in gold to the famous El Gallo for allowing himself to seem wounded by a beardless, callow boy."
"Item—one moon—" (MATT *looks up*.)
I see you spared no pains.

LUISA
You mean it wasn't real? The Bandit? The moonlight—?

MATT
Everything!

LUISA
But it isn't fair. We didn't need your moon, or bandits.
We're in love! We could have made our own moons!

BELL (*touched*)
My child.

MATT (*very bitter*)
We were just puppets!

BELL (*to* HUCK)
You see. You've spoiled everything!

HUCK
I told you it wouldn't work.

BELL
You told? *You?* Why, you liar.
Get out of my cumquat!

HUCK
Damn your cumquat!

(*He clips it down to the ground as* BELL *gasps in horror*.)

BELL
That does it! You're a murderer!

HUCK
And you're a fool.

BELL
Let go of my arm!

HUCK
Stop clipping my hat!

(*They struggle briefly*.)

BELL
By God, that does it! I'm going to build up my wall!

HUCK
I, too!

BELL
I'll lime mine up with bottles!

HUCK
I'll jag mine up with glass!

EL GALLO (*comes center to break up the fight*)

Pardon me.

FATHERS
Damn!

(*They exit*.)

MATT (*springs up*)
Wait!

LUISA
Oh, look! It's my bandit.

MATT
You are—(*Looks at the bill*.) El Gallo?

EL GALLO
Sometimes. (*And again he puts on the bandit hat*.)

MATT
About this bill. I think you earned it rather easily.

EL GALLO
You made it easy to earn.

MATT
That's true. But now I will make it harder.
Where is my sword! Somebody get me a
sword!

EL GALLO
Nice boy.

(*The* MUTE *hands* MATT *a sword—
a real one this time.*)

MATT
En garde!

(MATT *lunges forward furiously.*)

(EL GALLO *does not draw his sword,
but defends himself with his naked
hand, like a master giving a fencing
lesson.*)

EL GALLO
Up a bit with the wrist.
That foot back more.
Aim at the entrails.
That's good—encore!
Thrust One—Thrust Two;
Bend the knee—Thrust Three!

But then be sure to parry—
Like this, see.

(*He disarms* MATT *and throws the
sword back to the* MUTE.)

Another lesson?

MATT
God, I'm a fool!

LUISA
Always bragging.

MATT
Don't be sarcastic.

LUISA
I shall be sarcastic whenever I choose.

MATT
You think I couldn't do it?

LUISA
I think you'd better grow up.

MATT
Grow up! Grow up!
And this from a girl who is sixteen!

LUISA
Girls mature faster.

MATT
No. This can't be happening.
If I'm not mad,
If I'm not gloriously insane,
Then I'm just me again.
And if I'm me—
Then I can see.

LUISA
What?

MATT
Everything. All the flaws.
You're childish.

LUISA (*lightly*)
Childlike.

MATT
Silly.

LUISA
Soulful.

MATT
And you have freckles!

LUISA (*suddenly outraged*)
That's a lie!

MATT
I can see them under those pounds of
powder. Look (*Smears powder with his
thumb.*) Freckles!

LUISA
I hate you.

MATT
You see: self-deception. It's a sign of im-
maturity to wear lavender perfume before
you're forty.

LUISA
You're a poseur. I've heard you talking in
the garden, walking around reciting romantic poems about yourself. Ha—the
bold hero.

MATT
You're adolescent.

LUISA
Ahh!

(*She slaps him. There is a pause. Then as they speak, their anger is underscored by music.*)

MATT
Beyond that road lies adventure.

LUISA'
I'm going to take my hair down and go swimming in the stream.

MATT
You'll never hear of me again, my dear. I've decided to be bad.

LUISA
I'll sit up all night and sing songs to the moon.

MATT
I'll drink and gamble! I'll grow a moustache.
I'll find my madness—somewhere, out there.

LUISA
I'll find mine, too. I'll have an affair!

MATT
Good-bye forever!

LUISA
See if I care!

(*They break and start for different sides of the stage. But just before they exit, they suddenly stop—frozen in their tracks—as* EL GALLO *snaps his fingers. He looks at them understandingly, then he goes to* LUISA *and picks a tear from her cheek as the lights grow darker.*)

EL GALLO
This tear is enough—this tiny tear—
To save the entire world.

(*He carefully puts it in his pocket.*)

A boy may go;
The girl must stay.
Thus runs the world away.

(LUISA *walks up right, her back to the audience.* MATT *is still frozen front, caught in the middle of a dream.*)

See, he sees it.
And the world seems very grand.

(*The* MUSIC *has begun, and now* MATT *sings, as* EL GALLO *echoes him cynically.*)

["I Can See It"]

MATT
Beyond that road lies a shining world.

EL GALLO
Beyond that road lies despair.

MATT
Beyond that road lies a world that's gleaming—

EL GALLO
People who are scheming.

MATT
Beauty!

EL GALLO
Hunger.

MATT
Glory!

EL GALLO
Sorrow.

MATT
Never a pain or care.

EL GALLO
He's liable to find a couple of surprises there.

(*Now* EL GALLO *sings and* MATT *echoes.*)

EL GALLO
There's a song he must sing;
It's a well-known song
But the tune is bitter
And it doesn't take long to learn.

MATT
I can learn!

EL GALLO

That pretty little world that beams so
  bright.
That pretty little world that seems delightful
Can burn!

MATT

Let me learn!
Let me learn!

(*As the tempo picks up,* MATT *sings of
his vision.*)

For I can see it!
Shining somewhere!
Bright lights somewhere invite me to
  come there
And learn!
And I'm ready!

I can hear it!
Sirens singing!
Inside my ear I hear them all singing
Come learn!

Who knows—maybe—
All the visions that I see
May be waiting just for me
To say—take me there, and

Make me see it!
Make me feel it!
I know it's so, I know that it really
May be!
Let me learn!
I can see it!

EL GALLO

He can see it.

MATT

Shining somewhere!

EL GALLO

Shining somewhere.
Those lights not only glitter, but once
  there—
They burn!

MATT

I can see it!
I can hear it!

EL GALLO

He can hear it.

MATT

Sirens singing!

EL GALLO

Sirens singing.
Don't listen close or maybe you'll never
  return!

MATT

I can hear it.

BOTH

Who knows—may be—
All the visions he (I) can see—
May be waiting just for me
To say—take me there—and say

MATT

I can see it!
Shining somewhere!
Let me see it!
Take me there and make me part of it!

Make me see those shining sights inside
  of me!

EL GALLO

Make him see it!

MATT

Make me feel those lights inside don't
  lie to me!

EL GALLO

Make him feel it!

MATT

I know it's so, I know that it really
  may be.
It's what I've always waited for!
This is what my life's created for!

BOTH

Let me (him) learn!

EL GALLO (*speaks when the music is
over*)
The world will teach him
Very quickly
The secret he needs to know.
A certain parable about Romance;
And so—we let him go.

We commit him to the tender mercies
Of that most stringent teacher—Time.
But just so there's no slip-up
We'll add a bit—of spice.

(MUTE *opens the prop box and* MORTI-
MER *sticks his head out, dressed in pi-
rate garb with a patch across his eye.
He is joined soon by* HENRY, *in a lam-
entable long blond wig and carrying
a tambourine.*)

MORTIMER
Hold on there a minute, Matie!

MATT
What?

HENRY
And where may you be going, my fiery-
eyed young friend? Don't answer; I can
see it in your eyes.

MORTIMER
I see it too—them beady eyes!

HENRY
You go for the goose—the golden goose
that lays the platinum-plated egg, right?
Right! I am Lodevigo—just like yourself
—a young man looking for the pleasant
pinch of adventure.

MATT
Young man!

HENRY
Yes! And to your left, observe this seamy
individual; he is my companion who goes
by the name of—Socrates.

MORTIMER
I'm Roman.

HENRY
Romanoff, he means. A blue-blood.
He is descended from the Czars.

MATT
The Czars?

HENRY
He is, in fact, the noblest Romanoff of
them all.
But enough of chit-chat.

MORTIMER
Enough. Enough.

HENRY
You long for adventure? We will take
you, won't we, Socci?

MORTIMER
We'll take him, all right!

HENRY
To the places you've dreamed of—Venice
—Egypt! Ah—Egypt— (*He suddenly falls
and is caught by* MORTIMER.) "I am dying,
Egypt!"—that's a line from something. I
don't recall just what.

MATT
I thought I would—

HENRY
Seek your fortune! Exactly why we're
here. Right, Socci?

MORTIMER
Right, Loddi. We're going to give you the
works!

HENRY
The fireworks, he means.

MATT
It was my intention—

HENRY
Forget intentions! They paved the road to
hell. We'll see to your education.

MORTIMER
We know all the ropes!

HENRY
And the ropes to skip, as well!

MORTIMER
'Eathen idols!

HENRY
Whirling girlies!

MORTIMER
Tipsy gypsies!

HENRY
Fantastic beauty—just waiting to be unzipped!

MATT
But I—

HENRY (*clapping his hand over* MATT'*s
mouth*)
Don't bother to thank us!

MORTIMER (*doing likewise*)
Right! Let's hurry, Loddi— Hurry!

BOTH

(*singing as they upend him*)

Beyond that road—
Is an episode—
An episode—
An episode—
Beyond that road is an episode—
Look out, you nearly tripped!
Hip. Hip!
Beyond that road is an episode,
An episode, an episode—
Beyond that road is an episode—
Just waiting to be unzipped!
Hey!

(*They exit through the auditorium carrying* MATT.)

(*As* EL GALLO *continues to talk, the* MUTE *comes back in and begins to build a wall where the old one used to be. It might be of tissue—or of lights—or, simply the long wood bench placed center to stand for the wall.*)

EL GALLO
Now grant me in your minds a month.
October is over and the sky grows gray.
A month goes by,
It's a little bit colder.
A month goes by,
We're one month older.

(EL GALLO *steps back in the shadows. In just a moment,* BELLOMY *comes in, wearing his winter scarf.*)

BELL (*to* MUTE)
That's fine. There's nothing better than a good thick wall. Keep working, friend. Keep working!

(*He exits, and* HUCKLEBEE *comes in on his side. He too sports a winter scarf.*)

HUCK
Still progressing? Good. We want to get it finished before snowfall.

(*He exits, and* BELLOMY *returns, with a fur hat.*)

BELL
Hmmm. Getting colder. I'll just take a look at the wall. Fine! Keep on working— Lord, this weather makes a man feel old.

(*Exits. Enter* HUCKLEBEE, *with ear-muffs.*)

HUCK
Not a word. He's been gone for a month, and I haven't had a single word. (*To the* MUTE.) How's it going? Hmmm? Oh, I forgot. You're not supposed to talk.

(HUCKLEBEE *sits in his garden as* BELLOMY *reappears, all bundled up in a coat.*)

BELL
Luisa?—Now, dear, listen. It's silly to stand in the garden. You'll catch pneumonia. You'll catch asthma. Luisa? (*No response.*) Well, anyway—I brought you a little shawl.

(*The* FATHERS *see each other. They hesitate, and then bow gravely. Then they stand, face to face, watching the* MUTE *at work.*)

(*To the* MUTE.) I don't suppose you'd care to see my garden?

HUCK
He won't answer.

BELL
I don't recall addressing that remark to you, sir.

HUCK
He's not supposed to speak.

BELL
Oh— Oh, well.

(*They pace, then* BELLOMY *starts forward.*)

By the way—

HUCK (*eagerly*)
Yes?

BELL
Oh—nothing.

(They pace. And then HUCKLEBEE *begins to chuckle.)*

What's so funny?

HUCK
I was just thinking how we used to meet.

BELL *(smiles)*
Climbing over the wall.

HUCK
Secret meetings—

BELL
Just to play a little game of cards.

(They both laugh in delight.)

(Becoming serious.) How's your son?

HUCK
Not a word.

BELL
He'll come back—when he runs out of your money.

HUCK
Thank you. And your daughter?

BELL
Like a statue. Does nothing but dream all day.

HUCK
Pity.—How's your garden?

BELL
Growing!

HUCK
Mine, too.

BELL
So dependable.
Gardens go on growing.

HUCK
Yes, indeed, they do.

BELL
I tell you, I love vegetables.

HUCK
It's true. I love them, too.

(They shake hands and sing.)

["Plant a Radish"]

BOTH
Plant a radish;
Get a radish.
Never any doubt
That's why I love vegetables;
You know what you're about!

Plant a turnip; get a turnip.
Maybe you'll get two.
That's why I love vegetables;
You know that they'll come through!

They're dependable!
They're befriendable!
They're the best pal a parent's ever known!
While with children—
It's bewilderin'
You don't know until the seed is nearly grown
Just what you've sown.

So
Plant a carrot,
Get a carrot,
Not a brussel sprout.
That's why I love vegetables,
You know what you're about!

Life is merry,
If it's very
Vegetari-an.
A man who plants a garden
Is a very happy man!
    (This second chorus they sing like a vaudeville team, complete with little awkward dance steps.)
Plant a beanstalk;
Get a beanstalk.
Just the same as Jack.
Then if you don't like it,
You can always take it back!

But if your issue
Doesn't kiss you,
Then I wish you luck.
For once you've planted children,
You're absolutely stuck!

Every turnip green!
Every kidney bean!
Every plant grows according to the plot!

While with progeny,
It's hodge-podgenee,
For as soon as you think you know
    what kind you've got
It's what they're not!

So
Plant a cabbage;
Get a cabbage;
Not a sauerkraut!
That's why I love vegetables,
You know what you're about!

Life is merry
If it's very
Vegetari-an.
A man who plants a garden
Is a very happy man!

He's a vegetari-
Very merry—
Vegetari-an!

BELL (*when the song is over*)
Say, what about that game of pinochle?

HUCK
I prefer poker.

BELL
All right, but let's hurry!

HUCK
You still owe me from last time. (*To the*
MUTE.) You keep on working.

BELL (*as they exit*)
He's a nice chap.

    (*Now they are gone. The* MUTE *places
a stool or perhaps a ladder up center
for* EL GALLO *to sit on. Then the* MUTE
exits to the side. LUISA, *meanwhile, has
begun to come out of her trance.*)

LUISA
Oh! Oh! Oh!
    (*Sings.*)
I'd like to swim in a clear blue stream
Where the water is icy cold.
Then go to town in a golden gown
And have my fortune told.

    EL GALLO (*sings*)
Just once!
Just once!
Just once before I'm old!

LUISA (*looking up at him*)
It's my bandit!

EL GALLO
Your bandit, yes.

LUISA
What are you doing up in that tree?

EL GALLO
Growing ripe.

LUISA
Don't grow too ripe or you'll fall.

EL GALLO
Very wise.

LUISA
What do you see from up there?

EL GALLO
Everything.

LUISA
Really?

EL GALLO
Nearly.

LUISA
Do you see Matt?

EL GALLO
Do you care?

LUISA
No, I just wondered.
Can I climb up there beside you?

EL GALLO
You can if you can.

LUISA
    (*Climbs up beside him. The stage is
dark now, and only the* "TREE" *is lit.*)
There!
I don't see everything.

EL GALLO
It takes a little while.

LUISA
All I see is my own house. And Matt's.
And the wall.

EL GALLO
And that's all?

LUISA
All.
Is it fun to be a bandit?

EL GALLO
It has its moments.

LUISA
I think it must be fun.
Tell me,
Do you ride on a great white horse?

EL GALLO
I used to.

LUISA
But no longer?

EL GALLO
I developed a saddle rash.
Very painful.

LUISA
How unglamorous.
I never heard of a hero
Who had a saddle rash.

EL GALLO
Oh, it happens. Occupational hazard.

LUISA
Tell me,
What is your favorite plunder?

EL GALLO
Plunder?
I think that's Pirates.

LUISA
Well, then, booty.

EL GALLO
You've been reading too many books.

LUISA
Well, you must steal *something!*

EL GALLO
I steal fancies. I steal whatever is treasured
most.

LUISA
That's more like it—
Precious rubies!

EL GALLO (*looking at her necklace*)
Precious rhinestones.

LUISA
Rhinestones?

EL GALLO
Can be precious.
It depends on the point of view.

LUISA
Well, it doesn't sound very sound.
Economically, I mean.

EL GALLO (*touched, in spite of himself*)
Pretty child.

LUISA
Do you think so?
Do I attract you?

EL GALLO
Somewhat.

LUISA
Oh, but that's splendid!
Look, see this ribbon.
That's where you gave me a bruise.

EL GALLO
I'm so sorry. (*Gently he kisses her arm.*)

LUISA
Don't be silly. I adore it!
I kiss it three times every day.
Tell me,
Have you seen the world?

EL GALLO
A bit, yes.

LUISA
Is it like in the books?

EL GALLO
Depends on which books you read.

LUISA
The adventures. The Romances.
"Cast off thy name.
A rose by any other name—"
Do you know that?

EL GALLO
Sounds familiar.

LUISA
"Put up thy sword. The dew will rust it!"
That's Othello. He was older than Desde-
mona,

But she loved him because he had seen the
  world.
Of course he killed her.

EL GALLO (*dryly*)
Of course.

LUISA
"It's a far better thing that I do now
than I have ever done before!"
Isn't that beautiful? That man was beheaded.

EL GALLO
I'm not surprised.

LUISA
Take me there!

EL GALLO
Where?

LUISA
To the parties! To the world!

EL GALLO
But I'm a bandit.
There is a price upon my head.

LUISA
I was hoping that there would be!

EL GALLO
You and I!
Us together!

LUISA
Yes. Dancing forever and forever!

(MUSIC. *And as* EL GALLO *sings, he
holds his hand above her—her eyes
closed—as if casting her in a trance.*)

["Round and Round"]

EL GALLO (*sings*)
Round and round
Till the break of day.
Candles glow,
Fiddles play.
Why not be wild if we feel that way?
Reckless and terribly gay!

Round and round,
'Neath a magic spell.
Velvet gown,
Pink lapel.

Life is a colorful carousel.
Reckless and terribly gay!

(*He lifts her off their "tree" perch
onto the stage floor.*)

LUISA
I'm ready anytime.
If you'll take me, I'm
Ready to go!

So show the way to me,
I will try to be,
Ready to go!

EL GALLO
I seem to see Venice
We're on a lagoon.
A gondolier's crooning
A gondola tune.
The air makes your hair billow blue
  in the moon.

LUISA
I could swoon!

EL GALLO
You're so blue in the moon!

(*Now they begin to dance. The* MUTE
*hands her a mask—a paper mask of a
blank face; a laughing-hollow mask;
a stylish face that is frozen forever
into unutterable joy. This mask is
upon a little hand-stick—so that when
held in front of one's visage, it blocks
out any little telltale traces of compassion or of horror.*)

(*As* LUISA *and* EL GALLO *go on dancing,
we see—in a stylized blaze of light—*
MORTIMER *and* HENRY *up on the platform stage—waving "flames" of torn
red silk. At first they are gondoliers—
but as the action gets wilder, they
change into rioting peasants. In each
of these sequences, it is poor* MATT
who is the object of their fury.)

LUISA (*spoken*)
Look at the peasants.
They're lighting candelabras.
No, I believe they're lighting torches.
Yes, see—
They've started burning the palaces.
—There goes the Doge!

HENRY
A rivederci!

LUISA
Oh, what fun!
I *adore* pyrotechnics!

(*Suddenly* MORTIMER *and* HENRY *set*
MATT *on fire—in a bright red spot-*
light—and LUISA *gasps in horror.*)

LUISA
That man—look out; he's burning.
My God, he's on fire!

EL GALLO (*pleasantly*)
Keep on dancing.

LUISA
But he's burning—

EL GALLO
Just put up your mask—
Then it's pretty.

MATT
Help! Help!
(EL GALLO *raises the mask to her face,*
and—almost against her will, she be-
gins to laugh and babble.)

LUISA
Oh, yes, isn't he *beautiful!*
He's all sort of orange.
Red-orange.
That's one of my favorite colors!

MATT
Help!

LUISA
You look lovely!

(MORTIMER *and* HENRY *pull* MATT
down and out of sight as the MUTE
holds up a silk cloth to shield them—
the effect being rather like a Punch
and Judy show that is being per-
formed on the platform.)

EL GALLO
(*As* LUISA *sings a wild obbligato.*)

We'll just
Dance!
We'll kick up our heels to music
And dance!

Until my head reels with music
Like a lovely real romance.
All we'll do is daily dance.

All we'll do is just dance.
All we'll do is just dance.
All we'll do is just—

LUISA (*speaks*)
Whee. I'm exhausted.

EL GALLO (*speaks*)
But you can't be.
The evening's just started!
(MUSIC. *He starts singing again.*)
Round and round
Till the break of day.
Candles glow.
Fiddles play.
Why not be wild if we feel that way.
Reckless and terribly gay!

LUISA
I'm ready anytime,
If you'll take me, I'm
Ready to go!

So show the way to me,
I will try to be,
Ready to go!

EL GALLO
I seem to see Athens, it's terribly chic.
Atop the Acrop'lis, it's terribly Greek.
There's Venus, Adonis, 'n us—cheek
  to cheek.

LUISA
Oh how chic!

EL GALLO
To be Greek cheek to cheek!

(*Once more we see* MORTIMER *and*
HENRY *in colorful attire. And once*
more MATT *is along with them. He is*
ragged and disheveled—and he is
much the worse for wear.)

LUISA
Observe the friendly natives!
La, how gay.
Look, dear, they're beating a monkey.
Isn't that fun.
I wonder why anyone should be beating a
  monkey?
Oh, no, that's it.

It's not a monkey at all.
It's a man dressed in a monkey suit.
That man—they've hurt him!

EL GALLO
Put up the mask.

LUISA
But he is wounded.

EL GALLO
The Mask! The Mask!

MATT
Help!

(*Once more* EL GALLO *presses the sophisticated mask up to her face.*)

LUISA
Oh, isn't that cute.
They're beating a man in a monkey suit.
It's a show. La, how jolly.
Don't stop; it's charming.
Don't stop.

MATT
Help!

LUISA
That's it. Writhe some more.

(*The "puppets" disappear again, as
the* MUTE *holds up the cloth in front
of them.*)

EL GALLO
We'll just
Dance!
We'll kick up our heels to music
And dance!
Until my head reels with music
Like a lovely real romance.
All we'll do is daily dance.

All we'll do is just dance.
All we'll do is just dance.
All we'll do is just—

LUISA (*speaks*)
Couldn't we just sit this one out?

EL GALLO (*speaks*)
Ridiculous! When there's music to be
danced to—play, gypsies!

BOTH
(*With the whole company singing in
the background.*)

Round and round
'Neath a magic spell.
Velvet gown.
Pink lapel.
Life is a colorful carousel.
Reckless and terribly gay.

LUISA
I'm ready anytime.
If you'll take me, I'm
Ready to go!

So show the way to me,
I will try to be,
Ready to go!

EL GALLO
We'll be in Bengasi or maybe Bombay.
I understand Indja is terribly gay.
The natives assemble on Feast Day
and play

LUISA
With their snakes!

EL GALLO
What a racket it makes!

LUISA (*spoken*)
I think I'm going to love Indja.
Such a big population, and
I adore crowds!
Oh, look, there's a fakir—
Hi, Fakir!

HENRY (*a bit confused*)
A rivederci!

LUISA
See—he's there with his assistants.
They all know Yogi—
And they're just loads of fun!
There's one—a young one—
They're putting him down on some nails.
(*She puts down her mask.*)
If he fails,
He'll be cut to bits by those nails.

MATT
Help!

LUISA
Someone help him.

EL GALLO
The mask!

LUISA
But he's bleeding!

EL GALLO
Mask!

LUISA
Horrible!

EL GALLO
MASK!

> (*And he forces it up to her face. Once more, the transition.*)

LUISA
Go on. Sit down harder.
He's a sissy.
I don't believe he's a real fakir.
They never complain.
He's a fake fakir.

MATT
Help!

LUISA
Fake!

> EL GALLO, LUISA and COMPANY
We'll—
Just—
Dance—!
We'll kick up our heels to music
And dance!
Until my head reels with music.
Like a lovely real romance,
All we'll do is daily
    I can see the friendly natives!
All we'll do is just dance.
All we'll do is just dance.
All we'll do is just—round and round
  in a magic spell.
All we'll do is just; all we'll do is just;
  all we'll do is just—
Dance!

> (*At the end of the number,* HENRY, MORTIMER, *and* MATT *have gone, and* LUISA *and* EL GALLO *are back in the tree, exactly like the scene before.*)

EL GALLO
Now hurry. You must pack so that we may run away.

LUISA
Kiss me first.

EL GALLO
All right.

LUISA
Ahh.

EL GALLO
What is it?

LUISA
At last! I have been kissed upon the eyes. No matter what happens, I'll never never ever forget that kiss. I'll go now. (*She starts out.*)

EL GALLO
One word, Luisa, listen:
I want to tell you this—
I promise to remember too
That one particular kiss.
. . . And now hurry; we have a lifetime
  for kisses.

LUISA
True. You'll wait here?

EL GALLO
I promise.

LUISA
All right, then.

EL GALLO
Wait. Give me a trinket—to pledge that you will come back. That necklace—

LUISA (*instinctively, her hand goes up to guard it*)
Was my mother's.

EL GALLO
Good. It will serve as your pledge.

LUISA
All right. I leave you this necklace because it is my favorite thing. Here, guard it. I won't be long.
> (*She starts to go and then turns back.*)
It's really like that? The world is like you say?

EL GALLO
Of course.

(Suddenly we see MATT *coming back down the aisle where* HENRY *and* MORTIMER *had carried him off. He is in shadow, and neither* LUISA *nor* EL GALLO *take any notice of him as he sings.)*

["Beyond That Road Lies a Shining World"]

MATT
Beyond that road lies despair.

EL GALLO
Beyond that road lies a world that's gleaming.

MATT
People who are scheming.

EL GALLO
Beauty!

MATT
Hunger!

EL GALLO
Glory!

MATT
Sorrow!

EL GALLO
With never a pain or care.

MATT
She's liable to find a couple of surprises there.

LUISA
I'm ready. I won't be long. *(Once more, she turns back.)* You will be here?

EL GALLO
Right here. I promise.

(They have played this scene in a certain definite area of light.)

(When LUISA *has gone,* EL GALLO *slowly, sadly, turns to walk away from the spot. He is interrupted by* MATT, *who limps forward to stop him.)*

MATT
Wait.

EL GALLO
Well. The Prodigal Son comes home.

MATT
Don't leave her like that.
It isn't fair.

EL GALLO
It's her misfortune,
What do you care?

MATT
She's too young.
I said, don't leave her!

*(*MATT *tries to stop him. With the same slow deliberate sadness,* EL GALLO *raises his hand and hits the* BOY, *knocking him down to his knees, then* EL GALLO *moves on away.)*

*(*LUISA *returns. She calls out for* EL GALLO, *but he isn't there. She continues to call his name as she begins to realize that she has been left. Then slowly she sinks to her knees, on the opposite side of the stage from* MATT. *And the* MUTE, *with slow and deliberate compassion, reaches into his bag of stage tricks and with a sort of eerie grace, sprinkles them both with snow. As we see the children in this dim and winter light,* EL GALLO *addresses us directly.)*

EL GALLO
There is a curious paradox
That no one can explain.
Who understands the secret
Of the reaping of the grain?

Who understands why Spring is born
Out of Winter's laboring pain?
Or why we all must die a bit
Before we grow again.

I do not know the answer.
I merely know it's true.
I hurt them for that reason
And myself a little bit too.

(He steps back into the shadows.)

*(*MATT *looks over at the weeping* LUISA.)*

MATT
It isn't worth tears, believe me.
Luisa, please—don't cry.

LUISA
You look awful.

MATT
I know.

LUISA
What's that swelling?

MATT
That's my eye.

LUISA
Oh. And those scratches.
What in the world happened to you?

MATT
The world happened to me.

LUISA
Did you drink and gamble?

MATT
The first day, yes.
But the drink was drugged,
And the wheel kept hitting sixes.
Until I played a six.
And then it kept hitting sevens,
Until I played a seven.

LUISA
Did you serenade señoras?

MATT
I did for a little while.
Until I got hit.

LUISA
Hit?

MATT
With a slop pot.

LUISA
What?

MATT
A Spanish slop pot.
Believe me, it defies description.

(*She cannot help but smile at this.*)

LUISA (*trying to hide the smile*)
I'm sorry, Matt.

MATT
No. It's all right. I deserve it.
I've been foolish.

(MUSIC.)

LUISA
I have too. Believe me.
More than you.

(*Simply—very simply—they face each
other and sing:*)

["They Were You"]

MATT
When the moon was young,
When the month was May
When the stage was hung for my holi-
    day,
I saw shining lights
But I never knew
They were you
They were you
They were you.

LUISA
When the dance was done,
When I went my way
When I tried to find rainbows far
    away,
All the lovely lights seemed to fade
    from view,
They were you
They were you
They were you.

BOTH
Without you near me,
I can't see.
When you're near me
Wonderful things come to be.
Ev'ry secret prayer,
Every fancy free,
Ev'ry thing I dared for both you and
    me,
All my wildest dreams multiplied by
    two,
They were you
They were you
They were you.

MATT
They were you.

LUISA
They were you.

BOTH
They were you.

LUISA (*spoken as the music continues*)
I missed you, Matt.

MATT
I missed you, too. (*Sways.*)

LUISA
Oh, you've been hurt.

MATT
Yes.

LUISA
But you should have told me.
You should have told me that right away.
Here, sit down. Maybe I can bind it.

(*They sit on the platform, as the
MUTE stands above and behind them
and sprinkles them with paper
"snow."*)

MATT
You've been hurt, too.

LUISA
Yes.

MATT
It's beginning to snow.

LUISA
I know.

MATT
Here. Take my coat.

LUISA
No. Both.
There's room enough for both.

(*They pull close together and they
sing.*)

MATT and LUISA
Love.
You are love. (You are love)

Better far than a metaphor can ever,
   ever be.
Love—you are love. (You are love)
My mystery— (My mystery)
Of love—
   (*The* FATHERS, *who have been sitting
   upstage with their backs to us, now
   rise and come forward.*)

BELL
Look!

EL GALLO (*who has watched it all, steps
forward*)
Shh.

HUCK
They've come back.

BELL
It's a miracle. Let's take down the wall.

EL GALLO
No. Leave the wall.
Remember—
You must always leave the wall.
   (*Sings, as the others hum beneath
   him.*)
   Deep in December, it's nice to remem-
   ber
   Although you know the snow will fol-
   low.
   Deep in December, it's nice to remem-
   ber
   Without a hurt the heart is hollow.
   Deep in December, it's nice to remem-
   ber
   The fire of September that made us
   mellow.
   Deep in December, our hearts should
   remember
   And follow.

(*And as the* MUTE *gets the* FAN-
TASTICKS *drape from the prop box,
and he and* EL GALLO *carefully hang it
on the poles in front of the* PARENTS
and the LOVERS—*when the stage, in
fact, is as it was in the beginning, the
lights dim down. And the play, of
course, is done.*)

THE END

THE SIGN IN SIDNEY BRUSTEIN'S WINDOW

Lorraine Hansberry

For
ROBERT NEMIROFF
and
BURT D'LUGOFF
and
the committed everywhere

First presented by Burt C. D'Lugoff, Robert Nemiroff, and J. I. Jahre at the Longacre Theatre, New York City, on October 15, 1964, with the following cast:

SIDNEY BRUSTEIN   Gabriel Dell
ALTON SCALES   Ben Aliza
IRIS PARODUS BRUSTEIN   Rita Moreno
WALLY O'HARA   Frank Schofield
MAX   Dolph Sweet

MAVIS PARODUS BRYSON   Alice Ghostley
DAVID RAGIN   John Alderman
GLORIA PARODUS   Cynthia O'Neal
DETECTIVE   Josip Elic

Directed by Peter Kass
Scenery by Jack Blackman
Lighting by Jules Fisher
Costumes by Fred Voelpel

"The Wally O'Hara Campaign Song" by Ernie Sheldon
Production Associate: Alan Heyman
Associate to the Producers: Beverly Landau

SYNOPSIS OF SCENES

The action of the play takes place in the BRUSTEIN apartment and adjoining courtyard, in Greenwich Village, New York City.
ACT ONE. SCENE ONE: Time: This very present. Early evening, the late spring. SCENE TWO: Dusk. The following week.
ACT TWO. SCENE ONE: Just before daybreak. The following day. SCENE TWO: Evening. Late summer. SCENE THREE: Election Night. Early fall.
ACT THREE. SCENE ONE: Several hours later. SCENE TWO: Early the next morning.

© Copyright, 1965, 1966, by Robert Nemiroff as Executor of the Estate of Lorraine Hansberry. All rights, including the right of reproduction in whole or in part, in any form, are reserved under International and Pan-American Copyright Conventions.

CAUTION: Professionals and amateurs are hereby warned that *The Sign in Sidney Brustein's Window,* being fully protected under the Copyright Laws of the United States of America, the British Empire, including the Dominion of Canada, and all other countries of the Universal Copyright and Berne Conventions, is subject to royalty. All rights, including professional, amateur, motion picture, recitation, lecturing, public reading, radio and television broadcasting, and the rights of translation into foreign languages, are strictly reserved. Particular emphasis is laid on the question of readings, permission for which must be secured in writing. All inquiries should be addressed to Scott Meredith Literary Agency, Inc., 580 Fifth Avenue, New York, New York 10036, authorized agents for the Estate of Lorraine Hansberry and for Robert Nemiroff, Executor.

WHEN, on January 12, 1965, Lorraine Hansberry died of cancer, America and the world were robbed of a remarkable playwright. She was thirty-four at the time of her death. Born in Chicago of middle-class parents, she graduated from Englewood High School in 1948 and went to college at the University of Wisconsin.

Miss Hansberry was not the first black playwright to be produced on Broadway. As early as 1928 Frank Wilson's *Meek Mose* was produced at the Princess Theatre, and in 1933 Hall Johnson's *Run, Little Chillun* was also given on Broadway. It was, however, Langston Hughes, who died in 1967, who made the first major impact by a black playwright on the Broadway scene. His play *Mulatto* opened at the Vanderbilt Theatre in October, 1935, and played through December, 1937. However, for a number of reasons Miss Hansberry made an even stronger impression.

It was with her first Broadway success, *A Raisin in the Sun,* first given on March 11, 1959, that Miss Hansberry entered the theatre public's consciousness. That year she won the New York Drama Critics' Circle Award for the Best Play of the Year. Thus at twenty-nine she became the youngest American playwright, the fifth woman, and the only Negro ever to win the Critics' Award. The subsequent film, which like the play also starred Sidney Poitier, won the Cannes Film Festival Award.

Miss Hansberry was soon busy with projects for other plays, but the only other one to be produced in her short lifetime was *The Sign in Sidney Brustein's Window.* The play opened on October 15, 1964. On the day of her death it closed as a sign of respect, and the curtain never went up again. It had survived for 101 performances, which, while not sounding a particularly long run, in fact constituted a minor theatrical miracle.

Sidney Brustein was a play quite unlike *A Raisin in the Sun*. The latter was a wonderfully exciting evocation of the black experience, yet it remained a fairly conventional play. *Sidney Brustein* was far more controversial. There were variations in the writing, not so much in the style, but more in its tone. Some of the attitudes Miss Hansberry took up—her cool, although never unkind, neutrality toward homosexuality, for example—were not calculated to stir every liberal conscience, and her story was quite uncompromising in its efforts to discuss people rather than issues, life rather than causes.

Not unpredictably the play got what is known in the trade as "a mixed press." The sad economics of the Broadway theatre are such that when a serious play without well-known stars or, just possibly, a highly newsworthy theme, fails to get almost unanimously rave notices, its fate is virtually sealed. With a few exceptions, Miss Hansberry's play was respectfully, even warmly, received. They were the kind of notices that Off-Broadway or even in London's West End, might easily have guaranteed a run of anything between six months and a year. But Broadway is a tough world— *Sidney Brustein* cost $20,000 a week just to keep running and there was no advance sale at the box-office.

Surprisingly, the play simply refused to die. Money to keep it running came from many sources. From friends of the co-producer, Robert Nemiroff, husband of Miss Hansberry, from the theatrical community, even from the audience. At one memorable Sunday matinee the cast invited pledges from the audience and raised $5,000 to keep going. It was a remarkable and unusual theatrical saga.

It was a saga which, oddly enough, found a postscript. On January 2, 1969, Mr. Nemiroff saw his dramatic anthology *To Be Young, Gifted and Black* staged off-Broadway. This was an adaptation from the plays, letters, and speeches of Miss Hansberry. It was widely acclaimed and ran for more than a year before leaving New

York for a cross-country tour. The sensitivity, the warmth, the uncalculated passion of Lorraine Hansberry's writing and life-style were never more apparent. The evening included two scenes from *The Sign in Sidney Brustein's Window*. As ever, they were highly successful.

ACT ONE

Scene One

The setting is Greenwich Village, New York City—the preferred habitat of many who fancy revolt, or at least, detachment from the social order that surrounds us.

At the rear are all the recognizable sight symbols of the great city. They are, however, in the murk of distance and dominated by a proscenium foreground which is made up of jutting façades. These are the representative bits and pieces of architecture which seem almost inevitably to set the character of those communities where the arts and bohemia try to reside in isolation—before the fact of their presence tends to attract those others who wish to be in bohemia if not of it—and whose presence, in turn, paradoxically tends to drive the rents beyond the reach of the former. Tenements of commonplace and unglamorized misery huddle together with cherished relics of the beginning days of a civilization; the priceless and the unworthy leaning indiscriminately together in both arty pretentiousness and genuine picturesque assertiveness.

Thus, here is a renovation of a "Dutch farmhouse"; there, a stable reputed to have housed some early governor's horses; and here the baroque chambers of some famed and eccentric actor. And leading off, one or two narrow and twisty little streets with squared-off panes of glass that do, in midwinter, with their frosted corners, actually succeed in reminding one of Dickensian London. The studio apartment of the BRUSTEINS, at left, is the ground floor of a converted brownstone, which—like a few other brownstones in the Village—has an old-fashioned, wrought-iron outside staircase arching over a tiny patio where city-type vegetation miraculously and doggedly grows. Beneath the staircase landing is the BRUSTEINS's private entrance. Nearby, downstage right, is a tree.

In the cut-away interior of the apartment the walls are painted, after the current fashion in this district, the starkest white. To arrest the eye—because those who live here think much of such things—the colors which have been set against it are soft yellows and warm browns and, strikingly, touches of orange, vivid sharp orange, and that lovely blue associated with Navajo culture. We can see at once that the people who live here would not, even if they did have a great deal of money—which they certainly do not—spend it on expensive furnishings. They prefer by pocket book and taste—to the point of snobbery, perhaps—to scrounge about the Salvation Army bargain outlets; almost never the "Early American" shops which are largely if not entirely priced for the tourist trade. In any case, a few years ago most things would have been discernibly "do-it-yourself" modern in these rooms; but that mood is past now and there is not a single sling chair or low, sharply angled table. "Country things" have come with all their knocked-about air and utilitarian comfort. But there remain, still, crafted ceramic pots of massive rhododendrons in various corners and, everywhere, stacks of last year's magazines and a goodly number of newspapers. The result is that—while it is not a dirty place—clutter amounts almost to a motif. Prints range through reproductions of both the most obscure and the most celebrated art of human history, and these, without exception, are superbly and fittingly framed. And there is a sole expensive item: a well-arranged hi-fidelity unit, and, therefore, whole walls of long-playing records, and not one of them at an angle. Fighting them for supremacy of the walls, however, are hundreds and hundreds of books. And on one wall—SIDNEY's banjo.

In fine, it is to the eye and spirit an attractive place. Its carelessness does not make it less so. And, indeed, one might lounge here more easily than in some other contemporary rooms—and, perhaps, think more easily. Upstage center is the bedroom door. To its right, the bathroom. Downstage left is part of the kitchen area, which disappears offstage. And, dominating all, upstage left, the large irregularly shaped bay window, angled out from the building wall in a skylight effect, in which will presently hang—the Sign in SIDNEY BRUSTEIN's window.

TIME: This very present. Early evening, the late spring.

AT RISE: SIDNEY BRUSTEIN and ALTON SCALES enter, each burdened down with armloads, two or three each, of those wire racks of glasses such as are found in restaurants. They are heavy and the two men have carried them several blocks. They

*are very much out of breath and speak
haltingly as they struggle with the loads.*
SIDNEY BRUSTEIN *is in his late thirties and
inclined to no category of dress whatsoever
—that is to say, unlike his associates, who
tend to the toggle-coated, woven, mus-
tardy, corduroy appearance of the postwar
generation of intellectuals in Europe and
America. This has escaped* SIDNEY: *he
wears white dress shirts as often as not,
usually for some reason or other open at
the cuffs—but not rolled; old college shoes;
and whichever pair of trousers he has happened to put on with whichever jacket
he has happened to reach for that morning; and they will be more likely mismated
suit parts than sports outfits. It is not an
affectation; he does not care. He is of
medium build, vague carriage, tending to
shuffle a bit, except when in a fit of excitement. And his eyes are wider and more
childish than the sort generally associated
with the romance of the intellectual. His
sole attractive feature perhaps is a mat of
tight willful dark curls atop his head. He
does* not *wear glasses.* ALTON SCALES *is a
youth of about twenty-seven or so; lithe,
dark, with close-cropped hair. Unlike his
friend, he is dressed in the mustard, corduroy and sweatered manner of his milieu.*

———

SIDNEY. Never mind the kid's mother,
for Christ's sake. And never mind the
"great swelling crests of water" in his
girl's eyes. Don't bleed it. Write it like
you figure we already *care* without you
sending up organ music. Follow?

(*He puts down his load and fumbles for
his key;* ALTON *leans against the staircase
railing.*)

ALTON (*stiffly*). I hear what you are saying.

SIDNEY. But *compassion* is consuming
your heart and you want us to *know* it,
don't you? The old uptown sob sister
credo: "*In the beginning was the tear.*"

(*He picks up the glasses and they go
into the apartment. As the lights come up
on the interior,* SIDNEY *deposits his load on
the living-room floor.*)

ALTON. He may die. Mrs. Peretti said
Sal could still die.

(*He racks his glasses up on top of* SID-
NEY'S *and reels away with fatigue to the
couch, where he drops down, spent.*)

SIDNEY (*snatches out the page of newspaper copy to which he has been refer-*

ring). And this is going to save him? He
needs *this*? Look, baby, from now on,
when we write, let's forget we *absolutely
love* mankind. Don't venerate, don't celebrate, don't hallow what you take to be
—(*Facing out to the audience with a bit
of a smile.*)—the human spirit. Keep your
conscience to yourself. Readers don't want
it—they feel pretty damn sure that they
can't afford it. That's why Harvey had to
unload the paper. And that's why I am
now the proud owner, editor, publisher,
guiding light. (*With a flourish, returning
the copy to* ALTON.) Presume no commitment, disavow all engagement, mock all
great expectations. (*His eyes are now only
for the audience, scanning our reaction
with a wet-lipped savoring.*) And above
all else, avoid the impulse to correct: all
movements, causes, clubs and anti-clubs.
It's the only form of compassion left. (*He
lights a cigarette and wanders back to the
glasses, where he suddenly confronts them
with a mock funereal gravity, to the point
of making the sign of the cross.*) So—
there they are: the last remains of the
Silver Dagger.

ALTON. You're better off. What the hell
did you know about running a night club,
man?

SIDNEY. It wasn't *supposed* to be a night
club.

ALTON. That's right. It wasn't a night
club and it wasn't a coffeehouse or anything else that anybody ever heard of.

SIDNEY. I thought it was something people wanted. A place to listen to good folk
music. Without hoked-up come-ons. (*Puzzled, rubbing his face.*) I thought there'd
be an audience for it. For people like myself. There gotta be people like me somewhere, don't there?

ALTON. There are. And they don't go to
night spots—of whatever kind—just like
you don't.

SIDNEY (*moving toward the glasses
again*). You know what those glasses really
are, Alt? They're a testament to the release of Manny. He's free, now, my brother
Manny. Free of Sidney. Finally. Let's drink
to it. Drink to Manny's absolution.

(*He crosses downstage left to the counter. It is a combination bar and kitchen
surface, on either side of which stand two
unfinished wooden stools.*)

ALTON. Bourbon for me.

SIDNEY. You can have vodka *with* ice or

vodka without ice. (*Pouring.*) Good old absolved Manny. (*Crossing with a glass for* ALTON *and then turning and saluting the racks of glasses once again.*) The day he put up the money for the Silver Dagger he sat there with "End of Obligation" written all over him. An expression on his face which read: "This thing will be a failure. But having done this I will have done all I can for Sidney. After that I can call it quits in good conscience. You can do so much and then—well, that's it." So here's to you, Manny, you Prince of Philistines. Sidney the Kook has set you free! To hell with that. (*He puts down his glass, abruptly hauls out a huge pad of tracing paper and a big marking crayon, and sits down at his drafting table, which is framed by the window; it is angled almost horizontally to serve as his desk.*) Let's talk about the paper. (*With broad strokes he marks off apportionments of space on the sheets.*)

ALTON (*idle curiosity—that is not so idle*). Ahh—Sidney . . . Does Iris know you've *bought*—and I use the term loosely—the paper yet?

SIDNEY. No.

ALTON. Well, don't you think she oughta know?

SIDNEY. Yes, I'll tell her.

ALTON. When? It's been two weeks already.

SIDNEY (*trapped, therefore evasively*). When I get a chance, I'll tell her.

ALTON. She's going to have a lot of opinions about it.

SIDNEY. She always has opinions. If I paid them any attention I'd never accomplish anything. (*He looks back to his sheets.*) You know what? I think I'd like to try the next issue in reverse. You know, white on black. What's with this black on white jazz all the time? People get in ruts.

(IRIS, *his wife, enters with an armful of groceries. She has not yet reached thirty, is of ordinary prettiness of the sort one does not notice at a distance; but she is quick with a gamin vivacity that charms utterly the moment she speaks or one looks in her very large eyes. And true to a great number of the girls of the locale, she possesses vast quantities of long, long hair, presently done up in a French twist. It is dark brown. Life has already made* IRIS *too nervous and slightly inclined to hunch. But whatever her accomplish-*ments on stage, she is an actress, given to playful mimicry, and, at least with* SIDNEY, *she feels free to play this to the hilt. Between them, though this is not at all their actual relationship in years, there is more than a little of the adolescent girl showing off for father, seeking his approval, testing the limits of his knowledge and authority; and, especially of late, more than a little chafing at the bonds. He has been her lover, father, universe, god. But the man has feet of clay and, coupled with increasing dissatisfaction with her own state, there is the insistent, though as yet unidentified, need to break free. The tension between them bubbles freely to the surface; yet, save in their sharpest exchanges, there is still the element of banter and fun. At the click of the lock,* SIDNEY *thrusts his pad aside. She crosses to the bar, nodding to* ALTON; *stops momentarily at the glasses; throws a look at* SIDNEY; *deposits her groceries; stops again at the glasses; and takes off the raincoat she is wearing to reveal one of those hideous yellow and white uniforms of the kind that are invariably inflicted on counter waitresses in luncheonettes.*)

IRIS (*from the glasses to* SIDNEY). I don't want them in my living room.

SIDNEY. Where else can I put them?

IRIS. We're not going to have the residue of all your failures in the living room.

SIDNEY. Look. Don't start. It's all over. Isn't that enough?

(*He crosses to the phonograph and puts a record on.*)

ALTON. I just remembered a very pressing engagement someplace.

SIDNEY (*"Don't desert me"*). Where?

ALTON. I don't know, I'll think of it later.

(*He exits.*)

IRIS. It was all over *before* it started, if you ask me. (SIDNEY *does not rise to this; she goes into the kitchen. The music comes up. It is a white blues out of the Southland; a lyrical lament whose melody probably started somewhere in the British Isles more than one century ago and has crossed the ocean to be touched by the throb of black folk blues and then, finally, by the soul of backcountry crackers. It is, in a word, old, haunting, American, and infinitely beautiful; and, mingled with the voice of Joan Baez, it is a state-*

*ment which does not allow embarrass-
ment for its soaring and curiously ascen-
dant melancholy.* SIDNEY *busies himself
at the drawing board, with an occasional
side glance toward* IRIS. *The song, "Babe,
I'm Gonna Leave You," dominates utterly. Suddenly* IRIS *changes the subject.*)
Ben Asch was in for lunch.

SIDNEY. So?

IRIS (*turns off the phonograph*). He
said they're doing a tent production of
South Pacific out on the island this summer. Casting now. And guess who's doing it? Harry Maxton! Sidney, *Harry
Maxton*. Remember, he *loved* me when
I read for him that time!

(*She is up and at the mirror whipping
through a few of the hand gestures which
signified "Happy Talk" in the original
production. Her husband looks up at this
for a few seconds, sobers, and looks
away.*)
"Happy talk, keep talkin' happy talk
Talk about things you like to do . . ."

(*Wheeling and facing him exuber-
antly*). Remember—he really flipped for
my Liat!

SIDNEY. And he hired somebody else.
And you know perfectly well you won't
show up for the audition. (*He is immediately sorry.*)

IRIS (*frozen in the Liat pose*). You
rotten, cruel, sadistic, self-satisfying son
of a bitch! (*She exits into the bedroom.*)

SIDNEY. I'm sorry. I don't know why
I do that.

IRIS. Then why don't you find out and
give us both a break?

(*He fans that away dispiritedly.*)

SIDNEY. Does Steiner really tell you to
go around drumming up business for him
like that?

IRIS. I have *not* mentioned Dr. Steiner.
And I am *not* going to! I am not *ever*
going to mention Dr. Steiner in this
house again. *Or* my analysis. You don't
understand it. You can't—

SIDNEY *and* IRIS (*together, he wearily
with her*). "Unless you've been through
it yourself!"

IRIS (*reentering from bedroom; she has
changed into tight high-water pants and
a sweater*). That happens to be true!

SIDNEY. Iris, honey, you've been in
analysis for two years and the only difference is that before you used to cry all

the time and now you *scream* before you
cry.

IRIS. *You don't get better overnight,
Sidney, but it is helping me!* Do you
think that I would have been able to say
the things I just said if I weren't going
through a *tremendous* change?

SIDNEY (*genuinely*). What things?

IRIS. I just called you a sadistic, self-
satisfying, cruel son of a bitch to your
face instead of just thinking it. Don't
you remember when I couldn't say things
like that? Just think them and feel them
—but not *say* them?

SIDNEY. Which amounts to you paying
that quack twenty dollars a session to
teach you how to swear! Lots of luck!

IRIS. That's not the point!

SIDNEY. I'm sorry. Swear *out loud.*

IRIS (*through her teeth*). For someone
who thinks that they are the great intellect of all times, the top-heaviest son of
a bitch that ever lived—

SIDNEY (*dryly*). Another step toward
mental health—

IRIS. For someone who thinks that
they've got the most *open* mind that was
ever opened—you are the most narrow-
minded, provincial—

SIDNEY. —"insular and parochial—"

IRIS. —insular and parochial bastard
alive! And I'll tell you this: I may be
whacked up, sweetie, but I really would
hate to see the inside of *your* stomach. *Oh-
ho,* I really would! Saint John of the
Twelve Agonies, I'll tell you.

SIDNEY. I am not agonized.

IRIS. *Everyone* is agonized!

SIDNEY. How do you *know* this, Iris?

IRIS. *Everyone* knows it. *Der* (*She hesitates and mispronounces it.*) *Angst* is Everywhere. And I'll tell you this—if I had
all your hostilities—

SIDNEY. Look, Iris, three years ago you
practically tore up our marriage looking
for a sex problem, because one fine day
you decided we *had* to have one. We even
invented one for six months because you
knew we had to have one—because *everybody* did. Well, I promise you this time
we are not going to embark on the search
for my (*Correcting her.*) *Angst!*

IRIS (*darkly; sitting beside him on couch
and teasing*). I happen to know some
things about you *in bed* that you don't
know.

SIDNEY (*false and weary patience—but*

reaching out for her: he loves this girl).
Then tell me about them so we can discuss them.

IRIS (*an air of the holy*). Oh no! No
siree. Get thyself to a professional. You're
not going to catch *me* engaging in parlor
analysis!

SIDNEY. There was no psychiatric mystery about it! It was almost purely technical. There were just some things in bed
I wished you *wouldn't* do—(*Huskily.*)—
and some I wished you would. (*He holds
her in his arms.*)

IRIS (*in the sway of the moment*). That
just shows you: nothing about *sex* is *just*
technical. (*Sitting up*). And, I notice,
I'm not the one around here with an
ulcer. And I must say that for a *contented*
man, who just *happens* to have an ulcer,
you drink one hell of a lot!

SIDNEY. It's *my* ulcer! Moreover, I remember a time when, between the agonized and the contented, there was a
whole spectrum of humanity.

IRIS (*rather by rote*). Basically you are
an ambivalent personality. You can't admit to disorder of any sort because that
symbolizes weakness to you, and you
can't admit to health either because you
associate that with superficiality . . .

SIDNEY. Oh shut the hell up! I can't
stand it when you're on this jag! (*Reaching for her again: this precious foolishness is all a game he dearly loves.*)

IRIS (*shouting*). Then why didn't you
marry somebody you did like to talk to
then!

(*It hangs a second, is absorbed with
minor melancholy by the husband, who,
to rise above it, offers a parodied Elizabethan flourish.*)

SIDNEY. Because—(*Lifting a drink like
Cyrano.*) "what did please the morning's
academic ear did seem indeed—(*Bringing
the hand down defeated.*) to repel the
evening's sensuous touch. Think this poor
poet not cruel to say it; but—(*Concluding
the flourish.*) gentle Sid, be but a mortal
thing."

IRIS (*feminine cruelty*). Awwww, is
that what you told poor Evie when she
proposed?

SIDNEY. She didn't propose. Cut it out.

IRIS. You once told me she did.

SIDNEY. Bedroom boasts. You don't pretend to believe mine and I won't pretend
to believe yours. (*Holding her; in a
quieter tone*) What you were supposed
to say was, "In such regard and diluted
esteem doth my master hold his own
sweet Iris—"

IRIS (*looking up*). I don't know the
piece. What is it?

SIDNEY (*dully, staring off*). Nothing.

IRIS. What?

SIDNEY. Plutarch or some damn body!
What difference does it make *what* it's
from?

IRIS. Well, whatever it's from, it said
that you really do think I'm stupid!

SIDNEY (*hardly to her at all*). "My pardon on it, I will get me gone." (*A pause,
then to her*) It said: I love you. It said
I do not counsel reason or quarrel with
my nature. It said, girl, that I love my
wife. Curious thing. (*Stops her lips with
a kiss.*)

IRIS. Meaning frivolous mind and all.

SIDNEY. You make a silly fishwife. Stop
it.

IRIS. Can't I say *anything*?

SIDNEY. Not in this mood, it's driving
me crazy!

(*He gets up agitatedly and goes to the
window and looks out at the street.*)

IRIS (*resolute anger*). And one thing is
clear: You prefer picking at me to talking to me.

SIDNEY (*shouting*). I do not! And tell
that Steiner to take his love-hate obses-
sion and shove it!

IRIS. It is not something *you* can know
about, Sid. I am talking about *unconscious* motivation.

SIDNEY. If it is all that *"un"* then you
don't know about it either!

IRIS (*puzzled; caught*). I meant "sub."
A *sub*conscious motivation.

IRIS (*sore spot*). Sidney, why can't you
understand about to go to the audition.

IRIS (*sore spot*). Sidney, why can't you
understand about the blocks that people
have?

SIDNEY (*seated at his drawing board*).
I do understand about them and I know
that if they are nurtured enough they get
bigger and bigger and bigger.

IRIS (*in kind, through her teeth*). All
right, so I haven't worked out my life so
good. Have you? Or are those glasses
there a mere mirage I see before me?

SIDNEY. Aw, what do you know about
it?

IRIS (*undulating away with triumph*).

I know that there is no great wisdom in opening a folk-singing establishment where there are something like twenty of such establishments in a radius of four blocks square. I know that, darling-pie! And what the hell did you know about running a night club anyway?

(*She crosses into the bathroom to brush her teeth.*)

SIDNEY (*painfully: old refrain, lost cause*). It wasn't *supposed* to be a night club. (*A beat.*) It *would* have done okay if Bruno had done a better job on the publicity.

IRIS (*closes the bathroom door, and comes back*). He thought he should be paid.

SIDNEY. I offered him a quarter of the place!

IRIS. Who wants a quarter of a non-profit night club?

SIDNEY. *It wasn't a night club!*

IRIS. And what are you going to do with all those glasses?

SIDNEY. How do I know right now? There have to be other enterprises that need a hundred and fifty sturdy restaurant glasses, don't there?

IRIS. When they *audit* the place they're going to think it's awfully funny that there're no glasses. What are you going to say happened to them?

SIDNEY. How come I should know what happened to them? Why should I know every little detail. Maybe somebody broke in and took them or something.

IRIS. Auditors like to know about the details, Sid. They specialize in the details.

SIDNEY. And what are you worrying about that for? You oughta be glad I at least salvaged something out of it—that I had the get-up to go over there and get *something* out of there *before* they audit. Why can't you ever look at things that way? From the point of view of the things I do that have foresight. How come you gotta play wife-harpie all the time?

(IRIS *turns back the tracing paper on* SIDNEY's *board to reveal the masthead on which he had been working.*)

IRIS (*picking it up*). So now what? You're going to be an artist? This is *awful*. (*A fit of appropriate giggling.*)

SIDNEY. It's not supposed to be a drawing. It's the layout for the— (*He halts, not having meant to get into this just this way.*)

IRIS (*already expecting almost anything*). For the *what*, Sidney?

SIDNEY (*he exhales heavily*). Harvey Wyatt met some chick—

IRIS. Yes, *and*—

SIDNEY. —he decided to go live in Majorca. I mean forget the whole scene and just like that go live in Majorca . . .

IRIS (*sitting, one hand over her lips*). Oh, my God, no . . . Sidney—*no*.

SIDNEY (*shrugging*). So he *had* to unload the paper.

IRIS. No. God, don't let it be true. Unload it on—*whom?* Oh, Sidney, you haven't . . . ?

SIDNEY. I know it's hard for you, Iris. To understand what I'm all about—

IRIS (*slumping where she is*). I don't believe this. I don't believe that you could come out of—of *that*—(*Gesturing to the glasses.*) and get into *this*. Aside from anything else at the moment, what did you conceivably tell Harvey that you were going to pay him?

SIDNEY. We made an arrangement. Don't worry about it.

IRIS. What kind of arrangement, Sidney?

SIDNEY. *An arrangement.* That's all. I know what I arranged. I tell you, don't worry about it, that's all.

IRIS. Where in the name of God are you going to get the money to pay for a newspaper?

SIDNEY. It's a *small* newspaper. A weekly.

IRIS. Sidney, you can't afford a *yearly leaflet!*

SIDNEY (*quietly*). Why isn't it ever enough for me to tell you that I know what I'm doing? The money was not the important part of the deal one way or the other. This is a real rich babe Harvey's hooked up with so he's not worried about the money. Just yet.

IRIS. And when he is—? Where are you going to get it? That's what little old Iris is standing here with her barefaced everyday self wondering about.

SIDNEY. I'll raise it. That's all. I'll raise it. Period. Didn't I raise it for the Silver Dagger? Well, I'll raise it for this. In order to *do* things you have to *do* things. That's all.

(*During the above* WALLY O'HARA *and*

ALTON SCALES *have approached; the former is a conventionally dressed man, in his early forties, with rust-colored thinning hair; he carries several cardboard placards. For a moment the two stand in animated conversation, as if planning their next move. Now* ALTON *beats on the door.* IRIS *throws up her hands in disgust and admits them.*)

ALTON (*kissing her broadly. Gesturing toward* WALLY). Hey, look who I ran into.

WALLY (*shows a campaign poster to* SID *and* IRIS. *It reads:* VOTE O'HARA FOR REFORM). Hey, Sid.

SIDNEY (*standing stock-still, resolutely*). The answer is no.

ALTON (*yelling at him*). Don't be a clown! At least hear what the man has to say!

WALLY. Iris.

(*He kisses her. She goes into the kitchen to make a salad.*)

SIDNEY. I know what he has to say and I don't want to hear it. I'm out of it. Period. My little artsy-craftsy newspaper is going to stay clear of politics. *Any* kind of politics. Politics are for people who have those kinds of interests, that's all. I don't happen to have them any more.

WALLY (*as if he expected that; making himself comfortable*). Yes, I know. You've made yourself clear in the past: "Politics are a blight on the natural spirit of man. Politics are a cancer of the soul. Politics are dirty, fetid, compromise-ridden exercises in futility." Et cetera, et cetera, et cetera. (*Wandering over to the glass rocks and picking up a glass.*) A bunch of big drinkers here? (*Pouring a drink, then turning a knowing, skilled gaze on the editor.*) Nonetheless, Sidney—I've finally faced up to something that you've got to face up to; there is work to be done and someone has got to do it. Now, I'm taking time out from a busy law practice which is just beginning to build. I'm sticking my neck out to run, and all I'm asking from you is a little legwork, and the endorsement of—what I take it is now—your paper.

SIDNEY. Not even for you, Wally. My readers can do as they please. In my paper —no endorsements. And no editorials.

ALTON (*to* WALLY, *agitatedly*). You see! There it is, man! We are confronted with the great disease of the modern bourgeois intellectual: *ostrich*-ism. I've been watch-

ing it happen to this one; the great sad withdrawal from the affairs of men. (*With bitter facetiousness, pounding his breast—he pins up the poster on the bookshelves.*) It sort of gets me, *here.*

SIDNEY. Alton, do you know that it is an absolute fact that the one infallible way that one can always, and I mean *always,* tell an ex-Communist from ordinary human beings is by the sheer volume of his use of the word *bourgeois?*

ALTON. And do you know how one can always, infallibly, no matter what, tell a card-carrying phony? By the minuteness of the pretext on which he will manage to change the subject, *if* the subject is even remotely important.

WALLY (*laughing smoothly*). Why do you boys hang out together?

SIDNEY (*turning in kind on* ALTON). Yes, I suppose I *have* lost the pretensions of the campus revolutionary, Alton. I do admit that I no longer have the energy, the purity or the comprehension to— "save the world." (*Takes down* WALLY'S *poster. Looking at them with an internalized smile working the corners of his mouth.*) As a matter of fact, to get *real* big about it, I no longer even believe that spring must necessarily come at all. Or, that if it does, that it will bring forth anything more poetic or insurgent than —(*With a flourish.*) the winter's dormant ulcers.

WALLY (*getting up, crossing to* SIDNEY; *there is a pervasive assurance about him*). We're not talking about the world, we're talking about this community. It's like getting on the wagon, the way they tell you in the AA: Don't think about all the drinks you've got to give up, just concentrate on the next one. That's the trick, Sid. Don't think about the ailing world for the time being, just think about your own little ailing neighborhood, that's the point.

SIDNEY (*wandering away from him*). That's very impressive. (*Hands the poster back to* WALLY.) But the truth of the matter is, dear friends, I am afraid that I have experienced the *death* of the exclamation point. It has died in me. I no longer want to exhort anybody about anything. It's the final end of boyhood. (*Grinning wryly at his friends.*) Now, I admit that this is something that doesn't happen to everyone. Take old Alton here: one *long* exclamation point!

ALTON (*loftily*). Capitulation has one smell, one shape, one sound.

SIDNEY (*in kind*). Look, I'm not a neophyte. You wanna see my scrapbooks? Since I was eighteen I've belonged to every committee To Save, To Abolish, Prohibit, Preserve, Reserve and Conserve that ever was. And the result—(*With an almost rollicking flippancy.*) is that the mere thought of a "movement" to do *anything* chills my bones. I simply can no longer bear the spectacle of the hatchetry of power-driven insurgents trying at all costs to gain control—(*The coup de grâce.*) of the refreshment committee!

(*He crosses into the bathroom for a bottle of pills.*)

WALLY (*smiling easily*). I told you: Think only of not taking the next drink.

SYDNEY (*crossing back to the drawing board to take his pill with a drink*). You mean diddle around with the *little* things since we can't do anything about the *big* ones? Like the fact that I was born of a father who was maimed in one war, did some fighting of my own in another and have survived into the clear and present danger of a third? Forget about all that jazz, huh, and worry about—reforms in the traffic court or something?

WALLY (*putting his drink down, with vigor*). Christ, man, this is the second largest narcotics drop in the city, the outpost of every racket known to man! The syndicate thinks it owns this neighborhood, and there sits the regular machine—

SIDNEY. You kid yourself if you want to, Wally. *Do things* if it makes you happy. Just don't bug me about it. Iris, beer!

IRIS (*coming out from the kitchen*). All I've got to say, Sidney, is just mean what you say, that's all, just *mean* what you say.

WALLY (*strictly in jest*). All of which goes to prove that a woman's place is in the oven.

ALTON (*mugging*). *With* the door closed.

WALLY. I'm wondering, Sidney. In the clear and present danger—

(*The phone is ringing.*)

IRIS. Jesus, that'll be Mavis. I don't feel like Mavis tonight. Sid, you get it.

SIDNEY. I never feel like Mavis. You get it. (*Iris goes to answer.*) That Mavis,

boy—I *still* swear she is something Sinclair Lewis made up which has escaped the book! (*Looking at* ALTON *soberly.*) Speaking of Iris's sisters, I gather you've been seeing a lot of Gloria when she's in town.

(IRIS *at the phone, throws a swift pregnant glance at her husband.*)

ALTON (*mugging heavily and smacking his lips*). Yeaaahhhh.

SIDNEY. Yeah, well, take it from me and beware of the daughters of the House of Atreus.

(IRIS *looks daggers.*)

ALTON (*glibly, unaware of the byplay*). I'll take my chances. (*To* WALLY) You should *see* this one, man! (*Waving his fingers for the heat.*)

WALLY (*smiling*). I'd like to. (*Back to the attack*) Sidney, if you can't function—

ALTON. Only there's no point in your meeting her *now,* man. Like *I* have come into her vision and I am filling it out *entirely!*

WALLY. So where is this perfection? Why doesn't she drop by and help restore Sidney's vision?

IRIS (*cutting in, one hand cupping the receiver*). She's in Los Angeles. Travels a lot. She's a high-fashion model. (ALTON *passes a photo of* GLORIA *to* SID *and* WALLY.) I *am* listening to you, love. I don't care. Mav, that's all. Good-bye! (*As she hangs up the phone and wanders back to a position near her husband.*) Poor old Mavis. But you've got to admit that she doesn't give up. She's been trying to civilize me for years. Now she's got some dress for me.

SIDNEY. Dear old Mav, Mother of the Philistines. My brother is the Prince, but your sister is the Mother of them all!

(*He suddenly pulls the pins out of his wife's hair, causing it to fall down all over her. She is infuriated by this habit of his.*)

IRIS. Oh, damn it, Sid! Don't start that, I'm telling you! I mean it!

ALTON (*to* WALLY). If he had his way he'd have her running barefoot in a gingham dress with all that hair flying around. (*To* SIDNEY.) What are you, some kind of arrested rustic?

WALLY. I've often wondered how such a "nice middle-class Jewish boy" got so hung up on such a tired old Anglo-Saxon myth.

SIDNEY (*Western drawl*). I reckon my particular Jewish psyche was less discriminating than most.

WALLY (*pressing forward*). Sidney, if you can't function in one little community, then how—

SIDNEY (*escaping again*). Hey, honey, you know what I feel like? I am suddenly suffering from an all-consuming desire to take my books, my cameras, my records, and—my wife—and go—

IRIS, ALTON *and* WALLY (*together, in unison*). —up to the woods!

(*She, without appreciation, starts working at her hair, trying to get it back up.*)

SIDNEY (*painfully*). Yes. And stay . . . (*Pulling her head back hard and looking into her eyes.*) Forever.

(*She sighs.*)

ALTON (*to* WALLY). Man, you see what we are up against here? This clown is not only committed to the symbolic mountain tops. He goes in for the *whole real live physical thing.*

SIDNEY (*changing the subject; to* ALTON). By the way, I made an appointment with Mickey Dafoe for you. He expects you in his office at noon. Wear a tie and your best Establishment Ass-kissing Manner or something so you won't make him nervous.

ALTON. What do you mean you made an appointment for me? For what? What do I want to see Mickey Dafoe for?

SIDNEY. Gotta be you. Nobody else to go.

ALTON. Well, there's not me, I have nothing to say to people like Mickey Dafoe.

SIDNEY. You're right, you're wrong for it. Absolutely the wrong man to send. The Trade and Commerce Association is only responsible for like half of the advertising in the paper. We need somebody— (*Moving "aimlessly" toward* WALLY *so that at the last word they are face to face.* WALLY *is already shaking his head "no."*) smoooooth.

WALLY. Don't look at me.

SIDNEY. Why not, you fat cat you—?

WALLY. What makes you think you can always ask, ask, ask for things, Sid—and never give?

SIDNEY (*throwing up his hands*). Because before I am through my little artsy-craftsy newspaper is going—

IRIS. Oh, Sidney, newspaper, newspaper, newspaper! How long do you think that you're going to *have* a newspaper!

(*She disappears into the bedroom, putting her hair up.*)

ALTON. What's the matter with her lately?

SIDNEY (*a shrug*). Who knows? Maybe she's changing life.

WALLY. Come on, it's the Greek in her. You should know that. The triumph of the innate tragedy in her soul.

SYDNEY (*this entire exchange is for* IRIS *to hear*). She's only half Greek, so she should be only half tragic. Hey, Iris, when you come back out, turn up just one side of your face.

IRIS. Boy, are you fellows fun-nee! (*A wild cackle of sardonic laughter*)

WALLY. Hey, what is the other half?

SIDNEY. Irish 'n' Cherokee. I'm married to the only Greco-Gaelic-Indian hillbilly in captivity. If one can really think of Iris as being in captivity . . . Do your dance, honey. (*She snakes out promptly, hissing, in the dance steps of the Greek Miserlou— which turns into a jig and then into the usual stereotyped notion of some Indian war dance, concluding with a Marilyn Monroe freeze. Then she backs out.*) I taught her everything she knows! You should hear my mother on Iris. (*The inevitable*) "*Not* that I have anything against the *goyim,* Sidney, she's a nice girl, but the rice is too greasy. And *lamb* fat? For the *stomach?* With hominy grits? *Like a lump it sits.*"

WALLY (*nodding toward where* IRIS *is*). Any shows coming up?

SIDNEY (*softly, hand up to discourage the subject*). Don't bring it up.

ALTON (*who has been flipping the pages of a book on the coffee table in front of him*). One of your troubles is, Sid, that you admire the wrong parts of Thoreau.

SIDNEY (*who is deep in the chair; his back to* ALTON, *hand behind his head*). How do you know what parts of Thoreau I do or don't admire?

ALTON. You mark passages—(*He promptly starts to read aloud, while roaming the room, meaning in the beginning to inflict the facetious taunt on it, trilling his r's, but ultimately finding some difficulty in it, perhaps as the words have appeal even to him. As he reads we are aware of certain familiar colorings and inflections in his speech though we cannot presently place them*) ". . . In the coldest and bleakest places, the warmest charities still maintain a foothold. A cold and searching wind drives away all contagion, and nothing can withstand it but what has virtue in it. Whatever we meet in cold and bleak places, as the tops of mountains—" See! Always looking for them *mountain tops!* ". . . we respect for a sort of sturdy innocence. . . . It is invigorating to breathe the cleansèd air . . . and we fain would stay out long and late, that the gales may sigh through us, too, as through the lifeless trees, and fit us for the winter:—as if we hoped so to borrow some pure and steadfast virtue which will stead us in all seasons."

(SIDNEY *takes the book from him thoughtfully and a little defiantly, snaps it shut and returns it to its place on the shelf, then sits looking off.* IRIS *reappears in the bedroom doorway.*)

WALLY. All right—how's about the rest of Thoreau, Sidney boy? How's about the Thoreau of sublime social consciousness, the Thoreau who was standing in jail one day when that holy of holies, Mr. Ralph Waldo Emerson, comes strolling by and asks, "Well, Henry, what are you doing in there?" And Thoreau, who was "in there" for protesting the evils of his day, looked out at him and said—"The question is, Ralph, what are you doing (*New England old-timer inflection*) out *thay-ah?*"

(IRIS *knowing* SIDNEY *only too well and sensing the drift, starts humming "The Battle Hymn of the Republic" as she crosses into the kitchen.*)

SIDNEY. Cut it out.

(IRIS *enters with salad bowl and stands slicing vegetables at counter.*)

ALTON (*Coolly plunging in for the kill*). *Why*, Sid? She's right . . . Wally, stop that foolishness! Cool it, man. You're "venerating"! You're "celebrating the human spirit"! Your *"conscience* is showing"! Don't you know, Wally, "Readers —(*Indicating* IRIS) don't want it." The great untutored public—(*Indicating the window*) doesn't want it. And what's more, the exhausted insurgent—(*Indicating* SIDNEY) cannot afford it. 'S no use, Wally: the man's in mourning for his boyhood. Let's go before he sells you one hundred and fifty restaurant glasses.

(*He gets up.*)

SIDNEY (*stung*). Well, hooray the hell for you! . . . John the Baptist! (*He throws himself onto his knees and with outstretched arms offers a slow and very precise salaam.*) God bless your Saviour-type soul!

(*Hands fluttering holy-roller style, he begins a wailing chant, which peters out as* ALTON *stands over him, relentless.*)

ALTON. Look out, man, you're getting overinvolved. Too emotional; you might *shed a tear.* After all, what is it? Only one kid. One lousy junkie, all of seventeen. (*Brutally offhand*) What'd he do, sweep for you at the Silver Dagger, whatever his name is?

SIDNEY (*softly*). Sal Peretti . . .

ALTON. Oh yeah—Sal Peretti.

SIDNEY. I did what I could—

IRIS (*furious, pleading to hold back the inevitable*). Sidney, you gave him a job —you can't be responsible for *every* strange kid that walks in off the street!

SIDNEY. I tried to help.

ALTON. Let's go, Wally, we're wasting time. (*Pulling* WALLY *after him.*)

WALLY (*at the door*). I'm counting on you, Sid.

SIDNEY. *Don't.*

(*They exit. There is a long, pregnant beat as* SIDNEY *stands looking after them.* IRIS*'s eyes are immediately riveted to him from the counter, where she continues slicing salad—and they do not leave him, not for one instant, for the balance of the scene.* SIDNEY *stirs, wanders deep in thought about the room, back and forth, round and about. He takes up the poster, puts it on the coffee table, sits looking at it. He flops on the couch. Sits up. Flops back down again, looking off unseeing, then sits up and—at last—turns tentatively to* IRIS.)

IRIS (*as their eyes meet*). Sidney, I swear to heaven—I'll poison you!

BLACKOUT

SCENE TWO

TIME: *Dusk. The following week. In the darkness before the lights come up, once again the quarrelsome voices are heard.*

MAX (*round, juicy, gravel-voiced*). *Scarrew* Michelangelo! You and Michelangelo! You and Michelangelo all the time! Christ! Not again . . .

ALTON. Yes, again. The *larger* statement has to say it *all*—

(*The lights come up.* ALTON *and* MAX *are in the apartment. The latter's free-form paintings, laid out for inspection about the place, have inspired the present violent discussion.* MAX *is by all odds an original: middle-aged, gravel-voiced, squat, his salt-and-pepper short hair brushed dead forward; he wears sandals, stained jeans, a black turtleneck and a pained expression.*)

MAX. Your main trouble is that you are a literalist. You were born a literalist and you will die a literalist.

ALTON. And all I am saying is that decay is *not* the deepest damn thing going, you know? It's sick—so, like, it's supposed to be pro*found*? Too easy, baby. Death is too damn easy. Chaos is easier. And when you pretend that *that* is the scale of existence—

MAX (*gesture of the streets*). Go the hell away, Alton. You don't know a damn thing except *poster* art.

ALTON. What old poster art! Is Leonardo poster art?

MAX (*slamming down something with outrage*). I knew it, here we go again: back to the frigging Renaissance!

(SIDNEY *enters carrying a large banner.*)

SIDNEY. I got it.

ALTON. Great. Let's put it up, I've already got the nails in.

(SIDNEY *flings one end to* ALTON *and they hold it, for a moment unfurled. It reads:*

CLEAN UP COMMUNITY POLITICS
Wipe Out Bossism
VOTE REFORM

(*They stride to the window—where, presently, it hangs, face out to the street.*)

SIDNEY. All right, let's go to work. (*He sits at his board,* ALTON *at his side.* MAX *sits benignly apart: the "man of the hour," awaiting the call.*) Now, with a new masthead, the front page will stay pretty much as it is. Page two, some jumps and lesser items . . . page three, interviews, you know. Page four, letters to the editor and some weekly artwork.

ALTON (*winks—the victor*). *And* the editorials.

SIDNEY (*toss-off—who ever denied it?*; *then laughs*). And the editorials. Five and six: theatre, dance and movie reviews. By the way, I want to get rid of Dan Wallace and get Paul Russo. He's good.

ALTON. If you like obscurity, he's the best.

SIDNEY. Sure, Russo gets a little fuzzy, but you've got to admit the man knows films. (*As if this were somehow relevant.*) He's a very gentle man. Do you know he wanders around with little bits and pieces of paper in his pocket on which he writes down every single thing that moves him, good or bad, in a day?

ALTON. And at the end of the week he puts them in a hat and stirs them—and that's his movie review for the week!

SIDNEY. Oh, Alton, knock off! Where's the masthead, Max?

(MAX *rises and crosses ceremoniously with his portfolio; he opens it and places the masthead before them. Then, with a flourish, he flips off the tracing paper to unveil it, and stands back.*)

MAX (*modestly*). Here. It's a rough idea, you know.

(SIDNEY *and* ALTON *squint at it hard, look at each other, puzzled; the two turn it sidewise and upside down.* MAX *restores it rightside up. The two squint again. Finally,* ALTON *points to the bottom of the page.*)

SIDNEY. Three-point type for the nameplate of a newspaper? At the bottom of the page? Who's going to see it?

MAX (*Columbus Incarnate, Galileo, Copernicus, the Wright Brothers and Frank Lloyd, in one*). That's the whole point. You put it far right and low on the big field—and the eye *has* to follow. (*Professor to slow pupil, guides their eyes down and around the page with a finger. The other two men are silent;* MAX *is offended and starts to gather his things.*)

SIDNEY. Max, I like it—it just occurred to me—I like it!

MAX (*petulant, undeterred*). Look, I thought it was something different, something fresh.

(*He starts out.*)

SIDNEY. But, Max—

MAX. It's always that way. You revolutionaries are all the same. You start out full of fire and end up full of . . . shit!

(*He stamps out the door.* SIDNEY *rises to follow.*)

ALTON. Oh, Sidney! I'm telling you, it

looks like a bunch of art majors from Music and Art designed that page.

SIDNEY. Alton, will you please! (*Follows* MAX *out—takes the masthead from* MAX, *studies it.*) Max, you've done it again!

MAX (*one more moment of immovable glory; then relents*). As a matter of fact, Sid, let's change it every week. (SIDNEY *and* MAX *reenter and cross to the board.*) You know, a different type—Old English, Gothic, Bodoni. However we feel the day we're making it up.

SIDNEY. Max—you're so creative!

MAX. And in a different place! Locate it on a different place on the sheet every week!

ALTON (*suddenly shouting*). It's a newspaper! It's a goddamned newspaper—not an avant-garde toy!

MAX. He doesn't change, does he? You know, once you've had that Marxist monkey on your back you're hooked for life. To Alton—a newspaper's not an aesthetic adventure, it's—(*He tightens his face and balls his fist in a mock-serious gesture*) a weapon! (*Carried away by his idea, he leaps on the couch with an imaginary banner and sings.*)

   " 'Tis the final conflict
   Let each stand in his place—
   The Internationale—"

ALTON. Aw, go to hell.

MAX (*sings*). "Unites the human race!"

(IRIS *enters and halts at the sight. She is in her uniform, carrying paella in a brown paper bag.*)

IRIS (*violent facetiousness*). Well, *company*. And who have I invited to supper tonight?

(*She has their attention at last.*)

ALTON. Paella?

(*She nods "yes," with eyes closed, knowing that he will stay now. He puts his hand in the air to deliberately affect the class-room mannerism of a small child.*)

IRIS. Max?

MAX (*still on the couch*). Paella. Like crazy. (*Rubbing his head, stomach and consulting his watch, genuinely conflicted.*) But the problem is . . . there's this chick I was *supposed* to have met in the Black Knight—Jesus, an hour ago . . .

SIDNEY. There it is: the primeval decision, food or sex.

(MAX *closes his eyes to imagine a little of each presumably, caught in the pose of the true primitive.*)

ALTON (*going and leaning under* MAX *more or less to study the decision*). And let us watch *primitive* man decide—

(MAX *opens his eyes, steps down from the couch and begins to gather up his things in order to make the prior date.* IRIS *exits into the bedroom.*)

ALTON. The *loins* triumph! See, Max, you're *not* a true primitive or you would have put *food* first! You only *paint* like a savage. (*Pursuing* MAX *to the door.*) And—where the hell did you get that outfit, man? You look just like a put-up job for *Life*-Magazine-Visits-the-Left-Bank-and-all. Where's your goatee?

MAX (*staring him down—a squelch*). That's the difference between me and you, Alton: I have finally become a truly free man. I have even stopped worrying about *not* trying to look like a nonconformist *not* nonconforming. Dig?

(*He exits, giving* ALTON *one last baby chuck on the chin.* IRIS *reenters from bedroom in jeans and a sweater, with mail.*)

IRIS. Hey, I got a letter from Gloria.

ALTON. How is life in the pancake world, Iris, my light?

IRIS (*reading her mail*). Be still, I gotta read my mail. (ALTON *takes the banjo down, crosses to the rocker, begins to pick the banjo . . .* IRIS *looks up from the letter slowly, with astonishment and many confusions in her face.*) Why, Alton Scales . . . Gloria says that you asked her to marry you.

ALTON (*affecting the bashful teenager*). Yup.

SIDNEY (*looks up at him and then at his wife, and then back to his friend*). Are you for real?

ALTON (Ibid.). Yup.

SIDNEY. You're that gone on her?

ALTON (*sudden lover's hoarse sincerity*). In fact, I figure that if that babe doesn't hurry up and get herself back here —like I could flip.

SIDNEY. I'll be damned. (*To his wife.*) You never know.

IRIS (*in astonishment*). You never know.

SIDNEY. What did she say: "yes" or "no"?

ALTON. She didn't. She said she'd think about it while she was away—(*Strumming out an accompaniment on the banjo for emphasis*)—and like I have been *living* with tension for two weeks! (*Abruptly, his strum breaks into "The Midnight Special!" and he sings. After a few lines he stops. As the silence dawns on him—tensely.*) What's the matter? (*The other two avoid replying in an awkward moment of misunderstood discomfort. SIDNEY reconcentrates on his board; IRIS just sits, not knowing what to say. ALTON, tightly, with mounting anger, speaks directly to SIDNEY, crossing to him and standing fully in front of him; angrily.*) I said what's the matter, goddamnit! Come on, let's have it out, my little gray friends! This is like the moment of truth, old babies! Yeah, come on! Let's get to the nitty gritty, as it were! Let's blast all the crap away—

IRIS. Oh, Alton!

SIDNEY (*simply*). Why don't you take that damn tree off your shoulder, Alton? Frankly, it's embarrassing.

(*They glare at one another; ALTON softens to a different kind of embarrassment.*)

ALTON. Well, don't expect me to apologize . . . I have a right to think anything I want. In *this* world. Even of *you*—Sid.

SIDNEY. There are some misunderstandings that cost more than others, Alton.

IRIS. Besides, the point is—well for crying out loud—who'd expect that you two? Well, you know what I mean: You're so Paul P. Proletarian and all, and she's the Living Spirit of Madison Avenue.

ALTON. Well, hell, opposites attract and all, to coin a phrase. Besides, like— (*Slowly, real slow.*) I dig her!

SIDNEY (*with great sobriety*). That much?

ALTON (*a lover*). *That* much!

SIDNEY (*Russian accent*). Another Bolshevik bites the dust.

IRIS (*her eyes on him intently*). And that's all that we have to say about it, isn't it, Sidney?

SIDNEY (*considering swiftly and accepting this judgment*). That's all.

IRIS. Where's my *Variety*?

SIDNEY (*back with his board*). Under the apples.

IRIS (*a long afterthought*). And I don't like that expression, come to think of it.

SIDNEY. What expression?

IRIS (*shaking her finger, not serious*). About biting the dust. I know where that

came from. And on behalf of my Cherokee grandfather, I protest.

ALTON. I got your point, so knock it off.

IRIS (*turning on him*). You knock it off, sometimes, Alton! It's a bore. You and the causes all the time. It's phony as hell!

ALTON (*sharply, back at her*). I was born with *this* cause.

IRIS. That's what I mean! Fun with illusion and reality: white boy playing black boy all the time.

ALTON. I *am* a black boy. I didn't make up the game, and as long as a lot of people think there is something wrong with the fact that I *am* a Negro—I am going to make a point out of being one. Follow!

IRIS (*pragmatic bohemia*). But that's what makes it so phony. The country is full of people who dropped it when they could—what makes you so ever-loving different?

ALTON. It's something you either understand or don't understand.

(*He shrugs.*)

IRIS. Well, I guess everybody has to do *something* with their guilts.

ALTON (*flaring*). Guilt's got nothing to do with it . . .

SIDNEY. Come on, this is a stupid conversation. Be a Martian if you wanna.

IRIS (*settling down with her Variety; whistling it out*). Heroes, heroes, everywhere—and not a battle won! (*ALTON rises, abruptly—quickly crosses to the door.*) Alton?

ALTON (*turning at the door—gruff, indirect apology*). I'm going out for some wine for my contribution to the feed. Want something? Cigarettes?

SIDNEY (*grinning*). Nope.

ALTON. How about you, Laughing Tomahawk?

(*He exits.*)

IRIS. Flowers. For the table. (*Follows him out the door—calls after him.*) If you're going to be a brother-in-law you should try to get in with me. I know *plenty* about being a sister-in-law. Bring me flowers every day . . . (*At the top of her lungs.*) Lumumba. (*She ducks as the paperback he has been reading comes crashing against the door frame. She comes back in, closing the door. At once to her husband, sharply, wife-ishly.*) You just keep your mouth shut about Gloria, you hear!

SIDNEY. Did I say anything?

IRIS. No, but you sat there looking like death. Let them work it out, see! Let them work it out. Keep your mouth off it, I'm telling you.

SIDNEY (*almost screaming, as the point has been made*). Did I say anything, did I say anything, *shrew*?

IRIS (*turning back to her paper*). No, but I know you—the world's biggest busybody. (SIDNEY *rises, crosses, hands her the new masthead and, like the cat that swallowed the canary, unveils it with the same proud flourish as* MAX. IRIS *sits blankly, squints, looks at* SIDNEY, *turns it sidewise and upside down; finally he rights it and guides her eye in almost exact repetition of the prior sequence.*) You keeping it a secret? Looks arty.

SIDNEY (*furious*). All right—so it looks arty. What does that mean, do you know?

IRIS. Do I know what?

SIDNEY. Do you know what "arty" means? Or is it just some little capsule phrase thrown out to try to diminish me, since you have nothing genuinely analytical or even observant to say?

(*He is staring at her hard, angrily.*)

IRIS. I wasn't trying to be analytical. I was saying what I thought, which is that it looks arty.

SIDNEY. You mean that it looks different from other publications.

IRIS. No, I mean it looks different from other publications in a self-conscious sort of way. *Arty.*

SIDNEY. Iris, where did you get the idea you know enough about these things to pass judgment on them?

IRIS. From the same place you got the idea that you were an editor.

SIDNEY. Which happens at least to be more reasonable than the idea that you are anybody's actress.

IRIS (*putting down her paper, slowly, hurtfully*). Why don't you just hit me with your fists sometimes, Sid. (*Exits into the bathroom. Sobs are heard.*)

SIDNEY. I didn't mean that, baby. Come on. Do *South Pacific*. I'll hold the book for you.

IRIS. No. (*More sobs.*)

SIDNEY. Iris, honey, come on.

(*He opens the door—she pulls it shut. After a moment he tries again and she, clutching the inner knob, is tugged half into the room.*)

IRIS (*flaring irrationally, crossing out*

and down). Why should I go through all of that to read for something that I know I won't get in the first place. They don't want actresses, they just want easy lays, that's all. (*Snarling.*) That Harry Maxton, *please!* He's the biggest lech of them all. You want to know something, you really want to hear something I hope will burn your little ears off? That's why I didn't get the part before. I said "no"!

(SIDNEY *has halted and is standing, half turned from her, letting it pour out of her as he has many, many times before.*)

SIDNEY (*turning quietly, almost gently*). Iris, everybody knows that Harry Maxton is one of the most famous fags in America.

IRIS. All right, then. So everything goes with him! He just puts on the fag bit to cover up what he really is—

SIDNEY (*with proper incredulity*). You mean a lech?

IRIS (*with a wild, cornered gesture*). Sure, that's how twisted up they are in show business, you just don't know!

SIDNEY (*helplessly*). Even in show business—*that* twisted they're not. And making up sordid excuses to yourself is not the solution to your problem, so come off it!

IRIS. Leave me alone, Sidney. I don't want the part.

(*She has curled into a tight sulking ball.*)

SIDNEY (*continuing on, getting the book and then crossing back to her and kneeling in front of her*). Oh, Iris, Iris, Iris . . . (*He puts his head wearily on her knee.*) I want to help . . . so much . . . I'm on your side.

IRIS. I just don't have it. They say if you really have it—you stick with it no matter what—and that—that you'll do anything—

SIDNEY. That is one of the great romantic and cruel ideas of our civilization. A lot of people "have it" and they just get trampled to death by the mob trying to get up the same mountain.

IRIS. Oh—please, Sidney, don't start blaming everything on society. Sooner or later a person learns to hold *himself* accountable—that's what maturity is. If I haven't learned anything else in analysis I've sure learned that.

SIDNEY. Thank you, Dr. Steiner! Look, Iris, the world's finest swimmer cannot swim the Atlantic Ocean—even if analysis *does* prove it was his mother's fault!

IRIS. That's not an analogy. *Nobody* can swim the Atlantic Ocean—but some people *do* make it in the theatre. (*She smiles at him and puts her hand on his head and he settles at her feet.*) You make the lousiest analogies. Just like you can't add. I couldn't believe that at first.

SIDNEY. What?

IRIS. About your arithmetic. When I first met you I thought you were putting me on. You know, anybody all *that* brilliant who couldn't *add*. God, at home almost *nobody* could read—but *everybody* could add. (*Looking at him and playing with his hair a little.*) What's seven and seven—?

SIDNEY. Fourteen, naturally.

IRIS (*quickly*). And fourteen and fourteen?

SIDNEY (*hesitates; she giggles and he nestles playfully against her legs*). Twenty-eight.

IRIS. And twenty-eight and twenty-eight?

SIDNEY (*abruptly lost*). Oh, c'mon. That's calculus . . .

(*Both laugh; he comes into her arms.*)

IRIS. You don't know what it's like though—(*She is looking off, moving her fingers through his hair.*) God, to walk through those agency doors . . . There's always some gal sitting on the other side, at a desk, you know, with a stack of pictures practically up to the ceiling in front of her. And they're always sort of bored, you know. Even the polite ones, the nice ones, I mean, they can't help it. They've seen five million and two like you and by the time you come through that door they are *bored*. And when you get past them, into the waiting room, there they are—the five million and two sitting there, waiting to be seen, and they look scared and mean and as competitive as you do. And so you all sit there, and you don't know anything: how you look, how you feel, anything. And least of all do you know how they *want* you to read. And when you get inside, you know less. There are just those faces, Christ, half the time you almost wish that someone *would* make a pass or something; you could deal with that, you know—that's from *life*. You can deal with that and take your chances, but that almost never happens, at least not to me. All I ever see are those blank director-producer-writer faces just staring at you like a piece of unfinished wood, waiting for you to show them some-thing that will excite them, get them to arguing about you . . . And you just stand there knowing that you *can't*, no matter what, *do* it the way you *did* it at home in front of the mirror, the brilliant imaginative way you did it the night before. No matter what. All you can think is: What the hell am I doing standing here in front of these strangers, reading these silly words and jumping around for that fairy like some kind of nut . . . ? (*Looking up at him.*) Sidney, I wish I had it in me to—be *tougher*. (*Gently.*) Like—like Gloria, I guess.

SIDNEY. Gloria wasn't tough *enough*, but let's not get into that.

IRIS. No, let's not! Anyhow, this is all a waste of time. You know and I know that I will never show up for that audition. I just don't want to see those faces again—Jesus, do I ever feel *twenty-nine!*

SIDNEY. Take down your hair for me, Iris . . .

IRIS (*hoarsely, but not angrily*). Christ, you're still so hooked on my hair . . . (*Laughter through tears.*) It's spooky to be loved for your hair, don't you know that?

SIDNEY. Take down your hair . . . (*He reaches up behind and pulls the pins and it falls and there really is a great deal of it which almost covers her. Then he gets up and crosses to the phonograph, puts on a record and turns and waits; in a second or two a stinging mountain banjo hoe-down cuts into the silence. It swells and races: louder, swifter, filling room and theatre, this untamed music of the Blue-grass; in all the world there is none more vibrant.*) Dance for me, Iris Parodus . . . Come down out of the hills and dance for me, Mountain Girl.

IRIS (*lifting up her eyes to him from behind the hair*). I just don't feel Appalachian tonight, Sid. It just won't work tonight—(*They look at one another a long moment. The music continues. During the above,* MAVIS BRYSON, IRIS's *older sister, has crossed to the door. She is a heavier, red-headed version of* IRIS, *more uptown and fashionable. She knocks and* IRIS *gets up and opens the door—then, as swiftly, shuts and bars it with her outstretched body. Meaning the dress box which her sister is carrying.*) I don't want it, I don't need it and I won't take it.

MAVIS. Just try it on. That's all I ask.

(IRIS *reluctantly opens the door to admit her.*) Hello, Sid, darling.

SIDNEY. Hello, Mav.

MAVIS (*blithely opens the box*). Could you conceivably have the hootenanny at another time?

(*She turns off the phonograph.*)

IRIS. We don't go to cocktail parties, Mavis. At least the kind where you dress like *that*. I want to tell you from the top, Mavis. This is not a good time. I am in no mood for the big sister-little sister hassle today—that's all—

(MAVIS *crosses and maternally stops* IRIS's *mouth in mid-speech with one hand.*)

MAVIS. Just slip it on; I had it taken up for you. You'll look stunning in it. (*Confidentially, as she zips and buttons.*) What's that awful sign? Iris, it looks so vulgar to have writing in your window. (IRIS *points to* SID *as the culprit.*) What have you heard from Gloria?

IRIS. Not a word.

MAVIS. Here, let me smooth it down on you. Now, really, I can't tell a thing with those sticking out. (IRIS *pulls up her jeans as far as possible under the dress.*) It's stunning! (*As, in fact, it is, because, whatever else,* MAVIS's *taste is simple and elegant and the dress* will *be handsome on* IRIS.) Now, all you'll need for Easter is a new pair of sneakers.

SIDNEY (*appreciatively*). You're coming along, Mavis, you're coming along. How about a drink?

(*He goes to the bar.*)

MAVIS. You know, you're drinking a lot lately, Sidney. (*To* IRIS.) I thought you always said that the Jews didn't drink.

SIDNEY (*crossing from the bar*). Mavis, I'm assimilated!

MAVIS. Where was Gloria when you heard from her?

IRIS. Miami Beach. (*Then, angry with herself.*) And you're turning into a pure sneak—when it comes to digging.

MAVIS. And you weren't going to tell me. (*To* SIDNEY.) Why can't she tell me? Miami Beach, my God! (*A beat.*) Is she—?

IRIS. Of course she is, what do you think!

MAVIS (*covering her eyes*). The poor baby. All I can think of is that I am so glad Papa didn't live to—

IRIS. Look, Mavis, don't start. I just don't want the Gloria problem tonight.

No matter what else—she is living *her* life and we are living *ours*. (*A beat.*) So to speak.

(*She exits into the bedroom.*)

MAVIS. Is she coming any time soon?

IRIS. She didn't say.

(*She enters again.*)

MAVIS. When?

IRIS. Why can't you leave it alone, Mav? She won't see you when she does come. I guess she just can't take all those lectures any more.

MAVIS. And you don't lecture her—do you?

IRIS (*pouring a drink*). Mavis, if you weren't the world's greatest living anti-Semite you really should have married Sidney so that the two of you could have minded the world's business together. Jees!

MAVIS. That's not funny and I am not, for the four thousandth time, an anti-Semite. (*Swiftly.*) You don't think that about me, do you, Sid? Why?

IRIS. Now, come on: you nearly had a heart attack when we got married. In fact, that's when you went into analysis. Now either you were madly in love with *me* or you hate the Jews—*pick*!

MAVIS (*glaring at her*). Sometimes, Iris . . . (*A beat.*) Did she say if she needs anything?

IRIS. Now, what could *she* need? She's the successful one. As a matter of fact— (*Winks.*) I plan to put the old touch on her when she comes back.

MAVIS. Iris, you've gotten to be just plain dirty-minded.

IRIS. Look, I happen to have a sister who is a fancy call girl, a big-time, high-fashion whore. And I say so what? She's racking up thousands of tax-free dollars a year and it's her life so—who's to say?

(*Having done with responsibility, she shrugs with confidence.*)

MAVIS (*plaintively*). It's your baby sister —how can you talk like that?

IRIS. Look, Mav, you're all hung up in the puritan ethic and all. That's not my problem.

MAVIS (*gazing at her*). Is anything?

IRIS. Frankly, it's an anti-sex society—

SIDNEY (*exploding: enough is enough*). Oh, shut up! I can't stand it when you start prattling every lame-brained libertarian slogan that comes along, without knowing what the hell you're talking about.

IRIS (*with great indignation*). I am entitled to my opinion, Sid-nee!

SIDNEY (*riding over her*). You are *not!* Not so long as your opinion is based on stylish ignorance!

IRIS. Oh shut up, Sidney. On this subject you are the last of the Victorians.

SIDNEY. Not at all. You give old Victoria too much credit. If there was anything Victorians believed in it was that there *was* a place for the whore in society. The Victorians, sweet, were not against "sin," they were opposed to its *visibility*.

IRIS. All I know is this is an anti-sex soci—

SIDNEY. Look, Iris love—(*He grabs his head with frustration, wanting to make himself understood.*) how can I put it to you, in front of Mavis, so that you get it? (MAVIS *rolls her eyes offendedly.*) Victoria is dead so—like—it's just not that hard to *have* it, if you know what I mean, with your own girl friend. Dig? The guys running to the call girls are not pushing the sex revolution you think you are cheerleading—they are indulging in a medieval notion of its disrespectability! Aside from which, there ought to be some human relationships on which commerce cannot put its grisly paws, doncha think?

MAVIS. The *things* you *think* you have to talk about!

IRIS. Who cares? My whole point is that I just don't care.

MAVIS. Sidney, Gloria is a very sick girl. She's not bad. She's very, very sick.

IRIS. Well, she's in analysis, for crying out loud! (*Both turn and look at her,* MAVIS *blankly,* SIDNEY *triumphant.*) Well, she *says* he's helping her . . .

SIDNEY (*eyeing* MAVIS; *to* IRIS—*cat and mouse*). Oh, Iris, why don't you tell her the new development?

MAVIS (*to* SIDNEY). What?

IRIS (*to* SIDNEY). Fat mouth.

MAVIS (*wheeling to her sister*). What—?

IRIS (*to* MAVIS, *after another beat*). There's somebody we know who wants to marry her.

MAVIS (*closing her eyes and leaning back as if some particular prayer has been answered at exactly this moment*). Praise his name! (*Opening her eyes.*) Who? (*Anxiously—to* SIDNEY.) One of your friends?

(*He nods "yes." To* IRIS.) What does he do?

SIDNEY (*almost laughing*). Well, as a matter of fact, he works in a bookstore.

MAVIS. In a *what?*

SIDNEY. He works in a bookstore. Part time. (*Almost breaking up now.*) And as a matter of fact he used to be a Communist. (*His sister-in-law just stares at him with an open mouth and then looks to her sister; she then exhales a breath to demonstrate she feels that anything is possible here.*) But it's all right, Mav. He's strictly an NMSH-type Red.

MAVIS. What kind is that?

SIDNEY (*mugging*). "No-more-since-Hungary."

MAVIS. Does he know what—ah . . .

SIDNEY. Does he know what Gloria does for a living? No. She told him the model bit.

MAVIS (*hopefully*). Listen, people like that, I mean Communists and things—they're supposed to be very *radical* . . . about things . . . well . . . (*Pathetically.*) Well, aren't they?

SIDNEY. Who can say? There's "people like that" and "people like that."

MAVIS. Is he good-looking? What about Gloria? What does she . . . ?

SIDNEY (*deliberately playing it*). Uh, Mavis—

MAVIS. I knew this nightmare would have to end . . . It was just something that happened. It's the way the world is . . .

SIDNEY. He's also a Negro one, Mavis.

MAVIS. . . . these days. People don't know what to do with—(*Deep, guttural.*) A *Negro what*—?

SIDNEY (*still deliberately*). A Negro Communist. That is to say, that he's not a Communist any more—but he's still a Negro.

MAVIS (*looking from one to the other in open-mouthed silence*). Are you—(*A beat, as she turns her head back and forth again.*) Are you—(*Finally, composing herself, she crosses to* SIDNEY.) sitting there talking about . . . a *colored* boy?

SIDNEY (*rapidly, wagging his finger*). 1964, Mavis, 1964! "Uncommitted Nations," "Free World!" Don't say it, honey, don't say it! We'll think you're not chic!

MAVIS. I don't think you're funny worth a damn! (*Looking from one to the other.*) What do you think Gloria *is?!* (*The ques-*

tion hangs.) If this is your idea of some kind of bohemian joke I just don't think it's cute or clever or *anything*. I would rather see her—

SIDNEY (*finishing it for her*). —go on shacking up with any poor sick bastard in the world with a hundred bucks for a convention weekend!

(*They glare at one another.*)

MAVIS. Well now, listen, there are other men in the world! The last time I looked around me there were still some white men left in this world. Some fine ordinary up-standing plain decent very white men who were still looking to marry very white women . . .

(*During the above* DAVID RAGIN *has descended the stairway from his apartment overhead; now he pushes open the door and saunters in. An intense, slim, studied young man, of the latest fashionably casual dress and style; his mannerisms intend to suggest the entirely unmannered—but by choice. He is not in the least—"swish."*)

IRIS. Why hello, David, this is my sister, Mrs. Bryson.

MAVIS. How do you do.

(*He sits.*)

IRIS (*facetiously, to him*). I wouldn't bother, but she is from uptown where people knock on doors and all that jazz.

DAVID (*He ignores* MAVIS *completely—wearily*). You have any paper?

IRIS. The desk in the bedroom. (DAVID *exits into the bedroom.*) David is a playwright who lives upstairs. And we are the government—and we subsidize him.

(MAVIS *nods and turns to* SIDNEY.)

MAVIS. Well, *he's* sort of cute. Is he married?

SIDNEY (*simply*). David's gay. (MAVIS *doesn't get it.*) Queer. (*Still doesn't.*) Homosexual. (*Gets it, drawing back.*) Utterly.

MAVIS. Oh. (*Afterthought.*) Well, maybe she would want a rest . . . (DAVID *re-enters, crosses to the bar for a drink.* MAVIS *gathers up her things.*) Well, I should get on. I've got to meet Fred. Did I tell you the news, Iris? Fred's been put in charge of the Folk River Dam Project. Now, what do you think of that?

(SIDNEY *is struck by this.*)

IRIS. I think we are a talented family, obviously. Success in whatever we put our

—(*Holding—to outrage the sister.*) hands to.

MAVIS. Iris, not in front of people.

IRIS. David isn't people. He's a writer. And he worships prostitutes. He says they are the only *real* women—the core of life, as it were. Don't you, David?

MAVIS. The only thing about your flippancies, Iris, is that they don't solve any problems.

SIDNEY (*who has remained preoccupied by the earlier remark*). So old Fred is really doing all right for himself, huh?

(IRIS *lifts her eyes at this knowingly.*)

IRIS. Look out, Mavis, you're about to be tapped—

SIDNEY. You!

MAVIS (*pleasantly*). Now Sidney, you know Fred won't invest in a night club.

IRIS. The night club is dead. Long live the newspaper.

SIDNEY (*to* IRIS). It wasn't a *night club*.

MAVIS. A newspaper? (*Great intake of breath and, immediately, maternal exhalation.*) Oh, Sidney, Sidney, Sidney! You're thirty-seven years old. When are you going to grow up. (*Shaking her head.*) A *newspaper*.

SIDNEY (*tightly*). And what would a really "grown-up man" be doing with himself—in your enlightened opinion, Mavis?

MAVIS. Well, now, I know for a fact that your brother Manny has offered any number of times to get you a place in his firm. You're very lucky to have a brother in that kind of position, Sidney. A man like Fred had to do it all the hard way. I mean the *hard* way.

SIDNEY. And what will happen, Mavis, if I try, knowing better before I even open my mouth, to explain to you—that I consider my brother Manny a failure? I consider Fred a failure. I consider them to be men who accepted the alternatives that circumscribed them when they were born. I don't! I have a different set of alternatives—alternatives that I create! I either want to run my newspaper or—or go be an ambulance driver in Angola. I do not, for any reason, want to become part of Emmanuel Brustein, Inc.

MAVIS (*blinking, having heard nothing after "Angola"*). Be an ambulance driver —*where*, dear?

IRIS. But, Sidney, you can hardly drive . . .

SIDNEY. Oh, forget it!

IRIS (*hands on hips—to* DAVID). Talk about *bad* Hemingway.

MAVIS. Well, I really must go. (*To her sister, softly.*) You *will* let me know when Gloria is coming?

IRIS (*a great sigh*). Mavis—sooner or later you are going to have to learn that Gloria is living her life and doesn't want you to play Mama. Live and let live, that's all.

MAVIS. That's just a shoddy little way of trying to avoid responsibility in the world.

SIDNEY. Mavis—please go. It makes me *nervous* to be on your side! (*Bellowing.*)

MAVIS (*to* DAVID, *as she pulls on her gloves*). What are you writing, young man?

DAVID. Nothing you'd be interested in.

SIDNEY. Go on and tell her about your play, David. There is nothing else she can hear that's shocking today.

DAVID. Cool it, Sidney.

SIDNEY. David is engaged in the supreme effort of trying to wrest the theatre from the stranglehold of Ibsenesque naturalism, are you not, David? (DAVID *just stares indifferently at both of them. He is above, he feels, such repartee.*) As a matter of fact he has a play in production right now.

MAVIS. Oh, how nice! Is there something in it for Iris?

IRIS. You're not supposed to do that, Mavis.

SIDNEY. Besides, there are only two characters in David's play and they are both male and married to each other and the entire action takes place in a refrigerator.

MAVIS (*eyeing* DAVID *coolly and edging off a little*). I see.

DAVID. *I* didn't try to tell you what it was about. (*He has wandered to the sign. He studies it and turns to* SIDNEY, *shaking his head.*) And what have you got against the "machine" this week?

SIDNEY. Didn't you ever read *Huckleberry Finn,* David?

IRIS (*setting out the supper dishes; indicating her husband.*) He's Huck this week.

SIDNEY (*shouting: raspy-voiced, affecting Hal Holbrook affecting the garrulous old man of conscience*). And therefore "continually happy"! It's a machine, David! With a boss! A highly entrenched boss. Don't believe in bosses. Believe in independent men, like old Huckleberry!

DAVID (*shaking his head*). That's what I thought. Sidney, don't you know yet "the good guys" and "the bad guys" went out with World War II?

MAVIS. Well, sure. When you come right down to it, one politician *is* just like another.

SIDNEY (*rocking with his hands in prayerful fashion*). And a new religion is upon the West and it has only one hymn: (*Intoning a mock Mass.*) "We are all guilty . . . Father Camus, we are all guilty . . . *Ipso facto,* all guilt is equal . . . Therefore we shall in clear conscience abstain from the social act . . . and even the social thought . . ."

DAVID (*glaring at him*). Go ahead: kid it. It's easier to kid it than face the pain in it.

SIDNEY (*possessed by an all-consuming vision of the omnipotent catchword*). Ah, *"Pain!"* "Pain" in recognizing those dark tunnels which lead back to our primate souls, groveling about—(*He rises to a half stoop, arms dangling; and apelike throughout this speech, he crosses to, and up onto, the coffee table and then the sofa.*) in caves of sloth. The savage soul of man from whence sprang, in the first place, the Lord of the Flies, Beelzebub himself! (*Rather shouting.*) Man, dark gutted creature of ancestral—(*Leaping over the back of the sofa and lifting his hands in Bela Lugosi style.*) cannibalism and mysterious all-consuming eeevil! Ahhhhhh. (*Through the bars of the rocking chair he snarls and claws at all of them to burlesque this philosophy.*) Yahhhh! The Shadow knows.

MAVIS. I just said to Fred this morning: "Say what you like, it's always something different down at Iris and Sid's."

DAVID (*a little roused finally*). Well, what is the virtue of getting one boss out and putting another one in?

SIDNEY. The virtue—the virtue, my dear boy, if you will pardon the rhetoric, is to participate in some expression of the people about the way things are, that's all.

DAVID (*waving around, with derision*). Well, hel-lo, out there! (*He shakes his head.*) Well, that's what comes from reading too much Shaw.

SIDNEY (*angry*). Yah, well. Speaking of the drama, David, what *is* your play about?

DAVID. You read it. You tell me.

SIDNEY. No, you tell *me*.

DAVID. It's not for me to say.

SIDNEY (*for him*). ". . . each person will get from it what he brings to it?" Right?

DAVID (*as befits the present circumstance*). To be real simple-minded about it—yes.

SIDNEY. Then tell me this: What makes *you* the artist and the *audience* the consumer if they have to write your play for you?

DAVID. I know what it's about. (SIDNEY *merely looks at him—querulously.*) I told you, my plays have to speak for themselves.

SIDNEY. But to *whom*? For *whom*? For whom are they written, and, above all, *why* are they written?

DAVID (*getting up; his host is beyond belief*). You hate my kind of writing because it goes beyond the walls of Ibsen's prisons and Shaw's lectures—that's *your* problem, Sid.

MAVIS (*who has been turning from one to the other throughout, fascinated, incredulous, and trying all the while to get a word in edgewise herself*). I just don't know whatever happened to simple people with simple problems in literature.

SIDNEY (*riding right over her; to* DAVID, *grandiosely*). Oh come now, don't just choose the members of my team that you feel are most vulnerable. Go for my stars, too, David. Or are you afraid to tackle the masks of Euripedes and the shadows and hymns of Shakespeare?

(*They are almost toe to toe.*)

DAVID. Are you retreating from Ibsen and Shaw?

SIDNEY. *Not* on your life! But are you retreating before Euripedes and Shakespeare!

IRIS. I get so tired of this endless chess game!

DAVID (*heading for the door*). All I can say is that I write because I have to and what I have to. You don't know anything about it. Whatever you think of it, Sidney, I write. I squeeze out my own juices and offer them up. I may be afraid, but *I* write. (ALTON *reenters with paper bags and the flowers.*) Well, Dr. Castro, I presume.

ALTON (*in kind*). Jean Genet, as I live and breathe.

(*They shake hands.*)

SIDNEY (*taking the beer*). Did you bottle it yourself?

IRIS (*taking her flowers, and exchanging glances with her husband about what they are setting up*). David, are you going to stay to eat?

DAVID. Why not?

IRIS (*as they sit down to eat*). Mav?

MAVIS. No—dear! I've got to meet Fred. (*Reluctantly; her matchmaker eyes have not left* ALTON *since his entrance.*)

IRIS. Alton, I'd like you to meet my sister Mavis. Mavis, this is Alton Scales.

MAVIS. How do you do.

ALTON. How do you do.

(*As he crosses, she stands admiring him.*)

MAVIS (*to* SIDNEY). Is *he* married?

SIDNEY. No.

MAVIS. He isn't—ahhh—(*Meaning homosexual.*)

SIDNEY. We're not sure yet!

MAVIS (*a trill in her voice*). Good night, Mr. Scales.

ALTON. Good night.

SIDNEY (*with deliberate casualness*). Oh, Mavis, this is the chap we were just telling you about. (*She looks blank.*) From the bookstore.

(*There is silence; all except* DAVID *know the meaning of the moment for* MAVIS. *They variously concentrate on the food and exchange superior and rather childish glances; letting her live through the moment of discomfort. She turns slowly around to face the youth again. It is a contemporary confrontation for which nothing in her life has prepared her. There is silence and much deliberate chewing and eye-rolling. For his part,* ALTON *is prepared for virtually anything—to smile and kiss and be kissed, to scream or be screamed at, or to be struck and strike back. He is silent. Presently, this woman of conformist helplessness does the only thing she can, under these circumstances, she gags on her words so that they are hardly audible and repeats what she has already said.*)

MAVIS. Oh. How do you do.

ALTON (*raising his eyes evenly*). How do you do.

(*He turns and reaches for the food.* MAVIS *stands thoughtfully, watching this table in bohemia, the random art of the setting: a huge leafy salad, a bottle of wine, some candles, thick European bread; a portrait of diners who would sit down together only here: the taciturn young homosexual, the young Negro who is to be a kinsman, her sister, hair down, seemingly at home here; her brother-in-law, who presides.*)

SIDNEY (*swiftly, with open-hearted malice as she heads for the door*). Well, Alton, now you have met Mavis. There she is: the Bulwark of the Republic. The Mother Middleclass itself standing there revealed in all its towering courage. (*There are snickers of delight from the diners; he has even perhaps lifted his wineglass to her for these insults. Dismissal.*) Mavis, go or stay—but we're eating. (*Slapping at ALTON's paws.*) One to a man. One to a man!

(MAVIS *halts and turns to face them.*)

MAVIS (*she is silent so long that they look up at her, still with varying degrees of amusement; then—*). I am standing here and I am thinking: how smug it is in bohemia. I was taught to believe that —(*Near tears.*) creativity and great intelligence ought to make one expansive and understanding. That if ordinary people, among whom I have the sense at least to count myself, could not expect understanding from artists and—whatever it is that *you* are, Sidney—then where indeed might we look for it at all—in this quite dreadful world. (*She almost starts out, but thinks of the cap.*) Since you have all so busily got rid of God for us.

(*She turns and exits.*)

IRIS (*at once, unaffected by this eloquence, although* SIDNEY *is somewhat*). So—(*Knocking him in the ribs.*) put that in your pipe and smoke it, old dear!

DAVID (*also unaffected*). Some day I really must look into what it is that makes the majority so oppressively defensive under certain circumstances.

ALTON (*the most affected*). Oh quit it!

DAVID (*turning on him*). And now the gentle heart of the oppressed will also admonish us.

ALTON. Turn off, Fag Face!

DAVID (*glaring at him*). Isn't it marvelous, some people have their Altons and some have their Davids. You should be grateful to the Davids of the world, Alton: we at least provide a distraction from the cross you so nobly and (*Bitterly.*) so *deliberately* bear.

(ALTON *jumps up and heads for the door.*)

IRIS. Where are you going—?

ALTON. I'm sorry if it makes me un-

sophisticated in your eyes; but after a while, hanging out with queers gets on my nerves!

(ALTON *slams out of the house.* DAVID *puts down his fork slowly and sits quietly.* IRIS *notices and suddenly reaches out and touches him gently on the hand.*)

IRIS. Eat your supper, David. Alton's a big kid. You know.

DAVID (*turning his eyes on her slowly, steadily. A trap, casually*). You accept queers, don't you, Iris . . . ?

IRIS (*an innocent shrug*). Sure.

DAVID. Yes, because you accept *anything.* But—I am not *anything.* I hope he never has to explore the *why* of his discomfort. . .

SIDNEY (*winding up big*). Oh no . . . Come on, David! Don't start that jazz with me tonight. Is that the best you can do? I mean it! Is that really it? Anybody who attacks one—*is* one? Can it, boy!

IRIS (*a whine*). Sidney. Can't you be still sometimes . . . ?

SIDNEY (*raising his hand in a definite "stop" sign*). Oh no! I mean it. I have had it with that bit. I am bored with the syndrome.

IRIS. Who cares!

SIDNEY (*shouting at* IRIS). Is that all you can ever say? Who cares, who cares? Let the damn bomb fall, if somebody wants to drop it, 'tis the last days of Rome, so rejoice ye Romans and swill ye these last sick hours away! Well, I admit it: I *care!* I care about it all. It takes too much energy *not* to care. Yesterday I counted twenty-six gray hairs in the top of my head—all from trying *not* to care. And you, David, you have now written four-teen plays about not caring, about the isolation of the soul of man, the alienation of the human spirit, the desolation of all love, all possible communication. When what you really want to say is that you are ravaged by a society that will not sanctify your particular sexuality!

DAVID. It seems to have conveniently escaped your attention that *I* am the insulted party here.

SIDNEY. If somebody insults you—sock 'em in the jaw. If you don't like the sex laws, attack 'em, I think they're silly. You wanna get up a petition? I'll sign one. Love little fishes if you want. *But,* David, please get over the notion that your particular "thing" is something that only the deepest, saddest, the most nobly tortured can know about. It ain't—(*Spearing into the salad.*) it's just one kind of sex—that's all. And, in my opinion—(*Revolving his fork.*) the universe turns regardless.

(DAVID *looks at him for a long time, and then goes to the door.*)

IRIS (*going after* DAVID). What's the matter with everybody? David, come on, eat your supper.

DAVID. If you don't mind, I really can't stand the proud sociological oversimplifications which are beginning to abound—(*He nods to the sign in the window.*) in this house. I would rather eat alone.

(*He exits abruptly.*)

IRIS (*closing the door*). Well, that was some dinner party, thank you. What's with you lately, Sidney? Why do you have to pick at everybody? Where did you get the idea it was up to you to improve everybody? Leave people the hell alone!

SIDNEY (*in a fierce mood*). I don't try to improve people. Or, at least, you can't tell it by you.

IRIS (*properly hurt*). All right, Sid, one of these days you've got to decide who you want—Margaret Mead or Barbry Allen! I won't play both! As a matter of fact it's getting pretty clear—that I've got to decide too. (*Under her breath, to herself.*) God, have I got to decide!

SIDNEY. The least excuse and you haul up the old self-pitying introspection bit.

IRIS (*through her teeth*). What makes you think anybody can live with your insults?

SIDNEY. The world needs insults!

IRIS (*the last straw*). Sweet Heaven.

(*She starts to clear the table.*)

SIDNEY (*turning and noticing her exasperation with him*). I'm sorry. (*He moves to help; she rejects this. Several beats.*) There's a rally. You wanna go?

IRIS. I told you, don't expect me to get involved with that stuff!

SIDNEY. All right, all right. You wanna go over to the Black Knight and have a couple of beers?

IRIS. No, I don't want to go over to the Black Knight and have a couple of beers.

SIDNEY. Well then, suppose *you* just come up with *something, anything* that you would like to do. It will be your first achievement in this entire marriage.

IRIS. What does it do for you, Sid? Picking at me like that. Look, why don't you just go to your rally? And leave poor old Iris alone.

(*She turns on the phonograph.*)

SIDNEY (*grabs his jacket and heads for the door; then halts, hand on the knob, flings his jacket to the floor—helpless. More to himself than her*). Leave "poor old Iris alone"—and watch her turn quietly and willingly into a vegetable.

(IRIS *sits on the window seat, looking off, into the street—as a haunting guitar cuts the silence.*)

IRIS (*softly, fighting back tears*). It's getting different, Sidney, our fighting. Something's either gone out of it or come into it. I don't know which. But it's something that keeps me from wanting to make up with you a few hours later. That's bad, isn't it?

SIDNEY. Yeah, that's bad.

(*He turns and looks at his wife; she is crying—then picks up his jacket and starts out.*)

IRIS (*crying out*). Then let's put up a fight for it, Sidney! I mean it—let's fight like hell for it.

He halts at the outer staircase and stands clutching the rail and looking back toward the room where his wife sits looking after him, as the light fades on all but the two of them and the voice of Joan Baez, singing "All My Trials," fills the darkening stage.)

CURTAIN

ACT TWO

SCENE ONE

TIME: *Just before daybreak. The following day.*

AT RISE: *Only the faint light of pre-dawn illumines the outside staircase landing over the* BRUSTEIN *doorway; here* SIDNEY *lies, on his back, arms underhead, one leg doubled up and the other resting on his knee. New York at this hour is a world known to few of its inhabitants, and the silence of the great sleeping city is only accentuated by its few familiar sounds: the occasional moan of a foghorn on the Hudson or, now and then, the whirr of tires or clatter of a milk truck. The apartment is dark.*

Presently SIDNEY *sits up, picks up his*

banjo and, legs dangling over the patio, begins to pick it. The melody seems surely drawn from that other world which ever beckons him, a wistful, throbbing mountain blues. As he plays the lighting shifts magically, and nonrealistically, to create the mountain of his dreams. Gone is even the distant foghorn; he is no longer in the city. After several phrases of this, the music soars and quickens into a vibrant, stinging hoedown and the IRIS-of-his-Mind appears, barefooted, with flowing hair and mountain dress, and mounts the steps. She embraces him and then, as by the lore of hill people, is possessed by these rhythms, and dances in the shadows before him. The dance is a moving montage of all the bits and pieces of dance Americana: the dip for the oyster, the grand right and left. SIDNEY's banjo drives her on until both these spirits are exhausted and the mountain nymph gives him a final kiss and flees. He sits on, spent, plucks idly at the instrument. Now a light appears in the apartment's bedroom doorway and his wife enters through it, belting her robe, yawning, rubbing her eyes.

———

IRIS. Sid—? (*He does not reply or even hear her.*) Sidney? (*She switches on the lamp. For a moment stands blankly, then goes to the door and leans out.*) What are you doing up there? You'll wake the neighbors.

SIDNEY (*in the same unbroken reverie*). They can't hear me, Iris.

IRIS (*at the foot of the steps*). Oh, Sidney, you're a nut. C'mon down, I'll make you some coffee.

(*She fishes out her cigarettes and lights one.*)

SIDNEY (*shakes his head*). Listen! Do you hear the brook? There is nothing like clear brook water at daybreak. And when you drink, it gives back your own image.

IRIS (*charmed in spite of herself*). You'll catch cold, Sidney. It's too early for games. Come to bed.

SIDNEY. No, Iris. Come up. (*She does, as he speaks; and, finally, kneels beside him.*) Look at the pines—look at the goddamn pines. You can taste and feel the scent of them. And if you look down, down through the mist, you will make out the thin line of dawn far distant. There's not another soul for miles, and if you listen,

really listen—you might almost hear yourself think.

IRIS (*surveying the realm, gently laughing*). This is some mountain.

SIDNEY (*playful propriety pride*). It's a small mountain—but it's ours.

IRIS. Sidney . . . how much is fourteen and fourteen? (*She smiles and touches his face—and, for the moment, enters fully into his dream.*)

SIDNEY (*fondling her hair*). "Nymph in . . . all . . . my Orisons remembered."

IRIS (*looking up at him thoughtfully*). It really gets to you, doesn't it? Being here. You really are happy? You'd like to live right here, in the woods, wouldn't you?

SIDNEY. Yes. Yes. I would.

IRIS. And you're afraid to ask me to do something like that, aren't you? (*No answer.*) Afraid I'll look around at the woods and the brook and say, *"Here? Live?"* (*They both laugh at her mugging of her own attitude.*) And the worst of it is you'd be right. I would say exactly that. I wouldn't want to live here. (*Drooping her head a bit.*) I'm sorry. The truth is that I am cold and bored. I feel like watching television. I feel like having a swinging argument. I feel like sitting in a stupid movie or, or even a night club, a real stupid night club with dirty jokes and bad dancers. (*Looking at him.*) I've changed on you, haven't I, Sid? This particular mountain girl has been turning into an urban wastelander. (*Rather sweetly, still looking at him.*) Sorry. (*Several beats, she has been thinking of this.*) Most of all, I hate my hair. (*A beat.*) The things you don't know about me! (*A little laugh.*) Did you know, for instance, that you're the reason I wear it like this in the first place? (*Shaking her head with the little laugh again.*) There's a different style of "man trap" in every kind of woman. When I first came here, you know, I was working, dancing in this funny little old nothing of a sawed-off club, you know. And like I thought that the men who came there were not the ones that I came to the (*charade-style quote marks*) big city—to meet. I mean they were the kind that you could meet back home. So one of the girls who worked there and knew all the this-and-that listened to me and she said, "Well, honey, if that's what you're looking for, you've gotta go down to the

Black Knight Tavern and sit." (*Smiling.*) "Let your hair grow and go down to the Black Knight Tavern." Sounds like a folk song. Well, anyhow, the fourth time I went there, remember, it was about to . . . here. (*Marking off the shorter place.*) And there you were, just like that, sitting in that corner booth with—(*Remembering.*) Marty and Alt, wasn't it? Yes, it was Marty and Alt. And there you were sitting there, "holding forth." And I said to m'self: There's the one. After that I started eating vitamins to make m'hair grow faster. (*He laughs a soft, delighted "Oh, Iris!"*) So, s'help me! It's true! This same girl who told me everything, she got these vitamins for me too. And, well —*something* worked.

SIDNEY. I'm charmed.

IRIS. Women are a mess, aren't they? I mean they get these *fantastic* IDEAS about things, I mean life and all, when they're like three, you know. And nothing, I mean nothing gets it out of you. When I got off that train from Trenersville ten years ago I knew one thing in this world: I wanted to meet men who were as—as different from Papa as—as possible.

SIDNEY (*taking her hand*). Listen, Iris. Listen to the woods. Let's go for a walk.

IRIS (*huddling close*). It's too cold. And dark. And the woods frighten me.

SIDNEY. All right then, let's just go into the cabin and I'll make us a bang-up fire and some of the hottest coffee ever brewed. (*She just looks at him.*) You just want to go back to the city, don't you?

IRIS. Yes.

SIDNEY. You really hate it here in the woods?

IRIS. Yes. (*The tears come; tears of frustration, as she does not know exactly why. Gesturing around.*) I was born in country like this, you know, the real thing. I mean you didn't drive out anywhere to sort of *see* it. You just sat down on the back porch and—there it was. Something to run from; something to get the hell away from as fast as you could. All of us felt like that, me, Mav—Gloria.

SIDNEY. Then you've always hated coming up here. I didn't know that.

IRIS (*sort of a painful whine born of the effort to really make him finally understand*). No, I didn't *always* hate it . . . the first couple of years I just wanted to do what you wanted to do, be where

you were—you know, sort of wild and romantic the way it was supposed to be— (*A great burst of frustration.*) I mean, I thought it was going to be different. Papa was so crude and stupid . . . You know, I never heard my father make an abstract thought in his life; and, well, he had plenty of time to think, if you know what I mean. Didn't work that steady. And each of us; I think we've sort of grown up wanting some part of Papa that we thought was the thing missing in him. I wanted somebody who could, well, think; Mavis wanted somebody steady and ordinary. And Gloria, well, you know—rich men. Lots of them. (*Lifting up her hand anticipating.*) I know you're going to tell me that's parlor analysis, and it is, but—

SIDNEY. I'm not saying anything, Iris. I'm listening. I really am. I am listening to you.

IRIS. And now something is happening to me, changing me. Since we've been married. Sometimes, Sidney, I think if—if I hear any more talk from Alton and Max and David and—you—I'll shrivel up and die from it. You know what I want, Sidney? I am twenty-nine and I want to begin to know that when I die more than ten or a hundred people will know the difference. I want to *make* it, Sid. *Whatever* that means and *however* it means it: That's what I want. (*He is nodding; he genuinely understands and is deeply pained by it.*) Anyhow, what does it do for you, Sid? To come up here and talk to your—what do you call them—

SIDNEY (*smilingly*). My trolls.

IRIS. Yeah. 'Cause I tried having a few words with 'em and like what they had to say to me was nothing.

SIDNEY (*looking around*). Coming here makes me believe that the planet is mine again. In the primeval sense. Man and earth and earth and man and all that. You know. That we have just been born, the earth and me, and are just starting out. There is no pollution, no hurt; just me and this ball of minerals and gases suddenly shot together out of the cosmos.

IRIS (*looking at him, head tilted puppy style, mouth ajar*). Jeees.

SIDNEY. I love you very much.

(*They are quiet; he leans over gently and kisses her. After a long beat.*)

IRIS. Take me back to the city, please, Sid.

(He gets up and puts his banjo over his shoulder and takes her hand and they start down the steps—while at the same time the magic that is SIDNEY's *World fades and the lighting returns to normal. A passing truck guns its motor and day breaks on the city.)*

IRIS *(at the foot of the steps; remembering).* Sidney, it's Tuesday: you've got to move the car!

(They start to go in.)

DIMOUT

Scene Two

TIME: *Early evening in late summer.*

In the darkness—and in sharp contrast to the prior mood—a soundtruck loudspeaker blares out the buoyant, boisterous strains of "The Wally O'Hara Campaign Song"—sung by a folk group to the accompaniment of booming guitars and the occasional cheers and comments of the crowd, which joins in on the chorus.

"The Wally O'Hara Campaign Song"

Sing out the old, sing in the new,
It's your ballot and it's got a lot of work
    to do;
Sing out the old, sing in the new,
Wally O'Hara is the man for you!
  CHORUS. Wally O'Hara, Wally O'Hara
    Wally O'Hara is the man—for—you!
Sweep out the old, sweep in the new,
We've got a lot of sweeping to do;
Sweep out the old, sweep in the new,
Wally O'Hara is the man for you!
  CHORUS *(repeats).*
Who knows the people, every one?
(Wally! Wally!)
Who knows the job that must be done?
(Wally! Wally!)
Who is the man to beat the machine?
Who'll clean up this district and keep it
    clean?
(Wally! Wal-ly O'Hara!)
Vote out the old, vote in the new,
It's your ballot and it's got a lot of work
    to do;
Vote out the old, vote in the new,
Wally O'Hara is the man for you!
  CHORUS *(repeats).*

The song is not performed for its own sake, but rather as it might be by local talent from a touring vehicle in the campaign's heat; and, inevitably too, the speaker system is overworked, with resultant static and crackle from time to time. Still, what is lacking in polish is more than made up in fervor, and the tone is festive. The song should not be heard in its entirety, but gained in and out as indicated at appropriate moments. As the lights come up SIDNEY *and* WALLY *come on from the right in animated conversation. Each carries an armload of leaflets, and* SIDNEY, *a rolled-up flag.* WALLY *has his free arm about* SIDNEY's *shoulder and is agitated, moist-eyed.* SIDNEY *is more bemused. The soundtruck music moves off in the distance.*

WALLY *(with self-absorbed wonder).* No, Sid, I mean it. You can feel it in the air. There's a difference this time, a rumbling in the streets. My God, did you see the reception we got on Christopher Street? I tell you we really have underestimated the whole thing. *(Looking out at the audience.)* I mean it, we are going to win. Sidney, baby, we are going to win this thing, *I am going to win!*

(He slaps SIDNEY *on the back, crosses and exits with the flag.)*

SIDNEY *(with disbelieving eyes; to the audience).* It's a disease. We are at that point in a campaign which ushers in the dementia of the dark horse. Now comes the delusion, as ancient as elections themselves, which takes over the soul of the candidate. There is nothing to be done about it: it is in the nature of the type. He really thinks he is going to win. *(Whistling the campaign song, he balances his leaflets in the doorway and fishes for his keys—as* DAVID *enters, reading a newspaper and carrying a batch of others. To* DAVID.) So?

DAVID *(dryly, as if above self-appreciation).* "A complete unqualified hit."

(He hands SIDNEY *the paper.)*

SIDNEY. I'll be damned. Well, congratulations. Come on, I'll give you a drink.

(They enter.)

IRIS *(menacingly, from the bedroom).* Sid? Did you say it was all right for Alton to leave the loudspeaker system in the *bathtub?*

SIDNEY. That clown. *(The phone rings. He picks it up.)* No, no, no . . . *(Find-*

ing it on a wall map of the Village.)
You're in the Eighth Election District.
(*He hangs up.*)

IRIS (*over part of the above—in a tizzy*). And *who* gave this number as the *canvassing* headquarters? (*Shouting.*) I haven't been off the phone all afternoon!

SIDNEY (*to* IRIS, *changing the subject*). Did you see the reviews? We don't have to put on any more. We *know* a celebrity.

DAVID. Will you cut it out.

SIDNEY. Just listen—(*He reads aloud.*) ". . . Mr. Ragin has found a device which transcends language itself. In his work all façade fades, all panaceas dissolve, and the ultimate questions are finally asked of existence itself . . ." (*The obvious joke on himself.*) See. Just like I always said. (SIDNEY *gives him his drink. They toast.* SIDNEY *looks about the room for something. Then to* IRIS, *ever so sweetly, afraid of rousing the dead.*) Oh, Iris, did they leave the mailing piece? We've got all those envelopes to stuff.

IRIS (*shrieking, a veritable avenging Fury by now*). Sidney, if you don't get that trash out of here *today*, I'm going to *burn* the apartment down!!!

(SIDNEY *finds the enclosures, stacks them on the table and begins stuffing envelopes, whistling as he does—all but ignoring* DAVID.)

DAVID. By your recent antics I take it you believe there is something to be accomplished by all this? Presumably for the good?

SIDNEY (*not taking the bait, gaily*). C'mon, David. There is work to be done. Lend a hand. (*The phone rings. He answers*). Yes? No, it's *not* a mistake . . . Fourth Street *does* cross Eleventh Street.

(*He hangs up, goes back to work.*)

DAVID (*studying him as a specimen*). Well, I don't attack you for it. I know it is something most men, even thinking men, resist long after they know better.

SIDNEY (*between envelopes, not even raising his eyes*). You mean that Zarathustra has spoken—and God is dead?

DAVID. Yes.

SIDNEY. "Progress" is an illusion and the only reality is—nothing?

DAVID. You surprise me. Can one debate it?

SIDNEY (*finally sitting back for this; he feels himself in fine fettle*). One can observe that it is the debate which is, for all human purposes, beside the point. The *debate* which is absurd. The "why" of why we are here is an intrigue for adolescents; the "how" is what must command the living. Which is why I have lately become an insurgent again.

(*Back to work. The phone rings again —and this time* IRIS *comes shrieking out of the bedroom: one more call and she will* burn *the apartment down! She wears the dress* MAVIS *bought.*)

IRIS. Sid-nee—(*Noticing* DAVID *for the first time.*) David. (*Genuinely.*) My God, those reviews! It's marvelous. How do you feel?

SIDNEY (*on the phone*). You don't say? Right . . . right . . . right.

DAVID (*to* IRIS; *embarrassed by her display*). Please. Well, I've got to go to work.

IRIS. Work? Already? Aren't you just going to bask awhile or something?

DAVID (*sadly*). Doing what? See you. (*Exits.*)

SIDNEY (*hangs up*). You know what, the craziest thing is happening to Wally . . . that clown is actually—(*As the fact of* MAVIS's *dress dawns on him.*) Well, get you!

IRIS. I look pretty all right in this—huh, Sid?

SIDNEY. Sure, if you like the type. I like you in other things better.

IRIS. I know. I'm going out tonight, Sidney.

SIDNEY. Yeah? Where? (*Not thinking about that too much.*) You know not one, not one of the entire collection I've surrounded myself with . . .

IRIS. I talked to Lucille Terry today. She's having a cocktail party.

SIDNEY. Lucille Terry? *Lucille Terry!* Where in the name of God did she pop up from? I didn't know that you still saw each other.

IRIS. We haven't in years. But, you know, just like that people suddenly call each other up. So just like that she called me up last week about this party she was having.

SIDNEY (*his hand on the phone; he couldn't care less*). How is Lucy? Lemme see now, gotta call Mickey Dafoe, put on the old Establishment voice. "Hello, Mr. Dafoe, well, how are you, sir—" Fix me a drink, why doncha, honey?

IRIS (*crossing to the pantry; in a muted*

voice). Lucy didn't call me, Sid. I called her.

SIDNEY (*still thinking more about the call he has to make*). Yeah? You know I really hate to give fuel to Alton's narrow view of the world, but there is turning out to be a surprising amount of validity to his notions of base and superstructure. Two banks, a restaurant and three real estate firms have already canceled ads since we've come out for Wally . . .

IRIS (*disinterested, bringing him his drink*). Oh, really—(*The phone rings.*) Interesting.

SIDNEY (*picking it up*). Yes, Renee . . . She says what? . . . *Sure,* O'Hara could be an Italian name . . . Or his *mother's* Italian. (*Hangs up, to* IRIS.) Well, she *could* be. (*Noticing her standing there, finally just looking at him quietly.*) Aw, I'm sorry, honey, I really am, but I just don't feel like going to any party tonight. Especially the uptown scene. Not tonight. (*He is taking the entire situation lightly.*) Tell Lucy we love her but no.

IRIS (*starkly, staring down at him*). I wasn't asking you to come with me, Sidney.

(*He drinks, slowly absorbs this last remark and, for the first time, reacts with some sense of the portentousness of the moment.*)

SIDNEY. Oh?

IRIS. That's sort of the point. I—I am going alone.

SIDNEY. Oh. (*They are both quiet; neither looking at the other; the awkwardness shouts.*) Well, hell, so you're going to a party. Great. You should do things alone sometimes. Everybody should. What are we acting so funny about it for?

IRIS. Because we know it isn't just *a* party. It's the fact that I want to go. That I called Lucy.

SIDNEY (*very worried*). Well, don't worry about it. It's okay. Just have a nice time, that's all.

IRIS (*sadly*). Would you—would you like me to make you some supper before I go?

SIDNEY (*rising and crossing away not to face her*). Uh—no. No. Thanks. Wally and I are due on MacDougal Street in an hour. We'll go out with the kids after or something.

IRIS. You could have them here. There's

—there's a lot of stuff in the box and—plenty of beer.

SIDNEY (*getting it fully*). Is there?

IRIS. Yes. I'm sorry, Sid.

SIDNEY. You're planning on being late, aren't you?

IRIS. I think it'll be kind of late.

SIDNEY (*finally*). Who's going to be at this party, Iris?

IRIS. How do I know who's going to be there? Lucy's friends.

SIDNEY. Lucy's friends. The "would-be" set, as I recall it.

IRIS. Huh?

SIDNEY. The "would-be" set, would-be actresses, would-be producers. The would-bes tend to collect around Lucy a lot.

IRIS. Some of her friends are pretty successful.

SIDNEY. Like Ben Asch?

(*She wheels and they exchange a violent conversation without words.*)

IRIS (*getting into her shoes*). Look, Sid; let's make an agreement based on the recognition of reality. The reality being that the big thaw has set in with us and that we don't know what that means yet. So let's make some real civilized kind of agreement that until—well—until we know just what we feel, I mean about everything—let's not ask each other a whole lot of slimy questions.

SIDNEY. I'll ask all the slimy questions I want! Listen, Iris, have you been seeing this clown or something?

IRIS. Only once—after the time I told you.

SIDNEY. Once is all it takes.

IRIS. He thinks he can help me.

SIDNEY. Do what?

IRIS. Break in, that's what!

SIDNEY. Then why didn't he see *us?*

IRIS. I don't know, Sidney. I guess he was under the impression that I was a big girl now.

SIDNEY. I'll bet!

IRIS. But none of this is the main point, Sid. The main point is that I feel I want to do something else with my life. Other than—

SIDNEY. Other than what?

IRIS. Other than—this. Other than conversation about the Reformation; other than conversations about Albert Camus. Other than scraping together enough pancake money to study with every has-been actor who's teaching now because he can't work any more. There has to be another way.

SIDNEY. From the has-beens to the would-bes. I'll admit there is a progression there!

IRIS. Ben knows some extremely influential people. People who have been around —people who *do* the things they mean to do.

SIDNEY. Where?

IRIS. In the theatre and in politics too! Especially in politics. People who are not just talkers—but doers. Who do not take on a newspaper they cannot even afford and run it into the ground for a hopeless campaign. And for what? For Wally? If even half of what they say about Wally is true—

SIDNEY. Oh? And just what do "they" say?

(*He waits, knowing as he does, there is nothing she can say.*)

IRIS (*trapped*). Well, I don't know about any of this, but Lucy thinks—

SIDNEY (*holding up one hand; the issue is closed*). Right the first time, Iris! You *don't* know.

IRIS. Sidney, this is not the Silver Dagger you're getting into. These people are sharks.

SIDNEY (*with finality; father knows best*). Look, Iris, I'll make a deal with you: You let me fight City Hall and I'll stay out of Shubert Alley.

IRIS (*quietly; she has had it*). All right, Sidney.

SIDNEY. And stop ducking the main point: What is this glorious doer Ben Asch going to do for you?

IRIS. As a matter of fact he's already got me some work.

SIDNEY. Oh—why haven't you mentioned it? What show?

IRIS (*defensively*). It isn't exactly a show—but it *is* acting. Sort of. (*He stares at her.*) It's a TV commercial . . .

SIDNEY (*laughing*). Oh, Iris, Iris.

IRIS (*hotly*). Oh, aren't we better than everybody, Sidney Brustein! Aren't we above it! Well, I have news: If he gets me that job, I am going to take it. And when I'm doing it—I'll know that it beats hell out of slinging hash while I wait for "pure art" to come along.

SIDNEY. Iris, it's not just *what* you're getting into—it's *how*. You've got no business hanging out with Lucy and that crowd. How can it be that after five years of life with me you don't know better than this?

(*He has taken hold of her.*)

IRIS (*exploding, near tears*). I have learned *a lot* after five years of life with you, Sidney! When I met you I thought Kant was a stilted way of saying cannot; I thought Puccini was a kind of spaghetti; I thought the louder an actor yelled and fell out on the floor the greater he was. But you taught me to look deeper and harder. At everything: from Japanese painting to acting. Including, Sidney, my *own* acting. Thanks to you, I now know something I wouldn't have learned if it hadn't been for you. The fact . . . the *fact* that I am probably the world's *lousiest* actress . . . (*He releases her.*) So, there it is, the trouble with looking at ourselves honestly, Sidney, is that we come up with the truth. And, baby, the truth is a bitch.

(*Iris goes out the door.*)

SIDNEY (*going after her*). Iris, Iris, just listen—

IRIS (*facing him; resolutely; she will not be stopped*). All I know is that, from now on, I just want something to happen in my life. I don't much care *what*. Just something.

SIDNEY. I just want you to know that— whatever happens—you've been one of the few things in my life that made me happy.

IRIS (*an anguished voice—for both of them*). Oh, Sid, "happy." (*She reaches up, to touch his face a moment.*) Whoever started that anyhow? What little bastard was it? Teaching little kids there was such a thing?

(*She exits.* SIDNEY *goes back inside, sits, goes to the drawing board, then leaves that and picks up his banjo and then, with resolution, steps to the door and throws it open.*)

SIDNEY. Hey—David . . . David! Can you come down a sec—

(*But* DAVID *is right there, on his way out—rather sheepish, more boyish, genuine than in his prior scenes.*)

DAVID (*a grin*). Oh, you caught me. Waaaal, I decided to go out after all. Maybe I owe myself, under the circumstances, at least one night off. (*He continues, halts, comes back.* SIDNEY *hardly hears him; he is thinking of something intently*.) I'll tell you the truth . . . It— it seemed emptier than usual up there. I swore I wouldn't, you know—(*Embarrassed at the humanity of his present feelings*.) sort of go out and strut around . . . But by God, it's almost like I *have* to. Do you know what I mean? I mean— (*He laughs freely and drops his hands*.) I mean I *feel pretty good*.

SIDNEY (*half steering, half pushing him inside*). Well, why not! Who wouldn't? . . . C'mon in a sec . . .

DAVID (*suddenly, not aware that he is mainly talking to himself under the circumstances*). Don't make fun of me, Sidney! The truth is, today is not yesterday. Nothing could have made me believe this yesterday— But I am somebody else today. Inside. It's in my rooms upstairs, it's in my coat . . . it's in my skin. Christ, Sid—(*Pure unadulterated wonder*.) *I'm famous*. (*A grin*.) I have to go outside and find out what it's like to wear it in the streets. (*Sobering*.) As if I can't guess. Everybody will just be more self-conscious, phonier than they would have been yesterday. Just because my picture was in the papers. It's crazy. The phone keeps on ringing. For years I made fun of people who had unlisted numbers. First thing Monday—I'll have to get one. (*Final smile*.) G'night, Sid.

SIDNEY. No, wait a minute. Please. I'd like to talk to you. You want a drink?

DAVID. What do you want, Sidney? I'm in a hurry!

SIDNEY (*not looking at him*). Hey— David . . . it's as good as on, isn't it?

DAVID (*turning*). What—?

SIDNEY (*a little madly*). Your next play. It's as good as on—isn't it? Every producer in town will be looking for it, won't they?

DAVID (*annoyed to talk about this; a modest person in the true sense*). Well . . . my agent said there've been some calls already—(*A sigh about producers*.) First you can't get into their offices—

SIDNEY. You're very talented, David.

DAVID. I have to go.

(*He turns on his heels to leave*.)

SIDNEY. No. Look, remember we went once, together, to see that thing that Iris was in a couple of years ago?

DAVID. Yes?

SIDNEY. Well, you thought she was pretty good. Even better than I thought she was, didn't you? You said so.

DAVID. Those were my polite years. When I still cared what people thought about me.

SIDNEY. No, come on, you said that you thought what she did was pretty good.

DAVID. When she just danced. When she spoke, when she had lines, it was horrible.

SIDNEY. Well, now, *not horrible*. Just average.

DAVID. What do you want, Sidney?

SIDNEY. She's a hung-up kid, David. She needs something to happen for her, before she gets all turned around sideways.

DAVID (*unrelentingly*). What is it that you want, Sidney?

SIDNEY (*sitting and turning away from the other man*). Write her into your play, David. Something for her. Something simple that she can do. With dancing.

DAVID (*absorbing it; pressing his lips together with sadness and pulling his collar up about his ears*). I have to go now, Sid.

SIDNEY. It wouldn't have to be a big part, for Christ's sake! Look, she *needs* something to happen for her, don't you understand?

DAVID. You solve your marriage problems any way you have to, Sidney. I won't judge you, but don't bring them to me.

SIDNEY. I'll do the review—

(*Catching* DAVID *in the door*, SIDNEY *stops himself, amazed at the thought*.)

DAVID (*turning slowly back to him*). What did you say? (SIDNEY *is quiet, knowing the enormity of his error*.) Okay, I'll pretend I never heard you. I am going out now, Sidney. I don't need to experience the other part of this scene. The recovery of Morality and all that. That's *up*town drama. I can't stand those. I'll go and let you have this one all by yourself.

(*He starts out again, fast*. SIDNEY *grabs him*.)

SIDNEY. What's so awful about it? Can't you write about more than two characters at a time? How could it hurt?

DAVID. Just in case you don't understand me at all, Sidney, I'll tell you something. Prostitutes interest me clinically; I've not the least intention of ever becoming one. (*Crossing close to* SIDNEY *so that they are face to face.*) Now I'll tell you something else. Look into this cynic's eyes, Sidney. Go ahead, look! And finally understand what these pools of implacable cynicism stand for! It's integrity, Sidney.

SIDNEY (*in profound humiliation*). Don't feel so holy about it, David. I asked and you refused. Let's forget it. It was such a little—such a tiny little act on the part of a slightly desperate man.

DAVID. Such a tiny little corruption. Not three people in the whole world would ever really care whether or not my little insignificant play did or did not have its unities stretched to just happen to include a part for your wife in trade for a patch of glowing praise in your paper. Not three people in the whole world. That's the magic of the tiny corruptions, isn't it, Sidney? Their insignificance makes them so appealing.

SIDNEY (*profoundly embarrassed*). All right. I asked and you refused. Let's forget it.

DAVID (*all warmth has receded; his voice is tight, harsh and cold*). Well, thanks for something, anyway. I was really too mellow to go out in this world. Too vulnerable. I would have been torn to pieces. But you've fixed that. I'm ready for it now.

(WALLY *has crossed outside and enters in high jubilance, doing minstrel kicks, wiggling his hat above his head.*)

WALLY (*singing, clowning*).
"When the red, red, robin
Comes bob, bob, bobbin' along—!"

DAVID (*dryly*). Enter, the future.

WALLY (*halting the clowning; to* DAVID). Could be, could be. (*Facetiously, flippantly in high spirits.*) Allow me to offer the grim Past a leaflet. (*To* SIDNEY.) You should have seen the crowd on Hudson Street. Sidney, there is something *happening!*

DAVID (*demonstratively crumpling the leaflet and letting it fall to the floor*). It is my fondest hope and greatest expectation that one of these days the hoods will just get tired of you children and wrap you up in sacks and drop you in the river as in the old days.

WALLY. Well now—(*Nodding up and down, as if to encourage. Facetiously.*) There is an utterance from the very bowels of disenchantment. The only problem is, young man, you wear it badly. Those

French intellectuals you aim to be imitating have a few things weighing on them that you don't know very much about. Including two world wars and the loss of an empire. What's weighing *you* down, David? As far as I have ever been able to make out from your writings— some problem or other about your mother?

DAVID. Your friend—(*Angry, but not wishing to show it.*) is very clever, isn't he, Sidney? (*To* SIDNEY *alone.*) Put his remarks alongside the little proposition you just made me and see what you think of my disgust with both of you.

(*He turns and exits.*)

WALLY (*limp-wristedly*). "Well, I hope yew got that!"

SIDNEY. Cut it out. He's not swish. (*Dully.*) Aside from which, he's right.

WALLY. Ah me, ah me: pessimism is weighing heavily on the land. I wonder why. How's Iris?

SIDNEY. Fine.

WALLY. What's happening?

SIDNEY. What do you mean what's happening?

WALLY. She seems to be spending a lot of time lately with the girl friend of one of my poker-playing buddies, that's all.

SIDNEY. If you were married, you'd understand. Things get a little strained . . .

WALLY. Seems like a funny crowd for Iris. (*Noticing suddenly that* SIDNEY *is doubled over with pain.*) What's the matter?

SIDNEY. My ulcer is having a rock-and-roll party.

WALLY. Where's your medicine? I'll get it for you.

SIDNEY. In the bathroom. The brown bottle. (*Bitterly.*) They're tranquilizers.

WALLY (*reading from the bottle*). Says you're supposed to take one every morning. Didn't you take it?

SIDNEY. No.

WALLY. Why not?

SIDNEY. Because I hate them.

WALLY. Don't be such a nut. You should take them. It keeps you from getting upset about every little thing. That's the point of them.

(*He hands the pills to* SIDNEY, *who is sitting in the rocker.*)

SIDNEY (*turning his head slowly to his friend*). "Every little thing," huh, Wally? (*Reaching out and taking the pill and the water and setting them carefully in front of him on the table.*) Yes, by all means hand me the chloroform of my passions; the sweetening of my conscience; the balm of my glands. (*Lifting the pills like Poor Yorick's skull.*) Oh blessèd age! That has provided that I need never live again in the full temper of my rage. (*Rising and crossing to drawing board, he picks up a yardstick, which, in his hand, becomes the "sword" of the speech.*) In the ancient times, the good men among my ancestors, when they heard of evil, strapped a sword to their loins and strode into the desert; and when they found it, they cut it down —or were cut down and bloodied the earth with purifying death. But how does one confront these thousand nameless faceless vapors that are the evil of our time? Could a sword pierce it? (*Turning his eyes to* WALLY.) Look at me, Wally . . . Wrath has become a poisoned gastric juice in the intestine. One does not *smite* evil any more: one holds one's gut, thus —and takes a pill. (*As he rises suddenly to full Jovian stance.*) Oh, but to take up the sword of the Maccabees again! (*He closes down from the mighty gesture and sets down the "sword," then turns and lamely takes his pill and water.*) L'chaim!

QUICK FADEOUT

CURTAIN

Scene Three

TIME: *Election night. Early fall.*

In the darkness, the sounds of a not-too-far-distant victory celebration are heard: shouting, cheers and jubilation, the indistinct electronic mumble of a loudspeaker, and "The Wally O'Hara Campaign Song" —not sung this time by a few, but taken over by the whole crowd. Now and then a distinct shout "Wally!" or "O'Hara" can be heard to cut through.

AT RISE: SIDNEY *enters, in this spirit, and fumbles for his key in the entrance. The phone rings within. He leaves the door ajar as he crosses to the phone, snatching up glass and bottle en route. The sound dims somewhat but continues under.*

SIDNEY (*sheer exhilaration; he is heady with victory, not drink*). Oh—waaal, hello, dere, Mr. Dafoe! (*Fumbling with phone and bottle.*) Oh, I'm right here.

Right here! . . . Yes, yes . . . well, as I'm sure you can understand, we're in no mood to backtrack on anything today, Mr. Dafoe . . . Yes, by God, I am being smug, Mr. Dafoe! Wouldn't you be . . . Don't you realize what happened? Of all the crazy, impossible, illogical . . . Well, it *did* happen. We dead have in fact awakened, Mr. Dafoe! All right then, I will speak to you when I am sober. (*He hangs up and takes the first drink.* ALTON *has entered during the above and has stood quietly with his back to the door waiting for* SIDNEY *to finish.* SIDNEY *sees him—but not his expression.*) Alton, old baby, do you know the main trouble with us believers in this world? *We don't believe!* I didn't believe that what happened today could happen in a million years. That we would win. That little old ladies and big tough truck drivers and little skinny Madison Avenue ad men would all get up today and go out and wipe out the Big Boss in one fell stroke! Can you believe it? (*He sits and savors the wonder, shaking his head back and forth, then drinks again.*) You know what? We don't know anything about the human race, that's what. Not a damn thing when you come down to it. (*Suddenly thinking of a good taunt victim.*) Where's that David? (*Gets up and goes outside. The cheers and sound come up.*) Where is that sad-eyed little bastard today? Twenty years of political history overturned and he goes into hiding. (*shouting up.*) Hey, Strindberg! Where are you? What are you avoiding the partisans for today, huh?

ALTON (*dully*). Leave him alone.

SIDNEY. Leave him alone? I am going to make that sophomoric little elf eat his nineteenth-century profundities with a spoon! Do you know what we proved today, Alton? Do you *realize* what we proved? We proved that what the people need, what they want, is alternatives. Give them alternatives and all the dull stupid negative old shibboleths go up in smoke. Poof! (ALTON *is out of it; standing forlornly in a concentration of his own, not listening, not hearing.*) Look, Alt, do you know how *old* the world is? Not very damn old. Why, the whole frigging planetary system is only five billion years old. By eternity's measure—perhaps one day and one night! Do you get me? . . . And, look, it was only twenty-five million years ago that primitive apes were strolling around at a half stoop, you know what I mean, Alt. And they were apes, *not men,* apes. Just apes. (*Just a touch of liquor's fire as well as his own.*) By God, this is beautiful! Lucidity is positively flowing over me like the sweet oils of Persia! Apes! And between them and us came all the sub boys: Java, Peking, Neanderthal Man and then finally, a long, long time after, finally: Cro-Magnon Man. A mere, a lousy, a nothing of a teensy little thirty thousand years ago. Alton, *he's a baby!* He's an infant!

ALTON (*lifting bleary eyes wearily*). Who, Sidney?

SIDNEY. *Man! The human race!* Yesterday he made a wheel, and fire, so today we're all demanding to know why he hasn't made universal beauty and wisdom and truth too! (*Slumping down, spent.*) A few thousand lousy years he's had to figure out a calendar, and how to make the corn grow; a few lousy years to figure out—*everything.* And we give 'im hell. (*Lifting his eyes with plaintive joy.*) All he needs is a little more time . . . and he'll be all right, doncha think, Alt? Time and alternatives, like today? Maybe—maybe we could get through the whole thing then. You think? (*Noting the other's face finally, which is just staring at him.*) Were you pulling for the other side or something? (*Then rising and laughing and, lifting up his glass, singing Higgin's song from* My Fair Lady.) "I said to him we did it, we did it!" (*Then.*) What the hell is the matter with you?

ALTON (*his eyes trained on* SIDNEY). Is it true, Sid?

SIDNEY (*knowing at once*). Is what true—?

ALTON (*rising*). We've hung out together a long time; don't crap around. Is it true? Is it true she's a hooker? And you were going to let me marry her? (SIDNEY *says nothing; he sits, exhaling a great troubled sigh.*) Why didn't you tell me?

SIDNEY (*staring at the floor*). It wasn't my place to do so. It was for Gloria to tell you. People change. She'll change. She needs someone. Just don't make me sick today, Alton. Just don't act like a fraternity boy meeting his own girl under the lamppost.

ALTON. How would you act? (*They*

stare at one another.) When you go into the mines, Sid, you get coal in your skin; if you're a fisherman, you reek of fish! . . . She doesn't *know* how to love any more, it's all a performance. It has to be.

SIDNEY (*avoiding a direct reply*). If you could understand it, there is a great compliment to you in how I treated this, Alt. The compliment that I thought you could be man enough to absorb, and help Gloria like you wanted to help the rest of the world once. (ALTON *just laughs*)

ALTON. Talk to me man to man today, Sidney: Would you marry her?

SIDNEY. Alton, for Christ's sake! You were a revolutionary! Doesn't that stand for anything any more? It is one thing to take bread to the Bowery and another to eat it with them!

ALTON. *Would you marry her?*

SIDNEY. If I loved her . . . I don't know how to say it to you except that if I loved her . . .

ALTON (*screaming*). Don't you know some of the things these girls have to do?

SIDNEY. All right, I know. You are afire with all the images; every faceless man in the universe has become—

ALTON. Someone who has coupled with my love . . . used her like . . . an . . . inanimate object . . . a thing, an instrument . . . a commodity . . .

SIDNEY (*with supreme compassion for all*). In an effort to assuage something of his own pathetic needs, Alton . . .

ALTON. A commodity! (*Looking up at* SIDNEY.) Don't you understand, Sidney? (*Rubbing his head.*) Man, like I am spawned from commodities . . . and their purchasers. Don't you *know* this? I am running from being a commodity. How do you think I got the color I am, Sidney? Haven't you ever thought about it? I got this color from my grandmother being used as a commodity, man. The buying and the selling in this country began with *me.* Jesus, help me.

SIDNEY. All right.

ALTON. You don't understand . . . My father, you know, he was a railroad porter . . . who wiped up spit and semen, carried drinks and white man's secrets for thirty years . . . When the bell rang in the night he put on that white coat and his smile and went shuffling through the corridors with his tray and his whisk broom . . . his paper bags and his smile to wherever the white men were ringing . . . for thirty years. And my mother . . . she was a domestic. She always had, Mama did . . . bits of this and bits of that from the pantry of "Miss Lady," you know . . . some given, some stolen . . . And she would always bring this booty home and sit it all out on the kitchen table . . . So's we could all look at it . . . And my father . . . all the time he would stand there and look at it and walk away. And then one night, he had some kind of fit, and he just reached out and knocked all that stuff, the jelly, and the piece of ham; the broken lamp and the sweater for me and the two little vases . . . He just knocked it all on the floor and stood there screaming with the tears running down his face . . . "I ain't going to have the white man's leavings in my house, no mo'! I ain't going to have his *throw-away* . . . no mo'! . . ." And Mama, she just stood there with her lips pursed together and when he went to bed she just picked it all up, whatever hadn't been ruined or smashed, and washed it off and brushed it off and put it in the closet . . . and we *ate* it and *used* it . . . because we had to *survive,* and she didn't have room for my father's pride . . . I don't want white man's leavings, Sidney. I couldn't *marry* her. (*Getting up, and taking out a piece of paper.*) I wrote her a note.

SIDNEY. Aren't you even going to see her? (ALTON *drops his head.*) And if she was a black woman? (*It hangs.*) That's racism, Alt.

ALTON. I know it—(*Touching his head.*) here!

SIDNEY (*sadly, looking at him*). But— "A star has risen over Africa—"

ALTON (*looking back at him*). Yes.

SIDNEY. Over Harlem . . . over the south side . . .

ALTON. Yes.

SIDNEY. The new Zionism is raging . . . (ALTON *hands him the note, turns.*) Aren't you even going to see her?

ALTON (*from the door, in anguish*). No. I don't ever want to see her.

(*He runs off.* SIDNEY *follows him out.*)

SIDNEY. You are afraid that you would forgive her! And you don't want to do that, do you?

(*Stands looking after him as the sounds of the victory celebration—not the song*

now, *but the loudspeaker and crowd— envelop him. Presently* MAVIS *enters.*)

MAVIS. Sidney Brustein!

(*Arms outstretched, coming to him fast, sincerely impressed and overwhelmed. She steers him into the apartment, the closing door shuts out the sound.*)

MAVIS. Who'd of ever thought it! First thing when Fred saw the paper this afternoon, he called me from the office and said, "Mav, that brother-in-law of yours is some kind of political genius!" He's so excited. Why, he said that everybody is talking about you and the paper and Wally O'Hara. He said that it even went out on the national news. (*She has hugged and kissed him through most of this.*) Let's have a drink together, Sidney. I don't know how to tell you how proud I am. I just thought it was another one of those things that you are always doing—like with the night club—(*Correcting herself.*) I know, it wasn't a night club—and all. Where is everyone? . . . I thought this place would be—you know—

SIDNEY (*fixing her a drink*). —"jumping." I wasn't the candidate, Mav. Iris hasn't come in yet. Sometimes she stops off for the groceries . . .

MAVIS. Groceries! Aren't you kids going out and celebrate? Honest to God, you're so strange— You don't even look happy.

SIDNEY. Oh, I'm happy . . . It's kind of freakish though, you know, that we won. We never dreamed we would. (*To himself, with wonder.*) We never dreamed we would.

MAVIS (*takes a check out of her bag and puts it in* SIDNEY's *shirt pocket*). Here's a little present, for the paper. (*Noting his astonishment.*) From *Fred,* let's say. No, don't talk about it. Don't say a word. There it is. That's all.

SIDNEY (*looking at it*). This is a *lot* of money, honey.

MAVIS (*drinking*). I said let's not mention it and I mean it. When I—that is when *Fred*—decided that he would give it to you we agreed that we didn't want any chance whatsoever to feel good and gooey and Real Big about it. So—put it away.

SIDNEY (*looking at her, touched*). Well, thank—you—(*With great ostentation, this error.*) Oh, I mean, *Fred* for it.

MAVIS (*warmly*). Shut up. (*Looking at him, the liquor warming and freeing her.*)

I'm glad to have a chance to talk with you, Sidney. Alone. We've never really talked —I know that you don't like me—

SIDNEY (*because that remark must embarrass anyone*). Mavis—

MAVIS. No, it's all right. I know it. You know it. When you come down to it, what is there to like? Isn't it funny how different sisters can be?

SIDNEY. Yes, different. All of us. Everything.

MAVIS. Yeeesss, don't I know it. I was trying to explain that to Fred the other day. (*A little laugh.*) I don't mean I was trying to "explain" it . . . That sounds so funny: Fred isn't a stupid man, as we all know—but sometimes. Sometimes I get to thinking that certain kind of way. The way, you know, that *you* do—(*With her hands, a circle, and aptly, the universe.*) of a whole—

SIDNEY. In abstractions.

MAVIS. That's right. You won't believe it—but—I enjoy it when a person can say something so that it embraces a lot, so that it's in—in

SIDNEY (*staring at her*). Concepts.

MAVIS. Yes. I enjoy it. I've enjoyed the conversations I've heard down here. And, Sidney, I've understood some of them. (*There is a curious, believable and quite charming defiance in this announcement.*)

SIDNEY. Good for you, Mavis. Good for you.

MAVIS (*oddly*). But we get stuck, you know.

SIDNEY. Hmmm?

MAVIS. Some of us, we get stuck, in— (*Stiltedly.*) the original stimuli. Some of us never have a chance, you know—

SIDNEY (*nodding wearily, not wishing to hear this saga again*). I know—

MAVIS. Like Papa—he was such a dreamer. You know, sort of backwoods poet, kind of a cross between Willy Loman and Daniel Boone. He loved just sitting and thinking—

SIDNEY (*looking at her, stunned*). Didn't you and Iris have the same father?

MAVIS. Of course we had the same father! What do you think I'm talking about?

SIDNEY. *Rashomon*—what else?

MAVIS. He was a very wonderful man, very wonderful. And that's the joke on me—I thought, I thought I was marrying someone like Papa when I married Fred. Can you imagine—*Fred!*

SIDNEY. You mean you *wanted* him to be like your father?

MAVIS. Yes . . . and that's the way I thought Fred was, in those days. He *seemed* poetic—when he was young. Do you know that Fred used to drive in forty miles from Ellensville to see me when we were courting? Forty miles and then back forty, and in the world's worst car. That's what he was like then. Like Papa. (*A little high.*) Papa used to read the classics to us, you know, Greek tragedy. Sometimes in Greek.

SIDNEY (*wide-eyed*). You are pulling my leg.

MAVIS (*surprised*). Why? Oh, he didn't really know *classical* Greek, Sidney. Just everyday Greek from his folks, but that made it interesting . . . we used to do little productions in our living room. He would always let me be Medea, because he said I was strong—(*She rises and bellows forth in robust, dramatic and effective Greek the following, enriching it with not badly conceived if stagey classical stance and gesture.*) Ὁ πόνος μέ περικυκλώνει ἀπό ὅλες τίς μεριές καί ποιός μπορεῖ νά τό ἀμφισβητήση. Ἀλλά δέν χάθηκαν ἀκόμα ὅλα. Νομίζω ὄχι. (*Then in English, the first line or so, rather rattled off.*) "On all sides sorrow pens me in. Who can gainsay this? But all is not yet lost! Think *not* so. Still there are troubles in store for the new bride and for her bridegroom—" Well, *he* thought I was good.

SIDNEY. Mavis, I don't know you.

MAVIS. The ham part, I know. (*A little laugh.*) I know all the parts—and all the strophes. Sure, Papa was something! He was a man of great, great imagination. That's why he changed our name. It was plain old everyday Parodopoulos, you know—

SIDNEY. No, I didn't know.

MAVIS. But Papa wanted something, you know, *symbolic*. So he changed it to Parodus. You know what the parodus is in the development of Greek tragedy.

SIDNEY. Ah . . . no.

MAVIS (*proudly*). Sidney! Shame on you! The parodus is the chorus! And you know —no matter what is happening in the main action of the play—the chorus is always there, commenting, watching. He said that we were like that, the family, at the edge of life—not changing anything. Just watching and being.

SIDNEY (*struck*). I see.

MAVIS. That was Papa, dramatic as hell. (*Drinking her drink.*) I loved him very much. (*A beat.*) And Fred's no Papa.

SIDNEY. It's been one big disappointment, your marriage?

MAVIS (*dully*). Not for a minute. I knew by the time that Fred and I got married that he wasn't the Fred he seemed to be. I knew what I was marrying and I was right. Solid as a rock. Hah! (*Abruptly.*) We haven't touched each other more than twice since little Harry was born and that's . . . oh, six years now, isn't it? Harry will be six next month.

SIDNEY. Ah—by whose—

MAVIS. —design? Who knows? It just happens. (*Waving her hand.*) He doesn't suffer. He's got a girl.

SIDNEY (*gutturally*). Fred?

MAVIS (*looking at him*). Fred. (*Shaking her head.*) Sometimes I think you kids down here believe your own notions of what the rest of the human race is like. There are no squares, Sidney. Believe me when I tell you, everybody is his own hipster. Sure, for years now. Same girl, I'll say that for old Fred. I've met her.

SIDNEY (*he would genuinely like to seem blasé but he can't; he is truly astonished*). You have—?

MAVIS (*all with bitter restraint*). Oh sure. I went there. He has her all set up. Nothing fancy; Fred's strictly a family man, he puts the main money in the main place, our Fred. But decent, you know, respectable building, family people—a nice place for a single girl—(*The ultimate bitterness.*) with a kid. (*He absorbs this with a silent start but knows to say nothing.*) He's just a year younger than Harry. I saw him too. (*Now she is crying; SIDNEY is helpless in the face of this.*) You do find out. And I did the usual: I hired a sordid little man to find out for sure. He did. And so, one day, I did what a woman has to do: I went to see. Not the spooky thing, I didn't want to come in on them together or any of that junk. I know what a man and a woman do; I just wanted to meet her. So I got in a cab, got out, rang a bell and there she was. Nothing like expected! Not a chorine or something as you always think, even with Fred—in my mind I had decided it would be some cheap mess; but

no, there's this sandy-haired kid standing in pedal pushers and an apron, pregnant as all get-out. So I said I rang the wrong bell. And I went back, once, several months later—to see the baby. In the park. I had to see the baby. I didn't tell Fred about my knowing until after I saw the baby. And then, after that we went through the usual waltz . . . Divorce talk, all of it, you know.

SIDNEY. And then you decided against it.

MAVIS. Of course I decided against it. A divorce? For what? Because a marriage was violated? Ha! We've got three boys and their father is devoted to them; I guess he's devoted to all four of his boys. And what would I do? There was no rush years ago at home to marry Mavis Parodus; there was *just* Fred *then*. In this world there are two kinds of loneliness and it is given to each of us to pick. I picked. And, let's face it, *I* cannot type.

SIDNEY (*quietly shaking his head*). But you want only simple people and simple problems in literature . . .

MAVIS. Sure, isn't life enough?

SIDNEY. Does Iris know any of this?

MAVIS. What would I tell her for? Listen, we all play our roles. (*Long beat.*) Well, one thing is sure. I do not need another drop to drink. (*Fixing herself, compact in hand.*) So how is my cream-colored brother-in-law-to-be?

SIDNEY. He's not going to be.

MAVIS. Well, thank God for something. She broke it off, huh?

SIDNEY (*looking up, absorbing the assumption*). Yes . . . I guess so.

MAVIS (*blithe ignorance again*). It had to be. Look, the world's not ready. It just isn't. He seemed like a nice boy and all that, but it's just not possible. I mean in this world, you know. You have to think about children, you know. I knew Gloria would snap out of it. Why would she want to get into something like that? I mean he's very light, but—(*Halting.*) I'm not fooling you, am I?

SIDNEY. No.

MAVIS. I can't help it, Sid. It's the way I feel. You can't expect people to change that fast.

(*She gets up to go.*)

SIDNEY (*gently, more with wonder than assertion*). Mavis, the world is about to crack right down the middle. We've gotta change—or fall in the crack.

MAVIS (*not angrily*). Well, I think we are back to ourselves and you are probably starting to insult me again. I knew I was going to tell you about it though, Sid —one of these days. I always knew that. Since I first saw you I knew those eyes could find a place for anybody's tale. Don't talk to Iris about it . . . I know I don't have to ask it of you, but all the same. Don't, huh? She's a kid, Sidney. She doesn't know what she's all about yet. She will, she'll get herself together one of these days. (*Patting his cheek.*) And so will you. (*Looking at him.*) Gee, we're proud of you, Sid. I told Fred, "Say what you will, but the Jews have get-up!"

SIDNEY (*in that kind of mood*). Say what you will.

MAVIS. Now, there was nothing wrong with that, was there?

SIDNEY (*smiling*). Well, let's say there isn't. Today. (*A beat. She opens the door and we hear again the sounds of the rally.*) Mavis, what do you do . . . I mean . . . ?

MAVIS. To make up for Fred, you mean? (*As he follows her out, by the stairs.*) I take care of my boys. I shop and I worry about my sisters. It's a life.

SIDNEY (*a beat; gently, lifting his fists to the gods above; it is for their ears only*). "Witness you ever-burning lights above!" (*Then to her.*) You're tough, Mavis Parodus.

(*Kisses her—and, because she does have depth,* MAVIS *says nothing at all as she walks off.* SIDNEY *goes back in, pours a drink and stands looking out his window at the celebration. After a while* IRIS *enters. She looks completely different: she has been costumed somewhere in those precincts of the city where expressions of the couturier's need for yearly change of radical fashion are most evident. Her hair has been cut and teased to a stiff sculpture and tinted an entirely unnatural metallic yellow. She carries two shopping bags.* SIDNEY *is at the window and does not immediately see her.*)

IRIS. Well, congratulations, Sid.

SIDNEY. Your sister was here.

IRIS. Oh? Which one?

SIDNEY. What do you mean, which one?

IRIS. Gloria is due. I didn't get a chance to tell you, but she is in town and she's coming by tonight.

(IRIS *goes into the bedroom.*)

SIDNEY. Oh, my God, that's all I need.

IRIS. Since when aren't you glad to see Gloria?

SIDNEY. I'm always glad to see Gloria . . . Oh, never mind.

IRIS (*emerges with a traveling case*). What did Mavis want?

SIDNEY. Nothing. Just to talk. We talked.

(*He turns and rather freezes at the change in her, but not for comedy.*)

IRIS. I know. It looks pretty different. I won't ask if you like it. (*He is speechless and says nothing at all, merely stares as if he never really has seen her before. Brazening it out.*) I got the job. Just like that— (*A snap.*) they send you out to get fixed. (*She is putting on a new pair of shoes.*) Everything but the shoes. They say it's gauche to walk out of a store in a pair of shoes you've just bought. At least that's what poor people say. I guess nothing is gauche if you're rich enough. (*Wise afterthought.*) *Long* enough. Please don't stare at me like that, Sid. And let's don't discuss it.

SIDNEY (*with thoughtfulness*). Why did you always tell me all those stories about your father, Iris?

IRIS (*looking up*). You and Mavis had yourselves a real little old heart-to-heart, didn't you? What's the world coming to?

SIDNEY. Why did you make him out to be some kind of dull-witted nothing? What was the point of it?

IRIS (*irritably, swiftly, falsely*). Oh, why do you believe Mavis? She has some kind of transference about Papa. It's very complicated. When she talks about Papa she's really talking about this uncle of ours who—

SIDNEY (*knowing that she is going into a long involved lie*). Never mind, Iris. It doesn't matter.

IRIS (*sincerely*). I guess—I just tried to live up to your fantasy about me. All of it. People do that—

SIDNEY. Let's not talk about that—

IRIS. You did a terrific job on the election. You must feel good.

SIDNEY (*vaguely*). Yes, I feel good. (*A beat.*) Mavis said she thought we'd be going out to celebrate. You haven't told her anything then?

IRIS. No . . . who wants to hear all the wailing?

SIDNEY (*looking at her, slowly, with*

emphasis). I have a feeling she'd survive it.

IRIS. Mavis's idea of marriage is something you do at twenty—and it stays that way—*no matter what.* Everything else shocks.

SIDNEY. Sure. Dullsville. (*Several beats; as he studies her and the things she has brought in.*) What do you do? On the— (*Gestures "television."*) thing. I don't even know what the hell it is that you're actually—(*He holds this word for a fraction longer than ordinary meaning would dictate. She has not missed this and so signifies by a lift of brow without, however, comment.*) selling.

IRIS. Home permanents.

SIDNEY (*random gesture, not entirely innocent, circular waving of the hand*). Is that what—uh—they've used on you?

IRIS (*determined not to let him provoke her*). Don't be funny. This head has been in and out of all the booths in Mr. Lionel's for the last two and one half hours.

SIDNEY. But that's not what you are going to tell the people, is it? I mean you're not going to tell them that you got your—(*He reads from the label of a large, golden, elegantly lettered box.*) Golden Girl Curl by sitting in Mr. Lionel's for several hours, are you?

IRIS. No, Sid, that certainly is not what I am going to tell them. I am going— (*Getting up and advancing on the Golden Curl sample.*) to tell all the little housewifes that I just rolled it up on Golden Girl Curl . . . (*Before us, she assumes the manner of TV mannequins, holding up the box, with the slightest edge of hysteria just beneath the surface of her kidding.*) and rollers, using my magic Golden Girl Curl Box to hold everything just so . . . which you understand, is one of the main features of Golden Girl Curl Home Permanent.

SIDNEY. The box it comes in.

IRIS (*with genuine loathing for the whole nonsense, enunciating with contempt*). Yes! The box it comes in! (*She opens it—the bottom falls out and so do the rollers. Hurling it to the floor.*) Which also does not work! (*Wheeling, crying, shrieking.*) It's a job, Sidney! They do not pay you one hundred dollars an hour for hauling hamburgers at Hamlines. They do pay it for pretending that there is some difference between Golden Girl Curl and Wonder Curl, or between Wonder Curl and Home Perma Pearl, so what the hell do you want from me!

SIDNEY. It doesn't work . . .

IRIS (*precisely now in the manner of a defensive child*). It *does* work. It does work enough to justify it. They just send you to the hairdressers to play safe. They have to have everything just so when they tape things for television, Sidney. You don't realize how expensive it is to tape something. All those lights and cameras and technicians . . . they can't have your hair falling down from some . . . (*Swiping at Golden Girl Curl again.*) crappy old home permanent just when they're ready to shoot . . .

SIDNEY (*getting up and going to her and taking her in his arms*). What's the matter, baby, what's happening to you? What's it all about—? What is it you're going after now? What is it that's got you all turned around? Where do you think it's heading you?

IRIS (*in his arms entirely, sobbing out rapidly and incoherently virtually all of the irrelevant parts of her problem.*) Nothing . . . will put a curl in your hair . . . like this but . . . heat . . . But it works *some,* Sid, I did try it . . . Do you think the FTC would let them just put anything . . . on the air . . . like that . . . ?

SIDNEY. Baby—

IRIS (*shrieking—as the old comforting relationship threatens again*). I DON'T WANT TO PLAY APPALACHIAN ANY MORE!

SIDNEY. All right, honey, but there's no reason to get all tied up in new games . . . Iris . . .

IRIS (*shaking her head violently*). You don't understand, you still don't understand. I am not the same . . . I am different . . .

SIDNEY (*laughing, with wonder*). Dear, sweet God . . . I've been living with a little girl . . . Iris, you really *are* a child.

IRIS (*raising her face at that*). Sidney . . . *One* of us here is a child and it's not me . . . I've found out plenty about the world in the last few weeks, and it's nothing like you—or Papa—want it to be . . . Its not! It's not . . . There are things talked about . . . laughed about while you stand there framed by that sign . . . that make me wonder how I ever thought

you knew anything about this world at all
. . . *This* world, Sidney! It's so dirty.

SIDNEY (*rising now and crossing to her
again*). And what I am trying to tell you,
little girl, is that you are learning the
cynicism bit at the wrong time in our lives
. . . (*He is gesturing toward the sign in
the window. The crowd outside is heard
again, muffled cheers and the Campaign
Song.*) We *won* something today, Iris.
Not too much . . . just a little tiny part
of the world turned right side up . . .
Just listen . . .

IRIS (*the final outpouring*). Sidney! *Stop
it! I can't stand it!* You haven't won anything, Sid, they're all the same people!
(*The revelation does not penetrate.*) Don't
you hear me? I tried to tell you . . . They
own Wally . . . The people you've been
fighting . . . Own him completely: the
house he lives in, the clothes on his back,
the toothpaste he uses. *They own* him,
utterly, completely, entirely . . . (*Dragging him to the window.*) There it is,
Sid, the real world! Do you hear it? The
world you say was just turned right side
up!

(*A helpless hysterical gesture of flinging
it at him.*)

SIDNEY (*frantically, shaking his head
"no"—but his eyes saying "yes"*). What
kind of psychotic filth is this?

IRIS. It is filth. You don't know what
filth, you can't *imagine* what filth! But it's
not psychotic. Oh, Jesus, it's not even obscure . . . I have met people who didn't
believe that you didn't know this . . .
Jesus, Sid! I tried to tell you. Look, you
can count on it, in a few months he'll be
having press conferences to explain how
the pinkos and the bohemians duped him
in the first place and how he has found
his way back to the "tried and true leadership" of the . . . "mother party"! (*She
starts out, walking very much like the
dead, picking up her bags. As she opens
the door, the triumphant sounds of the
crowd fill the room.*) I would stay with
you awhile now . . . if it would help anything. But it wouldn't. (*Turning, weeping
freely.*) I'll send for my things some time
this week. Tell Gloria I'll phone her later.
(*Then, suddenly.*) For God's sake, Sidney,
take down that sign! *It's like spit in your
face!*

(*She exits. He reaches up and clutches
the sign for a long moment, the tension*

mounting within him—but then releases
it. Very much like a blind man, he moves
to the drawing board, where his hand
takes up the yardstick—the "sword of his
ancestors"—which he holds aloft before
him, saluting a foe that cannot be cut
down . . . then lets it slip through his
fingers. The sign pulses with a life on its
own; the roar of the crowd grows louder;
SIDNEY snaps the yardstick in half.*)

CURTAIN

ACT THREE

SCENE ONE

TIME: *Several hours later.*

AT RISE: *There is darkened gloom and
quiet in the room and the place is a mess.*
SIDNEY *is stretched out under the coffee
table, in considerable pain; one hand
clutches at a center spot in his lower chest.
An open whiskey bottle and glass are near.
In rough spasms, he harshly hums an old
Yiddish melody, "Rozhankis Mit Man-
dlen."*

Presently, his sister-in-law GLORIA *appears at the door, carrying a small valise.
She is about twenty-six, as lovely as we
have heard, but with surprising, fresh-
faced, wholesome, "all-American" looks.
She has a gleaming, casual, almost col-
legiate long bob, and the clothes are of
that kind of lively smartness rather than
dark elegance. With her valise she reminds
one of a coed home for the weekend and
no other thing. She knocks at the door;
finally tries it and comes in.*

GLORIA (*quizzically looking about in the
shadows*). Sidney? Sidney?

(*She turns on a lamp.*)

SIDNEY (*roaring drunk, as it were*). Stop
it . . . Let there be darkness! . . . Let
the tides of night fall upon us and envelop
us and protect us from the light . . . Shut
it out, shut out the light . . . How do you
like *them* apples, Goethe, old baby? Let
there be darkness, I say! Out, I say! (*Then,
recognizing her.*) Gloria!

GLORIA (*laughing*). You're a nut!

SIDNEY. Gloria! (*She picks him up—
drags him to couch.*)

GLORIA. Where's Iris?

SIDNEY (*singing "The Fireship" in reply: it is a song about a prostitute*).

"She had a bright and roving
　　eye-eye!
And her hair hung down in
　　ring-el-ets!"

(*He folds over and rather gags with pain.*)

"A nice girl, a proper girl, but
　　one of the roving kind!"

GLORIA. You're having an attack—aren't you?

(*Thinks of it, then crosses to the refrigerator and gets a container of milk.*)

SIDNEY. I'm all right!

(*Sings from the prone position.*)

"Her hair hung down in ring-
　　el-ets!"

(*Sitting up suddenly.*)

No, that's not the one.

(*Lifts his head like a howling dog and sings starkly "Come All Ye Fair and Tender Ladies."*)

"If I'da known before I started
I never would have courted none
I'da locked my heart in a box of
　　golden
and fastened it up with a silver
　　pin."

GLORIA (*offering the milk*). Come on, Sidney, you're not all that drunk. C'mon, drink this.

SIDNEY (*drinks, expecting liquor—spits out the milk*).

"Oh don't you remember the
　　days of our courtin'
When your head lay upon my
　　breast—"

GLORIA. What's going on, Sidney?

SIDNEY (*opening his eyes*). Can it be that the fall of man has entirely escaped even *your* notice?

GLORIA. What do you mean?

SIDNEY. All—all that sweat; all that up-all-night; all that, you should excuse the allusion—(*Hissing out the word.*) Passion. All for a mere flunky of Power. (*Gaily.*) Who cares anyhow? The world likes itself just fine the way it is, so don't pick at it. That's all you gotta know about anything: Don't pick at it! (*He has crossed on these lines to the door; he opens it and bellows up.*) Hey, Orpheus, come on down: I'm ready to cross over the Styx. (*He turns around and mugs heavily at* GLORIA.) Get it: I'm just going to hell with myself!

(*He slaps his thigh burlesquing that kind of humor thickly.*)

GLORIA. You need looking after. Where *is* Iris?

SIDNEY. Who? Oh, Iris. My wife. Who the hell knows. (*Wandering around.*) She was one of the lesser goddesses anyhow. A kind of "girl Friday for Zeus," as they put it in *Time* magazine. (*Posing.*) Lookit me, who am I? (*Stands on the couch—in Zeus pose;* GLORIA *can only laugh now.*) Come on, who am I? I'll give you a hint: I'm not Apollo. In fact, I am not a god. (*As Jimmy Durante would say it.*) Ignore my stately bearing for the time being and look in my eyes, and you will see there unmistakable— mortality. (*Collapses again.*) Here I am, Modern Man: flat on my back with an oozing intestine, a bit of a tear frozen in the corner of my eye, a glass of booze which will saturate without alleviating . . . and not the dimmest notion of what it is all about. (*He drinks and sits up.*) And my wife has run off to capture lightning bolts for Zeus. On account of he pays well and you get to meet all of the up and coming young gods and things.

DAVID (*entering, cooly*). Well, I see I have entered in a large moment.

SIDNEY. David, my boy! (*Throws the bottle*). The only man I happen to know personally who is unafraid of the dark. Have a drink.

DAVID. You're drunk and silly and I have a guest.

(*He starts out.*)

SIDNEY. Well, bring her—excuse me— *him* down and we'll have a happening or something.

DAVID. We're already having one, thank you.

SIDNEY (*grabbing hold of him*). All that motion, all that urgency . . . for nothing. That's the whole show, isn't it? A great plain where neither the wind blows, nor the rain falls, nor anything else happens. *Really happens,* I mean. Besides our arriving there and one day leaving again . . . That's what your plays are about, aren't they?

DAVID. Yes, I suppose so.

SIDNEY. Billy said it better than you though: ". . . a tale told by an idiot, full of sound and fury, signifying nothing." Billy said everything better.

DAVID. I won't argue. What's happened?

SIDNEY. Nothing . . . everything . . . And I won't argue with you any more either, David. You're right about everything.

DAVID. Well, at least you are learning.

SIDNEY. Oh yes, and to laugh! Finally. At the colossal absurdity. It's the only refuge, the only cove of endurance. To accept it all and offer back only a cold . . . shadowless stream of laughter. (*Does a vaudeville turn and strikes another especially ludicrous pose. Sings.*)

"Oh, we're lost—out here in the stars!"

(*Turning, as if seeing her for the first time.*) Gloria!

(*He holds out his arms to her. She goes to him and they embrace; there is a quite genuine affection between these two. He holds her rather desperately and, inadvertently, hurts her.*)

SIDNEY. What's the matter?

GLORIA (*covering quickly*). Some bruises. It's all right. Are *you* all right?

(SIDNEY *grabs his mouth; starts for the bathroom with great dignity which he cannot sustain; he breaks and runs in, closing door behind him. She notes* DAVID *fully for the first time.*)

GLORIA. And you must be—

DAVID. David Ragin. Hi.

GLORIA (*with recognition*). From upstairs. Hi. I'm—

DAVID. Gloria. The sister who—"travels a lot." (*As she clearly reacts to his emphasis.*) Oh, it's all right. I practically live here and it's, like, all in the family, no secrets. I do naughty things with boys only—so relax.

GLORIA. You're very free with personal information.

DAVID (*blithely*). Isn't it the great tradition for writers and whores to share the world's truths?

GLORIA (*spinning with astonishment and fury*). Listen, I don't like your language—or you.

DAVID. I'm sorry. I didn't know it would upset you.

GLORIA. Weren't you leaving?

DAVID. I said I was sorry. And I almost never apologize to anyone. I apologized to you—because I respect you.

GLORIA. I said, weren't you leaving?

DAVID. Look—it's okay with me. Relax. I'm writing about a—girl—like you. I cut away all the hypoc—

GLORIA. Look, little boy—(*Sudden strong,*

throaty tones.) I've never met you before, but I have met them like you a hundred times and I know everything you are about to say; because it's been asked and written four thousand times . . . anything I would tell you, you would believe it and put it down and feel like you'd been close to something old and deep and wise. Any bunch of lies I would make up. Well, these are not office hours. Now get the hell out of here!

(*Rising, she winces and catches her side.*)

DAVID. What's hurting you?

GLORIA (*in apparent physical pain*). Please be some kind of gentleman if you—think you can *swing* it and go away.

DAVID (*looking at her hard*). You really don't like your life?!

GLORIA (*her head back, her eyes closed*). The things people think in this world—!

DAVID. Can I get you something?

GLORIA. Just go away!

(*He exits.* SIDNEY *reenters, his head—and shirt—doused with water, affecting sobriety to little avail. He looks a state, crosses to* GLORIA *at the bar, carrying one shoe.*)

SIDNEY (*at the bottle*). Want a drink? Oh, I always forget—about you and your face, the tissues and all.

GLORIA. It's all right—I'm learning to like it. (*Slapping playfully at the under-chin and cheeks.*) Let the damn tissues fall! (*Looking up at him, softly.*) I've quit, Sid. *Really* quit.

SIDNEY (*changing the subject*). How did you—hurt yourself?

GLORIA. I didn't. That's the result of an evening spent with six and one-half feet of psycho. I happen to have a predi— What do you call it?

SIDNEY. Predilection?

GLORIA. Predilection for psychos and vice cops, it's quite amazing! To the point where some of the girls tease me about it. This last one . . . I think he was trying to kill me. It was his thing . . . you know, violence. (*Looking around.*) When's Iris coming? She must be working hard, this place is a wreck!

SIDNEY. She'll be along.

GLORIA (*grinning*). Hey—Sid, lookit me! (*Holding up the glass triumphantly.*) Whiskey. I've joined the human race. No more goofball pills—I'm kicking everything. (*She makes a comic face and their glasses clink.*) I did the whole gooey farewell bit with some of the kids. Adios, Muchachas! I'm going to marry him. Yes, I mean *after* we talk about it. I wouldn't unless I told him. I know girls who've done that. Doesn't work out. Never works out. You run into people. They make up all kinds of nutty things, but it doesn't work out. I'm going to sit down and say —(*A swinging recitation brimming over with confidence to conceal terror below: rehearsed too many times to perfection because she knows it won't work. The voice is bright with an assurance the eyes deny.*) "I was a nineteen-year-old package of fluff from Trenersville, Nowhere, and I met this nothing who took one look at this baby face of mine and said, 'Honey, there's a whole special market for you. Slink is on the way out; all-American wholesomeness is the rage. You've got it made! You'll be part of the aristocracy of the profession!' Which is true. Only it's the profession they don't exactly describe. After that you develop your own rationales to make it all right to yourself: a) It's old as time anyhow; (*They clink glasses loudly and laugh.*) b) (*Hand on heart—for God and country.*) It's a service to society; (*They clink again.*) and c) The *real* prostitutes are everybody else; especially housewives and career girls. (*Again they howl.*) We trade those gems back and forth for hours. Nobody believes it, but it helps on the bad days. And, sweetie, there are a lot of bad days.

SIDNEY. Gloria—no matter what happens, honey, you've got to stick to that.

GLORIA (*glass poised in midair, she lowers it slowly*). Okay, Sid, what is it— a letter or a phonograph record with violins?

SIDNEY. Gloria—

GLORIA (*supreme effort at self-control: to both steel herself for—and hold off— the inevitable*). I was on this date once, Sid. He had a book of reproductions by Goya. And there was this one—an etching, I think. Have you ever seen it? There's this woman, a Spanish peasant woman and she's standing like this— reaching out. And what she's reaching for are the teeth of a dead man. A man who'd been hanged. And she is rigid with—revulsion, but she wants his teeth, because it said in the book that in those days people thought that the teeth of the

dead were good luck. Can you imagine that? The things people think they have to do? To *survive?* Some day I'm going to buy that print. It's all about my life . . .

SIDNEY. He loves you, honey. He loves you terribly . . .

GLORIA (*tough, hoarse urgency: she is ready for it now*). Come on, Sidney! (SIDNEY *hands her the letter. There is presently in the silence only the single hurt outcry of any small creature of the forest, mortally struck. She crumples the letter in her hand. He crosses to her swiftly, tries to comfort her in his arms; she throws back a girlish head and emits now a cry deep, guttural and as primeval as the forest.*) Men! Oh God, men!

SIDNEY (*pouring a drink fast and trying to push it on her*). Come on—drink this for me—

GLORIA. Get that trash out of my face, Sidney. Get it away—(*She knocks it away and rises; he tries to block this, but the inner sense of futility makes it a half-hearted effort.*) Where's my handbag! Get out of my way, Sidney. Come on, who needs this world the way it is! (*Pulling free with a mighty jerk.*) Let go! (*She gets the bag and downs the pills, calming long before the effect, simply because she knows that they are inside.*) You see, no fuss, no muss . . . Drugs are the coming thing, Sid. Do you keep up with all the writings on mescaline and all? I find it fascinating . . . (*She lies down on the sofa. Her reversion is progressive; she is pushing hard for it; not letting the pills do it. Now she is drinking also.*) Ha— you want to hear something! I was going to marry that vanilla dinge! Do you know what some of the other girls do—they go off and they sleep with a colored boy— and I mean *any* colored boy so long as he is black—because they figure that is the one bastard who can't look down on them five seconds after it's over! And I was going to *marry* one!

SIDNEY (*crossing to* GLORIA). Maybe he'll change his mind. He was sort of in a state of shock about it. I mean, try to understand, it's very complicated about Alton—

GLORIA. Oh, so *he's* in a state of shock! Oh Jesus, that yellow-faced bastard! *He's* shocked. Look, Sid, I'll bet you two to one that at this instant he is lying dead drunk in the arms of the blondest or blackest two-bit hooker in town. *Nursing his shock! Telling his tale of woe! His tale!* She'll be telling it somewhere by morning to the girls and roaring with laughter . . . Like I'm doing. Aw, what the hell am I carrying on for—it wouldn't have worked. And besides, the life beats the hell out of that nine-to-five jazz. (*Suddenly a violent sob.*) *Sidney! What happened to my life!* (*He tries to go to her; she holds out a hand to stay him.*) I'll be twenty-six this winter and I have tried to kill myself three times since I was twenty-three . . . I was always awkward . . . But I'll make it. Or maybe a looney trick will be thorough some night. (*Sitting up.*) Well . . . that's enough gloom and doom, everybody! Come on, Sidney brother, cheer up. (*She rumples his hair, nuzzles playfully in a desperate effort at gaiety and release.*) After all, how many things could a nice normal healthy American girl kick all at one time—the racket and the pills? And take on integration, too? Tch! Tch! (*Weaving toward the phonograph.*) Let's have some music. And none of that creepy stuff my creepy father used to play. (*She puts on a record—some very modern jazz; it throbs low and warm and intense.*) Yeah . . . that's good. I have to have music . . . it helps to close things out. It envelops you. (*She beckons and* SIDNEY *moves into her arms; they begin to dance in a tight embrace, he in a bemused and delicious half-stupor; she as if, in the mere physical body contact, she were clinging to life. Now the denaturalization of these moments begins to heighten as per their state. A light, deathly blue, of great transparency, settles slowly and as imperceptibly as possible; it gives way to a hot and sensual fuchsia. The music follows suit—the more familiar jazz sounds going even beyond their own definitions. When each speaks it is stiffly and unnaturally, intoned with a heightened, fragmented delivery beyond sense or sequence, as if lucidity no longer required logic. An absurdist orgy is being created in front of us—a disintegration of reality to parallel the disintegration in* SIDNEY'S *world.*)

GLORIA (*as in a trance*). Things as they are are as they are and have been and will be that way because they got that way be-cause things were as they were in the first place.

(DAVID *reenters and slowly descends the stairs, glancing behind him several times. He stops halfway down to light a cigarette and stands—in silhouette—thoughtfully smoking, while the dialogue continues.*)

SIDNEY. "Society is based on complicity in the common crime . . ." (DAVID *continues down and stands just inside the door, watching* GLORIA *and* SIDNEY *as the sensual heat mounts between them.*) ". . . We all suffer from the murder of the primal father who kept all the females for himself and drove the sons away. So we murdered him and, cannibals that we are, ate him."

DAVID. Sidney, you've finally joined the human race! Welcome to the club.

SIDNEY (*to* DAVID). We are all guilty.

DAVID (*approaching them*). Therefore all guilt is equal.

GLORIA. Therefore none are innocent.

SIDNEY, DAVID *and* GLORIA (*together*). Therefore—

SIDNEY (*inspired*). None are guilty. (*He breaks from* GLORIA. *Facing audience, assumes his own parodied version of classic Hindu dance pose: standing on one foot, knee bent, the other up at right angles, toes turned out; one hand to chest in lotus position, the other at top of head, fingers pointing to sky; head moving from side to side. Deadpan.*) Any two of anything is totalitarian.

(*The beat picks up, he turns back and the three dance their own versions of the Frug, Watusi, Twist, etc.* GLORIA *weaves from one to the other, but they do not dance together: they face each other, but each is locked in the vacant isolation of a separate world, from which he speaks.*)

GLORIA. It is right and natural for the individual to be primarily concerned with himself.

DAVID. He must be dedicated to his own interests.

SIDNEY. There is a revolution in this idea.

SIDNEY, DAVID, GLORIA (*together*). Therefore—

SIDNEY. I shall make myself a magazine and build it like a brothel. The bricks will be old-fashioned: lovely bodies made dirty by the way I present them.

DAVID. But the mortar will be new: made of Great Names.

SIDNEY. So I will offer Rosemarie and Maryanne simply doing the splits—

DAVID. But leavened with Socrates on Punishment and William L. Shirer on the Blitz.

GLORIA. Oh, you'll show the boys Lucy Jones upside down—

SIDNEY. But only when she's back to back with a treatise on the excavation of an Etruscan town!

DAVID. It'll be a hell of a clever switch—

SIDNEY. But I'll prove I'm right—by growing rich!

SIDNEY, DAVID, GLORIA (*they sing in unison*).

"Ohhhhhhhh—
This is the way the cheese will rot!
The cheese will rot! The cheese will rot!
Oh this is the way the cheese will rot!
All on a Sunday morning!

(SIDNEY *moves away to lie down on the couch as* DAVID *melts into* GLORIA's *beckoning arms and they dance as did she and* SIDNEY *earlier.*)

GLORIA. Whaddaya do if your own father calls you a tramp . . . on his deathbed . . . huh? Whaddaya do?

SIDNEY (*on his back, rousing, with a flourish*). You only *think* that flowers are fragrant. 'Tis an illusion!

DAVID. Trying to live with your father's values can kill you. Ask me, I know.

GLORIA. No, Sweetie, living *without* your father's values can kill you. Ask *me, I* know.

SIDNEY (*sits up, cross-legged, Zen Buddhist fashion; pantomines*). Take a needle thus (*From lapel. Large gesture.*), peer through the eye. As much as you can see will be a part of the world. But it will be a true part, will it not? Therefore, set down what you have seen and call it the truth; if anyone argues with you, explain to the fool that it is harder to look *through* a needle than to look around one. (*He flops back.*)

DAVID. Any profession of concern with decency is the most indecent of all human affectations.

SIDNEY (*sits bolt upright; declaiming*). To be or not to be! (*A great pause, he sears us with his eyes—and falls back.*) Well, better leave *that* one alone!

SIDNEY, GLORIA and DAVID (*singing in disjointed unison*).

"Oh, who's afraid of Absurdity!
   Absurdity! Absurdity!
Who's afraid of Absurdity!
   Not we, not we, not we!"

(*As* SIDNEY *dozes off on the sofa,* GLORIA *stops* DAVID *with a long wet kiss, then steps back.* DAVID *is a little shaken. The music comes to an abrupt halt.*)

GLORIA. Where's the music . . . ? What happened to the music?

DAVID. Don't let's stop! . . . It was mah-velous. We were so completely outside of ourselves.

GLORIA (*crossing to the phonograph as the surreal fuchsia light fades back to white moonlight; drinking*). Sure, baby, a drunk, a hophead and a sick little boy could conjure up the Last Supper if they wanted. (*She turns it on and crosses to the bar. Sits and drinks. The music throbs softly.*)

DAVID (*following her; as much disengaged from her as she is from him; with wistful melancholy*). No, listen. All your life you want certain things and when you try to trace them back with the finger of your mind to where you believe you first started to want them, there is nothing but a haze . . . I was seven. So was Nelson. We were both exactly seven. We used to make a great deal out of that. We used to play all day in my yard. He had fine golden hair and a thin delicate profile—(*He traces her mouth with the fingers of one hand, touches her hair.*) and Mother always said: "Nelson is a real aristocrat." Then, just like that, one summer his family moved to Florence, Italy. Because that is the sort of thing that aristocrats do when they feel like it. And I never saw him again.

GLORIA (*nodding up and down drunkenly*). And you've been looking for him ever since.

DAVID. He never came back.

GLORIA. And now . . .

DAVID. There is a beautiful burnished golden boy very much like Nelson sitting on a chair upstairs. He is from one of the oldest, finest families in New England. He is exquisite. But great damage has been done to him—

GLORIA (*for this girl there are no surprises left*). He requires . . . the presence of a woman . . . Not just any girl, but someone young enough, fresh enough, in certain light, to make him think it is somebody of his own class—

DAVID. Yes. But—there is nothing to do. Apparently—it is merely a matter of—watching.

GLORIA (*raising her eyes pathetically*). And *you're* a friend of Sidney's . . .

DAVID. It's not for me. Perhaps you can understand: If he asked for the snows of the Himalayas tonight, I would try to get it for him. I thought—you might know of such things.

GLORIA (*agonized*). Oh . . . I know of such things!

DAVID. Will you come up—?

GLORIA (*a beat; not really to him*). Sure . . . why not?

DAVID. It's apartment 3-F.

(*He goes out and up.* GLORIA *stands for a long moment, looking after him, then crosses quickly to the phonograph, which she turns up louder, as if to drown out some voice that speaks only to her, till the persistent lonely chaos of the music fills the room. She tries to dance a little, that doesn't work; she downs more goofball pills with liquor. Then, snapping her fingers and undulating a little to the rhythms in the room, with a fixed smile, she goes out. But as she mounts the third step, she freezes in the grip of a physical revulsion she can no longer contain—then suddenly whirls.*)

GLORIA (*her words are a single guttural cry of pain*). Sick people belong in hospitals!!! (*For a long moment her eyes dart frantically and she whimpers, trapped, seeking refuge. There is none. At last she looks at the bottle of pills in her hand, walks slowly back and stands, spent, in the doorway. Then, resolutely.*) Papa—I *am* better than this! Now will you forgive me—?

(*She crosses to the bathroom, clutching the bottle, halts, terrified at the unseen presence there, turns away; but then, with a final lift of her head, she enters and closes the door. The phone begins to ring as the lights slowly dim.* SIDNEY *sleeps on.*)

DIMOUT

SCENE TWO

TIME: *Early the next morning.*

AT RISE: *There is now a stark, businesslike and cold atmosphere in the apartment, as* opposed to the tone of the last scene. It is just after dawn; in the course of this scene the blue-gray of the hour slowly lifts, until, at the end, the sun breaks full. A DETECTIVE, *with pad, routinely questions* IRIS, *who sits in the rocker facing front; slumped, in her coat, hands in pockets, eyes red and staring off at nothing in particular. For its part, the sign seems more naked now, more assertive, more dominating and, for all of its unnoticed presence, necessary. The bathroom door stands ajar.*

DETECTIVE. Age of the deceased?

IRIS. Twenty-six.

DETECTIVE. Your relationship?

IRIS. My sister.

DETECTIVE. Occupation? (SIDNEY *enters, in his coat, stands in the door for a moment, as if the mere fact of the apartment oppresses him.* IRIS *says nothing. The* DETECTIVE *coughs, tries again, anxious to get it over.*) Occupation of the deceased?

SIDNEY. Like, she was a member of the chorus.

DETECTIVE. Chorus girl—

(*He stars to write that;* IRIS *looks up but says nothing.*)

SIDNEY. No—no, she was a model.

DETECTIVE (*putting his book away*). All right. You know there's gonna be an inquest.

(IRIS *offers no response.* SIDNEY *finally nods. The* DETECTIVE *exits.*)

SIDNEY. I got them a cab. When they got home, Fred said, he'd call the doctor and have Mavis sedated. (*Paces agitatedly. Halting and looking at her.*) You should let it come, honey . . . Cry. It's worse if you do what you're doing . . . (*He spots* GLORIA's *headband on the floor, where she had dropped it; he picks it up, stands looking at the bathroom, then turns away —with a face contorted—to face his wife. A long beat. Then helplessly.*) You want a cup of tea or something? (IRIS *gives a quick, tight, little shake of her head "no."* WALLY *appears at the door, knocks, though it is ajar. He comes in, hat in hand, face cut with concern.* SIDNEY *just looks at him. A beat. Then grandly.*) I see, Wally: the drama has come of age! The deus ex machina no longer comes floating in with its heavenly resolution— or dissolution—it merely comes walking through the door—*like a man.*

WALLY (*to* IRIS). I heard about—your

sister. (*Awkwardly, sincerely.*) There's never anything to say, is there? But if there's anything I can do. (IRIS *does not respond in any way. To* SIDNEY *softly.*) She's in bad shape, Sidney. Why don't you call a doctor?

SIDNEY (*with an effort at restraint*). What do you want here, Wally?

WALLY. I know, Sidney, you think I'm the prince of all the bastards—

SIDNEY. No, as a matter of fact, it's been my opinion for some time now that the merely ambitious have enjoyed too much stature through the centuries: I think you're a rather rank-and-file bastard.

WALLY (*with a half smile*). It feels good, doesn't it, Sid? It must feel good: to be able to judge! One good betrayal vindicates all our own crimes, doesn't it? Well, I'm going to tell you something I learned a long time ago—

SIDNEY (*swiftly, angrily, as if by rote*). "If you want to survive you've got to swing the way the world swings!"

WALLY. It's true. You either negotiate or get out of the race. Face up, Sid—or is that too hard for you?—that I'm the same man I was a year ago. Two months ago. Last week. And I still believe I am making my contribution to changing things —but I happen to know that in order to get anything done, anything at all in this world, baby, you've got to know where the power is. That's the way it's always been and that's the way it always will be.

SIDNEY. How do you know?

WALLY (*as if there is no end to the innocence in this house*). Baby—I am *of* this world; it's something you know.

SIDNEY (*fingering* GLORIA'S *purse; a private irony*). And besides—(*Softly.*) "all the *real* prostitutes are everybody else."

WALLY (*ready for him*). Name calling is the last refuge of ineffectuals. You rage and I function. Study that sometimes, Sid. (*Crossing to the window.*) Look, you know that stop sign that the housewives have been trying to get at Macklin and Warren Streets? With the baby-carriage demonstrations and the petitions and all? Well, they'll get their stop sign now. *I'll* get it for them. But not as some wide-eyed reformer. And better garbage collection and the new playground and a lot of other things too.

SIDNEY (*half smile*). And the narcotic traffic? What about that?

WALLY (*a quick hand-waving*). That's more complicated. There's more involved. You don't go jumping into things.

SIDNEY (*instinctively, swiftly*). I see: We can go on stepping over the bodies of the junkies—but the trains will run on time!

(*He clicks his heels and throws off the Fascist salute smartly.*)

WALLY (*throwing his head back, just a little*). As a matter of fact, I knew it would be like this. That you would be standing there with that exact expression on your face, smoking a cigarette . . . filled with all the simple self-righteousness of bleeding innocence again betrayed. Well, I've only got this to say about it, Sid—

SIDNEY (*suddenly, without warning— the confrontation; the real one*). They're after my paper now, aren't they, Wally?

WALLY (*thrown; he would have preferred this on his own ground*). You don't understand. They don't want anything . . . Look, I told them not to expect to buy you, Sid. (*The latter smiles and nods his head throughout.*) I've made them understand that . . . Nothing changes. You go on exactly as before, that's all.

SIDNEY. Ah! I see: you mean covering the art shows, doing charming little photographic essays of the snow on our quaint little streets.

WALLY. Yes!

SIDNEY. And leave the world—to you?

WALLY. I didn't do you in, Sid. You did yourself in and there ought to be a lesson in it for you: stay up in the mountains with your banjos and your books where you belong.

SIDNEY. But should I persist?

WALLY. Sidney, I am talking to you as a friend . . .

SIDNEY. *Should I persist?*

WALLY (*had not wanted to say it like this*). Then the paper won't last six months.

SIDNEY (*with wonder—genuine wonder*). Wally, don't you know what kind of a house you've walked into? Didn't it hit you in the face? Didn't death breathe on you as you came through the door? What's the matter with you, man? While I lay stoned on that couch, a girl who tried to accept everything that you stand for died in that bathroom today. Do you think I haven't learned anything in the last few hours? The slogans of capitulation can *kill!* Every time we say "live and let live" —death triumphs!

WALLY. Sidney, what is it that you're trying to say?

SIDNEY. That I am going to fight you, Wally. That you have forced me to take a position. Finally—the one thing I never wanted to do. Just not being *for* you is not enough. Since that girl died—(*To* IRIS.) I'm sorry, honey, but I have to— since that girl died—I have been forced to learn I have to be *against* you. And, Wally, I'm against you—I swear it to you —and your machine. And what you have to worry about is the fact that some of us will be back out in those streets today. Only this time—thanks to you—we shall be more seasoned, more cynical, tougher, harder to fool—and therefore, less likely to quit.

WALLY (*the genuine passion of the compromised*). Sidney, you reek of innocence!

IRIS (*suddenly, turning*). The question is, Wally, what is it *you* reek of?

SIDNEY (*to* WALLY, *but the words are intended for* IRIS). I'll tell you what he reeks of: He reeks of accommodation. He reeks of collusion. He reeks of collaboration—with Power and the tools of Power . . . (*To* WALLY.) Don't you understand, man? Too much has happened to me! I love my wife—I want her back. I loved my sister-in-law. I want to see her alive. I—I love you—I should like to see you redeemed. But in the context in which we presently stand here I doubt any of this is possible. That which warped and distorted all of us is—(*Suddenly lifting his hands as if this were literally true.*) all around; it is in this very air! *This world*—this swirling, seething madness—which you ask us to accept, to help maintain—has done this . . . maimed my friends . . . emptied these rooms and my very bed. And now it has taken my sister. *This* world! Therefore, to live, to breathe—I shall *have* to fight it!

WALLY (*picking up his hat—shaking his head*). That's asking for it, Sidney . . .

SIDNEY. Then that should be the first thing I tell my readers—while I still can.

WALLY (*gesturing incredulously to* IRIS, *as if to an ally*). Am I really supposed to believe this—? (IRIS *slowly nods "yes"—then shrugs with innocence: What can she do with* SIDNEY? WALLY *turns back with genuine wonder.*) You really are a fool.

SIDNEY. Always have been. (*His eyes find his wife's.*) A fool who believes that death is waste and love is sweet and that the earth turns and men change every day and that rivers run and that people wanna be better than they are and that flowers smell good and that I hurt terribly today, and that hurt is desperation and desperation is—energy and energy can *move* things . . .

WALLY (*looking from one to the other; pronounced exasperation with "children"*). Let me know the time and place of the funeral, won't you? I'd like to send flowers.

(*He starts out, adjusts his hat, notes the sign, gazes at them and then wanders off.* IRIS *rises.*)

IRIS. For a long time now I've been wanting something. For a long time. I think it was for you to be all of yourself. I want to come home, Sidney. I want to come home but . . .

SIDNEY. We'll talk about it.

(*With a supreme mustering of will, and her whole body, she pushes shut the bathroom door, as if on the Past—and yet for a moment longer stands transfixed by it— then turns and crosses to* SIDNEY *on the couch.*)

IRIS (*holding her hands before her and turning them slowly*). When she was little . . . she had fat, pudgy hands . . . and I used to have to scrub them . . . because she couldn't get them clean. And so I would pretend that they were fish and I was the Fish Lady cleaning these little fish to sell them . . . That always tickled her so, and she would laugh and laugh and . . .

(*She gags on the first great sob, he folds her into his arms and, in the desperateness of this contact without words, the tears come freely now.*)

SIDNEY. Yes . . . weep now, darling, weep. Let us both weep. That is the first thing: to let ourselves feel again . . . Then, tomorrow, we shall make something strong of this sorrow . . . (*They sit spent, almost physically drained and motionless . . . as the clear light of morning gradually fills the room.*)

CURTAIN

THE LION IN WINTER

James Goldman

For BILL

First presented by Eugene V. Wolsk, Walter A. Hyman, and Alan King with Emanuel Azenberg at the Ambassador Theatre in New York City on March 3, 1966, with the following cast:

(*In order of appearance*)

HENRY II, King of England Robert Preston	RICHARD James Rado
ALAIS CAPET Suzanne Grossmann	ELEANOR OF AQUITAINE Rosemary Harris
JOHN Bruce Scott	PHILIP CAPET, King of France
GEOFFREY Dennis Cooney	Christopher Walken

Directed by Noel Willman
Scenery and costumes by Will Steven Armstrong
Lighting by Tharon Musser
Incidental music by Thomas Wagner
Production Manager, Jose Vega

SYNOPSIS OF SCENES

ACT ONE. SCENE ONE: Alais's chamber, late afternoon. SCENE TWO: A Reception Hall, immediately following. SCENE THREE: Eleanor's chamber, some time later. SCENE FOUR: The Reception Hall, immediately following. SCENE FIVE: Eleanor's chamber, shortly afterwards. SCENE SIX: Philip's chamber, immediately following.

ACT TWO. SCENE ONE: Henry's chamber, late at night. SCENE TWO: Alais's chamber, at dawn. SCENE THREE: The wine cellar, early morning.

THE TIME: Christmas, 1183.

THE PLACE: Henry's palace at Chinon, France.

THE SET: The palace at Chinon was famous for its grace and beauty. The arches, walls and columns of the set, though stone, are soft and light. There are no signs of royal wealth or pomp. The rooms in which the play occurs are simple, airy, clean and as free of furniture and things as possible.

Copyright © 1964, as an unpublished work, by James Goldman.
© 1966 by James Goldman.
Reprinted by permission of Random House, Inc.
All rights including the right of reproduction in whole or in part, in any form, are reserved under International and Pan-American Copyright Conventions. Published in New York by Random House, Inc., and simultaneously in Toronto, Canada, by Random House of Canada Limited.

CAUTION: Professionals and amateurs are hereby warned that *The Lion in Winter,* being fully protected under the Copyright Laws of the United States of America, the British Commonwealth, including the Dominion of Canada, and all other countries of the Berne and Universal Copyright Conventions, is subject to royalty. All rights, including professional, amateur, motion picture, recitation, lecturing, public reading, radio and television broadcasting, and the rights of translation into foreign languages, are strictly reserved. Particular emphasis is laid on the question of readings, permission for which must be secured in writing from the author's agent. All inquiries, Monica McCall Inc., 667 Madison Avenue, New York, N.Y. 10021.

JAMES GOLDMAN, it seems, started out his career with the noblest aspirations. He wanted to be a critic—only a music critic, to be sure, but the man's heart was in the right place. However, his postgraduate work at Columbia was interrupted by the draft. So he became a playwright, and a critic was lost to humanity.

Mr. Goldman was born in Chicago on June 30, 1927. He studied at the University of Chicago from 1947, receiving his M.A. in 1950. The same year he went to Columbia, until he was drafted in 1952.

It was in 1961 that he had his first play produced on Broadway. Collaborating with a younger brother, William Goldman, he offered *Blood, Sweat and Stanley Poole,* which was not anything like a success. The same year, although this time as a solo venture, Mr. Goldman had *They Might Be Giants* staged by Joan Littlewood for her Theatre Workshop in Stratford, London. It did not cause a great stir, and the following year found him once more collaborating on Broadway, this time on the book and lyrics of a musical called *A Family Affair,* working once more with his younger brother and on this occasion with John Kander. It flopped rather loudly.

Mr. Goldman, now living in New York, turned his attention to the novel, and in 1965 produced a novel, *Waldorf.* The following year, on March 3, 1966, his play *The Lion in Winter* opened on Broadway, starring Robert Preston and Rosemary Harris. Very well received by most of the critics, it regrettably did not settle down for a profitable run. Few people have ever had a *succés d'estime* on Broadway that has not cost him money. However, *The Lion in Winter* later became an Oscar-winning film starring Peter O'Toole and Katharine Hepburn, suggesting perhaps that movie audiences may be more sophisticated than those on Broadway.

The weakness of Mr. Goldman's play can be instantly perceived. It was put very well, in an opening-night notice, by Martin Gottfried of *Women's Wear Daily.* Mr. Gottfried wrote: "Goldman's play is the modern masquerading as the antique. *The Lion in Winter* has many qualities, but at its heart it is in disguise, and I think it knows it." I wish I had said that. It strikes at the root of the matter.

Mr. Goldman has written that rare, rare thing: an artistically acceptable historical play. It is a commonplace of dramaturgy that most historical plays are awful. For one thing, few playwrights know quite which tone to adopt. Here Mr. Goldman is writing about Henry II, a twelfth-century English king of formidable power and, apparently, wit. How do you write about him?

Shakespeare would have found no problem in this. He would have written about Henry II in the same style as he might write about Henry VI, for Shakespeare, in that beautiful blaze of theatrical innocence that was the Elizabethan theatre, knew nothing of anachronism, which is a grammatical usage that has been imposed upon us by scholars, grammarians, pedants, and critics. But *The Lion in Winter* is undoubtedly anachronistic.

There are many phrases here, indeed all through the play, that have the sound and heft of contemporary New York. Is this a fault? I think not. The play has occasionally been called Shavian, and certainly Mr. Goldman avails himself of Shaw's dramatic freedoms, if hardly equaling Shaw's dramatic wit or even dexterity. Mr. Goldman is not on that kind of level as a playwright; he is a frankly commercial writer whose quality is not to be found in what he does but in how well he does it.

In another opening-night notice, Stanley Kauffmann in the *New York Times* queried whether we could be interested in Henry's successor. Yet I think that this is not the point any more than is the play's obvious use of anachronism. You see, we *are* interested, and Mr. Goldman's overfamiliar and nudgingly jocular use of anachronisms is not only deliberate but vital. This is a play exquisitely designed for Broadway's menopausal audience of the 1960s. Henry is no Lear, for all Mr. Goldman's reference. He is a business executive, highly successful, and alive and moderately well in White Plains. He has a wife and a mistress, and problems with his sons over the estate.

Mr. Goldman writes the kind of plays that his audience can identify with. Yet *The Lion in Winter* is an altogether superior example of its admittedly raddled form. Which, probably, very probably, is why it had such a comparatively brief run on Broadway. For all its obvious failings, it was too good. Let the theatre historians eventually work that out.

HISTORICAL NOTE

The historical material on Henry's reign is considerable insofar as battles, plots, wars, treaties and alliances are concerned. This play, while simplifying the political maneuvering—and combining a meeting of the French and English Kings in 1183 with a Royal Court held at Windsor the following year into a Christmas Court that never was—is based on the available data.

The facts we have, while clear enough as to the outcome of relationships—such things as who kills whom and when—say little if anything about the quality and content of those relationships. The people in this play, their characters and passions, while consistent with the facts we have, are fictions.

There were no laws of primogeniture in Henry's time. It was a rare thing when the King was followed by his eldest son. When kings died, it was open season on the English throne, a fact responsible for much that Henry did.

ACT ONE

Scene One

ALAIS's *chamber. It is a small and graceful room, containing just a bench, a chest and a chair. Late afternoon light streams in through a window.*

As the curtain rises, ALAIS CAPET, *dressed for a state occasion, is removing a small crown from her exquisite head. She is twenty-three, serenely beautiful, and though glaring at him at the moment, unmistakably in love with* HENRY PLANTAGENET. *He has just turned fifty, an age at which, in his time, men were either old or dead. Not* HENRY. *Though arthritis comes occasionally and new battle wounds don't heal the way the old ones did, he still is very nearly all he ever was. He is enjoying that final rush of physical and mental vigor that comes to some men not before the end but just before the start of the decline. He wears, as always, plain and unimpressive clothes.*

As ALAIS *takes off her crown,* HENRY *turns to her and, with the beginning of impatience, speaks.*

———

HENRY. You must know that's a futile gesture. Come along.

ALAIS. No; I'll stay here and you can send reports.

HENRY. It's going to be a jungle of a day: if I start growling now, I'll never last.

ALAIS. You'll last. You're like the rocks at Stonehenge; nothing knocks you down.

HENRY. In these rooms, Alais, on this Christmas, I have all the enemies I need.

ALAIS. You have more than you think.

HENRY. Are you one? Has my willow turned to poison oak?

ALAIS. If I decided to be trouble, Henry, how much trouble could I be?

HENRY. Not much. You don't matter to the others; only me.

ALAIS. How great a matter am I?

HENRY. Alais, in my time I've known contessas, milkmaids, courtesans and novices, whores, gypsies, jades and little boys, but nowhere in God's Western world have I found anyone to love but you.

ALAIS. And Rosamund.

HENRY. She's dead.

ALAIS. And Eleanor.

HENRY. The new Medusa? My good wife?

ALAIS. How is your Queen?

HENRY. Decaying, I suppose.

ALAIS. You haven't seen her?

HENRY. No, nor smelled nor touched nor tasted. Don't be jealous of the gorgon; she is not among the things I love. How many husbands do you know who dungeon up their wives? I haven't kept the great bitch in the keep for ten years out of passionate attachment. Come. I've heard she's aging badly; let's go look.

ALAIS. Would it be troublesome if I betrayed you?

HENRY. We've no secrets, Eleanor and I. How can you possibly betray me?

ALAIS. I could give away your plans.

HENRY. You don't know what they are.

ALAIS. I know you want to disinherit Richard.

HENRY. So does Eleanor. She knows young Henry's dead. The Young King died in summer and I haven't named an heir. She knows I want John on the throne and I know she wants Richard. We are very frank about it.

ALAIS. Henry, I can't be your mistress if I'm married to your son.

HENRY. Why can't you? Johnny wouldn't mind.

ALAIS. I do not like your Johnny.

HENRY. He's a good boy.

ALAIS. He's got pimples and he smells of compost.

HENRY. He's just sixteen; he can't help the pimples.

ALAIS. He could bathe.

HENRY. It isn't such a dreadful thing to be a Queen of England. Not all eyes will weep for you.

ALAIS. Will yours?

HENRY. I don't know. Very likely.

ALAIS. All I want is not to lose you. Can't you hide me? Can't I simply disappear?

HENRY. You know you can't. Your little brother Philip's King of France now and he wants your wedding or your dowry back. I only took you for your dowry. You were seven. Two big knees and two big eyes and that's all. How was I to know?

ALAIS. Let Philip have the dowry back. It isn't much.

HENRY. I can't. The Vexin is a little county but it's vital to me.

ALAIS. And I'm not.

HENRY. It's been my luck to fall in love with landed women. When I married Eleanor, I thought: "You lucky man. The richest woman in the world. She owns the Aquitaine, the greatest province on the Continent—and beautiful as well." She was, you know.

ALAIS. And you adored her.

HENRY. Memory fails. There may have been an era when I did. (*Arranging a wisp of her hair.*) Let's have one strand askew; nothing in life has any business being perfect.

ALAIS. Henry, I was brought up to be dutiful. I smile a lot, bend easily and hope for very little. It is useful training and it's made a lot of hard things possible. But, Henry, not this thing.

HENRY. I've had them summoned and I'll have you by me. With the headdress or without it.

ALAIS. Oh, what difference does it make who's king?

HENRY. What difference?

ALAIS. Have you found religion, Henry? Are you going to look down from the clouds and see who's sitting in your place?

HENRY. I've got to know before I die. I've built an empire and I've got to know it's going to last. I've put together England and I've added to it half of France. I am the greatest power in a thousand years. And after me comes John. If I can't leave this state to John, I've lived for nothing.

ALAIS. John doesn't care for you at all.

HENRY. We love each other deeply.

ALAIS. None of them has any love for you.

HENRY. Because we fight? Tell me they all three want the crown, I'll tell you it's a feeble prince that doesn't. They may snap at me or plot and that makes them the kind of sons I want. I've snapped and plotted all my life: there is no other way to be a king, alive and fifty all at once.

ALAIS. I'm going to fight for you.

HENRY. Oh, fine.

ALAIS. When I was sixteen and we started this depraved relationship, I left everything to you. I lap sat, drank my milk and did what I was told. Not any more. Your cherub's twenty-three now and she's going to fight.

HENRY. With mace and chain?

ALAIS. With anything that I can think of.

HENRY. That's exactly what I need: another mind at work. Try; you can hear the thinking through the walls. There's Geoffrey, humming treachery. And Richard, growling out for gore. And Eleanor, she's thinking heavy thoughts like molten lead and marble slabs. My house is full of intellectual activity.

ALAIS. Add mine.

HENRY. Alais, Alais—I don't plan to give you up. I don't plan to give up anything. I'll make alliances and bargains, threaten, beg, break heads and hearts, and when I'm done, I'll make an heir of John, a petty prince of Richard and I'll still have you.

ALAIS. When can I believe you, Henry?

HENRY. Always; even when I lie.

ALAIS. How much is it safe to hope for?

HENRY. Everything.

ALAIS. But with so many enemies—

HENRY. I know—and some of them are smarter folk than I or crueler or more ruthless or dishonest. But not all rolled in one. The priests write all the history these days and they'll do me justice. Henry, they'll say, was a master bastard. (*Extending his arm.*) Come; let's go downstairs and meet the family.

(*She moves to join him.*)

DIM AND BLACKOUT

SCENE TWO

A Reception Hall, immediately following. It is a bright and spacious room. There is a bench, a large refectory table and a massive chair. A pile of holly boughs lies stacked in a corner.

*The young Plantagenets—*RICHARD, GEOFFREY *and* JOHN—*are entering as the lights rise.*

RICHARD LIONHEART, *at twenty-six, looks like his legend. He is handsome, graceful and impressive. He has been a famous soldier since his middle teens, and justly so; war is his profession and he is good at it.*

GEOFFREY, *Count of Brittany, is twenty-five. A man of energy and verve, he is attractive, charming and the owner of the best brain of a brainy family.*

JOHN, *at sixteen, does indeed have pimples. He is a charming-looking boy in spite of them, sweet-faced and totally adorable.*

They are bowing each other into the room when we see them.

————

JOHN. After you.

GEOFFREY. No; after you.

RICHARD. No; after you.

JOHN (*delighted with himself as he skips into the room*). Oh, have it your way; after me.

RICHARD (*following in, along with* GEOFFREY). You do keep growing, Johnny.

JOHN (*agreeing cheerfully*). Every way but up. Look: holly. (*Beginning to hang the holly boughs.*) I love Christmas.

GEOFFREY. Warm and rosy time. The hot wine steams, the Yule log roars and we're the fat that's in the fire. She's here, you know.

JOHN. Who?

RICHARD. Mother.

GEOFFREY. Since this morning.

RICHARD. Have you seen her?

GEOFFREY. Haven't you?

RICHARD. We're not as friendly as we were.

GEOFFREY. Does she still favor you?

RICHARD. Does she or doesn't she?

JOHN. If I'm supposed to make a fuss and kiss her hairy cheek, I won't.

RICHARD. What you kiss, little prince, is up to you.

JOHN. I'm Father's favorite; that's what counts.

RICHARD. You hardly know me, Johnny, so I beg you to believe my reputation: I'm a constant soldier and a sometime poet and I will be king.

JOHN. Just you remember: Father loves me best.

ELEANOR (*sweeping in*). The way you bicker it's a wonder that he cares for any of you.

(ELEANOR OF AQUITAINE *is sixty-one and looks nothing like it. She is a truly handsome woman of great temperament, authority and presence. She has been a queen of international importance for forty-six years and you know it. Finally, she is that most unusual thing: a genuinely feminine woman thoroughly capable of holding her own in a man's world.*)

GEOFFREY. Mother.

ELEANOR. Geoffrey—but I do have handsome children. John—you're so clean and neat. Henry takes good care of you. And Richard. Don't look sullen, dear; it makes your eyes go small and piggy and your chin look weak. Where's Henry?

RICHARD. Upstairs with the family whore.

ELEANOR. That is a mean and tawdry way to talk about your fiancée.

JOHN. My fiancée.

ELEANOR. Whosever fiancée, I brought her up and she is dear to me and gentle. Have we seen the French King yet?

GEOFFREY. Not yet.

ELEANOR. Let's hope he's grown up like his father—simon pure and simon simple. Good, good Louis; if I'd managed sons for him instead of all those little girls, I'd still be stuck with being Queen of France and we should not have known each other. Such, my angels, is the role of sex in history. How's your father?

JOHN. Do you care?

ELEANOR. More deeply, lamb, than you can possibly imagine. Is my hair in place? I've given up the looking glass; quicksilver has no sense of tact.

RICHARD. He still plans to make John king.

ELEANOR. Of course he does. My, what a greedy little trinity you are: king, king, king. Two of you must learn to live with disappointment.

HENRY (*entering, with* ALAIS). Ah—but which two?

ELEANOR. Let's deny them all and live forever.

HENRY. Tusk to tusk through all eternity. How was your crossing? Did the Channel part for you?

ELEANOR. It went flat when I told it to; I didn't think to ask for more. How dear of you to let me out of jail.

HENRY. It's only for the holidays.

ELEANOR. Like school. You keep me young. Here's gentle Alais. (*As* ALAIS *starts to curtsy.*) No, no; greet me like you used to. (*Hugging her.*) Fragile I am not: affection is a pressure I can bear.

HENRY. I've had the French King sent for. We will have a tactile conversation, like two surgeons looking for a lump. We'll state positions and I'll make the first of many offers. He'll refuse it, naturally, I'll make a better one and so on through the holidays until I win. For the duration of this joyous ritual, you will give, to your father, your support.

RICHARD. Why will I?

ELEANOR. Out of duty, dear. (*To* HENRY.) Tell me, what's Philip like? I hear he's quite impressive for a boy of seventeen—

HENRY (*as* PHILIP *enters*). My Lord.

ELEANOR. Oh—and you are. I'm Eleanor, who might have been your mother. All the others here you know.

PHILIP (PHILIP CAPET *is indeed impres-*

sive. He is tall, well-proportioned and handsome without being at all pretty. His manner is open, direct and simple and he smiles easily. He has been King of France for three years and has learned a great deal. He bows). Queen Eleanor—Your Grace.

HENRY. My Lord. Welcome to Chinon.

PHILIP. Sir.

HENRY. Your grievances, as we have understood them, have to do with Princess Alais and her dowry.

PHILIP. Sixteen years ago you made a treaty with us. It is time its terms were executed.

HENRY. We are willing to discuss it.

PHILIP. Our position comes to this: that you will either hold the marriage or return the Vexin. Alais marries Richard or we'll have the county back at once.

HENRY. That's clear, concise and well presented. My position is— Well, frankly, Philip, it's a tangle. Once I'm dead, who's to be king? I could draw papers till my scribes drop or the ink runs out and once I died, unless I've left behind me three contented sons, my lands will split three ways in civil war. You see my problem?

PHILIP. Clearly; but it's yours, not mine.

HENRY. Two years ago the Queen and I, for reasons passing understanding, gave the Aquitaine to Richard. That makes Richard very powerful. How can I give him Alais, too? The man she marries has you for an ally.

PHILIP. It's their wedding or the Vexin back. Those are the terms you made with Louis.

HENRY. True but academic, lad. The Vexin's mine.

PHILIP. By what authority?

HENRY. It's got my troops all over it: that makes it mine. Now hear me, boy. You take what memories you have of me and mark them out of date. I'm not your father's friend, now; I'm his son's opponent.

PHILIP. I'm a king: I'm no man's boy.

HENRY. A king? Because you put your ass on purple cushions?

PHILIP. Sir.

(*He turns on his heel and starts to go.*)

HENRY. Philip, you haven't got the feel of this at all. Use all your voices: when I bellow, bellow back.

PHILIP. I'll mark that down.

HENRY. This, too. We are the world in small. A nation is a human thing; it does what we do, for our reasons. Surely, if we're civilized, it must be possible to put the knives away. We can make peace. We have it in our hands.

PHILIP. I've tutors of my own. Will that be all?

HENRY. Oh, think. You came here for a reason. You've made demands of me. Now don't you want to ask me if I've got an offer?

PHILIP. Have you got an offer?

HENRY. Not yet—but I'll think of one. (PHILIP *starts off again.*) Oh, by the way . . . (*At the doorway,* PHILIP *turns.*) You're better at this than I thought you'd be.

PHILIP (*smiling*). I wasn't sure you'd noticed. (*He exits.*)

HENRY. Well—what shall we hang? The holly or each other?

ELEANOR. You can't read your sons at all. That isn't anger they're projecting; it's anxiety.

HENRY. I read them. I know Richard's moods and Johnny's faces and the thought behind the pitch of Geoffrey's voice. The trouble's at the other end; they don't know me. (*Turning to his sons.*) There is a legend of a king called Lear with whom I have a lot in common. Both of us have kingdoms and three children we adore and both of us are old. But there it stops. He cut his kingdom into bits. I can't do that. I've built this house and it will stand. What I have architected, you will not destroy.

RICHARD. Would you say, Father, that I have the makings of a king?

HENRY. A splendid king.

RICHARD. Would you expect me, Father, to be disinherited without a fight?

HENRY. Of course you'll fight. I raised you to.

RICHARD. I don't care what you offer Philip. I don't care what plans you make. I'll have the Aquitaine and Alais and the crown. I'll have them all.

JOHN. You're going to love my coronation.

RICHARD. I won't give up one to get the other. I won't trade off Alais or the Aquitaine to this (*Indicating* JOHN.)—this walking pustule. No, your loving son will not.

(*He exits.*)

JOHN. Did you hear what he called me?

ELEANOR. Clearly, dear. Now run along; it's nearly dinnertime.

JOHN. I only do what Father tells me.

HENRY. Go and eat.

JOHN. Did I say something wrong? I'm always saying something wrong. All right, I'll eat, I'll eat.

(*He exits.*)

ELEANOR. And that's to be the king.

GEOFFREY. And I'm to be his chancellor. Has he told you? John will rule the country while I run it. That's to say, he gets to spend the taxes that I get to raise.

ELEANOR. How nice for you.

GEOFFREY. It's not as nice as being king.

HENRY. We've made you Duke of Brittany. Is that so little?

GEOFFREY. No one ever thinks of crowns and mentions Geoff. Why is that? I make out three prizes here—a throne, a princess and the Aquitaine. Three prizes and three sons; but no one ever says, "Here, Geoff, here Geoff boy, here's a bone for you."

HENRY. I should have thought that being chancellor was a satisfying bone.

GEOFFREY. It isn't power that I feel deprived of; it's the mention that I miss. There's no affection for me here. You wouldn't think I'd want that, would you?

(*He exits.*)

ELEANOR. Henry, I have a confession.

HENRY. Yes?

ELEANOR. I don't much like our children. (*To* ALAIS.) Only you—the child I raised but didn't bear.

ALAIS. You never cared for me.

ELEANOR. I did and do. Believe me, Henry's bed is Henry's province: he can people it with sheep for all I care. Which, on occasion, he has done.

HENRY. Still that? When Rosamund's been dead for seven years?

ELEANOR. Two months and eighteen days. I never liked her much.

HENRY. You count the days?

ELEANOR. I made the numbers up. (*To* ALAIS.) He found Miss Clifford in the mists of Wales and brought her home for closer observation. Liking what he saw, he scrutinized her many years. He loved her deeply and she him. And yet, my dear, when Henry had to choose between his lady and my lands—

ALAIS. He'll leave me if he has to; I know that.

ELEANOR. Poor Alais.

ALAIS. There's no sport in hurting me; it is so easy.

ELEANOR. After all the years of love, the hair I've brushed and braided and the tears I've kissed away, do you think I could bring myself to hurt you?

ALAIS. Eleanor, with both hands tied behind you.

(*She exits.*)

HENRY. She is lovely, isn't she?

ELEANOR. Yes, very.

HENRY. If I'd chosen, who could I have picked to love to gall you more?

ELEANOR. There's no one. (*Moving to the holly boughs.*) Come on; let's finish Christmasing the place.

HENRY. Time hasn't done a thing but wrinkle you.

ELEANOR. It hasn't even done that. I have borne six girls, five boys and thirty-one connubial years of you. How am I possible?

HENRY (*joining her in hanging holly*). There are moments when I miss you.

ELEANOR. Many?

HENRY. Do you doubt it?

ELEANOR (*rumpling his hair*). That's my woolly sheep dog. So wee Johnny gets the crown.

HENRY. I've heard it rumored but I don't believe it.

ELEANOR. Losing Alais will be hard, for you do love her.

HENRY. It's an old man's last attachment; nothing more. How hard do you find living in your castle?

ELEANOR. It was difficult in the beginning but that's past. I find I've seen the world enough. I have my maids and menials in my courtyard and I hold my little court. It suits me now.

HENRY. I'll never let you loose. You led too many civil wars against me.

ELEANOR. And I damn near won the last one. Still, as long as I get trotted out for Christmas Courts and state occasions now and then—for I do like to see you—it's enough. Do you still need the Vexin, Henry?

HENRY. Need you ask?

ELEANOR. My strategy is ten years old.

HENRY. It is as crucial as it ever was. My troops there are a day away from Paris, just a march of twenty miles. I must keep it.

ELEANOR (*surveying the holly*). I'd say

that's all the jollying this room can stand.
I'm famished. Let's go in to dinner.

HENRY (*extending his arm*). Arm in
arm.

ELEANOR (*taking his arm and smiling at
him*). And hand in hand. You're still a
marvel of a man.

HENRY. And you're my lady.

ELEANOR. Henry, dear, if Alais doesn't
marry Richard, I will see you lose the
Vexin.

HENRY. Well, I thought you'd never say
it.

ELEANOR. I can do it.

HENRY. You can try.

ELEANOR. My Richard is the next king,
not your John. I know you, Henry. I know
every twist and bend you've got and I'll
be waiting round each corner for you.

HENRY. Do you truly care who's king?

ELEANOR. I care because you care so
much.

HENRY. I might surprise you. Eleanor,
I've fought and bargained all these years
as if the only thing I lived for was what
happened after I was dead. I've something
else to live for now. I've blundered onto
peace.

ELEANOR. On Christmas Eve.

HENRY. Since Louis died, while Philip
grew, I've had no France to fight. And in
that lull, I've found how good it is to write
a law or make a tax more fair or sit in
judgment to decide which peasant gets a
cow. There is, I tell you, nothing more
important in the world. And now the
French boy's big enough and I am sick
of war.

ELEANOR. Come to your question, Henry;
make the plea. What would you have me
do? Give out, give up, give in?

HENRY. Give me a little peace.

ELEANOR. A little? Why so modest? How
about eternal peace? Now there's a
thought.

HENRY. If you oppose me, I will strike
you any way I can.

ELEANOR. Of course you will.

HENRY (*taking her arm as before*). We
have a hundred barons we should look the
loving couple for.

ELEANOR (*smiling at him*). Can you read
love in that?

HENRY. And permanent affection.

ELEANOR (*as they start, grand and stately,
for the wings*). Henry?

HENRY. Madam?

ELEANOR. Did you ever love me?

HENRY. No.

ELEANOR. Good. That will make this
pleasanter.

DIM AND BLACKOUT

SCENE THREE

ELEANOR's *chamber, some time later. A
plain and pleasant room, it holds a chair,
a table and a low wood chest. Soft tapestries give warmth and color. As the lights
rise,* ELEANOR *is seated at the table wrapping Christmas presents. She looks up as*
RICHARD *appears.*

RICHARD. All right. I've come. I'm here.
What was it you wanted?

ELEANOR. Just to talk. We haven't been
alone, the two of us, in— How long is it,
lamb? Two years? You look fit. War
agrees with you. I keep informed. I follow
all your slaughters from a distance. Do sit
down.

RICHARD. Is this an audience, a goodnight
kiss with cookies or an ambush?

ELEANOR. Let us hope it's a reunion.
Must you look so stern? I sent for you to
say I want your love again but I can't say
it to a face like that.

RICHARD. My love, of all things. What
could you want it for?

ELEANOR. Why, for itself. What other
purpose could I have?

RICHARD. You'll tell me when you're
ready to.

ELEANOR. I scheme a lot; I know. I plot
and plan. That's how a queen in prison
spends her time. But there is more to me
than that. My mind's not disembodied.
Can't I say I love a son and be believed?

RICHARD. If I were you, I'd try another
tack. I have no dammed-up floods of passion for you. There's no chance I'll over-
flow.

ELEANOR. You are a dull boy.

RICHARD. Am I?

ELEANOR. Dull as plainsong: la, la, la,
forever on one note. I gave the Church
up out of boredom. I can do as much for
you.

RICHARD. You'll never give me up; not
while I hold the Aquitaine.

ELEANOR. You think I'm motivated by a
love of real estate?

RICHARD. I think you want it back. You're so deceitful you can't ask for water when you're thirsty. We could tangle spiders in the webs you weave.

ELEANOR. If I'm so devious, why don't you go? Don't stand there quivering in limbo. Love me, little lamb, or leave me.

RICHARD (*not moving*). Leave you, madam? With pure joy.

ELEANOR. Departure is a simple act. You put the left foot down and then the right.

JOHN (*entering, in high spirits, followed by* GEOFFREY). Mother—

ELEANOR. Hush, dear. Mother's fighting.

JOHN. Father's coming with the treaty terms.

ELEANOR. No doubt he's told you what they are.

JOHN. He doesn't have to. Don't you think I know which end is up?

ELEANOR. Of course you do, dear. Has he put the terms to Philip?

HENRY (*entering, with* ALAIS). Not yet, but we're shortly granting him an audience. I hope you'll all attend.

ELEANOR. Are we to know the terms or have you come to tease us?

HENRY. Not at all. The terms are these.

RICHARD. What are you giving up to Philip? What of mine?

JOHN. Whatever you've got goes to me.

GEOFFREY. And what's the nothing Geoffrey gets?

HENRY. For God's sake, boys, you can't all three be king.

RICHARD. All three of us can try.

HENRY. That's pointless now. The treaty calls for you to marry Alais and you shall. I want you to succeed me, Richard. Alais and the crown: I give you both.

RICHARD. I've got no sense of humor. If I did, I'd laugh.

HENRY. I've used you badly, haven't I?

RICHARD. You've used me cleverly and well.

HENRY. Not any more. I mean to do it.

JOHN. What about me? I'm your favorite, I'm the one you love.

HENRY. John, I can't help myself. Stand next to Richard. See how you compare. Could you keep anything I gave you? Could you beat him on the field?

JOHN. You could.

HENRY. But, John, I won't be there.

JOHN. Let's fight him now.

HENRY. How can I? There's no way to win. I'm losing too, John. All my dreams for you are lost.

JOHN. You've led me on.

HENRY. I never meant to.

JOHN. You're a failure as a father, you know that.

HENRY. I'm sorry, John.

JOHN. Not yet you're not. But I'll do something terrible and you'll be sorry then.

ELEANOR. Did you rehearse all this or are you improvising?

HENRY. Good God, woman, face the facts.

ELEANOR. Which ones? We've got so many.

HENRY. Power is the only fact. (*Indicating* RICHARD.) He is our ablest son. He is the strongest, isn't he? How can I keep him from the crown? He'd only take it if I didn't give it to him.

RICHARD. No—you'd make me fight to get it. I know you: you'd never give me everything.

HENRY. True—and I haven't. You get Alais and you get the kingdom but I get the one thing I want most. If you're king, England stays intact. I get that. It's all yours now—the girl, the crown, the whole black bloody business. Isn't that enough?

(*He exits.*)

ALAIS. I don't know who's to be congratulated. Not me, certainly. (*To* ELEANOR.) You got me for your Richard. How'd you manage it? Did you tell him he's your woolly lamb? Or say how much you like it in your castle?

ELEANOR. It's all lies but I told him.

ALAIS. Kings, queens, knights everywhere you look and I'm the only pawn. I haven't got a thing to lose: that makes me dangerous.

(*She exits.*)

ELEANOR. Poor child.

JOHN. Poor John—who says poor John? Don't everybody sob at once. My God, if I went up in flames, there's not a living soul who'd pee on me to put the fire out.

RICHARD. Let's strike a flint and see.

JOHN. He hates me. Why? What should he hate me for? Am I the eldest son? Am I the heir? Am I the hero? What's my crime? Is it some childhood score, some baby hurt? When I was six and you were sixteen, did I brutalize you? What?

ELEANOR. For whatever I have done to you, forgive me.

JOHN. What could you have done? You were never close enough.

ELEANOR. When you were little, you were torn from me: blame Henry.

JOHN. I was torn from you by midwives and I haven't seen you since.

ELEANOR. Then blame me if it helps.

RICHARD. No, it's the midwives' fault. They threw the baby out and kept the afterbirth.

JOHN. You're everything a little brother dreams of. You know that? I used to dream about you all the time.

ELEANOR. Oh, Johnny . . .

JOHN. That's right, Mother; mother me.

ELEANOR. Yes, if you'd let me.

JOHN. Let you? Let you put your arms around me just the way you never did? (*They are close.*) You can do it. Think I'm Richard. (*She puts her arms around him.*) That's it. That's the way. Now kiss my scabby cheek and run your fingers through my hair.

ELEANOR. John, John . . .

JOHN (*wrenching away*). No—it's all false. You know what I am? I'm the family nothing. Geoffrey's smart and Richard's brave and I'm not anything.

ELEANOR. You are to me.

JOHN. I'll show you, Eleanor. I haven't lost yet. (*Moving to go.*) Geoff.

GEOFFREY. In a minute.

JOHN. What's that?

GEOFFREY. Run along. I'm busy now.

JOHN. I give the orders. I'm the master. When I call, you come.

GEOFFREY. There's news in Chinon, John. That falling sound was you.

JOHN. The woods are full of chancellors.

GEOFFREY. And the castle's full of kings.

JOHN. Oh, you're not really leaving me?

GEOFFREY. No; I've already left.

JOHN. I don't care. I don't need anybody. (*He exits.*)

GEOFFREY. Well, Mummy, here I am.

ELEANOR. John's lost a chancellor, has he?

GEOFFREY. And you've gained one.

ELEANOR. It's a bitter thing your Mummy has to say.

GEOFFREY. She doesn't trust me.

ELEANOR. You must know Henry isn't through with John. He'll keep the Vexin till the moon goes blue from cold and as for Richard's wedding day, we'll see the second coming first; the needlework alone can last for years.

GEOFFREY. I know. You know I know. I know you know I know, we know that Henry knows and Henry knows we know it. We're a knowledgeable family. Do you want my services or don't you?

ELEANOR. Why are you dropping John?

GEOFFREY. Because you're going to win.

ELEANOR. I haven't yet.

GEOFFREY. You will with me to help you. I can handle John. He'll swallow anything I tell him and I'll take him by the hand and walk him into any trap you set.

ELEANOR. You're good, you're first class, Geoff. Did John agree?

GEOFFREY. To what?

ELEANOR. To making you his chancellor for betraying me?

GEOFFREY. I have some principles.

ELEANOR. Then how much did you get from Henry?

GEOFFREY. Get from Henry?

ELEANOR. What's the fee for selling me to him? Or have you found some way of selling everyone to everybody?

GEOFFREY. Not yet, Mummy, but I'm working on it. I don't care who's king but you and Henry do. I want to watch the two of you go picnicking on one another.

ELEANOR. Yes, it's true; you really mean it.

GEOFFREY. Do you blame me?

ELEANOR. You've a gift for hating.

GEOFFREY. You're the expert; you should know.

ELEANOR. You've loved me all these years.

GEOFFREY. Well, God forgive me, I've upset the Queen. Madam, may you rot.

ELEANOR. We need you. Help us.

GEOFFREY. What? And miss the fun of selling you?

ELEANOR. Be Richard's chancellor.

GEOFFREY. Rot.

(*He exits.*)

ELEANOR. Oh, Geoffrey. Well, that's how deals are made. We've got him if we want him. I should like some wine. Why did I have to have such clever children? He will sell us all, you know; but only if he thinks we think he won't. Scenes. I can't touch my sons except in scenes. (RICHARD *gives her a glass of wine.*) What's the matter, Richard?

RICHARD. Nothing.

ELEANOR. It's a heavy thing, your nothing. When I write or send for you or speak or reach, your nothings come. Like stones.

RICHARD. Don't play a scene with me.

ELEANOR. I wouldn't if I could.

RICHARD. There'd be no profit in it. That's my one advantage over you. You're wiser, shrewder, more experienced. I'm colder; I feel less.

ELEANOR. Why, you don't know yourself at all. I've known who I am some years now. I had, at one time, many appetites. I wanted poetry and power and the young men who create them both. I even wanted Henry, too, in those days. Now I've only one desire left: to see you king.

RICHARD. The only thing you want to see is Father's vitals on a bed of lettuce. You don't care who wins as long as Henry loses. You'd see Philip on the throne. You'd feed us to the Franks or hand us to the Holy Romans. You'd do anything.

ELEANOR (*nodding wearily*). That's good to know.

RICHARD. You are Medea to the teeth but this is one son you won't use for vengeance on your husband.

ELEANOR. I could bend you. I could wear you like a bracelet—but I'd sooner die.

RICHARD. You're old enough to die, in any case.

ELEANOR. How my captivity has changed you. Henry meant to hurt me and he's hacked you up instead. More wine. (*He takes the glass and goes to pour. She gazes at the hand that held the glass.*) Men coveted this talon once. Henry was eighteen when we met and I was Queen of France. He came down from the North to Paris with a mind like Aristotle's and a form like mortal sin. We shattered the Commandments on the spot. I spent three months annulling Louis and in spring, in May not far from here, we married. Young Count Henry and his Countess. But in three years' time, I was his Queen and he was King of England. Done at twenty-one. Five years your junior, General.

RICHARD. I can count.

ELEANOR. No doubt the picture of your parents being fond does not hang in your gallery—but we were fond. There was no Thomas Becket then, or Rosamund. No rivals—only me. And then young Henry came and you and all the other blossoms in my garden. Yes, if I'd been sterile, darling, I'd be happier today.

RICHARD. Is that designed to hurt me?

ELEANOR. What a waste. I've fought with Henry over who comes next, whose dawn is it and which son gets the sunset and we'll never live to see it. Look at you. I loved you more than Henry and it's cost me everything.

RICHARD. What do you want?

ELEANOR. I want us back the way we were.

RICHARD. That's not it.

ELEANOR. All right, then. I want the Aquitaine.

RICHARD. Now that's the mother I remember.

ELEANOR. No, it's not at all, but if you find her more congenial, she's the one you'll get. We can win. I can get you Alais. I can make the marriage happen—but I've got to have the Aquitaine to do it. I must have it back.

RICHARD. You were better in your scene with Geoffrey.

ELEANOR. Shall I write my will? "To Richard, everything." Would you believe me then? Where's paper?

RICHARD. Paper burns.

ELEANOR. And tears and turns to pudding in the rain. What can I do?

RICHARD. I did think Geoffrey put it nicely. You can rot.

ELEANOR. I love you.

RICHARD. You love nothing. You are incomplete. The human parts of you are missing. You're as dead as you are deadly.

ELEANOR. Don't leave me.

RICHARD. You were lovely once. I've seen the pictures.

ELEANOR. Oh, don't you remember how you loved me?

RICHARD. Vaguely—like a legend.

ELEANOR. You remember. We were always hand in hand.

(*Thrusting her hand in his.*) That's how it felt.

RICHARD. As coarse and hot as that.

ELEANOR (*snatching her hand away*). This won't burn. I'll scratch a will on this. (*Baring her forearm, with a small knife suddenly in her other hand.*) To Richard, everything.

RICHARD (*as she draws the blade across the flesh*). Mother!

ELEANOR. Remember how I taught you numbers and the lute and poetry.

RICHARD (*as they hold each other*). Mother.

ELEANOR. See? You do remember. I taught you dancing, too, and languages and all the music that I knew and how to love what's beautiful. The sun was warmer then and we were every day together.

DIM AND BLACKOUT

Scene Four

The Reception Hall, immediately following. A Christmas tree has been added to the room. JOHN *is drinking from a bottle as the lights rise.* GEOFFREY *enters, calling.*

———

GEOFFREY. John—there you are.

JOHN. Go find yourself another fool.

GEOFFREY. You're angry: good. Now, here's my plan.

JOHN. You are a rancid bastard. Want to fight?

GEOFFREY. John, use your head. Would I betray you?

JOHN. Why not? Everybody else does.

GEOFFREY. John, I only turned on you to get their confidence. It worked; they trust me.

JOHN. I tell you, your leg could fall off at the pelvis and I wouldn't trust the stump to bleed.

GEOFFREY. If you're not king, I'm nothing. You're my way to power, John.

JOHN. I still don't trust you.

GEOFFREY. Always put your faith in vices. Trust my slyness if you think I'm sly. Make use of me, deceive me, cast me off—but not until I've made you king.

JOHN. You think I can't outthink you, do you? All right, what's your plan?

GEOFFREY. We've got to make a deal with Philip.

JOHN. Why?

GEOFFREY. Because you're out and Richard's in.

JOHN. What kind of deal?

GEOFFREY. A war. If we three join and fight now, we can finish Richard off.

JOHN. You mean destroy him?

GEOFFREY. Yes.

JOHN. And Mother, too?

GEOFFREY. And Mother, too. Well, do we do it? Is it on?

JOHN. I've got to think.

GEOFFREY. We're extra princes now. You know where extra princes go.

JOHN. Down?

GEOFFREY. Very down.

PHILIP (*entering*). I see I'm early for my audience. Or am I late?

GEOFFREY. No, you're exquisitely on time. I feel the strangest sense of kinship with you, Philip.

PHILIP. So you've sensed it, too.

GEOFFREY. How far around the corner were you?

PHILIP. How'd you know?

GEOFFREY. You came in so conveniently.

PHILIP. I'll learn.

GEOFFREY. Well, was there anything you didn't overhear?

PHILIP. John's answer. Does he want a war or doesn't he?

GEOFFREY. Do you? If John asks for your soldiers, will he get them?

PHILIP. If John wants a war, he's got one.

GEOFFREY. John, you hear that?

JOHN. I'm still thinking.

GEOFFREY. Let me help. It's either Richard on the throne or you.

JOHN (*to* PHILIP). You think we'd win?

PHILIP. I know it.

JOHN. Father's coming.

GEOFFREY (*moving to exit*). This way. We've got plans to make. (*Turning back as* PHILIP *exits.*) John.

JOHN. In a minute.

(GEOFFREY *exits.*)

HENRY. (*entering with* ALAIS; *to* ALAIS). I'd appreciate a little quiet confidence. I have enough nits picking at me.

JOHN. Father, have you got a minute?

HENRY. What for?

JOHN. If you had a minute, we could talk.

HENRY. I'm busy now. Have you seen Philip?

JOHN. Look: you know that hunting trip we're taking on my birthday?

HENRY. Well?

JOHN. Forget it. I'm not going.

HENRY. Why not?

JOHN. I'm just not.

HENRY. But, John, the trip's all planned.

JOHN (*moving to go*). I'll go get Philip for you.

HENRY. You did have a good time last year, didn't you?

JOHN. I loved it.

HENRY. What's wrong, lad?

JOHN. You're busy.

HENRY. True enough but—

JOHN. You've got more important things to do.

HENRY. I can't make things all right if I don't know what's wrong.

JOHN. You're giving Richard everything.

HENRY. You think I'd do that?

JOHN. You don't love me any more.

HENRY. Don't pout—and stand up straight. How often do I have to tell you?

JOHN. When's my coronation?

HENRY. When I say so.

JOHN. That's no answer.

(*He starts off.*)

HENRY. John.

JOHN. Tell her how much you love her. You're a wonder with the women.

(*He exits.*)

HENRY. What in hell was that about?

ALAIS. He heard you disinherit him upstairs and wondered if you meant it.

HENRY. If I meant it? When I've fathered him and mothered him and babied him? He's all I've got. How often does he have to hear it? Every supper? Should we start the soup with who we love and who we don't?

ALAIS. I heard you promise me to Richard.

HENRY. You don't think I meant it?

ALAIS. I think you enjoy it, passing me from hand to hand. What am I to you—a collection plate? Or am I all you've got, like John?

HENRY. I've got to get the Aquitaine for John.

ALAIS. I talk people and you answer back in provinces.

HENRY. They get mixed up. What's the Aquitaine to Eleanor? It's not a province, it's a way to torture me. That's why she's upstairs wooing Richard, wheezing on the coals. She'll squeeze it out of him. God, but I'd love to eavesdrop. (*Doing* ELEANOR.) I taught you prancing, lamb, and lute and flute—

ELEANOR (*entering, carrying a great pile of Christmas boxes*). That's marvelous; it's absolutely me. (*He takes some from her.*) There you are. I thought as long as I was coming down I'd bring them. Where's the tree?

HENRY. (*leading the way to it*). Whatever are you giving me?

ELEANOR. You're such a child: you always ask.

HENRY (*reading from a package*). To Henry. (*Weighing it.*) Heavy. (*Delighted.*) It's my headstone. Eleanor, you spoil me.

ELEANOR. I never could deny you anything.

ALAIS. You've grown old gracefully, you two; I'll give you that.

HENRY (*as* ALAIS *starts to go*). Don't go. It nettles her to see how much I need you.

ALAIS. You need me, Henry, like a tailor needs a tinker's dam.

HENRY. Alais—

ALAIS. I know that look. He's going to say he loves me.

HENRY. Like my life. (*She turns sharply and exits.*) I talk like that to keep her spirits up. Well, how'd you do with Richard? Did you break his heart?

ELEANOR. You think he ought to give me back the Aquitaine?

HENRY. I can't think why he shouldn't. After all, I've promised him the throne.

ELEANOR. The boy keeps wondering if your promises are any good.

HENRY. There's no sense asking if the air's good when there's nothing else to breathe.

ELEANOR. Exactly what I told him.

HENRY. Have you got it? Will he give it back?

ELEANOR. How can you think I'd ever pass it on to John?

HENRY. It matters to me desperately.

ELEANOR. Why should it? Does it matter what comes after us?

HENRY. Ask any sculptor, ask Praxiteles, "Why don't you work in butter?" Eleanor, because it doesn't last.

ELEANOR. Is Johnny bronze? He'll go as green from mold as any of our sons.

HENRY. I know that. Richard gets the throne. You heard my promise. What else do you want?

ELEANOR. No Aquitaine for John.

HENRY. I've got to give him something. Isn't some agreement possible?

ELEANOR. Love, in a world where carpenters get resurrected, anything is possible.

HENRY. You bore him, dammit; he's your son.

ELEANOR. Oh, heavens yes. Two hundred eighty days I bore him. I recall them all. You'd only just found Rosamund.

HENRY. Why her so damn particularly? I've found other women.

ELEANOR. Countless others.

HENRY. What's your count? Let's have a tally of the bedspreads you've spread out on.

ELEANOR. Thomas Becket's.

HENRY. That's a lie.

ELEANOR. I know it. Jealousy looks silly on us, Henry.

HENRY. Doesn't it.

ELEANOR. You still care what I do.

HENRY. I want the Aquitaine for John. I want it and I'll have it.

ELEANOR. Is that menace you're conveying? Is it to be torture? Will you boil me or stretch me, which? Or am I to be perforated?

HENRY. I have the documents and you will sign.

ELEANOR. How can you force me to? Threats? Sign or I refuse to feed you? Tears? Oh, sign before my heart goes crack. Bribes, offers, deals? I'm like the earth, old man; there isn't any way around me.

HENRY. I adore you.

ELEANOR. Save your aching arches; that road is closed.

HENRY. I've got an offer for you, *ma jolie.*

ELEANOR. A deal, a deal. I give the richest province on the Continent to John for what? You tell me, mastermind. For what?

HENRY. Your freedom.

ELEANOR. Oh.

HENRY. Once Johnny has the Aquitaine, you're free. I'll let you out. Think: on the loose in London, winters in Provence, impromptu trips to visit Richard anywhere he's killing people. All that for a signature.

ELEANOR. You're good.

HENRY. I thought it might appeal to you. You always fancied traveling.

ELEANOR. Yes, I did. I even made poor Louis take me on Crusade. How's that for blasphemy? I dressed my maids as Amazons and rode bare-breasted halfway to Damascus. Louis had a seizure and I damn near died of windburn but the troops were dazzled. Henry, I'm against the wall.

HENRY. Because I've put you there, don't think I like to see it.

ELEANOR. I believe it; you do feel for me. To be a prisoner, to be bricked in when you've known the world—I'll never know how I've survived. These ten years, Henry, have been unimaginable. And you can offer me the only thing I want if I give up the only thing I treasure and still feel for me. You give your falcons more affection than I get.

HENRY. My falcons treat me better.

ELEANOR. Handle me with iron gloves, then.

HENRY. Sign the papers and we'll break the happy news. The Queen is free, John joins the landed gentry, Philip's satisfied and Richard gets a princess.

ELEANOR. Yes. Let's have it done. I'll sign. On one condition.

HENRY. Name it.

ELEANOR. Have the wedding now.

HENRY. What's that?

ELEANOR. Why, I've surprised you. Surely it's not sudden. They've been marching down the aisle for sixteen years and that's a long walk. John can be the best man—that's a laugh—and you can give the bride away. I want to watch you do it.

HENRY. Alais—I can live without her.

ELEANOR. And I thought you loved her.

HENRY. So I do.

ELEANOR. Thank God. You frightened me: I was afraid this wouldn't hurt.

HENRY. You fill me full of fear and pity. What a tragedy you are.

ELEANOR. I wonder, do you ever wonder if I slept with Geoffrey?

HENRY. With my father?

ELEANOR. It's not true but one hears rumors. Don't you ever wonder?

HENRY. Is it rich, despising me? Is it rewarding?

ELEANOR. No—it's terrible.

HENRY. Then stop it.

ELEANOR. How? It's what I live for.

HENRY. Rosamund, I loved you!

ELEANOR (*calling*). John—Richard—Geoffrey.

HENRY. Where's a priest? I'll do it. I'll show you. By Christ, I will. (*As* PHILIP, JOHN *and* GEOFFREY *enter from one side,* ALAIS *and* RICHARD *come in from the other.*) Somebody dig me up a priest.

JOHN. What for? What's happened?

ELEANOR. Richard's getting married.

JOHN. Now? He's getting married now?

ELEANOR. I never cease to marvel at the quickness of your mind.

JOHN. You can't hurt me, you bag of bile, no matter what you say. (*To* HENRY.) But you can. Father, why?

HENRY. Because I say so. (*To* GEOFFREY.) You. Bring me a bishop.

ELEANOR (*as* GEOFFREY *starts to go*). Get old Durham. He's just down the hall. (GEOFFREY *exits. To* ALAIS.) You'll make a lovely bride. I wonder if I'll cry.

ALAIS. You sound as if you think it's going to happen.

ELEANOR. And I do.

ALAIS. He's only plotting. Can't you tell when Henry's plotting?

ELEANOR. Not this time.

ALAIS. He'll never give me up.

HENRY. You think I won't?

ALAIS. Because you told me so.

HENRY. You're not my Helen; I won't fight a war to save a face. We're done.

ALAIS. I don't believe you.

HENRY. Wait ten minutes.

GEOFFREY (*entering*). I've sent word to Durham. He'll be waiting in the chapel.

HENRY. Good—let's get it over with.

ALAIS. Don't do this to me, Henry.

HENRY (*to* RICHARD). Take her.

ALAIS. No, wait. You don't want me, Richard.

HENRY (*to* ALAIS). Go to him.

ALAIS (*as a procession forms around her*). Not yet— (*To* PHILIP.) I am your sister. Can't you find some pity for me? (*To* ELEANOR.) *Maman,* you won't let this happen. (*Panic rising.*) Henry, if you ever loved me— (*At a gesture from* HENRY, *the procession starts to move.*) I won't do it. I won't say the words, not one of them. Henry, please. It makes no sense. Why give me up? What do you get? What are you gaining?

HENRY. Why, the Aquitaine, of course.

RICHARD (*stopping dead*). What's that?

HENRY. Your mother gets her freedom and I get the Aquitaine. (*To* ELEANOR.) That is the proposition, isn't it? You did agree.

RICHARD (*to* ELEANOR). Of course she did. I knew, I knew it. It was all pretense. You used me. God, and I believed you. I believed it all.

ELEANOR. I meant it all.

RICHARD. No wedding. There will be no wedding.

HENRY. But, my boy—

RICHARD. Not at this price.

HENRY. But Durham's waiting.

RICHARD. She's not worth the Aquitaine.

HENRY. You've simply got to marry her. It isn't much to ask. For my sake, Richard.

RICHARD. Never.

HENRY. But I've promised Philip. Think of my position.

RICHARD. Damn the wedding and to hell with your position.

HENRY. You don't dare defy me.

RICHARD. Don't I?

HENRY (*to* PHILIP). You're the King of France, for goodness' sake. Speak up. Do something.

RICHARD (*to* PHILIP). Make a threat, why don't you? Scare me.

PHILIP. Dunce.

RICHARD. Am I?

PHILIP. He never meant to have the wedding.

HENRY. Come again?

PHILIP. You're good at rage. I like the way you play it.

HENRY. Boy, don't ever call a king a liar to his face.

PHILIP. I'm not a boy. To you or anybody.

HENRY. Boy, you came here asking for a wedding or the Vexin back. By God, you don't get either one. It's no to both.

PHILIP. You have a pact with France.

HENRY. Then damn the document and damn the French. She'll never marry, not while I'm alive.

PHILIP. Your life and never are two different times.

HENRY. Not on my clock, boy.

(PHILIP *exits.*)

RICHARD. Listen to the lion. Flash a yellow tooth and frighten me.

HENRY. Don't spoil it, Richard. Take it like a good sport.

RICHARD. How's your bad leg?

HENRY. Better, thank you.

RICHARD. And your back and all the rest of it. You're getting old. One day you'll have me once too often.

HENRY. When? I'm fifty now. My God, boy, I'm the oldest man I know. I've got a decade on the Pope. What's it to be? The broadsword when I'm eighty-five?

RICHARD. I'm not a second son. Not now. Your Henry's in the vault, you know.

HENRY. I know; I've seen him there.

RICHARD. I'll have the crown.

HENRY. You'll have what Daddy gives you.

RICHARD. I am next in line.

HENRY. To nothing.

RICHARD. Then we'll have the broadswords now.

HENRY. This minute?

RICHARD. On the battlefield.

HENRY. So we're at war.

RICHARD. Yes, we're at war. I have two thousand men at Poitiers.

HENRY. Can they hear you? Call and see

who comes. You are as close to Poitiers as you're going to get.

RICHARD. You don't dare hold me prisoner.

HENRY. You're a king's son so I treat you with respect. You have the freedom of the castle.

RICHARD. You can't keep me here.

HENRY. Until we've all agreed that John comes next, I can and will.

RICHARD. The castle doesn't stand that holds me. Post your guards.

(*He exits.*)

JOHN. My God, I'm king again. Fantastic. It's a miracle. (*To* GEOFFREY, *who joins him.*) Are you happy for me, Geoff?

GEOFFREY (*as they exit together*). I'm happy for us both.

ELEANOR. I came close, didn't I? (*To* ALAIS.) I almost had my freedom and I almost had you for my son. I should have liked it, being free. (*To* HENRY.) You played it nicely. You were good.

HENRY. I really was. I fooled you, didn't I? God, but I do love being king.

ELEANOR. Well, Henry, liege and lord, what happens now?

HENRY. I've no idea. I know I'm winning and I know I'll win but what the next move is— (*Looking at her closely.*) You're not scared?

ELEANOR. No.

HENRY. I think you are.

ALAIS. I was. You mustn't play with feelings, Henry; not with mine.

HENRY. It wasn't possible to lose you. I must hold you dearer than I thought. (*To* ELEANOR.) You've got your enigmatic face on. What's your mood, I wonder.

ELEANOR. Pure delight. I'm locked up with my sons: what mother wouldn't dream of that? (*She moves to go, then stops in the doorway.*) One thing.

HENRY. Yes?

ELEANOR. May I watch you kiss her?

HENRY. Can't you ever stop?

ELEANOR. I watch you every night. I conjure it before I sleep.

HENRY. Leave it at that.

ELEANOR. My curiosity is intellectual: I want to see how accurate I am.

HENRY (*to* ALAIS). Forget the dragon in the doorway: come. (*Holding her.*) Believe I love you, for I do. Believe I'm yours forever, for I am. Believe in my contentment and the joy you give me and believe— (*To* ELEANOR.) You want more?

(*Their eyes burn at each other. Then, turning slowly back to* ALAIS.) I'm an old man in an empty place. Be with me.

(*They kiss.* ELEANOR *stands in the doorway, watching.*)

DIM AND BLACKOUT

SCENE FIVE

ELEANOR's *chamber, shortly afterward.* ELEANOR, *alone on stage, is seated at the table as the lights rise. A chest of jewels is on the table and she is feverishly covering herself with precious things.*

———

ELEANOR (*putting on a great bib necklace*). How beautiful you make me. What might Solomon have sung had he seen this? (*Picking up a mirror, unable to look.*) I can't. I'd turn to salt. (*Putting the mirror down.*) I've lost again. I'm done, for now. Well—there'll be other Christmases. (*Picking up another elaborate necklace.*) I'd hang you from the nipples but you'd shock the children. (*Putting it on.*) They kissed sweetly, didn't they? I'll have him next time. I can wait. (*Picking up a crown.*) Ah, there you are; my comfort and my company. We're locked in for another year: four seasons more. Oh, what a desolation, what a life's work. (*Putting it on as* GEOFFREY *enters.*) Is it too much? Be sure to squint as you approach. You may be blinded by my beauty.

GEOFFREY. Richard's raging all around the castle.

ELEANOR. Is he? Why?

GEOFFREY. He says it's got to do with being held a prisoner but I think he likes to rage.

ELEANOR. And John?

GEOFFREY. John's skipping after Richard, saying naughty things.

ELEANOR. And you?

GEOFFREY. I thought you might be lonely.

ELEANOR (*holding out the crown*). Here, Chancellor. Try it on for size.

GEOFFREY. Why do you think so little of me?

ELEANOR. Little? Never that. Whatever you are, you're not little.

GEOFFREY. I remember my third birthday. Not just pictures of the garden or the gifts, but who did what to whom and how it felt. My memory reaches back that far and never once can I remember anything from you or Father warmer than indifference. Why is that?

ELEANOR. I don't know.

GEOFFREY. That was not an easy question for me and I don't deserve an easy answer.

ELEANOR. There are times I think we loved none of our children.

GEOFFREY. Still too easy, don't you think?

ELEANOR. I'm weary and you want a simple answer and I haven't one. (*Starting to remove the jewelry.*) I was thinking earlier of Peter Abélard. I was a queen of fifteen in those days and on dull afternoons I'd go watch Héloïse watch Abélard spread heresy like bonemeal in the palace gardens. Here the Seine and there the cypress trees and how it bored me. Thought, pure thought, flashed clear as water all around me and all I could think about was how to make a Caesar of a monkish husband. I'd like to hear the old man talk again; I'd listen now. For my ambition's thin with age and all the mysteries are as plump as ever. (*Looking at* GEOFFREY.) I read minds. In yours, a shapely hand is writing, "Clever Mother, what's your clever reason for this clever talk?" It isn't clever but you'll make it so. (*Patting his cheek.*) I am so sick of all of you.

JOHN (*entering*). I thought I'd come and gloat a little.

ELEANOR. Mother's tired. Come stick pins tomorrow morning; I'll be more responsive then.

JOHN. It's no fun goading anyone tonight.

ELEANOR. Come, let me look at you. I'm full of looks this evening. I have looked a little in the mirror and I've read a passage in your brother's mind; what's there to see in you? A little me, a little Henry and a lot of someone I don't know. (*Turning away.*) Oh, John . . .

RICHARD (*entering*). The bastard's boxed us up.

ELEANOR. What's that, dear?

RICHARD. We're his prisoners, if that interests you.

ELEANOR. Why should it? I'm his prisoner anyway.

RICHARD. I've got to get to Poitiers. Henry wants a war, I'll give him one.

ELEANOR. I don't see how.

RICHARD. You seem to take that calmly.

ELEANOR. Well?

RICHARD. It was—correct me if I'm wrong, but it was my impression that you wanted Henry's throne for me.

ELEANOR. We've lost it this time, Richard. We can't win.

RICHARD. You think I'm finished, do you?

ELEANOR. So I do. I've suffered more defeats than you have teeth. I know one when it happens to me. Take your wormwood like a good boy. Swallow it and go to bed.

RICHARD. I will be king.

ELEANOR. And so you will. But not this year—and what's it matter to me anyway? The world stops when I die.

RICHARD. Yours does; mine doesn't.

ELEANOR. Leave it, Richard. Let it go for now. I have.

RICHARD. I can't.

JOHN. It's not so hard. Try saying after me: John wins, I lose.

RICHARD. What if John died?

JOHN. What's that?

RICHARD. What if he left us suddenly.

JOHN. You wouldn't dare.

RICHARD (*going for his dagger*). Why on earth wouldn't I?

JOHN. A knife—he's got a knife.

ELEANOR. Of course he has a knife. He always has a knife. We all have knives. It is eleven eighty-three and we're barbarians. How clear we make it. Oh, my piglets, we're the origins of war. Not history's forces nor the times nor justice nor the lack of it nor causes nor religions nor ideas nor kinds of government nor any other thing. We are the killers; we breed war. We carry it, like syphilis, inside. Dead bodies rot in field and stream because the living ones are rotten. For the love of God, can't we love one another just a little? That's how peace begins. We have so much to love each other for. We have such possibilities, my children; we could change the world.

GEOFFREY. And while we hugged each other, what would Philip do?

JOHN. Oh good God—Philip. We're supposed to start a war. If Father finds out, I'll be ruined.

GEOFFREY. Steady, John; don't panic.

JOHN. Some adviser you are.

GEOFFREY. Don't do anything without me. Let me handle it.

JOHN. If you're so smart, why am I always doing something dumb?

(*He exits.*)

ELEANOR (*alive again*). Well, Geoffrey. He's made a pact with Philip. You advised John into making war. That peerless boy; he's disinherited himself. When Henry finds out, when I tell him what John's done—I need a little time. Can you keep John away from Philip till I say so?

GEOFFREY. Anything you say.

(*He exits.*)

ELEANOR (*to* RICHARD). I want you out of here before this breaks. And that needs Philip. He has soldiers with him if he'll use them. Go to him, be desperate, promise anything: the Vexin, Brittany. Then once you're free and John is out of favor, we'll make further plans.

RICHARD. You talk to Philip. You're the diplomat; you see him.

ELEANOR. You're a friend. You know him; I don't. Quickly now. (*He moves to exit.*) And, Richard. (*He turns in the doorway.*) Promise anything. (*He exits.*) I haven't lost, it isn't over. Oh, I've got the old man this time. The damn fool thinks he loves John, he believes it. That's where the knife goes in. Knives, knives . . . it was a fine thought, wasn't it? Oh, Henry, we have done a big thing badly. (*Looking for her mirror.*) Where's that mirror? I am Eleanor and I can look at anything. (*Gazing into the mirror.*) My, what a lovely girl. How could her king have left her?

DIM AND BLACKOUT

SCENE SIX

PHILIP's *chamber, immediately following. It is a gracious room, its back wall lined with tapestries. A canopy bed, the curtains closed, stands at one side. A pair of chairs sit, one at each side of a low table on which there are two goblets and a wine decanter.*

———

As the lights rise, PHILIP *is preparing for bed. He turns as* GEOFFREY, *calling his name, comes skidding into the room.*

GEOFFREY. Philip, Philip—is John here?

PHILIP. Here? In my room?

GEOFFREY. Come on, Philip; this is me.

PHILIP. I've been expecting him.

GEOFFREY. The whole thing breaks tonight; we've reached the end of it.

PHILIP. If that's a warning, thank you.

GEOFFREY. What if it's an offer?

PHILIP. "What if" is a game for scholars: what if angels sat on pinheads?

GEOFFREY. What if I were king?

PHILIP. It's your game, Geoff; you play it.

GEOFFREY. All of England's land in France, from Normandy down to the Spanish border, once I'm king.

PHILIP. All that. What could I do that's worth all that?

GEOFFREY. By morning I can be the chosen son. The crown can come to me. But once it does, once Henry's favor falls my way, the war begins.

PHILIP. We have so many wars. Which one is this?

GEOFFREY. The one that Richard, John and Eleanor will make. I'll have to fight to keep what Henry, in his rage, is going to give me.

PHILIP. Yes, you will.

GEOFFREY. That's why I need you, Philip. Will you fight with me against them all?

PHILIP. Against them all?

GEOFFREY. Don't tell me it's a risk. I wouldn't hand you half of France to fight an easy war.

PHILIP. I wouldn't want you for an enemy.

GEOFFREY. Are we allies, then?

PHILIP. We were born to be.

GEOFFREY. I should say something solemn but I haven't time. I'm off to Father with the news that John's a traitor. After that—

JOHN (*bursting from behind the tapestry*). You stink, you know that? You're a stinker and you stink.

GEOFFREY. Come on. We're finished here.

JOHN. I'll kill you. Where's a dagger?

GEOFFREY. Hush, John, or you'll spoil everything.

JOHN. A sword, a spear, a candlestick. (*Reaching for a candlestick.*) It's lights out, stinker.

GEOFFREY (*stopping him*). Dumb. If you're a prince, there's hope for every ape in Africa. I had you saved. I wasn't on my way to Father—but he was. He would have gone to Henry and betrayed you. Look: it's in his face.

JOHN (*looking at* PHILIP *in dismay*). Oh. It's true. I don't know who my friends are.

RICHARD (*offstage, calling from a distance*). Philip.

GEOFFREY (*indicating the tapestry*). May we?

PHILIP. That's what tapestries are for.

JOHN (*as* GEOFFREY *disappears, with him, behind the tapestry*). I've ruined everything. I'll never learn.

PHILIP. Is someone there? I heard my name.

RICHARD (*entering*). I called it.

PHILIP. Richard. Hello, Richard.

RICHARD. You're halfway to bed. I'll wait for morning.

PHILIP. Come in.

RICHARD. Mother sent me.

PHILIP. Come in anyway. (*Filling glasses from the decanter.*) Our alchemists have stumbled on the art of boiling burgundy. It turns to steam and when it cools we call it brandywine.

RICHARD. I'm Henry's prisoner.

PHILIP. So you said you'd go to war and Henry drew the drawbridge on you.

RICHARD. Do you find that charming?

PHILIP. No.

RICHARD. Then why the charming smile?

PHILIP. I thought, I can't think why, of when you were in Paris last. Can it be two whole years ago?

RICHARD. It can. I need an army, Philip.

PHILIP (*handing him the brandy*). It will take the cold away.

RICHARD. I must have soldiers.

PHILIP. Have I aged? Do I seem older to you? They've been two fierce years: I've studied and I've trained to be a king.

RICHARD. I'll have your answer—yes or no.

PHILIP (*cold*). You'll have it when I give it. (*Warm again.*) See? I've changed. I'm not the boy you taught to hunt two years ago. Remember? Racing after boar, you flying first, me scrambling after, all day into dusk—

RICHARD (*turning to leave*). I'll try another time.

PHILIP. Don't go.

RICHARD. I must know: will you help me?

PHILIP. Sit and we'll discuss it. (RICHARD *sits.*) You never write.

RICHARD. To anyone.

PHILIP. Why should I make you King of England? Aren't I better off with John or Geoffrey? Why have you to fight when I could have the cretin or the fiend?

RICHARD. Would we fight?

PHILIP. We're fighting now. (*Terminating the interview.*) Good night.

RICHARD. You're still a boy.

PHILIP. In some ways. Which way did you have in mind?

RICHARD. You haven't asked how much you're worth to me.

PHILIP. You'll tell me.

RICHARD. You can have the Vexin back.

PHILIP. And what else?

RICHARD. All of Brittany.

PHILIP. That's Geoffrey's.

RICHARD. Does that matter?

PHILIP. Possibly to Geoffrey. And what else?

RICHARD. That's all your help is worth.

PHILIP. And in return, what do you want from me?

RICHARD. Two thousand soldiers.

PHILIP. And what else?

RICHARD. Five hundred knights on horse.

PHILIP. And what else?

RICHARD. Arms and siege equipment.

PHILIP. And what else?

RICHARD. I never wrote because I thought you'd never answer. (PHILIP *says nothing.*) You got married.

PHILIP. Does that make a difference?

RICHARD. Doesn't it?

PHILIP. I've spent two years on every street in hell.

RICHARD. That's odd: I didn't see you there. (PHILIP *takes* RICHARD'*s hand. They start moving to the bed.*) You haven't said you love me.

PHILIP. When the time comes.

HENRY (*offstage, calling*). Philip.

RICHARD. Don't go.

PHILIP. Hush.

(*He opens the bed curtains.*)

RICHARD. Philip . . . (*Climbing through the curtains.*) Hurry.

HENRY (*still offstage*). Philip, lad.

PHILIP (*closing the curtains*). Is someone there?

HENRY (*entering*). I am. It's not too late at night?

PHILIP. I've been expecting you.

HENRY. Oh, have you?

PHILIP (*indicating the glasses, his and* RICHARD'*s*). See—two glasses. I did hope you'd come.

HENRY. Good; we can't leave negotiations where they are. I've seen more royal rooms. Poor Chinon wasn't meant to sleep so many kings. I keep looking for your father in you.

PHILIP (*pouring brandy*). He's not there.

HENRY. I miss him. Has Richard or the Queen been here to see you?

PHILIP. Does it matter? If they haven't yet, they will.

HENRY. I want to reach a settlement. I left you with too little earlier.

PHILIP. Yes; nothing is too little.

HENRY. I am sorry you're not fonder of me, lad. Your father always said, "Be fond of stronger men."

PHILIP. No wonder he loved everyone.

HENRY. They'll offer you whole provinces to fight me.

PHILIP. Shocking. My advice to you is discipline your children.

HENRY. I came here to offer peace.

PHILIP. Piss on your peace.

HENRY. Your father would have wept.

PHILIP. My father was a weeper.

HENRY. Fight me and you'll lose.

PHILIP. I can't lose, Henry. I have time. Just look at you. Great heavy arms—they'd crush me like a leaf of lettuce. But each year they get a little heavier. The sand goes pit-pat in the glass. I'm in no hurry, Henry. I've got time.

HENRY. Suppose I hurry things along? What if I say that England is at war with France?

PHILIP. Then France surrenders. I don't have to fight to win. Take all you want—this county, that one. You won't keep it long.

HENRY. What kind of courage have you got?

PHILIP. The tidal kind: it comes and goes.

HENRY. By God, I'd love to turn you loose on Eleanor. More brandywine?

PHILIP. You recognize it?

HENRY. They were boiling it in Ireland before the snakes left. Well, things look a little bleak for Henry, don't they? You'll say yes to Richard when he comes; arms, soldiers, anything he asks for.

PHILIP. I'd be foolish not to.

HENRY. And withdraw it all before the battle ever started.

PHILIP. Wouldn't you, in my place?

HENRY. Why fight Henry when his sons will do it for you?

PHILIP. Yes, exactly.

HENRY. You've got promise, lad. That's first-class thinking.

PHILIP. Thank you, sir.

HENRY (*emptying his glass*). Good night.

PHILIP (*uncertain for the first time*). Good night? You're going? (HENRY *nods benignly*.) But we haven't settled anything.

HENRY. We open Christmas packages at noon. Till then.

PHILIP. You can't be finished with me.

HENRY. But I am. And it's been very satisfactory.

PHILIP. What's so satisfactory?

HENRY. Winning is. I did just win. Surely you noticed.

PHILIP. Not a thing. You haven't won a damn thing.

HENRY. I've found out the way your mind works and the kind of man you are. I know your plans and expectations. You have burbled every bit of strategy you've got. I know exactly what you will do and exactly what you won't. And I've told you exactly nothing. To these aged eyes, boy, that's what winning looks like. *Dormez bien*.

PHILIP. One time, when I was very small, I watched some soldiers take their dinner pig and truss it up and put the thing, alive and kicking, on the fire. That's the sound I'm going to hear from you.

HENRY. And I thought you lacked passion.

PHILIP. You—you made my father nothing. You were always better. You bullied him, you bellied with his wife, you beat him down in every war, you twisted every treaty, you played mock-the-monk and then you made him love you for it. I was there: his last words went to you.

HENRY. He was a loving man and you learned nothing of it.

PHILIP. I learned how much fathers live in sons. A king like you has policy prepared on everything. What's the official line on sodomy? How stands the Crown on boys who do with boys?

HENRY. Richard finds his way into so many legends. Let's hear yours and see how it compares.

PHILIP. He found me first when I was fifteen. We were hunting. It was nearly dark. I lost my way. My horse fell. I was thrown. I woke to Richard touching me. He asked me if I loved him—Philip, do you love me?—and I told him yes.

HENRY. I've heard much better.

PHILIP. You know why I told him yes? So one day I could tell you all about it. You cannot imagine what that yes cost. Or perhaps you can. Imagine snuggling to a chancred whore and, bending back your lips in something like a smile, saying,

"Yes I love you and I find you beautiful."
I don't know how I did it.

RICHARD (*charging from the bed*). No!
It wasn't like that.

PHILIP. But it was.

RICHARD. You loved me.

PHILIP. Never.

RICHARD. Get your sword. You've got
one. Pick it up.

PHILIP (*to* HENRY). He's your responsibility; you talk to him.

RICHARD (*to* HENRY). Get out. Please! I
don't want you here.

HENRY. It's no great joy to be here.

RICHARD. So the royal corkscrew finds
me twisted, does he?

HENRY. I'll go tell your mother: she'll be
pleased.

RICHARD. She knows: she sent me.

HENRY. How completely hers you are.

RICHARD. You've had four sons. Who do
you claim? Not Henry? Not my buried
brother. Not that monument to muck,
that epic idiot, oh, surely not.

HENRY. The boy is dead.

RICHARD. Let's praise him, then. Who can
forget his roquefort smile, his absent brow,
those apey eyes, that spoon-edged mind?
Why him? Why him and never me?

HENRY. He was the oldest. He came first.

RICHARD. Christ, Henry, is that all?

HENRY. You went with Eleanor.

RICHARD. You never called for me. You
never said my name. I would have walked
or crawled. I'd have done anything.

HENRY. It's not my fault. I won't be
blamed.

RICHARD. I only wanted you.

HENRY. No—it's my crown. You want
my kingdom.

RICHARD. Keep your kingdom.

HENRY. That I will.

RICHARD. I hope it kills you.

HENRY. I thank God I have another son.
Thank God for John.

GEOFFREY (*stepping from behind the
tapestry*). Who shall we thank for Geoffrey? (*To* HENRY.) You don't think much
of me.

HENRY. Much? I don't think of you at
all.

GEOFFREY. Nurse used to say I had your
hands; I might have more of you. Try
seeing me. I haven't Richard's military
skill; but he was here betraying you, not
I. I haven't John's I don't know what—
God knows what you can see in John—

and he's betrayed you, too. There's only
me.

HENRY. You think I'd ever make you
king?

GEOFFREY. You'll make me king because
I'm all you've got. (*Indicating* RICHARD.)
I was to be his chancellor. Ask him why.

HENRY. I've heard enough.

GEOFFREY. For moving John to treason.

HENRY. I don't doubt he offered, I don't
doubt you tried and I don't doubt John
loves me.

GEOFFREY. Like a glutton loves his lunch.
(*He pulls the tapestry from in front of*
JOHN.)

JOHN (*to* GEOFFREY). You turd.

HENRY. Well, John?

JOHN. It isn't what you think.

HENRY. What do I think?

JOHN. What Geoffrey said. I wouldn't
plot against you, ever.

HENRY. I know; you're a good boy.

JOHN. Can I go now, please? It's late. I
ought to be in bed.

HENRY. You fool.

JOHN. Me? What have I done now?

HENRY. Couldn't you wait? Couldn't you
trust me? It was all yours. Couldn't you
believe that?

JOHN. Will you listen to the grief?

HENRY. Who do you think I built this
kingdom for?

JOHN. Me? Daddy did it all for me?
When can I have it, Daddy? Not until we
bury you?

HENRY. You're just like them. And after
all I've given you.

JOHN. I got it; I know what you gave.

HENRY. I loved you.

JOHN. You're a cold and bloody bastard,
you are, and you don't love anything.

GEOFFREY. I'm it, I'm all that's left. Here,
Father; here I am.

HENRY. My life, when it is written, will
read better than it lived. Henry Fitz-
Empress, first Plantagenet, a king at
twenty-one, the ablest soldier of an able
time. He led men well, he cared for justice
when he could and ruled, for thirty years,
a state as great as Charlemagne's. He married, out of love, a woman out of legend.
Not in Alexandria or Rome or Camelot
has there been such a queen. She bore him
many children—but no sons. King Henry
had no sons. He had three whiskered
things but he disowned them. You're not
mine. We're not connected. I deny you.

None of you will get my crown. I leave you nothing and I wish you plague. May all your children breech and die. (*Moving unsteadily toward the door.*) My boys are gone. I've lost my boys. (*Stopping, glaring up.*) You dare to damn me, do you? Well, I damn you back. God damn you. All my boys are gone. I've lost my boys. Oh Jesus, all my boys.

BLACKOUT AND CURTAIN

ACT TWO

Scene One

HENRY's *chamber, late at night. It is a large room, unadorned and without ornament. There is a plain hard bed, an armchair and a charcoal brazier. As the curtain rises,* ALAIS, *dressed for bed, is crouching by the brazier, adding spices to a pot of mulled wine.*

———

ALAIS (*singing softly*).
    The Christmas wine is in the pot,
    The Christmas coals are red.
    I'll spend the day
    The lovers' way,
    Unwrapping all my gifts in bed.
(ELEANOR *appears behind her.*)
    The Christmas goose is on the spit,
    The Christmas . . .
(*She senses someone and turns.*)
ELEANOR. No one else is caroling tonight. It might as well be Lent. When I was little, Christmas was a time of great confusion for me: the Holy Land had two kings, God and Uncle Raymond, and I never knew whose birthday we were celebrating.
ALAIS. Henry isn't here.
ELEANOR. Good; we can talk behind his back.
ALAIS. He's outside, walking.
ELEANOR. In this cold?
ALAIS. He'll never notice it. What happened?
ELEANOR. Don't you know?
ALAIS. He came and stood awhile by the fire and went away. You would have liked the way he looked.
ELEANOR. There was a scene with beds and tapestries and many things got said. Spiced wine; I'd forgotten Henry liked it. May I stay?

ALAIS. It's your room just as much as mine: we're both in residence.
ELEANOR. Packed in, like the poor, three to a bed.
ALAIS. Did you love Henry—ever?
ELEANOR. Ever? Back before the flood?
ALAIS. As long ago as Rosamund.
ELEANOR. Ah, that's pre-history, lamb; there are no written records or survivors.
ALAIS. There are pictures. She was prettier than you.
ELEANOR. Oh, much. Her eyes, in certain light, were violet and all her teeth were even. That's a rare fair feature, even teeth. She smiled to excess but she chewed with real distinction.
ALAIS. And you hate her even now.
ELEANOR. No, but I did. He put her in my place, you see, and that was very hard. Like you, she headed Henry's table; that's my chair.
ALAIS. And so you had her poisoned.
ELEANOR. That's a folk tale. Oh, I prayed for her to drop and sang a little when she did but even Circe had her limits. No, I never poisoned Rosamund. Why aren't you happy? Henry's keeping you. You must be cleverer than I am.
ALAIS. Green becomes you. You must always wear it.
ELEANOR. Are you dressing me in envy?
ALAIS. I've tried feeling pity for you but it keeps on turning into something else.
ELEANOR. Why pity?
ALAIS. You love Henry but you love his kingdom, too. You look at him and you see cities, acreage, coastline, taxes. All I see is Henry. Leave him to me, can't you?
ELEANOR. But I left him years ago.
ALAIS. You are untouchable. And I thought I could move you. Were you always like this? Years ago, when I was young and worshiped you, is this what you were like?
ELEANOR. Most likely. Child, I'm finished and I've come to give him anything he asks for.
ALAIS. Do you know what I should like for Christmas? I should like to see you suffer.
ELEANOR (*nodding*). Alais, just for you.
ALAIS (*throwing herself into* ELEANOR's *arms*). Maman, oh, Maman.
ELEANOR (*singing softly*).
    The Christmas wine will make
        you warm—
Don't shiver, child.

ALAIS. I'm not.

ELEANOR.

>The Christmas logs will glow.
>There's Christmas cheer and com-
>   fort here—

Is that you crying?

ALAIS. *Non, Maman.*

ELEANOR. Hold close and never let me go. (HENRY *appears behind them.*)

HENRY. The sky is pocked with stars. What eyes the wise men must have had to spot a new one in so many.

ELEANOR. You look cold.

ALAIS. I've mulled some wine.

HENRY. I wonder, were there fewer stars then—I don't know. I fancy there's a mystery in it. (ALAIS *hands him a cup of wine.*) What's this?

ALAIS. Warm wine.

HENRY. Why, so it is. (*Cupping her face in his hands.*) You are as beautiful as I remembered. (*Briskly.*) Off to bed. My widow wants to see me.

ALAIS. Let me stay.

HENRY. Wait up for me. I won't be long.

ALAIS. She came to find out what your plans are.

HENRY. I know that.

ALAIS. She wants you back.

HENRY (*to* ELEANOR). Old as I am?

ELEANOR. Old as you are.

ALAIS. Oh, eat each other up for all I care. (*She starts to go, then stops and turns.*) I'm an orphan and I'll never have a husband and my lover's wife has fangs for teeth and everybody's going to die. We've got no Romans and no Christians but the rest of the arena, that we have. (*She exits.*)

ELEANOR. I'm rather proud; I taught her all the rhetoric she knows.

HENRY (*pouring wine for her*). So you want me back.

ELEANOR. She thinks I do. She thinks the need for loving never stops.

HENRY. She's got a point. I marvel at you: after all these years, still like a democratic drawbridge, going down for everybody.

ELEANOR (*he gives her wine*). At my age, there's not much traffic any more.

HENRY. To your interminable health. (*He drinks.*) Well, wife, what's on your mind?

ELEANOR. Oh, Henry, we have made a mess of it.

HENRY. Yes, haven't we.

ELEANOR. Could we have done it worse?

HENRY. You look like Doomsday.

ELEANOR. Late nights do that to me. Am I puffy?

HENRY. Possibly: it's hard to tell; there's all that natural sag.

ELEANOR. I've just seen Richard.

HENRY. Splendid boy.

ELEANOR. He says you fought.

HENRY. We always do.

ELEANOR. It's his impression that you plan to disinherit them.

HENRY. I fancy I'll relent. Don't you?

ELEANOR. I don't much care. In fact, I wonder, Henry, if I care for anything. I wonder if I'm hungry out of habit and if all my lusts, like passions in a poem, aren't really recollections.

HENRY. I could listen to you lie for hours. So your lust is rusty. Gorgeous.

ELEANOR. I'm so tired, Henry.

HENRY. Sleep, then. Sleep and dream of me with croutons. *Henri à la mode de Caen.*

ELEANOR. Henry, stop it.

HENRY. Eleanor, I haven't started.

ELEANOR. What is it you want? You want the day? You've carried it. It's yours. I'm yours.

HENRY. My what? You are my what?

ELEANOR. Your anything at all. You want my name on paper? I'll sign anything. You want the Aquitaine for John? It's John's. It's his, it's yours, it's anybody's. Take it.

HENRY. In exchange for what?

ELEANOR. For nothing, for a little quiet, for an end to this, for God's sake sail me back to England, lock me up and lose the key and let me be alone. (HENRY *applauds, louder and louder.*) You have my oath. I give my word. (*The applause stops. Sinking, bone-weary, into the chair.*) Oh. Well. Well, well.

HENRY. Would you like a pillow? Footstool? What about a shawl? (*She stares dully through him.*) Your oaths are all profanities. Your word's a curse. Your name on paper is a waste of pulp. I'm vilifying you, for God's sake. Pay attention. (*No response.*) Eleanor! (*She reaches out, takes his hand and kisses it.*) Don't do that.

(*She drops the hand.*)

ELEANOR (*flatly, from far away*). Like any thinking person, I should like to think there was—I don't care whose or which—

some God. Not out of fear: death is a lark; it's life that stings. But if there were some God, then I'd exist in his imagination, like Antigone in Sophocles'. I'd have no contraditions, no confusions, no waste parts or misplaced elements and then, oh, Henry, then I'd make some sense. I'd be a queen in Arcady and not an animal in chaos. How, from where we started, did we ever reach this Christmas?

HENRY. Step by step.

ELEANOR. What happens to me now?

HENRY. That's lively curiosity from such a dead cat. If you want to know my plans, just ask me.

ELEANOR. Conquer China, sack the Vatican or take the veil; I'm not among the ones who give a damn. Just let me sign my lands to John and go to bed.

HENRY. No, you're too kind. I can't accept.

ELEANOR. Oh, come on, man. I'll sign the thing in blood or spit or bright blue ink. Let's have it done.

HENRY. Let's not. No, I don't think I want your signature on anything.

ELEANOR. You don't?

HENRY. Dear God, the pleasure I still get from goading you.

ELEANOR. You don't want John to have my provinces?

HENRY. Bull's eye.

ELEANOR. I can't bear you when you're smug.

HENRY. I know, I know.

ELEANOR. You don't want Richard and you don't want John.

HENRY. You've grasped it.

ELEANOR. All right, let me have it. Level me. What do you want?

HENRY. A new wife.

ELEANOR. Oh.

HENRY. Aesthete and poetaster that you are, you worship beauty and simplicity. I worship with you. Down with all that's ugly and complex, like frogs or pestilence or our relationship. I ask you, what's more beautiful and simple than a new wife?

ELEANOR. So I'm to be annulled. Well, will the Pope annul me, do you think?

HENRY. The Pontiff owes me one Pontificate; I think he will.

ELEANOR. Out Eleanor, in Alais. Why?

HENRY. Why? Not since Caesar, seeing Brutus with the bloody dagger in his hand, asked, "You, too?" has there been a dumber question.

ELEANOR. I'll stand by it. Why?

HENRY. A new wife, wife, will bear me sons.

ELEANOR. That is the single thing of which I should have thought you had enough.

HENRY. I want a son.

ELEANOR. Whatever for? Why, we could populate a country town with country girls who've borne you sons. How many is it? Help me count the bastards.

HENRY. All my sons are bastards.

ELEANOR. You really mean to do it.

HENRY. Lady love, with all my heart.

ELEANOR. Your sons are part of you.

HENRY. Like warts and goiters—and I'm having them removed.

ELEANOR. We made them. They're our boys.

HENRY. I know. And good God, look at them. Young Henry: vain, deceitful, weak and cowardly. The only patriotic thing he ever did was die.

ELEANOR. I thought you loved him most.

HENRY. I did. And Geoffrey: there's a masterpiece. He isn't flesh: he's a device; he's wheels and gears.

ELEANOR. Well, every family has one.

HENRY. But not four. Then Johnny. Was his latest treason your idea?

ELEANOR. John has so few ideas; no, I can't bring myself to claim it.

HENRY. I have caught him lying and I've said he's young. I've seen him cheating and I've thought he's just a boy. I've watched him steal and whore and whip his servants and he's not a child. He is the man we've made him.

ELEANOR. Don't share John with me; he's your accomplishment.

HENRY. And Richard's yours. How could you send him off to deal with Philip?

ELEANOR. I was tired. I was busy. They were friends.

HENRY. Eleanor, he was the best. The strongest, bravest, handsomest and from the cradle on you cradled him. I never had a chance.

ELEANOR. You never wanted one.

HENRY. How do you know? You took him. Separation from your husband you could bear. But not your boy.

ELEANOR. Whatever I have done, you made me do.

HENRY. You threw me out of bed for Richard.

ELEANOR. Not until you threw me out

for Rosamund.

HENRY. It's not that simple. I won't have it be that simple.

ELEANOR. I adored you.

HENRY. Never.

ELEANOR. I still do.

HENRY. Of all the lies, that one is the most terrible.

ELEANOR. I know: that's why I saved it up for now. (*They throw themselves into each other's arms.*) Oh, Henry, we have mangled everything we've touched.

HENRY. Deny us what you will, we have done that. And all for Rosamund.

ELEANOR. No, you were right: it is too simple. Life, if it's like anything at all, is like an avalanche. To blame the little ball of snow that starts it all, to say it is the cause, is just as true as it is meaningless.

HENRY. Do you remember when we met?

ELEANOR. Down to the hour and the color of your stockings.

HENRY. I could hardly see you for the sunlight.

ELEANOR. It was raining but no matter.

HENRY. There was very little talk as I recall it.

ELEANOR. Very little.

HENRY. I had never seen such beauty— and I walked right up and touched it. God, where did I find the gall to do that?

ELEANOR. In my eyes.

HENRY. I loved you.

(*They kiss.*)

ELEANOR. No annulment.

HENRY. What?

ELEANOR. There will be no annulment.

HENRY. Will there not?

ELEANOR. No; I'm afraid you'll have to do without.

HENRY. Well . . . it was just a whim.

ELEANOR. I'm so relieved. I didn't want to lose you.

HENRY. Out of curiosity, as intellectual to intellectual, how in the name of bleeding Jesus can you lose me? Do you ever see me? Am I ever with you? Ever near you? Am I ever anywhere but somewhere else?

ELEANOR. I'm not concerned about your geographical location.

HENRY. Do we write? Do I send messages? Do dinghies bearing gifts float up the Thames to you? Are you remembered?

ELEANOR. You are.

HENRY. You're no part of me. We do not touch at any point. How can you lose me?

ELEANOR. Can't you feel the chains?

HENRY. You know enough to know I can't be stopped.

ELEANOR. But I don't have to stop you; I have only to delay you. Every enemy you have has friends in Rome. We'll cost you time.

HENRY. What is this? I'm not moldering; my paint's not peeling off. I'm good for years.

ELEANOR. How many years? Suppose I hold you back for one; I can—it's possible. Suppose your first son dies; ours did—it's possible. Suppose you're daughtered next; we were—that, too, is possible. How old is Daddy then? What kind of spindly, rickets-ridden, milky, semi-witted, wizened, dim-eyed, gammy-handed, limpy line of things will you beget?

HENRY. It's sweet of you to care.

ELEANOR. And when you die, which is regrettable but necessary, what will happen to frail Alais and her pruney prince? You can't think Richard's going to wait for your grotesque to grow?

HENRY. You wouldn't let him do a thing like that?

ELEANOR. Let him? I'd push him through the nursery door.

HENRY. You're not that cruel.

ELEANOR. Don't fret. We'll wait until you're dead to do it.

HENRY. Eleanor, what do you want?

ELEANOR. Just what you want: a king for a son. You can make more. I can't. You think I want to disappear? One son is all I've got and you can blot him out and call me cruel. For these ten years you've lived with everything I've lost and loved another woman through it all. And I'm cruel. I could peel you like a pear and God himself would call it justice. Nothing I could do to you is wanton; nothing is too much.

HENRY. I will die sometime soon. One day I'll duck too slow and at Westminster, they'll sing out *Vivat Rex* for someone else. I beg you, let it be a son of mine.

ELEANOR. I am not moved to tears.

HENRY. I have no sons.

ELEANOR. You've got too many sons. You don't need more.

HENRY. Well, wish me luck. I'm off.

ELEANOR. To Rome?

HENRY. That's where they keep the Pope.

ELEANOR. You don't dare go.

HENRY. Say that again at noon, you'll say it to my horse's ass. Lamb, I'll be rid of you by Easter: you can count your reign in days.

ELEANOR. You go to Rome, we'll rise against you.

HENRY. Who will?

ELEANOR. Richard, Geoffrey, John and Eleanor of Aquitaine.

HENRY. The day those stout hearts band together is the day that pigs get wings.

ELEANOR. There'll be pork in the tree-tops come the morning. Don't you see? You've given them a common cause: new sons. You leave the country and you've lost it.

HENRY. All of you at once.

ELEANOR. And Philip, too. He'd join us.

HENRY. Yes, he would.

ELEANOR. Now how's your trip to Rome?

HENRY. You'd truly do this to me?

ELEANOR. Oh, I've got you, got you, got you.

HENRY. Should I take a thousand men-at-arms to Rome or is that showy?

ELEANOR. Bluff away. I love it.

HENRY. Ah, poor thing. How can I break the news? You've just miscalculated.

ELEANOR. Have I? How?

HENRY. You should have lied to me. You should have promised to be good while I was gone. I would have let your three boys loose. They could have fought me then.

ELEANOR. You wouldn't keep your sons locked up here?

HENRY. Why the devil wouldn't I?

ELEANOR. You don't dare.

HENRY. Why not? What's to stop me? Let them sit in Chinon for a while.

ELEANOR. No; I forbid it!

HENRY. She forbids it!

ELEANOR. Did your father sleep with me, or didn't he?

HENRY. No doubt you're going to tell me that he did.

ELEANOR. Would it upset you?

HENRY. What about the thousand men? I say be gaudy and to hell with it.

ELEANOR. Don't leave me, Henry. I'm at rock bottom, I'll do anything to keep you.

HENRY. I think you think you mean it.

ELEANOR. Ask for something.

HENRY. Eleanor, we're past it; years past.

ELEANOR. Test me. Name an act.

HENRY. There isn't one.

ELEANOR. About my fornication with your father—

HENRY. Yes, there is. You can expire.

ELEANOR. You first, old man. I only hope I'm there to watch. You're so afraid of dying. You're so scared of it.

HENRY. Poor Eleanor; if only she had lied.

ELEANOR. She did. She said she never loved your father.

HENRY. I can always count on you.

ELEANOR. I've never touched you without thinking, "Geoffrey, Geoffrey."

HENRY. When you hurt me, I'll cry out.

ELEANOR. I've put more horns on you than Louis ever wore.

HENRY. Am I supposed to care?

ELEANOR. I'll kill you if you leave me.

HENRY. You can try.

ELEANOR. I loved your father's body. He was beautiful.

HENRY. It never happened.

ELEANOR. I can see his body now. Shall I describe it?

HENRY. Eleanor, I hope you die.

ELEANOR. His arms were rough, with scars here—

HENRY. Stop it!

ELEANOR. I can feel his arms. I feel them.

HENRY. AAH!

ELEANOR. What's that? Have I hurt you?

HENRY. Oh my God, I'm going to be sick.

ELEANOR (*hurling it after him as he exits*). We did it. You were in the next room when he did it! (*He is gone. Bleakly, in desolation.*) Well, what family doesn't have its ups and downs? (*At the brazier, spreading her hands over it.*) It's cold. I can't feel anything. (*Huddling close to the coals.*) Not anything at all. (*Hugging herself, arms around tight.*) We couldn't go back, could we, Henry?

DIM AND BLACKOUT

SCENE TWO

ALAIS's *chamber, at dawn.* ALAIS, *dressed for bed as we saw her last, sits deeply asleep in a chair.* HENRY *enters, moves to the window, and throws back the curtain. His spirits are too high; the man is fever-ish and a little frightening.*

———

HENRY. Get up, wake up, it's morning.

ALAIS (*startled*). Henry?

HENRY. When the King is off his ass, nobody sleeps.

ALAIS. What's wrong?

HENRY. We're packing up and moving out.

ALAIS. Is there a war? What's happened?

HENRY. Merry Christmas.

ALAIS. Henry, what's the matter?

HENRY. Nothing, for a change; would you believe it?

ALAIS. Where've you been all night?

HENRY. You know what a *mesnie* is? It's a train, an entourage. It's made of soldiers, cooks and clerics, wagons, barrows, linen, treasure, chickens, butts of wine and spices. I've been all night making one.

ALAIS. What for?

HENRY. We're off to Rome to see the Pope.

ALAIS. He's excommunicated you again.

HENRY. He's going to set me free. I'm having Eleanor annulled. The nation will be shocked to learn our marriage wasn't consummated.

ALAIS. What happened last night when I left?

HENRY. We hugged and kissed a little.

ALAIS. Oh, be serious.

HENRY. And then, I told her you and I were getting married.

ALAIS. Are we?

HENRY. By the Pope himself.

ALAIS. You mean it?

HENRY. Shall I kneel?

ALAIS. It's not another trick?

HENRY. The bridal party's drilling on the cobblestones.

ALAIS. She loves you, Henry.

HENRY. See for yourself.

ALAIS. She'll find a way to stop us.

HENRY. How? She won't be here. We're launching her for Salisbury Tower when the winds change. She'll be barging down the River Vienne by lunchtime.

ALAIS. If she doesn't stop us, Richard will.

HENRY. Suppose I do the worrying.

ALAIS. He won't like losing me.

HENRY. He's lost a damn sight more than you. I've corked him up.

ALAIS. You've what?

HENRY. He's in the cellar with his brothers and the wine. The royal boys are aging with the royal port. You haven't said "yes." Would you like a formal declaration? (*Kneeling, giving her his profile.*) There—my finest angle; it's on all the coins. Sad Alais, will you marry me?

ALAIS. I can't believe it.

HENRY. Be my Queen.

ALAIS. I never hoped for this. I mean, I always hoped but never thought—I mean—

HENRY. We'll love each other and you'll give me sons.

ALAIS. I don't know what I mean.

HENRY. Let's have five; we'll do Eleanor one better. Why, I'll even call the first one Louis if you like. Louis le Premier: how's that for a King of England?

ALAIS. Henry—you can't ever let them out.

HENRY. You've lost me. Let who out?

ALAIS. Your sons. You've put them in the dungeon and you've got to keep them there forever.

HENRY. Do I now?

ALAIS. If they're free when you die, it's the dungeon or the nunnery for me. I don't care which—a cell's a cell—but, Henry, what about the child?

HENRY. Don't bother me about the child. The damn thing isn't born yet.

ALAIS. If they're free, they'll kill it. I'm the one who'll live to see that and I will not see our children murdered.

HENRY. You don't make the ultimatums: I do.

ALAIS. Not this time. Either you keep them down forever or you find yourself another widow. I don't want the job.

HENRY. Do you know what you're asking me to do?

ALAIS. You locked your Queen up.

HENRY. But my boys—how can I?

ALAIS. That's for you to face.

HENRY. You have no children.

ALAIS. And I never will.

HENRY. But they're my sons.

ALAIS. I hate your sons. I'm not the one who wants a new line. If you want it, that's the price.

HENRY. You'll come to Rome if I say so. You'll marry me if I say so. The boys go free if I say so. My terms are the only terms. The difficulty is, you see, the difficulty is you're right. (*So weary.*) Incredible, but I have children who would murder children. Every time I've read *Medea*, I've thought: "No; the thing's absurd. Fish eat their young, and foxes: but not us." And yet she did it. I imagine she was mad;

don't you? Yes, mad she must have been.
(*He moves to go.*)

ALAIS. Henry—are you going down?

HENRY. Down? Yes.

ALAIS. To let them out or keep them in?

HENRY. Could you say, to a child of
yours, "You've seen the sunlight for the
last time?"

ALAIS. Can you do it, Henry?

HENRY. Well, I'd be a master bastard if
I did.

ALAIS. I must know. Can you?

HENRY. I shall have to, shan't I?
(*He goes.*)

DIM AND BLACKOUT

SCENE THREE

*The wine cellar, early morning. It is a
large, dark and vaulted place; its walls
and heavy door are offstage, lost in
shadow. Candles flicker in tall candlesticks. There are great casks of wine and
one small table in the cellar; nothing else.*

RICHARD, JOHN *and* GEOFFREY *are on
stage as the lights rise.* JOHN, *at a cask
of wine, is on the verge of replacing a
bung with a spigot.* RICHARD, *holding two
cups, stands by him.* GEOFFREY *stands
apart.*

———

JOHN. The trick is not to dribble when
you bang the bung. (*He bangs it and slips
the spigot into place.*) Voilà. I had an alcoholic Latin tutor—cup (RICHARD *hands
him a cup.*)—who taught me all he knew.

GEOFFREY. Which wasn't much.

JOHN. I know I might as well be drunk.

GEOFFREY. If I were you, I'd worry.

JOHN. You know me—cup (*He gives*
RICHARD *the full one and takes the empty.*)
—I'd just worry over all the wrong things.

GEOFFREY. Don't you know what's going
to happen?

JOHN. No, and you don't either. You
and your big cerebellum. (*Doing* GEOF-
FREY.) "I'm what's left. Here, Daddy; here
I am." And here you are.

RICHARD. But not for long.

GEOFFREY. You think we're getting out?

RICHARD. No; deeper in. The fortress at
Vaudreuil has dungeons down two hundred feet. That's where I'd keep us.

GEOFFREY. And if I were Father, I'm not
sure I'd keep the three of us at all. You

don't take prisoners; no, you don't. And
with good reason. Dungeon doors can
swing both ways but caskets have no
hinges.

JOHN. I know you. You only want to
frighten me.

GEOFFREY. John, the condition of your
trousers, be they wet or dry, could not concern me less. I think I'm apt to die today
and I am sweating, John. I'm sweating
cold.

JOHN. We've got friends.

GEOFFREY. Name one.

JOHN. Someone's got to rescue us.

GEOFFREY. I can't think who or how or
why.

RICHARD. He isn't going to see me beg.
He'll get no satisfaction out of me.

GEOFFREY. Why, you chivalric fool—as
if the way one fell down mattered.

RICHARD. When the fall is all there is, it
matters.

JOHN. Can't we run or hide or anything?

RICHARD. Just in the wine.

JOHN (*frightened by sounds of the cellar
door opening*). Geoff—

(ELEANOR *appears. She carries a large
covered breakfast tray. Like* HENRY, *she
hasn't slept.*)

ELEANOR. My barge is leaving at eleven
and I've come to say good-bye.

GEOFFREY. Does Henry know you're
here?

ELEANOR. The Queen still has some privileges. I bring you breakfast.

JOHN. I'm not hungry.

GEOFFREY. What's he planning?

RICHARD. Is he going to keep us here?

ELEANOR. First, have a little nourishment.

RICHARD. For God's sake, Mother—

ELEANOR. Eat.

(*She drops the tray on the table. It
makes a great metallic clatter.* RICHARD *removes the cover. The tray contains a stack
of daggers and short swords.*)

GEOFFREY. Well, Eleanor.

RICHARD. How heavy is the outside
guard?

ELEANOR. There's just the turnkey.

RICHARD. What about the courtyard and
the gates?

ELEANOR. They're putting Henry's train
together and it's chaos. You can walk right
out.

RICHARD. We'll go to Poitiers. He'll expect that but we'll meet him with an army when he comes. (*To* GEOFFREY *and* JOHN.) Keep close to me and when you run, run hard.

GEOFFREY. Why run at all? I think we ought to stay.

JOHN. Stay here?

GEOFFREY. Till Henry comes. (*To* ELEANOR.) He will come, won't he—and he'll come alone. (*To* RICHARD.) I count three knives to one.

RICHARD. You think we could?

JOHN. I'd only do it wrong. You kill him and I'll watch.

GEOFFREY. The three of us together: we must all three do it. I want us all responsible.

ELEANOR. Don't listen to him. Take the knives and run.

GEOFFREY. And miss this opportunity?

ELEANOR. Get out.

GEOFFREY (*to* RICHARD). I'll be behind the door with John. You'll want to do it from the front. (*To* ELEANOR.) And you, you lucky girl, you get to see the pageant.

ELEANOR. Mother's looking for a name for you—if English has one adequately foul.

GEOFFREY. Now hold on. I've been vilified enough. I've had enough of it. You brought the cutlery, you hauled it down here. Don't you dare tell me this wasn't in your mind.

ELEANOR. I tell you. I deny it.

GEOFFREY. Swear on something. I'm agog to hear what you consider holy.

(*She turns abruptly and starts to go.*)

RICHARD. Where are you going?

ELEANOR. Up for air.

GEOFFREY. (*to* RICHARD, *who moves to intercept her*). Don't stop her.

RICHARD. But she'll warn him.

GEOFFREY. Let her go. She isn't going to tell him anything.

ELEANOR. You think I'm going to let this happen?

GEOFFREY. Frankly, Mother, your position on the board is poorish. If you tattled, there would be a rash of executions and you don't want that. No, you don't want to lose a one of us: not even me.

ELEANOR. You're clever but I wonder if you're right.

GEOFFREY. Oh, lady, don't you know where you are? You're in stalemate. Warn him, it's the end of us: warn him not and it's the end of him. It's that clear.

ELEANOR (*not very loud*). Guard.

GEOFFREY. Go on, dear. Call again—and pitch it up a little.

ELEANOR. I'll have him take the knives away.

RICHARD. And be the one to put us in Vaudreuil, down two hundred feet?

ELEANOR. Then run away; escape. You've still got time.

RICHARD. No. Geoffrey's right; we'll stay.

ELEANOR. You, too? Oh, Richard.

RICHARD. Oh, oh, oh. There's nothing in your oh's: they're empty.

ELEANOR. You're not an assassin.

RICHARD. Look again.

ELEANOR. You're not. You're my Richard and you love me.

RICHARD. Let me kiss the nasty scratch and make it well.

ELEANOR. Yes, do. Come let me hold you.

RICHARD. You're more beautiful than ever. There is much that's beautiful in evil when it's absolutely pure. You are so foul you're fair. You stand there looking like a saint in pain when you brought us the knives to do your work.

ELEANOR. That's not true.

RICHARD. You did bring these things.

ELEANOR. Not for this.

RICHARD. Here—you want him dead, you do it.

ELEANOR. You unnatural animal.

RICHARD. Unnatural, Mummy? You tell me, what's nature's way? If poisoned mushrooms grow and babies come with crooked backs, if goiters thrive and dogs go mad and wives kill husbands, what's unnatural? Here stands your lamb. Come cover him with kisses; he's all yours.

ELEANOR. No, you're not mine. I'm not responsible.

RICHARD. Where do you think I learned this from? Who do you think I studied under? How old was I when you fought with Henry first?

ELEANOR. Young . . . I don't know.

RICHARD. How many battles did I watch?

ELEANOR. But those were battles, not a knife behind a door.

RICHARD. I've never heard a corpse ask how it got so cold. You've got a mind: you tell me, what was on it when you had your soldiers point their crossbows at him?

ELEANOR. That was in the field.

RICHARD. I don't care if it's in the dahlia bed. What were you thinking, Eleanor?

ELEANOR. Of you.

RICHARD. Of your unnatural animal?

ELEANOR. I did it all for you.

RICHARD. You wanted Father dead.

ELEANOR. No, never that.

RICHARD. You tried to kill him, didn't you?

ELEANOR. Yes.

RICHARD. Why? What did you want?

ELEANOR. I wanted Henry back.

RICHARD. You lie.

ELEANOR. I wanted Henry. Isn't there a chair?

JOHN (*handing her his cup of wine*). Here. (*She takes it and reaches out to touch his cheek. He draws away.*) None of that.

ELEANOR. I've done without it this long; I'll endure.

GEOFFREY. She'll warn him. I was wrong. She'll do it if she gets the chance.

ELEANOR. Then you're in stalemate, aren't you, lamb?

GEOFFREY. How so?

ELEANOR. You don't dare let me stay here and you don't dare let me out. Dear me, whatever shall we do with Mother?

GEOFFREY. Offhand there are several possibilities.

JOHN (*there are sounds of the door opening as he races to the table and slams the cover on the tray*). Watch it.

(HENRY *appears, carrying an armful of huge candles.* ALAIS *follows.*)

HENRY (*as he fills the empty candlesticks and* ALAIS, *with a taper, lights them*). It wants light. What we do in dungeons needs the shades of day. I stole the candles from the chapel. No one minded. Jesus won't begrudge them and the chaplain works for me.

ELEANOR. You look dreadful.

HENRY. So do you.

ELEANOR. I underslept a little.

HENRY. We can all rest in a little while. (*The candles are lit. The room is warm and cheery.*) That's better. Bright and clear, just like the morning.

ELEANOR. Here: I'll take the breakfast things.

RICHARD. Not yet.

ELEANOR. They've gotten cold.

RICHARD. They're good cold.

HENRY. Listen to me. What's the answer? Can I ever let you out?

RICHARD. What do you want from us? You must be mad. Why did you have to come here? Damn you, why'd you come?

HENRY. You think I want to lock you up?

RICHARD. You've got to. You can't let me out. You know you can't. I'll never stop.

HENRY. I can't stop either.

RICHARD. There's only fighting left.

HENRY. Not even that. What have you got to fight me with?

ELEANOR (*as* RICHARD *and* GEOFFREY *start for the tray*). My children. In the past, I've come and gone and loved you when it suited me. I never nursed you, warmed you, washed you, fed you, but today I felt such love for each of you and so I brought you breakfast.

RICHARD. Mother.

HENRY. Let her be.

ELEANOR (*removing the cover*). I thought I had no other choice but I was wrong again.

HENRY. Brave boys; that's what I have. Three warriors. Who had first crack? How was I divided up? Christ—

RICHARD. You drove us to it.

HENRY. Don't stop now. You're killers, aren't you? I am. I can do it. (*To* GEOFFREY.) Take a knife. (*To* RICHARD.) Come on. What is it? Come for me.

RICHARD. I can't.

HENRY. You're Richard, aren't you?

RICHARD. But you're Henry.

HENRY. Please. We can't stop and we can't go back. There's nothing else.

JOHN. Daddy? Take me back. Please. Can't we try again?

HENRY. Again?

JOHN. We always have before.

HENRY. Oh yes . . . we always have.

JOHN (*running toward him, arms outstretched*). Oh, Daddy—

(*He comes skidding to a stop as* HENRY *draws his sword and holds it leveled at* JOHN's *vitals.*)

ELEANOR. Go on. Execute them. You're the King. You've judged. You've sentenced. You know how.

HENRY. By God, I will. Come Monday and they'll hang you with the washing. There'll be princes swinging from the Christmas trees.

ELEANOR. Why wait? They are assassins, aren't they? This was treason, wasn't it? You gave them life—you take it.

HENRY. Who's to say it's monstrous? I'm the King. I call it just. (*To his sons.*)

Therefore, I, Henry, by the Grace of God King of the English, Lord of Scotland, Ireland and Wales, Count of Anjou, Brittany, Poitou and Normandy, Maine, Gascony and Aquitaine, do sentence you to death. Done this Christmas Day in Chinon in God's year eleven eighty-three. (*He moves to* RICHARD, *sword raised. He swings the sword through the air and brings it crashing to the cellar floor. Into the silence he speaks, softly and thoughtfully.*) Surely that's not what I intended. Children . . . Children are . . . They're all we have. (*Spent, shattered, unable to look at anyone or anything, he waves them from the room.*) Go on. I'm done, I'm done. I'm finished with you. Never come again.

(JOHN, GEOFFREY *and* RICHARD *exit.*)

ELEANOR. You spare the rod, you'll spoil those boys.

HENRY. I couldn't do it, Eleanor.

ELEANOR. Nobody thought you could.

HENRY. I did.

ALAIS. You saved them. You maneuvered it.

ELEANOR. Did I?

ALAIS. They're free because of you. They'll kill him one day; you know that.

ELEANOR. The next time or the next.

ALAIS. You always win, *Maman*.

ELEANOR. Except the prize.

ALAIS (*to* HENRY). Come rest.

HENRY. I want no women in my life.

ALAIS. You're tired.

HENRY. I could have conquered Europe, all of it, but I had women in my life.

ALAIS. I'll warm some wine.

HENRY. I've shot your world, you silly bitch, and there you stand, all honey and molasses. Sweet? You make my teeth ache.

(*They embrace.*)

ELEANOR. That's touching. Is it for my benefit?

HENRY. Your benefit? (*To* ALAIS.) Get out. Go on. Go.

ALAIS. When you want me, I'll be waiting.

(*She exits.*)

HENRY (*turning on* ELEANOR). For your benefit? I've done enough on your account. I should have killed you years ago.

ELEANOR. There's no one peeking. Do it now.

HENRY. I've wasted fortunes, squandered lives, spent everything—to buy this pit. I've got an eye for value. That is what I've made. I meant to do so much.

ELEANOR. Is this a play for pity?

HENRY. Not from you. You put me here. You made me do mad things. You've bled me.

ELEANOR. Shoulder it yourself. Don't put it on my back. You've done what you have done and no one but yourself has made you do it. Pick it up and carry it. I can. My losses are my work.

HENRY. What losses? I've been cheated, not you. I'm the one with nothing.

ELEANOR. Lost your life's work, have you? Provinces are nothing: land is dirt. I've lost you. I can't ever have you back again. You haven't suffered. I could take defeats like yours and laugh. I've done it. If you're broken, it's because you're brittle. You are all that I have ever loved. Christ, you don't know what nothing is. I want to die.

HENRY. You don't.

ELEANOR. I want to die.

HENRY. I'll hold you.

ELEANOR. I want to die.

HENRY. Stop saying that. Let me do something, damn you. This is terrible.

ELEANOR. Henry, I want to die.

HENRY. You will, you know. Wait long enough and it'll happen.

ELEANOR (*smiling*). So it will.

HENRY. We're in the cellar and you're going back to prison and my life is wasted and we've lost each other and you're smiling.

ELEANOR. It's the way I register despair. There's everything in life but hope.

HENRY. We have each other and for all I know that's what hope is.

ELEANOR. We're jungle creatures, Henry, and the dark is all around us. See them? In the corners, you can see the eyes.

HENRY. And they can see ours. I'm a match for anything. Aren't you?

ELEANOR. I should have been a great fool not to love you.

HENRY. Come along; I'll see you to your ship.

ELEANOR. So soon?

HENRY. There's always Easter Court.

ELEANOR. You'll let me out for Easter?

HENRY. Come the resurrection, you can strike me down again.

ELEANOR. Perhaps I'll do it next time.

HENRY. And perhaps you won't.

ELEANOR (*taking his arm, moving to*

go). It must be late and I don't want to miss the tide.

HENRY (*as they go*). You know, I hope we never die.

ELEANOR. I hope so, too.

HENRY. You think there's any chance of it?

CURTAIN

HUGHIE

Eugene O'Neill

First presented by Theodore Mann and Joseph E. Levine in association with Katzka-Berne at the Royale Theatre in New York City on December 22, 1964, with the following cast:

"ERIE" SMITH   Jason Robards   A NIGHT CLERK   Jack Dodson

Directed by José Quintero
Set and lighting by David Hays
Costume by Noel Taylor

Reprinted by permission of Carlotta Monterey O'Neill and Yale University Press.
Copyright © 1959 by Carlotta Monterey O'Neill.
All rights reserved under International and Pan-American Copyright Conventions.

CAUTION: Professionals and amateurs are hereby warned that *Hughie,* being fully protected under the copyright laws of the United States of America, the British Empire, including the Dominion of Canada, and all other countries of the copyright union, is subject to a royalty. All rights, including professional, amateur, motion picture, recitation, public reading, radio broadcasting, and the rights of translation into foreign languages, are strictly reserved. All inquiries regarding this play should be addressed to the Richard J. Madden Play Co., Inc., at 522 Fifth Avenue, New York City, N.Y.

AMERICA has produced many playwrights, but so far only one towering genius, Eugene O'Neill. The bare facts of his life are almost unimportant, for more than any of our playwrights, he has very properly passed into history. Born in New York City in 1888, died in Boston in 1953, studied at Princeton and Harvard, and, just to complete the Ivy League pattern, receiving an honorary degree from Yale, he was during his lifetime honored and reviled. He won three Pulitzer Prizes for Drama, in 1920, 1922, and 1928. In 1936 he won the Nobel Prize for Literature. He was honored.

Yet he was reviled. At the end of his career he found it difficult to have his plays produced, he found it difficult to write. He lived in that agony of the soul that was the motive force of his creation. The most curious thing of all is that his great plays, the masterpieces on which his reputation is likely to rest, were not the applauded hits of his early years but the tortured sublimities of his final plays, in their day either unproduced or found failures. There is an irony here that would appeal to any poet.

O'Neill was never an easy playwright; for that matter, he was never an easy writer. It is often the privilege of great writers to write badly on occasion, but it was a privilege O'Neill traded upon dangerously. Like most great artists he was prolific, but strangely enough there was little in his always competent, always exciting, and much praised early work to prepare the world for the blaze of genius he produced when the world itself had temporarily if not rejected him, at least pensioned him off to immortal mediocrity.

Great men are surprising creatures. At the end of a long, distinguished career, an aging Verdi unexpectedly produced *Otello* and *Falstaff,* the two great music dramas of all time. Verdi had been brilliant before, but nothing surpassed that final incandescence of his genius. O'Neill, when his reputation was at its height, had already done enough to be regarded as America's first significant playwright. To be sure, some of the plays were overrated, but as a body of work, even disregarding the last plays, they remain mightily impressive today. Even a partial list of them, *Mourning Becomes Electra, Anna Christie, Ah, Wilderness!* (surely the best of his early works), or the grandly styled *A Touch of the Poet*—these and others have their own integrity and their own value.

For all this O'Neill's reputation now seems likely to rest on three supreme works, *The Iceman Cometh, A Moon for the Misbegotten,* and *A Long Day's Journey into Night.* This is the great O'Neill, and a Broadway production in 1965 of *More Stately Mansions,* an unfinished play the poet had wished to be suppressed, only emphasized the wisdom of his choice and the care with which he realized his final work.

Perhaps one piece, a delicate one-act play, might be added to the big three as representing the pinnacle of O'Neill's genius. This is *Hughie,* a dialogue between a small-time gambler and a small-time hotel clerk. Somehow, in this very short, very simple play, O'Neill hits strong and deep at one of the subjects dear to his heart, the role of illusion in human survival. It is a beautiful piece, full of insight and with typical O'Neill feeling for language as it is spoken rather than how inferior playwrights imagine it is spoken.

Here is O'Neill's sweet compassion for the shabby, dog-eared corners of life. O'Neill is the poet for losers, and this spirit has never been more evocatively and certainly not so succinctly suggested. Anyone reading the play will realize—if only through the enormous and perhaps intransigent difficulties offered by the stage directions—the work's problems. The stage realization has somehow to convey thoughts in the Night Clerk's mind that O'Neill expresses so brilliantly between the dialogue. Yet this is a small major work. And so much more important than so many large minor works.

SCENE. *The desk and a section of lobby of a small hotel on a West Side street in midtown New York. It is between 3 and 4 A.M. of a day in the summer of 1928.*

It is one of those hotels, built in the decade 1900–10 on the side streets of the Great White Way sector, which began as respectable second class but soon were forced to deteriorate in order to survive. Following the First World War and Prohibition, it had given up all pretense of respectability, and now is anything a paying guest wants it to be, a third class dump, catering to the catch-as-catch-can trade. But still it does not prosper. It has not shared in the Great Hollow Boom of the twenties. The Everlasting Opulence of the New Economic Law has overlooked it. It manages to keep running by cutting the overhead for service, repairs, and cleanliness to a minimum.

The desk faces left along a section of seedy lobby with shabby chairs. The street entrance is off-stage, left. Behind the desk are a telephone switchboard and the operator's stool. At right, the usual numbered tiers of mailboxes, and above them a clock.

The NIGHT CLERK sits on the stool, facing front, his back to the switchboard. There is nothing to do. He is not thinking. He is not sleepy. He simply droops and stares acquiescently at nothing. It would be discouraging to glance at the clock. He knows there are several hours to go before his shift is over. Anyway, he does not need to look at clocks. He has been a night clerk in New York hotels so long he can tell time by sounds in the street.

He is in his early forties. Tall, thin, with a scrawny neck and jutting Adam's apple. His face is long and narrow, greasy with perspiration, sallow, studded with pimples from ingrowing hairs. His nose is large and without character. So is his mouth. So are his ears. So is his thinning brown hair, powdered with dandruff. Behind horn-rimmed spectacles, his blank brown eyes contain no discernible expression. One would say they had even forgotten how it feels to be bored. He wears an ill-fitting blue serge suit, white shirt and collar, a blue tie. The suit is old and shines at the elbows as if it had been waxed and polished.

Footsteps echo in the deserted lobby as someone comes in from the street. The

NIGHT CLERK *rises wearily. His eyes remain empty but his gummy lips part automatically in a welcoming The-Patron-Is-Always-Right grimace, intended as a smile. His big uneven teeth are in bad condition.*

ERIE SMITH *enters and approaches the desk. He is about the same age as the* CLERK *and has the same pasty, perspiry, night-life complexion. There the resemlance ends.* ERIE *is around medium height but appears shorter because he is stout and his fat legs are too short for his body. So are his fat arms. His big head squats on a neck which seems part of his beefy shoulders. His face is round, his snub nose flattened at the tip. His blue eyes have drooping lids and puffy pouches under them. His sandy hair is falling out and the top of his head is bald. He walks to the desk with a breezy, familiar air, his gait a bit waddling because of his short legs. He carries a Panama hat and mops his face with a red and blue silk handkerchief. He wears a light grey suit cut in the extreme, tight-waisted, Broadway mode, the coat open to reveal an old and faded but expensive silk shirt in a shade of blue that sets teeth on edge, and a gay red and blue foulard tie, its knot stained by perspiration. His trousers are held up by a braided brown leather belt with a brass buckle. His shoes are tan and white, his socks white silk.*

In manner, he is consciously a Broadway sport and a Wise Guy—the type of small-fry gambler and horse player, living hand to mouth on the fringe of the rackets. Infesting corners, doorways, cheap restaurants, the bars of minor speakeasies, he and his kind imagine they are in the Real Know, cynical oracles of the One True Grapevine.

ERIE *usually speaks in a low, guarded tone, his droop-lidded eyes suspiciously wary of nonexistent eavesdroppers. His face is set in the prescribed pattern of gambler's deadpan. His small, pursy mouth is always crooked in the cynical leer of one who possesses superior, inside information, and his shifty once-over glances never miss the price tags he detects on everything and everybody. Yet there is something phoney about his characterization of himself, some sentimental softness behind it which doesn't belong in the hard-boiled picture.*

ERIE *avoids looking at the* NIGHT CLERK, *as if he resented him.*

———

ERIE (*peremptorily*). Key. (*Then as the* NIGHT CLERK *gropes with his memory—grudgingly.*) Forgot you ain't seen me before. Erie Smith's the name. I'm an old timer in this fleabag. 492.

NIGHT CLERK (*in a tone of one who is wearily relieved when he does not have to remember anything—he plucks out the key*). 492. Yes, sir.

ERIE (*taking the key, gives the* CLERK *the once-over; he appears not unfavorably impressed but his tone still holds resentment*). How long you been on the job? Four, five days, huh? I been off on a drunk. Come to now, though. Tapering off. Well, I'm glad they fired that young squirt took on when Hughie got sick. One of them fresh wise punks. Couldn't tell him nothing. Pleased to meet you, Pal. Hope you stick around. (*He shoves out his hand. The* NIGHT CLERK *takes it obediently.*)

NIGHT CLERK (*with a compliant, uninterested smile*). Glad to know you, Mr. Smith.

ERIE. What's your name?

NIGHT CLERK (*as if he had half forgotten because what did it matter, anyway?*). Hughes. Charlie Hughes.

ERIE (*starts*). Huh? Hughes? Say, is that on the level?

NIGHT CLERK. Charlie Hughes.

ERIE. Well, I be damned! What the hell d'you know about that! (*Warming toward the* CLERK.) Say, now I notice, you don't look like Hughie, but you remind me of him somehow. You ain't by any chance related?

NIGHT CLERK. You mean to the Hughes who had this job so long and died recently? No, sir. No relation.

ERIE (*gloomily*). No, that's right. Hughie told me he didn't have no relations left—except his wife and kids, of course. (*He pauses—more gloomily.*) Yeah. The poor guy croaked last week. His funeral was what started me off on a bat. (*Then boastfully, as if defending himself against gloom.*) Some drunk; I don't go on one often. It's bum dope in my book. A guy gets careless and gabs about things he knows and when he comes to he's liable to find there's guys who'd feel easier if he wasn't around no more.

That's the trouble with knowing things. Take my tip, Pal. Don't never know nothin'. Be a sap and stay healthy. (*His manner has become secretive, with sinister undertones. But the* NIGHT CLERK *doesn't notice this. Long experience with guests who stop at his desk in the small hours to talk about themselves has given him a foolproof technique of self-defense. He appears to listen with agreeable submissiveness and be impressed, but his mind is blank and he doesn't hear unless a direct question is put to him, and sometimes not even then.* ERIE *thinks he is impressed.*) But hell, I always keep my noggin working, booze or no booze. I'm no sucker. What was I sayin'? Oh, some drunk. I sure hit the high spots. You shoulda seen the doll I made night before last. And did she take me to the cleaners! I'm a sucker for blondes. (*He pauses—giving the* NIGHT CLERK *a cynical, contemptuous glance.*) You're married, ain't you?

NIGHT CLERK (*long ago he gave up caring whether questions were personal or not*). Yes, sir.

ERIE. Yeah, I'd'a laid ten to one on it. You got that old look. Like Hughie had. Maybe that's the resemblance. (*He chuckles contemptuously.*) Kids, too, I bet?

NIGHT CLERK. Yes, sir. Three.

ERIE. You're worse off than Hughie was. He only had two. Three, huh? Well, that's what comes of being careless! (*He laughs. The* NIGHT CLERK *smiles at a guest. He had been a little offended when a guest first made that crack—must have been ten years ago—yes, Eddie, the oldest, is eleven now—or is it twelve?* ERIE *goes on with good-natured tolerance.*) Well, I suppose marriage ain't such a bum racket, if you're made for it. Hughie didn't seem to mind it much, although if you want my lowdown, his wife is a bum—in spades! Oh, I don't mean cheatin'. With her puss and figure, she'd never make no one except she raided a blind asylum. (*The* NIGHT CLERK *feels that he has been standing a long time and his feet are beginning to ache and he wishes 492 would stop talking and go to bed so he can sit down again and listen to the noises in the street and think about nothing.* ERIE *gives him an amused, condescending glance.*) How old are you? Wait! Let me guess. You look fifty or over but I'll lay ten to one you're forty-three or maybe forty-four.

NIGHT CLERK. I'm forty-three. (*He adds vaguely.*) Or maybe it is forty-four.

ERIE (*elated*). I win, huh? I sure can call the turn on ages, Buddy. You ought to see the dolls get sored up when I work it on them! You're like Hughie. He looked like he'd never see fifty again and he was only forty-three. Me, I'm forty-five. Never think it, would you? Most of the dames don't think I've hit forty yet. (*The* NIGHT CLERK *shifts his position so he can lean more on the desk. Maybe those shoes he sees advertised for fallen arches— But they cost eight dollars, so that's out— Get a pair when he goes to heaven.* ERIE *is sizing him up with another cynical, friendly glance.*) I make another bet about you. Born and raised in the sticks, wasn't you?

NIGHT CLERK (*faintly aroused and defensive*). I come originally from Saginaw, Michigan, but I've lived here in the Big Town so long I consider myself a New Yorker now.

(*This is a long speech for him and he wonders sadly why he took the trouble to make it.*)

ERIE. I don't deserve no medal for picking that one. Nearly every guy I know on the Big Stem—and I know most of 'em—hails from the sticks. Take me. You'd never guess it but I was dragged up in Erie, P-a. Ain't that a knockout! Erie, P-a! That's how I got my moniker. No one calls me nothing but Erie. You better call me Erie, too, Pal, or I won't know when you're talkin' to me.

NIGHT CLERK. All right, Erie.

ERIE. Atta Boy. (*He chuckles.*) Here's another knockout. Smith is my real name. A Broadway guy like me named Smith and it's my real name! Ain't that a knockout! (*He explains carefully so there will be no misunderstanding.*) I don't remember nothing much about Erie, P-a, you understand—or want to. Some punk burg! After grammar school, my Old Man put me to work in his store, dealing out groceries. Some punk job! I stuck it till I was eighteen before I took a run-out powder. (*The* NIGHT CLERK *seems turned into a drooping waxwork, draped along the desk. This is what he used to dread before he perfected his technique of not listening: The Guest's Story of His Life. He fixes his mind on his aching feet.* ERIE

chuckles.) Speaking of marriage, that was the big reason I ducked. A doll nearly had me hooked for the old shotgun ceremony. Closest I ever come to being played for a sucker. This doll in Erie—Daisy's her name—was one of them dumb wide-open dolls. All the guys give her a play. Then one day she wakes up and finds she's going to have a kid. I never figured she meant to frame me in particular. Way I always figured, she didn't have no idea who, so she holds a lottery all by herself. Put about a thousand guys' names in a hat—all she could remember—and drew one out and I was it. Then she told her Ma, and her Ma told her Pa, and her Pa come round looking for me. But I was no fall guy even in them days. I took it on the lam. For Saratoga, to look the bangtails over. I'd started to be a horse player in Erie, though I'd never seen a track. I been one ever since. (*With a touch of bravado.*) And I ain't done so bad, Pal. I've made some killings in my time the gang still gab about. I've been in the big bucks. More'n once, and I will be again. I've had tough breaks too, but what the hell, I always get by. When the horses won't run for me, there's draw or stud. When they're bad, there's a crap game. And when they're all bad, there's always bucks to pick up for little errands I ain't talkin' about, which they give a guy who can keep his clam shut. Oh, I get along, Buddy, I get along fine. (*He waits for approving assent from the* NIGHT CLERK, *but the latter is not hearing so intently he misses his cue until the expectant silence crashes his ears.*)

NIGHT CLERK (*hastily, gambling on "yes,"*). Yes, Sir.

ERIE (*bitingly*). Sorry if I'm keeping you up, Sport. (*With an aggrieved air.*) Hughie was a wide-awake guy. He was always waiting for me to roll in. He'd say, "Hello, Erie, how'd the bangtails treat you?" Or, "How's luck?" Or, "Did you make the old bones behave?" Then I'd tell him how I'd done. He'd ask, "What's new along the Big Stem?" and I'd tell him the latest off the grapevine. (*He grins with affectionate condescension.*) It used to hand me a laugh to hear old Hughie crackin' like a sport. In all the years I knew him, he never bet a buck on nothin'. (*Excusingly.*) But it ain't his fault. He'd have took a chance, but how could he with his wife keepin' cases on every nickel of his salary? I showed him lots of ways he could cross her up, but he was too scared. (*He chuckles.*) The biggest knockout was when he'd kid me about dames. He'd crack, "What? No blonde to-night, Erie? You must be slippin'." Jeez, you never see a guy more bashful with a doll around than Hughie was. I used to introduce him to the tramps I'd drag home with me. I'd wise them up to kid him along and pretend they'd fell for him. In two minutes, they'd have him hanging on the ropes. His face'd be red and he'd look like he wanted to crawl under the desk and hide. Some of them dolls was raw babies. They'd make him pretty raw propositions. He'd stutter like he was paralyzed. But he ate it up, just the same. He was tickled pink. I used to hope maybe I could nerve him up to do a little cheatin'. I'd offer to fix it for him with one of my dolls. Hell, I got plenty, I wouldn't have minded. I'd tell him, "Just let that wife of yours know you're cheatin', and she'll have some respect for you." But he was too scared. (*He pauses —boastfully.*) Some queens I've brought here in my time, Brother—frails from the Follies, or the Scandals, or the Frolics, that'd knock your eye out! And I still can make 'em. You watch. I ain't slippin'. (*He looks at the* NIGHT CLERK *expecting reassurance, but the* CLERK's *mind has slipped away to the clanging bounce of garbage cans in the outer night. He is thinking: "A job I'd like. I'd bang those cans louder than they do! I'd wake up the whole damned city!"* ERIE *mutters disgustedly to himself.*) Jesus, what a dummy! (*He makes a move in the direction of the elevator, off right front—gloomily.*) Might as well hit the hay, I guess.

NIGHT CLERK (*comes to—with the nearest approach to feeling he has shown in many a long night—approvingly*). Good night, Mr. Smith. I hope you have a good rest. (*But* ERIE *stops, glancing around the deserted lobby with forlorn distaste, jiggling the room key in his hand.*)

ERIE. What a crummy dump! What did I come back for? I shoulda stayed on a drunk. You'd never guess it, Buddy, but when I first come here this was a classy hotel—and clean, can you believe it? (*He scowls.*) I've been campin' here, off and on, fifteen years, but I've got a good no-

tion to move out. It ain't the same place since Hughie was took to the hospital. (*Gloomily.*) Hell with going to bed! I'll just lie there worrying—(*He turns back to the desk. The* CLERK's *face would express despair, but the last time he was able to feel despair was back around World War days when the cost of living got so high and he was out of a job for three months.* ERIE *leans on the desk—in a dejected, confidential tone.*) Believe me, Brother, I never been a guy to worry, but this time I'm on a spot where I got to, if I ain't a sap.

NIGHT CLERK (*in the vague tone of a corpse which admits it once overheard a favorable rumor about life*). That's too bad, Mr. Smith. But they say most of the things we worry about never happen. (*His mind escapes to the street again to play bouncing cans with the garbage men.*)

ERIE (*grimly*). This thing happens, Pal. I ain't won a bet at nothin' since Hughie was took to the hospital. I'm jinxed. And that ain't all— But to hell with it! You're right, at that. Something always turns up for me. I was born lucky. I ain't worried. Just moaning low. Hell, who don't when they're getting over a drunk? You know how it is. The Brooklyn Boys march over the bridge with bloodhounds to hunt you down. And I'm still carrying the torch for Hughie. His checking out was a real K.O. for me. Damn if I know why. Lots of guys I've been pals with, in a way, croaked from booze or something, or got rubbed out, but I always took it as part of the game. Hell, we all gotta croak. Here today, gone tomorrow, so what's the good of beefin'? When a guy's dead, he's dead. He don't give a damn, so why should anybody else? (*But this fatalistic philosophy is no comfort and* ERIE *sighs.*) I miss Hughie, I guess. I guess I'd got to like him a lot. (*Again he explains carefully so there will be no misunderstanding.*) Not that I was ever real pals with him, you understand. He didn't run in my class. He didn't know none of the answers. He was just a sucker. (*He sighs again.*) But I sure am sorry he's gone. You missed a lot not knowing Hughie, Pal. He sure was one grand little guy. (*He stares at the lobby floor. The* NIGHT CLERK *regards him with vacant, bulging eyes full of a vague envy for the blind. The garbage men have gone their predestined way.*

Time is that much older. The CLERK's *mind remains in the street to greet the noise of a far-off El train. Its approach is pleasantly like a memory of hope; then it roars and rocks and rattles past the nearby corner, and the noise pleasantly deafens memory; then it recedes and dies, and there is something melancholy about that. But there is hope. Only so many El trains pass in one night, and each one passing leaves one less to pass, so the night recedes, too, until at last it must die and join all the other long nights in Nirvana, the Big Night of Nights. And that's life. "What I always tell Jess when she nags me to worry about something: 'That's life, isn't it? What can you do about it?' "* ERIE *sighs again—then turns to the* CLERK, *his foolishly wary, wise-guy eyes defenseless, his poker face as self-betraying as a hurt dog's—appealingly.*) Say, you do remind me of Hughie somehow, Pal. You got the same look on your map. (*But the* CLERK's *mind is far away attending the obsequies of night, and it takes it some time to get back.* ERIE *is hurt—contemptuously.*) But I guess it's only that old night clerk look! There's one of 'em born every minute!

NIGHT CLERK (*his mind arrives just in time to catch this last—with a bright grimace*). Yes, Mr. Smith. That's what Barnum said, and it's certainly true, isn't it?

ERIE (*grateful even for this sign of companionship, growls*). Nix on the Mr. Smith stuff, Charlie. There's ten of *them* born every minute. Call me Erie, like I told you.

NIGHT CLERK (*automatically, as his mind tiptoes into the night again*). All right, Erie.

ERIE (*encouraged, leans on the desk, clacking his room key like a castanet*). Yeah. Hughie was one grand little guy. All the same, like I said, he wasn't the kind of guy you'd ever figger a guy like me would take to. Because he was a sucker, see—the kind of sap you'd take to the cleaners a million times and he'd never wise up he was took. Why, night after night, just for a gag, I'd get him to shoot crap with me here on the desk. With *my* dice. And he'd never ask to give 'em the once-over. Can you beat that! (*He chuckles—then earnestly.*) Not that I'd ever ring in no phoneys on a pal. I'm no heel. (*He chuckles again.*) And anyway, I

didn't need none to take Hughie because he never even made me knock 'em against nothing. Just a roll on the desk here. Boy, if they'd ever let me throw 'em that way in a real game, I'd be worth ten million dollars. (*He laughs.*) You'da thought Hughie woulda got wise something was out of order when, no matter how much he'd win on a run of luck like suckers have sometimes, I'd always take him to the cleaners in the end. But he never suspicioned nothing. All he'd say was "Gosh, Erie, no wonder you took up gambling. You sure were born lucky." (*He chuckles.*) Can you beat that? (*He hastens to explain earnestly.*) Of course, like I said, it was only a gag. We'd play with real jack, just to make it look real, but it was all my jack. He never had no jack. His wife dealt him four bits a day for spending money. So I'd stake him at the start to half of what I got—in chicken feed, I mean. We'd pretend a cent was a buck, and a nickel was a fin and so on. Some big game! He got a big kick out of it. He'd get all het up. It give me a kick, too—especially when he'd say, "Gosh, Erie, I don't wonder you never worry about money, with your luck." (*He laughs.*) That guy would believe anything! Of course, I'd stall him off when he'd want to shoot nights when I didn't have a goddamned nickel. (*He chuckles.*) What laughs he used to hand me! He'd always call horses "the bangtails," like he'd known 'em all his life—and he'd never seen a race horse, not till I kidnapped him one day and took him down to Belmont. What a kick he got out of that! I got scared he'd pass out with excitement. And he wasn't doing no betting either. All he had was four bits. It was just the track, and the crowd, and the horses got him. Mostly the horses. (*With a surprised, reflective air.*) Y'know, it's funny how a dumb, simple guy like Hughie will all of a sudden get something right. He says, "There're the most beautiful things in the world, I think." And he wins! I tell you, Pal, I'd rather sleep in the same stall with old Man o' War than make the whole damn Follies. What do you think?

NIGHT CLERK (*his mind darts back from a cruising taxi and blinks bewilderedly in the light: "Say yes,"*) Yes, I agree with you, Mr.—I mean, Erie.

ERIE (*with good-natured contempt*).

Yeah? I bet you never seen one, except back at the old Fair Grounds in the sticks. I don't mean them kind of turtles. I mean a real horse. (*The* CLERK *wonders what horses have to do with anything—or for that matter, what anything has to do with anything—then gives it up.* ERIE *takes up his tale.*) And what d'you think happened the next night? Damned if Hughie didn't dig two bucks out of his pants and try to slip 'em to me. "Let this ride on the nose of whatever horse you're betting on tomorrow," he told me. I got sore. "Nix," I told him, "if you're going to start playin' sucker and bettin' on horse races, you don't get no assist from me." (*He grins wryly.*) Was that a laugh! Me advising a sucker not to bet when I've spent a lot of my life tellin' saps a story to make 'em bet! I said, "Where'd you grab this dough? Outa the Little Woman's purse, huh? What tale you going to give her when you lose it? She'll start breaking up the furniture with you!" "No," he says, "she'll just cry." "That's worse," I said, "no guy can beat that racket. I had a doll cry on me once in a restaurant full of people till I had to promise her a diamond engagement ring to sober her up." Well, anyway, Hughie sneaked the two bucks back in the Little Woman's purse when he went home that morning, and that was the end of that. (*Cynically.*) Boy Scouts got nothin' on me, Pal, when it comes to good deeds. That was one I done. It's too bad I can't remember no others. (*He is well wound up now and goes on without noticing that the* NIGHT CLERK's *mind has left the premises in his sole custody.*) Y'know I had Hughie sized up for a sap the first time I see him. I'd just rolled in from Tia Juana. I'd made a big killing down there and I was lousy with jack. Come all the way in a drawing room, and I wasn't lonely in it neither. There was a blonde movie doll on the train—and I was lucky in them days. Used to follow the horses South every winter. I don't no more. Sick of traveling. And I ain't as lucky as I was— (*Hastily.*) Anyway, this time I'm talkin' about, soon as I hit this lobby I see there's a new night clerk, and while I'm signing up for the bridal suite I make a bet with myself he's never been nothin' but a night clerk. And I win. At first, he wouldn't open up. Not that he was cagey about gabbin' too much. But like he

couldn't think of nothin' about himself worth saying. But after he'd seen me roll in here the last one every night, and I'd stop to kid him along and tell him the tale of what I'd win that day, he got friendly and talked. He'd come from a hick burg upstate. Graduated from high school, and had a shot at different jobs in the old home town but couldn't make the grade until he was took on as night clerk in the hotel there. Then he made good. But he wasn't satisfied. Didn't like being only a night clerk where everybody knew him. He'd read somewhere—in the Suckers' Almanac, I guess—that all a guy had to do was come to the Big Town and Old Man Success would be waitin' at the Grand Central to give him the key to the city. What a gag that is! Even I believed that once, and no one could ever call me a sap. Well, anyway, he made the break and come here and the only job he could get was night clerk. Then he fell in love—or kidded himself he was—and got married. Met her on a subway train. It stopped sudden and she was jerked into him, and he put his arms around her, and they started talking, and the poor boob never stood a chance. She was a sales girl in some punk department store, and she was sick of standing on her dogs all day, and all the way home to Brooklyn, too. So, the way I figger it, knowing Hughie and dames, she proposed and said "yes" for him, and married him, and after that, of course, he never dared stop being a night clerk, even if he could. (*He pauses.*) Maybe you think I ain't giving her a square shake. Well, maybe I ain't. She never give me one. She put me down as a bad influence, and let her chips ride. And maybe Hughie couldn't have done no better. Dolls didn't call him no riot. Hughie and her seemed happy enough the time he had me out to dinner in their flat. Well, not happy. Maybe contented. No, that's boosting it, too. Resigned comes nearer, as if each was givin' the other a break by thinking, "Well, what more could I expect?" (*Abruptly he addresses the* NIGHT CLERK *with contemptuous good nature.*) How d'you and your Little Woman hit it off, Brother?

NIGHT CLERK (*his mind has been counting the footfalls of the cop on the beat as they recede, sauntering longingly toward the dawn's release; "If he'd only shoot it out with a gunman some night! Nothing exciting has happened in any night I've ever lived through!"; he stammers gropingly among the echoes of* ERIE's *last words*). Oh—you mean *my* wife? Why, we get along all right, I guess.

ERIE (*disgustedly*). Better lay off them headache pills, Pal. First thing you know, some guy is going to call you a dope. (*But the* NIGHT CLERK *cannot take this seriously. It is years since he cared what anyone called him. So many guests have called him so many things. The Little Woman has, too. And, of course, he has, himself. But that's all past. Is daybreak coming now? No, too early yet. He can tell by the sound of that surface car. It is still lost in the night. Flat wheeled and tired. Distant the carbarn, and far away the sleep.* ERIE, *having soothed resentment with his wisecrack, goes on with a friendly grin.*) Well, keep hoping, Pal. Hughie was as big a dope as you until I give him some interest in life. (*slipping back into narrative.*) That time he took me home to dinner. Was that a knockout! It took him a hell of a while to get up nerve to ask me. "Sure, Hughie," I told him, "I'll be tickled to death." I was thinking, I'd rather be shot. For one thing, he lived in Brooklyn, and I'd sooner take a trip to China. Another thing, I'm a guy that likes to eat what I order and not what somebody deals me. And he had kids and a wife, and the family racket is out of my line. But Hughie looked so tickled I couldn't welsh on him. And it didn't work out so bad. Of course, what he called home was only a dump of a cheap flat. Still, it wasn't so bad for a change. His wife had done a lot of stuff to doll it up. Nothin' with no class, you understand. Just cheap stuff to make it comfortable. And his kids wasn't the gorillas I'd expected, neither. No throwin' spitballs in my soup or them kind of gags. They was quiet like Hughie. I kinda liked 'em. After dinner I started tellin' 'em a story about a race horse a guy I know owned once. I thought it was up to me to put out something, and kids like animal stories, and this one was true, at that. This old turtle never wins a race, but he was as foxy as ten guys, a natural born crook, the goddamnedest thief, he'd steal anything in reach that wasn't nailed down— Well, I didn't get far. Hughie's wife butt in and stopped me cold. Told

the kids it was bedtime and hustled 'em off like I was giving 'em measles. It got my goat, kinda. I coulda liked her—a little—if she'd give me a chance. Not that she was nothin' Ziegfeld would want to glorify. When you call her plain, you give her all the breaks. (*Resentfully.*) Well, to hell with it. She had me tagged for a bum, and seein' me made her sure she was right. You can bet she told Hughie never invite me again, and he never did. He tried to apologize, but I shut him up quick. He says, "Irma was brought up strict. She can't help being narrow-minded about gamblers." I said, "What's it to me? I don't want to hear your dame troubles. I got plenty of my own. Remember that doll I brung home night before last? She gives me an argument I promised her ten bucks. I told her, 'Listen, Baby, I got an impediment in my speech. Maybe it sounded like ten, but it was two, and that's all you get. Hell, I don't want to buy your soul! What would I do with it? Now she's peddling the news along Broadway I'm a rat and a chiseler, and of course all the rats and chiselers believe her. Before she's through, I won't have a friend left." (*He pauses—confidentially.*) I switched the subject on Hughie, see, on purpose. He never did beef to me about his wife again. (*He gives a forced chuckle.*) Believe me, Pal, I can stop guys that start telling me their family troubles!

NIGHT CLERK (*his mind has hopped an ambulance clanging down Sixth, and is asking without curiosity: "Will he die, Doctor, or isn't he lucky?" "I'm afraid not, but he'll have to be absolutely quiet for months and months." "With a pretty nurse taking care of him?" "Probably not pretty." "Well, anyway, I claim he's lucky; and now I must get back to the hotel; 492 won't go to bed and insists on telling me jokes. It must have been a joke because he's chuckling." He laughs with a heartiness which has forgotten that heart is more than a word used in "Have a heart," an old slang expression*). Ha— Ha! That's a good one, Erie. That's the best I've heard in a long time!

ERIE (*for a moment is so hurt and depressed he hasn't the spirit to make a sarcastic crack; he stares at the floor, twirling his room key—to himself*). Jesus, this sure is a dead dump. About as homey as the Morgue. (*He glances up at the clock.*) Gettin' late. Better beat it up to my cell and grab some shut eye. (*He makes a move to detach himself from the desk but fails and remains wearily glued to it. His eyes prowl the lobby and finally come to rest on the* CLERK's *glistening, sallow face. He summons up strength for a withering crack.*) Why didn't you tell me you was deaf, Buddy? I know guys is sensitive about them little afflictions, but I'll keep it confidential. (*But the* CLERK's *mind has rushed out to follow the siren wail of a fire engine." A fireman's life must be exciting." His mind rides the engine, and asks a fireman with disinterested eagerness: "Where's the fire? Is it a real good one this time? Has it a good start? Will it be big enough, do you think?"* ERIE *examines his face—bitingly.*) Take my tip, Pal, and don't never try to buy from a dope peddler. He'll tell you you had enough already. (*The* CLERK's *mind continues its dialogue with the fireman: "I mean, big enough to burn down the whole damn city?" "Sorry, Brother, but there's no chance. There's too much stone and steel. There'd always be something left." "Yes, I guess you're right. There's too much stone and steel. I wasn't really hoping, anyway. It really doesn't matter to me."* ERIE *gives him up and again attempts to pry himself from the desk, twirling his key frantically as if it were a fetish which might set him free.*) Well, me for the hay. (*But he can't dislodge himself—dully.*) Christ, it's lonely. I wish Hughie was here. By God, if he was, I'd tell him a tale that'd make his eyes pop! The bigger the story the harder he'd fall. He was that kind of sap. He thought gambling was romantic. I guess he saw me like a sort of dream guy, the sort of guy he'd like to be if he could take a chance. I guess he lived a sort of double life listening to me gabbin' about hittin' the high spots. Come to figger it, I'll bet he even cheated on his wife that way, using me and my dolls. (*He chuckles.*) No wonder he liked me, huh? And the bigger I made myself the more he lapped it up. I went easy on him at first. I didn't lie—not any more'n a guy naturally does when he gabs about the bets he wins and the dolls he's made. But I soon see he was cryin' for more, and when a sucker cries for more, you're a dope if you don't let him have it. Every tramp I made got to be a Follies' doll. Hughie liked 'em to be Follies' dolls. Or in the Scandals or Frolics. He wanted me to be the Sheik of Araby, or something that any blonde'd go round-heeled about. Well, I give him plenty of that. And I give him plenty of gambling tales. I explained my campin' in this dump was because I don't want to waste jack on nothin' but gambling. It was like dope to me, I told him. I couldn't quit. He lapped that up. He liked to kid himself I'm mixed up in the racket. He thought gangsters was romantic. So I fed him some baloney about highjacking I'd done once. I told him I knew all the Big Shots. Well, so I do, most of 'em, to say hello, and sometimes they hello back. Who wouldn't know 'em that hangs around Broadway and the joints? I run errands for 'em sometimes, because there's dough in it, but I'm cagey about gettin' in where it ain't healthy. Hughie wanted to think it me and Legs Diamond was old pals. So I give him that too. I give him anything he cried for. (*Earnestly.*) Don't get the wrong idea, Pal. What I fed Hughie wasn't all lies. The tales about gambling wasn't. They was stories of big games and killings that really happened since I've been hangin' round. Only I wasn't in on 'em like I made out—except one or two from way back when I had a run of big luck and was in the bucks for a while until I was took to the cleaners. (*He stops to pay tribute of a sigh to the memory of brave days that were and that never were—then meditatively.*) Yeah, Hughie lapped up my stories like they was duck soup, or a beakful of heroin. I sure took him around with me in tales and showed him one hell of a time. (*He chuckles—then seriously.*) And, d'you know, it done me good, too, in a way. Sure. I'd get to seein' myself like he seen me. Some nights I'd come back here without a buck, feeling lower than a snake's belly, and first thing you know I'd be lousy with jack, bettin' a grand a race. Oh, I was wise I was kiddin' myself. I ain't a sap. But what the hell, Hughie loved it, and it didn't cost nobody nothin', and if every guy along Broadway who kids himself was to drop dead there wouldn't be nobody left. Ain't it the truth, Charlie? (*He again stares at the* NIGHT CLERK *appealingly, forgetting past rebuffs. The* CLERK's *face is taut with vacancy. His mind has been trying to fasten itself to some noise in the night, but a rare and threatening pause of silence has fallen on the city, and here he is, chained behind a hotel desk forever, awake when everyone else in the world is asleep, except Room 492, and he won't go to bed, he's still talking, and there is no escape.*)

NIGHT CLERK (*his glassy eyes stare through* ERIE's *face. He stammers deferentially*). Truth? I'm afraid I didn't get — What's the truth?

ERIE (*hopelessly*). Nothing, Pal. Not a thing. (*His eyes fall to the floor. For a while he is too defeated even to twirl his room key. The* CLERK's *mind still cannot make a getaway because the city remains silent, and the night vaguely reminds him of death, and he is vaguely frightened, and now that he remembers, his feet are giving him hell, but that's no excuse not to act as if the Guest is always right:* "I should have paid 492 more attention. After all, he is company. He is awake and alive. I should use him to help me live through the night. What's he been talking about? I must have caught some of it without meaning to." *The* NIGHT CLERK's *forehead puckers perspiringly as he tries to remember.* ERIE *begins talking again but this time it is obviously aloud to himself, without hope of a listener.*) I could tell by Hughie's face before he went to the hospital, he was through. I've seen the same look on guys' faces when they knew they was on the spot, just before guys caught up with them. I went to see him twice in the hospital. The first time, his wife was there and give me a dirty look, but he cooked up a smile and said, "Hello, Erie, how're the bangtails treating you?" I see he wants a big story to cheer him, but his wife butts in and says he's weak and he mustn't get excited. I felt like crackin', "Well, the Docs in this dump got the right dope. Just leave you with him and he'll never get excited." The second time I went, they wouldn't let me see him. That was near the end. I went to his funeral, too. There wasn't nobody but a coupla his wife's relations. I had to feel sorry for her. She looked like she ought to be parked in a coffin, too. The kids was bawlin'. There wasn't no flowers but a coupla lousy wreaths. It woulda been a punk showing for poor old Hughie, if it hadn't been for my flower piece. (*He swells with pride.*) That was some display, Pal. It'd knock your eye out! Set me back a hundred bucks, and no kiddin'! A big horseshoe of red roses! I knew Hughie'd want a horseshoe because that made it look like he'd been a horse player. And around the top printed in forget-me-nots was "Good-by, Old Pal." Hughie liked to kid himself he was my pal. (*He adds sadly.*) And so he was, at that—even if he was a sucker. (*He pauses, his false poker face as nakedly forlorn as an organ grinder's monkey's. Outside, the spell of abnormal quiet presses suffocatingly upon the street, enters the deserted, dirty lobby. The* NIGHT CLERK's *mind cowers away from it. He cringes behind the desk, his feet aching like hell. There is only one possible escape. If his mind could only fasten onto something 492 has said.* "What's he been talking about? A clerk should always be attentive. You even are duty bound to laugh at a guest's smutty jokes, no matter how often you've heard them. That's the policy of the hotel. 492 has been gassing for hours. What's he been telling me? I must be slipping. Always before this I've been able to hear without bothering to listen, but now when I need company—Ah! I've got it! Gambling! He said a lot about gambling. That's something I've always wanted to know more about, too. Maybe he's a professional gambler. Like Arnold Rothstein.")

NIGHT CLERK (*blurts out with an uncanny, almost lifelike eagerness*). I beg your pardon, Mr.—Erie—but did I understand you to say you are a gambler by profession? Do you, by any chance, know the Big Shot, Arnold Rothstein? (*But this time it is* ERIE *who doesn't hear him. And the* CLERK's *mind is now suddenly impervious to the threat of Night and Silence as it pursues an ideal of fame and glory within itself called Arnold Rothstein.*)

ERIE (*with mournful longing*). Christ, I wish Hughie was alive and kickin'. I'd tell him I win ten grand from the bookies, and ten grand at stud, and ten grand in a crap game! I'd tell him I bought one of those Mercedes sport roadsters with nickel pipes sticking out of the hood! I'd

tell him I lay three babes from the Follies
—two blondes and one brunette! (*The*
NIGHT CLERK *dreams, a rapt hero worship
transfiguring his pimply face: "Arnold
Rothstein! He must be some guy! I read
a story about him. He'll gamble for any
limit on anything, and always wins. The
story said he wouldn't bother playing in
a poker game unless the smallest bet you
could make—one white chip!—was a
hundred dollars. Christ, that's going
some! I'd like to have the dough to get
in a game with him once! The last pot
everyone would drop out but him and me.
I'd say, 'Okay, Arnold, the sky's the limit,'
and I'd raise him five grand, and he'd
call, and I'd have a royal flush to his four
aces. Then I'd say, 'Okay, Arnold, I'm a
good sport, I'll give you a break. I'll cut
you double or nothing. Just one cut. I
want quick action for my dough.' And
I'd cut the ace of spades and win again."
Beatific vision swoons on the empty pools
of the* NIGHT CLERK'*s eyes. He resembles
a holy saint, recently elected to Paradise.
Erie breaks the silence—bitterly resigned.*)
But Hughie's better off, at that, being
dead. He's got all the luck. He needn't
do no worryin' now. He's out of the
racket. I mean, the whole goddamned
racket. I mean life.

NIGHT CLERK (*kicked out of his dream
—with detached, pleasant acquiescence*).
Yes, it is a goddamned racket when you
stop to think, isn't it, 492? But we might
as well make the best of it, because—
Well, you can't burn it all down, can you?
There's too much steel and stone. There'd
always be something left to start it going
again.

ERIE (*scowls bewilderedly*). Say, what
is this? What the hell you talkin' about?

NIGHT CLERK (*at a loss—in much confusion*). Why, to be frank, I really don't—
Just something that came into my head.

ERIE (*bitingly, but showing he is com-
forted at having made some sort of contact*). Get it out of your head quick,
Charlie, or some guys in uniform will
walk in here with a butterfly net and
catch you. (*He changes the subject—earnestly.*) Listen, Pal, maybe you guess I was
kiddin' about that flower piece for Hughie
costing a hundred bucks? Well, I ain't!
I didn't give a damn what it cost. It was
up to me to give Hughie a big-time send-
off, because I knew nobody else would.

NIGHT CLERK. Oh, I'm not doubting

your word, Erie. You won the money
gambling, I suppose— I mean, I beg your
pardon if I'm mistaken, but you are a
gambler, aren't you?

ERIE (*preoccupied*). Yeah, sure, when
I got scratch to put up. What of it? But
I don't win that hundred bucks. I don't
win a bet since Hughie was took to the
hospital. I had to get down on my knees
and beg every guy I know for a sawbuck
here and a sawbuck there until I raised it.

NIGHT CLERK (*his mind concentrated on
the Big Deal—insistently*). Do you by any
chance know—Arnold Rothstein?

ERIE (*his train of thought interrupted
—irritably*). Arnold? What's he got to do
with it? He wouldn't loan a guy like me
a nickel to save my grandmother from
streetwalking.

NIGHT CLERK (*with humble awe*). Then
you do know him!

ERIE. Sure I know the bastard. Who
don't on Broadway? And he knows me—
when he wants to. He uses me to run
errands when there ain't no one else
handy. But he ain't my trouble, Pal. My
trouble is, some of these guys I put the
bite on is dead wrong G's, and they expect to be paid back next Tuesday, or
else I'm outa luck and have to take it on
the lam, or I'll get beat up and maybe
sent to a hospital. (*He suddenly rouses
himself and there is something pathetically but genuinely gallant about him.*)
But what the hell. I was wise I was takin'
a chance. I've always took a chance, and
if I lose I pay, and no welshing! It sure
was worth it to give Hughie the big send-
off. (*He pauses. The* NIGHT CLERK *hasn't
paid any attention except to his own
dream. A question is trembling on his
parted lips, but before he can get it out*
ERIE *goes on gloomily.*) But even that
ain't my big worry, Charlie. My big worry
is the run of bad luck I've had since
Hughie got took to the hospital. Not a
win. That ain't natural. I've always been
a lucky guy—lucky enough to get by and
pay up, I mean. I wouldn't never worry
about owing guys, like I owe them guys.
I'd always know I'd make a win that'd
fix it. But now I got a lousy hunch when
I lost Hughie I lost my luck—I mean,
I've lost the old confidence. He used to
give me confidence. (*He turns away from
the desk.*) No use gabbin' here all night.
You can't do me no good. (*He starts toward the elevator.*)

NIGHT CLERK (*pleadingly*). Just a minute, Erie, if you don't mind. (*With awe.*) So you're an old friend of Arnold Rothstein! Would you mind telling me if it's really true when Arnold Rothstein plays poker, one white chip is—a hundred dollars?

ERIE (*dully exasperated*). Say, for Christ's sake, what's it to you—? (*He stops abruptly, staring probingly at the* CLERK. *There is a pause. Suddenly his face lights up with a saving revelation. He grins warmly and saunters confidently back to the desk.*) Say, Charlie, why didn't you put me wise before, you was interested in gambling? Hell, I got you all wrong, Pal. I been tellin' myself, this guy ain't like old Hughie. He ain't got no sportin' blood. He's just a dope. (*Generously.*) Now I see you're a right guy. Shake. (*He shoves out his hand which the* CLERK *clasps with a limp pleasure.* ERIE *goes on with gathering warmth and self-assurance.*) That's the stuff. You and me'll get along. I'll give you all the breaks, like I give Hughie.

NIGHT CLERK (*gratefully*). Thank you, Erie. (*Then insistently.*) Is it true when Arnold Rothstein plays poker, one white chip—

ERIE (*with magnificent carelessness*). Sets you back a hundred bucks? Sure. Why not? Arnold's in the bucks, ain't he? And when you're in the bucks, a C note is chicken feed. I ought to know, Pal. I was in the bucks when Arnold was a piker. Why, one time down in New Orleans I lit a cigar with a C note, just for a gag, y'understand. I was with a bunch of high class dolls and I wanted to see their eyes pop out—and believe me, they sure popped! After that, I coulda made 'em one at a time or all together! Hell, I once win twenty grand on a single race. That's action! A good crap game is action, too. Hell, I've been in games where there was a hundred grand in real folding money lying around the floor. That's travelin'! (*He darts a quick glance at the* CLERK'*s face and begins to hedge warily. But he needn't. The* CLERK *sees him now as the Gambler in 492, the Friend of Arnold Rothstein—and nothing is incredible.* ERIE *goes on.*) Of course, I wouldn't kid you. I'm not in the bucks now—not right this moment. You know how it is, Charlie. Down today and up tomorrow. I got some dough ridin' on the nose of a turtle in the fourth at Saratoga. I hear a story he'll be so full of hop, if the joc can keep him from jumpin' over the grandstand, he'll win by a mile. So if I roll in here with a blonde that'll knock your eyes out, don't be surprised. (*He winks and chuckles.*)

NIGHT CLERK (*ingratiatingly pally, smiling*). Oh, you can't surprise me that way. I've been a night clerk in New York all my life, almost. (*He tries out a wink himself.*) I'll forget the house rules, Erie.

ERIE (*dryly*). Yeah. The manager wouldn't like you to remember something he ain't heard of yet. (*Then slyly feeling his way.*) How about shootin' a little crap, Charlie? I mean just in fun, like I used to with Hughie. I know you can't afford takin' no chances. I'll stake you, see? I got a coupla bucks. We gotta use real jack or it don't look real. It's all my jack, get it? You can't lose. I just want to show you how I'll take you to the cleaners. It'll give me confidence. (*He has taken two one-dollar bills and some change from his pocket. He pushes most of it across to the* CLERK.) Here y'are. (*He produces a pair of dice—carelessly.*) Want to give these dice the once-over before we start?

NIGHT CLERK (*earnestly*). What do you think I am? I know I can trust you.

ERIE (*smiles*). You remind me a lot of Hughie, Pal. He always trusted me. Well, don't blame me if I'm lucky. (*He clicks the dice in his hand—thoughtfully.*) Y' know, it's time I quit carryin' the torch for Hughie. Hell, what's the use? It don't do him no good. He's gone. Like we all gotta go. Him yesterday, me or you tomorrow, and who cares, and what's the difference? It's all in the racket, huh? (*His soul is purged of grief, his confidence restored.*) I shoot two bits.

NIGHT CLERK (*manfully, with an excited deadpan expression he hopes resembles Arnold Rothstein's*). I fade you.

ERIE (*throws the dice*). Four's my point. (*Gathers them up swiftly and throws again.*) Four it is. (*He takes the money.*) Easy when you got my luck—and know how. Huh, Charlie? (*He chuckles, giving the* NIGHT CLERK *the slyly amused, contemptuous, affectionate wink with which a Wise Guy regales a Sucker.*)

CURTAIN

THE TOILET

LeRoi Jones

First presented by Leo Garen and Stan Swerdlow in association with Gene Persson, Rita Fredericks, and the Theatre Vanguard, New York City, on December 16, 1964, with the following cast:

ORA (Big Shot), *short, ugly, crude, loud* James Spruill

WILLIE LOVE, *tall, thin; should have been sensitive; smiles* Gary Bolling

HINES, *big, husky, garrulous; he and* LOVE *are closest friends* D'Urville Martin

JOHNNY BOY HOLMES, *short, curly hair; bright, fast, likeable* Bostic Van Felton

PERRY, *tall, dark, somber, cynical* Norman Bush

GEORGE DAVIS, *tall, thin, crudely elegant; judicious* Antonio Fargas

SKIPPY, *quick, rather stupid but interested; someone to be trusted* Tony Hudson

KNOWLES, *large and ridiculous; a grinning ape* Walter Jones

DONALD FARRELL, *tall, thin, blonde, awkward, soft* Gary Haynes

FOOTS (Ray), *short, intelligent, manic; possessor of a threatened empire* Hampton Clanton

KAROLIS, *medium height; very skinny, and not essentially attractive, except when he speaks* Jaime Sanchez

Directed by Leo Garen
Designed by Larry Rivers
Associate Designer and lighting by Harold Baldrige
Sound by Art Wolff

The action takes place at the present time in a high school boys' toilet.

Copyright © 1964 by LeRoi Jones.
Reprinted by permission of The Sterling Lord Agency.

CAUTION: Professionals and amateurs are hereby warned that *The Toilet* is fully protected by the laws of copyright and is subject to royalty. All rights, including professional, amateur, motion picture, recitation, lecturing, public reading, radio and television broadcasting, the rights of translation into foreign languages, and quotation are strictly reserved. No part of this work may be used in any way without the written consent of the copyright holders. All inquiries concerning rights in the play should be addressed to the Sterling Lord Agency, 660 Madison Avenue, New York, N.Y. 10021.

LeRoi Jones is something else again in the history of American literature, in the history of the American theatre. The first black playwrights (and we have Lorraine Hansberry and James Baldwin represented in this volume) were concerned to express a black viewpoint in a white world. LeRoi Jones is something else again. LeRoi is black, militant, offers a hope to black audiences and a fierce challenge to white audiences. LeRoi Jones is a massive insult to white sensibility; he is also an American writer of quite unusual talent.

He was born in Newark, New Jersey, on October 7, 1934. His father was a postman (at one time it was a matter of pride to him that as long as he as a poet made less money than his father, the postman, he would never be in danger of knowing what luxury was) and he was educated at Howard University, Washington, D.C. He has taught at Columbia and elsewhere. He has been a poet and a playwright, and a militant black leader. His plays have never been meant simply as plays. They have been intended as inflammatory political tracts to further the political cause of black militancy.

In 1962 LeRoi Jones, in an address to the American Society for African Culture, declared that the true function of the black writer was to offer to society "the emotional history of the black man in this country: as its victim and its chronicler." As time has unfolded, Jones more and more has been both victim and chronicler himself.

His plays have all taken a rabidly racist stance, which I deplore but—okay, to an extent—can understand. This is simplification of the problem all decent white Americans face in confronting art works by any decent black American. The black feels anger and the white is expected to feel guilt (guilt usually on behalf of forefathers who were in Europe at the actual time of the crime), and from this transaction, and many like it, the black will be able to build up his racial pride, and will eventually be able to accept that white is also beautiful.

Jones, in his plays, in his poetry, in his essays, in his speeches, and also in his actions, represents a complex force in American society. In an introduction to *The Toilet,* Jones once wrote: "*The Toilet* is about the lives of black people. White people tell me it is not. They have no way of knowing, but they insist that they do." I do not insist: I believe that Jones writes with as much insight about his people as any black writer writing today. And his theme, so often, is the black as victim: the black as victim of violence, not only the violence done to him, but the violence he does to others.

His first play, adapted from a fictional work of his, was *Dante,* given a few Off-Broadway performances in 1961. But in 1964 the world broke out for LeRoi Jones as a dramatist: in New York there were productions of *The Baptism, The Toilet, Dutchman,* and *The Slave.*

Probably any of these plays—although I think *The Toilet* does have a literary advantage over the others—would have served to have given a sense of this very angry American, who writes with such passion, grace and understanding.

Racist anger is easily expressed. And even in those very, very rare cases (is there another?) where the anger is justified—yes, if I were black I would expect and hope to be every bit as militant as Jones—the resultant propagandist art is not of much value. Jones is an exception. He has a compassion for his white enemy he can never quite destroy, and this gives his work a nuance. He is also a quite wonderful, even if careless, writer, and this gives his work an advantage.

In the play *The Toilet,* you are encountering a complex mind grappling with two of the most complex themes of contemporary life. Jones is here talking about black and white, and the inevitabilities of fate that pigmentation places upon one, and simple human love. Jones's other plays, bitter, tragic, and as painful at the particularly personal level as an ingrowing toenail, all have their agonies and beauties.

For some years after this dramatic explosion, Jones was silent in the theatre, using other media to make his voice heard. Then in 1970 he staged *Slave Ship,* a vivid indictment of white imperialism. Once again Jones was bitter and angry in what was perhaps his clearest and most effective theatrical diatribe of them all.

Jones is a brilliant propagandist for his race. But he is also a poet. There lurks in all his work the ultimate compassion and comprehension of human poetry. Whatever you may hear to the contrary, LeRoi Jones is a good man. You have only to read him to know that.

The scene is a large bare toilet built of gray rough cement. There are urinals along one wall and a partition separating them from the commodes which are along the same wall. The toilet must resemble the impersonal ugliness of a school toilet or a latrine of some institution. A few rolls of toilet paper are spread out on the floor, wet through. The actors should give the impression frequently that the place smells.

———

ORA (*breaks through door grinning then giggling; looks around the bleak place, walks around, then with one hand on his hip, takes out his penis and urinates, still grinning, into one of the commodes, spraying urine over the seats*).

LOVE (*sticking his head through the door*). Big Shot! Hey, Big Shot! These guys say come and help them.

ORA (*zipping his fly and wiping the one hand on the back of his pants*). Yeh? (*Turning to* LOVE.) Yeh? They got him, huh?

LOVE (*pushing door open so his arm is straight*). Naw, they don't have him yet. He's on the second floor, running back and forth and hiding in empty rooms. But Knowles said for you to come help.

ORA (*flushing all the commodes and urinals in the row as he walks past*). Sheet! I'll catch that bastid in a second. (*Ducks under* LOVE's *arm to go out.*) Why the hell don't you get up there. You supposed to be faster than me.

LOVE. I'm s'posed to stay here and keep the place clear. (*Making a face.*) Damn. This place smells like hell.

ORA (*without turning around*). Yeh (*giggling.*) this must be your momma's house.

LOVE (*slipping inside the door and holding it against* ORA). Shit. At least I got one.

ORA (*thumps against the door, not really angry*). Bastid!

LOVE (*waits a few seconds, then pulls the door open slightly; then lets it shut and walks to a closed commode and noticing it's wet wipes it with some of the strewn toilet paper; he sits down and stretches his legs; then gets up and opens the commode to urinate.*) (*There are voices outside and then the door swings open and* HINES *and* HOLMES *come in.*)

HINES. Hey, Willie.

LOVE (*still urinating*). What you want? (*Comes out, zipping his pants.*)

HINES (*to* HOLMES). Man, this cat's in here pulling his whatchamacallit.

HOLMES (*to* LOVE). Yeh. Damn, Love, why don't you go get Gloria to do that stuff for you.

LOVE. She-et. (*Grinning.*) Huh. I sure don't need your ol' lady to be pullin' on my joint. (*Laughs.* HOLMES *begins to spar with him.*)

HINES. They didn't even catch that skinny nose punk yet.

LOVE. No? Why in hell not?

HOLMES. He's still running up and down the damn halls. I should go up there and drag that sonofabitch down. (HOLMES *and* HINES *begin to urinate also in the commodes.* LOVE *pulls open the door a small bit and looks out.*)

LOVE. Shit. Boy, all you slow ass cats. I'd catch that little skinny paddy boy in a second. Where's that little popeyed Foots?

HINES. Damn if I know. I think he's still in Miss Powell's class. You know if he missed her class she'd beat his head, and then get his ol' lady to beat his head again.

HOLMES. Shit. Skippy should've got hold of that damn Karolis by now. He ain't fast worth a bitch.

LOVE. Yeh, but he's so goddamned scary he might just jump out a goddamn window.

(HOLMES *finishes urinating and starts pushing* LOVE *and they begin to spar around.* HOLMES *is very funny, making boxerlike sounds and brushing his nose continuously with his thumbs.* LOVE *just stands straight with his left hand stiff and stabbing it out towards* HOLMES's *face.* HINES *finishes and gets in the action too. Both he and* HOLMES *are against* LOVE, *who starts to laugh and curse good-naturedly.*)

LOVE. Two a' you bastids, huh? I'll take you both. (*He starts kicking at them.*)

HINES. Boy, if you kick me, you'll die just like that . . . with your skinny ass leg up. They'll have to build a special coffin with a part for your leg.

HOLMES (*backing away and then turning on* HINES, *laughing*). Let's get this sum'bitch Willie.

HINES. (*Backing away, now kicking and swinging . . . but just timing blows so they won't strike anyone*). Goddam, Johnny Boy, you a crooked muthafucka.

You cats think you can mess with the kid? (*The two spar against* HINES *and then* LOVE *turns against* HOLMES.)

LOVE. Let's get this little assed cat. (HOLMES *kicks at them, then jumps up on the commodes in order to defend himself more "heroically."*

HOLMES. I'm gonna get your ass, Willie. I'm just trying to help you out and you gonna play wise. Ya' bastid.

HINES. Listen to that cat. (*Runs after* HOLMES.) I'm gonna put your damn head in one of those damn urinals. (*He and* LOVE *finally grab* HOLMES *and he begins struggling with them in earnest.*) Let's put this little bastard's head in the goddamn urinal!

HOLMES. You bastids! Let me go! Boy, I'm gonna cut somebody. Bastids!

(*The door opens and* ORA *comes in. His shirt is torn. But he rushes over laughing and starts punching everyone, even* HOLMES.)

HINES. Goddamn it, Big Shot, get the hell out of here.

HOLMES. Get 'em, Big Shot.

ORA (*pushes* HOLMES *who's still being held by* LOVE). I'm gonna punch you, you prick. Hold the cocksucker, Love.

LOVE (*releasing* HOLMES *immediately*). I ain't gonna hold him so you can punch him. (ORA *and* HOLMES *square off, both laughing and faking professional demeanor.*)

LOVE. Hey, Big Shot, what happened to your shirt?

ORA (*putting his hands down and handling the torn part of his shirt*). That muthafuckin' Karolis ripped it. (*The other three yowl.* HINES *puts his fingers to the hole as if to tear it again.*) Get outta here you black ass bastid. (*He squares off at* HINES, *then pushes him away.*) That paddy bastid! I had the cocksucker around the waist, and then he rips my shirt and scratches me. (*He holds up his wounded hand.*)

HINES. You let him get away?

ORA. No, hell. I punched the bastid right in his lip. But he was making so much noise we thought somebody'd come out and see us so Knowles and Skippy took him in the broom closet and I cut down the stairs. The stupid bastid was screaming and biting right outside of ol' lady Powell's room.

HOLMES. Did anybody come outta there?

ORA. You think I was gonna stay around and see? She and Miss Golden after me anyway.

LOVE. Did you see Foots in there?

ORA (*going to the door and peering out*). Yeh. And George Davis and Perry are in there too. (*He pushes door open and leans all the way out.*)

HINES. Shit. They're never gonna bring that sonofabitch down here. We ain't got all day.

ORA (*letting the door shut*). Yeh, Perry and Foots and them ought to be down here in a few minutes. It's almost three now.

LOVE (*pretending he has a basketball in his hands, he pretends to dribble and lunges forward simulating a fake at* HINES, *then he sweeps past* HINES *and leaps in the air as if making a layup shot*). Peed on you, just then, buddy.

HINES. Sheet, Man, you what you call a self-checker. I don't even have to block that shot. I just take it off the backboard like this. (*He spins around and leaps up at the imaginary basket and scoops the imaginary ball off, landing and shaking his head as if to shake off imaginary defenders.*) Another rebound! (*Makes motion of long pass down toward opposite "court."*) Now, the quick break! (*He moves in position for his own pass, receives it, makes one long stepping dribble and leaps as if dunking the ball in the basket.*) Two!

HOLMES. Boy, you guys sure play a lot of ball . . . off the court.

ORA (*opening the door again*). No shootin', cocksuckas.

LOVE (*still whirling and leaping as if he is making successful hook shots from an imaginary foul line*). Hey, what we gonna do to this cat when he gets here?

ORA (*leaning back in from the door though keeping it open with the fingers*). Damn, Love. You a stupid bastid. (*Peeks out door.*) We gonna kick that little frail bastid's ass.

HINES. In fact, you the one gonna do it, Willie.

HOLMES. Yeh, Love. (*Blocking one of* LOVE's *"shots."*)

LOVE. Shit. Karolis never bothered *me*. (*Faking* HOLMES *and swinging to shoot from the other side.*)

ORA (*looking back in and letting the door swing shut*). Damn, Willie (*In mock-*

ing seriousness.) Karolis is always telling everybody how he bangs the hell out of Caroline, every chance he gets. (*Begins to giggle.*)

HOLMES. Is that your mother's name, Love, Caroline?

HINES (*busy trying to lift a back window to look out on the yard*). What you mean, Johnny Boy, is that his mother's name? You the one told me.

LOVE (*swinging around as if to shoot again he suddenly punches* HOLMES *on the shoulder.* HOLMES *lets out a yelp of pain*). Uhhuh . . . I told you about messin' with me.

HOLMES (*holding his shoulder*). Shit. Why didn't you hit Big Shot, you bastard? He brought the shit up.

ORA (*has the door propped open again*). Shit. That narrow head bastid know better than to fuck with me. (*He peers out the door and as he does* LOVE *gestures as if to hit him in the back.*)

HOLMES (*to* LOVE). You scared ass bastard. Why don't you do it?

ORA (*turning around and throwing up his hands to defend himself*). Yeh, I wish you would, you bullet head sonofabitch.

(HOLMES *goes and sits on a radiator next to* HINES.)

LOVE. Man, nobody's thinking about you, Big Shot. (*He goes to urinate.*)

ORA (*pulling the door open again*). Here come Perry and them.

HOLMES (*jumping off the radiator still holding his shoulder*). Perry and who else?

ORA. George Davis and Donald Farrell.

HINES. Donald Farrell? What the hell's he doin' down here? Where the hell is Foots?

LOVE. Yeh, what the hell is Perry doing bringing Farrell down here with 'em? Shit.

(ORA *pulls the door open, and* PERRY, DAVIS, *and* FARRELL *come in.*)

PERRY. Hey, what's happening?

HOLMES. Shit. I should ask you. Where's Foots?

GEORGE. He had to stay upstairs for a while. Powell wanted to talk to him . . . or something.

ORA (*to* FARRELL). Man, whatta you want down here? Nobody asked you to come.

GEORGE. I told him he could come. Why not?

ORA. Whatta you mean, why not? You know goddamn well, why not. Silly sumbitch!

PERRY. Ah, Big Shot, why don't you be cool for a change, huh?

GEORGE. Yeh, man, Big Shot. Donald's not going to hurt anything.

ORA. No? (*Taking out a much smoked cigarette butt.*) Maybe you don't think so . . . but I do.

GEORGE. Oh, man, shit.

FARRELL. Why don't you want me here, Big Shot?

ORA (*glaring at* FARRELL). Man, don't be asking me questions.

FARRELL. Don't ask you questions? Why the hell not?

ORA (*menacingly at* FARRELL). Cause I said so, that's why. You don't like it, muthafucka?

PERRY (*stepping between them*). Goddamn it, Big shot, why don't you sit your ass down for a while and shut the hell up?

ORA (*turning to* PERRY). You gonna make me, muthafucka?

PERRY (*stepping to face* ORA). I can. And you better believe it, Baby!

ORA. Shit. (*Disparagingly; moving away from* FARRELL *and back to the center of the room.*) Well you damn sure got your chance right now, you black sonofabitch.

GEORGE (*moves between* PERRY *and* ORA). Oh, goddamnit why don't both you guys sit down. You too, Donald. (FARRELL *moves to sit on a radiator beside* HOLMES *and* HINES.) Ora, you wrong, man, and you know it.

ORA. How come I'm wrong, huh? You know goddamn well that skinny cocksucka over there (*At* FARRELL.) ain't got no business down here. He ain't gonna do a damn thing but stand around and look.

LOVE (*laughing*). That's all I'm gonna do.

HINES (*hunching* HOLMES *with his elbow*). Yeh, but that's okay for you, Willie. You so black, if you stand still nobody'll know you're standing there anyway. (*All laugh;* ORA *takes the opportunity to go to the door and crack it open.*)

PERRY. Where's the rest of those guys?

HINES. I guess they must still be upstairs in that broom closet.

PERRY. Broom closet? (*He and* DAVIS *lean against one of the walls and begin to smoke.*)

HINES. Yeh, Knowles and Skippy got

Karolis upstairs in a broom closet waiting till everybody leaves the floor I guess.

FARRELL. Jimmy Karolis?

HOLMES. Yeah, that's who we're waiting for. (*Giggles.*)

FARRELL. What the hell's gonna happen then?

ORA (*turning from door*). Man, what the hell you care, huh? Pee-the-bed-muthafucka!

HINES. Damn, George!

GEORGE. Damn, what?

HINES. Seems to me like Big Shot's right. You bring this cat down here and he doesn't even know what's happening.

ORA. You goddamn real I'm right. Simple ass cats.

FARRELL. What're you guys gonna gang Jimmy Karolis?

ORA. We gonna break that muthafucka's back.

FARRELL. For what?

ORA. Look man, why don't you shut up and get the hell out of here, huh?

FARRELL. You mean all you guys're gonna jump on Karolis?

ORA (*walking over to* FARRELL *and grabbing him by the shirt*). You gonna stick up for him? (FARRELL *tries to push* ORA'*s hands from his shirt, and though he is much taller than* ORA, ORA *pulls him from his seat.*)

FARRELL. Goddamn it, Ora, why don't you cut the shit?

GEORGE. Yeh, Ora, cut it out.

PERRY. Goddamn, that cat's always going for bad.

(GEORGE *come over to restrain* ORA, *but* ORA *succeeds in punching* FARRELL *in the stomach.* FARRELL *clutches his stomach and sinks to the floor groaning.*)

PERRY. You bastard. (*To* ORA. ORA *swings around to confront him.*)

ORA. You come on too, if you want to, you black sonofabitch!

(GEORGE *pushes them apart again and his push sends* ORA *rattling heavily against the door.*) Goddamnit, George, why don't you stay the fuck outta this?

GEORGE. Because there wasn't a goddamn reason in the world for you to hit Donald like that. (*Going to help* FARRELL *up.*) Damn, Ora, you're a wrong sonofabitch, you know that?

FARRELL (*still doubled up and holding his stomach. He pulls his arm back when* GEORGE *tries to help him up.*) No, man!

Lemme stay here. (*Still groaning.*) Ora, you dirty cocksucker.

ORA. Boy, you better shut up before I stomp mudholes in your pissy ass.

(*The door is suddenly pushed open and* KNOWLES *and* SKIPPY *come in holding* KAROLIS *by the arms.* KAROLIS'*s head is hanging, and he is crying softly and blood is on his shirt and face. His hair is mussed and standing all over his head.*)

LOVE. Ga-uh Damn! What'd you cats do?

KNOWLES (*giggling stupidly*). Love, now what the hell does it look like we did? Broke this muthafucka's jaw.

HINES. Damn. I thought we were just bringing the cat down here to fight Foots. I didn't know you guys were gonna break his head first.

SKIPPY. Well, he didn't wanna come. We had to persuade him.

KNOWLES. Shit, Skippy, whatta you mean "we?" I did all the persuading.

ORA. Aw, shit, Knowles. I bloodied the cat's lip. You trying to take all the credit.

SKIPPY. Yeh, Knowles. You didn't hit the cat but once, and that was on the goddamn shoulder. (*Letting* KNOWLES *drag* KAROLIS *into a corner where he lets him drop.*) You know what this cat was doing all the time we was in that goddamn broom closet? Tellin' jokes. (*Laughs.*) They must not a been funny either. Karolis didn't laugh once.

KNOWLES. What should I do with this guy. I gotta drag him everywhere.

ORA. Drop him in that goddamn corner. (*Walks over to corner and nudges* KAROLIS *with his foot.*) Hey, muthafucka. Hey! Why don't you straighten up?

SKIPPY (*noticing* FARRELL, *who is still crumpled in an opposite corner, but stirring*). Damn! What the hell happened to Donald?

PERRY. That goddamn Big Shot had to show how bad he was.

ORA (*laughing paradoxically*). He called me a nigger. (*All laugh.*)

LOVE. Well, what the hell are you? Wha's the matter, you shamed of your people?

ORA. Fuck you! (*He still stands over* KAROLIS, *nudging him with his foot.*) Hey, man, get up! (*Laughs.*)

HINES. Damn, Ora. Why don't you leave the cat alone?

ORA (*bending over as if to talk in* KA-

ROLIS's *ear*). *Hey, baby, why don't you get up?* I gotta nice fat sausage here for you.

GEORGE. Goddamn, Big Shot . . . You really a wrong sonofabitch!

ORA. Look man. (*Now kneeling over the slumped figure.*) If you want to get in on this you line up behind me. I don't give a shit what you got to say.

LOVE. Man, George, leave the cat alone. You know that's his stick. That's what he does (*Laughing.*) for his kicks . . . rub up against half dead white boys. (*All laugh.*)

ORA (*looking over his shoulder . . . grudgingly having to smile too*). I'd rub up against your momma too. (*Leaning back to* KAROLIS.) Come on, baby . . . I got this fat ass sa-zeech for you!

LOVE. Ora, you mad cause you don't have a momma of your own to rub up against. (*All laugh.*)

ORA (*turns again, this time less amused*). Fuck you, you boney head sonofabitch. As long as I can rub against your momma . . . or your fatha' (*Laughs at his invention.*) I'm doin' alright.

(*Door is pushed open suddenly and* FOOTS *comes in. He is nervous but keeps it hidden by a natural glibness and a sharp sense of what each boy in the room expects, singularly, from him. He is the weakest physically and smallest of the bunch, but he is undoubtedly their leader.*) (*When* FOOTS *comes in* KAROLIS *looks up quickly, then slumps again.*)

HINES. Man, where the hell you been?

FOOTS. That goddamn Van Ness had me in his office. He said I'm a credit to my race. (*Laughs and all follow.*) He said I'm smart-as-a-whip (*Imitating Van Ness.*) and should help him to keep all you unsavory (*Again imitating.*) elements in line. (*All laugh again.*)

LOVE. Yeh? What's he talking about?

FOOTS. Well, he seems to think that you guys . . . particularly that goddamn Big Shot and Knowles, are not good influences in this joint.

PERRY. Boy, you can say that again. Nutty muthafuckas!

ORA (*to* PERRY). Fuck you, tar baby!

FOOTS. Well, I'm supposed to make sure that you guys don't do anything bad to anybody. Especially to James Karolis. (*Laughing.*)

GEORGE. Oh yeh? He know about that?

FOOTS. Yeh, somebody told him Knowles

said he was gonna kick Karolis's ass. (*Seeing* KAROLIS *in the corner for the first time. His first reaction is horror and disgust . . . but he keeps it controlled as is his style, and merely half whistles.*) Goddamn! What the fuck happened to him? (*He goes over to* KAROLIS *and kneels near him, threatening to stay too long. He controls the impulse and gets up and walks back to where he was. He is talking throughout this action.*) Damn! What'd you guys do, kill the cat?

PERRY. Heavy-handed Big Shot again.

FOOTS (*looks at* ORA *quickly with disgust but softens it immediately to comic disdain*). What the hell you hit him with, Ora, a goddamn train?

ORA (*happy at the notice of his destruction*). No, man, I just bopped him in the mouth with the back of my hand.

FOOTS. Ga-uhd damn! You a rough ass cat, Shot. He sure don't look like he's in any way to fight anybody.

ORA (*laughing*). No, but he might be able to suck you off. Hee, hee.

LOVE. Shit. You the one that look like you want that, Big Shot.

FOOTS. Oh, shit. There wasn't any need of bringing the cat down here if you guys were gonna fuck him up before I got here. He was supposed to fight me. (*Almost angry.*)

HINES. Yeh, that's what I thought. You shouldn't of sent Ora and Knowles up after him then.

FOOTS. The only person I asked to go up was Skippy.

SKIPPY. Well, the sonofabitch wouldn't come . . . so, I got Superduck over there to help me. I didn't ask Ora to come. Knowles did.

KNOWLES. Oh, man, the cat's here. Get him up on his feet (*Laughs.*) then knock him down. That's all. That don't seem like no big problem to me. (*Through most of the action* KNOWLES *is drumming on the walls or the window or the door or the floor, in a kind of drum and bugle corps beat . . . also supplying the bugle parts vocally.*)

LOVE. Man, Knowles, why don't you stop being a goddamn Elk all the time. Damn. That cat's always drumming on something. Why don't you get a goddamn drum?

KNOWLES. I'm going to drum on your

boney head in a little while if you don't
shut up.

FOOTS. Well, I don't see any reason to
keep all this shit up. Just pour water on
the cat and let's get outta here.

ORA. What? You mean you made us go
through all this bullshit for nothing?

FOOTS. Well, what the hell am I gonna
do, beat on the guy while he's sprawled
on the floor. Damn, Ora, you're a pretty
lousy sonofabitch.

HINES. Man, Big Shot'd stomp anybody
in any damn condition. He likes it when
they're knocked out first, especially.

FOOTS. I'm pushed! There's no reason to
stay here. I can't fight the guy like he is.

FARRELL (*who has pushed himself up
and is leaning against the wall*). I sure
am glad somebody's got some sense here.

FOOTS (*seeing* FARRELL *for the first
time*). What the hell you doing here?
Who asked you to come here, huh? (*Embarrassed and angry.*)

ORA. That stupid ass Perry brought him.

PERRY. That's right. I just thought there
was gonna be a fight. I didn't know you
guys were gonna lynch anybody.

FOOTS. Lynch, your ass. Look, Donald,
why don't you leave, huh? Nobody needs
you here.

FARRELL (*slowly*). Yeh, okay, Ray. But
I just want to know why you're gonna
beat up on Jimmy like this. What the hell
did he do to you?

FOOTS (*almost indignantly*). None of
your goddamn business, Farrell. Just leave!

ORA. Yeh, man. I should've thrown your
ass out when you first come in here. Pee-
the-bed sonofabitch.

FARRELL. O.K. (*Stands up, still lightly
holding his stomach.*) O.K. but I want to
take Jimmy out of here with me. He can't
fight anybody.

ORA. Man, you better shut your goddamn mouth and get outta here!

FOOTS. Look, Donald, just leave, that's
all. You hear? (*Turns his back on* FAR-
RELL *and walks toward* KAROLIS, *then
thinking better of it turns towards* FAR-
RELL *again.*)

FARRELL. Ray! You're not gonna beat
the guy up when he's like that are you?

FOOTS. I don't need you to tell me what
to do. (*He goes over and pulls the door
open slightly.*) Just get out of here . . .
now!

FARRELL (*takes a step then looks towards* KAROLIS). But look at him, he can't
do anything. (*To* FOOTS.) Why do you
want to do this?

FOOTS. Goddamn it, get out!

FARRELL. That's no answer.

FOOTS. Man, I'll punch you in the belly
myself.

FARRELL. Shit. (*Disparagingly . . .
which makes* FOOTS *madder.*)

FOOTS (*in low horrible voice*). Goddamnit. You better get the fuck outta
here, right now!

FARRELL. Nobody's gonna tell me why?
(*He starts to move for the door.*)

PERRY. Look, Donald, you better cool
it, Buddy. You heard about that letter
didn't you?

FARRELL. Letter? What letter?

FOOTS. Man, I told you to leave. I'm not
gonna tell you again.

PERRY (*laughing*). The letter Karolis
sent Foots telling him he thought he was
"beautiful" . . . and that he wanted to
blow him. (*All giggle.*)

FARRELL (*turning sharply towards*
FOOTS). A letter?

ORA (*rushing at* FARRELL *from the side
and punching him*). Goddamn it! Didn't
you hear somebody say leave, pee ass?

FOOTS (*pushing between* FARRELL *and*
ORA). Cut it out, Ora!

FARRELL (*hurt again and slumping.*
ORA *tries to hit him again and the punch
is blocked by* FOOTS *who glares savagely
at* ORA). A letter? (*Groaning.*) Oh, Ray,
come on. Why don't you come off it?
(*He is looking up at* FOOTS.)

ORA (*leaps around* FOOTS *and pushes*
FARRELL *into the door*). Get out of here
you dumb bastid! (KNOWLES *pulls the
door open and shoves* FARRELL *through
it.*) Goddamn, what a stupid punk. (*He
laughs, as do some of the others.*)

FOOTS (*stares at the closed door for a
second, then he turns slowly to the others*).
Look, let's get out of here. This stuff is
finished.

KAROLIS (*has brought his head up during
the preceding scuffle, and has been staring
at* FOOTS; *as* FOOTS *and the others look
over towards him, he speaks very softly,
but firmly*). No. Nobody has to leave! I'll
fight you, Ray. (*He begins to pull himself
up. He is unsteady on his feet, but determined to get up . . . and to fight.*) I
want to fight you!

FOOTS (*startled and his eyes widen momentarily, but he suppresses it*).

HINES. Damn. Some guys don't know when they're well off.

ORA. Yeh. You little skinny muthafucka. You should've kept your mouth shut, and played dead.

KNOWLES. Goddamn. You mean that sonofabitch wasn' dead? Shit, Big Shot, you must hit like a girl.

ORA (*to* KNOWLES). Yeh? Well, let me hit you, you bastid.

KNOWLES (*disparagingly*). Shit.

KAROLIS (*pushing himself off the wall slightly and wiping his face with his sleeve*). No, Ray. Don't have them leave. I want to fight you.

FOOTS (*very silent and stiff, not wanting to be pushed*). Oh? (*Slowly.*) Well, that's damn fine with me.

ORA (*going behind* KAROLIS *and pushing him towards* FOOTS). You wanna fight? Well, go ahead, dick licker. (*Howls.*)

HINES. Yeh, get it on, fellas.

HOLMES. Karolis must be bad. (*Laughs.*)

GEORGE. Man, (*To* KAROLIS.) you sure you want to get in this? You look kinda shaky to me.

SKIPPY. Man, just sit down and watch. This might be good.

KAROLIS. Yes, Ray, I want to fight you, now. I want to kill you. (*His voice is still soft and terrible. The word "kill" is almost spit out.* FOOTS *does not move. He turns his head slightly to look* KAROLIS *in the eye, but he is motionless otherwise.*)

ORA. Goddamn it, fight! (*He pushes* KAROLIS *again. This time* KAROLIS *almost bumps* FOOTS *and* FOOTS *throws up his hands and pushes him away.*)

FOOTS. Goddamn you! Goddamn you! (*His body moves from being completely immobile to an angry snarling figure.*) You bastard! (*The others become animated, clapping their hands, shouting, whistling, and moving around as if they were also fighting.*)

KAROLIS. No, Ray. I want to fight you. (*He is moving around now, but his hands are still held tightly and awkwardly at his sides.*) I want to fight you.

FOOTS (*moving around with his hands up to fight; they both move around each other and* FOOTS *seems to get momentarily a change of heart*). Look now, Karolis . . . you're just gonna get your head blocked.

KAROLIS (*as if he didn't hear*). No. You have to fight me. I sent you a note, remember. That note saying I loved you. (*The others howl at this.*) The note saying you were beautiful. (*Tries to smile.*) You remember that note, Ray?

FOOTS. Goddamn it, if you're going to fight, fight you cocksucker!

KAROLIS. Yeh. That's what I'm going to do Ray. I'm going to fight you. We're here to fight. About that note, right? The one that said I wanted to take you into my mouth. (FOOTS *lunges at* KAROLIS *and misses.*) Did I call you Ray in that letter . . . or Foots? (*Trying to laugh.*) Foots! (*Shouts.*) I'm going to break your fucking neck. That's right. That's who I want to kill. Foots!

ORA (*pushing* KAROLIS *into* FOOTS). Fight, you goddamn sissy-punk bastid!

FOOTS (*slaps* KAROLIS *with his open hand*). You crazy bastard!

KAROLIS (*backing up . . . wanting to talk but still moving as if to fight*). Are you Ray or Foots, huh? (*The crowd begins to move forward to cut down the area of the match so that the two fighters will have to make contact.*)

HINES. Hit the sonofabitch, Foots!

FOOTS. Fight, you bastard!

KAROLIS. Yeh! That's why we're here, huh? I'll fight you, Foots! (*Spits the name.*) I'll fight you. Right here in this same place where you said your name was Ray. (*Screaming. He lunges at* FOOTS *and manages to grab him in a choke hold.*) Ray, you said your name was. You said Ray. Right here in this filthy toilet. You said Ray. (*He is choking* FOOTS *and screaming.* FOOTS *struggles and is punching* KAROLIS *in the back and stomach, but he cannot get out of the hold.*) You put your hand on me and said Ray!

SKIPPY. Goddamn, that bastid is choking the shit out of Foots. (*The two still struggle, with* KAROLIS *continuing to have the advantage.*)

HINES. That fuck is trying to kill Foots!

HOLMES. Goddamn it!

ORA (*suddenly leaping on* KAROLIS's *back, puts the same choke hold on him*). You cocksucka . . . how's that feel, huh? (*He pulls* KAROLIS *off of* FOOTS, *who falls to his knees.*) Huh?

KNOWLES. Let's kick this cocksucker's ass real good. (*He rushes up to help* ORA, *and the whole of the crowd surges into the center punching the fallen* KAROLIS *in the face.* KNOWLES *is screaming with laughter.*)

KAROLIS. No, no, his name is Ray, not Foots. You stupid bastards. I love somebody you don't even know. (*He is dragged to the floor. The crowd is kicking and cursing him.* ORA *in the center punching the fallen* KAROLIS *in the face.* KNOWLES *is screaming with laughter.*)

FOOTS (*now on his hands and knees but his head hangs limply and he is unaware of what is happening; he slumps again*).

(*They have beaten* KAROLIS *enough.* KAROLIS *is spread in the center of the floor and is unmoving.* ORA *drapes some of the wet toilet paper across his body and face.*)

ORA. Let's stick the sonofabitch's head in the damn toilet.

PERRY. Oh, man, fuck you. The cat's completely out. What more can you do to him?

GEORGE. Yeh, le's get Foots, and get outta here before somebody comes in.

ORA. Yeh. Hee, hee! Look at ol' Foots. That fuckin' paddy boy almost kilt him!

LOVE. Yeh. (*Laughing.*) I told you Karolis was probably bad!

(*All laugh.*)

KNOWLES. Nutty sonofabitch.

LOVE (*picking up* FOOTS *helped by* HINES *and* HOLMES). Hey, big eye! Get the hell up. (ORA *takes a paper cup and dips it in the commode and throws it in* FOOTS'S *face.*)

ORA. Yeh, get up, bad ass. (*Laughs.*) (*They all leave, as* FOOTS *begins to come to. All making noise, laughing, cursing.* KAROLIS *lies as before in the center of the room, motionless.*)

(*After a minute or so* KAROLIS *moves his hand. Then his head moves and he tries to look up. He draws his legs up under him and pushes his head off the floor. Finally he manages to get to his hands and knees. He crawls over to one of the commodes, pulls himself up, then falls backward awkwardly and heavily. At this point, the door is pushed open slightly, then it opens completely and* FOOTS *comes in. He stares at* KAROLIS'S *body for a second, looks quickly over his shoulder, then runs and kneels before the body, weeping and cradling the head in his arms.*)

BLACK

YOU KNOW
I CAN'T HEAR YOU
WHEN THE WATER'S RUNNING

(four one-act plays)

Robert Anderson

For AUDREY WOOD

First presented by Jack Farren and Gilbert Cates at the Ambassador Theatre in New York City on March 13, 1967, with the following cast:

(in order of appearance)

THE SHOCK OF RECOGNITION

A producer's office

JACK BARNSTABLE George Grizzard		DOROTHY Melinda Dillon
HERB MILLER Joe Silver		RICHARD PAWLING Martin Balsam

THE FOOTSTEPS OF DOVES

A basement showroom of a bedding store

SALESMAN George Grizzard		GEORGE Martin Balsam
HARRIET Eileen Heckart		JILL Melinda Dillon

I'LL BE HOME FOR CHRISTMAS

An apartment living room and kitchen

CHUCK Martin Balsam		CLARICE Melinda Dillon
EDITH Eileen Heckart		

I'M HERBERT

A side porch

HERBERT George Grizzard		MURIEL Eileen Heckart

Directed by Alan Schneider
Scenery designed by Ed Wittstein

Costumes designed by Theoni V. Aldredge
Lighting designed by Jules Fisher

Copyright © 1966, as an unpublished work, by Robert Woodruff Anderson.
© 1967 by Robert Anderson.
Reprinted by permission of Random House, Inc.
All rights including the right of reproduction in whole or in part, in any form, are reserved under International and Pan-American Copyright Conventions. Published in New York by Random House, Inc., and simultaneously in Toronto, Canada, by Random House of Canada Limited.

CAUTION: Professionals and amateurs are hereby warned that *You Know I Can't Hear You When the Water's Running,* being fully protected under the Copyright Laws of the United States of America, the British Commonwealth, including the Dominion of Canada, and all other countries of the Berne and Universal Copyright Conventions, is subject to royalty. All rights, including professional, amateur, motion picture, recitation, lecturing, public reading, radio and television broadcasting, and the rights of translation into foreign languages, are strictly reserved. Particular emphasis is laid on the question of readings, permission for which must be secured in writing, from the author's agent: Miss Audrey Wood, Ashley Famous Agency, Inc., 1301 Avenue of the Americas, New York, N.Y.

ROBERT ANDERSON was born in New York City on April 28, 1917, and graduated from Harvard, receiving his B.A. in 1939 and his M.A. a year later. His original intention was to be a teacher, and this was the career he started out on. However, the theatre proved more and more alluring.

During the Second World War he served as a naval officer, and during this time he wrote his first play, *Come Marching Home.* When this was submitted to a National Theatre Conference play contest for servicemen it won first prize, and a year later, in 1945, was produced by the Theater Department of Iowa University. Perhaps more important still, the play helped him win a Playwriting Fellowship from the National Theatre Conference.

In the summer of 1950 his play *Love Revisited* was tried out at Westport Country Playhouse, and in 1953 the Arena Theatre in Washington produced *All Summer Long,* a play that was subsequently given Off-Broadway.

The production that changed Anderson's life and established him as among the most successful of American playwrights was *Tea and Sympathy,* which, starring Deborah Kerr and the unrelated John Kerr, opened on September 30, 1953. Although it seems curious today, *Tea and Sympathy* in its time was something of a *succès de scandale,* for it was perhaps the first English-language play in modern times to deal with homosexuality in less than totally evasive terms. To be sure, these terms were nothing quite as frank as those that were to be used later by Mart Crowley in *The Boys in the Band.* However, the play seemed fairly strong for the nonpermissive theatre of 1953, and when the play was first produced in London four years later, it had the distinction of being banned by the censor—Britain's Lord Chamberlain—and, being cheated of a public performance, had to be produced by a theatre club.

After this great international hit—it was subsequently made into a very successful movie—Mr. Anderson wrote a number of plays and screenplays, including the plays *Silent Night, Lonely Night* in 1959, *The Days Between* in 1965, and the screenplays *Until They Sail* in 1957, *The Nun's Story* in 1959, and *The Sand Pebbles* in 1965. His next big Broadway hit came on March 13, 1967, with his evening of four one-act plays *You Know I Can't Hear You When the Water's Running.*

With an excellent cast led by Martin Balsam, George Grizzard, and Eileen Heckart, this four-in-hand evening soon established itself as one of the funniest shows in town. It was something of a surprise success, for it was offered to a number of Broadway producers before being accepted by two newcomers to Broadway, Jack Farren and Gilbert Cates, and had been written after Anderson's very serious drama *I Never Sang for My Father,* which was not produced until the following season.

Yet the success of *You Know I Can't Hear You When the Water's Running* was well deserved, for it was not only amusing, but it also had that undertone of seriousness that provides the essential difference between comedy and farce. Curiously enough, just as Anderson had anticipated in *Tea and Sympathy* the theatre's franker treatment of homosexuality, so in this new comedy he foresaw another new trend in the theatre—that toward nudity.

In the first play of the quartet—he calls the play *The Shock of Recognition*—Anderson has a playwright who wants to innovate male nudity on Broadway. All he wants is to have a husband come out of the bathroom, completely nude, say to his wife: "You know I can't hear you when the water's running," and return, having given the audience a very nasty shock of recognition. Interestingly, the whole turning point around which the play's humor revolves is the patent absurdity to the audience of any actor consenting to appear in the nude. Ironically, the very next Broadway season *Hair* opened, and what Anderson had postulated as a joke became a theatrical reality.

Apart from his writing activities, Anderson, who is married to the actress Teresa Wright, has been closely engaged in helping young playwrights. He has worked for the Dramatists Guild, initiated playwriting classes at the American Theatre Wing and the Actors Studio, and has also been a guiding light of the new Dramatists Committee, an organization pledged to assist aspiring playwrights.

THE SHOCK OF RECOGNITION

The action takes place in the office of a producer. There are doors to the left and right.

JACK BARNSTABLE, *the playwright—slight and intellectual—is waiting. In a moment,* HERB MILLER, *the producer, enters through the door right in a hurry. He is large, a rough diamond. He smokes a cigar.*

————

HERB. Sorry to keep you waiting, Jack. How are you?

(*They shake hands warmly.*)

JACK. I'm fine, Herb.

HERB. Good trip?

JACK. Great.

HERB. I'm damned excited about producing this play of yours.

(*He picks up a manuscript and waves it.*)

JACK. Good.

HERB. Did you order coffee? The girl can get you coffee.

JACK. No, thanks. I just finished breakfast.

HERB (*snaps on the intercom on his desk*). Dorothy?

DOROTHY (*her voice is heard*). Yes, Mr. Miller?

HERB. Any calls?

DOROTHY. No, Mr. Miller.

HERB. I don't want to be disturbed.

DOROTHY. Yes, Mr. Miller . . .

HERB (*sits at the desk*). Now, Jack . . . I've been talking to that agent of yours, and he says you mean it when you say in your script here . . . (*He reads.*) "Patrick, age forty-three, enters from the bathroom naked."

JACK. Well, sure. It's in the script.

HERB. I know. But I thought maybe it was there just to give an indication for the actor or director.

JACK. No. I mean it.

HERB. Well, Jack . . . I mean, hell! You've written a lot of plays. You know we can't do that.

JACK. Why not?

HERB. We'd be put in jail. You'd offend people.

JACK. Why should people be offended by a naked man?

HERB. Oh, come on . . .

JACK. Damn it, Herb, it's about time our theatre grew up . . . We got to let some air in here someplace . . . It's not as

though I were trying to do something sexy. Far from it . . . Look, when Ibsen put a real-life scene on the stage in 1889, the audience recognized their own lives and stood up and cheered.

HERB. Well, if you put a naked man onstage, they're gonna stand up and go home.

JACK. I'm not asking you to show a couple making love onstage.

HERB. That'll come next.

JACK. I just want the audience to get that shock of recognition . . . to feel at home . . . to say, "My God, that's just like us." Look, the wife's lying there in bed reading the morning newspapers . . . (HERB *suddenly looks at the script frantically.*) What's the matter?

HERB. I just thought I'd better check. Is she naked too?

JACK. No, Herb. For God's sake! She's lying there. She can be dressed six layers deep, as far as I'm concerned . . . and she's reading the papers and chattering away to her husband, who is in the bathroom . . . water running. Suddenly the water is turned off. Husband appears in the bedroom, . . . with toothbrush in his hand, naked, and says, "Honey, you know I can't hear you when the water's running." He stands there a moment . . .

HERB. Just long enough for everyone to faint.

JACK. . . . goes back in, and the next time we see him, he has a robe on, and that's that.

HERB. Why?

JACK. I told you. The shock of recognition. For the same reason they put running water onstage in *The Voice of the Turtle.*

HERB. Jack, baby, that was twenty-five years or more ago. We're in a different kind of theatre now.

JACK. Okay . . . I'll release you from your contract. What the hell . . .

HERB. Wait a minute, Jack . . .

JACK. It's important to me, Herb. This is not a sexy, muscular man . . . bare to the waist and full of erotic implications as to what he's got in his bulging blue jeans. I want to show man as he is . . . you . . . me . . .

HERB. Speak for yourself . . .

JACK. . . . what Shakespeare called a poor forked radish . . . with no implications except of mortality and ridiculousness.

HERB. You find a naked man ridiculous?

JACK. Mostly, yes. And so do you. I think the males in the audience will howl with delight and recognition.

HERB. At seeing this guy flapping in the breeze?

JACK. Yeah. A real man, naked. And, of course, in the play he's quite a guy. He's our hero.

HERB (*looking at the script*). You know, you didn't say in the script that not only do you want a naked man . . . you want a ridiculous-looking naked man.

JACK. That's the whole point. I don't want an Adonis onstage. That's what the movies and the other boys are getting at, the thing I'm trying to get away from.

HERB (*reads*). "He is touching in his nakedness . . ." Do you find a naked man "touching"?

JACK. Well . . . actually that was Sarah's expression. She finds a naked man . . . especially his rear end . . . "touching." When she said it, she called my attention to it, I took a look in the mirror.

HERB. And did you find your . . . tail . . . touching?

JACK. Look—

HERB. I think it's Sarah needs the analyst, not you. "Touching." Sounds kind of maternal, as though she wanted to use some baby powder on it . . . The last time I looked, I didn't find my behind touching . . . Nor does Gloria. She just finds it big . . . Mr. Big-Ass she calls me, if you'll excuse the expression. And I say, "Honey, you can't drive a spike with a tack hammer." Now, that's our relationship. Yours is obviously something else again.

JACK. Look, Herb—

HERB. Wait a minute, now. Let me suggest a compromise. If it's the rear end that's so touching, I mean . . . maybe we could get away with just showing that. They did that in *Marat-Sade* and got away with it.

JACK. No.

HERB. You want the whole works?

JACK. Yes.

HERB. I hesitate to ask you how your wife characterizes your . . . uh . . . your . . . Does she find that touching, too?

JACK. She finds it no work of art . . . nor does any woman, as I understand it, though I haven't done a house-to-house poll on it. It's the boys who find it a work of stunning magnificence . . . And I want to blast that. I want every man in the audience to want to reach out and shake my hand.

HERB. And every woman to reach out and pat your fanny.

JACK. I knew you'd give me a fight on this, Herb . . . so I brought some pictures.

HERB (*starts for the door, left*). Should I lock the door?

JACK. Come on now, look. (*He takes two pictures from a briefcase.*) Now that's what we're used to seeing . . . the idealized image of a naked man . . . fantasy! This is a normal, real man, naked.

HERB (*winces at the second picture*). I may be queer, but I like the first one better . . . Look upon this, dear mother . . . and on this . . . where the hell did you ever find a guy looked that pathetic? It's not you, is it? (*He steps back and looks.*) You take these pictures?

JACK. No.

HERB. I tell you what I think . . . I think the men are not going to reach out and shake your hand. They're gonna want to reach out and belt you one for showing up how ridiculous they are. Because no matter what your wife thinks, I don't think any man feels that his . . . thing . . . is ridiculous. I think he feels it's a formidable weapon, an awesome . . . thing.

JACK. Is that the way you think of it, something to attack with . . . aggressive . . . battering?

HERB. Well, I don't think of it as ridiculous.

JACK. I wonder what Gloria thinks of it.

HERB. I'm not going to ask her.

JACK. No. I wouldn't take the chance.

HERB. You know, Jack, I had Hank in mind for this part.

JACK. I think he'd be great.

HERB. You don't foresee any obstacle? Any eensy, weensy, ridiculous, pathetic obstacle?

JACK. How do you know that Hank wouldn't think it about time—

HERB. That someone saw him naked onstage? Somehow I don't think it's ever entered his mind. It's you who have this compulsion to exhibit yourself via some poor actor bastard . . . before the admiring public.

JACK. I don't want them to admire.

HERB. You want them to laugh. What masochism!

JACK. Okay, we'll get some unknown who'll leap at the chance to play a part like this.

HERB. I'm afraid if he leaps at the chance to appear naked on the stage, he's exactly the kind you don't want.

JACK. Well, somebody . . . My God.

HERB. I think an unknown would be ill-advised to do it, even for the chance to play the lead in a play of yours. Can't you see him for the rest of his career. Supposing he goes on to play Shakespeare, Hamlet, Lear, Oedipus. Nobody will ever be able to wipe out that touching image of him standing there naked with his toothbrush in his hand, saying, "Honey, you know I can't hear you when the water's running."

JACK. Look, Herb, haven't I earned the right to ask for this? The public knows me as a serious playwright . . . not someone just out for kicks and shocks. And if I feel that it's an important step forward in my playwriting, for all playwrights . . . I mean, are we going to let all the daring things be done in the wrong name because we're scared?

HERB. Jack, old friend, you have a fine play here. It's that rare combination . . . the public will love it, and the intellectuals won't be too contemptuous.

JACK. Why the hell should we in the theatre be so far behind the times? Have you read a book recently . . . what they put in books? Or seen a movie?

HERB. Look, it's already hard enough putting on a serious play this day and age. People say, "I got enough troubles in my life. Why come to the theatre to see the same thing?" Now you'll have them saying, "Look, I see my poor, pathetic, ridiculous husband walking around naked all the time. I don't want to come to the theatre to see another ridiculous naked man I don't even know."

JACK (*vehemently*). I want to say to that plain, ordinary man, her husband, I want to say to him in the audience . . . "Hello. We haven't forgotten you."

HERB. And he'll call back and say, "I wish the hell you would."

JACK. I want to say, "Hello. You're sick of seeing bizarre, way-out problems of men who aren't men and women who aren't women. Here you are!"

HERB. This is your life! Right down to your bare ass and pathetic—

JACK. Herb, you don't want to do this play?

(*He heads for his overcoat and starts to put it on.*)

HERB. Take it easy. Have you thought of the . . . uh . . . problem of casting . . . of auditioning for this part if Hank doesn't play it? I mean, actors are used to being turned down because they're too short or too tall. But to be turned down because their equipment is not ridiculous enough.

JACK. You're so damned prudish, you won't even call it by its right name . . . all these euphemisms . . . Equipment . . . Thing . . .

HERB. What would you like me to call it?

JACK. The technical word . . . the correct word . . . is penis.

HERB. If you go around calling it that, I understand why you think of it as pathetic and ridiculous. It's a ridiculous and belittling name. You call it what you want to call it, and I'll call it what I want to call it. But I've got to tell you something . . . I called it what I did partly because of you.

JACK. What do you mean?

HERB. All the years I've known you, I still find myself apologizing when I use a dirty word in front of you.

JACK. Oh, come on.

HERB. It's the truth. There's something about you. I always find myself saying "Sorry" . . . "Excuse it" . . . And that's another reason I think you're wrong to do this. The public doesn't see you as that kind of writer.

JACK. I'm sorry as hell I've been inhibiting you all these years, Herb. That's one of the most insulting things anyone has ever said to me.

HERB. I can't help it. It's true. Just something about you.

JACK. Would you care to explain that?

HERB (*at the intercom*). Dorothy?

DOROTHY (*on the intercom*). Yes, Mr. Miller.

HERB. Will you step in a minute? (*To* JACK.) You met her, didn't you?

JACK (*puzzled as to what this is all about*). When I came in, yes.

HERB. She's a Bennington girl doing her

three months' stint of learning about real
life.

(DOROTHY *enters*.)

HERB. Dorothy, you know Mr. Barnstable . . . (*To* JACK.) She's a great fan
of yours. (DOROTHY *is embarrassed*.) She
played in one of your plays at college.

DOROTHY. Oh, Mr. Miller. Really!

JACK (*trying to be pleasant*). Which
one?

DOROTHY. Oh, I was terrible!

JACK. I'm sure you weren't.

DOROTHY (*insistent*). I was! I was just
horrible!

JACK. What part?

DOROTHY. If I told you, you'd drop dead
right on the spot. Just awful!

HERB. Dorothy, tell me something. You
read Mr. Barnstable's play?

DOROTHY. Yes.

HERB. You liked it?

DOROTHY (*beams on* JACK). Oh, yes, I
did.

HERB. You read the stage directions?

DOROTHY. Well . . . yes.

HERB. The one in the beginning where
the man comes out of the bathroom naked
. . . You see, she's blushing just from my
reading the stage directions.

DOROTHY. I wasn't blushing.

HERB. You were. Mr. Barnstable here has
the idea he actually wants the man to come
out naked in that scene . . . (DOROTHY
giggles.) You see, deeper blushes.

DOROTHY (*giggling and angry*). I'm *not*
blushing.

HERB. Now here's a broad-minded educated girl . . . Her mind accepts the idea,
but her soul blushes.

DOROTHY (*put out*). Oh, Mr. Miller. I'm
not blushing.

HERB. Okay. Would you like to pay your
six-ninety to see a naked man onstage?

DOROTHY (*confused, she giggles*). It's not
a fair question.

HERB. Why not?

DOROTHY. Well, it just isn't.

HERB. Sounds like you got some kind of
conflict going there. You would like to
see him, but you don't want to admit it.

DOROTHY. Oh, no.

HERB. Do women get a boot out of seeing
naked men?

DOROTHY. Oh, Mr. Miller.

HERB. Do they or don't they? (DOROTHY
squirms.) Do you . . . or don't you?

DOROTHY. Mr. Miller!

(*She heads for the door, left*.)

HERB (*to* JACK). She's an incompetent
witness. She's never seen a naked man.

DOROTHY (*stops*). Mr. Miller!

HERB. Oh, then you have?

DOROTHY. You certainly don't expect a
person to anwer that.

HERB. All right, go out and pull yourself
together . . . I just wanted to demonstrate
to our playwright here what even the idea
of a naked man does to you.

DOROTHY. That's not fair.

HERB. There go your matinées . . .

JACK. Nonsense. I gave this to my grandmother to read, and her only comment was,
"Let me know when it opens and I'll be
there with my opera glasses." . . . Women
are bored with this respectability which
red-blooded but prudish men have forced
on them . . . They want to be let in on
the joke.

HERB. Dorothy, do you find a man's
sexual equipment ridiculous and pathetic?

DOROTHY. Mr. Miller!

(*She runs out gasping and in confusion*.)

HERB. Do you think she meant "yes" or
"no"?

JACK. You're a cruel bastard. That's a
cheap way of getting your kicks.

HERB. She's kind of cute, isn't she?

JACK. Getting yourself all worked up,
talking about the great Forbidden. That's
what I'm driving at.

HERB. I'm sorry if I didn't keep it on a
high intellectual plane . . . But people
just aren't going to. A baby . . . a naked
male boy, age two . . . they'll goo-goo
over, blush a little and say "Isn't it cute?"
But by age three it's already indecent.

JACK (*good-naturedly annoyed*). You
insist on thinking of it as sexy.

HERB. And you insist on pretending
we're in a laboratory where everyone is
going to be so high-minded. Look, we'll
get the designer to do the set so that the
bathroom is downstage . . . and there's
this piece of furniture just below it . . .
and he comes out just above it . . . and
he's covered to just below his belly button.
But we'll know he's naked, because she
says, "For God's sake, put something on."

JACK. You can hear a man's wife saying
that?

HERB. Yes.

JACK. What would her motive be?

HERB. She just wants him to put something on.

JACK. Come on, Herb . . . you've called me often enough on motivation . . . It would mean that the thing is some kind of monstrosity frightening to the eye . . . or that she's prudish and doesn't like her husband appearing naked in front of her. Neither of these things is true of my couple . . . You see, Herb . . .

HERB. Look, you got a lovely, sensitive play here, except for this one moment.

JACK. This one moment is what makes the whole play real . . . Look, people go to European movies, or art movies . . . not because of art but because of Life. They know there's some chance that the story will break through to the absurdities and truth of life . . . You want to know a scene I've got in my notebooks that I've never seen? I've lived it, but I've never seen it . . . A guy is giving a girl a snow job. He's almost got her where he wants her . . . and the timing is everything. He can't let a moment pass, or the mood change, or he's lost her. It's the end of the evening, and he's kissing her and fondling her . . . and she's smiling "yes" but telling him to run along home like a good boy. The only trouble is that this guy is running a race with his bladder . . . And he's finally got to go, and he's lost it . . . Didn't that ever happen to you? (HERB *gives him a look and turns away.*) Now that's real life . . . But when are we gonna see that scene in an American movie or in the American theatre? I feel like going to the edge of the stage, like Mary Martin in *Peter Pan* . . . and saying to the audience . . . "Do you believe in life as it is lived? . . . Don't you want to see it?" I think they want to see the ironies, the paradoxes . . . the absurdities . . . Hell, Life is a tragedy played by comedians. They know it. Let them see it onstage.

HERB. Look, Jack, you know more about tone than I do . . . TONE . . . You can't shift tone like that in a play.

JACK. You do it in life . . . at least in my house. One moment we're making love . . . the next minute we're wrangling about something . . . and then the dog gets excited and pees on the carpet . . . and we break up laughing.

HERB. That's your house! Your assumption is that what you experience in your house, they experience. I don't go around naked in my house. This is your assumption.

JACK. I would assume that at least in a man's bedroom and bathroom he goes naked occasionally. I don't walk around the living room or the kitchen, as a rule . . . I've done it a couple of times in the summer when the kids are away. It's okay . . . Gave me a feeling . . .

HERB (*flips on the intercom*). Dorothy.

DOROTHY (*over the intercom*). Yes, Mr. Miller?

HERB. Any actors out there?

DOROTHY (*over the intercom*). Yes, Mr. Miller.

HERB. Send one in.

JACK. What's this all about?

HERB. If we're gonna get this show on the road, we're gonna have to start seeing actors.

(JACK *takes off his coat.*)

DOROTHY (*enters from the door, left*). Mr. Richard Pawling

(*He doesn't follow at once. She calls him.*) Mr. Pawling!

(RICHARD PAWLING *enters. He is thirty-five. He is overeager, self-explaining, and anxious.* DOROTHY *exits.*)

HERB (*shaking hands*). Hello, Mr. Pawling.

PAWLING. How do you do?

HERB. This is Mr. Jack Barnstable.

PAWLING (*awed and pleased*). Oh . . . (*Crosses to shake hands very appreciatively with* JACK.) How do you do, Mr. Barnstable. It's a pleasure. A *real* pleasure! I . . . uh . . . didn't really expect to be seen by anyone . . . I was just bringing some new pictures of myself around for your files.

HERB. That's all right, Mr. Pawling. Please sit down.

PAWLING. Thank you . . . I've got my hair long because I'm up for a part in a Western series . . . but I can cut that . . . And the mustache is temporary . . . for a commercial. I'm a doctor, and I guess they feel it gives more dignity, you know. (*He rises.*) "One out of every two doctors recommends . . ." (*He laughs nervously and sits again.*) I . . . uh . . . worked for you once, Mr. Miller.

HERB. Oh?

PAWLING. About five years ago. I understudied Steiger . . .

HERB. (*not registering at all*). Oh, yes.

PAWLING (*there is awkward silence, as*

JACK *watches* HERB *and* HERB *waits.*) Uh . . . what kind of part is it, if I may ask?

HERB. It's a very good part . . . the lead.

(JACK *is aghast and goes to sit at one side of the room.*)

PAWLING (*worried that he is giving the wrong impression, he follows* JACK). I can be taller . . . I don't have my elevator shoes on . . . Or shorter. I mean . . . I can pretty well adapt. The hair is dark now, but you may remember, Mr. Miller, it was blond when I worked for you last.

HERB. Oh, yes.

PAWLING (*going on nervously*). I'm pretty well tanned up because of this Western . . . I told you . . . but if I stay away from the sunlamp for a couple of days . . . I . . . well . . . look more . . . intellectual, Mr. Barnstable . . . if that's what you're looking for. Also, I have my contact lenses in now, but I do have glasses, if that's closer to the image. (*He whips his glasses out and puts them on. He is thrown off balance by the two sets of lenses. After a moment, he takes them off.*) And, of course, I do have other clothes . . . And my weight's variable . . . I mean, if you're looking for someone thinner.

HERB. Actually, we're looking for someone rather . . . well, someone who can look a little pathetic and ridiculous.

PAWLING (*without a moment's hesitation*). That's me . . . I mean, put me in the right clothes . . . a little big for me . . . and I look like a scarecrow . . . I can shrink inside my clothes.

HERB. The question is, can you shrink inside your skin?

PAWLING (*looks from one to the other, smiling*). I can if I think it. If I can think it, I can be it . . . You see, here's my composites, the pictures I was leaving with the girl. (*Whips out a photo sheet and shows it to* HERB *at the desk.*) A doctor . . . a cowboy . . . a soldier . . . businessman . . . small-town grocer . . . You can't notice it, probably, but I'm wearing a hairpiece . . . I look quite different without it. Do you want me to . . .

(*He makes a move to strip off the very obvious hairpiece.*)

HERB. No, no. You don't have any pictures of you in a bathing suit, do you?

PAWLING. No. I . . . uh . . . When are you planning on doing the play?

HERB. No dates yet.

PAWLING. I could work out in a gym from now until then. I can put on quite a bit of muscle in a few months.

HERB. That wouldn't be necessary. "Ridiculous," I said.

PAWLING. Oh, yes. I forgot. Well, as I said, I *do* look ridiculous.

HERB. Jack, why don't you fill Mr. Pawling in? Take over. After all, it *is* your idea.

JACK. I don't think Mr. Pawling is exactly the type.

PAWLING (*coming to* JACK). I can look a lot younger. (*He "acts" younger.*)

JACK. It isn't that.

PAWLING. Or older.

(*He slumps.*)

HERB (*egging* JACK *on*). I think you owe it to Mr. Pawling to go into the part and the requirements. I mean, I don't think we should jump to any conclusion as to whether he's right or wrong. Particularly in this part, with its special requirements . . . I don't see how we can know until we've really seen Mr. Pawling.

PAWLING. Perhaps if I could read the script, I could come in looking more like . . . I mean, you know . . . dressed more for the part.

HERB (*seeing that* JACK *is not going to do anything*). Well, Mr. Pawling . . . this is an unusual part. It's a husband, and . . .

PAWLING. Well, I've been married three times.

(*He laughs nervously.*)

HERB. And in the opening scene, it's right after breakfast, and his wife's in bed, with the newspapers and coffee, and the husband is in the bathroom, which is adjacent to the bedroom . . . where the wife is lying in bed, having coffee, reading the papers. It's morning, you see, and she's having her morning coffee . . . and the husband is in the bathroom, and he's brushing his teeth, and the water's running . . . you know, while he's brushing his teeth . . . and she's talking to him . . . Why are you smiling?

PAWLING. Well, I mean . . . that's a situation I know like the back of my hand. My wives . . . they could never get it through their heads that you can't hear when the water's running.

HERB. That's his first line. He turns off the water, and he comes out and says, "Honey, you know I can't hear you when the water's running."

PAWLING. Well, you've got every husband with you from then on . . . I didn't say "honey," but I remember distinctly saying "For Christ's sake, how many times do I have to tell you I can't hear you when the goddamned water's running?" (*Turns to* JACK.) Excuse me, Mr. Barnstable.

JACK (*burning*). Why did you say "excuse me" to me?

PAWLING. I don't know.

(*Shrugs as if to say "Did I do something wrong?"*)

HERB. So the scene is familiar to you? (PAWLING *makes a gesture—"of course."*) What did you wear when you brushed your teeth?

PAWLING (*immediately*). I can wear anything you want.

HERB. But what did you wear?

PAWLING. It depends. Sometimes I sleep in my underwear . . . sometimes pajamas.

HERB. In this play the character wears nothing. He's brushing his teeth bare-assed.

PAWLING. I can do that. I've done that. Naturally. In the bathroom. Of course. Very good. Why not? The bathroom's offstage. Why not? But why is it important what the man is wearing if it's offstage?

HERB (*motions for* JACK *to take over*). Uh . . . Jack.

PAWLING. I mean, excuse me, I'm not questioning it. I can see where it helps the actor to understand the character. He's the kind of guy who brushes his teeth . . . (*He looks at* JACK.) in the nude. Yes. I can handle that . . . because I've done that.

HERB. He turns off the water, comes into the bedroom, and says the line you said . . . Only without the blasphemy, because Mr. Barnstable doesn't like blasphemy onstage.

PAWLING. Of course . . . I see, yes. He says the line . . .

HERB. Bare-assed. (PAWLING *looks from one to the other.*) How would you feel about that? The actor has to stand there naked . . . and say the line.

JACK (*getting angry, realizing that* HERB *is making a test case with this nonentity*). Look, let me explain it. This is not just for shock effect, or for thrills. There's nothing sexy about it. I just think that it's an added value for an audience to relate to a situation they know. The only shock would be

the pleasurable shock of recognition . . . the honesty and truthfulness of it. The man then goes back in the bathroom, and next time we see him, he's in a bathrobe, and we never see him naked again . . . I think it can be one of the great moments in the history of the theatre . . . Like Nora slamming the door in *A Doll's House.*

(PAWLING *has never heard of* A Doll's House.)

HERB (*to* PAWLING). How would you feel about that?

PAWLING (*looking from one to the other*). I have to apologize.

HERB (*thinking he has won his point, he speaks kindly*). I understand, Mr. Pawling.

(*He turns to smile his satisfaction at* JACK.)

PAWLING. I've got a hole in my sock. (*He takes off his coat and tie.*) I told you, I really didn't expect to see anyone. I was just dropping by to leave some new pictures . . . I didn't expect an interview. (*Goes on undressing. He takes off his shirt.*) How ridiculous do you want this man to look? I mean, I'm not a ninety-eight-pound weakling, but if I didn't eat anything for a while, and if I shaved the hair on my chest . . . is this guy supposed to be funny?

(JACK *won't answer; he looks at* HERB.)

HERB. No, he's the leading man. It's just that Mr. Barnstable wants to puncture this idea of the muscular and hefty man. He wants, in a sense, everyman.

PAWLING (*in his undershirt*). Well, that's me . . . I'm really the original anonymous man. People are all the time coming up to me and thinking they've met me . . . I got a face looks like everybody else's. (*Pulls off his undershirt.*) You see, I haven't got much muscle on my arms . . . and if I stand in a certain way, it even looks like less. (*He moves around demonstrating.*) The hair on the chest . . . I can shave that off and powder it down . . . and if I stand right . . . But then, they won't see that, I suppose. If I come in from downstage and look up at her in the bed (*He acts it out, going downstage and walking up.*) they'll only get a view of my tail and side . . . (*He is standing, trying this view out.*) Still, we ought to have that shaved.

HERB. But you see, Mr. Pawling, you

don't come in from downstage. You come in from upstage. I believe that's Mr. Barnstable's idea.

PAWLING (*stares out at the audience full-face, gradually getting the idea of what this involves*). Well . . .

(*He starts to take off his trousers.*)

JACK (*embarrassed*). I think that will be all, Mr. Pawling.

PAWLING (*sits down, slipping off his shoes so that he can get his trousers off; we see the hole in the sock*). My chest is misleading. That hair. But you see, my legs . . . (*As he strips off his trousers.*) I mean, I wouldn't want you to count me out because of that hair on my chest.

HERB (*watching* JACK's *embarrassment*). I think you're quite right, Mr. Pawling. Mr. Barnstable is out after a certain uncompromising effect, and I think we should see the whole works.

PAWLING (*the trousers are off; he stands there*). Well, the legs, as you see, are . . . well . . . ridiculous.

HERB. I think you're being modest, Mr. Pawling. But you see, I don't think the legs, or the hair on the chest, or anything like that really matters . . . Because when you come out onstage absolutely skinny, nobody is going to be looking at your legs, or your chest. So the question is . . . is the rest of you ridiculous? You see, Mr. Barnstable has the interesting theory that most women look upon that part of their men as ridiculous and pathetic . . . and he wants to present his man not as a stud, not as a romanticized phallic symbol, but as the miserable, laughable thing it is. Now, Mr. Pawling?

PAWLING. Well, I . . . It's embarrassing discussing this sort of thing, but . . . girls have sometimes . . . uh . . . laughed, or giggled . . . at first. Of course, it's not the look that counts. I mean, we all know that. (*They are all silent for a moment.*) Well, I've been turned down for parts because I was too short or too tall . . . too fat or too thin . . . too young or too old . . . But I never did or didn't get a part because of . . . (*He swings his arms in embarrassment.*) What the hell!

(*He starts to unbutton his shorts.*)

JACK. Hold it, Mr. Pawling!

(*He gathers up* PAWLING's *clothes.*)

PAWLING. But I agree with you completely, Mr. Barnstable. It's time the American theatre grew up.

JACK (*holding out his clothes to him*). Thank you for your cooperation, Mr. Pawling. You can dress in the next room. There's a door into the hall from there . . . (*Indicating the door, right.*) And we'll be in touch with you.

PAWLING (*not giving up*). But, I mean, if that's going to be the whole point of the thing . . .

JACK (*heading for the door, left*). I'm sure that that's as adaptable as the various other parts of your body . . .

HERB. But, Jack, I don't see how you're ever going to— (JACK *has turned and gone into the secretary's office, left.* PAWLING *looks after him, standing there in his shorts and socks, with his arms full of clothes.*) Well, thank you, Mr. Pawling. There's not much point without Mr. Barnstable.

(*He holds the other door for* PAWLING.)

PAWLING (*crossing to follow* JACK). I didn't say anything to . . . uh . . . ? I mean . . .

(*Catching him at the left door and ushering him back across to the right door.*)

HERB. No. Thank you very much. And I'd keep this all very much to myself, if I were you. We're thinking of you very seriously for the part.

PAWLING. You are! Well . . . Gee . . . Thank you for seeing me. It was a great honor meeting Mr. Barnstable . . . and to see you again.

(*There is a certain confusion with shaking hands with all the clothes, and saying goodbye, but finally* PAWLING *is out.* HERB *closes the door; he looks satisfied. He goes to the other door and opens it.*)

HERB. Ollie, Ollie, ocksin, all in free.

JACK (*comes in, mad; he goes for his coat*). I suppose you think you've won your point.

HERB. Theory is theory. Life is life.

JACK. That was no test. A man taking off his clothes in front of two guys is one thing—

PAWLING (*opens the door and steps in; he is still in shorts and socks*). Oh, Mr. Miller. Oh, excuse me.

(*He holds his undershirt to his bare chest.* JACK *stares at him and instinctively puts his overcoat over his chest.*)

HERB. Yes, Mr. Pawling?

PAWLING. Excuse me, but I've just had an idea. I've got a Polaroid camera . . . and I'll get my agent to take some pictures of me . . . uh . . . the way you want them, and I'll send them to you.

HERB. Not through the mails, please.

PAWLING. I'll bring them around, then.

HERB. "Attention Mr. Barnstable" . . . in a plain wrapper.

PAWLING. Right. Sorry about the holes in the socks.

(*He goes back into his room.*)

JACK (*putting on his coat*). You're a cruel bastard. You know we wouldn't even think of reading that guy . . .

HERB. Where you going?

JACK. I've got to have lunch with my lawyer and accountant.

HERB. Jack, I'll tell you what I'll do for the American theatre. What about a naked woman? Now, we put the man in bed, and the woman in the bathroom . . . naked. The water's running. And she's talking to him . . . And when she gets no answer from him, she comes out of the bathroom and says, "Did you hear what I said?" And she's naked.

JACK. And he says, "Honey, you know I can't hear you when you're naked."

(*He starts out the same door* PAWLING *used, checks himself, and crosses to the other door.*)

HERB (*acting as the businessman*). Okay, Jack. Let's quit the kidding around. Hank wants to do this part.

JACK (*stops in his tracks*). He does?

HERB. But he won't appear naked. I got an offer from Warner Brothers to pay $300,000 on a pre-production deal *if* Hank plays the part. Now you haven't had a hit in a while . . . Your share of $300,000 is . . .

JACK. That's insulting, Herb. You know that?

HERB. Yeah, I know. But how about it?

JACK (*ranting*). I turned down two movies could have earned me a fortune to write this play.

HERB. True. True.

JACK. For the privilege of saying what I want to say, the way I want to say it, in the only place I *thought* where you could still say it with some freedom.

HERB. You're right.

JACK. I mean, Herb . . . If we can't be bold in the theatre . . . where else? (*He calms down a moment.* HERB *waits.*) You asked Hank if he'd play the scene as written?

HERB. No. I just took it for granted what his answer would be. Anyway, I didn't know you really meant to play it . . . as written.

JACK. He didn't say anything about the scene?

HERB. Maybe he doesn't read stage directions.

JACK. On the other hand, Hank's a pretty gutsy guy. Maybe he just assumed we'd play it as written . . . You know, you bastard, you did prove one thing to me here just now . . . we couldn't play the scene with just anybody. It would have to be someone of Hank's stature . . . He'd bring his authority onstage with him . . .

HERB. So it really comes down to whether Hank with his authority . . .

JACK (*comes to* HERB). Will you put it on, as written, if Hank'll play it that way?

HERB. Sure.

JACK. Okay . . . I gotta get out of here, but after lunch, I'll call Hank. Let *me* talk to him . . . let me give him the background of my thinking . . . (*Heads for the door, stops, and turns.*) My God, we still got a problem.

HERB. What now?

JACK. We haven't any idea what Hank looks like naked.

HERB. Well, before we sign the contract, we could invite him to the Y for a swim.

(JACK *things about this a second, nods in assent, and leaves.*)

HERB (*shakes his head, smiling; he reaches for the phone and dials a number*). Hello, Hank . . . Herb Miller here . . . Sorry to call you at home, but I wanted to get to you fast. I'm going ahead with the play for sure this season . . . Barnstable's crazy to have you do it . . . He just left here . . . And he may be getting in touch with you, so I thought I ought to warn you about one thing and ask for your help. He's kind of a nut about that first scene. I don't know if you read all the stage directions, but the guy is supposed to be standing there in the bedroom naked . . . Oh, you did read that? Well, Barnstable's got the crazy idea he wants it played just like that . . . Naked. What? (*He rises.*) But good God, Hank. We can't do that! (*He continues to listen, consternation on his face.*) The shock of recognition.

(*He nods dully. The right door bursts open.*)

PAWLING (*his voice is heard*). Hey, Mr. Miller. Look!

(PAWLING's *right hand can be seen on the edge of the door.* HERB *dully motions* PAWLING *to go away, and barely gives him a glance. Then suddenly he realizes what he's seen. His head jerks up, straight front; then he does a slow turn to check out what he's seen.*)

PAWLING (*his voice*). I told you . . . Ridiculous!

(HERB's *eyes close, shutting out the sight of what he has seen. He is sinking to his chair as the lights go out.*)

CURTAIN

THE FOOTSTEPS OF DOVES

The scene is the basement of a store which sells nothing but beds, mattresses, springs, frames, and all the accouterments of the bedroom. Various beds are displayed. At one side there is the usual double bed: fifty-four inches. At another side, there are two single beds.

The SALESMAN *enters with* HARRIET *and* GEORGE. *The* SALESMAN *is a dried neuter of a man.* GEORGE *and* HARRIET *are an attractive, successful couple in their late forties. She wears a very nice suit, conservative hat and white gloves. He wears a gray flannel suit, button-down blue shirt, and brown felt hat. He has had one and one-third martinis.*

————

SALESMAN (*as they enter*). Downstairs here you have your better mattresses and springs. All sizes, shapes and degrees of firmness.

HARRIET (*moves past the double bed to the twin sizes*). We're interested in the twin size.

(GEORGE *stops at the fifty-four-inch double bed and stands and stares at it.*)

SALESMAN (*flat, not too interested*). Of course, your old classifications have broken down. Your twin used to mean thirty-six by seventy-five. Now you can get them in almost any dimension you want to suit your personal tastes. It's really just a matter of the price you want to pay, the dimensions and degree of firmness, and whether you want foam rubber or inner spring.

HARRIET (*looking at the beds*). I understand foam rubber is hot in summer.

SALESMAN. For some people . . . But then, some people are naturally warmer, some are colder. (*To* GEORGE, *who has sat on the double bed.*) That's your fifty-four. The twins are over here.

GEORGE. Good old fifty-four.

SALESMAN. A few people still ask for it.

GEORGE. We've slept in one for twenty-five years.

(SALESMAN *is confused. He looks to* HARRIET, *who has ignored* GEORGE—*and will continue to ignore him—elaborately.*)

HARRIET. How long is this one?

SALESMAN. That's our dimple model mattress . . . Apparently the buttons create dimples . . .

(GEORGE *has propped himself against the headboard of the double bed.*)

HARRIET. How long is it?

SALESMAN. That's your thirty-six by seventy-five.

HARRIET (*sitting on the bed*). I like a reasonably firm bed. George . . . Mr. Porter . . . likes a soft bed.

GEORGE. I'm Mr. Porter.

HARRIET. We've slept in a compromise for years, and neither one of us has been happy.

GEORGE. I've been happy.

HARRIET. George, is this long enough for you? (*He is still lying on the fifty-four-inch bed.*) George!

GEORGE. What?

HARRIET. See if this would be long enough for you, please. (GEORGE *saunters over and flops down, not at all interested. His hat topples off.*) Move up a little bit. (*He squirms up.*) That seems to be long enough. Are you comfortable? (GEORGE *shrugs.*) We should have measured the length of the old bed.

SALESMAN. If you've had it twenty-five years, it's probably seventy-five inches. (*As* HARRIET *sits on the bed.*) The only way to tell is to try . . . (HARRIET *is embarrassed.*) You don't have to take your shoes off . . . we have those protectors . . .

HARRIET (*embarrassed, she starts to lie down next to* GEORGE; *she has to squeeze*). George.

(*He moves a little. They both lie rigid, on their backs.*)

GEORGE. Put sides and a lid on it and bury us.

HARRIET (*sitting up*). This is how wide?

SALESMAN. That's your thirty-six. They come thirty-nine too. But of course, it's not meant to hold two people . . . except under . . . special circumstances.

GEORGE (*gets up*). That's what I'm interested in. The special circumstances. (*He moves to the fifty-four-inch bed and sits down on it, patting it.*) My mother and father had one bed, one of these . . . their whole married life. They both died in that bed.

HARRIET (*still aloof*). Your mother first, as I remember.

SALESMAN. People were smaller then.

GEORGE. And more loving. Now people are detached. They dance far away from each other. They want to sleep far away from each other . . . Sure, if you want to stay apart, a fifty-four-inch is too small. But that's not the idea. The idea is to get all mixed up with each other. You've seen cats sleeping together. (*He proceeds to demonstrate: cuddling his arms around his chest.* HARRIET *ignores him; she goes on reading labels and looking at ticking swatches, etc.*) Or puppies, or bears. One stirs, the other stirs . . . kind of slow and easy accommodation to each other. But they stay in a lump. For reassurance, comfort. All day you bump up against hard facts, hard edges, cold bodies. Good old fifty-four throws you up against something warm and round and soft . . . (*He looks at* HARRIET. *She looks away. He speaks to the* SALESMAN.) Are you married?

SALESMAN. No.

GEORGE. Let me tell you about twin beds . . . I tell you, the longest distance in the world is the distance between twin beds. I don't care if it's six inches or six feet. It's psychological distance . . . In an old fifty-four, you may get into bed. You don't know what you feel like . . . Then you roll up together . . . and you know . . . In twins, you got to make up your mind all by yourself, and then cross that damned gulf and find out if your twin feels like it. And then if you get there and find out you were wrong about yourself, well, it's a lot of embarrassment retreating. Or if you find out she's not in the mood . . . it's a big rejection. But in good old fifty-four,

you don't make a move until you're sure of yourself, and you can pretty well sense if she's in the mood . . . And if it still doesn't work out, what the hell, you just fall asleep, all wrapped around each other. No damage done.

HARRIET (*elaborately ignoring him*). The price is just for the mattress?

SALESMAN. Yes. In each case the box spring is available for the same price. Seventy-five dollars for the mattress . . . seventy-five for the box spring.

GEORGE. Same price for the double as for the single size. Right?

SALESMAN. Up to the fifty-four inches.

GEORGE. I've never understood that, but I've always thought it was damned nice. Somebody with a heart working there somewhere . . .

(*He shrugs, still not understanding how it happened.*)

SALESMAN. Our prices are competitive. I say that because people often come here and pick our brains and then go buy at discount houses.

HARRIET. Is this hair, kapok, cotton, or what?

SALESMAN. That is your sleepwell model. Fifty percent horsehair.

HARRIET. This seems very comfortable to me.

SALESMAN. Actually it's the one I have at home. Only I have it in the blue ticking . . . I've slept like a top for years.

HARRIET. Can you make arrangements to take the old bed away when you deliver the new?

SALESMAN. No. The federal law prohibits the resale of bedding. The best thing for you to do is to give it to a charity thrift shop and take a tax deduction.

GEORGE. That bed goes into the attic.

HARRIET (*not looking at him*). There is no room in the attic.

GEORGE. I will make room. You saved your wedding corsage. I can save our bed.

HARRIET (*blazing but smiling*). I will throw out my wedding corsage . . . gladly!

GEORGE. I will *not* throw out the bed!

HARRIET. Well, there's no need to discuss that here.

SALESMAN (*he has taken this all very coolly; he sees it every day*). Do you have any idea what kind of frame or headboard you would want?

HARRIET. I'd like to look at your head-boards. We don't want a footboard.

GEORGE. Harriet!

HARRIET (*burning, but controlled*). What?

GEORGE. I want a foot. I never said I'd do without a foot . . .

(HARRIET *is acutely embarrassed.*)

SALESMAN. Don't be embarrassed. We see this all the time. (*He moves to the stairs.*) Perhaps you'd like to discuss this alone for a few moments. I'll be upstairs if there are any questions. It's a difficult de-cision. Last week a couple broke off their engagement right here. (*He starts up the stairs.*) People have been known to go mad down here.

(*He exits.*)

HARRIET (*turning on* GEORGE). You're drunk.

GEORGE. On two martinis at lunch. And you drank most of the second one.

HARRIET. Yes, to try to prevent some-thing like this. Stop acting like a baby.

GEORGE. I am not acting like a baby.

HARRIET. Well, like a damned clown, then. We had this all out, over and over again at home. We've discussed it for months.

GEORGE. I've changed my mind.

HARRIET. It's too late to change your mind. My mind is made up. My God, hu-miliating me here in front of that man.

GEORGE. That man is of no importance to me. My marriage and my sex life are.

HARRIET. Yes. The whole store heard about your sex life in graphic detail. You painted me as a bitch who turns you down all the time, and yourself as a man very unsure of his power.

GEORGE. I did not.

HARRIET. That's the way it sounded. When it wasn't sounding like that, it was like babes in the woods, going to sleep all wrapped around each other.

(*She sits on the foot of a single bed.*)

GEORGE. Well, that's the way we do it. You know damned well you pull my left arm up over your shoulder like a blanket. It's your damned night-night, and you couldn't sleep without it.

(*He demonstrates, sitting beside her.*)

HARRIET. Night-night or no night-night, I haven't slept soundly in twenty years.

GEORGE. I'm fighting for our marriage, Harriet. You may not think I'm serious about it, but I am. Nietzsche said the big crises in our lives do not come with the sound of thunder and lightning, but softly like the footsteps of doves. That is not ex-act, but it is close enough.

HARRIET. Oh, honestly!

GEORGE. A man of forty-seven. It's a dangerous age. In a double bed he's got his wife there all the time, just the touch of her, the warmth, is exciting. After twenty-five years the image of the beloved wife is not always sexually stimulating in and of itself. But the touch always is.

HARRIET. The image of the beloved hus-band is not always so stimulating either.

GEORGE. I understand that. And I say we're taking a big chance. Across the room alone, a man could lie there night after night saying to himself . . . "Do I really feel like it? It's cold out there." And soon he just forgets about it more and more, and then that distance between them is like the Persian Gulf. And he finally decides he doesn't want to get his feet wet sloshing from bed to bed . . . and then they've had it. The family that lies together dies together.

HARRIET (*trying to reason with him, ap-pealing*). George, we've discussed this.

GEORGE. We've also discussed divorce . . . Three times. But when we came up to it, we couldn't do it. And I can't do this.

(*He gestures at the twin beds.*)

HARRIET. Well, I've got to. My back. The doctor said . . .

GEORGE. —That damned quack. *Our* doctor didn't say anything about it. But you trekked around to doctor after doctor till one told you . . . some faggot, no doubt . . . to get a single bed.

HARRIET. He's a perfectly good doctor.

GEORGE. He's a quack and a faggot who thinks it's disgusting for you to sleep with me anyway. What's he know about it? What are you going to do when you get up and go to the john?

HARRIET. Oh, for God's sake.

GEORGE. You know damned well you hurry back and snuggle up to me and say, "Oh, warm me up." You pull that old left arm over like a blanket.

(*He hugs her in demonstration.*)

HARRIET. George, that was all lovely. I'm not regretting any of that. Only times change. People change.

GEORGE. People change, and *go* through changes. I know. And I'm trying to be sympathetic about that. I know right now you feel kind of . . . you want to be left alone. But, Harriet, that's temporary. I know.

HARRIET. How do you know and what?

GEORGE (*being very considerate and delicate*). A woman comes back later with fierce desires!

HARRIET (*amused*). Who told you that?

GEORGE. I read it. The *Ladies' Home Journal*. (*Defensively.*) . . . I like to know. I like to be informed . . . what's going on inside your head. It's been very helpful to me on several occasions. "Can This Marriage Be Saved?"

HARRIET. —Now, George, please. Let's stick to facts. First, my back is breaking. Second, my nerves are shattered from sleeplessness. Third, you are a morning person, and I am a night person. I like to read in bed and sleep late. You like to go right to sleep and get up early. For twenty years I have turned out the light for you, and . . . Oh, this is nonsense. We've been over it all.

(*She rises and goes to the single beds.*)

GEORGE. What about a queen size or a king size?

HARRIET. We've discussed that. It won't fit in the bedroom. A fifty-four or twins along each wall is all that will fit.

GEORGE. Under the windows?

HARRIET. And drafts blowing down our necks?

GEORGE. Then let's sell the house.

HARRIET. Stop being ridiculous.

GEORGE. The house is meant to serve *our* purposes, not the other way around. That damned house. I've been breaking my ass to support it, and now it's going to separate me from my wife . . . I want a divorce!

HARRIET. All right.

GEORGE. You don't care. You don't take me seriously.

HARRIET. You have a right to say "I want a divorce" three times a day. I have a right not to take you seriously. Besides, you keep looking at it from your point of view . . . Old cuddly bears under a quilt . . . a couple of soup spoons nestled in a drawer . . . old night-night. A very romantic picture. Old ever-ready . . . Subconsciously I may be rebelling against that. I may want the space so that you'll have to make the effort, wade across the Persian Gulf. Get your feet wet . . . Not just sud-

denly decide you might as well since you hardly have to move to get it.

GEORGE. That's damned unfair. I have never taken you for granted. I have scrupulously concerned myself with your moods and preferences and responses . . . I could have been like some husbands who just use their wives . . . bang-bang! Thanks for the use of the hall. That's what some husbands do, in case you're interested.

HARRIET. Not in our cultural and educational bracket. I've read the articles too . . . so stop congratulating yourself.

GEORGE. You sound as though you'd had a miserable time.

HARRIET. I haven't, and you know it. Now stop acting like a martyr.

GEORGE. A martyr . . . a baby . . . a clown . . . It's lucky I have a fairly firm image of myself. It will be a miracle now if I can function at all.

HARRIET. Really . . .

GEORGE. Lying in a single bed . . . with seven feet between us. How do I feel tonight? She's lying there thinking of me as a baby, a clown, a martyr . . . and I've never given her anything more than every other man in my cultural and educational bracket gives his wife . . . Better not risk it.

HARRIET. Please decide what firmness of mattress you want. Because I would like to order and get this over with and get back to our right minds.

GEORGE. What happens six months from now when you return to combat with fierce desires? But I'm over the hill from disuse. Muscles atrophy, you know.

HARRIET. People will hear you.

GEORGE. I want people to hear me. Specifically, you!

HARRIET. I hear you.

GEORGE. You hear me, but you're not listening.

HARRIET (*low*). We'll get the thirty-nine-inch width. If you insist, we'll start the nights wrapped around each other . . . and then when you've decided what's playing or *not* playing that night, you can either stay for a while or go back to your own bed.

GEORGE. *I* get the cold bed.

HARRIET. *I'll* go to the other bed. My God!

GEORGE. How long do I get to make up my mind each night? Do we set an oven timer?

HARRIET. Now, I'm going to look at headboards. You decide on the firmness you want for your mattress.

(*She moves toward another showroom.*)

GEORGE. I warn you, Harriet. We are at the Rubicon.

HARRIET. I thought it was the Persian Gulf.

GEORGE. I can hear the doves!

(*But she is gone.* GEORGE, *disconsolate, walks around for a moment, looking at the beds; then picking up his hat, he gives a little kick to one of the single beds and saunters off in a different direction from the one* HARRIET *took. In a moment,* JILL *comes in. She is a swinging, charming, and disarming young woman of twenty-three dressed in a slack suit. She looks at the fifty-four-inch bed and smiles. She casually looks around the area and senses herself alone. She sits on the bed and bounces a few times. She puts down her purse, removes her jacket, leaving her dressed in sweater and slacks. She kicks off her shoes and lies down on the bed.* GEORGE *re-enters, staring off after* HARRIET, *scowling. He turns and sits on the single bed. He sees* JILL *across the way and rises in the same motion.* JILL *bounces up and down a couple of times, then turns over and lies on her stomach. She then assumes a couple of sleeping positions. She leans on one elbow and looks at the other side of the bed, as though she were looking down at another person. She smiles, as though in answer to something he had said, and gently moves a lock of hair from his imaginary face. She continues to size up the bed; then she sees* GEORGE.)

GEORGE (*waggling a finger at her*). Good morning. Sleep well? (JILL *sits up and smooths her sweater.*) I'm sorry. I didn't mean to embarrass you.

JILL. Why didn't you cough or something?

GEORGE. To be perfectly frank, I was enjoying watching you. You seem to have a true appreciation of good old fifty-four.

JILL. Of what?

GEORGE. Good old fifty-four. The width.

JILL. Oh. Well, I've always slept in a single.

GEORGE (*remembering her antics on the bed*). Oh? About to be married?

JILL. No. Just divorced.

GEORGE. Well, I don't wonder, sleeping together in a single bed.

(*He laughs at his bad joke.*)

JILL. We slept together in *two* single beds.

GEORGE. I see.

JILL. "So much better when either of you gets a cold," his mother said.

GEORGE. Do you get colds?

JILL. No. His mother got the colds. I got a divorce. (*She tests the bed by striking it in some way which* GEORGE *finds mysterious.*) He was a born bachelor. I think getting up and going back to his own bed gave him the comforting impression he wasn't really married.

GEORGE. This day and age, I'm surprised you didn't find that out before you were married.

JILL. That was my fault. I only had this thirty-inch bed. I couldn't very well expect him to spend the whole night in that.

GEORGE (*indicating the double bed*). I take it next time you're going to know beforehand.

JILL. What I'd really like is one of those old canopy beds, with curtains, or a big brass bed. I was born in an old brass bed. Conceived in it too.

GEORGE. I think you'll find this very congenial. It has my unqualified endorsement. My wife and I have slept on one for twenty-five years, and it would have held up for another ten at least, but my wife decided it was time for single beds.

JILL. You've been married for twenty-five years?

GEORGE. Yes.

JILL. Well, men *do* keep in better shape than women.

GEORGE (*pulls in his gut*). Yes . . . Well, I try to get to the club three times a week . . . play a little squash, keep down the old midriff.

JILL. I think men improve with age, mostly. They know what they want and how to get it, and what to do with it when they get it. Now, women . . . they get their men, feather their nests, and then let themselves go. That's cheating in my book. I'm not talking about your wife, of course.

GEORGE. Oh, Harriet's still—

JILL (*going right on*). It was all right when we were an agrarian society and women's function was to breed children to help on the farm. But now she has a responsibility to keep herself attractive. I wrote a paper on that in college.

GEORGE (*amused at her*). I'm sure the man gave you an A-plus.

JILL. It was a woman. She gave me a C-minus.

GEORGE. You sound very fair about the whole thing.

JILL. I should keep my mouth shut, but I think your wife is taking a terrible risk, an attractive man like you who plays squash.

GEORGE. Well, after all, times change. People change.

JILL. But the point is, you haven't changed. Things are very unfair in our society for men. They get these drives and urges when they're twelve or thirteen—

GEORGE. Twelve. Twelve.

JILL. And they keep them for years and years, and what are they supposed to do about them? A wider bed would be better, but I haven't the room for it.

GEORGE. One of those cookie-cutter apartments?

JILL. Never. An old brownstone. Way up at the top. A walk-up.

GEORGE. That's a curious location for a girl who admires older men.

JILL. I wouldn't be caught dead in one of those new places. The bedrooms are so gleaming and sharp and . . . antiseptic, a man wouldn't know if he was supposed to make love or operate.

GEORGE. My hopes for the younger generation are rising every minute. I lived in a brownstone once. East Fiftieth Street.

JILL (*fussing with swatches, not looking at him*). I'm on East Fifty-first.

GEORGE. I had a view of the river.

JILL. I don't.

GEORGE. I was between Second and First.

JILL. I'm between Second and Third.

GEORGE. Oh, I had a friend who lived at two forty-two.

JILL (*matter-of-factly*). Two twenty-six.

GEORGE. No. He was at two forty-two.

JILL. I'm at two twenty-six. (*She has been studying the mattress during this ritual of giving the address.*) I like a firm mattress.

GEORGE. So do I.

JILL. Do you call this firm?

GEORGE (*sits on the mattress and tests it.*) More or less.

JILL. How tall are you?

GEORGE. Five . . . uh . . . nine.

JILL. Weight?

GEORGE. One seventy-five . . . Stripped.

(*He beams.*)

JILL. Mmmmmmm. Could I be a nuisance and ask you to lie down?

(*She lies down.*)

GEORGE (*he hovers over the side of the bed she's lying on, awkward*). Of course.

JILL. What's the matter?

GEORGE. I . . . uh . . . This is usually my side of the bed.

(JILL *squirms across to the other side.* GEORGE *looks toward the various exits for signs of* HARRIET, *and then lies down, carefully keeping away from her.*)

JILL. Does this embarrass you?

GEORGE. No!

JILL. It doesn't seem to sag, does it?

GEORGE. No!

JILL. I mean, I don't roll downhill toward you?

GEORGE. Unfortunately not.

(*A quick laugh.*)

JILL. How much room do you have on that side, between you and the edge? (*She hitches up and leans over him to look at and feel the distance and measure it with her hand.*) Oh, quite a bit.

(*He suffers pleasantly from her hovering proximity.*)

GEORGE (*sits up*). I'm a little overweight at the moment. I should take off four or five pounds. But I haven't been able to exercise lately.

JILL. Oh?

GEORGE. I had an operation on my knee.

JILL. Torn cartilage?

GEORGE. Yes.

JILL. I have a bad knee the doctor's been itching to operate on, but I don't want my knee all scarred up. It does leave a nasty scar, doesn't it?

GEORGE. Well, it's not so bad.

(*He rolls up his trousers to show her his knee.*)

JILL. That's a very nice job he did. Anyway, scars on a man are rather attractive. I noticed you have a small scar on your upper lip. The war?

GEORGE (*looks at* JILL *a moment*). No. My dog bit me.

(JILL *lies down again.*)

GEORGE (*still sitting up*). Of course, the proper technique in a fifty-four-inch is not to lie like two mummies, but entwined.

JILL. Yes, all snuggled around each other. I'm an indiscriminate snuggler. Cats, dogs, dolls, stuffed animals, et cetera.

GEORGE. Are you a morning person or a night person?

JILL. What do you mean?

GEORGE. Some people are wide awake and full of vigor in the morning . . . others at night.

JILL. I guess you could say I'm a morning person . . . But I'm adaptable.

GEORGE. I'm a morning person.

JILL. *Are* you? (*Popping up.*) Well, this is all daydreaming anyway. (*She starts to put on her shoes and jacket.*) I can't afford a new bed yet. I'll probably have to wait till Mom and Dad die and I get the old brass one I was born in. Thank you very much. I have to be getting back to work.

GEORGE. What kind of work do you do?

JILL. I want to do something in design. But at the moment I do jobs of typing at home . . . manuscripts . . . short stories, novels . . . that sort of thing.

GEORGE. I see . . . I started a novel when I was in college.

JILL. Did you?

GEORGE. I never finished it.

JILL. That's too bad.

GEORGE. Maybe I ought to get back to it.

JILL. Well, if you want it typed, you have the address.

GEORGE. What? Oh. Oh, yes . . . two forty-two.

JILL. Two twenty-six . . . The name is Jill Hammond. (*Shaking hands.*) Thank you very much for your help. Your name is—

GEORGE. Uh . . . Porter. George . . . George Porter.

JILL. Good-bye, Mr. Porter . . . Good luck with your novel.

(*She smiles sweetly and leaves briskly.* GEORGE *remains at the foot of the stairs, wondering what has happened. He has a silly grin on his face.*)

HARRIET (*coming in*). George, I've picked the headboards . . . Very simple, clean lines.

GEORGE (*out of his reverie*). Okay.

HARRIET. Have you chosen the mattress you want?

GEORGE (*moving to the single bed*). Uh . . . well, yes. This one will be fine.

HARRIET. Look, George . . .

GEORGE. Yes?

HARRIET. I would like the twin beds. But if it's going to be so earthshaking for you, if it's going to make all that difference, I'll struggle on with the old bed for a while.

GEORGE (*looks at her a moment, genuinely touched, but also full of his new ideas*). That's very thoughtful of you, Harriet. But I've been thinking down here, and I think you're right. This will be fine.

(*He pats one of the singles, a little desperately.*)

HARRIET (*still sitting on the fifty-four-inch mattress*). I could get a better bed board and put it under my side so that I wouldn't—

GEORGE (*interrupting her, eager*). It's very generous of you, Harriet. Characteristically generous, but there's no question. You are right. These . . . these will be fine.

(*Standing between the two single beds, he pats both.*)

HARRIET. It's not the end of the world, you know.

GEORGE. I know. I know.

HARRIET. We've had twenty-five wonderful years wrapped around each other. But we *are* older now. At least I am, and I'm perfectly willing to admit it.

GEORGE. You're a good sport, Harriet.

HARRIET (*crossing and sitting on the single bed with him*). You'll see. It will be better. I can read late, and the light won't bother you. And you can come home as late as you want from your poker nights without disturbing me.

GEORGE. That's true.

HARRIET. You can play to your heart's content.

GEORGE. That's right.

HARRIET. And we'll have good times.

GEORGE. We sure will.

(*They kiss.*)

HARRIET. Well, let's go give the man the order then. (*She stands.*) George, if you want to keep the old bed up in the attic . . .

GEORGE. No. No. There's really no room for it. I'll just shove it in the station wagon and give it to some charity.

HARRIET. You should be able to get something for the brass frame.

GEORGE. I'll dicker.

HARRIET (*looking at the fifty-four-inch bed*). I'm not denying I'll miss it. (*She smiles.*) If we get lonesome for it, we can sneak off to a motel like a couple of kids.

(*They hug a moment.* HARRIET *starts for the stairs.*)

GEORGE (*takes a step toward the fifty-four-inch bed*). Good-bye, old friend. (*He moves a step toward the stairs, then turns.*) Be seeing you.

(HARRIET *laughs, reaches out her hand,* and they disappear up the stairs. The lights fade, but last of all on the fifty-four-inch bed.)

I'LL BE HOME FOR CHRISTMAS

The play takes place in the living room and kitchen of a modern apartment, represented by no more than a couple of flats, one with a door. The time is early spring, in the afternoon.

CHUCK BERRINGER *is lying full length on the couch. He is about forty-five, large and brawny. At the moment, he is smoking a cigar and balancing a bottle of beer on his chest. He is listening to a record on a record player within reach on a small table near the couch. The music is a series of songs popular during World War II. At the moment, "I'll Be Seeing You" is playing. From the way he smokes and drinks and stares off into space, it is clear that* CHUCK *has something on his mind. He is deeply troubled, and the music and the cigars and beer are a response to the trouble.*

After a few moments, his wife, EDITH, *comes into the apartment. She is about forty. Her hair is up in curlers, covered by a scarf. She is wearing an attractive blouse, a sweater and slacks. She is carrying a small bag from the market. Her approach to things is direct, hearty, no nonsense. She is apparently somewhat insensitive, though this may only be her way of coping with things that frighten her to death. She hears the music, stops, and frowns. Still carrying the bag, she goes to the living room door, shoves it open, and looks in.*

———

EDITH. Well, hello!

CHUCK. Hello.

EDITH (*looks at her watch*). Is my watch stopped or something?

CHUCK. I just thought I'd come home early.

EDITH. Something the matter?

CHUCK. I thought this was your afternoon with the girls.

EDITH. Wednesdays. Used to be Tuesdays. Tuesday's hair . . . and Fridays. (*Waves her hand to swish away the cigar smoke.*) Clarice is entertaining Teddy in here later on. (*She picks up an empty beer bottle.*) Go easy on the beer, huh? We got that thing for the crippled children tonight. (CHUCK *doesn't look at her. She looks at him for a worried moment; she goes with the bundle to the kitchen and sets it on a table.* CHUCK *gets up slowly, goes to the door and closes it. He moves back to the couch and takes up his position again.* EDITH, *puzzled and annoyed and disturbed, picks up the phone in the kitchen; perching on the wooden stool, she dials a number.*) Hello, Milly . . . Edith . . . Hi. Tell me something. Is Martin home? Well, Chuck's home, and I was wondering if the office was declaring a holiday or closed early or what? He's lying in the living room, smoking a cigar, drinking beer, listening to a record and staring into space . . . Some schmaltzy record he bought himself a couple of Christmases ago . . . songs from the War . . . (*In the living room, the music switches to "I'll Walk Alone."*) The only thing is that Chuck *doesn't* smoke cigars . . . he *doesn't* drink beer, and I don't know when he last listened to a record. No, forget I called, unless you hear something . . . Probably just one of his moods . . . (*She mimics broadly*) "What ever happened?" . . . "Where did it all go?" . . . He used to scare the bejesus out of me when he started wondering about the meaning of it all . . . I just don't listen any more . . . because I know that when he starts saying "What happened?" . . . he's really meaning "You happened." As though I were personally responsible for the high cost of living and the menopause . . . I tell you, kiddo, never marry a man at war with the inevitable . . . I'll let you know. 'Bye. (*She hangs up. Her heartiness disappears. She comes back to the living room door and finds it shut. She hesitates a moment, then opens it. She comes in, looks at* CHUCK *a moment, then.*) Did you see Clarice got a letter from Donny today? (*She gestures toward the table in the hall where the mail is left.*) If we get a letter from that boy once a month . . . I know you won't hear of it, but I'd stop his allowance . . . (*She moves an ashtray near him.*) Nothing happen at the office? (*He nods "No." She turns away from him. While she turns away, he takes a letter from the breast pocket of his shirt and casually stuffs it in his trouser pocket. He doesn't make any big thing of it.*) You still going away tomorrow on the sales trip? (*He nods his head.*) Would you pay the grocery bill before you go? I'm getting dirty looks down there . . . How long this time?

CHUCK. Two weeks.

EDITH (*his far-off mood scares her; she attacks on her own level before he can start—if he had any intentions of starting*). Look, I know this is probably not the right time, but it never seems to be the right time . . .

CHUCK. Couldn't it wait?

EDITH. Till when? (CHUCK *shrugs.*) Tonight it's "tomorrow" . . . and tomorrow, it's "tonight" . . . and then "when I come back." I'm sorry to break in one whatever's going on here, but I have to talk to you about these things. You're the father.

CHUCK (*looks at her, puzzled by this "hook"; he lifts the needle from the record*). What is it?

EDITH. One of the things is all your responsibility. The other I could make all mine, and never let you in on it. But I think you ought to know about it before . . . in case you have any opinions . . . (*Suddenly fanning the air.*) You don't smoke cigars. You don't drink beer.

CHUCK. Which thing is all my responsibility?

EDITH. I think Timmy is playing with himself. (CHUCK *takes the cigar from his mouth.*) Playing with himself.

CHUCK. I hope to God he is. If he isn't, he's a freak.

EDITH. Well, I'm sure he is. He moons around. He's losing weight.

CHUCK. You think perhaps he's in imminent danger of going blind or getting epilepsy?

EDITH. I think *he* might think that. He goes around sheepish, and full of some kind of guilt. I think you should have a talk with him.

CHUCK. To what end?

EDITH. I don't want his whole youth ruined by this stupid guilt. I think you should talk to Timmy and tell him it's okay.

CHUCK. Part of the reason a boy masturbates is in some kind of revolt or aggression against his parents. And if I say "Go ahead. It's all right with your mother and me," half the fun would be gone.

EDITH. I think if he knew that you had done it, and it didn't hurt you . . .

CHUCK. Oh, come on.

EDITH. Well, he looks at you like some kind of god, and he's ashamed in your presence because he's doing something you wouldn't do. It's a barrier between you. It's not fair, letting him go around with this image of you as perfect.

CHUCK. Somehow I question if that is the image of me prevailing in this house.

EDITH. Okay. Let your son suffer.

CHUCK. What do you mean, "suffer"?

EDITH. Fighting this impulse in himself.

CHUCK. I thought you said he wasn't fighting it.

EDITH. The other morning when I was making his bed, there was—

CHUCK (*sternly*). Edith!

EDITH. I'm telling you, that attached to the mattress of the upper bunk, on the underneath side, staring down at him . . .

CHUCK. A picture of a naked girl. Good. (*He turns away.*)

EDITH. A cardboard sign . . . about so big, and on it he'd printed in large letters the word WILLPOWER.

CHUCK. And you figured out from this . . .

EDITH. Yes.

CHUCK. Maybe the best thing for me to do would be just to turn the cardboard over and write ENJOY YOURSELF. How do you know this WILLPOWER doesn't apply to any number of other things? "Don't oversleep in the morning." . . . "Do your push-ups" . . . "Love your parents." You've got a dirty mind.

EDITH. That's exactly the point. I don't want him to look on it as dirty. I want him to look on it as a normal, healthy part of his life.

CHUCK. Edith, he may, in spite of your desire and efforts to give it the *Good Housekeeping* seal of approval . . . he may just crave a corner of dirtiness in his life.

EDITH. Okay. So you want him to marry the first girl he sleeps with out of gratitude for saving him from the "nasty habit" . . . and that has happened.

CHUCK. I'm sure.

EDITH. Donny up there at college . . . what do you suppose he's doing? He never writes about any girls. He never writes, but when he does, no girls . . . I'll bet you he marries the first girl . . . and all because you never talked to him about this. (CHUCK *turns away.*) I just want Timmy to look on it all as a natural hunger . . . and just as with our other appetites, we satisfy them as best we can . . . under the circumstances.

CHUCK. "The Loving Family" . . . Chapter Six.

(EDITH *starts taking curlers from her hair.*)

EDITH. You're always saying that you can't get close to your children. You try to have heart-to-heart talks with them about honesty and ideals and meaning . . . Try talking to Timmy about this. I can promise you, you'll have his undivided attention. (*There is no response from* CHUCK.) Well, then, I'll send him to the doctor and have him do it.

CHUCK. No!

EDITH. Times have changed since the doctor gave you that lecture and scared you so that you're still something of a problem in that area.

CHUCK. I do not consider myself a problem in that area.

EDITH. You have trouble being frank.

CHUCK. For which we should all be grateful.

EDITH. We're not discussing you now. We're discussing the children. Another generation.

CHUCK. I do not consider it prudish not to want to invade my son's pleasurable privacy. What do you want him to do? When he leaves the living room early some night, do you want him to say, "Good night, Mom . . . Good night, Dad. I think I'll mosey up to my room and . . ."

EDITH. Honestly!

CHUCK. A little mystery. A little snicker left in sex . . . please.

EDITH. Then I'll have to find a book.

CHUCK. No, dear God. I am the father here . . . good . . . bad . . . or indifferent. And if I feel my son needs to be wised up, I'll do it.

EDITH. You could put it in the form of an anecdote. You told me that during the war, you . . .

CHUCK. Thank you. I'll make my own occasion if I feel it's necessary.

EDITH. I mean, I think if it's tied in with the war like that. It's something that interests him now. It might come up quite naturally. Anyone who was a soldier is a hero to him, and if he knows that heroes did it . . .

CHUCK. Maybe we could persuade one of those TV shows about the war to slip it in casually . . .

EDITH. All right. Your embarrassment at talking to your own sons about something vital comes out in jokes and quips. I don't think they are very funny.

CHUCK. A little laughter, a little levity . . . leavening. Life is not, dear Edith, a desperate struggle and straining for the technically perfect orgasm . . . It's a laugh now and then. (EDITH *just stares at him.*) Look, I have made several sweeping statements to all concerned that I think sex is beautiful . . . one of the great blessings of mankind . . . in all its forms . . . as long as it involves no coercion, or injury, or pain . . . to anyone. Blessed be sex!

EDITH. You think general statements like that do any good? Time and again I give you all sorts of openings to go into some detail, and you side-step them . . . and it is your side-stepping makes them think that sex is dirty.

CHUCK. And I think it is your constant harping on the naturalness of sex that embarrasses the children. "Dear Lord, we thank you for this food which is about to be placed before us, and for the naturalness of sex . . ."

EDITH. You know what's going on in Timmy's mind? "I am doing injury to myself . . . to my future wife." You still feel guilty as hell about it, and that's why you can't talk to him about it.

CHUCK. I do not feel guilty about it. I just feel it is a private matter . . .

EDITH. You *do* have a feeling about it. If you'll remember during that period when I felt . . . well, after my operation, and I suggested to you—

CHUCK. Exactly! Like brushing my teeth or going to the john. It was for me to make that kind of decision, not you or some book you read.

EDITH. Well, it would have been better than all that mooning around and . . .

CHUCK. Mooning around and . . . longing . . . are sometimes better than meaningless . . . (*He doesn't go on.*) I don't want to talk any more about it.

EDITH. Your son knows how you are about these matters . . . Did you know he came to me to buy him his first jockstrap?

CHUCK. Oh, Lord, I have failed my own son because he went to his mother for his first jockstrap! As I remember, he came to me first, and I said he didn't need one yet.

EDITH. Well, I don't want to even begin to think what damage that did to him.

CHUCK. Edie, he didn't need one.

EDITH. But he wanted one. He felt it was time to be a man. Perhaps you could have used it as a cue to discuss other sex matters with him.

CHUCK. Did you?

EDITH. No. But when he got it, he strutted around in it, and I told him how fine he looked in it . . . You were away.

CHUCK. Thank God!

(*He puts the needle back on the record again. "I Should Care" is played.*)

EDITH. We have to discuss one more thing. (*She goes to the door and closes it.*) I don't want Clarice to hear us if she comes in . . . This thing of Clarice and Teddy . . . well . . . I've been keeping very close track of it . . . and I've been very honest with Clarice . . . (*She pushes the button on the recorder, stopping it.*) I mean, she knows about every thing I know. Of course, I still wish you would have an honest talk with her from the man's point of view.

CHUCK. Is that what we're going to start in on now?

EDITH. No. Because I know that that's impossible with you.

CHUCK. Damned right. I am not going to discuss with my daughter a man's . . . erogenous zones.

EDITH. All right. I gave that hope up a long time ago. But all I can say is, if I had known earlier in our marriage the peculiar little things you like, we would have been better off.

CHUCK. What do you mean, "peculiar little things"?

EDITH. Never mind.

CHUCK. What do you mean "peculiar," for God's sake?

EDITH. Well, perhaps not "peculiar"—special.

CHUCK. Why don't you have a talk with Donny about a woman's sexual responses?

EDITH. I *did*.

CHUCK. Oh? Complete with anatomical details?

EDITH. No. But I talked to him about a woman's feelings . . . her moods and inclinations and disinclinations . . . that a woman expects to accommodate herself to the needs of a man to a great extent, but . . .

CHUCK. It sounds as though you made a woman sound like a long-suffering animal. You've probably frightened him to death that he's imposing on a woman every time he wants to make love to her. "If it's not too much to ask." You know, Edith, with all the sex educating you've done around here, I don't know how you've had time to do the housework.

EDITH. Nature abhors a vacuum. And you have created a vacuum as far as the sex education of your children is concerned.

CHUCK (*serious*). Edith, for God's sake . . . I have told them all I think they want to hear from me. Can't you get it through your head that it's grotesque, us talking to them about sex. Sex to them is full of spring and beauty and something old people like you and me don't experience . . . It's absurd to them that we are capable of feeling the same thing they are feeling . . . And maybe we're not . . . They should feel something unique about love and sex . . . they should feel they're experiencing something unique and personal.

EDITH. Nevertheless . . .

CHUCK. They shouldn't be checking off their reactions on some grand universal checklist. "You know, Mom, that sensation you said I'd get? Well, I got it." . . . And "Ma, what do I do now? I pushed all the right buttons, and nothing happened."

EDITH. Nevertheless, there is something we must discuss. Though, as I said before, perhaps I shouldn't mention it and just go ahead.

CHUCK. If it's something you needn't mention, I'd appreciate your *not* mentioning it . . . at least today.

EDITH. It would be just great with you if we never mentioned anything disagreeable or difficult.

CHUCK. Is this disagreeable or difficult?

EDITH. Well, it's just a fact of life, and

it's not disagreeable or difficult if it's faced in a rational way.

CHUCK (*salutes*). Request permission to leave the ship.

EDITH. It's about Clarice.

CHUCK. She's pregnant.

EDITH. No. And I don't want her to be till she wants to be. That's the point.

CHUCK. Okay. I'm hooked. What is it?

EDITH. Clarice is going away to college next year. She'll be absolutely on her own, in a sense, and though we've done our best to give her standards, there will be pressures. Boys are not the same as they were in your day. They expect . . . They demand . . . from what I understand, talking with other mothers.

CHUCK. Those must be very titillating kaffee klatsches.

EDITH. You don't need to be sarcastic. We just exchange information we need. Don't tell me you men don't talk.

CHUCK. Believe it or not, we don't. There's more reticence among men. We may tell dirty jokes, but we do not go into the sex problems of our wives and sons and daughters . . . What are you getting at, Edie?

EDITH. Just that I think that Clarice needs more than information about sex now . . . I think, and please consider it quietly . . . rationally . . . I think I should take her to the doctor and arrange for . . . contraception. Now, please. Think about it, quietly.

CHUCK (*strong*). I think it's a lousy idea.

EDITH. You haven't thought.

CHUCK. I said "I *think* it's a lousy idea." It did not require a great deal of thought.

EDITH. But it does. Now, Chuck, you read. You know what's going on.

CHUCK. I read. That does not necessarily mean I know what's going on . . . in real life. I don't believe those kids you read about represent any more than five percent of . . . It's just not in the instincts.

EDITH. But it *is* the instincts. And now they're getting a chance.

CHUCK. There are other instincts . . . of tenderness and affection. They're not good copy . . . but they are there.

EDITH. A boy is out for everything he can get.

CHUCK. But I got news for you. With a girl he loves, he sometimes hopes he doesn't get it.

EDITH (*puzzled by this, she goes on*).

Clarice and Teddy have been going together for a year now . . .

CHUCK. Against my better judgment.

EDITH. You will not be choosing her bedmates. She will be choosing them.

CHUCK. Them? Do you think they'll be in the plural?

EDITH. They could well be, from what I understand.

CHUCK. I wish you would stop "understanding" and look at your own daughter. Do you think she'll be a bed-hopper?

EDITH. You imply that I'm insulting her if I say she might be. But she might be . . . I think . . . I won't say this to her, but I don't think it is necessarily a bad idea for her to . . . experiment . . . to know. So that she won't be stuck with the wrong man . . . the only man. I know it's distasteful for you to imagine your little girl in the arms of any man, let alone several . . .

CHUCK. Oh, come on.

EDITH. I knew I shouldn't have discussed it with you. You get so emotional about it.

CHUCK. There *are* emotions involved, you know. I mean, it isn't all a chart of erogenous zones. Don't settle for a four-zone man, honey, keep looking for a six-zone man.

EDITH. But I don't want her to be trapped, pregnant by some boy she doesn't even like.

CHUCK (*patiently*). I am trusting that her judgment, her emotions, will not let her get pregnant "by some boy she doesn't even like." If we haven't taught her that much in the way of standards . . .

EDITH. But you can't tell. Some night some boy might get her to drink too much. I've asked you repeatedly to teach her something about that, but again, "No." You—

CHUCK (*angry*). When's the last time, if ever, they caught us necking on this couch?

EDITH. What?

CHUCK. When's the last time we necked on this couch?

EDITH. Once a year you bring up this necking on the couch business . . .

CHUCK. When is the last time?

EDITH. We got the bed, for God's sake. Why the hell should we neck on the couch?

CHUCK. That's the demonstration we

should give them. Necking on the couch. Kissing.

(*He turns away.*)

EDITH. We haven't much time before she comes in from school. And you leave tomorrow.

CHUCK. Have you talked to her about this?

EDITH. Not yet.

CHUCK. No doctor is going to go along with you.

EDITH. Not that fossil Higgins. But some doctor who knows the score certainly will.

CHUCK. The pill isn't proved yet. There are possible side effects . . . and . . . my God, I forbid it!

EDITH. There's not just the pill. After all, we never used the pill . . .

CHUCK. But Clarice is a virgin. And as I understand it, a virgin can't be . . . can't use . . .

EDITH (*cutting in*). She is *not* a virgin.

CHUCK. How do you know?

EDITH. The doctor told me. He thought I should know.

CHUCK (*frowns and thinks*). Well, that doesn't necessarily mean . . . She's an active girl . . . sports . . . (EDITH *just stares him down.*) Well, it doesn't necessarily mean anything. Did you talk to her about it?

EDITH. No.

CHUCK. Did *he* talk to her about it?

EDITH. No.

CHUCK. Holy Christ, I hope it wasn't that Teddy.

EDITH. You see, it's impossible to discuss this with you without your getting emotional.

CHUCK (*accusing*). I said I never wanted them left alone in the house . . .

EDITH. Teddy drives a car.

CHUCK. They shouldn't let kids that age drive.

EDITH. Now calm down. Stop living in the olden days. At least now you may see the point of my wanting her . . . prepared.

CHUCK (*angry*). It is your job to prepare her up here . . . (*He points to his head.*) with a little less emphasis on the technical aspects of screwing.

EDITH. That's a charming word . . . I have tried to prepare her up here, but I am not going to be an ostrich about it.

CHUCK. Going through this . . . it's like inviting her to . . .

(*He doesn't go on.*)

EDITH. Her own body is inviting her. Her instincts are inviting her. Or did you want her to be a virgin when she married?

CHUCK. It is not what I want her to be, but what she wants to be. Has she asked for your help in this department?

EDITH. No, but she may be embarrassed.

CHUCK. Thank God for that. I should think you'd be embarrassed to mention it to her at this point.

EDITH. Didn't you talk to Donny about contraceptives when he went away to college?

CHUCK. Yes.

EDITH. Then why can't I discuss this with Clarice?

CHUCK. There is nothing wrong with discussing it. That is not what you suggested. Anyway, talking to Donny was another thing. It's a boy's . . . a man's responsibility. He should be prepared to handle it.

EDITH. And suppose he isn't?

CHUCK. Edith, I may not want to discuss a man's sexual attitudes with Clarice, but I don't mind discussing them with you. If a boy is out on a date with a girl, and suddenly the whole thing becomes . . . passionate . . . he does not like to hear from the girl . . . no matter how modern he is, no matter how many books on the subject he's read . . . "Go ahead, honey. It's all right. I'm prepared." If she said that, I'll tell you what goes through his head at that moment . . . "Does this mean she does this with all the boys? . . . Does it mean she took me for granted? . . . Does it mean if I hadn't made a pass, she would have thought me a shmo?"

EDITH. What is your solution?

CHUCK. The man makes the arrangements . . . at least the first time.

EDITH. You mean they stop while he goes hunting for a corner drugstore?

CHUCK. Well . . .

EDITH. Or does he just happen to have one . . . or an economy-size dozen, in his pocket? In which case, what does the girl think?

CHUCK. It's different. I can't explain why. But there's a nicety in it someplace . . .

EDITH. And what happens if they can't find a drugstore open . . . as we couldn't, if you'll remember . . . and the moment is possibly lost. You weren't prepared.

CHUCK. I was.

EDITH. We drove all over the damn

countryside looking for a drugstore that was open.

CHUCK. I had something in my wallet. Only by the time we got to the point, I loved you so much . . . I didn't want you to think I was the kind of guy who carried them around in his pocket . . . just in case.

EDITH. Well, that's very touching. Nowadays I think the girl would think you were a fink not to be prepared, after getting her all worked up.

CHUCK. I would think the girl might be flattered. To me, there is something sordid, at that moment, that beautiful moment, for the guy to go fishing in his wallet for some scruffy little paper packet he'd had hidden there for weeks.

EDITH. It would be a hell of a lot better than the ludicrous sight of you trying to keep me interested and at the same time driving around the countryside looking for an all-night drugstore . . . and not finding one. And you had something with you all the time!

CHUCK. I shouldn't have told you.

EDITH. Did you think I'd be shocked that you were prepared? My God, all girls don't have bashful fathers like you . . . I had a bashful mother who advised me to save my first kiss for the man I married . . . But not my father. He'd wised me up on what to expect . . . in very explicit terms.

CHUCK. I'm sorry if I disappointed your expectations.

EDITH. I don't know what your idea was, trying to appear so innocent that night. I knew there were other girls before me . . . that little romantic episode with that girl in London during the war . . .

CHUCK. The idea was the way I felt about you! Were you consulting with your father during those early days of our marriage? "What do I do now, Dad? I'm involved with an amateur who's still fumbling along by his instincts."

EDITH. Don't knock my dad. He opened my eyes to a great deal about life and love and the nature of man. With Mother's "disorders" he had a woman on the side. And he told me about it quite frankly . . . about the needs of a man, et cetera . . . He thought I should know this . . . And I'm damned glad he told me.

CHUCK (after a long moment of thinking this out). You sound as though his teaching you this . . . this matter of man's nature . . . woman on the side . . . infidelity . . . had stood you in good stead.

EDITH. Well, we're not discussing that.

CHUCK. I am . . . That's the goddamndest thing I've ever heard. Do you think I haven't been faithful to you?

EDITH. It's not worth discussing. It's not important.

CHUCK. Not important?

EDITH. It's only important not to discuss it . . . I think.

CHUCK. You have assumed bravely, stoically, armed with your daddy's sweeping wisdom about these matters, that I have been unfaithful to you?

EDITH. I find it embarrassing to discuss—

CHUCK. —I find it impossible not to discuss.

EDITH. I'm not making any accusations.

CHUCK. You are implying very heavily, and you seem to be decking yourself with some kind of sweet tolerance which I find disgusting . . . If you think I've been unfaithful to you, I'm appalled, frankly appalled, that you haven't stood up and shouted.

EDITH. That would be pretty ridiculous, wouldn't it? After all, what does it matter?

CHUCK. When? Please tell me when?

EDITH. You're away a great deal.

CHUCK. When?

EDITH. Long trips, extended periods. A woman would be foolish not to expect something to happen . . . Oh, meaningless, of course . . . But I'm trying to tell you, it doesn't matter.

CHUCK. Well, I'm sorry as hell to disappoint you, but there have been no little meaningless sexual skirmishes . . . My life is full enough of meaninglessness not to go looking for it in outlying districts.

EDITH. You don't have to defend yourself. Nobody is making any accusations.

CHUCK. You are making accusations. And you are infuriating me by your noble tolerance over something that has not taken place. And if it had taken place, I would expect you as a loving wife to stand up and howl.

EDITH. Difficult as it is for you to grasp, your virginity was not a concern of mine before we were married, and your strict fidelity is not a concern of mine now. I am not your jailer, and I am not stupid. The subject is closed as far as I am concerned.

(*She starts for the door.*)

CHUCK (*heads her off and grabs her*). Jesus Christ, men are not all like your father. All men do not relish meaningless rolls in the hay, in their own beds or other beds.

EDITH (*moves away from him, back into the room*). We were discussing the children.

CHUCK. I feel like clobbering you for assuming that I've laid every broad in every small town I've visited, all because your father gave you the lowdown. Why didn't he let you find out for yourself what your man . . . your husband would do? Because if it doesn't matter to you, it matters to me . . . It's hard as hell trying to keep any meaning going, but here, here in the most personal and private core of me, I insist that there be meaning, I want there to be meaning . . . I long for there to be meaning.

CLARICE (*offstage*). Hello.

EDITH (*moving from* CHUCK, *calling out*). Hello, dear.

CLARICE (*enters; she is eighteen and lovely; her arms are full of schoolbooks; she comes into the living room*). Hi.

(*She sees* CHUCK *and looks surprised.*) Hi . . . Surprise.

CHUCK (*as she comes to him, recovering from his anguish*). Hi, baby.

(*They embrace a second.*)

EDITH. I'll get the room aired out and cleaned for you and Teddy. Did you see you have a letter from Donny?

CLARICE. No . . .

(*She leaves and heads for the kitchen.* EDITH *has been gathering her purse, hair curlers, and various items.*)

CHUCK (*closing the door after* CLARICE). Edith! (EDITH *stops.*) I forbid this, Edith. There may not be many areas in my life where I can still act effectively, but here I can . . . and I forbid it.

EDITH (*moves past him to the door*). We'll talk about it again.

CHUCK. Don't you do anything while I'm away . . . Do you understand?

EDITH (*after a moment*). All right. But I wish to God you'd join the twentieth century.

(*She starts to open the door.*)

CHUCK. When Timmy comes in, send him to me, and I'll set his mind to rest about . . .

(EDITH *opens the door and leaves, closing the door after her. She stands for a moment in the shadows between the kitchen and the living room.*)

CHUCK (*slowly returns to the couch and sits, saddened by the scene he has just had; then he shifts his mood slightly*). You see, Timmy . . . many good men and true do that . . . soldiers, sailors, men at war . . . men on long trips into the Arctic . . . and other places. And, Timmy, there's nothing wrong with it . . . except it's awfully lonely.

(*He has said this last very simply. He turns and lies down on the couch, starts the record, and during the following, takes the letter from his pocket and rereads it.*)

EDITH (*now coming into the kitchen, where* CLARICE *has been looking at her letter*). What does Donny say?

CLARICE. Is that what you and Dad were talking about in there? Why he's home so early?

EDITH. What?

CLARICE. Donny's letter to Dad.

EDITH. What letter?

CLARICE (*reads*). "Dear Sis: Just so's you'll know what's going on. Here's a copy of a letter I've sent to Dad at his office. I'm sorry as hell to write like this, but I had to. It's cowardly to write and not face up to him on it, but we've never been able to talk . . ."

EDITH. What is this?

CLARICE. He didn't mention it?

(*Nodding toward* CHUCK.)

EDITH. What *is* it?

CLARICE. I haven't finished it yet, but Donny's leaving college.

EDITH. What?

CLARICE (*reads from Donny's letter*). "I'm leaving college, Dad. I don't know what I'll do, but this is all senseless to me. This and the kind of life it seems to be leading to. I don't know yet what I want to do with my life, and I'm not going to find out here. I think you've been preparing me for the only kind of life you know. Your kind of life. I don't want to hurt you, Dad, because you've always been a good Joe to me . . . but I could never take that kind of life. The life of your generation. You all fought a war. Nobody can take that away from you . . . But after that, what happened? (*She is finding the letter more difficult and painful to read.*) Whatever it was, it scares me, and I don't want it to happen to me . . .

Sometimes I don't know how you do it, Dad . . . Sometimes . . . (*She falters as her eyes read ahead, then.*) Sometimes I don't know how you have the courage to get up in the morning."

EDITH (*after a moment*). He wrote that to your father?

CLARICE (*saddened and disturbed by the letter*). I guess so.

(*She hands it over to* EDITH.)

EDITH (*looks at it a moment; then more in sympathy with* CHUCK *than anger at Donny*). Your father gets up in the morning . . . so that he can send your brother to a fine college so that he can write insulting letters like this.

(*She turns toward the living room and moves into the shadows by the door, her concern for* CHUCK *clearly showing on her face.*)

CHUCK (*he has finished rereading the letter; suddenly he starts to sing with the record*). "I'll be home for Christmas . . . if only in my—"

(*His voice breaks. He closes his eyes. The record finishes and the lights dim.*)

CURTAIN

I'M HERBERT

A very old man is sitting in one of two rocking chairs on a side porch. It is summer. He is bird-watching, his binoculars to his eyes.

———

HERBERT. Baltimore oriole. (*He shifts his glasses, scanning.*) Bobolink. (*Shifts again.*) Rose-breasted grosbeak. (*Shifts again and gets a little excited.*) A black-billed cuckoo. (*He speaks louder, to someone offstage.*) Grace, I saw a black-billed cuckoo.

MURIEL (*a very old woman, dressed with faded elegance, comes onstage carrying a rose*). My name is Muriel, foolish old man.

(*She sits in the other rocker.*)

HERBERT. I know your name is Muriel. That's what I called you.

MURIEL. You called me Grace. Grace was your first wife.

HERBERT. I called you Muriel. You're just hard of hearing and won't admit it . . . Grace . . . Grace . . . That's what I said!

MURIEL. There! You said it.

HERBERT. What?

MURIEL. Grace . . . You called me Grace.

HERBERT. Silly old woman. You call me Harry. But I call you Grace.

MURIEL. Can't you hear yourself?

HERBERT. What?

MURIEL. I said can't you hear yourself?

HERBERT. Of course I can hear myself. It's you that can't hear. I say you call me Harry. Sometimes. Your second husband . . . and sometimes George . . . your first.

MURIEL. I never did. You're saying that because you call me Grace . . . and once in a while Mary.

HERBERT. You just don't hear.

MURIEL. What's my name?

HERBERT. Silly question . . . Muriel. You're Muriel . . . Grace was my first wife. Mary was . . . way long ago.

MURIEL. Mary was before Grace.

HERBERT. No she wasn't.

MURIEL. She was.

HERBERT. I should know who was my first wife, God damn it, woman.

MURIEL. That's safe. Just call me "woman" . . . We won't get confused. It's not very flattering, but it's better than being called the names of your other wives. My name's Muriel. Your name's Harry.

HERBERT. Did you hear? You called me Harry. Pot calling the kettle black.

MURIEL. You got me confused, that's all. You always could mix me up. Back then when we were going to Europe . . .

HERBERT. We never been to Europe. That was Harry.

MURIEL. You and I went to Europe.

HERBERT. We did not. Grace and I went to Europe on our honeymoon. That's when I had money, before women had taken it all.

MURIEL. I've been to Europe with you.

HERBERT. You and Harry went to Europe.

MURIEL. I went to Europe with George, too.

HERBERT. Yes. Well, I'm Herbert.

MURIEL. We never been to Europe?

HERBERT. Singly, not together.

MURIEL. I think we have. You've forgotten.

HERBERT. I've got a perfectly good memory.

MURIEL. You can't even remember my name. (HERBERT *looks at her and blinks.*) You and I were in Venice together. You're ashamed to remember it because of the scandalous good times we had. You loved me then.

HERBERT. I didn't love you when you were in Venice having a scandalous good time with whichever one it was . . . George or Harry. Which was it?

MURIEL. It was you.

HERBERT. I've never been to Venice in my life.

MURIEL. Yesterday you said you'd never been to Chicago . . . and I proved you wrong on that. Your second daughter by your first wife died there. We went to the funeral.

HERBERT. Grace?

MURIEL. The daughter's name?

HERBERT. No. Grace's girl.

MURIEL. Grace wasn't your first wife. Mary was.

HERBERT. Were you there? . . . I tell you, one was enough. Two was more than plenty. I don't know what got into me to try it a third time.

MURIEL. You were sick and you were too tight to hire a nurse, so you married me.

HERBERT. I got well. Why didn't I kick you out? (MURIEL *starts to cry.*) Now don't cry. You know I don't mean it. You were always crying. Cried buckets at our son's wedding. Took on something awful.

MURIEL. We didn't have any children. And I don't cry. That was Mary. I'm Muriel.

HERBERT. It's no wonder I'm confused . . . which I'm not. But you all the time saying "Grace . . . Mary . . . Muriel."

MURIEL. I'm just trying to straighten you out.

HERBERT. What difference does it make? I answer when you call me Bernie.

MURIEL. I never called you Bernie. I maybe once or twice called you Harry, when I woke up sudden like and didn't know where I was. But I never knew a Bernie.

HERBERT. Bernie.

MURIEL. Never heard of him.

HERBERT. He'd be pleased to hear that.

MURIEL. Who was he?

HERBERT. You were carrying on with him when I met you.

MURIEL. I was married to Harry when you met me.

HERBERT. And carrying on with Bernie. But he cleared out.

MURIEL. That must have been Grace.

HERBERT. You were carrying on with?

MURIEL. No. Grace must have been carrying on with Bernie.

HERBERT. Grace wasn't married before. I was her first.

MURIEL. Not married . . . carrying on.

HERBERT. She was married to Harry and carrying on with Bernie.

MURIEL. You said she wasn't married before.

HERBERT. *You* were. *You* were.

MURIEL. What day of the week is it?

HERBERT. What's that got to do with it?

MURIEL. You can't remember anything any more. Senile old man. Bernie Walters!

HERBERT. That's him.

MURIEL. Who?

HERBERT. Bernie Walters.

MURIEL. I never heard of him.

HERBERT. You just said his name.

MURIEL. You've been saying it here for an hour. I just repeated it.

HERBERT. You said "Bernie Walters."

MURIEL. I said I never heard of him, and besides I wasn't married to Harry when I met you. It was George. If I'd been married to Harry, I wouldn't have looked at you. Fine, strapping man . . . may he rest in peace. Oh, what he did in Venice!

HERBERT. You see, it was Harry in Venice.

MURIEL. Of course it was Harry in Venice.

HERBERT. You said it was me.

MURIEL. You? Huh? You wouldn't have it in you to do a thing like that.

HERBERT. What? A thing like what?

MURIEL (*laughs*). Don't be jealous of a dead man. I've done my best to forget him, George, like I promised when I married you.

HERBERT. I'm Herbert.

MURIEL. Do you keep repeating it so you won't forget who you are?

HERBERT. You called me George just now.

MURIEL. A hearing aid's a cheap thing . . .

HERBERT. See here, Grace . . .

MURIEL. I'm Muriel.

HERBERT. You talk about me . . . What about you? "Muriel. I'm Muriel."

MURIEL. Cuckoo!

HERBERT (*he takes up his binoculars*). Where? I wouldn't call you Grace. Grace was soft and gentle and kind.

MURIEL. Why'd you leave her then?

HERBERT. I didn't. She died.

MURIEL. Mary died. Your first wife. You got sick of Grace and left her and married me.

HERBERT. Left Grace for you?

MURIEL. Yes, you silly old man.

HERBERT. All wrong. Grace was my darling.

MURIEL. She drove you crazy.

HERBERT. My first love.

MURIEL. Mary.

HERBERT. Mary drove me crazy.

MURIEL. She was your first love. You've told me about it often enough. The two of you young colts prancing around in the nude.

HERBERT. Mary?

MURIEL. Yes.

HERBERT. I never saw Mary naked. That was her trouble. Cold woman.

MURIEL. That was Grace.

HERBERT. Grace I saw naked. Oh, how naked! There was never anyone nakeder.

MURIEL. You can only be naked. You can't be more or less naked.

HERBERT. You didn't know Grace.

MURIEL. Mary. I did know Grace.

HERBERT. Naked?

MURIEL. Keep a civil tongue in your head.

HERBERT. I never saw you naked.

MURIEL. No, and not likely to. What'd be the point? You couldn't do anything about it.

HERBERT. Oh, that's what you think.

MURIEL. You married me at seventy . . . and you were through then . . . Except for dreaming.

HERBERT. You're lying. We had some good go's together, down by the beach.

MURIEL. You and I were never near a beach. And you were never near me in that way.

HERBERT. Old women forget . . . forget the joys of the flesh. Why is that?

MURIEL. I don't forget Bernie.

HERBERT. Who?

MURIEL. Bernie Walters.

HERBERT. Never heard of him.

MURIEL. My second husband. I was married to him when Harry came along . . . But Harry went away and then you came along . . . a long time after. Platonic marriage. That's what we've had, you and I, George. But it's all right.

HERBERT. Platonic under the willow tree that June?

MURIEL. What willow tree?

HERBERT. Oh, I've been good to you, Mary, for all your carping and your falling off in your old age, because I remember that willow tree. Muriel never knew about it. We were wicked.

MURIEL. If I thought you knew what you were talking about, I'd get mad. But I know you're just babbling. Babbling Bernie . . . That's you. Herbert used to say "How can you listen to him babble?"

HERBERT. I'm Herbert.

MURIEL. If it makes you feel more secure. Go on. Keep reminding yourself.

HERBERT. You called me Bernie.

MURIEL. Oh, sure, sure. And you've never been to Chicago.

HERBERT. I have so. I went there when my daughter died.

MURIEL. Well, I'm glad you admit it.

HERBERT. Why shouldn't I admit it? It's so. You just try to confuse me . . . Bernie, Harry, George, Grace, Mary.

MURIEL. You started a long time ago, slipping. Only then you were more honest about it. Very touching. When we went to Florida and you gave me the tickets and said, "Grace, my mind's slipping, take care of the tickets."

HERBERT. Your name's Muriel.

MURIEL. Yes, yes, lovey. My name's Muriel.

HERBERT. You referred to yourself as "Grace."

MURIEL (*sarcastic*). Oh, very likely. Very likely.

HERBERT. You said I gave you the tickets to Florida and said, "Grace, my mind's slipping."

MURIEL. Well, it was.

HERBERT. I've never been to Florida.

MURIEL. Ho-ho. Well, let's not go into it. The pongee suit.

HERBERT. I never owned a pongee suit.

MURIEL. You said it was the same suit you wore when you married Helen, and we had a long discussion about how ironic it was that you were wearing the same suit to run away with me.

HERBERT. Who's Helen?

MURIEL. You were married to her, silly.

HERBERT. I was running away to Florida with you and I was so old my mind was slipping and I couldn't remember the tickets?

MURIEL. Lovey, you're running a lot of things that happened at different times together now. Maybe you should just sit quietly for a while, Harry, till you get straightened out.

HERBERT. My name is Herbert.

MURIEL. That's right. We'll start from there. You're Herbert and I'm Grace.

HERBERT. You're Muriel.

MURIEL. That's right. Now let's just leave it at that now, or you won't sleep tonight.

HERBERT. I always sleep.

MURIEL. A fortune for sleeping pills.

HERBERT. I never had one in my life.

MURIEL. And you've never been to Chicago either, I suppose.

HERBERT. Never. Why should I have gone to Chicago?

MURIEL. Only because our daughter died there and we went to the funeral.

HERBERT. We had no children together.

MURIEL. I think we shouldn't talk any more now. You're getting confused.

HERBERT. You never let me near your lily-white body.

MURIEL. Ho-ho . . . and what about that afternoon under the willow tree? I think that's when we conceived Ralph.

HERBERT. Who is Ralph?

MURIEL. Ralph is your stepson. Good God!

HERBERT. I conceived my stepson under the willow tree?

MURIEL. I'd prefer it if we just remained quiet for a while. You can't follow a train of thought for more than a moment . . . and it's very tiring trying to jump back and forth with you. Just close your eyes and rest . . . Are your eyes hurting you?

HERBERT. No.

MURIEL. That medicine must be very good then.

HERBERT. What medicine?

MURIEL. You see, that's what I mean.

HERBERT. I never had any medicine for my eyes.

MURIEL. Yes, all right. All right. Let's not argue, George.

HERBERT. I'm Harry.

MURIEL. Yes, yes. All right. We'll just hold hands here, and try to doze a little . . . and think of happier days . . .

(*She takes his hand and they close their eyes and rock.*)

HERBERT (*after a long moment*). Mmmmm . . . Venice.

MURIEL (*dreamy*). Yes . . . Oh, yes . . . Wasn't that lovely . . . Oh, you were so gallant . . . if slightly shocking . . .

(*She laughs, remembering.*)

HERBERT. The beach . . .

MURIEL. The willow tree . . .

HERBERT (*smiling*). You running around naked . . . Oh, lovely . . . lovely . . .

MURIEL. Yes . . . lovely . . .

(*They go on rocking and smiling, holding hands as the lights dim.*)

CURTAIN

BENITO CERENO

Robert Lowell

First presented at the American Place Theatre, New York City, on November 1, 1964, with the following cast:

CAPTAIN AMASA DELANO Lester Rawlins
JOHN PERKINS Jack Ryland
DON BENITO CERENO Frank Langella
BABU Roscoe Lee Browne
ATUFAL Clayton Corbin
FRANCESCO Michael Schultz
AMERICAN SAILORS Conway W. Young, Robert Tinsley, Richard Kjelland, E. Emmet Walsch, Howard Martin

SPANISH SAILORS Luke Andreas, William Jacobson, James Zaferes
NEGRO SLAVES Woodie King, Lonnie Stevens, George A. Sharpe, Hurman Fitzgerald, Ernest Baxter, Aston Young, June Brown, Mary Foreman, Gene Foreman, Judith Byrd, M. S. Mitchell, Lane Floyd, Paul Plummer, Walter Jones, Ethan Courtney

Directed by Jonathan Miller

Copyright © 1964, 1965 by Robert Lowell. All rights reserved. Reprinted by permission of Farrar, Straus & Giroux, Inc., from *The Old Glory* by Robert Lowell.

CAUTION: Professionals and amateurs are hereby warned that *Benito Cereno,* being fully protected under the Copyright Laws of the United States of America, the British Commonwealth, including the Dominion of Canada, and all other countries of the Berne and Universal Copyright Conventions, is subject to royalty. All rights, including professional, amateur, motion picture, recitation, lecturing, public reading, radio and television broadcasting, and the rights of translation into foreign languages, are strictly reserved. Particular emphasis is laid on the question of readings, permission for which must be secured from the author's agent in writing. All inquiries concerning rights (other than amateur rights) should be addressed to the author's representative: Janet Roberts, London International Artists Ltd., 65 East Fifty-fifth Street, New York, N.Y. 10022.

The amateur acting rights of *Benito Cereno,* in the United States and Canada, are controlled exclusively by the Dramatists Play Service, Inc., 440 Park Avenue South, New York, N.Y. 10016. No amateur performance of the play in such territory may be given without obtaining permission of the Dramatists Play Service, and paying the requisite fee.

MANY people would call Robert Lowell America's leading poet. He is also the only significant contemporary poet, unless we count the Anglo-Americans T. S. Eliot and W. H. Auden, to show an interest in the theatre. Unlike Eliot, Lowell has yet to have a Broadway hit, but his contribution has been important. Perhaps more important is that it is now fully recognized.

Lowell was born in Boston—he *is* one of the Boston Lowells, those "who talk to the Cabots"—on March 1, 1917. He started at Harvard but, rejecting family tradition, transferred to Kenyon College in Ohio, where he graduated in 1940. That same year he became a convert to Roman Catholicism. At Kenyon College he came under the influence of the poets John Crowe Ransom and Randall Jarrell, and together they made the *Kenyon Review* an important platform for American poetry and criticism.

Lowell came from a naval family, and when the war came he tried to enlist in both the navy and the army, but he was physically unfit—his eyesight was not good enough, for one thing. As the war progressed Lowell became increasingly concerned about the death and destruction, particularly over the bombing of civilians in an indiscriminate fashion. In 1943 he received a draft notice which he refused on conscientious grounds, expressing his pain and sorrow in a personal letter to President Roosevelt. In October of that year he was sentenced to a year and a day imprisonment, although he served only five months.

This was perhaps one of the first public acts of independence of mind and spirit which have always characterized Lowell. This was the man who was later to reject an invitation sent by President Johnson to a White House garden party, or again to introduce a Soviet poet to a Manhattan audience with a warmly gratuitous attack upon both the American and Soviet governments, saying, in effect, a plague on both their houses.

Despite being a public figure who will on occasion find the necessity to speak out on public issues, he is also a very private man. His poetry has a private voice, even his conscience is private (a rare thing nowadays) until it breaks out into the open, sometimes explosively.

Over the years he has won all manner of prizes and received all manner of honors. He teaches, he writes poetry, and he—reluctantly perhaps—represents a certain moral force in our community. He is also a casual, if remarkable, playwright.

The intensely personal nature of his poetry has always made it difficult to write, a fact that Lowell has consistently acknowledged. The British poet and critic A. Alvarez once asked him whether he used playwriting to "alleviate" the strain of his poetry. Lowell replied: "Yes, and on a small scale. I mean, I don't know too much about writing plays. I found it a great relief to have a plot and people who aren't me at all. I could say things that were personal that I couldn't say in a confessional poem. I don't mean that I know how to write a play as well as a poem, but the medium gave a certain freedom."

For a man who has certain doubts on playwriting, Lowell has done remarkably well. As the old joke has it, you wonder how he would have done if he had known anything about it!

His major dramatic work is the trilogy *The Old Glory*. This consists of three plays, *Endecott and the Red Cross, My Kinsman, Major Molineux,* and *Benito Cereno*. It was originally intended that all three works should be staged together, but it would make a very long, if rewarding, evening. Consequently, when it was first given at the American Place Theatre in 1964, only the two final plays were produced. Four seasons later, also at the American Place, a revised version of *Endecott and the Red Cross* had its premiere. Meanwhile, in 1967, Lowell's version of *Prometheus* was given by the Yale Drama School Repertory Company.

Of all Lowell's plays, *Benito Cereno,* with its sweep and passion, its concern and poetic commitment, is the best. Based on a Herman Melville short novel, it takes a hard look at the American ambiguity toward freedom and slavery, and expresses its theme in dramatic poetry of unusual power.

SCENE. *About the year 1800, an American sealing vessel, the* President Adams, *at anchor in an island harbor off the coast of Trinidad. The stage is part of the ship's deck. Everything is unnaturally clean, bare and shipshape. To one side, a polished, coal-black cannon. The American captain,* AMASA DELANO, *from Duxbury, Massachusetts, sits in a cane chair. He is a strong, comfortable-looking man in his early thirties who wears a spotless blue coat and white trousers. Incongruously, he has on a straw hat and smokes a corncob pipe. Beside him stands* JOHN PERKINS, *his bosun, a very stiff, green young man, a relative of* DELANO's. *Three sailors, one carrying an American flag, enter.* EVERYONE *stands at attention and salutes with machinelike exactitude. Then the* THREE SAILORS *march offstage.* DELANO *and* PERKINS *are alone.*

———

DELANO
There goes the most beautiful woman in South America.

PERKINS
We never see any women, Sir;
just this smothering, overcast Equator,
a seal or two,
the flat dull sea,
and a sky like a gray wasp's nest.

DELANO
I wasn't talking about women,
I was calling your attention to the American flag.

PERKINS
Yes, Sir! I wish we were home in Duxbury.

DELANO
We are home. America is wherever her flag flies.
My own deck is the only place in the world
where I feel at home.

PERKINS
That's too much for me, Captain Delano.
I mean I wish I were at home with my wife;
these world cruises are only for bachelors.

DELANO
Your wife will keep. You should smoke, Perkins.
Smoking turns men into philosophers
and swabs away their worries.
I can see my wife and children or not see them
in each puff of blue smoke.

PERKINS
You are always tempting me, Sir!
I try to keep fit,
I want to return to my wife as fit as I left her.

DELANO
You're much too nervous, Perkins.
Travel will shake you up. You should let
a little foreign dirt rub off on you.
I've taught myself to speak Spanish like a Spaniard.
At each South American port, they mistake me for a
Castilian Don.

PERKINS
Aren't you lowering yourself a little, Captain?
Excuse me, Sir, I have been wanting to ask you a question.
Don't you think our President, Mr. Jefferson, is lowering himself
by being so close to the French?
I'd feel a lot safer in this unprotected place
if we'd elected Mr. Adams instead of Mr. Jefferson.

DELANO
The better man ran second!
Come to think of it, he rather let us down
by losing the election just after we had named this ship,
the *President Adams*. Adams is a nervous dry fellow.
When you've travelled as much as I have,
you'll learn that that sort doesn't export, Perkins.
Adams didn't get a vote outside New England!

PERKINS
He carried every New England state;
that was better than winning the election.
I'm afraid I'm a dry fellow, too, Sir.

DELANO

Not when I've educated you!

When I am through with you, Perkins,

you'll be as worldly as the Prince Regent
of England,

only you'll be a first-class American officer.

I'm all for Jefferson, he has the popular
touch.

Of course he's read too many books,

but I've always said an idea or two won't
sink our Republic.

I'll tell you this, Perkins,

Mr. Jefferson is a gentleman and an American.

PERKINS

They say he has two illegitimate Negro
children.

DELANO

The more, the better! That's the quickest
way

to raise the blacks to our level.

I'm surprised you swallow such Federalist
bilge, Perkins!

I told you Mr. Jefferson is a gentleman and
an American;

when a man's in office, Sir, we all pull behind him!

PERKINS

Thank God our Revolution ended where
the French one began.

DELANO

Oh, the French! They're like the rest of
the Latins,

they're hardly white people,

they start with a paper republic

and end with a toy soldier, like Bonaparte.

PERKINS

Yes, Sir. I see a strange sail making for the
harbor.

They don't know how to sail her.

DELANO

Hand me my telescope.

PERKINS

Aye, aye, Sir!

DELANO

(*With telescope*)

I see an ocean undulating in long scoops
of swells;

it's set like the beheaded French Queen's
high wig;

the sleek surface is like waved lead,

cooled and pressed in the smelter's mould.

I see flights of hurried gray fowl,

patches of fluffy fog.

They skim low and fitfully above the
decks,

like swallows sabering flies before a storm.

This gray boat foreshadows something
wrong.

PERKINS

It does, Sir!

They don't know how to sail her!

DELANO

I see a sulphurous haze above her cabin,

the new sun hangs like a silver dollar to
her stern;

low creeping clouds blow on from them to
us.

PERKINS

What else, Sir?

DELANO

The yards are woolly

the ship is furred with fog.

On the cracked and rotten head-boards,

the tarnished, gilded letters say, the *San
Domingo.*

A rat's-nest messing up the deck,

black faces in white sheets are fussing with
the ropes.

I think it's a cargo of Dominican monks.

PERKINS

Dominican monks, Sir! God help us,

I thought they were outlawed in the new
world.

DELANO

No, it's nothing. I see they're only slaves.

The boat's transporting slaves.

PERKINS

Do you believe in slavery, Captain Delano?

DELANO

In a civilized country, Perkins,

everyone disbelieves in slavery,

everyone disbelieves in slavery and wants
    slaves.
We have the perfect uneasy answer;
in the North, we don't have them and
    want them;
Mr. Jefferson has them and fears them.

PERKINS
Is that how you answer, Sir,
when a little foreign dirt has rubbed off on
    you?

DELANO
Don't ask me such intense questions.
You should take up smoking, Perkins.
There was a beautiful, dumb English ac-
    tress—
I saw her myself once in London.
They wanted her to look profound,
so she read Plato and the Bible and Ben-
    jamin Franklin,
and thought about them every minute.
She still looked like a moron.
Then they told her to think about nothing.
She thought about nothing, and looked
    like Socrates.
That's smoking, Perkins, you think about
    nothing and look deep.

PERKINS
I don't believe in slavery, Sir.

DELANO
You don't believe in slavery or Spaniards
or smoking or long cruises or monks or
    Mr. Jefferson!
You are a Puritan, all faith and fire.

PERKINS
Yes, Sir.

DELANO
God save America from Americans!

(*Takes up the telescope*)

I see octagonal network bagging out
from her heavy top like decayed beehives.
The battered forecastle looks like a raped
    Versailles.
On the stern-piece, I see the fading arms
    of Spain.
There's a masked satyr, or something
with its foot on a big white goddess.
She has quite a figure.

PERKINS
They oughtn't to be allowed on the ocean!

DELANO
Who oughtn't? Goddesses?

PERKINS
I mean Spaniards, who cannot handle a
    ship,
and mess up its hull with immoral statues.

DELANO
You're out of step. You're much too dry.
Bring me my three-cornered hat.
Order some men to clear a whaleboat.
I am going to bring water and fresh fish
    to the *San Domingo*.
These people have had some misfortune,
    Perkins!

PERKINS
Aye, aye, Sir.

DELANO
Spaniards? The name gets you down,
you think their sultry faces and language
make them Zulus.
You take the name *Delano*—
I've always thought it had some saving
Italian or Spanish virtue in it.

PERKINS
Yes, Sir.

DELANO
A Spaniard isn't a Negro under the skin,
particularly a Spaniard from Spain—
these South American ones mix too much
    with the Indians.
Once you get inside a Spaniard,
he talks about as well as your wife in Dux-
    bury.

PERKINS

(*Shouting*)

A boat for the captain! A whaleboat for
Captain Delano!

(*A bosun's whistle is heard, the lights
dim. When they come up, we are on
the deck of the* San Domingo, *the
same set, identical except for litter
and disorder.* THREE AMERICAN SAILORS

climb on board. They are followed by
PERKINS *and* DELANO, *now wearing a
three-cornered hat. Once on board, the*
AMERICAN SAILORS *salute* DELANO *and
stand stiffly at attention like toys.* NE-
GROES *from the* San Domingo *drift
silently and furtively forward.*)

DELANO
I see a wen of barnacles hanging to the
waterline of this ship.
It sticks out like the belly of a pregnant
woman.
Have a look at our dory Bosun.

PERKINS
Aye, aye, Sir!

(*By now, about twenty blacks and
two Spanish sailors have drifted in.
They look like some gaudy, shabby,
unnautical charade, and pay no attention to the Americans, until an unseen
figure in the rigging calls out a single
sharp warning in an unknown tongue.
Then they all rush forward, shouting,
waving their arms and making inarticulate cries like birds. Three shrill
warnings come from the rigging.
Dead silence. The men from the* San
Domingo *press back in a dense semi-
circle. One by one, individuals come
forward, make showy bows to* DE-
LANO, *and speak.*)

FIRST NEGRO
Scurvy, Master Yankee!

SECOND NEGRO
Yellow fever, Master Yankee!

THIRD NEGRO
Two men knocked overboard rounding
Cape Horn,
Master Yankee!

FOURTH NEGRO
Nothing to eat, Master Yankee!

NEGRO WOMAN
Nothing to drink, Master Yankee!

SECOND NEGRO WOMAN
Our mouths are dead wood, Master Yankee!

DELANO
You see, Perkins,
these people have had some misfortune.

(*General hubbub, muttering, shouts,
gestures, ritual and dumbshow of distress. The rigging, hitherto dark,
lightens, as the sun comes out of a
cloud, and shows* THREE OLD NEGROES,
*identical down to their shabby patches.
They perch on cat's-heads; their heads
are grizzled like dying willow tops;
each is picking bits of unstranded rope
for oakum. It is they who have been
giving the warnings that control the
people below. Everyone,* DELANO *along
with the rest, looks up.* DELANO *turns
aside and speaks to* PERKINS.)

It is like a Turkish bazaar.

PERKINS
They are like gypsies showing themselves
for money
at a county fair, Sir.

DELANO
This is enchanting after the blank gray roll
of the ocean!
Go tell the Spanish captain I am waiting
for him.

(PERKINS *goes off. Sharp warnings
from the* OAKUM-PICKERS. *A big black
spread of canvas is pulled creakingly
and ceremoniously aside.* SIX FIGURES
*stand huddled on a platform about
four feet from the deck. They look
like weak old invalids in bathrobes
and nightcaps until they strip to the
waist and turn out to be huge, shining
young Negroes. Saying nothing, they
set to work cleaning piles of rusted
hatchets. From time to time, they turn
and clash their hatchets together with
a rhythmic shout.* PERKINS *returns.*)

PERKINS
Their captain's name is Don Benito Cereno,
he sends you his compliments, Sir.
He looks more like a Mexican planter than
a seaman.
He's put his fortune on his back:

he doesn't look as if he had washed since
　they left port.

DELANO

Did you tell him I was waiting for him?
A captain should be welcomed by his fel-
　low-captain.
I can't understand this discourtesy.

PERKINS

He's coming, but there's something wrong
　with him.

　　(BENITO CERENO, *led by his Negro*
　　servant, BABU, *enters.* BENITO, *looking*
　　sick and dazed, is wearing a sombrero
　　and is dressed with a singular but
　　shabby richness. Head bent to one
　　side, he leans in a stately coma against
　　the rail, and stares unseeingly at DE-
　　LANO. BABU, *all in scarlet, and small*
　　and quick, keeps whispering, pointing
　　and pulling at BENITO'*s sleeve.* DELANO
　　walks over to them.)

DELANO

Your hand, Sir. I am Amasa Delano,
captain of the *President Adams,*
a sealing ship from the United States.
This is your lucky day,
the sun is out of hiding for the first time
　in two weeks,
and here I am aboard your ship
like the Good Samaritan with fresh food
　and water.

BENITO

The Good Samaritan? Yes, yes,
we mustn't use the Scriptures lightly.
Welcome, Captain. It is the end of the day.

DELANO

The end? It's only morning.
I loaded and lowered a whaleboat
as soon as I saw how awkwardly your ship
　was making for the harbor.

BENITO

Your whaleboat's welcome, Captain.
I am afraid I am still stunned by the storm.

DELANO

Buck up. Each day is a new beginning.
Assign some sailors to help me dole out my
　provisions.

BENITO

I have no sailors.

BABU

　　(*In a quick singsong*)

Scurvy, yellow fever,
ten men knocked off on the Horn,
doldrums, nothing to eat, nothing to drink!
By feeding us, you are feeding the King
　of Spain.

DELANO

Sir, your slave has a pretty way of talking.
What do you need?

　　(DELANO *waits for* BENITO *to speak.*
　　When nothing more is said, he shifts
　　awkwardly from foot to foot, then
　　turns to his SAILORS.)

Stand to, men!

　　(*The* AMERICAN SAILORS, *who have*
　　been lounging and gaping, stand in a
　　row, as if a button had been pressed.)

Lay our fish and water by the cabin!

　　(*The* SAILORS *arrange the watercans*
　　and baskets of fish by the cabin. A
　　sharp whistle comes from the OAKUM-
　　PICKERS. *Almost instantly, the provi-*
　　sions disappear.)

Captain Cereno, you are surely going to
　taste my water!

BENITO

A captain is a servant, almost a slave, Sir.

DELANO

No, a captain's a captain.
I am sending for more provisions.
Stand to!

　　(*The* AMERICAN SAILORS *stand to.*)

Row back to the ship. When you get there,
take on five hogsheads of fresh water,
and fifty pounds of soft bread.

　　(FIRST SAILOR *salutes and goes down*
　　the ladder.)

Bring all our remaining pumpkins!

(SECOND *and* THIRD *salute and go
down the ladder.*)

My bosun and I will stay on board,
until our boat returns.
I imagine you can use us.

BENITO
Are you going to stay here alone?
Won't your ship be lost without you?
Won't you be lost without your ship?

BABU
Listen to Master!
He is the incarnation of courtesy, Yankee
   Captain.
Your ship doesn't need you as much as we
   do.

DELANO
Oh, I've trained my crew.
I can sail my ship in my sleep.

(*Leaning over the railing and calling:*)

Men, bring me a box of lump sugar,
and six bottles of my best cider.

(*Turning to* BENITO:)

Cider isn't my favorite drink, Don Benito,
but it's a New England specialty;
I'm ordering six bottles for your table.

(BABU *whispers and gestures to* DON
BENITO, *who is exhausted and silent.*)

BABU
Une bouteille du vin.

(*To* NEGROES)

My master wishes to give you a bottle
of the oldest wine in Seville.

(*He whistles. A Negro woman rushes
into the cabin and returns with a dusty
beribboned bottle, which she holds
like a baby.* BABU *ties a rope around
the bottle.*)

BABU
I am sending this bottle of wine to your
   cabin.
When you drink it, you will remember us.
Do you see these ribbons? The crown of
   Spain is tied to one.
Forgive me for tying a rope around the
   King of Spain's neck.

(*Lowers the wine on the rope to the
whaleboat.*)

DELANO

(*Shouting to his* SAILORS:)

Pick up your oars!

SAILORS
Aye, aye, Sir!

DELANO
We're New England Federalists;
we can drink the King of Spain's health.

(BENITO *stumbles offstage on* BABU's
arm.)

PERKINS
Captain Cereno hasn't travelled as much
   as you have;
I don't think he knew what you meant by
the New England
Federalists.

DELANO

(*Leaning comfortably on the rail; half
to himself and half to* PERKINS:)

The wind is dead. We drift away.
We will be left alone all day,
here in this absentee empire.
Thank God, I know my Spanish!

PERKINS
You'll have to watch them, Sir.
Brown men in charge of black men—
it doesn't add up to much!
This Babu, I don't trust him!
Why doesn't he talk with a Southern ac-
   cent,
Like Mr. Jefferson? They're out of hand,
   Sir!

DELANO

Nothing relaxes order more than misery.
They need severe superior officers.
They haven't one.
Now, if this Benito were a man of energy . . .
a Yankee . . .

PERKINS

How can a Spaniard sail?

DELANO

Some can. There was Vasco da Gama and
Columbus . . .
No, I guess they were Italians. Some can,
but this captain is tubercular.

PERKINS

Spaniards and Negroes have no business
on a ship.

DELANO

Why is this captain so indifferent to me?
If only I could stomach his foreign reserve!
This absolute dictator of his ship
only gives orders through his slaves!
He is like some Jesuit-haunted Hapsburg
king
about to leave the world and hope the
world will end.

PERKINS

He said he was lost in the storm.

DELANO

Perhaps it's only policy,
a captain's icy dignity
obliterating all democracy—

PERKINS

He's like someone walking in his sleep.

DELANO

Ah, slumbering dominion!
He is so self-conscious in his imbecility . . .
No, he's sick. He sees his men no more
than me.
This ship is like a crowded immigration
boat;
it needs severe superior officers,
the friendly arm of a strong mate.
Perhaps, I ought to take it over by force.

No, they're sick, they've been through the
plague.

(BENITO *and* BABU *return.*)

I'll go and speak and comfort my fellow
captain.
I think you can help me, Captain. I'm feeling useless.
My own thoughts oppress me, there's so
much to do.
I wonder if you would tell me the whole
sad story of your voyage.
Talk to me as captain to captain.
We have sailed the same waters.
Please tell me your story.

BENITO

A story? A story! That's out of place.
When I was a child, I used to beg for
stories in Lima.
Now my tongue's tied and my heart is
bleeding.

(*Stops talking, as if his breath were
gone. He stares for a few moments,
then looks up at the rigging, as if he
were counting the ropes one by one.*
DELANO *turns abruptly to* PERKINS.)

DELANO

Go through the ship, Perkins,
and see if you can find me a Spaniard who
can talk.

BENITO

You must be patient, Captain Delano;
if we only see with our eyes,
sometimes we cannot see at all.

DELANO

I stand corrected, Captain;
tell me about your voyage.

BENITO

It's now a hundred and ninety days. . . .
This ship, well manned, well officered,
with several cabin passengers,
carrying a cargo of Paraguay tea and Spanish cutlery.
That parcel of Negro slaves, less than four
score now,
was once three hundred souls.
Ten sailors and three officers fell from the
mainyard off the Horn;

part of our rigging fell overboard with
    them,
as they were beating down the icy sail.
We threw away all our cargo,
Broke our waterpipes,
Lashed them on deck
this was the chief cause of our suffering.

DELANO

I must interrupt you, Captain.
How did you happen to have three officers
    on the mainyard?
I never heard of such a disposal,
it goes against all seamanship.

BABU

Our officers never spared themselves;
if there was any danger, they rushed in
to save us without thinking.

DELANO

I can't understand such an oversight.

BABU

There was no oversight. My master had
    a hundred eyes.
He had an eye for everything.
Sometimes the world falls on a man.
The sea wouldn't let Master act like a
    master,
yet he saved himself and many lives.
He is still a rich man, and he saved the
    ship.

BENITO

Oh, my God, I wish the world had fallen
    on me,
and the terrible cold sea had drowned me;
that would have been better than living
    through what I've
lived through!

BABU

He is a good man, but his mind is off;
he's thinking about the fever when the
    wind stopped—
poor, poor Master!
Be patient, Yankee Captain, these fits are
    short,
Master will be the master once again.

BENITO

The scurvy was raging through us.
We were on the Pacific. We were invalids
and couldn't man our mangled spars.

A hurricane blew us northeast through the
    fog.
Then the wind died.
We lay in irons fourteen days in unknown
    waters,
our black tongues stuck through our
    mouths,
but we couldn't mend our broken water-
    pipes.

BABU

Always those waterpipes,
he dreams about them like a pile of
snakes!

BENITO

Yellow fever followed the scurvy,
the long heat thickened in the calm,
my Spaniards turned black and died like
    slaves,
The blacks died too. I am my only officer
left.

BABU

Poor, poor Master! He had a hundred
    eyes,
he lived our lives for us.
He is still a rich man.

BENITO

In the smart winds beating us northward,
our torn sails dropped like sinkers in the
    sea;
each day we dropped more bodies.
Almost without a crew, canvas, water, or
a wind,
we were bounced about by the opposing
    waves
through cross-currents and the weedy
    calms,
and dropped our dead.
Often we doubled and redoubled on our
    track
like children lost in jungle. The thick fog
hid the Continent and our only port from
us.

BABU

We were poor kidnapped jungle creatures.
We only lived on what he could give us.
He had a hundred eyes, he was the master.

BENITO

These Negroes saved me, Captain.
Through the long calamity,

they were as gentle as their owner, Don
Aranda, promised.
Don Aranda took away their chains be-
fore he died.

BABU

Don Aranda saved our lives, but we
couldn't save his.
Even in Africa I was a slave.
He took away my chains.

BENITO

I gave them the freedom of my ship.
I did not think they were crates or cargo
or cannibals.
But it was Babu—under God, I swear I
owe my life to Babu!
He calmed his ignorant, wild brothers,
never left me, saved the *San Domingo.*

BABU

Poor, poor Master. He is still a rich man.
Don't speak of Babu. Babu is the dirt
under your feet.
He did his best.

DELANO

You are a good fellow, Babu.
You are the salt of the earth. I envy you,
Don Benito;
he is no slave, Sir, but your friend.

BENITO

Yes, he is salt in my wounds.
I can never repay him, I mean.
Excuse me, Captain, my strength is gone.
I have done too much talking. I want to
rest.

(BABU *leads* BENITO *to a shabby straw
chair at the side.* BENITO *sits.* BABU
fans him with his sombrero.)

PERKINS

He's a fine gentleman, but no seaman.
A cabin boy would have known better
than to send his three officers on the mainyard.

DELANO

(*Paying no attention:*)

A terrible story. I would have been un-
hinged myself.

(*Looking over toward* BABU *and*
BENITO)

There's a true servant. They do things
better
in the South and in South America—
trust in return for trust!
The beauty of that relationship is unknown
in New England. We're too much alone
in Massachusetts, Perkins.
How do our captains and our merchants
live,
each a republic to himself?
Even Sam Adams had no friends and only
loved the mob.

PERKINS

Sir, you are forgetting that
New England seamanship brought them
their slaves.

DELANO

Oh, just our Southern slaves;
we had nothing to do with these fellows.

PERKINS

The ocean would be a different place
if every Spaniard served an apprenticeship
on an American ship
before he got his captain's papers.

DELANO

This captain's a gentleman, not a sailor.
His little yellow hands
got their command before they held a
rope—
in by the cabin-window, not the hawse-
hole!
Do you want to know why
they drifted hog-tied in those easy calms—
inexperience, sickness, impotence and aristocracy!

PERKINS

Here comes Robinson Crusoe and his good
man Friday.

DELANO

We don't beat a man when he's down.

(BENITO *advances uncertainly on*
BABU*'s arm.*)

I am glad to see you on your feet again,
That's the only place for a Captain, sir!
I have the cure for you, I have decided
to bring you medicine and a sufficient sup-
    ply of water.
A first-class deck officer, a man from Salem,
shall be stationed on your quarter deck,
a temporary present from my owners.
We shall refit your ship and clear this mess.

BENITO

You will have to clear away the dead.

BABU

This excitement is bad for him, Yankee
    Master.
He's lived with death. He lives on death
    still;
this sudden joy will kill him. You've heard
how thirsty men die from overdrinking!
His heart is with his friend, our owner,
Don Aranda.

BENITO

I am the only owner.

(*He looks confused and shaken.* BABU
*scurries off and brings up the straw
chair.* BENITO *sits.*)

DELANO

Your friend is dead? He died of fever?

BENITO

He died very slowly and in torture.
He was the finest man in Lima.
We were brought up together,
I am lost here.

DELANO

Pardon me, Sir. You are young at sea.
My experience tells me what your trouble
    is:
this is the first body you have buried in the
    ocean.
I had a friend like yours, a warm honest
    fellow,
who would look you in the eye—
we had to throw him to the sharks.
Since then I've brought embalming gear
    on board.
Each man of mine shall have a Christian
    grave on land.
You wouldn't shake so, if Don Aranda
    were on board,

I mean, if you'd preserved the body.

BENITO

If he were on board this ship?
If I had preserved his body?

BABU

Be patient, Master!
We still have the figurehead.

DELANO

You have the figurehead?

BABU

You see that thing wrapped up in black
    cloth?
It's a figurehead Don Aranda bought us
    in Spain.
It was hurt in the storm. It's very precious.
Master takes comfort in it,
he is going to give it to Don Aranda's
    widow.
It's time for the pardon ceremony, Master.

(*Sound of clashing hatchets*)

DELANO

I am all for these hatchet-cleaners.
They are saving cargo. They make
an awful lot of pomp and racket though
about a few old, rusty knives.

BENITO

They think steel is worth its weight in
    gold.

(*A slow solemn march is sounded on
the gongs and other instruments. A
gigantic coal-black* NEGRO *comes up
the steps. He wears a spiked iron
collar to which a chain is attached
that goes twice around his arms and
ends padlocked to a broad band of
iron. The* NEGRO *comes clanking forward and stands dumbly and like a
dignitary in front of* BENITO. *Two
small black boys bring* BENITO *a frail
rattan cane and a silver ball, which
they support on a velvet cushion.*
BENITO *springs up, holds the ball, and
raises the cane rigidly above the head
of the Negro in chains. For a moment,
he shows no trace of sickness. The
assembled blacks sing, "Evviva, Benito!" three times.*)

BABU

(*At one side with the Americans, but keeping an eye on* BENITO:)

You are watching the humiliation of King
Atufal,
once a ruler in Africa. He ruled as much
land there as your President.
Poor Babu was a slave even in Africa,
a black man's slave, and now a white
man's.

BENITO

(*In a loud, firm voice.*)

Former King Atufal, I call on you to
kneel!
Say, "My sins are black as night,
I ask the King of Spain's pardon
through his servant, Don Benito."

(*Pause.* ATUFAL *doesn't move.*)

NEGROES
Your sins are black as night, King Atufal!
Your sins are black as night, King Atufal!

BENITO
What has King Atufal done?

BABU
I will tell you later, Yankee Captain.

BENITO
Ask pardon, former King Atufal.
If you will kneel,
I will strike away your chains.

(ATUFAL *slowly raises his chained
arms and lets them drop.*)

Ask pardon!

WOMAN SLAVE
Ask pardon, King Atufal.

BENITO
Go!

(*Sound of instruments. The* BLACK
BOYS *take* BENITO's *ball and cane. The
straw chair is brought up.* BENITO *sits.*
FRANCESCO *then leads him offstage.*)

BABU
Francesco!
I will be with you in a moment, Master.
You mustn't be afraid,
Francesco will serve you like a second
Babu.

BENITO
Everyone serves me alike here,
but no one can serve me as you have.

BABU
I will be with you in a moment.
The Yankee master is at sea on our ship.
He wants me to explain our customs.

(BENITO *is carried offstage.*)

You would think Master's afraid of dying,
if Babu leaves him!

DELANO
I can imagine your tenderness during his
sickness.
You were part of him,
you were almost a wife.

BABU
You say such beautiful things,
the United States must be a paradise for
people like Babu.

DELANO
I don't know.
We have our faults. We have many states,
some of them could stand improvement.

BABU
The United States must be heaven.

DELANO
I suppose we have fewer faults than other
countries.
What did King Atufal do?

BABU
He used the Spanish flag for toilet paper.

DELANO
That's treason.
Did Atufal know what he was doing?
Perhaps the flag was left somewhere it
shouldn't have been.
Things aren't very strict here.

BABU
I never thought of that.
I will go and tell Master.

DELANO
Oh, no, you mustn't do that!
I never interfere with another man's ship.
Don Benito is your lord and dictator.
How long has this business with King
    Atufal been going on?

BABU
Ever since the yellow fever,
and twice a day.

DELANO
He did a terrible thing, but he looks like
    a royal fellow.
You shouldn't call him a king, though,
it puts ideas into his head.

BABU
Atufal had gold wedges in his ears in
    Africa;
now he wears a padlock and Master bears
    the key.

DELANO
I see you have a feeling for symbols of
    power.
You had better be going now,
Don Benito will be nervous about you.

(BABU *goes off.*)

That was a terrible thing to do with a
    flag;
everything is untidy and unravelled here—
this sort of thing would never happen on
    the *President Adams.*

PERKINS
Your ship is as shipshape as our country,
    Sir.

DELANO
I wish people wouldn't take me as repre-
    sentative of our country:
America's one thing, I am another;
we shouldn't have to bear one another's
    burdens.

PERKINS
You are a true American for all your talk,
    Sir;

I can't believe you were mistaken for a
    Castilian Don.

DELANO
No one would take me for Don Benito.

PERKINS
I wonder if he isn't an impostor, some
    traveling actor from a circus?

DELANO
No, Cereno is a great name in Peru, like
    Winthrop or Adams with us.
I recognize the family features in our
    captain.

(*An* OLD SPANISH SAILOR, *grizzled and
dirty, is seen crawling on all fours
with an armful of knots toward the
Americans. He points to where* BENITO
and BABU *have disappeared, and whistles. He holds up the knots as though
he were in chains, then throws them
out loosely on the deck in front of
him. A* GROUP OF NEGROES *forms a
circle around him, holding hands and
singing childishly. Then, laughing,
they carry the* SPANIARD *offstage on
their shoulders.*)

These blacks are too familiar!
We are never alone!

(*Sound of gongs. Full minute's pause,
as if time were passing.* DELANO *leans
on the railing. The sun grows
brighter.*)

This ship is strange.
These people are too spontaneous—all
    noise and show,
no character!
Real life is a simple monotonous thing.
I wonder about that story about the calms;
it doesn't stick.
Don Benito hesitated himself in telling it.
No one could run a ship so stupidly,
and place three officers on one yard.

(BENITO *and* BABU *return.*)

A captain has unpleasant duties;
I am sorry for you, Don Benito.

BENITO

You find my ship unenviable, Sir?

DELANO

I was talking about punishing Atufal;
he acted like an animal!

BENITO

Oh, yes, I was forgetting. . . .
He was a King,
How long have you lain in at this island,
Sir?

DELANO

Oh, a week today.

BENITO

What was your last port, Sir?

DELANO

Canton.

BENITO

You traded seal-skins and American muskets
for Chinese tea and silks, perhaps?

DELANO

We took in some silks.

BENITO

A little gold and silver too?

DELANO

Just a little silver. We are only merchants.
We take in a dollar here and there. We
have no Peru,
or a Pizarro who can sweat gold out of
the natives.

BENITO

You'll find things have changed
a little in Peru since Pizarro, Captain.

(*Starts to move away.* BABU *whispers
to him, and he comes back abruptly,
as if he had forgotten something important.*)

How many men have you on board, Sir?

DELANO

Some twenty-five, Sir. Each man is at his
post.

BENITO

They're all on board, Sir, now?

DELANO

They're all on board. Each man is working.

BENITO

They'll be on board tonight, Sir?

DELANO

Tonight? Why do you ask, Don Benito?

BENITO

Will they all be on board tonight, Captain?

DELANO

They'll be on board for all I know.

(PERKINS *makes a sign to* DELANO.)

Well, no, to tell the truth, today's our
Independence Day.
A gang is going ashore to see the village.
A little diversion improves their efficiency,
a little regulated corruption.

BENITO

You North Americans take no chances.
Generally, I suppose,
even your merchant ships go more or less
armed?

DELANO

A rack of muskets, sealing spears and cutlasses.
Oh, and a six-pounder or two; we are a
sealing ship,
but with us each merchant is a privateer—
only in case of oppression, of course.
You've heard about how we shoot pirates.

BABU

Boom, boom, come Master.

(BENITO *walks away on* BABU's *arm
and sits down, almost offstage in his
straw chair. They whisper. Meanwhile, a* SPANISH SAILOR *climbs the
rigging furtively, spread-eagles his
arms and shows a lace shirt under
his shabby jacket. He points to* BENITO
and BABU, *and winks. At a cry from*
ONE OF THE OAKUM-PICKERS, THREE

NEGROES *help the* SPANIARD *down with servile, ceremonious attentions.*)

PERKINS
Did you see that sailor's lace shirt, Sir?
He must have robbed one of the cabin passengers.
I hear that people strip the dead
in these religious countries.

DELANO
No, you don't understand the Spaniards.
In these old Latin countries,
each man's a beggar or a noble, often both;
they have no middle class. With them it's customary
to sew a mess of gold and pearls on rags—
that's how an aristocracy that's going to the dogs
keeps up its nerve.

DELANO
It's odd, though,
that Spanish sailor seemed to want to tell me something.
He ought to dress himself properly and speak his mind.
That's what we do. That's why we're strong:
everybody trusts us. Nothing gets done
when every man's a noble. I wonder why
the captain asked me all those questions?

PERKINS
He was passing the time of day, Sir;
It's a Latin idleness.

DELANO
It's strange. Did you notice how Benito stopped rambling?
He was conventional . . . consecutive for the first time since we met him.
Something's wrong. Perhaps, they've men below the decks,
a sleeping volcano of Spanish infantry. The Malays do it,
play sick and cut your throat.
A drifting boat, a dozen doped beggars on deck,
two hundred sweating murderers packed below like sardines—
that's rot! Anyone can see these people are really sick,
sicker than usual. Our countries are at peace.

I wonder why he asked me all those questions?

PERKINS
Just idle curiosity. I hear
the gentlemen of Lima sit at coffee-tables from sun to sun,
and gossip. They don't even have women to look at;
they're all locked up with their aunts.

DELANO
Their sun is going down. These old empires go.
They are much too familiar with their blacks.
I envy them though, they have no character,
they feel no need to stand alone.
We stand alone too much,
that's why no one can touch us for sailing a ship;
When a country loses heart, it's easier to live.
Ah, Babu! I suppose Don Benito's indisposed again!
Tell him I want to talk to his people;
there's nothing like a well man to help the sick.

BABU
Master is taking his siesta, Yankee Master.
His siesta is sacred, I am afraid to disturb it.
Instead, let me show you our little entertainment.

DELANO
Let's have your entertainment;
if you know a man's pleasure
you know his measure.

BABU
We are a childish people. Our pleasures are childish.
No one helped us, we know nothing
about your important amusements,
such as killing seals and pirates.

DELANO
I'm game. Let's have your entertainment.

(BABU *signals. The gong sounds ten times and the canvas is pulled from the circular structure. Enclosed in a*

triangular compartment, an OLD SPAN-
ISH SAILOR *is dipping naked white
dolls in a tarpot.*)

BABU

This little amusement keeps him alive,
Yankee Master.
He is especially fond of cleaning the dolls
after he has dirtied them.

(*The* OLD SPANISH SAILOR *laughs hysterically, and then smears his whole
face with tar.*)

OLD SPANISH SAILOR

My soul is white!

BABU

The yellow fever destroyed his mind.

DELANO

Let's move on. This man's brain,
as well as his face, is defiled with pitch!

BABU

He says his soul is white.

(*The structure is pushed around and
another triangular compartment appears. A* NEGRO BOY *is playing chess
against a splendid Spanish doll with
a crown on its head. He stops and
holds two empty wine bottles to his
ears*).

This boy is deaf.
The yellow fever destroyed his mind.

DELANO

Why is he holding those bottles to his
ears?

BABU

He is trying to be a rabbit,
or listening to the ocean, his mother—
who knows?

DELANO

If he's deaf, how can he hear the ocean?
Anyway, he can't hear me.
I pass, let's move on.

(*The structure is pushed around to
a third compartment. A* SPANISH

SAILOR *is holding a big armful of
rope.*)

What are you knotting there, my man?

SPANISH SAILOR

The knot.

PERKINS

So I see, but what's it for?

SPANISH SAILOR

For someone to untie. Catch!

(*Throws the knot to* DELANO.)

BABU

(*Snatching the knot from* DELANO:)

It's dirty, it will dirty your uniform.

PERKINS

Let's move on. Your entertainment
is rather lacking in invention, Babu.

BABU

We have to do what we can
We are just beginners at acting.
This next one will be better.

(*The structure is pushed around and
shows a beautiful* NEGRO WOMAN. *She
is dressed and posed as the Virgin
Mary. A Christmas crèche is arranged
around her. A* VERY WHITE SPANIARD
*dressed as Saint Joseph stands behind
her. She holds a Christ-child, the same
crowned doll, only black, the* NEGRO
BOY *was playing chess against.*)

She is the Virgin Mary. That man is not
the father.

PERKINS

I see. I suppose her son is the King of
Spain.

BABU

The Spaniards taught us everything,
there's nothing we can learn from you,
Yankee Master.
When they took away our country, they
gave us a better world.

Things do not happen in that world as
   they do here.

PERKINS
That's a very beautiful,
though unusual Virgin Mary.

BABU
Yes, the Bible says, "I am black not white."
When Don Aranda was dying,
we wanted to give him the Queen of
   Heaven
because he took away our chains.

PERKINS
The Spaniards must have taught them
   everything;
they're all mixed up, they don't even
   know their religion.

DELANO
No, no! The Catholic Church doesn't just
   teach,
it knows how to take from its converts.

BABU
Do you want to shake hands with the
   Queen of Heaven, Yankee Master?

DELANO
No, I'm not used to royalty.
Tell her I believe in freedom of religion,
if people don't take liberties.
Let's move on.

BABU

   (Kneeling to the Virgin Mary:)

I present something Your Majesty has
   never seen,
a white man who doesn't believe in taking
   liberties,
Your Majesty.

   (The structure is pushed around and
   shows ATUFAL in chains but with a
   crown on his head.)

BABU
This is the life we believe in.
Ask pardon, King Atufal!
Kiss the Spanish flag!

DELANO
Please don't ask me to shake hands with
   King Atufal!

   (The canvas is put back on the structure.)

BABU
You look tired and serious, Yankee Master.
We have to have what fun we can.
We never would have lived through the
   deadly calms
without a little amusement.

   (Bows and goes off. The NEGROES
   gradually drift away. DELANO sighs
   with relief.)

DELANO
Well, that wasn't much!
I suppose Shakespeare started that way.

PERKINS
Who cares?
I see a speck on the blue sea, Sir,
our whaleboat is coming.

DELANO
A speck? My eyes are speckled.
I seem to have been dreaming. What's
   solid?

   (Touches the ornate railing; a piece
   falls onto the deck.)

This ship is nothing, Perkins!
I dreamed someone was trying to kill me!
How could he? Jack-of-the-beach,
they used to call me on the Duxbury
   shore.
Carrying a duck-satchel in my hand, I
   used to paddle
along the waterfront from a hulk to school.
I didn't learn much there. I was always
   shooting duck
or gathering huckleberries along the marsh
   with Cousin Nat!
I like nothing better than breaking myself
   on the surf.
I used to track the seagulls down the five-
   mile stretch of beach for eggs.
How can I be killed now at the ends of
   the earth
by this insane Spaniard?

Who could want to murder Amasa Delano?
My conscience is clean. God is good.
What am I doing on board this nigger-pirate ship?

PERKINS
You're not talking like a skipper, Sir.
Our boat's a larger spot now.

DELANO
I am childish.
I am doddering and drooling into my second childhood.
God help me, nothing's solid!

PERKINS
Don Benito, Sir. Touch him,
he's as solid as his ship.

DELANO
Don Benito? He's a walking ghost!

(BENITO *comes up to* DELANO. BABU *is a few steps behind him.*)

BENITO
I am the ghost of myself, Captain.
Excuse me, I heard you talking about dreams and childhood.
I was a child, too, once, I have dreams about it.

DELANO

(*Starting:*)

I'm sorry.
This jumping's just a nervous habit.
I thought you were part of my dreams.

BENITO
I was taking my siesta,
I dreamed I was a boy back in Lima.
I was with my brothers and sisters,
and we were dressed for the festival of Corpus Christi
like people at our Bourbon court.
We were simple children, but something went wrong;
little black men came on us with beetle backs.
They had caterpillar heads and munched away on our fine clothes.
They made us lick their horned and var-nished insect legs.
Our faces turned brown from their spit,
we looked like bugs, but nothing could save our lives!

DELANO
Ha, ha, Captain. We are like two dreams meeting head on.
My whaleboat's coming,
we'll both feel better over a bottle of cider.

(BABU *blows a bosun's whistle. The gongs are sounded with descending notes. The* NEGROES *assemble in ranks.*)

BABU
It's twelve noon, Master Yankee.
Master wants his midday shave.

ALL THE NEGROES
Master wants his shave! Master wants his shave!

BENITO
Ah, yes, the razor! I have been talking too much.
You can see how badly I need a razor.
I must leave you, Captain.

BABU
No, Don Amasa wants to talk.
Come to the cabin, Don Amasa.
Don Amasa will talk, Master will listen.
Babu will lather and strop.

DELANO
I want to talk to you about navigation.
I am new to these waters.

BENITO
Doubtless, doubtless, Captain Delano.

PERKINS
I think I'll take my siesta, Sir.

(*He walks off.* BENITO, BABU, *and* DELANO *walk toward the back of the stage. A scrim curtain lifts, showing a light deck cabin that forms a sort of attic. The floor is matted, partitions that still leave splintered traces have been knocked out. To one side, a small table screwed to the floor; on it, a dirty missal; above it, a small*

*crucifix, rusty crossed muskets on one
side, rusty crossed cutlasses on the
other.* BENITO *sits down in a broken
throne-like and gilded chair.* BABU
*begins to lather. A magnificent array
of razors, bottles and other shaving
equipment lies on a table beside him.
Behind him, a hammock with a pole
in it and a dirty pillow.*)

DELANO

So this is where you took your siesta.

BENITO

Yes, Captain, I rest here when my fate
will let me.

DELANO

This seems like a sort of dormitory, sitting-
room,

sail-loft, chapel, armory, and private bedroom all together.

BENITO

Yes, Captain: events have not been favorable

to much order in my personal arrangements.

(BABU *moves back and opens a locker.
A lot of flags, torn shirts and socks
tumble out. He takes one of the flags,
shakes it with a flourish, and ties it
around* BENITO's *neck.*)

BABU

Master needs more protection.
I do everything I can to save his clothes.

DELANO

The Castle and the Lion of Spain.
Why, Don Benito, this is the flag of Spain
you're using!
It's well it's only I and not the King of
Spain who sees this!
All's one, though, I guess, in this carnival
world.
I see you like gay colors as much as Babu.

BABU

(*Giggling:*)

The bright colors draw the yellow fever
from Master's mind.

(*Raises the razor.* BENITO *begins to
shake.*)

Now, Master, now, Master!

BENITO

You are talking while you hold the razor.

BABU

You mustn't shake so, Master.
Look, Don Amasa, Master always shakes
when I shave him,
though he is braver than a lion and
stronger than a castle.
Master knows Babu has never yet drawn
blood.
I may, though, sometime, if he shakes so
much.
Now, Master!
Come, Don Amasa, talk to Master about
the gales and calms,
he'll answer and forget to shake.

DELANO

Those calms, the more I think of them
the more I wonder.
You say you were two months sailing
here;
I made that stretch in less than a week.
We never met with any calms.
If I'd not heard your story from your lips,
and seen your ruined ship,
I would have said something was missing,
I would have said this was a mystery ship.

BENITO

For some men the whole world is a mystery;
they cannot believe their senses.

(BENITO *shakes, the razor gets out of
hand and cuts his cheek.*)

Santa María!

BABU

Poor, poor Master, see, you shook so;
this is Babu's first blood.
Please answer Don Amasa, while I wipe
this ugly blood from the razor and strop
it again.

BENITO

The sea was like the final calm of the
world

On, on it went. It sat on us and drank
  our strength,
crosscurrents eased us out to sea,
the yellow fever changed our blood to
  poison.

BABU

You stood by us. Some of us stood by you!

BENITO

Yes, my Spanish crew was weak and
  surly, but the blacks,
the blacks were angels. Babu has kept
  me in this world.
I wonder what he is keeping me for?
You belong to me. I belong to you forever.

BABU

Ah, Master, spare yourself.
Forever is a very long time;
nothing's forever.

(*With great expertness, delicacy and
gentleness,* BABU *massages* BENITO's
*cheeks, shakes out the flag, pours
lotion from five bottles on* BENITO's
*hair, cleans the shaving materials, and
stands off, admiring his work.*)

Master looks just like a statue.
He's like a figurehead, Don Amasa!

(DELANO *looks, then starts to walk out,
leaving* BENITO *and* BABU. *The curtain drops upon them.* DELANO *rejoins*
PERKINS, *lounging at the rail.*)

PERKINS

Our boat is coming.

DELANO

(*Gaily*)

I know!
I don't know how I'll explain this pomp
and squalor to my own comfortable family of a crew.
Even shaving here is like a High Mass.
There's something in a Negro, something
that makes him fit to have around your
  person.
His comb and brush are castanets.

What tact Babu had!
What noiseless, gliding briskness!

PERKINS

Our boat's about alongside, Sir.

DELANO

What's more, the Negro has a sense of
  humor.
I don't mean their boorish giggling and
  teeth-showing,
I mean his easy cheerfulness in every
  glance and gesture.
You should have seen Babu toss that Spanish flag like a juggler.
and change it to a shaving napkin!

PERKINS

The boat's here, Sir.

DELANO

We need inferiors, Perkins,
more manners, more docility, no one has
  an inferior mind in America.

PERKINS

Here is your crew, Sir.

(BABU *runs out from the cabin. His
cheek is bleeding.*)

DELANO

Why, Babu, what has happened?

BABU

Master will never get better from his sick-
  ness.
His bad nerves and evil fever made him
  use me so.
I gave him one small scratch by accident,
the only time I've nicked him, Don Amasa.
He cut me with his razor. Do you think
  I will die?
I'd rather die than bleed to death!

DELANO

It's just a pinprick, Babu. You'll live.

BABU

I must attend my master.

(*Runs back into cabin*)

DELANO

Just a pinprick, but I wouldn't have

thought

Don Benito had the stuff to swing a razor.

Up north we use our fists instead of knives.

I hope Benito's not dodging around some old grindstone

in the hold, and sharpening a knife for me.

Here, Perkins, help our men up the ladder.

(*Two immaculate* AMERICAN SAILORS *appear carrying great casks of water. Two more follow carrying net baskets of wilted pumpkins. The* NEGROES *begin to crowd forward, shouting, "We want Yankee food, we want Yankee drink!"* DELANO *grandiosely holds up a pumpkin; an* OLD NEGRO *rushes forward, snatches at the pumpkin, and knocks* DELANO *off-balance into* PERKINS's *arms.* DELANO *gets up and knocks the* NEGRO *down with his fist. All is tense and quiet. The* SIX HATCHET-CLEANERS *lift their hatchets above their heads.*)

DELANO

(*Furious*)

Americans, stand by me! Stand by your captain!

(*Like lightning, the* AMERICANS *unsling their muskets, fix bayonets, and kneel with their guns pointing at the* NEGROES. BENITO *and* BABU *appear.*)

Don Benito, Sir, call your men to order!

BABU

We're starving, Yankee Master. We mean no harm;

we've never been so scared.

DELANO

You try my patience, Babu.

I am talking to Captain Cereno;

call your men to order, Sir.

BENITO

Make them laugh, Babu. The Americans aren't going to shoot.

(BABU *airily waves a hand. The* NE-GROES *smile.* DELANO *turns to* BENITO.)

You mustn't blame them too much; they're sick and hungry.

We have kept them cooped up for ages.

DELANO

(*As the* NEGROES *relax*)

Form them in lines, Perkins!

Each man shall have his share.

That's how we run things in the States

to each man equally, no matter what his claims.

NEGROES

(*Standing back, bleating like sheep:*)

Feed me, Master Yankee! Feed me, Master Yankee!

DELANO

You are much too close.

Here, Perkins, take the provisions aft.

You'll save lives by giving each as little as you can,

Be sure to keep a tally.

(FRANCESCO, *a majestic, yellow-colored mulatto, comes up to* DELANO.)

FRANCESCO

My master requests your presence at dinner, Don Amasa.

DELANO

Tell him I have indigestion.

Tell him to keep better order on his ship.

It's always the man of good will that gets hurt;

my fist still aches from hitting that old darky.

FRANCESCO

My master has his own methods of discipline

that are suitable for our unfortunate circumstances.

Will you come to dinner, Don Amasa?

DELANO

I'll come. When in Rome, do as the Ro-

mans.
Excuse my quick temper, Sir.
It's better to blow up than to smoulder.

(*The scrim curtain is raised. In the cabin, a long table loaded with silver has been laid out. The locker has been closed and the Spanish flag hangs on the wall.* DON BENITO *is seated,* BABU *stands behind him. As soon as* DELANO *sits down,* FRANCESCO *begins serving with great dignity and agility.*)

FRANCESCO
A fingerbowl, Don Amasa.

(*After each statement, he moves about the table.*)

A napkin, Don Amasa.
A glass of American water, Don Amasa.
A slice of American pumpkin, Don Amasa.
A goblet of American cider, Don Amasa.
(DELANO *drinks a great deal of cider,* BENITO *hardly touches his.*)

DELANO
This is very courtly for a sick ship, Don Benito.
The Spanish Empire will never go down, if she keeps her chin up.

BENITO
I'm afraid I shan't live long enough to enjoy your prophecy.

DELANO
I propose a toast to the Spanish Empire on which the sun never sets;
may you find her still standing, when you land, Sir!

BENITO
Our Empire has lasted three hundred years,
I suppose she will last another month.
I wish I could say the same for myself.
My sun is setting,
I hear the voices of the dead in this calm.

DELANO
You hear the wind lifting;
it's bringing our two vessels together.

We are going to take you into port, Don Benito.

BENITO
You are either too late or too early with your good works.
Our yellow fever may break out again.
You aren't going to put your men in danger, Don Amasa?

DELANO
My boys are all healthy, Sir.

BENITO
Health isn't God, I wouldn't trust it.

FRANCESCO
May I fill your glass, Don Amasa?

BABU
New wine in new bottles,
that's the American spirit, Yankee Master.
They say all men are created equal in North America.

DELANO
We prefer merit to birth, boy.

(BABU *motions imperiously for* FRANCESCO *to leave. As he goes, bowing to the* CAPTAINS, FOUR NEGROES *play the* "*Marseillaise.*")

Why are they playing the "Marseillaise"?

BABU
His uncle is supposed to have been in the French Convention,
and voted for the death of the French King.

DELANO
This polite and royal fellow is no anarchist!

BABU
Francesco is very *ancien regime*,
he is even frightened of the Americans.
He doesn't like the way you treated King George.
Babu is more liberal.

DELANO
A royal fellow,
this usher of yours, Don Benito!

He is as yellow as a goldenrod.
He is a king, a king of kind hearts.
What a pleasant voice he has!

BENITO

(*Glumly*)

Francesco is a good man.

DELANO

As long as you've known him,
he's been a worthy fellow, hasn't he?
Tell me, I am particularly curious to
know.

BENITO

Francesco is a good man.

DELANO

I'm glad to hear it, I am glad to hear it!
You refute the saying of a planter friend
of mine.
He said, "When a mulatto has a regular
European face,
look out for him, he is a devil."

BENITO

I've heard your planter's remark applied
to intermixtures of Spaniards and Indians;
I know nothing about mulattoes.

DELANO

No, no, my friend's refuted;
if we're so proud of our white blood,
surely a little added to the blacks improves
their breed.
I congratulate you on your servants, Sir.

BABU

We've heard that Jefferson, the King of
your Republic,
would like to free his slaves.

DELANO

Jefferson has read too many books, boy,
but you can trust him. He's a gentleman
and an American!
He's not lifting a finger to free his slaves.

BABU

We hear you have a new capital modelled
on Paris,
and that your President is going to set up
a guillotine on the Capitol steps.

DELANO

Oh, Paris! I told you you could trust Mr.
Jefferson, boy,
he stands for law and order like your mulatto.
Have you been to Paris, Don Benito?

BENITO

I'm afraid I'm just a provincial Spaniard,
Captain.

DELANO

Let me tell you about Paris.
You know what French women are like—
nine parts sex and one part logic.
Well, one of them in Paris heard
that my ship was the *President Adams*.
She said,
"You are descended from Adam, Captain,
you must know everything,
tell me how Adam and Eve learned to
sleep together."
Do you know what I said?

BENITO

No, Captain.

DELANO

I said, "I guess Eve was a Frenchwoman,
the first Frenchwoman."
Do you know what she answered?

BENITO

No, Captain Delano.

DELANO

She said, "I was trying to provoke a philosophical discussion, Sir."
A philosophical discussion, ha, ha!
You look serious, Sir. You know, something troubles me.

BENITO

Something troubles you, Captain Delano?

DELANO

I still can't understand those calms,
but let that go. The scurvy,
why did it kill off three Spaniards in
every four,
and only half the blacks?
Negroes are human, but surely you
couldn't have favored them
before your own flesh and blood!

BENITO
This is like the Inquisition, Captain Delano.
I have done the best I could.

(BABU *dabs* BENITO's *forehead with cider*.)

BABU
Poor, poor Master; since Don Aranda died,
he trusts no one except Babu.

DELANO
Your Babu is an uncommonly intelligent fellow;
you are right to trust him, Sir.
Sometimes I think we overdo our talk of freedom.
If you looked into our hearts, we all want slaves.

BENITO
Disease is a mysterious thing;
it takes one man, and leaves his friend.
Only the unfortunate can understand misfortune.

DELANO
I must return to my bosun;
he's pretty green to be left alone here.
Before I go I want to propose a last toast to you!
A good master deserves good servants!

(*He gets up. As he walks back to* PERKINS, *the scrim curtain falls, concealing* BENITO *and* BABU.)

That captain must have jaundice,
I wish he kept better order.
I don't like hitting menials.

PERKINS
I've done some looking around, Sir. I've used my eyes.

DELANO
That's what they're for, I guess. You have to watch your step,
this hulk, this rotten piece of finery,
will fall apart. This old world needs new blood
and Yankee gunnery to hold it up.
You shouldn't mess around, though, it's their ship;

you're breaking all the laws of the sea.

PERKINS
Do you see that man-shaped thing in canvas?

DELANO
I see it.

PERKINS
Behind the cloth, there's a real skeleton,
a man dressed up like Don Benito.

DELANO
They're Catholics, and worship bones.

PERKINS
There's writing on its coat. It says,
"I am Don Aranda," and, "Follow your leader."

DELANO
Follow your leader?

PERKINS
I saw two blacks unfurling a flag,
a black skull and crossbones on white silk.

DELANO
That's piracy. We've been ordered
to sink any ship that flies that flag.
Perhaps they were playing.

PERKINS
I saw King Atufal throw away his chains,
He called for food, the Spaniards served him two pieces of pumpkin,
and a whole bottle of your cider.

DELANO
Don Benito has the only key to Atufal's padlock.
My cider was for the captain's table.

PERKINS
Atufal pointed to the cabin where you were dining,
and drew a finger across his throat.

DELANO
Who could want to kill Amasa Delano?

PERKINS
I warned our men to be ready for an emergency.

DELANO

You're a mindreader,
I couldn't have said better myself;
but we're at peace with Spain.

PERKINS

I told them to return with loaded muskets
and fixed bayonets.

DELANO

Here comes Benito. Watch how I'll humor
    him
and sound him out.

(BABU *brings out* BENITO'*s chair.*
BENITO *sits in it.*)

It's good to have you back on deck, Cap-
    tain.
Feel the breeze! It holds and will increase.
My ship is moving nearer. Soon we will
    be together.
We have seen you through your troubles.

BENITO

Remember, I warned you about the yellow
    fever.
I am surprised you haven't felt afraid.

DELANO

Oh, that will blow away.
Everything is going to go better and
    better;
the wind's increasing, soon you'll have no
    cares.
After the long voyage, the anchor drops
    into the harbor.
It's a great weight lifted from the cap-
    tain's heart.
We are getting to be friends, Don Benito.
My ship's in sight, the *President Adams!*
How the wind braces a man up!
I have a small invitation to issue to you.

BENITO

An invitation?

DELANO

I want you to take a cup of coffee
with me on my quarterdeck tonight.
The Sultan of Turkey never tasted such
    coffee
as my old steward makes. What do you
    say, Don Benito?

BENITO

I cannot leave my ship.

DELANO

Come, come, you need a change of cli-
    mate.
The sky is suddenly blue, Sir,
my coffee will make a man of you.

BENITO

I cannot leave my ship.
Even now, I don't think you understand
    my position here.

DELANO

I want to speak to you alone.

BENITO

I am alone, as much as I ever am.

DELANO

In America, we don't talk about money
in front of servants and children.

BENITO

Babu is not my servant.
You spoke of money—since the yellow
    fever,
he has had a better head for figures than
    I have.

DELANO

You embarrass me, Captain,
but since circumstances are rather special
    here,
I will proceed.

BENITO

Babu takes an interest in all our expenses.

DELANO

Yes, I am going to talk to you about your
    expenses.
I am responsible to my owners for all
the sails, ropes, food and carpentry I give
    you.
You will need a complete rerigging, almost
    a new ship, in fact,
You shall have our services at cost.

BENITO

I know, you are a merchant.
I suppose I ought to pay you for our lives.

DELANO

I envy you, Captain. You are the only owner
of the *San Domingo*, since Don Aranda died.
I am just an employee. Our owners would sack me,
if I followed my better instincts.

BENITO

You can give your figures to Babu, Captain.

DELANO

You are very offhand about money, Sir;
I don't think you realize the damage that has been done to your ship.
Ah, you smile. I'm glad you're loosening up.
Look, the water gurgles merrily, the wind is high,
a mild light is shining. I sometimes think
such a tropical light as this must have shone
on the tents of Abraham and Isaac.
It seems as if Providence were watching over us.

PERKINS

There are things that need explaining here, Sir.

DELANO

Yes, Captain, Perkins saw some of your men
unfurling an unlawful flag,
a black skull and crossbones.

BENITO

You know my only flag is the Lion and Castle of Spain.

DELANO

No, Perkins says he saw a skull and crossbones.
That's piracy. I trust Perkins.
You've heard about how my government blew
the bowels out of the pirates at Tripoli?

BENITO

Perhaps my Negroes . . .

DELANO

My government doesn't intend

to let you play at piracy!

BENITO

Perhaps my Negroes were playing.
When you take away their chains . . .

DELANO

I'll see that you are all put back in chains,
if you start playing pirates!

PERKINS

There's something else he can explain, Sir.

DELANO

Yes, Perkins saw Atufal throw off his chains
and order dinner.

BABU

Master has the key, Yankee Master.

BENITO

I have the key.
You can't imagine how my position exhausts me, Captain.

DELANO

I can imagine. Atufal's chains are fakes.
You and he are in cahoots, Sir!

PERKINS

They don't intend to pay for our sails and service.
They think America is Santa Claus.

DELANO

The United States are death on pirates and debtors.

PERKINS

There's one more thing for him to explain, Sir.

DELANO

Do you see that man-shaped thing covered with black cloth, Don Benito?

BENITO

I always see it.

DELANO

Take away the cloth. I order you to take away the cloth!

BENITO

I cannot. Oh, Santa María, have mercy!

DELANO

Of course, you can't. It's no Virgin Mary.
You have done something terrible to your
  friend, Don Aranda.
Take away the cloth, Perkins!

(*As* PERKINS *moves forward,* ATUFAL
*suddenly stands chainless and with
folded arms, blocking his way.*)

BABU

(*Dancing up and down and beside
himself*)

Let them see it! Let them see it!
I can't stand any more of their insolence;
the Americans treat us like their slaves!

(BABU *and* PERKINS *meet at the man-
shaped object and start pulling away
the cloth.* BENITO *rushes between them,
and throws them back and sprawling
on the deck.* BABU *and* PERKINS *rise,
and stand hunched like wrestlers,
about to close in on* BENITO, *who draws
his sword with a great gesture. It is
only a hilt. He runs at* BABU *and
knocks him down.* ATUFAL *throws
aside his chains and signals to the*
HATCHET-CLEANERS. *They stand behind*
BENITO *with raised hatchets. The*
NEGROES *shout ironically,* "Evviva
Benito!")

You too, Yankee Captain!
If you shoot, we'll kill you.

DELANO

If a single American life is lost,
I will send this ship to the bottom,
and all Peru after it.
Do you hear me, Don Benito?

BENITO

Don't you understand? I am as powerless
as you are!

BABU

He is as powerless as you are.

BENITO

Don't you understand? He has been holding a knife at my back.
I have been talking all day to save your
  life.

BABU

(*Holding a whip:*)

Do you see this whip? When Don Aranda
  was out of temper,
he used to snap pieces of flesh off us with
  it.
Now I hold the whip.
When I snap it, Don Benito jumps!

(*Snaps the whip.* DON BENITO *flinches.*)

DELANO

(*Beginning to understand*)

It's easy to terrorize the defenseless.

BABU

That's what we thought when Don
Aranda held the whip.

DELANO

You'll find I am made of tougher stuff
than your Spaniards.

ATUFAL

We want to kill you.

NEGROES

We want to kill you, Yankee Captain.

DELANO

Who could want to kill Amasa Delano?

BABU

Of course. We want to keep you alive.
We want you to sail us back to Africa.
Has anyone told you how much you are
worth, Captain?

DELANO

I have another course in mind.

BENITO

Yes, there's another course if you don't
  like Africa, there's another course.
King Atufal, show the Yankee captain

the crew that took the other course!

(*Three dead* SPANISH SAILORS *are brought onstage.*)

ATUFAL
Look at Don Aranda?

BABU
Yes, you are hot-tempered and discourteous, Captain.
I am going to introduce you to Don Aranda.
You have a new command, Captain. You must meet your new owner.

(*The black cloth is taken from the man-shaped object and shows a chalk-white skeleton dressed like* DON BENITO.)

Don Amasa, Don Aranda!
You can see that Don Aranda was a white man like you,
because his bones are white.

NEGROES
He is a white because his bones are white!
He is a white because his bones are white!

ATUFAL

(*Pointing to the ribbon on the skeleton's chest:*)

Do you see that ribbon?
It says, "Follow the leader."
We wrote it in his blood.

BABU
He was a white man
even though his blood was red as ours.

NEGROES
He is white because his bones are white!

BABU
Don Aranda is our figurehead,
we are going to chain him to the bow of our ship
to scare off devils.

ATUFAL
This is the day of Jubilee,
I am raising the flag of freedom!

NEGROES
Freedom! Freedom! Freedom!

(*The black skull and crossbones is raised on two poles. The* NEGROES *form two lines, leading up to the flag, and leave an aisle. Each man is armed with some sort of weapon.*)

BABU
Spread out the Spanish flag!

(*The Lion and Castle of Spain is spread out on the deck in front of the skull and crossbones.*)

The Spanish flag is the road to freedom.
Don Benito mustn't hurt his white feet on the splinters.

(*Kneeling in front of* BENITO:)

Your foot, Master!

(BENITO *holds out his foot.* BABU *takes off* BENITO's *shoes.*)

Give Don Benito back his sword!

(*The sword-hilt is fastened back in* BENITO's *scabbard.*)

Load him with chains!

(*Two heavy chains are draped on* BENITO's *neck. The cane and ball are handed to him.*)

Former Captain Benito Cereno, kneel!
Ask pardon of man!

BENITO

(*Kneeling*)

I ask pardon for having been born a Spaniard.
I ask pardon for having enslaved my fellow man.

BABU
Strike off the oppressor's chain!

(*One of* BENITO's *chains is knocked off, then handed to* ATUFAL, *who dashes it to the deck.*)

Former Captain Benito Cereno,
you must kiss the flag of freedom.

    (*Points to* DON ARANDA:)

Kiss the mouth of the skull!

    (BENITO *walks barefoot over the Spanish flag and kisses the mouth of* DON ARANDA.)

NEGROES
Evviva Benito! *Evviva* Benito!

    (*Sounds are heard from* PERKINS, *whose head has been covered with the sack.*)

ATUFAL
The bosun wants to kiss the mouth of freedom.

BABU
March over the Spanish flag, Bosun.

    (PERKINS *starts forward.*)

DELANO
You are dishonoring your nation, Perkins!
Don't you stand for anything?

PERKINS
I only have one life, Sir.

    (*Walks over the Spanish flag and kisses the mouth of the skull.*)

NEGROES
Evviva Bosun! *Evviva* Bosun!

DELANO
You are no longer an American, Perkins!

BABU
He was free to choose freedom, Captain.

ATUFAL
Captain Delano wants to kiss the mouth of freedom.

BABU
He is jealous of the bosun.

ATUFAL
In the United States, all men are created equal.

BABU
Don't you want to kiss the mouth of freedom, Captain?

DELANO
    (*Lifting his pocket and pointing the pistol:*)

Do you see what I have in my hand?

BABU
A pistol.

DELANO
I am unable to miss at this distance.

BABU
You must take your time, Yankee Master.
You must take your time.

DELANO
I am unable to miss.

BABU
You can stand there like a block of wood
as long as you want to, Yankee Master.
You will drop asleep, then we will tie you up,
and make you sail us back to Africa.

    (*General laughter. Suddenly, there's a roar of gunfire. Several* NEGROES, *mostly women, fall.* AMERICAN SEAMEN *in spotless blue and white throw themselves in a lying position on deck.* MORE *kneel above them, then* MORE *stand above these. All have muskets and fixed bayonets. The First Row fires. More* NEGROES *fall. They start to retreat. The Second Row fires. More* NEGROES *fall. They retreat further. The Third Row fires. The Three* AMERICAN LINES *march forward, but all the* NEGROES *are either dead or in retreat.* DON BENITO *has been wounded. He staggers over to* DELANO *and shakes his hand.*)

BENITO
You have saved my life.

I thank you for my life.

DELANO
A man can only do what he can,
We have saved American lives.

PERKINS

(*Pointing to* ATUFAL's *body:*)

We have killed King Atufal,
we have killed their ringleader.

(BABU *jumps up. He is unwounded.*)

BABU
I was the King. Babu, not Atufal,
was the king, who planned, dared and carried out
the seizure of this ship, the *San Domingo*.
Untouched by blood myself, I had all
the most dangerous and useless Spaniards
killed.
I freed my people from their Egyptian
bondage.
The heartless Spaniards slaved for me like
slaves.

(BABU *steps back, and quickly picks
up a crown from the litter.*)

This is my crown.

(*Puts crown on his head. He snatches*
BENITO's *rattan cane.*)

This is my rod.

(*Picks up silver ball.*)

This is the earth.

(*Holds the ball out with one hand
and raises the cane.*)

This is the arm of the angry God.

(*Smashes the ball.*)

PERKINS
Let him surrender. Let him surrender.
We want to save someone.

BENITO
My God how little these people understand!

BABU

(*Holding a white handkerchief and
raising both his hands:*)

Yankee Master understand me. The future
is with us.

DELANO

(*Raising his pistol:*)

This is your future.

(BABU *falls and lies still.* DELANO
*pauses, then slowly empties the five
remaining barrels of his pistol into
the body. Lights dim.*)

CURTAIN

FIDDLER ON THE ROOF

Joseph Stein

Based on Sholom Aleichem's Stories
Presented by Harold Prince at the Imperial Theatre, New York City, on September 22, 1964, with the following cast:

TEVYE, *a dairyman* Zero Mostel
GOLDE, *his wife* Maria Karnilova
TZEITEL ⎫
HODEL ⎪
CHAVA ⎬ *their daughters* ⎰ Joanna Merlin
SHPRINTZE ⎪ ⎱ Julia Migenes
BIELKE ⎭ Tanya Everett
Marilyn Rogers
Linda Ross
YENTE, *a matchmaker* Beatrice Arthur
MOTEL KAMZOIL, *a tailor* Austin Pendleton
SHANDEL, *his mother* Helen Verbit
PERCHIK, *a student* Bert Convy
LAZAR WOLF, *a butcher* Michael Granger
MORDCHA, *an innkeeper* Zvee Scooler
RABBI Gluck Sandor
MENDEL, *his son* Leonard Frey
AVRAM, *a bookseller* Paul Lipson
NAHUM, *a beggar* Maurice Edwards
GRANDMA TZEITEL, *Golde's grandmother*
Sue Babel

FRUMA-SARAH, *Lazar Wolf's first wife*
Carol Sawyer
YUSSEL, *a hatter* Mitch Thomas
CONSTABLE Joseph Sullivan
FYEDKA, *a young man* Joe Ponazecki
SASHA, *his friend* Robert Berdeen
THE FIDDLER Gino Conforti
VILLAGERS Tom Abbott, John C. Attle, Sue Babel, Sammy Bayes, Robert Berdeen, Lorenzo Bianco, Duane Bodin, Robert Currie, Sarah Felcher, Tony Gardell, Louis Genevrino, Ross Gifford, Dan Jasin, Sandra Kazan, Thom Koutsoukos, Sharon Lerit, Sylvia Mann, Peff Modelski, Irene Paris, Charles Rule, Carol Sawyer, Roberta Senn, Mitch Thomas, Helen Verbit

Music by Jerry Bock
Lyrics by Sheldon Harnick
Entire production directed and choreographed by Jerome Robbins
Settings by Boris Aronson
Costumes by Patricia Zipprodt
Lighting by Jean Rosenthal
Orchestrations by Don Walker
Musical Direction and Vocal Arrangements by Milton Greene
Dance Music arranged by Betty Walberg
Production Stage Manager, Ruth Mitchell

© 1964 by Joseph Stein
Music and Lyrics © 1964 by Sunbeam Music Corp.
Produced by special permission of the Estate of Olga Rabinowitz, Arnold Perl,
and Crown Publishers, Inc.

CAUTION: Professionals and amateurs are hereby warned that *Fiddler on the Roof* is fully
protected by the laws of copyright and is subject to royalty. All rights, including professional,
amateur, motion picture, recitation, lecturing, public reading, radio and television
broadcasting, the rights of translation into foreign languages, and quotation are strictly
reserved. No part of this work may be used in any way without the written consent of the
copyright holders. All inquiries concerning rights in the book should be addressed to
the William Morris Agency, 1740 Broadway, New York, N.Y. 10019, and all inquiries
concerning rights in the music and lyrics should be addressed to the Sunbeam Music Corp.,
22 West 48th Street, New York, N.Y. 10036.

A MUSICAL is always an act of collaboration, like a film or a ballet, rather than the product of one, or perhaps two, men. Also, by and large, the musical is more of a musical form than a literary form. There have been examples of musicals winning the Pulitzer Prize (*Of Thee I Sing* by George and Ira Gershwin was one), but normally people leave a musical humming the tunes rather than pondering on the story.

Another songwriting team to win a Pulitzer, however, was that of Jerry Bock (the music) and Sheldon Harnick (the lyrics), who achieved the distinction in 1959 with their smash-hit musical *Fiorello!* A few years after this they had the idea of basing a musical on the stories of the great Yiddish writer, Sholom Aleichem. They turned to the playwright Joseph Stein to provide the book, as they had worked with him on an earlier musical, *The Body Beautiful.*

It was Stein's task to adapt the Yiddish humor of Sholom Aleichem and his great character Tevye the milkman, and make it acceptable to a Broadway audience. This he undoubtedly achieved although admirers of the original Sholom Aleichem stories—most of the incidents here are taken from the book *Tevye's Daughters*—have occasionally suggested that the musical is a vulgarization of the original. But of course such objections are always raised when literature is used as a basis for a musical play—I have no doubt that Charles Gounod was more than once informed that *Faust* was a vulgarization of Goethe. What matters is not what has been lost, but what has been retained, and what has been created out of that.

Bock, Harnick, and Stein were not the only creative minds on this musical that came to be known as *Fiddler on the Roof.* Although he had no special creative function, the director and choreographer Jerome Robbins played a vital part in the shaping of the show.

It was Robbins, helped by the scenery of Boris Aronson and the costumes of Patricia Zipprodt, who was largely responsible for providing the musical with its remarkable ethnic atmosphere, and for re-creating the feeling of the small Russian village of Anatevka, where the musical is set.

Perhaps the most interesting aspect of *Fiddler on the Roof* was its lack of familiar commercial attributes. Here was a musical not only without its chorus line of pretty girls, but a musical stained with genuine tragedy, and ending on a note, at best, no more cheerful than pathos.

Yet there is real feeling here. Tevye's hot line to God, which he never ceases to use, his passion and humanity, his relationship with his daughters, and, most of all perhaps, his compassion and understanding for the world around him make him the most unforgettable character in the modern musical theatre.

Stein has done his work very smoothly and adroitly, but so too has Harnick. The lyrics are an integral part with the book, they both carry the action forward, and they go together with Bock's music to give the piece its authentic Yiddish feel. For example, how neat it is for the lyrics to introduce a Yiddish word, such as l'chaim or mazeltov, but in the same musical phrase also to provide it with its translation.

Fiddler on the Roof has shown—as did in a less original context the Shavian adaptation *My Fair Lady*—that a musical comedy can be possessed of marked literary value. It is revealing perhaps that this is the only musical to be included in this "crème de la crème," as Miss Jean Brodie would have said in her prime, of the American theatre. It is also ironic that *Fiddler* did not become the sixth musical in history to win a Pulitzer Prize. That is life, as Tevye would be the first to recognize.

C. B.

401

ACT ONE

THE PLACE: Anatevka, a village in Russia.
THE TIME: 1905, on the eve of the revolutionary period.

PROLOGUE

The exterior of TEVYE'S *house. A* FIDDLER *is seated on the roof, playing.* TEVYE *is outside the house.*

————

TEVYE. A fiddler on the roof. Sounds crazy, no? But in our little village of Anatevka, you might say everyone of us is a fiddler on the roof, trying to scratch out a pleasant, simple tune without breaking his neck. It isn't easy. You may ask, why do we stay up here if it's so dangerous? We stay because Anatevka is our home. And how do we keep our balance? That I can tell you in a word—tradition!
    VILLAGERS (*enter, singing*).
    Tradition, tradition—Tradition.
    Tradition, tradition—Tradition.

TEVYE. Because of our traditions, we've kept our balance for many, many years. Here in Anatevka we have traditions for everything—how to eat, how to sleep, how to wear clothes. For instance, we always keep our heads covered and always wear a little prayer shawl. This shows our constant devotion to God. You may ask, how did this tradition start? I'll tell you—I don't know! But it's a tradition. Because of our traditions, everyone knows who he is and what God expects him to do.
    TEVYE *and* PAPAS *sing:*
        ["Tradition"]

Who, day and night,
Must scramble for a living,
Feed a wife and children,
Say his daily prayers?
And who has the right,
As master of the house,
To have the final word at home?
    ALL.
    The papa, the papa—Tradition.
    The papa, the papa—Tradition.
    GOLDE *and* MAMAS.
    Who must know the way to make
        a proper home,
    A quiet home, a kosher home?
    Who must raise a family and run
        the home

So Papa's free to read the Holy
    Book?
ALL.
The mama, the mama—Tradition.
The mama, the mama—Tradition.
SONS.
At three I started Hebrew school,
At ten I learned a trade.
I hear they picked a bride for me.
I hope she's pretty.
ALL.
The sons, the sons—Tradition.
The sons, the sons—Tradition.
DAUGHTERS.
And who does Mama teach
To mend and tend and fix,
Preparing me to marry
Whoever Papa picks?
ALL.
The daughters, the daughters—
    Tradition.
The daughters, the daughters—
    Tradition.
(*They repeat the song as a round.*)
PAPAS.
The papas.
MAMAS.
The mamas.
SONS.
The sons.
DAUGHTERS.
The daughters.
ALL.
Tradition.
PAPAS.
The papas.
MAMAS.
The mamas.
SONS.
The sons.
DAUGHTERS.
The daughters.
ALL.
Tradition.
TEVYE. And in the circle of our little village, we have always had our special types. For instance, Yente, the matchmaker . . .
YENTE. Avram, I have a perfect match for your son. A wonderful girl.
AVRAM. Who is it?
YENTE. Ruchel, the shoemaker's daughter.
AVRAM. Ruchel? But she can hardly see. She's almost blind.

YENTE. Tell the truth, Avram, is your son so much to look at? The way she sees and the way he looks, it's a perfect match.

(*All dance.*)

TEVYE. And Reb Nahum, the beggar . . .

NAHUM. Alms for the poor, alms for the poor.

LAZAR. Here, Reb Nahum, is one kopek.

NAHUM. One kopek? Last week you gave me two kopeks.

LAZAR. I had a bad week.

NAHUM. So if you had a bad week, why should I suffer?

(*All dance.*)

TEVYE. And, most important, our beloved rabbi . . .

MENDEL. Rabbi, may I ask you a question?

RABBI. Certainly, my son.

MENDEL. Is there a proper blessing for the Tsar?

RABBI. A blessing for the Tsar? Of course. May God bless and keep the Tsar —far away from us!

(*All dance.*)

TEVYE. Then, there are the others in our village. They make a much bigger circle.

(*The* PRIEST, *the* CONSTABLE, *and other* RUSSIANS *cross the stage. The two groups nod to each other.*)

TEVYE. His Honor the Constable, his Honor the Priest, and his Honor—many others. We don't bother them, and, so far, they don't bother us. And among ourselves we get along perfectly well. Of course, there was the time (*pointing to the* TWO MEN) when he sold him a horse and he delivered a mule, but that's all settled now. Now we live in simple peace and harmony and—

(*The* TWO MEN *begin an argument, which is taken up by the entire group.*)

FIRST MAN. It was a horse.

SECOND MAN. It was a mule.

FIRST MAN. It was a horse!

SECOND MAN. It was a mule, I tell you!

VILLAGERS. Horse!

VILLAGERS. Mule!

VILLAGERS. Horse!

VILLAGERS. Mule!

VILLAGERS. Horse!

VILLAGERS. Mule!

VILLAGERS. Horse!

VILLAGERS. Mule!

EVERYONE.

Tradition, tradition—Tradition.
Tradition, tradition—Tradition.

TEVYE (*quieting them*). Tradition. Without our traditions, our lives would be as shaky as—as a fiddler on the roof!

(*The* VILLAGERS *exit, and the house opens to show its interior.*)

SCENE ONE

The kitchen of TEVYE's *house.* GOLDE, TZEITEL, *and* HODEL *are preparing for the Sabbath.* SHPRINTZE *and* BIELKE *enter from outside, carrying logs.*

SHPRINTZE. Mama, where should we put these?

GOLDE. Put them on my head! By the stove, foolish girl. Where is Chava?

HODEL. She's in the barn, milking.

BIELKE. When will Papa be home?

GOLDE. It's almost Sabbath and he worries a lot when he'll be home! All day long riding on top of his wagon like a prince.

TZEITEL. Mama, you know that Papa works hard.

GOLDE. His horse works harder! And you don't have to defend your papa to me. I know him a little longer than you. He could drive a person crazy. (*Under her breath.*) He should only live and be well. (*Out loud.*) Shprintze, bring me some more potatoes.

(CHAVA *enters, carrying a basket, with a book under her apron.*) Chava, did you finish milking?

CHAVA. Yes, Mama. (*She drops the book.*)

GOLDE. You were reading again? Why does a girl have to read? Will it get her a better husband? Here. (*Hands* CHAVA *the book.*)

(CHAVA *exits into the house.* SHPRINTZE *enters with a basket of potatoes.*)

SHPRINTZE. Mama, Yente's coming. She's down the road.

HODEL. Maybe she's finally found a good match for you, Tzeitel.

GOLDE. From your mouth to God's ears.

TZEITEL. Why does she have to come now? It's almost Sabbath.

GOLDE. Go finish in the barn. I want to talk to Yente alone.

SHPRINTZE. Mama, can I go out and play?

GOLDE. You have feet? Go.

BIELKE. Can I go too?

GOLDE. Go too.

(SHPRINTZE *and* BIELKE *exit.*)

TZEITEL. But Mama, the men she finds. The last one was so old and he was bald. He had no hair.

GOLDE. A poor girl without a dowry can't be so particular. You want hair, marry a monkey.

TZEITEL. After all, Mama, I'm not yet twenty years old, and—

GOLDE. Shah! (*Spits between her fingers.*) Do you have to boast about your age? Do you want to tempt the Evil Eye? Inside.

(TZEITEL. *leaves the kitchen as* YENTE *enters from outside.*)

YENTE. Golde darling, I had to see you because I have such news for you. And not just every-day-in-the-week news—once-in-a-lifetime news. And where are your daughters? Outside, no? Good. Such diamonds, such jewels. You'll see, Golde, I'll find every one of them a husband. But you shouldn't be so picky. Even the worst husband, God forbid, is better than no husband, God forbid. And who should know better than me? Ever since my husband died I've been a poor widow, alone, nobody to talk to, nothing to say to anyone. It's no life. All I do at night is think of him, and even thinking of him gives me no pleasure, because you know as well as I, he was not much of a person. Never made a living, everything he touched turned to mud, but better than nothing.

MOTEL (*entering*). Good evening. Is Tzeitel in the house?

GOLDE. But she's busy. You can come back later.

MOTEL. There's something I'd like to tell her.

GOLDE. Later.

TZEITEL (*entering*). Oh, Motel, I thought I heard you.

GOLDE. Finish what you were doing. (TZEITEL *goes out. To* MOTEL.) I said later.

MOTEL (*exiting*). All right!

YENTE. What does that poor little tailor, Motel, want with Tzeitel?

GOLDE. They have been friends since they were babies together. They talk, they play . . .

YENTE (*suspiciously*). They play? What do they play?

GOLDE. Who knows? They're just children.

YENTE. From such children, come other children.

GOLDE. Motel, he's a nothing. Yente, you said—

YENTE. Ah, children, children! They are your blessing in your old age. But my Aaron, may he rest in peace, couldn't give me children. Believe me, he was good as gold, never raised his voice to me, but otherwise he was not much of a man, so what good is it if he never raised his voice? But what's the use complaining. Other women enjoy complaining, but not Yente. Not every woman in the world is a Yente. Well, I must prepare my poor Sabbath table, so good-bye, Golde, and it was a pleasure taking our hearts out to each other. (*She starts to exit.*)

GOLDE. Yente, you said you had news for me.

YENTE (*returning*). Oh, I'm losing my head. One day it will fall off altogether, and a horse will kick it into the mud, and good-bye, Yente. Of course, the news. It's about Lazar Wolf, the butcher. A good man, a fine man. And I don't have to tell you that he's well off. But he's lonely, the poor man. After all, a widower . . . You understand? Of course you do. To make it short, out of the whole town, he's cast his eye on Tzeitel.

GOLDE. My Tzeitel?

YENTE. No, the Tsar's Tzeitel! Of course your Tzeitel.

GOLDE. Such a match, for my Tzeitel. But Tevye wants a learned man. He doesn't like Lazar.

YENTE. Fine. So he won't marry him. Lazar wants the daughter, not the father. Listen to me, Golde, send Tevye to him. Don't tell him what it's about. Let Lazar discuss it himself. He'll win him over. He's a good man, a wealthy man—true? Of course true! So you'll tell me how it went, and you don't have to thank me, Golde, because aside from my fee—which anyway Lazar will pay—it gives me satisfaction to make people happy—what better satisfaction is there? So good-bye, Golde, and you're welcome.

(*She goes out. Enter* TZEITEL.)

TZEITEL. What did she want, Mama?

GOLDE. When I want you to know, I'll tell you. Finish washing the floor.

(*She exits.* HODEL *and* CHAVA *enter with wash mop and bucket.*)

HODEL. I wonder if Yente found a husband for you?

TZEITEL. I'm not anxious for Yente to find me a husband.

CHAVA (*teasing*). Not unless it's Motel, the tailor.

TZEITEL. I didn't ask you.

HODEL. Tzeitel, you're the oldest. They have to make a match for you before they can make one for me.

CHAVA. And then after her, one for me.

HODEL. So if Yente brings—

TZEITEL. Oh, Yente! Yente!

HODEL. Well, somebody has to arrange the matches. Young people can't decide these things for themselves.

CHAVA. She might bring someone wonderful—

HODEL. Someone interesting—

CHAVA. And well off—

HODEL. And important—

["Matchmaker, Matchmaker"]

Matchmaker, Matchmaker,
Make me a match,
Find me a catch.
Catch me a catch.
Matchmaker, Matchmaker,
Look through your book
And make me a perfect match.

CHAVA.
Matchmaker, Matchmaker,
I'll bring the veil,
You bring the groom,
Slender and pale.
Bring me a ring for I'm longing
    to be
The envy of all I see.

HODEL.
For Papa,
Make him a scholar.

CHAVA.
For Mama,
Make him rich as a king.

CHAVA *and* HODEL.
For me, well,
I wouldn't holler
If he were as handsome as any-
    thing.
Matchmaker, Matchmaker,
Make me a match,
Find me a find,
Catch me a catch.
Night after night in the dark I'm
    alone,
So find me a match
Of my own.

TZEITEL. Since when are you interested in a match, Chava? I thought you just had your eye on your books. (HODEL *chuckles*.) And you have your eye on the rabbi's son.

HODEL. Why not? We only have one rabbi and he only has one son. Why shouldn't I want the best?

TZEITEL. Because you're a girl from a poor family. So whatever Yente brings, you'll take. Right? Of course right. (*Sings.*)
Hodel, oh Hodel,
Have I made a match for you!
He's handsome, he's young!
All right, he's sixty-two,
But he's a nice man, a good catch
    —true? True.
I promise you'll be happy.
And even if you're not,
There's more to life than that—
Don't ask me what.
Chava, I found him.
Will you be a lucky bride!
He's handsome, he's tall—
That is, from side to side.
But he's a nice man, a good catch
    —right? Right.
You heard he has a temper.
He'll beat you every night,
But only when he's sober,
So you're all right.
Did you think you'd get a prince?
Well, I do the best I can.
With no dowry, no money, no
    family background
Be glad you got a man.

CHAVA.
Matchmaker, Matchmaker,
You know that I'm
Still very young.
Please, take your time.

HODEL.
Up to this minute
I misunderstood
That I could get stuck for good.

CHAVA *and* HODEL.
Dear Yente,
See that he's gentle.
Remember,
You were also a bride.
It's not that
I'm sentimental.

CHAVA, HODEL, *and* TZEITEL.
It's just that I'm terrified!
Matchmaker, Matchmaker,
Plan me no plans,
I'm in no rush.

Maybe I've learned
Playing with matches
A girl can get burned.
So,
Bring me no ring,
Groom me no groom,
Find me no find,
Catch me no catch,
Unless he's a matchless match.

Scene Two

The exterior of TEVYE'*s house.* TEVYE
*enters, pulling his cart. He stops, and sits
on the wagon seat, exhausted.*

TEVYE. Today I am a horse. Dear God,
did you have to make my poor old horse
lose his shoe just before the Sabbath? That
wasn't nice. It's enough you pick on me,
Tevye, bless me with five daughters, a life
of poverty. What have you got against my
horse? Sometimes I think when things are
too quiet up there, You say to Yourself:
"Let's see, what kind of mischief can I
play on my friend Tevye?"
GOLDE (*entering from house*). You're
finally here, my breadwinner.
TEVYE (*to heaven*). I'll talk to You later.
GOLDE. Where's your horse?
TEVYE. He was invited to the black-
smith's for the Sabbath.
GOLDE. Hurry up, the sun won't wait for
you. I have something to say to you. (*Exits
into the house.*)
TEVYE. As the Good Book says, "Heal
us, O Lord, and we shall be healed." In
other words, send us the cure, we've got
the sickness already. (*Gestures to the door.*)
I'm not really complaining—after all, with
Your help, I'm starving to death. You
made many, many poor people. I realize,
of course, that it's no shame to be poor, but
it's no great honor either. So what would
have been so terrible if I had a small fortune?

["If I Were a Rich Man"]

If I were a rich man
Daidle deedle daidle
Digguh digguh deedle daidle
    dum,
All day long I'd biddy biddy
    bum,
If I were a wealthy man.

Wouldn't have to work hard,
Daidle deedle daidle
Digguh digguh deedle daidle
    dum,
If I were a biddy biddy rich
Digguh digguh deedle daidle
    man.

I'd build a big, tall house with
    rooms by the dozen
Right in the middle of the town,
A fine tin roof and real wooden
    floors below.
There would be one long stair-
    case just going up,
And one even longer coming
    down,
And one more leading nowhere
    just for show.

I'd fill my yard with chicks and
    turkeys and geese
And ducks for the town to see
    and hear,
Squawking just as noisily as they
    can.
And each loud quack and cluck
    and gobble and honk
Will land like a trumpet on the
    ear,
As if to say, here lives a wealthy
    man.
(*Sighs.*)

If I were a rich man,
Daidle deedle daidle
Digguh digguh deedle daidle
    dum,
All day long I'd biddy biddy
    bum,
If I were a wealthy man.

Wouldn't have to work hard,
Daidle deedle daidle
Digguh digguh deedle daidle
    dum,
If I were a biddy biddy rich
Digguh digguh deedle daidle
    man.

I see my wife, my Golde, looking
    like a rich man's wife,
With a proper double chin,
Supervising meals to her heart's
    delight.

I see her putting on airs and strutting like a peacock,
Oi! what a happy mood she's in,
Screaming at the servants day and
night.

The most important men in town
will come to fawn on me.
They will ask me to advise them
like a Solomon the Wise,
"If you please, Reb Tevye. Pardon
me, Reb Tevye,"
Posing problems that would cross
a rabbi's eyes.
(*He chants.*)

And it won't make one bit of dif-
f'rence
If I answer right or wrong.
When you're rich they think you
really know!

If I were rich I'd have the time
that I lack
To sit in the synagogue and pray,
And maybe have a seat by the
eastern wall,
And I'd discuss the Holy Books
with the learned men
Seven hours every day.
That would be the sweetest thing
of all.
(*Sighs.*)

If I were a rich man,
Daidle deedle daidle
Digguh digguh deedle daidle
dum,
All day long I'd biddy biddy
bum,
If I were a wealthy man.

Wouldn't have to work hard,
Daidle deedle daidle
Digguh digguh deedle daidle
dum,
Lord, who made the lion and the
lamb,
You decreed I should be what I
am,
Would it spoil some vast, eternal
plan—
If I were a wealthy man?

(*As the song ends,* MORDCHA, MENDEL,
PERCHIK, AVRAM, *and other* TOWNSPEOPLE
enter.*)

MORDCHA. There he is! You forgot my
order for the Sabbath!
TEVYE. Reb Mordcha, I had a little acci-
dent with my horse.
MENDEL. Tevye, you didn't bring the
rabbi's order.
TEVYE. I know, Reb Mendel.
AVRAM. Tevye, you forgot my order for
the Sabbath.
TEVYE. This is bigger news than the
plague in Odessa.
AVRAM (*waving the newspaper that he
holds*). Talking about news, terrible news
in the outside world—terrible!
MORDCHA. What is it?
MENDEL. What does it say?
AVRAM. In a village called Rajanka, all
the Jews were evicted, forced to leave their
homes.
(*They all look at each other.*)
MENDEL. For what reason?
AVRAM. It doesn't say. Maybe the Tsar
wanted their land. Maybe a plague . . .
MORDCHA. May the Tsar have his own
personal plague.
ALL. Amen.
MENDEL (*to* AVRAM). Why don't you ever
bring us some good news?
AVRAM. I only read it. It was an edict
from the authorities.
MORDCHA. May the authorities start itch-
ing in places that they can't reach.
ALL. Amen.
PERCHIK (*has quietly entered during
above and sat down to rest*). Why do you
curse them? What good does your cursing
do? You stand around and curse and chatter and don't do anything. You'll all chatter your way into the grave.
MENDEL. Excuse me, you're not from this
village.
PERCHIK. No.
MENDEL. And where are you from?
PERCHIK. Kiev. I was a student in the
university there.
MORDCHA. Aha! The university. Is that
where you learned to criticize your elders?
PERCHIK. That's where I learned that
there is more to life than talk. You should
know what's going on in the outside world.
MORDCHA. Why should I break my head
about the outside world? Let them break
their own heads.
TEVYE. He's right. As the Good Book
says, "If you spit in the air, it lands in your

face."

PERCHIK. That's nonsense. You can't close your eyes to what's happening in the world.

TEVYE. He's right.

AVRAM. He's right and he's right? How can they both be right?

TEVYE. You know, you're also right.

MORDCHA. He's right! He's still wet behind the ears! Good Sabbath, Tevye.

VILLAGERS. Good Sabbath, Tevye.

(*They take their orders and leave.* MEN-DEL *remains.*)

MENDEL. Tevye, the rabbi's order. My cheese!

TEVYE. Of course. So you're from Kiev, Reb . . .

PERCHIK. Perchik.

TEVYE. Perchik. So, you're a newcomer here. As Abraham said, "I am a stranger in a strange land."

MENDEL. Moses said that.

TEVYE (*to* MENDEL). Forgive me. As King David put it, "I am slow of speech and slow of tongue."

MENDEL. That was also Moses.

TEVYE. For a man with a slow tongue, he talked a lot.

MENDEL. And the cheese!

(TEVYE *notices that* PERCHIK *is eying the cheese hungrily.*)

TEVYE. Here, have a piece.

PERCHIK. I have no money. And I am not a beggar.

TEVYE. Here—it's a blessing for me to give.

PERCHIK. Very well—for your sake! (*He takes the cheese and devours it.*)

TEVYE. Thank you. You know, it's no crime to be poor.

PERCHIK. In this world, it's the rich who are the criminals. Someday their wealth will be ours.

TEVYE. That would be nice. If they would agree, I would agree.

MENDEL. And who will make this miracle come to pass?

PERCHIK. People. Ordinary people.

MENDEL. Like you?

PERCHIK. Like me.

MENDEL. Nonsense!

TEVYE. And until your golden day comes, Reb Perchik, how will you live?

PERCHIK. By giving lessons to children. Do you have children?

TEVYE. I have five daughters.

PERCHIK. Five?

TEVYE. Daughters.

PERCHIK. Girls should learn too. Girls are people.

MENDEL. A radical!

PERCHIK. I would be willing to teach them. Open their minds to great thoughts.

TEVYE. What great thoughts?

PERCHIK. Well, the Bible has many lessons for our times.

TEVYE. I am a very poor man. Food for lessons? (PERCHIK *nods.*) Good. Stay with us for the Sabbath. Of course, we don't eat like kings, but we don't starve, either. As the Good Book says, "When a poor man eats a chicken, one of them is sick."

MENDEL. Where does the Book say that?

TEVYE. Well, it doesn't exactly say that, but someplace it has something about a chicken. Good Sabbath.

MENDEL. Good Sabbath.

PERCHIK. Good Sabbath.

(MENDEL *exits as* TEVYE *and* PERCHIK *enter the house.*)

SCENE THREE

The interior of TEVYE's *house.* TEVYE's *daughters are there.* TEVYE *and* PERCHIK *enter.*

TEVYE. Good Sabbath, children.

DAUGHTERS (*running to him*). Good Sabbath, Papa.

TEVYE. Children! (*They all stop.*) This is Perchik. Perchik, this is my oldest daughter.

PERCHIK. Good Sabbath.

TZEITEL. Good Sabbath.

PERCHIK. You have a pleasant daughter.

TEVYE. I have five pleasant daughters. (*He beckons to the girls, and they run into his arms, eagerly, and* TEVYE *kisses each.*) This is mine . . . this is mine . . . this is mine . . . this is mine . . . this is mine . . .

(MOTEL *enters.* TEVYE *almost kisses him in sequence.*) This is not mine. Perchik, this is Motel Kamzoil and he is—

GOLDE (*entering*). So you did me a favor and came in.

TEVYE. This is also mine. Golde, this is Perchik, from Kiev, and he is staying the Sabbath with us. He is a teacher. (*To* SHPRINTZE *and* BIELKE.) Would you like to take lessons from him? (*They giggle.*)

PERCHIK. I am really a good teacher, a very good teacher.

HODEL. I heard once, the rabbi who must praise himself has a congregation of one.

PERCHIK. Your daughter has a quick and witty tongue.

TEVYE. The wit she gets from me. As the Good Books says—

GOLDE. The Good Book can wait. Get washed!

TEVYE. The tongue she gets from her mother.

GOLDE. Motel, you're also eating with us? (MOTEL *gestures, "Yes, if I may."*) Of course, another blessing. Tzeitel, two more. Shprintze, Bielke, get washed. Get the table.

TZEITEL. Motel can help me.

GOLDE. All right. Chava, you go too. (*To* PERCHIK.) You can wash outside at the well.

(*Exit the* DAUGHTERS, PERCHIK, *and* MO-TEL.) Tevye, I have something to say to you.

TEVYE. Why should today be different? (*He starts to pray.*)

GOLDE. Tevye, I have to tell you—

TEVYE. Shhh. I'm praying. (*Prays.*)

GOLDE (*having waited a moment*). Lazar Wolf wants to see you.

(TEVYE *begins praying again, stopping only to respond to* GOLDE, *then returning to prayer.*)

TEVYE. The butcher? About what? (*Prays.*)

GOLDE. I don't know. Only that he says it is important.

TEVYE. What can be important? I have nothing for him to slaughter. (*Prays.*)

GOLDE. After the Sabbath, see him and talk to him.

TEVYE. Talk to him about what? If he is thinking about buying my new milk cow (*prays*) he can forget it. (*Prays.*)

GOLDE. Tevye, don't be an ox. A man sends an important message, at least you can talk to him.

TEVYE. Talk about what? He wants my new milk cow! (*Prays.*)

GOLDE (*insisting*). Talk to him!

TEVYE. All right. After the Sabbath, I'll talk to him.

(TEVYE *and* GOLDE *exit. He is still praying.* MOTEL, TZEITEL, *and* CHAVA *bring in the table.* CHAVA *exits.*)

TZEITEL. Motel, Yente was here.

MOTEL. I saw her.

TZEITEL. If they agree on someone, there will be a match and then it will be too late for us.

MOTEL. Don't worry, Tzeitel. I have found someone who will sell me his used sewing machine, so in a few weeks I'll have saved up enough to buy it, and then your father will be impressed with me and . . .

TZEITEL. But, Motel, a few weeks may be too late.

MOTEL. But what else can we do?

TZEITEL. You could ask my father for my hand tonight. Now!

MOTEL. Why should he consider me now? I'm only a poor tailor.

TZEITEL. And I'm only the daughter of a poor milkman. Just talk to him.

MOTEL. Tzeitel, if your father says no, that's it, it's final. He'll yell at me.

TZEITEL. Motel!

MOTEL. I'm just a poor tailor.

TZEITEL. Motel, even a poor tailor is entitled to some happiness.

MOTEL. That's true.

TZEITEL (*urgently*). Will you talk to him? Will you talk to him?

MOTEL. All right, I'll talk to him.

TEVYE (*entering*). It's late! Where is everybody? Late.

MOTEL (*following him*). Reb Tevye—

TEVYE (*disregarding him*). Come in, children, we're lighting the candles.

MOTEL. Reb Tevye. (*Summoning courage.*) Reb Tevye, Reb Tevye.

TEVYE. Yes? What is it? (*Loudly.*) Well, Motel, what is it?

MOTEL (*taken aback*). Good Sabbath, Reb Tevye.

TEVYE (*irritated with him*). Good Sabbath, Good Sabbath. Come, children, come.

(TEVYE's *family,* PERCHIK, *and* MOTEL *gather around the table.* GOLDE *lights the candles and says a prayer under her breath.*)

TEVYE *and* GOLDE (*sing to* DAUGHTERS).
["Sabbath Prayer"]

May the Lord protect and defend
    you,
May He always shield you from
    shame,
May you come to be
In Yisroel a shining name.

May you be like Ruth and like
    Esther,
May you be deserving of praise.
Strengthen them, O Lord,
And keep them from the stran-
    ger's ways.

May God bless you
And grant you long lives.
(*The lights go up behind them, showing
other families, behind a transparent cur-
tain, singing over Sabbath candles.*)
  GOLDE.
    May the Lord fulfill our Sabbath
      prayer for you.
TEVYE *and* GOLDE.
    May God make you
    Good mothers and wives.
TEVYE.
    May He send you husbands who
      will care for you.
TEVYE *and* GOLDE.
    May the Lord protect and defend
      you,
    May the Lord preserve you from
      pain.
    Favor them, O Lord,
    With happiness and peace.
    O hear our Sabbath prayer.
    Amen.

SCENE FOUR

The inn, the following evening. AVRAM,
LAZAR, MENDEL, *and several other people
are sitting at tables.* LAZAR *is waiting impatiently, drumming on the tabletop,
watching the door.*

———

LAZAR. Reb Mordcha.
MORDCHA. Yes, Lazar Wolf.
LAZAR. Please bring me a bottle of your
best brandy and two glasses.
AVRAM. "Your best brandy," Reb Lazar?
MORDCHA. What's the occasion? Are you
getting ready for a party?
LAZAR. There might be a party. Maybe
even a wedding.
MORDCHA. A wedding? Wonderful. And
I'll be happy to make the wedding merry,
lead the dancing, and so forth. For a little
fee, naturally.
LAZAR. Naturally, a wedding is no wed-
ding without you—and your fee.
(FYEDKA *enters with several other* RUS-

SIANS.)
FIRST RUSSIAN. Good evening, Innkeeper.
MORDCHA. Good evening.
FIRST RUSSIAN. We'd like a drink. Sit
down, Fyedka.
MORDCHA. Vodka? Schnapps?
FYEDKA. Vodka.
MORDCHA. Right away.
(TEVYE *enters.* LAZAR, *who has been
watching the door, turns away, pretending
not to be concerned.*)
TEVYE. Good evening.
MORDCHA. Good evening, Tevye.
MENDEL. What are you doing here so
early?
TEVYE (*aside to* MENDEL). He wants to
buy my new milk cow. Good evening,
Reb Lazar.
LAZAR. Ah, Tevye. Sit down. Have a
drink. (*Pours a drink.*)
TEVYE. I won't insult you by saying no.
(*Drinks.*)
LAZAR. How goes it with you, Tevye?
TEVYE. How should it go?
LAZAR. You're right.
TEVYE. And you?
LAZAR. The same.
TEVYE. I'm sorry to hear that.
LAZAR (*pours a drink*). So how's your
brother-in-law in America?
TEVYE. I believe he is doing very well.
LAZAR. He wrote you?
TEVYE. Not lately.
LAZAR. Then how do you know?
TEVYE. If he was doing badly, he would
write. May I? (*Pours himself another
drink.*)
LAZAR. Tevye, I suppose you know why
I wanted to see you.
TEVYE (*drinks*). Yes, I do, Reb Lazar,
but there is no use talking about it.
LAZAR (*upset*). Why not?
TEVYE. Why yes? Why should I get rid
of her?
LAZAR. Well, you have a few more with-
out her.
TEVYE. I see! Today you want one. To-
morrow you may want two.
LAZAR (*startled*). Two? What would I
do with two?
TEVYE. The same as you do with one!
LAZAR (*shocked*). Tevye! This is very
important to me.
TEVYE. Why is it so important to you?
LAZAR. Frankly, because I am lonesome.
TEVYE (*startled*). Lonesome? What are

you talking about?

LAZAR. You don't know?

TEVYE. We're talking about my new cow. The one you want to buy from me.

LAZAR (*stares at* TEVYE, *then bursts into laughter*). A milk cow! So I won't be lonesome! (*He howls with laughter.* TEVYE *stares at him.*)

TEVYE. What's so funny?

LAZAR. I was talking about your daughter. Your daughter, Tzeitel! (*Bursts into laughter.* TEVYE *stares at him, upset.*)

TEVYE. My daughter, Tzeitel?

LAZAR. Of course, your daughter, Tzeitel! I see her in my butcher shop every Thursday. She's made a good impression on me. I like her. And as for me, Tevye, as you know, I'm pretty well off. I have my own house, a good store, a servant. Look, Tevye, why do we have to try to impress each other? Let's shake hands and call it a match. And you won't need a dowry for her. And maybe you'll find something in your own purse, too.

TEVYE (*shouting*). Shame on you! Shame! (*Hiccups.*) What do you mean, my purse? My Tzeitel is not the sort that I would sell for money!

LAZAR (*calming him*). All right! Just as you say. We won't talk about money. The main thing is, let's get it done with. And I will be good to her, Tevye. (*Slightly embarrassed.*) I like her. What do you think?

TEVYE (*to the audience*). What do I think? What do I think? I never liked him! Why should I? You can have a fine conversation with him, if you talk about kidneys and livers. On the other hand, not everybody has to be a scholar. If you're wealthy enough, no one will call you stupid. And with a butcher, my daughter will surely never know hunger. Of course, he has a problem—he's much older than her. That's her problem. But she's younger. That's his problem. I always thought of him as a butcher, but I misjudged him. He is a good man. He likes her. He will try to make her happy. (*Turns to* LAZAR.) What do I think? It's a match!

LAZAR (*delighted*). You agree?

TEVYE. I agree.

LAZAR. Oh, Tevye, that's wonderful. Let's drink on it.

TEVYE. Why not? To you.

LAZAR. No, my friend, to you.

TEVYE. To the both of us.

LAZAR. To our agreement.

TEVYE. To our agreement. To our prosperity. To good health and happiness. (*Enter* FIDDLER.) And, most important (*sings*):

["To Life"]

To Life, to Life, L'Chaim.

TEVYE *and* LAZAR.
    L'Chaim, L'Chaim, To Life.

TEVYE.
    Here's to the father I've tried to
        be.

LAZAR.
    Here's to my bride to be.

TEVYE *and* LAZAR.
    Drink, L'Chaim,
    To Life, to Life, L'Chaim.
    L'Chaim, L'Chaim to Life.

TEVYE.
    Life has a way of confusing us,

LAZAR.
    Blessing and bruising us,

TEVYE *and* LAZAR.
    Drink, L'Chaim, to Life.

TEVYE.
    God would like us to be joyful,
    Even when our hearts lie panting
        on the floor.

LAZAR.
    How much more can we be joyful
    When there's really something
    To be joyful for!

TEVYE *and* LAZAR.
    To Life, to Life, L'Chaim.

TEVYE.
    To Tzeitel, my daughter.

LAZAR.
    My wife.
    It gives you something to think
        about,

TEVYE.
    Something to drink about,

TEVYE *and* LAZAR.
    Drink, L'Chaim, to Life.

LAZAR. Reb Mordcha.

MORDCHA. Yes, Lazar Wolf.

LAZAR. Drinks for everybody.

MENDEL. What's the occasion?

LAZAR. I'm taking myself a bride.

VILLAGERS. Who? Who?

LAZAR. Tevye's eldest, Tzeitel.

VILLAGERS. Mazeltov. . . . Wonderful.

. . . Congratulations. . . . (*Sing.*)
    To Lazar Wolf.

TEVYE.
  To Tevye.
VILLAGERS.
  To Tzeitel, your daughter.
LAZAR.
  My wife.
ALL.
  May all your futures be pleasant
      ones,
  Not like our present ones.
  Drink, L'Chaim, to Life,
  To Life, L'Chaim,
  L'Chaim, L'Chaim, to Life.
  It takes a wedding to make us
      say,
  "Let's live another day,"
  Drink, L'Chaim, to Life.
  We'll raise a glass and sip a drop
      of schnapps
  In honor of the great good luck
  That favored you.
  We know that
  When good fortune favors two
      such men
  It stands to reason we deserve it,
      too.
  To us and our good fortune.
  Be happy, be healthy, long life!
  And if our good fortune never
      comes,
  Here's to whatever comes.
  Drink, L'Chaim, to Life.
  Dai-dai-dai-dai-dai-dai-dai.
(*They begin to dance. A* RUSSIAN *starts
to sing, and they stop, uncomfortable.*)
RUSSIAN.
  Za va sha, Zdarovia,
  Heaven bless you both, Nazdro-
      via,
  To your health, and may we live
      together in peace.
  Za va sha, Zdarovia,
  Heaven bless you both, Nazdro-
      via,
  To your health, and may we live
      together in peace.
OTHER RUSSIANS.
  May you both be favored with the
      future of your choice.
  May you live to see a thousand
      reasons to rejoice.
  Za va sha, Zdarovia,
  Heaven bless you both, Nazdro-
      via,
  To your health, and may we live
      together in peace.

Hey!
(*The* RUSSIANS *begin to dance, the*
OTHERS *join in and they dance to a wild
finale pileup on the bar.*)
TEVYE (*from the pileup*).
  To Life!
(*Blackout.*)

SCENE FIVE

*The street outside the inn. Entering
through the inn door are the* FIDDLER,
LAZAR, TEVYE, *the other* VILLAGERS, *and the*
RUSSIANS, *singing "To Life."*

———

LAZAR. You know, Tevye, after the mar-
riage, we will be related. You will be my
papa.
TEVYE. Your papa! I always wanted a
son, but I wanted one a little younger
than myself.
(*The* CONSTABLE *enters.*)
CONSTABLE. Good evening.
FIRST RUSSIAN. Good evening, Constable.
CONSTABLE. What's the celebration?
FIRST RUSSIAN. Tevye is marrying off his
oldest daughter.
CONSTABLE. May I offer my congratula-
tions, Tevye?
TEVYE. Thank you, your Honor.
(*All but* TEVYE *and the* CONSTABLE *exit.*)
CONSTABLE. Oh, Tevye, I have a piece of
news that I think I should tell you, as a
friend.
TEVYE. Yes, your Honor?
CONSTABLE. And I'm giving you this
news because I like you. You are a decent,
honest person, even though you are a
Jewish dog.
TEVYE. How often does a man get a
compliment like that? And your news?
CONSTABLE. We have received orders
that sometime soon this district is to have
a little unofficial demonstration.
TEVYE (*shocked*). A pogrom? Here?
CONSTABLE. No—just a little unofficial
demonstration.
TEVYE. How little?
CONSTABLE. Not too serious—just some
mischief, so that if an inspector comes
through, he will see that we have done
our duty. Personally, I don't know why
there has to be this trouble between people, but I thought I should tell you, and
you can tell the others.

TEVYE. Thank you, your Honor. You're a good man. If I may say so, it's too bad you're not a Jew.

CONSTABLE (*amused*). That's what I like about you, Tevye, always joking. And congratulations again, for your daughter.

TEVYE. Thank you, your Honor. Goodbye. (*The* CONSTABLE *exits.* TEVYE *turns to heaven.*) Dear God, did You have to send me news like that, today of all days? It's true that we are the Chosen People. But once in a while can't You choose someone else? Anyway, thank You for sending a husband for my Tzeitel. L'Chaim.

(*The* FIDDLER *enters, he circles* TEVYE, *and they dance off together.*)

SCENE SIX

Outside TEVYE'S *house.* PERCHIK *is teaching* SHPRINTZE *and* BIELKE *while they peel potatoes at a bench.* HODEL *is cleaning pails at the pump.*

———

PERCHIK. Now, children, I will tell you the story from the Bible, of Laban and Jacob, and then we will discuss it together. All right? (*They nod.*) Good. Now Laban had two daughters, Leah and the beautiful Rachel. And Jacob loved the younger, Rachel, and he asked Laban for her hand. Laban agreed, if Jacob would work for him for seven years.

SHPRINTZE. Was Laban a mean man?

PERCHIK (*dryly*). He was an employer! Now, after Jacob worked seven years, do you know what happened? Laban fooled him, and gave him his ugly daughter, Leah. So, to marry Rachel, Jacob was forced to work another seven years. You see, children, the Bible clearly teaches us, you must never trust an employer. Do you understand?

SHPRINTZE. Yes, Perchik.

BIELKE. Yes, Perchik.

PERCHIK. Good, now—

GOLDE (*entering from the barn*). Papa isn't up yet?

HODEL. No, Mama.

GOLDE. Then enough lessons. We have to do Papa's work today. How long can he sleep? He staggered home last night and fell into bed like a dead man. I couldn't get a word out of him. Put that away and clean the barn. (SHPRINTZE *and* BIELKE *exit into the barn. To* HODEL.) Call me when Papa gets up. (GOLDE *exits.* HODEL *pumps a bucket of water.*)

HODEL. That was a very interesting lesson, Perchik.

PERCHIK. Do you think so?

HODEL. Although I don't know if the rabbi would agree with your interpretation.

PERCHIK. And neither, I suppose, would the rabbi's son.

HODEL. My little sisters have big tongues.

PERCHIK. And what do you know about him, except that he is the rabbi's son? Would you be interested in him if he were the shoemaker's son, or the tinsmith's son?

HODEL. At least I know this, he does not have any strange ideas about turning the world upside down.

PERCHIK. Certainly. Any new idea would be strange to you. Remember, the Lord said, "Let there be light."

HODEL. Yes, but He was not talking to you personally. Good day. (*Starts off.*)

PERCHIK. You have spirit. Even a little intelligence, perhaps.

HODEL. Thank you.

PERCHIK. But what good is your brain? Without curiosity it is a rusty tool. Good day, Hodel.

HODEL. We have an old custom here. A boy acts respectfully to a girl. But, of course, that is too traditional for an advanced thinker like you.

PERCHIK. Our traditions! Nothing must change! Everything is perfect exactly the way it is!

HODEL. We like our ways.

PERCHIK. Our ways are changing all over but here. Here men and women must keep apart. Men study. Women in the kitchen. Boys and girls must not touch, should not even look at each other.

HODEL. I am looking at you!

PERCHIK. You are very brave! Do you know that in the city boys and girls can be affectionate without permission of a matchmaker? They hold hands together, they even dance together—new dances—like this. (*He seizes her and starts dancing, humming.*) I learned it in Kiev. Do you like it?

HODEL (*startled*). It's very nice.

PERCHIK (*stops dancing*). There. We've just changed an old custom.

HODEL (*bewildered*). Yes. Well, you're welcome—I mean, thank you—I mean, good day.

PERCHIK. Good day!

(TEVYE *enters, suffering from a headache.*)

TEVYE. Bielke, Shprintze, what's your name?

HODEL. Hodel, Papa.

TEVYE. Where is Tzeitel?

HODEL. She's in the barn.

TEVYE. Call her out. (HODEL *exits into the barn.*) Reb Perchik. How did the lesson go today?

PERCHIK (*watching* HODEL's *exit*). I think we made a good beginning.

(*Enter* GOLDE.)

GOLDE. Ah, he's finally up. What happened last night, besides your drinking like a peasant? Did you see Lazar Wolf? What did he say? What did you say? Do you have news?

TEVYE. Patience, woman. As the Good Book says, "Good news will stay and bad news will refuse to leave." And there's another saying that goes—

GOLDE (*exasperated*). You can die from such a man!

(TZEITEL *enters from the barn.* HODEL *and* CHAVA *follow her.*)

TEVYE. Ah, Tzeitel, my lamb, come here. Tzeitel, you are to be congratulated. You are going to be married!

GOLDE. Married!

TZEITEL. What do you mean, Papa?

TEVYE. Lazar Wolf has asked for your hand.

GOLDE (*thrilled*). I knew it!

TZEITEL (*bewildered*). The butcher?

GOLDE (*enraptured*). My heart told me this was our lucky day. O dear God, I thank Thee, I thank Thee.

TEVYE. And what do you say, Tzeitel?

GOLDE. What can she say? My first-born, a bride! May you grow old with him in fortune and honor, not like Fruma-Sarah, that first wife of his. She was a bitter woman, may she rest in peace. Not like my Tzeitel. And now I must thank Yente. My Tzeitel, a bride! (*She hurries off.*)

HODEL *and* CHAVA (*subdued*). Mazeltov, Tzeitel.

TEVYE. You call that a Mazeltov? (HODEL *and* CHAVA *exit.*) And you, Reb Perchik, aren't you going to congratulate her?

PERCHIK (*sarcastic*). Congratulations, Tzeitel, for getting a rich man.

TEVYE. Again with the rich! What's wrong with being rich?

PERCHIK. It is no reason to marry. Money is the world's curse.

TEVYE. May the Lord smite me with it! And may I never recover! Tzeitel knows I mean only her welfare. Am I right, Tzeitel?

TZEITEL. Yes, Papa.

TEVYE. You see.

PERCHIK. I see. I see very well. (*He exits.*)

TEVYE. Well, Tzeitel, my child, why are you so silent? Aren't you happy with this blessing?

TZEITEL (*bursts into tears*). Oh, Papa, Papa.

TEVYE. What is it? Tell me.

TZEITEL. Papa, I don't want to marry him. I can't marry him. I can't—

TEVYE. What do you mean, you can't? If I say you will, you will.

TZEITEL. Papa, if it's a matter of money, I'll do anything. I'll hire myself out as a servant. I'll dig ditches, I'll haul rocks, only don't make me marry him, Papa, please.

TEVYE. What's wrong with Lazar? He likes you.

TZEITEL. Papa, I will be unhappy with him. All my life will be unhappy. I'll dig ditches, I'll haul rocks.

TEVYE. But we made an agreement. With us an agreement is an agreement.

TZEITEL (*simply*). Is that more important that I am, Papa? Papa, don't force me. I'll be unhappy all my days.

TEVYE. All right. I won't force you.

TZEITEL. Oh, thank you, Papa.

TEVYE. It seems it was not ordained that you should have all the comforts of life, or that we should have a little joy in our old age after all our hard work.

(*Enter* MOTEL, *breathless.*)

MOTEL. Reb Tevye, may I speak to you?

TEVYE. Later, Motel. Later.

MOTEL. I would like to speak to you.

TEVYE. Not now, Motel. I have problems.

MOTEL. That's what I want to speak to you about. I think I can help.

TEVYE. Certainly. Like a bandage can help a corpse. Good-bye, Motel. Good-bye.

TZEITEL. At least listen to him, Papa.

TEVYE. All right. You have a tongue, talk.

MOTEL. Reb Tevye, I hear you are arranging a match for Tzeitel.

TEVYE. He also has ears.

MOTEL. I have a match for Tzeitel.

TEVYE. What kind of match?

MOTEL. A perfect fit.

TEVYE. A perfect fit.

MOTEL. Like a glove.

TEVYE. Like a glove.

MOTEL. This match was made exactly to measure.

TEVYE. A perfect fit. Made to measure. Stop talking like a tailor and tell me who it is.

MOTEL. Please, don't shout at me.

TEVYE. All right. Who is it?

MOTEL. Who is it?

TEVYE (*pauses*). Who is it?

MOTEL. Who is it?

TEVYE. Who, is it?

MOTEL. It's me—myself.

TEVYE (*stares at him, then turns to the audience, startled and amused*). Him? Himself? (*To* MOTEL.) Either you're completely out of your mind or you're crazy. (*To the audience.*) He must be crazy. (*To* MOTEL.) Arranging a match for yourself. What are you, everything? The bridegroom, the matchmaker, the guests all rolled into one? I suppose you'll even perform the ceremony. You must be crazy!

MOTEL. Please don't shout at me, Reb Tevye. As for being my own matchmaker, I know it's a little unusual.

TEVYE. Unusual? It's crazy.

MOTEL. Times are changing, Reb Tevye. The thing is, your daughter Tzeitel and I gave each other our pledge more than a year ago that we would marry.

TEVYE (*stunned*). You gave each other your pledge?

TZEITEL. Yes, Papa, we gave each other our pledge.

TEVYE (*looks at them, turns to the audience. Sings*).

["Tradition" Reprise]

They gave each other a pledge.
Unheard of, absurd.
You gave each other a pledge?
Unthinkable.
Where do you think you are?
In Moscow?
In Paris?
Where do they think they are?
America?

What do you think you're doing?
You stitcher, you nothing!
Who do you think you are?
King Solomon?
This isn't the way it's done,
Not here, not now.
Some things I will not, I cannot,
    allow.
Tradition—
Marriages must be arranged by
    the papa.
This should never be changed.
One little time you pull out a
    prop,
And where does it stop?
Where does it stop?

(*Speaks.*) Where does it stop? Do I still have something to say about my daughter, or doesn't anyone have to ask a father anymore?

MOTEL. I have wanted to ask you for some time, Reb Tevye, but first I wanted to save up for my own sewing machine.

TEVYE. Stop talking nonsense. You're just a poor tailor.

MOTEL (*bravely*). That's true, Reb Tevye, but even a poor tailor is entitled to some happiness. (*Looks at* TZEITEL *triumphantly.*) I promise you, Reb Tevye, your daughter will not starve.

TEVYE (*impressed, turns to the audience*). He's beginning to talk like a man. On the other hand, what kind of match would that be, with a poor tailor? On the other hand, he's an honest, hard worker. On the other hand, he has absolutely nothing. On the other hand, things could never get worse for him, they could only get better. (*Sings.*)

They gave each other a pledge—
Unheard of, absurd.
They gave each other a pledge—
Unthinkable.
But look at my daughter's face—
She loves him, she wants him—
And look at my daughter's eyes,
So hopeful.

(*Shrugs. To the audience.*)
Tradition!

(*To* TZEITEL *and* MOTEL.) Well, children, when shall we make the wedding?

TZEITEL. Thank you, Papa.

MOTEL. Reb Tevye, you won't be sorry.

TEVYE. I won't be sorry? I'm sorry already!

TZEITEL. Thank you, Papa.

MOTEL. Thank you, Papa.

TEVYE. Thank you, Papa! They pledged their troth! (*Starts to exit, then looks back at them.*) Modern children! (*Has a sudden thought.*) Golde! What will I tell Golde? What am I going to do about Golde? (*To heaven.*) Help! (*Exits.*)

TZEITEL. Motel, you were wonderful!

MOTEL. It was a miracle! It was a miracle. (*Sings.*)

["Miracle of Miracles"]

Wonder of wonders, miracle of
  miracles,
God took a Daniel once again,
Stood by his side, and miracle of
  miracles,
Walked him through the lion's
  den.
Wonder of wonders, miracle of
  miracles,
I was afraid that God would
  frown.
But, like He did so long ago in
  Jericho,
God just made a wall fall down.
When Moses softened Pharoah's
  heart,
That was a miracle.
When God made the waters of
  the Red Sea part,
That was a miracle, too.
But of all God's miracles large
  and small,
The most miraculous one of all
Is that out of a worthless lump
  of clay
God has made a man today.
Wonder of wonders, miracle of
  miracles,
God took a tailor by the hand,
Turned him around, and, miracle
  of miracles,
Led him to the Promised Land.
When David slew Goliath, yes!
That was a miracle.
When God gave us manna in the
  wilderness,
That was a miracle, too.
But of all God's miracles, large
  and small,
The most miraculous one of all
Is the one I thought could never
  be—
God has given you to me.

SCENE SEVEN

TEVYE's *bedroom. The room is in complete darkness. A groan is heard, then another, then a scream.*

———

TEVYE. Aagh! Lazar! Motel! Tzeitel!

GOLDE. What is it? What?

TEVYE. Help! Help! Help!

GOLDE. Tevye, wake up! (GOLDE *lights the lamp. The light reveals* TEVYE *asleep in bed.*)

TEVYE (*in his sleep*). Help! Help!

GOLDE (*shaking him*). Tevye! What's the matter with you? Why are you howling like that?

TEVYE (*opening his eyes, frightened*). Where is she? Where is she?

GOLDE. Where is who? What are you talking about?

TEVYE. Fruma-Sarah. Lazar Wolf's first wife, Fruma-Sarah. She was standing here a minute ago.

GOLDE. What's the matter with you, Tevye? Fruma-Sarah has been dead for years. You must have been dreaming. Tell me what you dreamt, and I'll tell you what it meant.

TEVYE. It was terrible.

GOLDE. Tell me.

TEVYE. All right—only don't be frightened!

GOLDE (*impatiently*). Tell me!

TEVYE. All right, this was my dream. In the beginning I dreamt that we were having a celebration of some kind. Everybody we knew was there, and musicians too.

(*As he speaks,* MEN, *including a* RABBI, WOMEN, *and* MUSICIANS *enter the bedroom.* TEVYE, *wearing a nightshirt, starts to get out of bed to join the dream.*) In the middle of the dream, in walks your Grandmother Tzeitel, may she rest in peace.

GOLDE (*alarmed*). Grandmother Tzeitel? How did she look?

TEVYE. For a woman who is dead thirty years, she looked very good. Naturally, I went up to greet her. She said to me—

(GRANDMA TZEITEL *enters, and* TEVYE *approaches her and greets her in pantomime.* GRANDMA *sings.*)

["The Tailor, Motel Kamzoil"]

GRANDMA TZEITEL.
  A blessing on your head,

RABBI.

Mazeltov, Mazeltov.

GRANDMA TZEITEL.

To see a daughter wed.

RABBI.

Malzeltov, Mazeltov.

GRANDMA TZEITEL.

And such a son-in-law,
Like no one ever saw,
The tailor Motel Kamzoil.

GOLDE (*bewildered*). Motel?

GRANDMA TZEITEL.

A worthy boy is he,

RABBI.

Mazeltov, Mazeltov.

GRANDMA TZEITEL.

Of pious family.

RABBI.

Mazeltov, Mazeltov.

GRANDMA TZEITEL.

They named him after my
Dear Uncle Mordecai,
The tailor Motel Kamzoil.

GOLDE. A tailor! She must have heard wrong. She meant a butcher.

(TEVYE, *who has returned to* GOLDE, *listens to this, then runs back to* GRANDMA TZEITEL.)

TEVYE.

You must have heard wrong,
    Grandma,
There's no tailor,
You mean a butcher, Grandma,
By the name of Lazar Wolf.

GRANDMA TZEITEL (*flies into the air, screaming angrily*). No!!
(*Sings.*)

I mean a tailor, Tevye.
My great grandchild,
My little Tzeitel, who you named
    for me,
Motel's bride was meant to be.
For such a match I prayed.

CHORUS.

Mazeltov, Mazeltov,

GRANDMA TZEITEL.

In heaven it was made.

CHORUS.·

Mazeltov, Mazeltov,

GRANDMA TZEITEL.

A fine upstanding boy,
A comfort and a joy,
The tailor Motel Kamzoil.

GOLDE (*from bed*). But we announced it already. We made a bargain with the butcher.

TEVYE.

But we announced it, Grandma,
To our neighbors.
We made a bargain, Grandma,
With the butcher, Lazar Wolf.

GRANDMA TZEITEL (*Again flies into the air, screaming angrily*). No!!
(*Sings.*)

So you announced it, Tevye,
    That's your headache.
But as for Lazar Wolf, I say to
    you,
Tevye, that's your headache, too.

CHORUS.

A blessing on your house, Mazel-
    tov, Mazeltov,
Imagine such a spouse, Mazeltov,
    Mazeltov,
And such a son-in-law,
Like no one ever saw,
The tailor Motel Kamzoil.

TEVYE (*speaks*). It was a butcher!

CHORUS.

The tailor Motel Kamzoil.

TEVYE (*speaks*). It was Lazar Wolf.
(*Sings.*)

The tailor Motel Kam . . .

CHORUS.

Shah! shah!
Look!
Who is this?
Who is this?
Who comes here?
Who? who? who? who? who?
What woman is this
By righteous anger shaken?

SOLO VOICES.

Could it be?
Sure!
Yes, it could!
Why not?
Who could be mistaken?

CHORUS.

It's the butcher's wife come from
    beyond the grave.
It's the butcher's dear, darling,
    departed wife,
Fruma-Sarah, Fruma-Sarah.
Fruma-Sarah, Fruma-Sarah, Fru-
    ma-Sarah.

FRUMA-SARAH.

Tevye! Tevye!
What is this about your daugh-
    ter marrying my husband?

CHORUS.

Yes, her husband.

FRUMA-SARAH.
　Would you do this to your friend
　　and neighbor,
　　　　　　Fruma-Sarah?
CHORUS.
　　　　　Fruma-Sarah.
FRUMA-SARAH.
　Have you no consideration for a
　　woman's feelings?
CHORUS.
　　　Woman's feelings.
FRUMA-SARAH.
　Handing over my belongings to
　　a total stranger.
CHORUS.
　　　　Total stranger.
FRUMA-SARAH.
　　How can you allow it, how?
　How can you let your daughter
　　take my place?
　Live in my house, carry my keys,
　And wear my clothes, pearls—
　　how?
CHORUS.
　How can you allow your daughter
　　　To take her place?
FRUMA-SARAH.
　　　　　Pearls!
CHORUS.
　　　　　House!
FRUMA-SARAH.
　　　　　Pearls!
CHORUS.
　　　　　Keys!
FRUMA-SARAH.
　　　　　Pearls!
CHORUS.
　　　　　Clothes!
FRUMA-SARAH.
　　　　　Pearls!
CHORUS.
　　　　　How?
FRUMA-SARAH.
　　　　　Tevye!!
CHORUS.
　　　　　Tevye!!
FRUMA-SARAH.
　Such a learned man as Tevye
　　wouldn't let it happen.
CHORUS.
　　　Let it happen.
FRUMA-SARAH.
　Tell me that it isn't true, and
　　then I wouldn't worry.
CHORUS.
　　　Wouldn't worry.
FRUMA-SARAH.
　Say you didn't give your blessing
to your daughter's
　　marriage.
CHORUS.
　　Daughter's marriage.
FRUMA-SARAH.
　Let me tell you what would fol-
　　low such a fatal wedding.
CHORUS.
　　　Fatal wedding.
　　　　Shh!
FRUMA-SARAH.
　If Tzeitel marries Lazar Wolf,
　　I pity them both.
　She'll live with him three weeks,
　And when three weeks are up,
　　I'll come to her by night,
　I'll take her by the throat, and
　　　. . .
　　This I'll give your Tzeitel,
　　That I'll give your Tzeitel,
　　This I'll give your Tzeitel,
(*Laughs wildly.*) Here's my wed-
ding present if she marries Lazar Wolf!
(*She starts choking Tevye. The* CHORUS
exits screaming.)
GOLDE (*while* TEVYE *is being choked*).
It's an evil spirit: May it fall into the
river; may it sink into the earth. Such a
dark and horrible dream! And to think
it was brought on by that butcher. If my
Grandmother Tzeitel, may she rest in
peace, took the trouble to come all the
way from the other world to tell us about
the tailor, all we can say is that it is all
for the best, and it couldn't possibly be
any better. Amen.

TEVYE. Amen.

GOLDE (*sings*).
　A blessing on my head, Mazel-
　　tov, Mazeltov,
　Like Grandma Tzeitel said, Maz-
　　eltov, Mazeltov.
　　We'll have a son-in-law,
　　Like no one ever saw,
　　The tailor Motel Kamzoil.

TEVYE.
　We haven't got the man,
GOLDE.
　　Mazeltov, Mazeltov.
TEVYE.
　We had when we began.
GOLDE.
　　Mazeltov, Mazeltov.
TEVYE.
　But since your Grandma came,

She'll marry what's his name?
GOLDE.
    The tailor Motel Kamzoil.
TEVYE *and* GOLDE.
    The tailor Motel Kamzoil,
    The tailor Motel Kamzoil,
    The tailor Motel Kamzoil.

(GOLDE *goes back to sleep.* TEVYE *mouths the words "Thank You" to God, and goes to sleep.*)

SCENE EIGHT

The village street and the interior of MOTEL's *tailor shop.* MOTEL *and* CHAVA *are in the shop.* VILLAGERS *pass by.*

———

MAN. Bagels, fresh bagels.

WOMAN (*excited*). Did you hear? Did you hear? Tevye's Tzeitel is marrying Motel, not Lazar Wolf.

VILLAGERS. No!

WOMAN. Yes.

MENDEL. Tzeitel is marrying Motel?

WOMAN. Yes!

VILLAGERS. No! (*They rush into the shop and surround* MOTEL. MORDCHA *enters the street.*) Mazeltov, Motel. Congratulations.

MORDCHA. What's all the excitement?

AVRAM. Tevye's Tzeitel is going to marry—

MORDCHA. I know. Lazar Wolf, the butcher. It's wonderful.

AVRAM. No. Motel, the tailor.

MORDCHA. Motel, the tailor, that's terrible! (*Rushes into the shop.*) Mazeltov, Motel.

WOMAN (*to* SHANDEL, *exiting from the shop*). Imagine! Tzeitel is marrying Motel. I can't believe it!

SHANDEL (*outraged*). What's wrong with my son, Motel?

WOMAN. Oh, excuse me, Shandel. Mazeltov.

VILLAGERS (*inside the shop*). Mazeltov, Mazeltov.

MOTEL. Yussel, do you have a wedding hat for me?

YUSSEL. Lazar Wolf ordered a hat but it's not cheap.

MOTEL. I got his bride, I can get his hat!

YUSSEL. Then come, Motel, come.

MOTEL. Chava, can you watch the shop for a few minutes? I'll be back soon.

CHAVA. Of course.

MOTEL. Thank you, Chava. (*They all exit from the shop, calling Mazeltovs.*)

VILLAGERS (*to* CHAVA). We just heard about your sister. . . . Mazeltov, Chava. . . . Mazeltov, Chava.

CHAVA. Thanks—thank you very much.

(*All but* CHAVA *exit.* FYEDKA, SASHA, *and another* RUSSIAN *enter at the same time. They cross to* CHAVA, *blocking her way into the shop.*)

SASHA *and* RUSSIAN (*mockingly, imitating others, with a slight mispronunciation*). Mazeltov, Chava. Mazeltov, Chava.

CHAVA. Please may I pass.

SASHA (*getting in her way*). Why? We're congratulating you.

RUSSIAN. Mazeltov, Chava.

FYEDKA (*calmly*). All right, stop it.

SASHA. What's wrong with you?

FYEDKA. Just stop it.

SASHA. Now listen here, Fyedka—

FYEDKA. Good-bye, Sasha. (SASHA *and the* RUSSIAN *hesitate.*) I said good-bye! (*They look at* FYEDKA *curiously, then exit.*) I'm sorry about that. They mean no harm.

CHAVA. Don't they? (*She enters shop. He follows her.*) Is there something you want?

FYEDKA. Yes. I'd like to talk to you.

CHAVA. I'd rather not. (*She hesitates.*)

FYEDKA. I've often noticed you at the bookseller's. Not many girls in this village like to read. (*A sudden thought strikes him. He extends the book he is holding.*) Would you like to borrow this book? It's very good.

CHAVA. No, thank you.

FYEDKA. Why? Because I'm not Jewish? Do you feel about us the way they feel about you? I didn't think you would. And what do you know about me? Let me tell you about myself. I'm a pleasant fellow, charming, honest, ambitious, quite bright, and very modest.

CHAVA. I don't think we should be talking this way.

FYEDKA. I often do things I shouldn't. Go ahead, take the book. It's by Heinrich Heine. Happens to be Jewish, I believe.

CHAVA. That doesn't matter.

FYEDKA. You're quite right. (*She takes the book.*) Good. After you return it, I'll ask you how you like it, and we'll talk about it for a while. Then we'll talk about life, how we feel about things, and it can all turn out quite pleasant.

(CHAVA *puts the book on the table as* MOTEL *enters.*)

MOTEL. Oh, Fyedka! Can I do something for you?

FYEDKA. No, thank you. (*Starts to leave.*)

MOTEL. Oh, you forgot your book.

CHAVA. No, it's mine.

MOTEL. Thank you, Chava. (CHAVA *takes the book and leaves the shop with* FYEDKA.)

FYEDKA (*outside*). Good day, Chava.

CHAVA. Good day.

FYEDKA (*pleasantly*). Fyedka.

CHAVA. Good day, Fyedka. (*They exit.* MOTEL *puts on his wedding hat.*)

SCENE NINE

Part of TEVYE's *yard. Night.* TZEITEL, *in a bridal gown, enters, followed by* TEVYE, GOLDE, HODEL, BIELKE, CHAVA, SHPRINTZE, *and* RELATIONS. MOTEL *enters, followed by his* PARENTS *and* RELATIONS. *Many* GUESTS *enter, carrying lit candles. The men take their places on the right, as a group, the women on the left;* TZEITEL *and* MOTEL *stand in the center;* TZEITEL *and* MOTEL *places a veil over* TZEITEL's *head.* FOUR MEN *enter, carrying a canopy. They are followed by the* RABBI. *The canopy is placed over* MOTEL *and* TZEITEL. GUESTS *start singing.*

["Sunrise, Sunset"]

TEVYE.
　　Is this the little girl I carried?
　　Is this the little boy at play?
GOLDE.
　　I don't remember growing older.
　　　　When did they?
TEVYE.
　　When did she get to be a beauty?
　　When did he grow to be so tall?
GOLDE.
　　Wasn't it yesterday when they
　　　　were small?
MEN.
　　　　Sunrise, sunset,
　　　　Sunrise, sunset,
　　　　Swiftly flow the days.
　　Seedlings turn overnight to sun-
　　　　flowers,
　　　　Blossoming even as we gaze.

WOMEN.
　　　　Sunrise, sunset,
　　　　Sunrise, sunset,
　　　　Swiftly fly the years.
　　One season following another,
　　Laden with happiness and tears.
TEVYE.
　　What words of wisdom can I
　　　　give them?
　　How can I help to ease their
　　　　way?
GOLDE.
　　Now they must learn from one
　　　　another
　　　　　　Day by day.
PERCHIK.
　　They look so natural together.
HODEL.
　　Just like two newlyweds should
　　　　be.
PERCHIK *and* HODEL.
　　Is there a canopy in store for me?
ALL.
　　　　Sunrise, sunset,
　　　　Sunrise, sunset,
　　　　Swiftly fly the years.
　　One season following another,
　　Laden with happiness and tears.

(*During the song, the following mime is performed. The* RABBI *lifts* TZEITEL's *veil. He prays over a goblet of wine and hands it to the bride and groom. They each sip from it.* TZEITEL *slowly walks in a circle around* MOTEL. MOTEL *places a ring on* TZEITEL's *finger. The* RABBI *places a wine-glass on the floor. The song ends. A moment's pause.* MOTEL *treads on the glass.*)

ALL (*at the moment the glass breaks*). Mazeltov!

SCENE TEN

The set opens to show the entire yard of TEVYE's *house. Part of it is divided down the center by a short partition. Several tables are set up at the rear of each section. The* MUSICIANS *play, and all dance and then seat themselves on benches at the tables. The women are on the left, the men on the right. As the dance concludes,* MORDCHA *mounts a stool and signals for silence. The noise subsides.*

ALL. Shah. Shah. Quiet. Reb Mordcha. Shah. Shah.

MORDCHA. My friends, we are gathered here to share the joy of the newlyweds, Motel and Tzeitel. May they live together in peace to a ripe old age. Amen.

ALL. Amen.

(*The* RABBI *slowly makes his way to the table, assisted by* MENDEL.)

MORDCHA. Ah, here comes our beloved rabbi. May he be with us for many, many years.

RABBI (*ahead of the others*). Amen.

ALL. Amen.

MORDCHA. I want to announce that the bride's parents are giving the newlyweds the following: a new featherbed, a pair of pillows—

GOLDE (*shouting from the women's side*). Goose pillows.

MORDCHA. Goose pillows. And this pair of candlesticks.

ALL. Mazeltov!

MORDCHA. Now let us not in our joy tonight forget those who are no longer with us, our dear departed, who lived in pain and poverty and hardship and who died in pain and poverty and hardship. (*All sob. He pauses a moment.*) But enough tears. (*The mourning stops immediately.*) Let's be merry and content, like our good friend, Lazar Wolf, who has everything in the world, except a bride. (*Laughter.*) But Lazar has no ill feelings. In fact, he has a gift for the newlyweds that he wants to announce himself. Come, Lazar Wolf.

LAZAR (*rising*). Like he said, I have no ill feelings. What's done is done. I am giving the newlyweds five chickens, one for each of the first five Sabbaths of their wedded life. (*Murmurs of appreciation from all.*)

TEVYE (*rising*). Reb Lazar, you are a decent man. In the name of my daughter and her new husband, I accept your gift. There is a famous saying that—

LAZAR. Reb Tevye, I'm not marrying your daughter. I don't have to listen to your sayings.

TEVYE. If you would listen a second, I was only going to say—

LAZAR. Why should I listen to you? A man who breaks an agreement!

(*Murmurs by the assemblage.*)

MENDEL. Not now, Lazar, in the middle of a wedding.

LAZAR. I have a right to talk.

TEVYE (*angry*). What right? This is not your wedding.

LAZAR. It should have been!

(*Murmurs by the assemblage.*)

MENDEL. Reb Lazar, don't shame Reb Tevye at his daughter's wedding.

LAZAR. But he shamed me in front of the whole village!

(*An argument breaks out. Everyone takes sides.*)

ALL. That's true. . . . The rabbi said . . . It was a shame . . . He has no feelings . . . This is not the place—

MENDEL. Shah. Shah. Quiet. The rabbi. The rabbi, the rabbi.

RABBI (*rising, as the noise subsides*). I say—Let's sit down. (*Sits.*)

TEVYE. We all heard the wise words of the rabbi.

(*Everyone returns to his seat.*)

MORDCHA. Now, I'd like to sing a little song that—

TEVYE (*bursting out*). You can keep your diseased chickens!

LAZAR. Leave my chickens out of this. We made a bargain.

TEVYE. The terms weren't settled.

LAZAR. We drank on it—

FIRST MAN. I saw them, they drank on it.

SECOND MAN. But the terms weren't settled.

SHANDEL. What's done is done.

TEVYE. Once a butcher, always a butcher.

GOLDE. I had a sign. My own grandmother came to us from the grave.

YENTE. What sign? What grandmother? My grandfather came to me from the grave and told me that her grandmother was a big liar.

LAZAR. We drank on it.

(*Bedlam.* MORDCHA *tries to quiet the guests.* PERCHIK *climbs onto a stool, banging two tin plates together.*)

MORDCHA. Quiet, I'm singing.

TEVYE. The terms weren't settled.

GOLDE. I had a sign.

YENTE. An agreement is an agreement.

PERCHIK (*silences them*). Quiet! Quiet! What's all the screaming about? "They drank on it—" "An agreement—" "A sign." It's all nonsense. Tzeitel wanted to marry Motel and not Lazar.

MENDEL. A young girl decides for herself?

PERCHIK. Why not? Yes! They love

each other.

AVRAM. Love!

LAZAR. Terrible!

MENDEL. He's a radical!

YENTE. What happens to the matchmaker?

(*Another violent argument breaks out.*)

RABBI. I say—I say—(*They all turn to him.*)

TEVYE. Let's sit down? (*Rabbi nods.*)

MORDCHA. Musicians, play. A dance, a dance! (*The music starts, but no one dances.*) Come on, dance. It's a wedding.

YENTE. Some wedding!

(PERCHIK *crosses to the women's side.*)

AVRAM. What's he doing?

TEVYE. Perchik!

FIRST MAN. Stop him!

PERCHIK (*to* HODEL). Who will dance with me?

MENDEL. That's a sin!

PERCHIK. It's no sin to dance at a wedding.

AVRAM. But with a girl?

LAZAR. That's what comes from bringing a wild man into your house.

TEVYE (*signaling* PERCHIK *to return to the men's side*). He's not a wild man. His ideas are a little different, but—

MENDEL. It's a sin.

PERCHIK. It's no sin. Ask the rabbi. Ask him. (*They all gather around the* RABBI.)

TEVYE. Well, Rabbi?

RABBI (*thumbs through a book, finds the place*). Dancing—Well, it's not exactly forbidden, but—

TEVYE. There, you see? It's not forbidden.

PERCHIK (*to* HODEL). And it's no sin. Now will someone dance with me? (HODEL *rises to dance.*)

GOLDE. Hodel!

HODEL. It's only a dance, Mama.

PERCHIK. Play! (PERCHIK *and* HODEL *dance.*)

LAZAR. Look at Tevye's daughter.

MENDEL. She's dancing with a man.

TEVYE. I can see she's dancing. (*Starts toward them as if to stop them. Changes his mind.*) And I'm going to dance with my wife. Golde! (*Golde hesitates, then dances with him.*)

SHANDEL. Golde! (MOTEL *crosses to* TZEITEL.) Motel!

(TZEITEL *dances with* MOTEL. *Others join them. They all dance, except for* LAZAR

and YENTE, *who storm off. As the dance reaches a wild climax, the* CONSTABLE *and his* MEN *enter, carrying clubs. The dancers see them and slowly stop.*)

CONSTABLE. I see we came at a bad time, Tevye. I'm sorry, but the orders are for tonight. For the whole village. (*To the* MUSICIANS.) Go on, play, play. All right, men.

(*The* RUSSIANS *begin their destruction, turning over tables, throwing pillows, smashing dishes and the window of the house. One of them throws the wedding-gift candlesticks to the ground, and* PERCHIK *grapples with him. But he is hit with a club and falls to the ground. The* GUESTS *leave.*)

HODEL (*rushes to* PERCHIK). No, Perchik!

(*The* GUESTS *have left during the above action.*)

CONSTABLE (*to his* MEN). All right, enough! (*To* TEVYE.) I am genuinely sorry. You understand. (TEVYE *does not answer. To his* MEN.) Come. (*The* CONSTABLE *and his* MEN *exit.*)

GOLDE. Take him in the house. (HODEL *helps* PERCHIK *into the house.*)

TEVYE (*quietly*). What are you standing around for? Clean up. Clean up.

(*They start straightening up, picking up broken dishes, bringing bedding back to the house.* TZEITEL *picks up candlesticks, one of which is broken. They freeze at sudden sounds of destruction in a nearby house, then continue straightening up as the curtain falls.*)

ACT TWO

PROLOGUE. *The exterior of* TEVYE's *house.* TEVYE *is sitting on a bench.*

———

TEVYE (*to heaven*). That was quite a dowry You gave my daughter Tzeitel at her wedding. Was that necessary? Anyway, Tzeitel and Motel have been married almost two months now. They work very hard, they are as poor as squirrels in winter. But they are both so happy they don't know how miserable they are. Motel keeps talking about a sewing machine. I know You're very busy—wars and revolutions, floods, plagues, all those little things that bring people to You—couldn't You take a second away from Your catastrophes and get it for him? How much trouble would it be? Oh, and while You're in the neighborhood, my horse's left leg—Am I bothering You too much? I'm sorry. As the Good Book says—Why should I tell You what the Good Book says? (*Exits.*)

SCENE ONE

The exterior of TEVYE's *house. Afternoon.* HODEL *enters, petulantly, followed by* PERCHIK.

———

PERCHIK. Please don't be upset, Hodel.

HODEL. Why should I be upset? If you must leave, you must.

PERCHIK. I do have to. They expect me in Kiev tomorrow morning.

HODEL. So you told me. Then good-bye.

PERCHIK. Great changes are about to take place in this country. Tremendous changes. But they can't happen by themselves.

HODEL. So naturally you feel that you personally have to—

PERCHIK. Not only me. Many people. Jews, Gentiles, many people hate what is going on. Don't you understand?

HODEL. I understand, of course. You want to leave. Then good-bye.

PERCHIK. Hodel, your father, the others here, think what happened at Tzeitel's wedding was a little cloudburst and it's over and everything will now be peaceful again. It won't. Horrible things are happening all over the land—pogroms, violence—whole villages are being emptied of their people. And it's reaching everywhere, and it will reach here. You understand?

HODEL. Yes, I—I suppose I do.

PERCHIK. I have work to do. The greatest work a man can do.

HODEL. Then good-bye, Perchik.

PERCHIK. Before I go (*he hesitates, then summons up courage*), there is a certain question I wish to discuss with you.

HODEL. Yes?

PERCHIK. A political question.

HODEL. What is it?

PERCHIK. The question of marriage.

HODEL. This is a political question?

PERCHIK (*awkwardly*). In a theoretical sense, yes. The relationship between a man and woman known as marriage is based on mutual beliefs, a common attitude and philosophy toward society—

HODEL. And affection.

PERCHIK. And affection. This relationship has positive social values. It reflects a unity and solidarity—

HODEL. And affection.

PERCHIK. Yes. And I personally am in favor of it. Do you understand?

HODEL. I think you are asking me to marry you.

PERCHIK. In a theoretical sense, yes, I am.

HODEL. I was hoping you were.

PERCHIK. Then I take it you approve? And we can consider ourselves engaged, even though I am going away? (*She nods.*) I am very happy, Hodel. Very happy.

HODEL. So am I, Perchik.

PERCHIK (*sings*).

["Now I Have Everything"]

I used to tell myself
That I had everything,
But that was only half true.
I had an aim in life,
And that was everything,
But now I even have you.
I have something that I would
    die for,
Someone that I can live for, too.
Yes, now I have everything—
Not only everything,
I have a little bit more—
Besides having everything,
I know what everything's for.
I used to wonder,
Could there be a wife
To share such a difficult, wand-
    'ring kind of life.

HODEL.

I was only out of sight,
    Waiting right here.

PERCHIK.

Who knows tomorrow
Where our home will be?

HODEL.

I'll be with you and that's
    Home enough for me.

PERCHIK.

Everything is right at hand.

HODEL *and* PERCHIK.

Simple and clear.

PERCHIK.

I have something that I would
        die for,
Someone that I can live for, too.
Yes, now I have everything—
        Not only everything,
I have a little bit more—
Besides having everything,
I know what everything's for.

HODEL. And when will we be married,
Perchik?

PERCHIK. I will send for you as soon
as I can. It will be a hard life, Hodel.

HODEL. But it will be less hard if we
live it together.

PERCHIK. Yes.

(TEVYE enters.)

TEVYE. Good evening.

PERCHIK. Good evening. Reb Tevye, I
have some bad news. I must leave this
place.

TEVYE. When?

PERCHIK. Right away.

TEVYE. I'm sorry, Perchik. We will all
miss you.

PERCHIK. But I also have some good
news. You can congratulate me.

TEVYE. Congratulations. What for?

PERCHIK. We're engaged.

TEVYE. Engaged?

HODEL. Yes, Papa, we're engaged. (Takes
PERCHIK's hand.)

TEVYE (pleasantly, separating them). No,
you're not. I know, you like him, and he
likes you, but you're going away, and
you're staying here, so have a nice trip,
Perchik. I hope you'll be very happy, and
my answer is no.

HODEL. Please, Papa, you don't understand.

TEVYE. I understand. I gave my permission to Motel and Tzeitel, so you feel
that you also have a right. I'm sorry,
Perchik. I like you, but you're going
away, so go in good health and my answer is still no.

HODEL. You don't understand, Papa.

TEVYE (patiently). You're not listening.
I say no. I'm sorry, Hodel, but we'll find
someone else for you, here in Anatevka.

PERCHIK. Reb Tevye.

TEVYE. What is it?

PERCHIK. We are not asking for your
permission, only for your blessing. We are
going to get married.

TEVYE (to HODEL). You're not asking
for my permission?

HODEL. But we would like your blessing, Papa.

TEVYE.

["Tradition" Reprise]

I can't believe my own ears. My
        blessing? For What?
For going over my head? Impos-
        sible.
At least with Tzeitel and Motel,
        they asked me,
They begged me.
But now, if I like it or not,
She'll marry him.
So what do you want from me?
        Go on, be wed.
And tear out my beard and un-
        cover my head.
Tradition!
They're not even asking permis-
        sion
From the papa.
What's happening to the tradi-
        tion?
One little time I pulled out a
        thread
And where has it led? Where has
        it led?
Where has it led? To this! A man
        tells me he is getting mar-
        ried.
He doesn't ask me, he tells me.
        But first, he abandons her.

HODEL. He is not abandoning me, Papa.

PERCHIK. As soon as I can, I will send
for her and marry her. I love her.

TEVYE (mimicking him). "I love her."
Love. It's a new style. On the other hand,
our old ways were once new, weren't they?
On the other hand, they decided without parents, without a matchmaker. On
the other hand, did Adam and Eve have
a matchmaker? Yes, they did. Then it
seems these two have the same matchmaker. (Sings.)

They're going over my head—
Unheard of, absurd.
For this they want to be
        blessed?—
Unthinkable.
I'll lock her up in her room.
I couldn't—I should!—
But look at my daughter's eyes.
She loves him.
Tradition!

(*Shrugs.*) Very well, children, you have my blessing and my permission.

HODEL. Oh, thank you, Papa. You don't know how happy that makes me.

TEVYE (*to the audience*). What else could I do?

PERCHIK. Thank you, Papa.

TEVYE (*worried*). "Thank you, Papa." What will I tell your mother? Another dream?

PERCHIK. Perhaps if you tell her something—that I am going to visit a rich uncle—something like that.

TEVYE. Please, Perchik. I can handle my own wife. (PERCHIK *and* HODEL *exit. He calls aggressively.*) Golde! Golde! (*She enters from the house. He speaks timidly.*) Hello, Golde. I've just been talking to Perchik and Hodel.

GOLDE. Well?

TEVYE. They seem to be very fond of each other—

GOLDE. Well?

TEVYE. Well, I have decided to give them my permission to become engaged. (*Starts into the house.*)

GOLDE (*stopping him*). What? Just like this? Without even asking me?

TEVYE (*roaring*). Who asks you? I'm the father.

GOLDE. And who is he? A pauper. He has nothing, absolutely nothing!

TEVYE (*hesitating*). I wouldn't say that. I hear he has a rich uncle, a very rich uncle. (*Changes the subject.*) He is a good man, Golde. I like him. He is a little crazy, but I like him. And what's more important, Hodel likes him. Hodel loves him. So what can we do? It's a new world, a new world. Love. (*Starts to go, then has a sudden thought.*) Golde—(*Sings.*)
["Do You Love Me?"]

Do you love me?

GOLDE.
Do I what?

TEVYE.
Do you love me?

GOLDE.
Do I love you?
With our daughters getting married
And this trouble in the town,
You're upset, you're worn out,
Go inside, go lie down.
Maybe it's indigestion.

TEVYE. Golde, I'm asking you a question—

Do you love me?

GOLDE.
You're a fool.

TEVYE. I know—
But do you love me?

GOLDE.
Do I love you?
For twenty-five years I've washed
your clothes,
Cooked your meals, cleaned your
house,
Given you children, milked the
cow.
After twenty-five years, why talk
about
Love right now?

TEVYE.
Golde, the first time I met you
Was on our wedding day.
I was scared.

GOLDE.
I was shy.

TEVYE.
I was nervous.

GOLDE.
So was I.

TEVYE.
But my father and my mother
Said we'd learn to love each other.
And now I'm asking, Golde,
Do you love me?

GOLDE.
I'm your wife.

TEVYE. I know—
But do you love me?

GOLDE.
Do I love him?
For twenty-five years I've lived
with him,
Fought with him, starved with
him.
Twenty-five years my bed is his.
If that's not love, what is?

TEVYE.
Then you love me?

GOLDE.
I suppose I do.

TEVYE.
And I suppose I love you, too.

TEVYE *and* GOLDE.
It doesn't change a thing,
But even so,
After twenty-five years,
It's nice to know.

Scene Two

The village street. YENTE, TZEITEL, *and other villagers cross.* YENTE *and* TZEITEL *meet.)*

———

FISH SELLER. Fish! Fresh fish!

YENTE. Oh, Tzeitel, Tzeitel darling. Guess who I just saw! Your sister Chava with that Fyedka! And it's not the first time I've seen them together.

TZEITEL. You saw Chava with Fyedka?

YENTE. Would I make it up? Oh, and Tzeitel, I happened to be at the post office today and the postman told me there was a letter there for your sister Hodel.

TZEITEL. Wonderful, I'll go get it. (*Starts off.*)

YENTE. I got it! It's from her intended, Perchik. (*Hands letter to* TZEITEL.)

TZEITEL. Hodel will be so happy, she's been waiting—But it's open.

YENTE. It happened to be open. (TZEITEL *exits.* YENTE *watches her leave, then turns to a group of* VILLAGERS.) Rifka, I have such news for you.

["I Just Heard"]

Remember Perchik, that crazy
    student?
Remember at the wedding,
When Tzeitel married Motel
And Perchik started dancing
With Tevye's daughter Hodel?
Well, I just learned
That Perchik's been arrested, in
    Kiev.

VILLAGERS.
No!

YENTE.
Yes!

(YENTE *and the* FIRST GROUP *exit. A* WOMAN *crosses to a* SECOND GROUP.)

FIRST WOMAN. Shandel, Shandel! Wait till I tell you—
Remember Perchik, that crazy
    student?
Remember at the wedding,
He danced with Tevye's Hodel?
Well,
I just heard
That Hodel's been arrested, in
    Kiev.

VILLAGERS.
No! Terrible, terrible!

(*The* SECOND GROUP *exits. A* SECOND WOMAN *crosses to a* THIRD GROUP.)

SECOND WOMAN. Mirila!
Do you remember Perchik,
That student, from Kiev?
Remember how he acted
When Tzeitel married Motel?
Well, I just heard
That Motel's been arrested
For dancing at the wedding.

VILLAGERS.
No!

SECOND WOMAN.
In Kiev!

(*The* THIRD GROUP *exits.* MENDEL *crosses to a* FOURTH GROUP.)

MENDEL. Rabbi! Rabbi!
Remember Perchik, with all his
    strange ideas?
Remember Tzeitel's wedding
Where Tevye danced with Golde?
Well I just heard
That Tevye's been arrested
And Golde's gone to Kiev.

VILLAGERS.
No!

MENDEL.
God forbid.

VILLAGERS.
She didn't.

MENDEL.
She did.

(*The* FOURTH GROUP *exits.* AVRAM *crosses to the* FIFTH GROUP. YENTE *enters and stands at the edge of the* GROUP *to listen.*)

AVRAM. Listen, everybody, terrible news —terrible—
Remember Perchik,
Who started all the trouble?
Well, I just heard, from someone
    who should know,
That Golde's been arrested,
And Hodel's gone to Kiev.
Motel studies dancing,
And Tevye's acting strange.
Shprintze has the measles,
And Bielke has the mumps.

YENTE.
And that's what comes from men
    and women dancing!

Scene Three

The exterior of the railroad station. Morning. HODEL *enters and walks over to a bench.* TEVYE *follows, carrying her suitcase.*

———

HODEL. You don't have to wait for the train, Papa. You'll be late for your customers.

TEVYE. Just a few more minutes. Is he in bad trouble, that hero of yours? (*She nods.*) Arrested? (*She nods.*) And convicted?

HODEL. Yes, but he did nothing wrong. He cares nothing for himself. Everything he does is for humanity.

TEVYE. But if he did nothing wrong, he wouldn't be in trouble.

HODEL. Papa, how can you say that, a learned man like you? What wrongs did Joseph do, and Abraham, and Moses? And they had troubles.

TEVYE. But why won't you tell me where he is now, this Joseph of yours?

HODEL. It is far, Papa, terribly far. He is in a settlement in Siberia.

TEVYE. Siberia! And he asks you to leave your father and mother and join him in that frozen wasteland, and marry him there?

HODEL. No, Papa, he did not ask me to go. I want to go. I don't want him to be alone. I want to help him in his work. It is the greatest work a man can do.

TEVYE. But, Hodel, baby—

HODEL. Papa—(*Sings.*)

["Far From the Home I Love"]

How can I hope to make you understand
Why I do what I do,
Why I must travel to a distant land
Far from the home I love?
Once I was happily content to be
As I was, where I was,
Close to the people who are close to me
Here in the home I love.
Who could see that a man would come
Who would change the shape of my dreams?
Helpless, now, I stand with him
Watching older dreams grow dim.
Oh, what a melancholy choice this is,
Wanting home, wanting him,
Closing my heart to every hope

but his,
Leaving the home I love.
There where my heart has settled long ago
I must go, I must go.
Who could imagine I'd be wand'ring so
Far from the home I love?
Yet, there with my love, I'm home.

TEVYE. And who, my child, will there be to perform a marriage, there in the wilderness?

HODEL. Papa, I promise you, we will be married under a canopy.

TEVYE. No doubt a rabbi or two was also arrested. Well, give him my regards, this Moses of yours. I always thought he was a good man. Tell him I rely on his honor to treat my daughter well. Tell him that.

HODEL. Papa, God alone knows when we shall see each other again.

TEVYE. Then we will leave it in His hands. (*He kisses* HODEL, *starts to go, stops, looks back, then looks to heaven.*) Take care of her. See that she dresses warm. (*He exits, leaving* HODEL *seated on the station platform.*)

SCENE FOUR

The village street, some months later. The VILLAGERS *enter.*

———

AVRAM. Reb Mordcha, did you hear the news? A new arrival at Motel and Tzeitel's.

MORDCHA. A new arrival at Motel and Tzeitel's? I must congratulate him.

AVRAM. Rabbi, did you hear the news? A new arrival at Motel and Tzeitel's.

RABBI. Really?

MENDEL. Mazeltov.

FIRST MAN. Mazeltov.

SECOND MAN. Mazeltov.

(SHANDEL *crosses quickly, meeting a* WOMAN.)

WOMAN. Shandel, where are you running?

SHANDEL. To my boy, Motel. There's a new arrival there.

VILLAGERS. Mazeltov, Mazeltov, Mazeltov, Shandel.

SCENE FIVE

MOTEL's *tailor shop.* MOTEL *and* CHAVA *are in the shop.* GOLDE *and the* VILLAGERS *crowd around* MOTEL, *congratulating him. They fall back, revealing a used sewing machine.*

———

VILLAGERS. Mazeltov, Motel. We just heard. Congratulations. Wonderful.

MOTEL. Thank you, thank you very much.

(TZEITEL *enters.*)

AVRAM. Mazeltov, Tzeitel.

TZEITEL (*ecstatic*). You got it!

MOTEL. I got it!

TZEITEL. It's beautiful.

MOTEL. I know!

TZEITEL. Have you tried it yet?

MOTEL (*holds up two different-colored pieces of cloth sewn together*). Look.

TZEITEL. Beautiful.

MOTEL. I know. And in less than a minute. And see how close and even the stiches are.

TZEITEL. Beautiful.

MOTEL. I know. From now on, my clothes will be perfect, made by machine. No more handmade clothes.

(*The* RABBI *enters.*)

MORDCHA. The rabbi, the rabbi.

MOTEL. Look, Rabbi, my new sewing machine.

RABBI. Mazeltov.

TZEITEL. Rabbi, is there a blessing for a sewing machine?

RABBI. There is a blessing for everything. (*Prays.*) Amen.

VILLAGERS. Amen. . . . Mazeltov. (VILLAGERS, RABBI *exit.*)

GOLDE. And the baby? How is the baby?

TZEITEL. He's wonderful, Mama.

(FYEDKA *enters. There is an awkward pause.*)

FYEDKA. Good afternoon.

MOTEL. Good afternoon, Fyedka.

FYEDKA. I came for the shirt.

MOTEL. It's ready.

TZEITEL. See, it's my new sewing machine.

FYEDKA. I see. Congratulations.

MOTEL. Thank you.

FYEDKA (*after another awkward moment*). Good day. (*Leaves the shop.*)

MOTEL. Good day.

GOLDE. How does it work?

MOTEL. See, it's an amazing thing. You work it with your foot and your hand.

(CHAVA *exits from the shop and meets* FYEDKA *outside.*)

FYEDKA. They still don't know about us? (*She shakes her head.*) You must tell them.

CHAVA. I will, but I'm afraid.

FYEDKA. Chava, let me talk to your father.

CHAVA. No, that would be the worst thing, I'm sure of it.

FYEDKA. Let me try.

CHAVA. No, I'll talk to him. I promise.

(TEVYE *enters.*)

FYEDKA (*extending his hand*). Good afternoon.

TEVYE (*takes the hand limply*). Good afternoon.

FYEDKA (*looks at* CHAVA). Good day. (*Exits.*)

TEVYE. Good day. What were you and he talking about?

CHAVA. Nothing, we were just talking. (TEVYE *turns to go into* MOTEL's *shop.*) Papa, Fyedka, and I have known each other for a long time and—and

TEVYE (*turning back*). Chava, I would be much happier if you would remain friends from a distance. You must not forget who you are and who that man is.

CHAVA. He has a name, Papa.

TEVYE. Of course. All creatures on earth have a name.

CHAVA. Fyedka is not a creature, Papa. Fyedka is a man.

TEVYE. Who says that he isn't? It's just that he is a different kind of man. As the Good Book says, "Each shall seek his own kind." Which, translated, means, "A bird may love a fish, but where would they build a home together?" (*He starts toward the shop, but* CHAVA *seizes his arm.*)

CHAVA. The world is changing, Papa.

TEVYE. No. Some things do not change for us. Some things will never change.

CHAVA. We don't feel that way.

TEVYE. We?

CHAVA. Fyedka and I. We want to be married.

TEVYE. Are you out of your mind? Don't you know what this means, marrying outside of the faith?

CHAVA. But, Papa—

TEVYE. No, Chava! I said no! Never talk about this again! Never mention his name again! Never see him again! Never! Do you understand me?

CHAVA. Yes, Papa. I understand you.

(GOLDE *enters from the shop, followed* by SHPRINTZE *and* BIELKE.)

GOLDE. You're finally here? Let's go home. It's time for supper.

TEVYE. I want to see Motel's new machine.

GOLDE. You'll see it some other time. It's late.

TEVYE. Quiet, woman, before I get angry. And when I get angry, even flies don't dare to fly.

GOLDE. I'm very frightened of you. After we finish supper, I'll faint. Come home.

TEVYE (*sternly*). Golde. I am the man in the family. I am head of the house. I want to see Motel's new machine, now! (*Strides to the door of the shop, opens it, looks in, closes the door, turns to* GOLDE.) Now, let's go home! (*They exit.* CHAVA *remains looking after them.*)

SCENE SIX

A road. Late afternoon. TEVYE *is pushing his cart.*

———

TEVYE (*sinks down on the cart*). How long can that miserable horse of mine complain about his leg? (*Looks up.*) Dear God, if I can walk on two legs, why can't he walk on three? I know I shouldn't be too upset with him. He is one of Your creatures and he has the same rights as I have: the right to be sick, the right to be hungry, the right to work like a horse. And, dear God, I'm sick and tired of pulling this cart. I know, I know, I should push it a while. (*He starts pushing the cart.*)

GOLDE (*offstage*). Tevye! (*She enters, upset.*) Tevye!

TEVYE (*struck by her manner*). What? What it is?

GOLDE. It's Chava. She left home this morning. With Fyedka.

TEVYE. What?

GOLDE. I looked all over for her. I even went to the priest. He told me—they were married.

TEVYE. Married! (*She nods.*) Go home, Golde. We have other children at home. Go home, Golde. You have work to do. I

have work to do.

GOLDE. But, Chava—

TEVYE. Chava is dead to us! We will forget her. Go home. (GOLDE *exits.* TEVYE *sings.*)

["Chavaleh"]

Little bird, little Chavaleh,
    I don't understand what's happening today.
Everything is all a blur.
All I can see is a happy child,
The sweet little bird you were,
Chavaleh, Chavaleh.
Little bird, little Chavaleh,
    You were always such a pretty little thing.
Everybody's fav'rite child,
Gentle and kind and affectionate,
What a sweet little bird you were,
Chavaleh, Chavaleh.

(CHAVA *enters.*)

CHAVA. Papa, I want to talk with you. Papa, stop. At least listen to me. Papa, I beg you to accept us.

TEVYE (*to heaven*). Accept them? How can I accept them? Can I deny everything I believe in? On the other hand, can I deny my own child? On the other hand, how can I turn my back on my faith, my people? If I try to bend that far, I will break. On the other hand . . . there is no other hand. No Chava. No—no—no!

CHAVA. Papa. Papa.

VILLAGERS (*seen behind a transparent curtain, sing as* CHAVA *exits slowly*).
    Tradition. Tradition. Tradition.

SCENE SEVEN

TEVYE's *barn.* YENTE *enters with two* BOYS, *teen-age students, who are obviously uncomfortable in the situation.*

———

YENTE. Golde, are you home? I've got the two boys, the boys I told you about.

(GOLDE *enters, followed by* SHPRINTZE *and* BIELKE.) Golde darling, here they are, wonderful boys, both learned boys, Golde, from good families, each of them a prize, a jewel. You couldn't do better for your girls—just right. From the top of the tree.

GOLDE. I don't know, Yente. My girls are still so young.

YENTE. So what do they look like, grandfathers? Meanwhile they'll be engaged, nothing to worry about later, no looking around, their future all signed and sealed.

GOLDE. Which one for which one?

YENTE. What's the difference? Take your pick.

GOLDE. I don't know, Yente. I'll have to talk with—

(*Enter* LAZAR WOLF, AVRAM, MENDEL, MORDCHA, *and other* VILLAGERS.)

AVRAM. Golde, is Reb Tevye home?

GOLDE. Yes, but he's in the house. Why, is there some trouble?

AVRAM (*to* BIELKE *and* SHPRINTZE). Call your father. (*They exit.*)

YENTE (*to the* BOYS). Go home. Tell your parents I'll talk to them. (*They exit.*)

GOLDE. What is it? Why are you all gathered together like a bunch of goats? What's—

(TEVYE *enters.*)

AVRAM. Reb Tevye, have you seen the constable today?

TEVYE. No. Why?

LAZAR. There are some rumors in town. We thought because you knew him so well, maybe he told you what is true and what is not.

TEVYE. What rumors?

AVRAM. Someone from Zolodin told me that there was an edict issued in St. Petersburg that all—Shh. Shh.

(*He stops as the* CONSTABLE *enters with* TWO MEN.)

TEVYE. Welcome, your Honor. What's the good news in the world?

CONSTABLE. I see you have company.

TEVYE. They are my friends.

CONSTABLE. It's just as well. What I have to say is for their ears also. Tevye, how much time do you need to sell your house and all your household goods? (*There is a gasp from the* VILLAGERS. *They are stunned. They look to* TEVYE.)

TEVYE. Why should I sell my house? Is it in anybody's way?

CONSTABLE. I came here to tell you that you are going to have to leave Anatevka.

TEVYE. And how did I come to deserve such an honor?

CONSTABLE. Not just you, of course, but all of you. At first I thought you might be spared, Tevye, because of your daughter Chava, who married—

TEVYE. My daughter is dead!

CONSTABLE. I understand. At any rate, it affects all of you. You have to leave.

TEVYE. But this corner of the world has always been our home. Why should we leave?

CONSTABLE (*irritated*). I don't know why. There's trouble in the world. Troublemakers.

TEVYE (*ironically*). Like us!

CONSTABLE. You aren't the only ones. Your people must leave all the villages— Zolodin, Rabalevka. The whole district must he emptied. (*Horrified and amazed exclamations from the* VILLAGERS.) I have an order here, and it says that you must sell your homes and be out of here in three days.

VILLAGERS. Three days! . . . Out in three days!

TEVYE. And you who have known us all your life, you'd carry out this order?

CONSTABLE. I have nothing to do with it, don't you understand?

TEVYE (*bitterly*). We understand.

FIRST MAN. And what if we refuse to go?

CONSTABLE. You will be forced out.

LAZAR. We will defend ourselves.

VILLAGERS. Stay in our homes . . . Refuse to leave . . . Keep our land.

SECOND MAN. Fight!

CONSTABLE. Against our army? I wouldn't advise it!

TEVYE. I have some advice for you. Get off my land! (*The* VILLAGERS *crowd toward the* CONSTABLE *and his* MEN.) This is still my home, my land. Get off my land! (*The* CONSTABLE *and his men start to go. The* CONSTABLE *turns.*)

CONSTABLE. You have three days! (*Exits.*)

FIRST MAN. After a lifetime, a piece of paper and get thee out.

MORDCHA. We should get together with the people of Zolodin. Maybe they have a plan.

FIRST MAN. We should defend ourselves. An eye for an eye, a tooth for a tooth.

TEVYE. Very good. And that way, the whole world will be blind and toothless.

MENDEL. Rabbi, we've been waiting for the Messiah all our lives. Wouldn't this be a good time for him to come?

RABBI. We'll have to wait for him someplace else. Meanwhile, let's start packing. (*The* VILLAGERS *start to go, talking together.*)

VILLAGERS. He's right. . . . I'll see you

before I go.

FIRST MAN. Three days!

MORDCHA. How will I be able to sell my shop? My merchandise?

THIRD MAN. Where can I go with a wife, her parents, and three children?

(*Exit all but* YENTE, GOLDE, AVRAM, LAZAR, MENDEL, *and* TEVYE.)

YENTE. Well, Anatevka hasn't been exactly the Garden of Eden.

AVRAM. That's true.

GOLDE. After all, what've we got here? (*Sings.*)

["Anatevka"]

A little a bit of this,
A little bit of that,

YENTE.
A pot,

LAZAR.
A pan,

MENDEL.
A broom,

AVRAM.
A hat.

TEVYE.
Someone should have set a match to this place long ago.

MENDEL.
A bench,

AVRAM.
A tree,

GOLDE.
So what's a stove?

LAZAR.
Or a house?

MENDEL (*speaks*). People who pass through Anatevka don't even know they've been here.

GOLDE.
A stick of wood,

YENTE.
A piece of cloth.

ALL.
What do we leave?
Nothing much,
Only Anatevka. . . .
Anatevka, Anatevka,
Underfed, overworked Anatevka,
Where else could Sabbath be so
   sweet?
Anatevka, Anatevka,
Intimate, obstinate Anatevka,
Where I know everyone I meet.
Soon I'll be a stranger in a strange
   new place,

Searching for an old familiar face
From Anatevka.
I belong in Anatevka,
Tumbledown, workaday Ana-
   tevka,
Dear little village, little town of
   mine.

GOLDE. Eh, it's just a place.

MENDEL. And our forefathers have been, forced out of many, many places at a moment's notice.

TEVYE (*shrugs*). Maybe that's why we always wear our hats.

SCENE EIGHT

Outside TEVYE's *house.* MOTEL *and* TZEITEL *are packing baggage into a cart and a wagon.* SHPRINTZE *and* BIELKE *enter with bundles.*

———

SHPRINTZE. Where will we live in America?

MOTEL. With Uncle Abram, but he doesn't know it yet.

SHPRINTZE. I wish you and the baby were coming with us.

TZEITEL. We'll be staying in Warsaw until we have enough money to join you.

GOLDE (*entering, with goblets*). Motel, be careful with these. My mother and father, may they rest in peace, gave them to us on our wedding day.

TZEITEL (*to* BIELKE *and* SHPRINTZE). Come, children, help me pack the rest of the clothes. (*They exit into house.*)

YENTE (*enters*). Golde darling, I had to see you before I left because I have such news for you. Golde darling, you remember I told you yesterday I didn't know where to go, what to do with these old bones? Now I know! You want to hear? I'll tell you. Golde darling, all my life I've dreamed of going to one place and now I'll walk, I'll crawl, I'll get there. Guess where. You'll never guess. Every year at Passover, what do we say? "Next year in Jerusalem, next year in the Holy Land."

GOLDE. You're going to the Holy Land!

YENTE. You guessed! And you know why? In my sleep, my husband, my Aaron, came to me and said, "Yente, go to the Holy Land." Usually, of course, I wouldn't listen to him, because, good as he was, too much brains he wasn't blessed with. But in my sleep it's a sign. Right? So, somehow or other, I'll get to the Holy Land. And you want to know what I'll do there? I'm a matchmaker, no? I'll arrange marriages, yes? Children come from marriages, no? So I'm going to the Holy Land to help our people increase and multiply. It's my mission. So good-bye, Golde.

GOLDE. Good-bye, Yente. Be well and go in peace. (*They embrace.*)

YENTE (*exiting*). Maybe next time, Golde, we will meet on happier occasions. Meanwhile, we suffer, we suffer, we suffer in silence! Right? Of course, right. (*She exits.* GOLDE *sits on a large straw trunk, sadly wrapping a pair of silver goblets.* TEVYE *enters, carrying a bundle of books, and puts them on the wagon.*)

TEVYE. We'll have to hurry, Golde. (*She is looking at the goblets.*) Come, Golde, we have to leave soon.

GOLDE. Leave. It sounds so easy.

TEVYE. We'll all be together soon. Motel, Tzeitel, and the baby, they'll come too, you'll see. That Motel is a person.

GOLDE. And Hodel and Perchik? When will we ever see them?

TEVYE. Do they come visiting us from Siberia every Sabbath? You know what she writes. He sits in prison, and she works, and soon he will be set free and together they will turn the world upside down. She couldn't be happier. And the other children will be with us.

GOLDE (*quietly*). Not all.

TEVYE (*sharply*). All. Come, Golde, we have to get finished.

GOLDE. I still have to sweep the floor.

TEVYE. Sweep the floor?

GOLDE. I don't want to leave a dirty house. (*She exits behind the house as* LAZAR *enters, carrying a large suitcase.*)

LAZAR. Well, Tevye, I'm on my way.

TEVYE. Where are you going?

LAZAR. Chicago. In America. My wife, Fruma-Sarah, may she rest in peace, has a brother there.

TEVYE. That's nice.

LAZAR. I hate him, but a relative is a relative! (*They embrace.*) Good-bye, Tevye. (LAZAR *exits.* TEVYE *enters the house, passing* TZEITEL, *who enters with a blanket and a small bundle.*)

TEVYE. Tzeitel, are they finished inside?

TZEITEL. Almost, Papa. (TZEITEL *puts the blanket on* MOTEL's *wagon, kneels down, and begins rummaging in the bundle.* CHAVA *and* FYEDKA *enter.* TZEITEL *turns to enter the house, and sees them.*) Chava! (CHAVA *runs to her. They embrace.* TZEITEL *looks toward the house.*) Papa will see you.

CHAVA. I want him to. I want to say good-bye to him.

TZEITEL. He will not listen.

CHAVA. But at least he will hear.

TZEITEL. Maybe it would be better if I went inside and told Mama that—

(GOLDE *comes round the side of the house.*)

GOLDE. Chava!

(*She starts toward her as* TEVYE *enters from the house with a length of rope. He sees them, turns, reenters house, returns, and bends down to tie up the straw trunk, his back to* CHAVA *and* FYEDKA.)

CHAVA. Papa, we came to say good-bye. (TEVYE *does not respond, but goes on working.*) We are also leaving this place. We are going to Cracow.

FYEDKA. We cannot stay among people who can do such things to others.

CHAVA. We wanted you to know that. Good-bye, Papa, Mama. (*She waits for an answer, gets none, and turns to go.*)

FYEDKA. Yes, we are also moving. Some are driven away by edicts, others by silence. Come, Chava.

TZEITEL. Good-bye, Chava, Fyedka.

TEVYE (*to* TZEITEL, *prompting her under his breath as he turns to another box*). God be with you!

TZEITEL (*looks at him, then speaks to Chava, gently*). God be with you!

CHAVA. We will write to you in America. If you like.

GOLDE. We will be staying with Uncle Abram.

CHAVA. Yes, Mama. (CHAVA *and* FYEDKA *exit.* TEVYE *turns and watches them leave. There is a moment of silence; then he turns on* GOLDE.)

TEVYE (*with mock irritation*). We will be staying with Uncle Abram! We will be staying with Uncle Abram! The whole world has to know our business!

GOLDE. Stop yelling and finish packing. We have a train to catch.

(MOTEL, SHPRINTZE, *and* BIELKE *enter from the house.*)

TEVYE. I don't need your advice, Golde. Tzeitel, don't forget the baby. We have to catch a train, and a boat. Bielke, Shprintze, put the bundles on the wagon.

(TEVYE *moves the wagon to the center of the stage, and* MOTEL *puts the trunk on it.* TZEITEL *brings the baby out of the house. They turn to one another for good-byes.*)

TZEITEL. Good-bye, Papa. (*They embrace.*)

GOLDE. Good-bye, Motel.

MOTEL. Good-bye, Mama.

(TZEITEL *and* GOLDE *embrace.*)

TEVYE. Work hard, Motel. Come to us soon.

MOTEL. I will, Reb Tevye. I'll work hard. (TEVYE *takes one last look at the baby, then* TZEITEL *and* MOTEL *exit with their cart. When they are gone,* TEVYE *turns to the wagon.*)

TEVYE (*picking up pots*). Come, children. Golde, we can leave these pots.

GOLDE. No, we can't.

TEVYE. All right, we'll take them. (*Puts them back.*)

BIELKE (*childishly, swinging around with* SHPRINTZE). We're going on a train and a boat. We're going on a—

GOLDE (*sharply*). Stop that! Behave yourself! We're not in America yet!

TEVYE. Come, children. Let's go.

(*The stage begins to revolve, and* TEVYE *begins to pull the wagon in the opposite direction. The other* VILLAGERS, *including the* FIDDLER, *join the circle. The revolve stops. There is a last moment together, and the* VILLAGERS *exit, at different times and in opposite directions, leaving the family on stage.* TEVYE *begins to pull his wagon upstage, revealing the* FIDDLER, *playing his theme.* TEVYE *stops, turns, beckons to him. The* FIDDLER *tucks his violin under his arm and follows the family upstage as the curtain falls.*)

SLOW DANCE ON THE KILLING GROUND

William Hanley

First presented by Hume Cronyn-Allen–Hodgon Inc.–Stevens Productions Inc.–Bonfils-Seawell Enterprises at the Plymouth Theatre in New York City on November 30, 1964, with the following cast:

(*In order of appearance*)

GLAS George Rose ROSIE Carolan Daniels
RANDALL Clarence Williams III

Directed by Joseph Anthony
Set designed by Oliver Smith
Costumes by Ann Roth
Lighting by Jack Brown

SYNOPSIS OF SCENES

The play happens on the night of June 1, 1962, in a small store in a district of warehouses and factories in Brooklyn, and in the kitchen of the apartment adjoining the store. In the surrounding streets the buildings are squat and dark, the street lamps unlit. Viewed from a distance, the dim glow cast into the street through the window of the lighted store would be seen to be the only light in a great, stone darkness.

But for a lapse of some five minutes or so between the first and second scenes of Act Two, the action is continuous.

Copyright © 1964 by William Hanley.
Reprinted by permission of Random House, Inc.

CAUTION: Professionals and amateurs are hereby warned that *Slow Dance on the Killing Ground* is subject to a royalty. It is fully protected under the copyright laws of the United States of America, and of all countries covered by the International Copyright Union (including the Dominion of Canada and the rest of the British Commonwealth), and of all countries covered by the Pan-American Copyright Convention and the Universal Copyright Convention, and of all countries with which the United States has reciprocal copyright relations. All rights, including professional, amateur, motion picture, recitation, lecturing, public reading, radio broadcasting, television, and the rights of translation into foreign languages, are strictly reserved. Particular emphasis is laid on the question of readings, permission for which must be secured from the author's agent in writing.

All inquiries concerning rights (other than amateur rights) should be addressed to the author's agent, Hayden Griffin, Hesseltine, Bookman and Seff, Ltd., 157 West 57th Street, New York, N.Y. 10019, without whose permission in writing no performance of the play may be made.

The amateur production rights of *Slow Dance on the Killing Ground* are controlled exclusively by the Dramatists Play Service, Inc., 440 Park Avenue South, New York, N.Y. 10016. No amateur performance of this work may be given without obtaining in advance the written permission of the Dramatists Play Service, Inc., and paying the requisite fee.

IT IS almost axiomatic that an American playwright is born in New York City—it must have something to do with the pollution—but William Hanley was born in Lorain, Ohio, on October 22, 1931. He, of course, lives in New York City.

Mr. Hanley studied at Cornell University and at the American Academy of Dramatic Arts. His first break came in 1962 when two of his one-act plays, *Whisper into My Good Ear* and *Mrs. Dally Has a Lover,* were produced Off-Broadway and won the Vernon Rice Award. (In 1965 they were given a new Broadway staging.) The following year Mr. Hanley offered *Today Is Independence Day.* And then, on November 30, 1964, *Slow Dance on the Killing Ground* opened on Broadway at the Plymouth Theatre.

In January of 1968 Mr. Hanley had his next major play, *Flesh and Blood,* diverted from Broadway and given a network telecast on NBC Television. This unusual procedure was explained subsequently by the playwright himself when this play (about a family clinging to a solitary apartment in an otherwise empty tenement scheduled for demolition) was eventually published in book form.

Mr. Hanley commented that during the 1965–1966 Broadway season there were twenty plays on Broadway that might be called dramas—"no singing, no dancing, not too many laughs." He noted that some of the plays were obviously inferior and undeserving and had been properly and instantly put out of their misery by the critics. "But," Mr. Hanley continues, "there were favorable, in some cases glowing, reviews for a number of those plays, despite which only two of them were running at the season's end and neither of those survived the summer that followed."

Which is why Mr. Hanley is turning to television. *Flesh and Blood,* incidentally, is intended as part of a dramatic trilogy called *The Times We Had.* The second play of the trilogy is *The Summer Before the War,* but whether these are intended for Broadway or television seems to be not yet known.

However for all of this television excursion, which received a very mixed reception from the television critics, Mr. Hanley's major reputation is so far based on *Slow Dance on the Killing Ground,* which was revived Off-Broadway in 1970.

Slow Dance, which has proved popular with repertory groups throughout the country, is an excellent example of that genre that Broadway desperately needs for its sustenance, the "good-bad play." It is not the nature of the theatre to produce a whole series of masterpieces. How many plays, domestic or foreign, written in the past ten years, or fifteen years, or twenty years, are going to be added to that tiny store of classics we regard as our permanent dramatic literature?

Yet the theatre has to be kept going, plays have to be produced, the works have to be kept oiled. Most plays are by the natural way of things bad. This is true of music, of painting, of dance, indeed of any art form. What you are looking for is not the work of blazing genius—O'Neills are rare—but the totally professional work, enjoyable on its own unpretentious terms. *Slow Dance* fits this bill.

It is a fairly simple, even if tricksy, melodrama. Three characters, a guilt-ridden ex-Communist German owning a small store in Brooklyn, an antic black murderer on the run from the cops, and, finally, a poor, misunderstood, plain girl seeking an abortion from a pregnancy arising from her very first sexual experience, meet, discuss, and settle their differences with the world. Mr. Hanley has a dozen themes running through his play and all of them are obvious, yet the author knows what he is doing and he has created three very fine vehicles for his actors. For this reason if no other I suspect that *Slow Dance on the Killing Ground* will enjoy quite a long life in the American theatre.

ACT ONE: Pas de Deux

The shop is the kind of place usually referred to in New York City as a candy store but whose merchandise and function cover a much wider range in service and activity than that term would suggest.

The entrance to the store is in the left center wall. To the right of this door there is a very large plate-glass window, unwashed and clouded. The door opens onto a low landing, bounded on the left by a guard-rail, two steps lead down to the floor-level of the store. Below the window, and running parallel to the upper wall, is the counter-top of a soda fountain, in front of which are several wooden stools. To the left of the street entrance, downstage, there is a single small table with chairs. Part of the right wall, to a height of six feet or so from the floor, is covered with racks for magazines and garish paperbound books. In front of these racks downstage is a low bench for the display of newspapers; above the racks, too high to reach without the aid of a ladder, there are shelves and cabinets, crammed with a miscellany of merchandise: most everything from shaving supplies to stationery. Against the left wall, downstage, there is a jukebox, glittering new, in jarring conflict with its surroundings. In the right wall an open doorway gives access to a dimly lit hallway which leads to the kitchen. Next to the doorway there is a wall telephone. The kitchen occupies the far right of the stage and is unlit now. The store is lit with a number of hanging lightbulbs covered with conical green metal shades.

It is a moment before GLAS *enters, through the doorway at the right, carrying an eight-foot stepladder on his shoulder.* GLAS *is a man of sixty-five, slow of movement, but with an intimation of strength about him. His very erect bearing is marred only by a mild but very definite limp. He is an unusually alert and observant man but a silent one by nature; so that, although he absorbs all that goes on about him, he does not ordinarily feel compelled to comment upon it.*

He opens the legs of the ladder and settles them in front of the magazine racks. He ascends the ladder and thoughtfully regards the contents of the cabinet, descends the ladder and moves to the rear of the soda fountain. He stoops, is out of

sight for a moment, then reappears holding a large ledger and a clipboard, to which are fastened several sheets of paper. He places these on the countertop and moves around the counter. He opens the ledger, finds the page, returns to the ladder and ascends it. He removes a box from the cabinet, counts its contents, descends the ladder and makes a notation on the inventory sheet attached to the clipboard. He ascends the ladder again and is in the process of counting the contents of a second box when the door is jolted open and RANDALL *bounds in from the street.*

RANDALL *is a Negro boy of eighteen, slim, wiry, handsome. He is wearing a close-fitting suit with a somewhat short jacket and velvet collar, a narrow-brimmed hat with a high crown, and a rather voluminous cape that falls to his hips. He carries a tightly rolled umbrella. The overall effect is somewhat Edwardian but for the dirty white sneakers on his feet and the dark glasses he wears.*

At the sound of his entrance, GLAS *has turned, unseen by* RANDALL, *to watch the boy.* RANDALL *is breathless, as from a long run, and highly agitated. He closes the door behind him and rests his back upon it. He looks about quickly and believes the place to be deserted. After a moment, he calms and relaxes, but even then his movements are relatively quick and tense. Throughout, he has been humming a tune, quietly, absently. He looks quickly about the place and takes only a single step before* GLAS *speaks.*

———

GLAS. So? (RANDALL *starts, almost violently, and it is a moment, a split second, before he discovers* GLAS *atop the ladder. His demeanor changes instantly to an attitude of breeziness, near-gaiety.*)

RANDALL. *Hey,* daddy! (GLAS *merely gazes, silent.*) Didn't see you up there! Pretty neat, yes indeedy!

GLAS. Neat?

RANDALL. I mean, you pretty much able to keep your eye on matters from up there, right? Panoramic view. Pan-o-ramic! Neat.

GLAS (*confused, gesturing with the box*). No, I'm only—

RANDALL (*downstage to table*). Man! it's hot, ain't it?

GLAS (*descending the ladder; crossing behind counter*). What can I do for you?

RANDALL (*turns to* GLAS). Oh, well now! that there's a question, ain't it!

GLAS. What?

RANDALL. I mean, what can you *do* for me. (*Crosses right to telephone.*) The possibilities are endless, know what I mean? Right? But we start with somethin' easy. (*Turns to* GLAS, *points with umbrella.*) Gimme a . . . gimme an egg cream.

GLAS. Chocolate?

RANDALL. That's a nice flavor.

GLAS (*halts abruptly, remembering*). I can't.

RANDALL. Can't what.

GLAS. Make an egg cream. My seltzer water, the tap's broken.

RANDALL. Now, ain't that the way? Ain't that always the way? (*Crosses upstage to stool.*) You ask me what can you do for me, I give you somethin' real easy to start with and you got a busted tap on your seltzer water. Man, oh, man. How you fixed for a bottle of lemon-soda, say?

GLAS. Lemon soda I got.

RANDALL. Crazy. (*Sits stool facing counter. While* GLAS *takes the soda from the freezer behind the counter, removes the cap and gives the bottle to* RANDALL, RANDALL *puts coin on counter.*) You open kinda late, aintcha?

GLAS. I don't know.

RANDALL. You don't know?

GLAS. What time is it? (*Takes money.*)

RANDALL. 'Cordin' to my twenny-one jewel, Swiss movement chronometer calendar watch it now six minutes after ten o'clock P.M. June the first, nineteen sixty-two. (*Takes a drink.*)

GLAS. Yes.

RANDALL. Hmm?

GLAS (*turns to register;* RANDALL *looks out window;* GLAS *puts change on counter and goes to ladder*). Yes, I'm open late. (GLAS *moves to resume his inventory and is constantly ascending and descending the ladder throughout what follows while* RANDALL, *nervous, peering out the window and the door, is moving always. He hums again for a moment the same tune.*)

RANDALL. About what time you figurin' on closin' up? I mean, approximate? (*Puts change in his pocket.*)

GLAS (*ascends ladder—counts contents in box*). Oh . . . sooner or later. No hurry.

RANDALL. Well, what I mean, you gotta go to *sleep* sometime, right?

GLAS. I don't sleep much.

RANDALL. Oh, that right?

GLAS. I don't like to sleep.

RANDALL (*off stool downstage to bench, picks up magazine*). You of European abstraction.

GLAS. I beg your pardon?

RANDALL. Your accent. Originally you speak another tongue, I mean you come from across the sea, right?

GLAS. Oh. *Ex*-traction.

RANDALL (*turns to* GLAS). Sir?

GLAS. You said *ab*straction. The word is *ex*traction. European *ex*traction.

RANDALL. Oh. Yeah . . . well, I stand corrected, daddy.

GLAS (*definitely, pressing the point*). *Ex*traction.

RANDALL. You the precise type, I be sure to watch my step with you—linguistically speakin'. (*Drops magazine and crosses upstage to counter, gets soda, crosses left to door.* GLAS *descends ladder.* RANDALL *prowls for a moment and moves to door, singing quietly to himself the tune recognizable as the one he has been humming.*) "I went to the rock to hide my face, / The rock cried out, no hiding place . . ." (*From the street, footsteps are heard on the pavement, approaching.* RANDALL *tenses and becomes still. This is seen by* GLAS *but* RANDALL *is unaware of being observed: the footsteps, it seems, are more important. The steps grow louder until a figure is dimly seen through the window, passing in the street. The footsteps fade.* RANDALL *calms.*) You know there ain't a single light out there atall? For about twenny blocks? I mean, the streetlights, daddy, they all *out!*

GLAS. Repairing the power lines. They've been digging up the street for about two weeks now.

RANDALL (*crosses downstage to table; puts down soda*). Well, dig they must, daddy, dig they must. This is a kinda kooky place for a store though, ain't it.

GLAS (*downstage picks up magazine and puts it back on rack.*) Why?

RANDALL (*crosses to jukebox*). Well, I mean, it is what you might say, off the beaten track, somewhat removed from the bustling lanes of commerce.

GLAS. Only at night. In the daytime I do okay with the factory people. At night it's quiet. I like it that way.

RANDALL. You ain't afraid to go home this late at night?

GLAS (*crosses to chair*). You ask a lot of questions, sonny.

RANDALL (*turns to* GLAS). Well, it's just that I'm of the inquirin' type of mind. No offense intended, I hasten to assure you, sir. (*A pause, during which* GLAS *studies* RANDALL *and mistakenly interprets his answer to be sincere.*)

GLAS (*turns, starts right*). This is home. (*Pointing.*) In the back.

RANDALL. Crazy.

GLAS (*stops; turns to* RANDALL). What's crazy about it?

RANDALL. No, there do seem to be some misunderstandin' here this evenin'. Crazy: that means, uh . . . that's all right, that's good.

GLAS (*upstage to stool*). What's all right?

RANDALL (*sits chair*). That you *live* here, daddy. I mean, it is an excellent *i-dea!*

GLAS. Ah.

RANDALL (GLAS *ascends ladder*). You'll see: pretty soon we be understandin' each other perfect. You mind if I ask you another little question? One which might prove to be to your definite benefit?

GLAS. Mm?

RANDALL. You climb up to the top of that there ladder, right? Then you count the stuff in one a them boxes, right? Then you—(GLAS *descends ladder.*) climb down the ladder and write on that there paper, right?

GLAS (*crosses behind counter to ledger*). Inventory, yeah.

RANDALL. Yeah, but it'd be a lot faster you took the paper up there on the ladder. (*Pause.*)

GLAS (*looks at ladder*). What's the hurry?

RANDALL. Oh. Well, now you got a point there. Long as you ain't in no hurry.

GLAS (*crosses left to platform*). I don't see you around here before, sonny.

RANDALL. You like to do me a little favor?

GLAS. What.

RANDALL. Don't call me sonny.

GLAS. What's your name?

RANDALL (*stands, moves above chair; after a pause*). Why.

GLAS (*downstage to table picks up cups and napkins; obviously*). You don't want me to call you sonny, what should I call you?

RANDALL (*leans on railing*). Winston.

GLAS (*takes newspaper from chair*). Winston. Okay.

RANDALL. Winston Churchill. (*Pause.*)

GLAS. This is a joke?

RANDALL. You don't think I look like my name could be Winston Churchill?

GLAS. It makes no difference to me one way or the other.

RANDALL. Tell you the truth, my name is Franz . . . Franz Kafka. (*Pause.*)

GLAS (*stops, turns*). You should be on the TV with your funny line of jokes—sonny. (*Takes cup from counter. Throws his collection in can behind counter and picks up rag.*)

RANDALL. You know Franz Kafka? I don't mean, did you know him personally, I mean you know who he was? (*Crosses to telephone. No response.*) You know that story he write where this fella wake up one mornin' and find out he turned into a *bug*? You know that story? That actually happen to me. (GLAS *crosses left to table and wipes it.*)

GLAS (*drily*). Is that right.

RANDALL (*upstage to left end counter; puts down soda*). Yeah. One mornin' I wake up and I realize I'm actually a *bug*. I *look* the same, like always, you know, but actually I'm a *bug*.

GLAS. How is that.

RANDALL (*continues to move upstage as far as he can then turns downstage*). Oh well, it a little too complicated to explain just at the present moment. Some other time, maybe.

GLAS (*crosses to center*). Don't you ever stand still, boy?

RANDALL (*downstage to stool, turns left, crosses to center a few feet from* GLAS). Stand still! Baby, get *me* to stand still they gonna have to nail my feet to the floor! *To the floor!* (*He hurls his umbrella, like a spear, at the floor. The stem, apparently sharpened to a point, pierces the wood and the umbrella stands of itself.*) Know what I mean? (*Pause.*)

GLAS. That's dangerous. (RANDALL *retrieves the umbrella and cleans the point caressingly in the palm of his hand.*)

RANDALL. Ain't it now? You know I got a IQ of a hundred and eighty-seven? Yeah. A hundred and eighty-seven. Fact.

GLAS (*smiling*). Oh, yeah?

RANDALL. Yeah, that the reaction that information usually get. It a true statement, nevertheless. Eighteen years old and a IQ of a hundred and eighty-seven. (*Crosses upstage to stool.*) When I was a little kid they used to be always givin' me a lotta these here tests, you know? (GLAS *crosses left to behind counter. Puts rag on fountain. Crosses to ladder.*) They take me up to Columbia University and all these cats be sittin' around puffin' on their pipes and askin' me a lotta questions, you know, tryin' to figure out how it could happen I be so smart. But that just the way it is: a genius is what I am. I got a photographic memory, you know? (GLAS *moves ladder downstage to doorway and ascends.*) Sometimes known as total recall. Like for instance, would you care to hear me quote some of the book *War and Peace* by Count Leo Tolstoy? I couldn't quote you nothin' past page one hundred and forty-six, though, 'cause that's as far as I got in that particular book, it actually a rather borin' book, if you know what I mean. (GLAS *smiles.*) What's so amusin'?

GLAS (*turns to* RANDALL). It happens to be one of the greatest books.

RANDALL. Yeah, I heard that. Bored the shit outta *me*.

GLAS. When you get older you'll be able to appreciate it.

RANDALL. You think so, uh? (GLAS *nods.*) You read that book, then, uh? (RANDALL *picks up umbrella, moves downstage to ladder.*)

GLAS (*descends ladder*). Mm.

RANDALL (*leans on ladder*). Mm. So anyway, here I am with this here fantastic IQ (GLASS *crosses to counter between stools —turns ledger around.*), you see what I mean? Of course, as is clear and apparent to the naked eye, I am, withal, a young gentleman of some color—which limits my horizons considerable in this here present society we got, notwithstandin' IQ's and all. (RANDALL *turns to* GLAS.)

GLAS (*turns*). Not necessarily. If you're as smart as you say, you could do great things.

RANDALL. For my race?

GLAS. What?

RANDALL (*downstage to stool*). That's what they used to be tellin' me all the time when I was on the inside. With a mind like you got, Randall, you could be doin' great things for your race. Unquote.

GLAS (*downstage to left of stool*). Inside where?

RANDALL (*sits, leans back against ladder; feet up on bench*). Oh, you know: a reform school here, a co-rectional institution there, a work farm for minor offenders upstate I was on for a while, *that* was very nice, lotsa fresh air, you know? They was always sayin' that: with a mind like you got, Randall, you could be doin' great things for your race. It never occurred to them to say I could be doin' great things for *me*. Not that I got a mind to do that neither, but it woulda been a nice change from all that jazz about great things for my race. (GLAS *turns away.* RANDALL *stands. Stops him.*) My name is Randall. I mean, that my true name. 'Cause I don't want you callin' me sonny or boy or nothin' like that. Okay? Randall. . . . Okay?

GLAS. Okay. (GLAS *moves upstage to counter.*)

RANDALL. What's yours? (RANDALL *moves upstage sits stool.*)

GLAS. What?

RANDALL. Your name, I mean. (GLAS *gazes at him for a moment before answering.*)

GLAS (*crosses right to ladder*). Glas.

RANDALL. Glass?

GLAS. With one *s*.

RANDALL. What kinda name is that, Glas with one *s*?

GLAS (*turns to* RANDALL). German for the Glas with two esses. (GLAS *ascends ladder.*)

RANDALL. Oh, I dig. German. (*Points to the window.*) Glass with two esses. (*Points to* GLAS.) Glas with one *s*. Neat. Short and sweet. (GLAS *counts contents of cigar box.*) Actually the point is already made by the time one gets to the first, so that other *s* just kinda *dangle* there doin' *nothin*. I like that. Glas with one *s*. (RANDALL *looks out window.*) And now that my attention been called to it, and you don't mind me sayin', but the glass with two esses here could use a little washin', I do believe.

GLAS. Why? (*Turns to* RANDALL.)

RANDALL. Why! Well, daddy, you can't hardly even see *through* it. It downright *dirty,* that glass with two esses.

GLAS. There's nothing out there I particularly want to see.

RANDALL. Is that right?

GLAS. That's right.

RANDALL (*sits*). You don't like the nature of things out there particularly?

GLAS (*descends ladder*). Exactly.

RANDALL (*stands; moves downstage of stool.*) Well now, you see? I had a feelin', I just *knew* we was brothers under the skin, somehow. I hasten to repeat (GLAS *crosses left to ledger between stools.*) *under* the skin, no offense intended, no indeed, sir. But I know exactly what you mean, exactly! I mean, it is grotesque out there, ain't it, now? It is . . . (RANDALL *crosses downstage to left end of bench. Sits.*) bizarre! You know what that is out there, daddy? You know? That is the *killing* ground out there.

GLAS (*turns to* RANDALL). The what?

RANDALL (*stands; moves upstage to* GLAS). I mean that's No Man's Land out there, daddy! (*Crosses left to door.*) That somebody *elses* turf, a regular *mine field*, you gotta step *carefully*, they *kill* you out there, know what I mean?

GLAS (*crosses between stools watching right*). Not exactly.

RANDALL. Butcher shop. It a regular butcher shop out there. (*Turns to* GLAS.) You know what happened out there just last year alone?

GLAS. Do I know what *happened*?

RANDALL. Just last year alone.

GLAS. What happened?

RANDALL (*downstage to chair; sits, umbrella on table*). What happened out there —and I quote—what happened out there was four hundred and eighty-three homicides! (GLAS *leans on counter and watches* RANDALL *who closes his eyes and recites, from memory.*) "Contrary to public impression, most homicides are spontaneous and are committed in the home; they are not the result of gangland reprisals but of family disputes. These facts about murder were revealed today by Police Commissioner Michael J. Murphy in releasing a report by his department's Statistical and Records Bureau in a dossier of such crimes during 1961. Out of four hundred and eighty-three homicides last year, an increase of ninety-three over the preceding year, eighty-seven and four-tenths percent were solved or cleared by arrests. A study of them discloses the following: fifty-three percent of the homicides occurred between seven P.M. and three A.M. Two hundred and thirty-nine were committed in Manhattan. One hundred and fifty were committed in Brooklyn. Sixty in the Bronx. Twenty-nine in Queens. Five in Richmond. Fifteen husbands were slain by their wives. Eighteen wives were slain by their husbands . . . ten sons were slain by their mothers . . . two sons were slain by their fathers . . . six daughters were slain by their mothers . . . (GLAS *moves downstage watching* RANDALL.) . . . four daughters were slain by their fathers . . . one father was killed by his daughter . . . two mothers were killed by their sons . . . four stepfathers were killed by their stepsons . . . one stepfather was killed by his stepdaughter . . . two sisters killed their brothers . . . three brothers killed their brothers . . . one son-in-law killed his father-in-law . . . one father-in-law killed his son-in-law . . . one son-in-law killed his mother-in-law . . . one despondent mother drowned her three children in the East River . . . another despondent mother drowned her three children in a bathtub . . . one child was killed for bedwetting. . . ." (*Pause.*) Oh, man, man. . . . (RANDALL *slumps on table. There is a long silence.* GLAS *appears to be quite absorbed in the recitation.* RANDALL *seems not to be present at all. For a moment or so the sound of an approaching truck is heard, it slows outside the store and there is the sound of two heavy thumps on the sidewalk. The sound brings* GLAS *and* RANDALL *out of their immobility,* RANDALL *starts and becomes alerted, an action that does not go unnoticed by* GLAS *as he moves toward the door.* RANDALL *stands above table. Points umbrella at* GLAS. GLAS *moves to door. Truck pulls away loudly.* GLAS *opens the door and exits.* RANDALL *moves upstage behind door, waits, tensed, until* GLAS *re-enters carrying two bundles of tabloid newspapers tied with heavy cord.*)

GLAS (*drops bundles*). I've been meaning to ask you something.

RANDALL. Yeah?

GLAS. About your eyes.

RANDALL (*right hand on door*). What about 'em?

GLAS. Is there something wrong with them?

RANDALL. Ain't nothin' wrong with my eyes.

GLAS. Oh. (*He has cut the cord on one of the bundles and taken up the top newspaper. He peruses the front page for a moment—a huge headline—emits a grunt and tosses the paper aside on the counter-top. The remaining newspapers he begins to arrange on the bench in front of the magazine rack.*)

RANDALL. What makes you think there somethin' wrong with my eyes?

GLAS. I wondered why you wear sunglasses in the middle of the night.

RANDALL. Oh. Well, I like 'em. *You* know.

GLAS (*sits on stool looking at headline*). Ah.

RANDALL. Except maybe it's because I like the nighttime (RANDALL *pushes door closed.*) and sometimes it ain't nighttime enough . . . know what I mean?

GLAS (*after a moment*). Yes.

RANDALL (*crosses to counter; he takes up the newspaper from the counter, off-handedly*). I see where they really hung his ass, hah? (*No response from* GLAS.) This here Nazi cat, I mean. Them Jews really hung his ass, *after* all. How you pronounce that name? (GLAS *turns to resume his work.*)

GLAS (*over his shoulder*). Eichmann.

RANDALL (*reproducing the sound with precision*). Eichmann. Adolf Eichmann. Them German names gimme a lotta trouble. German and Russian, they very tough to pronounce. I do very good with the French, though. Baudelaire. That's a French name. (*Turns left. And, more carefully, savoring it.*) Baudelaire . . . I guess you know he was one a them unhappy French poets. (*Crosses right to center with paper.*) Why you figure they done that anyway?

GLAS (*looking at headline*). What?

RANDALL. The Jews. Why you figure they hung this here Eichman chap?

GLAS (*stands; spreads out papers on bench*). Look, sonny—

RANDALL. Oh now, Mister Glas, sir, there you go *again*. (*Upstage to counter. Drops paper beside ledger.*) Sonny. What is it, you don't like to get on first name basis, uh—certain types, shall we say?

GLAS (*cuts cord on second bundle*). What do you mean, certain types?

RANDALL (*his back to counter*). You know what I mean. I mean me bein' a young gentleman of some color.

GLAS (*spreads second bundle*). Sonny, I don't care if you'd be purple with orange stripes.

RANDALL. Oh, now *that's* a clashy combination. That's all we'd need, things ain't tough enough.

GLAS. Yeah, sure.

RANDALL (*downstage to bench*). I do perceive you ain't got much sympathy for some a the various and sundry dilemmas currently facin' mankind, then?

GLAS (*turns right with string*). I stay right here and I watch the world go by and I don't get in its way.

RANDALL. Yeah, but you can't do that, daddy.

GLAS. Why not?

RANDALL. Because . . . well . . . because you can't.

GLAS. You're a genius, you can't think of a better reason than that? (*Crosses left, picks up other string. Goes behind counter.*)

RANDALL. Well, what I mean, because sooner or later it gonna come walkin' right in that door there. With a gun in its hand or somethin' maybe.

GLAS (*drops string in trash*). What?

RANDALL (*turns left to* GLAS). Well, that just a figure of speech. What I mean, the whole world got a gun in its hand. Like what I was sayin' before. You see what I mean atall? (*Pause. Upstage to stool.*) Yeah, I see you see what I mean.

GLAS. In that case I got one too. (*He reaches beneath the counter and comes up with a revolver in his left hand.*) Hah? (*Pause.*)

RANDALL (*quietly*). Well now, well now. I thought you wasn't a member of the club, you been sayin'. You a member in good standin', dues all paid up.

GLAS. No.

RANDALL. Oh, come on now, daddy, *I* dig. You got yours, I got mine. (*Puts point of umbrella on counter beside gun.*) We prepared!

GLAS (*puts gun away*). No. (*Pause. They gaze, taking each other's measure. Glas leans on counter.*) What were you running away from?

RANDALL. Sir?

GLAS. When you came in here: what were you running away from?

RANDALL (*closer to counter*). Where'd you get an idea like that, baby? Where in the world?

GLAS. I'll give you some advice.

RANDALL (*sits stool facing downstage*). Oh, boy.

GLAS. You got trouble out there, don't bring it in here.

RANDALL. You barkin' up the incorrect tree, daddy.

GLAS (*crosses right to ladder*.) I got the right tree, all right.

RANDALL. Your mistake is in a definite misinterpretation of my basic approach. (GLAS *ascends ladder*.) You see? What I mean, that just the manner in which I happen to come on: like gangbusters.

GLAS. I don't know what you're talking about, the way you talk, I'm just telling you— (*Puts cigar box on ladder flap*.)

RANDALL. You don't understand?

GLAS. I'm just telling you—

RANDALL. Which part?

GLAS. What?

RANDALL. Which part? I mean, which portion of my previous statements there don't you understand? I be glad to explain it to you in more detail. (*Pause*.)

GLAS (*quietly*). Maybe you better leave now, hah?

RANDALL. Leave? *Leave?*

GLAS (*descends ladder*). Out.

RANDALL. What is it you got against me, anyway?

GLAS (*reaches for soda*; RANDALL *grabs it*). Out.

RANDALL. You prejudiced, aintcha?

GLAS (*crosses to center*). Out.

RANDALL. Actually, I seen it right the minute I come in the door. We can always tell, you know. Always tell.

GLAS (*testily*). Tell what! (*Moves upstage to counter*.)

RANDALL (*smiling, conspiratorial*). You know.

GLAS. Now look, sonny, I already told—

RANDALL (*turns left*). Like that: see what I mean? You absolutely and categorically refuse to address me by my proper and true name. (GLAS *writes in ledger*.) Little things like that, see what I mean? Little things like that's how we can always tell. Sonny. Boy. Little things like that. I guess you be prejudiced against the Jews, too, if you wasn't one yourself. (*Silence*. GLAS *smiles, the smile broadens and ends in a short laugh*.)

GLAS (*turns to* RANDALL). What makes you think I'm a Jew? (*Moves downstage with clipboard*.)

RANDALL. There's ways, daddy.

GLAS. What ways?

RANDALL. Well, man, if there's one thing I can tell right off when I see one, it's a Jew.

GLAS. Oh?

RANDALL. Sure.

GLAS. That's very interesting.

RANDALL. Oh, yeah.

GLAS. How?

RANDALL. Mmm?

GLAS (*moves downstage to bench*). How do you go about it?

RANDALL. Oh, well, man, it a little too subtle and complicated to go into just at the present moment. (GLAS *takes cigar box from ladder*.)

GLAS. You said that before.

RANDALL. Said what?

GLAS (*puts cigar box on bench and sits on stool*). That it's too complicated to explain.

RANDALL. No, man, we ain't been talkin' about Jews before just now.

GLAS (*turns to* RANDALL). About something else you said it.

RANDALL. Oh, yeah?

GLAS. When you said you were a bug.

RANDALL. Oh. Yeah. Truly.

GLAS. Why did you say that?

RANDALL. That I'm a bug? (GLAS *nods*.) Because I am. We are *all* bugs. You, me. Everybody!

GLAS. Bugs.

RANDALL. Just waitin' to be squashed.

GLAS. By whom?

RANDALL. Bigger bugs. You see, baby, what is euphimistly called life is actually—

GLAS (*checking contents of cigar box; writing on clipboard*). Euphemistically.

RANDALL. Euphemistically. Actually, you bein' very helpful to fillin' in the small gaps in my education. Yeah, so what is *euphemistically* called life is actually just one big bug-house and you either gotta grow up to be one a them big bugs or you gotta scurry. Know what I mean? *Scurry*. You stand still and you find yourself bein' *squashed*. That one of my philosophies of life. What's one of yours? (RANDALL *reaches behind counter for gun*.)

GLAS. What?

RANDALL (*pulls hand back*). Philosophies of life.

GLAS. I have none. (*He turns his attention to the inventory, his back to* RANDALL.)

RANDALL. Sure you do, you already told me one. You said to me, you said, uh . . . *you* know, that you was gonna cool it right in here and you wasn't gettin' in nobody's way. (*Reaches again. Misses.*) That's one philosophy of life, but I mean, what's another one of your favorites?

GLAS (*amused*). I have to have more than one?

RANDALL. Oh, well, man, certainly! (*While he speaks,* RANDALL *quickly and quietly gropes behind the counter and comes up with the gun in his hand, it disappears into a pocket within the cape.*) I mean you got only one philosophy of life and then the situation changes, *then* where are you? Know what I mean? I mean, you gotta have several diverse philosophies to operate on, dependin' on the various situations that you find yourself meetin' up with. (*Pause.* GLAS *turns.* RANDALL *sits stool, his hand still in pocket.* GLAS *takes up box and approaches him.* RANDALL *pulls out his hand. There is an apple in it.*)

GLAS (*turns, ascends ladder*). Aren't you hot with all them clothes on? (*Puts box back on shelf.*)

RANDALL. What'd you have in mind I was runnin' away from? (*Crosses left to between stools—turns his back to counter.*)

GLAS (*writing on clipboard*). How would I know?

RANDALL. True. 'Course there's a lotta possibilities. Lemme see, now . . . could be I knocked over my friendly neighborhood grocery store to get me an apple and a little loose change? . . . Or perhaps I am a remnant of one of our local altercations commonly known as the gang rumble, in which several children have been left slain, slain on the field of battle? . . . That don't appeal to you, neither? Well, lemmee see, now . . . could be I just recently committed a criminal assault on a white lady of middle age in the dark and deserted end (*Turns left.*) of a subway station plaform? (*Turns back to Glas.*) . . . No? . . . Or perhaps, *perhaps* (*Sits stool.*) —this a good one—perhaps I just up and done away with my momma, stabbin' her numerous times about the breast and abdomen with a ice pick. (*From within the cape, an ice pick appears in his hand, he drives it into the seat of the stool. Pause. Takes bite of apple.* GLAS *turns slowly and descends ladder with clipboard and crosses left and stops a few feet from stool. The ice pick between* RANDALL *and him.*)

GLAS. You could be arrested for having a thing like that.

RANDALL. I could be arrested for jaywalkin'. It all relative, know what I mean?

GLAS. What are you doing with such a thing?

RANDALL (*tosses apple on counter*). Well . . . you can't never tell when I'm gonna run into a block of ice. Like I was sayin' earlier on, I like to be prepared for all and sundry eventualities. Looked upon in a certain way, and dependin' on the use to which it is put, a ice pick is also a philosophy of life. Never fear, however, you can be certain that if I committed one of them depredations just enumerated, you can be certain that sooner or later the sword of justice will pierce my heart. Sooner or later. (*He returns the ice pick to a pocket within the cape.*) Actually, as a matter of fact, I am the possessor (GLAS *sits stool—puts clipboard on counter.*) of a rather *unique* and *original* type of heart. (*Pause.*)

GLAS. What were you running away from? (*Pause.*)

RANDALL. You the persistent type, though, ain't you, daddy. Ain't always a good idea to be too persistent, though, you know? . . . I mean, (*Crosses left to above table.*) . . . what is Truth, said Jesting Pilate and would not stay for an answer. You know who said that? You know? (*No response from* GLAS.) Francis Bacon was the one who said that. Would you care (*Turns to* GLAS.) for me to tell you about my unique and original type of heart? (*Puts foot upon chair, takes a handful of wooden kitchen matches and strikes one holding it up before him, regarding the flame.*) Got a hole in it.

GLAS. A hole.

RANDALL. Born like that, a little old hole in my heart.

GLAS (*drily*). That certainly is a unique and original type of heart.

RANDALL (*blows out match*). 'm I confusin' you?

GLAS (*confused; stands; moves downstage of counter*). No, no.

RANDALL. You lookin' at me in a very puzzled tone of voice. You probably thinkin' it a lotta shit about me bein' born with a hole in my heart, right? (RANDALL *lights another match.* GLAS *stares.*) Doubting Thomas . . . I'd let you stick your finger in *my* wound, 'cept it be somewhat difficult.

GLAS. What are you supposed to be, the Statue of Liberty, or what?

RANDALL. Fire, daddy, fire! Hot!

GLAS (*gestures taking in the store*). Look, sonny, it ain't much, but I like it. So stop with the matches!

RANDALL (*throws match over his shoulder; a caricature*). Yassah, boss, yassah! Tote that barge! Lift that bale! Get a little drunk and they hang you on a nail! If you're *white,* you're *right!* (*Crosses right to counter.*) Shuffle, shuffle, shuffle!

GLAS (*turns to* RANDALL; *points*). I don't like that kind of talk!

RANDALL. What kinda talk is that, daddy?

GLAS. And stop calling me daddy! (*Crosses to ladder. Pushes it upstage beside gum ball machine. The steps now face downstage. Crosses left to counter.*)

RANDALL. No offense intended, sir, I assure you. It is definitely not my intention to impugn the purity of your ancestral heritage, seein' as how I heard that a lotta you German (GLAS *turns ledger and clipboard around.*) folks was unusually sensitive to that topic at one time in the not-too-distant past. (*Crosses right to stool.*) Course, you bein' a Jew and all I been inclined to think of you bein' somewhat *less* sensitive in that there area.

GLAS. I'm not a Jew. (*Crosses left, goes behind counter and tosses apple in trash.*)

RANDALL. You ain't?

GLAS. Why don't you go home now, sonny.

RANDALL. I'm already there, baby.

GLAS. Oh? Your trunks are arriving later? (RANDALL *sits stool.*)

RANDALL. Oh-oh. There you go again, slashin' away at me with your (GLAS *picks up rag, wipes his hands then leans on elbows at left end of counter and watches* RANDALL.) biting and satirical wit. No, but what I mean, any particular place I happen to find myself, that's home. My walls are the space around me and heaven is my roof. Poetic like that. I live in my skin, baby, like everyone else. And anything I happen to need I got right here, of course. (*He opens his cape, which is lined, top to bottom, with zippered pockets.*) You name it, I got it. No need for me to be borin' you with a complete and exhaustive inventory but like for an exam-

ple, I just earlier this evenin' acquired me this battery-operated toothbrush even. (*He displays this, switching it on and off.*) Cain't hardly wait till tomorra mornin', see how it works. It either gonna give my teeth one hell of a brushin' or it gonna *elect*rocute me.

GLAS. I suppose you sleep walking around too, hah?

RANDALL (*he returns the gadget to the pocket of the cape*). Oh, well, no, baby, I ain't quite perfected my organism to that level of development as yet. Of course, I got certain physical requirements that requires me to grab forty, fifty winks now and again. But there's lottsa places for that if one is smart and uses the natural intelligence. For instance, I can always go down into the subway and get me the local to Pelham Bay Park and back again, which take about three days, sleepin' all the way. Then sometimes I spend the night in the Egyptian Room of the Metropolitan Museum of Art. Very nice. Also, occasionally, the Cloisters. You know the Cloisters?

GLAS. The what?

RANDALL. The Cloisters. Uptown.

GLAS. No.

RANDALL. That's the best place. Absolutely. It's a place they built like where them monks used to live a long time ago, you know? A monastery. All stone and cool and quiet with a lotta old wooden statues of saints and Jesus Christ and people like that. That's the best place to sleep.

GLAS. They don't catch you?

RANDALL. No, I hide pretty good. They ain't never caught me yet. . . . Yeah, I sure woulda liked to be one a them monks way back then. You believe in reincarnation?

GLAS. Reincarnation?

RANDALL. Yeah.

GLAS. No.

RANDALL (*picks up soda*). Ah. Well, *I* do. It can be a great comfort on occasion in this vale of tears, you be surprised. (*Moves downstage to bench.*) I was a courtier in the court of Lorenzo de Medici one a my other times. Fifteenth century . . . yeah . . . (GLAS *puts rag away and crosses to right end of counter. Pause. For a moment* RANDALL *is far away.*) So anyway, now I think I'm beginnin' to understand. (*Turns to* GLAS.)

GLAS. Hmm?

RANDALL. I mean, you not bein' a Jew and all. Here I been goin' on the false assumption that you was. Is. A Jewish man. That bein' the case, it been hard for me to reconcile the fact that you ain't been givin' a shit one way or the other about old Adolf here, (GLAS *picks up newspaper.*) swayin' gently to and fro, as they say, with a broken neck, ruptured larynx, deceased. (*Turns upstage.*) But you *not* bein' a Jew, I now comprehend totally. Your indifference. (RANDALL *sits stool.*)

GLAS. You think only Jews care? (*Moves left behind counter with paper.*)

RANDALL. They do seem to be the ones most upset and distraught by the matter, yeah. I mean, they 'as the ones who *hung* him. Seem to me somewhat bloodthirsty.

GLAS (*crosses to above table*). What do *you* know about it?

RANDALL. What I read in the newspapers, baby.

GLAS (*drops newspaper on table*). There's more to know than what you read in the newspapers, believe me.

RANDALL. Why?

GLAS. Because there is.

RANDALL. I mean why should I believe you?

GLAS. Because I know.

RANDALL. What do you know, daddy?

GLAS (*turns to* RANDALL). I was there.

RANDALL. Where?

GLAS. Germany. In the camps.

RANDALL (*stands; crosses left to center*). Mm-hm. Thought you said you wasn't a Jew.

GLAS (*moves downstage of chair*). You didn't have to be a Jew.

RANDALL. What else could you be to be allowed inta one a them camps?

GLAS (*turns to* RANDALL). What do you mean, *allowed* in? What do you think, they were private hotels or something? (*Then shouting.*) What do you think! (*Pause.*)

RANDALL (*points umbrella at* GLAS; *quietly*). Don't be hollerin' at me, Mister Glas, sir. One thing do get me all upset and nervous is for someone to be hollerin' at me. (GLAS *backs away. Sits chair. Turns downstage.*) I mean we gettin' along just fine, so long as we be nice to each other and don't go raisin' our voices in the heat of anger, know what I mean? (RANDALL *crosses left above table. Puts soda on table.*

GLAS *does not appear intimidated by the menace in* RANDALL's *tone.*)

GLAS (*over his shoulder*). You're a real sensitive type, you are.

RANDALL (*sits chair facing* GLAS; *puts umbrella on table*). So what was you doin' in the concentration camp, then? If you wasn't a Jew? (*Pause.*)

GLAS. I was a political prisoner, a communist. (*He speaks this very quickly and turns away.*)

RANDALL. Oh, man! That's *worse!* You was really a commonist?

GLAS. That's right.

RANDALL. You still? A commonist?

GLAS. No.

RANDALL. Uh, huh. So, what was it like, bein' in one a them concentration camps?

GLAS. You don't know?

RANDALL. How would *I* know? *I* ain't never been in one. (GLAS *turns to him.*) Been in one or two places bearin' a close *resemblance* to concentration camps, but I am otherwise without firsthand knowledge of their true nature. So this here is a ideal opportunity for you to fill in one a them gaps in what might be referred to as my smorgasbord education. (GLAS *smiles.*) You got a real nice smile, Mister Glas, sir. You smiled more often you'd be winnin' friends and influencin' people all over the place.

GLAS. I'm not interested in—

BOTH (*unison*). Winning friends and influencing people.

RANDALL (*nodding*). I know, I know. So what was it like, then. (*Pause.* GLAS, *when he speaks, is without emotion, his face a mask, his voice flat and dull.*)

GLAS (*grabs his left knee*). They smashed my leg. In four places. Starting at the ankle and working their way up.

RANDALL (*matter-of-factly, seemingly unmoved*). Why'd they do that?

GLAS. Why?

RANDALL. I mean, was it just it was a slow afternoon like and they had nothin' better to do, or what?

GLAS (*after a pause, as though he had not heard*). And there was a time we found out that one of the prisoners had acquired some parts of a dead body and given them to the cook in return for certain favors. The cook kept the regular meat ration for himself and put the human flesh in the stew, which the prisoners ate.

RANDALL (*quietly*). Oh, man.

GLAS. When we found out, first we killed the cook. We stuffed his mouth with the meat, the human flesh, and pushed his head into the stewpot and held him under until he was dead. (GLAS *stands. Crosses right to ladder.*) The next night we killed the other one, the prisoner. We picked him up, four of us, and threw him against the fence. (*Pause.*)

RANDALL. Yeah?

GLAS (*going up ladder*). Mm.

RANDALL. So?

GLAS. What?

RANDALL. What then? I mean, you threw him against the fence? That's all? (GLAS *reaches into box of candles.*)

GLAS. It was wired, the fence. He was electrocuted. (*Pause.*)

RANDALL (*stands*). *That's* cool.

GLAS (*turns; a candle in his left hand*). But you don't have to go back to those days and those places to find Nazis. It was Nazis put *that* there.

RANDALL. Which? (GLAS *crosses to center.* RANDALL *turns to him.*)

GLAS. That. That monstrosity, that noise box. (RANDALL *turns to jukebox.*) What do you think it's doing here? One day two men come in and look around and ask me how would I like a jukebox, give the place a little class? I say no, thanks just the same, I don't need no jukeboxes today. They say, sure I do, they can tell just by looking at me that I need a jukebox. I say no, still very polite. They say yes, only not so nice this time. I say no again, they say yes, I say definitely no. (*Points at window.*) So the next night a brick through the window, glass flying all over the place, a cut on my head. So I have a jukebox. (*Moves down center.*) And those men, they wear white ties with their black shirts, but around the eyes—just like the Nazis.

RANDALL (*moves above table*). You shoulda reported those gentlemen to your local law enforcement authorities.

GLAS (*turns; moves upstage to counter.*) That's the first funny joke you made yet, sonny. (*Absently, a candle in his hand.*) They light a candle.

RANDALL. Say again?

GLAS (*crossing to right end of counter*). A candle. Every year a bunch of Jewish people get together and light a fat candle for the six million Jews the Nazis killed. A candle. (*Turns left, puts candle on counter.*) For six million people you light the sun, maybe. But a candle?

RANDALL. Even a fat candle?

GLAS (*angrily*). You even make a joke about that? (RANDALL *turns away, quickly, removes his glasses, his hat. When he speaks now, the dialect is gone, there is no trace of the distorted speech rhythm, the frenetic delivery and the level of the voice is lower and normal.*)

RANDALL (*sits chair*). Perhaps a candle would do for the living, Mister Glas. (*Pause.* GLAS *is clearly puzzled.*)

GLAS (*turns to* RANDALL). What?

RANDALL (*puts glasses in hat, puts hat on table*). What I mean to say is that if the dead require the sun, perhaps a mere candle would do for the living. Like you. Or me. Tell you what (GLAS *crosses slowly right*): the first chance I get, I'll light a candle for you. Place a small sign on it, perhaps: This candle for Mr. Glas, exclusively. (GLAS *moves downstage.*) One of the living. Don't be confused, Mister Glas, sir. (*Turns to* GLAS.) It's just that sometimes . . . I run out of gas, so to speak.

GLAS. Gas? What gas? Listen—

RANDALL. Well, I mean, energy. What I mean to say is that it requires a great deal of energy to be what one is not. For any extended length of time. You'd be surprised how much energy is required. (GLAS *approaches* RANDALL.) Which cannot be sustained indefinitely. Also, it always bores me finally.

GLAS. You talk different.

RANDALL. True. True. Precisely.

GLAS (*stops beside* RANDALL). What are you, some kind of an actor or something?

RANDALL. Not exactly, no.

GLAS. What do you mean, not exactly? What kind of funny business—?

RANDALL. I mean only to the extent that we all are. Do you know what I mean? (*Pause.* GLAS *backs away to far stool.*)

GLAS. I don't know and I don't care. There's the door, sonny. You go out just the way you come in and we won't have any trouble around here, okay?

RANDALL (*stands; in dialect again*). You gettin' me all wrong, daddy. Ain't gonna be no trouble, nohow. (*Pause.*)

GLAS. I think maybe I call the cops. (*He turns toward the telephone on the wall but, before he can take a second step,*

RANDALL *is there; he rips the receiver from the box, returns to* GLAS *and hands it to him, the cord dangling.*)

RANDALL. Say hello for *me*. (GLAS *stares*.) You can go and get them if you like, of course. The police. I won't stop you. (RANDALL *crosses left to end of counter. Stands on first step and turns to* GLAS. *Again in the dialect*.) 'Course they ain't no tellin' how far *away* they be. And there ain't no way of tellin' what this place look like by the time you get back. And they ain't *absolutely* no way of tellin' where *I* be by that time. (RANDALL *watches closely, smiling, waiting for* GLAS *to make the next move and knowing what it will be*. GLAS *makes it: a lunge behind the counter, groping. He comes up in a rage.*)

GLAS. Where is it?

RANDALL (*turns away*). What's that.

GLAS (*knowing already*). The gun, God damn it!

RANDALL. Oh, that. That's in my pocket, yes.

GLAS. Stupid!

RANDALL. Me?

GLAS (*after a pause, grinning humorlessly*). No, not you. What do you want? (GLAS *moves left to center of counter*.) Tell me what you want, you take it and you leave, hah? (*Turns upstage*.) Just go away and leave me alone. I don't want any trouble. (RANDALL *is at the street door, looking into the street*.)

RANDALL. If *I* were you I'd write a letter to the mayor or something about that. (RANDALL *off platform to table*.) No street lights: very bad for business, no street lights. (GLAS *turns to* RANDALL.) Who wants to walk down a dark street, anymore? (*He adds, in the dialect*.) 'Ceptin' maybe chaps like me. (*Picks up hat— puts glasses on*.) I mean, there is a certain fear and tension amongst the populace, you know what I mean? And a reluctance to venture down dark streets. (*Moves up on platform. Then again, naturally, quietly*.) A reluctance to venture down dark streets. (*Pulls door ajar. He begins to hum again the same tune. Closes door, moves left, leans against wall*.)

GLAS (*moves to stool*). What's the idea with you, anyway? The funny talk and the phony stories. What's the idea with all that? (*Sits stool*.)

RANDALL (*still at the door, his back to* GLAS). You do me wrong, Mister Glas, sir: I speak only the truth.

GLAS. All that about being a genius, that's the truth, hah? (RANDALL *nods, indifferently*.) I suppose you were born with a hole in your heart, too.

RANDALL (*turns, crosses right to counter; puts down hat and umbrella; leans toward* GLAS). True, all true. Truly. Actually it's the only thing in my life for which I have an explanation, the hole in my heart. (*Turns left. Takes off glasses*.) Randall, you see, was conceived of a union between his mother and one of the numberless men she never saw again, his mother being a prostitute by profession. Conceived of lust and the natural hungers of the flesh, but without love. It was that absence of love that left the hole in Randall's heart, no mistake. I mean (*Turns back to* GLAS. *Takes off cape, puts it on counter*.), picture, if you will, Randall, at the age of approximately six months when his momma discovered that (*Downstage to above stool*.) his heart hadn't healed up all the way, like it was supposed to, like everyone else's, while he was still in his momma's womb. A comparatively rare occurrence, indeed. So they excuted with great skill and care a delicate operation and sewed up that nasty hole in Randall's wee heart. A colloquial expression, that, a hole in the heart, but true. True. She used it often, his momma did. It got so that Randall began to think if he heard that expression one more time he be about ready to cut somebody's throat, it being a toss-up whether it would be his own or his momma's. (*Sits stool down right, starts to rock*.) He was saved from the perpetration of that rash act, however, by the fact that about that time his momma was apprehended for offerin' her charms to a officer of the law. Funny thing is he didn't arrest her until after he'd accepted her offer. Know what I mean? Reason I know is, I was in the closet at the time, watchin', unbeknownst to momma and her gentleman visitor who proved subsequently to be an officer of the law. (*Stops rocks, turns downstage*.) I was seven years old at the time, and fond of playin' in momma's closet. Poor momma. That old cop gettin' up offa her and pullin' up his pants and flashin' his shiny old badge, was she surprised. Mad too, of course, but mostly surprised, I remember that very clear. That was her third arrest for lewd and lascivious behavior and (*Off stool. Crosses to above table. Faces down left.*) she got detained for ninety days in the Women's House of Detention. It was durin' that time of her detention that somebody or other took high offense at the fact of me striking one of my playmates lightly on the face without first taking the precaution of removing the beer can opener from my hand, an oversight which made for quite a little bit of a mess so far as the little chap's face was concerned. (*Looks at* GLAS. *Crosses right to down center facing down right.*) So, my momma bein' elsewhere occupied and me bein' otherwise kinless, they up and put me in a kinda (*Turns downstage.*) home. That's where they first discovered about me bein' so smart and all 'cause at the time I was carryin' in my pocket a book of poems which I had acquired free of charge under somewhat surreptitious circumstances and which had been authored by someone whose name I couldn't pronounce and they said what was I doin' with that book, a book like that, and I said readin' it. (*Crosses upstage right to ladder looking into hallway.* GLAS *turns to him.*) Then after a while, they let me go back to my momma who was free and swingin' again. Now you have a kinda montage effect showin' momma plyin' her trade and Randall gettin' the picture very gradual but very clear and this goes on for several years, Randall listenin' to the men clompin' up the stairs with his momma and down again alone, leavin' momma in the bedroom with the sound of running water. (*Turns left and leans toward* GLAS.) About that time was when she stopped usin' that expression. You know: about the hole in Randall's heart? She stopped usin' it and Randall started. Had a nice ring to it, that expression, and it explained a lotta things just right. Like for instance, the time (*Moves downstage to bench.*) Randall is in the process of fleein' the scene of a crime, as they say, when a thirty-eight caliber bullet fired from the gun bein' held steadily in the hand of one of New York's Finest, marksmen all, when that bullet entered his back just under the left shoulder blade (*Slumps as imaginary bullet hits.*) and lodged against the back side of a rib, the force of the blow propelling Randall some ten feet or so right into the gutter on his face. And there Randall lay with his mouth in a little river of rainwater, shot through the heart. (*Turns to* GLAS.) Oh, you know what the doctors said, naturally they said that bullet had struck him just an inch *below* the heart but he knew better, Randall did. He knew goddamned well that little old bullet had passed right through the hole in his heart and out the other side. (*Crosses left, sits on end of bench facing down left.*) Follows two years of restitution for Randall in a woodsy little correctional farm for Youthful Offenders in the upper reaches of New York State. And wouldn't you know that on attainin' his freedom, who should be standin' there to greet him at the train station but his dear little momma? His momma who wrote him three letters in two years and never did manage to make him a visit in the flesh. (*Turns head downstage.*) But there she is, standin' in a silky green dress and a white hat, sayin' welcome home, Randall, you lookin' just fine. And Randall just look at her right in the eye for about a minute or two and says real quiet, go away, momma. Which disturbs her no end, for some reason or other and sets her to screaming on a graduated scale of pitch and intensity, following Randall across the marble vastness of the Grand Central Station and all the folks lookin' on and listenin' to the flashy, colored lady makin' all that racket, they're so uninhibited and spontaneous, those people. Her screamin' I'm your momma, Randall, I'm your momma no matter what, and various and assorted other demands of endearment. And the last thing Randall hears before he hit the top of the stairs, leavin' his mother puffin' at the bottom, the last he hears was her screamin', you got no love in you, Randall, you're all mean and black inside and you got no love in you! Which was all too true, of course. Because that piece which had never grown into Randall's heart? . . . That was the place where love is. Of course. (GLAS *rises turns up leans on counter. Pause.* RANDALL *turns to* GLAS.) Never make a long story short, that's my motto. (*Stands, moves upstage to between stools. Pause.*) Is your silence a profound one, Mister Glas? (RANDALL *picks up his hat.* GLAS *only gazes.* RANDALL *speaks again in the dialect.*) Well, silence also speaks, daddy. (*Sings quietly. Puts*

*on his glasses and cape. Picks up his um-
brella.*) I went to the rock to hide my
face, the rock cried out, no hiding place.
. . . (*Crosses left to door. The door bursts
open.* RANDALL *jumps off platform and behind door.* GLAS *whirls around toward
door. Standing in the doorway is a girl
of nineteen, singularly plain-looking with
orange hair that falls to her shoulders,
and eyeglasses. She is wearing a blue
denim skirt and a black cotton pullover
and sandals. Her name is* ROSIE.)

ROSIE (*with mingled rage and frustration, imploringly, near to tears*). Where
the hell is the goddamn Brooklyn Bridge?
(*She releases her hold on the knob of the
door, staggers, falls on stool and pulls it
down with her as she faints.* RANDALL *and*
GLAS *are as still as she while the curtain
falls on Act One.*)

ACT TWO: Pas de Trois

SCENE ONE

*A moment has passed; all are as before.
Then* GLAS *moves, stooping to the girl.*

———

GLAS. Miss? . . . Miss! (*Distraught, he
slaps her face lightly, tentatively. He looks
about for a moment, disorganized. Then
he gets to his feet and exits quickly into
the kitchen, ignoring* RANDALL. RANDALL's
*eye falls upon the ladder and he moves
to it. He looks up, then climbs to the very
top, pulls the light cord, and sits, his chin
in his hands, surveying the scene.* GLAS
re-enters carrying a large bottle. He notes
RANDALL's *absence and looks around
quickly, but not up, and assumes him to
be gone. He stoops to the girl, removes
the cap from the bottle, lifts her head
and holds the bottle under her nose, waft-
ing it. She comes awake choking and
coughing.*)

ROSIE. Jesus! (*She sits up, grasps the
bottle, looking at the label, pushing it
away.*) Ammonia! Jesus!

GLAS. Are you all right?

ROSIE (*sitting up now, groggy*). I
fainted.

GLAS. Yes. Are you all right?

ROSIE. I know it sounds corny as hell
but where am I?

GLAS (*puts stool back in place; rests

ammonia bottle on it*). My name is Glas.
This is my place, my store.

ROSIE. I *am* in Brooklyn, though, right?

GLAS. Oh, yes.

ROSIE. I got lost. Goddamned BMT.

GLAS. You're looking for the Brooklyn
Bridge?

ROSIE. Yeah. At this point I'm strongly
considering jumping off it.

GLAS. I beg your pardon?

ROSIE. I think I can get up now. (GLAS
assists her to her feet.)

GLAS. Maybe you better sit here for a
little bit, hah? (*She sits in chair at the
table. Picks up the newspaper, glances at
the headline.*)

ROSIE. Oh, they hung the bastard, huh?
Good. (*She drops the paper.*)

GLAS (*picks up ammonia bottle and gets
cap from floor*). I should call a doctor for
you maybe, hah?

ROSIE. No, no, that won't be necessary.
But listen, I'll tell you something that
would help out a lot.

GLAS (*turns to Rosie*). Yeah?

ROSIE. Is there a bathroom around?

GLAS. You're going to be sick?

ROSIE. Well no. It's just I've been walking all over Brooklyn for hours and I
have to go to the bathroom pretty bad.

GLAS. Oh, I see. Oh . . . well, yes, I
got a bathroom sure. Straight back through
there, the second door on the left hand
side of the hallway. (*Points off right.*)

ROSIE. Thank you very much. (*She goes
to the door and exits.* GLAS *watches after
her for a moment, then his attention is
caught by* RANDALL's *empty soda bottle
on table left. He picks it up. Goes to the
door and looks into the street.* RANDALL
blows his nose. GLAS *whirls and discovers*
RANDALL *atop the ladder.*)

GLAS (*after a pause*). I don't know what
to do about you. (*Moves down to steps.*)
What do you want here?

RANDALL (*in dialect*). What is it make
you think I gotta be *wantin'* somethin'?
I asked you for anything yet? *Nothin'.* So
what so difficult to understand about that?
(GLAS *puts ammonia behind counter.*) I
merely come trippin' merrily into here,
real casual-like, to pass the time of the
evenin' and right away you figurin' me to
cut you up and *rob* you, or somethin'!
You been watchin' too much of the TV,
that the problem with you, I think, and

lettin' your imagination run *riot,* as they say.

GLAS (*crosses right to center*). I don't have a TV.

RANDALL. Whooee, you a difficult man, indeed.

GLAS. In the first place, you didn't come in here casual, you came in here running. I saw you.

RANDALL. We already decided that to be a matter of opinion, I been thinkin'—the truth not always bein' found in the eye of the beholder. What about in the second place?

GLAS (*crosses down right to stool*). In the second place, someone who destroys my property and steals my pistol which I had to apply for a special permit at the Police Department (*Picks up receiver and puts it on bookshelf. Moves left.*), otherwise it's against the law— Not to mention the fact of all this funny talk when you can speak as good as me. That's in the third place. Why do you talk like that if you can talk properly?

RANDALL. A matter of self-induced schizophrenia, purely. (GLAS *moves upstage to counter.*) You lookin' at the Doctor Jekyll and Mister Hyde of the Negro race, daddy.

GLAS (*sits stool facing counter*). You mock yourself.

RANDALL (*naturally*). Perhaps not myself. (*Pause. Dialect.*) So whatta you figure *she* wants, then? . . . The little chick with the orange hair currently occupyin' your bathroom.

GLAS. How do I know what she wants? The Brooklyn Bridge, she says.

RANDALL. Which sound to me suspicious in the *extreme.* Don't it hit you somewhat suspicious? (*Before* GLAS *can reply, the glow from a flashing red light is thrown into the store from the street and with it a very brief groan of a siren: a police car has parked at the curb and announced its presence.* GLAS *stands.* RANDALL *scrambles down the ladder, then stands very still.*) I do believe that be the cops. (GLAS *moves toward the door.* RANDALL *lunges to the door, holding it shut with the point of his umbrella.* GLAS *stops and regards* RANDALL *and the umbrella.*)

GLAS. They won't come in if I go out. (*Silence.*) They come every night—for a bottle of soda and an ice cream pop. They don't come in, I take it out to them. Curb

service, hah? (RANDALL *is not amused.*) They won't come in if I go out. (RANDALL *relents finally.* GLAS *opens the door and calls out.*) I'll be right with you, hah? (*He moves to the rear of the counter, gets two bottles of soda, opens them, and two ice cream pops; he exits into the street.* RANDALL *moves silently across the store to the hallway and stands motionless, waiting.* GLAS *reappears in the doorway and returns* RANDALL's *gaze. The police car is heard pulling away.* GLAS *closes the door.* RANDALL *steps out of the hallway.*)

RANDALL (*naturally*). You're a very confusing man, Mister Glas.

GLAS (*crosses right behind counter*). It's a confusing life, sonny. (RANDALL *moves upstage to stool, takes the revolver from within the cape and places it on the counter.*) The bullets? You don't want to take the bullets out? (RANDALL *regards the gun a moment before turning slowly reascending the ladder.* GLAS *takes the revolver and replaces it on its hook beneath the counter.*) What have you done, Randall? (*Door slams off right,* ROSIE *enters, freshened.*)

ROSIE (*stops right end of counter*). Well, that's a vast improvement.

GLAS. How do you feel?

ROSIE. Well, the truth is, all that's the matter with me is I haven't eaten anything in about twenty-four hours. (*Sits stool.*) You don't happen to have any food here, do you? Like a sandwich or something?

GLAS. Candy and ice cream. Soda. Coffee. Pastry—but it's stale.

ROSIE. Is there anyplace around here I could get something to eat?

GLAS. Not this time of night. You really haven't eaten anything in all that time?

ROSIE. No. What time is it, anyway?

RANDALL (*Turns light on.*) 'Cordin' to my twenny-one jewel, Swiss movement chronometer (ROSIE *turns to* RANDALL *startled.*) watch it is now seventeen and a half minutes past eleven o'clock in the evenin' of June the the first, nineteen hundred and sixty two.

ROSIE. Who's he?

RANDALL. Randall.

GLAS. *This* week. (*The private joke is acknowledged between* RANDALL *and* GLAS, *leaving* ROSIE *somewhat confused, but she lets it pass.*) Don't pay any attention to him.

ROSIE. It's a little hard not to pay any

attention to a guy with an umbrella and sunglasses sitting on top of a ladder in a candy store (*Turns to* GLAS.), but I'll try if you think it's the best thing. (*She looks up at* RANDALL.) Randall, was it?

RANDALL. Hidi, little chick!

ROSIE. Rosie. .

RANDALL. Rosie. Welcome back to the realm of the conscious, Rosie.

ROSIE. Thank you very much.

GLAS. All right, stop that talk will you, goddamnit! (GLAS *crosses right to ladder. To* ROSIE.) He doesn't really talk that way.

ROSIE. I beg your pardon?

GLAS. He doesn't really talk that way. (*Bangs ladder.*) Come down off the goddamn ladder now! (*Pause.* GLAS *is glaring at* RANDALL. RANDALL *is wiping the lenses of his glasses with a handkerchief—without removing them from his eyes, however.* ROSIE *looks from one to the other, and wants no part of either of them.*)

ROSIE. Well, I guess I'll be going, then, okay?

GLAS (*turns to* ROSIE). No, wait. I think you should rest maybe for—

ROSIE. Look, I don't know what kind of a nuthouse I fell into here, but I'm just not really in the mood for it tonight. (GLAS *crosses down right to doorway.*) Any other night, okay, it might prove to be interesting, but tonight, no, definitely no. (*She takes two steps and again becomes faint.*) Oh, boy. (ROSIE *sits stool.*)

GLAS (*moving quickly to her aid*). You're not well, miss.

ROSIE. It's all right. I'll be okay in no time at all. What time did you say it was? Just the hour, I *know* what year it is. (GLAS *downstage sits stool facing upstage.*)

RANDALL. 'leven thirty.

ROSIE. Well, it's too late now even if I could find it. (*She takes a slip of paper from her purse, hands it to* GLAS.) You know where that is, that address?

GLAS. Never heard of that street.

RANDALL. Lemme see there. (*He descends the ladder, takes the paper, looks at it a moment, thinks.*) Oh, yeah, yeah. That right near by to the Brooklyn Bridge. (*Gives paper back to* ROSIE.) You a *long* way from the Brooklyn Bridge, little chick, a *long* way.

ROSIE (*puts paper in bag*). I already figured that out, thanks.

RANDALL (*crosses left to center*). Ain't surprised you couldn't find that there place, though, it one a them funny streets, maybe two, three blocks long, you know? (*Turns to* ROSIE.) Also a pretty wild neighborhood for a little chick like yourself to be lookin' for in the middle of a night. (*Crosses left to end of counter.*) A unsavory locale, you might say.

ROSIE (*off stool; downstage to* GLAS). Yeah, well it's too late now, I was supposed to be there three hours ago. I should have known better than to have ever set my foot in Brooklyn. (RANDALL *moves downstage left to chair. Puts foot upon chair.*)

GLAS. Where are you from, miss?

ROSIE. A million miles away—the Bronx. Riverdale, actually. You know Riverdale?

GLAS. No.

ROSIE. Don't bother. (ROSIE *sits left end of bench.*) If I don't get something to eat pretty soon I'm going to faint dead away on your floor again. (*Searching in her purse for change.*) I'll have a couple of candy bars, at least, and maybe a bottle of soda.

RANDALL (*picks up soda bottle*). I recommend the lemon.

GLAS (*stands; turns to* ROSIE). No. I'll fix you something decent to eat. Come on.

ROSIE (*stands*). Where?

GLAS. In back.

ROSIE (*instantly suspicious, of course*). What's in back?

GLAS (*crosses right enters hallway*). My house. (*Switches on kitchen light.*) My kitchen.

ROSIE (*backs up to center*). Oh. Well, listen, you don't have to go to all that— (RANDALL *crosses left stage of chair.*)

GLAS (*in doorway*). You haven't eaten in twenty-four hours?

ROSIE. Something like that, but—

GLAS. You take a sandwich and a glass of milk.

ROSIE. Well, if it's not too much trouble. . . .

GLAS (*enters store*). No trouble. Then you go back to Riverside and get a good night's sleep.

ROSIE. Yeah. River*dale*.

GLAS. River*dale*. (*He waits.*) So?

ROSIE. Okay. Thanks very much. (*She moves to the door where* GLAS *waits; passes him and enters the kitchen.* GLAS *gazes at* RANDALL *for a moment.*)

GLAS. All right, come on. (GLAS *turns,*

followed by RANDALL, *and enters the kitchen. It is an ordinary, clean, well-kept place. The refrigerator and stove are on the right wall; downstage right there is a neatly made-up cot. Downstage left a table with two chairs. There is a covered canary cage on a stand and, on the refrigerator, a bowl with several goldfish.* RANDALL *remains at the door, lounging, not entering the room for a moment.* GLAS *speaks to* ROSIE.) Sit. (*She does and* GLAS *makes preparations to serve her food.*)

ROSIE (*puts bag on floor beside her*). Where'd you get that outfit, Randall? Barney's Boys Town?

RANDALL (*hangs hat on hook above sink; smiles*). You very sharp, you know it, little chick? (GLAS *takes cheese and milk from refrigerator.*)

ROSIE. I know. Like my stepfather says, sharp as a tack and just as flatheaded. He's full of terribly clever remarks like that.

RANDALL. I didn't say nothin' about the shape of your head, I only said you was very sharp, which is true. (*He leans on sink.*)

ROSIE. Yeah, well, for once he was right.

RANDALL. Hm?

ROSIE. My stepfather.

RANDALL. Ah.

ROSIE. I certainly appreciate this.

GLAS. What's the idea of going such a long time without eating, hah?

ROSIE. Well, the doctor told me I wasn't supposed to eat anything for eight hours, at least, so, true to my fashion, I overdid it—like everything else.

GLAS. What doctor?

ROSIE. The doctor I had the appointment with tonight who lives on the street nobody ever heard of. (*Drinks milk.*)

GLAS (*brings bread and cheese to table*). A Doctor tells you not to eat? What kind of a doctor is that?

ROSIE. Well, he's an abortionist, as a matter of fact. (*Making sandwich.*) He probably engages in a number of other unsavory medical practices (GLAS *puts knife and plate on table.*) but my particular business with him is in his capacity as an abortionist.

RANDALL (*moves downstage to bed*). It would appear, then, that you stubbed your toe, so to speak, while makin' your way along life's highway?

ROSIE (*cuts sandwich*). Very well put.

GLAS. You're, uh . . . you're going to a doctor?

ROSIE (*eating*). It's either that or get myself a knitting needle and have a go at it myself, which I'm told is an ill-advised solution. . . .

GLAS (*turns to* ROSIE). But, what I mean . . . you don't want the child?

ROSIE. *Hell,* no.

RANDALL. You a pretty outspoken type, ain't you, little chick?

ROSIE. Am I shocking you? (*Turns to* GLAS *without waiting for an answer.*) It happens every day, you know. And I have no patience with all the whispered-behind-the-hand hypocrisy about the facts of life, however sordid they may sometimes be. Right out in the open, that's my motto. *Right out in the open.* What camp were you in Mister Glas?

GLAS. Mmm?

ROSIE. In Germany. What concentration camp were you in?

GLAS (*sits chair left*). How do you know I was in a camp?

ROSIE. The tattoo. (GLAS *glances briefly at the number tattooed on the inside of his left forearm.*)

RANDALL. Oh, man, is that what that is? Here I been thinkin' maybe it been his Social Security number, or somethin'.

ROSIE (*turns to* RANDALL). Oh, that's funny, that's really funny. You're a regular three-act comedy.

GLAS. He isn't as stupid as he would like you to think. Pay no attention to him. (RANDALL *turns away, angrily.* ROSIE *looks at* RANDALL; *then at* GLAS, *then again, at* RANDALL. *She is apparently disinclined to pursue the matter and resumes eating.*)

ROSIE. A lot of my grandfather's family were in the camps. But they didn't make it out. Their name was Kasner. Ever run across them? (GLAS *shakes his head.*) You're not Jewish, are you?

GLAS. No.

ROSIE. Political then, huh?

RANDALL (*turns to* GLAS). He a commonist, Mister Glas is.

ROSIE. Are you?

GLAS. I was at the time.

RANDALL. Once a commonist, always a commonist.

ROSIE (*over her shoulder*). That's an interesting political philosophy. (*To* GLAS.) I'm doing a thesis on the camps.

GLAS. Hmmm?

ROSIE. A thesis. *You* know, a college term paper, Modern History.

GLAS. Ah.

ROSIE. Maybe you'd like to contribute.

GLAS. Contribute?

ROSIE. Well, I've been interviewing some survivors, you know? Getting some fantastic stories, actually. (RANDALL *moves below bed*.) I mean, it's one thing to read about the kinds of things that went on in the camps, you know, but to hear it, to watch someone's lips speaking the words, to see the eyes. The worst thing I've heard about was the cannibalism. Only one man that I've interviewed so far, but even one. He said it seemed more terrible in retrospect than it did at the time. I can see how that might be true. An interesting thing about that particular man, though: he doesn't eat pork. It occurred to me, so I asked him. You know what I mean? He ate human flesh once, but he won't eat pork because it's against his religion, of course. Anyway, maybe you could answer a few questions about your experience. I've been getting mostly Jews, very few political prisoners.

GLAS. No, no questions.

ROSIE. Oh . . . may I ask why?

GLAS. I got no answers.

ROSIE. Oh. Well, I understand. (GLAS *gazes at her*.)

RANDALL. "Please do not understand me too quickly." Andre Gide said that. (ROSIE *is mildly impressed at this*.) Where you in attendance at college, little chick?

ROSIE. NYU. Where else? (*Still intrigued at* RANDALL'*s knowledge of Gide, she turns to* GLAS.) He wanted to send me to Vassar, old stepdaddy, but I wasn't having any of that, thankyouverymuch. All those trees, all that ivy, it would've driven me right out of my skull. I'm strictly a city girl. New York, New York where the natives talk like machine guns, that's for me.

GLAS. Listen, uh—Rosie. About this other business. I mean, this—doctor, the . . .

ROSIE. The abortion, you mean.

GLAS. Yes, abortion.

ROSIE. You don't like the word.

GLAS. It's an ugly word.

ROSIE. There are no ugly words, Mister Glas. It's a perfectly good word. *Abortion*. See? The roof didn't fall in. What about it?

GLAS. It's not a good thing.

ROSIE. Good, bad. It's necessary. You know?

GLAS. Why?

ROSIE. Why?! Well, I'm not married for one thing.

GLAS. You couldn't get married?

ROSIE. Oh boy! Who'd marry *me*?

RANDALL. I'd marry you, little chick.

ROSIE. Thanks anyway, we both have enough problems.

GLAS. What do you mean, who would marry you? Why not?

ROSIE. Take a good look at me, Mister Glas. Homely is homely no matter how you slice it; I'm nobody's dream girl.

RANDALL. Everybody is *some*body's dream girl, little chick.

ROSIE. Look—uh, Randall: be anything you like but don't be naive, okay? *Naiveté* is a bore. You know how in the movies this girl with glasses takes them off and suddenly everybody in the room falls down at the sheer beauty of her?

RANDALL. I seen that picture, yeah.

ROSIE. Look. (*She removes her eyeglasses. Turns to* GLAS *and then back to* RANDALL. *Pause*.)

RANDALL. I see what you mean, yeah. (*She replaces the eyeglasses*.)

GLAS. What about the young man?

ROSIE. The responsible party?

GLAS. Yes.

ROSIE. As a way out, my way is better. *Believe* me.

GLAS. You couldn't be married to him?

ROSIE. No.

GLAS. He won't, hah?

ROSIE. What, marry me? (GLAS *nods*.) I don't know, I haven't asked him.

RANDALL. 'Cordin' to my understandin' of the usual procedure, it supposed to be the other way around.

ROSIE. I don't think either of you are quite grasping the picture here. In the first place, the guy doesn't even know about it, that I'm pregnant. In the second place I haven't *seen* him since the afternoon of our Grand Passion. In the third place I wouldn't tell him I was pregnant if I *did* see him. Besides which, I have no intention of getting married. Even if he were to make the offer, which I doubt. And I *certainly* have no intention of having a kid, since I have other plans, careerwise.

GLAS. Ah.

ROSIE. I'm going to be a writer, you see, and—

RANDALL. That a fact?

ROSIE. And obviously a child at this time could not possibly be on the agenda.

RANDALL. What kinda books you gonna write, little chick?

ROSIE. Good ones.

GLAS. Listen, Rosie . . . how about you tell this young man about . . . your condition, hah?

ROSIE. Mister Glas, I appreciate your interest and concern, but there's no point in pursuing these hypothetical conjectures, there really isn't. I know what I'm doing.

GLAS. Listen, Rosie, you got to think, in the long run—

ROSIE. Oh, the *long* run, the *long* run! That's all I ever hear! The long run this, the long run that! What about the *short* run! I mean what do you know about it? I'm the one with this, this *thing* floating blissfully around in my womb, feeding off me, draining me of all the juices of my life, ruining all my plans! Don't talk to me about *long* runs! (*An abrupt silence; all are still.*) I'm sorry.

GLAS (*patting her hand.*) That's all right . . . it's all right. (GLAS *stands, moves upstage right to stove. Gets cup and spoon.* ROSIE *removes her hair which proves to be a wig.* RANDALL *is silent, but fascinated.* GLAS, *his back to the girl, does not immediately see.* ROSIE *takes a comb from her purse and proceeds to comb the wig.* GLAS *turns to the table and is brought up short; in his surprise, drops the spoon, picks it up, wipes it on pants.*)

ROSIE. One of my attempts at glamor. I like to think it helps, but I guess not; one has to remember the line about silk purses out of sow's ears. Face it, I'm a sow's ear of the first water. (GLAS *puts cup and spoon on table left of* ROSIE. *Returns to stove to make coffee.*)

RANDALL. You know what they say about beauty, little chick.

ROSIE (*without looking at him*). You tell me beauty is only skin-deep, Randall, and I'll belt you right in the mouth. . . . Can you imagine me wearing this thing tonight? Of all nights? (*Puts comb away.*) I mean, I only wear it on special occasions, you know? Some special occasion. (*Drops wig on table.*) At first, earlier this evening, I got all dressed up, my best dress, with matching shoes, pearl earrings, the works.

There I was, looking myself over in the full-length mirror, seeing how I looked and then I realized where I was going. Getting all dressed up to go to an abortion . . . what a stupid life. What a stupid, stupid life.

GLAS (*down to table, pours coffee*). Have some coffee.

ROSIE. What do you think, Mister Glas? Stupid?

GLAS. I have no opinion.

RANDALL (*moves upstage to sink.*) Mister Glas a pretty difficult man to pin down, you find. Matter of fact, it been startlin' to me these here past few minutes that he been devotin' any attention atall to your present predicament. (GLAS *picks up a plate and moves toward stove. To* GLAS.) Here I been thinkin' you to be merely a watcher of the go-bye world, Mister Glas, sir, lackin' the inclination or desire to be, uh—*involved.*

GLAS (*angrily*). You stay out of this, hah! (RANDALL *turns away, angrily. Faces left.* GLAS *puts pot on stove and goes to table.*)

ROSIE. If you knew me better, you'd see that this is exactly the kind of thing that's likely to happen to me. (*She resumes combing of the wig.*) Getting knocked up, I mean. The point is it was my first time, I was a virgin before that. Wouldn't you know it, I'd get caught? Aside from everything else, I'm not lucky either. (GLAS *puts butter in refrigerator.*) You see, if I was lucky, Harold and I could've succumbed to our silly little passion and that would've been that, the end of it. (GLAS *downstage, sits on end of bed and watches* ROSIE.) And New Rochelle, of all places. At least if it'd been in some nice apartment in the Village, say, with the sounds coming through the window of traffic and people, the breeze blowing the curtain over the bed, like in the movies. But, no. I lost my virginity in the attic of an old house in New Rochelle. Harold's grandmother's house. On a rainy day in spring on the floor of the attic in his grandmother's house, listening to the rain on the roof, breathing the dust of old things. . . . And what comes next but his grandmother who was supposed to be in the city for the day. But instead she's suddenly standing in the door to the attic, attracted there, no doubt, by the scuffling sounds of the imminent consummation. So she's standing there,

screaming (ROSIE *bangs on the table.*):
"Stop that! Stop that this instant!" (GLAS
turns away.) Needless to say, it was out
of the question. Stopping. At that particular moment. I mean, sex is like a flight
over the sea, one reaches the point of no
return. . . . I guess it sounds funny now,
but, you know, at the time . . . it was
pretty rotten. Sordid, I mean . . . it wasn't
at all the way it's supposed to be. (RAN-
DALL *moves downstage to chair left.*) And
Harold, of all people. A girl finds herself
in this predicament, this condition, she'd
at least like to be able to think of the
cause of it as being some clever, handsome
guy with charm and experience, just returned from spending a year in Rome,
say, on a Guggenheim fellowship. But
Harold, . . . Harold is six foot two, about
a hundred and twenty-five pounds, tops,
an Economics major at CCNY . . . That's
about the best I'll ever be able to do,
I know it. (*She smiles and snorts.*) Ever
since I found out I was pregnant I've been
walking around with a face down to here
and my mother kept saying, "What's the
matter with you, anyway, I just don't
know what's gotten into you lately." So,
finally, I told her: a kid named Harold,
as a matter of fact. . . . (*Picks up bag
and takes out compact. Wipes her mouth.*)
Oh, well, I just keep telling myself: "Remember Rosie, like in the song . . . someday my prince will come . . . Snow
White. . . ." (*Pause.*)

RANDALL. Don't worry, little chick:
someday your prince'll come.

ROSIE. Sure, sure.

GLAS. You say your mama knows?
About this?

ROSIE (*puts away compact; bag back on
floor*). Oh, yeah.

GLAS. She knows what you're going to
do and she doesn't . . . she doesn't care?

ROSIE. Oh, sure. She cares. Certainly.
But she's realistic. I'll say that much for
her.

GLAS. And your father too?

ROSIE. Not my father. My stepfather.
My real father is dead, you see.

GLAS. Ah, I'm sorry to hear.

ROSIE. Thank you, yeah, some island
out in the middle of the Pacific Ocean.
(*Wryly.*) Remember that war they had?

GLAS. I remember several.

ROSIE. Yeah. So Harvey Kasner, age
nineteen, gets killed on a stupid sunny day
on some stupid island out in the middle of
the Pacific Ocean, nineteen forty-three. I
would like to've known Harvey Kasner,
my mother says he was a pretty nice kid.
He never even knew I existed. The letter
my mother wrote to tell him she was going to have me came back. He was dead
before it got there, it came back unopened
with the rest of his stuff, personal effects.

GLAS. Mm.

ROSIE. And for what? After all the
noise dies down and the dead are buried,
the politicians come out from under the
rocks and split the take, am I right?

RANDALL (*to GLAS*). She somethin' *else,*
ain't she?

ROSIE. What does that mean, I'm something else?

RANDALL. Well, *you* know. . . . *Style,*
Rosie! You got *style!*

ROSIE (*contemptuously*). Style! This
isn't style! This is *front!* All front! But you
hit it right on the head. A style is what
you need in this life. You have to find a
style and stick to it. That's my whole problem: I haven't been able to find a style yet.
(*A brief pause. She sighs.*) Well, at least
I don't laugh at everyone's jokes anymore.
I used to laugh at everybody's jokes, you
know. Funny or not.

GLAS. Why?

ROSIE. So they'd like me.

GLAS. Really?

ROSIE. It's nice to be liked.

GLAS. Did it work?

ROSIE. What?

GLAS. Laughing at everybody's jokes.
Did it work? Did they like you? (*Pause.*)

ROSIE (*thoughtfully*). I don't know.
They didn't say. (*Pause.*)

GLAS. If I was to make a joke and you
didn't laugh that would be okay. I like
you anyway.

RANDALL (*crosses right to bed above
GLAS*). You have captured Mister Glas's
heart, little pussycat. Which is no mean
trick, I can assure you, indeed. Like I
been tryin' all a my life.

ROSIE. You know each other a long
time, huh?

GLAS. I know him about an hour.

ROSIE. Oh. (*Confused she looks to* RAN-
DALL.)

RANDALL. Skip it, Rosie. That were
merely a private little joke, understood
only by me, the significance of which
would be somewhat obscure to others, I

admit. He's right. He knows me about a hour. Howsomever— (*To* GLAS.) "I do desire we may be better strangers." (*To* ROSIE.) You know who said that?

ROSIE (*shakes her head*). You seem to be unusually well read. (*Pause.*)

RANDALL (*moves downstage of table; with a sudden edge*). You mean, for uh —someone like me?

ROSIE. What?

RANDALL (*crosses left below table to chair.*) *You* know: unusual, you mean, for a young chap of my color and station in life?

ROSIE. Your color! Who said anything about your *color*? Listen, buster, you could be yellow-polka-dots for all I care one way or another. All I said was—

RANDALL (*turns to* ROSIE). We do seem to be comin' up with some *unusual* alternate color schemes this evenin'.

ROSIE. I don't know what that's supposed to mean, all I said was—

RANDALL. Mister Glas's color scheme was, I think, uh—purple with orange stripes, which also has its points.

ROSIE (*to* GLAS). What's he talking about, do *you* know?

GLÁS. Don't pay any attention to him.

RANDALL (*leaning over table, points umbrella at* GLAS; *violently*). Now you knock that off, you hear! Knock that off about not payin' any attention! Knock it off! And you! (*He wheels on* ROSIE.) Don't you be askin' *him* what I'm talkin' about! You ask *me* what I'm talkin' about! Hear? I be glad to explain it to you, but you ask *me*!

ROSIE (*unintimidated*). What are you getting so excited about? All I said—

GLAS. All right, wait a *minute,* wait a *minute!* (*Silence. All are still.*) Everybody relax! No trouble!

RANDALL (*crosses right above table to* GLAS; *quietly*). Mister Glas, sir, you got a absolutely *morbid* fear of trouble, aintcha. (*To* ROSIE.) I don't need nobody doin' any explainin' for me, little chick. I don't need nobody doin' *nothin'* for me. You dig? (*No response from* ROSIE. *She only returns his gaze steadily. Leans over, his face close to* ROSIE's.) You dig?

GLAS. Tell him all right, Rosie. (ROSIE *looks at* GLAS, *then back to* RANDALL.) Tell him all right.

ROSIE (*finally*). All right, Randall. (RANDALL *moves upstage to doorway. Takes hat off hook. He relents and the tension leaves him.* ROSIE's *attention remains fixed on him, nevertheless, as he begins concentratedly to clean his glasses.*) I didn't mean to insult you or anything like that, Randall. It might have sounded patronizing but I didn't mean it that way, honestly.

RANDALL (*downstage to* ROSIE; *with a beaming, totally insincere smile*). Tha's okay, little chick. Tha's okay. We jus' drop the whole matter, right? (*Pause.* ROSIE *gazes at him.*)

ROSIE (*stands; coldly*). Listen, you nervy bastard, who do you think you are?

RANDALL. Say again?

ROSIE (*pushes chair against table; furious*). Giving *me* that Uncle Tom shuffle-and-smile routine?

GLAS (*apprehensive*). Rosie . . . (RANDALL's *smile fades to one of more natural proportions.*)

ROSIE (*upstage right to stove and back down again.*) Talk about insulting! I just apologize for sounding patronizing and you come right back and patronize *me*? Who do you think you are!

GLAS. Listen, Rosie . . .

RANDALL (*leans on wall; takes off glasses; his voice normal*). Well, if the truth be told, Rosie, I haven't quite decided yet. (ROSIE *turns to* GLAS, *opens her mouth to speak, but closes it again. Pause.*)

ROSIE. What did you say?

RANDALL. I said, I haven't quite decided yet. I am, however, working on it constantly. (ROSIE *nods. Pause.*)

ROSIE. What's the idea, Randall?

RANDALL. Would you care to explain it to her, Mister Glas?

GLAS (*grabs* ROSIE's *bag and slams it on chair; flatly*). Sometimes he runs out of gas. (*She waits for some elaboration of that cryptic remark, but none comes.*)

ROSIE. As an explanation that leaves a lot to be desired. What's with you, you get your kicks going around putting people on?

RANDALL. If I disguise my voice to speak the truth, Rosie, it is no less the truth.

ROSIE (*drily*). Who said that. (RANDALL *places his hand gently upon his breast. He turns and exits.* ROSIE *looks after him in silence for a moment. He reappears in the store as* ROSIE *turns to* GLAS.) What's the idea with him? (*The lights fade on the kitchen while, in the store,* RANDALL

*moves to the street door and stands, look-
ing out into the darkness. He begins to
hum the tune again: "No Hiding Place."
The lights fade to black.*)

ACT TWO

Scene Two

*The lights rise again on the store. Some
minutes have elapsed. In the kitchen, GLAS
is at the sink, his back to ROSIE who is
seated at the table, absorbed. RANDALL is
as before, gazing into the street. ROSIE rises
and moves from the kitchen, stands in the
doorway to the store, watching RANDALL.
She steps into the room.*

———

RANDALL. Where is our good samaritan?
(*Throughout now, except where otherwise indicated,* RANDALL's *voice and actions
are natural, the parody is gone.*)

ROSIE (*with a vague gesture toward the
kitchen*). Washing the dishes.

RANDALL. Fastidious.

ROSIE. Yeah. (*She places her handbag
and wig on the counter.*) He's been telling me about you.

RANDALL. He knows little.

ROSIE. Very interesting, though. I mean,
do you really have an IQ of a hundred
and eighty-seven? (*Sits stool.*)

RANDALL. So they tell me. (*In the
kitchen* GLAS *moves down to table, sits.
He faces out, still, absorbed in thought.*)

ROSIE. That's some fantastic IQ.

RANDALL (*takes off cape*). You're envious, Rosie?

ROSIE. Well, not envious exactly. I
wouldn't mind having a mind like that,
though. I mean, with a mind like that one
could do anything. You. You could do
great things.

RANDALL (*hangs cape on post; opens his
jacket; already anticipating the answer*).
For whom?

ROSIE. Well . . . for anyone. For your
race, for one thing. Certainly for your
race. (RANDALL *smiles, having gotten the
answer.*) You don't agree?

RANDALL (*crosses right to telephone;
takes book from rack, his back to* ROSIE).
You're a splendid girl, Rosie. A little on
the square side, but a splendid girl.

ROSIE. Why? What's square about that?

RANDALL. I'm a freak, Rosie. You've

heard the expression: in the country of
the blind the one-eyed man is king? (*He
shakes his head.*) In the country of the
blind the one-eyed man is a freak.

ROSIE. Depends on how you look at it.

RANDALL (*sits on stool facing downstage*). Through my single, freak's eye.
What else did he tell you?

ROSIE (*turns left*). Oh . . . that you
don't have any place to live and that
you've been in trouble with the police and
that you have some kind of heart condition and about your mother being a . . .
well, about your mother.

RANDALL. Prostitute.

ROSIE. Yes.

RANDALL. I thought you were unafraid
of the right words, Rosie. What else?

ROSIE. What?

RANDALL. What else did he tell you?

ROSIE. Well . . . that you're probably
in trouble right now. (RANDALL *smiles.*)
That you were running away from something when you came in here tonight.
(*Turns to* RANDALL.) *Are* you in some
kind of trouble? (*Pause.*)

RANDALL (*stands; puts book on rack*).
When are you going to start writing your
books, Rosie? (*Pause. She acknowledges
the evasion with a wry smile and is prepared to submit to it for the moment, but
her question remains unanswered and her
eyes never leave him.*)

ROSIE. I've already started.

RANDALL. Ah?

ROSIE. I've begun my first novel.

RANDALL. Well, now. What's it about?

ROSIE. I don't know yet.

RANDALL (*upstage to ladder*). You've
already begun it and you don't know
what its about?

ROSIE. I'll find out as I move along.

RANDALL (*crosses right to stool; leans on
counter*). Well, I'll be sure to keep my
eyes open for a book written by Rosie
Kasner.

ROSIE. Rosalind.

RANDALL (*looks up at* ROSIE). Hm?

ROSIE. My full name is Rosalind.

RANDALL. Oh. That's a nice name, Rosalind. Rosie's a nice name, but Rosalind is
nicer. Beautiful, actually. You ought to
call yourself Rosalind.

ROSIE (*turns downstage; snorts*). Open
your eyes, Randall: do I look like a Rosalind?

RANDALL. What does a Rosalind look

like? (*A pause, finally, her eyes leave him. Shrugs.*) I wish I was beautiful to match my beautiful name. (RANDALL *snatches up the wig, moves downstage to bench, puts it on and postures, an attempt to distract her from thoughts of absent beauty.*) Hey! Do I look like a Rosalind?

ROSIE (*drily*). You look like a colored queen.

RANDALL (*crosses left to table, removing the wig, and in the dialect; putting wig on bottle*). Least I don't have *that* problem. Gotta be thankful for small favors, like they say. (*Then, naturally. Sits chair.*) Do you want to know a secret, as a matter of fact?

ROSIE (*picks up bag*). About what?

RANDALL. About me.

ROSIE. What?

RANDALL. I'm a virgin, as a matter of fact. (*Pause.*)

ROSIE. Oh?

RANDALL (*nods*). I've been saving it all up.

ROSIE (*apprehensively*). I beg your pardon?

RANDALL. I've been saving it all up.

ROSIE. Saving what all up?

RANDALL. My passion.

ROSIE (*off stool, moves downstage center*). Oh . . . really? Well . . . that's very interesting, isn't it?

RANDALL. Why?

ROSIE. Well, because . . . I don't know . . . it's (*Crosses left to end of counter.*) . . . well, I guess it's not really all *that* interesting, I just meant (*Leans on counter.*) . . . well, Jesus, *I* don't know! What do you mean, *why!* (*Crosses left to jukebox.*) What are you telling *me* for?

RANDALL (*after a brief pause*). I thought it would be interesting. In the meantime, I had been studying up on it.

ROSIE (*turns to* RANDALL). On what?

RANDALL. The Art. The Art of Love. You know: the uses of the flesh.

ROSIE (*sits chair*). Studying up?

RANDALL. Many books on that subject now. And when the time were to come, what a truly cataclysmic explosion of Love it would be! But it looks as though the matter will end this way.

ROSIE. What way?

RANDALL. That I will end a stranger to the ways and uses of the flesh, Rosie. (GLAS *stands, leaves kitchen and enters store.*)

ROSIE. Why?

RANDALL. No hiding place, Rosie.

ROSIE. What?

RANDALL. My soul is corrupt, Rosie, but oh, my flesh is pure.

ROSIE. What are you talking about, Randall? (GLAS *crosses left to center.*)

RANDALL. I'm still here, Mister Glas.

GLAS (*stops*). So I see.

RANDALL. I'll go if you want me to go.

GLAS. Yeah, sure.

RANDALL. Truly. (*Pause.* GLAS *regards him for a moment.*)

GLAS (*moves upstage right to below stool*). Go, stay, it makes no difference to me.

RANDALL. Actually, I find myself suddenly very tired and would very much like to sit quietly for a bit. What are *your* immediate plans, Rosie?

GLAS. You finally decided to talk right and stop with the funny stuff, hah?

ROSIE. Yeah, why *do* you do that, Randall?

RANDALL. I don't know.

ROSIE (*impatiently*). Well, you *must* know.

RANDALL. Why?

ROSIE (*annoyed*). Oh, come on.

RANDALL (*in the dialect*). You a college-educated person, little Rosie, why not *you* tell *me?* You could write us a watchama-callit, a thesis on it, even. (*Pause.*)

ROSIE (*turns away*). You win.

GLAS. He always wins. (GLAS *crosses right stage to ladder. His back to* RANDALL.)

RANDALL. Do you really want to know? (ROSIE *gazes at him, wanting to know.*) It is my what you might call insulation against the fire of life. (*He smiles.*) Mister Glas spells his name with one *s*, did you know that? German for the glass with two esses.

ROSIE. That's an exciting bit of information.

RANDALL. Well, I only wanted to be sure you spelled it right in your thesis on camp survivors.

GLAS (*turns to* RANDALL; *alerted*). What?

ROSIE. No, I'm not—

RANDALL (*to* GLAS). I said I wanted to be sure she spelled your name correctly in her thesis.

GLAS (*moves downstage center*). Wait a minute, no name, you don't use my name, you know.

ROSIE (*stands*). Of course not. (*To* RANDALL.) What are you getting everybody excited for? (*To* GLAS.) I don't use anyone's name, Mister Glas. (*Crosses right below table to left end of counter.*) Of course not. (*To* RANDALL.) What are you trying to do, make trouble or something?

RANDALL (*stands*). Why don't you want her to use your name, Mister Glas? (GLAS *moves downstage near telephone.*)

ROSIE. I *don't use names.* Will you stop? (*Puts bag on counter.*)

RANDALL. What *is* your story, Mister Glas?

GLAS. What story?

RANDALL. Who you are: *that* story.

GLAS (*his back to* RANDALL). I thought you said you were very tired and wanted to sit quiet for a while? So why don't you sit quiet for a while?

RANDALL (*crosses right to center*). There are many people in this world, Rosie, with a *Do Not Disturb* sign hung around their necks. Invisible, but present. Mister Glas is one of those. "Among wolves one must howl a little," Mister Glas. (*He turns to* ROSIE.) Have you ever heard that, Rosie? (*She nods.* GLAS *moves upstage to doorway.*) Mister Glas has never learned to howl. (RANDALL *upstage to stool.*) You see? He has no talent for it, you see? The wolves are howling their heads off out there and Mister Glas is in here keeping his trap strictly shut. True, Mister Glas? (GLAS *stares at him.*) Why?

GLAS (*turns to* RANDALL). I told you why already once.

RANDALL. To watch the world go by and keep out of its way? That's no answer, Mister Glas. Survival. That's why.

ROSIE (*moves between stools;* GLAS *crosses behind counter*). I don't follow this at all.

RANDALL. Survival, Mister Glas? True?

GLAS (*turns to* RANDALL). You said yourself, they kill you out there.

RANDALL. But survival is possible for a time even out there. (*Downstage to bench.*) Behold Randall: *I* survive.

GLAS. With an ice pick? With a gun?

ROSIE. *What* ice pick?

RANDALL. One chooses one's means, Mister Glas.

ROSIE. *What* gun?

RANDALL. We're all going to fall on the killing ground one day or another, Mister Glas. At least, I'll die in action. (*Turns upstage.*) And it's you who has the gun, remember? You're in no position to look with contempt upon those of us who choose to defend ourselves: it's *you* who has the gun. (GLAS *reaches below the counter, comes up with the revolver in his hand and throws it with contempt onto the counter.* ROSIE *is, of course, startled. Backs up to left of stool.*)

GLAS. Empty. (*Pause.*)

RANDALL. Empty?

GLAS. To frighten someone who means me harm, maybe, yes. To kill with, never.

ROSIE. What the hell *is* this?

RANDALL (*upstage to ladder*). Before— when you asked me to empty the gun— what was that?

GLAS. A little joke on you.

ROSIE. Listen . . .

RANDALL. You fascinate me, Mister Glas. From the start here tonight, you've fascinated me. (*Moves down near stool.*)

GLAS. I got a fascinating personality.

RANDALL. You also confuse me, of course.

GLAS (*puts gun away*). So you said.

ROSIE. Would someone explain to me what exactly is going on here? (*Pause.* RANDALL *gazes at her.*)

RANDALL (*sits on stool*). Rosie, if I were dying right now would you save my life? (*A short pause.*)

ROSIE. *I* don't know. Maybe, if I could. Why?

RANDALL. How far would you go? To what extent?

ROSIE. How far would I *have* to go?

RANDALL. Would you die *for* me? Would you go that far? (*Pause.*)

ROSIE. No.

RANDALL. Why not?

GLAS. There was only one Jesus Christ, sonny.

RANDALL. And they don't make them like *that* any more, Mister Glas, sir. (*To* ROSIE). But you'd try, then, hm?

ROSIE. Try what?

RANDALL. To save my *life*. If I were *dying*.

GLAS. Don't play with her, Randall.

ROSIE (*cautiously*). Yes, I'd try.

RANDALL (*turns downstage away from* ROSIE). Take a good look at me, Rosie. (*He waits.*) Are you looking?

ROSIE. Of course I'm looking.

RANDALL. All right, I'm dying. Save me. (*Pause.*)

ROSIE (*backs up to between stools*). I don't understand.

GLAS (*crosses right, comes from behind counter*). Leave her alone, Randall. (*To* ROSIE.) Randall has done some terrible thing tonight, Rosie.

ROSIE (*alarmed*). What has he done?

GLAS. I don't know. Some terrible thing.

ROSIE. Randall? What have you done? (*No response from* RANDALL.)

GLAS. The police are after him, perhaps. Or someone else. But, whoever it is will kill him for what he has done. (*Downstage behind* RANDALL.)

ROSIE. Kill him?

RANDALL (*turns to* GLAS). I've known from the very first instant, Mister Glas, that we—understood. Each other.

GLAS. I can't save you. A little bit, maybe, like before with the cops. But finally—no. (*Crosses right to telephone. Pause.* RANDALL *flings himself away.*)

RANDALL (*in the dialect*). 'Course you can't!

ROSIE (*turns to* RANDALL). What is it you've done, Randall?

RANDALL (*turns to* ROSIE). How do *you* feel about death, Rosie?

ROSIE (*drily*). I'm against it.

RANDALL. I want to know, Rosie! (GLAS *downstage to bench, his back to them. Pause.*)

ROSIE. Well . . . I can't conceive of death. Death is not-feeling, I can't conceive of not-feeling. Those people who donate their bodies to science after they're dead? I could never do that. They'd come at my dead body with a knife and I'd *feel* it, I *know* I would.

RANDALL (*picks up umbrella, turns left away from* ROSIE). Dead is dead, Rosie, and only then the knife holds no pain.

ROSIE (*crosses to right of stool*). What is it you've done, Randall?

RANDALL (*in the dialect*). Sweetie, I'm what the psychologists call a "unreachable youth." You tryin' to reach me?

GLAS. Don't tease her, Randall.

ROSIE. It's all right, I'm used to it. (*To* RANDALL.) You don't want to pursue this, then, right?

RANDALL (*hangs umbrella on post*). No.

ROSIE. Just don't forget I offered.

GLAS. There's nothing you could do for him, Rosie. And he knows it.

ROSIE. How do you *know* there's noth-ing I could do for him? (*To* RANDALL.) How do you *know*?

RANDALL (*turns to* ROSIE). What could you do, Rosie? Give me a for instance.

ROSIE. Well . . . well, I don't know! I could give you an alibi! I could do that!

RANDALL. An alibi for what?

ROSIE. For whatever it is you've done, goddamnit. What do you think for what?

RANDALL. How do you know I've done anything?

ROSIE. You just said you did!

RANDALL. That gentleman there said I did.

ROSIE. You agreed with him!

RANDALL. Mister Glas, did I agree with you?

GLAS. Leave her alone, Randall. (*Exploding.*) LEAVE HER ALONE, NOW!

ROSIE (*off stool moves downstage right with bag*). Oh, forget it.

GLAS (*violently*). Is that the kind of books you're going to write, Rosie! Books about how people save each other's lives? Don't you believe it, Rosie! Nobody saves nobody! (*Crosses left above* ROSIE.) Right, Randall?

RANDALL (*moves left of table; sits chair*). An indisputable truth.

ROSIE (*to* RANDALL). That's one hell of an attitude! (*To* GLAS.) Just because *you* don't care?

GLAS (*turns back to* ROSIE). You want to save somebody, Rosie? (*Pointing to her abdomen.*) Save *that* life, then! Save what you *can* save!

ROSIE. Shut up about that! We're not talking about that!

GLAS. No?

ROSIE. What do you know about it! (*She turns away, quickly, holding herself, protecting herself.*)

GLAS. *I* know! (*Turns left crosses to left end of counter.*) I know!

RANDALL (*quietly*). What do you know, Mister Glas, sir?

GLAS (*after a pause, quietly*). I know.

RANDALL. Of course you do, we know that. But what, exactly? (*He grins.*) Your turn to speak, Mister Glas . . . our turn to listen. (*A long pause.* RANDALL *waits, watching* GLAS. GLAS *returns his gaze, then looks to* ROSIE *who, still angry, is turned away. He looks again to* RANDALL. *Finally, his gaze shifts from* RANDALL. *He moves downstage to table and takes up the newspaper, looks at the headline.*)

GLAS. This man . . . do you know what they say? They say that when they arrested him he appeared to be relieved. Not frightened. Not angry. Not defiant. They say he appeared to be—*relieved!* (*Crosses right to center.*) . . . Do you know why? I'll tell you why. Because all these years he knew, you see. He waited, and he knew that sooner or later it would happen: the discovery that would mean his judgment and his death. And the anticipation of a blow is always, somehow, more terrible that the blow itself when it finally comes. (*Turns upstage.*) So, one can understand his relief. When the blow finally came.

ROSIE (*sits left end of bench; puts her bag beside her; hostile*). He doesn't deserve anything so comforting as relief. He deserves what he got. (GLAS *upstage to counter, sits stool facing counter.*)

RANDALL (*quietly, his eyes on* GLAS). Bloodthirsty, Rosie.

ROSIE. When it comes to the Eichmanns of this world I get very Jewish. (*To* GLAS.) I should think you'd feel the same.

RANDALL (*still on* GLAS, *waiting*). Mister Glas isn't a Jew.

GLAS (*puts paper on counter, turns downstage*). But I had a wife who was a Jew. And a son who was a Jew—for his mother's sake. Ten years old he was then. Nineteen thirty-eight. To be married to a Jew in Germany in nineteen thirty-eight, Rosie, a man might as well have been a Jew himself: the Nazis made no distinctions. And, of course, to have been a Jew then was to wait for the day they opened your door and took you away. They opened so many doors . . . so many doors . . . and came out with Jews in their fists. . . . (*Turns to* RANDALL.) . . . Most men, you know, most men can live all of their lives with the conviction that they have honor, and they can go to their graves with that conviction without ever having been put to the test of it. I envy them, the ones who escape the test. Not me. (*Turns downstage.*) In the summer of nineteen thirty-eight I had my test, my choice to make: to wait until I was taken to a concentration camp as a Jew with my Jewish wife and my Jewish son . . . or to live as a Communist and fight for my country, my Germany, against the Nazis. (*Stands. Moves downstage to* ROSIE.) Sure, you can say: where is the choice there, where is the choice to make against

loyalty to your wife, to your son? Easy to say. Even for me, easy to say now. (*Downstage below* ROSIE.) But not then. Because, you see, the Party, belief in the Party was above all. Of course, this is impossible to believe, I know, for anyone who was not of it. But it was true: the Party was God, the defeat of Nazism our Paradise to be attained on earth, our German earth. And, to save my life for that fight, I abandoned them, my wife and my child, in the middle of a night, without a word. I went to another city, I took another name. (*Turns left, crosses to above chair.*) I was a railroad engineer in those days, and the war was coming, and the trains were rolling day and night in Germany, then, day and night. For nearly a year I carried freight between Hamburg and Cologne: chemicals, machinery, armaments. From time to time, I would get news of home, from comrades, that my wife and son were well, were safe yet. (*Sits chair.*) . . . And then I was transferred to another run, to a place called Mauthausen, and the freight was people. . . . Three trips I made in two months and I carried hundred and hundreds of people, Jews, to the concentration camp at Mauthausen. . . . Until August, nineteen thirty-nine, and Stalin made his pact with Hitler. Communism embraced Nazism, my god kissed Satin and called him friend. In that moment there was a new truth: that I had abandoned my wife and my son of the wolves and saved myself for nothing. For *nothing!* My life, without them, had been without meaning. And their death without me, when it came, would be equally without meaning. Unless . . . unless, it was not too late, hah? Of course! I could go back! With what dignity and honor there was left to me! I could go back to my wife—whether she would forgive me or not, whether she would have me or not. (*Stands, crosses left to center.*) I would live with her again, and with my son, as the husband of a Jew, as the father of a Jew and wait for them to open our door and take us! Together. . . . And I went back. . . . (*Turns downstage.*) . . . And in the house the windows were smashed . . . and the door was open . . . and they were gone. (*Pause.*) I left Germany then. (*Turns upstage then turns to* ROSIE.) Save what you *can* save, Rosie. I know.

ROSIE (*ignoring this, perhaps not hearing it, quietly*). You were never in a concentration camp. (*Silence from* GLAS. *He turns away.*) Your arm, the number.

GLAS. A tattoo fellow did it for me. Here in Brooklyn.

ROSIE. But *why?*

GLAS (*turns to* ROSIE). I don't know . . . it was *supposed* to be there, it *should* have happened. . . . Do you understand?

RANDALL (*without looking at* GLAS; GLAS *moves upstage to right of stool*). The leg, Mister Glas? That they were supposed to have broken up?

GLAS (*turns to* RANDALL). A railroad accident.

RANDALL. And the stories about the camp you were supposed to have been in?

GLAS. Everyone knows those stories. They are all true. Not my truth . . . but the truth.

ROSIE. Jesus.

GLAS (*closes newspaper*). For this man . . . the waiting is over. He committed a crime for which a punishment has been named, you see. (*Turns downstage.*) But me. Who will judge *me?* Who will condemn *me*, and by what law? (*He moves to the door, opens it, looks out into the street.*) The first time I told my truth in twenty-three years. (*He moves out.*)

RANDALL (*with irony*). And the truth shall make him free. (*After a moment,* ROSIE *moves to the door. Pause.*) What is he doing?

ROSIE. Sitting on the curb.

RANDALL. Mm.

ROSIE (*back against door*). Randall?

RANDALL. Hmm?

ROSIE. I think he's crying.

RANDALL. Mm, hm.

ROSIE. Yes, he is. He's crying. (RANDALL *takes up the wig from the table.*) Shouldn't we do something?

RANDALL (*his attention on the wig*). You amaze me, Rosie, you truly do. (*Stands. Puts on wig.*) You always think there's something to be *done.*

ROSIE (*still at door, looking out*). Jesus.

RANDALL. Mourn not, little Rosie, mourn not. (*He turns to jukebox, inserts a coin in the slot, the machine comes alive in colored lights.*) Maybe we'll think of something, Rosie. (*Crosses right to center.*)

ROSIE (*without turning*). What?

RANDALL. I said: maybe we'll think of something. To be done. (*The record begins: it is the voice of Frank Sinatra singing "You Go To My Head."* RANDALL *crosses right to stool. Sits facing downstage.* ROSIE *at the door. Turns, faces left. At the end of the first few bars of the song the curtain falls on Act Two. The music continues behind the curtain, and fades out slowly as the house lights come up.*)

ACT THREE: Coda

Before the rise, the music is again heard, continuing. At the rise, the scene is revealed as before; several moments have elapsed. ROSIE *is still at the door,* RANDALL *on the stool. The last few bars of the song are sung, the record ends. Silence.*

ROSIE *turns and moves, despondently, downstage to railing. Turns to* RANDALL.

———

ROSIE. You look ridiculous.

RANDALL (*absently*). Hmmmm?

ROSIE. Will you take the wig off, this is hardly the time for jokes. (RANDALL, *still absorbed. Pause.* ROSIE *moves right to counter.*) I feel very sorry for him, Randall.

RANDALL (*turns to* ROSIE). You do seem to be missing the point, sweet Rosie. He doesn't want you to feel *sorry* for him, he doesn't want your *pity*. Save your pity for those who want it, Rosie, don't piddle it away on those who don't.

ROSIE (*Downstage to chair; a rhetorical question*). Well, what are you supposed to do, a man dumps a story like that right in your lap? (*Pause.*)

RANDALL. Stand up. (RANDALL *stands. Moves down puts wig on stool.*)

ROSIE. Haven't you any compassion at all?

RANDALL (*with mock interest*). What is that: compassion. (RANDALL *takes off jacket. Drops it on bench.*) I mean, that compassion, that's okay up to a point, little Rosie, that's what you do until the doctor comes, (*Upstage to counter. Picks up newspaper.*) but it doesn't do much good, you know, finally.

ROSIE. I suppose not.

RANDALL (*looks at ladder*). So I suppose it's time we did something, then.

ROSIE. About what?

RANDALL (*moves ladder downstage above stool; steps of ladder facing right*). He still there?

ROSIE. Yes. Now what. (RANDALL *moves stool down left of ladder.*)

RANDALL (*crosses left to cape*). You said what could we do, Rosie, and I said perhaps we'll think of something.

ROSIE. So?

RANDALL. So, I've thought of something and we'll do it, then. (*Picks up cape and puts it on.*)

ROSIE. What.

RANDALL. Mister Glas is a victim of every man's unfortunate need to be judged, Rosie. (*Shuts off light over table.*)

ROSIE. Oh, yeah?

RANDALL. So, we'll do that little thing, Rosie.

ROSIE. What little thing?

RANDALL (*offering his hand*). Be seated, Rosie, be seated.

ROSIE. What?

RANDALL. Sit. (*Lifts* ROSIE *onto counter. Goes behind counter. Pulls down shade over window.*) Here.

ROSIE. What the hell for? What are you doing, anyway? Now, listen, Randall—!

RANDALL (*crosses right, shuts off light upstage right*). Ssh! (*A single light burning: it illuminates in a circle of light, the area around the ladder, the stool, and* ROSIE *on the counter.*)

ROSIE. What exactly is this game called? (RANDALL *downstage to stool. Puts on wig.*)

RANDALL. It has no name, I just invented it. (RANDALL *ascends the ladder—stands on fourth step.*) It's the game without a name.

ROSIE. Okay, I'll bite. What now?

RANDALL. We wait. For the principal party in these proceedings. (*On cue,* GLAS *appears in the doorway.*)

GLAS. What's going on?

RANDALL. Short wait. (*There is a change in* GLAS: *his erect carriage is no more; he is hunched, slumped. It is as though his secret had been the core of him, the force sustaining him, that which has held him erect. Having divulged his secret at last, the core has been drawn out, the shell is collapsed.*)

GLAS (*closes door*). What's all this here? (*Moves downstage above table.*) What are you doing up there? Why are the lights out? Rosie, what's this?

ROSIE (*embarrassed suddenly*). I don't really know, Mister Glas. I'm sorry. (*She moves as if to leave the counter.*)

RANDALL. *Sit,* Rosie! (*She stays.*)

ROSIE. Listen, you nut—

RANDALL (*using ice pick as gavel, bangs once on ladder top; in the dialect*). You stand accused, Mister Glas, sir!

GLAS (*downstage of chair*). What, what?

RANDALL. Accused, yes!

ROSIE. He's crazy, Mister Glas. I'm convinced.

RANDALL (*bangs "gavel" three times; his voice like a machine gun*). Hear ye! Hear ye! God bless all here! We are gathered together here for certain special and particular purposes, to wit: to determine the guilt or innocence (GLAS *moves right watching* RANDALL. *Stops above stool.*) of one, Glas, first name unknown and immaterial, brought forward here and now before this here qualified tri-bunal—that's me—with the view in mind to settin' his heretofore troubled conscience at rest concernin' a certain matter, to wit: his need to be judged. (GLAS *turns downstage.*) The jury—that's you, Rosie—may consider itself duly sworn to deliver at the requisite time the proper various verdicts which are demanded by the laws previously set down by this here society regardin' the execution of justice in all its forms. (*Bangs "gavel" once.*)

ROSIE (*turns away*). Jeee*sus.*

RANDALL. The jury is pushin' for a charge of contempt by this here court unless it be more circumspect and reserved in its reactions to the procedure herein bein' carried out. Be warned, jury. (*Returning to* GLAS.) The first charge to be considered before this tri-bunal here convened is that of, uh—abandonment. Specifically, the, the abandonment aforethought of the family of the accused, specifically, one wife and one son, aged, uh—ten? (GLAS *nods.*) Yeah, ten years of age. How do you plead? (GLAS *folds his hands in front of him.*) Guilty or not guilty?

ROSIE (*pause*). Should I call a cop, Mister Glas? (*She moves to descend from the counter, when* GLAS *speaks, stopping her.*)

GLAS. Guilty.

ROSIE (*sits back*). Mister Glas . . . ?

RANDALL. How say the jury? (*Silence.* ROSIE *is gazing at* GLAS *who waits, motionless.*) How says the jury!

ROSIE (*to* RANDALL). If I had a mind to,

I could point out a very basic little flaw in this whole farce, you know? The fact is, he already said he was guilty, so you don't need any opinion from the jury, or whatever it is I'm supposed to be. That's if I had a mind to. Which I haven't.

RANDALL. The accused's own opinion and hearsay evidence is naturally prejudiced and inadmissible for the purposes of this tri-bunal. Guilty or not guilty, jury? Of the charge of abandonment?

GLAS (*turns to* ROSIE). Say, Rosie! (*Pause. She gazes at* GLAS.)

ROSIE. You too?

GLAS (*more quietly*). Say, Rosie. (*Pause. She looks at* RANDALL, *at* GLAS *again*.)

ROSIE. You already said you were guilty. (*To* RANDALL.) He already said—

RANDALL. The jury do seem to be losin' sight and grasp of the main issue at hand here. Certainly *he* said it. Nobody *else* said it, however. *Yet.* That the issue at hand which we takin' care of now in this here tri-bunal.

GLAS (*still more quietly, insistent*). Say, Rosie. (*Pause.*)

ROSIE (*quietly*). Guilty, yes. Mister Glas . . . ?

GLAS. Ssh, Rosie. (*Turns downstage again. Bows his head.*)

RANDALL. We can now proceed to the more difficult and complex matters been laid before this tri-bunal, to wit: is this here defendant guilty of a certain what might be called *moral deformity* currently to be found present in certain types of individuals now resident within the context of this, uh—society that we got goin' for us at the moment! You will recall, if you will, the defendant's testimonial that some time after the abandonment of his family, he found himself present in another somewhat tricky situation, to wit: employment as the uh—driver of a train that were engaged in the transport of certain parties, namely the Jews, to the place called . . . uh . . . uh . . .

ROSIE. Mauthausen.

RANDALL. Correct. Mauthausen. Now. Did the defendant know—I mean, *know*—whether or not these here parties, namely the Jews, were maybe criminal types convicted by the laws of that time and place? The answer is clear here: no. Definitely. It bein' a matter of record accordin' to the accused's own testimonial that he knew them people to be Jews merely and no

criminal types convicted of crimes against the state by due process of law. Correct? (GLAS *nods*.) Correct. Furthermore, did the accused here before us know that the parties were bein' transported to the place of their ultimate and inescapable death? The answer, in the very words of the accused, is yes. Definitely. How do the accused plead? Guilty or not guilty?

GLAS (*raises his head*). Guilty.

RANDALL. How do the jury find? (*Silence.*) *How do the*—

ROSIE (*lowers her head*). Guilty, yes.

RANDALL. We movin' nicely right along here now. (*Bangs the "gavel."*) This bring us to the very brink of a most ticklish aspect of this case, to wit: the subsequent disposition of the defendant's Self *by* hisself. Did the accused, upon learnin' of its true nature, *refuse* the employment which tended to incriminate him as a direct accomplice in the unspeakable deaths inflicted upon many hundreds of innocent persons, namely the Jews? Did he refuse? He did not. Definitely. On the contrary, jury, *on the contrary*. What he did was, he donned his overhalls and chugged his choo-choo right on inta that place, Mauthausen, keepin' his mouth strictly shut, as we have discovered to be his habit and approach to life. And, subsequent to that, havin' discovered the folly of his havin' deserted his wife and his child for the sake of a *Cause,* to wit: the Commonists, the folly of aiding and abetting in the act of murder for the sake of that *Cause,* when it turn right around, somewhat confusingly, and kiss and make up with its up-till-then sworn enemy, the *other* Cause, to wit: the Nazis. True, we gotta reserve a little bit of sympathy for the accused at this point 'cause we gotta admit there ain't nothin' quite so upsettin' as discoverin' you been believin' in the *wrong Cause.* Which brings us back to the original matter under consideration, to wit: the disposition of the defendant's Self *by* hisself upon discoverin' the Folly of his Ways. Did he, in expiation, for his crimes, throw hisself beneath (GLAS *whirls around to* RANDALL.) the wheels of that very same choo-choo that he'd been runnin' back and forth to the place called Mauthausen? He did not. As is plain to see. *Au contraire,* jury, *au contraire.* He *es-caped,* is what he did. He *withdrew* from the *field* of *battle*. He *lived*. (GLAS *sinks forward. His hands on stool*.)

ROSIE. He tried to go back to his family first.

RANDALL. A gesture which we must be constrained to look upon with caution, jury, if not with outright suspicion. A somewhat *tardy* gesture, if you will. (*A crack of the "gavel."*) Therefore. The defendant stands accused of the charge of continuing. Continuing to maintain himself in a aura of public innocence. Continuing not to seek out punishment for his crimes. Continuing, in short, to live. How do you plead?

GLAS. Guilty.

RANDALL. Jury? Guilty or not guilty?

ROSIE (*looks up*). Of what?

RANDALL. Of *continuing*, jury. To *live*. (*Pause*.)

ROSIE (*lowers her head*). Guilty.

RANDALL (*raps "gavel" once*). The jury havin' voiced no dissent with, and bein' in agreement with, the judgment of the defendant—and also, I might add, with the privately held and hitherto undivulged opinions of this court, namely me—all that bein' the case, this court find the defendant guilty on all counts here before it this evenin' and, havin' no alternative, do sentence the defendant to death in the first degree. Done. *Done*, then! (*A crack of the "gavel."* RANDALL *descends the ladder and moves to the rear of the counter, removing the wig. He drives ice pick into the countertop. He puts on the dark glasses and takes the gun from its place, laying it gently on the countertop*.)

ROSIE (*upon seeing the gun*). Randall!! (RANDALL *leaps in a slow, graceful handspring, over the counter, coming to rest behind* GLAS. *He puts the muzzle of the gun to the base of* GLAS's *skull*.) Randaaal!

RANDALL (*quietly*). Sshh. (ROSIE *is wide-eyed, transfixed.* GLAS *is motionless.* RANDALL *pulls the trigger and the hammer falls, audibly, on the empty chamber. Silence*.) Done, then. . . . (*Moves upstage below stool*.) You got a short span of memory, little chick. It empty, you recall? (*He points the gun at her breast and pulls the trigger: another click*.) You recall now? (*He places the muzzle at his own temple, pulls the trigger. Then again, pointing it this time, but not touching* GLAS's *head and again pulls the trigger.* GLAS *drops his hands to his side.* RANDALL *crosses upstage,*

drops gun beside ROSIE. *Crosses left to chair*.) It's done, Rosie. (RANDALL *turns on light over table. Pause.* ROSIE *is badly shaken*.)

ROSIE. *What's* done?

RANDALL (*sits chair, faces left; with a shrug*). Something. (GLAS *crosses right to ladder, leans on it*.) You know: the *something* you spoke of? (*Takes off glasses puts them on table. Loosens cape and drapes it over back of chair*.)

ROSIE. You almost scared me to death, you bastard, you *nut!*

RANDALL. Well, it make as much sense as *some* trials I could mention. (GLAS *speaks without looking at* RANDALL.)

GLAS (*sits stool facing right*). It should have been loaded, hah? Randall? (*Pause*.)

RANDALL. No sword of justice will pierce *your* heart, Mister Glas. (ROSIE *picks up the gun. On her face there appears a look of disturbance, puzzlement*.)

ROSIE. Randall. . . .

RANDALL. Hmm?

ROSIE. You didn't really know, did you?

RANDALL. Know what, little Rosie?

ROSIE. About the gun. I mean, you didn't really know it wasn't loaded.

RANDALL. Sure I did, Rosie. Didn't he say so?

ROSIE. But you didn't really *know*. He might not have been telling you the truth when he said it wasn't loaded. You didn't look to see, or anything. It *could* have been loaded. (*Pause*.)

RANDALL. You asking a lot of questions, Rosie, without the answers to match.

ROSIE (*off counter, crosses left to* RANDALL). It's true, isn't it?

RANDALL. Wha's true?

ROSIE. That you didn't really know. Suppose it *had* been? Suppose it *had* been loaded?

RANDALL (*turns to* ROSIE). Well, then, that woulda been another contingency which we woulda—

ROSIE (*thrusting the revolver beneath his eyes*). Suppose it had been *loaded*, Randall! (*Pause.* ROSIE *is terrified at the possibilities, the implications. Her eyes well with tears. She backs up to stool*.) I don't understand.

RANDALL (*turns away*). Well, it's a clock shop, little Rosie, we're all telling a different time. (*Turns to* GLAS.) Isn't that right, Mister Glas?

GLAS. That's right, Randall.

ROSIE (*turns to* GLAS; *puts gun on counter; hysterically*). But, Mister Glas! He didn't *know!* (*Crosses right to ladder.*) He didn't *know* it wasn't loaded. He could've *killed* you! You could be *dead!* Don't you understand!

GLAS (*rises; calmly*). Of course, I understand, Rosie.

ROSIE. Well, *I* don't. I really don't. (*She weeps.*)

GLAS. I knew it wasn't loaded, Rosie.

ROSIE (*grabs ladder*). But, *he* didn't, goddamnit! *He* didn't know! Why won't you listen! He could've been killing you, for all he knew!

GLAS (*crosses to center*). He was, Rosie, he was. Sshh. Don't cry. (*She is unconsolable.*) Randall, tell her you knew it wasn't loaded.

RANDALL (*readily*). I knew it wasn't loaded.

ROSIE (*moves downstage of ladder*). You're lying! You're lying!

GLAS (*turns to* ROSIE). Sshh. It doesn't matter, Rosie, it doesn't matter.

ROSIE. Of course, it matters! Jesus Christ!

GLAS (*crosses upstage left to end of counter*). Not to me, Rosie. Not to Randall.

ROSIE (*screaming*). *It matters to me!*

RANDALL (*stands, crosses to stool center*). Why, Rosie?

ROSIE (*crosses downstage left, sits end of bench*). *I don't know!* (*Pause.*)

GLAS (*picks up gun, goes behind counter and puts it away right*). Won't they be missing you at home, Rosie?

ROSIE. No.

RANDALL (*moves to ladder; folds it; puts it upstage right against back wall*). I should think they'd be missing you at home at this late hour, Rosie. (GLAS *crosses left to chair. Sits facing upstage.*)

ROSIE. I'm supposed to be staying with a friend tonight.

RANDALL (*moves left end of counter; leans on it*). Ah. (ROSIE *is despondent now; her "front" is gone, her responses are dead and flat.*)

ROSIE. I didn't want to go home—after the doctor. So I told them I'd be staying at a friend's. Now I'll have to go through the whole thing all over again, all the arrangements and everything.

RANDALL (*turns to* ROSIE). You're really going to do that thing, then, hah, Rosie?

ROSIE. Of course I'm going to do it. Why not?

RANDALL. Ah. (*Pause.*) Well, it'll be a new experience for you, Rosie, you'll be able to put it in one of those books you're going to write.

ROSIE. That's not very funny.

RANDALL (*his attitude changes suddenly to one of quiet intensity; moves downstage beside* ROSIE). Rosie . . . don't do it, Rosie.

ROSIE. What? (*Pause.*) What do you mean, don't do it? What's it to you, anyway?

RANDALL (*in the dialect*). Ain't nothin' ta me (*Backs away. Grabs stool. Returns it to its place. Sits facing left.*), little chick, nothin' atall.

ROSIE. It's easy for you to say, isn't it. Don't do it. Just like that, don't do it.

RANDALL. We don't have to pursue the matter, Rosie, if you don't care to. (*Pause. She studies him.*)

ROSIE. You're judging *me* now, aren't you. Like *him.* (*She points at* GLAS *who is silent, motionless.*)

RANDALL. Not at all, Rosie.

ROSIE (*rises, holding bag*). You think I *want* to do it?

RANDALL (*turns to* ROSIE). That's a very tricky question, Rosie, I decline to answer. I'm told we do what we most want to do. (*Turns away.*)

ROSIE (*crosses left to* RANDALL). Well, of course, I *want* to. But I don't *really* want to. I have no choice.

RANDALL. Of course.

ROSIE. I *don't!*

RANDALL (*stands, whirls on her*). You *do!* (*Pause.*)

ROSIE (*turns away; quietly*). But not one that I care to take. (GLAS *looks at her.*)

RANDALL (*crosses below* ROSIE *to bench; turns to* GLAS). Ah. Ah, yes. Yes, yes, yes. Did you hear, Mister Glas?

GLAS. Yes.

ROSIE. I have to do it. (*Sits stool. Pause.*) You understand, don't you, Randall? (RANDALL *turns away. She turns to* GLAS.) Mister Glas? (GLAS *turns away.*)

RANDALL (*turns downstage*). What does it matter whether or not we understand, Rosie? (*Pause.*)

ROSIE (*with all the "front" at her command and for what is probably the last time in her life*). That's right! What does it matter! (*Drops bag on floor.*) It happens every day, right? (*Leans back against counter.*) And I have no patience with all the whispered-behind-the-hand hypocrisy about the facts of life, however *sordid* . . . (*Then quietly, quickly.*) they may sometimes be. (ROSIE *turns to counter. Her head on her arm. Pause.*)

RANDALL (*upstage to stool*). You angry with me, Rosie? (*Pause.*)

ROSIE (*sits up, turns downstage*). No, I'm not angry with you. A little frightened of you, maybe.

RANDALL. Why frightened, Rosie?

ROSIE. Because you confuse me. I have to know who people are or else I become confused and I tend to be frightened by things that confuse me. (*Turns to RANDALL.*) I don't think *you* even know who you are, Randall. I don't think you even *think* you know who you are.

RANDALL. Think, Rosie? *Think.* I know not *think.* You know that saying: "I think, therefore I am"? It's a bunch of *bosh,* baby. (*Leans to ROSIE.*) I *feel,* therefore I am: *that's* the truth.

ROSIE. What do you feel, Randall?

RANDALL (*downstage to bench*). Oh, many things.

ROSIE. Easy answer, Randall. What things?

RANDALL. Private things.

ROSIE. Phony.

RANDALL (*turns to ROSIE*). Hm?

ROSIE. You. *"Private things."* Bullshit, Randall. Phony.

RANDALL (*moves upstage; seizing her he pulls her off stool*). Not phony! Not! Not! You want to know what I feel? (GLAS *rises watches them from jukebox.*) You want to *know?* There is a *passion* loose in the world, little chick! A passion for the sounds of violence, for the sight of pain! A passion for death and disaster! We're up to the eyeballs in blood, little chick: you gotta swim in it or drown in it, one or the other. Listen! You hear that? You hear that long, faint, faraway roar out there? You gotta listen good and you'll hear it. (*Releases her, crosses downstage left below chair.*) Listen! Hear it? You know what that is? That's the Yahoos screaming for blood out there! Isn't that right, Mister Glas?

GLAS (*without turning*). That's right, Randall.

RANDALL. It's a butcher shop, little Rosie! (*Upstage to door. Grabs screen. Hanging on door. He turns to ROSIE.*) Where's your cleaver!

ROSIE. I'll never take up a cleaver.

RANDALL. Then you gotta be fast on your feet, little chick! Fast, *fast* on your feet! (*Then, more quietly.*) Unless you want to be like Mister Glas and bury yourself in a hole and wait for someone to come along and execute you with an imaginary bullet in the brain. That's also a way. (*Backs up against door.*) But, ever which way, it all comes to the same thing in the end, Rosie: no hiding place.

ROSIE (*crosses to left end of counter above stool*). From what, Randall?

RANDALL. From what?

GLAS. Tell us, Randall. It's time.

RANDALL (*downstage to steps*). Is it? Is it that time already?

GLAS. You owe it to us, Randall.

RANDALL. Do I. (*Turns to ROSIE. GLAS nods.*) Yes, I suppose I do, all things considered, mm, hm. (*Downstage to beside chair. Pause. He begins to go off into a dreamlike state.*)

GLAS (*backs up to jukebox*). Go on, Randall. (*Pause.*)

RANDALL (*sits chair; ROSIE and GLAS watch him*). Up the stairs, first. One flight, two flights, three flights, four. Through the door. Into the room. Dark. Sit. Wait. Noises in the bedroom, familiar noises in the bedroom. Creak, moan. Creak, moan. Creak, moan. Momma moaning, giving value for money. Wait. Quiet. Dark. Clock, tickticktick, clock, tickticktick. Fire engine. Clock, tickticktick. He comes out of the bedroom, head down, faceless man, buttoning, shoelaces clicking on the linoleum. Out the door. Slam. Quiet. Wait. Bedspring creaks. Match strikes in the bedroom. Exhalation. Don't smoke in bed, momma: everybody says. Randall stands up. Into the bedroom. Mama on the bed, black on white. Screams. Covers up. No words. (GLAS *turns away upstage.* ROSIE *backs up to stool.*) Screams when the knife comes down. Screams when the knife comes down. Screams when the knife comes down. Many times. Knife breaks. Ice pick. Small round holes in the white sheet pumping blood. No screams . . . no screams no more . . . no momma no more, no momma no more. . . . (*Pause.*)

ROSIE (*picks up her bag*). Ohmygod . . . ohmygod . . . Mister Glas, he . . .

GLAS. I heard, Rosie. (*She weeps.*)

RANDALL (*stands, crosses right to bench*). Do you know the Cloisters, Rosie? (*Picks up his jacket.*)

ROSIE (*turns to* RANDALL). They'll catch you, Randall, they'll kill you.

RANDALL (*putting jacket on*). That's a quiet place, the Cloisters, like where them monks used to live long ago. I sure woulda liked to be one a them monks. Maybe next time.

ROSIE. Oh, Randall, Randall, there won't be any next time! They'll kill you for what you've done!

RANDALL (*looks at* ROSIE). Of course, but I mean after that. The next time I come back. I neglected to tell you, Rosie, you see, I believe in the Resurrection and the Life—in the truest sense. Surely, this isn't the only crack we get at it? (*Buttons jacket.*) Surely not. How absurd that would be. (*Crosses upstage to counter between stools.*) So, I figure maybe next time I be a monk . . . and live in a quiet place. . . . (GLAS *crosses right to platform.*)

ROSIE (*desperately; turns to* RANDALL). Maybe they won't catch you, Randall! That's right! How will they know it was you!

RANDALL. Well, a couple of people saw me, you know? Who know me. (*Pulls ice pick from counter—puts it in pocket.*) Also, the knife, that's still there, my fingerprints firmly impressed upon the handle. (ROSIE's *body is convulsed with a shudder.*)

ROSIE (*crosses downstage right above bench; leans against bookcase*). God, God. . . .

RANDALL (*turns to* ROSIE). The one thing worries me a bit is that I might go to Hell. Of course, you must understand, Rosie, my conception of Hell is not that of others, the Eternal Flames and all. (*Turns downstage.*) There are no flames involved, in Hell. What Hell really is is the denial of rebirth. The soul is a ghost, adrift. Adrift and aware of life looking for a new body to inhabit, a new flesh, looking for a way back into the world, into life. And being denied it. That's Hell, little chick. No flames involved. No flames atall.

GLAS. Randall. (GLAS *moves up onto platform.*) Which way I fly is Hell; myself am Hell.

RANDALL. *Very good*, Mister Glas, sir! Who said that?

GLAS (*shrugs, shakes his head, moves behind counter*). Someone.

RANDALL (*picks up hat*). Ah. (*He turns again to* ROSIE.) And heaven, Rosie— (*Moves downstage center.*) Heaven is that first filling of the lungs with that first breath of a new life.

ROSIE (*crosses left sets stool facing left*). Mister Glas! Can't we *do* something?

RANDALL (*crosses left to above chair; grinning*). There you go again, Rosie.

GLAS (*crosses right behind counter to ledger, closes it*). Why don't you see, Rosie . . . he *must* die, in violence, because of what he is and because of what he has done. Just as I must *live,* without violence, because of what I am and what I have done. . . . (*Crosses left to end of counter beside stool.*) Just as you, Rosie . . . just as you will go to your doctor, up that dark street, and afterward . . . write books, maybe . . . about how people should save each other. . . . We choose, Rosie. We choose the dark streets up which we walk. We choose them. (*Turns to* RANDALL.) And if we are guilty of the denial of life . . . who is there to save us from that . . . but ourselves? (*Pause. She looks at* GLAS, *at* RANDALL.)

ROSIE. *God damn it!* (*She turns away, downstage. Drops bag on floor. Bangs fists on bench. Pause.*)

RANDALL (*turns to* ROSIE). A splendid chick, don't you think, Mister Glas?

GLAS. Are you going to make them look for you, Randall?

RANDALL (*puts on hat*). Yeah, I think I'll give 'em a little bit of a run for their money. You know me.

GLAS. Yes.

RANDALL (*takes cape from back of chair; puts it on*). Of course, when they catch up with me, though, that'll have to be the end of the story, I'll have to make sure of that. The other alternatives are—unthinkable.

ROSIE (*turns to* RANDALL). Don't talk like that, Randall!

RANDALL (*picks up umbrella*). So this'll have to be the end of this particular time around. (*Puts on glasses.*)

GLAS. That will be the best way, yes.

RANDALL (*moves up on platform*). So I guess I better get crackin'.

GLAS. Good luck, then, hah, Randall?

(RANDALL *moves to the door, opens it and stands there looking out, his back to* GLAS *and* ROSIE. ROSIE *turns away right.*)

RANDALL. Man! Man! I sure don't like it out there.

GLAS. Randall . . . maybe next time . . . maybe next time, a quiet place. (*Silence.* GLAS *takes up the candle, a remnant of the never-completed inventory. He holds the candle in his hand a moment,* then strikes a match and lights the wick. He drops a bit of melted wax on the countertop and fastens the candle to it. He gazes into the flame. All three are back to back now. A moment, and RANDALL turns in a final look around the room, then bolts through the door and is gone into the darkness. GLAS *and* ROSIE *are motionless.*)

CURTAIN

IN WHITE AMERICA

Martin B. Duberman

For LU and IRV with love

First presented by Judith Rutherford Marechal on October 31, 1963, at the Sheridan Square Playhouse, New York City, with the following cast *:

(In order of appearance)

GLORIA FOSTER	CLAUDETTE NEVINS
JAMES GREENE	MICHAEL O'SULLIVAN
MOSES GUNN	FRED PINKARD

Directed by Harold Stone
Designed by Robin Wagner
Costume Supervision, Patricia Quinn Stuart
Musical Direction, Oscar Brand
Music performed by Billy Faier

Copyright © 1964 by Martin B. Duberman.
Reprinted by permission of the Houghton Mifflin Company.
All rights reserved.

CAUTION: Professionals and amateurs are hereby warned that *In White America* is subject to a royalty. It is fully protected under the copyright laws of the United States of America, the British Empire, including the Dominion of Canada, and all other countries of the Copyright Union. All rights, including professional, amateur, motion pictures, recitation, lecturing, public reading, radio broadcasting, television and the rights of translation into foreign languages are strictly reserved. In its present form the play is dedicated to the reading public only.

For all other rights than those stipulated above, apply to The Sterling Lord Agency, Attention Claire S. Degener, 75 E. 55th Street, New York, N.Y. 10022.

Copying from this book in whole or in part is strictly forbidden by law, and the right of performance is not transferable.

The songs in this script were selected and edited by Oscar Brand. Lyrics copyright © 1963 by O. Brand.

* The actors played so many roles because of the documentary nature of this play, the original playbill did not specify the roles played by the actors.

MARTIN DUBERMAN lives an interesting double life, for he is both a successful playwright and professor of history at Princeton. For recreation he has moonlighted as a drama critic for such publications as the *Partisan Review* and *Show* magazine.

Duberman was born on August 6, 1930, in New York City. He was educated at Yale, where he took his B.A., and received his M.A. and Ph.D. from Harvard, where he started his academic career as a teaching fellow. He moved to Princeton in 1962 and became professor in 1967.

As a historian he has had a most impressive career. In 1962 he published *Charles Francis Adams, 1807–1886,* which won the Bancroft Prize that same year, and four years later his study *James Russell Lowell* was a nominee for the National Book Award. In 1965 he edited *The Anti-Slavery Vanguard: New Essays on the Abolitionists,* and in 1969 he produced a book of essays he called *The Uncompleted Past,* in which he queried certain aspects of history, black power, and university dissent.

In White America was Duberman's first play. It had its first performance at the Sheridan Square Playhouse on October 31, 1963, and ran for over 500 performances, winning the 1963/64 Vernon Rice Award, given by the Drama Desk. He has subsequently had other plays produced. In May, 1968, his sketch, *Metaphors,* a sinisterly shaded account of an entrance interview at Yale, was given as part of *Collision Course,* a dramatic anthology by some of the best young playwrights in America, and in 1969 the playwright's unit of the Actors Studio offered *The Colonial Dudes.* Soon after this a double bill of plays, *The Memory Bank,* was produced Off-Broadway, receiving most thoughtful and respectful notices, although the evening did not settle down for a long run.

The phrase "the theatre of fact" has been coined by a group of German playwrights led by Rolf Hochhuth, who in plays such as *The Deputy* and *Soldiers* has sought to give dramatic form to historical, on occasion controversially historical, facts and suppositions.

Duberman, both historian and playwright, is naturally fascinated by such possibilities. In an essay called "History as Theater" in *The Uncompleted Past,* Duberman makes his position clear enough. First he admits that: "Almost all combinations of history and theater have been made by dramatists, with the result . . . that historical episodes have been used, shaped and embellished for imaginative purposes. The past event becomes the occasion for a statement not in itself strictly historical.

"This is in accord with the writer's usual procedure; he transposes the raw material of experience, he makes it his own and, if he has sufficient insight and artistry, everyone's."

In recent years we have heard many defenses of the theatre of fact, but none I think more commonsensically persuasive than this. The theatre provides fact with the same purple privilege as if it were fiction. Our audiences do not go to the theatre for, primarily, a political discussion, but when that political discussion is draped out with all the exciting trappings of theatricality, then all of us can be moved.

In White America is an avowedly political play. It seeks to demonstrate the black experience to all of us with a white cracker lurking at the edges of our sensibility. Duberman has done a great job. He is a very shrewd editor, and he also happens to be a very fine historian.

Where Duberman differs from the German school of "dramatists of fact," is in his strict allegiance to his documents. In his first preface to *In White America,* he wrote: "I chose to tell this story on the stage, and through historical documents, because I wanted to combine the evocative power of the spoken word with the confirming power of historical fact."

This combination given here has made a truly powerful play, and one of the first attempts to place the black man in his tragic American landscape. There is no real anger here, more the objective recounting of ice-cold facts. Yet cumulatively they make *In White America* into an extraordinary theatrical experience.

AUTHOR'S PREFACE

Plays do not usually require prefaces—unless, like Mr. Shaw, we are not yet certain if the point has been won. The reason for this note is less combative: I would like to explain why I tried to make a "play" out of historical documents.

My starting point was the wish to describe what it has been like to be a Negro in this country (to the extent that a white man can describe it). Neither popular journalism nor professional history has made much effort to tell this story. Both have been dominated by whites, and the whites, whether from guilt, indifference, or hostility, have been slow to reveal the American Negro's past. The revelations are painful, but they must be faced if the present is to be understood, and the future made more tolerable.

Negroes are themselves often unfamiliar with their history. The truth has not been easy to come by in a society dominated by whites, nor easy to digest; old wounds, old degradations, must in the name of self-respect be avoided. Yet if there is much in this history to enrage or sadden the Negro, there is also much to make him proud: here is a people who maintained their humanity while being treated inhumanly, who managed to endure as men while being defined as property.

I chose to tell this story on the stage, and through historical documents, because I wanted to combine the evocative power of the spoken word with the confirming power of historical fact. The spoken word is able to call forth the binding emotions of pity and sympathy. Men would feel, not merely understand the Negro's story. His experience might thereby become our own, past reality might enter into present consciousness. The resulting compassion would be further validated by the documentary format. Americans, admirers of "fact," would have difficulty discounting their concern if based solidly on the "stuff" of history.

It was easier to formulate these goals than to find the materials to meet them. To some extent professional history, which aims at the comprehensive, and professional theatre, which relies on the selective, are at cross-purposes. Yet a "documentary play" on the Negro, to deserve that title, must somehow be both good history and good theatre, must try to be a genuinely representative sample of Negro life and at the same time a vivid and moving one. This best of all possible worlds can only be approximated. How close I have come, I cannot say. I have gone through hundreds of sources and thousands of notes, but diligence and good intentions, however much they may solace the Puritan heart, have never yet guaranteed success. All I am sure of is that the documentary technique in the theatre is worth exploring, and, even more, that the story of being black "in white America" desperately needs telling.

AUTHOR'S NOTE ON THE TEXT AND PRODUCTION OF PLAY

Except for introductory narratives, the material is presented as originally written or spoken. None of the documents, of course, has been used in its entirety, but in editing I have not added or paraphrased except in those very few cases where a word or two was absolutely necessary for clarity or transition.

The production should be mounted in the simplest possible manner, with a minimum of props and "effects." In the original production each scene was staged and acted out rather than simply read from stools or lecterns. But no costumes or elaborate scenery was used. The actors dressed in contemporary street clothes, and the "set" consisted only of a plain, black backdrop, and a series of raised wooden floor boards, so that scenes could be played on various levels. There were also eight chairs in various positions on the stage so that those actors not performing in a given scene could remain seated. An antique table was placed center stage and covered with old books and documents, in order to suggest the historical basis of the readings. Scenes were sometimes begun by an actor taking a book or document from the table, reading a few lines from it, and then easing from that into acting out the scene.

The company should consist of three Negro and three white actors, two men and one woman in each case. The actors alternate the reading of the narratives, rather than one actor reading all of them. In the original production, the musical material was performed by one banjo-guitarist, but future productions might wish to experiment both with musicians and with the choice of songs. The songs herein listed are meant as suggestions only; they are those used in the original production.

ACT ONE

ON STAGE: *three Negro and three white actors, two men and one woman in each case, and a guitarist.*

WHITE MAN *comes forward, picks newspaper off table and reads aloud from it the current date.*

————

WHITE MAN. [January 12, 1964] If God had intended for the races to mix, he would have mixed them himself. He put each color in a different place.

NEGRO MAN. The American white man has a conscience, and the nonviolent method appeals to that conscience.

WHITE WOMAN. Negroes are demanding something that isn't so unreasonable—to get a cup of coffee at a lunch counter, to get a decent job.

NEGRO WOMAN. What they really feels on the inside never changes. Eventually they'll wind up calling you a nigger.

WHITE MAN. Negro impatience can be readily understood, but defiance breeds doubt, and riots breed hatred.

NEGRO MAN. Sure I love my white brother, but I watch him!

NEGRO MAN. To integrate with evil is to be destroyed with evil. We want an area of this land we can call our own.

WHITE WOMAN. My children won't be taking sides—unless we idiots tell them there are sides to take.

NEGRO MAN. After four hundred years of barbaric treatment, the American Negro is fed up with the unmitigated hypocrisy of the white man.

WHITE MAN (*reading again from newspaper*). If they got guts enough to come down here all they'll get is a load of buckshot. The white people have shown remarkable restraint in not killing niggers wholesale.
[January 12, 1964]

NEGRO ACTRESS (*sings*).
Oh, freedom, Oh, freedom,
Oh, freedom, over me!
And before I'll be a slave,
I'll be buried in my grave,
And go home to my Lord
And be free.

NARRATOR. (*Throughout the play the delivery of the narratives is alternated among the actors.*) *The story of the Negro in the United States begins with the slave trade. A ship's doctor aboard a slave vessel in the mid-eighteenth century described his impressions.*

SHIP'S DOCTOR. The slave ships lie a mile below the town, in Bonny River, off the coast of Guinea. Sometimes fifteen sail meet here together. Scarce a day passes without some Negroes being purchased and carried on board . . .

The wretched Negroes are immediately fastened together, two and two, by handcuffs on their wrists and by irons rivetted on their legs. They are then sent down between the decks and placed in a space partitioned off for that purpose. They are frequently stowed so close as to admit of no other position than lying on their sides. Nor will the height between decks allow them to stand.

The diet of the Negroes while on board, consists chiefly of horsebeans boiled to the consistence of a pulp.

Upon the Negroes refusing to take food, I have seen coals of fire, glowing hot, put on a shovel and placed so near their lips as to scorch and burn them. I have also been credibly informed that a certain captain in the slave-trade, poured melted lead on such of his Negroes as obstinately refused their food.

On board some ships the common sailors are allowed to have intercourse with such of the black women whose consent they can procure. The officers are permitted to indulge their passions among them at pleasure.

The hardships suffered by the Negroes during the passage are scarcely to be conceived. The exclusion of fresh air is the most intolerable. Whenever the sea is rough and the rain heavy it becomes necessary to shut every conveyance by which air is admitted. The Negroes' rooms very soon grow intolerably hot. The confined air produces fevers and fluxes which carry off great numbers of them. The floor of their rooms can be so covered with blood and mucus in consequence of the flux, that it resembles a slaughterhouse. Last week by only continuing among them for about a quarter of an hour, I was so overcome with the heat, stench, and foul air that I nearly fainted; and it was only with assistance that I could get on deck . . .

One evening while the ship lay in Bonny River, one of the Negroes forced his way through the network on the larboard side of the vessel, jumped overboard and was devoured by the sharks. Circumstances of this kind are very frequent.

Very few of the Negroes can bear the loss of their liberty and the hardships they endure.

NEGRO ACTRESS (*sings*).
> And before I'll be a slave,
> I'll be buried in my grave,
> And go home to my Lord
> And be free.

QUAKER WOMAN (*reads aloud from parchment*). February 11, 1790. To the Senate and House of Representatives of the United States: The Address of the people called Quakers, in their annual assembly convened.

Firmly believing that unfeigned righteousness in public, as well as private stations, is the only sure ground of hope for the Divine blessing, we apprehend ourselves religiously bound to request your serious christian attention, to the gross national iniquity of trafficking in the persons of fellow-men.

Many are the enormities abhorrent to common humanity, and common honesty, which we judge it not needful to particularise to a body of men, chosen as eminently distinguished for wisdom as extensive information. But we find it indispensably incumbent on us, to attempt to excite your attention to the affecting subject, that a sincere and impartial inquiry may take place, whether it be not in reality within your power to exercise justice and mercy, which, if adhered to, we cannot doubt, must produce the abolition of the slave trade.

FIRST CONGRESSMAN. Mr. President, this petition prays that we should take measures for the abolition of the slave trade. This is desiring an unconstitutional act, because the Constitution secures that trade to the States, independent of Congressional restrictions, for a term of twenty-one years. Therefore, it ought to be rejected as an attempt upon the virtue and patriotism of the House.

SECOND CONGRESSMAN. I think it is incumbent upon every member of this House to sift the subject well, and ascertain what can be done to restrain a practice so nefarious. The Constitution has authorized us to levy a tax upon the importation of such persons. I would willingly go to that extent; and if anything further can be devised to discountenance the trade, consistent with the terms of the Constitution, I shall cheerfully give it my assent and support.

FIRST CONGRESSMAN. I fear that if Congress takes any measures indicative of an intention to interfere with the kind of property alluded to, it would sink in value very considerably, and might be injurious to a great number of citizens, particularly in the Southern States.

SECOND CONGRESSMAN. I think the gentleman carries his apprehensions too far. It appears to me, that if the importation was crushed, the value of a slave would be increased instead of diminished.

FIRST CONGRESSMAN. I differ much in opinion. If through the interference of the General Government the slave trade was abolished, it would evince to the people a disposition towards a total emancipation, and they would hold their property in jeopardy. The petitioners may as well come forward and solicit Congress to interdict the West India trade, because from thence we import rum, which has a debasing influence upon the consumer. But, sir, is the whole morality of the United States confined to the Quakers? Do they understand the rights of mankind, and the disposition of Providence, better than others? If they were to consult that Book, which claims our regard, they will find that slavery is not only allowed but commended. And if they fully examine the subject, they will find that slavery has been no novel doctrine since the days of Cain; but be these things as they may, I hope the House will order the petition to lie on the table, in order to prevent alarm to our Southern brethren.

NARRATOR. *The Quaker petition on the slave trade was tabled. Yet the whole question of the Negro's place in American life continued to disturb a few thoughtful men. Among them was Thomas Jefferson.*

JEFFERSON. The love of justice and the love of country plead equally the cause of these people, and it is a moral reproach to us that they should have pleaded it so long in vain. Yet the hour of emancipation is advancing. Nothing is more certainly written in the book of fate, than that these people are to be free; nor is it less certain that the two races, equally free, cannot live in the same government. Nature, habit, opinion, have drawn indelible lines of distinction between them. (*Coming forward.*)

The blacks are at least as brave, and more adventuresome. But this may perhaps proceed from a want of forethought, which prevents their seeing a danger till it be present. They are more ardent after their female; but love seems with them to be more an eager desire than a tender delicate mixture of sentiment and sensation. Their griefs are transient. Those numberless afflictions, which render it doubtful whether heaven has given life to us in mercy or in wrath, are less felt, and sooner forgotten with them. In general, their existence appears to participate more of sensation than reflection. It appears to me that in memory they are equal to the whites; in reason much inferior, as I think one could scarcely be found capable of tracing and comprehending the investigations of Euclid. It will be right to make great allowances for the difference of condition, of education, of conversation, of the sphere in which they move. Yet we know that among the Romans, the condition of their slaves was much more deplorable than that of the blacks on the continent of America. Notwithstanding, their slaves were often their rarest artists. They excelled too in science . . . But they were of the race of whites.

To justify a general conclusion, requires many observations. I advance it, therefore, as a suspicion only, that the blacks, whether originally a distinct race, or made distinct by time and circumstances, are inferior to the whites in the endowments both of body and mind.

NEGRO ACTOR (*sings*).

My old missus promised me,
Hmm-mm-mm,
When she die, gonna set me free,
Hm-mm-mm.

Missus die nine years ago,
Hmm-mm-mm,
Here ah is in the same old row,
Hm-mm-mm.

NARRATOR. *White men rarely heard the slaves themselves talk about their condition. One of the few exceptions was a conversation recorded by a Northern journalist, Frederick Law Olmsted, with a house servant named William.*

OLMSTED (*to audience*). After leaving a plantation near New Orleans, I was driven about twenty miles in a buggy, by one of the house servants. He was inclined to be talkative and as he expressed great affection and respect for his owner, I felt at liberty to question him on some points upon which I had always previously avoided conversing with slaves. (*Crossing to where the slave,* WILLIAM, *is seated.*) He first said that he came from Virginia . . .

WILLIAM. I reckon there is no brack folks anywhere so well made as those who was born in Virginny. Is you from New Orleans, massa?

OLMSTED. No, I live in the North.

WILLIAM. Da's great many brack folks dah, massa?

OLMSTED. No; very few.

WILLIAM. Da's a great many in Virginny.

OLMSTED. But I came from beyond Virginia—from New York.

WILLIAM. If I was free, I would go to Virginny, and see my old mudder. I don't well know, exactly, how old I is; but I rec'lect, de day I was taken away, my ole mudder she tell me I was tirteen years old. I felt dreadful bad, but now I like it here. De people is almost all French. Is dere any French in New York?

OLMSTED. Yes, but not as many as in Louisiana.

WILLIAM. I s'pose dah is more of French people in Lusiana den dah is anywhar else in all de world—a'nt dah, massa?

OLMSTED. Except in France.

WILLIAM. Wa's dat, sar?

OLMSTED. France is the country where all the Frenchmen came from, in the first place.

WILLIAM. Wa's dat France, massa?

OLMSTED. France is a country across the ocean, the big water, beyond Virginia, where all the Frenchmen first came from; just as the black people all came first from Africa, you know.

WILLIAM. *Is* de brack folks better off to be here, massa?

OLMSTED. I think so.

WILLIAM. *Why is it,* then, massa, when de brack people is free, dey wants to send 'em away out of dis country?

OLMSTED (*taken aback*). Some people think Africa is a better place for you. (*Changing the subject.*) What would you do, if you were free?

WILLIAM. If I was free, massa; *if I was free* . . . I would—Well, sar, de fus thing I would do, if I was free, I would go to work for a year, and get some money for myself,—den-den-den, massa, dis is what I do—I buy me, fus place, a little house, and little lot land, and den-no; den-den-I would go to old Virginny, and see my old mudder. Yes, sar, I would like to do dat fus thing; den, when I com back, de fus thing I'd do, I'd get me a wife; den, I'd take her to my house, and I would live with her dar; and I would raise things in my garden, and take 'em to New Orleans, and sell 'em dar, in the market. Dat's de way I would live, if I was free.

OLMSTED. Well, now, wouldn't you rather live on a plantation with a kindly master like yours than to be free, William?

WILLIAM. Oh! no, sir, I'd rather be free! Oh, yes, sir, I'd like it better to be free; I would dat, master.

OLMSTED. Why would you?

WILLIAM. Why, you see, master, if I was free—if I was *free,* I'd have all my time to myself. I'd rather work for myself. Yes. I'd like dat better.

OLMSTED. But then, you know, you'd have to take care of yourself, and you'd get poor.

WILLIAM. No, sir, I would not get poor, I would get rich; for you see, master, then I'd work all the time for myself.

OLMSTED. You don't suppose there would be much sugar raised, do you?

WILLIAM. Why, yes, master, I do. Why not, sir? What would de brack people do? Wouldn't dey hab to work for dar libben? and de wite people own all de land—war dey goin' to work? Dey hire demself right out again, and work harder dan dey do now to get more wages—a heap harder. I tink so, sir. I would do so, sir.

OLMSTED. The black people talk among themselves about this, do they; and they think so generally?

WILLIAM. Oh! yes, sir; dey talk so; dat's wat dey tink.

OLMSTED. Then they talk about being free a good deal, do they?

WILLIAM. Yes, sir. Dey—(*suddenly on guard*) dat is, dey say dey wish it was so; dat's all dey talk, master—dat's all, sir.

(*The light fades.*)

NARRATOR. *Some of William's fellow slaves were interviewed many years later about their recollections of slavery.*

MAN. I sets and 'members the times in the world. I 'members now clear as yesterday things I forgot for a long time. I 'members 'bout the days of slavery, and I don't 'lieve they ever gwine have slaves no more on this earth. I think God done took that burden offen his black children, and I'm aiming to praise Him for it to His face in the days of glory.

WOMAN. I's hear tell of them good slave days, but I ain't never seen no good times then. One time Aunt Cheyney was just out of bed with a suckling baby and she run away. Old Solomon gits the nigger hounds and takes her trail. They gits near her and she grabs a limb and tries to hist herself in a tree, but them dogs grap her and pull her down. The men hollers them onto her, and the dogs tore her naked and et the breasts plumb off her body. She got well and lived to be a old woman, but 'nother woman has to suck her baby, and she ain't got no sign of breasts no more.

MAN. Sometimes I wishes that I could be back to the old place, 'cause we did have plenty to eat, and at hog-killing time us had more'n a plenty. Old Master kill eight or ten set-down hogs at one time . . . What a set-down hog? It's a hog what done et so much corn he got so fat that he feets can't hold him up, and he just set on he hind quarters and grunts and eats, and eats and grunts, till they knock him in the head.

MAN. Talking 'bout victuals, our eating was good. Can't say the same for all places. Some of the plantations half starved their niggers till they wasn't fitting for work. They had to slip about to other places to piece out their meals.

WOMAN. I recollects once when I was trying to clean the house like Ole Miss tell me, I finds a biscuit, and I's so hungry I et it, 'cause we never see such a thing as a biscuit . . . and she comes in and say, "Where that biscuit?" I say, "Miss, I et it 'cause I's so hungry." Then she grabs that broom and start to beating me over the head with it and calling me lowdown nigger, and I guess I just clean lost my head 'cause I knowed better than to fight her if I knowed anything 't all, but I start to fight her, and the driver, he comes in and he grabs me and starts beating me with that cat-o'-nine-tails, and he beats me till I fall to the floor nearly dead. He cut my back all to pieces, then they rubs salt in the cuts for more punishment. Lord, Lord, honey! Them was awful days.

MAN. The niggers didn't go to the church building; the preacher came and preached to them in their quarters. He'd just say, "Serve your masters. Don't steal your master's turkey. Don't steal your master's chickens. Don't steal your master's hogs. Don't steal your master's meat. Do whatsomever your master tells you to do." Same old thing all the time.

MAN. My white folks didn't mind their niggers praying and singing hymns, but some places wouldn't 'low them to worship a-tall, and they had to put their heads in pots to sing or pray.

WOMAN. Once Massa goes to Baton Rouge and brung back a yaller gal dressed in fine style. She was a seamster nigger. He builds her a house 'way from the quarters. This yaller gal breeds fast and gits a mess of white young-uns. She larnt them fine manners and combs out their hair.

Oncet two of them goes down the hill to the dollhouse, where the Missy's children am playing. They wants to go in the dollhouse and one of the Missy's boys say, "That's for white children." They say, "We ain't no niggers, 'cause we got the same daddy as you has, and he comes to see us near every day." They is fussing, and Missy is listening out her chamber window . . .

When Massa come home his wife hardly say nothing to him, and he asks her what the matter, and she tells him, "Since you asks me, I'm studying in my mind 'bout them white young-uns of that yaller nigger wench from Baton Rouge." He say, "Now, honey, I fotches that gal just for you, 'cause she a fine seamster." She say, "It look kind of funny they got the same kind of hair and eyes as my children, and they got a nose look like yours." He say, "Honey, you just paying 'tention to talk of little children that ain't got no mind to what they say." She say, "Over in Mississippi I got a home and plenty with my daddy, and I got that in my mind."

Well, she didn't never leave, and Massa bought her a fine, new span of surrey hosses. But she don't never have no more children, and she ain't so cordial with the Massa. That yaller gal has more white young-uns, but they don't never go down the hill no more.

MAN. One thing what make it tough on the niggers was them times when a man and he wife and their children had to be taken 'way from one another, sold off or taken 'way to some other state. They was heaps of nigger families that I know what was separated in the time of bondage that tried to find they folkses what was gone. But the mostest of 'em never git together again even after they sot free 'cause they don't know where one or the other is.

MAN. Slavery time was tough, boss. You just don't know how tough it was. I can't 'splain to you just how bad all the niggers want to get they freedom.

NEGRO ACTRESS (*sings*).

Right foot, left foot,
Along the road,
Follow the drinking gourd.

Up to the North,
Drop your load,
Follow the drinking gourd.

NARRATOR. *Slaves constantly tried to flee the plantation and head North to freedom. Efforts by their masters to trace them led, in a few rare cases, to an exchange of letters.*

JOURDAN ANDERSON. To My Old Master, Colonel P. H. Anderson, Big Spring, Tennessee.

Sir: I got your letter, and was glad to find that you had not forgotten Jourdon, and that you wanted me to come back and live with you again. Although you shot at me twice before I left you, I am glad you are still living.

I want to know particularly what the good chance is you propose to give me. I am doing tolerably well here. I get twenty-five dollars a month, with victuals and clothing; have a comfortable home for Mandy,—the folks call her Mrs. Anderson, —and the children—Milly, Jane, and Grundy—go to school and are learning well. The teacher says Grundy has a head for a preacher. They go to Sunday school, and Mandy and me attend church regularly. We are kindly treated.

Mandy says she would be afraid to go back without some proof that you were disposed to treat us justly and kindly; and we have concluded to test your sincerity by asking you to send us our wages for the time we served you. This will make us forget and forgive old scores, and rely on your justice and friendship in the future. I served you faithfully for thirty-two years, and Mandy for twenty years. At twenty-five dollars a month for me, and two dollars a week for Mandy, our earnings would amount to eleven thousand six hundred and eighty dollars. Add to this the interest for the time our wages have been kept back, and deduct what you paid for our clothing, and three doctor's visits to me, and pulling a tooth for Mandy, and the balance will show what we are in justice entitled to. Please send the money by Adam's Express, in care of V. Winters, Esq., Dayton, Ohio.

Say howdy to George Carter, and thank him for taking the pistol from you when you were shooting at me.

From your old servant,
Jourdon Anderson

MRS. SARAH LOGUE. To Jarm: . . . I write you these lines to let you know the situation we are in,—partly in consequence of your running away and stealing Old Rock, our fine mare. Though we got the mare back, she never was worth much after you took her. If you will send me one thousand dollars, and pay for the old mare, I will give up all claim I have to you. In consequence of your running away, we had to sell Abe and Ann and twelve acres of land; and I want you to send me the money, that I may be able to redeem the land. If you do not comply with my request, I will sell you to someone else, and you may rest assured that the time is not far distant when things will be changed with you. A word to the wise is sufficient . . . You know that we reared you as we reared our own children.

Yours, etc.
Mrs. Sarah Logue

JARM. Mrs. Sarah Logue: . . . had you a woman's heart, you never could have sold my only remaining brother and sister, because I put myself beyond your power to convert me into money.

You sold my brother and sister, Abe and Ann, and twelve acres of land . . . Now you ask me to send you $1000 to enable you to redeem the *land,* but not to redeem my poor brother and sister! You say that you shall sell me if I do not send you $1000, and in the same breath you say, "You know we raised you as we did our own children." Woman, did you raise your *own children* for the market? Did you raise them for the whipping post? Did you raise them to be driven off, bound to a coffle in chains? Where are my poor bleeding brothers and sisters? Can you tell? Who was it that sent them off into sugar and cotton fields, to be kicked and cuffed, and whipped, and to groan and die . . . ?

Did you think to terrify me by present-ing the alternative to give my money to you, or give my body to slavery? Then let me say to you, that I meet the proposition with scorn and contempt. I will not budge one hair's breadth. I will not breathe a shorter breath . . . I stand among free people.

NARRATOR. *Some Negroes reacted to slavery not by fleeing, but by rising in rebellion. In 1831, the slave Nat Turner, and his followers, turned on their masters in Southampton County, Virginia.*

NAT TURNER. I was thirty-five years of age the second of October last, and born the property of Benjamin Turner. In my childhood a circumstance occurred which made an indelible impression on my mind . . . Being at play with other children, when three or four years old, I was telling them something, which my mother, over-hearing, said had happened before I was born. I stuck to my story, however, and re-lated some other things which went, in her opinion, to confirm it. Others being called on, were greatly astonished, and caused them to say, in my hearing, I surely would be a prophet . . .

I studiously avoided mixing in society, and wrapped myself in mystery, devoting my time to fasting and prayer. I obtained influence over the minds of my fellow-servants—(not by the means of conjuring and such-like tricks—for to them I always spoke of such things with contempt), but by the communion of the Spirit . . . they believed and said my wisdom came from God.

About this time I had a vision—I saw white spirits and black spirits engaged in battle, and the sun was darkened—the thunder rolled in the heavens, and blood flowed in streams—and I heard a voice saying, "Such is your luck, such you are called to see; and let it come rough or smooth, you must surely hear it." I com-municated the great work laid out for me to do. It was quickly agreed, neither age nor sex was to be spared.

It was my object to carry terror and dev-astation wherever we went. We killed Mrs. Waller and ten children. Then we started for Mr. William Williams . . . Mrs. Wil-liams fled, but she was pursued, overtaken, and after showing her the mangled body of her lifeless husband, she was told to get down and lay by his side, where she was shot dead. The white men pursued and fired on us several times. Five or six of my men were wounded, but none left on the field. . . . Finding myself defeated . . . I gave up all hope for the present . . . I was taken, a fortnight afterwards in a little hole I had dug out with my sword. I am here loaded with chains, and willing to suffer the fate that awaits me.

NEGRO ACTOR (*sings*).

For the old man is a waitin!
For to carry you to freedom
If you follow the drinking gourd.

NARRATOR. *In the North, although the Negroes were free, they were segregated and despised. The Reverend Samuel J. May described their treatment in Canterbury, Connecticut.*

MAY. In the summer or fall of 1832 I heard that Miss Prudence Crandall, an excellent, well-educated Quaker, had been induced by a number of ladies and gentlemen of Canterbury, Connecticut, to establish her boarding and day school there.

For a while the school answered the expectations of its patrons, but early in the following year, trouble arose. Not far from Canterbury there lived a colored man named Harris. He had a daughter, Sarah, a bright girl about seventeen years of age. She had passed, with good repute as a scholar, through the school of the district and was hungering for more education. Sarah applied for admission into this new Canterbury school and Miss Crandall admitted her.

The pupils, I believe, made no objection. But in a few days the parents of some of them called and remonstrated. "They would not have it said that their daughters went to school with a nigger girl." Miss Crandall was assured that, if she did not dismiss Sarah Harris, her white pupils would be withdrawn from her.

She could not comply with such a demand . . . Accordingly, she gave notice that next term her school would be opened for "young ladies and little misses of color." The whole town was in a flame of indignation. Miss Crandall begged me to come to her as soon as my engagements would permit. When I arrived I was informed that a town-meeting was to be held. She requested that I might be heard as her attorney.

The Honorable Andrew T. Judson was undoubtedly the chief of Miss Crandall's persecutors. He was the great man of the town, much talked of by the Democrats as soon to be Governor, and a few years afterwards was appointed Judge of the United States District Court.

JUDSON. Mr. May, we are not merely opposed to the establishment of this school in Canterbury; we mean there shall not be such a school set up anywhere in our State. The colored people never can rise from their menial condition in our country; they ought not to be permitted to rise here. They are an inferior race of beings, and never can or ought to be recognized as the equals of the whites. Africa is the place for them.

MAY. Mr. Judson, there never will be fewer colored people in this country than there are now. Of the vast majority of them this is the native land, as much as it is ours. The only question is, whether we will recognize the rights which God gave them as men.

JUDSON. That nigger school shall never be allowed in Canterbury, nor in any town of this State.

MAY (*to audience*). Undismayed by such opposition, Miss Crandall received early in April fifteen or twenty colored young ladies from Philadelphia, New York, Providence, and Boston. At once all accommodations at the stores in Canterbury were denied her. She and her pupils were insulted whenever they appeared in the streets. The doors and doorsteps of her house were besmeared; her well was filled with filth. Finally the house was assaulted by a number of persons with heavy clubs and iron bars; five window-sashes were demolished and ninety panes of glass dashed to pieces.

For the first time Miss Crandall seemed to quail, and her pupils had become afraid to remain another night under her roof. The front rooms of the houses were hardly tenantable; and it seemed foolish to repair them only to be destroyed again. After due consideration, therefore, it was determined that the school should be abandoned. The pupils were called together, and I was requested to announce to them our decision. Twenty harmless, well-behaved girls, whose only offence was that they had come together there to obtain useful knowledge, were to be told that they had better go away. The words almost blistered my lips. I felt ashamed of Canterbury, ashamed of

Connecticut, ashamed of my country, ashamed of my color.

NARRATOR. *Many Northern Negroes were active in the antislavery struggle, and some took part in other reform movements as well. One of the most famous was the illiterate ex-slave Sojourner Truth, who in 1851 unexpectedly rose at a Woman's Rights Convention.*

SOJOURNER TRUTH. Wall, chilern, whar dar is so much racket dar must be somethin' out o' kilter. I tink dat 'twixt de black folks of de Souf and de womin at de Norf, all talkin' 'bout rights, de white men will be in a fix pretty soon. But what's all dis here talkin' 'bout?

Dat man ober dar say dat womin needs to be helped into carriages, and lifted ober ditches, and to hab de best place everywhar. Nobody eber helps me into carriages, or ober mud-puddles, or gibs me any best place! And a'n't I a woman? Look at me! Look at my arm! I have ploughed, and planted, and gathered into barns and no man could head me! And a'n't I a woman? I have borne thirteen children, and seen 'em mos' sold off to slavery, and when I cried out with my mother's grief, none but Jesus heard me! And a'n't I a woman?

Den dey talks 'bout dis ting in de head; what dis dey call it? (*A voice whispering:*) Intellect.

Dat's it, honey. What's dat got to do wid womin's rights? If my cup won't hold but a pint, and yourn holds a quart, wouldn't ye be mean not to let me have my little half-measure full?

Den dat little man in black dar, he say women can't have as much rights as men, 'cause Christ wan't a woman! Whar did your Christ come from? Whar did your Christ come from? From God and a woman! Man had nothin' to do wid Him!

If de fust woman God ever made was strong enough to turn de world upside down all alone, dese women togedder ought to be able to turn it back, and get it right side up again! And now dey is asking to do it, de men better let 'em.

CAST (*sings*).
God's gonna set this world on fire,
God's gonna set this world on fire
One of these days, halleluja!
God's gonna set this world on fire,
Gonna set this world on fire one of
    these days.

NARRATOR. *In 1859, John Brown, who has alternately been called a saint and a madman, made an unsuccessful attempt at Harpers Ferry, Virginia, to free the slaves. Brought to trial and sentenced to death, John Brown addressed the court.*

JOHN BROWN. I have, may it please the Court, a few words to say.

In the first place, I deny everything but what I have all along admitted,—the design on my part to free the slaves. I never did intend murder, or treason. Had I interfered in behalf of the rich, the powerful, the intelligent, the so-called great, it would have been all right; and every man in this court would have deemed it an act worthy of reward rather than punishment.

This court acknowledges, as I suppose, the validity of the law of God. I see a book kissed here which I suppose to be the Bible. That teaches me that all things whatsoever I would that men should do to me, I should do even so to them. It teaches me, further, to "remember them that are in bonds, as bound with them." I endeavored to act up to that instruction. I say, I am yet too young to understand that God is any respecter of persons. I believe that to have interfered as I have done —as I have always freely admitted I have done—in behalf of His despised poor, was not wrong, but right. Now, if it is deemed necessary that I should forfeit my life for the furtherance of the ends of justice, and mingle my blood further with the blood of millions in this slave country—I submit; so let it be done!

NARRATOR. *Just before John Brown was led from his cell to the gallows, he handed a guard this last message.*

JOHN BROWN. "I, John Brown, am now quite *certain* that the crimes of this *guilty land* will never be purged away but with *blood.* I had, as I now think vainly, flattered myself that without very much bloodshed it might be done."

(*Guitar chords of "John Brown's Body"*)

NARRATOR. *Civil war broke out in April 1861. Mary Boykin Chesnut, wife of the Senator from South Carolina, described in her diary the onset of war. April 8, 1861 . . .*

MRS. CHESNUT. Talbot and Chew have come to say that hostilities are to begin. The men went off almost immediately, and I crept silently to my room where I sat down to a good cry . . . Mrs. Wigfall came in and we had it out, on the subject of civil war. We solaced ourselves with dwelling on all its known horrors, and then we added some remarks about what we had a right to expect with Yankees in front and Negroes in the rear. "The slave owners must expect a servile insurrection, of course," said Mrs. Wigfall.

NARRATOR. *April 13, 1861 . . .*

MRS. CHESNUT. Fort Sumter has been on fire . . . Not by one word or look can we detect any change in the demeanor of these Negro servants. Lawrence sits at our door, as sleepy and as respectful and as profoundly indifferent. So are they all. They carry it too far. You could not tell they even hear the awful noise that is going on in the bay, though it is dinning in their ears night and day. And people talk before them as if they were chairs and tables, and they make no sign. Are they stolidly stupid, or wiser than we are, silent and strong, biding their time.

NARRATOR. *August 1863, Portland, Alabama . . .*

MRS. CHESNUT. Dick, the butler here, reminds me that when we were children, I taught him to read as soon as I could read myself . . . but he won't look at me now. He looks over my head, he scents freedom in the air. He always was very ambitious.

He is the first Negro that I have felt a change in. They go about in their black masks, not a ripple or an emotion showing; and yet on all other subjects except the War they are the most excitable of all races. Now Dick might make a very respectable Egyptian Sphynx, so inscrutably silent is he.

(*Guitar effect of drum rolls*)

NARRATOR. *The first regiment of ex-slaves was mustered into the service of the Union Army in 1862. It was under the command of a white officer from Boston, Colonel Thomas Wentworth Higginson.*

HIGGINSON. November 24, 1862 . . . Reporting to General Saxton, I had the luck to encounter a company of my destined command, marched in to be mustered into the United States service. The first to whom I spoke had been wounded in a small expedition after lumber, in which he had been under fire.

NEGRO SOLDIER *steps forward and stands at attention.*)

(*To* NEGRO SOLDIER.) Did you think that more than you bargained for, my man?

NEGRO SOLDIER. I been a-tinking, Mas'r, *dat's jess what I went for.*

HIGGINSON (*to audience*). I thought this did well enough for my very first interchange of dialogue with my recruits. (*Consulting his diary.*) December 5, 1862. This evening, after working themselves up to the highest pitch, a party suddenly rushed off, got a barrel, and mounted some man upon it, who brought out one of the few really impressive appeals for the American flag that I have ever heard . . .

(*The lights dim on* HIGGINSON *and come up on another* NEGRO SOLDIER.)

NEGRO SOLDIER. Our mas'rs dey hab lib under de flag, dey got dere wealth under it, and ebryting beautiful for dere chilen. Under it dey hab grind us up, and put us in dere pocket for money. But de fus' minute dey tink dat ole flag mean freedom for we colored people, dey pull it right down, and run up de rag ob dere own. But we'll nebber desert de ole flag, boys, neber; we hab lib under it for *eighteen hundred sixty-two years,* and we'll die for it now.

(*Lights fade on the* SOLDIER *and come up on* HIGGINSON.)

HIGGINSON. Their religious spirit grows more beautiful to me in living longer with them. Imbued from childhood with the habit of submission, they can endure everything. Their religion also gives them zeal, energy, daring. They could easily be made fanatics, if I chose; but I do not choose. Their whole mood is essentially Mohammedan, perhaps, in its strength and its weakness. The white camps seem rough and secular, after this; and I hear our men talk about "a religious army," "a Gospel army," in their prayer-meetings. They are certainly evangelizing the chaplain, who was rather a heretic at the beginning . . .

1ST NEGRO SOLDIER (*praying*). Let me lib dat when I die I shall *hab manners,* dat I shall know what to say when I see my Heabenly Lord.

2ND NEGRO SOLDIER (*praying*). Let me lib wid de musket in one hand an' de Bible in de oder,—dat if I die at de muzzle ob de musket, I may know I hab de blessed Jesus in my hand, an' hab no fear.

3RD NEGRO SOLDIER (*praying*). I hab lef' my wife in de land o' bondage; my little ones dey say eb'ry night, Whar is my fader? But when I die, when I shall stan' in de glory, den, O Lord, I shall see my wife an' my little chil'en once more.

HIGGINSON. Expedition up the St. Mary's River: This morning, my surgeon sent me his report of killed and wounded: "One man killed instantly by a ball through the heart, and seven wounded, one of whom will die. Robert Sutton, with three wounds, —one of which, being on the skull, may cost him his life—would not report himself till compelled to do so by his officers."

(*He puts away the surgeon's report.*)

And one of those who were carried to the vessel—a man wounded through the lungs—asked only if I were safe, the contrary having been reported. An officer may be pardoned some enthusiasm for such men as these . . .

(*He turns to another page in the diary.*)

January 1, 1863. Today we celebrated the issuance of President's Lincoln's Proclamation of Emancipation. It was read by Dr. W. H. Brisbane. Then the colors were presented to us by the Reverend Mr. French. All this was according to the programme. Then, the very moment the speaker had ceased, and just as I took and waved the flag . . .

NEGRO SINGERS (*breaking in*).
> My Country, 'tis of thee,
> Sweet land of liberty,
>   Of thee I sing!

(*The singing continues quietly under the rest of the speech.*)

HIGGINSON. Firmly the quavering voices sang on, verse after verse; others of the colored people joined in; some whites on the platform began, but I motioned them to silence. I never saw anything so electric; it made all other words cheap; it seemed the choked voice of a race at last unloosed. Just think of it!—the first day they had ever had a country, the first flag they had ever seen which promised anything to their people! When they stopped, there was nothing to do for it but to speak, and I went on; but the life of the whole day was in those unknown people's song.

(*The singing swells.*)

SINGERS.
> . . . From every mountainside
> Let freedom ring!

ACT TWO

NEGRO ACTOR.
> No more auction block for me,
> No more, no more,
> No more auction block for me,
> Many thousand gone.
>
> No more pint of salt for me,
> No more, no more,
> No more pint of salt for me,
> Many thousand gone.

NEGRO MAN. We was free. Just like that, we was free. Right off colored folks started on the move. They seemed to want to get closer to freedom, so they'd know what it was—like it was a place or a city . . .

NEGRO WOMAN. A heap of people say they going to name theirselves over. They name theirselves big names. Some of the names was Abraham, and some called theirselves Lincum. Any big name 'cepting their master's name.

NEGRO MAN. The slaves don't know where to go. They's always 'pend on Old Marse to look after them. Three families went to get farms for theyselves, but the rest stay on for hands on the old place.

NEGRO WOMAN. I remember someone asking—"You got to say 'Master'?" And somebody answered and said, "Naw." But they said it all the same. They said it for a long time.

NEGRO MAN. They makes us git right off the place, just like you take a old hoss and turn it loose. That how us was. No money, no nothing.

NEGRO MAN. What I likes best, to be slave or free? Well, it's this way. In slavery I owns nothing and never owns nothing. In freedom I's own the home and raise the family. All that cause me worriment, and in slavery I has no worriment, but I takes the freedom.

NARRATOR. *The whites reacted to the Negroes' freedom in a variety of ways. A Northern woman, Elizabeth Bothume, went South to teach the ex-slaves.*

ELIZABETH BOTHUME. On October 25, 1864, I received the following communication:—"You are hereby appointed by the New England Freedman's Aid Society a teacher of freed people at Beaufort, South Carolina." I found my location was to be at Old Fort Plantation. A large number of colored refugees had been brought here and I was impatient to begin. Each hour showed me that at the North we had but a faint conception of the work to be done.

While the zeal of these people for learning never flags, they have no possible conception of time. Men, women, and children hurry to the schoolhouse at all hours and at most unseasonable times, expecting "to catch a lesson." Reproof is unheeded, or not understood; "Us had something *particular* to do," is the invariable excuse.

I must confess, the ignorance of some of the visitors in regard to the condition of the freedman is positively astounding. Some officers belonging to the "Tenth Army Corps" of Sherman's army visited the school. I was expecting them, and had examined the children a little upon general subjects. Imagine my surprise, when they had sung and answered a few general questions, to have one of the visitors get up and ask, "Children, who is Jesus Christ?" For a moment the whole school seemed paralyzed. Then an older boy sprang up, and exclaimed, "Him's Massa Linkum" . . .

Then General Howard made a short address, in which he gave them a motto, "To try hard." This all could understand. So when he asked what he should tell their friends at the North about them, they all answered, "Tell 'em we'se goin' to try hard."

At another school General Howard asked this question, and a little boy answered, "Massa, tell 'em we is rising."

NARRATOR. *The Negroes' freedom disrupted the pattern of Southern life, as a Georgia woman, Eliza Andrews, noted in her diary.*

ELIZA ANDREWS. Washington, Georgia. No power on earth can raise an inferior, savage race above their civilized masters and keep them there. No matter how high a prop they build under him, the Negro is obliged, sooner or later, to find his level. The higher above his natural capacity they force the Negro in their rash experiments, the greater must be his fall in the end, and the more bitter our sufferings in the meantime.

The town is becoming more crowded with "freedmen" every day, and their insolence increases with their numbers. We have not even an errand boy now, for George, the only child left on the place, is going to school! . . . Everybody is doing housework. Father says that this is what

has made the Anglo-Saxon race great; they are not afraid of work. But it does seem to me a waste of time for people who are capable of doing something better to spend their time sweeping and dusting while scores of lazy Negroes that are fit for nothing else are lying around idle. Dr. Calhoun suggested that it would be a good idea to import some of those apes from Africa and teach them to take the place of the Negroes, but Henry said that just as soon as we had got them tamed, and taught them to be of some use, those crazy fanatics at the North would insist on coming down here to emancipate them and give them universal suffrage. A good many people seem to think that the Yankees are never going to be satisfied till they get the Negroes to voting. Father says it is the worst thing we have to fear now.

(Guitar chords of "Dixie")

NARRATOR. *By 1866, the voting question was paramount. On February 7, Frederick Douglass, the chief spokesman for his race, and George T. Downing, another prominent Negro leader, brought the issue to Andrew Johnson, President of the United States.*

GEORGE T. DOWNING. We present ourselves to Your Excellency in the name of the colored people of the United States. We are Americans, native-born Americans. We are citizens. On this fact, and with confidence in the triumph of justice, we cherish the hope that we may be fully enfranchised.

PRESIDENT JOHNSON. I do not like to be arraigned by some who can get up handsomely rounded periods and deal in rhetoric. While I say I am a friend of the colored man, I do not want to adopt a policy that I believe will end in a contest between the races, in the extermination of one or the other. God forbid that I should be engaged in such a work!

FREDERICK DOUGLASS. Mr. President, do you wish—

PRESIDENT JOHNSON. I am not quite through yet . . . The query comes up, whether these two races without time for passion and excitement to be appeased, and without time for the slightest improvement, are to be thrown together at the ballot box.

Will you say a majority of the people shall receive a state of things they are opposed to?

DOUGLASS. That was said before the war.

JOHNSON. I am now talking about a principle; not what somebody else said.

DOWNING. Apply what you have said, Mr. President, to South Carolina, where a majority of the inhabitants are colored.

JOHNSON. That doesn't change the principle at all. It is for the people to say who shall vote, and not for the Congress of the United States. It is a fundamental tenet in my creed that the will of the people must be obeyed. Is there anything wrong or unfair in that?

DOUGLASS (*smiling*). A great deal that is wrong, Mr. President, with all respect.

JOHNSON. It is the people of the States that must for themselves determine this thing.

God knows that anything I can do to elevate the races I will do, and to be able to do so is the sincere desire of my heart. (*Abruptly.*) I am glad to have met you, and thank you for the compliments you have paid me.

DOUGLASS. I have to return to you our thanks, Mr. President, for so kindly granting us this interview. We did not come here expecting to argue this question with Your Excellency . . . if you would grant us permission, of course we would endeavor to controvert some of the positions you have assumed.

JOHNSON. I thought you expected me to indicate what my views were on the subjects touched upon by your statement.

DOWNING. We are very happy, indeed, to have heard them.

DOUGLASS. If the President will allow me, I would like to say one or two words in reply. You enfranchise your enemies and disfranchise your friends.

JOHNSON. All I have done is to indicate what my views are, as I supposed you expected me to, from your address.

DOUGLASS. But if Your Excellency will be pleased to hear, I would like to say a word or two in regard to enfranchisement of the blacks as a means of *preventing* a conflict of races.

JOHNSON. I repeat, I merely wanted to indicate my views, and not to enter into any general controversy.

Your statement was a very frank one, and I thought it was due to you to meet it in the same spirit.

DOUGLASS. Thank you, sir.

JOHNSON. If you will all inculcate the idea that the colored people can live and advance to better advantage elsewhere than in the South, it would be better for them.

DOUGLASS. But we cannot get away from the plantation.

JOHNSON. What prevents you?

DOUGLASS. The Negro is divested of all power. He is absolutely in the hands of those men.

JOHNSON. If the master now controls him or his action, would he not control him in his vote?

DOUGLASS. Let the Negro once understand that he has an organic right to vote, and he will raise up a party in the Southern States among the poor, who will rally with him.

JOHNSON. I suggest emigration. If he cannot get employment in the South, he has it in his power to go where he can get it.

DOUGLASS (*to his fellow delegates*). The President sends us to the people, and we go to the people.

JOHNSON. Yes, sir; I have great faith in the people. I believe they will do what is right.

(*Music—guitarist*)

> I am a good old Rebel,
> And that's just what I am.
> And for this land of liberty,
> I do not give a damn.
> I'm glad I fought against it—
> I only wish we'd won,
> And I ain't askin pardon,
> For what I been or done.

(*As the lights fade on the scene, they come up on the figure of a man wearing the hood of the Ku Klux Klan.*)

NARRATOR. *In 1866, the Radical wing of the Republican party gained control of Congress and gave the Negro the right to vote. At once, the Ku Klux Klan rose to power in the South . . .*

THE HOODED FIGURE. *Before the immaculate Judge of Heaven and Earth, and upon the Holy Evangelists of Almighty God, I do, of my own free will and accord, subscribe to the sacredly binding obligation: We are on the side of justice, humanity, and constitutional liberty, as bequeathed to us in its purity by our forefathers. We oppose and reject the principles of the Radical party.*

(*Music—guitarist*)

> I hate the Freedmen's Bureau

And the uniform of blue,
I hate the Declaration of Independ-
ence, too.
I hate the Constitution
With all its fume and fuss,
And them thievin', lyin' Yankees,
Well, I hate 'em wuss and wuss.

NARRATOR. *Acts of violence by the Klan were investigated by the Federal government in a series of hearings and trials.*

PROSECUTOR. What was the purpose of the Ku Klux Klan? What were the raids for?

KLANSMAN. To put down Radicalism, the raids were for.

PROSECUTOR. In what way were they to put down Radicalism?

KLANSMAN. It was to whip them and make them change their politics.

PROSECUTOR. How many raids have you been on by order of the Chief?

KLANSMAN. Two, sir.

PROSECUTOR. Now, will you state to the jury what was done on those raids?

KLANSMAN. Yes, sir. We were ordered to meet at Howl's Ferry, and went and whipped five colored men. Presley Holmes was the first they whipped, and then went on and whipped Jerry Thompson; went then and whipped Charley Good, James Leach, and Amos Lowell.

PROSECUTOR. How many men were on these raids?

KLANSMAN. I think there was twenty in number.

PROSECUTOR. How were they armed and uniformed?

KLANSMAN. They had red gowns, and had white covers over their horses. Some had pistols and some had guns.

PROSECUTOR. What did they wear on their heads?

KLANSMAN. Something over their heads came down. Some of them had horns on.

PROSECUTOR. Disguises dropped down over their faces?

KLANSMAN. Yes, sir.

PROSECUTOR. What was the object in whipping those five men you have named?

KLANSMAN. The object, in whipping Presley Holmes, was about some threats he had made about him going to be buried in Salem graveyard.

PROSECUTOR. What was the first to occur?

KLANSMAN. Well, sir, Webber—he was leading the Klan—ran into the yard and kicked down the door, and dragged him out, and led him off about two hundred yards, and whipped him.

PROSECUTOR. How many lashes did they give him?

KLANSMAN. I cannot tell you how many.

PROSECUTOR. Did they whip him severely or not?

KLANSMAN. His shirt was stuck to his back.

PROSECUTOR. What occurred at the next place?

KLANSMAN. They whipped Jerry Thompson at the next place; told him never to go to any more meetings; to stay at home and attend to his own business.

PROSECUTOR. What was done at the next place?

KLANSMAN. They went there and whipped Charley Good. They whipped him very severe; they beat him with a pole and kicked him down on the ground.

PROSECUTOR. What did they tell him?

KLANSMAN. To let Radicalism alone; if he didn't his doom would be fatal.

(*The lights fade. They come up immediately on another examination. A Negro woman,* HANNAH TUTSON, *is being questioned.*)

LAWYER. Are you the wife of Samuel Tutson?

MRS. TUTSON. Yes, sir.

LAWYER. Were you at home when he was whipped last spring?

MRS. TUTSON. Yes, sir; I was at home.

LAWYER. Tell us what took place then, what was done, and how it was done.

MRS. TUTSON. That night, just as I got into bed, five men bulged right against the door, and it fell in the middle of the floor. George McRae ran right to me. As I saw him coming I took up the child—the baby —and held to him. I started to scream, and George McRae catched me by the throat and choked me. And he catched the little child by the foot and slinged it out of my arms. They got me out of doors. The old man was ahead of me, and I saw Dave Donley stamp on him. They carried me to a pine, and then they tied my hands there. They pulled off all my linen, tore it up so that I did not have a piece of rag on me as big as my hand. I said, "Men, what are you going to do with me?" They said, "God damn you, we will show you; you are living on another man's premises." I said, "No; I am living on my own premises; I gave $150 for it and Captain Buddington

and Mr. Mundy told me to stay here."
They whipped me for a while. Then
George McRae would say, "Come here,
True-Klux." Then the True-Klux would
step off about as far as (*pointing to a
member of the committee*) that gentleman
and whisper; when they came back they
would whip me again. Every time they
would go off, George McRae would make
me squat down by the pine, and he would
get his knees between my legs and say,
"Old lady, if you don't let me have to do
with you, I will kill you." I said, "No";
they whipped me. There were four men
whipping me at once.

LAWYER. How many lashes did they give
you in all?

MRS. TUTSON. I cannot tell you, for they
whipped me from the crown of my head to
the soles of my feet. I was just raw. After
I got away from them that night I ran
to my house. My house was torn down.
I went in and felt where my bed was. I
could not feel my little children and I
could not see them.

LAWYER. Did you find your children?

MRS. TUTSON. I did next day at twelve
o'clock.

LAWYER. Where were they?

MRS. TUTSON. They went out into the
field.

LAWYER. Did the baby get hurt—the one
you had in your arms when they jerked it
away?

MRS. TUTSON. Yes, sir; in one of its hips.
When it began to walk one of its hips was
very bad, and every time you would stand
it up it would scream. But I rubbed it and
rubbed it, and it looks like he is outgrow-
ing it now.

(*Music—guitarist*)

You've got to cross that lonesome
valley,
You've got to cross it by yourself.
There ain't nobody can do it for you,
You've got to cross it all alone.

NARRATOR. *The Federal investigations
were not followed by effective Federal action. From 1878 to 1915 over three thousand Negroes were lynched in the South—
a necessary protection, it was said, against
Negro rapists. Yet most lynchings were
either for no offense or for such causes as
"Insult," "Bad Reputation," "Running
Quarantine," "Frightening Children by
Shooting at Rabbits," or "Mistaken Identity."*

*On January 21, 1907, United States
Senator Ben Tillman, of South Carolina,
gave his views on the subject from the
Senate floor.*

SENATOR TILLMAN. Mr. President, a word
about lynching and my attitude toward it.
A great deal has been said in the newspapers, North and South, about my responsibility in connection with this matter.

I have justified it for one crime, and one
only. As governor of South Carolina I
proclaimed that, although I had taken the
oath of office to support law and enforce
it, I would lead a mob to lynch any man
who had ravished a woman.

Mr. President . . . When stern and sad-
faced white men put to death a creature in
human form who has deflowered a white
woman, they have avenged the greatest
wrong, the blackest crime in all the category of crimes.

The Senator from Wisconsin prates
about the law. Look at our environment
in the South, surrounded, and in a very
large number of counties outnumbered, by
the Negroes—engulfed, as it were, in a
black flood of semi-barbarians. For forty
years these Negroes have been taught the
damnable heresy of equality with the white
man. Their minds are those of children,
while they have the passions and strength
of men.

Let us carry the Senator from Wisconsin
to the backwoods in South Carolina, put
him on a farm miles from a town or railroad, and environed with Negroes. We
will suppose he has a fair young daughter
just budding into womenhood; and recol-
lect this, the white women of the South
are in a state of siege . . .

That Senator's daughter undertakes to
visit a neighbor or is left home alone for a
brief while. Some lurking demon who has
watched for the opportunity seizes her; she
is choked or beaten into insensibility and
ravished, her body prostituted, her purity
destroyed, her chastity taken from her, and
a memory branded on her brain as with a
red-hot iron to haunt her night and day as
long as she lives.

In other words, a death in life. This
young girl thus blighted and brutalized
drags herself to her father and tells him
what has happened. Is there a man here
with red blood in his veins who doubts
what impulses the father would feel? Is it
any wonder that the whole countryside

rises as one man and with set, stern faces, seek the brute who has wrought this infamy? And shall such a creature, because he has the semblance of a man, appeal to the law? Shall men coldbloodedly stand up and demand for him the right to have a fair trial and be punished in the regular course of justice? So far as I am concerned he has put himself outside the pale of the law, human and divine. He has sinned against the Holy Ghost. He has invaded the holy of holies. He has struck civilization a blow, the most deadly and cruel that the imagination can conceive. It is idle to reason about it; it is idle to preach about it. Our brains reel under the staggering blow and hot blood surges to the heart. Civilization peels off us, any and all of us who are men, and we revert to the original savage type whose impulse under such circumstances has always been to "kill! kill! kill!"

NARRATOR. *The Negro's intimidation was reflected in the views of Mr. Booker T. Washington, the most prominent Negro at the turn of the century, when he addressed a predominantly white audience at Atlanta.*

WASHINGTON. The Negroes' greatest danger is, that in the great leap from slavery to freedom we may overlook the fact that the masses of us are to live by the production of our hands. It is at the bottom of life we must begin, and not the top. You can be sure in the future, as you have been in the past, that you and your families will be surrounded by the most patient, faithful, law-abiding, and unresentful people that the world has seen.

In all things that are purely social we can be as separate as the fingers, yet one as the hand in all things essential to mutual progress.

The wisest among my race understand that the agitation of questions of social equality is the extremest folly. It is important and right that all privileges of the law be ours, but it is vastly more important that we be prepared for the exercise of those privileges. The opportunity to earn a dollar in a factory just now is worth infinitely more than the opportunity to spend a dollar in an opera house.

NARRATOR. *W. E. B. Du Bois, later one of the founders of the N.A.A.C.P., was not satisfied with Mr. Washington's leadership.*

DU BOIS. One hesitates to criticise a life which, beginning with so little, has done

so much. And yet the time is come when one may speak in all sincerity and utter courtesy of the mistakes and shortcomings of Mr. Booker T. Washington. Mr. Washington represents in Negro thought the old attitude of adjustment and submission. He practically accepts the alleged inferiority of the Negro races and withdraws many of the high demands of Negroes as men and American citizens. Mr. Washington asks that black people concentrate all their energies on industrial education, the accumulation of wealth and the conciliation of the South.

We do not expect that the free right to vote, to enjoy civic rights, and to be educated, will come in a moment; we do not expect to see the bias and prejudices of years disappear at the blast of a trumpet; but we are absolutely certain that the way for a people to gain their reasonable rights is not by voluntarily throwing them away and insisting that they do not want them; that the way for a people to gain respect is not by continually belittling and ridiculing themselves: that, on the contrary, Negroes must insist, in season and out of season, that voting is necessary to modern manhood, that color discrimination is barbarism, and that black boys need education as well as white boys.

NARRATOR. *The segregation of Federal employees became widespread for the first time during Woodrow Wilson's administration. To protest this policy, a delegation of Negro leaders, led by Monroe Trotter, called upon President Wilson in November 1914.*

MONROE TROTTER. Mr. President, one year ago we came before you and presented a national petition, signed by colored Americans in thirty-eight states, protesting against the segregation of employees of the National Government as instituted under your administration. We come to you, Mr. President, a year after to renew the protest and appeal.

PRESIDENT WILSON. After our last visit, I and my cabinet officers investigated as promised, and my cabinet officers told me the segregation was caused by friction between colored and white clerks, and not done to injure or humiliate the colored clerks, but to avoid friction. Members of the cabinet have assured me that the colored clerks would have comfortable conditions, though separated. The white people of the country, as well as I, wish to see the colored people progress, admire the progress they have already made, and want to see them continue along independent lines. There is, however, a great prejudice against colored people, and we must deal with it as practical men. Segregation is not humiliating but a benefit, and ought to be so regarded by you gentlemen. If your organization goes out and tells the colored people of the country that it is a humiliation, they will so regard it.

TROTTER (angrily). Mr. President, it is not in accord with known facts to claim that segregation was started because of race friction of the white and colored clerks, for the simple reason that for fifty years white and colored clerks have been working together in peace and harmony and friendliness, doing so even through two Democratic administrations. Soon after your inauguration began segregation was drastically introduced.

WILSON. If this organization is ever to have another hearing before me it must have another spokesman. Your manner offends me.

TROTTER. In what way?

WILSON. Your tone, with its background of passion.

TROTTER. But I have no passion in me, Mr. President, you are entirely mistaken; you misinterpret my earnestness for passion. We cannot control the minds of the colored people and would not if we could on the segregation question. Two years ago you were regarded as a second Abraham Lincoln.

WILSON. I want no personal reference.

TROTTER. Sir, if you will allow me to continue you will see my intent.

WILSON. I am the one to do the interrupting, Mr. Trotter.

TROTTER. We colored leaders are denounced in the colored churches as traitors to our race.

WILSON. What do you mean by traitors?

TROTTER. Because we supported the Democratic ticket in 1912.

WILSON. Gentlemen, the interview is at an end.

NARRATOR. *During World War I the French, at the request of the American authorities, issued a directive concerning Negro American Troops.*

FRENCH OFFICER. To the French Military Mission stationed with the American Army. August 7, 1918. Secret information concerning the Black American Troops.

It is important for French officers who have been called upon to exercise command over black American troops, or to live in close contact with them, to recognize that American opinion is unanimous on the "color question," and does not admit of any discussion.

The French public has become accustomed to treating the Negro with familiarity and indulgence.

These are matters of grievous concern to the Americans. They consider them an affront to their national policy. It is of the utmost importance that every effort be made to avoid profoundly estranging American opinion.

We must not eat with the blacks, must not shake hands or seek to talk or meet with them outside of the requirements of military service. Americans become greatly incensed at any public expression of intimacy between white women with black men.

Military authority cannot intervene directly in this question, but it can through the civil authorities exercise some influence on the population.

[Signed] Linard

(*Guitar—"Mademoiselle from Armentières"*)

NARRATOR. *After World War I, Negro resentment became more vocal. Marcus Garvey's movement of Black Nationalism, a forerunner of today's Black Muslims, attracted hundreds of thousands of followers.*

MARCUS GARVEY. We are too large and great in numbers not to be a great people, a great race, and a great nation. We are the descendants of a suffering people. We are the descendants of a people determined to suffer no longer. The time has now come when we must seek our place in the sun. If Europe is for the Europeans, then Africa shall be for the black peoples of the world. We are not asking all the Negroes of the United States to leave for Africa. The majority of us may remain here, but we must send our scientists, our mechanics, and our artizans, and let them build railroads, let them build the great educational and other institutions necessary, and when they are constructed, the time will come for the command to be given, "Come Home!"

The hour has come for the Negro to take his own initiative. No more fear, no more cringing, no more sycophantic begging and pleading. Destiny leads us to liberty, to freedom; that freedom that Victoria of England never gave; that liberty that Lincoln never meant; that freedom, that liberty, that will see us men among men, that will make us a great and powerful people.

NEGRO ACTRESS (*sings*).

I'm on my way
To Canaan's land,
I'm on my way
To Canaan's land.

I'm on my way
To Canaan's land,
I'm on my way,
Good Lord, I'm on my way.

NARRATOR. *Out of the difficult years of the Depression emerged the colorful personality of Father Divine. His blend of religion, charity, and personal drama brought him thousands of Negro and white followers.*

MISS BEAUTIFUL LOVE.

Peace, my dearest Father:
I thank You for allowing me to write as it is my deepest desire to try to please You more each minute. I thank You for Your world at large and Your beautiful, sweet Peace that You have given to all of the children.

I thank you to report some cases of retribution, Father.

There is one whose name is Yaddy, who used dirty words. He stated You were a little bigger sport than he was. His wife has given birth to a baby who has never closed its mouth. I saw the baby when it was about 9 months old and its mouth hung open very wide.

There is one whose name is Mr. James Barr, who also thinks he is cursing You. He and his truck fell 20 feet below the level . . . He was sent to the hospital . . . now he is going blind.

Father, I will try to please you each day. I will try to make you as happy as the rambling piano keys on Easter Sunday morning, or a happy angel when she does a holy dance.

Very truly yours,
Miss Beautiful Love

FATHER DIVINE.
My dear Miss Love:
You can see in every instance that those who tried to measure ME with the measure of a man received the reward meted out to finite man.

In the case of the man, who you say, classed ME with himself, retribution came to him. For it was retribution when his child was born its mouth wide open and cannot close it.

The man, who you say thought he could curse ME, suffered retribution and is going blind. Things don't just happen, but they happen Just! What he intended for me came to him heaped up, pressed down, and running over.

Thus, retribution rolls on, striking here and there at those who think they can criticize and slander ME, but none can reach ME. Hence, it does not pay to defy MY Name, for this leaves ME, as I AM ever Well, Healthy, Joyful, Peaceful, Lively, Loving, Successful, Prosperous and Happy in Spirit, Body and Mind and in every organ, muscle, sinew, joint, limb, vein, and bone and even in every ATOM, fiber and cell of MY BODILY FORM.

Respectfully and Sincere, I AM
REV. M. J. DIVINE, MsD., D.D.
(Better know as FATHER DIVINE)
(*Guitar—reprise of "I'm on My Way"*)

NARRATOR. *As the rest of the nation began to recover from the Depression, Negroes continued to be economically exploited.*

LABORER. I was born in Elbert County, Georgia. I never went to school a day in my life. When I reached twenty-one I signed a contract—that is, I made my mark—to work on a farm for one year. My white employer was to give me $3.50 a week, and furnish me a little house on the plantation. All the people called him Senator. At the end of the first year, the Senator suggested that I sign up a contract for ten years; then, he said, we wouldn't have to fix up papers every year. I asked my wife about it; she consented; and so I made a ten-year contract.

It was then made plain to us that, in the contracts, we had agreed to be locked up in a stockade at any time the Senator saw fit. And if we got mad and ran away, we could be run down by bloodhounds, and the Senator might administer any punishment he thought proper. What could we do about it? We shut our mouths, and went to work.

But at the close of the ten-year period, to a man, we all wanted to quit. We refused to sign new contracts—even for one year. But two or three years before, the Senator had started a large store, which was called the commissary. All of us laborers were forced to buy our supplies—food, clothing and so on—from that store. We were charged all sorts of high prices.

Well, at the close of the tenth year, when we meant to leave, the Senator said to some of us with a smile—and I never will forget that smile—I can see it now . . .

(*Lights up on two white men, the* SENATOR *and his* STOREKEEPER. *The* STOREKEEPER *is holding an account book.*)

SENATOR. Boys, I'm sorry you're going to leave me. I hope you will do well in your new places—so well that you will be able to pay the little balances which most of you owe me.

(*He turns to the* STOREKEEPER, *who steps forward and reads from the account book.*)

STOREKEEPER. Frank Raines: One hundred and seventy-three dollars. Joe Simpson: One hundred and forty-six dollars. Cato Brown: One hundred and ninety-eight dollars . . .

(*The lights fade on the two white men.*)

LABORER. According to the books there was no man who owed less than $100. I owed $165, according to the bookkeeper. No one of us would have dared to dispute a white man's word. We were told we might go, if we signed acknowledgments. We would have signed anything, just to get away. So we stepped up and made our marks. The next morning it was explained to us that in the papers we had signed we had not only made acknowledgments of our debt, but had also agreed to work for our employer until the debts were paid by hard labor. And from that day forward we were treated just like convicts. Really we had made ourselves slaves, or peons, as the laws called us.

The working day on a peon farm begins with sunrise and ends when the sun goes down. Hot or cold, sun or rain, this is the rule. It was a hard school that peon camp was. A favorite way of whipping a man was to strap him down to a log and spank him fifty or sixty times on his bare feet with a piece of plank. I could tell more, but I've said enough . . .

But I didn't tell you how I got out. When I had served for nearly three years—and you remember I owed them only $165—one of the bosses came up to me and said that my time was up. He was the one who was said to be living with my wife. He took me in a buggy into South Carolina, set me down and told me to "git." I been here in the Birmingham district since and I reckon I'll die either in a coal mine or an iron furnace. It don't make much difference which. Either is better than a Georgia peon camp.

(*Guitar—a few bars of "Sometimes I Feel Like a Motherless Child"*)

NARRATOR. *When the Second World War began, segregation was still the official policy of the United States armed forces. It remained so throughout the war. Persistent rumors of conflict between Negro and white troops reached Walter White, Secretary of the N.A.A.C.P., who went overseas to investigate. Among the places he visited was Guam.*

WALTER WHITE. There were no Negro combat troops in Guam, only service units. Negro resentment at this would probably never have been translated into action had not a long series of unchecked and unpunished insults and attacks been made upon these Negroes. Stones, empty beer bottles, and other missiles were thrown from trucks into the Negro camp accompanied by such epithets as "niggers," "nightfighters" and "black sons-of-bitches." Twice hand grenades were hurled into the Negro camp. Small gangs of Marines began to run Negroes out of Agana, the largest town on Guam.

On the afternoon of Christmas Day, 1944, two intoxicated Marines shot and killed a Negro sailor. Neither of them was even arrested . . .

Around nightfall, a jeep with a machine gun mounted on it drove past firing into the Negro camp. By this time the camp was in a state of almost hysterical apprehension. Negroes climbed aboard two trucks and set out for Agana. A roadblock was thrown up and all of the Negro

men—forty-four in number—were arrested . . .

Among the crimes charged against them
were unlawful assemblage, rioting, theft of
government property, and attempted murder. The recommendations of the Board
of Inquiry, despite the evidence, resulted
in courts-martial and the sentencing of all
forty-four men to prison terms. Happily
these were later reversed when we ap-
pealed the convictions. But we had to take
the cases all the way to the Secretary of the
Navy and the White House to achieve
this.

It was this pattern which was responsible for the cynical remark I heard so often
from Negro troops—"We know that our
battle for democracy will begin when we
reach San Francisco on our way home!"

NARRATOR. *There was no major breakthrough until 1954, when the Supreme
Court declared segregation in public
schools unconstitutional. Southern resistance to the court's decision came to a head
three years later at Little Rock, Arkansas,
when a fifteen-year-old girl tried to go to
school at Central High.*

GIRL. The night before I was so excited
I couldn't sleep. The next morning I was
about the first one up. While I was pressing my black and white dress—I had made
it to wear on the first day of school—my
little brother turned on the TV set. They
started telling about a large crowd gathered
at the school. The man on TV said he
wondered if we were going to show up
that morning. Mother called from the
kitchen, where she was fixing breakfast,
"Turn that TV off!" She was so upset and
worried. I wanted to comfort her, so I
said, "Mother, don't worry!"

Dad was walking back and forth, from
room to room, with a sad expression. He
was chewing on his pipe and he had a
cigar in his hand, but he didn't light
either one. It would have been funny,
only he was so nervous.

Before I left home Mother called us into
the living room. She said we should have
a word of prayer. Then I caught the bus
and got off a block from the school. I saw
a large crowd of people standing across the
street from the soldiers guarding Central.
As I walked on, the crowd suddenly got
very quiet. For a moment all I could hear
was the shuffling of their feet. Then someone shouted, "Here she comes, get ready!"

The crowd moved in closer and then began to follow me, calling me names. I still
wasn't afraid. Just a little bit nervous.
Then my knees started to shake all of a
sudden and I wondered whether I could
make it to the center entrance a block
away. It was the longest block I ever
walked in my whole life.

Even so, I still wasn't too scared because all the time I kept thinking that
the guards would protect me.

When I got right in front of the school,
I went up to a guard. He just looked
straight ahead and didn't move to let
me pass him. I stood looking at the school
—it looked so big! Just then the guards let
some white students go through.

The crowd was quiet. I guess they were
waiting to see what was going to happen.
When I was able to steady my knees, I
walked up to the guard who had let the
white students in. He too didn't move.
When I tried to squeeze past him, he
raised his bayonet and then the other
guards closed in and they raised their
bayonets.

They glared at me with a mean look
and I was very frightened and didn't
know what to do. I turned around and
the crowd came toward me. They moved
closer and closer. Somebody started yelling, "Lynch her!" "Lynch her!"

I tried to see a friendly face somewhere
in the mob—someone who maybe would
help. I looked into the face of an old
woman and it seemed a kind face, but
when I looked at her again, she spat on
me.

They came closer, shouting, "No nigger
bitch is going to get in our school. Get out
of here!" Then I looked down the block
and saw a bench at the bus stop. I thought,
"If I can only get there I will be safe." I
don't know why the bench seemed a safe
place to me, but I started walking toward
it. I tried to close my mind to what they
were shouting, and kept saying to myself,
"If I can only make it to the bench I will
be safe."

When I finally got there, I don't think
I could have gone another step. I sat down
and the mob crowded up and began shouting all over again. Someone hollered,
"Drag her over to this tree! Let's take
care of the nigger." Just then a white man
sat down beside me, put his arm around
me and patted my shoulder.

(*During last part of speech, white actor sits beside her on bench.*)

WHITE MAN. She just sat there, her head down. Tears were streaming down her cheeks. I don't know what made me put my arm around her, saying, "Don't let them see you cry." Maybe she reminded me of my fifteen-year-old daughter.

Just then the city bus came and she got on. She must have been in a state of shock. She never uttered a word.

GIRL. I can't remember much about the bus ride, but the next thing I remember I was standing in front of the School for the Blind, where Mother works. I ran upstairs and I kept running until I reached Mother's classroom.

Mother was standing at the window with her head bowed, but she must have sensed I was there because she turned around. She looked as if she had been crying, and I wanted to tell her I was all right. But I couldn't speak. She put her arms around me and I cried.

WHITE ACTOR (*sings*).
  They say down in Hines County
  No neutrals can be met,
  You'll be a Freedom Rider,
  Or a thug for Ross Barnett.

(WHOLE CAST, *looking at each other, not the audience, quietly sings four lines of* "Which Side Are You On.")

NARRATOR. *After 1957, the Negro protest exploded—bus boycotts, sit-ins, Freedom Rides, drives for voter registration, job protests.*

NEGRO MAN. After four hundred years of barbaric treatment, the American Negro is fed up with the unmitigated hypocrisy of the white man.

WHITE MAN. The Negroes are demanding something that isn't so unreasonable.

NEGRO MAN. To have a cup of coffee at a lunch counter.

WHITE MAN. To get a decent job.

NEGRO WOMAN. The Negro American has been waiting upon voluntary action since 1876.

WHITE MAN. If the thirteen colonies had waited for voluntary action this land today would be part of the British Commonwealth.

WHITE WOMAN. The demonstrations will go on for the same reason the thirteen colonies took up arms against George III.

NEGRO MAN. For like the colonies we have beseeched.

NEGRO WOMAN. We have implored.

NEGRO MAN. We have supplicated.

NEGRO MAN. We have entreated.

NEGRO WOMAN. We are writing our declaration of independence in shoe leather instead of ink.

WHITE MAN. We're through with tokenism and gradualism and see-how-far-you've-comeism.

WHITE MAN. We're through with we've-done-more-for-your-people-than-anyone-elseism.

NEGRO WOMAN. We can't wait any longer.

NEGRO MAN. *Now* is the time.

WHITE ACTOR (*stepping forward, reads from document*). We the people of the United States, in Order to form a more perfect Union . . .

NEGRO ACTRESS (*sings under* "We the people . . . ," *slowly building in volume*).
  Oh, freedom—
  Oh, freedom—
  Oh, freedom over me!
  And before I'll be a slave,
  I'll be buried in my grave,

WHITE ACTOR (*cont'd*). . . . . establish Justice, insure domestic Tranquility, provide for the common defence, promote the general Welfare, and secure the Blessings of Liberty to ourselves and our Posterity, do ordain and establish this Constitution for the United States of America . . .

WHOLE CAST (*Sings*).
  . . . And go home to my Lord
  And be free!

THE OWL AND THE PUSSYCAT

Bill Manhoff

First presented by Philip Rose, Pat Fowler, and Seven Arts Productions at the ANTA Theatre in New York City on November 18, 1964, with the following cast:

F. SHERMAN   Alan Alda   DORIS W.   Diana Sands

Directed by Arthur Storch

SYNOPSIS OF SCENES

The action takes place in an apartment in San Francisco.

ACT ONE. After Midnight.

ACT TWO. SCENE ONE: The next morning. SCENE TWO: Four o'clock that afternoon. SCENE THREE: The next morning. SCENE FOUR: Two A.M. the following morning. SCENE FIVE: The following evening. SCENE SIX: Three weeks later.

ACT THREE. One week later.

THE OWL AND THE PUSSYCAT, by Bill Manhoff.
Copyright © 1965 by Topaz Productions, Inc.
Reprinted by permission of Doubleday & Company, Inc.
All rights reserved.

CAUTION: Professional and amateurs are hereby warned that *The Owl and the Pussycat* is subject to a royalty. It is fully protected under the copyright laws of the United States of America, the British Empire, including the Dominion of Canada, and all other countries of the Copyright Union. All rights, including professional, amateur, motion pictures, recitation, lecturing, public reading, radio broadcasting, television and the rights of translation into foreign languages are strictly reserved. In its present form the play is dedicated to the reading public only.

Stock royalty quoted on application to Samuel French, Inc.

For all other rights than those stipulated above, apply to General Artists Corporation, 640 Fifth Avenue, New York, N.Y. 10019.

Copying from this book in whole or in part is strictly forbidden by law, and the right of performance is not transferable.

BILL MANHOFF is one of the many comedy writers who first cut his teeth on radio and television. He was born in Newark, New Jersey, in 1919, and studied at City College in New York City. From 1944 until 1946 he was associated with the radio program "Duffy's Tavern," and he later produced TV scripts for Danny Thomas among others.

The Owl and the Pussycat was his first play to be produced on Broadway, or, indeed, anywhere else. Directed by Arthur Storch, it was a first-time hit, and later became a film directed by Herbert Ross and starring Barbra Streisand, offering Miss Streisand her first dramatic role in the cinema.

Following the success of *The Owl and the Pussycat,* Mr. Manhoff wrote a new comedy, originally announced for the 1967/68 season and called variously *Simple Simon* or *The Unemployed*. It concerns a delicatessen owner in love with a married woman, but at time of writing it has yet to be produced.

The Owl and the Pussycat was not only a Broadway hit; it has since proved enormously popular in stock all over the country. A two-character play, cleverly scripted, with an undertone of sexual naughtiness, it was first given on Broadway on November 18, 1964.

The play concerns a bookstore clerk and prostitute—except not quite. Because the bookstore clerk imagines he's really a writer, and the prostitute imagines she is really a model. They meet when she has been thrown out of her apartment after a complaint by him to the landlord over her peripheral activities, particularly when the blinds are up. He has a pair of binoculars and an overdeveloped sense of public duty.

It is a modest little play, almost an archetypal Broadway comedy of its period, and yet better crafted than most: the man, the girl, the classic duet involving sexual appetite and human understanding. Here there is a special dimension in the play with two people finding out the truth about their pretenses and, eventually, hopefully even if tentatively, clinging to it.

One aspect of the play's Broadway success was its almost chance introduction to the New York theatre of casual, officially almost unnoticeable, but in fact extraordinarily noticeable, miscegenation. The roles of Felix (the none-too-wise young owl) and Doris (the sweet yet alley-minded pussycat) have been given no ethnic definition by the author. However, on Broadway they were first played by white Alan Alda and black Diana Sands, and at that place and at that time it did offer, I think, a liberal frisson of integration. Sadly, it would be less true today. Indeed, it would probably be unrealistic to cast a white boy and a black girl in a play nowadays without making an issue of it. Interestingly, apart from an intriguing performance of Saint Joan (where classicism covered everything), Miss Sands's next Broadway role was in *The Gingham Dog,* a play by Lanford Wilson about the breakup of a mixed marriage. We had gone a long sad journey between 1964 and 1969.

ACT ONE

SCENE: *Felix Sherman's apartment in San Francisco. A third floor walk-up with a partly obstructed view of the Golden Gate Bridge through a large leaded window. It is the room of a self-advertising intellectual—indifferently furnished in a purely functional, almost Spartan way. There's a fireplace; a closet door and doors leading to the bedroom and bathroom on the right; the door to the hall on the left; a portable typewriter on a small table at the window. An open dictionary, etc. Slightly at odds with the informality of the furnishings is the precise formality of their arrangement: chairs are lined up, books precisely arranged. A dedicated orderliness has done its best with discouraging material.*

AT RISE: *The only light comes through the window from the moon. There is an insistent knocking at the door right. There is no response.*

———

DORIS. Mr. Sherman! . . . Mr. Sherman! . . . (*Etc., etc.*)

(*Through the door to the bedroom comes* FELIX SHERMAN. *He's tying the belt of a robe he has slipped on over his pajamas. He's in his middle thirties. He turns on a lamp and goes toward the door.*)

FELIX. Yes? Who is it?

DORIS (*offstage*). Mr. Sherman?

FELIX. Who's there?

DORIS (*off*). I have to see you, Mr. Sherman.

FELIX (*somewhat reassured at finding the caller is female, he goes closer to the door*). Who are you—what is it?

DORIS (*off*). You don't know me, but it's terribly important.

FELIX. It's very late. I never open the door to strangers at this hour.

DORIS (*off*). I'll only be a minute—please—please, it's a matter of life and death.

FELIX. Are you alone?

DORIS (*off*). Yes, I am. I'm just a little girl and I'm all alone, and I need your help.

FELIX (*he goes to the door*). What's it about? Is anybody chasing you?

DORIS (*off*). No, no, I just can't discuss it through the door—it's extremely personal. Please—I beg you.

FELIX. Swear to me that you're alone.

DORIS (*off*). What did you say? Swear to you?

FELIX. Say, "As God is my judge I am all alone."

DORIS (*off*). As God is my judge I am only a little girl all alone here in the hall—and I'm not running away from anybody. (*Obviously with great misgivings,* FELIX *opens the door.* DORIS WAVERLY *enters. She is twenty-six, hard, alert, protected at every human point by a thick shell and physically sturdier than* FELIX. *As soon as* FELIX *sees her he tries to close the door but she forces her way past him.* FELIX *retreats in nervous confusion.* DORIS *follows him.*) Hello, Pansy—rat-fink pansy!

FELIX. You lied about your size!

DORIS. You spider—you cockroach!

FELIX. You're making a mistake. I'm afraid you have the wrong apartment.

DORIS. I just wanted to get a look at you.

FELIX. It's a mistake!

DORIS. Oh will you listen to her! Mistake! You didn't spy on me from your window and call my landlord, huh?

FELIX. I don't know you.

DORIS. Well, I should have known! Any queer who peeps at girls through his window like a dirty weasel wouldn't be man enough to admit it.

FELIX. You gained entry here under false pretenses— You have no right—

DORIS. Was it fun? Did you wish you could do what the big boys were doing?

FELIX. I have no idea what you're talking about.

DORIS. "I have no idea what you're talking about." Come on, don't give me that! He told me. You're the one that called all right. "Sherman."

FELIX. If you leave immediately—I won't call the police—

DORIS. Call them. You said you would. You told Gould you were gonna call the police . . . you know you told him that, you slimy snail—you bedbug . . . you cockroach.

FELIX. I advise you to curb your foul mouth and stop making obscenities out of God's harmless little creatures.

DORIS. Why don't you curb your foul rotten mind? Try to be a man for once.

FELIX. Now listen to me—

DORIS. You're lucky I'm too refined to beat you up—the way I feel—

FELIX. Will you listen to me . . . you're insane!

DORIS. You're lucky I can't stand physical violence.

FELIX. Now look—something has happened to you obviously—

DORIS (*starting to get weepy*). What has happened is that I have been thrown out of my room. At two o'clock in the morning.

FELIX. He did that? That was unnecessary.

DORIS. Then you admit it. You called Gould, right?

FELIX. I don't have to admit anything.

DORIS (*going to window*). I don't know how you even saw anything this far away. You must have eyes like a vulture. Why did you pick on me? (*The flood of anger is running out, leaving her weak.*) How dare you do something like this? I get sick when I think there are people like you! I took money from a couple of gentlemen—did that hurt you?

FELIX (*condescending*). You must expect a certain number of people to respect the laws. That's what holds society together.

DORIS. Three cheers for you! And I'm not society, huh? I don't have to get held together?

FELIX. My dear woman, you were breaking the law. If you find yourself in trouble it is only—

DORIS (*she notices a pair of field glasses; she picks them up*). So this is how you saw! Oh now it's bad enough with the naked eye—but with spyglasses—now that is just plain dirty, Mister. I'm sorry! When you work at it this hard—filthy, Mister! Filthy, filthy!

FELIX (*defensive*). I'm a writer. A writer is an observer. I have a right to those.

DORIS. You want me to tell you what you're full of?

FELIX. I wouldn't expect you to understand.

DORIS. You are nothing but a dirty, filthy Peeping Tom!

FELIX. Why don't you ever pull down your window shade?

DORIS. I never pull down my window shade. I hate window shades.

FELIX. That's your privilege, by all means.

DORIS. I keep forgetting the world is full of finks. That's my trouble. I ought to get

it tattooed on the back of my hand— "Watch out for Finks." (*Annoyed,* FELIX *suddenly sits at the typewriter and types rapidly on a white card which he then pins to the bulletin board.*) What are you doing? (*Reading it.*) "A rule worth making is worth keeping." What is that?

FELIX. That's to remind me never to open my door after midnight.

DORIS. Why don't you make one to remind you to stop being a fink?

FELIX. I wish you would stop using that ugly word.

DORIS. You don't like it? Too bad! Fink. Pansy fink, Queer fink, Peeping Tom fink, fink fink, you fink!

FELIX. Feel better? (*He goes to the door and opens it.*) If you're sure your poison sacs are empty you can go.

DORIS. Just tell me where I'm supposed to go?

FELIX. Don't you have a friend you could stay with?

DORIS. Not that I can move in on at two A.M.

FELIX. How about a hotel?

DORIS. I got seventy-two cents. The son-of-a-bitch took all of my money.

FELIX. Who did?

DORIS. Barney Gould, the landlord.

FELIX. How could he do that?

DORIS. While he was helping you hold society together with one hand—he was robbing me with the other. He said you saw me take money from a couple of— and you were gonna call the cops and if I gave him the money he'd cover up with the cops—that's how could I!

FELIX. He was lying to you. All I did was ask him if he knew what was going on in his building.

DORIS. Gee, that was big of you!

FELIX. Well, I felt he should know. For his own protection.

DORIS. Oh, sweet! You're just a big mother, aren't you? Now will you lend me five bucks so I can get a room? I'll pay you back.

FELIX. I don't have any money. I got paid today and haven't cashed my check.

DORIS. I never knew a fink that did have any money.

FELIX. Don't you know anybody you could call? (*DORIS has fallen onto a chair. She's defeated and near tears.*) Don't you have any family? (*Looking at the couch.*) You can't stay here!

DORIS. I'd rather sleep in the gutter.

FELIX. It's a matter of taste, I suppose. (*On her last line,* DORIS *has gone to the door. She brings in a large suitcase and a portable TV set.*) What are you doing?

DORIS. Get me a sheet and a blanket for that couch.

FELIX. You're not staying here. Oh, no—no!

DORIS. Naturally I'm staying. Where have I got to go?

FELIX. I thought you were looking forward to a night in the gutter.

DORIS. Just get a blanket, will you please . . . and stop being so goddam bitchy! Come on, come on.

FELIX. Very well, you may stay the night.

DORIS. Thanks for nothing. (FELIX *starts to answer. Changes his mind. Goes to the bedroom.* DORIS *takes off her coat, tosses it carelessly onto the coffee table, sets the suitcase on the sofa and she opens it; takes a nightgown out of the suitcase and closes it.* FELIX *comes from the bedroom with one folded sheet, a blanket, and dumps the sheet and blanket on the sofa. He glares at her.* DORIS *plugs in the television set.*) What kind of reception do you get?

FELIX. I wouldn't know. I've never had a television set.

DORIS. Oh, that's right—you got your spy-glasses! By the way, how was I on the late, late show?

(FELIX *goes to the coffeepot and pours coffee into a plastic cup.*)

FELIX. You're not planning to watch television at this hour?

DORIS (*tucking sheet under sofa cushion*). It's the only way I can get to sleep —I won't play it loud— Listen—I don't want to be here—if you had kept your mouth shut—

FELIX. And if you had kept your window shade down—

DORIS. You got a sweetheart in there? Some bouncy young boy or do you dig the rough trade—

FELIX. You're an alley cat, aren't you? On your back and rip out their guts with your hind claws.

DORIS. And what do you do, lover? Pull their hair and scratch out their eyes? Give me some of that coffee . . . please. (FELIX *starts to pour cup for her.*) No. A whole cup'll keep me awake. Just give me a sip of yours. Do you ever write for television?

FELIX. No, thank you.

(FELIX *crosses to her and she takes his cup; takes two sips, watching him.*)

DORIS. What kind of a writer are you? Did I ever hear of you?

FELIX. No.

DORIS. Did anybody?

FELIX. Voices like mine are drowned out by the clatter of the cash register. That's *two* sips—

(DORIS *gives him back the cup.* FELIX *starts to drink, switches the cup, and drinks from the other side.*)

DORIS. Now, what was that you just did?

FELIX. What?

DORIS. Drinking out of the other side like that—

FELIX. Oh—I always do that—it's a reflex—

DORIS. Yeah—sure it is.

FELIX. Really—I'm a hypochondriac.

DORIS. You make me feel like I'm a cockroach and I just crawled into your clean little house and you're trying to get up the nerve to squash me—that's the way you make me feel.

FELIX. Oh my God, you're crazy!

DORIS. Listen, Mister—I don't want to see that in your eyes when you look at me —I am a model. I have been in many television commercials at a time when I weighed 105, which unfortunately I don't any more. So don't you dare turn that cup around, you hear? You don't catch anything from a model—do you hear me— I may turn a trick or two but *I am a model!* (DORIS's *voice has risen hysterically. At this point there's a* KNOCK *at the wall.*)

FELIX. Listen—you can't stay here. Why don't you try the YWCA?—

DORIS. With seventy-two cents? That Christian the YWCA is not—

FELIX. Will you try to be quiet—there's an old man downstairs.

DORIS. And you don't want him to think you switched to girls, right?

FELIX. Now look—

DORIS (*interrupting as she exits to bathroom*). Don't worry about it—just leave me alone. I'll try to get out of here before you wake up. (*He starts to bedroom. From offstage.*) Do me a favor—if you wake up and I'm still here, yell before you come out so I can close my eyes. I don't wanna have to look at you first thing in

the morning. Where's the john? Excuse
me—the jane?—the bathroom!

FELIX. It's in there. Good night.

DORIS (off). Good night, fink.

(FELIX *exits to the bedroom. We hear
the* SOUNDTRACK *of the movie clearly now.*)

OLD WOMAN'S VOICE. Then you knew—
all the time.

OLD MAN'S VOICE. Yes—I knew he was
guilty.

OLD WOMAN'S VOICE. Then why, Ben?

OLD MAN'S VOICE. Why did I let them
convict me for his crime?

OLD WOMAN'S VOICE. Thirty years—thirty
long years—why, Ben? Why?

(DORIS *enters from the bathroom wearing her nightgown; she watches the movie
for a couple of lines of dialogue.*)

OLD WOMAN'S VOICE. You had so much to
live for—the governorship. There were
those who thought you had a chance for
the White House.

OLD MAN'S VOICE. Yes—there were those
who said that—

OLD WOMAN'S VOICE. And you threw it
all away, Ben, to save him. Why? He was
a thief and a drunkard.

OLD MAN'S VOICE. Why? Because a girl
with cornflower blue eyes and yellow hair
loved him.

OLD WOMAN'S VOICE. Oh Ben, my eyes
are still cornflower blue, but my hair is all
white now.

OLD MAN'S VOICE. Not to me—Alice—
to me it'll always be yellow.

OLD WOMAN'S VOICE. Ben—you mean—
oh no!

OLD MAN'S VOICE. Then they didn't tell
you? Yes, Alice—I'm blind, an accident
in the prison library.

OLD WOMAN'S VOICE. No, you're not
blind, Ben, for as long as I live, you have
two cornflower blue eyes—

OLD MAN'S VOICE. Alice—

OLD WOMAN'S VOICE. Oh Ben—

(*And the music comes up for a big
finish.* DORIS *crosses to the set.*)

ANNOUNCER. And that concludes the late,
late show. Well—

(*The voice is killed as* DORIS *turns off
the* SET. *She turns on the radio; it doesn't
work; she shakes it; desperately.*)

DORIS (*shouts*). God damn it! Hey fink,
fink!

(FELIX *enters.*)

FELIX. Now what?

DORIS. My radio won't work. I must
have banged it coming up the stairs!

FELIX. Do you really have to—?

DORIS. It's the only way I can go to
sleep. You got a radio?

FELIX. No.

DORIS. What'll I do now? Why did I
have to come up here?

FELIX. Why not correct your mistake?
Leave!

DORIS. I should have just given a certain
friend of mine a dollar to beat you up.

FELIX. A dollar? Can't be much of a
beating.

DORIS. He's a friend. He would do it for
nothing, but I make him take a dollar.

FELIX. I see.

DORIS (*calls*). What's so goddam funny?
I'll send him around tomorrow. I guaran-
tee you won't think it's so funny. Now
I'll never get to sleep.

FELIX. Why can't you sleep?

DORIS. I'm very high-strung.

FELIX. I don't have any sleeping pills
or I'd—

DORIS. I don't take sleeping pills. I never
take them. They're enervating.

FELIX. How about a hot bath? That'll
relax you.

DORIS (*talking in a compulsive rush*). I
never take baths. They're enervating too.
You know that word—"enervating"?
Most people think it means just the opposite of what it really means. (FELIX *walks
back toward the bedroom in the middle
of her speech, yawning, yearning for sleep.*
DORIS *raises her voice to a shout.* FELIX
stops.) Another word that kills me is
naive—I always thought it was "nave"
you know. How do you pronounce it?

FELIX. I never use it.

DORIS. I mean I heard the word na'ive,
but—

(*The* KNOCK *is heard again.*)

FELIX. What's the matter with you?
What are you trying to do? I got up at
five-thirty this morning.

DORIS. Listen, I know this sounds crazy,
but will you sit here for a little while and
talk to me?

FELIX. You act as though you were
afraid to be alone.

DORIS. I usually fall asleep with the television on or the radio—but now my radio's
on the fritz and it's too late for TV.

FELIX. It's too late for me, too. I'm
signing off. (*Sings.*)

Oh say can you see by the dawn's
early light—
This is Channel Sherman signing off
for the night.

DORIS (*laughs much too hard*). That's
pretty funny. I never would have thought
you had a sense of humor.

FELIX. I'm a funny fink.

DORIS. Just goes to show you never can
tell about people. (*As she talks* FELIX *turns
and makes another try for the bedroom.
Without a pause and without changing
her tone or her volume,* DORIS *goes on.*)
If you take one more step I'm gonna
scream at the top of my lungs.

FELIX. For God's sake—

DORIS. I can't help it. Do you think I can
help it? I can't fall asleep unless I'm listening to something. Read me something
—you got any magazines?

FELIX. Isn't there any other way for you
to get to sleep?

DORIS. There's only one other way.

FELIX. That wouldn't interest me.

DORIS. That is not what I meant—evil-
minded!

FELIX. Listen—I must get some sleep.

DORIS. So must I—which I would if not
for some dirty rotten bastard who you and
I both know. Pardon my language.

FELIX (*humoring a child*). All right—
all right. What do you want?

DORIS. Read to me. Read me anything
and I'll fall asleep. Nothing with big
words. I hate big words. (FELIX *looks
around the room, looks at* DORIS, *looks at
his books; looks back at* DORIS, *obviously
decides he has nothing suitable.*) Well?

FELIX. We're out of bedtime stories.
What was the other way you have of
falling asleep?

DORIS. Huh? Oh—that's only in the
winter when it's real cold—I huddle myself down in bed under about a million
blankets—it's a wonder I don't suffocate
—come on read to me—anything.

(FELIX *picks up a small bronze bust,
for a second considers hitting her with it.*)

FELIX. I could put you to sleep with
Shakespeare.

DORIS. Shakespeare gives me a headache.

FELIX. I don't have anything you'd like.
I don't have any comic books, movie magazines or any other literature of that nature!

DORIS (*yawning*). Don't stop—your
voice is very enervating. You know what

that means? Oh yeah—I told you before.
Come on—keep talking—

FELIX (*looks about desperately, picks up
the box of breakfast food, reads the label*).
Ingredients: oat flour—wheat starch—
sugar, salt, cinnamon, sodium phosphate,
calcium carbonate, artificial coloring, iron,
niacin, thiamine and riboflavin, caramel,
vegetable oil with freshness preserved by
Butylated Hydroxelene and—

DORIS. No—that's no good—I'm getting
hungry. Hey—read me one of your stories.
Read me your latest one.

FELIX. You wouldn't like it. (*Remembering.*) Four score and seven years ago
our fathers brought forth on this continent
a new nation—conceived in liberty and
dedicated to the proposition that all men
were created equal—equal— (*Stops, stuck;
he sits on the end of the sofa, exhausted.*)

DORIS. Don't stop—that's nice—the Declaration of Independence—right?

FELIX. No, Custer's farewell address to
the Indians.

DORIS. Oh, yes—that's right—why'd you
stop?

FELIX. I don't remember any more. Listen—I'm exhausted—

DORIS. Why wouldn't I like your story?

FELIX. It has no rape scene, no beautiful
people, and no happy ending.

DORIS. Let's hear it. Maybe I can spot
where you went wrong.

FELIX. You ought to be ashamed of
yourself! A big girl like you afraid to be
alone— (*He yawns.*)

DORIS. Isn't that ridiculous! Ever since
I was a kid—I tell you it's not being alone
that's scary—I wouldn't mind being alone
—but there's somebody there—I can hear
him breathing—he just stands there breathing and it just panics me—I had this analysis you know for six months and the
doctor told me— (*Stops.*) Hey— (*He's
dozed off.*)

FELIX. Oh—what were you saying?

DORIS. About being alone—my analyst
said—

FELIX. You were analyzed?

DORIS. Of course.

FELIX. Really?

DORIS. There's a brain in there—honest!

FELIX. What kind of a doctor?

DORIS. Jewish.

FELIX. No. I mean—never mind. What
did he say?

DORIS. Oh, I hate that!

FELIX. What?

DORIS. "Never mind" like "forget it, you're too dumb to understand."

FELIX. Oh no—it was just a foolish question on my part.

DORIS. Really?

FELIX. Sure. That's why I said "never mind." What did he tell you?

DORIS. He said I was afraid to be alone because of unconscious guilt.

FELIX. Guilt is very bad.

DORIS. It's enervating.

FELIX. If you don't let me go to sleep you're gonna be completely enervated by guilt feelings tomorrow.

DORIS. Never mind, wise guy! Read me your story.

FELIX (*picks up typewriter script*). You won't like it.

DORIS. If it puts me to sleep I'll love it.

FELIX (*reading*). Scream—

DORIS. "Scream." That's the title, right —"Scream."

FELIX. Yes.

DORIS. That's a wild title.

FELIX. Thank you. (*Reads.*) The sun spit morning into Werner's face—one eyelid fluttered—dragging the soul back screaming from its stealthy flight to death—

DORIS (*sitting up*). The sun spit morning into this guy's face?

FELIX. Yes.

DORIS. You were right.

FELIX. When?

DORIS. I don't like it. I hate it.

FELIX. It wasn't written for you to like.

DORIS. Why wasn't it written for me to like? I'm the public—

FELIX. You're raising your voice.

DORIS. The sun spit morning into his face!

FELIX. Shh! What are you getting angry about?

DORIS. What right do you have to put down a terrible thing like that in a story —"The sun spit morning in a man's face."

FELIX. All right—you don't like it—but calm down.

DORIS. Yeah—look at me! I always get mad at stuff like that.

FELIX. Just because you don't understand it?

DORIS. It makes me feel shut out—you know? It makes me mad as hell! You know once I threw a clock at the TV.

FELIX. Really?

DORIS. I swear to God. It was Maurice Evans in something—poetry—I don't know—and all of a sudden—bam—sixty-three bucks for a new tube.

FELIX. And with just the turn of a knob you could have had the reassurance of mediocrity.

DORIS. Damn it, are you talking to me or not?

FELIX. Why do you get so angry at anything that's over your head?

DORIS. I can't help it. When I was going to this head shrinker—every once in a while he'd start talking big words and I'd get so boiling mad! Once I put my dress on inside out—

FELIX. You took psychiatric sessions with your dress off?

DORIS. Oh hell—why did I let that slip out! (*Hiccups.*)

FELIX. It's perfectly all right. The barter system is time-honored.

DORIS (*getting angry*). Now I don't know what that means either, Mister—

FELIX. Take it easy now—

DORIS. You know what you are? You're inflabious. (*Hic.*)

FELIX. Inflabious?

DORIS. Yeah.

FELIX. What does that mean?

DORIS (*thumbing her nose*). Ah ha! How does it feel? I'm not gonna tell you!

FELIX. You just made up a word?

DORIS. How do I know you're not making up yours?

FELIX. Mine are in the dictionary.

DORIS. That's *your* story!

FELIX. I suppose it never occurred to you that as an alternative to getting angry you might make some attempt to understand whatever it is that confuses you?

DORIS. Why? Why should I? What about people making some attempt to not confuse me? (*Hic.*)

FELIX. Because progress does not lie in the pampering of the brainless.

DORIS. Drop— (*Hic.*) dead! Damn it!

FELIX. Hold your breath.

DORIS. Hold yours . . .

FELIX. Maybe you can hiccup yourself to sleep.

DORIS. You better not be so damn funny —people have been known to— (*Hic.*) die from the hiccups.

FELIX. Drink a glass of water.

DORIS. That never works with me. Only

one thing works with me—you gotta scare me.

FELIX. How the devil am I gonna scare a holy terror like you?

DORIS (*hic*). I get them very deep—it's a strain on the heart, so stop fooling around and scare me— (*Hic.*) or I'll scream. (FELIX *turns and walks around the sofa—suddenly pounces with clawed hands snarling like a tiger.*) Oh come— (*Hic.*) on! (FELIX *drops down behind sofa—*DORIS *hiccups twice.* FELIX *suddenly appears on all fours around the end of the sofa rising menacingly and hissing like a snake.*) It's no use. I was expecting it. You have to do it when I'm not— (*Hic.*) expecting it.

FELIX. Oh, that's ridiculous! How can I do that? You're waiting for me to frighten you.

DORIS. Well, make me— (*Hic.*) forget about it—stupid. Then when my mind is on— (*Hic.*) something else—then do it!

FELIX. When your mind is on something else!

DORIS. Of course, stupid! Change the subject—put me off my— (*Hic.*) guard.

FELIX. Some weather we're having. It's a wonderful summer, isn't it?

DORIS. Beautiful. (*Hic.*)

FELIX. I think it's quite a bit warmer than it was last year at this time. Don't you?

DORIS. I was in Chicago— (*Hic.*) last summer.

FELIX. That's an interesting city, Chicago.

DORIS. I didn't— (*Hic.*) like it. Come on, will you—you want me to hiccup to death? (*Hic.*)

FELIX. I'm putting you off your guard!

DORIS. I'm off my— (*Hic.*) guard by now. Stupid!

FELIX. You're expecting it now.

DORIS. I am not. (*Hic.*) Come on, will you! (FELIX *gives a hideous roar.* DORIS *looks at* FELIX *for a second, then.*) You're right. I was— (*Hic.*) expecting it.

FELIX. Listen—I'm through—I'm finished—I'm exhausted. I'm going to bed—I don't care what you do—you can scream yourself sick—I just don't care! (FELIX *exits to bedroom.* DORIS *turns facing audience.*)

DORIS. Dirty son of— (*Hic.*) bitch! Cockroach! (*Behind her* FELIX *creeps on tiptoe from the bedroom.*) Rotten—

(*Hic.*) pervert. I could die for all he cares. (*Hic.*) I could die right—

(*At this point, unheard by her,* FELIX *is right behind* DORIS. *Suddenly he growls and puts his hands around her neck.* DORIS *jumps in terror. She turns and clouts* FELIX *in the face.*)

FELIX. What's the idea!

DORIS. You wanna give somebody a heart attack? You maniac, you wanna kill me?

FELIX (*nursing his face*). You're out of your mind!

DORIS. Do you know how dangerous that is—to scare somebody like that. My heart is pounding like crazy.

FELIX. You asked me to scare you—

DORIS. I didn't ask for a heart attack. I'm fainting! Do you have any vodka?

FELIX. No—all I have is a little cooking sherry. What you need now is sleep—I'll leave you alone so you can drop off.

DORIS. Cooking sherry! You know you're not real.

FELIX. Wait a minute. I think I have a little Scotch.

DORIS. That's better.

FELIX (*looking in cupboard*). Unless I gave it away— (THE NEIGHBOR *knocks and shouts "Quiet down"*) no here it is. (*He takes out a bottle with about two inches of liquor—pours her a drink.*)

DORIS. That's good—hurry up—will you? (FELIX *hands her the glass. She drinks.*) Ugh—what is it—cooking Scotch?

FELIX. Someone left it here. Your hiccups are gone.

DORIS. My whole insides are gone.

FELIX. Now how about going to sleep? I can't stand up any more— Good night. (*He starts toward bedroom.*)

DORIS (*screams*). Don't you leave me alone!

(*There's one knock on wall then.*)

OLD MAN'S VOICE. Quiet down or I'll call the police.

FELIX (*yells*). Call them! It's a good idea!

DORIS. Shh! Not so loud.

FELIX (*still yelling*). I'm the one who should be calling the police. I'm an idiot.

DORIS. Stop yelling.

FELIX. Tyrannized in my own home by an ignorant whore! What's the matter with me?

DORIS (*angry, but starting to cry*). You were just being nice to an unfortunate person because it's your fault she's unfortunate.

FELIX. No—I've been on the defensive—I've actually been apologetic because I did my duty as a citizen.

DORIS (*shouting through her tears*). All right, Citizen—shoot me, Citizen! Call the cops, Citizen! Save America, Citizen!

FELIX (*shouting*). It's not my fault you're a whore.

DORIS. Stop calling me that! I'm a model, and an actress.

FELIX. You're not what you call yourself, you're what you are!

DORIS. Will you stop yelling? He'll call the cops.

FELIX (*still yelling*). He can't. He doesn't have a phone.

DORIS. Well, stop yelling. A gentleman doesn't yell at a lady.

FELIX (*sarcastic*). Excuse me, Lady—

DORIS. Listen, you—you don't know anything about me. You have no right to even talk to me—because you don't even know who I am! So what right have you got? Do you know that I never take a trick to whom I have not been properly introduced? You can't just pick me up on the street—

FELIX (*sarcastic*). Pardon me—is that so?

DORIS. You bet your ass that's so! I may be a prostitute—but I am not promiscuous!

FELIX. Oh, what a nice distinction!

DORIS. You bet it is! Did you know I was in two TV commercials? A Dazzle Laundry Soap and a Platzburg Beer? No! You don't know anything about me. Nothing! But you sound off your big mouth!

FELIX. Look—I've got a couple of dollars—maybe you can get a room down on Van Ness.

DORIS. Call the cops—

FELIX. Look— I'm exhausted.

DORIS. Call the cops—I want you to—I don't care any more.

FELIX. I don't want to call the police. Look, Doris.

DORIS. Who told you my name is Doris?

FELIX. It's on your nightgown.

DORIS. Who gave you permission to read my nightgown? (*Turning away from him.*) Don't call me "Doris"—you don't know who I am. Don't talk to me.

FELIX. All right—Miss—whoever you are—your staying here is no good for either one of us.

DORIS (*quiet now*). Nobody knows who I am. Wouldn't it be funny if I didn't know who I was either?

FELIX. All you need is some sleep. You'll feel better.

DORIS. Oh, I feel better—I'm okay— (*She sighs deeply and shudders.*)

FELIX (*sudden attack of guilt*). Listen—I want you to know I'm really sorry I did what I did—I mean telling your landlord.

DORIS. Forget it. Maybe it's for the best—it was time I got out of that crummy room. Anyway I've had it with Frisco. I think I'll move to LA and change my name. Maybe I can get a job—I know a guy in an advertising agency in LA.

FELIX. Can you do secretarial work?

DORIS. I can't spell. I'm so dumb—

FELIX. You're not dumb at all.

DORIS. Who's not dumb, me? You really mean that? I know you do, otherwise you would never say it, right?

FELIX. That's right.

DORIS. You're the type. I feel dumb though.

FELIX. You just don't think. You live almost exclusively in the atmosphere of your emotions, reacting to everything emotionally—don't you?

DORIS. I guess so. Like getting so mad when I don't understand something—right?

FELIX. Right.

DORIS. Could a person get over something like that?

FELIX. I would say there's a lot more hope for you than there would be for a girl who was left completely unmoved by what she didn't understand.

DORIS. You know you talk great, you really do.

FELIX. Language is my business.

DORIS. You make any money at it?

FELIX. I don't write to make money.

DORIS. You'd take money if they gave it to you, naturally, right?

FELIX. If they gave it to me for writing my way. The trouble is they only give you money for writing their way.

DORIS. Yeah, well I guess they figure it's their money.

FELIX. I think that's the way they figure, yes.

DORIS. Go argue with that! Anyway, you sure do know a lot of words!

FELIX. You like words, don't you?

DORIS. When I understand them.

FELIX. You should stop running away from your mind. It won't bite you.

DORIS. Is that what I'm doing?

FELIX. Most of the world is. Fleeing the pain of thought.

DORIS (*reverently*). "Fleeing the pain of thought." Did you make that up?

FELIX. It's from a poem I wrote.

DORIS (*savoring it*). "Fleeing the pain of thought." (*She suddenly turns her head—puts the handkerchief to her face.*) You wanna make love to me?

FELIX. No, I don't.

DORIS (*sudden rush of embarrassment*). Oh, my God!

FELIX. What?

DORIS. Nothing. I just thought of how I came in here before, screaming such terrible language.

FELIX. You were pretty angry.

DORIS. I'm so ashamed. I know you'll never believe it but when I'm not mad, I'm very refined.

FELIX. I believe it. I think you have to be very tough because you're very soft.

DORIS. Gee, that's nice. Thank you. It doesn't make sense. But thank you.

FELIX. You're welcome. It makes sense.

DORIS. Anyway, I have this horrible temper. It makes me into a completely different person.

FELIX. I'm sorry I told your landlord. I really am. It was an act of self-righteousness. I don't often do things like that.

DORIS. Oh, listen—what the hell. (*Correcting herself immediately.*) What the devil. You had a strong feeling that it was the right thing to do—so you did it. You can't help those things.

FELIX. You're very gracious.

DORIS. I am, really? Gracious?

FELIX. Yes.

DORIS. You know I once wrote an essay in high school and the teacher thought it was so good she made me read it to the class. The subject was "How I Feel Motion Pictures and Television Have Affected My Life." She sent it to a couple of magazines but they sent it back.

FELIX. I know the feeling.

DORIS. *Reader's Digest* and some other one. I never should have left school—only my mother got sick and my father started drinking again and my goddam brother —pardon the language—joined the Navy and to tell you the truth, I figured what did an actress need with a high school diploma anyway, and this agent felt he could get me into this semi-professional theatre group which never got off the ground, as it turned out. I had two copies of the essay, but I lost them both.

FELIX. What essay?—Oh, yes—

DORIS. "How I Feel Motion Pictures and Television Have Affected My Life." I thought I would write it out again but I can't remember it. Let me ask you something—are there books you can read that will increase your intelligence?

FELIX. Not really.

DORIS. That was a stupid question, wasn't it?

FELIX. No.

DORIS. Then what are you smiling at?

FELIX. I don't know. (DORIS *leans forward suddenly and kisses* FELIX *on the lips. After a frozen beat.*) Reading books can only add to your information.

DORIS. I have always felt it was really like a sickness, being you know—queer. It's certainly nothing to be ashamed of or looked down on. (Like my goddam brother loves to beat them up.) Did you have a bed experience with a girl? Is that what did it?

FELIX. What makes you so sure I'm queer? Isn't it possible I'm just not interested.

DORIS. You mean I'm not your type?

FELIX. I don't mean that—

DORIS. Do you think I'm pretty?

FELIX. Yes, I do.

DORIS. I'm not really. I just make you think I am.

FELIX. How do you do that?

DORIS. It's just a trick. You just gotta act pretty—it's hard to explain.

FELIX. In other words, you're not pretty —you're just a good actress.

DORIS. Well, I'm not a dog—but, well— yeah I never thought about it—but it is—it's acting—watch—now I look pretty —right?

FELIX. Uh huh.

DORIS. Okay—now watch— (DORIS *lets her face and body slump into vacant stupidity.*)

FELIX. That's amazing! Like two different girls!

DORIS. *Now* you're putting me on!

FELIX. No—I'm not!

DORIS. It's hard to tell with you . . . anyway—what's your name?

FELIX. Sherman.

DORIS. I know that from the doorbell. F. Sherman. What does the F. stand for?

FELIX. "Fink."

DORIS. Come on!

FELIX. "Felix."

DORIS. "Felix." Ugh! It sounds like stepping on snails.

FELIX. What's your name?

DORIS. Doris.

FELIX. Doris what?

DORIS. I don't know. I'm between names right now. I've been using "Waverly," but it's been bad luck. I gotta change it— You know I got a feeling I've seen you some place.

FELIX. At the bookshop possibly—the Beacon of Light Bookshop on Polk. That's where I work.

DORIS. That's it. Sure—I think I once paid you for a *Reader's Digest.*

FELIX. Very possibly. I never look at the customers. Especially *Reader's Digest* customers.

DORIS. What's wrong with the *Reader's Digest?*

FELIX. Oh, God—not now.

DORIS. What's the matter? The sun doesn't spit in anybody's face in the *Reader's Digest,* right?

FELIX. No. In the *Reader's Digest* mediocrity drools all over itself!

DORIS. I don't know what *that* means! . . . What do you think of Washington?

FELIX. What?

DORIS. "Doris Washington." (*She tries it with different inflections.*) Doris. Doris Washington . . . Miss Doris Washington. That's very common, isn't it?

FELIX. No question. I notice you favor the initial W.

DORIS. That's because my real name is Wilgus. It's a terrible name, but I would never think of giving up that W.

FELIX. Respect for family tradition. Good for you! What about "Wadsworth"?

DORIS. I used that. I was Doris Wadsworth for two weeks once, in Vegas, was it? Yeah, Vegas.

FELIX. I was Sigmund Freud in a girl's apartment one night for three hours.

DORIS. You know that's the second thing you said I didn't understand and I didn't get mad.

FELIX. What was the first?

DORIS. *Reader's Digest* drooling or something. I think I'm falling in love with you.

FELIX. With me—? Come on now—

DORIS. Believe it or not, you're my type. All the guys I fall in love with are weak in the body and strong in the head. And half the time they turn out to be—gay. That's my luck. You wanna kiss me?

FELIX. No.

DORIS. Try it.

FELIX. No thank you.

DORIS (*sighs*). Here I go again!

FELIX. You don't see any middle ground between no sex at all and wholesale copulation, do you?

DORIS. What does that mean, Baby?

FELIX. You can make me very grateful to you by not calling me "Baby."

DORIS. Okay, Lover—how does "Lover" strike you?

FELIX. I don't care for any of those amorous generic labels. I am an individual named Felix.

DORIS. I wouldn't say that name for a million dollars. You would make me very grateful by not saying it again. Also by not using those big words. You'll make me sore.

FELIX (*amused*). I'll watch it.

DORIS. I think you need a new name. It'll be good for you. You're an "M"— "Mark"—no—"Michael"—Michael, that's it!

FELIX. I'm staying with Felix—thank you.

DORIS. You're cute as hell— Did you ever go with a girl?

FELIX. As a matter of fact, I've been seeing one girl for almost two years.

DORIS. No kidding. Where is she?

FELIX. She's in New York right now.

DORIS. What does she look like?

FELIX. I'll show you. (*Picks up a slim book from the mantel.*)

DORIS. She' a writer?

FELIX. She's one of the finest poetesses in the country.

DORIS (*looking at the book*). Anne— (*mispronouncing it*) Weyderhaus?

FELIX. Weyderhaus.

DORIS (*turns book over, reads*). "September Leaves"—she looks very brainy.

FELIX. She is.

DORIS. She knows how to look it. That's for sure! I'm trying to picture her with a girl's hairdo.

FELIX. She likes to wear her hair that way. I assure you she's very much a woman.

DORIS. Well, okay. Who said she wasn't?

FELIX (*caught on the limb*). Well, I just wanted you to know.

DORIS (*shrugs*). That's between you and her. There's more than one way to skin a cat.

FELIX. Now what does that mean?

DORIS (*opening a book*). Just a saying. (*Looks at it.*) It don't rhyme, honey.

FELIX. No. In that respect it doesn't come up to Mother Goose.

DORIS. She'll flip when she hears about you having a girl in your place all night—

FELIX. No she won't. We don't have that kind of relationship.

DORIS. I bet. I can't wait to tell her, anyway—

FELIX. You're not serious.

DORIS. It's my duty. Guy cheating on his girl. Gotta hold society together.

FELIX. Now listen, you can't do that!

DORIS. What's the matter—you got no sense of humor?

FELIX. I thought you were serious.

DORIS. It's hard to tell when I'm kidding. I'm such a good actress.

FELIX. You really are.

DORIS. People are always saying to me, "Gee, Doris, we never know when you're kidding." And listen—about your story— I get sore at Shakespeare too—so it's probably a sign you're a genius—let's kiss and make up. (*And before* FELIX *can move* DORIS *has thrown her arms around him.* FELIX *responds and the kiss develops some heat.* FELIX *leans over her getting lost in the kiss—then catches himself and breaks out of it. He's badly disturbed. He's lost the smug upper hand and is battling for his life from now on.*) Hey! Whatever gave you the idea you were gay?

FELIX. I never had that idea. You had it.

DORIS. Wow! That's all I can say—wow! Where you running?

FELIX. I have to be at work at eight-thirty.

DORIS. We got plenty of time. Kiss me again.

FELIX. I've got to get some sleep—listen, I have an idea—there's a radio in my bedroom—

DORIS (*happily*). Good!

FELIX. It's built into the headboard— so why don't you sleep in my bed?

DORIS (*happily*). Crazy.

FELIX. I'll sleep out here.

DORIS (*distastefully*). Swell! What's wrong, Baby? I know you want to.

FELIX. I happen to be an intellectual. That means that I am not at the mercy of what I *want* to do.

DORIS. Groovy!

FELIX. Only animals are controlled by their appetites. Go on now. You can let the radio put you to sleep.

(DORIS *rises, showing him her legs.* FELIX *is on the ropes and* DORIS *knows it. She exits and he goes back to the sofa, sits down.* DORIS *appears at the door. She's teasing him now.*)

DORIS. Hey—it's a double bed.

FELIX. I know.

DORIS. I always feel so selfish sleeping alone in a double bed—when there are people in China sleeping on the ground.

FELIX. Please go to sleep.

(*She shrugs and exits. He lies down, turns over restlessly, looks to the bedroom. His eye falls on the book of poetry. He puts the book away from him.*)

DORIS (*off*). How do you turn it on?

FELIX. Second knob from the right.

DORIS (*off*). Good night.

FELIX. Good night.

DORIS (*off*). Is that too loud?

FELIX. I can't even hear it.

DORIS (*off, singing it lovingly*). Good night.

FELIX. Good night!

(*He turns over, turns over again, sits up, picks up the book of poetry. He rises suddenly, goes to the bookcase, shoves the book into it and comes back to the sofa.* DORIS *appears at the bedroom door.*)

DORIS. Michael, honey— (FELIX *ignores her.*) Honey— (*He flops over restlessly on the sofa.*) When you come in bring that blanket with you, will you, honey?

(DORIS *disappears into the bedroom.* FELIX *sits up. He realizes he's going into the bedroom; he panics suddenly in the realization of defeat.*)

FELIX (*shouting*). I am not an animal. I am a man of intellect. You can't do this to me.

DORIS. Hey, Baby—not so loud!

FELIX. I am not "Baby." I am not "Honey." I am Felix, Felix, Felix, Felix, Felix! (*Exhausted by the outburst he flops on the sofa as the* MAN *next door knocks on the wall.* FELIX *addresses the wall, shouting.*) Felix! (*He stops, sighs. Looks at the blanket. Slowly he reaches for it and starts for the bedroom.*)

BLACKOUT

ACT TWO

SCENE ONE

Morning LIGHT *through the window. The phone is ringing.* FELIX *staggers sleepily out of the bedroom, picks up the phone.*

———

FELIX. Hello—what? Oh, Victor—what time is it? . . . Oh—no—I'm not coming in today, Victor—yes . . . I don't know what it is . . . I think I'm fighting off a bug . . . no—I'll call one—yes—yes I will. Goodbye, Victor. (*He hangs up—looks around the room.*)

DORIS (*off, sleepily*). Michael!

FELIX. Yes?

DORIS (*off*). What time is it?

FELIX. Nine forty-five.

DORIS (*off*). Who was that?

FELIX. Victor—the fellow who owns the bookshop.

(DORIS *appears at the door in her nightgown; she stretches in traditional feline contentment.* FELIX *prepares the coffee pot and takes oranges out of a bag. She goes to* FELIX.)

DORIS. What did you tell him?

FELIX (*pulling away from her*). That I'm fighting off a bug.

DORIS. What are we doing today?

FELIX. I'm doing some research at the library.

DORIS. Let me do that— (*She takes the knife from* FELIX's *hand and cuts the oranges.*) You sore at me?

FELIX. Of course I'm not sore at you.

DORIS. You hate yourself in the morning?

FELIX. No, I don't hate myself. Stop being foolish.

DORIS. I don't know about anybody else, but I'm in love. (*Singing.*) I'm in love with a wonderful guy. (FELIX *has opened the door, taken in a bottle of milk and a newspaper; he folds newspaper open at the classified section.*) Did you hear what I said? Hey, sexy—did you hear me?

FELIX (*running down the columns*). Unfurnished — unfurnished — furnished rooms—

DORIS (*hurt, trying to hide it*). I guess you don't want me to stay here—that's pretty obvious.

FELIX. Don't be ridiculous.

DORIS. Frankly I don't like this place very much. I mean the way you got it fixed. It isn't very inviting.

FELIX. You weren't very invited.

DORIS. I liked you better last night. You're a very changeable fella, you know that?

FELIX (*he finishes the coffee preparation and straightens the room under dialogue.*) Do you always wake up overflowing with unsolicited character analysis?

DORIS (*an explosion of temper*). You watch your language, damn you! Far as I'm concerned you are talking to yourself and frankly I find you very enervating.

FELIX. Let me do that—you get dressed.

DORIS (*pushing him away*). I'm doing it. I'll be dressed and out of here in no time at all—I assure you. (*As* FELIX *goes back to what he was doing, turning his back to her.*) I can't stand people who don't look you in the eye when you're talking to them! (*There's a moment of cold silence as* DORIS *squeezes the oranges and* FELIX *cleans ash trays. Then, her voice trembling.*) I should of slept in the park last night!

FELIX. Have you ever tried letting thirty seconds go by without talking?

DORIS. Have you ever tried dropping dead?

FELIX. What a rare combination of ladylike delicacy and penetrating wit. And to reply to it on its own high intellectual level— (*Strums his lower lip with his forefinger and exits to bathroom.*)

DORIS. Go on—play with yourself. Nobody cares—

FELIX (*off*). You know something—the quality of your conversation makes it hard to tell whether you're talking or vomiting.

DORIS. Now, that's clever. That should go in a story—right after the sun spits in the man's face. (DORIS *finishes one glass of juice, starts the second.*) I fall in love three or four times a week. It doesn't mean a thing. You hear me? You should see some of the stupid jerks I fall in love with! (*There's the sound of the toilet flushing from the bathroom.*) The same to you, Mister! And you're so lousy in bed it's funny!

FELIX (*off*). I didn't hear you laughing.

DORIS. I was just showing common courtesy. I was acting.

FELIX (*off*). I've seen the role played much better.

DORIS. Drop dead!

FELIX (*off*). I've got the perfect name for you— Doris Watercloset.

DORIS. I've got the perfect name for you too—Felix Fruit! I can't wait to get out of here—you make me sick.

FELIX (*off*). The nauseation is mutual.

DORIS. That's your story! (*The juice is finished. She picks up the newspaper and looks at the ads, running her finger down the column; suddenly she stops. The classified ads have thrown her back into the bleak pattern of her days.* FELIX *appears at the bathroom door. He's buttoning his shirt.*)

FELIX. Listen, would you go to see somebody about a job if I gave you a name and an address?

DORIS. I can get along very well without any help from you.

FELIX. That suits me.

DORIS (*mimicking him*). "That suits me." You sound like my goddam brother. What kind of a job?

FELIX. Working on hats?

DORIS. What kind of hats?

FELIX. Women's hats. A customer of mine—Mrs. Lucillian makes hats to order —she has a shop on Columbus—she was in yesterday and mentioned that she needs a girl to help her.

DORIS. I don't know the first thing about hats.

FELIX. You don't have to. I don't think. She shows you what to do. Why don't you go and see her?

DORIS. It sounds like a drag. Working on hats.

FELIX. Forgive me—I forgot you have easier ways of earning money.

DORIS (*rising, livid*). I will not take that from you. I am a model. You get that through your big stupid brain and don't you ever forget it.

FELIX. All I said was—

DORIS. Whatever I might do on the side to stay alive is not what I am.

FELIX (*calmly smug*). I'm afraid it's what you do to pay your rent that classifies you. (FELIX *throws his smug line as*

he goes to the bedroom tucking in his shirt.)

DORIS. All right—then what are you? What does that make you? (FELIX *stops at the bedroom door momentarily.* DORIS *has struck a nerve. He exits to the bedroom. Calling.*) Hey, clerk! Clerk! *Reader's Digest,* please! Hey, boy—which comic book do you recommend?

(*There is a silence from the bedroom.* DORIS *slumps unhappily on the sofa.* FELIX *enters from the bedroom looking grim. He's putting on a coat sweater. Under following dialogue he picks up a yellow legal pad and puts it into a leather envelope.*)

FELIX. You can take your time getting out. I won't be home until four.

DORIS. How could you be as sweet as you were last night and then wake up like such a monster? Would you mind very much telling a poor dumb girl just what happened so she'll know?—Did I say something? I say dopey things sometimes but I don't mean anything by it. (*She follows him as he crosses toward the door right in stony silence.*) You said something so beautiful to me—I bet you don't remember. It was the most beautiful thing anybody ever said to me. And I turned on the light so I could see your face. (*He opens the door, exits. She holds it open, calling after him, angry.*) You looked happy! You looked happy—you fink!

BLACKOUT

ACT TWO

SCENE TWO

Four o'clock that afternoon. Door opens and FELIX *enters, takes off sweater, opens the closet door. Just as he does,* DORIS *pops out. She's determinedly gay.*

———

DORIS. Surprise!

FELIX. What are you doing here?

DORIS. I couldn't find a room.

FELIX. You mean you didn't look for one.

DORIS. Hey—you think that could have anything to do with it? (FELIX *glares at her, goes into the bedroom and returns with the TV set and starts for the door.* DORIS *pushes him. There's a short wres-*

tling match. FELIX *is no match for her. He falls helpless and winded on the sofa.*) The first thing you're gonna do is join a gym. (*As* FELIX *takes his briefcase and starts to pack it.*) Where are you going?

FELIX. If you can't get the vermin out of your house, then you move out and leave the vermin in possession. You have no choice.

DORIS. What's the vermin? Is that me?

FELIX. Vermin—that means crawling insects.

DORIS. I know, but you can't insult me—it's impossible, you know why?

FELIX. Why are you doing this—why don't you get out? What's it going to get you?

DORIS. It's all your fault.

FELIX. All right—but—

DORIS. Oh, I don't mean getting me thrown out of my room. I mean it's your fault I'm in love.

FELIX. You're insane.

DORIS. It's true—you made me love you. (*Sings.*)

> I didn't want to do it—
> I didn't want to do it—

FELIX. What do I have to do to get rid of you? I'll give you ten dollars.

DORIS. Make it fifty million—that's how much it'll cost you to get rid of me—not a penny less. Hey—I thought you were going to move out and leave the vermin in possession—what happened?

FELIX. No. I will not let you put me out of my home.

DORIS. Good for you! I would have lost all respect for you if you left.

FELIX. How long are you planning to stay?

DORIS. How should I know? I'm stuck here. (*Sings.*) I'm just a prisoner of love. Notice I'm singing all the time—I always do that when I'm in love.

FELIX. You're an imbecile.

DORIS. Okay. Fine! See—you can't insult a person who's in love. You can't do anything to them, because they're so light—you can throw them off the roof and they'll float to the ground.

FELIX. Will you stop talking about love? I've never heard such mindless drivel in my life.

DORIS. Listen, I know a lot about love.

FELIX. That thing you fall in and out of three or four times a week is not love. Neither is that thing you sell.

DORIS. Now don't be nasty, honey. This is different. I love you in a very deep quiet way—like a river.

FELIX. Like a river! (*Shouting.*) You mean like a sewer!

DORIS. Now don't get worked up, darling. You tell me what love is. Go ahead, sweetheart—I'm listening. Is it when you get mad and yell at somebody like you're yelling at me?

FELIX (*shouting*). No it is not!

DORIS. You better calm down . . .

FELIX (*fighting for self-control*). You upset me. I admit it. You're an animal. You're so foreign to anything that's important to me. Don't you understand? You personify what I hate.

DORIS. You didn't hate it last night.

FELIX. That's what disgusts me. All my life I fought that animal taint. It's like finding a fungus you loathe growing on your own skin!

DORIS (*shaken badly*). Oh, that's a disgusting thing to call somebody—"fungus"!

FELIX. I didn't call you that.

DORIS. Sure—I'm some slimy moldy fungus, right?

FELIX. I didn't say that.

DORIS. Oh yes, you did say that!

FELIX. All right, I said it! I mean it! Now will you get out—will you go?

DORIS. I never met anybody in my life that made me feel so cheap and dirty.

FELIX. Then get out of here.

DORIS. I don't understand why I love you.

FELIX. Get out! I hate you!

DORIS. Not as much as I hate you!

FELIX. Then get out! Get out!

DORIS. No! I'm gonna stay here and hate you right to your face!

FELIX. All right, then I'm going.

DORIS. Fine. Great. Go on.

FELIX. It's the only way.

DORIS. Well, go on—get out.

FELIX. What do you mean, "Get out"? This is my home. I live here. Don't you tell me to get out.

DORIS. Well, I'm not getting out. You can try to throw me out if you want to.

FELIX. I wouldn't dirty my hands.

DORIS. I wouldn't want your slimy hands on me.

FELIX. I ought to turn you over to the police.

DORIS. Fine. Why don't you?

FELIX. That's what I should do.

DORIS. Go ahead. Call them.

FELIX. That's what I'll do. That's just what I'll do!

DORIS. Go ahead.

FELIX. That's just exactly what I'm going to do!

DORIS. All right. Fine. You do that.

FELIX. You bet I will. You can just bet on it!

DORIS. You call the police. You do that. It's fine with me.

FELIX. Don't you for a moment think I won't!

DORIS. Oh, you'd do it!

FELIX. You bet I would. And that's just what I'm going to do.

DORIS. Fine. You turn me in. You do that. You're the man to do it.

FELIX. I most certainly am, and that's what I'm going to do!

BLACKOUT

ACT TWO

SCENE THREE

FELIX (*on telephone; the stage is in darkness*). Nothing serious, Victor. No—I'm a little tired. I had a very bad time last night. No—I hate to take them, they're enervating. Thank you, but I'll be fine by twelve or so. I'll come in then.

(LIGHTS *come up slowly. Morning light through the window.* DORIS *stands near* FELIX *peering at him through the binoculars.*)

———

DORIS. Ooh, look at the big man. (*He ignores her.*) Don't you love me? Oh, that's right—only in the bedroom. I forgot—it depends on what room we're in. Let's take a shower together. I want to find out how you feel about me in the bathroom.

FELIX. Doris—I'm not coming back to this apartment tonight. I mean it.

DORIS. Honey—what are you fighting? Why don't you take it easy? (*She tries to embrace him. He pushes her off, knocking the orange out of her hand.* DORIS *laughs, picks up the orange.*) You better bring some more oranges. We're running out.

FELIX. I won't be coming back. Did you hear me?

DORIS (*humoring a child*). Sure. You'll be back after work to pack your things, though? (*Silence from* FELIX.) Would you like me to pack for you and have it ready?

FELIX. Shut up.

DORIS. I could put it all outside the door so you wouldn't even have to come inside.

FELIX. Your humor is like you are—crude and clumsy.

DORIS (*going to him—tenderly*). Baby—why don't you stop—?

FELIX. If you call me "baby" once more, I'll— (*Looks around desperately.*) I'll smash your television set.

DORIS (*goes to him, feels his head*). I think you've got a fever.

FELIX (*looking to heaven*). Oh God! Are you listening—are you laughing? She says I've got a fever.

DORIS. You're not going to work today—you're getting right back into bed.

FELIX (*to heaven*). Do you hear? The tower of my mind is crashing down—wrecked by a termite—and now the termite is putting me to bed! God—do something!

(*She's pushing and pulling him to the sofa.*)

DORIS. Don't talk to God that way. He'll strike you dead.

FELIX. Oh no! Not while He's having so much fun with me!

(*She pushes him down on the sofa—feels his head again.*)

DORIS. Does it hurt any place?

FELIX. Listen—I'm going to beg you—please—go away—please leave me alone.

DORIS (*feeling his throat*). Does this hurt?

FELIX. You're grinding your heel in my raw soul. That is what hurts.

DORIS. Wow! That's good! You ought to use that in a story.

FELIX (*weakly*). You must go away. Why won't you go away? Tell me why!

DORIS. Because, sweetheart—I can make you happy—I do make you happy—if you'll only let me—

FELIX. No—no—you make me miserable.

DORIS. But, baby . . .

FELIX. "Baby," you make happy, yes—but "Felix" you make miserable, and that's me—Felix—I am Felix. Will you listen to me? I am not "Baby." I don't want to be "Baby."

DORIS. I wish you'd go to bed. Do you have a thermometer?

FELIX. It's a nightmare—I'm caught in a fog—I'm screaming! But I can't make a sound!

DORIS. Lie down on the sofa.

FELIX (*limp, he flops down on the sofa*). What's the use?

DORIS. That's my boy.

FELIX. Yes. That's your boy. I confess. Felix unmasked. Felix captured and brought to justice—"Baby—honey—sweetheart" alias "Felix."

DORIS. Now just relax. (*She feels his forehead again.*) Does it hurt any place?

FELIX. No. All the nerves have died.

DORIS. Now be serious. Is your throat sore? Do you have a headache? Should I call the doctor?

FELIX. That's ridiculous! The disease never calls the doctor.

DORIS. Now don't say nasty things! Be nice.

FELIX (*rising hysteria*). Nice? You're absolutely right! Now that I have come to live in Niceville I must do as the nice people do—I must be nice. "Baby sweetheart" must be nice.

DORIS (*beginning to be afraid*). You're absolutely crazy. I never heard such crazy talk in my life.

FELIX. You're right again. Baby must not speak the language of Felix. Felix the mind is dead. Long live Baby!

DORIS. Please stop it.

FELIX. Call me "Baby"—say "please stop it, Baby"—go on.

DORIS. I don't want to.

FELIX. Why not? That's who I am—I'm Baby.

DORIS. Please, honey, you're scaring me.

FELIX. Yes—yes—sorry—that's because I'm not talking Baby's language. How's this? (*Tough.*) What do you say we feed the face, Sweetie, and then we can hop into the sack and knock off a quickie. Let's ball. Let's get down in the slime and roll around in it. Let's have a little poontang. Let's hump. (*As* DORIS *withdraws from him.*) That's it, hump, hump, hump.

DORIS (*completely depressed by now*). All right—all right, you win.

FELIX. I win? What do I win?

DORIS. I'm going. (*She exits to bedroom; then, from offstage.*) I'll come back later to get my things. When you're not here.

FELIX (*calls*). Are you really going, Baby?

DORIS. That's what you want, isn't it?

FELIX. It's not my first choice. My first choice is for you never to have come. Could I have that?

DORIS. You sure fooled me. I thought I had you figured.

FELIX. You did—I'm the one I had fooled.

DORIS (*she opens the door*). I'll call you tonight when I get set and let you know where I am.

FELIX. Don't call.

DORIS. Don't be such a baby. You can always hang up on me if you don't want to talk to me.

FELIX. I won't be here.

DORIS. You better take care of yourself or you're gonna be sick. You hear me?

FELIX (*wryly*). I'll take an aspirin.

DORIS. Good idea—no—there's some fizz powder on the dresser. It gets into the bloodstream seconds faster than aspirin.

FELIX. I grew up with aspirin. I refuse to believe there's a short-cut aspirin doesn't know about.

DORIS. Just the same—take that powder. And I'll call you tonight.

FELIX (*shouting as* DORIS *exits*). I won't be here! (*Alone now,* FELIX *sits for a moment staring at the floor. He puts his hands to his face in a stab of panic. He rises and paces rapidly. He goes to the window. His eyes fall on the binoculars. He picks them up, turns them over, carries them to the stage left platform and lays them on the corner. He goes to the sink and opens the drawer. Takes out a hammer and goes to them. He kneels and systematically pounds the binoculars to pieces as:*)

CURTAIN FALLS

ACT TWO

SCENE FOUR

Two A.M. *the following morning. The room is dark. We hear* FELIX's *footsteps and his key in the lock. The door opens and he enters. Turns on the light. His eyes go first to the bedroom door. Then to the floor where Doris's television set still occupies its spot.*

FELIX (*addressing the bedroom door as he crosses to it*). I see you couldn't find a room again. I should have known you were lying. What made me think you'd keep your word? You don't know how to— (*He has exited to bedroom on the last words. There's a pause. From offstage.*) Doris! Doris—? (FELIX *comes slowly out of the bedroom. He goes to the closet door, opens it, looks inside; then opens the bathroom door and looks inside; closes the door.* DORIS *has gone. He goes to the sofa, sits, looking at the TV set. The phone rings. He reaches for it, pulls back; he rises and lights a cigarette nervously as the phone continues to ring. It's a slow patient ring with all the time in the world. Finally* FELIX *picks it up with an impulsive swoop. Angry; into phone.*) Hello— Oh—nothing, Victor—I just got home.—I went to a movie. . . . Angry?—Why should I get angry at a telephone? Helpless tool of a monopoly? What? . . . Oh—when did she call? What was the number? 4–6792. (*He writes it down. Then to* VICTOR.) Good night. (*Hangs up. He paces, miserable. He stops at the phone, picks it up, picks up the phone number, puts it down. Picks it up again and dials; waits. He hears* DORIS *say "Hello" and he panics.*) Wrong number. (*He slams the receiver down and paces, raging at himself. Stops at the phone. Picks it up again, dials, waits, and panics once more.*) Wrong number! (*Slams down the receiver. He's so angry with himself he slaps his face hard enough to stagger himself. Then gathers all his courage. Deliberately and resolutely picks up the phone and dials.*) Hello, Doris? . . . Felix. I hope I didn't wake you. . . . No! Wrong numbers, huh? . . . That's a shame. I guess at this hour of the morning there's an awful lot of drunk dialing. Drunk dialing! You know, like drunk driving—it's a joke. I know there's nothing funny about drunk driving. That isn't what I meant—Oh, forget it. Well I just got home. You left your television set . . . Oh . . . Tell him to come after three . . . How do you like your room? That's a shame! Well, don't let it depress you— you'll be on your feet again in no time . . . No, it was not a crack! You mustn't be so damn sensitive . . . All right, all right. Listen I've been doing a lot of thinking and I wanted to talk to you. . . . Not on the phone . . . Well, I've been think-

ing and I realized that we got off on the wrong foot, you and I, and it was silly and I think we can be friends and I think our relationship must be re-established on a different basis . . . No. They just sound big over the phone. Look, I thought if you weren't doing anything right now . . . (*He gets a disappointing response to this.*) Oh . . . yes—well how about having lunch with me? . . . Oh . . . well what are you doing for—? . . . I see. Yes . . . Yes . . . That won't give us much time . . . Yes. All right, I'll look for you around six . . . I hope you don't . . . Doris? . . . Hello . . . Doris? (*Doris has hung up.* FELIX *replaces the receiver. He sighs deeply. Looks around the room. He crosses right, turns on the table lamp. Crosses down to straighten out the coffee table, sits on the couch. Takes radio off the coffee table and places it on the floor. As the radio touches the floor it bursts into sound: a rock and roll recording from an all-night disc jockey. And as the music drones on,* FELIX *lies on the sofa on his side, wide-eyed and sleepless.*)

BLACKOUT

ACT TWO

SCENE FIVE

Six P.M. that day. The room is empty. The front door is ajar. There's a knock and DORIS *sticks her head through.*

DORIS. Anybody home?
FELIX (*in bathroom*). Is it still raining?
DORIS (*still at door*). No, it stopped.
FELIX (*off*). Paper said it would rain all night.
DORIS. Yeah.
FELIX (*off*). I guess the rain doesn't read the paper. There's some Scotch on the table.
DORIS. Where'd you get this?
FELIX (*off*). Bought it.
DORIS. How come?
FELIX (*off*). Not enough nerve to steal it, I suppose. Take your coat off. (*He enters from bedroom. His hair slicked for the occasion.*) I like your dress.
DORIS. The color's good, but it flattens me out a little in the bust. You don't look so good.

FELIX. I had a hard day. Listen—I wanted to talk to you, Doris. It's a little embarrassing—I wanted to apologize for my emotional behavior yesterday morning.

DORIS. Forget it. It was my fault—I guess I needled you.

FELIX. No. The lance is not the cause of the infection it exposes. The fact that—

DORIS (*stopping him*). Wait a minute— (*Thinks for a second—then triumphantly.*) You know, I understand that!

FELIX. Of course—naturally. Doris, you're a bright girl. Remember I told you that soon after we met?

DORIS. Yes, you did. You said I wasn't dumb.

FELIX. And that's exactly what I want to talk to you about. After you left I used some good solid logic. It saved my life.

DORIS. That sounds good.

FELIX. Well, the fact is, I have lived almost thirty years as a logical man. My religion was the reason. The mind. It's the only thing I believe in. And it has given me a lonely life.

DORIS. I thought you were older than thirty.

FELIX. I'll be thirty in October. Fact number two—I felt a very powerful attraction to a girl—you—very powerful, all right—put the facts through the logic—there's only one answer—I had to be attracted by one thing in you.

DORIS. Well, listen—

FELIX. Your mind!

DORIS. You're kidding.

FELIX. Doesn't it sound logical?

DORIS. It may be logical, but it doesn't make sense.

FELIX. I realized suddenly that I'm not attracted to you at all as an animal. Don't you see—I couldn't be. It's your trapped intelligence calling out for help that drew me so strongly.

DORIS. You're all excited and happy. Gee, I'm glad. You were in such bad shape yesterday, you had me scared.

FELIX. That was insane grief. Premature grief for Felix the mind. I was very rough on you. I feel like dying when I think of the things I said to you. Can you forgive me? Can we be friends—non-physical friends, of course?

DORIS. Non-physical?

FELIX. I'm going to save you, Doris.

DORIS. May I ask from what?

FELIX. From circumstances that have kept you from using your mind. You're in a jungle. I'm going to cut through all that rotting growth and rescue you.

DORIS. I feel like Sleeping Beauty with that forest around her.

FELIX. Yes—yes—that's wonderful! The sleeping beauty of the mind.

DORIS. Wonderful?

FELIX. Without training—your unhindered natural imagination reaches for metaphor—oh, Doris—do you know how exciting that is to a man of intellect?

DORIS. What's "metaphor"?

FELIX. Metaphor is—no—there— (*Points to the dictionary.*) Look it up for yourself. Go—discover a word! M-e-t-a-p-h-o-r.

DORIS. Not me—I hate dictionaries.

FELIX. Why? You like words.

DORIS. Yeah, but in the dictionary they're so, I don't know—dead.

FELIX. Dead—oh, my God, of course! Laid out—dissected—by the cataloguing mind! A mortuary of words—Doris, that's wonderful!

DORIS. You mean I did it again? I can't tell you how surprised I am.

FELIX. I felt it in you—I sensed it, didn't I?

DORIS. Yes, you did—you said something about it.

FELIX. I know—I know.

DORIS (*catching the artificial excitement*). It was very smart of you to notice —most people don't notice—I never noticed! Gosh, think of all the smart things I must of said without realizing!

FELIX. Yes—a flower born to blush unseen—wasting your sweetness on the desert air.

DORIS. That's like poetry.

FELIX. It is poetry. Famous poetry.

DORIS. Hey—I spotted it, didn't I?

(*As* DORIS *starts to sparkle with excitement,* FELIX *is aroused.*)

FELIX. Of course you spotted it. Like a thirsty root spots water—

DORIS. Did I ever tell you about the essay I wrote in school?

FELIX. I'd love to read it.

DORIS. I lost it.

FELIX. That's all right—you'll write others.

DORIS. You think so?

FELIX. Why not? Why not?

DORIS. I used to think I had a brain. But people keep calling you stupid, you know—year after year.

FELIX. Stupid people.

DORIS. My goddam brother. From morning to night—"stupid-stupid-stupid." Well, after a while you figure where there's smoke there's fire—you know?

FELIX. Of course. A sensitive nature like yours is no match for a bully.

DORIS. Sensitive! Boy, you put your finger on it! How did you know I was sensitive?

FELIX. You had to be—that's the price of a thinking mind—sensitivity.

DORIS. It is?

FELIX. Yes.

DORIS. Well, I'm sure sensitive, all right. I cry at the drop of a hat. Well, you saw the way I carried on here yesterday—

FELIX. Yes.

DORIS. Over nothing at all. Did you ever see sensitive like that?

FELIX. I should have known. I should have realized why I was drawn to you.

DORIS. I was always ashamed of myself for crying so much. That means you're smart, huh?

FELIX. It means—that's right—it means you're smart.

DORIS. I always thought I was such a dope—crying over nothing.

FELIX. Dopes don't cry. They have no pride. Dopes are not vulnerable.

DORIS. Pride—I got a lot of that.

FELIX. Of course you have.

DORIS. My brother always said to me that I had too much pride.

FELIX. Is that the "goddam" brother?

DORIS. No—the older one.

FELIX. Well, you can't have too much pride. Pride constructs dignity and lives in it.

DORIS. "Pride constructs dignity and lives in it"? Poetry—right?

FELIX. It's from an essay of mine.

DORIS. Oh. Well, it sounds like poetry.

FELIX. Thank you.

DORIS. I'll bet you're a wonderful writer.

FELIX. You didn't care for my short story. Remember?

DORIS. When? Oh—the sun spitting in the guy's face—well, I was mad at you —I was just getting back at you.

FELIX. Well, it doesn't matter.

DORIS. It grows on you. I can see it, you know—

FELIX. What's that?

DORIS (acting out the rising sun). The sun—like a big face. It looks up real slow over the edge of the world and it goes— pttt. (She makes a soft spitting sound with her lips.)

FELIX. That's very imaginative of you.

DORIS. Well, it's just good writing, that's all—it makes you see it.

FELIX. Thank you.

DORIS. Gee, I'm so excited! I'm shivering—look at me.

FELIX. Would you like a drink?

DORIS. I got one.

FELIX (putting his arm around her). Are you cold?

DORIS. No—I don't know what it is— excitement, I guess.

FELIX. I know what it is. It's the first shock of childbirth.

DORIS. Bite your tongue!

FELIX (fondles and nuzzles her). No—I mean you're being born. You—

DORIS. Yeah—I see what you mean—I'm being born—you know what I'm doing? I'm entering into a new world. (He kisses her on the cheek.) You didn't hear what I said—

FELIX. What?

DORIS. I'm entering into a new world.

FELIX. I heard you. It's true, welcome to the world of the intellect. (He kisses her on the neck.)

DORIS. I'm beginning to talk like you a little—did you notice—? Hey—what are you doing? I wanna talk.

FELIX (continuing to make love to her). I want to hear you talk, don't stop.

DORIS. Felix—cut that out—

FELIX. Talk—I'm listening.

DORIS. We're intellectuals—we're non-physicals, remember?

FELIX. This isn't physical. That's what makes it so exciting—don't you see?

DORIS. I don't think so.

FELIX. That's what draws us together— not the attraction of bodies, but the excitement of two live—healthy—exuberant minds—calling hungrily to one another!

DORIS. Oh.

FELIX. It's an irresistible intellectual attraction. (He throws himself at her hungrily.)

DORIS. Is that what this is—intellectual?

FELIX. Of course.

DORIS. It's our minds?

FELIX (in a frenzy of self-delusion). Yes —yes.

DORIS (*starting to respond*). It's not the usual thing?

FELIX. No—no—of course not—

DORIS. You know something—it's every bit as good!

ACT TWO

SCENE SIX

Three weeks later. Nobody home. The TV set is back. We hear running footsteps up the stairs. The door is opened with a key and DORIS *bursts into the room. She's carrying an expensive portable radio. She shoves the radio under the coffee table, pulls off her sweater, throws it onto a chair, snatches up a book. We hear* FELIX's *footsteps on the stairs outside as* DORIS *falls onto the sofa and becomes absorbed in the book.* FELIX *opens the door with his key and enters.*

——

DORIS. Hi, sweetie.

FELIX (*very quiet. He's holding down the lid on boiling indignation*). Hello.

DORIS. Hey, what's this? We've only been living in sin for three weeks and already you don't kiss me "hello" any more?

FELIX. I had a hard day. Have you been out?

DORIS. Only for lunch. Hey, you wanna check the breakfast dishes? I'll give you a half a buck you find any dirt or any dried soap this time!

FELIX. Later. I saw somebody enter the building as I got off the bus. I thought it was you.

DORIS. Must have been the girl downstairs. You hungry, sweetie?

FELIX. No, I've got a headache. (*Looking at her book.*) Still on chapter two?

DORIS. I had an awful lot of words to look up.

FELIX (*going to the dictionary, looks at it*). It wasn't the girl downstairs.

DORIS. Who? Oh—you want something for your headache?

FELIX. No, thank you. I'm enjoying it.

DORIS. Honest—some of the things you say sometimes.

FELIX. Have you been working with your word for the day?

DORIS. Oh—"impeccable"—sure—(*Sneaking a look at her pad.*) "Impeccable without a fault—incapable of doing wrong." Now, used in a sentence—let's see. (*Looking around.*) Oh—when the typewriter got back from the repair shop, it was impeccable.

FELIX. No—that's wrong.

DORIS. Why?

FELIX. In three weeks I don't think you've assimilated two new words.

DORIS. Oh, come on—sure I have. Hey what's the matter with you tonight?

FELIX. Have you been to the dictionary today?

DORIS. Sure—I told you.

FELIX. Yes— (*He's been taking off his tie. He sees the radio under the coffee table. He stands up.*) Where'd you get the radio.

DORIS. Oh—I picked it up at the junk shop—three bucks.

FELIX (*going to bedroom*). Good.

DORIS. I don't even know if it works.

FELIX (*exits to bedroom*). It looks brand new to me.

DORIS (*drags the set out, dumps the ashtray on it, rubs in the ashes, spits, scratches it with the ashtray as she talks*). It's practically an antique—made in the year one. I think I got taken but I needed a radio for out here. You have to play that one in the bed so loud if you wanna hear it out here and my other one keeps conking out—so I figured—what the hell—I'd take a chance—sometimes these old beat-up sets play as good as a new one.

(*She abruptly drops the aging process as* FELIX *comes out of the bedroom. He has taken off his coat.*)

FELIX. How many times did you say you used the dictionary today?

DORIS. I don't know. What's wrong, honey?

FELIX. Please go over to the dictionary and look at it closely.

DORIS (DORIS *goes and looks at the dictionary*). What am I supposed to see?

FELIX. Look at the edges—at the top—

DORIS. What's this? (*Peeling off a strip of Scotch tape.*)

FELIX. That is a strip of Scotch tape. It's been there for two days. Undisturbed. Where were you this afternoon?

DORIS. That's such a nasty thing to do.

FELIX. Where were you yesterday afternoon?

DORIS. I do not care for the tone of your voice.

FELIX. Where did you get the dirty but brand-new radio?

DORIS. I'm warning you—stop it—this warning will not be repeated.

FELIX. We're not going to fight. We're going to have an honest unemotional discussion.

DORIS. Yeah? So you start out by calling me a liar.

FELIX. I did not call you a liar. I'm not going to lose my temper.

DORIS. You might as well. I'm gonna lose mine!

FELIX. Would you care to tell me what's wrong?

DORIS. What's wrong? You're a creep that puts Scotch tape on the dictionary—you know that word—"creep"? Used in a sentence: "Fred Sherman is a big creep."

FELIX (*starting at "Fred"*). What did you call me?

DORIS. It's your name. Fred—Freddie—I thought that would jar your apricots! I found your yearbook from school—Fred Sherman. You didn't tell me you changed your name, did you? You creep. I'm sorry—pardon my language, but you are a creep.

FELIX. It's all right—it's a step up from "fink." Congratulations—now—I'd like to hear why you feel you have to sneak out afternoons and lie to me.

DORIS. I just got bored. I had to get out. Look—I tried working on hats. I tried looking for a job, right? I tried.

FELIX. Have you been plying your old trade?

DORIS. Have I been what? No, I haven't. I told you I was through doing that.

FELIX. Where'd you get the radio?

DORIS. I collected some money. Somebody owed me some money and they paid me.

FELIX. I see. Why didn't you tell me that?

DORIS. Because I knew you wouldn't believe it. I knew what you'd think.

FELIX. I see.

DORIS. Don't say "I see," like you were looking through your lousy spyglasses. Listen—why don't you stop trying to make out like you're a human being? I mean the strain must be terrible—why don't you just relax and admit you're God and you know all about everything?

FELIX. Why did you have to lie? I just want to know why you lied to me about going out and about looking up words.

DORIS. Because I'm a liar, okay?

FELIX. Why didn't you tell me?

DORIS. Why didn't you tell me you changed your name from "Fred" to "Felix"?

FELIX (*ignoring her question*). I'm very sad. You had a chance to do something important for yourself and you're quitting. You're not giving yourself a chance.

DORIS. I gave myself a chance—you had me going there for a while, but it's silly. I'm a dope and that's all there is to it.

FELIX. You're not a dope. You're a bright girl.

DORIS. Not when it comes to dictionaries and the history of philosophy, I'm not. (*Indicates the book she was reading.*)

FELIX. You have a potential capacity for—

DORIS (*interrupting*). No, I don't have any potential anything.

FELIX (*losing the fight against his temper*). Don't interrupt me—who do you think is better qualified to judge mental capacity—you or I?

DORIS. You—

FELIX. Then why are you arguing with me?

DORIS. Felix, I—

FELIX. Would I be wasting my time with you if you didn't have a brain?

DORIS. Felix—

FELIX. Do you think an intellectual such as myself would waste his time with a dumbbell?

DORIS. Felix, I know myself—you can't tell me—

FELIX. I tell you you're a very intelligent girl, and you'd know it yourself if you weren't so damned stupid!

DORIS. I am not stupid! I've got good healthy everyday brains. I haven't got your kind of brains and I'm glad, because I'm gonna tell you something—I think your brains are rotten!

FELIX. Ah—the cat turns inevitably and bares her atavistic fangs.

DORIS. To use those ugly, lonely words nobody else uses—that's all your brains are good for. To keep people away because you're scared to death of people!

FELIX. She spits in inarticulate fury.

DORIS. You know what your brains are good for? To make up your own lousy little language that the rest of the world can't even understand.

FELIX. Well, all right—stay with the rest of the world—don't let anybody make you a foreigner there by teaching you to speak the English language!

DORIS (*going to closet*). What a dope I was to listen to you. (*Mimicking him.*) I'm gonna save you, Doris! (*In her own voice.*) You are such a phony, I can't believe it. You don't write for money but you keep sending your junk to magazines, don't you? And you keep getting it sent back, don't you? Meanwhile all you got is a phony job, a phony girl friend, a phony apartment and a phony bunch of words! (*She has taken the suitcase from the closet and started to throw garments into it as she talks.*)

FELIX. What are you doing?

DORIS. What does it look like I'm doing?

FELIX (*quietly*). Now don't get washed away. Think, Doris. Try to understand one basic thing. Try to hold on to what I see in you.

DORIS (*yelling*). You see nothing! You don't see me at all! You don't see anything. Because even your eyes are phony! (KNOCK *on the wall.* DORIS *addresses the wall; yelling.*) I'll be through in a minute! (*To* FELIX.) You know what you see in me? You never had a girl that made you feel like a big man in bed—that's all.

FELIX. Doris—

DORIS (*interrupting*). Well, I want to tell you something about what a hot stud you think you are in the sack—

FELIX. Don't say it, Doris—

DORIS. You leave me cold, Fred. You're nothing at all.

FELIX. You're raising your voice.

DORIS. You do nothing to me, Freddie —you only think you do. You know why?

FELIX. I know—you're a great actress and to you that bed is theatre in the round —I know all about it—well, now I'm going to tell you something—I don't *leave* you cold—I *find* you cold—"frigid"—is that word in your meager stock?

DORIS. Drop dead.

FELIX. Sure you're an actress in bed— because you can't be a woman.

DORIS. With a man I can, Fred—Freddie, it takes a man.

FELIX. Sometimes. Even with fantasies, and dirty words and the guilty stink of the sewer you can only sometimes whip

yourself into a parody of passion—sometimes! Isn't that right?

DORIS. Stop yelling. Nobody's listening to you. (*She's closing the suitcase.*)

FELIX. All right. You're lost. Goodbye. I tried.

DORIS. Now try shutting up. I'll send for the TV. I'll send a man! (*Takes a good look at him.*)

FELIX (*follows her to the door*). No matter where you go or what you do or what you call yourself—you are now and forever a whore named Doris Wilgus.

DORIS. Okay. And what are you now and forever? A miserable magazine peddler named Freddie Sherman and a lousy writer and you always will be and you wanna know why—? (*Hitting him deliberately with every word.*) Because, God damn it! The—sun—does—not—spit!

BLACKOUT

ACT THREE

One week later. Afternoon. FELIX *is asleep on the couch, face down, all his clothing on; the bottle of Scotch is on the floor, all gone but for an inch or so.* FELIX *stirs and awakens painfully. He takes four or five oranges from a drawer and cuts one in half, cuts his finger, drops the knife, looks at the cut, puts the finger in his mouth and crosses to the bathroom. Just after he exits to the bathroom, there's a knock at the door.*

FELIX. Come in. (*There's a key in the lock and the door opens and* DORIS *enters. She comes into the room as* FELIX *enters from the bathroom, his finger in his mouth, holding a Band-Aid in his other hand. They look at each other for a frozen instant.*) I cut myself.

DORIS (*reaching for the Band-Aid*). Let me open that.

FELIX (*handing it to her*). Thank you.

DORIS. How'd you do it?

FELIX. Cutting oranges.

(*In this exchange,* DORIS's *eyes are lowered to the cut finger.* FELIX *looks at her face.*)

DORIS. Orange juice at five o'clock in the afternoon?

FELIX. I was thinking of having shredded wheat for dinner.

DORIS (*putting the Band-Aid on the cut*). Did you put anything on it?

FELIX. No. It's a medicated Band-Aid.

DORIS. Do you have a lot of confidence in medicated Band-Aids? I don't. This friend of mine got an infection from a Band-Aid once.

FELIX. I'm very fatalistic about those things.

DORIS. Oh.

FELIX. I figure a Band-Aid's either got your name on it or it hasn't.

DORIS. You're probably right. I'm a terrible worrier.

FELIX. No, you're right. It's better to be safe than sorry.

DORIS. Yes, but it's no good to live in fear. You can get killed crossing the street.

FELIX. Fools rush in where angels fear to tread.

DORIS. I beg your pardon—I don't follow that.

FELIX. I didn't follow it either.

DORIS. Let me make your orange juice for you.

FELIX. No—don't—don't bother—

DORIS (*starts to make juice*). I got time —I found this key to the apartment. I was in the neighborhood and I thought you might be needing an extra key.

FELIX. I've been getting by with the one. How's Allen?

DORIS. Allen?

FELIX. That nice-looking fellow who picked up your television set.

DORIS. Oh, "Aaron"—you said "Allen." He's all right. He's married to my friend Barbara.

FELIX. Oh, nice chap.

DORIS. Yes—how's Anne? Back from New York yet?

FELIX. Yes. She's fine—I guess. I haven't seen her.

DORIS. By the way, do you like this suit? (*She turns away from the squeezer to show it.*)

FELIX. Very much. Is it new?

DORIS. Yes— I found this little shop on Philbert. It's real small but they have impeccable taste. (*A side glance to see the effect of "impeccable" on* FELIX.)

FELIX. That's very good.

DORIS. You notice I've assimilated "impeccable."

FELIX. Very good.

DORIS. I had to get some clothes for my new job. I'm a receptionist.

FELIX. Oh—good.

DORIS. It's a place called Ganshaver Brothers. Custom wallpaper. It's supposed to be for decorators only, but anybody can get in really.

FELIX. It sounds fine.

DORIS. And of course it gives me plenty of time for my reading. By the way, have you read *Oliver Twist* by Charles Dickens?

FELIX. Yes.

DORIS. He writes somewhat on the style of Somerset Maugham, don't you think?

FELIX. I think he steals from him.

DORIS. Yes, I think so, too. And, oh yes, I met this photographer who's taking pictures of me—you know for the model agencies. He's only charging me for his materials and labor and he really digs me —he's doing a layout—six different expressions—he wants to put it in a folder and call it "Doris Wheeler—Girl of a Thousand Moods." (*Pouring the juice from the squeezer.*) What do you think of "Wheeler"?

FELIX. I like it.

(*There's more juice than the glass will hold;* DORIS *takes another glass and pours the small surplus into it. She hands the full glass to* FELIX. *All this under dialogue.*)

DORIS. And what's new with you? How's your writing?

FELIX. It's legible.

DORIS. Oh, good—I guess— (*Sipping her juice.*) Boy, you're right about fresh orange juice. It has an impeccable taste.

(DORIS *looks at* FELIX *over the edge of the glass; she covers her nervousness by sipping the juice.* FELIX *looks at her steadily for a moment. She smiles a nervous hopeful confused little smile.*)

FELIX. Why did you come back?

DORIS. I've assimilated three new words —"intricate"—"belligerent" and "embellish"— You wanna hear me use them in a sentence?

FELIX. No.

DORIS. It's not hard. You were right. I wasn't giving myself a chance. (*She has gone to the table; picks up a manuscript with a letter attached.*) Oh, you finally got your story back from that big shot. With a letter and everything. (*She reads the letter.*)

FELIX. Doris—why did you come back?

DORIS. What does he mean, "counterfeit emotions and artificial images"?

FELIX. He means the sun doesn't spit.

DORIS (*reading*). He's sorry! (*Throws down the manuscript.*) Who the hell does he think he is!?

FELIX. Doris, why did you come back?

DORIS (*looking away from him*). I never had anybody like you in love with me before. I'll never find anybody like you again.

FELIX. You mean somebody who'll try to change you and then say rotten things to you because he can't change you?

DORIS. Oh, I don't care about that—I think you're a talented sweet wonderful man.

FELIX. You are disgusting, do you know that?

DORIS. Don't be mean to me—please.

FELIX. Why not? That's what you came for. Don't you know you came back for that?

DORIS. No, I didn't—

FELIX. Of course you did—why else but to be insulted? "Sweet wonderful man" she calls me! Have you forgotten the things we said to each other? Didn't any of it register on your thirty-nine-cent-plastic-made-in-Japan brain?

DORIS. Why can't we be nice to one another? We could if we tried.

FELIX. Oh God, listen to her! Don't you know that you're a criminal and an animal—how can I be nice to you?

DORIS. But you care for me. I know you care for me.

FELIX (*shouting*). That's what I'm talking about. I care for you!

DORIS. You see—you said it! You said you care for me.

FELIX. And you're so pleased by the words that choke me!

DORIS. Felix, please don't talk that way. You love me and I love you. You can't control those things. It's not your fault.

FELIX. No. Nature finds your level for you. You're right. I'm just shocked to see my level—excuse me.

DORIS. I know I'm nothing compared to you. I know that. But that doesn't mean you're like me just because you love me.

FELIX. It doesn't? Are you sure it doesn't? Doesn't your instinct tell you I'm your equal—the mate for you? Of course it tells you that!

DORIS. Oh, Baby— Not my equal. I'm nothing compared to you.

FELIX. Nothings can only be loved by other nothings. It's axiomatic.

DORIS. Don't say that. Maybe it isn't love — You could just be sorry for me—or maybe you love me the way you love a pet.

FELIX. There's a thought!

DORIS. Why not? A pet doesn't have any brains—you don't have anything in common with it—but you love it, don't you?

FELIX. Is that what you want to be—my pet?

DORIS. Now don't start twisting everything.

FELIX. No, no, that sounds good—you could be my pet whore.

DORIS. Felix . . .

FELIX. Would you sleep in a box in the corner? Would you wear a collar? Would you run around the neighborhood nights? Yes, you probably would. Well, I could have you spayed, couldn't I? (*DORIS sits looking at him helplessly.*) Well?

DORIS. Well, what?

FELIX. I don't feel any reaction from you, how about it?

DORIS. Don't do that, Felix.

FELIX. It was your idea. Don't you even want to give it a chance? You could do it. I think you could. You're already house-broken. I'm sure you could learn a few simple tricks. Going to the market, cleaning the apartment. Give it a try. What have you got to lose? Doris . . . try it. (*Calling a dog.*) Here Doris, here girl. (*Whistles.*) Come on Doris, come on, good girl, Doris—pretty Doris. (*DORIS starts to cry quietly.*) Damn it, I'm serious about this, you stupid bitch. Don't stand there like a human being!

DORIS. I don't understand what you want me to do. If you could explain it to me, I know I'd feel better.

FELIX. I want you to be a nice girl and give me your paw. Come on, give Daddy your paw.

DORIS. Don't forget—I assimilated "impeccable."

FELIX. If you don't give me your paw I'm going to give you away. Now give me your paw—come on.

DORIS. You're scaring me. Why do you want to do that?

FELIX. Do you want me to give you away? Well, do you? Answer me! Do you want me to give you to some poor family who'll beat you? Answer me— (*She shakes her head.*) Is that so hard to do?—is that such a difficult trick for a full-grown dog? Answer me! Can't you tell me—is it hard to do? (DORIS *shakes her head*.) Well, then, why won't you do it?

DORIS. If I do will you stop acting like this?

FELIX. We make no deals with pets here! Give me your paw, God damn it. (DORIS *looks at him in helpless surrender. Slowly she raises her right hand and puts it into* FELIX's *hand. He looks at her for a moment then he melts. He bends and kisses her hand*.) I'm sorry—I'm so sorry, Doris. Doris, please forgive me.

DORIS. It's okay. I just get a little scared, that's all. It's okay. I'd get used to it. Listen, Felix—you'd never have to even talk to me. If you felt like going out you could just get up and walk out without even saying goodbye. I wouldn't even say anything— Like if you said to me when we got up—"Doris, no talking today," I wouldn't even open my mouth. (*She stops.* FELIX *looks at her*.) Felix—

FELIX. You're very sweet.

DORIS. And another thing—

FELIX. Wait— Let me think for a moment.

DORIS. It's about that thinking. If it keeps hanging you up like this, maybe it isn't good for you.

FELIX. No, you're right. It's obsolete. The world has long since given it up—and here I stand, a foolish, lonely anachronism—the last of the dodo birds.

DORIS. Felix—you stop that.

FELIX. Listen to me. I'm going to be very calm and quiet and I want you to try to understand me—all right?

DORIS. Don't use any big words.

FELIX. I won't. Now listen—although you can't possibly see the reason for it—you must take my word—there's only one thing for me to do now. I've got to kill myself.

DORIS. Oh, don't talk that way. You kidding?

FELIX. I'm very serious.

DORIS. But why? Why?

FELIX. Didn't I just say you can't possibly understand why?

DORIS. But sweetheart—listen—

FELIX (*interrupting*). Didn't I say that?

DORIS. Yes—

FELIX. Didn't I ask you to take my word for it? Can't you do that much for me?

DORIS. But I don't—Felix, I— (*Frustrated*.) Oh, I could just kill you, sometimes!

FELIX (*sits at typewriter—puts in paper*). Just love me as you do, mindlessly, and see that this suicide note doesn't get lost . . . (*Thinking*.) "To Whom It May Concern" . . .

DORIS. Oh, Felix—I don't want to live without you! I'll never find anybody else like you.

FELIX. You'll settle for less. (*Thinking*.) "To Whom It May Concern—but never does—"

DORIS. I'll never be happy. I know I won't. Didn't I try to get along without you? Why do you think I came back?

FELIX. It was only a week—

DORIS. It wouldn't make any difference how long it was. I know. I could see what kind of a life I would have. I couldn't stand it. Not now. Before I met you I could have stood it—

FELIX. Will you please shut up? I'm trying to work.

DORIS. Then just tell me—can I commit suicide with you?

FELIX. No, you can't.

DORIS. Please Felix—why not?

FELIX. Because—I'm doing it alone—

DORIS. Will it hurt if I do it with you?

FELIX. Yes.

DORIS. Why?

FELIX. Because with me it's an affirmation of principle—a rebuke to the world—with you it would just be "monkey see—monkey do"!

DORIS. No, it wouldn't. I would be doing it for the same reason you would.

FELIX. Yours would dilute mine.

DORIS. It would not!

FELIX. How can I make her understand? Yours would be meaningless—you don't have a good reason.

DORIS. I can't live without you.

FELIX. That's a silly, sentimental suicide—that's just weakness and failure.

DORIS. And what about yours?

FELIX. Mine will be a proud taunting challenging suicide—a thought—provoking suicide.

DORIS. Who'll know the difference?

FELIX. My note will explain the difference— (*Thinking*.) Because truth is dead. (*Starting to type*.) Because moral courage

is dead—I, Felix Sherman, choose to die
—(*Weighing it.*) have chosen to die—

DORIS. Why can't I, Doris Wheeler, have
chosen to die also?

FELIX. Doris, will you please shut up?

DORIS. You're making me real sore now.
If I want to commit suicide you can't stop
me—it's a free country!

FELIX (*very reasonbly*). That's true! I
only ask that you don't louse up mine!

DORIS. But I don't want to do it alone.
I want to do it with you.

FELIX. Well, you can't and that's all
there is to it.

DORIS. You're nothing but a mean selfish
son of a bitch. (*She sits, angry.*) I'll fix
you—I'll tear your suicide note.

FELIX. You couldn't do a thing like that.

DORIS. I will unless you let me do it
with you.

FELIX. You couldn't be so heartless.

DORIS. Look who's talking about heartless. You want to leave me all alone, don't
you? You'd do that to me, wouldn't you?
You don't care about me at all! Nobody
does.

FELIX (*relenting*). Doris—darling—listen—

DORIS. It feels like a hot shower when
you call me darling.

FELIX. My dear strange child—please
try to understand why I have to do this
alone—I want it to have a certain impact.
I want to hit out through every morning
newspaper at all—

DORIS (*interrupting*). You're very foolish from a newspaper standpoint.

FELIX. I'm trying to force the public to
think about—(*Stops.*) What did you say?
The newspaper standpoint?

DORIS. Certainly. What's one fellow committing suicide? You can find that in the
paper any day—in the back pages—but a
good suicide pact is front-page news—

FELIX (*impressed with this; then, dis-
carding it*). Oh—but it's so cheap, it's—

DORIS. Cheap? Listen, what about that
beautiful note you're writing? You want
that mentioned on page thirty-two?
"There was a piece of paper with writing
on it on the jerk's body." Or you want it
on the front page? "The dead lovers were
both clutching a brilliant suicide note
which said"—and so forth—

FELIX. "Nos Morituri—Te Salutamus."
I think you're right.

DORIS. What is that?

FELIX. We who are about to die, salute
you. Latin.

DORIS. Oh, Felix, really—"we"? Oh,
honey, thank you!

FELIX (*at the typewriter*). "To Whom
It May Concern—we who are about to
die, salute you—" Good, Doris—you're
right!—you're instinctively right!

DORIS. I guess it's the actress in me.
How are we going to do it?

FELIX. Do what? Oh—I don't know.

DORIS. Sleeping pills are the nicest, but
they're hard to get.

FELIX. Sweetheart—please let me concentrate—

DORIS. Well, I could be handling the
details if you'll just give me a minute to
make a decision—

FELIX. Shhh— (*Writing.*) "Because
truth is dead—"

DORIS. I can't decide this all by myself—

FELIX (*rises and paces*). It needs a
finish—

DORIS. Why don't you knock off five
minutes and we'll work this out?

FELIX. Work what out?

DORIS. Then I could be making the
arrangements.

FELIX. Arrangements?

DORIS. My absent-minded professor—
how are we gonna do it?—gun—knife?

FELIX. Oh, no!

DORIS. I couldn't agree with you more—
but what then? We could never get
enough sleeping pills.

FELIX. No—not sleeping pills. Sleeping
pills have such a neurotic connotation.

DORIS. Well, we can't get them anyway
—what else is nice and painless and—?
Hey—right under our noses—(*Points to
the stove.*)

FELIX. Gas? No—

DORIS. Why not?

FELIX. Gas is negative. Gas is passive
defeat.

DORIS. Well, I give up. What do you
suggest?

FELIX. Hemlock is what we need!

DORIS. Hemlock?

FELIX. That would be perfect. It would
be eloquent!

DORIS. Hang ourselves from a hemlock
tree?

FELIX. Hang ourselves? Oh no—hemlock is the poison of Socrates.

DORIS. Poison? I'm sorry—no sir! Not
me!

FELIX. What's your objection to poison?

DORIS. Because I don't wanna burn up my insides and have cramps and like that—

FELIX. You can get painless poisons.

DORIS. Where—at the drugstore?

FELIX. Yes, as a matter of fact. You can buy poison to exterminate pests, can't you?

DORIS (laughing). I can just see us sitting here spraying each other with bug bombs.

FELIX. This is no joke, Doris.

DORIS. I'm sorry—but what do we say? "Pardon me, sir—we want to kill some rats, but we don't want to hurt them, they're so cute"? Now listen to Doris—Gas!

FELIX. All right— I suppose it is the only sensible way—

DORIS. Of course, dopey! And you were gonna do this alone!

FELIX. I'll finish the note.

DORIS (going to the stove). Now how will we work this?

FELIX (getting a thought). How does this sound—?

DORIS. Honey, we got problems—

FELIX. What?

DORIS. Only one burner works. That's not much gas.

FELIX. It will work. We'll have to plug up the door. It will take time—

DORIS. We can't do that—let this whole big room fill up with gas?

FELIX. Why not?

DORIS. We can't waste all that gas!

FELIX. Damn it! If you're not serious about this, Doris—

DORIS. Sure I'm serious about it.

FELIX. "Waste all that gas"?

DORIS. I'm sorry—it's the way I was brought up—I can't help it.

FELIX. Well, we can't do it anyway, not really.

DORIS. What do you mean?

FELIX. Too many chinks in those old windows—too much of a draft in here—the only way gas will work in this thing is to stick your head in the oven.

DORIS. I don't think it's big enough.

FELIX. Yes, it is.

DORIS. Not for both of us.

FELIX. No, but we could take turns.

DORIS. Oh, yeah? No thank you. We're doing it together. "Two-gether"—not "one gether."

FELIX. But what's the difference? I'd let you go first, naturally.

DORIS. Thanks a lot! And then you change your mind and I'm dead all by myself! . . . No thank you!

FELIX. All right. I'll go first.

DORIS. And I'm gonna sit here waiting and check you to see if you're done! . . . Forget it!

FELIX. Well, maybe we can do it together. Let's see—(They get down on their knees and try to fit their heads into the oven. There are ad-lib "Wait," "Here," "Now," "No, no, sideways," "Look out for my nose," etc. They exhaust every possible combination of positions. DORIS starts to giggle. Deeply hurt.) Doris, why don't you just go home and forget all about it?

DORIS. I'm sorry, honey, It just struck me funny!

FELIX. You'd think you were playing some kind of a birthday party game. We're committing suicide, God damn it!

DORIS. I know it, Felix—I'm sorry I laughed.

FELIX. Are you sincere about this? Now really—if you're not—

DORIS. Of course I am.

FELIX. Are you sure? I hope you are.

DORIS. I am, honey. I just wanna make sure we go together—that's all—wouldn't that be best?

FELIX. I suppose so. (Interrupting.) Wait a minute! Oh—that's it! Of course!

DORIS. What?

FELIX. It combines painlessness and dramatic impact.

DORIS. What, what?

FELIX. A jump—hand in hand from a public building—

DORIS. I don't know—a jump?

FELIX. It's perfect! Talk about news value—talk about the front page—

DORIS. It sounds kind of scary!

FELIX. Why?—An exhilarating flight through space and then oblivion.

DORIS. Well, I guess you wouldn't feel anything. (Puts her hand between her knees.) Except a very cold breeze.

FELIX. What a gesture—what a stage setting for my note.

DORIS. What building though? This one isn't high enough—

FELIX. No—not this kind of a building —an office building. One of man's monuments to his false gods—one located in the center of town.

DORIS. We couldn't get into an office building at this hour, could we?

FELIX. No—you're right—a hotel—that's it! A hotel!

DORIS. Yeah—we could check into a room on the top floor— Oh—I've got it—I've got it! Perfect—

FELIX. What?

DORIS. The Top of the Mark.

FELIX. The Top of the Mark?

DORIS. You know the bar—the Top of the Mark.

FELIX. Yes, of course—look—a couple strolls in at the height of the evening's revelry. Quietly they ask for a table at the window—twenty floors above the shining city. They sit for a moment—perhaps they order a drink—the man takes an envelope from his pocket and props it against his glass. Then they rise. They turn to the noisy, laughing room. In a loud voice the man calls out: Goodbye, Gomorrah!"

DORIS. Do I say anything?

FELIX. What?—You don't say anything.

DORIS. It was my idea, you know.

FELIX. All right—okay—you say something too—and then—

DORIS. What do I say?

FELIX. Whatever you want to—

DORIS. Could I say what you said: "Goodbye Tomorrow"?

FELIX. "Goodbye Gomorrah."

DORIS. What does that mean?

FELIX. Don't you remember Sodom and Gomorrah from the Bible?

DORIS. Oh yes—the two wicked cities—sure—I get it. That's good. Hey—how about "Farewell, cruel world."

FELIX. Shut up.

DORIS. Why?

FELIX. Just shut up. Then together we yell—"Goodbye, Gomorrah," and before their horrified eyes we turn to the window—and, hand in hand, we jump—

DORIS. We ought to kiss first and blow kisses to the whole room— (FELIX gives her a disgusted look.) You know—goodbye kisses . . . You know the trouble with you? You only like your own ideas.

FELIX. You just don't understand this—you don't get the values involved— It's useless! I can't work with you.

DORIS (interrupting). Okay—okay—don't lecture me—we'll do it your way.

FELIX. Now let me finish this note.

DORIS (sudden thought). Oh, my God!

FELIX. What is it?

DORIS. Felix—the Top of the Mark is out.

FELIX. What?

DORIS. We can't do it from the Top of the Mark.

FELIX. Why not?

DORIS. They won't allow ladies wearing slacks.

FELIX. You're not wearing slacks.

DORIS. No, I have to go home and change to slacks before we jump.

FELIX. Change to slacks—why?

DORIS. Because I loaned my imported French panties to my friend Anne for a date and all my others are at the laundry except one pair with holes in them and I am not jumping twenty stories in a skirt with ratty panties on.

FELIX. I don't believe my ears! I just don't believe you said that!

DORIS. Now don't panic.

FELIX. Now, wait a minute! Are you actually concerned about your panties?

DORIS. Not if I can jump in slacks, I'm not. In a skirt, yes—absolutely.

FELIX. It's too much—I can't bear it.

DORIS. Felix, will you calm down—we'll figure out another way.

FELIX. What's the use—I should have known you'd wreck it. I think I knew it all along.

DORIS. Oh, you're so stubborn! That's all. You got your heart set on the Top of the Mark. (Sighs.) Okay—I'll see if I can reach Anne and get my panties back. (She dials.)

FELIX. I should have done it alone. (FELIX sits looking at DORIS in mute despair.)

DORIS (into phone). Hello, Janice? This is Doris—listen, it's very urgent that I contact Anne— Have you any idea where she went with her date? Well, will you—ask Patty? (Covers mouthpiece and addresses FELIX.) I'd borrow a pair from her, but she buys her lingerie at Woolworth's—she's a Communist or— Hello?—yeah? You're kidding! You sure? Thanks, Janice. (She hangs up.) You'll never guess in a million years where Anne is right now with her date—in my panties—

FELIX (lifelessly). The Top of the Mark.

DORIS. How did you know—is that fantastic? Is that fate! Now here's what we'll do—I'll run home and change into a skirt —meanwhile you can change your shirt and put on a tie—why don't you put on your blue suit and that silver tie?—then we'll go up to the Mark and we'll find Anne and her date. I'll take Anne to the ladies' room and get my panties from her— Gee, what'll I tell her why I want them. I'll just say it's my first date with you and I wanna make a good impression —meanwhile you could be— (*She stops;* FELIX *has quietly started to tear up the suicide note.*) What are you doing? (FELIX *turns away from her. She goes to him.*)

FELIX. Go away.

DORIS. What's wrong?

FELIX. Nothing. You destroyed my life —why not my death? It's symmetrical.

DORIS. Is it off? Sweetheart—just tell me —I don't understand. I just wanted to help you.

FELIX (*shouting*). Will you get out of here? Get out of my sight.

DORIS (*picking up the coffee jar*). You're out of coffee. (*She puts on her coat.*) I'll be right back.

FELIX. Where are you going?

DORIS. To get some coffee.

FELIX. Not now.

DORIS. It'll just take a minute. You need a hot cup of coffee.

FELIX (*a touch of panic*). No—don't leave! Don't leave me.

DORIS. Okay—take it easy, baby— Don't be afraid. (*She sits and puts her arms around him.*)

FELIX. Doris, what am I going to do?

DORIS. You know something I just realized?

FELIX. What?

DORIS. You're as bad as I am—you're scared of everything you don't understand.

FELIX (*looking heavenward*). When? When are you going to let me out? (*Listens.*) Uh-huh.

DORIS. What'd He say?

FELIX. Don't call us, we'll call you.

DORIS (*laughing*). You big dope.

FELIX. No, the word for me is failure— rat-fink failure.

DORIS. We're not licked yet. We'll try again after dinner.

FELIX. Forget it, honey—it's no use.

DORIS. Listen, don't feel bad. If I hadn't been here you'd be in the papers by now —I loused you up. It was just me and my silly panties. But you can do anything, Felix, anything you want to do.

FELIX. No—no—don't feed me that. I can't live on that—wait. Wait—I wonder if—I bet that's it.

DORIS. What, Felix?

FELIX. Now listen, pay attention. My name is Fred Sherman. I'm a clerk in a bookstore. I have a pocketful of talent, but it's counterfeit. Now who are you?

DORIS. You're nuts.

FELIX. Who are you?

DORIS. Doris Wheeler.

FELIX. The model?

DORIS. And actress.

FELIX. Like hell you are! No sir! Now, who are you?

DORIS. Why are we doing this?

FELIX. Who are you?

DORIS. I don't understand.

FELIX. Never mind. Now, who are you? Take your time. Who are you really?— don't be afraid.

DORIS. Doris Wilgus?

FELIX. Very good. And what do you do? Easy now?

DORIS. I'm a receptionist. I was formerly a prostitute—but also I was in two television commercials—

FELIX (*holding out his hand, smiling*). I thought you looked familiar. How do you do?

DORIS (*taking his hand*). Very nice meeting you, Fred. Actually it was only one commercial.

(*They hold hands lightly.*)

CURTAIN FALLS

THE ODD COUPLE

Neil Simon

First presented by Saint Subber on March 10, 1965, at the Plymouth Theatre in New York City, with the following cast:

(In order of appearance)

SPEED Paul Dooley	OSCAR MADISON Walter Matthau
MURRAY Nathaniel Frey	FELIX UNGAR Art Carney
ROY Sidney Armus	GWENDOLYN PIGEON Carole Shelley
VINNIE John Fiedler	CECILY PIGEON Monica Evans

Written by Neil Simon
Directed by Mike Nichols
Set designed by Oliver Smith
Lighting by Jean Rosenthal
Costumes by Ann Roth

SYNOPSIS OF SCENES

The action takes place in an apartment on Riverside Drive in New York City.
ACT ONE. A hot summer night.
ACT TWO. SCENE 1: Two weeks later, about eleven at night. SCENE 2: A few days later, about eight P.M.
ACT THREE. The next evening, about seven-thirty.

Copyright © 1966 by Nancy Enterprises, Inc.
Reprinted by permission of Random House, Inc.
All rights including the right of reproduction in whole or in part, in any form, are reserved under International and Pan-American Copyright Conventions. Published in New York by Random House, Inc., and simultaneously in Toronto, Canada, by Random House of Canada Limited.

CAUTION: Professionals and amateurs are hereby warned that *The Odd Couple* is fully protected under the Universal Copyright Convention, Berne Convention and Pan-American Copyright Convention and is subject to royalty. All rights are strictly reserved, including professional, amateur, motion picture, television, radio, recitation, lecturing, public reading and foreign language translation, and none of such rights can be exercised or used without written permission from the copyright owner. All inquiries for licenses and permissions should be addressed to:—

International Authors Society, Ltd.
c/o Albert I. DaSilva
4 West 56th Street
New York, N.Y. 10019

Neil Simon was born with success in his mouth rather than a silver spoon, and it has never hurt him a bit. He was also born, just like Yankee Doodle Dandy, on the Fourth of July—the Fourth of July in question coming in 1927. He started to write with his brother Danny, and produced revue sketches and the like, to say nothing of a widely acclaimed first play, *Come Blow Your Horn,* first given in 1961.

From then onward Mr. Simon has never looked sideways, let alone back. He has become one of the most successful comedy writers of all time, and the natural inheritor of the old Broadway writers of the twenties and thirties.

In a way Mr. Simon was the first writer to cut his teeth artistically in television. It gave him two things—one good and one bad. The good thing was his ear for the speech of the people, his total empathy with their wit, his perhaps dangerously accurate assessment of the joke and sentiment that will corral in the ratings. What was bad in fact was merely a mirror image of what was good. His very adroitness played enemy to his brilliance.

What at first perhaps happened was that his humanity never quite lived up to his wit. He has a simply god-given talent to make jokes. His situations are funny enough in all conscience, but he can back it up with a crackling wit that obtains its crackle simply from its unassailable likelihood. One of Mr. Simon's most popular plays was the brilliantly, almost indecently, funny *Plaza Suite.* In the first play, where a Peter Pan suburban husband tries to find a lost youth with his secretary rather than recognizing reality with his wife, he aims dead center at life. He misses, not because his people are not real—they are, they even chatter with the red blood of life—but because the situation itself is so real it is a cliché.

Simon's problem is not that he is not as good as his glorious predecessors in the history of American comedy, but that he is so much better. In plays like *Barefoot in the Park,* or musicals such as the woefully underrated *Little Me,* the surprisingly overrated *Sweet Charity,* and the altogether blissful *Promises, Promises,* Simon has set up a standard of verbal wit and sheer literacy that almost seems its own worst enemy.

He is so sharp—the jokes have such a beautiful, seemingly machine-made precision—that you wonder what lies behind the superficial glitter. And frankly, if you are human and you envy any man that funny, you probably presume but little. Only serious men get themselves taken seriously, which is probably why they are serious. But Neil Simon is not just content to stand up and make jokes, to tease and titillate a loyal public into delightedly shocked laughter. Mr. Simon wants, deserves, and needs to be taken seriously.

The first play of *Plaza Suite,* with its derelict marriage floating out to a lost sea, is an example of this very important element in Simon's playwrighting. Even at its most outrageously witty, when the jokes are falling like snow in December, Mr. Simon's play itself takes more pride in its humanity than in its humor. This same element of seriousness made itself felt in Simon's next two plays, *Last of the Red Hot Lovers* and, more particularly, *The Gingerbread Lady.*

Of Simon's many plays and musical books, *The Odd Couple* is clearly among his best. The jokes and wisecracks are, of course, all present and correct and only waiting to be counted. But, more surprisingly, this comedy of two grass widowers setting up house together has a great deal more than its wit to keep it warm. In this story of a man and his maladjustment with another man—that historic encounter between the social slob and the social saint—Simon creates a genuine comedy of manners. It would be easy to say "Go and Enjoy," but beyond your immediate enjoyment note the strange intensity of the writing, and the delicacy of the situations as well as the sharpness of the wit. Mr. Simon has written a comedy so perfectly of its time and place that it seems safe to say that it will survive every change of fashion, as have the best of the old Broadway comedies of the past.

C.B.

ACT ONE

It is a warm summer night in OSCAR
MADISON's *apartment. This is one of those
large eight-room affairs on Riverside Drive
in the upper eighties. The building is
about thirty-five years old and still has
vestiges of its glorious past—high ceilings,
walk-in closets and thick walls. We are in
the living room with doors leading off to
the kitchen, a bedroom and a bathroom,
and a hallway to the other bedrooms.*

*Although the furnishings have been
chosen with extreme good taste, the room
itself, without the touch and care of a
woman these past few months, is now a
study in slovenliness. Dirty dishes, dis-
carded clothes, old newspapers, empty bottles, glasses filled and unfilled, opened and
unopened laundry packages, mail and dis-
arrayed furniture abound. The only cheerful note left in this room is the lovely view
of the New Jersey Palisades through its
twelfth-floor window. Three months ago
this was a lovely apartment.*

*As the curtain rises, the room is filled
with smoke. A poker game is in progress.
There are six chairs around the table but
only four men are sitting. They are* MUR-
RAY, ROY, SPEED *and* VINNIE. VINNIE, *with
the largest stack of chips in front of him,
is nervously tapping his foot; he keeps
checking his watch.* ROY *is watching* SPEED
and SPEED *is glaring at* MURRAY *with incredulity and utter fascination.* MURRAY *is
the dealer. He slowly and methodically
tries to shuffle. It is a ponderous and painful business.* SPEED *shakes his head in disbelief. This is all done wordlessly.*

SPEED (*cups his chin in his hand and
looks at* MURRAY). Tell me, Mr. Maverick,
is this your first time on the riverboat?

MURRAY (*with utter disregard*). You
don't like it, get a machine.

(*He continues to deal slowly.*)

ROY. Geez, it stinks in here.

VINNIE (*looks at his watch*). What time
is it?

SPEED. Again what time is it?

VINNIE (*whining*). My watch is slow.
I'd like to know what time it is.

SPEED (*glares at him*). You're winning
ninety-five dollars, that's what time it is.
Where the hell are you running?

VINNIE. I'm not running anywhere. I
just asked what time it was. Who said
anything about running?

ROY (*looks at his watch*). It's ten-thirty.

(*There is a pause.* MURRAY *continues to
shuffle.*)

VINNIE (*after the pause*). I got to leave
by twelve.

SPEED (*looks up in despair*). Oh, Christ!

VINNIE. I told you that when I sat
down. I got to leave by twelve. Murray,
didn't I say that when I sat down? I said
I got to leave by twelve.

SPEED. All right, don't talk to him. He's
dealing. (*To* MURRAY.) Murray, you wanna
rest for a while? Go lie down, sweetheart.

MURRAY. You want speed or accuracy,
make up your mind.

(*He begins to deal slowly.* SPEED *puffs
on his cigar angrily.*)

ROY. Hey, you want to do me a really
big favor? Smoke toward New Jersey.

(SPEED *blows smoke at* ROY.)

MURRAY. No kidding, I'm really worried
about Felix. (*Points to an empty chair.*)
He's never been this late before. Maybe
somebody should call. (*Yells off.*) Hey,
Oscar, why don't you call Felix?

ROY (*waves his hand through the
smoke*). Listen, why don't we chip in
three dollars apiece and buy another window. How the hell can you breathe in
here?

MURRAY. How many cards you got,
four?

SPEED. Yes, Murray, we all have four
cards. When you give us one more, we'll
all have five. If you were to give us two
more, we'd have six. Understand how it
works now?

ROY (*yells off*). Hey, Oscar, what do
you say? In or out?

(*From offstage we hear* OSCAR's *voice.*)

OSCAR (*offstage*). Out, pussycat, out!

(SPEED *opens and the others bet.*)

VINNIE. I told my wife I'd be home by
one the latest. We're making an eight
o'clock plane to Florida. I told you that
when I sat down.

SPEED. Don't cry, Vinnie. You're forty-
two years old. It's embarrassing. Give me
two . . .

(*He discards.*)

ROY. Why doesn't he fix the air conditioner? It's ninety-eight degrees, and it
sits there sweating like everyone else. I'm
out.

(*He goes to the window and looks out.*)

MURRAY. Who goes to Florida in July?

VINNIE. It's off-season. There's no crowds and you get the best room for one-tenth the price. No cards . . .

SPEED. Some vacation. Six cheap people in an empty hotel.

MURRAY. Dealer takes four . . . Hey, you think maybe Felix is sick? (*He points to the empty chair.*) I mean he's never been this late before.

ROY (*takes a laundry bag from an arm-chair and sits*). You know, it's the same garbage from last week's game. I'm beginning to recognize things.

MURRAY (*throwing his cards down*). I'm out . . .

SPEED (*showing his hand*). Two kings . . .

VINNIE. Straight . . .

(*He shows his hand and takes in the pot.*)

MURRAY. Hey, maybe he's in his office locked in the john again. Did you know Felix was once locked in the john overnight. He wrote out his entire will on a half a roll of toilet paper! Heee, what a nut!

(VINNIE *is playing with his chips.*)

SPEED (*glares at him as he shuffles the cards*). Don't play with your chips. I'm asking you nice; don't play with your chips.

VINNIE (*to* SPEED). I'm not playing. I'm counting. Leave me alone. What are you picking on me for? How much do you think I'm winning? Fifteen dollars!

SPEED. Fifteen dollars? You dropped more than that in your cuffs!

(SPEED *deals a game of draw poker.*)

MURRAY (*yells off*). Hey, Oscar, what do you say?

OSCAR (*enters carrying a tray with beer, sandwiches, a can of peanuts, and opened bags of pretzels and Fritos*). I'm in! I'm in! Go ahead. Deal!

(OSCAR MADISON *is forty-three. He is a pleasant, appealing man who seems to enjoy life to the fullest. He enjoys his weekly poker game, his friends, his excessive drinking and his cigars. He is also one of those lucky creatures in life who even enjoys his work—he's a sportswriter for the New York Post. His carefree attitude is evident in the sloppiness of his household, but it seems to bother others*

more than it does OSCAR. *This is not to say that* OSCAR *is without cares or worries. He just doesn't seem to have any.*)

VINNIE. Aren't you going to look at your cards?

OSCAR (*sets the tray on a side chair*). What for? I'm gonna bluff anyway. (*Opens a bottle of Coke.*) Who gets the Coke?

MURRAY. I get a Coke.

OSCAR. My friend Murray the policeman gets a warm Coke.

(*He gives him the bottle.*)

ROY (*opens the betting*). You still didn't fix the refrigerator? It's been two weeks now. No wonder it stinks in here.

OSCAR (*picks up his cards*). Temper, temper. If I wanted nagging I'd go back with my wife. (*Throws them down.*) I'm out. Who wants food?

MURRAY. What have you got?

OSCAR (*looks under the bread*). I got brown sandwiches and green sandwiches. Well, what do you say?

MURRAY. What's the green?

OSCAR. It's either very new cheese or very old meat.

MURRAY. I'll take the brown.

(OSCAR *gives* MURRAY *a sandwich.*)

ROY (*glares at* MURRAY). Are you crazy? You're not going to eat that, are you?

MURRAY. I'm hungry.

ROY. His refrigerator's been broken for two weeks. I saw milk standing in there that wasn't even in the bottle.

OSCAR (*to* ROY). What are you, some kind of a health nut? Eat, Murray, eat!

ROY. I've got six cards . . .

SPEED. That figures—I've got three aces. Misdeal.

(*They all throw their cards in.* SPEED *begins to shuffle.*)

VINNIE. You know who makes very good sandwiches? Felix. Did you ever taste his cream cheese and pimento on date-nut bread?

SPEED (*to* VINNIE). All right, make up your mind, poker or menus. (OSCAR *opens a can of beer, which sprays in a geyser over the players and the table. There is a hubbub as they all yell at* OSCAR. *He hands* ROY *the overflowing can and pushes the puddle of beer under the chair. The players start to go back to the game only to be sprayed again as* OSCAR *opens another beer can. There is another outraged cry as they try to stop* OSCAR *and mop up the beer on the table with a towel which was hanging on the standing lamp.* OSCAR, *undisturbed, gives them the beer and the bags of refreshments, and they finally sit back in their chairs.* OSCAR *wipes his hands on the sleeve of* ROY's *jacket which is hanging on the back of the chair.*) Hey, Vinnie, tell Oscar what time you're leaving.

VINNIE (*like a trained dog*). Twelve o'clock.

SPEED (*to the others*). You hear? We got ten minutes before the next announcement. All right, this game is five card stud. (*He deals and ad libs calling the cards, ending with* MURRAY's *card.*) . . . And a bullet for the policeman. All right, Murray, it's your bet. (*No answer.*) Do something, huh.

OSCAR (*getting a drink at the bar*). Don't yell at my friend Murray.

MURRAY (*throwing in a coin*). I'm in for a quarter.

OSCAR (*proudly looks in* MURRAY's *eyes*). Beautiful, baby, beautiful.

(*He sits down and begins to open the can of peanuts.*)

ROY. Hey, Oscar, let's make a rule. Every six months you have to buy fresh potato chips. How can you live like this? Don't you have a maid?

OSCAR (*shakes his head*). She quit after my wife and kids left. The work got to be too much for her. (*He looks on the table.*) The pot's shy. Who didn't put in a quarter?

MURRAY (*to* OSCAR). You didn't.

OSCAR (*puts in money*). You got a big mouth, Murray. Just for that, lend me twenty dollars.

(SPEED *deals another round.*)

MURRAY. I just loaned you twenty dollars ten minutes ago.

(*They all join in a round of betting.*)

OSCAR. You loaned me *ten* dollars *twenty* minutes ago. Learn to count, pussycat.

MURRAY. Learn to play poker, chicken licken! Borrow from somebody else. I keep winning my own money back.

ROY (*to* OSCAR). You owe everybody in the game. If you don't have it, you shouldn't play.

OSCAR. All right, I'm through being the nice one. You owe me six dollars apiece for the buffet.

SPEED (*dealing another round of cards*). Buffet? Hot beer and two sandwiches left over from when you went to high school?

OSCAR. What do you want at a poker game, a tomato surprise? Murray, lend me twenty dollars or I'll call your wife and tell her you're in Central Park wearing a dress.

MURRAY. You want money, ask Felix.

OSCAR. He's not here.

MURRAY. Neither am I.

ROY (*gives him money*). All right, here. You're on the books for another twenty.

OSCAR. How many times are you gonna keep saying it?

(*He takes the money.*)

MURRAY. When are you gonna call Felix?

OSCAR. When are we gonna play poker?

MURRAY. Aren't you even worried? It's the first game he's missed in over two years.

OSCAR. The record is fifteen years set by Lou Gehrig in 1939! I'll call! I'll call!

ROY. How can you be so lazy?

(*The phone rings.*)

OSCAR (*throwing his cards in*). Call me irresponsible, I'm funny that way.

(*He goes to the phone.*)

SPEED. Pair of sixes . . .

VINNIE. Three deuces . . .

SPEED (*throws up his hands in despair*). This is my last week. I get all the aggravation I need at home.

(OSCAR *picks up the phone.*)

OSCAR. Hello! Oscar the Poker Player!

VINNIE (*to* OSCAR). If it's my wife tell her I'm leaving at twelve.

SPEED (*to* VINNIE). You look at your watch once more and you get the peanuts in your face. (*To* ROY.) Deal the cards!

(*The game continues during* OSCAR's *phone conversation, with* ROY *dealing a game of stud.*)

OSCAR (*into the phone*). Who? Who did you want, please? *Dabby? Dabby who?* No, there's no Dabby here. Oh, *Daddy!* (*To the others.*) For crise sakes, it's my kid. (*Back into the phone, he speaks with great love and affection.*) Brucey, hello, baby. Yes, it's Daddy! (*There is a general outburst of ad libbing from the poker players. To the others.*) Hey, come on, give me a break, willya? My five-year-old kid is calling from California. It must be costing him a fortune. (*Back into the phone.*) How've you been, sweetheart? Yes, I finally got your letter. It took three weeks. Yes, but next time you tell Mommy to give you a stamp. I know, but you're not supposed to draw it on. (*He laughs. To the others.*) You hear?

SPEED. We hear. We hear. We're all thrilled.

OSCAR (*into the phone*). What's that, darling? What goldfish? Oh, in your room! Oh, sure. Sure, I'm taking care of them. (*He holds the phone over his chest*). Oh, God, I killed my kid's goldfish! (*Back into the phone.*) Yes, I feed them every day.

ROY. Murderer!

OSCAR. Mommy wants to speak to me? Right. Take care of yourself, soldier. I love you.

VINNIE (*beginning to deal a game of stud*). Ante a dollar . . .

SPEED (*to* OSCAR). Cost you a dollar to play. You got a dollar?

OSCAR. Not after I get through talking to this lady. (*Into the phone with false cheerfulness.*) Hello, Blanche. How are you? Err, yes, I have a pretty good idea why you're calling. I'm a week behind with the check, right? *Four* weeks? That's not possible. Because it's not possible. Blanche, I keep a record of every check and I *know* I'm only *three* weeks behind! Blanche, I'm trying the best I can. Blanche, don't threaten me with jail because it's not a threat. With my expenses and my alimony, a prisoner takes home more pay than I do! Very nice, in front of the kids. Blanche, don't tell me you're going to have my salary attached, just say goodbye! Goodbye! (*He hangs up. To the players.*) I'm eight hundred dollars behind in alimony so let's up the stakes.

(*He gets his drink from the poker table.*)

ROY. She can do it, you know.

OSCAR. What?

ROY. Throw you in jail. For nonsupport of the kids.

OSCAR. Never. If she can't call me once a week to aggravate me, she's not happy. (*He crosses to the bar.*)

MURRAY. It doesn't bother you? That you can go to jail? Or that maybe your kids don't have enough clothes or enough to eat?

OSCAR. Murray, *Poland* could live for a year on what my kids leave over from lunch! Can we play cards?

(*He refills his drink.*)

ROY. But that's the point. You shouldn't *be* in this kind of trouble. It's because you don't know how to manage anything. I should know; I'm your accountant.

OSCAR (*crossing to the table*). If you're my accountant, how come I need money?

ROY. If you need money, how come you play poker?

OSCAR. Because I need money.

ROY. But you always lose.

OSCAR. That's why I need the money! Listen, *I'm* not complaining. *You're* complaining. I get along all right. I'm living.

ROY. Alone? In eight dirty rooms?

OSCAR. If I win tonight, I'll buy a broom. (*MURRAY and SPEED buy chips from VINNIE, and MURRAY begins to shuffle the deck for a game of draw.*)

ROY. That's not what you need. What you need is a wife.

OSCAR. How can I afford a wife when I can't afford a broom?

ROY. Then don't play poker.

OSCAR (*puts down his drink, rushes to ROY and they struggle over the bag of potato chips, which rips, showering everyone. They all begin to yell at one another*). Then don't come to my house and eat my potato chips!

MURRAY. What are you yelling about? We're playing a friendly game.

SPEED. Who's *playing*? We've been sitting here talking since eight o'clock.

VINNIE. Since *seven*. That's why I said I was going to quit at *twelve*.

SPEED. How'd you like a stale banana right in the mouth?

MURRAY (*the peacemaker*). All right, all right, let's calm down. Take it easy. I'm a cop, you know. I could arrest the whole lousy game. (*He finishes dealing the cards.*) Four . . .

OSCAR (*sitting at the table*). My friend Murray the Cop is right. Let's just play cards. And please hold them up; I can't see where I marked them.

MURRAY. You're worse than the kids from the PAL.

OSCAR. But you still love me, Roy, sweety, right?

ROY (*petulant*). Yeah, yeah.

OSCAR. That's not good enough. Come on, say it. In front of the whole poker game. "I love you, Oscar Madison."

ROY. You don't take any of this seriously, do you? You owe money to your wife, your government, your friends . . .

OSCAR (*throws his cards down*). What do you want me to do, Roy, jump in the garbage disposal and grind myself to death? (*The phone rings. He goes to answer it.*) Life goes on even for those of us who are divorced, broke and sloppy. (*Into the phone.*) Hello? Divorced, Broke and Sloppy. Oh, hello, sweetheart. (*He becomes very seductive, pulls the phone to the side and talks low, but he is still audible to the others, who turn and listen.*) I told you not to call me during the game. I can't talk to you now. You *know* I do, darling. All right, just a minute. (*He turns.*) Murray, it's your wife.

(*He puts the phone on the table and sits on the sofa.*)

MURRAY (*nods disgustedly as he crosses to the phone*). I wish you *were* having an affair with her. Then she wouldn't bother *me* all the time. (*He picks up the phone.*) Hello, Mimi, what's wrong?

(SPEED *gets up, stretches and goes into the bathroom.*)

OSCAR (*in a woman's voice, imitating* MIMI). What time are you coming home? (*Then imitating* MURRAY.) I don't know, about twelve, twelve-thirty.

MURRAY (*into the phone*). I don't know, about twelve, twelve-thirty! (ROY *gets up and stretches.*) Why, what did you want, Mimi? "A corned beef sandwich and a strawberry malted!"

OSCAR. Is she pregnant again?

MURRAY (*holds the phone over his chest*). No, just fat! (*There is the sound of a toilet flushing, and after* SPEED *comes out of the bathroom,* VINNIE *goes in. Into the phone again.*) What? How could you hear that, I had the phone over my chest? Who? Felix? No, he didn't show up tonight. What's wrong? You're kidding! How should I know? All right, all right, goodbye. (*The toilet flushes again, and after* VINNIE *comes out of the bathroom,* ROY *goes in.*) Goodbye, Mimi. Goodbye. (*He hangs up. To the others.*) Well, what did I tell you? I knew it!

ROY. What's the matter?

MURRAY (*pacing by the couch*). Felix is missing!

OSCAR. Who?

MURRAY. Felix! Felix Ungar! The man who sits in that chair every week and cleans ashtrays. I told you something was up.

SPEED (*at the table*). What do you mean, missing?

MURRAY. He didn't show up for work today. He didn't come home tonight. No one knows where he is. Mimi just spoke to his wife.

VINNIE (*in his chair at the poker table*). Felix?

MURRAY. They looked everywhere. I'm telling you he's missing.

OSCAR. Wait a minute. No one is missing for one day.

VINNIE. That's right. You've got to be missing for forty-eight hours before you're missing. The worst he could be is lost.

MURRAY. How could he be lost? He's forty-four years old and lives on West End Avenue. What's the matter with you?

ROY (*sitting in an armchair*). Maybe he had an accident.

OSCAR. They would have heard.

ROY. If he's laying in a gutter somewhere? Who would know who he is?

OSCAR. He's got ninety-two credit cards in his wallet. The minute something happens to him, America lights up.

VINNIE. Maybe he went to a movie. You know how long those pictures are today.

SPEED (*looks at* VINNIE *contemptuously*). No wonder you're going to Florida in July! Dumb, dumb, dumb!

ROY. Maybe he was mugged?

OSCAR. For thirty-six hours? How much money could he have on him?

ROY. Maybe they took his clothes. I knew a guy who was mugged in a doctor's office. He had to go home in a nurse's uniform.

(OSCAR *throws a pillow from the couch at* ROY.)

SPEED. Murray, you're a cop. What do you think?

MURRAY. I think it's something real bad.

SPEED. How do you know?

MURRAY. I can feel it in my bones.

SPEED (*to the others*). You hear? Bulldog Drummond.

ROY. Maybe he's drunk. Does he drink?

OSCAR. Felix? On New Year's Eve he has Pepto-Bismol. What are we guessing? I'll call his wife.

(*He picks up the phone.*)

SPEED. Wait a minute! Don't start anything yet. Just 'cause we don't know where he is doesn't mean somebody else doesn't. Does he have a girl?

VINNIE. A what?

SPEED. A girl? You know. Like when you're through work early.

MURRAY. Felix? Playing around? Are you crazy? He wears a vest and galoshes.

SPEED (*gets up and moves toward* MURRAY). You mean you automatically know who has and who hasn't got a girl on the side?

MURRAY (*moves to* SPEED). Yes, I automatically know.

SPEED. All right, you're so smart. Have I got a girl?

MURRAY. No, you haven't got a girl. What you've got is what *I've* got. What you *wish* you got and what you *got* is a whole different civilization! *Oscar* maybe has a girl on the side.

SPEED. That's different. He's divorced. That's not on the side. That's in the middle.

(*He moves to the table.*)

OSCAR (*to them both as he starts to dial*). You through? 'Cause one of our poker players is missing. I'd like to find out about him.

VINNIE. I thought he looked edgy the last couple of weeks. (*To* SPEED.) Didn't you think he looked edgy?

SPEED. No. As a matter of fact, I thought *you* looked edgy.

(*He moves down to the right.*)

OSCAR (*into the phone*). Hello? Frances? Oscar. I just heard.

ROY. Tell her not to worry. She's probably hysterical.

MURRAY. Yeah, you know women.

(*He sits down on the couch.*)

OSCAR (*into the phone*). Listen, Frances, the most important thing is not to worry. Oh! (*To the others.*) She's not worried.

MURRAY. Sure.

OSCAR (*into the phone*). Frances, do you have *any* idea where he could be? He what? You're kidding? Why? No, I didn't know. Gee, that's too bad. All right, listen, Frances, you just sit tight and the minute I hear anything I'll let you know. Right. G'bye.

(*He hangs up. They all look at him expectantly. He gets up wordlessly and crosses to the table, thinking. They all*

watch him a second, not being able to stand it any longer.)

MURRAY. Ya gonna tell us or do we hire a private detective?

OSCAR. They broke up!

ROY. Who?

OSCAR. Felix and Frances! They broke up! The entire marriage is through.

VINNIE. You're kidding!

ROY. I don't believe it.

SPEED. After twelve years?

(OSCAR *sits down at the table.*)

VINNIE. They were such a happy couple.

MURRAY. Twelve years doesn't mean you're a *happy* couple. It just means you're a *long* couple.

SPEED. Go figure it. Felix and Frances.

ROY. What are you surprised at? He used to sit there every Friday night and tell us how they were fighting.

SPEED. I know. But who believes Felix?

VINNIE. What happened?

OSCAR. She wants out, that's all.

MURRAY. He'll go to pieces. I know Felix. He's going to try something crazy.

SPEED. That's all he ever used to talk about. "My beautiful wife. My wonderful wife." What happened?

OSCAR. His beautiful, wonderful wife can't stand him, that's what happened.

MURRAY. He'll kill himself. You hear what I'm saying? He's going to go out and try to kill himself.

SPEED (*to* MURRAY). Will you shut up, Murray? Stop being a cop for two minutes. (*To* OSCAR.) Where'd he go, Oscar?

OSCAR. He went out to kill himself.

MURRAY. What did I tell you?

ROY (*to* OSCAR). Are you serious?

OSCAR. That's what she said. He was going out to kill himself. He didn't want to do it at home 'cause the kids were sleeping.

VINNIE. Why?

OSCAR. Why? Because that's Felix, that's why. (*He goes to the bar and refills his drink.*) You know what he's like. He sleeps on the window sill. "Love me or I'll jump." 'Cause he's a nut, that's why.

MURRAY. That's right. Remember he tried something like that in the army? She wanted to break off the engagement so he started cleaning guns in his mouth.

SPEED. I don't believe it. Talk! That's all Felix is, talk.

VINNIE (*worried*). But is that what he

said? In those words? "I'm going to kill myself?"

OSCAR (*pacing about the table*). I don't know in what words. She didn't read it to me.

ROY. You mean he left her a note?

OSCAR. No, he sent a telegram.

MURRAY. A *suicide telegram?* Who sends a suicide telegram?

OSCAR. Felix, the nut, that's who! Can you imagine getting a thing like that? She even has to tip the kid a quarter.

ROY. I don't get it. If he wants to kill himself, why does he send a telegram?

OSCAR. Don't you see how his mind works? If he sends a note, she might not get it till Monday and he'd have no excuse for not being dead. This way, for a dollar ten, he's got a chance to be saved.

VINNIE. You mean he really doesn't want to kill himself? He just wants sympathy.

OSCAR. What he'd really like is to go to the funeral and sit in the back. He'd be the biggest crier there.

MURRAY. He's right.

OSCAR. Sure I'm right.

MURRAY. We get these cases every day. All they want is attention. We got a guy who calls us every Saturday afternoon from the George Washington Bridge.

ROY. I don't know. You never can tell what a guy'll do when he's hysterical.

MURRAY. Nahhh. Nine out of ten times they don't jump.

ROY. What about the tenth time?

MURRAY. They jump. He's right. There's a possibility.

OSCAR. Not with Felix. I know him. He's too nervous to kill himself. He wears his seatbelt in a drive-in movie.

VINNIE. Isn't there someplace we could look for him?

SPEED. Where? Where would you look? Who knows where he is?

(*The doorbell rings. They all look at* OSCAR.)

OSCAR. Of course! If you're going to kill yourself, where's the safest place to do it? With your friends!

(VINNIE *starts for the door.*)

MURRAY (*stopping him*). Wait a minute! The guy may be hysterical. Let's play it nice and easy. If *we're* calm, maybe *he'll* be calm.

ROY (*getting up and joining them*).

That's right. That's how they do it with those guys out on the ledge. You talk nice and soft.

(SPEED *rushes over to them, and joins in the frenzied discussion.*)

VINNIE. What'll we say to him?

MURRAY. We don't say nothin'. Like we never heard a thing.

OSCAR (*trying to get their attention*). You through with this discussion? Because he already could have hung himself out in the hall. (*To* VINNIE.) Vinnie, open the door!

MURRAY. Remember! Like we don't know nothin'.

(*They all rush back to their seats and grab up cards, which they concentrate on with the greatest intensity.* VINNIE *opens the door.* FELIX UNGAR *is there. He's about forty-four. His clothes are rumpled as if he had slept in them, and he needs a shave. Although he tries to act matter-of-fact, there is an air of great tension and nervousness about him.*)

FELIX (*softly*). Hi, Vin! (VINNIE *quickly goes back to his seat and studies his cards.* FELIX *has his hands in his pockets, trying to be very nonchalant. With controlled calm.*) Hi, fellas. (*They all mumble hello, but do not look at him. He puts his coat over the railing and crosses to the table.*) How's the game going? (*They all mumble appropriate remarks, and continue staring at their cards.*) Good! Good! Sorry I'm late. (FELIX *looks a little disappointed that no one asks "What?" He starts to pick up a sandwich, changes his mind and makes a gesture of distaste.*) Any Coke left?

OSCAR (*looking up from his cards*). Coke? Gee, I don't think so. I got a Seven-Up!

FELIX (*bravely*). No, I felt like a Coke. I just don't feel like Seven-Up tonight!

(*He stands watching the game.*)

OSCAR. What's the bet?

SPEED. You bet a quarter. It's up to Murray. Murray, what do you say? (MURRAY *is staring at* FELIX.) Murray! Murray!

ROY (*to* VINNIE). Tap his shoulder.

VINNIE (*taps* MURRAY's *shoulder*). Murray!

MURRAY (*startled*). What? What?

SPEED. It's up to you.

MURRAY. Why is it always up to me?

SPEED. It's not always up to you. It's up

to you now. What do you do?

MURRAY. I'm in. I'm in.

(*He throws in a quarter.*)

FELIX (*moves to the bookcase*). Anyone call about me?

OSCAR. Er, not that I can remember. (*To the others.*) Did anyone call for Felix? (*They all shrug and ad lib "No."*) Why? Were you expecting a call?

FELIX (*looking at the books on the shelf*). No! No! Just asking.

(*He opens a book and examines it.*)

ROY. Er, I'll see his bet and raise it a dollar.

FELIX (*without looking up from the book*). I just thought someone might have called.

SPEED. It costs me a dollar and a quarter to play, right?

OSCAR. Right!

FELIX (*still looking at the book, in a sing-song*). But, if no one called, no one called.

(*He slams the book shut and puts it back. They all jump at the noise.*)

SPEED (*getting nervous*). What does it cost me to play again?

MURRAY (*angry*). A dollar and a quarter! *A dollar and a quarter!* Pay attention, for crise sakes!

ROY. All right, take it easy. Take it easy.

OSCAR. Let's calm down, everyone, heh?

MURRAY. I'm sorry. I can't help it. (*Points to* SPEED.) He makes me nervous.

SPEED. I make *you* nervous. You make *me* nervous. You make *everyone* nervous.

MURRAY (*sarcastic*). I'm sorry. Forgive me. I'll kill myself.

OSCAR. Murray!

(*He motions with his head to* FELIX.)

MURRAY (*realizes his error*). Oh! Sorry.

(SPEED *glares at him. They all sit in silence a moment, until* VINNIE *catches sight of* FELIX, *who is now staring out an upstage window. He quickly calls the others' attention to* FELIX.)

FELIX (*looking back at them from the window*). Gee, it's a pretty view from here. What is it, twelve floors?

OSCAR (*quickly crossing to the window and closing it*). No. It's only eleven. That's all. Eleven. It says twelve but it's really only eleven. (*He then turns and closes the other window as* FELIX *watches him.* OSCAR *shivers slightly.*) Chilly in here. (*To the others.*) Isn't it chilly in here?

(*He crosses back to the table.*)

ROY. Yeah, that's much better.

OSCAR (*to* FELIX). Want to sit down and play? It's still early.

VINNIE. Sure. We're in no rush. We'll be here till three, four in the morning.

FELIX (*shrugs*). I don't know; I just don't feel much like playing now.

OSCAR (*sitting at the table*). Oh! Well, what *do* you feel like doing?

FELIX (*shrugs*). I'll find *something*. (*He starts to walk toward the other room.*) Don't worry about me.

OSCAR. Where are you going?

FELIX (*stops in the doorway. He looks at the others who are all staring at him*). To the john.

OSCAR (*looks at the others, worried, then at* FELIX). Alone?

FELIX (*nods*). I always go alone! Why?

OSCAR (*shrugs*). No reason. You gonna be in there long?

FELIX (*shrugs, then says meaningfully, like a martyr*). As long as it takes.

(*Then he goes into the bathroom and slams the door shut behind him. Immediately they all jump up and crowd about the bathroom door, whispering in frenzied anxiety.*)

MURRAY. Are you crazy? Letting him go to the john alone?

OSCAR. What did you want me to do?

ROY. Stop him! Go in with him!

OSCAR. Suppose he just has to go to the john?

MURRAY. Supposing he does? He's better off being embarrassed than dead!

OSCAR. How's he going to kill himself in the john?

SPEED. What do you mean, how? Razor blades, pills. Anything that's in there.

OSCAR. That's the kids' bathroom. The worst he could do is brush his teeth to death.

ROY. He could jump.

VINNIE. That's right. Isn't there a window in there?

OSCAR. It's only six inches wide.

MURRAY. He could break the glass. He could cut his wrists.

OSCAR. He could also flush himself into the East River. I'm telling you he's not going to try anything!

(*He moves to the table.*)

ROY (*goes to the doorway*). Shhh! Listen! He's crying. (*There is a pause as all listen as* FELIX *sobs.*) You hear that. He's crying.

MURRAY. Isn't that terrible? For God's sakes, Oscar, do something! Say something!

OSCAR. What? What do you say to a man who's crying in your bathroom?

(*There is the sound of the toilet flushing and* ROY *makes a mad dash back to his chair.*)

ROY. He's coming!

(*They all scramble back to their places.* MURRAY *gets mixed up with* VINNIE *and they quickly straighten it out.* FELIX *comes back into the room. But he seems calm and collected, with no evident sign of having cried.*)

FELIX. I guess I'll be running along.

(*He starts for the door.* OSCAR *jumps up. So do the others.*)

OSCAR. Felix, wait a second.

FELIX. No! No! I can't talk to you. I can't talk to anyone.

(*They all try to grab him, stopping him near the stairs.*)

MURRAY. Felix, please. We're your friends. Don't run out like this.

(FELIX *struggles to pull away.*)

OSCAR. Felix, sit down. Just for a minute. Talk to us.

FELIX. There's nothing to talk about. There's nothing to say. It's over. Over. Everything is over. Let me go!

(*He breaks away from them and dashes into the stage-right bedroom. They start to chase him and he dodges from the bedroom through the adjoining door into the bathroom.*)

ROY. Stop him! Grab him!

FELIX (*looking for an exit*). Let me out! I've got to get out of here!

OSCAR. Felix, you're hysterical.

FELIX. Please let me out of here!

MURRAY. The john! Don't let him get in the john!

FELIX (*comes out of the bathroom with* ROY *hanging onto him, and the others trailing behind*). Leave me alone. Why doesn't everyone leave me alone?

OSCAR. All right, Felix, I'm warning you. Now cut it out!

(*He throws a half-filled glass of water, which he has picked up from the bookcase, into* FELIX's *face.*)

FELIX. It's *my* problem. I'll work it out. Leave me alone. Oh, my stomach.

(*He collapses in* ROY's *arms.*)

MURRAY. What's the matter with your stomach?

VINNIE. He looks sick. Look at his face.

(*They all try to hold him as they lead him over to the couch.*)

FELIX. I'm not sick. I'm all right. I didn't take anything. I swear. Ohh, my stomach.

OSCAR. What do you mean you didn't take anything? What did you take?

FELIX (*sitting on the couch*). Nothing! Nothing! I didn't take anything. Don't tell Frances what I did, please! Oohh, my stomach.

MURRAY. He took something! I'm telling you he took something.

OSCAR. What, Felix? *What?*

FELIX. Nothing! I didn't take anything.

OSCAR. Pills? Did you take pills?

FELIX. No! No!

OSCAR (*grabbing* FELIX). Don't lie to me, Felix. Did you take pills?

FELIX. No, I didn't. I didn't take anything.

MURRAY. Thank God he didn't take pills.

(*They all relax and take a breath of relief.*)

FELIX. Just a few, that's all.

(*They all react in alarm and concern over the pills.*)

OSCAR. He took pills.

MURRAY. How many pills?

OSCAR. What kind of pills?

FELIX. I don't know what kind. Little green ones. I just grabbed anything out of her medicine cabinet. I must have been crazy.

OSCAR. Didn't you look? Didn't you see what kind?

FELIX. I couldn't see. The light's broken. Don't call Frances. Don't tell her. I'm so ashamed. So ashamed.

OSCAR. Felix, how many pills did you take?

FELIX. I don't know. I can't remember.

OSCAR. I'm calling Frances.

FELIX (*grabs him*). No! Don't call her. Don't call her. If she hears I took a whole bottle of pills . . .

MURRAY. A whole bottle? *A whole bottle of pills?* (*He turns to* VINNIE.) My God, call an ambulance!

(VINNIE *runs to the front door.*)

OSCAR (*to* MURRAY). You don't even know what *kind!*

MURRAY. What's the difference? He took

a whole bottle!

OSCAR. Maybe they were vitamins. He could be the healthiest one in the room! Take it easy, will you?

FELIX. Don't call Frances. Promise me you won't call Frances.

MURRAY. Open his collar. Open the window. Give him some air.

SPEED. Walk him around. Don't let him go to sleep.

(SPEED *and* MURRAY *pick* FELIX *up and walk him around, while* ROY *rubs his wrists.*)

ROY. Rub his wrists. Keep his circulation going.

VINNIE (*running to the bathroom to get a compress*). A cold compress. Put a cold compress on his neck.

(*They sit* FELIX *in the armchair, still chattering in alarm.*)

OSCAR. One doctor at a time, heh? All the interns shut the hell up!

FELIX. I'm all right. I'll be all right. (*To* OSCAR *urgently.*) You didn't call Frances, did you?

MURRAY (*to the others*). You just gonna stand here? No one's gonna do anything? I'm calling a doctor.

(*He crosses to the phone.*)

FELIX. No! No doctor.

MURRAY. You *gotta* have a doctor.

FELIX. I don't need a doctor.

MURRAY. You gotta get the pills out.

FELIX. I got them out. I threw up before! (*He sits back weakly.* MURRAY *hangs up the phone.*) Don't you have a root beer or a ginger ale?

(VINNIE *gives the compress to* SPEED.)

ROY (*to* VINNIE). Get him a drink.

OSCAR (*glares angrily at* FELIX). He threw up!

VINNIE. Which would you rather have, Felix, the root beer or the ginger ale?

SPEED (*to* VINNIE). Get him the drink! Just get him the drink.

(VINNIE *runs into the kitchen as* SPEED *puts the compress on* FELIX's *head.*)

FELIX. Twelve years. Twelve years we were married. Did you know we were married twelve years, Roy?

ROY (*comforting him*). Yes, Felix. I knew.

FELIX (*with great emotion in his voice*). And now it's over. Like that, it's over. That's hysterical, isn't it?

SPEED. Maybe it was just a fight. You've had fights before, Felix.

FELIX. No, it's over. She's getting a lawyer tomorrow. My cousin. She's using *my* cousin! (*He sobs.*) Who am *I* going to get?

(VINNIE *comes out of the kitchen with a glass of root beer.*)

MURRAY (*patting his shoulder*). It's okay, Felix. Come on. Take it easy.

VINNIE (*gives the glass to* FELIX). Here's the root beer.

FELIX. I'm all right, honestly. I'm just crying.

(*He puts his head down. They all look at him helplessly.*)

MURRAY. All right, let's not stand around looking at him. (*Pushes* SPEED *and* VINNIE *away.*) Let's break it up, heh?

FELIX. Yes, don't stand there looking at me. Please.

OSCAR (*to the others*). Come on, he's all right. Let's call it a night.

(MURRAY, SPEED *and* ROY *turn in their chips at the poker table, get their coats and get ready to go.*)

FELIX. I'm so ashamed. Please, fellas, forgive me.

VINNIE (*bending to* FELIX). Oh, Felix, we—we understand.

FELIX. Don't say anything about this to anyone, Vinnie. Will you promise me?

VINNIE. I'm going to Florida tomorrow.

FELIX. Oh, that's nice. Have a good time.

VINNIE. Thanks.

FELIX (*turns away and sighs in despair*). We were going to go to Florida next winter. (*He laughs, but it's a sob.*) Without the kids! Now they'll go without me.

(VINNIE *gets his coat and* OSCAR *ushers them all to the door.*)

MURRAY (*stopping at the door*). Maybe one of us should stay?

OSCAR. It's all right, Murray.

MURRAY. Suppose he tries something again?

OSCAR. He won't try anything again.

MURRAY. How do you *know* he won't try anything again?

FELIX (*turns to* MURRAY). I won't try anything again. I'm very tired.

OSCAR (*to* MURRAY). You hear? He's very tired. He had a busy night. Good night, fellows.

(*They all ad lib goodbyes and leave.*

The door closes, but opens immediately and ROY *comes back in.)*

ROY. If anything happens, Oscar, just call me.

(He exits, and as the door starts to close, it reopens and SPEED *comes in.)*

SPEED. I'm three blocks away. I could be here in five minutes.

(He exits, and as the door starts to close, it reopens and VINNIE *comes back in.)*

VINNIE. If you need me I'll be at the Meridian Motel in Miami Beach.

OSCAR. You'll be the first one I'll call, Vinnie.

*(*VINNIE *exits. The door closes and then reopens as* MURRAY *comes back.)*

MURRAY *(to* OSCAR*).* You're sure?

OSCAR. I'm sure.

MURRAY *(loudly to* FELIX, *as he gestures to* OSCAR *to come to the door).* Good night, Felix. Try to get a good night's sleep. I guarantee you things are going to look a lot brighter in the morning. *(To* OSCAR, *sotto voce.)* Take away his belt and his shoe laces.

(He nods and exits. OSCAR *turns and looks at* FELIX *sitting in the armchair and slowly moves across the room. There is a moment's silence.)*

OSCAR *(he looks at* FELIX *and sighs).* Ohh, Felix, Felix, Felix, Felix!

FELIX *(sits with his head buried in his hands. He doesn't look up).* I know, I know, I know, I know! What am I going to do, Oscar?

OSCAR. You're gonna wash down the pills with some hot, black coffee. *(He starts for the kitchen, then stops.)* Do you think I could leave you alone for two minutes?

FELIX. No, I don't think so! Stay with me, Oscar. Talk to me.

OSCAR. A cup of black coffee. It'll be good for you. Come on in the kitchen. I'll sit on you.

FELIX. Oscar, the terrible thing is, I think I still love her. It's a lousy marriage but I still love her. I didn't want this divorce.

OSCAR *(sitting on the arm of the couch).* How about some Ovaltine? You like Ovaltine? With a couple of fig newtons or chocolate mallomars?

FELIX. All right, so we didn't get along. But we had two wonderful kids, and a beautiful home. Didn't we, Oscar?

OSCAR. How about vanilla wafers? Or Vienna fingers? I got everything.

FELIX. What more does she want? What does *any* woman want?

OSCAR. I want to know what *you* want. Ovaltine, coffee or tea. Then we'll get to the divorce.

FELIX. It's not fair, damn it! It's just not fair! *(He bangs his fist on the arm of the chair angrily, then suddenly winces in great pain and grabs his neck.)* Oh! Ohh, my neck. My neck!

OSCAR. What? What?

FELIX *(he gets up and paces in pain. He is holding his twisted neck).* It's a nerve spasm. I get it in the neck. Oh! Ohh, that hurts.

OSCAR *(rushing to help).* Where? Where does it hurt?

FELIX *(stretches out an arm like a halfback).* Don't touch me! Don't touch me!

OSCAR. I just want to see where it hurts.

FELIX. It'll go away. Just let me alone a few minutes. Ohh! Ohh!

OSCAR *(moving to the couch).* Lie down; I'll rub it. It'll ease the pain.

FELIX *(in wild contortions).* You don't know how. It's a special way. Only Frances knows how to rub me.

OSCAR. You want me to ask her to come over and rub you?

FELIX *(yells).* No! No! We're getting divorced. She wouldn't want to rub me anymore. It's tension. I get it from tension. I must be tense.

OSCAR. I wouldn't be surprised. How long does it last?

FELIX. Sometimes a minute, sometimes hours. I once got it while I was driving. I crashed into a liquor store. Ohhh! Ohhh!

(He sits down, painfully, on the couch).

OSCAR *(getting behind him).* You want to suffer or do you want me to rub your stupid neck?

(He starts to massage it.)

FELIX. Easy! Easy!

OSCAR *(yells).* Relax, damn it: relax!

FELIX *(yells back).* Don't yell at me! *(Then quietly.)* What should I do? Tell me nicely.

OSCAR *(rubbing the neck).* Think of warm jello!

FELIX. Isn't that terrible? I can't do it. I can't relax. I sleep in one position all night. Frances says when I die on my tombstone it's going to say, "Here Stands

Felix Ungar." (*He winces.*) Oh! Ohh!

OSCAR (*stops rubbing*). Does that hurt?

FELIX. No, it feels good.

OSCAR. Then say so. You make the same sound for pain or happiness.

(*Starts to massage his neck again.*)

FELIX. I know. I know. Oscar—I think I'm crazy.

OSCAR. Well, if it'll make you feel any better, I think so too.

FELIX. I mean it. Why else do I go to pieces like this? Coming up here, scaring you to death. Trying to kill myself. What is that?

OSCAR. That's panic. You're a panicky person. You have a low threshold for composure.

(*He stops rubbing.*)

FELIX. Don't stop. It feels good.

OSCAR. If you don't relax I'll break my fingers. (*Touches his hair.*) Look at this. The only man in the world with clenched hair.

FELIX. I do terrible things, Oscar. You know I'm a cry baby.

OSCAR. Bend over.

(FELIX *bends over and* OSCAR *begins to massage his back.*)

FELIX (*head down*). I tell the whole world my problems.

OSCAR (*massaging hard*). Listen, if this hurts just tell me, because I don't know what the hell I'm doing.

FELIX. It just isn't nice, Oscar, running up here like this, carrying on like a nut.

OSCAR (*finishes massaging*). How does your neck feel?

FELIX (*twists his neck*). Better. Only my back hurts. (*He gets up and paces, rubbing his back.*)

OSCAR. What you need is a drink.

(*He starts for the bar.*)

FELIX. I can't drink. It makes me sick. I tried drinking last night.

OSCAR (*at the bar*). Where *were* you last night?

FELIX. Nowhere. I just walked.

OSCAR. All night?

FELIX. All night.

OSCAR. In the rain?

FELIX. No. In a hotel. I couldn't sleep. I walked around the room all night. It was over near Times Square. A dirty, depressing room. Then I found myself looking out the window. And suddenly, I began to think about jumping.

OSCAR (*he has two glasses filled and crosses to* FELIX). What changed your mind?

FELIX. Nothing. I'm still thinking about it.

OSCAR. Drink this.

(*He hands him a glass, crosses to the couch and sits.*)

FELIX. I don't want to get divorced, Oscar. I don't want to suddenly change my whole life. (*He moves to the couch and sits next to* OSCAR.) Talk to me, Oscar. What am I going to do? What am I going to do?

OSCAR. You're going to pull yourself together. And then you're going to drink that Scotch, and then you and I are going to figure out a whole new life for you.

FELIX. Without Frances? Without the kids?

OSCAR. It's been done before.

FELIX (*paces around*). You don't understand, Oscar. I'm nothing without them. I'm—*nothing!*

OSCAR. What do you mean, nothing? You're something! (FELIX *sits in the armchair.*) A person! You're flesh and blood and bones and hair and nails and ears. You're not a fish. You're not a buffalo. You're *you!* You walk and talk and cry and complain and eat little green pills and send suicide telegrams. No one else does that, Felix. I'm telling you, *you're the only one of its kind in the world!* (*He goes to the bar.*) Now drink that.

FELIX. Oscar, you've been through it yourself. What did you do? How did you get through those first few nights?

OSCAR (*pours a drink*). I did exactly what you're doing.

FELIX. Getting hysterical!

OSCAR. No, drinking! *Drinking!* (*He comes back to the couch with the bottle and sits.*) I drank for four days and four nights. And then I fell through a window. I was bleeding but I was forgetting.

(*He drinks again.*)

FELIX. How can you forget your kids? How can you wipe out twelve years of marriage?

OSCAR. You can't. When you walk into eight empty rooms every night it hits you in the face like a wet glove. But those are the facts, Felix. You've got to face it. You can't spend the rest of your life crying. It annoys people in the movies! Be a good boy and drink your Scotch.

(*He stretches out on the couch with his head near* FELIX.)

FELIX. I can imagine what Frances must be going through.

OSCAR. What do you mean, what *she's* going through?

FELIX. It's much harder on the woman, Oscar. She's all alone with the kids. Stuck there in the house. She can't get out like me. I mean where is she going to find someone now at her age? With two kids. Where?

OSCAR. I don't know. Maybe someone'll come to the door! Felix, there's a hundred thousand divorces a year. There must be *something* nice about it. (FELIX *suddenly puts both his hands over his ears and hums quietly.*) What's the matter now?

(*He sits up.*)

FELIX. My ears are closing up. I get it from the sinus. It must be the dust in here. I'm allergic to dust.

(*He hums. Then he gets up and tries to clear his ears by hopping first on one leg then the other as he goes to the window and opens it.*)

OSCAR (*jumping up*). What are you doing?

FELIX. I'm not going to jump. I'm just going to breathe. (*He takes deep breaths.*) I used to drive Frances crazy with my allergies. I'm allergic to perfume. For a while the only thing she could wear was my after-shave lotion. I was impossible to live with. It's a wonder she took it this long.

(*He suddenly bellows like a moose. He makes this strange sound another time.* OSCAR *looks at him dumbfounded.*)

OSCAR. What are you doing?

FELIX. I'm trying to clear my ears. You create a pressure inside and then it opens it up.

(*He bellows again.*)

OSCAR. Did it open up?

FELIX. A little bit. (*He rubs his neck.*) I think I strained my throat.

(*He paces about the room.*)

OSCAR. Felix, why don't you leave yourself alone? Don't tinker.

FELIX. I can't help myself. I drive everyone crazy. A marriage counselor once kicked me out of his office. He wrote on my chart, "Lunatic!" I don't blame her. It's impossible to be married to me.

OSCAR. It takes two to make a rotten marriage.

(*He lies back down on the couch.*)

FELIX. You don't know what I was like at home. I bought her a book and made her write down every penny we spent. Thirty-eight cents for cigarettes; ten cents for a paper. Everything had to go in the book. And then we had a big fight because I said she forgot to write down how much the book was. Who could live with anyone like that?

OSCAR. An accountant! What do I know? We've not perfect. We all have faults.

FELIX. Faults? Heh! Faults. We have a maid who comes in to clean three times a week. And on the other days, Frances does the cleaning. And at night, after they've both cleaned up, I go in and clean the whole place again. I can't help it. I like things clean. Blame it on my mother. I was toilet-trained at five months old.

OSCAR. How do you remember things like that?

FELIX. I loused up the marriage. Nothing was ever right. I used to recook everything. The minute she walked out of the kitchen I would add salt or pepper. It's not that I didn't trust her, it's just that I was a better cook. Well, I cooked myself out of a marriage. (*He bangs his head with the palm of his hand three times.*) God damned idiot!

(*He sinks down in the armchair.*)

OSCAR. Don't do that; you'll get a headache.

FELIX. I can't stand it, Oscar. I hate me. Oh, boy, do I hate me.

OSCAR. You don't hate you. You love you. You think no one has problems like you.

FELIX. Don't give me that analyst jazz. I happen to know I hate my guts.

OSCAR. Come on, Felix; I've never *seen* anyone so in love.

FELIX (*hurt*). I thought you were my friend.

OSCAR. That's why I can talk to you like this. Because I love you almost as much as *you* do.

FELIX. Then help me.

OSCAR (*up on one elbow*). How can I help you when I can't help myself? You think *you're* impossible to live with? Blanche used to say, "What time do you want dinner?" And I'd say, "I don't know. I'm not hungry." Then at three o'clock in the morning I'd wake her up and say, "Now!" I've been one of the highest paid sportswriters in the East for the past fourteen years, and we saved eight and a half dollars—in pennies! I'm never home, I gamble, I burn cigar holes in the furniture, drink like a fish and lie to her every chance I get. And for our tenth wedding anniversary, I took her to see the New York Rangers–Detroit Red Wings hockey game where she got hit with a puck. And I *still* can't understand why she left me. That's how impossible *I* am!

FELIX. I'm not like you, Oscar. I couldn't take it living all alone. I don't know how I'm going to work. They've got to fire me. How am I going to make a living?

OSCAR. You'll go on street corners and cry. They'll throw nickels at you! You'll work, Felix; you'll work.

(*He lies back down.*)

FELIX. You think I ought to call Frances?

OSCAR (*about to explode*). What for? (*He sits up.*)

FELIX. Well, talk it out again.

OSCAR. You've *talked* it all out. There are no words left in your entire marriage. When are you going to face up to it?

FELIX. I can't help it, Oscar; I don't know what to do.

OSCAR. Then listen to me. Tonight you're going to sleep here. And tomorrow you're going to get your clothes and your electric toothbrush and you'll move in with me.

FELIX. No. no. It's your apartment. I'll be in the way.

OSCAR. There's eight rooms. We could go for a year without seeing each other. Don't you understand? I *want* you to move in.

FELIX. Why? I'm a pest.

OSCAR. I *know* you're a pest. You don't have to keep telling me.

FELIX. Then why do you want me to live with you?

OSCAR. Because I can't stand living alone, that's why! For crying out loud, I'm proposing to you. What do you want, a ring?

FELIX (*moves to* OSCAR). Well, Oscar, if you really mean it, there's a lot I can do around here. I'm very handy around the house. I can fix things.

OSCAR. You don't have to fix things.

FELIX. I want to do *something*, Oscar.

Let me do something.

OSCAR (*nods*). All right, you can take my wife's initials off the towels. Anything you want.

FELIX (*beginning to tidy up*). I can cook. I'm a terrific cook.

OSCAR. You don't have to cook. I eat cold cuts for breakfast.

FELIX. Two meals a day at home, we'll save a fortune. We've got to pay alimony, you know.

OSCAR (*happy to see* FELIX's *new optimism*). All right, you can cook.

(*He throws a pillow at him.*)

FELIX (*throws the pillow back*). Do you like leg of lamb?

OSCAR. Yes, I like leg of lamb.

FELIX. I'll make it tomorrow night. I'll have to call Frances. She has my big pot.

OSCAR. *Will you forget Frances!* We'll get our own pots. Don't drive me crazy before you move in. (*The phone rings.* OSCAR *picks it up quickly.*) Hello? Oh, hello, Frances!

FELIX (*stops cleaning and starts to wave his arms wildly. He whispers screamingly*). I'm not here! I'm not here! You didn't see me. You don't know where I am. I didn't call. I'm not here. I'm not here.

OSCAR (*into the phone*). Yes, he's here.

FELIX (*pacing back and forth*). How does she sound? Is she worried? Is she crying? What is she saying? Does she want to speak to me? I don't want to speak to her.

OSCAR (*into the phone*). Yes, he is!

FELIX. You can tell her I'm not coming back. I've made up my mind. I've had it there. I've taken just as much as she has. You can tell her for me if she thinks I'm coming back she's got another think coming. Tell her. Tell her.

OSCAR (*into the phone*). Yes! Yes, he's fine.

FELIX. Don't tell her I'm fine! You heard me carrying on before. What are you telling her that for? I'm not fine.

OSCAR (*into the phone*). Yes, I understand, Frances.

FELIX (*sits down next to* OSCAR). Does she want to speak to me? Ask her if she wants to speak to me?

OSCAR (*into the phone*). Do you want to speak to him?

FELIX (*reaches for the phone*). Give me

the phone. I'll speak to her.

OSCAR (*into the phone*). Oh. You don't want to speak to him.

FELIX. She doesn't want to speak to me?

OSCAR (*into the phone*). Yeah, I see. Right. Well, goodbye.

(*He hangs up.*)

FELIX. She didn't want to speak to me?

OSCAR. No!

FELIX. Why did she call?

OSCAR. She wants to know when you're coming over for your clothes. She wants to have the room repainted.

FELIX. Oh!

OSCAR (*pats* FELIX *on the shoulder*). Listen, Felix, it's almost one o'clock.

(*He gets up.*)

FELIX. Didn't want to speak to me, huh?

OSCAR. I'm going to bed. Do you want a cup of tea with Fruitanos or Raisinettos?

FELIX. She'll paint it pink. She always wanted it pink.

OSCAR. I'll get you a pair of pajamas. You like stripes, dots, or animals?

(*He goes into the bedroom.*)

FELIX. She's really heartbroken, isn't she? I want to kill myself, and she's picking out colors.

OSCAR (*in the bedroom*). Which bedroom do you want? I'm lousy with bedrooms.

FELIX (*gets up and moves toward the bedroom*). You know, I'm glad. Because she finally made me realize—it's over. It didn't sink in until just this minute.

OSCAR (*comes back with pillow, pillowcase, and pajamas*). Felix, I want you to go to bed.

FELIX. I don't think I believed her until just now. My marriage is *really* over.

OSCAR. Felix, go to bed.

FELIX. Somehow it doesn't seem so bad now. I mean, I think I can live with this thing.

OSCAR. Live with it tomorrow. Go to bed tonight.

FELIX. In a little while. I've got to think. I've got to start rearranging my life. Do you have a pencil and paper?

OSCAR. Not in a little while. Now! It's my house; I make up the bedtime.

(*He throws the pajamas to him.*)

FELIX. Oscar, please. I have to be alone for a few minutes. I've got to get organized. Go on, you go to bed. I'll—I'll clean up.

(*He begins picking up debris from the floor.*)

OSCAR (*putting the pillow into the pillowcase*). You don't have to clean up. I pay a dollar fifty an hour to clean up.

FELIX. It's all right, Oscar. I wouldn't be able to sleep with all this dirt around anyway. Go to bed. I'll see you in the morning.

(*He puts the dishes on the tray.*)

OSCAR. You're not going to do anything big, are you, like rolling up the rugs?

FELIX. Ten minutes, that's all I'll be.

OSCAR. You're sure?

FELIX (*smiles*). I'm sure.

OSCAR. No monkey business?

FELIX. No monkey business. I'll do the dishes and go right to bed.

OSCAR. Yeah.

(*Crosses up to his bedroom, throwing the pillow into the downstage bedroom as he passes. He closes his bedroom door behind him.*)

FELIX (*calls him*). Oscar! (OSCAR *anxiously comes out of his bedroom and crosses to* FELIX.) I'm going to be all right! It's going to take me a couple of days, but I'm going to be all right.

OSCAR (*smiles*). Good! Well, good night, Felix.

(*He turns to go toward the bedroom as* FELIX *begins to plump up a pillow from the couch.*)

FELIX. Good night, Frances.

(OSCAR *stops dead.* FELIX, *unaware of his error, plumps another pillow as* OSCAR *turns and stares at* FELIX *with a troubled expression.*)

ACT TWO

SCENE ONE

Two weeks later, about eleven at night. The poker game is in session again. VINNIE, ROY, SPEED, MURRAY *and* OSCAR *are all seated at the table.* FELIX's *chair is empty.*

There is one major difference between this scene and the opening poker-game scene. It is the appearance of the room. It is immaculately clean. No, not clean. Sterile! Spotless! Not a speck of dirt can be seen under the ten coats of Johnson's Glo-Coat that have been applied to the floor in the last three weeks. No laundry bags, no dirty dishes, no half-filled glasses.

Suddenly FELIX *appears from the kitchen. He carries a tray with glasses and food—and napkins. After putting the tray down, he takes the napkins one at a time, flicks them out to full length and hands one to every player. They take them with grumbling and put them on their laps. He picks up a can of beer and very carefully pours it into a tall glass, measuring it perfectly so that not a drop spills or overflows. With a flourish he puts the can down.*

———

FELIX (*moves to* MURRAY). An ice-cold glass of beer for Murray.

(MURRAY *reaches up for it.*)

MURRAY. Thank you, Felix.

FELIX (*holds the glass back*). Where's your coaster?

MURRAY. My what?

FELIX. Your coaster. The little round thing that goes under the glass.

MURRAY (*looks around on the table*). I think I bet it.

OSCAR (*picks it up and hands it to* MURRAY). I knew I was winning too much. Here!

FELIX. Always try to use your coasters, fellows. (*He picks up another drink from the tray.*) Scotch and a little bit of water?

SPEED (*raises his hand*). Scotch and a little bit of water. (*Proudly.*) And I have my coaster.

(*He holds it up for inspection.*)

FELIX (*hands him the drink*). I hate to be a pest but you know what wet glasses do?

(*He goes back to the tray and picks up and wipes a clean ashtray.*)

OSCAR (*coldly and deliberately*). They leave little rings on the table.

FELIX (*nods*). Ruins the finish. Eats right through the polish.

OSCAR (*to the others*). So let's watch those little rings, huh?

FELIX (*takes an ashtray and a plate with a sandwich from the tray and crosses to the table*). And we have a clean ashtray for Roy (*handing* ROY *the ashtray*). Aaaaand—a sandwich for Vinnie.

(*Like a doting headwaiter, he skillfully places the sandwich in front of* VINNIE.)

VINNIE (*looks at* FELIX, *then at the sandwich*). Gee, it smells good. What is it?

FELIX. Bacon, lettuce and tomato with mayonnaise on pumpernickel toast.

VINNIE (*unbelievingly*). Where'd you get it?

FELIX (*puzzled*). I made it. In the kitchen.

VINNIE. You mean you put in toast and cooked bacon? Just for me?

OSCAR. If you don't like it, he'll make you a meat loaf. Takes him five minutes.

FELIX. It's no trouble. Honest. I love to cook. Try to eat over the dish. I just vacuumed the rug. (*He goes back to the tray, then stops.*) Oscar!

OSCAR (*quickly*). Yes, sir?

FELIX. I forgot what you wanted. What did you ask me for?

OSCAR. Two three-and-a-half-minute eggs and some petit fours.

FELIX (*points to him*). A double gin and tonic. I'll be right back. (FELIX *starts out, then stops at a little box on the bar.*) Who turned off the Pure-A-Tron?

MURRAY. The what?

FELIX. The Pure-A-Tron! (*He snaps it back on.*) Don't play with this, fellows. I'm trying to get some of the grime out of the air.

(*He looks at them and shakes his head disapprovingly, then exits. They all sit in silence a few seconds.*)

OSCAR. Murray, I'll give you two hundred dollars for your gun.

SPEED (*throws his cards on the table and gets up angrily*). I can't take it any more. (*With his hand on his neck.*) I've had it up to here. In the last three hours we played four minutes of poker. I'm not giving up my Friday nights to watch cooking and housekeeping.

ROY (*slumped in his chair, head hanging down*). I can't breathe. (*He points to the Pure-A-Tron.*) That lousy machine is sucking everything out of the air.

VINNIE (*chewing*). Gee, this is delicious. Who wants a bite?

MURRAY. Is the toast warm?

VINNIE. Perfect. And not too much mayonnaise. It's really a well-made sandwich.

MURRAY. Cut me off a little piece.

VINNIE. Give me your napkin. I don't want to drop any crumbs.

SPEED (*watches them, horrified, as* VINNIE *carefully breaks the sandwich over* MURRAY's *napkin. Then he turns to* OSCAR).

Are you listening to this? Martha and Gertrude at the Automat. (*Almost crying in despair.*) What the hell happened to our poker game?

ROY (*still choking*). I'm telling you that thing could kill us. They'll find us here in the morning with our tongues on the floor.

SPEED (*yells at* OSCAR). Do something! Get him back in the game.

OSCAR (*rises, containing his anger*). Don't bother me with your petty little problems. You get this one stinkin' night a week. I'm cooped up here with Dione Lucas twenty-four hours a day.

(*He moves to the window.*)

ROY. It was better before. With the garbage and the smoke, it was better before.

VINNIE (*to* MURRAY). Did you notice what he does with the bread?

MURRAY. What?

VINNIE. He cuts off the crusts. That's why the sandwich is so light.

MURRAY. And then he only uses the soft, green part of the lettuce. (*Chewing.*) It's really delicious.

SPEED (*reacts in amazement and disgust*). I'm going out of my mind.

OSCAR (*yells toward the kitchen*). Felix! Damn it, *Felix!*

SPEED (*takes the kitty box from the bookcase, puts it on the table, and puts the money in*). Forget it. I'm going home.

OSCAR. Sit down!

SPEED. I'll buy a book and I'll start to read again.

OSCAR. Siddown! Will you siddown! (*Yells.*) Felix!

SPEED. Oscar, it's all over. The day his marriage busted up was the end of our poker game. (*He takes his jacket from the back of the chair and crosses to the door.*) If you find some real players next week, call me.

OSCAR (*following him*). You can't run out now. I'm a big loser.

SPEED (*with the door open*). You got no one to blame but yourself. It's all your fault. You're the one who stopped him from killing himself.

(*He exits and slams the door.*)

OSCAR (*stares at the door*). He's right! The man is absolutely right.

(*He moves to the table.*)

MURRAY (*to* VINNIE). Are you going to

eat that pickle?

VINNIE. I wasn't thinking of it. Why? Do you want it?

MURRAY. Unless you want it. It's your pickle.

VINNIE. No, no. Take it. I don't usually eat pickle.

(VINNIE *holds the plate with the pickle out to* MURRAY. OSCAR *slaps the plate, which sends the pickle flying through the air.*)

OSCAR. Deal the cards!

MURRAY. What did you do that for?

OSCAR. Just deal the cards. You want to play poker, deal the cards. You want to eat, go to Schrafft's. (*To* VINNIE.) Keep your sandwich and your pickles to yourself. I'm losing ninety-two dollars and everybody's getting fat! (*He screams.*) Felix!

(FELIX *appears in the kitchen doorway.*)

FELIX. What?

OSCAR. Close the kitchen and sit down. It's a quarter to twelve. I still got an hour and a half to win this month's alimony.

ROY (*sniffs*). What is that smell? Disinfectant! (*He smells the cards.*) It's the cards. He washed the cards!

(*He throws down the cards, takes his jacket from the chair, and moves past the table to put his money into the kitty box.*)

FELIX (*comes to the table with* OSCAR's *drink, which he puts down; then he sits in his own seat*). Okay. What's the bet?

OSCAR (*hurrying to his seat*). I can't believe it. We're gonna play cards again. (*He sits.*) It's up to Roy. Roy, baby, what are you gonna do?

ROY. I'm going to get in a cab and go to Central Park. If I don't get some fresh air, you got yourself a dead accountant.

(*He moves toward the door.*)

OSCAR (*follows him*). What do you mean? It's not even twelve o'clock.

ROY (*turns back to* OSCAR). Look, I've been sitting here breathing Lysol and ammonia for four hours! Nature didn't intend for poker to be played like that. (*He crosses to the door.*) If you wanna have a game next week (*He points to* FELIX.) either Louis Pasteur cleans up *after* we've gone, or we play in the Hotel Dixie! Good night!

(*He goes and slams the door. There is a moment's silence.* OSCAR *goes back to the table and sits.*)

OSCAR. We got just enough for handball!

FELIX. Gee, I'm sorry. Is it my fault?

VINNIE. No, I guess no one feels like playing much lately.

MURRAY. Yeah. I don't know what it is, but something's happening to the old gang.

(*He goes to a side chair, sits and puts on his shoes.*)

OSCAR. Don't you know what's happening to the old gang? It's breaking up. Everyone's getting divorced. I swear, we used to have better games when we couldn't get out at night.

VINNIE (*getting up and putting on his jacket*). Well, I guess I'll be going too. Bebe and I are driving to Asbury Park for the weekend.

FELIX. Just the two of you, heh? Gee, that's nice! You always do things like that together, don't you?

VINNIE (*shrugs*). We have to. I don't know how to drive! (*He takes all the money from the kitty box and moves to the door.*) You coming, Murray?

MURRAY (*gets up, takes his jacket and moves toward the door*). Yeah, why not? If I'm not home by one o'clock with a hero sandwich and a frozen éclair, she'll have an all-points out on me. Ahhh, you guys got the life.

FELIX. Who?

MURRAY (*turns back*). Who? You! The Marx Brothers! Laugh, laugh laugh. What have you got to worry about? If you suddenly want to go to the Playboy Club to hunt Bunnies, who's gonna stop you?

FELIX. I don't belong to the Playboy Club.

MURRAY. I know you don't, Felix, it's just a figure of speech. Anyway, it's not such a bad idea. Why don't you join?

FELIX. Why?

MURRAY. Why! Because for twenty-five dollars they give you a key—and you walk into Paradise. *My* keys cost thirty cents—and you walk into corned beef and cabbage. (*He winks at him.*) Listen to me.

(*He moves to the door.*)

FELIX. What are you talking about, Murray? You're a happily married man.

MURRAY (*turns back on the landing*). I'm not talking about *my* situation. (*He puts on his jacket.*) I'm talking about *yours!* Fate has just played a cruel and rotten trick on you, so enjoy it! (*He turns to go, revealing "PAL" letters sewn on the back of his jacket.*) C'mon, Vinnie.

(VINNIE *waves goodbye and they both exit.*)

FELIX (*staring at the door*). That's funny, isn't it, Oscar? They think we're happy. They really think we're enjoying this. (*He gets up and begins to straighten up the chairs.*) They don't know, Oscar. They don't know what it's like.

(*He gives a short, ironic laugh, tucks the napkins under his arm and starts to pick up the dishes from the table.*)

OSCAR. I'd be immensely grateful to you, Felix, if you didn't clean up just now.

FELIX (*puts dishes on the tray*). It's only a few things. (*He stops and looks back at the door.*) I can't get over what Murray just said. You know I think they really envy us. (*He clears more stuff from the table.*)

OSCAR. Felix, leave everything alone. I'm not through dirtying-up for the night.

(*He drops some poker chips on the floor.*)

FELIX (*putting stuff on the tray*). But don't you see the irony of it? Don't you see it, Oscar?

OSCAR (*sighs heavily*). Yes, I see it.

FELIX (*clearing the table*). No, you don't. I really don't think you do.

OSCAR. Felix, I'm telling you I see the irony of it.

FELIX (*pauses*). Then tell me. What is it? What's the irony?

OSCAR (*deep breath*). The irony is—unless we can come to some other arrangement, I'm gonna kill you! That's the irony.

FELIX. What's wrong?

(*He crosses back to the tray and puts down all the glasses and other things.*)

OSCAR. There's something wrong with this system, that's what's wrong. I don't think that two single men living alone in a big eight-room apartment should have a cleaner house than my mother.

FELIX (*gets the rest of the dishes, glasses and coasters from the table*). What are you talking about? I'm just going to put the dishes in the sink. You want me to leave them here all night?

OSCAR (*takes his glass, which FELIX has put on the tray, and crosses to the bar for a refill*). I don't care if you take them to bed with you. You can play Mr. Clean all you want. But don't make *me* feel guilty.

FELIX (*takes the tray into the kitchen, leaving the swinging door open*). I'm not asking you to do it, Oscar. You don't have to clean up.

OSCAR (*moves up to the door*). That's why you make me feel guilty. You're always in my bathroom hanging up my towels. Whenever I smoke you follow me around with an ashtray. Last night I found you washing the kitchen floor, shaking your head and moaning, "Footprints, footprints!"

(*He paces around the room.*)

FELIX (*comes back to the table with a silent butler. He dumps the ashtrays, then wipes them carefully*). I didn't say they were yours.

OSCAR (*angrily sits down in the wing chair*). Well, they *were* mine, damn it. I have feet and they make prints. What do you want me to do, climb across the cabinets?

FELIX. No! I want you to walk on the floor.

OSCAR. I appreciate that! I really do.

FELIX (*crosses to the telephone table and cleans the ashtray there*). I'm just trying to keep the place livable. I didn't realize I irritated you that much.

OSCAR. I just feel *I* should have the right to decide when my bathtub needs a going over with Dutch Cleanser. It's the democratic way!

FELIX (*puts the silent butler and his rag down on the coffee table and sits down glumly on the couch*). I was wondering how long it would take.

OSCAR. How long *what* would take?

FELIX. Before I got on your nerves.

OSCAR. I didn't say you get on my nerves.

FELIX. Well, it's the same thing. You said I irritated you.

OSCAR. *You* said you irritated me. *I* didn't say it.

FELIX. Then what *did* you say?

OSCAR. I don't know *what* I said. What's the difference what I said?

FELIX. It doesn't make any difference. I was just repeating what I thought you said.

OSCAR. Well, don't repeat what you *thought* I said. Repeat what I *said!* My God, that's irritating!

FELIX. You see! You *did* say it!

OSCAR. I don't believe this whole conversation.

(*He gets up and paces by the table.*)

FELIX (*pawing with a cup*). Oscar, I'm —I'm sorry. I don't know what's wrong with me.

OSCAR (*still pacing*). And don't pout. If you want to fight, we'll fight. But don't pout! Fighting *I* win. Pouting *you* win!

FELIX. You're right. Everything you say about me is absolutely right.

OSCAR (*really angry, turns to* FELIX). And don't give in so easily. I'm *not* always right. Sometimes *you're* right.

FELIX. You're right. I do that. I always figure I'm in the wrong.

OSCAR. Only this time you *are* wrong. And I'm right.

FELIX. Oh, leave me alone.

OSCAR. And don't sulk. That's the same as pouting.

FELIX. I know. I know. (*He squeezes his cup with anger.*) Damn me, why can't I do one lousy thing right?

(*He suddenly stands up and cocks his arm back, about to hurl the cup angrily against the front door. Then he thinks better of it, puts the cup down and sits.*)

OSCAR (*watching this*). Why didn't you throw it?

FELIX. I almost did. I get so insane with myself sometimes.

OSCAR. Then why don't you throw the cup?

FELIX. Because I'm trying to control myself.

OSCAR. Why?

FELIX. What do you mean, why?

OSCAR. Why do you have to control yourself? You're angry, you felt like throwing the cup, why don't you throw it?

FELIX. Because there's no point to it. I'd still be angry and I'd have a broken cup.

OSCAR. How do you *know* how you'd feel? Maybe you'd feel *wonderful*. Why do you have to control every single thought in your head? Why don't you let loose *once* in your life? Do something that you *feel* like doing—and not what you *think* you're supposed to do. Stop keeping books, Felix. Relax. Get drunk. Get angry. C'mon, *break the goddamned cup!*

(FELIX *suddenly stands up and hurls the cup against the door, smashing it to pieces. Then he grabs his shoulder in pain.*)

FELIX. Oww! I hurt my arm!

(*He sinks down on the couch, massag-*)

ing his arm.)

OSCAR (*throws up his hands*). You're hopeless! You're a hopeless mental case!

(*He paces around the table.*)

FELIX (*grimacing with pain*). I'm not supposed to throw with that arm. What a stupid thing to do.

OSCAR. Why don't you live in a closet? I'll leave your meals outside the door and slide in the papers. Is that safe enough?

FELIX (*rubbing his arm*). I used to have bursitis in this arm. I had to give up golf. Do you have a heating pad?

OSCAR. How can you hurt your arm throwing a cup? If it had coffee in it, that's one thing. But an empty cup . . .

(*He sits in the wing chair.*)

FELIX. All right, cut it out, Oscar. That's the way I am. I get hurt easily. I can't help it.

OSCAR. You're not going to cry, are you? I think all those tears dripping on the arm is what gave you bursitis.

FELIX (*holding his arm*). I once got it just from combing my hair.

OSCAR (*shaking his head*). A world full of room-mates and I pick myself the Tin Man. (*He sighs.*) Oh, well, I suppose I could have done worse.

FELIX (*moves the rag and silent butler to the bar. Then he takes the chip box from the bar and crosses to the table*). You're darn right, you could have. A *lot* worse.

OSCAR. How?

FELIX. What do you mean, how? How'd you like to live with ten-thumbs Murray or Speed and his complaining? (*He gets down on his knees, picks up the chips and puts them into the box.*) Don't forget I cook and clean and take care of this house. I save us a lot of money, don't I?

OSCAR. Yeah, but then you keep me up all night counting it.

FELIX (*goes to the table and sweeps the chips and cards into the box*). Now wait a minute. We're not always going at each other. We have some fun too, don't we?

OSCAR (*crosses to the couch*). Fun? Felix, getting a clear picture on Channel Two isn't my idea of whoopee.

FELIX. What are you talking about?

OSCAR. All right, what do you and I do every night?

(*He takes off his sneakers and drops them on the floor.*)

FELIX. What do we do? You mean after dinner?

OSCAR. That's right. After we've had your halibut steak and the dishes are done and the sink has been Brillo'd and the pans have been S.O.S.'d and the leftovers have been Saran-Wrapped—what do we do?

FELIX (*finishes clearing the table and puts everything on top of the bookcase*). Well, we read, we talk . . .

OSCAR (*takes off his pants and throws them on the floor*). No, no. *I* read and *you* talk! I try to work and you talk. I take a bath and you talk. I go to sleep and you talk. We've got your life arranged pretty good but I'm still looking for a little entertainment.

FELIX (*pulling the kitchen chairs away from the table*). What are you saying? That I talk too much?

OSCAR (*sits on the couch*). No, no. I'm not complaining. You have a lot to say. What's worrying me is that I'm beginning to listen.

FELIX (*pulls the table into the alcove*). Oscar, I told you a hundred times, just tell me to shut up. I'm not sensitive.

(*He pulls the love seat down into the room, and centers the table between the windows in the alcove.*)

OSCAR. I don't think you're getting my point. For a husky man, I think I've spent enough evenings discussing tomorrow's menu. The night was made for other things.

FELIX. Like what?

(*He puts two dining chairs neatly on one side of the table.*)

OSCAR. Like unless I get to touch something soft in the next two weeks, I'm in big trouble.

FELIX. You mean women?

(*He puts two other dining chairs neatly on the other side of the table.*)

OSCAR. If you want to give it a name, all right, women!

FELIX (*picks up the two kitchen chairs and starts toward the landing*). That's funny. You know I haven't even *thought* about women in weeks.

OSCAR. I fail to see the humor.

FELIX (*stops*). No, that's really strange. I mean when Frances and I were happy, I don't think there was a girl on the street I didn't stare at for ten minutes. (*He crosses to the kitchen door and pushes it open with his back.*) I used to take the wrong subway home just following a pair of legs. But since we broke up, I don't even know what a woman looks like.

(*He takes the chairs into the kitchen.*)

OSCAR. Well, either I could go downstairs and buy a couple of magazines—or I could make a phone call.

FELIX (*from the kitchen, as he washes the dishes*). What are you saying?

OSCAR (*crosses to a humidor on a small table and takes out a cigar*). I'm saying let's spend one night talking to someone with higher voices than us.

FELIX. You mean go out on a date?

OSCAR. Yah . . .

FELIX. Oh, well, I—I can't.

OSCAR. Why not?

FELIX. Well, it's all right for you. But I'm still married.

OSCAR (*paces toward the kitchen door*). You can *cheat* until the divorce comes through!

FELIX. It's not that. It's just that I have no—no *feeling* for it. I can't explain it.

OSCAR. Try!

FELIX (*comes to the doorway with a brush and dish in his hand*). Listen, I intend to go out. I get lonely too. But I'm just separated a few weeks. Give me a little time.

(*He goes back to the sink.*)

OSCAR. There isn't any time left. I saw *TV Guide* and there's nothing on this week! (*He paces into and through the kitchen and out the kitchen door onto the landing.*) What am I asking you? All I want to do is have dinner with a couple of girls. You just have to eat and talk. It's not hard. You've eaten and talked before.

FELIX. Why do you need me? Can't you go out yourself?

OSCAR. Because I may want to come back here. And if we walk in and find you washing the windows, it puts a damper on things.

(*He sits down.*)

FELIX (*pokes his head out of the kitchen*). I'll take a pill and go to sleep.

(*He goes back into the kitchen.*)

OSCAR. Why take a pill when you can take a girl?

FELIX (*comes out with an aerosol bomb held high over his head and circles around the room, spraying it*). Because I'd feel guilty, that's why. Maybe it doesn't make any sense to you, but that's the way I feel.

(*He puts the bomb on the bar and takes the silent butler and rag into the kitchen. He places them on the sink and busily begins to wipe the refrigerator.*)

OSCAR. Look, for all I care you can take her in the kitchen and make a blueberry pie. But I think it's a lot healthier than sitting up in your bed every night writing Frances's name all through the crossword puzzles. Just for one night, talk to another girl.

FELIX (*pushes the love seat carefully into position and sits, weakening*). But who would I call? The only single girl I know is my secretary and I don't think she likes me.

OSCAR (*jumps up and crouches next to* FELIX). Leave that to me. There's two sisters who live in this building. English girls. One's a widow; the other's a divorcée. They're a barrel of laughs.

FELIX. How do you know?

OSCAR. I was trapped in the elevator with them last week. (*Runs to the telephone table, puts the directory on the floor, and gets down on his knees to look for the number.*) I've been meaning to call them but I didn't know which one to take out. This'll be perfect.

FELIX. What do they look like?

OSCAR. Don't worry. Yours is very pretty.

FELIX. I'm not worried. Which one is mine?

OSCAR (*looking in the book*). The divorcée.

FELIX (*goes to* OSCAR). Why do I get the divorcée?

OSCAR. I don't care. You want the widow?

(*He circles a number on the page with a crayon.*)

FELIX (*sitting on the couch*). No, I don't want the widow. I don't even want the divorcée. I'm just doing this for you.

OSCAR. Look, take whoever you want. When they come in the door, point to the sister of your choice. (*Tears the page out of the book, runs to the bookcase and hangs it up.*) I don't care. I just want to have some laughs.

FELIX. All right. All right.

OSCAR (*crosses to the couch and sits next to* FELIX). Don't say all right. I want you to promise me you're going to try to have a good time. Please, Felix. It's important. Say, "I promise."

FELIX (*nods*). I promise.

OSCAR. Again!

FELIX. I promise!

OSCAR. And no writing in the book, a dollar thirty for the cab.

FELIX. No writing in the book.

OSCAR. No one is to be called Frances. It's Gwendolyn and Cecily.

FELIX. No Frances.

OSCAR. No crying, sighing, moaning or groaning.

FELIX. I'll smile from seven to twelve.

OSCAR. And this above all, no talk of the past. Only the present.

FELIX. And the future.

OSCAR. That's the new Felix I've been waiting for. (*Leaps up and prances around.*) Oh, is this going to be a night. Hey, where do you want to go?

FELIX. For what?

OSCAR. For dinner. Where'll we eat?

FELIX. You mean a restaurant? For the four of us? It'll cost a fortune.

OSCAR. We'll cut down on laundry. We won't wear socks on Thursdays.

FELIX. But that's throwing away money. We can't afford it, Oscar.

OSCAR. We have to eat.

FELIX (*moves to* OSCAR). We'll have dinner here.

OSCAR. *Here?*

FELIX. I'll cook. We'll save thirty, forty dollars.

(*He goes to the couch, sits and picks up the phone.*)

OSCAR. What kind of a double date is that? You'll be in the kitchen all night.

FELIX. No, I won't. I'll put it up in the afternoon. Once I get my potatoes in, I'll have all the time in the world.

(*He starts to dial.*)

OSCAR (*pacing back and forth*). What happened to the new Felix? Who are you calling?

FELIX. Frances. I want to get her recipe for London broil. The girls'll be crazy about it.

(*He dials as* OSCAR *storms off toward his bedroom.*)

CURTAIN

SCENE TWO

It is a few days later, about eight o'clock. No one is on stage. The dining table looks like a page out of House and Garden. *It is set for dinner for four, complete with linen tablecloth, candles and wine glasses. There is a floral centerpiece and flowers about the room, and crackers and dip on the coffee table. There are sounds of activity in the kitchen.*

The front door opens and OSCAR *enters with a bottle of wine in a brown paper bag, his jacket over his arm. He looks about gleefully as he listens to the sounds from the kitchen. He puts the bag on the table and his jacket over a chair.*

———

OSCAR (*calls out in a playful mood*). I'm home, dear! (*He goes into his bedroom, taking off his shirt, and comes skipping out shaving with a cordless razor, with a clean shirt and a tie over his arm. He is joyfully singing as he admires the table.*) Beautiful! Just beautiful! (*He sniffs, obviously catching the aroma from the kitchen.*) Oh, yeah. Something wonderful is going on in that kitchen. (*He rubs his hands gleefully.*) No, sir. There's no doubt about it. I'm the luckiest man on earth. (*He puts the razor into his pocket and begins to put on the shirt.* FELIX *enters slowly from the kitchen. He's wearing a small dish towel as an apron. He has a ladle in one hand. He looks silently and glumly at* OSCAR, *crosses to the armchair and sits.*) I got the wine. (*He takes the bottle out of the bag and puts it on the table.*) Batard Montrachet. Six and a quarter. You don't mind, do you, pussycat? We'll walk to work this week. (FELIX *sits glumly and silently.*) Hey, no kidding, Felix, you did a great job. One little suggestion? Let's come down a little with the lights (*he switches off the wall brackets*) —and up very softly with the music. (*He crosses to the stereo set in the bookcase and picks up some record albums.*) What do you think goes better with London broil, Mancini or Sinatra? (FELIX *just stares ahead.*) Felix? What's the matter? (*He puts the albums down.*) Something's wrong. I can tell by your conversation. (*He goes into the bathroom, gets a bottle of after-shave lotion and comes out putting it on.*) All right, Felix, what is it?

FELIX (*without looking at him*). What is it? Let's start with what time do you think it is?

OSCAR. What time? I don't know. Seven thirty?

FELIX. Seven thirty? Try eight o'clock.

OSCAR (*puts the lotion down on the small table*). All right, so it's eight o'clock. So?

(*He begins to fix his tie.*)

FELIX. So? You said you'd be home at seven.

OSCAR. Is that what I said?

FELIX (*nods*). That's what you said. "I will be home at seven" is what you said.

OSCAR. Okay, I said I'd be home at seven. And it's eight. So what's the problem?

FELIX. If you knew you were going to be late, why didn't you call me?

OSCAR (*pauses while making the knot in his tie*). I couldn't call you. I was busy.

FELIX. Too busy to pick up a phone? Where were you?

OSCAR. I was in the office, working.

FELIX. Working? Ha!

OSCAR. Yes. Working!

FELIX. I called your office at seven o'clock. You were gone.

OSCAR (*tucking in his shirt*). It took me an hour to get home. I couldn't get a cab.

FELIX. Since when do they have cabs in Hannigan's Bar?

OSCAR. Wait a minute. I want to get this down on a tape recorder, because no one'll believe me. You mean now I have to call you if I'm coming home late for dinner?

FELIX (*crosses to* OSCAR). Not *any* dinner. Just the ones I've been slaving over since two o'clock this afternoon—to help save *you* money to pay your wife's alimony.

OSCAR (*controlling himself*). Felix, this is no time to have a domestic quarrel. We have two girls coming down any minute.

FELIX. You mean you told them to be here at eight o'clock?

OSCAR (*takes his jacket and crosses to the couch, then sits and takes some dip from the coffee table*). I don't remember what I said. Seven thirty, eight o'clock. What differences does it make?

FELIX (*follows* OSCAR). I'll tell you what difference. You told me they were coming at seven thirty. You were going to be here at seven to help me with the hors d'oeuvres. At seven thirty they arrive and we have cocktails. At eight o'clock we have dinner. It is now eight o'clock. *My London broil is finished!* If we don't eat now the whole damned thing'll be *dried out!*

OSCAR. Oh, God, help me.

FELIX. Never mind helping *you*. Tell Him to save the meat. Because we got nine dollars and thirty-four cents worth drying up in there right now.

OSCAR. Can't you keep it warm?

FELIX (*pacing*). What do you think I am, the Magic Chef? I'm lucky I got it to come out at eight o'clock. What am I going to do?

OSCAR. I don't know. Keep pouring gravy on it.

FELIX. What gravy?

OSCAR. Don't you have any gravy?

FELIX (*storms over to* OSCAR). Where the hell am I going to get gravy at eight o'clock?

OSCAR (*getting up*). I thought it comes when you cook the meat.

FELIX (*follows him*). When you *cook* the meat? You don't know the first thing you're talking about. You have to make gravy. It doesn't come!

OSCAR. You asked my advice, I'm giving it to you.

(*He puts on his jacket.*)

FELIX. Advice? (*He waves the ladle in his face.*) You didn't know where the kitchen was till I came here and showed you.

OSCAR. You wanna talk to me, put down the spoon.

FELIX (*exploding in rage, again waving the ladle in his face*). Spoon? You dumb ignoramus. It's a ladle. You don't even know it's a ladle.

OSCAR. All right, Felix, get a hold of yourself.

FELIX (*pulls himself together and sits on the love seat*). You think it's so easy? Go on. The kitchen's all yours. Go make a London broil for four people who come a half hour late.

OSCAR (*to no one in particular*). Listen to me. I'm arguing with him over gravy.

(*The bell rings.*)

FELIX (*jumps up*). Well, they're here. Our dinner guests. I'll get a saw and cut the meat.

(*He starts for the kitchen.*)

OSCAR (*stopping him*). Stay where you are!

FELIX. I'm not taking the blame for this dinner.

OSCAR. Who's blaming you? Who even *cares* about the dinner?

FELIX (*moves to* OSCAR). *I* care. I take *pride* in what I do. And you're going to explain to them exactly what happened.

OSCAR. All right, you can take a Polaroid picture of me coming in at eight o'clock! Now take off that stupid apron because I'm opening the door.

(*He rips the towel off* FELIX *and goes to the door.*)

FELIX (*takes his jacket from a dining chair and puts it on*). I just want to get one thing clear. This is the last time I ever cook for you. Because people like you don't even appreciate a decent meal. That's why they have TV dinners.

OSCAR. You through?

FELIX. I'm through!

OSCAR. Then smile. (OSCAR *smiles and opens the door. The girls poke their heads through the door. They are in their young thirties and somewhat attractive. They are undoubtedly British.*) Well, hello.

GWENDOLYN (*to* OSCAR). Hallo!

CECILY (*to* OSCAR). Hallo.

GWENDOLYN. I do hope we're not late.

OSCAR. No, no. You timed it perfectly. Come on in. (*He points to them as they enter.*) Er, Felix, I'd like you to meet two very good friends of mine, Gwendolyn and Cecily . . .

CECILY (*pointing out his mistake*). Cecily and Gwendolyn.

OSCAR. Oh, yes. Cecily and Gwendolyn . . . er (*trying to remember their last name*). Er . . . Don't tell me. Robin? No, no. Cardinal?

GWENDOLYN. Wrong both times. It's Pigeon!

OSCAR. Pigeon. Right. Cecily and Gwendolyn Pigeon.

GWENDOLYN (*to* FELIX). You don't spell it like Walter Pidgeon. You spell it like "Coo-Coo" Pigeon.

OSCAR. We'll remember that if it comes up. Cecily and Gwendolyn, I'd like you to meet my room-mate, and our chef for the evening, Felix Ungar.

CECILY (*holding her hand out*). Heh d'yew dew?

FELIX (*moving to her and shaking her hand*). How do you do?

GWENDOLYN (*holding her hand out*). Heh d'yew dew?

FELIX (*stepping up on the landing and shaking her hand*). How do you do you?

(*This puts him nose to nose with* OSCAR, *and there is an awkward pause as they look at each other.*)

OSCAR. Well, we did that beautifully. Why don't we sit down and make ourselves comfortable?

(FELIX *steps aside and ushers the girls down into the room. There is ad libbing and a bit of confusion and milling about as they all squeeze between the armchair and the couch, and the* PIGEONS *finally seat themselves on the couch.* OSCAR *sits in the armchair, and* FELIX *sneaks past him to the love seat. Finally all have settled down.*)

CECILY. This is ever so nice, isn't it, Gwen?

GWENDOLYN (*looking around*). Lovely. And much nicer than our flat. Do you have help?

OSCAR. Er, yes. I have a man who comes in every night.

CECILY. Aren't you the lucky one?

(CECILY, GWENDOLYN *and* OSCAR *all laugh at her joke.* OSCAR *looks over at* FELIX *but there is no response.*)

OSCAR (*rubs his hands together*). Well, isn't this nice? I was telling Felix yesterday about how we happened to meet.

GWENDOLYN. Oh? Who's Felix?

OSCAR (*a little embarrassed, he points to* FELIX). He is!

GWENDOLYN. Oh, yes, of course. I'm so sorry.

(FELIX *nods that it's all right.*)

CECILY. You know it happened to us again this morning.

OSCAR. What did?

GWENDOLYN. Stuck in the elevator again.

OSCAR. Really? Just the two of you?

CECILY. And poor old Mr. Kessler from the third floor. We were in there half an hour.

OSCAR. No kidding? What happened?

GWENDOLYN. Nothing much, I'm afraid.

(CECILY *and* GWENDOLYN *both laugh at her latest joke, joined by* OSCAR. *He once again looks over at* FELIX, *but there is no response.*)

OSCAR (*rubs his hands again*). Well, this really is nice.

CECILY. And ever so much cooler than our place.

GWENDOLYN. It's like equatorial Africa on our side of the building.

CECILY. Last night it was so bad Gwen and I sat there in nature's own cooling ourselves in front of the open fridge. Can you imagine such a thing?

OSCAR. Er, I'm working on it.

GWENDOLYN. Actually, it's impossible to get a night's sleep. Cec and I really don't know what to do.

OSCAR. Why don't you sleep with an air conditioner?

GWENDOLYN. We haven't got one.

OSCAR. I know. But we have.

GWENDOLYN. Oh, you! I told you about that one, didn't I, Cec?

FELIX. They say it may rain Friday.

(*They all stare at* FELIX.)

GWENDOLYN. Oh?

CECILY. That should cool things off a bit.

OSCAR. I wouldn't be surprised.

FELIX. Although sometimes it gets hotter after it rains.

GWENDOLYN. Yes, it does, doesn't it?

(*They continue to stare at* FELIX.)

FELIX (*jumps up and, picking up the ladle, starts for the kitchen*). Dinner is served!

OSCAR (*stopping him*). No, it isn't!

FELIX. Yes, it is!

OSCAR. No, it isn't! I'm sure the girls would like a cocktail first. (*To the girls.*) Wouldn't you, girls?

GWENDOLYN. Well, I wouldn't put up a struggle.

OSCAR. There you are. (*To* CECILY.) What would you like?

CECILY. Oh, I really don't know. (*To* OSCAR.) What have you got?

FELIX. London broil.

OSCAR (*to* FELIX). She means to drink. (*To* CECILY.) We have everything. And what we don't have, I mix in the medicine cabinet. What'll it be?

(*He crouches next to her.*)

CECILY. Oh, a double vodka.

GWENDOLYN. Cecily, not before dinner.

CECILY (*to the men*). My sister. She watches over me like a mother hen. (*To* OSCAR.) Make it a *small* double vodka.

OSCAR. A small double vodka! And for the beautiful mother hen?

GWENDOLYN. Oh, I'd like something cool. I think I would like to have a double Drambuie with some crushed ice, unless you don't have the crushed ice.

OSCAR. I was up all night with a sledge hammer. I shall return!

(*He goes to the bar and gets bottles of vodka and Drambuie.*)

FELIX (*going to him*). Where are you going?

OSCAR. To get the refreshments.

FELIX (*starting to panic*). Inside? What'll *I* do?

OSCAR. You can finish the weather report.

(*He exits into the kitchen.*)

FELIX (*calls after him*). Don't forget to look at my meat! (*He turns and faces the girls. He crosses to a chair and sits. He crosses his legs nonchalantly but he is ill at ease and he crosses them again. He is becoming aware of the silence and he can no longer get away with just smiling.*) Er, Oscar tells me you're sisters.

CECILY. Yes. That's right.

(*She looks at* GWENDOLYN.)

FELIX. From England.

GWENDOLYN. Yes. That's right.

(*She looks at* CECILY.)

FELIX. I see. (*Silence. Then, his little joke.*) We're not brothers.

CECILY. Yes. We know.

FELIX. Although I am a brother. I have a brother who's a doctor. He lives in Buffalo. That's upstate in New York.

GWENDOLYN (*taking a cigarette from her purse*). Yes, we know.

FELIX. You know my brother?

GWENDOLYN. No. We know that Buffalo is upstate in New York.

FELIX. Oh!

(*He gets up, takes a cigarette lighter from the side table and moves to light* GWENDOLYN's *cigarette.*)

CECILY. We've been there! Have you?

FELIX. No! Is it nice?

CECILY. Lovely.

(FELIX *closes the lighter on* GWENDOLYN's *cigarette and turns to go back to his chair, taking the cigarette, now caught in the lighter, with him. He notices the cigarette and hastily gives it back to* GWENDOLYN, *stopping to light it once again. He puts the lighter back on the table and sits down nervously. There is a pause.*)

FELIX. Isn't that interesting? How long have you been in the United States of

America?

CECILY. Almost four years now.

FELIX (*nods*). Uh huh. Just visiting?

GWENDOLYN (*looks at* CECILY). No! We live here.

FELIX. And you work here too, do you?

CECILY. Yes. We're secretaries for Slenderama.

GWENDOLYN. You know. The health club.

CECILY. People bring us their bodies and we do wonderful things with them.

GWENDOLYN. Actually, if you're interested, we can get you ten per cent off.

CECILY. Off the price, not off your body.

FELIX. Yes, I see. (*He laughs. They all laugh. Suddenly he shouts toward the kitchen.*) Oscar where's the drinks?

OSCAR (*offstage*). Coming! Coming!

CECILY. What field of endeavor are you engaged in?

FELIX. I write the news for CBS.

CECILY. Oh! Fascinating!

GWENDOLYN. Where do you get your ideas from?

FELIX (*he looks at her as though she's a Martian*). From the news.

GWENDOLYN. Oh, yes, of course. Silly me . . .

CECILY. Maybe you can mention Gwen and I in one of your news reports.

FELIX. Well, if you do something spectacular, maybe I will.

CECILY. Oh, we've done spectacular things but I don't think we'd want it spread all over the telly, do you, Gwen?

(*They both laugh.*)

FELIX (*he laughs too, then cries out almost for help*). Oscar!

OSCAR (*offstage*). Yeah, yeah!

FELIX (*to the girls*). It's such a large apartment, sometimes you have to shout.

GWENDOLYN. Just you two baches live here?

FELIX. Baches? Oh, bachelors! We're not bachelors. We're divorced. That is, Oscar's divorced. I'm *getting* divorced.

CECILY. Oh. Small world. We've cut the dinghy loose too, as they say.

GWENDOLYN. Well, you couldn't have a *better* matched foursome, could you?

FELIX (*smiles weakly*). No. I suppose not.

GWENDOLYN. Although technically I'm a widow. I was divorcing my husband, but he died before the final papers came

through.

FELIX. Oh, I'm awfully sorry. (*Sighs.*) It's a terrible thing, isn't it? Divorce.

GWENDOLYN. It can be—if you haven't got the right solicitor.

CECILY. That's true. Sometimes they can drag it out for months. I was lucky. Snip, cut and I was free.

FELIX. I mean it's terrible what it can do to people. After all, what is divorce? It's taking two happy people and tearing their lives completely apart. It's inhuman, don't you think so?

CECILY. Yes, it can be an awful bother.

GWENDOLYN. But of course, that's all water under the bridge now, eh? Er, I'm terribly sorry, but I think I've forgotten your name.

FELIX. Felix.

GWENDOLYN. Oh, yes. Felix.

CECILY. Like the cat.

(FELIX *takes his wallet from his jacket pocket.*)

GWENDOLYN. Well, the Pigeons will have to beware of the cat, won't they?

(*She laughs.*)

CECILY (*nibbles on a nut from the dish*). Mmm, cashews. Lovely.

FELIX (*takes a snapshot out of his wallet*). This is the worst part of breaking up.

(*He hands the picture to* CECILY.)

CECILY (*looks at it*). Childhood sweethearts, were you?

FELIX. No, no. That's my little boy and girl. (CECILY *gives the picture to* GWENDOLYN, *takes a pair of glasses from her purse and puts them on.*) He's seven, she's five.

CECILY (*looks again*). Oh! Sweet.

FELIX. They live with their mother.

GWENDOLYN. I imagine you must miss them terribly.

FELIX (*takes back the picture and looks at it longingly*). I can't stand being away from them. (*Shrugs.*) But—that's what happens with divorce.

CECILY. When do you get to see them?

FELIX. Every night. I stop there on my way home! Then I take them on the weekends, and I get them on holidays and July and August.

CECILY. Oh! Well, when is it that you miss them?

FELIX. Whenever I'm not there. If they didn't have to go to school so early, I'd go over and make them breakfast. They love my French toast.

GWENDOLYN. You're certainly a devoted father.

FELIX. It's Frances who's the wonderful one.

CECILY. She's the little girl?

FELIX. No. She's the mother. My wife.

GWENDOLYN. The one you're divorcing?

FELIX (*nods*). Mm! She's done a terrific job bringing them up. They always look so nice. They're so polite. Speak beautifully. Never, "Yeah." Always, "Yes." They're such good kids. And she did it all. She's the kind of woman who— Ah, what am I saying? You don't want to hear any of this.

(*He puts the picture back in his wallet.*)

CECILY. Nonsense. You have a right to be proud. You have two beautiful children and a wonderful ex-wife.

FELIX (*containing his emotions*). I know. I know. (*He hands* CECILY *another snapshot.*) That's her. Frances.

GWENDOLYN (*looking at the picture*). Oh, she's pretty. Isn't she pretty, Cecy?

CECILY. Oh, yes. Pretty. A pretty girl. Very pretty.

FELIX (*takes the picture back*). Thank you. (*Shows them another snapshot.*) Isn't this nice?

GWENDOLYN (*looks*). There's no one in the picture.

FELIX. I know. It's a picture of our living room. We had a beautiful apartment.

GWENDOLYN. Oh, yes. Pretty. Very pretty.

CECILY. Those are lovely lamps.

FELIX. Thank you! (*Takes the picture.*) We bought them in Mexico on our honeymoon. (*He looks at the picture again.*) I used to love to come home at night. (*He's beginning to break.*) That was my whole life. My wife, my kids—and my apartment.

(*He breaks down and sobs.*)

CECILY. Does she have the lamps now too?

FELIX (*nods*). I gave her everything. It'll never be like that again. Never! I— I—(*He turns his head away.*) I'm sorry. (*He takes out a handkerchief and dabs his eyes.* GWENDOLYN *and* CECILY *look at each other with compassion.*) Please forgive me. I didn't mean to get emotional. (*Trying to pull himself together, he picks up a bowl from the side table and offers it to the girls.*) Would you like some potato chips?

(CECILY *takes the bowl.*)

GWENDOLYN. You mustn't be ashamed I think it's a rare quality in a man to be able to cry.

FELIX (*puts a hand over his eyes*). Please.. Let's not talk about it.

CECILY. I think it's sweet. Terribly, terribly sweet.

(*She takes a potato chip.*)

FELIX. You're just making it worse.

GWENDOLYN (*teary-eyed*). It's so refreshing to hear a man speak so highly of the woman he's divorcing! Oh, dear. (*She takes out her handkerchief.*) Now you've got me thinking about poor Sydney.

CECILY. Oh, Gwen. Please don't.

(*She puts the bowl down.*)

GWENDOLYN. It was a good marriage at first. Everyone said so. Didn't they, Cecily? Not like you and George.

CECILY (*the past returns as she comforts* GWENDOLYN). That's right. George and I were never happy. Not for one single, solitary day.

(*She remembers her unhappiness, grabs her handkerchief and dabs her eyes. All three are now sitting with handkerchiefs at their eyes.*)

FELIX. Isn't this ridiculous?

GWENDOLYN. I don't know what brought this on. I was feeling so good a few minutes ago.

CECILY. I haven't cried since I was fourteen.

FELIX. Just let it pour out. It'll make you feel much better. I always do.

GWENDOLYN. Oh, dear; oh, dear; oh, dear.

(*All three sit sobbing into their handkerchiefs. Suddenly* OSCAR *bursts happily into the room with a tray full of drinks. He is all smiles.*)

OSCAR (*like a corny M.C.*). Is ev-rybuddy happy? (*Then he sees the maudlin scene.* FELIX *and the girls quickly try to pull themselves together.*) What the hell happened?

FELIX. Nothing! Nothing!

(*He quickly puts his handkerchief away.*)

OSCAR. What do you mean, nothing? I'm gone three minutes and I walk into a funeral parlor. What did you say to them?

FELIX. I didn't say anything. Don't start in again, Oscar.

OSCAR. I can't leave you alone for five seconds. Well, if you really want to cry, go inside and look at your London broil.

FELIX (*he rushes madly into the kitchen*). Oh, my gosh! Why didn't you call me? I told you to call me.

OSCAR (*giving a drink to* CECILY). I'm sorry, girls. I forgot to warn you about Felix. He's a walking soap opera.

GWENDOLYN. I think he's the dearest thing I ever met.

CECILY (*taking the glass*). He's so sensitive. So fragile. I just want to bundle him up in my arms and take care of him.

OSCAR (*holds out* GWENDOLYN's *drink. At this, he puts it back down on the tray and takes a swallow from his own drink*). Well, I think when he comes out of that kitchen you may have to.

(*Sure enough,* FELIX *comes out of the kitchen onto the landing looking like a wounded puppy. With a protective kitchen glove, he holds a pan with the exposed London broil. Black is the color of his true love.*)

FELIX (*very calmly*). I'm going down to the delicatessen. I'll be right back.

OSCAR (*going to him*). Wait a minute. Maybe it's not so bad. Let's see it.

FELIX (*shows him*). Here! Look! Nine dollars and thirty-four cents worth of ashes! (*Pulls the pan away. To the girls.*) I'll get some corned beef sandwiches.

OSCAR (*trying to get a look at it*). Give it to me! Maybe we can save some of it.

FELIX (*holding it away from* OSCAR). There's nothing to save. It's all black meat. Nobody likes black meat!

OSCAR. Can't I even look at it?

FELIX. No, you can't look at it!

OSCAR. Why can't I look at it?

FELIX. If you looked at your watch before, you wouldn't have to look at the black meat now! Leave it alone!

(*He turns to go back into the kitchen.*)

GWENDOLYN (*going to him*). Felix! Can *we* look at it?

CECILY (*turning to him, kneeling on the couch*). Please? (FELIX *stops in the kitchen doorway. He hesitates for a moment. He likes them. Then he turns and wordlessly holds the pan out to them.* GWENDOLYN *and* CECILY *inspect it wordlessly, and then turn away sobbing quietly. To* OSCAR) How about Chinese food?

OSCAR. A wonderful idea.

GWENDOLYN. I've got a better idea. Why don't we just make pot luck in the kitchen?

OSCAR. A *much* better idea.

FELIX. I used up all the pots!

(*He crosses to the love seat and sits, still holding the pan.*)

CECILY. Well, then we can eat up in *our* place. We have tons of Horn and Hardart's.

OSCAR (*gleefully*). That's the best idea I ever heard.

GWENDOLYN. Of course it's awfully hot up there. You'll have to take off your jackets.

OSCAR (*smiling*). We can always open up a refrigerator.

CECILY (*gets her purse from the couch*). Give us five minutes to get into our cooking things.

(GWENDOLYN *gets her purse from the couch.*)

OSCAR. Can't you make it four? I'm suddenly starving to death.

(*The girls are crossing to the door.*)

GWENDOLYN. Don't forget the wine.

OSCAR. How could I forget the wine?

CECILY. And a corkscrew.

OSCAR. *And* a corkscrew.

GWENDOLYN. And Felix.

OSCAR. No, I won't forget Felix.

CECILY. Ta, ta!

OSCAR. Ta, ta!

GWENDOLYN. Ta, ta!

(*The girls exit.*)

OSCAR (*throws a kiss at the closed door*). You bet your sweet little crumpets, "Ta, Ta!" (*He wheels around beaming and quickly gathers up the corkscrew from the bar, and picks up the wine and the records.*) Felix, I love you. You've just overcooked us into one hell of a night. Come on, get the ice bucket. Ready or not, here we come.

(*He runs to the door.*)

FELIX (*sitting motionless*). I'm not going!

OSCAR. What?

FELIX. I said I'm not going.

OSCAR (*crossing to* FELIX). Are you out of your mind? Do you know what's waiting for us up there? You've just been invited to spend the evening in a two-bedroom hothouse with the Coo-Coo Pigeon Sisters! What do you mean you're not going?

FELIX. I don't know how to talk to them. I don't know what to say. I already told them about my brother in Buffalo. I've used up my conversation.

OSCAR. Felix, they're crazy about you. They told me! One of them wants to wrap you up and make a bundle out of you. You're doing better than I am! Get the ice bucket.

(*He starts for the door.*)

FELIX. Don't you understand? I cried! I cried in front of two women.

OSCAR (*stops*). And they *loved* it! I'm thinking of getting hysterical. (*Goes to the door.*) Will you get the ice bucket?

FELIX. But why did I cry? Because I felt guilty. Emotionally I'm still tied to Frances and the kids.

OSCAR. Well, untie the knot just for tonight, will you!

FELIX. I don't want to discuss it any more. (*Starts for the kitchen.*) I'm going to scrub the pots and wash my hair.

(*He goes into the kitchen and puts the pan in the sink.*)

OSCAR (*yelling*). Your greasy pots and your greasy hair can wait. You're coming upstairs with me!

FELIX (*in the kitchen*). I'm not! *I'm not!*

OSCAR. What am I going to do with two girls? Felix, don't do this to me. I'll never forgive you!

FELIX. I'm not going!

OSCAR (*screams*). All right, damn you, I'll go without you! (*And he storms out the door and slams it. Then it opens and he comes in again.*) Are you coming?

FELIX (*comes out of the kitchen looking at a magazine*). No.

OSCAR. You mean you're not going to make any effort to change? This is the person you're going to be—until the day you die?

FELIX (*sitting on the couch*). We are what we are.

OSCAR (*nods, then crosses to a window, pulls back the drapes and opens the window wide. Then he starts back to the door.*) It's twelve floors, not eleven.

(*He walks out as FELIX stares at the open windows.*)

CURTAIN

ACT THREE

The next evening about 7:30 P.M. *The room is once again set up for the poker game, with the dining table pulled down, the chairs set about it, and the love seat moved back beneath the windows in the alcove.* FELIX *appears from the bedroom with a vacuum cleaner. He is doing a thorough job on the rug. As he vacuums around the table, the door opens and* OSCAR *comes in wearing a summer hat and carrying a newspaper. He glares at* FELIX, *who is still vacuuming, and shakes his head contemptuously. He crosses behind* FELIX, *leaving his hat on the side table next to the armchair, and goes into his bedroom.* FELIX *is not aware of his presence. Then suddenly the power stops on the vacuum, as* OSCAR *has obviously pulled the plug in the bedroom.* FELIX *tries switching the button on and off a few times, then turns to go back into the bedroom. He stops and realizes what's happened as* OSCAR *comes back into the room.* OSCAR *takes a cigar out of his pocket and as he crosses in front of* FELIX *to the couch, he unwraps it and drops the wrappings carelessly on the floor. He then steps up on the couch and walks back and forth mashing down the pillows. Stepping down, he plants one foot on the armchair and then sits on the couch, taking a wooden match from the coffee table and striking it on the table to light his cigar. He flips the used match onto the rug and settles back to read his newspaper.* FELIX *has watched this all in silence, and now carefully picks up the cigar wrappings and the match and drops them into* OSCAR's *hat. He then dusts his hands and takes the vacuum cleaner into the kitchen, pulling the cord in after him.* OSCAR *takes the wrappings from the hat and puts them in the butt-filled ashtray on the coffee table. Then he takes the ashtray and dumps it on the floor. As he once more settles down with his newspaper,* FELIX *comes out of the kitchen carrying a tray with a steaming dish of spaghetti. As he crosses behind* OSCAR *to the table, he indicates that it smells delicious and passes it close to* OSCAR *to make sure* OSCAR *smells the fantastic dish he's missing. As* FELIX *sits and begins to eat,* OSCAR *takes a can of aerosol spray from the bar, and circling the table, sprays all around* FELIX, *then puts the can down next to him and goes back to his newspaper.*

———

FELIX (*pushing the spaghetti away*). All right, how much longer is this gonna go on?

OSCAR (*reading his paper*). Are you talking to me?

FELIX. That's right, I'm talking to you.

OSCAR. What do you want to know?

FELIX. I want to know if you're going to spend the rest of your life not talking to me. Because if you are, I'm going to buy a radio. (*No reply.*) Well? (*No reply.*) All right. Two can play at this game. (*Pause.*) If you're not going to talk to me, I'm not going to talk to you. (*No reply.*) I can act childish too, you know. (*No reply.*) I can go on without talking just as long as you can.

OSCAR. Then why the hell don't you shut up?

FELIX. Are you talking to me?

OSCAR. You had your chance to talk last night. I begged you to come upstairs with me. From now on I never want to hear a word from that shampooed head as long as you live. That's a warning, Felix.

FELIX (*stares at him*). I stand warned. Over and out!

OSCAR (*gets up, takes a key out of his pocket and slams it on the table*). There's a key to the back door. If you stick to the hallway and your room, you won't get hurt.

(*He sits back down on the couch.*)

FELIX. I don't think I gather the entire meaning of that remark.

OSCAR. Then I'll explain it to you. Stay out of my way.

FELIX (*picks up the key and moves to the couch*). I think you're serious. I think you're really serious. Are you serious?

OSCAR. This is my apartment. Everything in my apartment is mine. The only thing here that's yours is you. Just stay in your room and speak softly.

FELIX. Yeah, you're serious. Well, let me remind you that I pay half the rent and I'll go into any room I want.

(*He gets up angrily and starts toward the hallway.*)

OSCAR. Where are you going?

FELIX. I'm going to walk around your bedroom.

OSCAR (*slams down his newspaper*). You stay out of there.

FELIX (*steaming*). Don't tell me where to go. I pay a hundred and twenty dollars a month.

OSCAR. That was off-season. Starting tomorrow the rates are twelve dollars a day.

FELIX. All right. (*He takes some bills out of his pocket and slams them down on the table.*) There you are. I'm paid up for today. Now I'm going to walk in your bedroom.

(*He starts to storm off.*)

OSCAR. Stay out of there! Stay out of my room!

(*He chases after him.* FELIX *dodges around the table as* OSCAR *blocks the hallway.*)

FELIX (*backing away, keeping the table between them*). Watch yourself! Just watch yourself, Oscar!

OSCAR (*with a pointing finger*). I'm warning you. You want to live here, I don't want to see you, I don't want to hear you and I don't want to smell your cooking. Now get this spaghetti off my poker table.

FELIX. Ha! Ha, ha!

OSCAR. What the hell's so funny?

FELIX. It's not spaghetti. It's linguini!

(OSCAR *picks up the plate of linguini, crosses to the doorway and hurls it into the kitchen.*)

OSCAR. Now it's garbage!

(*He paces by the couch.*)

FELIX (*looks at* OSCAR *unbelievingly: what an insane thing to do*). You are crazy! I'm a neurotic nut but *you are crazy!*

OSCAR. *I'm* crazy, heh? That's really funny coming from a fruitcake like you.

FELIX (*goes to the kitchen door and looks in at the mess. Turns back to* OSCAR). I'm not cleaning that up.

OSCAR. Is that a promise?

FELIX. Did you hear what I said? I'm not cleaning it up. It's your mess. (*Looking into the kitchen again.*) Look at it. Hanging all over the walls.

OSCAR (*crosses to the landing and looks in the kitchen door*). I like it.

(*He closes the door and paces around.*)

FELIX (*fumes*). You'd just let it lie there, wouldn't you? Until it turns hard and brown and . . . Yich, it's disgusting. I'm cleaning it up.

(*He goes into the kitchen.* OSCAR *chases after him. There is the sound of a struggle and falling pots.*)

OSCAR. *Leave it alone!* You touch one strand of that linguini—and I'm gonna punch you right in your sinuses.

FELIX (*dashes out of the kitchen with* OSCAR *in pursuit. He stops and tries to calm* OSCAR *down*). Oscar, I'd like you to take a couple of phenobarbital.

OSCAR (*points*). Go to your room! Did you hear what I said? *Go to your room!*

FELIX. All right, let's everybody just settle down, heh? (*He puts his hand on* OSCAR'*s shoulder to calm him but* OSCAR *pulls away violently from his touch.*)

OSCAR. If you want to live through this night, you'd better tie me up and lock your doors and windows.

FELIX (*sits at the table with a great pretense of calm*). All right, Oscar, I'd like to know what's happened?

OSCAR (*moves toward him*). What's *happened?*

FELIX (*hurriedly slides over to the next chair*). That's right. Something must have caused you to go off the deep end like this. What is it? Something I said? Something I did? Heh? What?

OSCAR (*pacing*). It's nothing you said. It's nothing you did. It's *you!*

FELIX. I see. Well, that's plain enough.

OSCAR. I could make it plainer but I don't want to hurt you.

FELIX. What is it, the cooking? The cleaning? The crying?

OSCAR (*moving toward him*). I'll tell you exactly what it is. It's the cooking, cleaning and crying. It's the talking in your sleep, it's the moose calls that open your ears at two o'clock in the morning. I can't take it any more, Felix. I'm crackin' up. Everything you do irritates me. And when you're not here, the things I know you're gonna do when you come in irritate me. You leave me little notes on my pillow. I told you a hundred times, I can't stand little notes on my pillow. "We're all out of Corn Flakes. F.U." It took me three hours to figure out that F.U. was Felix Ungar. It's not your fault, Felix. It's a rotten combination.

FELIX. I get the picture.

OSCAR. That's just the frame. The picture I haven't even painted yet. I got a typewritten list in my office of the "Ten Most Aggravating Things You Do That Drive Me Berserk." But last night was the topper. Oh, that was the topper. Oh, that was the ever-loving lulu of all times.

FELIX. What are you talking about, the London broil?

OSCAR. No, not the London broil. I'm talking about those two lamb chops. (*He points upstairs.*) I had it all set up with that English Betty Boop and her sister, and I wind up drinking tea all night and telling them *your* life story.

FELIX (*jumps up*). Oho! So *that's* what's bothering you. That I loused up your evening!

OSCAR. After the mood you put them in, I'm surprised they didn't go out to Rockaway and swim back to England.

FELIX. Don't blame me. I warned you not to make the date in the first place.

(*He makes his point by shaking his finger in* OSCAR'*s face.*)

OSCAR. Don't point that finger at me unless you intend to use it!

FELIX (*moves in nose to nose with* OSCAR). All right, Oscar, get off my back. Get off! Off!

(*Startled by his own actions,* FELIX *jumps back from* OSCAR, *warily circles him, crosses to the couch and sits.*)

OSCAR. What's this? A display of temper? I haven't seen you really angry since the day I dropped my cigar in your pancake batter.

(*He starts toward the hallway.*)

FELIX (*threateningly*). Oscar, you're asking to hear something I don't want to say. But if I say it, I think you'd better hear it.

OSCAR (*comes back to the table, places both hands on it and leans toward* FELIX). If you've got anything on your chest besides your chin, you'd better get it off.

FELIX (*strides to the table, places both hands on it and leans toward* OSCAR. *They are nose to nose*). All right, I warned you. You're a wonderful guy, Oscar. You've done everything for me. If it weren't for you, I don't know what would have happened to me. You took me in here, gave me a place to live and something to live for. I'll never forget you for that. You're tops with me, Oscar.

OSCAR (*motionless*). If I've just been told off, I think I may have missed it.

FELIX. It's coming now! You're also one

of the biggest slobs in the world.

OSCAR. I see.

FELIX. And completely unreliable.

OSCAR. Finished?

FELIX. Undependable.

OSCAR. Is that it?

FELIX. And irresponsible.

OSCAR. Keep going. I think you're hot.

FELIX. That's it. I'm finished. *Now* you've been told off. How do you like that?

(*He crosses to the couch.*)

OSCAR (*straightening up*). Good. Because now I'm going to tell *you* off. For six months I lived alone in this apartment. All alone in eight rooms. I was dejected, despondent, and disgusted. Then *you* moved in—my dearest and closest friend. And after three weeks of close, personal contact—I am about to have a nervous breakdown! Do me a favor. Move into the kitchen. Live with your pots, your pans, your ladle and your meat thermometer. When you want to come out, ring a bell and I'll run into the bedroom. (*Almost breaking down.*) I'm asking you nicely, Felix—as a friend. Stay out of my way!

(*And he goes into the bedroom.*)

FELIX (*is hurt by this, then remembers something. He calls after him*). Walk on the paper, will you? The floors are wet. (OSCAR *comes out of the door. He is glaring maniacally, as he slowly strides back down the hallway.* FELIX *quickly puts the couch between him and* OSCAR.) Awright, keep away. Keep away from me.

OSCAR (*chasing him around the couch*). Come on. Let me get in one shot. You pick it. Head, stomach or kidneys.

FELIX (*dodging about the room*). You're gonna find yourself in one sweet law suit, Oscar.

OSCAR. It's no use running, Felix. There's only eight rooms and I know the short cuts.

(*They are now poised at opposite ends of the couch.* FELIX *picks up a lamp for protection.*)

FELIX. Is this how you settle your problems, Oscar? Like an animal?

OSCAR. All right. You wanna see how I settle my problems. I'll show you. (*Storms off into* FELIX's *bedroom. There is the sound of falling objects and he returns with a suitcase.*) I'll show you how I settle them. (*Throws the suitcase on the table.*) There! That's how I settle them!

FELIX (*bewildered, looks at the suitcase*). Where are you going?

OSCAR (*exploding*). Not me, you idiot! You. You're the one who's going. I want you out of here. Now! Tonight!

(*He opens the suitcase.*)

FELIX. What are you talking about?

OSCAR. It's all over, Felix. The whole marriage. We're getting an annulment! Don't you understand? I don't want to live with you any more. I want you to pack your things, tie it up with your Saran Wrap and get out of here.

FELIX. You mean actually move out?

OSCAR. Actually, physically and immediately. I don't care where you go. Move into the Museum of Natural History. (*Goes into the kitchen. There is the crash of falling pots and pans.*) I'm sure you'll be very comfortable there. You can dust around the Egyptian mummies to your heart's content. But I'm a human, living person. (*Comes out with a stack of cooking utensils which he throws into the open suitcase.*) All I want is my freedom. Is that too much to ask for? (*Closes it.*) There, you're all packed.

FELIX. You know, I've got a good mind to really leave.

OSCAR (*looking to the heavens*). Why doesn't he ever listen to what I say? Why doesn't he hear me? I know I'm talking —I recognize my voice.

FELIX (*indignantly*). Because if you really want me to go, I'll go.

OSCAR. Then go. I want you to go, so go. When are you going?

FELIX. When am I going, huh? Boy, you're in a bigger hurry than Frances was.

OSCAR. Take as much time as she gave you. I want you to follow your usual routine.

FELIX. In other words, you're throwing me out.

OSCAR. Not in other words. Those are the perfect ones. (*Picks up the suitcase and holds it out to* FELIX.) I am throwing you out.

FELIX. All right, I just wanted to get the record straight. Let it be on *your* conscience.

(*He goes into his bedroom.*)

OSCAR. What? What? (*Follows him to the bedroom doorway.*) Let what be on my conscience?

FELIX (*comes out putting on his jacket and passing by* OSCAR). That you're throwing me out. (*Stops and turns back to him.*) I'm perfectly willing to stay and clear the air of our differences. But you refuse, right?

OSCAR (*still holding the suitcase*). Right! I'm sick and tired of you clearing the air. That's why I want you to leave!

FELIX. Okay, as long as I heard you say the words, "Get out of the house." Fine. But remember, what happens to me is your responsibility. Let it be on *your* head.

(*He crosses to the door.*)

OSCAR (*follows him to the door and screams*). Wait a minute, damn it! Why can't you be thrown out like a decent human being? Why do you have to say things like, "Let it be on your head"? I don't want it on my head. I just want you out of the house.

FELIX. What's the matter, Oscar? Can't cope with a little guilt feelings?

OSCAR (*pounding the railing in frustration*). Damn you. I've been looking forward to throwing you out all day long, and now you even take the pleasure out of that.

FELIX. Forgive me for spoiling your fun. I'm leaving now—according to your wishes and desires.

(*He starts to open the door.*)

OSCAR (*pushes by* FELIX *and slams the door shut. He stands between* FELIX *and the door.*) You're not leaving here until you take it back.

FELIX. Take what back?

OSCAR. "Let it be on your head." What the hell is that, the Curse of the Cat People?

FELIX. Get out of my way, please.

OSCAR. Is this how you left that night with Frances? No wonder she wanted to have the room repainted right away. (*Points to* FELIX's *bedroom.*) I'm gonna have yours dipped in bronze.

FELIX (*sits on the back of the couch with his back to* OSCAR). How can I leave if you're blocking the door?

OSCAR (*very calmly*). Felix, we've been friends a long time. For the sake of that friendship, please say, "Oscar, we can't stand each other; let's break up."

FELIX. I'll let you know what to do about my clothes. Either I'll call—or some-

one else will. (*Controlling great emotion.*) I'd like to leave now.

(OSCAR, *resigned, moves out of the way.* FELIX *opens the door.*)

OSCAR. Where will you go?

FELIX (*turns in the doorway and looks at him*). Where? (*He smiles.*) Oh, come on, Oscar. You're not really interested, are you?

(*He exits.* OSCAR *looks as though he's about to burst with frustration. He calls after* FELIX.)

OSCAR. All right, Felix, you win. (*Goes out into the hall.*) We'll try to iron it out. Anything you want. Come back, Felix. Felix? *Felix?* Don't leave me like this— you louse! (*But* FELIX *is gone.* OSCAR *comes back into the room closing the door. He is limp. He searches for something to ease his enormous frustration. He throws a pillow at the door, and then paces about like a caged lion.*) All right, Oscar, get a hold of yourself! He's gone! Keep saying that over and over. He's gone. He's really gone! (*He holds his head in pain.*) He did it. He put a curse on me. It's on my head. I don't know what it is, but something's on my head. (*The doorbell rings and he looks up hopefully.*) Please let it be him. Let it be Felix. Please give me one more chance to kill him.

(*Putting the suitcase on the sofa, he rushes to the door and opens it.* MURRAY *comes in with* VINNIE.)

MURRAY (*putting his jacket on a chair at the table*). Hey, what's the matter with Felix? He walked right by me with that "human sacrifice" look on his face again.

(*He takes off his shoes.*)

VINNIE (*laying his jacket on the love seat*). What's with him? I asked him where he's going and he said, "Only Oscar knows. Only Oscar knows." Where's he going, Oscar?

OSCAR (*sitting at the table*). How the hell should I know? All right, let's get the game started, heh? Come on, get your chips.

MURRAY. I have to get something to eat. I'm starving. Mmm, I think I smell spaghetti.

(*He goes into the kitchen.*)

VINNIE. Isn't he playing tonight?

(*He takes two chairs from the dining alcove and puts them at the table.*)

OSCAR. I don't want to discuss it. I don't

even want to hear his name.

VINNIE. Who? Felix?

OSCAR. I told you not to mention his name.

VINNIE. I didn't know what name you meant.

(*He clears the table and places what's left of* FELIX's *dinner on the bookcase.*)

MURRAY (*comes out of the kitchen*). Hey, did you know there's spaghetti all over the kitchen?

OSCAR. Yes, I know, and it's not spaghetti; it's linguini.

MURRAY. Oh. I thought it was spaghetti. (*He goes back into the kitchen.*)

VINNIE (*taking the poker stuff from the bookcase and putting it on the table*). Why shouldn't I mention his name?

OSCAR. Who?

VINNIE. Felix. What's happened? Has something happened?

(SPEED *and* ROY *come in the open door.*)

SPEED. Yeah, what's the matter with Felix?

(SPEED *puts his jacket over a chair at the table.* ROY *sits in the armchair.* MURRAY *comes out of the kitchen with a six-pack of beer and bags of pretzels and chips. They all stare at* OSCAR *waiting for an answer. There is a long pause and then he stand up.*)

OSCAR. We broke up! I kicked him out. It was my decision. I threw him out of the house. All right? I admit it. Let it be on my head.

VINNIE. Let what be on your head?

OSCAR. How should I know? *Felix put it there!* Ask him! (*He paces around to the right.*)

MURRAY. He'll go to pieces. I know Felix. He's gonna try something crazy.

OSCAR (*turns to the boys*). Why do you think I did it? (MURRAY *makes a gesture of disbelief and moves to the couch, putting down the beer and the bags.* OSCAR *moves to him.*) You think I'm just selfish? That I wanted to be cruel? I did it for you—I did it for all of us.

ROY. What are you talking about?

OSCAR (*crosses to* ROY). All right, we've all been through the napkins and the ashtrays and the bacon, lettuce and tomato sandwiches. But that was just the beginning. Just the beginning. Do you know what he was planning for next Friday night's poker game? As a change of pace.

Do you have any idea?

VINNIE. What?

OSCAR. A Luau! An Hawaiian Luau! Spareribs, roast pork and fried rice. They don't play poker like that in Honolulu.

MURRAY. One thing has nothing to do with the other. We all know he's impossible, but he's still our friend, and he's still out on the street, and I'm still worried about him.

OSCAR (*going to* MURRAY). And I'm not, heh? I'm not concerned? I'm not worried? Who do you think sent him out there in the first place?

MURRAY. Frances!

OSCAR. What?

MURRAY. Frances sent him out in the first place. *You* sent him out in the second place. And whoever he lives with next will send him out in the third place. Don't you understand? It's Felix. He does it to himself.

OSCAR. Why?

MURRAY. I don't know why. *He* doesn't know why. There are people like that. There's a whole tribe in Africa who hit themselves on the head all day long.

(*He sums it all up with an eloquent gesture of resignation.*)

OSCAR (*a slow realization of a whole new reason to be angry*). I'm not going to worry about him. Why should I? He's not worrying about me. He's somewhere out on the streets sulking and crying and having a wonderful time. If he had a spark of human decency he would leave us all alone and go back to Blanche.

(*He sits down at the table.*)

VINNIE. Why should he?

OSCAR (*picks up a deck of cards*). Because it's his wife.

VINNIE. No, Blanche is your wife. His wife is Frances.

OSCAR (*stares at him*). What are you, some kind of wise guy?

VINNIE. What did I say?

OSCAR (*throws the cards in the air*). All right, the poker game is over. I don't want to play any more.

(*He paces around on the right.*)

SPEED. Who's playing? We didn't even start.

OSCAR (*turns on him*). Is that all you can do is complain? Have you given one single thought to where Felix might be?

SPEED. I thought you said you're not

worried about him.

OSCAR (*screams*). I'm not worried, damn it. I'm not worried. (*The doorbell rings. A gleeful look passes over* OSCAR's *face.*) It's him. I bet it's him! (*The boys start to go for the door.* OSCAR *stops them.*) Don't let him in; he's not welcome in this house.

MURRAY (*moves toward the door*). Oscar, don't be childish. We've got to let him in.

OSCAR (*stopping him and leading him to the table*). I won't give him the satisfaction of knowing we've been worrying about him. Sit down. Play cards. Like nothing happened.

MURRAY. But, Oscar . . .

OSCAR. Sit down. Everybody. Come on, sit down and play poker.

(*They sit and* SPEED *begins to deal out cards.*)

VINNIE (*crossing to the door*). Oscar . . .

OSCAR. All right, Vinnie, open the door.

(VINNIE *opens the door. It is* GWENDOLYN *standing there.*)

VINNIE (*surprised*). Oh, hello. (*To* OSCAR.) It's not him, Oscar.

GWENDOLYN. How do you do.

(*She walks into the room.*)

OSCAR (*crosses to her*). Oh, hello, Cecily. Boys, I'd like you to meet Cecily Pigeon.

GWENDOLYN. Gwendolyn Pigeon. Please don't get up. (*To* OSCAR.) May I see you for a moment, Mr. Madison?

OSCAR. Certainly, Gwen. What's the matter?

GWENDOLYN. I think you know. I've come for Felix's things.

(OSCAR *looks at her in shock and disbelief. He looks at the boys, then back at* GWENDOLYN.)

OSCAR. Felix? My Felix?

GWENDOLYN. Yes. Felix Ungar. That sweet, tortured man who's in my flat at this moment pouring his heart out to my sister.

OSCAR (*turns to the boys*). You hear? I'm worried to death and he's up there getting tea and sympathy.

(CECILY *rushes in dragging a reluctant* FELIX *with her.*)

CECILY. Gwen, Felix doesn't want to stay. Please tell him to stay.

FELIX. Really, girls, this is very embarrassing. I can go to a hotel. (*To the boys.*)

Hello, fellas.

GWENDOLYN (*overriding his objections*). Nonsense. I told you, we've plenty of room, and it's a very comfortable sofa. Isn't it, Cecy?

CECILY (*joining in*). Enormous. And we've rented an air conditioner.

GWENDOLYN. And we just don't like the idea of you wandering the streets looking for a place to live.

FELIX. But I'd be in the way. Wouldn't I be in the way?

GWENDOLYN. How could you possibly be in anyone's way?

OSCAR. You want to see a typewritten list?

GWENDOLYN (*turning on him*). Haven't you said enough already, Mr. Madison? (*To* FELIX.) I won't take no for an answer. Just for a few days, Felix.

CECILY. Until you get settled.

GWENDOLYN. Please. Please say, "Yes," Felix.

CECILY. Oh, please—we'd be so happy.

FELIX (*considers*). Well, maybe just for a few days.

GWENDOLYN (*jumping with joy*). Oh, wonderful.

CECILY (*ecstatic*). Marvelous!

GWENDOLYN (*crosses to the door*). You get your things and come right up.

CECILY. And come hungry. We're making dinner.

GWENDOLYN (*to the boys*). Good night, gentlemen; sorry to interrupt your bridge game.

CECILY (*to* FELIX). If you'd like, you can invite your friends to play in our flat.

GWENDOLYN (*to* FELIX). Don't be late. Cocktails in fifteen minutes.

FELIX. I won't.

GWENDOLYN. Ta, ta.

CECILY. Ta, ta.

FELIX. Ta, ta.

(*The girls leave.* FELIX *turns and looks at the fellows and smiles as he crosses the room into the bedroom. The five men stare dumbfounded at the door without moving. Finally* MURRAY *crosses to the door.*)

SPEED (*to the others*). I told you. It's always the quiet guys.

MURRAY. Gee, what nice girls.

(*He closes the door.* FELIX *comes out of the bedroom carrying two suits in a plastic cleaner's bag.*)

ROY. Hey, Felix, are you really gonna move in with them?

FELIX (*turns back to them*). Just for a few days. Until I find my own place. Well, so long, fellows. You can drop your crumbs on the rug again.

(*He starts toward the door.*)

OSCAR. Hey, Felix. Aren't you going to thank me?

FELIX (*stopping on the landing*). For what?

OSCAR. For the two greatest things I ever did for you. Taking you in and throwing you out.

FELIX (*lays his suits over the railing and goes to* OSCAR). You're right, Oscar. Thanks a lot. Getting kicked out twice is enough for any man. In gratitude, I remove the curse.

OSCAR (*smiles*). Oh, bless you and thank you, Wicked Witch of the North.

(*They shake hands. The phone rings.*)

FELIX. Ah, that must be the girls.

MURRAY (*picking up the phone*). Hello?

FELIX. They hate it so when I'm late for cocktails. (*Turning to the boys.*) Well, so long.

MURRAY. It's your wife.

FELIX (*turning to* MURRAY). Oh? Well, do me a favor, Murray. Tell her I can't speak to her now. But tell her I'll be calling her in a few days, because she and I have a lot to talk about. And tell her if I sound different to her, it's because I'm not the same man she kicked out three weeks ago. Tell her, Murray; tell her.

MURRAY. I will when I see her. This is Oscar's wife.

FELIX. Oh!

MURRAY (*into the phone*). Just a minute, Blanche.

(OSCAR *crosses to the phone and sits on the arm of the couch.*)

FELIX. Well, so long, fellows.

(*He shakes hands with the boys, takes his suits and moves to the door.*)

OSCAR (*into the phone*). Hello? Yeah, Blanche. I got a pretty good idea why you're calling. You got my checks, right? Good. (FELIX *stops at the door, caught by* OSCAR's *conversation. He slowly comes back* into the room to listen, putting his suits on the railing, and sitting down on the arm of the armchair.*) So now I'm all paid up. No, no, I didn't win at the track. I've just been able to save a little money. I've been eating home a lot. (*Takes a pillow from the couch and throws it at* FELIX.) Listen, Blanche, you don't have to thank me. I'm just doing what's right. Well, that's nice of you too. The apartment? No, I think you'd be shocked. It's in surprisingly good shape. (FELIX *throws the pillow back at* OSCAR.) Say, Blanche, did Brucey get the goldfish I sent him? Yeah, well, I'll speak to you again soon, huh? Whenever you want. I don't go out much any more.

FELIX (*gets up, takes his suits from the railing and goes to the door*). Well, good night, Mr. Madison. If you need me again, I get a dollar-fifty an hour.

OSCAR (*makes a gesture to stop* FELIX *as he talks on the phone*). Well, kiss the kids for me. Good night, Blanche. (*Hangs up and turns to* FELIX.) Felix?

FELIX (*at the opened door*). Yeah?

OSCAR. How about next Friday night? You're not going to break up the game, are you?

FELIX. Me? Never! Marriages may come and go, but the game must go on. So long, Frances.

(*He exits, closing the door.*)

OSCAR (*yelling after him*). So long, Blanche. (*The boys all look at* OSCAR *a moment.*) All right, are we just gonna sit around or are we gonna play poker?

ROY. We're gonna play poker.

(*There is a general hubbub as they pass out the beer, deal the cards and settle around the table.*)

OSCAR (*standing up*). Then let's play poker. (*Sharply, to the boys.*) And watch your cigarettes, will you? This is my house, not a pig sty.

(*He takes the ashtray from the side table next to the armchair, bends down and begins to pick up the butts. The boys settle down to play poker.*)

CURTAIN

THE SUBJECT WAS ROSES

Frank D. Gilroy

For MY MOTHER and MY FATHER

First presented by Edgar Lansbury at the Royale Theatre, New York City, on May 25, 1964, with the following cast:

(*In order of appearance*)

JOHN CLEARY   Jack Albertson   TIMMY CLEARY   Martin Sheen
NETTIE CLEARY   Irene Dailey

Directed by Ulu Grosbard
Scenery designed by Edgar Lansbury
Lighting by Jules Fisher
Costumes by Donald Foote
Production Stage Manager, Paul Leaf

SYNOPSIS OF SCENES
The action takes place in a middle-class apartment, May, 1946.
ACT ONE. SCENE ONE: Saturday morning. SCENE TWO: Saturday afternoon.
SCENE THREE: Two A.M. Monday morning.
ACT TWO. SCENE ONE: Sunday morning. SCENE TWO: Sunday evening. SCENE
THREE: Two A.M. Monday morning. SCENE FOUR: Nine A.M. Monday morning

---

From ABOUT THOSE ROSES AND THE SUBJECT WAS ROSES, by Frank D. Gilroy.
Copyright © 1965 by Frank D. Gilroy.
Reprinted by permission of Random House, Inc.
All rights including the right of reproduction in whole or in part, in any form, are reserved under International and Pan-American Copyright Conventions. Published in New York by Random House, Inc., and simultaneously in Toronto, Canada, by Random House of Canada Limited.

CAUTION: Professionals and amateurs are hereby warned that *The Subject Was Roses,* being fully protected under the Copyright Laws of the United States of America, the British Empire, including the Dominion of Canada, and all other countries of the Berne and Universal Copyright Conventions, is subject to royalty. All rights, including professional, amateur, motion picture, recitation, lecturing, public reading, radio and television broadcasting, and the rights of translation into foreign languages, are strictly reserved. Particular emphasis is laid on the question of readings, permission for which must be secured from the author's agent in writing. All inquiries should be addressed to the author's agent, Blanche Gaines, 350 West 57th Street, New York, N.Y. 10019.

The amateur acting rights of *The Subject Was Roses* are controlled exclusively by Samuel French, 25 West 45th Street, New York, N.Y., without whose permission in writing no amateur performance of it may be made.

DURING the Golden Age of television—those days when there were still fugitive hopes that it might one day establish itself if not as an art form then at least as some means of artistic communication—a number of writers for the theatre cut their teeth on the new medium. Some of them were comic writers, such as Neil Simon, while others were more dramatically inclined. Prominent among the latter group was Frank D. Gilroy.

Gilroy was born in New York City on October 13, 1925. He fought in the army for two and a half years during the Second World War, returning home in 1946, when he attended Dartmouth College and started writing. Graduating from Dartmouth in 1950, he won a year's postgraduate study at the Yale School of Drama, and established himself as a TV writer in 1952. For television his credits included almost all of the major dramatic shows, and he also started to write for movies, notably writing the scripts for *The Fastest Gun Alive* with Glenn Ford, and *The Gallant Hours* with James Cagney.

He wrote his first stage play *Who'll Save the Plowboy?*, in 1957, but it was not until January 9, 1962, that it was produced Off-Broadway by the Phoenix Theatre. It was quite clear from this play that the theatre had acquired an important new voice with a gift for natural dialogue and that feeling for human behavior that was probably characteristic of early television drama at its best. The play caused quite a stir, and it was the winner of the Obie Award given for the best American play of that year. With this modest yet marked success behind him, it might have been imagined by anyone unaware of the ways and byways of the American theatre that the production of his next play would be a comparatively simple matter. It was not.

When the original text of *The Subject Was Roses* was published by Random House, Gilroy appended a book-length essay that he called *About Those Roses or How Not to Do a Play and Succeed*. In this he chronicles in diary form the trials and tribulations of the play from its genesis to its first night. As a theatrical horror story it almost ranks with William Gibson's classic saga about *Two for a Seesaw,* which he calls *The Seesaw Log*. Mr. Gilroy did not take his play out of town, but for a play that was eventually to win drama's triple crown in 1965—the Pulitzer Prize, the New York Drama Critics' Award for the Best Play, and the Tony Award for the Best Play—and later become a successful movie, it certainly had a lot of trouble in reaching that first night on May 25, 1964.

Gilroy wrote his play between screen jobs in Hollywood, from the winter of 1960 to the fall of 1961. He revised it the following winter and sent it off to his agent in the spring of 1962. For two years the struggle continued. Curiously enough, it was not particularly difficult to get backing, although at times it appeared as though the producers interested in producing it were playing a game of musical chairs around Gilroy. But, even more, the difficulty stemmed from casting the play's three roles. Actor after actor read the play and for some reason or another turned it down. It is interesting that in considering the risks encountered on Broadway by playwrights and producers, we sometimes forget the risks also taken by actors. They, of course, do not forget, and this makes them very choosy.

When *Roses* eventually was funded, cast, and produced, it came in at the very end of the 1963/64 Broadway season, and opened with an advance sale of $165. Helped by absolutely glowing notices from the critics, it still had to work its way through Broadway's traditionally treacherous summer before it could start bringing in money. Indeed it was not until its 136th performance that it had a sold-out house.

The play amply confirmed the promise of *Plowboy*. It proved a tightly written, subtly characterized family drama of a young soldier coming home from the war in 1946. It is the drama of the inarticulate, the drama of people who have feelings but are uncertain how to convey them.

A couple of seasons later Gilroy tried again with *The Only Game in Town*. Once more it was bedeviled with casting difficulties, once more it had a cast of three, once more it was the final play of the season. The resemblances ended there. It was blasted by the critics, and had only a run of a few days. However, even if it didn't get a Pulitzer it did win a $500,000 movie sale. But will it also have discouraged Gilroy from working again in the theatre? It is to be hoped not. The theatre needs him.

ACT ONE

SCENE ONE

SCENE: *The kitchen and living room of a middle-class apartment in the West Bronx. A doorway links the two rooms; an invisible wall divides them. The living room is furnished with the heavy uphol- stered pieces (replete with antimacassars) considered fashionable in the late twen- ties and early thirties. There is evidence of a party given the night before: a beer keg, a stack of camp chairs, a sagging banner that is hand lettered—"Welcome Home, Timmy."*

TIME: *A Saturday morning in May of 1946.*

AT RISE: *A man stands alone in the kitchen, lost in contemplation of an army jacket hanging from the door. The man,* JOHN CLEARY, *is fifty. The army jacket bears an infantry division patch, corporal chevrons, service ribbons (including the ETO with two battle stars, and a presi- dential unit citation), four "Hershey Bars" marking two years of overseas duty, and the "Ruptured Duck" signifying re- cent discharge.* JOHN CLEARY'S *expression as he regards the jacket is one of almost reverent curiosity. He touches the jacket, feels the material, traces the outline of the chevrons inquiringly. Now, on an impulse, he takes the jacket from the hanger, dons it furtively, is enjoying what is obviously a secret moment when he hears a key turn in the front door. Quickly returning the jacket to the hanger, he takes a seat at the kitchen table and appears engrossed in a newspaper as the door opens and his wife,* NETTIE, *forty-five, enters with a bundle of groceries.*

NETTIE. It's a lovely day . . . Timmy still asleep?

JOHN. Haven't heard him . . . Better give me mine.

NETTIE. I thought we'd all have break- fast together.

JOHN. I have to go downtown.

NETTIE. Today?

JOHN. Ruskin wants to see me. (*She re- gards him a moment, then begins to set the food before him.*) I'm going to stop at Saint Francis on the way . . . to offer a prayer of thanks.

NETTIE. Toast?

JOHN. Yes . . . All those casualties and he never got a scratch. We're very lucky.

NETTIE. What do you want on it?

JOHN. Marmalade . . . The Freeman boy dead. The Mullin boy crippled for life . . . Makes you wonder . . . Think he enjoyed the party?

NETTIE. He seemed to.

JOHN. First time I ever saw him take a drink.

NETTIE. He drank too much.

JOHN. You don't get out of the army every day.

NETTIE. He was sick during the night.

JOHN. Probably the excitement.

NETTIE. It was the whiskey. You should have stopped him.

JOHN. For three years he's gotten along fine without anyone telling him what to do.

NETTIE. I had to hold his head.

JOHN. No one held his head in the army.

NETTIE. That's what *he* said.

JOHN. But that didn't stop *you*.

NETTIE. He's not in the army any more.

JOHN. It was a boy that walked out of this house three years ago. It's a man that's come back in.

NETTIE. You sound like a recruiting pos- ter.

JOHN. *You* sound ready to repeat the old mistakes.

NETTIE. Mistakes?

JOHN. Pardon me.

NETTIE. You said mistakes.

JOHN. Slip of the tongue.

NETTIE. I'd like to know what mistakes you're referring to.

JOHN. The coffee's excellent.

NETTIE. I'd really like to know.

JOHN. He was eighteen when he went away. Until that time, he showed no spe- cial skill at anything, but you treated him like he was a protégé.

NETTIE. I think you mean prodigy.

JOHN. What I really mean is baby.

NETTIE. For a baby he certainly did well in the army.

JOHN. I didn't say he *was* a baby. I said you treated him like one.

NETTIE. You were surprised he did well. You didn't think he'd last a week.

JOHN. Bless us and save us, said Mrs. O'Davis.

NETTIE. Do you know why you were surprised?

JOHN. Joy, joy, said Mrs. Malloy.

NETTIE. Because you never understood him.

JOHN. Mercy, mercy, said old Mrs. Percy.

NETTIE. I never doubted that he'd do as well as anyone else.

JOHN. Where he's concerned you never doubted, period. If he came in here right now and said he could fly, you'd help him out the window.

NETTIE. If you're saying I have confidence in him, you're right. And why not? Who knows him better?

JOHN. Is there more coffee?

NETTIE. He's exceptional.

JOHN. Here we go again.

NETTIE. Yes—exceptional!

JOHN. In what way?

NETTIE. I refuse to discuss it.

JOHN. A person who's going to be famous usually drops a *few* clues by the time they're twenty-one.

NETTIE. I didn't say famous—I said exceptional.

JOHN. What's the difference?

NETTIE. You wouldn't understand.

JOHN. Here's something you better understand—you can't treat him as though he'd never been away. He's not a kid.

NETTIE. If you had stopped him from drinking too much that would have been treating him like a kid?

JOHN. This is where I came in.

NETTIE. He was trying to keep up with you and you knew it.

JOHN. You sound like you're jealous.

NETTIE. The two of you so busy drinking you hardly paid attention to anyone else.

JOHN. You *are* jealous!

NETTIE. Don't be absurd.

JOHN. He and I got along better yesterday than we ever did before and you're jealous. (*She turns away.*) Well, well, well.

(*He finishes the last of his coffee. Rises to leave.*)

NETTIE. Can't Ruskin wait till Monday?

JOHN. No. And don't pretend you're disappointed. What a charming little breakfast you and he will have together.

NETTIE. You're welcome to stay.

JOHN. My ears are burning already.

NETTIE. I've never said a word against you and you know it.

JOHN. Don't forget my excursion to Montreal.

NETTIE. It was always your own actions that turned him against you.

JOHN. And the convention—don't leave that out.

(*He starts from the room.*)

NETTIE. The curtains. (*He regards her.*) The curtains for Timmy's room. They're coming today.

JOHN. I don't know anything about curtains.

NETTIE. Yes, you do.

JOHN. I do not.

NETTIE. They'll be ten dollars.

JOHN. What's the matter with the old ones?

(TIMMY CLEARY, *twenty-one, wearing army suntans, open at the neck, emerges from his room, starts toward the kitchen, is arrested by their voices. He stops, listens.*)

NETTIE. They're worn out.

JOHN. They look all right to me.

NETTIE. They aren't all right.

JOHN. Ten dollars for curtains.

NETTIE. Timmy will want to bring friends home.

JOHN. The old squeeze play.

(TIMMY *puts his hands over his ears.*)

NETTIE. Are you going to give me the money?

(JOHN *extracts a bill from his wallet, slaps it on the table.*)

JOHN. Here!

NETTIE. I need five dollars for the house.

JOHN. I gave you fifteen yesterday.

NETTIE. That went for the party.

JOHN. That party cost close to a hundred dollars.

NETTIE. It was worth it.

JOHN. Did I say it wasn't? (*He takes another bill from his wallet and puts it down.*) There.

(TIMMY *goes back, slams the door of his room to alert them, then approaches the kitchen.* NETTIE *and* JOHN *compose themselves cheerfully as* TIMMY, *equally cheerful, enters.*)

TIMMY. Good morning.

JOHN. Champ.

NETTIE. Morning, son.

(TIMMY *shakes hands with his father; kisses his mother on the cheek.*)

JOHN. We thought you were going to sleep all day.

TIMMY. I smelled the coffee.

JOHN. Mother said you were sick during the night.

TIMMY. I'm fine now.

JOHN. I was a little rocky myself.

TIMMY. I wonder why.

(*They both laugh.*)

NETTIE (*to* JOHN). What time is your appointment?

JOHN. Eleven-fifteen.

NETTIE. It's twenty-five of.

JOHN (*to* TIMMY). Mr. Ruskin wants to see me.

TIMMY. That's too bad.

JOHN. Why?

TIMMY. Thought we might take in the Giant game.

NETTIE (*to* JOHN). Why don't you?

JOHN. You know I can't. (*To* TIMMY.) This thing with Ruskin means a sure sale.

TIMMY. I understand.

JOHN. We'll go tomorrow.

NETTIE. My mother expects us for dinner tomorrow.

(JOHN *looks at* NETTIE *as though he might say something, thinks better of it, turns to* TIMMY.)

JOHN. How about *next* Saturday?

TIMMY. All right.

JOHN. We'll get box seats—the works.

TIMMY. Sounds fine.

JOHN. Swell.

NETTIE. What time will you be home?

JOHN. I'll call you.

NETTIE. I'll be at my mother's.

JOHN (*appraising* TIMMY). I understand none of your old clothes fit.

TIMMY. That's right.

JOHN. Meet me downtown on Monday and we'll get you some new ones.

TIMMY. Okay.

(JOHN *feints a jab.* TIMMY *covers up. They spar good-naturedly until* TIMMY *drops his hands.*)

JOHN. I still think I can take you.

TIMMY. I wouldn't be surprised.

JOHN. See you later.

TIMMY. Right.

(JOHN *moves toward the door, stops before the army jacket, indicates one of the ribbons.*)

JOHN. What did you say this one was for?

TIMMY. It's a combat infantry badge.

JOHN. How about that?

TIMMY. It's not as important as it sounds.

JOHN. We'll have to sit down and have a real talk. I want to hear all about it.

TIMMY. All right.

JOHN. It's great to have you home.

TIMMY. It's great to be home.

JOHN. The Mullin boy crippled. The Freeman boy dead. We're very lucky.

TIMMY. I know.

JOHN. I'm stopping off at St. Francis this morning to offer a prayer of thanks . . . See you later.

TIMMY. Right.

(JOHN *exits from the apartment.* TIMMY *looks after him.*)

NETTIE. How did you sleep?

TIMMY. Fine . . . How's he feeling?

NETTIE. All right.

TIMMY. He looks a lot older.

NETTIE. It's been two years . . . It must have seemed strange. (*He glances at her.*) Sleeping in your own bed.

TIMMY (*turning away again*). Yes . . . How's his business?

NETTIE. Who knows?

TIMMY. The coffee market's off.

NETTIE. I hope you're hungry.

TIMMY. I can't get over the change in him.

NETTIE. Guess what we're having for breakfast.

TIMMY. It's not just the way he looks.

NETTIE. *Guess what we're having for breakfast.* (*He turns to her.*) Guess what we're having.

TIMMY. What?

NETTIE. Guess.

TIMMY. I don't know.

NETTIE. Yes, you do.

TIMMY. No.

NETTIE. Sure you do.

TIMMY. What is it?

NETTIE. You're fooling.

TIMMY. What is it?

NETTIE. What's your favorite?

TIMMY. Bacon and eggs?

NETTIE. Now I know you're fooling.

TIMMY. No.

NETTIE. I forgot what a tease you were.

TIMMY. I'm not teasing.

NETTIE. Waffles. We're having waffles.

TIMMY. Fine.

NETTIE. You used to be crazy about waffles.

TIMMY. I still am.

NETTIE. I've got the waffle batter ready.

TIMMY. Swell.

NETTIE. Your first morning home, you're entitled to whatever you want.

TIMMY. I want waffles.

NETTIE. I used the last egg in the batter.

TIMMY. *I want waffles.*

NETTIE. Really?

TIMMY. Cross my heart.

NETTIE. All right.

(*While she prepares things, he goes to a window, gazes out.*)

TIMMY. I see a new butcher.

NETTIE. Quite a few new stores.

TIMMY. Pop said the Bremens moved.

NETTIE. And the Costellos . . . Remember old Zimmer the tailor?

TIMMY. Sure.

NETTIE. A few weeks ago a woman brought him a coat she wanted altered. Zimmer started to fix it, then very politely excused himself, went up to the roof and jumped. No one knows why.

TIMMY. Who was the woman?

NETTIE. Mrs. Levin.

TIMMY. That explains it.

NETTIE. That's not funny.

TIMMY. Sorry.

NETTIE. What a thing to say.

TIMMY. I said I'm sorry.

NETTIE. I'm surprised at you.

TIMMY. Bless us and save us.

NETTIE. *What?*

TIMMY. Bless us and save us. As in "Bless us and save us, said Mrs. O'Davis; Joy, joy, said Mrs. Malloy . . ." (*She regards him incredulously.*) What's the matter?

NETTIE. I never expected to hear that nonsense from *you!*

TIMMY. It beats swearing.

NETTIE. You used to cover your ears when your father said it.

TIMMY (*with mock solemnity*). I'll never say it again.

NETTIE. *Don't talk to me like that!* . . . I'm sorry. I don't know what's wrong with me this morning. I don't think I slept well . . . Too much excitement—the party and all. (*She resumes the preparation of breakfast: pours batter on the waffle iron while he, still not recovered from her outburst, studies her.*) Will you have bacon with it?

TIMMY. Just the waffles will be fine.

NETTIE. Did you like the party?

TIMMY. Yes.

NETTIE. I wish the house had looked better.

TIMMY. What's wrong with it?

NETTIE. It needs painting. The sofa's on its last legs. And the rugs . . . Well, now that you're here I'll get it all fixed up.

TIMMY. It looks fine to me.

NETTIE. I still can't believe you're here.

TIMMY. I find it a little hard to believe myself.

NETTIE. You *are* here?

TIMMY. Want to pinch me? . . . Go ahead. (*She hesitates. He holds out his hand.*) Go on. (*She takes his hand.*) Believe it now? (*She continues to hold his hand. He becomes uneasy.*) Hey. (*Oblivious to his resistance, she still clings to his hand.*) What are you doing? (*She persists. His agitation mounts.*) Cut it out . . . Cut it out! (*He jerks free of her; immediately tries to make light of it.*) One pinch to a customer . . . House rule. (*She regards him mutely.*) The waffles must be ready; the light on the iron went out. (*She just looks at him.*) Isn't that what it means when that little light goes out? (*She looks at him a moment more, then goes to the waffle iron, lifts the cover, starts to remove the waffles, stops, moves to a chair, sits, folds her hands in her lap and begins to cry.*) What's the matter? . . . What's wrong? . . . What is it? . . . *What is it?*

NETTIE (*continuing to cry*). They stuck.

TIMMY. What?

NETTIE. Why did they have to stick today?

TIMMY. The waffles?

NETTIE. I can't remember the last time they stuck.

TIMMY. What's that to cry about?

NETTIE. I've looked forward to this morning for three years and nothing's right.

TIMMY. Why do you say that?

NETTIE. Not one thing.

TIMMY. What isn't right?

NETTIE. Not one single thing.

TIMMY. Will you please stop?

NETTIE. The things you've been saying—your attitude.

TIMMY. What things? What attitude?

NETTIE. You haven't even asked about Willis.

TIMMY. . . . How is he?

NETTIE. Every time I look at you, you avoid me.

TIMMY (*turning away*). That's ridiculous.

NETTIE. You're doing it now.

TIMMY. I am not!

NETTIE. How could you forget waffles were your favorite?

TIMMY. I just forgot.

NETTIE. Then you must have forgotten a lot of things.

TIMMY. *I'll tell you one thing I didn't forget.* (*She looks at him.*) The dance. (*No reaction from her.*) The one we were going to have the first morning I was home.

NETTIE. What made you think of that?

TIMMY. It's been on my mind all along.

NETTIE. I'll bet.

TIMMY. I was about to turn the radio on when you started crying.

NETTIE. I'll bet.

TIMMY. If you're through, I'll do it now. Are you through?

NETTIE. I haven't danced in so long I've probably forgotten how.

(*He goes to the living room, snaps on the radio, dials to a band playing a slow fox trot, returns to the kitchen.*)

TIMMY. Shall we have a go at it?

NETTIE. I can't remember the last time I danced.

TIMMY. Come on.

NETTIE. You really want to?

TIMMY. Yes.

NETTIE (*rising*). You asked for it.

TIMMY. That-a-girl. (*He puts his arms about her.*) Here we go. (*They move smoothly, gracefully.*) Forgot how to dance—who you kidding?

NETTIE. I guess it's one of those things you never forget.

TIMMY. Remember this? (*He goes into a maneuver that she follows perfectly.*) You've been taking lessons.

NETTIE. Of course.

(*They dance from the kitchen into the living room.*)

TIMMY. Come here off-ten?

NETTIE. Foist time.

TIMMY. Me likewise . . . By yuhself?

NETTIE. Widda goil friend.

(*The song ends.*)

ANNOUNCER'S VOICE. That's all the time we have on Dance Parade this morning. I hope—

(TIMMY *goes to the radio, dials, picks up a polka band going full blast.*)

TIMMY. What do you say?

NETTIE. The spirit's willing.

TIMMY. Let's go! (*They take off.*) Not bad . . . not bad.

NETTIE. What will the neighbors think?

TIMMY. The worst. (*The rhythm begins to accelerate.*) We're coming into the home stretch. Hang on.

(*They move faster and faster.*)

NETTIE. I'm getting dizzy.

(*As they whirl about the room they begin to laugh.*)

TIMMY. Hang on.

NETTIE. I can't do any more.

(*The laughter grows.*)

TIMMY. Hang on!

NETTIE. I can't!

(*The laughter becomes hysterical.*)

TIMMY. Hang on! Hang on!

NETTIE. I can't! I . . .

(*They trip, collapse to the floor.*)

TIMMY. You all right?

NETTIE. I think so.

(*Both breathe laboredly. The laughter subsides. He snaps the radio off, then sits on the floor facing her.*)

TIMMY. I'm dead . . . absolutely dead.

NETTIE. So am I.

TIMMY. I can't remember the last time I laughed like that.

NETTIE. I can . . . We were driving to the lake and stopped at that dinky carnival.

TIMMY. The time I got you to go on that ride.

NETTIE. Your father thought we'd lost our minds. He kept begging the man to stop the engine.

TIMMY. Which made us laugh all the harder.

NETTIE. Know something?

TIMMY. What?

NETTIE. I really believe you're here now.

TIMMY. So do I.

NETTIE. What are you going to do today?

TIMMY. I don't know.

NETTIE. Why don't you come to Mama's with me?

TIMMY. We're going there for dinner tomorrow.

NETTIE. Willis would love to see you.

TIMMY. I'll see him tomorrow.

NETTIE. When we told him you were coming home he began to sing. It's the first time he's done that in months.

TIMMY. All right, I'll go.

NETTIE. We won't stay long.

TIMMY. All right.

(*The door opens and* JOHN *enters, sees them on the floor.*)

JOHN. Well, hello (TIMMY *rises.*) Don't get up on my account.

TIMMY. We were dancing and fell down.

NETTIE (*to* JOHN). What did you forget?

JOHN. Nothing.

NETTIE (*rising*). Why did you come back?

JOHN. I changed my mind. (*To* TIMMY.) If you still want to go to the ball game, it's a date.

NETTIE. What about Ruskin?

JOHN. The hell with him. (*To* TIMMY.) Still want to go?

TIMMY. Yes.

NETTIE. What about Willis?

JOHN. What *about* Willis?

NETTIE. Timmy was going to see him this afternoon.

TIMMY. I'll see him tomorrow.

NETTIE. I told him you'd be over today.

TIMMY. Before you even asked me?

NETTIE. I thought sure you'd want to.

TIMMY. You had no right to do that.

NETTIE. What will I tell him?

TIMMY. Tell him I'll be there tomorrow.

NETTIE. He'll be disappointed.

TIMMY. That's not my fault.

JOHN. The game starts at twelve.

TIMMY. Just have to get my tie.

NETTIE. You haven't eaten.

TIMMY. We'll grab something on the way. (*He exits.*)

JOHN. I came out of Saint Francis and started for the subway. Was halfway there when I thought of Mr. Freeman: What wouldn't *he* give to be able to spend a day with his son? . . . It made me turn around and come back. (*She just looks at him.*) You're mad. (*No reply.*) You told me to take him to the game.

NETTIE. And you always do what I tell you.

JOHN. Bless us and save us.

(TIMMY, *knotting his tie, reappears, puts on his jacket, snaps to attention.*)

TIMMY. Corporal Cleary reporting for duty.

JOHN. Kiss your mother good-bye.

TIMMY. That's not a duty. (*He kisses* NETTIE *on the cheek. She receives the kiss impassively.*) So long, Mom.

JOHN. We won't be late.

(*He and* TIMMY *exit. She stands as she is.*)

CURTAIN

SCENE TWO

TIME: *Late afternoon—the same day.*

AT RISE: JOHN *and* TIMMY *enter the apart-* ment. TIMMY *carries a bouquet of red roses.* JOHN *has just concluded a joke and they are both laughing.*

JOHN. I haven't told that one in years.

TIMMY. I was considered a very funny fellow. Thanks to you.

JOHN. Hello? . . . Anybody home? (*No answer.*) Still at her mother's.

TIMMY (*indicating the roses*). I better put these in water.

(*They move into the kitchen.*)

JOHN. Stand another beer?

TIMMY. Sure.

(*While* TIMMY *puts the roses in a vase,* JOHN *gets two cans of beer from the refrigerator.*)

JOHN (*opening the beers*). How did you remember all those jokes of mine?

TIMMY. Just came to me.

JOHN. I don't remember most of them myself . . . (*Hands* TIMMY *a beer.*) Here you go.

TIMMY. Thanks.

JOHN. What'll we drink to?

TIMMY. The Chicago Cubs.

JOHN. Think it'll help them?

TIMMY. Can it hurt?

JOHN (*raising the can*). To the Cubs.

TIMMY. To the Cubs.

(*They both drink.*)

JOHN. Sixteen to three.

TIMMY. I'm still glad we went.

JOHN. So am I. (*Drinks.*) That was a beautiful catch Ott made.

TIMMY. Yes.

JOHN. For a moment I thought he lost it in the sun.

(TIMMY *says nothing.* JOHN *drinks.*) So they really went for the old man's jokes?

TIMMY. Especially the ones about Uncle Mike.

JOHN. Such as?

TIMMY. The Pennsylvania Hotel gag.

JOHN. Columbus told that one to the Indians.

TIMMY. Uncle Mike was a famous man in our outfit.

JOHN. Joking aside, he was quite a guy. Stood six three. Weighed close to two fifty.

TIMMY. I remember his picture.

JOHN. He was in the Spanish American War.

TIMMY. I know.

JOHN. Got hit by a bullet once that knocked him out. When he came to, he was lying in a field full of wounded men. The ones that were sure goners were marked with yellow tags so no one would waste time on them. The others had blue tags. Mike found a yellow tag around his wrist. The fellow next to him who was unconscious had a blue one. Quick as a wink Mike switched the tags and . . . How about that? I'm telling *you* war stories. Go on—you do the talking.

TIMMY. About what?

JOHN. You must have seen some pretty bad things.

TIMMY. Not as much as a lot of others.

JOHN. Maybe you'd rather not talk about it.

TIMMY. I don't mind.

JOHN. I'd like to hear what you have to say.

TIMMY. I don't know how to begin.

JOHN. Anything that comes to mind.

TIMMY. Want to hear the bravest thing I ever did?

JOHN. Yes.

TIMMY. The first night we were in combat I slept with my boots off.

JOHN. Go on.

TIMMY. That's it.

JOHN. You slept with your boots off?

TIMMY. Doesn't sound like much, does it?

JOHN. Not offhand.

TIMMY. The fellows who eventually cracked up were all guys who couldn't sleep. If I hadn't decided to take my boots off I'd have ended up being one of them.

JOHN. I see.

TIMMY. Want to know the smartest thing I did?

JOHN. Sure.

TIMMY. I never volunteered. One day the lieutenant bawled me out for it. I said, "Sir, if there's anything you want me to do, you tell me and I'll do it. But if you wait for me to volunteer you'll wait forever."

JOHN. What did he say to that?

TIMMY. Nothing printable. The fact is I wasn't a very good soldier, Pop.

JOHN. You did everything they asked you.

TIMMY. The good ones do more. You'd have been a good one.

JOHN. What makes you say that?

TIMMY. I can tell.

JOHN. Well, thanks.

TIMMY. You're welcome.

JOHN. It's one of the big regrets of my life that I was never in the service.

TIMMY. I know.

JOHN. The day World War One was declared I went to the recruiting office. When they learned I was the sole support of the family, they turned me down.

TIMMY. I know.

JOHN. A lot of people made cracks. Especially guys like Clayton and Harper who waited to be drafted and then wangled safe jobs at Governors Island and the Navy Yard . . . I fixed their wagons one night —sent the army flying one way and the navy the other. That was the last about slacking I heard from *them* . . . Still it bothers me—missing out on the whole thing . . . I keep wondering what difference it might have made in my life . . . And then I wonder how I'd have made out . . . I wouldn't have settled for a desk job. I'd have gotten to the front.

TIMMY. I'm sure of that.

JOHN. But once there, how would I have done?

TIMMY. Fine.

JOHN. How do you know?

TIMMY. You're a born fighter.

JOHN. They say a lot of fellows who were terrors as civilians turned to jelly when they heard those bullets.

TIMMY. Not you.

JOHN. It doesn't seem so. But you can't be sure . . . That's always bothered me. (*Drinks the last of his beer.*) How about another?

TIMMY. Fine.

JOHN. Maybe we shouldn't.

TIMMY. Why?

JOHN. Your mother blames me for your getting sick last night; says I encouraged you to drink too much.

TIMMY. It wasn't what I drank. It was the excitement.

JOHN. That's what I told her.

TIMMY. *I'll* open two more.

JOHN. All right. (*While* TIMMY *gets the beers,* JOHN *regards the roses.*) Her father used to send her roses every birthday . . . A dozen red ones . . . Never missed . . . Even at the end.

TIMMY. Tell her they were your idea.

JOHN. What?

TIMMY. Tell her the roses were your idea.

JOHN. Why?

TIMMY. She'll get a kick out of it . . . All right?

JOHN. If you like.

TIMMY (*handing him a beer*). Here you go.

JOHN. Thanks.

TIMMY. You call it this time.

JOHN (*raising his beer*). To the two nicest fellows in the house.

TIMMY. I'll buy that. (*They drink.* TIMMY *regards the can.*) Funny how you acquire a taste for things.

JOHN. Yes.

TIMMY. When I was a kid I couldn't even stand the smell of beer.

JOHN. Believe it or not I was the same.

TIMMY. We seem to have gotten over it.

JOHN. Yes . . . Can I say something to you?

TIMMY. Sure.

JOHN. You won't take it the wrong way?

TIMMY. No.

JOHN. I owe you an apology.

TIMMY. For what?

JOHN. You were always sick; always home from school with one thing or another. I never thought you'd last in the army.

TIMMY. Neither did I.

JOHN. Really?

TIMMY. Really.

JOHN. When Dr. Goldman heard they took you he said it was ridiculous. When they put you in the infantry he said it was inhuman.

TIMMY. And when I survived?

JOHN. He said it was a miracle. (*They both laugh.*) I don't think it was a miracle. I think we just underestimated you . . . Especially me . . . That's what I wanted to apologize for.

TIMMY. Remember that corny thing you used to recite—about how a boy thinks his father is the greatest guy in the world until he's fifteen. Then the doubts start. By the time he's eighteen he's convinced his father is the worst guy in the world. At twenty-five the doubts start again. At thirty it occurs to him that the old man wasn't so bad after all. At forty—

JOHN. What about it?

TIMMY. There's some truth to it.

JOHN. I think you've had too much to drink.

TIMMY. I'm not saying you're a saint.

JOHN. That's a relief.

TIMMY. But taking into account where you started from, and the obstacles you had to overcome, what you've done is something to be proud of.

JOHN. Well, thank you.

TIMMY. How many guys that you grew up with even turned out legitimate?

JOHN. Not many.

TIMMY. And most of *them* are still scraping along where they started.

JOHN. That's true.

TIMMY. How many years of school did you have?

JOHN. I had to quit after the fourth grade.

TIMMY. I've met college graduates who don't know nearly as much as you about the things that really count.

JOHN. Must have been Yale men.

TIMMY. I'm serious.

JOHN. Speaking of college . . . If you get into one of those big ones and it's more than the G.I. Bill pays for, I'll help you out.

TIMMY. Thanks.

JOHN. That's just between you and me.

TIMMY. Why?

JOHN. I don't want people getting wrong notions.

TIMMY. About what?

JOHN. That I'm loaded.

TIMMY. *Are* you loaded?

JOHN. Don't be ridiculous.

TIMMY. That doesn't answer my question.

JOHN. The question's ridiculous.

TIMMY. That's still no answer.

JOHN. No, I'm not loaded.

TIMMY. How much do you have?

JOHN. What?

TIMMY. How much money do you have?

JOHN. Is this your idea of a joke?

TIMMY. No.

JOHN. Then why are you doing it?

TIMMY. I don't want to take money from you if you can't afford it.

JOHN. I can afford it.

TIMMY. Some of the places I applied at are pretty expensive.

JOHN. I can afford it!

TIMMY. Then you must be loaded.

JOHN. *I am not loaded!*

TIMMY. We have a summer place, a car. Now you tell me you can afford any school in the country. You must be fairly loaded.

JOHN. *If I hear that word once more, I'm marching right out the door!*

(TIMMY *is unable to suppress his laughter any longer.*)

TIMMY. You haven't changed a bit. (JOHN *regards him uncertainly.*) You look as though I'd asked you to betray your country.

(JOHN, *against his will, smiles.*)

JOHN. You son of a gun.

TIMMY. I really had you going.

JOHN. Some joke.

TIMMY. Oh, say, Pop.

JOHN. What?

TIMMY. How much *do* you have?

JOHN. *Enough's enough!* (TIMMY *laughs anew.*) I think we better change the subject.

TIMMY. How did you meet Mother? (JOHN *regards him.*) You said change the subject.

JOHN. You know all about that.

TIMMY. Just that you picked her up on the subway.

JOHN. It wasn't like that at all.

TIMMY. Then I don't know all about it.

JOHN. "Picked her up" makes it sound cheap.

TIMMY. Sorry.

JOHN. The first time I spoke to her was on the subway but there's more to it.

TIMMY. Tell me.

JOHN. Why?

TIMMY. I might become a writer and want to do a story about it someday.

JOHN. A writer?

TIMMY. Maybe.

JOHN. Well, that's the first I heard about that.

TIMMY. Me, too. Must be the beer . . . What year was it you met her?

JOHN. Nineteen twenty-one . . . A writer?

TIMMY. A writer . . . Where were you working then?

JOHN. At Emerson's . . .

TIMMY. And?

JOHN. One morning I saw her walk by. That afternoon she passed again. Same the next day. Turned out she worked around the corner. I . . . You sure you want to hear this?

TIMMY. Uh-huh.

JOHN. One evening I happened to be leaving at the same time she did. Turned out we took the same subway. She got off at Seventy-second Street . . . To make a long story short, I got a seat next to her one day and we started talking.

TIMMY. That's it?

JOHN. Yes.

TIMMY. Sounds like an ordinary pickup to me.

JOHN. *Well, it wasn't* . . . I left some things out.

TIMMY. Such as?

JOHN. I don't remember . . . It was twenty-five years ago.

TIMMY. The way I heard it, you followed her for a month before you finally got the nerve to speak.

JOHN. I thought you didn't know the story.

TIMMY. To convince her your intentions were honorable, you asked if you might call at her home. True or false? . . . Well?

JOHN. True. (*Chuckles.*) You wouldn't believe how nervous I was. And she didn't make it any easier . . . Pretended the whole thing was a complete surprise. Bernhardt couldn't have done it nicer . . . Or looked nicer . . . All in blue . . . Blue dress, blue hat, blue shoes . . . Everything blue . . . Light blue . . . And dignified . . . One look at her, you knew she was a lady . . . My family *called* her The Lady. To their minds it was an insult. (*Regards* TIMMY.) How did we get on this?

TIMMY. You were—

(*He is interrupted by the opening of the outside door.* NETTIE *enters.*)

JOHN. Join the party.

(*She enters the kitchen.*)

TIMMY. We're having a little hair of the dog.

NETTIE. How was the game?

JOHN. One-sided.

TIMMY. Pop was just telling me how you and he met.

(NETTIE *turns to* JOHN *questioningly.*)

JOHN. He asked me.

TIMMY (*to his mother, indicating his father*). His version is a little different from yours.

NETTIE. What do you mean?

TIMMY. He says *you* chased *him.*

NETTIE. That'll be the day.

TIMMY. Says you did everything but stand on your head to attract his attention. (NETTIE *is not sure now whether he's kidding or not.*) That's what he said.

(NETTIE *looks uncertainly from* TIMMY *to* JOHN. *They break up simultaneously.*)

NETTIE. You two.

JOHN. How about a beer?

NETTIE. No thanks.

JOHN. Come on—

TIMMY. Be a sport.

NETTIE. All right.

JOHN. That-a-girl.

NETTIE. Just a glass. (*To* TIMMY, *while* JOHN *gets the beer.*) What *did* he tell you?

TIMMY. He said you were dressed in blue and nobody ever looked nicer.

NETTIE. I'll bet.

TIMMY (*to* JOHN). Didn't you say that?

JOHN. I'm a stranger here.

NETTIE. Did he tell you how he used his friend Eddie Barnes?

JOHN. Bless us and save us.

NETTIE. Every night they'd get on the subway, stand right in front of me, and have a loud conversation about how well they were doing in business.

JOHN. It wasn't every night.

NETTIE. Poor Eddie had to go an hour out of his way.

TIMMY. That's what I call a friend.

JOHN. The best I ever had. (*Extends a glass of beer to* NETTIE.) Here you go. (*She stares past him.*) Here's your beer.

(*She continues looking off. He follows her gaze to the roses.*)

NETTIE. Where did they come from?

TIMMY. Pop got them . . . for you.

NETTIE (*to* JOHN). You did?

JOHN. Yes.

(*She goes to the roses.*)

NETTIE. They're beautiful . . . Thank you.

JOHN. You're welcome.

NETTIE. What made you do it?

JOHN. We happened to pass a place and I know you like them.

NETTIE. I haven't had red roses since Papa died. (*To* TIMMY.) He used to send me a dozen on my birthday. Never missed.

TIMMY. I remember.

NETTIE (*to* JOHN). Thank you.

JOHN. You're welcome.

NETTIE. I'm going to cry.

(*She does.*)

JOHN. You don't bring flowers—they cry. You do—they cry.

NETTIE. I'm sorry.

TIMMY. What's to be sorry?

NETTIE. He was the kindest, gentlest man that ever lived.

TIMMY. I know.

NETTIE. I'm all right now.

JOHN (*handing her the glass of beer*). Here's what you need.

NETTIE. Maybe so.

TIMMY (*raising his beer*). To happy days.

JOHN and NETTIE. To happy days.

(*They all drink.*)

NETTIE (*regarding the roses*). They're just beautiful.

JOHN (*anxious to change the subject*). Talking of Eddie Barnes before, God rest his soul, reminds me of the time old Emerson put up a second-hand car for the man who sold the most coffee over a three-month period. I won it, but couldn't drive. Eddie said he'd teach me. We didn't get two blocks from the office when he ran broadside into an ice truck.

NETTIE. How about that ride to Connecticut? He practically killed us all.

JOHN. What was the name of the place we stayed at?

NETTIE. The Rainbow Grove.

JOHN. That's right. Big fat red-haired dame ran it.

NETTIE. Mrs. Hanlon.

JOHN (*mimicking Mrs. Hanlon à la Mae West*). "My friends all call me Daisy." (*He and* NETTIE *laugh.*) I dubbed her the Will Rogers of Connecticut—she never met a man she didn't like.

(*They all laugh.*)

NETTIE. Remember the night you, Eddie, and a couple of others picked her up, bed and all, and left her sleeping in the middle of the baseball field.

JOHN. In the morning when we went out to play, she was still there.

TIMMY. What did you do?

JOHN. We ruled that any ball hitting her on the fly was a ground rule double. (*They all laugh.*) We had a lot of fun at that place.

NETTIE. Yes.

JOHN. I wonder if it's still there.

NETTIE. I wonder.

JOHN. Let's take a ride someday and see.

NETTIE. All right.

(*She starts to rise.*)

JOHN. Where you going?

NETTIE. Have to start supper.

JOHN. Forget it—we're eating out!

NETTIE. I bought a steak.

JOHN. It'll keep. (*To* TIMMY.) Where would you like to go, Champ?

NETTIE. Maybe he has a date.

JOHN. Bring her along.

TIMMY. I don't have a date.

NETTIE. I thought you'd be seeing that Davis girl?

TIMMY. That's finished.

NETTIE. She was a nice girl.

JOHN. She was a dunce.

NETTIE. John!

TIMMY. Pop's right.

NETTIE. You men are terrible.

TIMMY. You're too kind.

JOHN. Well, where are we going?

TIMMY. You two settle it while I see a man about a dog.

(*He exits.*)

JOHN. How about the Concourse Plaza?

NETTIE. All right.

JOHN. I had a nice day today.

NETTIE. I'm glad.

JOHN. He's quite a boy.

NETTIE. That's what I've been telling you for years.

JOHN. We talked about things. Really talked. The way Eddie and I used to . . . The hell with the Concourse Plaza! Let's go downtown! Let's go to the New Yorker!

NETTIE. You *are* in a good mood.

JOHN. Because I want to go downtown?

NETTIE. That and the roses.

JOHN. Are you going to talk about those roses all night?

NETTIE. I just wanted to thank you for them.

JOHN. You already have.

NETTIE. You sound as though you're sorry you got them.

JOHN. Don't be ridiculous.

NETTIE. Then what are you angry about?

JOHN. I'm just tired of hearing about them. A guy gets some roses—big deal.

NETTIE. You're embarrassed.

JOHN. I am not.

NETTIE. You did something nice and you're embarrassed.

JOHN. You don't know what you're talking about.

NETTIE. Don't worry, I won't tell anyone.

JOHN. *Nettie, please.*

NETTIE. All right, but I want to let you know how much I appreciate it.

JOHN. Good. I'm glad.

NETTIE. I do . . . I really do. (*On an impulse she touches his shoulder. The contact is mutually startling. Flustered, she turns away.*) We haven't been to the New Yorker in years . . . I wonder if they still have the ice show? . . . Do you suppose we'll have any trouble getting in on a Saturday night?

(TIMMY *enters.*)

TIMMY. What did you decide?

JOHN. We're going to the Hotel New Yorker.

TIMMY. Well, digga digga doo.

JOHN. After that we're going to the Diamond Horseshoe. And then the Sawdust Trail.

TIMMY. Sounds like our night to howl.

JOHN. That's what it is.

(*He howls.*)

TIMMY. You call that a howl?

(*He howls louder. Now* JOHN *howls. Now* TIMMY. *Now* JOHN. *Now* TIMMY. *Each howl is louder than the last.*)

CURTAIN

Scene Three

TIME: *Two* A.M. *Sunday morning.*

AT RISE: *The apartment is in darkness. From the hallway outside the apartment, we hear* TIMMY *and* JOHN *in loud but dubious harmony.*

TIMMY *and* JOHN (*offstage*). "Farewell, Piccadilly . . . Hello, Leicester Square . . . It's a long, long way to Tipperary . . . But my heart's right there."

NETTIE (*offstage*). You'll wake the Feldmans.

JOHN (*offstage*). Nothing could wake the Feldmans.

(TIMMY *and* JOHN *laugh.*)

NETTIE (*offstage*). Open the door.

JOHN (*offstage*). Can't find my keys.

TIMMY (*offstage—giggling*). I can't find the door.

NETTIE (*offstage*). Honestly.

JOHN (*offstage*). Where would you be if you were my keys?

NETTIE (*offstage*). Here—I'll do it.

JOHN (*offstage*). Did you ever see such pretty hair?

NETTIE (*offstage*). Stop.

TIMMY (*offstage*). Beautiful hair.

NETTIE (*offstage*). Will you please let me open this door?

(*A key turns. The door opens.* NETTIE, *followed by* JOHN *and* TIMMY, *enters. She turns on the lights.*)

JOHN. Home to wife and mother.

NETTIE (*to* JOHN). Someday we'll break our necks because you refuse to leave a light.

TIMMY (*sings*). "By the light . . . (JOHN *joins in.*) Of the silvery moon—"

NETTIE. That's just enough.

JOHN. Whatever you say, Antoinette.

NETTIE. I say to bed.

JOHN. Shank of the evening. (*He grabs her around the waist and manages a squeeze before she breaks away. Ignoring the look of censure she directs at him, he turns to* TIMMY.) No sir, you can't beat a law degree. Springboard for anything.

TIMMY. So they say.

NETTIE (*to* JOHN). Anyone can be a lawyer. How many people become writers?

JOHN. That's my point.

NETTIE. You should be proud to have a son who wants to try something different.

JOHN. Did I say I wasn't proud of him?

TIMMY. Abra ka dabra ka deedra slatter-in. (*They regard him.*) The fellow in the red jacket who leads the horses to the post at Jamaica always says that when they reach the starting gate. Abra ka dabra ka deedra slatter-in. And here are your horses for the fifth race . . . Long as you can say it, you're not drunk . . . *Abra ka dabra ka deedra slatter-in.*

JOHN. Abra ka dabra . . .

TIMMY. Ka deedra slatter-in.

NETTIE. Honestly.

JOHN. Ka zebra—

TIMMY. Not zebra. Deedra . . . Ka deedra slatter-in . . . Abra ka dabra ka deedra slatter-in.

JOHN. Abra . . . ka dabra . . . ka deedra . . . slatter-in.

TIMMY. Faster.

JOHN. Abra, ka dabra, ka deedra, slatter-in.

TIMMY. Faster.

JOHN. Abra ka dabra ka deedra slatter-in.

NETTIE. Have you both lost your minds?

JOHN. Nothing wrong with us that a little nightcap wouldn't cure.

(*He enters the kitchen.*)

NETTIE (*following him*). I'll nightcap you.

TIMMY. I can't bear to hear married people fight.

JOHN (*to* NETTIE). We ought to go dancing more.

NETTIE. Now I know you're drunk.

TIMMY (*calling from the living room*). Who was it that used to call us The Four Mortons?

JOHN (*calling back*). Harold Bowen.

TIMMY (*staring at the audience*). I wish we were.

JOHN (*to* NETTIE). Remember the first dance I took you to?

NETTIE. Of course.

JOHN. I'll bet you don't.

NETTIE. Of course I do.

TIMMY (*lost in contemplation of the audience*). I have this magical feeling about vaudeville.

JOHN (*to* NETTIE). Where was it, then?

NETTIE. The Crystal Terrace.

JOHN. And what was the first song?

NETTIE. It's too late for quiz games.

TIMMY. It doesn't matter how cheap and tinny the show is . . . Soon as the house lights go down and the band starts up, I could cry.

JOHN (*to* NETTIE). The first song we ever danced to was "Pretty Baby." A blond guy crooned it.

NETTIE. Through a gold megaphone.

JOHN. You *do* remember.

NETTIE. Of course.

(JOHN *moves to touch* NETTIE. *To elude him, she re-enters the living room. He follows.*)

TIMMY (*to the audience—à la Smith and Dale*). "I've got snew in my blood" . . . "What's snew?" . . . "Nothing. What's snew with you?"

NETTIE (*to* JOHN—*indicating* TIMMY). What's he doing?

JOHN. Playing the Palace.

TIMMY (*to the audience*). "Take off the coat, my boy . . . Take . . . off . . . the . . . coat . . . Tay-ake . . . o-f-f-f-f . . . the coat-t-t-t-t."

JOHN and TIMMY. "The coat is off."

NETTIE (*to* TIMMY). Will you please go to bed?

TIMMY (*to the audience*). In closing I would like to do a dance made famous by the inimitable Pat Rooney.

(*Nods to* JOHN.) Maestro, if you please.

(JOHN *begins to hum "The Daughter of Rosie O'Grady" as both he and* TIMMY *dance in the manner of Pat Rooney.*)

NETTIE. John! Timmy! (*They stop dancing.*) Mama expects us at twelve.

TIMMY (*to the audience*). We're running a bit long, folks: No dance tonight. My mother thanks you. My father thanks you. My sister thanks you. And the Feldmans thank you. (*He goes into Jimmy Durante's closing song.*) "Good night . . . Good night . . . Good night—"

NETTIE. *Good night.*

TIMMY (*kisses* NETTIE). Good night, Mrs. Cleary—whoever you are.

NETTIE. Good night, dear.

TIMMY. (*to* JOHN—*indicating the audience*). Tough house, but I warmed them up for you.

JOHN. Thanks.

TIMMY. Don't look now, but your leg's broken.

JOHN. The show must go on.

TIMMY (*to* NETTIE—*indicating* JOHN). Plucky lad. (*Extends his hand to* JOHN.) Honor to share the bill with you.

JOHN (*shaking with him*). Likewise.

TIMMY. Sleep well, chaps.

JOHN. Night, Champ.

NETTIE. Sure you don't want an Alka Seltzer?

TIMMY Abra ka dabra ka deedra slatter-in . . . see you in the morning.

JOHN. With the help of God.

TIMMY (*moving toward his room*). Abra ka dabra ka deedra slatter-in . . . Abra ka dabra ka deedra slatter-in . . . And here are your horses for . . .

(*He enters his room, closes the door.*)

NETTIE. Home two days and both nights to bed like that.

JOHN. He's entitled. You should hear some of the things he's been through. They overran one of those concentration camps—

NETTIE I don't want to hear about it now.

JOHN. You're right. It's no way to end a happy evening.

NETTIE. I think we have some aspirin in the kitchen.

(*She moves into the kitchen. He follows, watches her take a bottle of aspirin from a cabinet.*)

JOHN. You didn't say anything before about a headache.

NETTIE. I don't have a headache.

JOHN. Then what—

NETTIE. I read that if you put an aspirin in cut flowers they keep longer. (*She drops an aspirin in the vase, regards the roses.*) I wonder what made you get them?

JOHN. I don't know.

NETTIE. There must have been some reason.

JOHN. I just thought it would be nice to do.

(*She turns to him.*)

NETTIE. It was.

(*They regard each other a moment.*)

JOHN. I like your dress.

NETTIE. You've seen it before.

JOHN. It looks different . . . Everything about you looks different.

NETTIE. What Mass are you going to?

JOHN. Ten o'clock.

NETTIE (*picking up the vase of roses and starting toward the living room*). I better set the alarm.

JOHN. Nettie? (*She turns to him.*) I had a good time tonight.

NETTIE. So did I.

(NETTIE *enters the living room and places the roses on a table.*)

JOHN (*following her into the living room*). Did you really? Or were you putting it on for his sake?

NETTIE. I really did.

JOHN. So did I.

NETTIE. I'll set the alarm for nine-fifteen. (*She starts away again.*)

JOHN. Now that he's back we'll have lots of good times.

(*She stops.*)

NETTIE. What's wrong between you and I has nothing to do with him.

JOHN. I didn't say it did.

NETTIE. We have to solve our own problems.

JOHN (*coming up behind her*). Of course.

NETTIE. They can't be solved in one night.

JOHN (*touching her*). I know.

NETTIE. One nice evening doesn't make everything different.

JOHN. Did I say it did?

(*His lips brush the nape of her neck.*)

NETTIE. I guess you don't understand.

JOHN. I forgot how nice you smelled.

NETTIE. You'll spoil everything.

JOHN. I want things right between us.

NETTIE. You think this is going to make them right?

JOHN (*his hand moving to her breasts*). We have to start some place.

NETTIE (*breaking away*). Start?

JOHN. Bless us and save us.

NETTIE. *That's not my idea of a start.*

JOHN. Nettie, I want you . . . I want you like I never wanted anything in my life.

NETTIE (*covering her ears*). Stop.

JOHN. *Please?*

NETTIE. You're drunk.

JOHN. *Do you think I could ask again if I wasn't?*

NETTIE. I'm not one of your hotel lobby whores.

JOHN. If you were I wouldn't have to ask.

NETTIE. A couple of drinks, a couple of jokes, and let's jump in bed.

JOHN. Maybe that's my mistake.

NETTIE. How do you suppose Ruskin managed without you today?

JOHN. Maybe you don't want to be asked!

(*He seizes her.*)

NETTIE. Let me alone.

JOHN (*as they struggle*). *You've had the drinks! You've had the jokes!*

NETTIE. *Stop!*

(*She breaks free of him; regards him for a moment, then picks up the vase of roses and hurls them against the floor. The impact is shattering. They both freeze. For a moment there is silence. Now* TIMMY's *door opens.*)

TIMMY (*entering*). What happened?

NETTIE. The roses . . . I knocked them over.

TIMMY. Sounded like a bomb.

NETTIE. I'm sorry I woke you. (TIMMY *bends to pick up a piece of the vase.*) Don't . . . I'll clean up. You go back to bed. (*He hesitates.*) Please.

TIMMY. All right . . . Good night.

NETTIE. Good night.

TIMMY. Good night, Pop.

(JOHN, *his back to* TIMMY, *remains silent.* TIMMY *hesitates a moment, then goes off to his room and closes his door.*)

NETTIE (*to* JOHN). You moved me this afternoon . . . When you brought the roses, I felt something stir I thought was dead forever. (*Regards the roses on the floor.*) And now this . . . I don't understand.

JOHN (*without turning*). I had nothing to do with the roses . . . They were *his* idea.

(*She bends and starts to pick up the roses.*)

CURTAIN

ACT TWO

SCENE ONE

TIME: *Nine-fifteen* A.M. *Sunday morning.*
AT RISE: JOHN *and* NETTIE *are at the breakfast table.*

JOHN. Coffee's weak.

NETTIE. Add water.

JOHN. I said *weak* . . . Waste of time bringing good coffee into this house . . . (*He looks for a reaction. She offers none.*) I'm thinking about renting the lake house this summer . . . (*Still no reaction from her.*) Business is off . . . (*Still no reaction.*) Well, what do you say?

NETTIE. About what?

JOHN. Renting the lake house.

NETTIE. Timmy will be disappointed.

JOHN. How about you?

NETTIE. I'm in favor of it.

JOHN. Of course you are.

NETTIE. I wonder why.

(TIMMY *enters.*)

TIMMY. Morning.

NETTIE. Good morning.

(TIMMY *kisses her.*)

TIMMY (*to* JOHN). Morning.

JOHN. Nice of you to join us.

TIMMY. My pleasure.

JOHN. This isn't a hotel. We have our meals at certain times.

(TIMMY *now senses his father's irritation.*)

TIMMY. You should have woke me.

NETTIE (*to* TIMMY). It's all right.

JOHN. Of course it is.

NETTIE (*to* TIMMY, *who regards his father puzzledly*). Sit down. (TIMMY *sits.*) What do you want?

TIMMY. Coffee.

NETTIE. Just coffee?

TIMMY. Stomach's a bit shaky.

NETTIE. You should have taken that Alka Seltzer.

TIMMY. I'll be all right.

JOHN. Two days—two hangovers. Is that what they taught you in the army?

TIMMY (*to* JOHN). Cream, please? (JOHN *passes the cream.*) Thank you.

JOHN. I'm thinking of renting the lake house.

TIMMY. How come?

JOHN. I can use the money.

TIMMY. Oh . . .

JOHN. That all you're going to say?

TIMMY. What do you expect me to say?

JOHN. I thought that house meant something to you.

TIMMY. It does. But if you need the money—

JOHN. A bunch of strangers sleeping in our beds, using our things—doesn't bother you at all?

TIMMY. If it has to be it has to be.

JOHN. Of course! I forgot! What's a little summer cottage, after the earth-shattering things you've been through?

TIMMY (to NETTIE—*holding up the cream pitcher*). Do you have more cream?

NETTIE (*taking the pitcher*). Yes.

JOHN. What do you want more cream for?

TIMMY. Coffee's strong.

JOHN. It's weak.

TIMMY. It's too strong for me. (NETTIE *returns the refilled pitcher to him.*) Thanks.

(*He adds cream to his coffee.*)

JOHN. A few months in the army and they're experts on everything. Even coffee.

TIMMY. Who said that?

JOHN. By the time I was your age I was in the coffee business nine years . . . Nine years . . . When I was seventeen they sent me to Brazil for three months.

TIMMY. I know.

JOHN. I'd never even been out of New York before but I went down there on my own and did my job.

TIMMY. For Emerson, wasn't it?

JOHN. No uniform. No buddies. No Uncle Sam to lean on. Just myself . . . All alone in that strange place.

TIMMY. That's the time you grew the mustache to look older.

JOHN. Who's telling the story?

TIMMY. Sorry.

JOHN. Thirty-five years in the business and *he's* going to tell me about coffee.

TIMMY. I wasn't telling you anything about anything. I just said that for me, the coffee was too strong.

JOHN. It isn't strong!

TIMMY (to NETTIE). What time's dinner?

NETTIE. Mama expects us at twelve.

JOHN. I suppose you'll wear your uniform.

TIMMY. It's the only thing I have that fits.

JOHN. Are you sure? I mean maybe you haven't grown as much as you think.

(TIMMY, *studiously trying to avoid a fight, turns to* NETTIE.)

TIMMY. Ravioli?

NETTIE. And meat balls.

JOHN. G.I. Bill, home loans, discharge bonus, unemployment insurance—you boys did pretty well for yourselves.

NETTIE. They did pretty well for us, too.

JOHN (*sings*). "Oh, say can you see."

TIMMY. What's your point, Pop?

JOHN. The war's over.

TIMMY. I'll buy that.

JOHN. The world doesn't owe anyone a living—including veterans.

TIMMY. I'll buy that too.

JOHN. Let the Jews support you.

TIMMY. Come again?

JOHN. Wasn't for them we wouldn't have gotten in it in the first place.

TIMMY. I thought you broke that record.

JOHN. Lousy kikes.

NETTIE. John!

TIMMY (to NETTIE). I changed my mind —I'll have some toast.

JOHN (to TIMMY). Don't tell me you've lost your great love for the Jews?

NETTIE. *Stop it!*

TIMMY (to NETTIE). It's all right.

JOHN. How nice of you to let me talk in my own house. And me not even a veteran.

TIMMY. Would you mind telling me what you're mad about?

JOHN. Who's mad?

NETTIE (to TIMMY). Anything on the toast?

TIMMY. Honey, if you've got it.

JOHN. A man states a few facts and right away he's mad.

NETTIE (*at the cupboard*). How about strawberry jam?

TIMMY. No.

JOHN. If I get a halfway decent offer I might sell the lake house.

NETTIE. Peach?

TIMMY. All right.

JOHN. Hurry up with your breakfast.

TIMMY. What for?

JOHN. Mass starts in twenty minutes and you're not even dressed.

TIMMY. Mass?

JOHN. Mass.

TIMMY. I haven't been to Mass in over two years. You know that.

JOHN. Lots of bad habits you boys picked up that you'll have to get over.

TIMMY. Not going to Mass isn't a habit I picked up. It's a decision I came to after a lot of thought.

JOHN. What way is that for a Catholic to talk?

TIMMY. I haven't considered myself a Catholic for quite a while.

JOHN. Must be something wrong with my ears.

NETTIE (to JOHN). You knew this was coming. Why pretend it's such a shock?

JOHN. Now there's a familiar alliance. (*To* TIMMY.) So you've outgrown the Faith?

TIMMY. It doesn't answer my needs.

JOHN. Outgrown your old clothes and outgrown the Faith.

TIMMY. Pop, will you listen to me—

JOHN. Billions of people have believed in it since the beginning of time but it's not good enough for you.

TIMMY. It's not a question of good enough.

JOHN. What do you say when people ask what religion you are?

TIMMY. Nothing.

JOHN. You say you're nothing?

TIMMY. Yes.

JOHN. The Clearys have been Catholics since . . . since the beginning of time. And now you, a Cleary, are going to tell people that you're nothing?

TIMMY. Yes.

JOHN. *You're an atheist!*

NETTIE. John!

JOHN. When you come to the blank after religion on those college applications, put down atheist. Make a big hit in those Ivy League places, from what I hear.

TIMMY. I'm not an atheist.

JOHN. Then what are you?

TIMMY. I don't know . . . But I'd like a chance to find out.

JOHN. You don't know what you believe in?

TIMMY. Do *you?*

JOHN. Yes.

TIMMY. Tell me . . . Well, go on!

JOHN. I believe in the Father, the Son and the Holy Ghost . . . I believe that God created man in his own image . . . I—

TIMMY. Pop, look . . . if your faith works for you, I'm glad. I'm very glad. I wish it worked for me . . . But it doesn't.

JOHN. Do you believe in God—yes or no?

TIMMY. I don't believe in Heaven, or Hell, or Purgatory, or—

JOHN. *Yes or no?*

TIMMY. I believe there's something bigger than myself. What you call it or what it is I don't know.

JOHN. Well, this is a fine how-do-you-do.

NETTIE (*to* JOHN). Yesterday you said he was a man. A man has a right to decide such things for himself.

JOHN. "Good morning, Father Riley." "Good morning, Mr. Cleary. I understand your boy's out of service." "Yes, Father." "Where is he this fine Sunday morning, Mr. Cleary?" "Home, Father." "Is he sick, Mr. Cleary?" "No, Father." "Then why isn't he here in church, Mr. Cleary?" "He's become an atheist, Father."

TIMMY. I'm not an atheist!

JOHN. Whatever you are, I won't have it! I'm the boss of this house. If you want to go on living here you'll do as I say. And I say you're going to church with me this morning.

NETTIE (*to* JOHN). *Do you know what you're doing?*

JOHN (*to* NETTIE). Keep out! (*To* TIMMY.) Well?

NETTIE (*to* TIMMY). Don't pay any attention to him.

TIMMY (*to* NETTIE). It's all right. (*To* JOHN.) I'll go to church with you. (*Rises.*) Be out in a minute.

(*He starts from the room.*)

JOHN. Forget it!

TIMMY. What?

JOHN. I said forget it. The Lord doesn't want anybody in His house who has to be dragged there. (*To* NETTIE *as he puts on his jacket.*) Score another one for your side.

TIMMY. It has nothing to do with her.

JOHN (*to* TIMMY). Wait till you're down on all fours someday—you'll be glad to see a priest then.

(*He starts out.*)

NETTIE. We'll meet you at Mama's.

JOHN. I won't be there.

NETTIE. She expects us.

JOHN. We all have our disappointments.

TIMMY. I said I'd go with you.

(JOHN *exits, slamming the door.*)

NETTIE. Now what was that all about?

TIMMY (*furious with himself*). I should have gone with him.

NETTIE. I'll never understand that man.

TIMMY. Why didn't I just go? Why did I have to make an issue?

NETTIE. It wasn't your fault.

TIMMY. It never *is.*

NETTIE. When he's in one of those moods there's nothing anyone can do.

TIMMY. The alliance, he called us.

NETTIE. Everyone's entitled to their own beliefs.

TIMMY. That's what we must seem like

to him—an alliance. Always two against one. Always us against him . . . Why?

NETTIE. If you're through eating, I'll clear the table.

TIMMY. Didn't you hear me?

NETTIE. Evidently your father's not the only one who got up on the wrong side of the bed this morning.

TIMMY. *I'm not talking about this morning.*

NETTIE. There's no need to shout.

TIMMY. You, and him, and me, and what's been going on here for twenty years . . . It's got to stop.

NETTIE. What's got to stop?

TIMMY. *We've* got to stop ganging up on him.

NETTIE. Is that what we've been doing?

TIMMY. You said you've never understood him.

NETTIE. And never will.

TIMMY. Have you ever really tried? . . .

NETTIE. Go on.

TIMMY. Have you ever tried to see things from his point of view?

NETTIE. What things?

TIMMY. The lake house, for instance.

NETTIE. The lake house?

TIMMY. It's the pride and joy of his life and you're always knocking it.

NETTIE. Do you know why?

TIMMY. Because he bought it without consulting you.

NETTIE. Drove me out to this Godforsaken lake. Pointed to a bungalow with no heat or hot water and said, "That's where we'll be spending our summers from now on."

TIMMY. An hour's ride from New York City isn't exactly Godforsaken.

NETTIE. It wasn't an hour's ride twenty years ago.

TIMMY. The point is, would he have gotten it any other way? If he had come to you and said he wanted to buy a cottage on a lake in New Jersey, would you have said yes?

NETTIE. I might have.

TIMMY. No. Not if it had been a palace with fifty servants.

NETTIE. I don't like the country.

TIMMY. We'd have spent every summer right here.

NETTIE. My idea of a vacation is to travel —see something new.

TIMMY. You had a chance to see Brazil.

NETTIE. That was different.

TIMMY. The fellow who took that job is a millionaire today.

NETTIE. And still living in Brazil.

TIMMY. Which is not to be compared with the Bronx.

NETTIE. So it's my fault we're not millionaires.

TIMMY. Who knows—your mother might have loved Brazil! (*This causes her to turn from him.*) You violently objected to moving from Yorkville to the Bronx . . . Why?

NETTIE (*clearing the table in an effort to avoid him*). I hate the Bronx.

TIMMY (*pursuing her*). But you insisted that your mother move up here.

NETTIE. They tore down her building. She had to move somewhere.

TIMMY. Except for summers at the lake, have you ever gone two days without seeing her?

NETTIE. Only because of Willis. (*He starts from the room.*) Where are you going?

TIMMY. To get dressed. Then I'm going to church and apologize to him for acting like a fool.

NETTIE. You'll be at Mama's for dinner?

TIMMY. Only if he'll come with me.

NETTIE. You disappointed Willis yesterday. You can't do it again.

TIMMY. Oh yes I can!

NETTIE. How cruel.

TIMMY. Not as cruel as your dragging me over there every day when I was little. And when I was bigger, and couldn't go every day, concentrating on Sunday. "Is it too much to give your crippled cousin one day a week?" And when I didn't go there on Sunday, I felt so guilty that I couldn't enjoy myself anyway . . . I hate Sunday, and I don't think I'll ever get over it. But I'm going to try.

NETTIE. How fortunate for the cripples in this world that everyone isn't as selfish as you.

TIMMY. Why do you keep calling him a cripple? That's not the worst thing wrong with Willis. It's his mind. He's like a four-year-old.

NETTIE. Can a four-year-old read a book?

TIMMY (*pressing his attack relentlessly*). Yes, he reads. After you drilling him every day for twenty years. But does he have any idea what he's reading about? . . . If you and the rest of them over there want to throw your lives away on him, you go ahead and do it! But don't try and sacrifice me to the cause! (NETTIE, *stunned by* TIMMY'S *assault, exits from the kitchen, disappears into the bedroom. Immediately regretful at having vented his feelings so strongly,* TIMMY *moves into the living room; is pondering the best way to apologize, when* NETTIE, *carrying a pocketbook, appears, takes a coat from the hall closet, puts it on.*) Where are you going? (*No answer.*) Your mother doesn't expect us till twelve. (*No answer.*) Give me a minute to dress and I'll go with you. (*No answer.*) Now look—(As NETTIE *reaches for her pocketbook,* TIMMY *also reaches for it in an effort to prevent her departure. He wrests it from her. As he does so, his face registers surprise.*) This is like lead. (*He opens the bag, regards the contents, looks at her puzzledly.*) You've got all your coins in here . . . You're taking your coins . . . What for? (*She extends her hand for the bag. He surrenders it. She moves toward the door.*) Will you please say something?

NETTIE. Thank you for the roses.

(*She exits.*)

CURTAIN

SCENE TWO

TIME: *Ten P.M. Sunday.*

AT RISE: TIMMY, *highball glass in hand, whiskey bottle on the coffee table before him, sits on the sofa in the living room. It is plain that he has been drinking for some time.* JOHN, *cold sober, moves about the room nervously.*

———

TIMMY. I remember sitting here like this the night she went to have John.

JOHN. Why would she just walk out and not tell anyone where she was going?

TIMMY. I was six.

JOHN. Without any reason.

TIMMY. Dr. Goldman came at midnight and took her to the hospital.

JOHN. It doesn't make sense.

TIMMY. After they left, I started to cry. You did too.

JOHN. It's not like her.

TIMMY. I asked you if you loved her. You nodded. I asked you to say it. You hesitated. I got hysterical. To quiet me you finally said, "I love her."

JOHN. Maybe she's at Sophie's.

TIMMY. No. (JOHN *regards him questioningly.*) I called Sophie.

JOHN (*looking at a pocket watch*). It's after ten.

TIMMY. I called everybody.

JOHN. She's been gone twelve hours.

TIMMY. They all said they'd call back if they heard from her.

JOHN. If she's not here by eleven o'clock I'm calling the police.

TIMMY. I wonder what difference it would have made if John lived.

JOHN. I wonder what department you call.

TIMMY. I remember you and I going to visit her at the hospital on a Sunday afternoon. I had to wait downstairs. First time I ever heard the word incubator . . . Incubator.

JOHN. I guess you call Missing Persons.

TIMMY. As we left the hospital and started down the Concourse, we ran into an exotic Spanish-looking woman whom you'd met on one of your trips to Brazil. She was a dancer. Very beautiful. You and she spoke awhile and then you and I went to a movie. Fred Astaire and Ginger Rogers in *Flying Down to Rio.*

JOHN. What are you talking about?

TIMMY. I always thought that was a coincidence—meeting a South American woman and then seeing a picture about Rio . . . *Was* it a coincidence?

JOHN. What?

TIMMY (*sings*). "Hey Rio, Rio by the sea-o. Got to get to Rio and I've got to make time."

JOHN. You're drunk.

TIMMY. Abra ka dabra ka deedra slatter-in.

JOHN. Fine time you picked for it.

TIMMY. A bunch of chorus girls stood on the wings of a silver plane singing that song—"Hey Rio. Flying down to Rio—"

JOHN. You're the last one who saw her. The police will want to question you.

TIMMY. She left the house at ten A.M., your Honor. Didn't say boo but I assumed she was going to her mother's. Brown coat. Brown hat. When I got to her mother's, she wasn't there. They hadn't seen her—hadn't heard from her. I had two helpings of ravioli and meat balls. Came back here to wait. When she didn't call by three o'clock I started to worry—

JOHN. And drink.

TIMMY. *When she didn't call by three*

o'clock I started to worry . . . I tried to get in touch with my father. Called all the bars I could think of—"Is Mr. Cleary there?" . . . "If he comes in would you please tell him to call his house?" . . . It was like old times.

JOHN. I told you—I had dinner and went to a movie.

TIMMY. "*Is* Mr. Cleary there?"—Shows how long I've been away. You never say, "*Is* Mr. Cleary there?" You say, "Let me speak to Mr. Cleary." As though you *knew* he was there.

JOHN. I was at a movie.

TIMMY. Did it have a happy ending?

JOHN. *Gilda,* with Rita Hayworth and Glenn Ford.

TIMMY. I didn't ask you what it was.

JOHN. At the Loew's Paradise.

TIMMY. *I didn't ask you what it was!*

JOHN. What's the matter with you?

TIMMY (*about to pour another drink*). Join me?

JOHN. No, and I think you've had enough.

TIMMY. First time I ever saw you refuse a drink.

JOHN. I want you to stop.

TIMMY. But you're powerless to stop me. It's a lousy position to be in, *I* know.

JOHN. That's your last one.

(*He starts to remove the bottle.*)

TIMMY. Take it and I leave!

(JOHN *hesitates, puts the bottle down.*)

JOHN. Joy, joy, said Mrs. Malloy.

TIMMY. Louder louder, said Mrs. . . . What rhymes with louder?

JOHN. You were sick Friday night. Sick last night.

(*The phone rings. By the time* TIMMY *gets to his feet* JOHN *is picking up the receiver.*)

JOHN (*on the phone*). Hello? . . . Oh . . . (*The abrupt disinterest in his voice causes* TIMMY *to sit down.*) Nothing . . . I said we haven't heard anything . . . I know how long she's been gone . . . Of course I'm concerned . . . *I don't care how I sound—I'm concerned* . . . If she's not here by eleven, that's what I'm going to do . . . That's a comforting bit of information. (*He hangs up, returns to the living room.*) Her mother again. Wanted to let me know how many muggings there's been lately.

TIMMY. I've got it! Earl Browder.

JOHN. What?

TIMMY. Louder, louder, and Mrs. Earl Browder.

JOHN. I'm glad you can take the whole thing so calmly.

TIMMY. To quote a famous authority: "I don't care how I sound—I'm concerned."

JOHN (*regards his watch*). Ten after ten.

TIMMY. Trouble with you is you haven't had enough experience in these matters.

JOHN. Where the devil can she be?

TIMMY. I'm an old hand.

JOHN. Never done anything like this before in her life.

TIMMY. All those nights I lay in bed waiting for your key to turn in the door. Part of me praying you'd come home safe, part of me dreading the sound of that key because I knew there'd be a fight.

JOHN. I'll give her a few minutes more.

TIMMY. All those mornings I woke up sick. Had to miss school. The boy's delicate, everyone said, has a weak constitution.

JOHN. I'll give her till half-past.

TIMMY. From the day I left this house I was never sick. Not once. Took me a long time to see the connection.

JOHN. Where can she go? She has no money.

TIMMY. Wrong.

JOHN. What?

TIMMY. Nothing.

JOHN. You said wrong.

TIMMY (*sings*). "Hey Rio. Rio by the—"

JOHN. I want to know what you meant.

TIMMY. She took her coins. (JOHN *goes into the bedroom.*)

TIMMY (*quietly*). "Hey Rio. Rio by the sea-o."

(JOHN *reappears.*)

JOHN. Why didn't you mention it before?

TIMMY. Slipped my mind.

JOHN. Over fifty dollars in dimes and quarters, and she took them all.

TIMMY. Person could go quite a ways with fifty dollars.

JOHN. You saw her take them?

TIMMY. Yes.

JOHN. Didn't it strike you as peculiar?

TIMMY. Everything strikes me as peculiar.

JOHN. There's something you're not telling me.

TIMMY. We all have our little secrets.

JOHN. There *is* something!

TIMMY. Take you and your money for instance.

JOHN. I want to know what it is.

TIMMY. For all I know, we're millionaires.

JOHN. I want to know why she walked out.

TIMMY. Just between us chickens, how much do you have?

(TIMMY *reaches for the bottle to pour another drink, but* JOHN *snatches it out of his reach.*)

JOHN. Answer me.

TIMMY. If you don't put that bottle down, I'm leaving.

JOHN. I want an answer!

TIMMY (*rising*). See you around the pool hall.

JOHN (*shoving him down hard on the sofa*). *I want an answer!*

TIMMY. Hell of a way to treat a veteran.

JOHN. I've taken all the crap from you I'm going to.

TIMMY. You want an answer. I want a drink. It's a deal.

(*He reaches for the bottle but* JOHN *keeps it from him.*)

JOHN. First the answer.

TIMMY. I forget the question.

JOHN. Why did your mother leave this house? . . . Well?

TIMMY. We had an argument.

JOHN. About what?

TIMMY. I don't remember.

JOHN. Probably something to do with your drinking.

TIMMY. Yes, that's what it was. She said I drank too much.

JOHN. She's right.

TIMMY. Yes.

JOHN. I never thought I'd see the day when you and she would argue.

TIMMY. Neither did I.

JOHN. She didn't say where she was going? Just took the coins and left?

TIMMY. That's right.

JOHN. Beats me.

(*He starts toward the kitchen.*)

TIMMY. Where you going?

JOHN. To get something to eat.

TIMMY. *Eat?*

JOHN. I didn't have any supper.

TIMMY. A minute ago you were so worried you couldn't even sit down.

JOHN. I'm just going to have a sandwich.

TIMMY. Have a banquet!

JOHN. What are you getting mad at *me* for? You're the one who argued with her.

TIMMY. Which absolves you completely! She might jump off a bridge but *your* conscience is clear!

JOHN. A person doesn't take a bunch of change along if they're planning to do something like that.

TIMMY. *She thanked me for the roses!* (JOHN *just looks at him.*) Don't you have any consideration for other people's feelings?

JOHN. Consideration?

TIMMY. Don't you know how much it pleased her to think they were from you?

JOHN. *You* talk about consideration?

TIMMY. How could you do it?

JOHN. Do you have any idea how I looked forward to this morning? To Mass, and dropping in at Rafferty's afterwards with you in your uniform?

TIMMY. Always the injured party.

JOHN. You'll be the injured party in about two minutes.

TIMMY. I already am.

JOHN. Real rough you had it. Good food. Good clothes. Always a roof over your head.

TIMMY. Heigh-ho, everybody, it's count-your-blessings time.

JOHN. I'll tell you what rough is—being so hungry you begged. Being thrown out in the street with your few sticks of furniture for all the neighbors to enjoy. Never sleeping in a bed with less than two other people. Always hiding from collectors. Having to leave school at the age of ten because your father was crippled for life and it was your job to support the house . . . You had it rough, all right.

TIMMY. The subject was roses.

JOHN. Where I couldn't have gone with your advantages . . . What I couldn't have been.

TIMMY. I still want to know why you told her about the roses.

JOHN. We were having words and it slipped out.

TIMMY. Words about what? . . . Well?

JOHN. Stop pushing or I'll tell you.

TIMMY. Go on! Go on!

JOHN. *The humping I'm getting is not worth the humping I'm getting.*

TIMMY (*rising*). You pig.

JOHN. I'm warning you!

TIMMY. *You pig.* (JOHN's *right hand shoots out, catches* TIMMY *hard across the*

side of his face. NETTIE *enters.*) *Bon soir.*
(NETTIE *regards them with an air of de-
tached curiosity.*) Had one too many . . .
Lost my ka deedra slatter-in.
(NETTIE *removes her hat and coat.*)

JOHN. Where have you been? (NETTIE
*lays her hat, coat and pocketbook on a
chair in the foyer.*) I was about to call the
police. (NETTIE *gives no indication that she
even hears him.*) I want to know where
you've been. (NETTIE *moves through the
living room, stops in front of* TIMMY, *who
has just poured himself another drink.*)
Are you going to tell me where you've
been?

NETTIE. You wouldn't believe me.

JOHN. Of course I'd believe you.

NETTIE (*to* TIMMY). You don't look well.

TIMMY. Appearances are deceiving—I
feel terrible.

JOHN. Why wouldn't I believe you?

NETTIE. You just wouldn't.

JOHN. Tell me and see.

NETTIE. I went to the movies.

JOHN. Go on.

NETTIE. That's it.

JOHN. You just went to the movies?

NETTIE. That's right.

JOHN. You've been gone over twelve
hours.

NETTIE. I stayed for several shows.

JOHN. Are you trying to tell me you
were at a movie for twelve hours?

NETTIE. I knew you wouldn't believe me.

TIMMY. *I* believe you.

NETTIE. Thank you.

TIMMY. What did you see?

NETTIE. That means you *don't* believe
me.

TIMMY. No, I guess not.

JOHN. I demand to know where you
were.

NETTIE. I went to the Hotel Astor, picked
up a man, had a few drinks, a few jokes,
went to his room and—

JOHN. Stop it!

NETTIE. I was just getting to the best
part.

JOHN. You're making a fool of yourself.

NETTIE. Is there anything I could say
that you *would* believe?

TIMMY. Say you took a bus downtown,
walked around, visited a museum, had
dinner, went to Radio City, and came
home.

NETTIE. I took a bus downtown, walked
around, visited a museum, had dinner . . .

TIMMY. Went to Radio City and came
home.

NETTIE. Went to Radio City and came
home.

TIMMY. I'll buy that. (*To* JOHN.) If you
had any sense you'd buy it, too.

JOHN. I don't have any sense. I'm just a
poor, ignorant slob whose wife's been missing twelve hours—and I want to know
where she was.

TIMMY. What difference does it make?

JOHN. Stay out of this!

TIMMY. How?

JOHN (*to* NETTIE). What are you going
to tell your mother?

NETTIE. Nothing.

JOHN. The poor woman's almost out of
her mind.

TIMMY. There's a joke there some place.

JOHN. At least call her and say you're
home.

NETTIE. She'll want an explanation.
When I tell her, she won't believe me **any**
more than you did.

JOHN. I'll believe you when you tell the
truth.

TIMMY. What *is* truth? (JOHN *shoots
him a furious glance.*) Sorry.

NETTIE. I'll tell you this . . . In all my
life, the past twelve hours are the only
real freedom I've ever known.

TIMMY. Did you enjoy it?

NETTIE. Every moment.

TIMMY. Why did you come back?

NETTIE. I'm a coward.

JOHN. *Will somebody tell me what's
going on?*

TIMMY (*to the audience*). You heard the
question. (*He peers out into the theatre,
points.*) Up there in the balcony. The
bearded gentleman with the . . . (*He
stops abruptly, rubs his stomach, regards
the audience wanly.*) Sorry, folks, but I'm
about to be ill.

(*He hastens offstage.* NETTIE *follows
him.* JOHN *takes advantage of her absence
to examine her pocketbook, is going
through it when she returns.*)

NETTIE. He wouldn't let me hold his
head, ordered me out of the bathroom,
locked the door.

JOHN. What happened to your coins?

NETTIE. I spent them.

JOHN. How?

NETTIE. I took a bus downtown, walked
around, visited a museum—

(JOHN *interrupts her by slamming the pocketbook to the table.*)

JOHN. Wasn't for his drinking, none of this would have happened.

NETTIE. Why do you say that?

JOHN. If he didn't drink, you and he wouldn't have argued. (*She regards him uncomprehendingly.*) Isn't that why you left? Because you had an argument about his drinking?

NETTIE. We had an argument, but it wasn't about drinking.

JOHN. What was it about?

NETTIE. You, mostly.

JOHN. Go on.

NETTIE. He thinks I don't give you enough credit . . . Feels you're quite a guy . . . Said we had to stop ganging up on you.

(JOHN *turns away.*)

CURTAIN

SCENE THREE

TIME: *Two* A.M. *Monday.*

AT RISE: *The apartment is in darkness. Now a crack of light appears beneath the door to* TIMMY'*s room. The door opens.* TIMMY, *in pajamas, emerges, goes to the living room, turns on a lamp which reveals* NETTIE, *in nightgown and robe, sitting on the sofa.*

NETTIE. I couldn't sleep.

TIMMY. Neither could I. Came out to get a magazine.

NETTIE. You feel all right?

TIMMY. Yes.

(*He looks through a pile of magazines, selects one.*)

NETTIE. What time is it?

TIMMY. Almost two . . . Are *you* all right?

NETTIE. Yes.

TIMMY. Well, I guess I'll turn in. (*She offers no comment.*) Good night.

(*Again, no response. He starts away.*)

NETTIE. Isn't there something you want to tell me?

TIMMY. As a matter of fact there is . . . but it'll keep till morning.

NETTIE. You've decided to leave.

TIMMY. Yes.

NETTIE. When?

TIMMY. It's not a sudden decision.

NETTIE. When are you leaving?

TIMMY. In the morning. (*He looks for a comment from her, but she remains silent.*) This fellow I went to high school with has a flat on Twenty-second Street. His roommate just got married and he's looking for a replacement. I figured . . . (*He becomes aware that she isn't listening.*) Hey . . . (*Still no reaction.*) Hey. (*She regards him absently.*) Give you a penny for them.

NETTIE. An apple core.

TIMMY. What?

NETTIE. An apple core . . . I was due to start working for a law firm. Passed all the interviews and had been notified to report for work the following Monday . . . On Sunday, my sister and I were walking in the park when a blond boy who had a crush on me but was too bashful to speak, demonstrated his affection by throwing an apple core which struck me here. (*She indicates the area beneath her left eye.*) When I woke up Monday morning, I had the most beautiful black eye you ever saw. Too embarrassed to start a new job looking like that, I called in sick. They called back to say the position had been filled by someone else . . . The next job I found was the one that brought your father and I together . . . I often think of that apple core and wonder what my life would be like if it had never been thrown.

TIMMY. Everyone wonders about things like that.

NETTIE. I was going in early to type up some dictation I'd taken the night before . . . Front Street was deserted . . . As I walked, I had the sensation of being watched . . . I glanced up at the office I was passing and saw this young man, your father, staring down . . . He regarded me intensely, almost angrily, for a moment, then suddenly realized I was looking back at him and turned away . . . In that moment, I knew that that young man and I were not suited to each other . . . And at the same time I knew we would become involved . . . that it was inevitable.

TIMMY. Why? You had others to choose from.

NETTIE. Oh yes . . . All gentle, considerate men. All very much like my father . . . One of them was the baker from Paterson, New Jersey, that we always joke about.

TIMMY. The fellow who brought a hatbox full of pastries whenever he called on you.

NETTIE. Yes . . . What a sweet man . . . How he begged me to marry.

TIMMY. What was it that drew you to Pop?

NETTIE. I think it was his energy . . . a certain wildness. He was not like my father at all . . . I was attracted . . . and I was afraid. I've always been a little afraid of him . . . And then he was clearly a young man who was going places. Twenty-four when I met him and making well over a hundred a week. Great money in those days and his prospects were unlimited . . . Money was never plentiful in our house. We weren't poor like his people, you understand. Never without rent, or food, or tickets to the opera, or nice clothes. But still we weren't well-to-do . . . My father brought home stories from the hotel about the various bigwigs who came in and what they wore and how they talked and acted. And we went to the opera. And we had friends who were cultured. Musical Sunday afternoons. Those were Papa's happiest moments . . . Yes, I liked good things. Things that the baker from Paterson and the others could never give me . . . But your father surely would. The way he was going he would be a millionaire . . . That was his dream, you know—to be a millionaire by the time he was forty . . . Nineteen twenty-nine took care of that. He was never quite the same afterwards . . . But when I met him he was cock of the walk. Good-looking, witty young Irishman. Everyone liked him and those who didn't at least feared him because he was a fierce fellow. Everyone wanted to go into business with him. Everyone wanted to be social with him . . . He was immediately at home on a ship, a train . . . in any bar. Strangers thought he was magnificent. And he *was* . . . as long as the situation was impersonal . . . At his best in an impersonal situation . . . But that doesn't include the home, the family . . . The baker from Paterson was all tongue-tied outside, but in the home he would have been beautiful . . . Go to bed now.

(*He kisses her on the forehead.*)

TIMMY. Want the light off?

NETTIE. Please.

(*He moves to the lamp, is about to turn it off, hesitates.*)

TIMMY. When I left this house three years ago, I blamed *him* for everything that was wrong here . . . When I came home,

I blamed *you* . . . Now I suspect that no one's to blame . . . Not even me. (*He turns the light off.*) Good night.

NETTIE. Good night.

(TIMMY *exits into his room, closes the door. For a moment there is silence. Then . . .*)

NETTIE. "Who loves you, Nettie?" . . . "You do, Papa." . . . "Why, Nettie?" "Because I'm a nice girl, Papa."

CURTAIN

SCENE FOUR

TIME: *Nine* A.M. *Monday.*

AT RISE: JOHN *and* NETTIE *are in the kitchen.*

———

JOHN. One word from you . . . That's all it would take.

NETTIE. I'm not so sure.

JOHN. Try.

NETTIE. No.

JOHN. Do you want him to go?

NETTIE. No.

JOHN. Then say something before it's too late.

NETTIE. What do you want for breakfast?

JOHN. Who cares about breakfast?

NETTIE. Timmy's having scrambled eggs.

JOHN. *Am I the only one who's upset by what's going on here?*

NETTIE. No.

JOHN. Then how can you just stand there?

NETTIE. Would you feel better if I wept?

JOHN. You'll weep when he's gone.

NETTIE. But not now.

JOHN. All I want you to do is tell him how you feel.

NETTIE. He knows that.

JOHN. You won't speak to him.

NETTIE. I can't.

JOHN. You're the one who'll miss him most . . . With me it's different. I've got my business.

NETTIE. I envy you.

JOHN. Just ask him to wait a couple of days and think it over.

NETTIE. After a couple of days, we'd be used to having him around. It would be that much harder to see him leave.

JOHN. He might change his mind. Might not want to leave.

NETTIE. He has to leave sometime.

JOHN. But not now. Not like this.

NETTIE. Twenty-second Street isn't the end of the world.

JOHN. If he leaves this house today I don't want to see him ever again!

NETTIE. If you say that to him, make it clear that you're speaking for yourself.

JOHN. Who's this fellow he's moving in with?

NETTIE. A boy he knew at high school.

JOHN. Everything he wants right here—food, clothing, a room of his own. And he has to move into a dirty coldwater flat.

NETTIE. I think I understand his feeling.

JOHN. Home two days and gone again. The neighbors will have a field day.

NETTIE. I'm going in to call him now.

JOHN. I want to see him alone.

NETTIE. If you're wise you won't start a row.

JOHN. *I want to see him alone.*

NETTIE. All right.

(*She goes inside, knocks at* TIMMY'*s door.*)

TIMMY'S VOICE. Come in.

(*She enters the room, closes the door after her.*)

JOHN (*addresses* TIMMY'*s place at the table*). I understand you've decided to leave us . . . (*Not satisfied with this opening, he tries another.*) What's this nonsense about your leaving? . . . (*And another.*) Your mother tells me you're moving out. I would like to know why. (*The first part of this opening pleases him, the last part doesn't. He tries variations on it.*) I de- mand to know why . . . Would you be so good as to tell me why? . . . *Why, God-damn it?*

(*He is puzzling over these various ap- proaches when* TIMMY *enters the kitchen.*)

TIMMY. Good morning.

JOHN. Morning.

TIMMY. Mother said you wanted to see me.

JOHN. Sleep well?

TIMMY. Yes.

JOHN. Good . . .

TIMMY. You wanted to see me?

JOHN. Mother says you're leaving.

TIMMY. Yes.

JOHN. Rather sudden, isn't it?

TIMMY. Not really.

JOHN. Mind telling me why?

TIMMY. I just think it's best.

JOHN. For who?

TIMMY. Everyone.

JOHN. Crap! (TIMMY *starts from the room.*) *Wait.* (*The note of entreaty in his voice causes* TIMMY *to halt.*) I didn't mean that . . . The fact is I don't blame you for wanting to leave. I had no business hitting you.

TIMMY. That's not why I'm going.

JOHN. If there was any way I could undo last night, I would.

TIMMY. It's not a question of last night.

JOHN. If I had to do it over again I'd cut my arm off.

TIMMY. Pop, listen—

JOHN. I don't know what gets into me sometimes.

TIMMY. Pop! (JOHN *looks at him.*) I'm not leaving because of anything that hap- pened last night . . . I always intended to leave.

JOHN. You never mentioned it.

TIMMY. I planned to stay a couple of weeks and then go.

JOHN. A couple of days isn't a couple of weeks.

TIMMY. It's not like I'm going to China.

JOHN. Why two days instead of two weeks?

TIMMY. Because I know that if I stay two weeks I'll *never* leave.

JOHN. If it's what I said yesterday, about me being the boss and you'd have to do what I said—forget it.

TIMMY. It's not that.

JOHN. I was just letting off steam.

TIMMY. *It's not that.*

JOHN. As far as I'm concerned you're a man—you can come and go as you please, do as you please. That goes for religion, drinking, anything.

TIMMY. How can I make you under- stand?

JOHN. Even girls. I know how it is to be your age. Give me a little advance notice and I'll see that you have the house to yourself whenever you want.

TIMMY. Pop, for Chrisake.

JOHN (*flares momentarily*). *What kind of language is that?* (*Then hastily.*) I'm sorry. I didn't mean that. Talk any way you want.

TIMMY. I don't know what to say to you.

JOHN. What I said yesterday about the Jews, I was just trying to get a rise out of you.

TIMMY. I know.

JOHN. The time those bums from Saint Matthew's jumped the I-cash-clothes man, I was the one who saved him.

TIMMY. I know.

JOHN. Whole crowd of people watching but I was the only one who did anything.

TIMMY. Do you think I could forget that?

JOHN. Stay another week. Just a week.

TIMMY. I can't.

JOHN. Stay till Wednesday.

TIMMY. No.

JOHN. Do you have any idea how your mother looked forward to your coming home?

TIMMY. Yes.

JOHN. Then how can you do it?

TIMMY. We're just going around in circles.

JOHN. What happens to the lake house?

TIMMY. What do you mean?

JOHN. Without you, what's the good of it?

TIMMY. I'll be spending time there.

JOHN. I thought we'd have a real summer together like before the war.

TIMMY. You're making this a lot tougher than it has to be.

JOHN. *Did you expect me to say nothing? Like her?* . . .

TIMMY. Are you through?

JOHN (*trying a new tack*). I know what the trouble is. You know what the trouble is? You're like me . . . Stubborn . . . All the Clearys are stubborn . . . Would rather die than admit a mistake . . . Is that a fact? Yes or no?

TIMMY. I don't know.

JOHN (*points to himself*). Well, here's one donkey who's seen the light. I've been wrong in my dealings with you and I admit it.

TIMMY. Pop—

JOHN. Not just wrong last night, but all along. Well, those days are gone forever, and I'll prove it . . . You know how much money I have?

TIMMY. I don't want to know.

JOHN. Fourteen thousand three hundred and fifty-seven dollars.

TIMMY. Pop!

JOHN. Plus a bit more in stocks . . . Now *you* admit that *you* made a mistake—admit you don't really want to leave and we'll forget the whole thing.

TIMMY. I *don't* want to leave.

JOHN. See—

TIMMY. But I'm leaving.

JOHN (*turning away*). *Then go and good riddance!*

TIMMY. Listen to me.

JOHN. The sooner the better.

TIMMY. *Listen to me!* (*Pauses—then goes on quietly, intensely.*) There was a dream I used to have about you and I . . . It was always the same . . . I'd be told that you were dead and I'd run crying into the street . . . Someone would stop me and ask why I was crying and I'd say, "My father's dead and he never said he loved me."

JOHN (*trying unsuccessfully to shut out* TIMMY's *words*). I only tried to make you stay for her sake.

TIMMY. I had that dream **again** last night . . . Was thinking about it this morning when something occurred to me that I'd never thought of before.

JOHN. She's the one who'll miss you.

TIMMY. It's true you've never said you love me. But it's also true that I've never said those words to you.

JOHN. I don't know what you're talking about.

TIMMY. I say them now—

JOHN. *I don't know what you're talking about.*

TIMMY. I love you, Pop. (JOHN's *eyes squeeze shut, his entire body stiffens, as he fights to repress what he feels.*) I love you. (*For another moment,* JOHN *continues his losing battle, then, overwhelmed, turns, extends his arms.* TIMMY *goes to him. Both in tears, they embrace.* NETTIE *emerges from* TIMMY's *room, closes the door with emphasis to alert them to her approach.* TIMMY *and* JOHN *separate hastily.*)

JOHN. What I said about the money—that's strictly between us.

TIMMY. I understand.

(NETTIE *enters the kitchen. If she is aware of anything unusual in their appearance or manner, she doesn't show it.*)

NETTIE. Ready for breakfast? (*They nod.*) Sit down.

(*They sit. She pours the coffee.*)

NETTIE (*to* TIMMY). Your bag is packed and ready to go.

TIMMY. I've changed my mind.

NETTIE. What?

TIMMY. I've changed my mind. I'm going to stay a few more days.

JOHN. I'm afraid that's out of the question. (TIMMY *and* NETTIE *regard him incredulously.*) When you said you were going, I called the painters. They're coming in to do your room tomorrow . . . You know how hard it is to get the painters. If we don't take them now, it'll be months before they're free again.

TIMMY. Then I guess I better leave as scheduled.

JOHN. I think so. (*To* NETTIE.) Don't you?

NETTIE. . . . Yes.

(JOHN *tastes the coffee—scowls.*)

JOHN. I don't know why I bother to bring good coffee into this house. If it isn't too weak, it's too strong. If it isn't too strong, it's too hot. If it isn't . . .

CURTAIN